"Although it is difficult to paint a portrait of a living science that often refuses to sit still long enough, psychology always sits well for those really determined to discover the secrets of its true character. I hope you will become one of those adventurous explorers of human nature."

from the Preface

Psychology and Life

Eleventh Edition

Psychology and Life

Eleventh Edition

Philip G. Zimbardo

Stanford University

Scott, Foresman and Company

Glenview, Illinois   London, England

*Dedicated to my children, Adam, Zara, and Tanya—
with hope that the best is yet to come; to my wife
and colleague, Christina Maslach—with delight for
sharing the joy that is now; and to my editor and
friend, Marguerite Clark—with gratitude for having
contributed so much to this and many previous editions
of* Psychology and Life.

Credit lines for the photos, illustrations, and other copyrighted materials appearing in this work are placed in the *Acknowledgments* section beginning on page LI. This section is to be considered an extension of the copyright page.

Library of Congress Cataloging in Publication Data

Zimbardo, Philip G.
  Psychology and life.

  Bibliography: p.
  Includes index.
  1. Psychology. I. Title.
BF121.Z54 1985   150   84—14185
ISBN 0—673—15418—1
2 3 4 5 6-RRW-89 88 87 86 85

To the Instructor

Although there are over 160 other textbooks written for this course, *Psychology and Life* is unique. The first edition was written in 1937 by Floyd Ruch. Since then, it has become the model that has been imitated by a large share of the basic texts that have followed—for its student orientation, its eclectic, unbiased presentation of different viewpoints, its combining of scientific rigor with relevance to life concerns, and its creative use of graphics and pedagogical features that make complex material more accessible to the reader.

Psychology and Life ranks first in seniority among textbooks in psychology. However, its continuing success comes from never resting on our laurels, but always striving to provide a fresh, contemporary perspective on the state of psychological knowledge. This 11th Edition has been totally rewritten over the last four years to bring you the most comprehensive and accurate picture possible of the field of psychology today. Since I also teach the introductory psychology course (and have enjoyed doing so for over twenty-five years now), I am able to keep in touch with changing student values and backgrounds.

Can the serious, research-based core of psychological knowledge be presented not as a catalogue of dry facts but as an exciting process of discovery that is alive with challenges for the curious investigator? I believe it can. Can this scientific enterprise be presented as an approach to understanding the human condition that nevertheless retains its wonder at the marvels of individual functioning and its compassion for individual malfunctioning? I believe it can. And can psychology be scientific and serious yet still be a source of endless enjoyment for the researcher, teacher, and student of psychology? I know it can. These concerns have been the guiding force that directed every stage in the development of *Psychology and Life*.

Wherever possible, important concepts are presented in a context that ties them to their historical origins, or to their significance within the dynami-

cally changing field of psychology, or to their possible operation in our lives. Many chapters are entirely new, while all the rest have undergone major renovations. These changes were made to reflect the dramatic transformations that have taken place in many areas of psychological investigation over the past five years. This revision is different from past editions (and from most comparable texts) in trying to integrate knowledge across diverse areas of psychology by building conceptual bridges between regions usually treated as separate. It is the cumulative development of information and the fertilization of ideas across once independent territories that are the hallmark of contemporary psychology—and of this new edition of *Psychology and Life*.

For example, physiological psychology with its new methods for probing brain mechanisms and processes now more clearly informs the study of sensation, perception, learning, memory, attention, motivation, stress, and mental disorders. So, too, cognitive psychology is becoming more central in areas as disparate as social psychology, psychotherapy, stress, emotion, and artificial intelligence. I have also tried to show that the study of such phenomena as consciousness and stress is basic to understanding human nature, and that these are not simply high interest topics thrown in for "relevance." *Psychology and Life 11th* reflects these and other exciting trends in our field.

In addition to fundamental changes in the content of every chapter, other improvements characterize this new edition. The basic conceptual approaches to psychological knowledge—psychobiological, psychodynamic, behavioral, cognitive, and existential-humanistic—are outlined in the first chapter and then reappear many times as alternative perspectives on motivation, stress, personality, therapy, and other areas of study. Other organizing principles help make the content of *Psychology and Life 11th* more accessible to the reader, such as the use of overviews of what is to come and cogent summaries of the ground that we have covered. Definitions of key terms, major concepts, and factual knowledge are more clearly presented "up front," while the interpretations, implications, and generalizations that add essential depth are kept distinguishable from this basic core of information. Another distinctive feature of this text is found in places where a body of knowledge is organized in original tables, figures, or sets of comparisons and contrasts (for example, the flow chart of memory, the factors in stress, and the good-evil sides of human attributes). There are also places where the author talks directly to the reader to offer advice about a variety of student concerns, such as stress management, mental health, or resisting pressures toward conformity and obedience. But always the central focus is on the research foundation of psychological knowledge, what we know from "classic" studies, as well as what we are discovering from current research.

Our presentation of each area includes some historical background, a sampling of current theoretical approaches, and representative research methods and findings, with emphasis on how these concepts are related to ideas in other chapters and how these processes function in the individual's overall, continuing task of coping with life demands. We start with three foundation chapters (the approach of psychology, a survey of life-span development, and the biological bases of all our behavior), then follow with three sections on processes that occur within individuals (perceptual processes, action processes, and cognitive processes). Next come two sections on personality processes (theories and assessment of personality) and pathological processes (stress, behavior disorders, and therapy) and finally a section on social and group processes, and the power of the social situation—for good or ill. Included in the book but not in the mainstream of the chapters is a concise appendix on designing research and using basic statistical techniques for analyzing research data.

Although it is difficult to paint a portrait of a living science that often refuses to sit still long enough, psychology always sits well for those really determined to discover the secrets of its true character. I hope you will become one of those adventurous explorers of human nature.

The total *Psychology and Life* program

To encourage greater efficiency in studying, learning, retention, and test taking, we have prepared two student-focused supplements. *Working with Psychology,* co-authored with Scott Fraser of the University of Sourthern California, will be a valuable aid for any student who wishes to more fully develop his or her proficiency as a learner and academic performer. It contains many features (such as guided reviews and self-scored tests) that enable students to take better control of their education and gain greater competence in acquiring and demonstrating their knowledge of introductory psychology. *Working with Psychology* is also available in a computerized format.

The *Psychology and Life Unit Mastery System (PLUMS) Student's Guide,* prepared by Karl Minke and John Carlson of the University of Hawaii, provides a self-paced study program. It includes exercises for mastering chapter specifics and mastering chapter concepts, as well as self-quizzes over each unit of material.

Giving credit where it is deserved

Students have helped improve the quality of *Psychology and Life* by sending us feedback about what worked for them, as well as constructive feedback of what we can do better next time around. Please carry on this tradition by noting your reaction to each chapter on the evaluation form at the back of this book. Please do so soon after reading each chapter. Then, as soon as your course has ended, just drop the postage-paid form in the mail. Thanks in advance; I read each one personally and revise the book in part based on that input.

I also have received an enormous amount of help from my own students, colleagues, and expert critical reviewers who have insisted on the highest standards of scholarship. They have taught me much in the process, and indirectly will contribute to your learning and enjoyment of this new edition of *Psychology and Life.* To each of them I am grateful and offer a measure of the thanks they deserve by noting their contributions here.

Collaborating on the preparation of the manuscript were a number of my colleagues. Stephen Palmer (University of California, Berkeley) drafted the sensation and perception chapters and reviewed many other key chapters. Others who assisted in the drafting of material were: Frank Halasz (Stanford University), cognition; Joan Linsenmeier, Research Appendix; Christina Maslach (University of California, Berkeley), sex roles and social psychology; Carlo Piccione, consciousness; and Antonette Zeiss, stress, personality, and abnormal.

Valuable critical feedback on every chapter has come from Scott Fraser (University of Southern California), my former student, a model teacher, and co-author of *Working with Psychology* and also from Sandra Holmes (University of Wisconsin). Input that has helped improve the text was also provided by Karl Minke and John Carlson (University of Hawaii), the authors of the *Psychology and Life Unit Mastery System,* and by Terry Maul (San Bernardino Valley College), co-author of the *Instructor's Resource Book.*

My colleagues at Stanford University have helped with reviews of material in their respective areas of expertise: Sophia Cohen, Maureen Callanan, Nelson Donegan, Phoebe Ellsworth, John Flavell, George Quattrone, Robert Mauro, David Rosenhan, and Barbara Tversky. Students Glen Hallam and Chris Dickerson diligently tracked down references, while Chris also teamed with Elaine Vaughan in helping to prepare the glossary.

The many drafts of our many chapters were typed primarily by Rosanne Saussotte with assistance from time to time from Paola Coda-Nunziante, Teresa Putnam, Nellie Yoshida, and Iris Ganz.

My favorite publisher, Scott, Foresman, supported these efforts fully. The College Division staff were patient in providing the extra time required to do this edition right and without any compromises. Heading the editorial team that shaped a sometimes overweight manuscript into a trim, solid book was Joanne Tinsley. Her perceptive editing was ably aided and abetted by Paula Fitzpatrick, Louise Howe, Marguerite Clark, and Joan Linsenmeier. Credit for design and illustrations goes to a creative artist, Juan Vargas, and to Sandy Schneider, picture editor.

And finally, there are the many academic reviewers chosen because of their reputation as either teachers of introductory psychology or specialists in a content area covered by our text. Some reviewed chapters of the 10th Edition, others read drafts of the 11th Edition. Although they sometimes battered my self-esteem, they always bettered my presentation of psychology as science and as a vital subject in a student's intellectual development. I hope they will see how their feedback has made this a much better book for their students and for you. They are listed alphabetically:

Judith P. Allik
 University of Dayton
Robert Arkin
 University of Missouri-Columbia
Pietro Badia
 Bowling Green State University
Linda Musun Baskett
 University of Arkansas
Major Johnston Beach
 U.S. Military Academy, West Point
Hal S. Bertilson
 Weber State College
Jay Braun
 Arizona State University
Gary P. Brown
 Kellogg Community College
James N. Butcher
 University of Minnesota
Jay Caldwell
 California State University, Chico
A. Charles Catania
 University of Maryland
Garvin Chastain
 Boise State University
Charles Cofer
 University of North Carolina, Chapel Hill
Ann Sloan Devlin
 Connecticut College
Thomas K. Eckle
 Modesto Junior College
Randall W. Engle
 University of South Carolina
Laura Frishman
 Northwestern University
Gabriel P. Frommer
 Indiana University
Frederick P. Gault
 Western Michigan University
Alan G. Glaros
 University of Florida
Anthony Grasha
 University of Cincinnati
Richard A. Griggs
 University of Florida
Ronald L. Growney
 University of Connecticut

Arthur Gutman
Florida Institute of Technology

Charles G. Halcomb
Texas Tech University

Richard Halgin
University of Massachusetts

David W. Ingersol
Fordham University

Will Kenny
Formerly at University of Minnesota

Dan Landis
University of Mississippi

Joan B. Lauer
Indiana University

Laurence La Voie
University of Miami

Rob Linsenmeier
Northwestern University

Charles Lord
Princeton University

Neil S. Lutsky
Carleton College

Wesley Lynch
Montana State University

Daniel P. Murphy
Creighton University

Steve A. Nida
Franklin University

William B. Pavlik
University of Georgia

Blaine Peden
University of Wisconsin, Eau Claire

Clark Presson
Arizona State University

Duane H. Reeder
Glendale Community College

Joan Rosen
Miami-Dade Community College, South

Milton E. Rosenbaum
University of Iowa

William B. Rucker
Mankato State University

William Schicht
Virginia Polytechnic Institute

David J. Schneider
University of Texas

Kenneth Schweller
Buena Vista College

Wayne Sjoberg
Northern Arizona University

Stuart Solomon
Southern Connecticut State University

Richard Teevan
SUNY, Albany

Alexandra Teguis
Manchester Community College

Robert H. Terborg
Calvin College

Joseph Thorpe
University of Missouri-Columbia

Michael Walraven
Jackson Community College

W. Beryl West
Middle Tennessee State University

Margaret H. White
California State, Fullerton

A. Bond Woodruff
Northern Illinois University

Everett L. Worthington, Jr.
Virginia Commonwealth University

Fred L. Yaffee
Washburn University of Topeka

Philip B. Young
Towson State University

Shelley Zedeck
University of California, Berkeley

My heartfelt thanks and deep appreciation go out to each and every critical reviewer, encouraging colleague, dedicated editor, and supportive friend who enabled me to put more life into this rendering of psychology and also contribute more meaningful psychology to our life.

Welcome aboard! You are about to begin a special journey that should be fascinating, challenging, and enjoyable. You have chosen to discover the reasons why we think, feel, and act as we do. You want to know what causes your behavioral patterns and those that you observe in others. You are curious about how the human mind functions. You wonder about how much of what you are is due to what you inherited at birth from your parents and ancestors and also how much is due to what you've learned through personal experience. You may even be concerned about your uniqueness from, yet similarity to, other people and even other animal species. Well, then you've come to the right place to start getting answers, suggestions, and clues.

Your teacher serves as your guide, the trip director, while this text is your tour book—your field notes. Together we hope to be able to share with you some of our enthusiasm and love for the study of psychology. But our task won't be easy.

Unlike many other college courses, the introductory psychology course is one that many students enter believing they already know a great deal about the subject. After all, if psychology is the study of individual behavior, aren't you a behaving individual? And haven't you studied how other individuals behave—members of your family, teams, clubs, friends, and public figures? Moreover, you've seen psychology in the news and in various media accounts of the motivations of someone's actions, the causes of one person's success, another's suicide, a senseless murder, or a heroic sacrifice. You've probably even heard of the names of some of the major contributors to psychological knowledge—Sigmund Freud, Ivan Pavlov, and B. F. Skinner. What's left to learn? The simple answer is "a lot."

The range of material we will be covering is probably greater than in any other introductory level course you will take. You will be investigating the secrets of behavior as they are revealed in the functioning of the brain and its chemical transmitters of information, but then you will also be examining much broader issues, such as the nature of violence and ways to improve cooperation among nations. You will study the development of language and thinking in children and also the breakdown of human potential in stress reactions, mental disorders, and processes of dehumanization. You will learn how our senses enable us to make such precise contact with the environment and also how our personal biases distort reality.

So the challenge lies in opening yourself to a vast new realm of knowledge with many technical terms, definitions, concepts, and principles to be mastered—in the limited time available for any one course in your schedule. You will probably have to put in more dedicated study time on this course than you anticipated if you want to get out of it much of the rich core of information that is available for the serious traveler. If you do, it will be worth the effort.

GETTING THE MOST OUT OF THIS BOOK

Here are some suggestions for getting the best return on the time you invest in studying *Psychology and Life.* They are intended to promote comprehension and efficiency and make you aware of the features that have been built into each chapter to help you.

- Set aside sufficient time to study for this course; there is much new technical information that will require careful reading and reflection.
- Find a study place with minimal distractions; reserve this spot for study and do nothing there other than reading, note-taking, and reviewing your course material.
- Keep a record or log of the number of hours (in half-hour intervals) that you put in studying for this course. Chart it on a cumulative graph (one that adds each new study time to the prior total).

- Begin each chapter by looking over its outline. It shows you the topics that will be covered, their sequence, and how they are related to one another.
- Next, skip to the end of the chapter and read the Summary. It will flesh out the outline by indicating the important themes, concepts, and conclusions, as well as their sequence of appearance.
- Read the Opening Case on the tinted pages at the beginning of the chapter. It will give you a perspective on the central theme(s) in the chapter.
- Continue using the *SQ3R* method (which you've already actually begun):

  Survey: Skim the sections noted above to get the "gist" of the chapter.

  Question: Write out a brief list of questions you want to be able to answer about the content of this chapter.

  Read: Now dig in and read the chapter. Outline key points, paraphrase them in your own words. Become an active note-taker—the more active the better.

  Recite: When you finish each chapter, repeat *aloud* all the points you can remember.

  Review: After at least an hour, actively review all you can remember by writing out or reciting the major points of the chapter. Repeat and space these active reviews several times before an examination.
- Bear in mind as you study that the test questions that accompany this text ask you to demonstrate your mastery of the material in the following four ways:

  Definitions: recall or recognition of verbatim statements, meanings of terms, concepts, and processes described in the text.

  Factual information: recall or recognition of information about different approaches to psychological issues, theories, models, research, and important individuals.

  Comparisons: recall of relationships between or among content presented at different points of the chapter, even though the connections may not have been made explicitly; ability to make judgments about differences, similarities, and contrasts of ideas.

  Extensions and applications: reasoning ability to go beyond what is given to form generalizations, to make predictions or derivations, and to illustrate some general principle or concept with a specific example.

Psychology and Life has been carefully designed to facilitate your learning experience. As you read, be sure to note these features:

- The different type styles of the various headings indicate the structure of the chapter and show the relationships among the concepts. They should help you plan your reading and can serve as convenient break points for each period of study.
- The most important terms and concepts appear in **boldface** type and are also gathered alphabetically in the *Glossary* at the end of the book. (Each definition in the *Glossary* is followed by the number of the text page on which the term is discussed in context.) *Italicized* terms are also significant; some of them too are defined in the *Glossary*.
- Detailed reports of particular studies are indented to distinguish them from the body of the text.
- Close-ups are set off by rules from the flow of the text. They contain ideas that extend the information being presented in special ways. Some are more in-depth presentations of research; others give applications or suggest items of possible personal relevance to you.
- When a name and date are given in parentheses after a statement or conclusion, they identify the person whose research is being cited and the date of his or her publication. (The word "see" before a citation indicates that it is a more general source of relevant information). An alphabetical list of these authors and their publications, which form the scholarly foundation of *Psychology and Life,* is found at the end of the book. This enables you or your instructor to go directly to the source for more complete information on any of these ideas.
- The back of the book contains other useful reference information. There is an *Appendix* on designing research and analyzing it statistically that you may find useful even if it is not required reading for your course. And there are both a *Subject Index* of important concepts discussed in the text and a *Name Index* of all the individuals whose work is cited.

I believe you will find *Psychology and Life* a valuable reference source that will be useful in other courses for term papers or background information. I hope you will want to keep it as an addition to your personal library of intellectual resource materials.

OVERVIEW

PROLOGUE by Neal Miller

PART ONE FOUNDATIONS

1 PROBING THE MYSTERIES OF MIND AND BEHAVIOR
2 LIFE-SPAN PSYCHOLOGICAL DEVELOPMENT
3 THE BIOLOGY OF BEHAVIOR

PART TWO PERCEPTUAL PROCESSES

4 SENSATION
5 PERCEPTION
6 THE NATURE OF CONSCIOUSNESS

PART THREE ACTION PROCESSES

7 CONDITIONING AND LEARNING
8 MOTIVATION AND EMOTION

PART FOUR COGNITIVE PROCESSES

9 REMEMBERING AND FORGETTING
10 THINKING AND COMMUNICATING

PART FIVE PERSONALITY PROCESSES

11 UNDERSTANDING HUMAN PERSONALITY
12 ASSESSING INDIVIDUAL DIFFERENCES

PART SIX PATHOLOGICAL PROCESSES

13 UNDERSTANDING AND MANAGING STRESS
14 ABNORMAL PSYCHOLOGY
15 THERAPIES FOR PERSONAL CHANGE

PART SEVEN SOCIAL PROCESSES

16 THE SOCIAL BASES OF BEHAVIOR
17 EXPLORING SOCIAL ISSUES

POSTSCRIPT
APPENDIX UNDERSTANDING RESEARCH

CONTENTS

PROLOGUE by Neal Miller   xix

PART ONE   FOUNDATIONS   1

1   PROBING THE MYSTERIES OF MIND AND BEHAVIOR   2

PSYCHOLOGY: DEFINITIONS AND GOALS   6
   What psychology is
   What psychology tries to do
RESEARCH FOUNDATIONS   11
   Basic methods for gathering data
   Enhancing objectivity
   Going beyond the facts
ALTERNATIVE PERSPECTIVES   22
   Differing assumptions and approaches
   Psychological models as maps
   Using psychological models
PLANS FOR OUR PSYCHOLOGICAL
JOURNEY   28
SUMMARY   30

2   LIFE-SPAN PSYCHOLOGICAL DEVELOPMENT   32

THE LIFE-SPAN APPROACH   36
   How development is studied
   Basic concepts
THE LIFE CYCLE BEGINS   40
   Genetic influences on behavior
   What can babies do?
   The beginning of language acquisition
COGNITIVE DEVELOPMENT   50
   Piaget's insights into mental growth
   Modern perspectives on cognitive development

SOCIAL AND EMOTIONAL DEVELOPMENT   55
   Socialization
   Gender roles
   Moral development
   Psychosexual and psychosocial development
THE CYCLE EXTENDS . . . AND ENDS   66
   Adolescence
   Adulthood
   The later years
SUMMARY   71

3   THE BIOLOGY OF BEHAVIOR   72

WHAT MAKES BEHAVIOR "WORK"?   74
   Mind and brain
   Nerve energy
   Special cells for special jobs
HOW DO CELLS COMMUNICATE WITH ONE
ANOTHER?   78
   The central and peripheral nervous systems
   Behavioral regulation by the endocrine system
   Neurons as building blocks
HOW DOES THE BRAIN CONTROL
BEHAVIOR?   93
   Development of the brain
   Functional organization of the human brain
HOW IS THE BRAIN STUDIED?   101
   Touching a sensitive nerve
   Lesions are forever
   Recording the activity of neurons
   Looking at living brains
SUMMARY   106

PART TWO   PERCEPTUAL PROCESSES   107

4   SENSATION   108

SENSORY KNOWLEDGE OF THE WORLD   110
Reality and illusion
Sensation, perception, and classification
FROM PHYSICAL ENERGY TO MENTAL
EVENTS   113
Psychophysics
Constructing psychophysical scales
THE VISUAL SYSTEM   119
The eye
Processing in the retina
Pathways to the brain
DIMENSIONS OF VISUAL EXPERIENCE   122
Color
Spatial properties
Time and motion
HEARING   134
The physics of sound
Psychological dimensions of sound
The physiology of hearing
OTHER SENSES   141
The chemical senses
The body senses
The pain sense
SUMMARY   148

5   PERCEPTION   150

THE TASK OF PERCEPTION   152
Interpreting retinal images
Evidence from ambiguous figures
Theories of visual perception
PERCEPTUAL PROCESSES   161
Organizational processes
Depth perception
Perceptual constancies

CLASSIFICATION PROCESSES   176
"Bottom-up" and "top-down" processes
Pattern recognition
The influence of contexts and expectations
The role of personal and social factors
SUMMARY   185

6   THE NATURE OF CONSCIOUSNESS   186

THE PSYCHOLOGY OF CONSCIOUSNESS   188
Consciousness as an aid to survival
The changing scientific status of consciousness
Psychological studies of attention
Mental processing without consciousness
THE DUALITY OF CONSCIOUSNESS   197
Two minds in one brain?
Complementary orientations to the world?
EVERYDAY CHANGES IN CONSCIOUSNESS   200
Daydreaming and fantasy
Sleeping and dreaming
EXTENDED STATES OF CONSCIOUSNESS   207
Hallucinations
Hypnosis
Mind alteration with drugs
CONSCIOUSNESS: THE ORDINARY AND THE
EXTRAORDINARY   219
SUMMARY   220

PART THREE **ACTION PROCESSES** 221

7 **CONDITIONING AND LEARNING** 222

THE STUDY OF LEARNING 224
Philosophical assumptions
What is learning?
CLASSICAL CONDITIONING: LEARNING BASED ON SIGNALS 226
Pavlov's discovery
The classical conditioning paradigm
The anatomy of classical conditioning
OPERANT CONDITIONING: LEARNING ABOUT CONSEQUENCES 234
Thorndike and the law of effect
Skinner's experimental analysis of behavior
The operant conditioning paradigm
Properties of reinforcers
The mechanics of reinforcers
NEW DEVELOPMENTS IN LEARNING THEORY 250
Biological constraints on conditioning
Cognitive influences on conditioning
What is learned in conditioning?
SUMMARY 258

8 **MOTIVATION AND EMOTION** 260

UNDERSTANDING MOTIVATION 263
Why use motivational concepts?
Using motivational concepts in research
THEORETICAL PERSPECTIVES 268
Instincts as motivators
Drive theory and learning
Deficiency and growth motivation
Cognitions, expectations, and attributions
HUNGER AND EATING 275
The search for feeding regulators
A multiple-system approach
SEX AND SEXUALITY 280
Sexual arousal
Human sexuality
ACHIEVEMENT AND WORK 286
Achievement motivation
Work motivation
Motivation and the future
EMOTION 294
Are emotions innate or learned?
What starts an emotion?
Which is "primary"—thought or feeling?
SUMMARY 301

PART FOUR COGNITIVE PROCESSES 303

9 REMEMBERING AND FORGETTING 304

WHAT IS MEMORY? 306
An information-processing view
Encoding, storage, and retrieval
Three memory systems
SENSORY MEMORY 310
Encoding for sensory memory
Storage: how much and how long?
Processing for transfer to short-term memory
SHORT-TERM MEMORY 313
Encoding in short-term memory
Storage in short-term memory
Processing in short-term memory
Retrieval from short-term memory
LONG-TERM MEMORY 318
Encoding for long-term memory
Storage in long-term memory
Retrieval from long-term memory
Two memories versus multiple levels
REMEMBERING AS A CONSTRUCTIVE PROCESS 328
Schemas
Eyewitness testimony
WHY DO WE FORGET? 332
Explanations of forgetting
The physical bases of forgetting—and remembering
SUMMARY 337

10 THINKING AND COMMUNICATING 338

STUDYING THINKING 340
Cognition and the cognitive approach
Studying the unobservable
MENTAL STRUCTURES FOR THINKING 346
Concepts
Propositions
Schemas and scripts
Visual images and cognitive maps
KEYS TO COMPREHENSION 355
Integrating the unknown into the known
Revising mental structures and reducing discrepancy
MAKING DECISIONS AND JUDGMENTS 358
Utility and probability
Sources of error in decision making
SOLVING PROBLEMS 361
Well-defined and ill-defined problems
Understanding the problem
Finding the best search strategy: algorithms or heuristics?
IMPROVING COGNITIVE SKILLS 364
Acquiring and perfecting skills
Becoming an expert
Metacognitive knowledge
COMMUNICATING THOUGHTS 371
Verbal and nonverbal communication
The relation between language and thought
Criteria for "true" language
Is language uniquely human?
SUMMARY 375

PART FIVE **PERSONALITY PROCESSES** 377

11 **UNDERSTANDING HUMAN PERSONALITY** 378

STUDYING PERSONALITY 381
Research strategies
Theories about personality
TYPE AND TRAIT THEORIES 386
Categorizing with types
Describing with traits
Criticisms of type and trait theories
PSYCHODYNAMIC THEORIES 391
Freudian psychoanalysis
Neo-Freudian theories
Criticisms of Freudian theory
HUMANISTIC THEORIES 400
A person-centered approach
Self theory
Criticisms of humanistic theories
LEARNING THEORIES 404
A strict behavioristic approach
Reconciling the analytic and behavioral
approaches
Bandura's social learning theory
Criticisms of learning theories
COGNITIVE THEORIES 409
Personal construct theory
Cognitive social learning theory
Criticisms of cognitive theories
COMPARING THEORIES 411
SUMMARY 412

12 **ASSESSING INDIVIDUAL DIFFERENCES** 414

WHAT IS ASSESSMENT? 416
METHODS OF ASSESSMENT 418
Basic features of formal assessment
Sources of information
ASSESSING INTELLIGENCE 424
Historical context
IQ tests
What is intelligence?
The use and misuse of IQ
ASSESSING PERSONALITY 435
Objective measures
Projective tests
ASSESSING CREATIVITY 441
What qualifies as creative?
Correlates of creativity
ASSESSMENT AND YOU 445
Vocational interests and aptitudes
Social strengths and weaknesses: shyness
Political and ethical issues
SUMMARY 451

PART SIX PATHOLOGICAL PROCESSES 453

13 UNDERSTANDING AND MANAGING STRESS 454

THE CONCEPT OF STRESS 456
Meanings of "stress"
The role of cognitive appraisal
PHYSIOLOGICAL STRESS REACTIONS 458
Emergency reactions to external threats
The general adaptation syndrome
Stress and disease
PSYCHOLOGICAL STRESS REACTIONS 466
Behavioral patterns
Emotional aspects of the stress response
Cognitive effects of stress
SOURCES OF STRESS 471
Major life stressors
Life's little hassles
Catastrophic events
Chronic societal sources of stress
VULNERABILITY AND RESISTANCE 475
Common coping strategies
Supportiveness of the environment
MANAGING STRESS BETTER 481
Altering bodily reactions
Modifying cognitive strategies
Stress control and your mental health
SUMMARY 486

14 ABNORMAL PSYCHOLOGY 488

THE PROBLEM OF MENTAL DISORDERS 490
CLASSIFYING MENTAL DISORDERS 492
What is abnormal?
DSM-III
MAJOR TYPES OF MENTAL DISORDER 494
Personality disorders
Anxiety disorders
Somatoform disorders
Dissociative disorders
Psychosexual disorders
Affective disorders
Paranoid disorders
Schizophrenic disorders
UNDERSTANDING MENTAL DISORDERS 512
Major models of mental disorder
Using the models to make sense of schizophrenia
Making judgments about individuals
SUMMARY 524

15 THERAPIES FOR PERSONAL CHANGE 526

THE THERAPEUTIC CONTEXT 529
Overview of kinds of therapy
Entering therapy
Goals and settings
Healers and therapists
HISTORICAL CONTEXT 532
PSYCHODYNAMIC THERAPIES 534
Freudian psychoanalysis
Beyond Freud
BEHAVIOR THERAPIES 539
Counterconditioning
Contingency management
Social learning therapy
Generalization techniques
COGNITIVE THERAPIES 547
Cognitive behavior modification
Changing false beliefs
EXISTENTIAL-HUMANISTIC THERAPIES 549
Group therapies
Marital and family therapy
BIOMEDICAL THERAPIES 553
Psychosurgery and electroconvulsive therapy
Chemotherapy
THERAPEUTIC EFFECTIVENESS 557
PROMOTING MENTAL HEALTH 562
SUMMARY 563

PART SEVEN **SOCIAL PROCESSES** 565

16 **THE SOCIAL BASES OF BEHAVIOR** 566

THE APPROACH OF SOCIAL PSYCHOLOGY 569
  The person in the social environment
  The importance of social reality
  Social applications
SOCIAL PERCEPTION 573
  Impression formation
  Attribution
ATTITUDES AND PERSUASION 580
  The nature of attitudes
  Persuasive communications
INTERPERSONAL ATTRACTION 585
  Reasons for affiliation
  Liking
  Loving
GROUP PROCESSES 592
  Group form and function
  Group influence
  Group leadership
  Intergroup relations
SUMMARY 606

17 **EXPLORING SOCIAL ISSUES** 608

HUMAN POTENTIAL AND SOCIAL INFLUENCE 611
  The puzzle of human nature
  Individuation and deindividuation
DEHUMANIZED RELATIONSHIPS 618
  The functions of dehumanization
  Dehumanization techniques
OBEDIENCE TO AUTHORITY
  Milgram's obedience paradigmAuthority systems, disobedience, and you
HUMAN AGGRESSION AND VIOLENCE 627
  Aggression as inborn
  Physiological bases of aggression
  The frustration-aggression hypotheses
  Agression as provoked readiness
  Aggression as socially learned
  The violence of pornography
PSYCHOLOGY BEYOND THE INDIVIDUAL 634
  Social dilemmas
  Areas of application
SUMMARY 639

A POSTSCRIPT: PSYCHOLOGY AND YOU 640
APPENDIX: UNDERSTANDING RESEARCH 641
GLOSSARY III
REFERENCES XIX
ACKNOWLEDGMENTS LI
NAME INDEX LIX
SUBJECT INDEX LXIX

INTRODUCTION TO THE PROLOGUE
by Phil Zimbardo

In each of our lives, special events occur that we remember with a vividness that grows rather than dims over the years. Often they are experiences of significant learning, times when we have discovered in ourselves or in others some source of knowledge that influences the paths we travel in our journey through life.

One of those prized times happened for me when, as an undergraduate, I attended my first psychology convention. It was the 1954 annual meeting of the American Psychological Association at which investigators doing basic and applied research presented their latest findings. The very first talk I attended was about the lecturer's research on the role of motivation and reward in learning. That was my special time out-of-ordinary-time. I began to sense that I was experiencing something novel yet fundamental, something profound yet simple, something exciting yet ordinary.

This "peak experience" was not inspired by the charismatic style of the lecturer; to the contrary, his presentation made no attempt to be "flashy." Rather, what I heard was an eloquently clear and concise summary of a Yale University professor's attempt to discover some basic principles that explained how organisms learn.

My reaction was also not attributable to the obvious relevance of the findings to my personal life. His subjects were white laboratory rats; to a youngster raised in a New York City ghetto, rats were not supposed to go to Ivy League colleges where they learned to be smart—they were just rotten rodents to be exterminated.

What was so captivating then? It was the vision of this researcher systematically going about the task of uncovering clues to some of nature's well-guarded secrets. What he communicated to me was a total commitment to a life's work of finding the right questions to ask, developing methods for getting some good answers, and using that new information as a lever to pry loose the next clue to the mystery of human and animal behavior.

After hearing that lecture by Neal Miller, I knew that I wanted "a piece of the action." So instead of going to work, I went to Yale Graduate School to study under Professor Miller and become a research psychologist.

The enthusiasm for research that Miller displayed during that convention lecture paled in comparison to the excitement and delight he expressed openly in class or in the laboratory over an interesting idea that could be tested in an experiment or a hot piece of evidence that supported a theoretical prediction. The more I learned about this modest, unassuming master psychologist, the deeper became my respect for what he represented.

The country boy twang in his voice gave little indication of the sophistication of his thinking nor of his ready willingness to entertain new and different ideas. For example, Miller received his Ph.D. from Yale, where he was influenced by Clark Hull applying Pavlov's principles of conditioning to Thorndike's trial-and-error learning. (These names you will come to know as you read on in this text). But then he went to Vienna for psychoanalytic training, where he was analyzed by Heinz Hartmann, an analyst recommended by Sigmund Freud. During World War II he studied fear and courage in aerial combat, extending ideas from his laboratory research on learned fear and conflict. He went on to study social learning and imitation and then attempted to show that neurotic behavior could be understood, researched, and treated as a special case of general principles of learning. His book, Personality and Psychotherapy, written with John Dollard, encouraged psychologists to think more broadly about investigating normal and abnormal aspects of human behavior.

While I was at Yale, I saw this pioneering behavioral researcher take a new path, one literally into the dark recesses where all learning takes place—the brain. Miller and his team of talented students performed the first experiments in which learning was influenced by direct stimulation of deep areas of the brain. From then until now, Neal Miller has studied many forms of learning, both from the inside out and outside in—being as interested in physiological mechanisms as in environmental influences. His work has always been guided by the twin goals of using rigorous scientific methods to discover basic laws of behavior and mental processes, and applying the results of such research to improve the quality of human functioning.

I have invited him to share with me the pleasure of introducing you to psychology as science, and psychology as vital in everyday life. Professor Miller has elected to discuss how basic research motivated by intellectual curiosity and applied research motivated by the desire to solve a problem unexpectedly came together in the discovery of a revolutionary treatment for mental disorders. Since he modestly avoids mention of how his own work illustrates this same basic theme, I shall add a postscript that does so.

△ ▮ *Neal Miller and Phil Zimbardo*

PROLOGUE
by Neal Miller

In a world in which science is increasingly affecting all of our lives, it is important for the citizens of a democracy to understand how scientific research leads to increased knowledge and how this increased knowledge leads to practical applications. I shall attempt to illustrate this, first by a simple analogy and then by a few concrete examples.

A great puzzle

To begin with the simple analogy, scientific research is like trying to put together the pieces of a large and complicated jigsaw puzzle. At the very beginning, one could set oneself the goal of making a narrow path straight across the center of the puzzle from a specific point on one side to a specific one on the other. That task would be like applied research directed at a very special goal, such as a cure for cancer or the prevention of strokes. Some people think we should concentrate on this type of research because it has immediate relevance. However, in the early stages of working on a large and complex puzzle, such a strategy is likely to be extremely inefficient, and indeed may be impossible. It is much better to proceed by looking for pieces that fit together, perhaps beginning with the margins where the problem is simpler because some pieces have straight sides. Similarly in scientific research it often is more efficient to be guided by how the facts of nature fit together, rather than by a highly specific goal. Research guided primarily by how the facts of nature fit together, rather than by particular utility, is called *basic research*.

But after a whole section of the puzzle is almost solved, a person who wants to complete a specific line across the puzzle may find it efficient to look for the one or two missing pieces whose shapes and colors now are defined by the already completed parts. By that time, it also will be possible to complete many other paths across the puzzle.

Given a large complex puzzle in various stages of solution, should we not concentrate on looking for places where only a few missing pieces are needed to complete a path to a highly desirable goal? Indeed we should, and indeed we do. The rewards for putting in those last few pieces are so high that usually there is no shortage of ambitious young scientists and engineers eager to fill in the last gap. Furthermore, usually there is no shortage of money; appropriate organizations ranging from private foundations, to governmental operating agencies, to private businesses such as drug companies are looking for just such opportunities. And to give the contributions of such agencies their due credit, the pieces they add to the puzzle for the immediate practical payoff may also be valuable as points of departure for further basic research leading off in quite unexpected directions.

The analogy I have given you is imperfect because a puzzle has definite known boundaries, so that from the beginning it is possible to draw a line across it as the path toward a specific goal. Actually, science is more like exploring an endless, unknown continent, so that in the beginning one may not even be able to see the most important goals. On the new continent, explorers may not have any idea what they are going to discover until they are already within sight of it. They must be guided by what they find. It may be far more efficient to follow the path of a crooked river than to decide in advance to go in a straight line in a certain direction before one knows whether or not that will lead into the cliffs of a mountain. And, again, once one has made the unexpected discovery of nuggets of gold in a stream bed, there is no shortage of prospectors eager to rush into that area.

Because basic research involves exploring the unknown, one cannot predict what one is going to discover—something of immediate value or that one has entered a blind alley. At other times, what one discovers may seem to have no practical use but may turn out to be an important step on a long path that unexpectedly leads to something of great practical value. But history has proved again and again that in the long run the process of discovery, seeking new knowledge for its own sake, contributes to enough practical results that supporting it is an extremely profitable investment.

Now let us turn to a real example of a remarkable behavioral change produced by scientific research.

A remarkable behavioral change

Thirty years ago, the conditions in the disturbed wards of large mental hospitals were incredibly horrible. Day and night there were moans of despair, meaningless babblings, and subhuman screams of fear and rage. The stench of urine and feces was nauseating. The largest group of patients were schizophrenic and were considered to be completely hopeless; they would never leave the mental hospital to live with their loved ones again.

These terrible conditions have been dramatically changed. Patients now go to the bathroom, remain clothed, do not annoy each other, and can be given psychotherapy. Cases of schizophrenia are no longer considered to be hopeless. The use of new types of drugs made these revolutionary changes possible. *Chlorpromazine* was one of the first and most important of these drugs that led to these merciful practical benefits.

How was chlorpromazine developed? The Committee of Brain Sciences got money for a historian of science, Dr. Judith Swazey, to find out. I shall summarize the main findings of her search, the details of which can be found in her fascinating and instructive book.* I shall add, too, a few observations from my own experience.

The first pieces of a great puzzle

As you know, alchemists began by setting themselves the very practical task of finding a way to change cheap metals into gold. Gradually, they became more interested in discovering the laws of how different amounts of different elements combined, and they became known as chemists. One British chemist tried to alter the composition of a coal-tar product to form a medicine, which seemed to have a somewhat similar composition; he failed to do that but produced instead the first artificial dye, a purple one. As the British dye industry became profitable, the interest in chemistry increased. But the chemists in the British dye industry were almost exclusively interested in practical ways to make dyes. In Germany and Switzerland, by contrast, there was a closer association between the dye industry and the universities, and more emphasis on basic research. The German chemists became interested in the problem of how compounds made of exactly the same elements could be so different. They gradually discovered that these differences were caused by the fact that the same group of atoms could be put together in different patterns; for example, in a straight chain or in

different kinds of rings. Because of their emphasis on basic research to get such types of knowledge, the supremacy of the dye and other chemical industries passed from England to Germany and Switzerland.

A little over 100 years ago, a German research chemist was investigating the structure of two dyes, a violet and a blue one. He found that they both had the same central structure of three rings. The different colors were caused by the different short chains of atoms that were attached to the outside of these three rings. At that time there was no reason to suspect that these three rings would be the basis for a drug that would have the dramatic effect of improving conditions in mental hospitals.

From a deadly fungus to antihistamines

Another set of parts that begin to fit together in our great jigsaw puzzle involves a strange fungus, called *ergot,* that poisons grain but had been used to stop bleeding and to produce contractions of the uterus. A British scientist discovered that one of the chemicals he purified from the poisonous mixture produced by ergot was especially effective in producing contractions in strips of tissue from a cat's intestine or uterus. He called this chemical histamine, and started to study it systematically. If he had stopped with its effects on isolated tissues, he would have failed to see its most significant effects. But he discovered that when he injected it into the veins of an anesthetized dog or cat, its action of causing contractions in the smooth muscle of the gut was accompanied by the *opposite* effect of producing *relaxation* of the smooth muscle of small arteries and capillaries. This second effect caused a quick fall in blood pressure; the animal went into a state of shock and died. This shock was similar to that of a severe allergic reaction. A long line of subsequent research showed that histamine is released in the body during allergic reactions such as asthma, hives, or hay fever.

Once the effects of histamine were known, it was logical to look for a drug that would block these effects, an *antihistamine.* A French scientist measured three criteria to determine the antihistamine activity of the many drugs he tested: (a) ability to stop the contractions produced by histamine in a strip of intestine, (b) ability to protect animals from the asthma-like symptoms produced by inhaling a spray of histamine, and (c) ability to prevent the fatal shock

---

*Swazey, J. P. (1974). *Chlorpromazine in psychiatry. A study of therapeutic innovation.* Cambridge, Mass.: MIT Press.

produced by injecting histamine into a vein. Such tests, of course, could not be performed on people; in each case, guinea pigs were used. Testing a large number of plausible compounds in this way, the French scientist discovered two that had the effect of blocking histamine. But both of them were too poisonous to be used with people. At this point, a French drug firm joined in the research; by 1944 they found some antihistamines that they could sell for purposes such as drying up runny noses produced by hay fever and for treating asthma.

Back to the three-ringed structure

Now the story returns to the blue dye built around the three central rings. This dye had been found to have some action against malaria. Therefore, the pharmacologists at the French drug company started on a program to see if they could change the outer structure of this dye molecule to make it into a better cure for malaria. They built many new molecules around the central three rings and tested the ability of the new substances to cure animals experimentally infected with malaria. During routine tests of some of the new drugs, they found some that blocked histamine, even though their structure was different from that of the early antihistamines. Therefore, they changed the direction of their research and started looking for drugs based on the central three rings that would have a stronger effect against histamine. Eventually, they created a drug that could be sold as an antihistamine and that also was found to help in the treatment of motion sickness.

Evidence of behavioral effects

One of the difficulties with the antihistamines was that they made people sleepy. The pharmacologists at the drug companies were interested in getting rid of this troublesome side effect. In order to find out quickly and efficiently which changes in the outer structure of the drug molecule could reduce this sleepiness, they needed a test that would work with animals such as rats or mice. Finally, they found a good one that enabled them to evaluate many different chemicals that had the effect of blocking histamine. They gave the animals a barbiturate, which is a sleep-producing drug, and found out how much

was added to the time that the animal remained asleep if it also received a dose of the antihistamine. Unfortunately for their present goal, the new antihistamine based on the three rings had an especially strong effect of adding to the sleeping time.

Thus far, the side effect of producing drowsiness had been considered to be undesirable. But Dr. Henri Laborit, a French naval surgeon, was interested in using drugs to try to combat surgical shock, a significant cause of death in severely injured patients. He tried to put animals, and later patients, into a state of "artificial hibernation." He thought the drowsiness and certain other effects produced by the antihistamine with three rings would be especially useful. When he tested it on patients, he found that it produced a state of happy, calm drowsiness. This was the first hint that this kind of drug might have any effect that could be useful in mental hospitals.

Development of tests of animal learning

At this point, we need to go back to what had happened at another part of our huge jigsaw puzzle. Darwin's theory of evolution had caused biologists to look for similarities between the behavior of animals and people. There was a burst of stories about animals who did clever things, such as opening gates as if they really understood how the latch held the gate shut.

In a series of experiments at the end of the nineteenth century, an American psychologist, Edward L. Thorndike, showed that animals could learn to do such things by a much less glamorous process that he called trial-and-error learning. A hungry cat was locked up inside a cage, with a dish of tempting food set outside. The cat would push, pull, and bite at various parts of the apparatus in a more-or-less random manner. If some series of movements happened by chance to open the door, the cat would dash out rewarded by freedom and food. On the next trial, the movements rewarded by escape and food were more likely to be repeated, until finally the cat learned to perform promptly the acts that led most directly to the reward. This basic research was the beginning of the systematic study of animal learning.

Soon other experimenters developed different devices. One of these was a maze in which the problem was to see how the animals stopped entering into blind alleys and learned to use the shortest path to the goal of food. Another was a test of muscular strength and coordination in which rats were trained to climb up a rope to get food on a platform at the top. Some experimenters began using these methods to study the effects of antihistamine drugs on rats and found that they interfered with the maze more than with the rope-climbing test. This result suggested that these drugs affected some higher brain function more than they did muscular strength and coordination. Yet other work showed that the antihistamine drugs that had the greatest effect on sleeping time were *not* those that had the greatest effect on the tests of learned behavior. These results suggested that the drugs might have two different types of effects on the brain.

Decision to look for larger behavioral effects

By 1950, the French drug company was impressed enough by the evidence for behavioral effects of antihistamines that they thought it would be worthwhile to look for the ones that produced the largest such effects. This time many drugs were tested for their effects on adding to the barbiturate sleeping time, adding to the effects of pain-killing drugs, and disrupting rope-climbing and maze behaviors. From this program, which used animal subjects, they hoped to discover drugs that might be useful in surgical anesthesia, in treating epilepsy, or in psychiatry.

Their screening tests showed that one of the compounds with the three central rings which they had discarded earlier because it had only weak antihistamine effects had the strongest effects in the behavioral tests. Changing a few of the outer atoms in this compound produced a drug—**chlorpromazine** (abbreviated as CPZ)—that had exceptionally strong behavioral effects. The company then proceeded to more thorough animal studies of its various actions on the body and on behavior. Since none of these was harmful, they gave it human clinical trials. The hope grew that this new drug might be useful in surgery, in medicine and obstetrics, and in psychiatry to interrupt maniacal outbursts of extremely active behavior.

Resistance to evidence for drug treatment of mental illness

Dr. Laborit used CPZ in combination with other drugs to help in his procedure of artificial hibernation. He observed a "disinterestedness" in his patients and suggested that the drug might be of psychiatric use in making therapy by prolonged sleep safer. Neither artificial hibernation nor prolonged sleep was particularly successful but, during 1952 and 1953, evidence gradually accumulated that CPZ was remarkably effective in treating certain cases of psychosis. Its use met strong resistance, however. The general feeling was that it was incredible, impossible, that a drug could modify a mental disorder which is such a complex phenomenon of neural, biochemical, and social factors. Actually, some of the most spectacular results came accidentally, as told by a Canadian psychiatrist:

> "At that time we thought we were just treating excited states with CPZ and attributed the improvement that the schizophrenics showed to that effect of the drug. But then, about three months after the trial had ended, we discovered that some of the chronic back-ward schizophrenics had been accidentally left on large doses of CPZ. And incredibly, to us, four or five of the back-ward patients were getting better. No one believed that a pill could cause remission in schizophrenia, and we seemed to be getting the best results with chronic paranoids, the group most refractory to treatment" (in Swazey, p. 157).

Two American drug companies refused a chance to acquire CPZ. The management did not want to gamble on a drug that had no clear-cut chance of large sales. At that time, Dr. Leonard Cook, a pharmacologist working with Smith Kline & French was on a project of comparing the behavioral effects of barbiturates used in sleeping pills with other compounds that might turn out to be new types of sleeping pills. He used a test in which a rat stood on a grid floor through which an electric shock could be given to its feet. Rats could climb a pole to escape the electric shock. A buzzer signaled that the shock was coming; by responding promptly the rat could completely avoid the shock. After training, normal rats would climb the pole promptly when either the buzzer or the shock was turned on. When different groups of rats were tested after receiving increasingly strong doses of barbiturates, they would continue to respond to the buzzer alone as well as to the shock alone until the dose was so large that they could not climb the pole. With CPZ, however, the situation was strikingly different. Animals stopped responding to the buzzer at doses much lower than those required to prevent them from responding to the shock. A similar difference appeared in tests of exploratory behavior; the CPZ animals became quiet long before they showed any signs of difficulty in walking, whereas the barbiturate animals continued to explore until it was difficult for them to walk. These tests clearly showed that CPZ had a type of action on the brain that was strikingly different from that of the barbiturates.

As a result of both clinical and experimental evidence, the officers at Smith Kline & French decided to acquire the American rights to the new drug and make a major effort to promote it.

The resistance to trying out any drug for treating mental patients was still strong; it was hard for the drug company to get leaders of American psychiatry to start clinical trials. But the conditions in the disturbed wards in the large state mental hospitals were desperate, so CPZ was tried out there. As it proved to be effective, its use in such hospitals increased. But old patterns of thought are hard to change. Although psychiatrists and psychologists were forced to admit that the new drugs were useful, many of them said the drugs were nothing more than a substitute for the straitjacket used for the complete physical restraint of violent patients. Thus, the idea persisted that nothing as simple as a drug could possibly have any real effects on anything as complex as a mental illness.

Some crucial tests

The success of the drugs in relieving the horrible conditions in the disturbed back wards of the large mental hospitals enabled some of the more farsighted workers in mental health to persuade Congress to give funds to support a large increase in research on psychopharmacology, the effect of drugs on behavior. Part of the increased money was used to develop better methods of measuring symptoms of mental disease, especially of schizophrenia, the most serious and expensive of the major psychoses.

First the Veterans Administration and then the National Institute of Mental Health organized studies in which a number of different hospitals agreed to cooperate in applying the same experimental designs and measures of symptoms to study the effects of the new drugs. The clear-cut conclusion of these studies was that CPZ relieves some of the most trou- blesome symptoms of schizophrenia, such as hallucinations (hearing voices or seeing things that were not there), peculiar associations between words, inappropriate expressions of strong emotions, and delusions (such as believing that an evil secret gang is using radar beams to spy on and persecute you). CPZ does not merely have a general calming effect; along with quieting down extreme states of agitation, extremely withdrawn patients become more normally responsive to events and people in the real world. In short, CPZ has specific antischizophrenic effects.

Although it is not a complete cure, CPZ goes a long way toward enabling the patients to ignore or control troublesome symptoms, such as hallucinations. It makes the patients accessible to social retraining and psychotherapy. Given in smaller doses to patients released from the mental hospitals, it definitely reduces a tendency for them to break down again so that they must be readmitted. Most of the terrible conditions in the disturbed wards of the large mental hospitals are now but a dim memory of a horrid past.

In addition to the relief of incredible suffering by schizophrenic patients and their loved ones, the money saved by avoiding many years of hospitalization and by return of many (but far from all) patients to productive work has been enough to repay many times over all of the money that ever has been invested in research on it.

The demonstration that a drug can have a major effect on mental illness resulted in increased investments in psychopharmacology by drug firms and by the government, primarily via the National Institute of Mental Health. This has led to the discovery of drugs to help in the treatment of other conditions— for example, the excruciating torture of mental depressions that can drive patients to suicide. Furthermore, the usefulness of the drugs led to additional funds for basic research that have produced exciting advances in physiological psychology and neuroscience.

But more remains to be accomplished. We do not yet understand the causes of schizophrenia well enough to prevent it, and the drugs that we have are not a complete cure. A certain percentage of the patients who are kept on CPZ and similar drugs for a long time develop disturbing, uncontrollable movements. While many patients have been returned to their loved ones, and a significant number to productive work, unfortunately others who do not have loving families or are less able to cope have been turned out on the streets. Thus, although an enormous amount of misery has been relieved, much more remains to be done by additional research and by more humane social actions.

A summarizing look backward

A number of lessons may be learned from the history I have just described. Many crucial discoveries along many different pathways led in ways that could not have been predicted to the making of CPZ. Some of the research, like Thorndike's work on animal learning, was purely basic, exploring the unknown for the sake of discovering new knowledge rather than to achieve any given practical goal. Other research, like studying the effects of compounds derived from ergot, was searching for knowledge without any very specific goal in mind, but in an area that seemed likely to lead to practical results because, in addition to being a poison, the complex mixture of chemicals in ergot did have some uses. Yet other research was distinctly applied, such as trying to find a drug that would block the effects of histamine. In one case, the discovery that it was difficult to achieve the goal of reducing the undesirable side effects, like the drowsiness produced by antihistamine drugs, led to the decision to reverse the direction of research toward the opposite goal of trying to increase these effects. This reversal of direction produced profitable results—a new type of sleeping pill, and also eventually a powerful drug to treat schizophrenia. This latter discovery was so unexpected, and most specialists thought that it was so impossible, that it took strong evidence, some of it secured by accident, to convince them that it had been done. Until near the very end, nobody could have predicted that any of these discoveries would lead to a treatment for mental disorder.

The details will be somewhat different in other examples of the process by which research leads to valuable applications. But, in general, the lesson of the importance of basic research is much the same. For example, Comroe and Dripps (1977)* made a study of the ten advances that leading physicians treating the heart and lungs said had done the most to relieve the suffering and save the lives of their patients. Tracing back the 663 pieces of research essential for these ten major advances, they found that 42 percent had been carried out by scientists whose goal at the time was unrelated to the later clinical advances—scientists who were seeking knowledge for the sake of knowledge. Without this basic research,

many crucial parts of it on animals, the practical applications, such as open-heart surgery, would have been impossible.

A catastrophic effect on motor coordination

In other parts of the great puzzle, other pieces are still just beginning to fit together. One of my close friends was a skillful skier. Suddenly he found his skill slipping away; he began to take nasty spills on trails that had never bothered him before. Next, his hands began to tremble. Then, a rigid muscular tension developed, making his movements stiff and awkward. Furthermore, each simple task that he previously had performed automatically now required his full attention, so that he could not do two things at once. For example, if he was holding his lunch in a brown bag and turned his attention to opening the door to his car, he dropped his lunch. He said: "It is like a lot of circuits are being removed from my computer." He had the classic symptoms of Parkinson's disease.

The happier part of this story begins with the fact that basic research on animals, stimulated by the successful application of CPZ and other drugs, had discovered that a certain chemical, dopamine, is used to transmit messages across tiny gaps in the connections between nerve cells in a part of the brain that is involved in motor coordination. Then studies of the brains of Parkinson patients killed in accidents found that they had much less dopamine in this part of the brain. After that discovery, a logical idea was to try to supply the missing dopamine, but other research on animals had revealed a barrier that prevents certain substances, such as dopamine, from entering the brain. Still other studies on animals had found that (a) L-dopa is a building block of dopamine; (b) when more of it is present, more dopamine is made; and (c) L-dopa can get through the barrier and into the brain. Fitting these separate pieces of knowledge together led to the use of large doses of L-dopa to treat Parkinson's disease.

This treatment made my friend mercifully much better for approximately 10 years until his brain's ability to make dopamine became too low to be helped. And now to the final part of my story.

---

*Comroe, J. H., & Dripps, J.D. (1977, January 31). *The top ten clinical advances in cardiovascular-pulmonary medicine and surgery, 1945–1975 (Final report).* Bethesda, MD: National Heart, Lung, and Blood Institute.

Some hints toward a hypothesis about schizophrenia

Whenever my friend was given doses of L-dopa that were too large, he began to have hallucinations, to see and hear things that were not there, somewhat like a schizophrenic person. But if patients are given too much CPZ for the treatment of schizophrenia, they may develop symptoms like those of Parkinson's disease. Furthermore, the drugs that are most effective against schizophrenia are also most effective in producing the Parkinson-like side effects of uncontrollable movements. These facts suggest that schizophrenia may involve an overactivity of dopamine in some part of the brain. Thus, schizophrenia and Parkinson's disease may represent changes in opposite directions from normal.

There is another interesting fact. If patients who have been immobilized by Parkinson's disease for many years are suddenly subjected to a severe stress, such as a fire, they may suddenly leap out of their wheelchairs and run to safety. After the extreme stress is over, they lose all their motor coordination again. Apparently, extreme stress can compensate for a lack of dopamine. On the other side of the picture, it is generally believed that, in a susceptible person, severe stress can precipitate the onset of schizophrenia. And even with apparently normal people, the extraordinary stress of combat in war can produce schizophrenia-like symptoms. The suggestion is that stress and dopamine may summate so that stress will correct for a deficiency but also can produce the same effect as an oversupply.

The description I have just recounted is oversimplified. There are a number of pieces which, while they come tantalizingly close to fitting into the puzzle, definitely do not quite fit. We shall have to try to arrange them in somewhat different ways or find other missing pieces. Some challenging questions are: Why do drugs that have a profound effect on motor coordination also have a profound effect on thoughts and perceptions? Do the Parkinson patients suffer from too little activity in the brain mechanisms involved in certain inborn organized patterns of motor behavior? And do schizophrenic patients suffer from too much activity (or too little inhibitory control of) the mechanisms responsible for certain innately organized patterns of thought and perception? We cannot say—yet.

POSTSCRIPT
by Phil Zimbardo

Neal Miller's recent research has provided a new window through which we can see more clearly how our physiological processes, such as blood pressure, and even the complex action of the immune system, can be influenced by reinforcement—just as simple responses of his rats were reinforced. He and others are showing how we learn to get reinforcement for being sick—physically and psychologically—and are pointing the way toward new directions of reinforcing "wellness behaviors." His ideas have been important in the development of a new area of research and application, behavioral medicine—an interdisciplinary field where issues in psychology and medicine intersect.

The work of Miller and his students on visceral learning and stress has helped provide the scientific foundation for the development of biofeedback. This technique detects small bodily changes, amplifies them and "feeds them back" to the person via visual or auditory signals. Through this means, the person learns to control a variety of internal "problem" behaviors, such as headaches or abnormal blood pressure. Miller and his colleagues have applied this method to help patients with broken spinal cords sit up, stand, and leave the hospital for the first time. Before training, these patients would ordinarily faint as their blood pressure dropped when they sat up. They were trained to detect small changes in their blood pressure and were reinforced for slight increases until they were able to be erect without fainting. In turn, basic research on these patients has shown that they can control blood pressure directly rather than affecting it indirectly by changing their breathing or tensing their muscles. Learning such direct control had been believed to be impossible.

Witnessing the emergence of the personal control and pride that accompany such a big change in a patient's behavior is a source of great joy to Miller and his colleagues. In this and other ways, Neal Miller sets a special example for psychologists and other researchers of how research and practice can go hand in hand so that we may know more about ourselves and care better for each other.

Part One

Foundations

Chapter One
Probing the Mysteries of Mind and Behavior

Chapter Two
Lifespan Psychological Development

Chapter Three
The Biology of Behavior

PROBING THE MYSTERIES OF MIND AND BEHAVIOR

■ PSYCHOLOGY: DEFINITIONS AND GOALS
What psychology is
What psychology tries to do
■ RESEARCH FOUNDATIONS
Methods for gathering data
Enhancing objectivity
Going beyond the facts
■ ALTERNATIVE PERSPECTIVES
Differing assumptions and approaches
Psychological models as maps
Using psychological models
■ PLANS FOR OUR PSYCHOLOGICAL JOURNEY
■ SUMMARY

Welcome to the start of what I hope will prove an exciting journey for you as we explore together many fascinating aspects of human nature. We will try to unravel some of the mysteries of why people behave, think, and feel as they do. In addition to learning *what* psychologists have found about these mysteries, you will discover much about *how* they have done so.

Psychology and Life is more than a textbook filled with the facts of psychological research. It is also a guidebook for appreciating how one asks psychological questions, seeks answers, and evaluates conclusions. Whether or not you choose psychology as a career, you cannot avoid using it informally in your everyday life. Even without further formal training, a careful reading of this introduction to psychology should increase your curiosity about the origins of behaviors you observe, broaden your theories about human nature, and sharpen your predictions about how you and others might act in future situations.

Our exploration of psychology will follow many different paths. It will take us to research laboratories throughout the world, to mental hospitals, nurseries, schools, factories, and many other places where we can observe psychology in action.

Every scientific journey begins with an adventurer puzzled enough by some uncertainty to ask, "I wonder why . . . ?"

> All persons are puzzles until
> at last we find in some word or
> act the key to the man, to the
> woman: straightway all their past
> words and actions lie in light
> before us.
>
> Ralph Waldo Emerson, *Journals*

The following three *Opening Cases* offer a sampling of the adventures ahead.

Tina: A terribly good mother turkey

Turkeys are generally good mothers. They spend much time caring for their young—cleaning, warming, and feeding them. Young chicks respond by chirping contentedly with a characteristic loud and clear "cheep-cheep" sound. But a researcher observing the behavior of turkeys noticed one day that a turkey chick stopped making its usual sound; it still walked around actively, but it did not chirp. Tina, its formerly affectionate mother, stopped tending it, ignored it, and finally killed it! Why did this female turkey murder her own helpless chick? Could the maternal behavior of mamma turkey have been influenced by that "cheep-cheep" sound?

Yes indeed; it has been found that this particular sound triggers an automatic reaction in all mother turkeys. To demonstrate how "blindly automatic" that response is, the researcher put a stuffed polecat near Tina. She furiously attacked this creature, who is a natural enemy. But when the stuffed polecat made the "cheep-cheep" baby turkey sound (from a tape recorder planted inside it), Tina gathered it to her bosom, giving it all the love that only a mother turkey can. Later, when the tape-recorded "cheep" stopped, Tina turned terrible, tearing apart the silent polecat (Fox, 1974).

Many other species also exhibit mechanical patterns of behavior during episodes of courtship, mating, maternal care, or aggression. Such unlearned behavior—which is released by some specific object or event in the environment, such as a particular color, shape, sound, or smell—is called a *fixed action pattern*. It is an inborn response to a given type of stimulation that is typical of a given species in its natural habitat. A blueprint for this instinctive behavior is genetically transmitted from one generation to the next, presumably because of its survival value among those animals who respond to the correct signals from nature.

Imo from Koshima

Much behavior is molded by basic biological needs for survival, but this is less so with animal species higher on the evolutionary ladder. When we observe primates such as monkeys, chimpanzees, apes, and people, we see cultural experiences coming to play a significant role.

Imo was a young female macaque living on the offshore Japanese island of Koshima. For years researchers had tried in vain to observe the life-style of her elusive troop of free-ranging monkeys. They finally enticed them out of the forest by leaving sweet potatoes and other treats as bait on an open beach, where observations could be made more easily.

Careful observation revealed that different subgroups had their own dietary preferences. Some ate meat, some fish, others roots; some ate fruit with the pit; others threw the pit away. Eating, then, was not a matter of simply using what was available to satisfy hunger. It was dictated partly by the customs of each monkey troop.

When the researchers' goodies were first put out, the older monkeys resisted sampling them at all. It was the younger ones who were more adventurous and took the risk, after which the elders followed their example.

Then the young female, Imo, did something no other monkey had done. She began carrying her sweet potatoes to a pool to wash off the sand before eating them. In a few weeks her playmates began copying her; soon her siblings and other close associates regularly washed their potatoes, too. After a while, Imo introduced a new ritual—taking potatoes that had already been cleaned in the fresh-water pool and washing them in the sea. Presumably the salt water added flavor or salt they needed in their diet. When the researchers returned ten years later, the habit of washing sweet potatoes in the sea had spread to two thirds of all the monkeys. This habit of sweet-potato washing had become "completely established as an element in the troop's cultural life."

In order to keep the troop in the open area for more extensive observations, the researchers now changed the diet to unhusked rice, since the monkeys took longer to sift the rice grains out of the sand before eating them. But the researchers had not reckoned with Imo's inventiveness. She scooped up handfuls of rice and sand and threw the whole lot into the water. The sand sank, the rice floated, and Imo skimmed off her fast-food snacks. Again, her

△ ▌ *A macaque washing fruit.*

discovery was copied by her companions, and the new eating habit soon became ingrained in the life of the group (Itani, 1961).

For reasons unknown, Imo was a more radical, creative thinker than her peers. But the ability of the others to learn by watching her resulted in shared skills, shared knowledge, and new ritualized ways of behaving for the whole group. What Imo and her monkey troop from Koshima had done was to create a simple culture, a prototype of human cultures, in which learned skills and preferences for particular ways of doing things are shared with others and even with later generations, supplementing inborn, genetically programmed abilities.

◁ ▌ *Dan W. before the murders.*

Killer Dan
Generations of readers have been fascinated by Robert Louis Stevenson's tale of the mild-mannered Dr. Jekyll, whose personality is suddenly transformed into that of a fiendish maniac, Mr. Hyde, when he drinks a chemical potion. This fictional portrait leads readers to pause and wonder about the stability of their own personalities and to reconsider whether deep within the ordinary sophisticated self they present to the world may lurk a "darker," more primitive side of their nature. The recent, strange-but-true case of "killer Dan" raises these doubts anew.

Dan W. was an all-American boy. This good-looking, robust family man had been a policeman and a heroic firefighter, and though quite young, had won election to a position in his city's government on a law-and-order platform. He was an advocate of strict morality and opposed liberalizing the restrictions against the city's large homosexual population. He was sometimes at odds with another city official who represented that group of citizens.

One day, Dan unexpectedly resigned from his office, claiming he could not afford to continue to support his family in that low-paying position. Then he abruptly changed his mind and asked the mayor to reinstate him. The mayor refused. Shortly thereafter, Dan smuggled a pistol into City Hall and killed the mayor with a barrage of bullets fired at point-blank range. He then reloaded his gun, went to the office of his gay opponent, and shot him to death. A little later, he surrendered to the police. He admitted his guilt but offered no explanation of the reasons behind his sudden personality change. How could he have gone from being a conservative, religious, law-supporting "pillar of the community" to a cold-blooded murderer who showed no remorse?

At his trial, a number of possible motives surfaced, and others were offered. Might his violence have been triggered by motives of frustration, revenge, hatred for homosexuals, or even latent homosexual tendencies in himself that he was unconsciously trying to reject? Some argued that he was overwhelmed by the build-up of stressful circumstances in his life. Others felt he was simply playing out the American macho male stereotype, in which might makes right, especially with a gun in hand.

Did these murders really show a change in personality? Had he not shown the same trait of *impulsivity* earlier in his heroic rescues during fires, and in his sudden public resignation and quick reversal? Maybe he hadn't really changed, but was only showing his impulsiveness in a different kind of setting.

Dan's lawyer was able to present a defense for this confessed murderer of two city officials that got him off with a light sentence of 7 years, 8 months. The jury accepted the argument that Dan's capacity to reason, plan, and comprehend the full meaning of his actions had been diminished by the large amounts of junk foods he ate during bouts of depression! This "Twinkies defense" was accepted by jury and judge as a physiological basis for the violent behavioral acts. It was a new version of the insanity defense. Needless to say, many people in San Francisco, where the dual murders took place, were outraged by this lenient sentence— and 5 years later by Dan's early parole in 1984. (For more details on this case, see Weiss, 1984.)

Dan's case raises many puzzling issues— about his motivation, his state of mind at the time he was facing each of his victims, the extent to which his deeds were premeditated or driven by uncontrollable impulse or passion, and whether this was a real-life parallel to the fictional case of Dr. Jekyll and Mr. Hyde. It also sensitizes us to the operation of psychological concepts in legal principles and judicial decisions. *Should* there be a defense that absolves murderers from full criminal responsibility? Under what circumstances, if any, might *your* actions no longer be governed by ordinary considerations of morality? Are there any circumstances under which *you* might become an assassin?

You will need to learn much more psychology before beginnng to get some answers to such big questions. This text will help you do so, though you will see, too, that psychology itself is a long way from having all the answers.

PSYCHOLOGY: DEFINITIONS AND GOALS

You now have a few clues as to what a course in psychology is about. In this section we'll look at some formal definitions of what psychology is to psychologists and preview what psychologists are trying to accomplish.

What psychology is

Psychology began as the study of mental events—what was happening in the human mind. With roots in philosophy and physiology, psychology did not emerge as a science in its own right until a little over a hundred years ago. The first formal experimental laboratory was established in 1879 in Leipzig, Germany, by Wilhelm Wundt; a smaller, less formal one was established at about the same time in the United States by William James at Harvard University.

Wundt and James differed strikingly in their approaches. Wundt was a precise experimentalist whose focus was on analysis of separate sensations, as reported by subjects trained to analyze the elements of their own consciousness. James, on the other hand, did little formal research. He was a philosopher-psychologist trained in medicine, and his interests ranged widely, including topics as diverse as habit, emotion, and religious experience. James believed in free will and wrote about inner experience as an ongoing, flowing process not divisible into independent sensations.

Early in the twentieth century, American psychologists sought to develop a more objective science by investigating only outer actions observable to everyone. For many years thereafter, psychology was defined as the *scientific study of the behavior of organisms.* The observable behavior of both humans and other species became its subject matter, and the precision and objectivity demanded in other sciences were now demanded in psychology.

As the field of psychology has matured, it has become clear that we cannot understand actions without some understanding of mental processes. At the same time, as we shall see, investigators have devised new ways of studying mental events that are indirect but much more objective than the older method of simply having subjects try to analyze their

◁ *Wilhelm Wundt (1832–1920).*

◁ *William James (1842–1910).*

own consciousness. As a result, many psychologists now define **psychology** as the *scientific study of behavior and mental processes.* This is the definition we will use throughout this text. We will see, however, that the concept of mental processes, or ''mind,'' is regarded differently by psychologists from different backgrounds.

Psychology today is a way of thinking broadly about how living creatures cope with their environment and interact with each other. It is a behavioral science at the intersection of philosophy, biology, sociology, physiology, and cultural anthropology. Though psychologists observe *specific instances* of behavior, what they are interested in discovering are *general laws of behavior.* Laws of behavior are statements that describe how the average individual is likely to behave under a specified set of conditions.

Psychologists ask such questions as, What would happen to behavior Z if stimulus X were changed? (e.g., How hard would you study if the teacher began to reward you with a gold star?) Does Y really make a difference in how organisms react? (e.g., Does your perception of how much control you have affect how happy and healthy you are?) How do personality traits A and B fit together? (e.g., How are shyness and aggressiveness related?)

If the storehouse of psychological knowledge is filled with observations and research findings derived

Test your "commonsense knowledge" of psychology on the 15 selected statements below. Mark *T* before those you think are true as stated and *F* before those statements you believe are false. Then check the footnote on page 8 for the answers (from Vaughan, 1977).

_____ 1. To change people's behavior toward members of ethnic minority groups, we must first change their attitudes.

_____ 2. Memory can be likened to a storage chest in the brain into which we deposit material and from which we can withdraw it later if needed. Occasionally, something gets lost from the "chest," and then we say we have forgotten.

_____ 3. The basis of the baby's love for its mother is the fact that the mother fulfills its physiological needs for food, etc.

_____ 4. The more highly motivated you are, the better you will do at solving a complex problem.

_____ 5. The best way to ensure that a desired behavior will persist after training is completed is to reward the behavior every single time it occurs throughout training (rather than intermittently).

_____ 6. A schizophrenic is someone with a split personality.

_____ 7. Fortunately for babies, human mothers have a strong maternal instinct.

_____ 8. Biologists study the body; psychologists study the mind.

_____ 9. Psychiatrists are defined as medical people who use psychoanalysis.

_____ 10. Children memorize much more easily than adults.

_____ 11. Boys and girls exhibit no behavioral differences until environmental influences begin to produce such differences.

_____ 12. Genius is closely akin to insanity.

_____ 13. The unstructured interview is the most valid method for assessing someone's personality.

_____ 14. Under hypnosis, people can perform feats of physical strength which they could never do otherwise.

_____ 15. Children's IQ scores have very little relationship with how well they do in school.

_____ TOTAL CORRECT

from tested theories, then the entrance key is shaped by good questions from curious minds. Usually these questions are stimulated by an observation that something doesn't make sense, jars with our expectations, or challenges our notions of how individuals ought to behave—like the *Opening Cases* that began our chapter.

Abnormal psychology is a topic many students want to learn more about because of a fascination with the change from normality to abnormality—as witnessed in the case of Dan W. But many less dramatic phenomena that we will study can be fascinating as well. Where are your memories stored—in what part of your brain and in what form? How can you see a three-dimensional, stable world full of color when the image on the sensitive surface of your eye is two-dimensional, shaky, and colorless? What type of therapy works best to relieve severe mental depression? These are but a few of the many interesting questions psychologists have asked in the course of conducting research. Perhaps your ques-

tions too will serve as a key to discoveries of new psychological knowledge in the future. For now, try your answers to the questions in the **Close-up, "Commonsense" Psychology Quiz,** on this page.

What psychology tries to do

For the psychologist conducting basic research, the goals are to describe, explain, predict, and control behavior. For the applied psychologist, there is a fifth goal—*to improve the quality of human life*. These five goals form the foundation of the psychological enterprise. Let's examine each of them.

Describe what happens. The first task in psychology, as in other sciences, is to "get the facts"—to collect the relevant data. **Data** are reports of observations (the singular of data is **datum**). A person's

feelings of anxiety are not data because they cannot be observed by others. On the other hand, a person's restless behavior, oversecretion of adrenaline, or verbal report of anxiety could all be observed or measured and reported by others, and thus could be data.

Descriptions in psychology are statements about the behavior of organisms and the conditions under which the behavior occurs. Psychologists call the behavior a **response** and the related environmental conditions **stimuli** (the singular of stimuli is **stimulus**). A researcher may observe a sequence of ongoing behaviors, such as the development of the sweet-potato washing ritual by Imo and her troop, or only a single event, such as someone signing (or refusing to sign) a petition. What psychologists look for are consistent relationships between stimuli and responses or between particular responses.

Describing events objectively is not as simple as you might think. For example, how would you describe the action in the picture on this page? In an objective description you would note gestures, facial expressions, objects and people present, actions being performed. But if you say that a person is showing anger or fear or arrogance or timidity, you are inferring inner states, not simply describing behavior that you can see. Your descriptions of behavior—your data—can include only external features that can be perceived by others, such as what a person said, what movements were made, what score a person got, or how many people indicated agreement with a decision.

Explain what happens. Though description must stick to perceivable information, explanation deliber-

ately goes beyond what can be perceived to try to uncover a principle or process or relationship that could account for it. Thus the observation that the turkey chick was silent before Tina killed it led to the tentative explanation that the cheep-cheep sound might be a trigger for maternal behavior. Subsequent research did indeed show such a relationship.

Though inferring inner states or underlying relationships is "out of bounds" during description, inferences and speculations are extremely useful when it comes to looking for explanations. You wonder if two things you saw are related. If you find first-born children as a group are more intelligent than later-born children (on average they are), you start looking for a reason.

Sometimes researchers make an inference (an educated guess) about something that is happening inside the organism, something that makes the observed behavior more understandable. This inner, unseen condition is called an **intervening variable.** It may be a physiological condition (such as hunger) or a psychological process (such as an expectation). Intervening variables are *not* "interfering" variables, as some students might mistakenly think; rather they are processes that are assumed to link observable stimulus input with measurable response output. Intervening variables are recognized as part of the explanation of how stimuli and responses might be related.

Psychologists distinguish between overt and covert behaviors. **Overt behaviors** are responses that are visible to observers. **Covert behaviors** are unseen psychological processes such as expecting, interpreting, or deciding. As indicated above, covert behaviors may be postulated as intervening variables to help make observed behavior more understandable. Many psychologists are primarily interested in these inner behaviors, although they can be studied only indirectly through inferences based on observation of some kind of overt behavior. Several ingenious ways of studying covert processes have been devised, and we will discuss them in detail in Chapter 10.

*The 15 items in the Commonsense Quiz were answered incorrectly by more than half of a group of introductory psychology students at the University of Pittsburgh. All items are false as stated, though many reflect widespread popular beliefs (Vaughan, 1977).

Predict what will happen. Predictions are statements of the likelihood that a certain event will occur, or that a given relationship will be found. Some predictions are based on applying information about the past to future situations or on the belief that a knowledge of the future is available through oracles, astrology, or psychic revelation. In science, by contrast, predictions are based on an understanding of how events are related.

An inference that you make to explain your data is only a hunch until you test it by predicting something that will happen if it is true. A specific prediction about behavior is called a **hypothesis**: it is a testable statement that an expected outcome will result from specific conditions. The investigator's hunch that Tina's unmotherly behavior was related to the absence of the cheep-cheep sound led to the hypothesis that even a stuffed polecat would call forth maternal behavior if it made the right sound. A hypothesis must be about conditions and outcomes that can be observed and must be specific enough that the evidence obtained can support or challenge it.

Once basic relationships are understood, other predictions can be made. A college admissions officer can predict students' college grades from their SAT scores, and psychologists can predict less self-confidence in students who define themselves as shy. Predictions can even be made of events that have never been observed. For example, from your understanding of Tina's behavior, you would predict that other mother turkeys would behave the same way, and you might also predict that a mother turkey whose hearing was destroyed would kill her chicks even if they were cheeping loudly. You might be right or wrong, depending on whether other, nonauditory cues were available. But your prediction of something you had never seen would come from your understanding that this fixed action pattern is released by the cheep-cheep sound.

While some psychologists are content with explaining a relationship as the goal of their inquiry, others insist that if you cannot predict the conditions under which a given behavior will appear or change, you simply have not understood it. At least, they say, you cannot be sure your explanation is correct unless you can use it to predict what will happen or what will make it happen. When different explanations are put forward to account for some behavior or relationship, they are usually judged on the basis of which one can make the most accurate and comprehensive predictions.

Control what happens. For many psychologists, control is the central, most powerful goal. Controlling behavior goes beyond predicting behavior by making it happen or not happen—starting it, maintaining it, stopping it, and influencing its form or strength or rate.

The ultimate test of any causal explanation of behavior lies in being able to demonstrate the conditions under which the behavior can be controlled. In the development of the drug chlorpromazine (see *Prologue*), the researchers could be sure of the power of chlorpromazine only by demonstrating that a characteristic "euphoric quietude" could be started, stopped, maintained, or changed by changes in the administration of chlorpromazine. Only by such demonstrations can we establish that the conditions we think are responsible for a behavior are in fact both necessary and sufficient conditions, and that other available conditions are not causing the effect we observe.

The ability to control behavior is important because it gives psychologists ways of changing behavior to help people. In this respect, psychologists are a rather optimistic group; many believe that virtually any undesired behavior pattern can be modified. Control in the form of intervention to change a destructive behavior pattern is at the heart of all programs of psychological treatment or therapy.

Serious ethical issues can arise, however, when one person tries to control another person's behavior. This is true wherever the attempt to control takes place—for example, in psychotherapy, in a psychological experiment with prisoners subjected to behavior modification, or in an urban relocation plan that disrupts an old neighborhood for the sake of "progress." It is interesting to note here that *understanding*—rather than control—tends to be the goal of psychologists in many Asian and African countries.

As the field of psychology has grown, there has been among psychologists an increased awareness and sensitivity to the range of situations that can involve potential violations of ethical principles. Those working with clients or patients often draw up working contracts that explicitly outline the rights, obligations, and reasonable expectations of each party. In research, the well-being of those who participate as subjects in experiments—humans and animals—is now protected by formal ethical standards and committees of the American Psychological Association and by explicit policies and procedures at most local institutions as well.

Improve the quality of life. Many of the findings of psychology are being applied to the solution of human problems. Some of these findings have come from *applied research,* in which the goal was to find solutions to particular practical problems. Other findings have come from *basic research,* in which a phenomenon or process is studied originally for accurate and comprehensive knowledge without regard to possible later applications.

Applied researchers have always had improvement of the quality of life as an important goal. Basic researchers, on the other hand, have generally felt that their responsibility lay in the scientific enterprise of getting objective facts and drawing accurate conclusions from them—but not necessarily in applying their findings to improve things for the general populace. For basic researchers, often knowing the answer was enough. And even though psychologists have historically pursued more basic than applied research, both approaches have yielded many discoveries of far-reaching importance to society.

Over time, as awareness has increased that psychological findings are often used to change people's lives, the demand has grown for psychologists to be more than just "objective" scientists. They have a responsibility for trying to see that their findings are not misinterpreted by policy makers and that they are used for socially responsible, constructive purposes that will enrich the lives of those affected. Indeed, no matter how objective psychologists are in gathering data, their personal values are likely to influence their choice of what to investigate and their recommendations for action based on their findings.

There are many different kinds of applied psychologists who work in a variety of settings. For example, clinical psychologists work in hospitals, clinics, or private therapy to counsel or try to change the behavior patterns of people with mental and behavioral disorders. Industrial psychologists often work in organizational settings to discover how to improve worker morale while increasing productivity and efficiency as well. Educational psychologists may help in the design of school curricula and child-care programs. Environmental psychologists may work with architects and urban planners to design housing projects that facilitate the needs of the residents rather than just serve as spaces in which to "store" people. In addition, some are studying ways to promote behaviors that will conserve energy or reduce pollution.

Health psychologists are collaborating with medical researchers to understand better how behavior

▽ **Figure 1.1A** *Specialty Areas of Psychologists*

Shown here are percentages of psychologists by specialty area (A) and work setting (B), based on a random survey in 1978 of 6,551 members of the American Psychological Association holding doctorate degrees in psychology. (Based on Stapp & Fulcher, 1981)

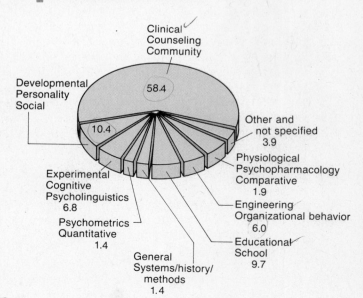

and life-style affect physical health and how behavioral principles can be used to aid medical treatment—to get patients to comply with the doctor's orders and follow a prescribed routine, for example. Forensic, or legal, psychologists apply psychological knowledge to human problems in the field of law enforcement. They may work with the courts, trying to determine the mental competency of defendants; or they may be involved in counseling inmates in prison rehabilitative programs. Psychologists are also working with computer scientists at both basic and applied levels to try to understand human problem solving better and to help develop increasingly sophisticated "computer thinking." For a schematic representation of the many fields and settings in which psychologists can work, see **Figures 1.1A** and **1.1B.**

With this brief overview of the goals of psychology, we are ready to look at how psychologists go about working toward those goals. In the next section we will look at some of the ways in which psychologists gather data, what they do to ensure objectivity in their data gathering, and how they go beyond data to build generalizations and theories.

▽ ▍**Figure 1.1B** *Work Settings of Psychologists*

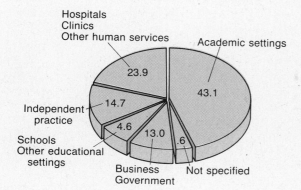

Hospitals
Clinics
Other human services

Academic settings

23.9

43.1

Independent practice

14.7

4.6 13.0 .6

Schools
Other educational
settings

Business
Government

Not specified

RESEARCH FOUNDATIONS

Research in science is a systematic search for information. It is based on the **scientific method,** which is a set of attitudes and procedures for gathering and interpreting objective information in such a way as to minimize sources of error and yield dependable generalizations. Scientific knowledge is built on a base of **empirical** evidence—that is, evidence obtained through the observation of perceivable events, or *phenomena,* rather than just from opinions or beliefs or statements by an authority.

Psychological research is the *how* of what is known in psychology. Basic to research in psychology, as in other sciences, are (a) keeping complete records of observations and data analysis in a format that other researchers can understand and evaluate; (b) communicating one's findings and conclusions in ways that allow independent observers to **replicate** (repeat) the findings; and (c) building knowledge as new findings are integrated into previous ones.

Psychology is a *behavioral* science because what is observed is either actual behavior, as when the speed of responding to a stimulus is measured, or the products of behavior, as when the drawings of children are observed. But behavior occurs in many forms and guises that often elude any ready explanation. Researchers ideally will insist on adequate supporting evidence for any conclusion while being open to the possibility that what is already "known" may turn out to be inaccurate.

Strictly speaking, the empirical results of any research are limited to the reactions actually recorded from particular individuals in a specific context. But the researcher is always looking for general principles. So from what has been observed from this small sample of behavior by a sample of individuals in a sample situation, the researcher makes generalizations about the larger population of reactions, organisms, and situations from which the samples came. Some of the procedures researchers use to increase their confidence in making generalizations involve both methods for choosing the sample and special statistical methods for analyzing the data.

In this section we will look first at several of the research methods in psychology. Then we will examine some requirements for ensuring objectivity—whatever the research method used—and some conceptual issues involved in going beyond specific findings to draw generalizations, build theories, and talk about causation. More information about planning and conducting research and drawing statistically justified conclusions is presented in the *Understanding Research Appendix.*.

Basic methods for gathering data

All research methods in psychology are based on observation of behavior. They range from observation of natural, ongoing behavior in unrestricted settings to observation under focused, highly controlled, artificial conditions where the researcher changes the stimulus conditions and limits the responses that are possible. The five methods most often used in psychological research are naturalistic observation, surveys, interviews, tests, and controlled experiments. In addition, there are some combined and special methods, five of which we will review briefly here.

Naturalistic observation. Observing some naturally occurring behavior with no attempt to change or interfere with it is called **naturalistic observation.** For example, you might sit behind a one-way glass and observe preschoolers' play without their knowing you were there. You might simply record the ongoing behavior you noticed and considered worth recording. Or you might focus on particular factors in the situation, such as how often each child initiates an interaction with another or how often each child is chosen as a play partner. Any such factor that varies in amount or kind is called a **variable.** You would find that the children differ greatly regarding these variables. From your observations of each child's interaction patterns, you might make inferences about popularity or social isolation. Or you might look for other variables in the situation—for example, other behaviors or stimulus conditions that were often associated with initiating play behavior or being chosen.

Naturalistic observation can be conducted in the laboratory or in the "field," which is any setting outside the laboratory where there is ongoing, "natural" behavior to be observed. The *Opening Case* of Imo's sweet-potato washing was a field study carried out by naturalistic observation. Some kinds of human behavior can be studied only through naturalistic observation because it would be unethical or impractical to tamper with the situation.

Naturalistic observation is especially useful in the early stages of an investigation for discovering the extent of some phenomenon or getting an idea of what the important variables and relationships might be. The data from naturalistic observation often provide clues for the investigator to use in formulating a hypothesis to test by other research methods.

Surveys. A survey is a method of gathering information from a large number of people. Self-report information is gathered in response to a list of questions that follows a fixed format. Questioning may be done face-to-face or by mail or telephone. The information gathered is fairly superficial and easily scorable. Questions may be about the individuals' knowledge, attitudes, opinions, feelings, expectations, or behavior.

Surveys can be helpful in establishing how strong a particular reaction is among a given population of people, how widespread a problem is, or what the significant issues are from the viewpoint of the public. A summary of survey data on what types of people and situations make college students feel shy is shown in **Table 1.1.**

Interviews. An **interview** is a face-to-face dialogue between a researcher and an individual for the purpose of obtaining detailed information about the individual. Interviews conducted for research purposes are interactive, in that the researcher varies the questioning to follow up on what the individual says; nonverbal behavior such as fidgeting, hesitation, or emotionality are also part of the data recorded. The

◁ *By sitting behind a one-way mirror, the psychologist can observe the child at play and record his observations without influencing or interfering with the child's behavior.*

Table 1.1   *What Makes You Shy?*

Situations	Percentage of Shy Students
Where I am focus of attention—large group (as when giving a speech)	73%
Of lower status	56%
Social situations in general	55%
New situations in general	55%
Requiring assertiveness	54%
Where I am being evaluated	53%
Where I am focus of attention—small group	52%
One-to-one different-sex interactions	48%
Of vulnerability (need help)	48%
Small task-oriented groups	28%
One-to-one same-sex interactions	14%
Other People	
Strangers	70%
Opposite sex	64%
Authorities by virtue of their knowledge	55%
Authorities by virtue of their role	40%
Relatives	21%
Elderly people	12%
Friends	11%
Children	10%
Parents	8%

Philip G. Zimbardo. Shyness: What It Is, What to Do About It, Copyright © 1977, Addison-Wesley, Reading, Mass.

interviewer is sensitive to the process of the interaction as well as to the information revealed.

Good interviewers are able to establish *rapport,* a positive social relationship with the interviewee that encourages trust and sharing of personal information. In some cases, data may be accumulated over many interviews.

Psychological tests. Psychological tests are measuring instruments used to assess an individual's standing relative to others on some mental or behavioral characteristic, such as intelligence, vocational interests, values, aptitudes, or scholastic achievement.

▷ *The controlled experiment conducted in the laboratory may involve the use of complex equipment for recording responses.*

Each test consists of a set of questions, problems, or activities, the responses to which are assumed to be indicators of a particular psychological function. Where feasible, group tests permit information to be obtained quickly from large numbers of people without the cost of trained individuals to administer the tests.

Typically, test performance is used to predict how the person will probably behave in a particular later situation. For example, SAT scores are predictors of grades in college; scores on a test of mechanical ability indicate which individuals are highest in the abilities needed for mechanical work. Because the use of psychological tests of intelligence, personality, and vocational interests is so widespread in our society, we will study in detail how they are constructed, used, and at times, abused, in Chapter 12.

The controlled experiment. The observation of the silent turkey chick being killed by its mother was an example of naturalistic observation. But when the presence or absence of the cheep-cheep sound was systematically varied, an experiment was taking place. Here the investigator intervened and changed the stimulus conditions instead of just recording what was happening naturally.

A **controlled experiment** is a research method in which observations are made of specific behavior under systematically varied conditions. The investigator manipulates one or more stimulus variables and observes the effects on one or more behaviors. Controlled experiments are used for testing hypotheses. They help determine how two or more variables are related and whether there is a cause-effect

Aging, Health, and a Sense of Control

It has long been assumed that the health problems that accompany growing old are genetically programmed into the species. But consider an alternate hypothesis—namely, that age-related decline in health is in part psychologically determined and not solely biological in origin. Can it in fact be shown that environment and psychological factors (psychosocial variables) play a significant role in the health of older people? If so, might biological declines in the elderly even be reversible by psychosocial intervention?

Clues to the likely answers to such questions have been provided by research showing that elderly people who perceive that they have a choice about whether to enter a retirement home fare better subsequently than those who perceive that they have no choice.

In one carefully documented study of 40 people whose applications were received by a nursing home in Cleveland, Ohio, 23 died within a month of mailing the application. It turned out that of those who had died, the vast majority were applicants whose families had made the application for them, as opposed to their making the application for themselves (Ferrare, 1962).

This result is very provocative, but it is a correlational finding, showing the relation between two classes of responses. In order to demonstrate a *causal* connection between health and a sense of control, it is necessary to manipulate a stimulus condition that affects people's perceptions of their choice and control and then assess the consequences on their health. Psychologist Judith Rodin (1983) and her colleagues have done just that in an extended series of studies. We will cite one of her experiments to illustrate the sequence of events in a controlled experiment.

Rodin hypothesized that training which increased subjects' sense of control and reduced their feelings of lack of control would result in a variety of changes in three classes of variables: attitudes, behavior, and health status. Four months before the experimental treatment was to begin, 40 elderly female residents in a nursing home were selected and given extensive interviews covering issues related to perceived control, stress, and personal problems. In addition, behavioral observations were made, blood pressure and urine tests were given, and general ratings of health status were recorded. (None of the patients was acutely ill, and all were able to walk without assistance.)

The subjects were matched on age and length of residence and then randomly assigned to one of three groups: the experimental group, which would receive training; an "attention" control group, which would receive no training but spend the same amount of time with a psychologist just talking about problems of the elderly; and a second control group, which would receive no special attention. The training was the *independent variable;* perceived sense of control, a hypothesized *interven-*

relationship between them—that is, between a particular condition and a later response.

In the simplest experiment, the form or amount of one stimulus variable is changed systematically under carefully controlled, often quite restrictive, conditions, and a response variable is observed to see if it changes, too. The stimulus that is changed and used to predict the response is called the **independent variable.** The response is the unit of behavior whose form or amount is expected to *depend* on the changes in the independent variable; it is called the **dependent variable**. In the turkey experiment, for example, the stimulus of the cheeping sound was the independent variable and maternal behavior the dependent variable.

To determine that it is *only* the independent variable, and not other factors, that is causing the behavioral change, the experimenter attempts to control or at least account for the effect of all extraneous conditions. This can be done in three ways: through the use of experimental and control groups, random assignment, and controlled procedures.

The **subjects** in an experiment are the individuals whose behavior is being observed. They are assigned to either the **experimental group**—the group exposed to the independent variable—or to the **control group**—the group exposed to all the conditions of the experiment *except for* the independent variable. Subjects are assigned to group by a chance procedure called **random assignment** (similar to

ing variable; and measures of attitudes, behavior, and health, the *dependent variables,* which were expected to change for the experimental group.

The experimental group received two sessions of training for three weeks by psychologists who were unaware of the pretest data. The training procedure taught these elderly patients to minimize negative self-statements and use positive self-statements. They were also given training in how to be more active contributors to their own experience and how to solve problems regarding potential health hazards. It was hypothesized that this training would affect the intervening variable, *sense of control.*

One month after the experimental period, the pretest procedures were repeated as a posttest. An estimate of stresses that had occurred naturally in the residential setting was also made. As predicted, the women in the experimental group, on the average, were better able than those in the control groups to deal with stresses in their environment and better able to modify conditions that gave rise to problems. They participated more in activities, were more happy, social, and energetic, and felt that they had more freedom to effect change and determine relevant outcomes in their environment. Levels of stress-related hormones in the urine were also significantly reduced, and their general health patterns were shown to be improved. On several of the posttest measures, the attention control group were slightly better than the no-attention control group, but the differences were not statistically significant. On measures taken eighteen months later, the improvement of the experimental group had continued.

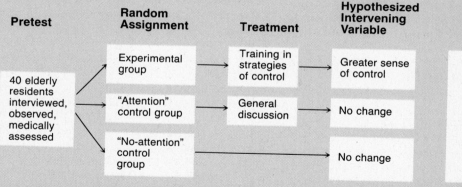

Pretest	Random Assignment	Treatment	Hypothesized Intervening Variable	Posttest of Dependent Variables
40 elderly residents interviewed, observed, medically assessed	Experimental group	Training in strategies of control	Greater sense of control	Four classes of variables measured 1. Self-reported attitudes and feelings 2. Behavior, activity 3. Physiological changes 4. Ratings of general health
	"Attention" control group	General discussion	No change	
	"No-attention" control group		No change	

flipping a coin). Each subject thus has an equal chance of being in either the experimental or the control group. The purpose of random assignment is to make the different groups in the experiment as similar as possible before they are exposed to the independent variable. In this way, if behavioral differences are found between these groups, the differences can be attributed to the presence or absence of the independent variable and not to some initial difference in ability or experience, for example.

Another aspect of control in scientific experiments is the use of **controlled procedures,** procedures that attempt to hold constant all variables and conditions other than those related to the hypothesis being tested. Instructions, temperature, time allowed, how the responses are recorded, and so on need to be as similar as possible for all subjects to ensure that their experience is the same *except for* the difference in the independent variable.

An example of a controlled experiment is outlined in the **Close-up** above. Problems that can arise in conducting experiments, and some of the ways of counteracting them are discussed further in the *Research Appendix.*

Although we learn about behavior from a number of sources, the cornerstone of scientific psychology is the controlled experiment. Yet it is not always possible to perform experiments to test hypotheses. Sometimes the phenomenon is too broad to be reduced to specific variables that can be manipulated (e.g., mob behavior or the effects of excessive environmental overload). Or the independent variable cannot be manipulated for practical reasons (e.g., the effects of being in love or of being divorced) or for ethical reasons (e.g., heredity in humans or reactions to extreme stress).

Combined and special methods. Some research methods in psychology combine two or more procedures from the five basic methods, while others have a special feature that makes them uniquely suited for particular uses. Five such methods to be considered here are case studies, longitudinal studies, archival research, cross-cultural research, and evaluation research. Other methods that have been developed for research in special areas of psychology will be described in later chapters.

Case studies are scientific biographies of selected individuals. They are a method for trying to capture the richness and uniqueness of human personality. The data that go into a case study may come from many sources, such as the person's own recollections, the researcher's observations, interviews with others who know the person, and any available information from psychological tests. This research method is often used with mentally ill patients by clinical psychologists interested in understanding abnormal behavior. It was the primary method used by Sigmund Freud.

Many behaviors change with age. One way of studying these changes is by **longitudinal studies,** in which a researcher observes selected responses of the same individuals at two or more different times in their lives. Some longitudinal studies have followed people's development over many years. Notable here is the research of Lewis Terman, which was begun soon after World War I on subjects who were classified as "geniuses" when they were children. These subjects have been followed systematically through their adult life; some of the findings will be discussed in Chapter 2.

Sometimes psychologists collect information by analyzing existing data or investigating products of behavior that were made at some time in the past. **Archival research** is the use of previously published findings or of data about behavioral processes or psychological environments gathered from books, documents, and other records or cultural artifacts. Examining different conceptions of the brain or of insanity from different historical records is an exam-

ple of archival research. So is counting the frequency of sexist jokes in popular magazines from 1940 to the present. In one archival study, the frequency of achievement-oriented themes in children's stories was assessed in different time periods. Relationships were then found between those themes and indicators of economic achievement in the society thirty years later (De Charms & Moeller, 1962).

Cross-cultural research is used to discover whether some behavior found in one culture also occurs in other cultures. In cross-cultural research the unit of analysis is a culture or a society rather than individuals, although the data are observations of individual reactions. Cross-cultural researchers may use field observations, surveys, interviews, tests, archival data, or controlled experiments. The cross-cultural method has been used to compare diverse sexual patterns, perceptual differences in reactions to illusions, and, recently, cultural factors that influence productivity (Hofstede, 1984).

An important new type of research in psychology, called **evaluation research,** focuses on evaluation of whether a particular social program or type of therapy does what it is supposed to do and whether it is cost-effective. Do particular laws or regulations or personnel practices have the hoped-for results, are the benefits worth the costs, financially and psychologically, and how might a program be changed to function more effectively? New data may be collected from interviews, surveys, and observations and combined with already existing data (from archives, experiments, or other sources) within the program being evaluated. Results may be stated in terms of cost effectiveness—how much a program costs in money and effort to produce a particular outcome (Kosecoff & Fink, 1982). For example, a current, large-scale government-sponsored study is investigating the results and costs of several methods of treating depression. That research will be described more fully in Chapter 15 on therapy.

Whatever the method used, it is not enough to collect data unless we have some assurance that the procedures we use are giving us data that are reliable and valid. **Reliability** means that data are consistent; **validity** means that the data are measures of what we think they are. For example, a score on a driver's test is reliable if retesting would give the same score. It is valid if it really is an indication of the person's driving ability. Reliability and validity are important concepts in psychology, as we shall see. Both—but in particular, reliability—are buttressed by the procedures for enhancing objectivity to be discussed next.

Enhancing objectivity

When as ordinary citizens, we hear or read "Research shows . . .," we tend to accept at face value the conclusion that follows. Why *are* we more ready to believe in the truth of such statements than of most other claims? It is probably because we know that the scientific method, if followed, enhances objectivity and minimizes bias. It is our assumption of objectivity behind such reports that gives them tremendous power and potential for influencing what we think. So as researcher-consumers in our experimenting society, we need to know what some of these objectivity-enhancing procedures are. We can then be alert to cases where claims prefaced by those magic words "Research shows . . ." are not in fact justified. Here we will touch on a few important ways of ensuring objectivity, whatever research method is used.

Clearly defined variables. In any study, the variables of interest need to be clearly defined in terms of something that the researcher can observe. If you want to study shyness, you have to state what observable behavior you will take as your definition of shyness. It might be withdrawal behavior in a social situation, or critical self-statements about one's social skill, or failure to make eye contact with friendly people. If you wanted to study aggressive behavior, you might define aggression as behavior that injures another person, or as a score on a test of aggressiveness. Definitions like these are called **operational definitions** because they define the variable in terms of specific operations the investigator uses to determine its presence. Operational definitions avoid the ambiguity of everyday descriptive terms and ensure that both the stimulus variables and the response variables are observable events.-

Even inner processes can be studied by being defined in terms of something that can be observed. For example, hunger, an inner state, might be operationally defined as "24 hours without food," or "15 percent loss of body weight in a given time period." The experimenter could then study the effects of hunger, defined in that particular way, on various behaviors.

Operational definitions enable the experimenter to be very explicit "for the record" about what is being studied. Another researcher who wants to replicate the study or build on its findings needs to know how the variables were defined. Sometimes when different researchers report contradictory findings about behavior like shyness or aggressiveness, it turns out that they have used different definitions of the terms and hence have not been measuring the same behaviors.

Standardization. Standardization is a technique of using uniform procedures for administering tests, interviews, surveys, and experiments. The investigator plans the exact manner in which to treat and observe each participant and to record the behavior so that the conditions of data collection are the same for everyone. In controlled experiments, for example, instructions may be presented on tape, stimuli displayed on video screens, and responses made by depressing a given button, which feeds directly into a computer as part of the uniform procedures regularly followed. That way each subject experiences exactly the same experimental conditions. Standardization minimizes unwanted *variability* in the behavior of research subjects—which would occur if the questions were asked differently or other conditions during the experiment were changed, or if there were not a consistent way to score responses. As we shall see in Chapter 12, standardization is especially important in both constructing and using psychological tests.

Avoidance of bias. Even with standardized procedures, bias can inadvertently be introduced by either the subjects or the researcher. For example, a subject who dislikes females in authority could introduce bias by not paying attention to the instructions of a female experimenter and thus respond differently than other subjects in the same experimental condition. Or a subject who wants to make a good impression could bias the results by giving the responses he or she thinks the experimenter wants.

Examples of unwitting researcher-caused bias are many. Like the rest of us, researchers are human: they tend to see what they expect to see, despite their commitment to objectivity. Even worse, their expectations may prompt changes in the behavior of the subjects they are supposedly just observing.

In a study of unintentional researcher-caused bias, students were hired to act as "experimental assistants" in studying how reliably people could determine from a photo whether the person pictured was experiencing success or failure. Their "subjects" were to look at a series of photos and rate each one on a scale from +10 (extreme success) to −10 (extreme failure). Actually, all the photos had earlier been rated as neutral in expression. Half of the "experimental assistants" were then led to believe that the subjects they observed would give ratings that averaged about +5, while the other half were led to expect average ratings of −5. Both groups then read the same instructions to their "subjects."

As you can now probably anticipate, both sets of "experimental assistants" found the effect they were expecting. In some subtle, nonverbal way, even though they had read standardized instructions and supposedly just watched while the photos were being judged, they had communicated their expectations to their "subjects" and then observed them doing just as expected.

Similar results were found with rats as subjects. When experimenters were led to believe that one group of rats was smarter than another, they later reported observing superior performance by the supposedly smarter but actually similarly ordinary rodents (Rosenthal, 1966).

This unconscious biasing of data because of the experimenter's expectations about what the data *ought* to be is called the "experimenter expectancy bias effect." It has been studied extensively by psychologist Robert Rosenthal as an interesting problem in how subtle forms of interpersonal communication can lead to self-fulfilling prophecies. In one particularly dramatic demonstration, teachers were led to believe that certain students would be "late bloomers." Sure enough, those students did do better as the year wore on; yet they were ordinary students who had been picked at random (Rosenthal & Jacobson, 1968).

We often see what we expect to see, but this form of bias can be controlled in several ways. Both subjects and experimental assistants can be kept unaware of ("blind to") which subjects get which treatment. Bias due to emphasis, tone, manner, or gestures of the experimenter may be eliminated by using standardized, impersonal testing procedures such as presenting instructions on tape or on computer consoles.

Independent replication. If a research finding cannot be replicated by another researcher from an independent laboratory, it cannot be considered reliable. Thus, it is important that the researcher clearly communicate the exact manner in which experimental procedures were used, so that independent investigators can precisely replicate the original experiment. Furthermore, if the findings of a study are likely to have a substantial impact on people, it would be wise to have a number of separate repli-

cations before any action is taken or any policy made which is based on the research findings. Typically, other researchers will try to both reproduce the original finding and refine and extend it by adding conditions or new measures or other improvements.

These are only some of the ways researchers try to reduce ambiguity and subjectivity and avoid bias. Use of such procedures enables us to be confident that the results are not unduly influenced by uncontrolled factors or by subjective or personal values of the experimenter. It does *not* mean that the findings are true, since experimenters can always make "honest" mistakes. But it provides a reasonable assurance that given the way the variables were defined and the study was carried out, the data can be trusted as objective.

Going beyond the facts

Well-designed, carefully executed research can yield trustworthy facts, but then new issues arise as the researcher seeks to go beyond the specific observations to inferences and generalizations. Two of these conceptual issues center on fundamental concerns of scientific research: probability and causality.

"I THINK YOU SHOULD BE MORE EXPLICIT HERE IN STEP TWO."

Probability versus certainty. Suppose you find a difference between the scores of your experimental group and those of your control group at the end of an experiment. How sure can you be that it is a real difference, caused by exposure to the independent variable, and that you would find the same difference if you repeated the experiment? Could it have been due to chance factors?

Psychologists use a statistical inference procedure that gives them an estimate of the probability that an observed difference could have occurred by chance. This computation is based on the size of the difference and the spread of the scores. By common agreement, they accept a difference as "real" when the probability that it might be due to chance is less than 5 in 100 (indicated by the notation $p<.05$). In most research a **significant difference** is one that meets this criterion, though in some cases an even stricter one, $p<.01$ (less than 1 in 100), is used. (This and other statistical methods of gauging the trustworthiness of particular findings are discussed in more depth in the Research Appendix.)

With a statistically significant difference in hand, the researcher can draw a conclusion about the behavior that was under investigation. But the conclusion is a statement of the *probable* relationship between the events that were investigated, never one of certainty. Truth in science is provisional, always open to revision by later data from better studies, developed from better hypotheses.

Confidence in any conclusion increases over time as supporting evidence accumulates. When this occurs, it becomes ever more probable that the data reflect an accurate description of "the way things really are." As data meet the test of replication, they become part of a general principle, a statement that a behavioral response is consistently related to another response or to a stimulus in a certain way. Gradually, principles are incorporated into **theories,** groups of interrelated principles that explain and/or predict behavior. A psychological theory makes conjectures about some behavioral or mental process at a more general level than hypotheses do. Some hypotheses are testable propositions derived from theory, while others are based on empirical observations from which a theory may be developed.

Good theories are powerful tools for integrating what is known, helping to make sense of many different relationships among variables, and suggesting

▷ *Minimum fact, maximum explanation.*

where to look for further information. But theories, like hypotheses, can never be proved once and for all. Any science is a method of "successive approximations," in which explanations are refined or replaced as new evidence accumulates, bringing us gradually closer, we hope, to accurate statements about what is true. But because all evidence is of necessity based on particular examples, using particular subjects, in a particular set of circumstances, all generalizations are leaps beyond the observed to the realm of the probable—and they may be wrong.

Inaccurate theories can retard scientific development by causing researchers to search in the wrong places or to think inaccurately about why behavior has occurred. When new, replicated data are inconsistent with a theory, the theory should be modified to accommodate them. Less scientifically but more typically, the data are simply ignored. For example, Ptolemy's theory that the earth was the center of the universe persisted long after Copernicus' rival theory was shown to be a better model of planetary motion (see Conant, 1958).

When inaccurate theories have practical consequences, they can do more than mislead us—they can be destructive. For example, false theories about the causes of stuttering have led to many useless remedies (Van Riper, 1970), as have many theories about mental disorders. Theories about the supposed genetic inferiority of racial or ethnic groups have also led to destructive consequences; we'll discuss these in later chapters.

Correlation, causation, and coincidence. We all want to know what things are related and particularly what will bring the results we want and what

will not—so as to have some control over our lives. But when we note that two things seem to be regularly related to each other—close in time and place—can we assume that the earlier one is causing the later one? Unfortunately, the answer is "No, not necessarily." The one may indeed cause the other; or they may be related in some *other* consistent, meaningful way; or the association between them may be just coincidence.

Take coincidence first. If you get a good grade on three tests in a row using a particular pen, you may be tempted to use that "lucky pen" for tests in the future; but you really know—deep down—that the pen couldn't have caused the good grades (though expecting that it will, as an intervening variable, may now affect your level of confidence and result in your doing better). The original relationship between using the pen and getting good grades would have been just coincidence.

Moving beyond coincidence, we find that sometimes, over a period of time, two things show a statistical relationship to each other when there is no apparent or proven reason why they should be related. This is called an *actuarial* relationship. For example, did you know that there has been a statistically significant relationship between Super Bowl winners and stock prices since the Super Bowl began in 1966? It seems that over 90 percent of the time, when the winning team has been from the old National Football League or the new National Conference (like the Dallas Cowboys), Standard and Poor's index of 500 Common Stocks has gone up in the following twelve months. It has declined when the winning team was from the American Football Conference (like the Miami Dolphins).

Actuarial prediction—prediction based on statistically established past relationships—has many practical uses. There is probably some causal link between accident rates and the age and sex of drivers, but insurance companies do not have to know what the causal link is or even if there is one. They predict accident rates by age and sex group and set insurance premiums accordingly just on the basis of the fact that age and sex *are* consistently related to accident rates.

A **correlation** is a consistent relationship between variables. Much research in psychology is a search for correlations—between socioeconomic conditions and psychological development, between particular personality characteristics and various behaviors, between cheep-cheep noises and mothering behavior, between a sense of control and physical health in the elderly, for example. By tapping large enough samples and using adequate controls, researchers hope to find relationships that are not just coincidental, nor simply actuarial; their ultimate aim is to identify *cause-and-effect* relationships. They want to go beyond knowing just that two variables are related to knowing *how* they are related. But the correlation itself does not provide any causal information. When two variables are found to be correlated (and you think you've eliminated the possibility of coincidence), one may cause the other, or they both may be caused by a third variable, or they may be related in some other way. You just do not know from only the correlational information.

What *does* a correlation tell you? In the first place, a correlation is always a relationship between sets of measures, not between a single pair of measures. When you say that SAT scores of high-school seniors are *positively correlated* with their college grades later, you mean that people with high scores on the SAT generally get high grades. If the reverse were true, you would say they were *negatively correlated* and would predict that people who got high scores on one measure would tend to have low scores on the other. You would expect a negative correlation between test measures of shyness and measures of assertive behavior, for example. The higher the correlation—either positive or negative—the closer the relationship and the more accurately you can predict one measure knowing the other. In both cases the two sets of measures vary together in a systematic way. (Correlations are discussed further in the *Research Appendix*.)

In these cases, one behavior (SAT scores or shyness) is being used as a predictor of another behavior (college grades or assertive behavior). In correlational studies, where researchers are seeking consistent relationships between different variables, both the independent variable (predictor) and the dependent variable (that which is predicted) are typically responses.

Since correlations are relationships between *sets* of measurements, predictions based on them are *group* predictions. Correlations cannot always be accurate predictions for individuals (except in the rare cases where there is a perfect correlation). For example, a positive correlation between heavy smoking and incidence of cancer tells us that there will be more cancer among heavy smokers than among

Table 1.2 Relationship of TV Viewing and Grades on Achievement Tests

Hours of TV watched daily	Test Scores	
	Reading	Math
0–½	75	69
½–1	74	65
1–2	73	65
2–3	73	65
3–4	72	63
4–5	71	63
5–6	70	62
6+	66	58

A consistent negative relationship is seen here: The fewer the hours spent watching TV, the higher the grades in both reading and math. Does this prove that watching TV causes poor grades? How would you find out? What other explanations might there be for the correlation between TV watching and grades? (California Department of Education, 1982)

nonsmokers but does not tell us whether any particular individual will get cancer.

Though SAT scores are highly correlated with college grades, you would never make the mistake of assuming that your SAT scores *caused* your grades in college. But in other cases the fallacy of inferring causation from correlation is not so obvious. It is an error that can have serious consequences, as we shall see in many instances throughout the text. Serious or not, it is a trap that is easy to fall into. For an example of a correlation that people might misinterpret causally, see **Table 1.2.**

To demonstrate a causal relationship, one must be able to control the variables in question. The following conditions must be met: (a) the behavior can be started or stopped by presenting or withholding the independent variable (or the *amount* of the behavior can be changed by making corresponding changes in the amount of the independent variable); and (b) these changes in behavior occur in this context *only* following manipulation of the independent variable.

When the causal relationship between an independent variable and a dependent variable has been demonstrated, we can conclude only that *changes* in the first cause *changes* in the second *when other broad classes of independent variables are held constant.* Psychologists see behavior as a function of (caused by) two general classes of independent variables: *factors in the organism* at a particular time in its life and *stimulus factors,* including the context in which a specific stimulus occurs. These relationships can be expressed in the following formula:

$$B = f(O_t \times S_c)$$

This can be read as, "Behavior is a function of organism factors at a given time in the organism's life *interacting with* stimulus factors within a particular context."

In a given study, the independent variable may be chosen from any of these factors, with the others held constant. In the coming chapters we will see that in different areas of psychological research, certain of these independent variables are emphasized more than others. For example, in developmental psychology, time variables are central; in the study of learning, specific stimulus variables are central. But regardless of which variable is manipulated and which ones are held constant, all continue to influence the behavior.

A hypothetical example in which the variables can be observed is the behavior of a 6-year-old student whose teacher puts a gold star on his forehead as a prize for good performance. No one else in the class gets a star. The child smiles, spends more hours studying, and reports that he likes school. Now consider how these behaviors might change as a function of:

- *changed organism*—child expects a prize of more value;
- *changed time*—student is 18 years old;
- *changed stimulus*—teacher puts a question mark instead of a star on the student's forehead;
- *changed context*—everyone in the class gets a star.

Our understanding of the determinants of behavior involves knowing about all these variables and how they function to generate behavior that we can observe or measure in some way.

Because there are usually many factors that can influence a complex behavior, the effect of one independent variable often depends on that of a second independent variable. This joint effect is called an **interaction**.

Data gathering and explanation build on each other. Most psychologists would agree on the basic points we have been making about ensuring objectivity in data gathering and about building explanations and generalizations from them. However, they differ considerably in the particular perspectives they have developed for exploring and explaining behavior. Our next task is to examine some of these.

ALTERNATIVE PERSPECTIVES

Psychological research has included studies of instinctive behavior in lower animals, studies of skill development, studies of particular processes in humans (such as sensation, learning, and attitude change), studies of neurobiological functions, studies of the development and course of mental disorders, studies of conformity pressures—and much more. It is hardly surprising that curious investigators, focusing on different kinds or aspects of behavior and using different research methods, have developed different perspectives from which to explain the behaviors they were studying.

Differing assumptions and approaches

All psychologists adopt philosophical assumptions which then influence the kinds of questions they raise and the focus and methods of their research. Some of these assumptions are choices about enduring controversies, such as whether humans are inherently good or evil, and whether they have free will or simply act out a script imposed by their heredity (biological determinism) or their environment (environmental determinism). Other assumptions are especially related to psychology, such as whether organisms are basically active or reactive, whether psychological and social phenomena can ultimately be explained in terms of physiological processes, and whether a complex behavior is just the sum of many smaller components or has new, emergent qualities.

The assumptions psychologists adopt from among these and other options determine what they will study, what organisms they will use for subjects, the degree to which they will try to control what happens, and the level of analysis they will find most appropriate.

The level of analysis may range from micro to molecular to molar. On the *micro level,* psychologists study fine-grained, small units of behavior such as biochemical activities in a nerve cell. On the *molecular level,* they are concerned with somewhat larger, though still precisely defined units of behavior, such as responding to a sound of a certain intensity. On the *molar level,* they study behavior of the whole functioning organism in a complex environment, such as gender-role behaviors of men and women in different cultures. The level of analysis also varies in its temporal focus. Some psychologists focus on the present situation, such as how organisms learn; others look for causes of behavior in the past, such as the influence of a traumatic loss in early childhood; still others study the importance of future events such as the influence of goal setting on performance.

Psychological models as maps

Most researchers base their work on a conceptual **model,** a simplified way of thinking about the basic components and relationships in their field of knowledge. Often models are based on an analogy between the processes to be explained and a system already understood. Early psychologists used the analogy of a telephone switchboard as a model for trying to explain processes in the brain. Models are useful in any field where much remains to be discovered because they provide a framework in which investigators can formulate new hypotheses to be tested, plan research, and evaluate their findings.

Among the current models being used by psychologists, five predominate: the psychophysiological, the psychodynamic, the behavioristic, the cognitive, and the humanistic. They vary in how specific and precise they try to be and in their dependence on research findings or theory. Also, they overlap at certain points, and most psychologists probably find useful concepts in more than one. But the five are based on quite different sets of assumptions and are distinct enough to have given rise to many lively controversies among psychologists. Research in a number of areas is organized around one or another of these general models, and you will be reading about their contributions at a number of other points in our journey.

Because any model selectively focuses on certain content while ignoring other kinds of information, it sacrifices some of the richness of the remarkable creatures being studied. Psychoanalytic thinker Carl Jung, himself a creative model builder, had this to say about models:

''Learn your theories as well as you can, but put them aside when you touch the miracle of life.''

The psychophysiological model. The word fragment *psych* refers to mental processes, *physio* to bodily ones. The psychophysiological model guides the work of most physiological psychologists as they try to find the links between brain and nervous system functioning and behavior, both overt and covert. According to this biologically based model, functioning of the organism is explained in terms of the physical structures and processes that make it work. Visual sensation is explained in terms of processes in the eyes, optic nerve, and brain. Nerve impulses are explained in terms of chemical and electrical processes in and between nerve cells. Four assumptions are implicit: that psychological and social phenomena can be understood in terms of biochemical processes; that complex phenomena can be understood by analysis into smaller units; that all behavior—or behavior potential—is determined by physical structures and largely hereditary processes; and that experience can modify behavior by altering these underlying structures and processes. The task of researchers is to understand behavior at the most precise possible micro or molecular level of analysis.

Physiological psychologists are among a growing number of neuroscientists from many disciplines—including biology, chemistry, physiology, and pharmacology—all of whom do work related to brain functioning. Neuroscientists study subjects ranging from simple organisms like crawfish to complex organisms like human beings; and their research is conducted in both laboratories and clinical settings. For example, in a hospital they might study patients with brain disease or patients suffering a memory loss following an accident.

Neuroscientists have won Nobel Prizes in physiology for illuminating how we hear (George von Békésy), how we see features of the environment

▷ *Nobel Prize-winning neuroscientists David Hubel (left) and Torsten Wiesel. They have investigated how the brain processes visual information so that we see forms.*

(David Hubel and Torsten Wiesel), and how the brain functions when the two halves are split (Roger Sperry). We will have more to say about their discoveries in later chapters.

The psychodynamic model. According to the psychodynamic model, all behavior is driven, or motivated, by powerful inner forces. In this view, our actions stem from inherited instincts, biological drives, and attempts to resolve conflicts between personal needs and social requirements. We act because we feel. Action is the product of tension, and its purpose is to reduce tension. Motivation is the key concept in the psychodynamic model. As coal fuels a steam locomotive, so deprivation states, physiological arousal, conflicts, and frustrations provide the power for behavior. In this model, the organism stops reacting when its needs are satisfied and its drives reduced.

◁ *Sigmund Freud (1856–1939).*

Psychodynamic principles of motivation were most fully developed by Viennese physician Sigmund Freud in the late nineteenth and early twentieth century. Freud's ideas grew out of his work with mentally disturbed patients, but he believed that the same principles applied to both normal and abnormal behavior. According to Freud's theory, what we are is fully determined by our heredity in combination with early childhood experiences. The infant, driven by unlearned instincts for self-preservation and desires for pleasure, experiences conflicts and traumatic experiences, such as parental taboos, that fully determine his or her personality thereafter. Often the early experiences continue to influence behavior in disguised ways that the person does not understand.

The psychodynamic view of Freud usually adopts a molar level of analysis, with the person seen as pulled and pushed by a complex network of forces. The nature of the human organism is seen as basically evil, with violence a natural means of expressing primitive sexual and aggressive urges. Strong societal controls are assumed to be needed if people are to be saved from their own passions for pleasure and destructiveness.

Freud's ideas have had a greater influence on many areas of psychological thought than those of any other individual. You will encounter different aspects of his contributions to psychology as you read about child development, dreaming, forgetting, unconscious motivation, personality, neurotic disorders, and psychoanalytic therapy. His ideas will appear as frequent markers on our psychological journey.

In addition, many psychologists since Freud have taken the psychodynamic model in new directions. Notably, some theorists here have moved away from a primary focus on the influence of instincts and drives on psychological development to a focus on social influences and interactions. For example, Erik Erikson (whom you will meet in Chapter 2) theorized that certain developmental stages are based on psychosocial development. And Margaret Mahler has studied how children establish a sense of self separate from others with whom they interact.

The behavioristic model. The behavioristic model is concerned with neither biochemical processes nor hypothetical inner motivations but with outer, visible behavior and its relationships to environmental stimulation. The behaviorally oriented psychologist uses data that are specific, measurable responses, such as blinking an eye, pressing a lever, or saying "yes" following an identifiable stimulus (e.g., a light or a bell). The main objective of behavioristic analysis is to understand how particular environmental stimuli control particular kinds of behavior. The level of analysis is thus molecular: the responses studied, such as learned habits, are broader than the responses of a neuron but narrower than the response of a person developing defenses for meeting inner needs.

According to the behavioristic model, behavior is assumed to be wholly determined—in this case, by conditions in the environment—and people are assumed to be neither good nor evil but simply reactive and modifiable by the proper arrangement of environmental conditions. Though heredity may place some limits on what environment can accomplish, behaviorally oriented psychologists assume that what we become is largely the result of nurture, not nature.

Behaviorists have typically collected their data from controlled laboratory experiments; they may use electronic apparatus and computers to present stimuli and record responses. They insist on very precise operational definitions and rigorous standards of evidence, usually in quantifiable form. Often they study animal subjects because control of all the conditions can be much more complete than with human subjects and because the basic processes they investigate occur in simpler form in subhuman species.

The view that only the overt behavior of organisms is the proper subject of scientific study is called **behaviorism.** It began early in this century with the work of John B. Watson. Watson was an American

psychologist who was influenced by a concept of learning developed by the Russian physiologist Ivan Pavlov. Pavlov had discovered that a physiological response, such as salivation, would come to follow not only the presence of food in the mouth but also the sight or sound of anything that was regularly followed by food. But whereas Pavlov's primary interest was in the physiology of the learned relationship,

△ | *John B. Watson (1878–1958).*

Watson's interest was in the learned association itself, the new relationship established between the response and the stimulus in the environment. He was reacting against the then-prevalent belief in the importance of instincts, unobservable hereditary mechanisms that were being postulated to explain personality and behavior. If behavior could be shown to be due to learning, it would open up new possibilities for changing undesirable behavior. Watson established a new direction in psychology—a search for causes in the environment—and was the first to insist that psychologists should study only observable behavior.

Watson believed that mental events could not be studied scientifically. Other behaviorists went further, asserting, as B. F. Skinner does, that no concepts about inner, unseen processes are needed to explain behavior.

For much of this century the behavioristic model has been dominant in American psychological research and thinking. Its impact, through its emphasis on the need for rigorous experimentation and operationally defined variables, has been felt in most areas of psychology. Its contribution to our understanding of learning will be taken up in Chapter 7, and many applications of its principles will be seen in other chapters.

The cognitive model. According to the cognitive model, *cognition*—the processes of knowing, which includes attending, thinking, remembering, expecting, fantasizing, and consciousness itself—is not just an intervening variable linking stimuli to responses but is itself a key causal factor in behavior. We act because we think. The way we process and recall the information we receive is believed to be as important as the stimulus input in determining what we do. Furthermore, we are not simply *reactive* in this process but also *active* in scanning the environment for what we need and transforming both information and physical objects to suit our purposes. According to the cognitive model, our behavior is only partly determined by preceding events. It is partly a phenomenon that emerges because we can think in totally novel ways, not predictable from the past. Both inherited structures and environmental input influence us but neither one wholly determines the evaluations, definitions, and decisions that will be created in our experience. We start life as neither good nor evil but with potential for both.

In Wundt's laboratory a hundred years ago, conscious processes were studied by introspection. As the term suggests, **introspection** is a method of gathering data in which trained subjects report their current conscious experience as accurately as they can. Wundt used the method to study sensations; he was trying to relate sensations to particular stimuli.

This type of introspection is not widely used today, and the focus has shifted. Cognitive psychologists of the 1980s are interested in questions about how people *interpret* the stimulus environment and *decide* what to do, based on *memories* of what worked in the past and *expectations* of desired or undesired consequences. But instead of depending on subjects' own reports of feelings or thoughts, they look for outer behaviors that are indicators of the inner processes. They create situations in which different responses will result from different thought processes and then watch to see which response occurs. Their data are measures of these outer behaviors—and thus verifiable by others who follow the same procedures. But their hypotheses and theories are about the unobservable, covert processes.

Cognitive psychologists see thoughts as both results and causes of overt actions. For example, when you hurt someone, you may regret it (thought as result); when you regret your actions, you may apologize for them (thought as cause). They study thought processes at both molecular and molar levels. For example, they may examine the speed with which different types of sentences are understood (molecular) or a subject's recollection of an early childhood event (molar). Psychologist Herbert Simon won a Nobel Prize in economics for his theory and research on how people make decisions under conditions of uncertainty.

With the development of new, more objective methods for studying mental processes (which we'll examine more fully in later chapters), some behavioristically oriented researchers have shifted to a more cognitive emphasis. Two of these are Albert Bandura, who incorporates cognitive events in his explanations of social learning, and Donald Meichenbaum, whose cognitive behavioral therapy trains people to change the statements they make about themselves. The approach of these researchers weds the behavioristic insistence on rigorous research methodology and standards of evidence with the renewed interest in inner experience.

Many psychologists see the new cognitive orientation as dominant in psychology today. Contributions of the cognitive orientation will be our primary focus in Chapters 9 and 10 but will also figure prominently in other chapters.

The humanistic model. Sometimes called the "third force," humanistic psychology evolved in the 1950s and 1960s as an alternative to the pessimism and determinism of the psychodynamic and the behavioristic models. According to the humanistic model, people are neither driven by powerful, instinctive forces nor manipulated by their environment. They are active creatures who are innately good and capable of choice. They strive for growth and development of their potentials, seek change, and can plan and restructure their lives.

The humanistic psychologist studies behavior not by reducing it to components, elements, and subprocesses but by trying to see the *patterns in life histories* of people in their everyday environments. Thus the level of analysis is a molar one. In sharp contrast to the behaviorists, humanistic psychologists focus on the *phenomenal* world, the subjective world experienced by the individual, rather than the objective world seen by external observers and researchers. Unlike the cognitively oriented research psychologist who ties postulated inner processes to specific behavioral indicators, humanistic psychologists are more interested in how these inner processes lead to new insights and value choices.

The humanistic model is less a research-based model, and it developed less as a theory to explain behavior in general, than as an approach for helping normal people lead fuller, richer lives. It was this intent that gave rise to encounter groups and other types of personal growth groups in the 1960s and 70s. Three important contributors have been Carl Rogers, Rollo May, and Abraham Maslow. Rogers

Abraham Maslow (1908–1970).

Carl Rogers (1902–   ).

Table 1.3 *Comparison of Models*

	Psychophysiological	Psychodynamic	Behavioristic	Cognitive	Humanistic
Focus of study	Brain and nervous system processes	Unconscious drives, conflicts	Specific overt behaviors	Mental processes, language	Human potentials
Level of analysis	Micro to molecular	Molar	Molecular	Molecular to molar	Molar
Predominant research approach	Study relationships between physiological and psychological processes	Study behavior as expression of hidden motives	Study behavior as it relates to stimulus conditions	Study mental processes through behavior indicators	Study life patterns, values, goals
View of human nature	Passive and mechanistic	Instinct-driven	Reactive and modifiable	Active and reactive	Active and unlimited in potential
Predominant determinants of behavior	Hereditary and biochemical processes	Heredity and early experience	Environment and stimulus conditions	Stimulus conditions and mental processes	Potentially self-directed

has emphasized the individual's natural tendency toward psychological growth and health, and the importance of a positive self-concept in this process. May was one of the first psychologists to explore phenomena such as anxiety from the perspective of the individual. Maslow postulated the need for self-actualization and studied the characteristics of people he judged to be self-actualized. We will learn more about their ideas in later chapters.

Using psychological models

Each of the models rests on a different set of assumptions and implies a different way of looking for answers to questions about behavior, as summarized in **Table 1.3**. Let's look at how psychologists using the different models might deal with the question of why people act aggressively:

- *Psychophysiological*—study the role of particular brain regions in aggression by electrically stimulating them and observing when destructive actions are elicited.
- *Psychodynamic*—analyze aggression as the person's reactions to frustrations caused by barriers to pleasure, such as poverty or unjust authority.

- *Behavioristic*—identify rewards that may have followed past aggressive responses, such as extra attention given to a child who hit a classmate. Or look for rewards the aggressive person is getting *now* for aggressive acts.
- *Cognitive*—ask the person about the hostile thoughts and fantasies he or she experiences while watching aggressive scenes, noting aggressive imagery and intentions to harm others.
- *Humanistic*—look for personal values and social conditions that foster self-limiting, aggressive perspectives instead of growth-enhancing, sharing experiences.

All these approaches have been used in the effort to understand why people behave aggressively and how such behavior can be changed. In Chapter 17 we will see what has been learned about the sources of aggression.

But it is not only professional psychologists who have theories about why people do what they do. Don't you already have some convictions about whether behavior is more influenced by heredity or environment, whether people are basically good or evil, and whether or not they have free will? As you read about the findings based on these formal models, keep checking the conclusions against your own views of behavior. In doing so, examine where your personal views have come from and where they may need to be broadened or changed.

© 1979 United Feature Syndicate, Inc.

Psychological claims are an unavoidable aspect of the daily life of any thinking, feeling, acting person in this psychologically sophisticated society. Every day you address the same issues psychologists do: you ask questions about your own behavior or that of other people, you seek answers from your theories or observations or what "authorities" say, and you check out the answers against the evidence available to you.

What authorities do you accept? How skeptical are you of reports in the press about what research has supposedly shown? Do you ask whether terms were operationally defined, observations standardized, experimental controls present, bias avoided? When a product is billed as "37 percent more effective," do you ask, "compared to what other treatment?" When "4 out of 5 doctors recommend X," do you question whether the survey included only 5 doctors—who might be prejudiced because they happen to be employed by the company that produces X? When someone presents you with "established conclusions" about the "obvious inferiority" of some social or ethnic group, do you ask to see the evidence supporting such statements? I hope that the things you learn from reading *Psychology and Life* will make you a more informed citizen, one who is sensitive to the pitfalls of erroneous reporting and conclusion-drawing. A goal for each of us is to develop a personal model of human behavior based on carefully weighed evidence.

PLANS FOR OUR PSYCHOLOGICAL JOURNEY

Although I have been teaching, conducting research, and writing about psychology for a quarter of a century, my enthusiasm for this journey becomes greater with each new venture. I hope that with the combined resources of this text as road map and your instructor as guide, you will emerge from this introduction to psychology filled with enthusiasm for further study and personal involvement in the field. First, let's have a brief overview of the route we will follow.

In Chapter 2 we begin by examining the psychological development of ourselves, the versatile *Homo sapiens,* over the life span—from infancy through childhood, adulthood, and old age. What transformations take place that enable a biological organism, starting with only a set of genetic blueprints, to evolve into a thinking, feeling person? The basic psychological processes surveyed here for their role in the development of the individual will be analyzed in greater detail in subsequent chapters. Before getting into each of these specific processes, however, we will show how the structures and functioning of the nervous system are ultimately responsible for the wonderful things we can do and experience (Chapter 3).

The first process we will examine in detail is sensation. How do we connect with the sensory world for nourishment and stimulation, as well as for pleasure and avoidance of pain (Chapter 4)? The study of sensation helps us understand how we see, hear, smell, taste, and feel our way around. But we are not just sensation-programmed robots: our perceptions are interpretations of the messages from our environment based on our past experience, the current context, and our needs, goals, and expectations (Chapter 5). Our ability to sense and perceive contributes to our uniqueness on a further dimension: we have a conscious awareness of ourselves and an ability to go beyond the givens of experience in extending the limits of our consciousness (Chapter 6).

Whenever we learn something new, we are profiting from experience by changing our ability to adapt to our environment. We transcend our genetic inheritance by using our potential for a remarkable range of learning. Learning frees us from stereotyped automatic reactions (like the mother turkey's instinctive response to cheep-cheep sounds) by enabling us to develop adaptive, novel behavior sequences (like Imo's potato washing). We learn to predict what events tend to go together, as well as what the consequences of our actions will be (Chapter 7). In fact, the nervous system is designed for learning, for being changed by virtually all that we experience.

But this great potential for learning did not develop just so we could sit under an apple tree and daydream. Humans are also designed for action, to survive by getting what they need—like harvesting apples to satisfy hunger—or by avoiding what is dangerous—like a falling branch from the apple tree.

Like other species, we humans are motivated by basic drives like hunger and such (or is it ''sex''?), but we are also motivated by personal and social needs to develop our potentials, to achieve, and sometimes to have power over others. Some of us develop such strong motivation for work that we become workaholics. And accompanying these sources of action are diverse feelings, emotions, and moods that appear to be distinctly human qualities (Chapter 8).

We also need to keep a record of our experiences and anticipate the challenges we will be meeting. Memory is the living library of all references to our past (Chapter 9). Much of it is available to help us deal with problems of the present or make future decisions—as long as we have access to the material that is stored there. When we do, we are able to go beyond what is given in our current experience to become powerful information processors—thinking, reasoning, judging, problem-solving, creating individuals (Chapter 10). And when we add our unique ability for language, we can learn secondhand from the experiences of others, and also communicate to others what's in or on our minds.

Up to this point, in looking at separate processes, we will have been searching for laws of uniformity—how different individuals respond to the same situations in the same general ways—through perceiving, learning, remembering, and so on. Now our focus will shift back again to the whole functioning personality as we ask how and why people respond differently to the same situations. We'll look at several theories about personality (Chapter 11) and then at how personality, intelligence, and creativity are assessed by psychologists and those whose decisions affect our lives—school administrators and prospective employers, among others (Chapter 12).

Unfortunately, the circumstances of life are never completely ideal. We need to know what challenges are likely to upset our optimal functioning and how we can manage stress more effectively (Chapter 13). When things are *not* managed well, we may become overwhelmed with extreme anxiety and tension. Or we may suffer more serious mental disorders. We will want to know the forms these disorders can take and the tolls they can extract from us (Chapter 14). But we also need to discover what kinds of therapy can help restore optimal mental health (Chapter 15).

The final phase of our journey acknowledges that there is no such thing as an isolated individual. Each one of us exists because other people mated, nourished us, protected us, taught us, and gave us values, purposes, and goals. So we inquire into the social nature of the human animal (Chapter 16) and into what aspects of the social environment can serve to impoverish or dignify the quality of human life (Chapter 17). How can the bond that forms the human connection be strengthened so that no person becomes isolated from the network of social support essential for individuals to realize their fullest potential? Answering that question will be a life's work for you—begun here but followed on new paths in other places.

That is the travel plan that has been laid out for you. Your instructor may schedule some detours or rearrange the sequence to match the course syllabus better or to fit time constraints or a personal preference for an alternative route. Your instructor may also have a preference for whether or when to use the special sections we have supplied—the *Prologue* by Neal Miller on the often unexpected bonuses derived from basic research; and the *Understanding Research Appendix* which extends the information given on research methods in this chapter and tells you a little about analysis of research data.

The *Opening Case* that begins each chapter serves to start you thinking about important concepts relevant to the core ideas of the chapter. These brief encounters along our psychological journey are meant both to pique your interest and to serve as a constant reminder that psychology is the study of the behavior of individuals, of living beings—not just abstract concepts.

OK, then, you're on your way. Hope it will be a worthwhile "journey." The Italian in this author says, "Andiamo!" Let's go!

SUMMARY

■ Scientific psychology started a little over a hundred years ago as an attempt to study elements of inner consciousness. Later, its focus was on outer, observable actions. Today, its subject matter includes the study of both outer behavior and mental processes.

■ The goals of psychology are to describe, explain, predict, and control behavior, as well as to improve the quality of life.

■ The objective data of psychology are observable stimuli and observable responses. Explanation identifies relationships and underlying processes that make sense of behavioral observations.

■ Psychological research is based on the scientific method, a set of attitudes and procedures for ensuring objectivity in gathering empirical information and for minimizing error.

■ Five basic research methods in psychology are naturalistic observation, surveys, interviews, psychological tests, and controlled experiments. Combined and special methods include case studies, longitudinal studies, archival research, cross-cultural research, and evaluation research.

■ A controlled experiment is a procedure for testing a hypothesis about a possible causal relationship between two or more variables. The experimenter manipulates an independent variable and notes the effects on a dependent variable (some observable response). All conditions except the independent variable are held constant for all subjects. Subjects may be randomly assigned to an experimental group (which is exposed to the independent variable) or a control group (which is not exposed).

■ Whatever the research method, objectivity is enhanced through use of clearly defined, observable variables; standardized procedures for giving instructions, presenting stimulus conditions, and scoring responses; avoidance of bias by a variety of techniques, including keeping researchers and subjects "blind" to which subjects are given which treatments; and independent replications of the same findings by different investigators.

■ Conclusions from research are statements of probability, never certainty. Accumulating consistent evidence leads to general principles and eventually to broad theories, but it is always possible that new evidence may disprove them. Science is a method of "successive approximations" to discovering the actual relationships that exist.

■ Correlations are consistent patterns of relationship between two sets of measures. The higher the correlation, either positive or negative, the stronger the relationship. A high positive correlation indicates that high scorers on one measure will tend also to be high scorers on the other; with negative correlations, scoring high on one measure is associated with scoring low on the other.

■ A causal relationship is indicated if an investigator can start, stop, maintain, or change a behavior by changes in the independent variable and if those changes occur only under those conditions. Correlations cannot be assumed to be causal relations.

■ When a causal relationship is found, one can conclude only that the *change* in the stimulus conditions caused the *change* in the response, with other conditions held constant. Behavior is believed to be a function of (caused by) factors in the organism at a particular time in its life interacting with stimulus factors within a particular context. The independent variable in a given study may come from any of these classes.

■ Five theoretical models cover much of the ground to be followed on our psychological journey. They have evolved from the work of investigators studying very different kinds of problems in diverse research settings.

■ Psychologists trying to find relationships between behavior and brain mechanisms generally follow the psychophysiological model. It is based on the assumption that each level of functioning can be described more precisely in terms of the biological structures and processes that make it work.

■ According to the psychodynamic model, behavior is driven by instinctive forces, inner conflicts, and motivation that can be unconscious as well as conscious. Early traumatic experiences influence behavior throughout life, often in disguised ways. Social mechanisms are developed to restrain the individual's selfish, destructive impulses.

■ According to the behavioristic model, behavior (the response) is determined by external stimulus conditions. The psychologist's task is to identify the functional relationships between behavior and stimuli. This model has been predominant in American psychology for much of this century.

■ For psychologists who adopt the cognitive model, it is important to study the mental processes that intervene between stimulus input and response initiation. How information is processed influences the options organisms have in adapting to their environment and the symbolic ways they can transform it. Many areas of contemporary psychology use a cognitive approach.

■ The humanistic model is a perspective on human nature that emphasizes the individual's inherent capacity to make rational choices. This approach suggests directions for therapy and self-improvement based on self-regulation of behavior and the development of human potential.

2

LIFE-SPAN PSYCHOLOGICAL DEVELOPMENT

■ THE LIFE-SPAN APPROACH
How development is studied
Basic concepts
■ THE LIFE CYCLE BEGINS
Genetic influences on behavior
What can babies do?
The beginning of language acquisition
■ COGNITIVE DEVELOPMENT
Piaget's insights into mental growth
Modern perspectives on cognitive development
■ SOCIAL AND EMOTIONAL DEVELOPMENT
Socialization
Gender roles
Moral development
Psychosexual and psychosocial development
■ THE CYCLE EXTENDS . . . AND ENDS
Adolescence
Adulthood
The later years
■ SUMMARY

Imagine that you have been asked to help decide what should be done with a wild creature captured by hunters in a French forest. He does not speak, but grunts and communicates only with eye movements and gestures. He tries to escape, running on all fours, and will bite or scratch anyone who gets too close. But this creature is a human child, a boy of about 12.

You are observing a *feral*—uncivilized—child, whose behavior appears more animal than human. He is described by his caretakers as "equally wild and shy." He seems frightened and "always impatient and restless," continually seeking escape "back to the freedom of his forest home and family of wild animals."

Suppose further that you have been faced with the task the French Government presented to young Dr. Jean Marc Itard: educate and civilize this savage child. Where would you begin? How would you discover what the child already knows? What would you try to teach him—and how?

Dr. Itard accepted this challenge, in part, as a test of the "new science of mental medicine." The year was 1800 and psychology was not yet a formal field of study. The influence of the mind on behavior was a subject of great interest to educators, philosophers, and some physicians, but as yet there had been no research to test their ideas.

A century earlier, in 1690, English philosopher John Locke had speculated that at birth the infant's mind was a blank slate, a *tabula rasa,* on which experience would inscribe knowledge. This *empiricist* view, that all knowledge comes from experience, was later opposed by the *nativist* view of French philosopher Jean Jacques Rousseau in the mid-1700s. Rousseau believed that inheritance was the key

△ Dr. Jean Marc Itard at about age 40.

to human development and that, in fact, human potential was corrupted by civilizing social influences. So Itard's little pupil, covered with animal scars, became the test case for these lofty philosophical ideas about human development.

Itard supported the empiricist view. He named the boy Victor and set out to demonstrate that "only in the heart of society" could Victor learn how to become fully human.

Success and enthusiasm filled the first years of Itard's patient and inventive training of his pupil. Victor learned to speak a few words—*lait* ("milk") and *O Dieu* ("Oh God")—and to comprehend many instructions and commands. He learned to keep himself clean and became affectionate and well mannered.

△ A portrait of Victor, the "Wild Boy of Aveyron."

But sadly, this initial spurt in Victor's cognitive and moral development sputtered and stalled. Five years later he had not progressed much further. Although he had learned to use symbols in thinking, to relate to other people, and to show pleasure in doing things well or shame at mistakes, he had not learned to talk or behave in all the ways that would make him like other young people. Most troubling to Itard was Victor's explosive, uncivilized sexuality.

Disappointed, the teacher-researcher called off this "natural experiment." Victor spent his remaining years in Paris, cared for by Dr. Itard's housekeeper. He died in 1828 at about age 40, ten years before his teacher.*

---

*For more details about this unique student-teacher relationship, you might want to read the accounts by Dr. Itard, reprinted in 1962, or Harlan Lane's more recent analysis (1976).

Why was Itard not more successful with his pupil? Were his methods at fault or was his pupil unable to learn? Probably both. Itard's first experiment in "behavior modification" could have profited from advances made years later in the education of the deaf; and Victor's learning may have been limited because he was retarded or had passed an age critical for learning basic skills. His prolonged isolation had also "deprived him of the crucial skill by which children and adults profit from social experiences that are not explicitly designed for their instruction, namely the skill of imitation" (Lane, 1976, p. 182).

But we must acknowledge the legacy of Victor and the contribution Itard made to shaping the modern education of retarded and deaf children. Itard's ideas also influenced the development of normal preschool education, in particular the "Montessori" method of Maria Montessori. Many children since have succeeded where Victor failed in part because of this pioneering study of human nature.

The *Opening Case* of Victor, who came to be known as the "Wild Boy of Aveyron," offers a challenging start for our psychological journey. The basic questions it raised are still of fundamental concern to psychologists. To what extent is any behavior or characteristic due to heredity or environment? How important are early life influences in shaping development? Is there a "developmental timetable" that regulates when particular aspects of functioning ordinarily appear, or are they always modifiable by education? And then there is the most profound question of all: How does a newborn baby turn into a sophisticated, complex adult capable of doing so much?

Think back to your first day of elementary school. What are all the ways you have changed over the years since then—in size, body build, and strength; in what you could understand and do; and in your interactions with your physical and social environment? How might you be different today if you had grown up among a tribe of Amazon Indians, been adopted by a royal family, never gone to school, or been tutored from birth on by a team of education specialists?

Consider two more questions. Is there anything about you that is still the *same* now as it was when you were five years old? And when you think about your parents or guardians, how have *they* changed from your earliest recollections of them to your most recent? In each instance, you are dealing with questions of *developmental change*—how you and other organisms change over time. To some extent, you are a unique creature without an exact duplicate anywhere. Yet your development has involved many systematic changes that were predictable for you and others of your species, culture, sex, and age.

In this chapter we will explore **developmental psychology,** the branch of psychology that is concerned with the processes and stages of growth and with changes in physical and psychological functioning from conception across the life span. Though we will touch on the major psychological changes and challenges unique to each successive period of life, we will focus on psychological development and primarily on the early years, when the transformations are so rapid and varied. Our plan is to see here an intact, whole organism functioning and changing in many ways—acquiring language, learning to reason, and developing emotional and social patterns of behavior. These and other strands of development correspond with the separate content areas of psychology that will be our focus in subsequent chapters, before we again return to the whole person in Chapter 11 where we'll examine personality in depth.

THE LIFE-SPAN APPROACH

Until recently, developmental psychologists limited their domain to three periods of major growth—infancy, childhood, and adolescence. Adulthood was long considered to be primarily a period of stability between the growth of youth and the decline of old age. But this assumption has been challenged by the new view that development is a lifelong process beginning at conception and ending at death (Baltes et al., 1980; Honzik, 1984). New tasks, different challenges, and characteristic sources of delight and frustration mark each period of our lives.

Since the beginning of a science of developmental psychology in the 1920s, two different focuses have emerged on the issue of what to study: *processes* or *age-specific life periods.* Some developmental psychologists study particular aspects of development—changes in processes such as learning, language, or moral reasoning. Others focus on the whole developing person; they study what human beings are like during different life periods.

How development is studied

What research method developmental psychologists choose depends on whether they are seeking to describe or explain the behavior under study. Descriptive information is provided by normative studies, while cause-effect information is provided by experimental studies. Within each of these, in turn, three types of time-based research designs are possible: cross-sectional, longitudinal, and sequential.

Normative investigations. The aim of normative investigations is to describe something that is characteristic of a specific age or developmental stage. From systematic testing of individuals of different ages, researchers can determine developmental landmarks, such as those listed in **Table 2.1** for mental and motor development during the first 8 months after birth. These are **norms,** standard patterns of development or achievement based on observation of many children at various ages. They indicate the average age at which the children performed the behaviors tested.

A good example of a normative investigation is a study conducted by Nancy Bayley (1969). She tested 100 infants at monthly intervals up to the age of 2 on a series of tests of mental and motor development. From her findings she constructed a set of norms for infant development over this entire period, which are known today as the "Bayley Scales of Infant Development." Scales such as Bayley's can help give parents an idea of when they might expect to see certain behaviors in their infant. However, it is very important for anyone using these scales to remember that the figures are simply averages; in no sense do they dictate when a particular child *should* show a particular behavior.

Experimental investigations. Many babies develop "stranger anxiety," a distress response to unfamiliar people. A normative study could provide information about when this behavior most often appears—it begins at about 8 months and can last for some time—but not an explanation for it. To get at the causes, we would need to conduct an experiment in which we systematically vary specific conditions that we suspect may influence the behavior. For example, we might plan a study to find out whether the anxiety is a response to all strangers or only to those with certain characteristics.

One such study was done with 14 children between 1 to 2 1/2 years of age as subjects. In one experimental condition, a research assistant was trained to act either "positive-nice" or "negative-nasty" toward each subject; in another condition he was instructed either to make eye contact with the subject or to avoid doing so. Under these varying conditions the subjects responded differently. They avoided or reacted negatively to the "nasty" stranger and also to the one who ignored them—that is, their behavior was typical of a stranger-anxiety response. But they did not make this response to the unfamiliar "nice" person. In the situations when the stranger merely made eye contact with the children, "this behavior opened lines of communication between them. Then, the children not only looked at the stranger but also vocalized, smiled, and approached" (Clarke-Stewart, 1978, p. 124).

With a better understanding of what causes particular behavior to occur or fail to occur, the developmental psychologist acquires new tools for improving healthy development and correcting or avoiding unhealthy development. "Thus, where it was once necessary to chart the *typical,* the challenge for many has now become to discover the possible" (Lipsitt & Reese, 1979, pp. 22–23).

Table 2.1   *Norms for Infant Mental and Motor Development*

One Month	Five Months
Responds to sound Becomes quiet when picked up Follows a moving person with eyes Retains a large easily grasped object placed in hand Vocalizes occasionally	Discriminates strange from familiar persons Makes distinctive vocalizations (e.g., pleasure, eagerness, satisfaction) Makes effort to sit independently Turns from back to side Has partial use of thumb in grasp
Two Months	Six Months
Smiles socially Engages in anticipatory excitement (to feeding, being held, and so on) Recognizes mother Inspects surroundings Blinks to object or shadow (flinches) Lifts head and holds it erect and steady	Reaches persistently, picks up cube deftly Transfers objects hand to hand Lifts cup and bangs it Smiles at mirror image and likes frolicking Reaches unilaterally for small object
Three Months	Seven Months
Vocalizes to the smiles and talk of an adult Searches for sound Makes anticipatory adjustments to lifting Reacts to disappearance of adult's face Sits with support, head steady	Makes playful responses to mirror Retains two of three cubes offered Sits alone steadily and well Shows clear thumb opposition in grasp Scoops up pellet from table
Four Months	Eight Months
Head follows dangling ring, vanishing spoon, or ball moved across table Inspects and fingers own hands Shows awareness of strange situations Picks up cube with palm grasp Sits with slight support	Vocalizes four different syllables (e.g., da-da, me, no) Listens selectively to familiar words Rings bell purposely Attempts to obtain three presented cubes Shows early stepping movements (prewalking progression)

This table shows the average age at which each behavior is performed up to 8 months. Individual differences in rate of development are considerable, but most infants follow this sequence. (From Lipsitt & Reese, 1979, p. 18)

Time-based designs. Most research on development uses a **cross-sectional design,** in which groups of subjects of different chronological ages are observed and compared. The researcher can then draw conclusions about behavioral differences that may be related to those age differences.

An *advantage* of a cross-sectional design is that an entire age range can be investigated at one time. A *disadvantage* is that since the groups being compared differ in year of birth, differences in the social or political conditions they've experienced—rather than age—may be responsible for their differences in behavior. For example, a group of 16-year-olds who have grown up during a period of severe economic depression or political turmoil may reflect attitudes that are not typical of 16-year-olds born earlier or later.

In a **longitudinal design,** the same subjects are observed repeatedly—sometimes over many years. An *advantage* of longitudinal research is that since the subjects have lived through the same socioeconomic period, age-related changes cannot be confused with differences due to differing socioeconomic circumstances. A *disadvantage* is that only individuals born at about the same time are tested, so that the generalizability of the results to people born at some different time will be unknown. Another problem with the longitudinal study is the amount of time required to complete it if the age span to be covered is large. It is also difficult and expensive to keep in contact with the subjects for repeated measurements that can last a lifetime.

One of the most ambitious longitudinal studies was begun soon after World War I by Lewis Terman and is still being carried on after 60 years. Over 1500 boys and girls, mainly in grades 3 through 8 (born about 1910) were selected on the basis of high intelligence scores (in the genius range). They have been tested at regular intervals ever since—first, to see how they compared to youngsters in general, then to see if their intellectual superiority would be maintained, and finally to discover the conditions and experiences that contributed to life satisfaction and to different styles of handling important life problems.

The first data were secured by survey questionnaires, interviews, and rating scales by parents and teachers. Initial follow-ups used the same data sources, but after 1936, questionnaires were sent regularly by mail to the subjects themselves. In the 1940s the young adults were gathered at testing centers and given several kinds of tests.

About 75 percent of those believed to be living are still returning questionnaires every ten years. Since Terman's death in 1956, the research has been carried on by Robert and Pauline Sears of Stanford University. Some of their findings in regard to life happiness, as assessed when the subjects were in their early sixties will be described on page 70 (P. Sears & Barbee, 1977; R. Sears, 1977; Terman, 1925; Terman & Oden, 1947, 1959).

The best features of the cross-sectional and longitudinal approaches are combined in a **sequential design,** in which subjects span a certain, usually small, age range and are grouped according to year of birth; then the groups are observed repeatedly over several years. Individuals born the same year are said to belong to the same **birth cohort.** By choosing cohorts whose ages will overlap during the course of the study, the researcher avoids both the confusion of effects of age and time of birth of the cross-sectional approach and the generalizability problem of the longitudinal approach. In addition, overlapping the age ranges of the different cohorts allows the researcher to study a fairly broad age range in less time than would be required by the longitudinal method alone.

In one sequentially designed study, four groups were selected, consisting of cohorts born in 1954, 1955, 1956, and 1957 who were 15, 14, 13, and 12, respectively, at the time of first testing. Each was tested for achievement motivation three times over a three-year period. This design allowed the researchers not only to compare several groups at the same age but also to follow the development of each group over the three-year period, while obtaining data covering the five-year age span from ages 12 to 17 (see **Figure 2.1**).

These observations began in 1970, following several years of strong youth protest and development

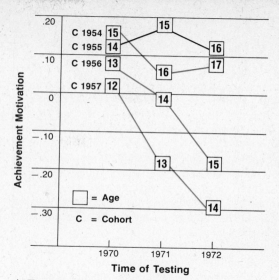

Figure 2.1 *Sequential Study of Adolescents' Personalities*

Four groups of adolescents, born in successive years 1954 through 1957, were tested for achievement motivation in 1970, 1971, and 1972. These observations followed several years of strong youth protest and the development of a counterculture that ridiculed an achievement orientation. The two later-born cohorts showed big declines in their achievement motivation while the other two remained more stable. Differences among the 14-year-olds born different years were especially striking. Apparently, even a two-year difference in time of birth can constitute a "generation gap" for some behaviors. (Adapted from Nesselroade & Baltes, 1974)

of a counterculture that ridiculed the achievement orientation and rationality of the "older generation." The two younger cohorts (born in 1957 and 1956) showed big declines in their motivation to achieve as they grew older, while the other two cohorts were more stable. Small differences between the cohorts at the beginning widened by the end of the study to become substantial. Some differences in this personality measure were even greater for groups of the same age (14-year-olds born in different years) than for the same groups at different ages (the 1954 or 1955 cohorts). So even a two-year difference in time of birth can constitute a "generation gap" for some behaviors (Nesselroade & Baltes, 1974).

Basic concepts

In studies of development, age itself is the usual independent variable; the dependent variable is the behavior whose changes are being studied at various ages. But age is really an indicator of underlying physiological and psychological changes that are presumed to be taking place and causing or making possible the changes in behavior. So age is also called an **index variable**—a variable that indicates the presence of other variables. It can be used as an independent variable because it is regularly associated with the underlying changes, much like certain blips on a sonar screen indicate the presence of a submarine. Index variables may also be responses, as when slips of the tongue are taken as indicators of unconscious wishes.

Although psychologists usually use **chronological age,** the number of months or years since birth, as their independent variable, they make a distinction between it and **developmental age,** which is the chronological age at which most children show a particular level of physical or mental development. For example, a 3-year-old child who has verbal skills typical of most 5-year-olds is said to have a developmental age of 5 for verbal skills. As you will see in Chapter 12, the familiar concept of IQ is based on the ratio of the overall mental developmental age to chronological age.

An important issue in developmental psychology is the extent to which development is characterized by *continuity* or *discontinuity*. Some psychologists take the position that development is essentially continuous, occurring through accumulation of *quantitative* changes. According to this continuity view, we become more skillful in thinking or talking or using our muscles much as we become gradually taller—through cumulative action of the same continuing processes.

Other psychologists see development as a succession of reorganizations with behavior *qualitatively* different in different life periods. In their view, particular aspects of development are discontinuous, although development as a whole is a continuous process. Thus, newborns are seen as not merely less

dependent on the mother than before birth (a quantitative change) but rather as dependent in totally different ways: physical dependence is different and a new dimension of psychological dependence has been added, both of which are qualitative changes. Another example of qualitative change is seen in the use of language by a 7-year-old: language not only is used more skillfully but also reflects different patterns of thought.

Psychologists who see development as discontinuous speak of **developmental stages,** qualitatively different levels of development. They believe that different behaviors appear at different ages or in different life periods because different underlying causes are operating. The term *stage* is reserved for an interval of time in which there are some qualitative differences in physical, mental, or behavioral functioning from times before and after it. The concept of stages also implies a progression toward an expected end state (Cairns & Valsinger, 1984). Developmental stages are assumed to occur always in the same sequence, with each stage a necessary building block for the next. The concept of stages is important in developmental psychology and appears in several of the major theories we will examine.

Related to the concept of developmental stages is that of critical periods. A **critical period** is a sensitive time during development when the organism is optimally ready to acquire a particular behavior. But certain stimuli and experiences must occur for this to happen. If they do not and the organism does not develop the new behavior, it will be difficult and perhaps impossible to do so later.

Experimental evidence supports the idea that critical periods occur in animals and humans. For example, salamander tadpoles usually start swimming immediately. If they are prevented from swimming for their first eight days by being kept in an anesthetizing solution, they swim normally when they are released. If kept in the solution four or five days longer, they are never able to do so; the critical period has passed (Carmichael, 1926). Likewise, dogs and monkeys raised in isolation for a few months after birth behave in bizarre ways throughout their lives, even if later reared with other normal animals (Scott, 1963). The brain of a human infant is most vulnerable to malnutrition shortly before birth and for a few months thereafter, when it is growing rapidly. Malnutrition can impair mental capacities permanently when it occurs during this period but not when it occurs later in life (Wurtman, 1982). It seems

◁ *This seventeenth-century drawing of a sperm cell by Niklaas Hartsoeker shows a tiny, completely formed human being inside it. It reflects the old belief that the child is a miniaturized adult, changing only by getting bigger—a quantitative change.*

reasonable to conclude that there are times in the early life of most organisms when optimum development is vulnerable to these critical-period effects. If there is a critical period for language development in humans, perhaps Itard failed because his instruction of Victor began after that period.

Developmental psychologists currently divide the human life span into nine periods, beginning with the prenatal period and ending with death. **Table 2.2** lists all nine periods, along with the time span and major characteristics of each. Death is included as the last period because it exerts considerable influence on our earlier development and because adjustment to its inevitability is one of our major developmental tasks, especially near the end of our life span.

In the remainder of this chapter, we will look both at the individual during different life periods and at several basic psychological processes that change over the life span. Beginning with prenatal development and with what infants can do, we will then examine in some detail the development of language, mental functioning, and social and emotional patterns. Finally we will discuss the later periods of the life cycle, focusing on the problems, choices, and satisfactions of those years.

THE LIFE CYCLE BEGINS

An energetic sperm cell discovers a receptive egg cell; united, they follow a trail as old as life itself to become a newborn human being in a mere nine months. This marvelous transformation is guided by principles of evolution and shaped by individual genetic influences. We prefer to think of human nature as somehow above and free from the biological processes that so clearly direct animal behavior. Indeed, we tend to believe that each baby comes into the world totally unequipped to deal with its environment. Even William James, one of psychology's most significant early contributors, held the traditional view of the infant as a know-nothing, do-nothing organism. He wrote that the infant is so ''assailed by eyes, ears, nose, skin and entrails at once'' that it experiences its world as ''one great blooming, buzzing confusion'' (1890).

Research in the past two decades has challenged this view of the newborn. Babies start with remarkable know-how and can use many of their senses to

Table 2.2 *Stages in Life-Span Development*

Stage	Age Period	Some Major Characteristics	Stage	Age Period	Some Major Characteristics
1. Prenatal Stage	Conception to birth	Physical development	5. Adolescence	About 13 to about 20 years	Highest level of cognitive capacity reached; independence from parents; sexual relationships
2. Infancy	Birth at full term to about 18 months	Locomotion; rudimentary language; social attachment	6. Young Adulthood	About 20 to about 45 years	Career and family development
3. Early Childhood	About 18 months to about 6 years	Language well established; gender typing; group play; ends with ''readiness'' for schooling	7. Middle Age	About 45 to about 65 years	Career reaches highest level; self-assessment; retirement
4. Late Childhood	About 6 to about 13 years	Many cognitive processes become adult except in speed of operation; team play	8. Old Age	About 65 years to death	Enjoy family, achievements; dependency; widowhood; poor health
			9. Death		A ''stage'' in a special sense, see text.

take in information virtually from the beginning. We might better think of them as prewired ''friendly computers,'' well equipped to respond to the adults who care for them. We will review here some of the ways in which human development is influenced by the genes we inherit from our parents, as well as some of the evidence that these genetic influences provide the potential for those little brains to start functioning much earlier than most adults realize.

Genetic influences on behavior

Our body build, behavior, and development were all determined to some extent at the moment the sperm and egg cells of our parents united in conception. Our genetic inheritance imposes certain constraints on our bodies, brains, and behavior—but it also makes certain behavior possible for us that is not possible for members of other species. Heredity provides the potentials with which environmental influences interact to enable each species to adapt to its own habitat. But all we actually inherit are chromosomes and genes.

Chromosomes and genes. Chromosomes are double strands of DNA (deoxyribonucleic acid) in the nucleus of the cells. All normal human body cells have 46 chromosomes. As cells divide, each chromosome strand splits down the middle, with half going to each new cell. Each half then acts as a template for replacing the missing half out of materials in the surrounding tissue. In contrast to body cells, the **germ cells,** spermatozoa and ova, contain only 23 chromosomes because they remain at half strength in their final division. When male and female germ cells unite, they form 23 pairs, to provide the 46 chromosomes that later will be found in all the body cells of the child. Thus the child receives half its chromosomes—a random selection—from each parent (see **Figure 2.2**).

The **genes** are segments along these chromosome strands that contain the ''blueprint'' for our development. They also set the timetables for different aspects of development. The genes provide the instructions for the development of our physical characteristics and even some of our psychological attributes. An amazing fact to consider is that a baby born with the normal complement of 46 chromosomes has somewhere between 30,000 and 100,000 genes in *each* cell.

An organism's full set of genes—all of the genes inherited from both parents—is called the **genotype.** The set of characteristics the organism actually develops—its observable features such as body build and eye color—is called the **phenotype.** A whole new field of research called **behavior genetics** is focused on attempts to identify the genetic components in behavioral traits, such as intelligence, mental disorders, and altruism (Fuller, 1982; McLearn & DeFries, 1973).

Most human characteristics in which heredity plays a role are **polygenic** (poly = many), meaning that they are dependent on a combination of genes. Genes that are always expressed in the individual's development are called **dominant** genes. Those that are expressed only when paired with a similar gene are called **recessive** genes. All-or-nothing characteristics like eye color may be controlled by a single gene or pair of genes. Characteristics that vary in degree, like height, are thought to be controlled by several genes. Complex characteristics, including some psychological attributes such as emotionality, are believed to be controlled or influenced by many groups of genes.

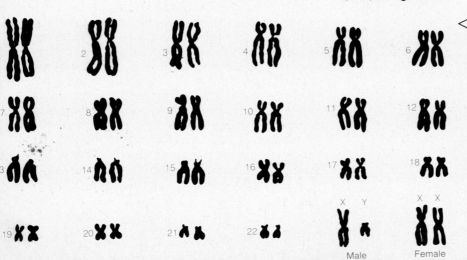

◁ **Figure 2.2**

Shown here are the twenty-three pairs of chromosomes each normal baby is born with. In both males and females, twenty-two pairs are the same. The twenty-third pair determines the sex of the child. Males have one X chromosome and one smaller Y chromosome, or an XY pair. Females have two X chromosomes, or an XX pair.

Only about 10 percent of the genes we inherit will be used in the course of our lives. The unused genetic potential in our genotype is like a trust fund, available if our usually constant environment changes in significant ways.

An interesting perspective on the relation between genes, evolution, and behavior is provided by behavior geneticist Myron Hofer:

''The genes that have been selected for us in the process of evolution are a series of hedged bets as to environments that may be encountered and the behavioral strategies that will be required to deal with them. The information is essentially historical— what worked in the past. . . . Not only does our genetic makeup contain hidden potential that awaits new environments to be expressed, but the behavioral capacities that we are predisposed to acquire also allow us different behavioral options at any moment in time'' (1981, p. 191).

When the environmental requirements are specific and predictable, behavior is rigidly programmed by the genes. We then see stereotyped, unlearned behavioral patterns, such as the fixed-action patterns of Tina, the mother turkey we met in the *Opening Case* in Chapter 1. Animals that are higher on the phylogenetic (animal development) scale face more varied environmental challenges and have replaced the stereotyped behavior patterns seen in lower animals with patterns more complex and changeable through experience. In the case of humans, an almost limitless diversity of behavioral traits can emerge as genetic predispositions interact with experience in varied physical, social, and cultural environments.

There are many steps between the action of a gene in organizing assemblies of protein molecules and the final structure of an organ or any behavioral function. At each of these steps environmental influences also help determine the outcome. For example, at the very first step in the long process of development, neighboring genes regulate whether a particular gene will be turned on or off. In the following two or three months, environmental factors such as malnutrition, radiation, or certain drugs can prevent the normal formation of organs and body structures. A tragic case occurred in the early 1960s, when several hundred women who had taken a tranquilizer called *thalidomide* early in pregnancy gave birth to babies whose arms and legs had not developed beyond stumps. The environmental factor of maternal malnutrition during pregnancy may also lead to mental retardation and to low birth weight, which is associated with later health problems.

Physical growth and maturation. The blueprint provided by the genes directs the physical development of the organism in a predictable sequence and also is responsible for the appearance of certain behaviors at roughly the same time for all normal members of the species, though there are some cultural variations. Some, like sucking, are totally unlearned. Others follow inner promptings but need a bit of refinement through experience. For example, most children sit without support by 7 months of age, pull themselves up to a standing position a month or two later, and walk soon after they are a year old. Once the underlying physical structures are sufficiently developed, these behaviors require only a minimally adequate environment and a little practice for proficiency. They seem to ''unfold from within,'' following an inner, genetically determined timetable that is characteristic for the species. This process of organizational changes in bodily functioning, through the continuing action of heredity, is called **maturation**. The characteristic sequences of both physical and mental growth are programmed by maturation (see, for example, the sequence for locomotion in **Figure 2.3**).

Genetic factors are considered to be the instigators of maturational changes, which in turn make the individual ready for new experience and learning. It is also true, however, that certain kinds of experience may influence physiological functioning and thus biological development. For example, although no amount of practice or encouragement can teach children to walk or talk or read before they are maturationally ready, cross-cultural research findings reveal variations in the *timing* of some maturational changes. These differences can presumably be attributed to different cultural experiences.

The influence of maturation is most apparent in early development, but it continues throughout life. It is maturation in the nervous system that changes the amount and type of sleep we need at different stages of life (Chapter 6), maturation in the endocrine system that brings on the rapid development of the sex organs and secondary sex characteristics at puberty (e.g., voice change).

Different aspects of development follow different maturational timetables. The earliest behavior of any kind is the heartbeat, the action of the heart muscle. It begins in the *prenatal* period, before birth, when

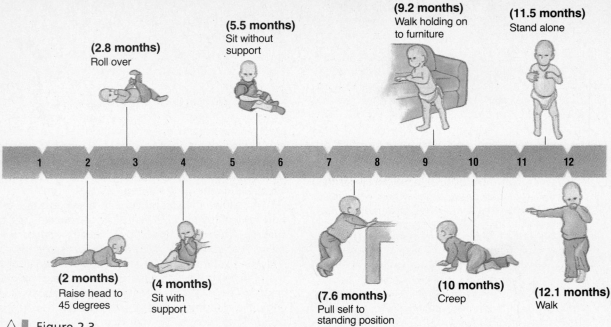

(2.8 months)
Roll over

(5.5 months)
Sit without
support

(9.2 months)
Walk holding on
to furniture

(11.5 months)
Stand alone

1 2 3 4 5 6 7 8 9 10 11 12

(2 months)
Raise head to
45 degrees

(4 months)
Sit with
support

(7.6 months)
Pull self to
standing position

(10 months)
Creep

(12.1 months)
Walk

△ Figure 2.3

*The development of walking requires no special teaching. It follows a fixed time-ordered sequence
that is typical for all physically capable members of our species. In cultures where there is more
stimulation of walking, children begin to walk sooner than in ours. The Hopi Indian practice of
carrying babies in tightly bound back cradles retards walking, but once the child is released, the
same sequence is seen. What is remarkable about walking is that it should occur at all. The
crawling infant successfully getting around must suffer frustration in the early attempts to walk.
Yet the effort persists. Ultimately the child reaps the evolutionary reward of greater flexibility and
adaptability than is possible with four-legged locomotion. (After Shirley, 1931)*

the embryo is about three weeks old and a sixth of
an inch long. Responses to stimulation have been
observed as early as the sixth week, when the embryo is not yet an inch long. Spontaneous movements have been observed by the eighth week (Carmichael, 1970; Humphrey, 1970).

After the eighth week the developing embryo is
called a **fetus.** The mother feels movement of the
fetus about the sixteenth week after conception, although fetal movements may be heard with a steth-
oscope a week or two earlier. At these ages, the fetus is somewhere around 7 inches long (the average
length at birth is 20 inches).

Babies seem to be all head. At birth a baby's head
is already about 60 percent of its full adult size and
measures a quarter of the whole body length (Bayley, 1956). The neural tissue of the brain grows at an
astonishing rate, increasing by 50 percent in the first
two years, 80 percent above birth size in the next
two, and leveling off by about 11 years of age. The
infant's body weight doubles in the first 6 months
and triples by its first birthday. By the age of 2, the
child's trunk is about half of its adult length.

Genital development is on a quite different developmental program. Genital tissue shows little change
until the teenage years, then develops rapidly in only
a few years to adult proportions. **Figure 2.4** shows
the systematic, though different, patterns of growth
for neural and genital tissues, as compared with
overall body growth.

By birth or soon after, genetic and early environmental influences have resulted in the development
of basic physical and psychological characteristics like

◁ *A human embryo at six weeks,
actual size.*

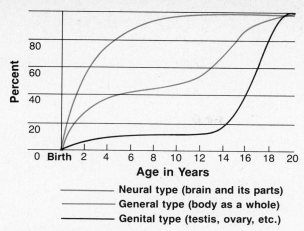

Percent (y-axis): 80, 60, 40, 20

Age in Years (x-axis): 0 Birth 2 4 6 8 10 12 14 16 18 20

— Neural type (brain and its parts)
— General type (body as a whole)
— Genital type (testis, ovary, etc.)

body build, temperament, and predispositions to certain physical and mental illnesses. These are called **constitutional factors.** They are presumed to be largely hereditary and remain fairly consistent throughout a person's lifetime. Even at birth, constitutional factors are apparent in the child's body type, characteristic physiological functioning, and basic reaction tendencies. For example, some babies are more sensitive to stimulation than others; some have a high energy level; some are placid, not easily upset. Basic reaction tendencies such as these, present at birth, affect the way children *interact* with their environment and thus the experiences they will have and what they will learn. But it is still possible for experience to modify the way a constitutional factor is expressed.

Nature and nurture. To what extent is human behavior determined by heredity (nature) and to what extent is it learned (nurture)? The controversy over the relative importance of nature and nurture has been of central importance in the study of development. Itard had hoped to shed light on this controversy by successfully educating Victor.

The extreme positions of Locke and Rousseau, described on page 33, do injustice to the richness of behavior. Almost any complex action is shaped by both inherited biological influences and experience, including learning. Not only that, but they have a continuing mutual influence on each other, in which each one makes possible certain further advances in the other but also limits the contributions the other can make.

Heredity sets upper limits to what can develop; experience and practice determine how closely the limits are approached. For example, your heredity determines how tall you *could* grow; how tall you actually become depends partly on nutrition, an environmental factor. Similarly, the level of mental ability that a person develops seems to depend on both genetic potential and environmental opportunity.

Genetic influences have been found for many psychological characteristics. For example, males, on the average, do better than females on tests of visual spatial abilities; females do better on tests of perceptual speed. These are evidently genetic differences (Rose et al., 1979). Certain reading disabilities, too,

Is depth perception innate or learned? The apparatus below was designed to study this. A board laid across a piece of heavy glass has a checkered pattern appearing just below it on one side but dropping away on the other to form a "visual cliff." Will subjects move onto the "steep" side when encouraged to do so? Most infants avoid this side from the time they can move about: chicks and goats within 1 day of birth, cats at 3 to 4 weeks, and humans at 6 to 10 months. Though the human infant might have learned this perception, it seems unlikely that the goat could have done so (Gibson & Walk, 1960).

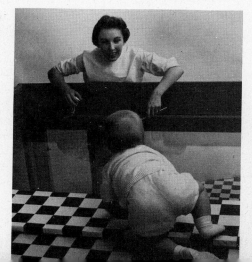

Books in Transit: Up-front or Down-side?

You can conduct a simple observational study that reveals how one kind of behavior you probably engage in without much thought is influenced by your heredity and your environment.

Question: When you carry books (without a book bag), do you carry them:

_____ at your side?
_____ in front, against your chest?

Task: Observe 10 males and 10 females about your age and record whether each is a side-carrier or a front-carrier. Record your observations in the matrix below.

	Side carriers	Front carriers
males **n = 10**	n =_____ _____%	n =_____ _____%
females **n = 10**	n =_____ _____%	n =_____ _____%

Your conclusion:

Research shows that the way we carry books varies according to sex. Most school-age girls and women clasp books against their chests; boys and men generally hold them at their sides. During the first two years of school, both sexes carry books as older males do: about 8 out of 10 are side carriers. Males become even more so, reaching nearly 100 percent in junior high school. Females shift from side to front carrying as they mature, with a marked switch at the seventh grade level. By high school, nearly all of them have become front carriers (see **Figure** and photo).

According to Jenni and Jenni (1976), this carrying style is a behavioral difference that is mainly due to differences in skeletal-muscle development and learned conformity to one's peer groups. This dramatic difference is slightly less by college age, but still about 80 percent of the women are front carriers and 90 percent of the men are side carriers.

Next, try a little experiment by getting a group of your friends to reverse this behavior for a week and see if they can influence others to switch unconsciously.

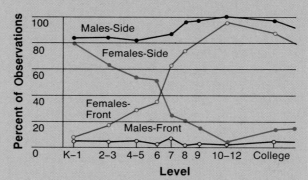

appear to have a significant genetic component (De Fries & Decker, 1982). There is evidence that some forms of mental disorder have a genetic component. And some traits of temperament found in one identical twin predictably occur in the other as well, even when the twins are reared in quite different environments (Floderus-Myrhed et al., 1980). Findings with regard to intelligence and the statistical technique for calculating the contribution of heredity in that case will be discussed in Chapter 12.

The debate continues, and you can participate by conducting the experiment described in the **Close-up** at top of page. But many investigators today are even more interested in identifying *how* heredity and environment and their interaction contribute to development than in trying to weigh their relative importance.

What can babies do?

How do babies organize their early experiences and what can they do? These questions are at the core of a virtual explosion of research on the *infancy period,* which lasts for about the first 18 months of life, while the child is "incapable of speech" (the Latin meaning of *infancy*). Much of this research is focused on the **neonate,** the newborn baby up to a month old.

Responding and adapting. Even within the first few hours of life, it is clear that the newborn infant, given an appropriate stimulus, is capable of a variety of built-in responses. If placed upon the mother's abdomen, the baby will usually make crawling motions. The baby will turn its head toward anything that scratches its cheek—a nipple or a finger—and begin to suck it. Sucking is an exceedingly complex but already highly developed behavior pattern, involving intricate coordination of tongue and swallowing movements, synchronization of the baby's breathing with the sucking and swallowing sequence, and tactile stimulation from the nipple. Yet it appears that most babies "know how to do it" from the start.

Also, from the earliest moments of taking in fluid, sucking is an *adaptable* behavior that can be changed by its *consequences.* The rapidity of sucking, for example, is dependent on the sweetness of the fluid being received. The sweeter the fluid, the more continuously—and also the more forcefully—the infant will suck (Lipsitt et al., 1976).

In fact, the sucking rate even depends on the *pattern* of sweetness over time, rather than simply the absolute amount of sweetness at the moment.

A group of newborns who were given a sucrose-sweetened solution through an automated nipple apparatus responded at the rate of 55 sucks per minute, compared with 46 sucks per minute for a group that received water. A third group, which had sucrose first and then water, matched the rate of the first group while they were getting sucrose. But when the sucrose changed to water, their rate fell below that of the water-only group. Not only did they respond differently to the different tastes, but the experience of the sweet solution in the preceding five minutes weakened their response to the water solution (Kobre & Lipsitt, 1972).

▷ Newborns prefer human faces to other patterns. Their intent gazing primes infants for social interaction with their caregivers.

Infants apparently come into the world preprogrammed to like and seek pleasurable sensations, such as sweetness, and to avoid or escape from unpleasant stimulation, such as loud noises, bright lights, strong odors, and painful stimuli. They also prefer novel stimuli to familiar ones (Cohen & Gelber, 1975). How these inborn preferences and response tendencies can lead to the learning of new responses will be discussed in Chapter 7. For now, the important point is that they generate behavior that affects the environment (faster sucking produces more sweets), and this consequence, in turn, changes the subsequent behavior. Even the hour-old newborn is primed to interact with its environment and prepared to learn from its experiences. It is through such interactions of inherited response tendencies and learned experiences that naive babies, in time, become worldly individuals.

Interacting socially. Most of all, babies are designed to be *sociable.* They prefer human voices to other sounds and human faces to most other patterns (Fantz, 1963). As early as one week of age, they can distinguish their mother's voice from that of other women. In another week, they perceive her voice and face as part of a total unit, and get upset when experimenters pair one of them with a stranger's voice or face (Carpenter, 1973).

Babies not only respond to but also *interact* with their caregivers. High-speed film studies of this interaction reveal a remarkable degree of *synchronicity*—gazing, vocalizing, touching, and smiling of mothers and infants are closely coordinated (Martin, 1981). Babies respond and learn, but they also send out messages to those willing to listen and to love them.

Not only have the behaviors of mothers and infants been shown to be linked, but their feelings are also matched. A three-month old infant may laugh when its mother laughs and frown or cry in response to her negative **affect**—emotion or mood (Tronick et al., 1980).

Skeels Stimulates Environment Stimulates IQ

During the 1930s, two baby girls neglected by their mentally retarded mothers were committed to an Iowa orphanage. When first observed by psychologist Harold Skeels, they were physically sick and clearly retarded in mental development. At 15 and 18 months of age, respectively, they were transferred to an institution for the retarded. When Skeels saw them six months later, they were alert and healthy, and their intelligence test scores had increased. Skeels attributed the change to the fact that these little waifs had been "adopted" by the nurses and patients and given a loving, stimulating environment.

Skeels set about testing this chance observation in a systematic fashion. A total of 13 similarly neglected children, averaging 19 months of age with a mean IQ score of 64, far below the "normal" IQ of 100, were sent from the orphanage to a home for mental retardates as "house guests." Each child in the experimental group was quickly "adopted" by an older woman, and warm personal relationships developed. These were supported by the other patients and staff members. What were the effects of this tender, loving care?

About three years later, their IQs had gained an average of 28 points, increasing from an average of 64 to 92. A comparable amount had been *lost* by a comparison group of orphans who had started with an initial average IQ 23 points higher but had stayed in the overcrowded orphanage. After two more years, 11 of the special-care children were considered adoptable (children with very low IQs were considered unadoptable) and indeed had been adopted.

In what amounts to a developmental psychologist's *tour de force,* Skeels went out years later, after the children were grown, and located *every one from the original study,* except for one of the control group, who had died at age 15. The differences he found in the adult lives of the two groups were enormous. All the children who had received the special care, on a one-to-one basis from an attentive "aunt," had become self-supporting adults; none was a ward of any institution. In contrast, 5 of the 11 surviving comparison individuals were still institutionalized. The average income of the 6 employed comparison individuals was only one-quarter that of the special-care group. In the latter group 8 of the 13 had graduated from high school, and 5 had gone to college. The average educational attainment of the special-care group was the eleventh grade, while that of the comparison group was only the fourth grade. Eleven of the special-care group had married, and among them had had 28 children whose IQs averaged a normal 104. None of them showed signs of mental retardation (Skeels, 1966).

This research was honored by an award for excellence by the Kennedy Foundation, and the award was presented to Dr. Skeels by a young man then completing his master's degree in business administration. Although the young man did not know it until this time, he had been one of the infants whom Skeels had assigned to special care.

Young children can be helped along the route of interaction and learning through enriched environments that stimulate their senses and encourage responding. For a look at the importance of early stimulation and interaction for both intellectual and social development, see the **Close-up** above.

In general, developmental psychologists currently studying what babies can do are becoming ever more impressed with how precocious they are. They seem to come equipped to accomplish three basic tasks of survival: sustenance (feeding), maintenance of contact with other people (for protection and care), and defense against harmful stimuli (withdrawing from pain or threat). But to do so requires perceptual skills, some ability to understand their experiences with people and objects, and basic thinking skills that very early combine the brain's information from different senses, such as vision and touch, to aid in grasping moving objects (von Hofsten & Lindhagen, 1979).

Some investigators have concluded that children are born with the ability to distinguish between things they experience and then to put this information into categories. Being able to categorize the flow of conscious experience is essential for building a knowledge base that grows by fitting the novel into familiar slots and adding new categories when a better fit is called for (see Masters, 1981). Given their limited education, infants are remarkably sophisticated young beings.

The beginning of language acquisition

The difficulty Dr. Itard had in teaching Victor to use the French language was probably not too much greater than that which many foreign-language teachers experience regularly in trying to teach American college students to communicate in French or any other foreign language. Despite their advanced cognitive development, college students are usually unable to do what the average preschool child does with ease: quickly acquire and be able to use a vocabulary of about 2000 words to express thoughts and feelings.

Young children's acquisition of language is one of the most remarkable achievements of the human species. In the span of a few years, with little formal instruction, and often in spite of faulty information (parents talking "baby talk," for example), young children become superb linguists. By the age of 5, normal children can analyze language into its minimal separable units of sounds and meaning, use rules they have *discovered independently* for combining sounds into words and words into meaningful sentences, and also take an active part in conversations.

Though language structure is not our focus here, **Table 2.3** summarizes various aspects of structure, in order to illustrate the complexity of what young children learn. But how do they learn? How do they become able to use language to express novel ideas with word combinations they may never have heard—the test of true language mastery?

Stages in natural language learning. The answer to the above questions will come in part from a look at what the child does at each of four stages in language acquisition: the babbling stage, the one-word stage, the two-word stage, and the telegraphic-speech stage.

1. The babbling stage. Even before the vocal apparatus is completely formed, a baby begins to make vowel-like sounds. Cooing sounds begin in the second month, and babbling at four to five months; such sounds are considered important precursors of language. Even babies born deaf babble until about six months; then they stop and are unable to speak without intensive training.

To speak, one must hear language spoken, and the language the child hears is the one that will be acquired. Infants appear to be ready to learn *any* language they hear. For example, babies of English-speaking parents produce not only speech sounds

---

Table 2.3   *The Structure of Language*

Grammar is the field of study which seeks to describe the way language is structured and used. It includes several domains:

1. **Phonology**—the study of the way sounds are put together to form words.

   A **phoneme** is the smallest unit of speech that distinguishes between any two utterances. For example, *b* and *p* distinguish *bin* from *pin*.

   A **morpheme** is the minimum distinctive unit of grammar that cannot be divided without losing its meaning. The word *bins* has two morphemes, *bin* and *s*, indicating the plural.

   Phonetics is the study and classification of speech sounds.

2. **Syntax**—the way in which words are strung together to form sentences. For example, subject ("I") + verb ("like") + object ("you") is one standard English word order.

3. **Semantics**—the study of the meanings of words and their changes over time. **Lexical meaning** is the dictionary meaning of a word. Meaning is sometimes conveyed by the *context* of a word in a sentence ("Run *fast*" versus "Make the knot *fast*") or the *inflection* with which it is spoken (try emphasizing different words in the phrase, "a white house cat").

4. **Pragmatics**—rules for participating in conversations, social conventions for communicating, sequencing sentences, responding appropriately to others.

---

found in English but also sounds that occur in other languages, too. These "foreign" sounds gradually drop out of the baby's repertoire, and then only the sounds used in English remain.

Another aspect of this early period of babbling is infants' ability to *recognize* sounds before being able to produce them. Even one-month-old infants are able to distinguish between different types of consonants, as shown by changes in their rate of nipple sucking that occur in response to hearing different consonants. (Eimas et al., 1971).

Beyond babbling, infants also vocalize in response to the sounds made by their parents. Sometimes they do so simultaneously; sometimes they alternate their sounds with their parents', in a conversation without words. In doing this, the infants are learning sound patterns and intonations. As they near the end of the first year, they begin to imitate the intonation pattern of their parents' language. Though no words are produced, the sounds of an American child are those of American English, while those of a Japanese child begin to sound Japanese (Glucksberg & Danks, 1975).

2. The one-word stage. The beginnings of patterned, "true" speech occur some time near the end of the first year, as the child's first recognizable words begin to appear. These first words are usually concrete nouns or verbs. They are used to *name* things that stand out in the perceptual world because they move, make a noise, or can be manipulated—*Mama, ball, dog,* for instance. Later they are used to make *requests: milk, cookie, bed.* The child not only is learning the meaning of these single words, but also is using them in a sequence of one-word utterances in conversations that convey more complex meanings. A child hearing a car go by says: "Car." Parent: "What?" Child: "Go." Parent: "What?" Child: "Bus." The parent interprets this to mean that the child is recalling a bus ride taken the previous day—a memory probably triggered by the sound of the car. In this one-word stage, the child is actively developing hypotheses about how to use words together in sentences. Not used at this time are words for relationships, internal states, or passive objects that do not stand out in the child's perception.

3. The two-word stage. For adults to understand the child's two-word utterances such as "Tanya ball," they must know the *context* in which the words are spoken. "Tanya ball" could mean Tanya wants the ball or throws the ball, depending on who has it. In turn, the child comes to appreciate the importance of context for understanding meaning.

Many of young children's first word combinations are used as an aid in categorizing objects into a variety of classes—for their own information rather than as a means of communicating with others (Halliday, 1975). Language aids this categorizing, but the cognitive ability to put objects, events, sounds, and people into categories begins in infancy even before any words are used. Before they are a year old, children group objects on the basis of similarity of form, color, and especially function (Cohen & Strauss, 1979; Nelson, 1979).

All children speak in one-word utterances before putting two-words together. But they do not go through a three-word stage. After two words, sentence size varies considerably. By age 2, vocabulary has expanded to about 50 words; it then explodes to 1000 words by age 3 (Lenneberg, 1969).

4. The telegraphic-speech stage. Beyond the two-word stage, speech becomes **telegraphic:** filled with short, simple sentences with many content words (mostly nouns and verbs) but lacking tense endings, plurals, and **function words** like *the, and,* and *of,* which help express the relationships between other words. "Bill hit ball window break" is a telegraphic message. The full message is, "Bill hit the ball that broke the window." In most languages that have been studied, function words are added in a predictable order as the language user matures.

By the age of 2, English-speaking children have learned that word order is important and that the three critical elements are actor-action-object usually arranged in that order. They typically misinterpret "Mary was followed by her little lamb to school" as "Mary" *(actor)* "followed" *(action)* "her lamb" *(object),* ignoring the function words.

At the telegraphic-speech stage, language becomes a tool with multiple uses. Speech helps the child differentiate the physical world of spaces and objects from the social-personal realm of attachments, emotions, and the regulation of behavior. It is also a vehicle for getting the attention of others (there is less crying), as well as for showing feelings and expressing needs.

Language becomes more complex in the maturing child for many reasons. Obviously, it reflects the child's growing vocabulary (see **Figure 2.5**). Coupled with this is the child's increasingly sophisticated memory and ability to reason and use abstract ideas. Furthermore, the child is discovering that there is more to life than meets the eye. There are processes of change as well as objects that change; there are memories of the past and expectations of the future and much that cannot be seen—like fear and trust—but needs to be communicated.

Hypotheses and rules. From a study of the regular patterns of errors that most children make in using language at each stage of development, it is apparent that they are trying out hypotheses about how sounds and words ought to go together to convey meaning and about the rules of phonology, syntax, and semantics. Sometimes, of course, the hypotheses children come up with are wrong.

One of the most common errors is **overregularization,** in which a rule is applied too widely, resulting in incorrect linguistic forms. For example, once a child learns the past-tense rule for most verbs (add *ed* to the verb), the *ed* will be added to *all* verbs. The result is words such as "doed" and "breaked". As the child learns the rule for plurals (add the sound *s* or *z* to the end of the word), again there is overex-

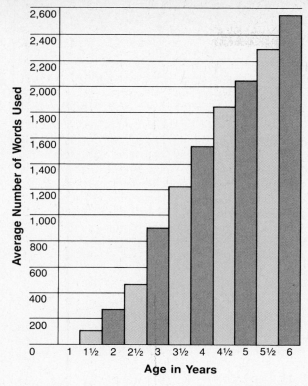

◁ **Figure 2.5** *Children's Growth in Vocabulary*

The number of words a child can use increases rapidly between the ages of 1½ and 6. Shown here are average vocabularies found in one study in each half yearly interval.

(From "The Acquisition of Language" by B. A. Moskowitz, *Scientific American,* Nov. 1978. Copyright © 1978 by Scientific American, Inc. All rights reserved. Reprinted by permission.)

tension of the rule, resulting in words like "foots" and "mouses."

When a word first appears in a child's vocabulary—"moon," for example—it may mean only one feature of the moon, such as roundness; and clocks, cakes, the letter *O,* or any circular object may also then be called "moon." Gradually, the word is associated with other characteristics of the moon (rises at night, shines, varies in shape) until the word is applied only to the moon (Clark, 1973).

Overregularization is an especially interesting error to psychologists because it usually appears after the child has learned and used the correct forms of the verbs and nouns. That is, the child first uses the correct verb forms, "came" and "went," apparently because they were learned as separate vocabulary items. But when the general rule for past tenses is learned later, it is immediately extended to all verbs. The child says "comed" and "goed," even though he or she has never heard other people say such words. Such mistakes are evidence that language learning depends on acquisition of general rules rather than just accumulation of specific bits of information.

Acquiring language: nature or nurture? As a child acquires language, systems involved in *comprehending* language, such as memory and cognitive strategies for self-monitoring of speech, are being coordinated with systems that *produce* speech. De-

spite the rapidity with which speech appears, this coordination takes time and the different parts of it develop at different rates (Clark & Hecht, 1983).

Our sketch of *what* young children can do with—and to—language at different stages has not answered our initial question of *how* they acquire language. Do they learn it from experiences of imitating the sounds, words, and sentences they hear being corrected, and then making the necessary modifications? This *nurture* viewpoint, as argued by B. F. Skinner (1957), regards language acquisition as a learned skill like any other.

Environmental influences do indeed play a role in shaping language. Preverbal sounds children utter but do not hear used by adults will drop out of their repertoire. The dependence of language acquisition on social interaction is seen in the case study of a boy with normal hearing born to deaf parents.

The parents spoke only in American Sign Language but exposed the child to a daily diet of television viewing. He was sickly and confined to his home, so that while he heard people talking on TV, the only real people he had contact with were his parents. By the age of 3 he was able to use sign language fluently—but could not speak or understand spoken English. The researcher concluded a child can learn a language only if there are chances for interaction with real people who speak the language (Moskowitz, 1978).

The bulk of the evidence, however, suggests that the primary role in both steering and timing speech acquisition is played by nature, through maturation. According to this view, children come to the language acquisition situation not as blank slates but rather with biologically predetermined mental structures that facilitate the comprehension and production of speech by limiting the hypotheses they generate about the grammar of language (Chomsky, 1965, 1975). As soon as the brain is sufficiently developed to send out its nerve signals, their language acquisition "program" is partly written. Language emerges and evolves at particular periods that correspond more closely with the child's physical and cognitive maturation than with particular learning experiences—always assuming opportunities to interact with speaking humans (Lenneberg, 1969).

Children learn to speak in a highly methodical way, by breaking down the language they hear into its simplest parts and then developing rules that put the parts together to communicate thoughts and feelings (Moskowitz, 1978). They produce words they have never heard when they misuse certain grammatical rules; later they produce sentences that they have never heard. Moreover, they usually receive very little systematic teaching from parents, tend to ignore corrections, and do not benefit much from additional practice. All of this evidence seems to indicate that children are born to be competent in using language.

As we mature, many new language skills are added. We learn to use language to inform, to persuade, to flatter, to conceal. As we elaborate our language into rhetoric, we seek to make it a thing of beauty by using elegant poetic variations, inventing new words and ways of expressing familiar ideas as well as giving verbal expression to our fears and fantasies. To carry on a simple conversation requires mastering many skills: monitoring the sequence and pacing of exchanges and how much time each person has spoken, interrupting, giving and receiving compliments, changing the topic, paraphrasing, and more. When we then integrate "body language" of nonverbal gestures to our spoken language, the complexity of message sending (encoding) and receiving (decoding) becomes enormous. But we do it, usually well, without a single course in the art of conversational communication.

Life without language would be more than an inconvenient deficit. It would be life without connection to ideas and to people. Language is a vehicle for meeting our need to know, to belong, and to express what we know and feel. It is fundamental to our humanity.

Having outlined some aspects of early development, we next examine two of the major strands of development that continue throughout the life cycle: cognitive development—how we become able to use ideas and process information—and social-emotional development—how we form the bonds of the human connection and become socialized.

COGNITIVE DEVELOPMENT

How the processes of knowing develop—including perceiving, reasoning, imagining, and problem solving—is referred to as **cognitive development**. Studies of cognitive development tend to focus on such topics as what and how children remember, how children develop expectations and a sense of the future, and how children sort experiences into categories. Many of the current attempts to discover how mental processes develop derive from the pioneering work of the late Swiss psychologist Jean Piaget.

Piaget's insights into mental growth

No one has contributed more to our knowledge of how children think, reason, and solve problems than Jean Piaget. For nearly fifty years he devoted his career to observing children's intellectual development. Piaget began by carefully observing the behavior of his own children from an early age. He would pose problems for them, observe their response, alter the situation slightly, and again see how they would respond. Experimental psychologists today study information processing in laboratory settings by designing complex experiments that yield simple, specific conclusions. Piaget used simple demon-

△ Jean Piaget (1896–1980).

strations and interviews with one child at a time to draw complex generalizations.

Piaget was interested primarily in the changes that take place in a child's mental processes during the course of cognitive development. How does a child transform specific, concrete information gathered through sensory experience into general, abstract concepts that are not limited to any immediate stimulus situation? To answer this question, Piaget studied how children perceive certain situations and how they come to "think about" and "know about" physical reality. His interest was not in how much children knew but in how their thinking and inner representations of outer reality changed at different stages in their development.

Assimilation and accommodation. According to Piaget, there are two processes at work in cognitive growth. He called the first process **assimilation,** in which we fit new information into what we already know, modifying it as necessary. He called the second process **accommodation,** in which we restructure or modify what we already know so that new information can fit in better.

For example, consider the transitions a baby must make in changing from breast to bottle and then to cup. The initial sucking response, as we have seen, is present at birth. In adapting to a bottle, the infant still uses many parts of the sequence unchanged (assimilation) but must grasp and draw on the rubber nipple somewhat differently and learn to hold the bottle up at an appropriate angle (accommodation). The step from bottle to cup requires more accommodation but still will rely on earlier skills of sucking in fluid and swallowing it.

Piaget saw cognitive development as the result of the constant interweaving of assimilation and accommodation in an upward, spiraling process. Assimilation keeps and adds to what exists, thereby connecting the present with the past. Accommodation results from problems posed by the environment, perceptions that do not fit with what we know and think. These discrepancies between our ideas and what we see are an important influence in cognitive development. They force the child to develop more adaptive inner structures and processes, making possible creative and more appropriate action to meet future challenges. So both assimilation and accommodation are needed, but in balance.

Through these two processes we become increasingly less dependent on perceiving and more dependent on thinking. Mental growth always includes going from reliance on *appearances* to reliance on *rules.*

According to Piaget, the earliest mental structures, which he called **schemes,** simply guide sensorimotor sequences such as sucking, looking, grasping, pushing, and so forth, probably with little or no "thought" as we know it. These sensorimotor sequences are dependent on the presence of classes of objects—things that can be sucked, or watched, or grasped, for example. But thereafter, mental structures increasingly incorporate symbolic representations of outer reality which, in turn, make possible increasingly complex mental operations (Gallagher & Reid, 1981; Piaget, 1977).

Stages in cognitive development. Piaget identified four qualitatively different stages of cognitive growth in the continuing upward spiral of assimilation and accommodation. He believed that all children progress through these stages in the same sequence, although they differ in their rate of development. He called the four stages the *sensorimotor stage* (infancy), the *preoperational stage* (early childhood), the *concrete operational stage* (middle childhood), and the *formal operational stage* (adolescence). Distinctive styles of thinking emerge at each stage.

1. The sensorimotor stage (roughly from birth to age 2). So many new cognitive achievements appear during the first two years that Piaget subdivided the sensorimotor stage itself into six substages. We will summarize here only the two main trends in this period: the change in adaptive responses and the development of object permanence.

In the early months the infant "knows" only "in the sense of recognizing or anticipating familiar, recurring objects and happenings and 'thinks' in the sense of behaving toward them . . . in predictable, organized, and often adaptive ways" (Flavell, 1977, p. 16). But during the first year the sensorimotor sequences are improved, combined, coordinated, and integrated (sucking and grasping, looking and manipulating, for example). They become more varied as the infant tests different aspects of the environment, discovers that actions have an effect on outer events, and begins to perform what look like intentional, cognitively directed behaviors toward clear goals. By the end of the second year, the capacity to represent absent events symbolically is clearly present, as shown by the child's ability to name an object not present.

Part of this development of the child's adaptive responses is a gradual development of a concept of **object permanence**—that is, of objects as existing and behaving independently of his or her action or awareness. The child progresses from merely following a moving object visually (soon after birth), to continuing to look where the object has gone out of sight (2–3 months), to watching for its reappearance at a different spot or visually searching for it (4–8 months), to retrieving it from out-of-sight positions under increasingly different and less vision-dependent conditions (8–18 months). By about age 2 the child "will grin with anticipation, and then search

◁ As children move through the sensorimotor stage of development, they explore the environment, learning that their actions have consequences. They also become aware through this constant testing of their environment that they are separate from the things they perceive.

systematically each possible hiding place. . . . He may also spontaneously try the same game on you, with him doing the hiding and you doing the finding. . .'' (Flavell, 1977, p. 47). Clearly children at this age now have an internal symbolic representation of the object as independent of their perception of it or action toward it.

2. The preoperational stage (roughly 2 to 7 years). Young children start life as naive realists. That is, they believe in what they see. But like scientists, who look for regularities in the flux and variety of individual events, young children gradually become aware of *invariants* in their environment, things that do not change their identity despite changes in appearance. Their mastery of the concept of object permanence enables them to go on to discover other invariants—first to discover that objects not only have continuing identity but the *same qualitative* identity despite changes in appearance.

Early in the preoperational period, children may believe that a boy could become a girl if he played with dolls or wore girls' clothes; by the end of the period, they are likely to know better. In one study, 3-year-old children who watched the hind end of a cat while a dog mask was put over its head thought the cat had become a dog; 6-year-olds were more likely to believe that a cat could not turn into a dog (DeVries, 1969).

Their previous mastery of object permanence also readies children for representative thinking during this period, thinking dependent on symbols rather than on sensorimotor relationships. But their thinking is still more dependent on appearances than on concepts and rules, which prevents them from carrying out certain mental operations; hence the name *preoperational* to characterize the thought processes of this period.

Thinking at the beginning of this period is characterized by **centrism,**—that is, the child cannot take more than one perceptual factor into account at the same time. One aspect of centrism is **egocentrism,** not self-centeredness but difficulty in imagining a scene from someone else's viewpoint. Piaget used a three-dimensional, three-mountain scene and asked children what a teddy bear standing on the far side would see; his subjects could not describe the scene accurately until about age 7 (Piaget & Inhelder, 1967). In more recent research, however, using scenes more familiar to children, children of 3 and 4 were able to turn a movable version of the scene to show someone else's view, though they did poorly with a scene like the one Piaget used (Borke, 1975).

In general, **decentration**—the ability to take into account two or more physical dimensions at once—does not come until later. This ability is illustrated in Piaget's classic lemonade study. When an equal amount of lemonade is poured into two glasses 5-, 6-, and 7-year-old children all report that the glasses contain the same amount. But when the lemonade from one glass is poured into a tall, thin glass, they have differing opinions.

The 5-year-olds know it is the same lemonade in the tall glass (qualitative identity) but believe that

△ The 5-year-old girl in the photo is aware that the two containers have the same amount of colored liquid. But when the liquid from one is poured into a taller container, she then indicates that there is more in the taller one. She has not yet grasped the concept of conservation.

somehow it has become *more.* The 6-year-olds are uncertain but also say the tall glass has more. The 7-year-olds ''know'' there is no difference. The younger children are still relying on appearance; the older ones, on a rule. They are also taking into account two dimensions, height and width, while the younger children are considering only height, a normally useful cue for ''more.''

3. Concrete operations (roughly 7 to 11 years).
The 7-year-olds in the lemonade study have achieved an understanding of what Piaget called **conservation.** This is the understanding that physical properties do not change when nothing is added or taken away, even though appearances change. The lemonade example showed conservation of volume. During the concrete operational period, children develop other kinds of conservation, such as conservation of number and area. They are ready at last for what Piaget called **mental operations**—they can mentally transform information and then mentally reverse the sequence. They can depend on concepts rather than on perceptual evidence from looking at and touching things.

But though these children become able to use logic and inference in solving concrete problems, the symbols they use in reasoning are still symbols for concrete objects and events, not yet abstractions. Their limitations are shown in the familiar game of ''20 Questions,'' in which the task is to identify what is being thought by asking the fewest possible questions. The child of 7 or 8 usually sticks with specific questions which, if correct, could solve the task (Is it a bird? Is it a cat?). A few years later children will approach the task systematically, going from general categories (Is it animal?) to subcategories and then specific guesses, which means asking several questions at first that could not themselves answer the ''What is it?'' question (Bruner et al., 1966).

4. The formal operational stage (roughly age 11 on).
In Piaget's final stage of cognitive growth, logical operations are no longer bound by concrete problems. It is now possible to deal with abstractions, consider hypothetical questions (What if a man had eyes in the back of his head?), and design formal ways to test abstract ideas. Most young adolescents have acquired all the mental structures needed to go from naive thinker to expert.

The approach of adolescents and adults to the ''20 Questions'' game demonstrates this ability to use abstractions and to adopt an information-processing strategy that is not limited by the questions posed to them. They impose their own structure on the task, starting with broad categories, and then formulate and test hypotheses in the light of their knowledge of categories and relationships.

Modern perspectives on cognitive development

There is no question of the importance of Piaget's contribution in focusing attention on the development of cognitive processes in children. The questions he asked, the phenomena he studied, and the conceptual insights he offered remain significant. His theory of the dynamic interplay of assimilation and accommodation is generally accepted as a valid account of how a child's mind develops. The general features of his cognitive stages have also been supported by independent investigators.

On the other hand, many of Piaget's testing situations were loose, unstructured, and poorly controlled. Since his formulation of stages was based largely on observation of his own three children, it is difficult to rule out the influence of Piaget the father on Piaget the data gatherer. In addition, Piaget relied heavily on children's descriptions of their thought processes, whereas a child may understand something but not be able to explain it. So it is not surprising that other researchers are supplementing and in some cases challenging some of Piaget's findings.

For example, there is growing evidence that children possess some cognitive capacities earlier than Piaget believed possible (Selman, 1980). It has been shown that first-graders can understand how to do conservation of quantity tasks by imitating the reasoning of children who are conservers (Botvin & Murray, 1975). Using tasks and procedures different from Piaget's, researchers have also found that preschoolers can deal with limited number sets (up to 5), can do some ordering and classification of objects, and as we have seen, can switch to take the perspective of others under certain conditions (Borke, 1975; Lempers et al., 1977). And evidence is accumulating that preschool children have a good understanding of cause-and-effect relationships when they are tested with objects familiar to them and when they can show their understanding

through behavior instead of having to make verbal responses (Pines, 1983).

In current research on cognitive development there is more emphasis on the acquisition of language, memory, and reading skills and more intense study of adolescent thought processes. Studies today are also more likely to include the personal, social, and ecological (environmental) contexts in which the individual's behavior occurs (Posner, 1982; Rogoff, 1982). Such studies have found that a child who is unable to recall a short list of arbitrarily designated words in a memory test somehow can recall a large number of names of classmates and lines from many songs. New strategies for organizing material for memory and recall become possible when the material has *significance.* For example, classmates' names are remembered well when the child constructs a mental organization of the class seating plan or of functional groupings such as reading groups (Bjorklund & Zeman, 1982). Likewise, there is a growing recognition that developing competence in specific domains (like chess) requires practice and the building of a large knowledge base, not simply more complex mental operations.

Much research has found discrepancies between children's verbal reports about their thought processes and performance measures of them. Understanding the reasons for these discrepancies may help us understand better how children and adults become aware of their own cognitions, as well as the processes that generate ''thoughtful'' behavior (Schneider, 1984).

At a more fundamental level, theorists are questioning the extent to which mental activity is qualitatively different at different stages of cognitive development. Some argue that an important aspect of intellectual development consists of learning how to organize existing knowledge better rather than the unfolding of new capacities. For example, a child may organize knowledge into subroutines—coherent units of information and systematic ways of using them. Subroutines increase the child's efficiency in carrying out arithmetical functions, comprehending stories, and other mental tasks. With practice, the child also develops greater ability to gain swift access to these stored subroutines (Rozin, 1976). These advances may be due simply to quantitative learning rather than to new inner cognitive potential.

SOCIAL AND EMOTIONAL DEVELOPMENT

A child competent in language and cognitive skills would still be deficient without corresponding social and emotional development. Although developmental psychologists have tended to focus on the growth of mental processes, children do not thrive solely by becoming smart: they must form relationships with other people and they must be in touch with their own feelings.

In this section we will examine some aspects of these strands of development: how children form relationships with others (parents most significantly), how parenting styles affect the child's behavior and personality; how gender roles develop. Then we will look at the development of moral understanding and end with a brief discussion of stages of sexual and social orientation, as described by two influential theorists: Sigmund Freud and Erik Erikson.

Socialization

Socialization is the name given to the lifelong process whereby an individual's behavioral patterns, values, standards, skills, attitudes, and motives are shaped to conform to those regarded as desirable in a particular society (Hetherington & Parke, 1975). Many people are involved in this social learning—mother, father, siblings, relatives, friends, and co-workers. Institutions, including the school, the church, and the legal and penal systems, also exert pressure toward certain values and compliance with certain standards of conduct. But the family is the most influential shaper and regulator of socialization. Here the basic patterns of responsiveness to others are formed. These in turn form the basis of consistent styles of relating to other people throughout life.

Parents' goals in socializing their children range from the specific—saying "please" and "thank you" and not talking with a mouth full of food—to the general—being cooperative, honest, and responsible. Overall, parents are concerned with fostering the optimal development of their children into well-functioning adults (see **Table 2.4**). In our society, one of the values associated with a desirable adult role is the ability to form bonds of intimacy and stability with others (Maccoby & Martin, 1983).

Attachment and loving relationships. Social development begins with the establishment of a close emotional relationship between the child and the mother or other regular caretaker. This intense, enduring relationship is called **attachment.** For the child to develop attachment, sensory and response systems must be sufficiently mature, and there must

Table 2.4 *Types of Tasks of Early Childhood Socialization in the Family*

Parental Aim or Activity	Child's Task or Achievement
1. Provision of nurturance and physical care	Acceptance of nurturance (development of trust)
2. Training and channeling of physiological needs in toilet training, weaning, provision of solid foods, etc.	Control of the expression of biological impulses; learning acceptable channels and times of gratification
3. Teaching and skill-training in language, perceptual skills, physical skills, self-care skills in order to facilitate care, insure safety, etc.	Learning to recognize objects and cues; language learning; learning to walk, negotiate obstacles, dress, feed self, etc.
4. Orienting the child to immediate world of kin, neighborhood, community, and society, and to his or her own feelings	Developing a cognitive map of one's social world; learning to fit behavior to situational demands
5. Transmitting cultural and subcultural goals and values and motivating the child to accept them for his or her own	Developing a sense of right and wrong; developing goals and criteria for choices, investment of effort for the common good
6. Promoting interpersonal skills, motives, and modes of feeling and behaving in relation to others	Learning to take the perspective of another person; responding selectively to the expectations of others
7. Guiding, correcting, helping the child to formulate own goals, plan own activities	Achieving a measure of self-regulation and criteria for evaluating own performance

(From Clausen, 1968, p. 141)

be close interaction with a parent or other caregiver during the critical period of the first year. Attachment is usually apparent by the time the infant is 6 to 9 months old and is promoted by circumstances that extend the duration and/or frequency of close physical contact. It has been found that conditions for attachment are often best for first-born children and for infants who are at risk (premature or sick).

We can infer the child's development of attachment from several behaviors. The child seeks to be near the parent (or caregiver), resists separation from the parent, uses the parent as a secure base when exploring unfamiliar situations, and clings to the parent when afraid. Further, the child seeks both attention and signs of approval from the parent or caregiver (Brackbill, 1979). The baby may gain closeness and attention through a variety of behaviors, such as smiling, vocalizing, looking at the parent's face, and crying.

Attachment behaviors occur in many species. In some, the forming of the relationship is aided by chemical effects from the mother's licking the newborn, eating the placenta, and giving off odors called *pheromones* that are attractive to the young. It is guided by a timetable associated with the stage at which the infant animal begins to move about.

In some species, attachment is called **imprinting;** it is a primitive form of learning in which the infant animal physically follows and forms an attachment to the first moving object it sees and/or hears (Johnson & Gottleib, 1981). Usually this object is the mother—

but not always. Young geese raised by a human will learn to follow that person instead of one of their own kind (Lorenz, 1937). A monkey raised by a dog will become more strongly attached to its foster mother than to other monkeys (Mason & Kenney, 1974).

In animals, this basic first attachment is the mechanism by which the young establish their identification as members of their species. Extensive animal research on attachment has demonstrated an upper age limit for developing the relationship, as well as the results of a failure to develop it. For example, puppies that do not form an attachment to other dogs by 14 weeks of age have difficulty ever doing so (Scott et al., 1974). But even attachment to the mother is not enough for healthy social development. Young monkeys—despite the formation of strong attachment to a mother substitute—have trouble forming normal social and sexual relationships in adulthood *if* they have been deprived of chances to interact with other monkeys in their early lives (see the **Close-up** on pp. 58–59).

With human infants, the more immediate effects of lack of close, loving relationships—on physical growth and even on life itself—has been shown in many studies. In 1915, a doctor at Johns Hopkins Hospital reported that despite adequate physical care, 90 percent of the infants admitted to orphanages in Baltimore died within the first year. Studies of hospitalized infants over the next thirty years found that despite adequate nutrition, the children often developed respiratory infections and fevers of unknown origin, failed to gain weight, and even showed signs of physiological deterioration, such as diarrhea, decrease in muscle tone, and eating difficulties (see Bowlby, 1969; Sherrod et al., 1978). A study of 91 infants in foundling homes in the United States and Canada reported evidence of anxiety, sadness, physical retardation, insomnia, stupor, and abnormal weight loss among the children—and the death of over a third of them, most between the

◁ Konrad Lorenz, the researcher who pioneered in the study of imprinting, graphically demonstrates what can happen when young animals (in this case, goslings) become imprinted on someone other than their mother.

seventh and twelfth month of life, despite good food and medical care (Spitz & Wolf, 1946). And as we will see in Chapter 3, family environments marked by emotional detachment and hostility can lead to low weight and retarded bone development; children begin to grow when they are removed from the hostile environment, but their growth again becomes stunted if they are returned to it (Gardner, 1972).

It seems clear that early deprivation can slow physical, mental, and social development, producing lasting handicaps (Kagan & Klein, 1973). Yet some children are resilient in the face of severe life stresses. Why?

> A longitudinal study of a group of 690 Hawaiian children from very poor families followed their development from soon after conception to age 20. In their life of poverty, these children experienced many stressful events and one in five developed serious behavior problems at some time during the 20-year period. Boys suffered most from illnesses, learning problems, and problems in controlling aggression; girls suffered most from dependency problems.
>
> Those who showed effective coping patterns were physically robust, very active, and responsive to other people. Furthermore, they had developed a sense of self-confidence and coherence in their positive relationships to their families. Strong bonds had been forged between infant and primary caregiver. The child was rarely separated from the family, was given much attention, and was part of a multigenerational social support network of family and friends (Werner & Smith, 1982).

A close interactive relationship with loving adults is the child's first step toward healthy physical growth and normal socialization. As the original attachment to the primary caregiver extends to other family members, they too become models for new ways of thinking and behaving. From these early attachments the child then develops the tendency to adapt to the needs of others in a socialized world.

Parenting styles.

> "I am very pro-American. I have a small son and have hopes that when he grows up he will join one of the armed forces. To ensure this, I have thought of talking to him while he is sleeping—no great speech, but a little patriotism and the suggestion that an army career would be good. Can this type of suggestion help, or will it cause him to rebel?" (Caplan, 1969, p. 65)

This father's request for advice, though unusual, highlights a central issue in socialization: How far can parents go in conveying their own values, beliefs, and even prejudices to their children? This concern raises a second issue: How does childrearing shape and control what the child learns and does?

Ideas about what is required of a good parent have varied greatly at different times in our history. Today we have the advantage of being able to find out from empirical studies what results to expect from different kinds of parent-child interactions. To a considerable extent, the answer seems to depend on the age of the child.

> One study found that optimal parental care in *infancy* consists of providing a stimulating social and physical environment, being responsive to the child's needs, and expressing much love with physical contact. But permissive parenting is not as effective in the *preschool* years (2 to 5) and may have negative consequences for the child (Clarke-Stewart, 1973).
>
> In another study nursery-school children were observed by raters and evaluated by their teachers on a variety of dimensions. Three personality patterns emerged. *Mature* children were high on self-reliance, self-control, exploration, and positive affect. *Disaffiliated* children showed little positive affect or curiosity and had few friends. *Immature* children were dependent on others and low on self-reliance and self-control measures.

Attachment Is Not Enough

An extensive program of research on the role of mothering in monkeys has provided intriguing and unexpected answers to basic questions about the mother-child relationship. Although the findings cannot be applied directly to humans, they suggest useful lines of human research.

The generally accepted theory at the beginning was that infants develop attachment and affection for a caretaker in response to having physical needs met, especially the need for food. But when macaque monkeys were separated from their mothers at birth and placed in cages where they had access to two artificial "mothers"—a wire one and a terrycloth one, the babies nestled close to the cloth mother and spent little

time on the wire one, even when it was the wire one that gave milk: the one that provided contact comfort was preferred over the one that provided food.

The terrycloth mother was also used as a base of operations in exploring new stimuli. When stimuli known to produce curious and manipulative responses were introduced, the baby monkeys would gradually venture out to explore, then return to her before exploring further. When a fear stimulus (a toy bear beating a drum) was introduced, the baby monkeys would run to her; when new stimuli were presented in her absence, they would often freeze in a crouched position or run from object to object screaming and crying. When a cloth diaper was one of the objects, they would often clutch it, but it never pacified them (Harlow & Zimmerman, 1958).

Did the monkeys with terrycloth mothers develop normally, as it appeared? At first, the experimenters thought so, but a very different picture emerged when it became time for females raised in this way to become mothers. First, despite elaborate arrangements, it took many months to get any of them inseminated; success was finally achieved with 4 of the 18.

◁ *The baby monkeys nestled close to the cloth mother and spent little time near the wire one, regardless of which one gave milk.*

Other observers then interviewed the parents of these children, asking them questions about four dimensions of their parenting: *control* (number of rules and follow-through on getting compliance to their directives); *maturity demands* (requirements for the child to behave appropriately for his or her age); *communication* (discussion of family rules and general nature of parent-child dialogue); *nurturance* (display of affection toward the child and a conflict-free home atmosphere).

It was found that *permissive* parents (low on control and maturity demands) tended to have *immature* children, *authoritarian* parents (low on commu-

nication and nurturance) had *disaffiliated* children, and *authoritative* parents (relatively high on all dimensions) were most likely to have *mature* preschoolers. Evidently the ideal parenting style during this difficult period of major social and emotional change is a style that provides structure, discipline with love, and a willingness to discuss problems and decisions with the child (Baumrind, 1967; 1973).

In an ongoing longitudinal study with a larger group of children, the same investigator found similar relationships at age 4. When the children were observed five years later at age 9, the authoritative parenting pattern was still associated with competence, assertiveness, and social responsibility in the children. Despite arguments by one critic (Lewis,

"After the birth of her baby, the first of these un-mothered mothers ignored the infant and sat relatively motionless at one side of the living cage, staring fixedly into space hour after hour. If a human observer approached and threatened either the baby or the mother, there was no counter-threat. . . . As the infant matured and became mobile, it made continual, desperate attempts to effect maternal contact. These attempts were consistently repulsed by the mother. She would brush the baby away or restrain it by pushing the baby's face to the woven-wire floor" (Harlow, 1965, pp. 256–57).

When other "motherless monkeys" were artificially inseminated, most were either indifferent and unresponsive to their babies or brutalized them, biting off their finger or toes, pounding them, and nearly killing them until caretakers intervened.

One of the most interesting findings was that despite the consistent punishment, the babies persisted in their attempts to make maternal contact. In the end, "it was a case of the baby adopting the mother, not the mother adopting the baby" (Harlow, 1965, p. 259). And fortunately, with successive pregnancies, the maternal behavior of these mothers improved.

In subsequent studies, the Harlows found that the monkeys who had only terrycloth mothers showed adequate, but considerably delayed, heterosexual adjustment if they were given ample opportunity to interact with other infant monkeys as they were growing up. As with human babies, the development of normal socialization and communication in monkeys seems to require experiences of *interaction* with other members of their species (Harlow & Harlow, 1966).

◁ *Monkeys who were separated from their mothers at birth and who were prevented from observing behavior in others of their species subsequently either rejected or ignored their own babies and repulsed attempts by the babies to make maternal contact.*

1981) that some of the findings could be reinterpreted as child-to-parent effects rather than parent-to-child effects, the investigator argues otherwise. She states that her findings are inconsistent with that interpretation, and that the data are better explained by attributing the children's behavior to the combination of firm control and emotional responsiveness represented in the authoritative pattern. (Baumrind, 1984).

This research makes an important new distinction between *authoritarian* parenting, (restrictive control without warmth or open parent-child dialogue) and *authoritative* parenting, in which firm parental control is combined with warmth, open communication, and shared decisions. It is consistent with an earlier study of the parenting styles related to self-esteem in boys 9 to 11.

The boys with *low* self-esteem came from homes where little affection was shown to them. They were often neglected, few rules or limits were imposed, and there was little discussion but frequent physical punishment for annoying the parents. *Medium* levels of self-esteem were associated with getting more affection and having both more rules and more shared

decision-making, but also having little privacy and being overly protected. *High* self-esteem was found in children whose parents provided love with reasonable discipline, where rules were applied carefully and consistently, privacy was allowed, and independence was encouraged (Coopersmith, 1967).

We may conclude that parents' behavior toward their children and the system of rules, rewards, and communication they establish in the home all influence the child's social and emotional growth. Permissive-indulgent parenting seems best in infancy, whereas an authoritative, reciprocal, interactive style of parenting is more likely to prove optimal from preschool years up to adolescence. There is no evidence for positive results from the authoritarian or autocratic parenting style as practiced within our democratic society. It is not yet known what works best during adolescence or in cultures with different social-political structures from ours.

It is also important not to underestimate the child's impact on the parent's behavior. For example, active, aggressive children may induce quite different reactions in their parents from those called forth by quiet, gentle children. In addition, we should note that the complex process of socialization is affected by many influences other than parent-child relationships that cannot be considered here, such as socioeconomic class, ethnic-cultural differences, mother's age, family size, and being raised by one parent instead of two.

Gender roles

It is no secret that males and females are different. Not only do they have different physical characteristics, but they often behave in different ways and play different roles in society. While some of these differences are linked to biology, far more are the result of socialization processes.

Sex refers to the biologically based characteristics that distinguish males from females—in this context, especially those that are necessary for reproduction. These characteristics enable males to produce sperm and ejaculate, and females to menstruate, ovulate, gestate (carry a fetus), and lactate (nurse a child). These differences are universal, biologically determined, and unchanged by social influence. **Gender,** by contrast, is a psychological phenomenon; it refers to learned sex-related behaviors and attitudes of males and females. Differences beyond those that are biologically based—much of what we consider masculine or feminine—are variable and are learned, influenced, and shaped by the particular culture in which we live (Williams, 1983).

Gender identity is one's sense of maleness or femaleness; usually it includes an awareness and acceptance of one's biological sex. (For transsexual individuals, there is a disparity between sex and gender identity: they feel they are one sex "trapped" in a body of the other sex.) **Gender roles** are patterns of behavior regarded as appropriate for males and females in a particular society. They provide the definitions for "masculinity" and "femininity" in the society and are highly variable from one society to the next.

Gender-role socialization begins at birth. In one study, parents described their newborn daughters as little, beautiful, delicate, and weak and their newborn sons as firm, alert, strong, and coordinated, even though the babies showed no obvious differences in weight, height, or health (Rubin et al., 1974). These different perceptions influence how parents actually treat their sons and daughters as they are growing up. They dress them differently, give them different types of toys to play with, and communicate with them differently. For example, research by naturalistic observation has shown that male infants are held more and given more physical stimulation. Parents also pay more attention to sons' vocalizations and signals for food (Parke & Sawin, 1976; Yarrow, 1975). In addition, boys are given more freedom to explore and to go a distance from home, while girls are encouraged to stay closer to their mothers and to carry out more supervised activities within the home (Fagot, 1978; Saegert & Hart, 1976).

This pattern of differential gender-role socialization continues to be seen in research that examines how parents teach their children new skills. Even if they are teaching the same thing to their sons and daughters, they use different teaching styles. With a son, they are likely to set higher standards and emphasize mastering the situation and achieving the goal, in spite of any difficulties he may encounter. With a daughter, they are likely to emphasize the interpersonal aspect of the teaching situation, joking and giving her encouragement and emotional support for her efforts. Should she have problems, the parents are apt to be protective and not push her to keep striving. Thus, the message for boys is one of mastery and achievement, while the message for girls focuses on nurturance and social relationships (Block et al., 1975).

Several kinds of learning processes are involved in gender-role socialization. First, children learn much about gender roles through rewards and punishment: they find that if they engage in gender-appropriate behavior, they are likely to receive praise, gifts, and affection, whereas they may be punished, ridiculed, or ostracized for behaving in gender-inappropriate ways. Second, children also learn about gender roles through watching what other people are doing and then imitating that behavior, even if there is no immediate reward for doing so. Third, based on their observations and experience, they develop certain beliefs and formulate rules about gender and gender-appropriate behavior: girls wear dresses and have long hair and boys wear pants and have short hair. Beliefs and general understanding about gender are dependent on the child's age and level of cognitive ability.

The result of gender-role socialization is that boys and girls grow up in different *psychological* environments which shape how they view the world and deal with its problems. A variety of socializing agents—teachers, peers, and the mass media, as well as parents—consistently and subtly reinforce these alternate conceptions of what is important in

the male's and female's world view. For men, the unstated socialization goals are to be bold, to seek freedom, and to "dare to be great." For women, the goals are to be content with achieving security and a conflict-free life, while hoping to be good. It is in this sense that psychologist Jeanne Block (1983) concludes that parents give their girls "roots" to build homes and families, but give their boys "wings" to soar to new adventures.

✓ Moral development

Morality is a system of beliefs, values, and underlying judgments about the rightness or wrongness of acts. One function is to ensure that individuals will act to keep their obligations to others in the society and will behave in ways that do not interfere with the rights and interests of others.

Babies are *amoral*—neither moral nor immoral but simply lacking in any understanding of people's responsibilities to each other. The development of this understanding is an important part of socialization.

Early approaches to the study of moral development. In the 1920s a team of Yale University behaviorists set out to study moral knowledge and its relation to moral behavior in children ages 6 to 14. They administered tests of moral knowledge to large numbers of children and observed their behavior in a number of situations where there was a chance to be either honest or dishonest. The data were unexpected. Most children were honest in some situations, dishonest in others. Instead of being guided by a general trait of honesty or dishonesty, behavior seemed to depend more on the situation—how attractive the reward was and how likely the child was to get caught. Also, moral or immoral behavior showed little relation to moral knowledge, which was generally high, and there was no evidence of greater moral development with age. These experimenters concluded that morality was not a stable quality in people, but a response that varied with the demands of the situation (Hartshorne & May, 1928).

Sigmund Freud (1913/1976) took a different approach. His interest was in the development of *motivation* for moral behavior rather than in the behavior itself. Freud believed that children learn to

◁ *Parents socialize their children into different gender roles. Little boys are encouraged to master situations and achieve goals and little girls to nurture and establish social relationships.*

internalize certain moral principles that then guide their actions; they learn not to act in ways that will be punished or threaten their security. Freud argued that most people behave morally most of the time because of the inhibiting effects of their conscience or the guilt they feel when they do something wrong. Freud's ideas on this topic will be elaborated in Chapter 11.

Piaget (1960), in a third approach, sought to tie the development of moral judgment to the child's general cognitive development, which we have already described. As children progress through the stages of cognitive growth, they put differing relative weights on the consequences of an act versus the actor's intentions. For example, to the preoperational child, someone who breaks several cups accidentally is judged to be "naughtier" than one who breaks one cup intentionally. A little later, the actor's intentions will weigh more heavily in the child's judgment.

Kohlberg's stages. The best-known psychological approach to moral development today is that of Lawrence Kohlberg (1964). Like Piaget, Kohlberg has focused on the development of *moral reasoning* and proposes several qualitative stages. Each stage is characterized by a different basis for moral judgments. For example, at Stage 2, a person's moral judgments tend to be based on a calculation of personal risks and benefits; at Stage 3, moral judgments are based on a desire for acceptance from others.

According to Kohlberg's original formulation, people can be categorized as being at one of six stages of moral development. Since then, he has theorized that an even higher moral stage (Stage 7) exists, although it is rarely found. Unlike Piaget's stages, Kohlberg's stages are not related to particular ages. And though moral reasoning at the upper levels is not possible before cognitive maturity, there is no automatic unfolding of these stages of moral reasoning. In fact, only about a quarter of the adults in our society seem to rise past Stage 4 of Kohlberg's ladder (Kohlberg, 1973).

To assess individual subjects, Kohlberg devised a series of moral dilemmas in which different moral principles are pitted against one another. In one dilemma, for example, a man is trying to help his wife obtain a certain drug needed to treat her cancer. An unscrupulous druggist will sell it to him only for much more than it cost him—more money than the man can raise. Should the man steal it? Why or why not? The interviewer probes the reasons for the sub-

ject's decision and then scores the answers. The scoring is based on the *reasons* that are given rather than on which decision is made (Kohlberg, 1964, 1967).

Kohlberg claims that (a) any individual can be characterized as being at one of these stages at a given time; (b) everyone goes through the stages in the same order; (c) the higher stages are more comprehensive and complex; and (d) the same stages occur in any culture. There is empirical evidence to support these theoretical claims (Kohlberg, 1981).

Are women less moral than men? Despite the evidence for these stages, there is still considerable debate about a number of aspects of Kohlberg's concepts including the reliability and validity of his classification (Rosen, 1980). Additional controversy centers around the problem of sexual bias in Kohlberg's conception of moral reasoning (Loevinger & Knoll, 1983), a bias that makes men seem to be more moral than women.

Kohlberg has found that most men reach Stage 4 in moral reasoning on his dilemmas test, while most women stop at Stage 3. As you can see in **Table 2.5,** Stage 4 has a law-and-order orientation involving maintenance of the society's institutions and rules, while Stage 3 reasoning involves living up to the conventions of "good" behavior approved by others in the social group. Other research, however, has found women to be more politically liberal than men. And in Kohlberg's scheme, liberal ideology is associated with higher levels of morality which involve extending the same principles of fairness to groups beyond one's own (Holstein, 1978).

Two Australian researchers decided to explore the question of sex differences in morality by seeing whether differences in moral judgments would occur if the major character in Kohlberg's stories were female instead of male. When this character was a woman, the scores of male subjects dropped to the Stage 3 level. (Women scored at Stage 3 regardless of the sex of the story character.) The investigators saw these changes in male scores as evidence that certain types of behavior and reasoning are seen as appropriate for women in our society. That is, women are expected to make judgments from an emotional perspective (Bussey & Maughan, 1982).

If girls are given "roots" and boys "wings" in our society, perhaps it is not surprising that they also develop different patterns of moral reasoning.

In a study of men's and women's moral development during the early adult years, convincing evi-

Table 2.5   *Kohlberg's Stages of Moral Reasoning*

Levels and Stages	Reasons for Moral Behavior
I Preconventional Morality Stage 1 Pleasure/pain orientation Stage 2 Cost-benefit orientation; reciprocity—an eye for an eye	To avoid pain, not get caught To get rewards
II Conventional Morality Stage 3 Good child orientation Stage 4 Law and order orientation	To gain acceptance, avoid disapproval To follow rules, avoid censure by authorities
III Principled Morality Stage 5 Social contract orientation Stage 6 Ethical principle orientation Stage 7 Cosmic orientation	To promote the society's welfare To achieve justice, avoid self-condemnation To be true to universal principles, feel oneself part of cosmic direction that transcends social norms

(Based on Kohlberg, 1964, 1981)

dence was found that socialization into male and female gender roles in our society had created different patterns of social and moral understanding and a different hierarchy of values in the men and women subjects. The men's sense of self-worth seemed to come from being autonomous and independent, whereas the women's sense of self was based on interdependence. The experimenter saw the first as an overemphasis on self-integrity, the second as an overemphasis on attachment—both essential aspects of balanced development. For the men, this had led to a morality based on equal rights and devotion to abstract principles even at the sacrifice of people's well-being. For the women, it had led to a morality based on caring, in which increasing maturity broadened the scope of the person's sense of responsibility and compassion. For mature women, the goal became not equality but equity, in responding to people's differing needs (Gilligan, 1977, 1982).

In keeping with the attachment versus independence contrast in the general socialization of men and women is a study comparing the social competence of men and women who scored high on the Kohlberg scale. The high-scoring women were judged to be verbally skilled, interpersonally competent, honest, emotionally expressive, and psychologically healthy. The high-scoring men, by contrast were judged to be socially inept, withdrawn, anxious, engaging in fantasy, and self-centered (Lifton, 1983). Apparently the men were at a disadvantage in situations emphasizing social interaction and sensitivity to other people's feelings.

Kohlberg's concept of a single hierarchy of stages in moral development needs to be reexamined in the light of these more recent findings. There is consid-

erable evidence that the moral reasoning of men and of women develops differently, based on different principles.

Here again we see an important benefit of the scientific method: the ability of successive studies to build on, refine, and modify earlier conclusions. Research does more than merely support or question a hypothesis. It can point to limitations of the conclusions or variables involved. While *moral judgment* has been shown to be largely developmental, *moral action* may not be on a developmental timetable. And *moral feeling*, which seems to be critical for moral action, has not even been studied. Neither has moral giftedness of individuals like Gandhi or collective moral action of groups of citizens facing common problems (Social Science Research Council, 1984).

Psychosexual and psychosocial development

Two other aspects of social and emotional development are the changes in the child's sexuality and in personal and social orientations in different life periods. We will look at one theory regarding each aspect; again, the theories are cast in terms of qualitatively different stages of development.

Freud's psychosexual stages. Freud (1905/1976) postulated what he called **psychosexual stages,** involving successive ways of satisfying instinctual biological urges through stimulation of different areas of the body: the mouth, the anus, and the genitals. Here we will discuss the stages briefly; later, in Chapter 11, we will see how they fit into Freud's broader theory of personality.

The most primitive stage of psychosexual development is the *oral stage,* in which the mouth region is the primary source of gratification—from nourishment, stimulation, and making contact with the environment. For example, infants and toddlers spend a great proportion of their time in nonnutritive sucking activities, such as thumb or finger sucking, and in mouthing toys and other objects.

In the *anal stage,* which follows at about age 2, gratification comes first from elimination of feces and then from retention of them. Social demands in most cultures challenge the child's pleasure from both the process and the products of excretion and eventually suppress and regulate it.

The *phallic stage,* from about ages 3 to 5, centers around the exploration and stimulation of one's own body, especially the penis or the clitoris. In Freudian theory, the child is assumed to experience sexual love toward the parent of the opposite sex during this period. During the *latency stage,* from about age 6 to puberty, satisfaction is gained from exploring the environment and developing skills. Puberty then ush-

ers in the *genital stage,* which involves moving toward sexual contact with others.

According to Freud, either too much gratification or too much frustration at one of the early stages leads to **fixation,** which means that the child is unable to progress normally to the next stage. Such fixations then hamper the child's subsequent development. For example, *oral fixation* is alleged to lead to dependency on others, drug addiction, compulsive eating, and even tendencies toward verbal fluency and sarcasm. *Anal fixation* is presumed to result in a stubborn, compulsive, stingy, excessively neat individual.

Freud's concept of psychosexual stages has been found useful by many clinicians in guiding their treatment of patients with certain mental disorders. On the other hand, he arrived at his ideas through analytical introspection and through interviews with adult patients, *not* by studying children. Attempts to find experimental confirmation for his predictions have had mixed results at best.

Erikson's psychosocial stages. Also based on clinical observations rather than experimental research is a formulation of psychosocial stages of development by present-day theorist Erik Erikson (1963). **Psychosocial stages** are successive orientations toward oneself and toward others. Each stage requires a new level of social interaction; success or failure in achieving it can change the course of subsequent development in a positive or negative direction. Unlike Freud, Erikson sees development as continuing throughout life.

Erikson identified eight psychosocial stages, in the life cycle. At each stage a particular conflict comes into focus, as shown in **Table 2.6.** Although the conflict continues in different forms and is never resolved once and for all, it needs to be sufficiently resolved at this stage if the individual is to cope successfully with the conflicts of later stages.

For example, in the first stage, the infant needs to develop a basic sense of trust in its environment through interaction with its caregivers. Trust is a natural accompaniment of a strong attachment relationship with a parent who provides food, warmth, and the comfort of physical closeness. But a child whose basic needs are not met, who experiences inconsistent handling, lack of physical closeness and warmth, and frequent absence of a caring adult, may develop a pervasive sense of mistrust, insecurity, and anxiety—and be unready for the venturesomeness that will be required in the next stage.

"First of all class—some food for thought: Let me say that I have consumed vast quantities of the psychodynamic literature and, after chewing it over, I still find it difficult to swallow this garbage about there really being such a thing as an 'oral dependent personality'..."

Table 2.6 *Erikson's Psychosocial Stages*

Approximate Age	Crisis	Adequate Resolution	Inadequate Resolution
0–1½	Trust vs. mistrust	Basic sense of safety	Insecurity, anxiety
1½–3	Autonomy vs. self-doubt	Perception of self as agent capable of controlling own body and making things happen	Feelings of inadequacy to control events
3–6	Initiative vs. guilt	Confidence in oneself as initiator, creator	Feelings of lack of self-worth
6–puberty	Competence vs. inferiority	Adequacy in basic social and intellectual skills	Lack of self-confidence, feelings of failure
Adolescent	Identity vs. role confusion	Comfortable sense of self as a person	Sense of self as fragmented; shifting, unclear sense of self
Early adult	Intimacy vs. isolation	Capacity for closeness and commitment to another	Feeling of aloneness, separation; denial of need for closeness
Middle adult	Generativity vs. stagnation	Focus of concern beyond oneself to family, society, future generations	Self-indulgent concerns; lack of future orientation
Later adult	Ego-integrity vs. despair	Sense of wholeness, basic satisfaction with life	Feelings of futility, disappointment

(Based on Erikson, 1963)

With the development of walking and the beginnings of language, there is expansion of the child's exploration and manipulation of objects (and sometimes people!). With these activities should come a comfortable sense of autonomy and of adequacy as a capable and worthy person. Excessive restriction or criticism at this second stage may lead instead to self-doubts, while demands beyond the child's ability, as in too-early or too-severe demands for toilet training, can discourage efforts to persevere in mastering new tasks. They also can lead to stormy scenes of confrontation, disrupting the close, supportive parent-child relationship that the child still needs for accepting risks and meeting new challenges. The two-year-old who insists that a particular ritual be followed precisely or demands the right to do something without help is acting out of a need to affirm his or her autonomy and adequacy. The message being communicated is: "Don't treat me like a baby—unless I ask to be!"

Toward the end of the preschool period, the child who has developed a basic sense of trust, first in the immediate environment and then in himself or herself, has become a person who can now initiate both intellectual and motor activities. The ways in which parents respond to the child's self-initiated activities either encourage a sense of freedom and self-confidence needed for the *next* stage or produce a sense of guilt and a feeling of being an inept intruder in an adult world.

During the elementary-school years, the child who has successfully resolved the crises of the earlier stages is ready to go beyond random exploring and testing to the systematic development of competencies. School and sports offer arenas for learning intellectual and motor skills, and interaction with peers offers an arena for developing social skills. Other opportunities come through special lessons, organized group activities, and individual perseverance in following an interest. Successful efforts in these pursuits lead to feelings of competence. Some youngsters, however, become spectators rather than performers or experience enough failure to give them a sense of inferiority, leaving them handicapped for meeting the demands of the next life stages.

Erikson's formulation has been widely accepted because it has helped us see the life cycle as a whole, putting both the changes and the overall continuity into perspective. The first four stages are part of the socialization of the child; the last four are landmarks in the continuing socialization of the adult. These will be discussed in the remainder of the chapter.

THE CYCLE EXTENDS . . . AND ENDS

Though childhood years are the formative ones, we have a remarkable capacity for change across the entire life span (Brim & Kagan, 1980). Though early infant and childhood experiences are extremely important, their long-term effects for different individuals are highly variable (Henderson, 1980; Simmel, 1980).

Beyond childhood come choices about sexual partners, education, career, marriage, family, leisure time, and more. Obligations and commitments multiply as time seems to become scarcer. We begin to "live for the future" and be nostalgic about the past. We lose the child's delight in becoming absorbed in the present moment, and stress becomes a more constant companion. In this concluding section, we can only consider briefly some theories and research about certain aspects of the human life span beyond the childhood years.

Adolescence

At the beginning of adolescence, the individual is still essentially a child. In our society, most young adolescents live at home, are financially and emotionally dependent on their parents, and follow a structured schedule revolving around school and organized group activities often supervised by adults. By the end of the period, though financial dependence and education may be continuing, there is far less adult planning or supervision, and the young person may have "left home" emotionally and perhaps physically.

During adolescence, family ties become less intense as more time is spent outside the home. In our society this typically means less structure and adult guidance, exposure to new and perhaps conflicting values, strong peer pressure for conformity in behavior and dress—coupled with a great need for peer

support and acceptance—and many situations calling for personal decisions. Physical maturity far outruns psychological maturity.

The young person can now see things from another's point of view and behave differently in different situations according to what is seen as socially appropriate. But in trying out different roles in different settings, there is a danger of becoming confused as one tries to fulfill roles that may be conflicting. Erikson called this *role confusion*. The young person is testing different possibilities about who he or she is and what he or she wants to stand for, extremely difficult tasks for many young people. Adolescence is often a time of moodiness, ambivalence, self-centeredness, and rebellion, with the young person trying to achieve independence and at the same time cling to the security of dependence.

The need at this stage is to establish an integrated, "centered" identity that is coherent and personally acceptable—rather than merely put on a socially acceptable mask. According to Erikson, this identity must have four components: (a) an acceptance of one's adult sexuality; (b) becoming a person on one's own rather than just being "the son or daughter of Dr. Z"; (c) committing oneself to basic beliefs; and (d) deciding on a preferred social and vocational role. There are two dangers—either that no stable identity will develop or that the young person will accept a *negative identity,* a socially unacceptable role, such as that of "speed freak" or "bully." A negative identity can either be imposed on the person by others (e.g., delinquent) or chosen by the young person to get even with others who have been obstacles or otherwise caused pain (e.g., rebel).

Depending on the culture, social class, and availability of jobs, adolescence in our society is either a period of indulgent nonparticipation in the adult world or one in which continued education combines with or is replaced by work experience. In societies where it is clear from early childhood what one's adult role will be and where a single set of values is shared by old and young, there may be a sense of approaching fulfillment and self-validation rather than the stress and turmoil so common among our young people.

◁ *Adolescence in the United States is marked by loosening of family ties, intense concern over and often ambivalence about being independent, and strong peer pressure.*

Conditions in the United States and Italy provide an interesting contrast in adolescent experience. For American adolescents, autonomy is greatly facilitated by their family experiences but often coupled with some emotional indifference or aloofness between parents and adolescent children. The typical Italian adolescent experiences greater warmth and concerned interest—along with attempts to control his or her behavior by parents whose overprotective affection can become intrusive (Palmonari & Ricci Bitti, 1981; Petter, 1968). This is but one example of the cross-cultural variations in developmental patterns that need to be studied empirically before we can know which phenomena of social development in adolescence are universal (Triandis & Heron, 1981).

Adulthood

The transition into young adulthood is marked by decisions about advanced education, vocation, intimate relationships, and for many, marriage. In the United States, where many students leave home to live in a college dormitory, they never really go home again, but set out on a path of self-determination. By contrast, most European college students continue to live at home and remain more closely tied to family values and constraints.

Among college-age youth concern shifts from wanting to be liked by everyone to needing to love and be loved by a special someone. But only the person who has developed a clear and comfortable sense of his or her own identity is ready for the risks and potentials of intimacy. Erikson defines *intimacy* as a full commitment—sexual, emotional, and moral—to another person. Intimacy requires openness, courage, ethical strength, and usually some sacrifice and compromise of one's personal preferences. Intimacy can occur in other close relationships besides marriage. The alternative to intimacy, according to Erikson, is *isolation,* lack of a secure sense of connectedness, a feeling of being essentially alone.

Those who do find a supportive partner with whom to share personal feelings, fears, and successes have been found to be both happier and physically healthier than those who fail to do so. We shall see throughout our journey that anything that isolates individuals from social support puts them "at risk" for both physical and mental problems.

For those who meet the challenge of intimacy successfully, the next opportunity—and challenge—is *generativity.* The focus of concern becomes a commitment beyond oneself—to family, work, society, or future generations. This is typically a crucial step in development in one's thirties and forties.

Those who have not successfully resolved the crises of identity and intimacy may still be trying to do so during this period, perhaps with an increasing sense of insecurity and failure. If they have children, they may be unable to give them the steady acceptance, emotional support, and guidance that the children will need to weather their own storms and crises of development.

Systematic studies of personality development in adulthood are comparatively recent and are still mapping unmarked territory. And two of the best known, by social psychologist Daniel Levinson (1978) and psychoanalytically oriented G. E. Vaillant (1977), studied only men (see the **Close-up** on p. 68).

For men, the twenties seem to be a period of hope and optimism, of beginnings of an independent life, with full responsibility for oneself and for one's choice of life-style. Early in the thirties, there may be a period of reassessment, of questioning basic directions set in the twenties and either affirming them or "adjusting course" to follow new inner imperatives. The later thirties are often a time of consolidation and satisfaction. Between 40 and 50 what has come to be known as a "mid-life crisis" may occur, in which again one's past choices and present contributions and commitments are questioned. Life is half over; has freedom been given up for security? Intimacy for career success? There is a new concern about a genuine identity, which can be seen as a later version of the adolescent's search for identity. Depending on how one adapts to the stress of this inner turmoil, one may renew commitments, make changes, or become resigned to an unfulfilling life situation.

In general, even less is known about adult personality development of women than of men, especially about the different effects of being a homemaker or a career person or combining the two. Not surprisingly, Gail Sheehy (1976), in interviews, found greater uncertainty among women than among men about vocational choice. Among many of those whose vocation was exclusively homemaking, she found feelings of being isolated or diminished and separated from former friends and family, with frustration and some guilt at not doing any of the things for which their education had prepared them.

Behavioral options available to women—and feelings about what is desirable—are determined largely by values in the society. According to polls of wom-

Male Personality Development in Adulthood: Two Studies

Daniel Levinson (1978) studied intensively a group of 40 men from all walks of life between the ages of 35 and 45. In reconstructing their lives, he discovered a pattern of age-linked developmental periods which he called "seasons in a man's life."

A surprising finding was the importance of *mentor* relationships to men during their early twenties and thirties. Mentors were teachers, co-workers, neighbors, or relatives who acted as sponsors, introducing the young men into new social and business worlds. They provided counsel and support in times of stress and served as models for achievements and life-style. When the mentor relationship ended, the younger man, having internalized the mentor's qualities, often became a mentor himself.

For many of these men there was also a "special woman," whose function, in the men's descriptions, seemed to be mainly to support the man's search for fulfillment of his "dream." This dream seemed to be basically one of achievement, integrity, and personal fulfillment.

G. E. Vaillant (1977) has written about the personality development of 95 highly intelligent men who were interviewed and observed systematically for 30 years following their graduation from college in the mid-1930s. He found great changes in many of the men, often quite unpredictable from their behavior in college.

Vaillant's interviews covered physical health, social relationships, and career achievement. At the end of the 30-year period, he identified the 30 men with the best outcomes and the 30 with the worst outcomes and compared them in a number of ways, including their evidence of their maturity in terms of Erikson's psychosocial stages. The table compares the scores of the two groups on several items from the interviews that were indicative of psychosocial maturity. By middle life, the best-outcome men were carrying out *generativity* tasks of assuming responsibility for others and giving some of themselves back to the world. Even the adjustment of their children seemed to be associated

with the fathers' maturity: the more mature fathers were more able to give children the help *they* needed in adjusting to the world.

From the study, Vaillant concluded that personality growth ceases only when one is unable to replace one's losses. Most poignant were the cases of a few whom he called "perpetual boys." They had suffered severe losses in grade school and had not developed competencies beyond the kind of things they were good at then.

Differences between Best- and Worst-Outcome Subjects on Factors Related to Psychosocial Maturity

	Best Outcomes (30 men)	Worst Outcomes (30 men)
Childhood environment poor	17%	47%
Pessimism, self-doubt, passivity, and fear of sex at 50	3%	50%
In college personality integration put in bottom fifth	0	33%
Subjects whose career choice reflected identification with father	60%	27%
Dominated by mother in adult life	0	40%
Failure to marry by 30	3%	37%
Bleak friendship patterns at 50	0	57%
Current job has little supervisory responsibility	20%	93%
Children admitted to father's college	47%	10%
Children's outcome described as good or excellent	66%	23%
Average yearly charitable contribution	$3,000	$500

(From Vaillant, 1977)

---

en's preferences taken in 1970 and 1983, motherhood was regarded as the best part of being a woman by 53 percent of young women in the earlier poll. Only 26 percent for the later generation of young women reported this feeling. In addition, the later poll showed that a majority of working women

(58 percent) regarded independence and being employed as satisfying and preferable to being at home. Furthermore, 59 percent of all women polled thought employed women are as good mothers, if not better, than women who stay at home ("U.S. Women," 1983).

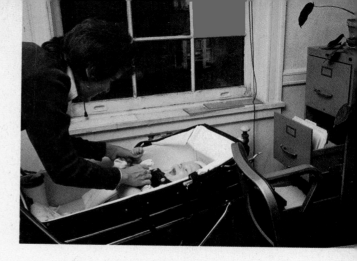

Carol Gilligan's challenge to Kohlberg's male-based theory of moral development was discussed earlier (p. 63). Gilligan holds that personality development through the adult years continues to progress differently for men and women because of their basically different earlier socialization—toward separateness for men, toward attachment for women. She sees both trends as one sided and cites evidence that in mid-life, many men and women try to establish a better balance, the men moving toward more attachment, the women toward greater self-identity (Gilligan, 1982).

The later years

In Erikson's eighth and final stage of psychosocial development, the crisis revolves around the meaning of life—life in general and one's own life in particular. If adequate solutions were found at each of the preceding stages, older adults can enjoy a sense of fulfillment and wholeness. They can look back gladly on what has been their part in a larger plan, and can look ahead comfortably to the unknown of death. People who achieve this sense of *ego-integrity* are likely also to achieve Kohlberg's higher stages of morality. On the other hand, a sense that one's life has been unsatisfying or misdirected leads to feelings of despair and futility.

Increasing age brings sensory deficits and increasing health problems. Although adults over 70 represent only about a tenth of the United States population, they receive nearly a fourth of all medical prescriptions, most frequently for tranquilizers. Bodily illnesses and mental deterioration are closely correlated, each kind of negative change being a catalyst for the other (Habot & Libow, 1980). Depression is a central problem for many older people, marked by feelings of loneliness, rejection, apathy, anxiety about health, irritability, and social withdrawal. Suicide becomes more probable among older white males. But the variables that contribute to suicide and suicide attempts are many and complex (Stenback, 1980).

Cognitive functioning. On the positive side, there is evidence that some aspects of intellectual functioning are equal or even superior in older people, while there is little to support the stereotype of cognitive decline in the later years. For example, 70-year-olds score higher than college-age individuals on tests of vocabulary and information. Their memory is poorer for recall of lists of numbers but not for recognition of words or for several other kinds of memory tasks.

Tests that involve speed of response, on the other hand, put the elderly at a disadvantage, and cognitive abilities are impaired by the presence of physical problems, such as cardiovascular disorders, or by living in unstimulating or socially deprived environments. Obsolescence can also handicap the elderly: on some kinds of problem-solving tasks they may do as well as they ever did but younger subjects may do better because they have a better background in current technology. A general conclusion is that from the early sixties to the mid-seventies "there is a normal decline in some but not all individuals for some but not all abilities, but beyond 80 decrement is the rule for most individuals" (Schaie, 1980, p. 279).

Additional conclusions, summarized by Bernice Neugarten (1976) are:

1. Old people who remain physically and mentally active perform better than those who become inactive.
2. Educational level predicts performance in old age; the higher the education attained, the better the performance.

3. Intellectual decline seems to be inversely related to longevity; the less bright die younger.
4. Intellectual decline is greater in old men than in old women.

Satisfaction with life. Looking back, how do older people evaluate their life satisfactions, and what earlier factors were predictive of satisfaction with life? Some interesting answers emerge from longitudinal studies of men and women who have been investigated over much of their life span.

Among the wives in one study, marital compatibility and satisfaction with the husband's job at age 30 predicted (was correlated with) general satisfaction at age 70. Among the husbands the characteristics at age 30 that were predictive of general satisfaction later were good health, stamina, high energy level, job satisfaction, and having an emotionally stable wife (Mussen et al., 1982).

The longitudinal Terman study of high-IQ boys and girls (mentioned at the beginning of this chapter) explored life satisfaction when the subjects had reached an average age of 62.

Among the men, satisfaction was assessed in relation to occupation, working into their sixties, family life, and broken or unbroken marriage. Most satisfaction was derived from occupation and family life. Occupational satisfaction, in turn, was related to several feelings expressed at age 30: ambition, liking for work, living up to one's potential, and having actively chosen one's occupation. Affective qualities at age 30 that had persisted for the next three decades

of their lives were ''optimism about life, an enjoyment of occupational combat, and a feeling of self-worth (R. Sears, 1977, p. 123).

Among the women, greatest satisfaction with their work was found among subjects who had had careers (whether single or married), but broader measures of satisfaction were reported among the homemakers. Earlier conditions that were correlated with high *general* satisfaction later in life for the group as a whole were positive relations with their parents, early self-confidence, good health, marriage, children, social contacts, community service, and work in a professional field (P. Sears & Barbee, 1977).

There seems to be stability over time in general emotional-motivational orientation that can give direction and meaning to one's life—or, when negative or lacking, can lead to unhappiness and despair.

With old age comes the inevitability of death. The realization that life is finite and that one's days are numbered can have an important influence on one's mental health and behavior. Depending on the strategies developed to cope with that knowledge of mortality, there can be a renewed assault on life goals, an attempt to live the remaining time to the fullest, or denial or other defenses.

When death comes at the end of an illness, even the process of dying can be seen in terms of a sequence of stages that may include denial, anger, bargaining, and acceptance (Kübler-Ross, 1969). But other researchers studying the reactions of dying people have observed more fluidity and complexity than is suggested in Kübler-Ross' fixed stages. Some see ''a hive of affect'' with an interplay of hope and disbelief, of anguish, terror, rage, and envy, alternating with acquiescence, boredom, surrender, and even yearning for death (Schneidman, 1976).

After death, the individual's memory lives on in all those that were somehow touched by his or her presence during that lifetime. Handling that death becomes a new part of their developmental challenges—and in that sense the life cycle is never ending.

SUMMARY

■ Developmental psychology is concerned with changes in physical and psychological functioning across the life span. Some developmental psychologists study processes or strands of development, such as cognitive or social development; others study the challenges and characteristics of whole individuals at different life periods.

■ Normative studies are descriptive; experimental studies provide information about causes. Each may involve cross-sectional, longitudinal, or sequential designs.

■ Inheritance occurs through genes received at conception, half from each parent. Maturation programs many characteristic sequences of physical and mental change throughout life. Most complex actions are shaped by both nature (heredity) and nurture (experience and learning).

■ Newborns respond to patterns of stimulation, change their responses as a result of experience, and interact actively with the mother or other caregiver.

■ Acquisition of language proceeds through babbling, one-word, two-word, and telegraphic-speech stages. Analysis of children's speech errors reveals that they actively test hypotheses and develop rules about language. Maturation plays a key role in shaping and timing language development.

■ As described by Piaget, cognitive growth comes about through a continuing interaction of the processes of assimilation and accommodation. Assimilation fits the new into what is already known; accommodation changes the known to adapt to the new information or experience.

■ Piaget, like Freud, Kohlberg, and Erikson, stressed the role of distinct stages in development. Each of these periods occurs in a fixed sequence that is qualitatively different from the others. He proposed four stages of cognitive growth: sensorimotor, preoperational, concrete operational, and formal operational. Current researchers are exploring additional facets of cognitive growth and change throughout the life span.

■ A child acquires roles, behavior, and attitudes expected of individuals in society through the process of socialization. Normal socialization begins with formation of an attachment between the infant and the caregiver. Failure to establish attachment in infancy is associated with physical and psychological problems.

■ A permissive parenting style is optimal during infancy. During early and middle childhood an authoritative style is more effective than either a permissive or an authoritarian one.

■ Sex differences are physical differences; gender differences are psychological, learned differences associated with "masculinity" and "femininity." Individuals learn both a gender identity and a gender role. Researchers have found that parents and teachers treat boys and girls differently, giving girls "roots" in social relationships and boys "wings" of independence.

■ Kohlberg's stages of moral reasoning show a developmental progression toward greater concern for universal rights and abstract ethical priciples, though men's and women's development differs. Women progress toward a broader sense of responsibility and compassion, while men progress toward greater devotion to abstract principles based on equal rights.

■ Psychosexual development, according to Freud, proceeds through an oral stage, an anal stage, a phallic stage, a latency stage, and a genital stage. These stages involve successive sources of gratification of instinctual urges. Failure to progress through this sequence is assumed to hamper personality development and cause specific psychological disorders.

■ According to Erikson, there are eight stages of psychological development that extend throughout life. These mark changes in one's orientation to oneself and others; each represents resolution of a particular crisis and is essential for success in later stages. Adequate resolution brings trust, autonomy, initiative, and competence in the childhood years, identity in adolescence, intimacy in young adulthood, generativity in middle adulthood, and finally ego-integrity in old age.

■ Adolescence is a period of growing independence and separation from family, often with ambivalence and considerable stress. The experience of adolescence varies among cultures.

■ Middle adulthood and old age present new challenges and bring continuing change. Intellectual ability in the later years depends on the individual's past and present physical activity and on continuing mental involvement in life. It has been found, through longitudinal studies, that general life satisfaction of the elderly can be predicted from their emotional and motivational characteristics at around age 30, and that this satisfaction involves somewhat different factors for men and women.

3

THE BIOLOGY OF BEHAVIOR

WHAT MAKES BEHAVIOR "WORK"?
Mind and brain
Nerve energy
Special cells for special jobs

HOW DO CELLS COMMUNICATE WITH ONE ANOTHER?
The central and peripheral nervous systems
Behavioral regulation by the endocrine system
Neurons as building blocks

HOW DOES THE BRAIN CONTROL BEHAVIOR?
Development of the brain
Functional organization of the brain

HOW IS THE BRAIN STUDIED?
Touching a sensitive nerve
Lesions are forever
Recording the activity of neurons
Looking at living brains

SUMMARY

We are in the operating room of the Montreal Neurological Institute observing brain surgery on Buddy, a young man suffering from epilepsy. Before the surgeon can remove the tumor causing Buddy's uncontrollable seizures, he must discover what the consequences would be of removing portions of the tissue around it. In effect, he must draw a *map* of part of Buddy's brain—a map relating particular areas to the mental and behavioral functions they affect or control. The surgeon relies generally on previously drawn maps of the typical human brain, but must plot more precise information for each uniquely individual brain.

First, the surgeon removes part of the thick, bony layer of skull that shields and protects the brain. We can now see the outermost, deeply wrinkled surface of the brain, called the *cortex.* With the point of a thin wire, an *electrode,* the surgeon gently touches one area of the cortex, stimulating it with small amounts of electrical current. There is no pain receptivity in the brain; thus an electrical current can be used to stimulate activity in the brain without causing discomfort to the patient. Buddy remains conscious under local anesthesia and can report what he experiences as the surgeon probes his brain.

"Nil, nil, no reaction noted," states a nurse. The surgeon then carefully places the electrode on another spot only millimeters away. "Fist clenching, hand raising, twitching reaction observed." The surgeon stimulates the same area again, and the nurse reports a similar motor reaction. This procedure of stimulating one area after another and observing the behavior elicited allows the surgeon to put together the map he must follow to guide his operation.

Suddenly, an unexpected response occurs.

"The patient is grinning, he is smiling; eyes opening when that area is stimulated."

"Buddy, what happened, what did you just experience?"

"Doc, I heard a song, or rather a part of a song, a melody."

"Buddy, have you heard it before?"

"Yes, I remember having heard it a long time ago, but I can't remember the name of the tune."

When a different brain site is stimulated, the patient recalls in vivid detail a thrilling childhood experience. As if by pushing an electronic memory button, the surgeon, Dr. Wilder Penfield, has touched memories stored silently for years in the recesses of his patient's brain (Penfield & Baldwin, 1952).

This type of neurosurgery (*neuro* means "relating to the nervous system," of which the brain is a part) contributes to our understanding of how the brain functions. But it also helps relieve human suffering by applying knowledge gained from basic research in physiological psychology and related fields to human problems.

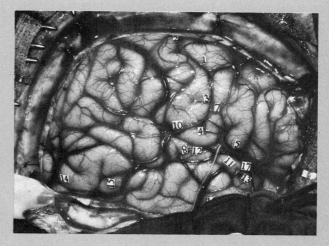

△ *Shown here is the right cerebral cortex of an epileptic patient, exposed for surgery with the patient fully conscious. The numbers indicate spots at which electrical stimulation produced positive responses—simple sensory and motor responses at spots 3, 4, 7, and 8 and flashback experiences at spots 11, 12, 14, and 15. For example, when spot 11 was stimulated, the patient reported hearing a neighborhood mother calling her little boy. She identified the experience as "something that happened years ago" (Penfield, 1958).*

Physiological psychology is the branch of psychology that studies the physical and chemical factors involved in behavior. A general objective of physiological psychologists is to relate anatomical structures and physiological processes in the brain and other parts of the body to psychological experience and behavior. Among other psychologists who share this interest in the physical and chemical factors involved in behavior are psychophysiologists, neuropsychologists, and psychobiologists. In this approach, humans are studied as biological organisms who have much in common with other species. What is special about the human organism is its specialized brain.

In Buddy's case, it might appear that the brain is passive, being acted upon by the surgeon's electrical wand. But Buddy's brain and yours were designed for action. Although the brain receives a steady stream of signals from the senses, which inform it of changes in the environment, it is also the nervous system's "central command station": it interprets the input and directs the glands and muscles as the organism acts upon its world. But *how* does stimulation of some piece of brain tissue lead to action of a particular muscle? And how did the psychological experience Buddy reported get into his brain and get held there for years? Answers to these questions will come as part of a broader understanding of the physiological bases of behavior that you will begin to gain as we explore four major questions in this chapter: (a) What makes behavior "work?" (b) How do cells communicate with one another? (c) How does the brain control behavior? (d) How is the brain studied?

Francis Crick, who, along with James Watson, discovered DNA, believes that: "There is no scientific study more vital to man than the study of his own brain. Our entire view of the universe depends on it" (1979, p. 232). But be cautioned. Despite enormous recent advances in the scientific analysis of the brain, there are vast regions yet uncharted.

WHAT MAKES BEHAVIOR "WORK"?

This question rephrased in the current idiom of physiological psychology would be: What are the internal mechanisms and physical structures that determine how any given behavioral sequence operates? But it is an old question, phrased differently in different times, yet fundamental to any basic conception of human nature. We will briefly examine how ancient philosophers and religious scholars asked what proved to be the wrong questions, how a philosophical assumption about mind and body allowed scientific study of the nervous system to begin, and what happened when conclusions based on scientific observations replaced conclusions supported only by authority or logic.

Mind and brain

According to prescientific thinking, behavior was brought about by some inner spirit, some *anima* (life force) in the person or sometimes by divine or demonic possession. In this *animistic* explanation, the same kinds of spiritual forces thought to live in rivers and clouds were believed to guide living creatures also. This belief was in keeping with the early distinction by philosophers between the realm of the mind, where ideas reigned, and the domain of the body, where physical sensation and movements took place. The same separation of the nonmaterial mind and soul from the physical was also assumed by early theologians, who searched for "the seat of the soul," the place within the human body where the divine spirit might guide bodily actions.

For the Greek philosopher Aristotle, "the seat of the soul," the place where the mind's powers ruled the body's passions, was in the heart. Though not supported by any data, this view is revived annually on Valentine's Day when we pay homage to the heart as the symbol of true love and affectionate understanding. It also underlies the symbolism of the Purple Heart medal awarded to wounded soldiers for their courage in battle.

The Greek physician Galen integrated—in a curious fashion—Aristotle's notions about the importance of the heart with his own pioneering observations of the nerves of dissected brains. Because hydraulic models for pumping fluid through hollow tubes were popular in his time, he mistakenly assumed that nerves must operate on a hydraulic principle. He decided that blood flowed into the heart where it was converted to "vital spirits," which were then pumped to the brain, and from there to specific muscles and sense organs.

The soul and the machine. It was the French philosopher and mathematician René Descartes who began to ask the right questions in the early 1600s. He put forth the view that the body was an "animal machine" that could be understood scientifically—that is, by discovering natural laws through empirical observation. He then raised purely physiological questions, questions of bodily mechanics of motion, that could be separated from psychological questions about consciousness and perception. These, in turn, were separated from religious questions of how divine laws govern human conduct. Descartes' insistence upon reducing complex sensory processes to their underlying physical basis has been termed the *mechanistic* approach to the study of physiological processes. It was a breakthrough in its time, at last allowing scientific study of bodily processes.

Descartes (1646, 1662) held that behavior "works" as a mechanical reaction to physical energies in the environment that excite the senses. He too believed that this excitation flowed in hollow tubes as "animal spirits" which were transmitted to the brain and then reflected back again to contract specific muscles. The notion of a *reflex* in which an external stimulus leads to a response is still an important physiological concept though we now know that nerves are not hydraulic tubes and that the incoming sensory signals and the outgoing motor signals to the muscles travel along different nerve pathways.

Because Descartes was a devoutly religious man, he could not dispense with the soul in his theory of bodily functioning. Yet because of his belief in the appropriateness of a mechanistic view of perception and other sensory processes, he could not accept the soul as the director of such processes. How did he resolve this dilemma?

Descartes' intellectual feat was postulating a *dualism* to separate the action of the mechanistic body and brain from that of the spiritual soul and ephemeral mind. If the soul could act upon all parts of the body, the body would not be a perfect machine but rather an "unaccountable mechanism." So Descartes theorized that the soul and body interact at only one spot: the centrally located *pineal gland,* thought to be the only part of the brain that is not duplicated in its two halves (actually, the pituitary gland is another). His view was that the soul was not confined to this space, but could act upon the extended substance of the body only at this one point.

Mind as an evolved ability of brains. In the physiological research that followed Descartes' breakthrough, any ideas about the soul were quickly banished from the enterprise. In our own century, behavioral psychologists went further, looking for lawful relationships between behavior and environmental stimuli and disregarding what went on in the "black box" that lay between them.

Descartes' dualism has continued to the present, however, in the position of those who see an active, *teleological* (purposeful), immaterial mind somehow acting upon a passive, reactive, mechanistic brain and giving behavior its direction (Rychlak, 1979). Such an approach implies that the complex behavior of the whole organism can be understood only "from the top down."

Physiological psychologists, by contrast, have tried to understand behavior "from the bottom up," hop-

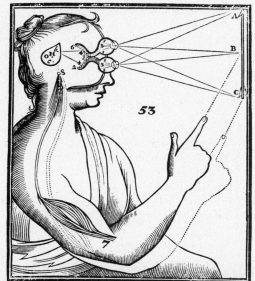

◁ *As portrayed in this 1686 woodcut, Descartes believed that information about the outside world was received by the eyes and transmitted by "strings in the brain" to the all-important pineal gland. This gland, he explained, was filled with "animal humors" that poured out whenever a light stimulus made contact with the pineal gland, causing it to tilt downward. The humors then flowed through "hollow tubes" (nerves) until they reached muscles, causing them to expand or contract in response to the environmental input. Despite his picturesque concepts of strings and tubes, both Descartes' concept of reflex action and his association of the pineal gland with response to light were remarkably close to the truth.*

ing ultimately to understand complex mental processes by understanding the biochemical processes that underlie both actions and thoughts. In rejecting Descartes' dualism, in which mind is somehow above natural law, they have assumed a *monism,* in which mind and brain are seen as aspects of a single reality, with mind nothing more (nor less) than the evolved ability of complex brains to think. Donald Hebb, an eminent Canadian physiological psychologist, has argued for this viewpoint.

"Mind is the capacity for thought, and thought is the integrative activity of the brain—that activity up in the control tower that, during waking hours, overrides reflex response and frees behavior from sense dominance. . . . Free will is not a violation of scientific law, it doesn't mean indeterminism, it's not mystical. What it is, simply, is a control of behavior by the thought process" (1974, p. 75).

In this view, the basis of all behavior, including thinking, lies in the nervous system: mental processes still derive from a *neural substrate* even though they show characteristics that are not predictable when one looks at neural functioning (Glassman, 1983). Consciousness depends on the brain and is changed when brain functioning is changed, but consciousness is not the brain. Thoughts are created by neural events in some incredibly complex combinations that we do not yet understand, and they cannot happen without that neural activity. Yet thoughts are not nerve impulses. Their content, their sequences, and their contribution to survival are characteristics not predictable from the processes in and between neurons. Though mind cannot function independently of brain, mental and neural events can be studied separately. This recognition paves the way for a "new dualism," not in terms of basic reality or kinds of "stuff" in the universe, but in terms of levels of analysis. How this new dualism has legitimized and made possible the study of consciousness will be discussed in Chapter 6.

Nerve energy

By the nineteenth century, the scientific orientation toward the inner determiners of behavior brought the view that (a) the brain was the important center for controlling action; (b) this control was exercised through networks of nerves which transmitted electrical signals from the brain to muscles; and (c) the functions of brain and nerves were orderly and could

be understood solely in terms of physics, chemistry, and biology. Scientists from many nations contributed to this view of "what makes behavior work." Three of the most noteworthy were Johannes Müller, Hermann von Helmholtz, and Sir Charles Sherrington.

Müller discovered that the different senses are served by different nerves. But his **law of the specific energy of nerves** held that all nerve impulses are virtually identical, and the quality of each sensory experience is determined by the specific type of receptor that is stimulated. He hypothesized that the brain does not receive light or sound, for example, but only a common kind of nerve signal. Nerve signals are interpreted as light when they are transmitted by nerves from the eyes, and as sound when they come from the ears.

Is the "will to act" the same as the act itself? Only if nerve impulses are instantaneous, as fast as the speed of light—which many nineteenth century investigators believed. Using electricity to stimulate successive points along the nerve of a frog, the German physiologist Helmholtz measured the time that elapsed before the corresponding muscle twitched. He then stimulated a man on the toe and the thigh and observed the differences in time required for reaction to this stimulation. In both cases, he found that it took *time* for the stimulation to produce a reaction—and more time when the distance was greater. In fact, to everyone's surprise, it turned out that the transmission of the nerve impulse was relatively slow (less than 90 feet per second in the frog's motor nerve).

Of Helmholtz's demonstration, a modern experimentalist and historian of psychology, E. G. Boring, wrote: "To separate the movement in time from the event of will that caused it was in a sense to separate the body from the mind, and almost from the personality or self" (1950, p. 42). Helmholtz paved the way for research that used *reaction time* to measure how long thinking and other mental events took (as we will see in Chapter 10). And he raised deeper issues; it was obvious that response to stimulation was being delayed in the nervous system. But where and how? A whole new set of questions began to be asked by researchers studying mechanisms of coordination and control within the nervous system.

To Sherrington (1906) goes credit for showing that there are direct connections in the nervous system between nerve pathways carrying incoming sensory information and pathways sending outgoing motor signals (signals to muscles). These *reflex arcs* form the basis of much behavior with survival value, where fast responding is essential, as in withdrawing a limb in response to a painful stimulus, or blinking when an irritant gets in the eye. Sherrington's study of reflexes also led to the concept that the nervous system involves not just excitation but inhibition as well. While *excitation* of a nerve increases activity within the nervous system, *inhibition* of a nerve can reduce or even block activity. We now know that a major task of the nervous system is the continuing integration of a great many excitatory and inhibitory signals.

Special cells for special jobs

The complexity that is *you* evolved from a simple one-celled organism, such as a *paramecium* (which you have probably seen swimming about on the stage of a microscope in a biology classroom). But in your brain alone there are on the order of a hundred billion (10^{11}) cells—about the same number as the stars in our galaxy (Stevens, 1979). Why wasn't the one-celled organism sufficient to meet nature's demands? And what brought about this enormous increase in the number of cells that are required to make behavior work?

Single-celled organisms would seem to contain all the material necessary for survival: (a) **cytoplasm,** which is the substance in which most of the cell's biochemical reactions take place and in which the breakdown of nutrients into body energy (**metabolism**) occurs; (b) an *outer membrane,* which keeps the internal contents separate from the external environment and, through its contractions, provides one means of locomotion; and (c) a **nucleus,** which contains DNA and directs the activities in the cytoplasm through the production of various nucleic acids. The cell can also divide to reproduce and perpetuate itself.

But a single cell is not designed to adapt to changes in the environment that interfere with its usual functioning. A cell's mobility is too limited when rapid motion is required, and it may have nutritional problems because it is not flexible enough to synthesize new substances when its regular food supply is unavailable. And the duplicates of itself that it produces will be no better suited to a changing, hostile environment than is the parent cell.

Cell differentiation, specialization, and redundancy. For greater complexity and flexibility, a multi-celled organism with cells specialized to perform particular functions is the only answer. Every cell in your body still has cytoplasm, a membrane, and a nucleus, which perform the general functions described above, but what the cells themselves do, and hence their makeup and ways of functioning, has become specialized.

Within different body systems, the various cells have developed widely differing capabilities. Thus some cells have specialized for detecting different kinds of sensory energy. Nerve cells have specialized to transmit information throughout the body—without themselves actually moving about. And cells that form muscle tissue can engage in substantial transformation of chemical energy—to get the work done.

These highly specialized functions of individual types of cells are duplicated innumerable times in many cells as a kind of "margin of safety"—guaranteeing that the specific job will get done even if some cells are damaged. This duplication, or *redundancy,* increases the organism's flexibility for dealing with extreme environmental challenges, while its cell specialization has increased the variety of situations to which it can respond or adapt.

But at what cost have these positive features been added? To gain these advantages, what price was paid?

The need for coordination. When you increase the number of cells and give them specialized jobs, new problems arise. The major problem is that the cells can no longer work independently, but must operate in a coordinated fashion. While you are reading this, your eyes and head are moving; if you are taking notes, your fingers and hand are working. But you are also breathing, swallowing, blinking, and digesting food, while trying to memorize some of the printed information before you. This concert of separate functions must somehow be orchestrated into a coordinated whole. Some actions are given priority over others ("keep reading, stop snacking"); sudden stimulus events must be attended to immediately while repeated ones can be put "on hold." How is this complex coordination and control of multiple inputs and outputs accomplished?

Effective functioning of any multicellular organism demands that its component cells coordinate their activities through some system of communication. Information must be transferred between cells in widely separated parts of the body. Two systems have evolved to enable this to happen: the *endocrine system* with its hormonal messengers and the *nervous system* with its neural messengers. We will study each in some detail; here we will simply provide an overview of how they are alike and different.

Hormonal and neural messengers. The endocrine and nervous systems have four common features: a messenger molecule is released from one cell, travels a long or short distance within the organism, and interacts with the surface of a second cell, leading to a change in the internal chemistry of that second cell. They differ in how the messengers travel and how they communicate.

Hormones are substances secreted into the bloodstream from specialized cells in various glands of the body (such as "sex" hormones secreted by the testes or ovaries). They are carried in the blood until they attach themselves to the surface of a target tissue that is especially responsive to a given hormone. When this happens, they regulate many *biochemical* processes in these target cells, contributing to a variety of biological and psychological reactions, such as sexual arousal or fear.

The nervous system is a vast network of nerve cells, *neurons,* highly specialized to perform the function of rapid communication of information between adjacent cells. These nerve cells are designed first to transmit *electrochemical* impulses down their length, then to secrete a messenger molecule—a *neurotransmitter*—which crosses a tiny gap between two nerve cells. This chemical substance attaches itself to the membrane of the next cell and produces a change in its electrical activity, exciting or inhibiting it. All intercellular communication that results in some type of behavior is the result of either the hormonal or the neural messenger system—sometimes both. Because they play such a central role in making behavior "work," we will have a much closer look at how they function in the sections that follow.

HOW DO CELLS COMMUNICATE WITH ONE ANOTHER?

What a piece of work is man! how noble in reason! how infinite in faculties! in form and moving how express and admirable!

Shakespeare, *Hamlet*

The human nervous system provides for the flexible functioning of a biological organism that faces constant challenge from an ever changing environment. It can draw from past experience to respond swiftly to present demands while anticipating future possibilities—even its own eventual death. It is the physical entity that makes it possible for us to flee or fight danger, to seek a mate and reproduce our kind, and sometimes to build a better mousetrap, if not a brave new world.

The nervous system is the biological machinery for intelligent life. In humans this structure is remarkably complex. The complexity comes from the huge number of cells it contains, their diversity, the intricate ways in which they are organized into functional units, and the ways in which they can communicate with one another. We will first consider how the nervous system is organized into central and peripheral components; then we will look briefly at its supplementary messenger service, the endocrine system. Finally, we will examine the basic unit of the nervous system, the nerve cell, or neuron.

The central and peripheral nervous systems

The nervous system of all vertebrates (organisms with a backbone or spinal column) is made up of a central nervous system and a peripheral nervous system.

The **central nervous system** (CNS) consists of the brain and the spinal cord. It integrates and coordinates the various functions of the body by processing incoming and outgoing messages. The central nervous system is the intermediary between all stimulus input and response output, from the reflex contraction of the pupil of the eye in bright light to the creative production of a poem or computer program. Since we will focus on the brain in detail later, we will outline only the role of the spinal cord here.

The **spinal cord** is a trunkline of nerve cells connecting the brain with the rest of the body through the peripheral nervous system. It is housed in the hollow tube formed by the spinal column, or vertebrae. Between each pair of vertebrae, spinal nerves branch out from the spinal cord and eventually connect with sensory receptors or muscles or glands. The spinal cord also coordinates the activity of the left and right sides of the body, and is responsible for some primitive reflexes that require no brain processing. For example, it is possible for an animal whose spinal cord has been separated from its brain to perform a *spinal* reflex action, such as withdrawing a limb from a painful stimulus. Though normally the brain is "notified," the action is completed without directions from higher up. Damage to the nerves of the spinal cord can result in paralysis of the legs or trunk, as seen in *paraplegic* individuals who have suffered spinal cord injuries.

Despite its commanding position, the central nervous system is isolated from any direct contact with the outside world. It would be little more than stuffing in the black box were it not for the **peripheral nervous system** (PNS), which is the interface between the central nervous system and the environment. The peripheral nerves located throughout the body have two functions: (a) some carry information from each of the sensory receptors (in the eye, ear, skin, and so on) to the brain and (b) some carry messages from the brain and spinal cord out to the

muscles and glands (see **Figure 3.1**). The central and peripheral nervous systems are continually communicating with each other.

Part of the peripheral nervous system, called the **somatic nervous system,** is under voluntary control. It controls the skeletal muscles of the body ("make a fist," "release it"). The **autonomic nervous system** is the other part of the peripheral nervous system; it governs activity not normally under the individual's direct control. It must work even when you are asleep, and it sustains life processes during anesthesia and prolonged coma states. The somatic and autonomic systems are directed by different structures in the brain.

The autonomic nervous system deals with "survival" matters of two kinds: those involving threats to the organism and those involving bodily maintenance. Two divisions within the autonomic system "work together in opposition" to accomplish these survival tasks. The **sympathetic division** deals with emergency responding, while the **parasympathetic division** deals with internal monitoring and regulation of a variety of functions. (see **Figure 3.2**).

The *sympathetic* division can be regarded as a trouble shooter: when you face an emergency or a challenge, it mobilizes the brain for arousal and the body for action. Digestion stops, blood flows away from internal organs to the muscles, oxygen transfer is increased, heart rate increases, the endocrine system is stimulated to activate a variety of motor responses. To relax, calm down, and "mellow out" after the danger is over, the *parasympathetic* division decelerates these processes. Digestion resumes, heartbeat slows, breathing is relaxed, and so forth. Basically, the parasympathetic division carries out the body's nonemergency "housekeeping chores," such as elimination of bodily wastes, protection of the visual system (through tears and pupil constriction),

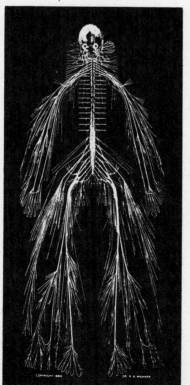

◁ **Figure 3.1**

All main motor and sensory nerves in the peripheral nervous system are shown here as they were dissected out by Dr. R. G. Weaver of Philadelphia, a famous nineteenth-century anatomist. Nerves in the spinal cord connect them with the brain.

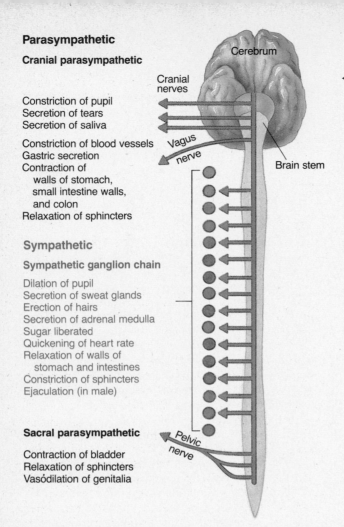

Parasympathetic

Cranial parasympathetic

Constriction of pupil
Secretion of tears
Secretion of saliva

Constriction of blood vessels
Gastric secretion
Contraction of
  walls of stomach,
  small intestine walls,
  and colon
Relaxation of sphincters

Cerebrum

Cranial
nerves

Vagus
nerve

Brain stem

Sympathetic

Sympathetic ganglion chain

Dilation of pupil
Secretion of sweat glands
Erection of hairs
Secretion of adrenal medulla
Sugar liberated
Quickening of heart rate
Relaxation of walls of
  stomach and intestines
Constriction of sphincters
Ejaculation (in male)

Sacral parasympathetic

Pelvic
nerve

Contraction of bladder
Relaxation of sphincters
Vasodilation of genitalia

◁ **Figure 3.2** *The Autonomic Nervous System*

This is a highly simplified diagrammatic portrayal of the parts of the autonomic nervous system—where the major nerves originate and what their main functions are. For simplicity, the system on only one side of the body is shown. Parasympathetic parts and functions are labeled in black and sympathetic ones in color. Note that the sympathetic nerves pass through or have connections in a chain of ganglia (clusters of nerve cell bodies) lying directly outside the spinal cord.

propranol or a placebo was given to student musicians before they performed in front of a small audience or a TV crew. As gauged by a variety of measures, the drug eliminated the physical symptoms that impede performance (including dry mouth), reduced nervousness, and even improved the quality of musical performance as judged by experienced critics. (Another drug, which *stimulates* that part of the sympathetic nervous system, was found to *increase* stage fright symptoms.)

The investigators recommend that propranol be taken only under medical supervision and as part of a retraining program that attempts to modify both the psychological and physiological reactions associated with stage fright (Brantigan et al., 1982; Noyes, 1982).

Behavioral regulation by the endocrine system

The endocrine system, too, is under the control of the structures in the brain. It complements, and often works in conjunction with, the autonomic nervous system. It carries out long-term regulation of basic body functions and helps the organism deal with stressful situations.

The **endocrine system** (see **Figure 3.4**) consists of ductless glands, located in many parts of the body, that secrete hormones directly into the bloodstream. A **hormone** is a chemical messenger carried by the circulation of the blood throughout the body to act on tissue distant from its origin. Each hormone exerts a specific effect only on tissue that is genetically programmed to be responsive to its messenger molecules. By influencing diverse but specific target organs or tissue, hormones can regulate an enormous range of biochemical processes. They do so by influencing the activity and rate at which enzymes and other proteins are manufactured, or by altering

and long-term conservation of body energy. **Figure 3.3** is a schematic representation of the components of the nervous system.

Sometimes the sympathetic nervous system overreacts to a situation as if it were a threat requiring mobilization of flight or fight reactions—when it is not actually life threatening. For example, many people, including experienced performers, suffer from *stage fright,* disabling feelings of anxiety accompanied by palpitating heart, tremors, sweating, and dry mouth—and sometimes temporary loss of memory. Some performers use alcohol or tranquilizers to keep calm but these can impair performance and become addicting. An apparent cure for stage fright has been reported in the form of a pill that has the effect of preventing the unwanted physiological arousal without undesirable side effects.

The generic drug *propranol* (a commonly prescribed version is called *Inderal*) was found to block the action of the hormone noradrenalin that usually speeds up the heart and causes other physical symptoms of stage fright. In a double-blind study, either

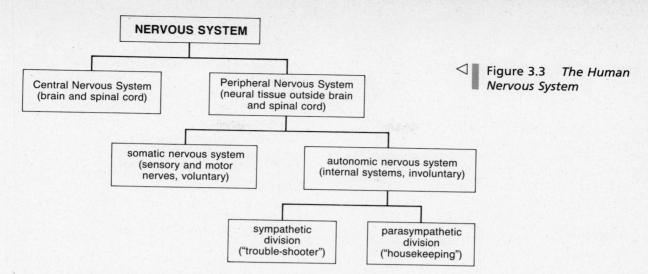

Figure 3.3 *The Human Nervous System*

NERVOUS SYSTEM

Central Nervous System (brain and spinal cord)

Peripheral Nervous System (neural tissue outside brain and spinal cord)

somatic nervous system (sensory and motor nerves, voluntary)

autonomic nervous system (internal systems, involuntary)

sympathetic division ("trouble-shooter")

parasympathetic division ("housekeeping")

cell membranes, permitting or restricting passage of various substances into target cells.

Endocrine glands respond to the levels of chemicals in the bloodstream, or are stimulated by other hormones or by nerve impulses from the brain. This multiple-action communication system allows for control of slow, continuous processes such as maintenance of blood-sugar levels and calcium levels, metabolism of carbohydrates, and general body growth. It can also respond with gusto to crises—for exam-

ple, by energizing the muscular system through release of the hormone adrenalin into the bloodstream—so we can run faster toward the finish line or away from danger. The endocrine system also promotes the survival of the organism by helping fight infections or disease, and the survival of the species through regulation of sexual arousal, production of reproductive cells, and production of milk in nursing mothers.

This "cross-talk" between the autonomic nervous system and the endocrine system contributes to the vital function of homeostasis. **Homeostasis** means constancy or equilibrium of the internal conditions of the body. It is also thought of as the tendency of organisms to maintain their equilibrium and resist change. Homeostatic mechanisms are complex and

Pineal gland

Pituitary gland (the "master gland")

Parathyroids
Thyroid

Thymus

Adrenals

Islets of Langerhans
Ovaries (in the female)

Testes (in the male)

Figure 3.4 *The Endocrine System*

The locations of the various endocrine glands are shown in the diagram. The pituitary gland produces the growth hormone and directs the activity of other glands. The thyroids principally affect metabolism and growth; a thyroid deficiency impairs learning ability and the development of intelligence. The parathyroids regulate calcium and phosphorus levels in the blood. The adrenal medulla produces adrenalin and noradrenalin, both important in emotion; hormones from the adrenal cortex affect general body activity, secondary sex characteristics, and reactions to prolonged stress. The ovaries and testes are vital to sexual development, sexual drive, and reproduction. The islets of Langerhans secrete insulin, which controls the sugar level in the blood. The thymus plays a role in bodily immunities and the pineal gland in regulation of bodily cycles.

Psychosocial Dwarfism

One of the clearest, most dramatic—and saddest—instances of the interplay of physiological and psychological factors comes from studying children who are "psychosocial dwarfs." In the syndrome of *psychosocial dwarfism,* there is a failure in growth resulting from the child's prolonged exposure to emotionally stressful environmental conditions. Children who have been isolated, confined to a limited space, untouched, and unloved stop growing physically or grow much more slowly than normal. One such adolescent of nearly 14 had the body size of a child less than 7 years old (Curtis, 1977).

A natural experiment demonstrated clearly the relationship between lack of normal affectional bonds and failure of normal physical growth.

An intensive study was made of 6 "thin dwarfs," children who were underweight and short and had retarded skeletal development and a "bone age" much less than their chronological age. All had lived in family environments marked by emotional detachment and hostility. The children gained weight and began to grow when they were removed from the hostile environment but their growth again be-

came stunted if they were returned to it. Extended exposure to such deprivation in early life left a permanent mark on body size, intellect, and personality (Gardner, 1972).

Normally, the pituitary gland is stimulated to produce its growth hormone by a brain structure just above it, the *hypothalamus.* But with emotional starvation, the hypothalamus, which is important in emotional arousal, fails to have its usual stimulating effect. Analyses of the blood of some emotionally deprived children have found virtually no release of growth hormones. One mechanism by which the release of growth hormone is suppressed appears to be disturbed sleep patterns these children typically experience. Normally, growth hormones circulate in large amounts during deep sleep; anything that disrupts the normal proportion of deep sleep will then result in less growth hormone and can lead to psychosocial dwarfism.

Fortunately, these effects are reversible. Removing children from environments that create prolonged psychological stress leads to a resumption of growth (Brasel & Blizzard, 1974).

subtle self-regulating mechanisms that keep many internal conditions within the limits necessary for the body's well-being, much as a thermostat in a heating system maintains a constant temperature.

The **pituitary gland** is called the "master gland" because it secretes at least ten hormones that influence the secretions of the other endocrine glands, as well as a growth hormone that promotes protein synthesis and influences our stature. Absence of this growth hormone results in dwarfism, its excess in gigantic growth (see **Close-up** above). In males pituitary secretions activate the testes to secrete testosterone, which is responsible for such sex-linked characteristics of males as beard, deep voice, prominent muscles, and broad shoulders. Testosterone may also have the behavioral effects of increasing aggression, boisterous activity, and sexual drive. In females another pituitary hormone stimulates production of *estrogen,* which is essential to the hormonal chain reaction that triggers the release of eggs from a female's ovaries, making her fertile. Cer-

tain birth-control pills work by blocking the mechanism in the pituitary that controls this hormone flow, thus preventing the eggs from reaching the stage of development where they can be fertilized.

The **pineal gland,** Descartes' candidate for "seat of the soul," turns out to be an endocrine gland that secretes the hormone *melatonin.* This is one of the chemicals responsible for the human ability to get a suntan—hardly the most wonderful of divine gifts to the human species. In animals melatonin synthesis is regulated by the light in day-night light cycles. In animal research where melatonin was administered experimentally, sleep was induced and the female's ovulation was inhibited. Thus fundamental cycles of mammals' behavior—sleep, hibernation, and mating—may somehow be turned on and off by this silent switch (Wurtman, 1979).

Neurons as building blocks

All behavior begins with the action of neurons. A **neuron** is a cell specialized to receive, process, and/or transmit information to other cells within the body. Neurons, or nerve cells, form the basic building blocks of the nervous system. They are both numerous and varied. We have as many neurons in our brain as there are stars in our galaxy. Neurons vary in shape, size, chemical composition, and function; over 200 different types have been identified in mammal brains.

A typical neuron gathers information at one end and transmits signals at the other. The part of the cell that receives incoming signals is a set of branched fibers called **dendrites** that extend from the cell body. The dendrites spread out to receive input from hundreds or thousands of other neurons. The cell body, or **soma,** contains the nucleus of the cell and the cytoplasm that sustains the cell's life. The soma combines and averages all the information coming in from its dendrites (or in some cases directly from another neuron) and passes it on to an extended fiber, the **axon.** The axon takes this combined signal and conducts it along its length (which can be more than a meter or less than a millimeter). Axons end in swollen, bulb-like structures called *axon boutons* or **terminal buttons.** These provide the mechanism for getting the signal across from the axon of one neuron to the dendrites or soma of neighboring neurons. The structure of a typical neuron is shown in **Figure 3.5.**

The neuron's signal is an electrical event. It is produced when *ions,* electrically charged particles, flow through the membrane of a cell, changing its *polarity,* and thereby its capacity to conduct electrochemical signals. Neurons transmit information in only one direction, according to the **law of forward conduction:** from the axon of one neuron to the dendrites or cell bodies of others.

Three major classes of neurons can be identified according to the types of cells to which they send or from which they receive information. **Sensory neurons** carry messages toward the central nervous system from cells in the periphery that are sensitive to light, sound, body position, and the like. **Motor neurons** carry messages away from the central nervous system to the muscles and glands. They are also called *afferent* (''carrying toward'') and *efferent* (''carrying away'') neurons, respectively.

Sensory neurons rarely communicate directly with motor neurons, however. Between them is usually a third class of neurons called **interneurons.** The bulk of the billions of neurons in the brain are interneurons that make many contacts with each other be-

▽ Figure 3.5 *The Neuron*

Shown here is a motor neuron, one of the three main types of neuron in the human body. Nerve impulses are received by branched areas called dendrites and transmitted to the cell body or soma, where life-sustaining metabolic activity also takes place. The transmitting end of the neuron is the elongated axon, which is often enclosed in a fatty myelin sheath. Terminal buttons at the branched endings of axons transmit impulses to the next neurons in the chain.

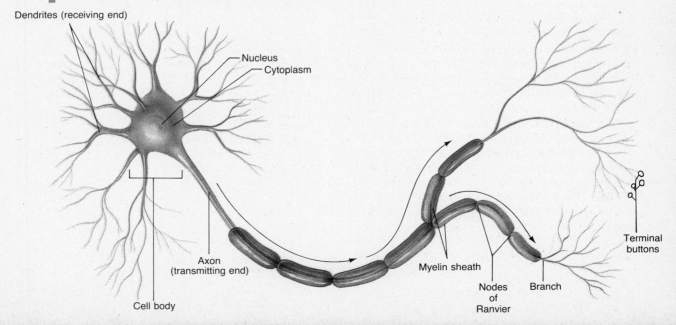

Dendrites (receiving end)

Nucleus
Cytoplasm

Axon
(transmitting end)

Cell body

Myelin sheath

Nodes
of
Ranvier

Branch

Terminal
buttons

fore reaching a motor neuron. For every motor neuron there are as many as 5000 interneurons in the great intermediate net—the computational system of the brain (Nauta & Feirtig, 1979).

At birth or shortly afterward the brain has all the neurons it is ever going to have. After that, neurons do not divide to form new cells. But they die in astonishing numbers, estimated to be about 10,000 every day throughout life. Fortunately, because we start with so many, we will lose less than 2 percent of our original supply in seventy years, unless we suffer from a brain disease. The deteriorated brain functioning that sometimes comes in old age is usually due not to fewer neurons but to degenerative changes in the neurons themselves or in the chemical substances that carry signals between neurons.

Interspersed among the neurons are about ten times as many **glial cells (glia).** The word *glia* is derived from the Greek word for "glue," and one function of these cells is to hold neurons close together, though they do not actually touch. While their other functions are not yet entirely clear, glial cells appear to act as conduits between blood vessels and neurons, and thus may transport nourishment to the latter (see **Figure 3.6**). They may also be the medium through which hormones and drugs can reach neurons in the brain. Though glia do not directly transmit information, they facilitate this task by forming a sheath that insulates the axons of some neurons, speeding conduction of the electrochemical impulse, as we shall see.

Nerve conduction: Sending the message out.

We can think of neurons as "salt-water bags" floating in a different kind of "salt-water soup." The cell membrane plays the critical role in keeping the ingredients of the two fluids apart or letting them mix a little. Both fluids contain **ions** (electrically charged particles) of sodium, chloride, and potassium, but when the neuron is inactive, there are ten times as many potassium ions *inside* the neuron as sodium and chloride ones *outside* it. The potassium ions are held there by the negative charge of protein molecules. Because of this imbalance, there is a negative electrical charge inside the neuron and a positive one outside it, and the membrane is said to be in a polarized state. This is called a **resting potential,** but it is no resting *state*. It is like a taut, drawn bow, ready to fire instantly when it is released—in this case, when a message from an adjoining neuron arrives.

The key to neural transmission is the selective permeability of the membrane—different permeabil-

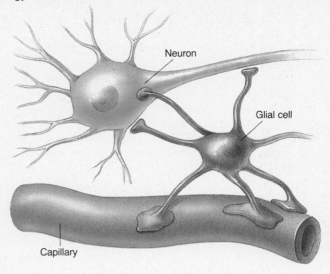

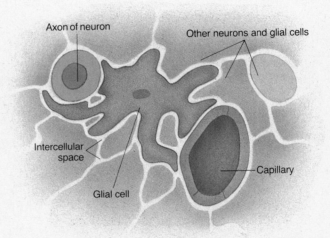

△ **Figure 3.6**

The top drawing shows a single glial cell located between a neuron and a capillary (a tiny blood vessel). The bottom drawing shows a thin slice of brain tissue as seen through an electron microscope. The brain is packed with neurons and glia, separated by narrow channels. These channels, the extracellular space of the brain, are filled with cerebrospinal fluid.

ity to different ions—and the fact that this permeability can change. When the neuron is inactive, the membrane is more permeable to potassium ions than to sodium ones, but there is some leakage in both directions, and pumps must function continuously to send them back. One such pump exchanges three sodium ions that have leaked in for two potassium ions that have leaked out, thus maintaining the preponderance of potassium ions inside. **Figure 3.7** is a diagrammatic sketch of a sodium pump. A large share of the energy used in the nervous system goes into this maintenance of the polarized state of readiness. The maintenance of this differential charge, in turn, provides a reserve of energy ready to be used during neural transmission (Kalat, 1984).

Changes in the permeability of the membrane of a neuron to these ions are responsible for all electrical signals in the nervous system, and new research is revealing the molecular basis of this process (Stevens, 1979; Catterall, 1984). Two kinds of signals occur: *graded potentials* and *action potentials*.

Graded potentials are the spreading, graded activity in the dendrite or cell body membrane produced by external stimulation from another neuron. At the point of stimulation sodium ions flow into the cell, and the resting potential is disturbed: the cell is *depolarized*. This local depolarization spreads like ripples on a pond caused by a pebble. The greater the stimulation, the larger the graded potential signal that is sent along the membrane of the dendrite and

cell body. But this spreading wave weakens with distance and fades unless combined with other comparable waves. The cell body acts like a computer, combining and summing all the graded potentials that are reaching it. If the total is above a certain magnitude, or *threshold,* the graded potential that reaches the axon activates an **action potential,** or *nerve impulse.*

What happens now is that sodium ions flood into the cell, causing a sudden, dramatic "collapse" of the resting potential—depolarization of the axon membrane—and a powerful electrical signal along it. Because the resting potential of the membrane collapses completely, each nerve impulse is total and equal in size. Thus, the axon fires according to an *all-or-none principle:* once its threshold has been reached by the incoming graded potential, a uniform action potential is generated; if the threshold is not reached, there is no nerve impulse.

The nerve impulse races down the length of the axon like a flame along a fuse. Successive sections of the membrane become permeable to sodium, then to potassium—and then quickly recover fully (in one millisecond) and are ready to be fired again. Once started, the nerve impulse is *self-propagating:* it keeps going until it reaches the terminal buttons. Unlike the graded potential in the dendrites, the axonal impulse does *not* vary in size or speed as it travels along. **Figure 3.8** illustrates both graded potentials and nerve impulses.

Different neurons conduct at different speeds; the fastest have signals that move at the rate of 200 meters per second, the slowest plod along at 10 centimeters per second (Bullock et al, 1977). The axons

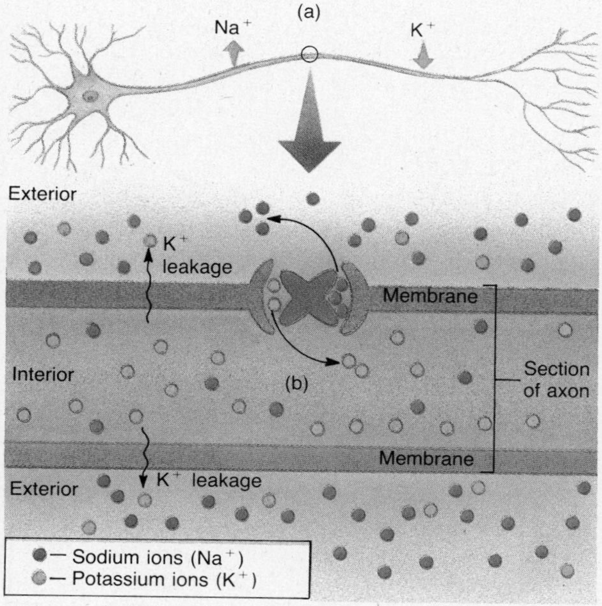

Figure 3.7 *A Sodium Pump*

This highly diagrammatic view of an axon section suggests the mechanism by which sodium pumps function to maintain the resting potential of a neuron. When the neuron is at rest, there is a high concentration of sodium (Na+) ions on the outside and potassium (K+) ions on the inside. Since potassium ions are continually leaking out through the membrane, a "pump" mechanism functions to exchange potassium for sodium, thus keeping the neuron in a state of readiness to fire. (For the sake of simplicity, the chloride ions which are also present have been omitted from the diagram.)

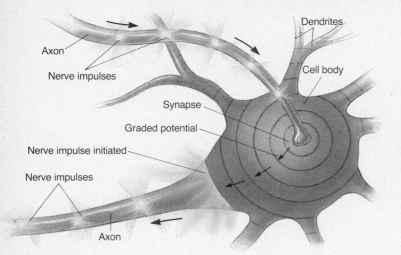

Axon

Nerve impulses

Dendrites

Cell body

Synapse

Graded potential

Nerve impulse initiated

Nerve impulses

Axon

◁ **Figure 3.8** *Graded Potentials and Nerve Impulses*

Here an axon from one neuron is shown making a synapse on the cell body of another neuron. Excitation by the first initiates a graded potential in the second. This diagram also shows the two types of electrical potential changes which are the basis of all neural activity. Graded potentials develop relatively slowly and are local and graded in intensity; like ripples on a pond, they are strongest at their source and diminish with distance. Graded potentials are converted by axons into brief, all-or-none bursts of electrical activity called action potentials *or nerve impulses, which travel without getting smaller all the way to the end of the axon. Axons in our bodies can transmit impulses at rates of up to a thousand per second. Normally, there are thousands of synapses on a neuron, but only one is shown here. Stimulation through the synapses is a common source of graded potentials, but some neurons generate such potentials spontaneously.*

of the fastest neurons are covered with a **myelin sheath,** a covering that insulates the axon. The myelin looks something like long beads on a string. The tiny breaks between the "beads" are called **nodes of Ranvier.** In neurons whose axons have this myelin covering, the fast-moving impulse skips along from one node to the next like an express train passing local stations. Damage to this coating throws off the delicate timing of nerve impulses. Multiple sclerosis, for example, is a disease of the myelin sheath that results in double vision, tremors, and eventual paralysis.

You may wonder how a uniform, all-or-none nerve impulse can transmit information about differences in intensity of stimulation. A more intense stimulus does two things to make its presence known. It triggers more frequent nerve impulses in each neuron, and also triggers impulses in more neurons. Somewhere in the brain this information about rate and quantity is combined and encoded, resulting in an appropriate sensation.

Synapses and neurotransmitters: Getting the message across. When an impulse arrives at the axon terminal, it cannot keep going because neurons do not touch each other. There is a gap between the end of each neuron and the start of the next. This junction, known as the **synapse,** is the neurons' "point of indirect contact," and the fluid that fills it acts as an insulator, not permitting the electrical activity to pass across it.

To bridge the gap and get the neural message across to the next neurons in line, electrical conduction is changed to chemical transmission. The neural signal is carried by chemical messengers from one side of the synapse—the *presynaptic membrane* of the terminal button—across the gap to the *postsynaptic membrane* of the dendrites or soma of the next

neuron. There it triggers a graded potential and the next electrical signal travels on.

When a nerve impulse reaches the end of an axon, small, precisely measured amounts of transmitter chemicals are released into the synaptic gap from **synaptic vesicles,** tiny sacs in the terminal buttons of the axon, as shown in **Figure 3.9.** These chemicals diffuse across the gap and attach to receptors in the postsynaptic membrane. The amount of chemical released corresponds to the number of incoming impulses: each impulse releases one vesicle. Thus more frequent signals (from more intense stimulation) trigger a greater amount of synaptic chemicals.

These chemical messengers are called **neurotransmitters;** they interact with receptors on the postsynaptic cell membrane to change its electrical potential and thus its ability to generate a graded potential. Then the neurotransmitter substance is either broken down or taken back into the terminal button (this is called **reuptake**), leaving the synapse ready for its next assignment. Anything that interferes with this process either keeps impulses flowing or prevents new messages from getting across.

Specific transmitter substances have now been found in the brain, in the spinal cord, in the peripheral nerves, and even in certain glands. Some occur primarily in one location, while others are more widespread. More than 30 substances are known or

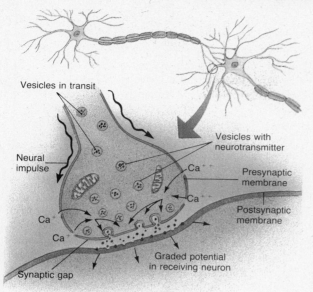

Vesicles in transit

Neural impulse

Ca⁺

Ca⁺

Synaptic gap

Vesicles with neurotransmitter

Ca⁺⁺

Ca⁺⁺

Presynaptic membrane

Postsynaptic membrane

Graded potential in receiving neuron

◁ **Figure 3.9** *The Synapse*

Activity at a synapse begins when a nerve impulse reaches the terminal button of an axon. The depolarizing action opens calcium ion (Ca^{++}) gates in the membrane of the terminal button, admitting the positive ions. The presence of calcium ions causes the synaptic vesicles to rupture, releasing neurotransmitter molecules into the gap between the neurons. If enough of these molecules bind to receptor sites on the postsynaptic membrane, a graded potential will be initiated in the second neuron.

suspected to be transmitters in the brain. Some chemicals, like epinephrine and norepinephrine, serve as neurotransmitters and also are secreted as hormones by endocrine glands. Some of the chemicals believed to function as neurotransmitters are described in **Table 3.1.**

Some synapses are excitatory: the transmitter substance causes the postsynaptic neuron to generate impulses at a higher rate. Others are inhibitory: the transmitter substance reduces the rate of impulses or prevents new impulses in the postsynaptic cell. But it is the receptor rather than the transmitter substance that determines what the effect will be: the same transmitter substance may be excitatory at one synapse, inhibitory at another. Synapses on dendrites tend to be excitatory; synapses on the cell body tend to be inhibitory. It is the sum of the excitatory and inhibitory effects on a neuron that determines whether it will fire and if it does, the rate of firing.

Table 3.1 *Chemicals Thought to Be Neurotransmitters*

For a chemical to be designated a neurotransmitter, several criteria must be met. It must be manufactured in the presynaptic terminal of a neuron and be released when a nerve impulse reaches the terminal. Its presence in the synaptic gap must generate a biological response in the next neuron, and if its release is blocked, there must be no subsequent response. Among the chemicals so far identified as neurotransmitters are the following:

Acetylcholine ("asséetil-cóleen")—found in many synapses of the central and peripheral nervous systems and the parasympathetic division. Excitatory at most central synapses and neuro-muscular synapses; inhibitory at heart and some other autonomic nervous system synapses.

Serotonin—produced in the central nervous system, involved in circuits that influence sleep and emotional arousal. Can be either excitatory or inhibitory.

Catecholamines—three chemicals found in synapses in the central nervous system and sympathetic division.

Dopamine—found in circuits involving voluntary movement, learning, memory, and emotional arousal. Inhibitory.

Norepinephrine or chemically similar noradrenalin—both a hormone and a transmitter. Found in circuits controlling arousal, wakefulness, eating, learning, and memory. Can be either excitatory or inhibitory.

Epinephrine or chemically similar adrenalin—both a hormone and a transmitter. Either excitatory or inhibitory; actions include increased pulse and blood pressure.

Amino acids—widely found in brain.

GABA—the main inhibitory transmitter in the brain.

Glutamic acid—possibly the chief excitatory transmitter in the brain.

Neuropeptides—chains of amino acids found in the brain.

Enkephalins—mostly inhibitory, as in pain relief, but excitatory in some locations.

Beta-endorphin—the most powerful pain reliever produced in the brain. Mostly inhibitory but excitatory in some locations; contained in the stress hormone, ACTH.

(Adapted from Rosenzweig & Leiman, 1982, p. 159)

For the billions of neurons in the brain there are trillions of synapses. One estimate suggests that there are 10^{14}, a hundred trillion synapses all told (Hubel, 1979). Some neurons have as many as 100,000 synapses with other neurons. Much of the subtle modulation of behavioral response patterns results from the overlaying of these chemically coded systems on the neuronal networks of the brain (Iversen, 1978).

Of the special significance of the synapse in human evolution, neurobiologist Steven Rose has said: "Consciousness, learning and intelligence are all synapse-dependent. It is not too strong to say that the evolution of humanity followed the evolution of the synapse" (1973, p. 65).

Drugs and synapses: Tampering with signals.
Many drugs exert their effects on behavior, mood, and thinking by influencing synaptic transmission. Chemical assault may interfere with any of the four steps in transmission: (a) release of the neurotransmitter from the presynaptic terminal; (b) binding of the transmitter on the postsynaptic membrane; (c) the opening of channels to allow ion exchange; or (d) the reuptake or neutralizing of substances of the transmitter that remain in the gap.

For example, curare, the poison used by South American natives in their blowgun darts, kills by blocking the postsynaptic receptor sites for the muscles. The transmitter acetylcholine is released by efferent nerves but cannot be bound to the plugged up receptors in the muscle cells. The poisoned animal dies—often from inability to breathe—because its muscles stop responding to signals from the nervous system.

Amphetamines are "uppers," drugs that increase alertness, counteract fatigue, and enhance feelings of well-being. They enhance transmission at those synapses where the transmitter norepinephrine is released. Their action is to release norepinephrine, block its reuptake, and prevent it from being broken down after it binds to the receptor. Thus the synapse is flooded with the transmitter, which keeps triggering the postsynaptic neurons—sometimes late into the night before an exam. It now appears that even a single low dose of amphetamine can permanently change certain nerve cells, increasing their long-term sensitivity to subsequent exposure (Robinson et al., 1982). Barbiturates are "downers," drugs that inhibit the transmission of norepinephrine at synapses, slowing down or blocking the process of information exchange across the synapse.

The street drug called "angel dust" or PCP causes sudden increases in muscle strength along with bizarre changes in behavior resembling those seen in severe mental disorders—and can result in death. Recently the mechanism by which PCP affects the brain has been identified (Albuquerque et al., 1983). PCP binds to the potassium channel of the presynaptic axon membrane and prevents the sodium ion flow from being reversed. The axon then keeps firing impulses and releasing transmitters into the synapse. In motor cells this produces extraordinary physical strength; in brain cells it can result in hallucinations and other abnormal mental functioning.

Many disorders of the brain are being traced to disturbances in the synthesis, release, or inactivation of a specific transmitter, or in the receptivity of postsynaptic membranes. For example, in Parkinson's disease, or shaking palsy, there is a deficiency of the transmitter dopamine in the synapses of the part of the brain that controls movement. Administration of the drug *L-dopa* has been found to facilitate the manufacture of dopamine, dramatically relieving the symptoms of this lethal disease.

Unfortunately, the same drugs that improve the symptoms of one disorder can also create other symptoms. For example, drugs that relieve severe depression elevate the levels of dopamine and serotonin. Symptoms of schizophrenia are *worsened* by an excess of dopamine; they are relieved by drugs that *suppress* the action of dopamine synapses (Kety, 1979). But drugs that remove dopamine and serotonin from the synapses can cause depression. (See **Close-up** on p. 89.)

Understanding the chemistry of synapses may one day be the key to unravelling some of the profound mysteries of mental disorders.

Neuroregulators: Making a lasting impression. Besides the neurotransmitters and the hormones, which act as "first messengers," there is a "second messenger" system of **neuroregulators.** These are chemicals activated by both neurotransmitters and hormones that work inside the receiving cell. They amplify the effect of the transmitter or hormone and can change the electrical potential of the membrane and alter the internal biochemistry of the cell. Evidently a stimulant like caffeine prolongs the action of these "second messengers." Neuroregulators work more slowly than the "first messengers" and may be involved in longer-lasting actions.

The Keys to Paradise

The poet De Quincy wrote, "Thou hast the keys to Paradise, O just, subtle, and mighty opium." Those "keys" open the doors to feelings of euphoria and analgesia (relief from pain). But opium—and its derivatives, morphine and heroin—can also open the way to addiction.

Opium, which comes from the juice of a poppy plant, exerts its powerful effect by acting on the central nervous system. But its derivative morphine comes in two forms: one, the powerful drug; the other a totally inert and ineffective substance nearly identical in molecular structure. Somehow one can act on the nerve cells but not the other. The question for researchers was how the nerve cells can tell them apart.

One hypothesis proposed was that there must be specialized receptors on some neurons that can accept the active form of morphine but not the inactive one, much as a lock can be opened by the right key but not by wrong ones. But why should the brain have receptor sites to fit the juice of the poppy plant? One answer could be that the brain itself produces a similar key—its own opiates.

A search for these "keys" in the brain was undertaken, and in 1975 two pharmacologists isolated substances in the brains of pigs that activate the same receptor sites as morphine and have a similar effect. These pain-relieving substances, produced by the brain itself, were called *enkephalins* ("in the head") (Hughes et al., 1975). Enkephalins were later found in the brains of other mammals and in many different brain regions. They act as neurotransmitters and also can increase or decrease the action of other transmitters—making them very powerful brain agents (Snyder & Childers, 1979). They occur in several amino acid chains which have collectively been given the name *endorphins,* a contraction of the words *endogenous*

("from within") and *morphine.* Like morphine, endorphins can be addictive as well as relieve pain when administered from the outside.

The wide-ranging effects of endorphins have been studied by means of a research strategy based on the action of another chemical, *naloxone.* Morphine addicts suffering from near-lethal drug overdoses are helped instantly by injections of naloxone. In just 30 seconds naloxone reverses morphine's effects by preventing morphine from binding to its usual receptor sites—in effect, plugging up the locks so the opiate key can no longer get in. Naloxone has no other known effect on the brain's functioning.

Naloxone has been found to have the same effect in reversing the effects of endorphins. Pain relief usually brought about by endorphins following stimulation by acupuncture needles or electrical stimulation is blocked or reduced by naloxone. The presence of endorphins can thus be studied indirectly by observing the effects of naloxone.

Endorphins are now known to be stored in the pituitary glands. Besides relieving pain (to be discussed more fully in the next chapter), they play a role in the regulation of body temperature, respiration, hypertension, epileptic seizures, eating, memory, mood, and sexual behavior (Bolles & Fanelow, 1982). The most powerful analgesic produced by the brain, called *beta-endorphin,* has been synthesized by biochemists and given to human subjects.

Endorphin therapy is being developed to try to help drug addicts, chronic pain sufferers, and some types of mental patients. Perhaps some of the keys to human nature, if not Paradise, will be found in the mighty endorphins.

One hypothesis is that the mechanism for permanently altering the electrical properties of the receiving neuron works by sustaining the activity of a synapse over a relatively long time, through the action of a small molecule called *cyclic AMP.* This molecule, produced in the cell by stimulation from the first messengers, is the means by which neuroregulators exert their effects. This could be the basis for synthesis of new protein molecules that store information in a lasting form. It may be that such alteration of the biochemistry of a neuron and its synaptic connections is the basis for memory (Nathanson & Greengard, 1977). How we learn and how we store what we have learned for later use are questions of great current interest to psychologists working at different levels of analysis, as you will see in coming chapters.

Neural networks: Acting in concert. Up to now we have been looking at how the nervous system *transmits* information. Its other major task is to *process* information. The first level of processing is seen in the combining of graded potentials in the cell body and the modification of synaptic transmission that inhibits or increases nerve cell activity. Higher levels of complexity in information processing require circuits, systems of neurons functioning together to perform tasks that individual cells cannot carry out alone.

The simplest ones are reflex arcs, which may involve only a sensory neuron and a motor neuron, or these two plus an interneuron between them in the spinal cord. Reflex arcs provide for automatic, rapid, simple response to specific types of stimulation, such as the knee jerk in response to pressure below the kneecap (see **Figure 3.10**). Just as a secretary processes routine calls without disturbing the boss, the body's system of reflex arcs operate largely independent of brain involvement when the health and safety of the organism can benefit from a simple, swift response (Woolridge, 1963).

In addition, many reflex arcs contain interneurons, that make connections with the brain. The brain is notified of reflex responses and *can* alter them, as you can demonstrate by trying *not* to respond to a tap below the kneecap: probably you can't prevent the reflex response altogether but can lessen it. Though a single reflex arc is a simple mechanism, a reflex *action* involves many reflex arcs and other interconnections and may be quite complex. For example, the pupil-contraction reflex involves several interneurons before the information about light intensity even leaves the eye.

Neural networks follow a basic principle of nature: all life processes are organized *hierarchically*. This means that simpler units, structures, and processes are organized into levels of ever greater complexity, with higher ones exercising some control over lower ones. At each level of complexity there are limits and constraints that can be overcome only by a more complex system (Jacob, 1977). Just as new capabilities become available at each level from molecule to cell to organ to organism, new potential for information processing becomes available with increasingly complex neural networks.

Early mechanisms for control of regions of the organism, or of particular specialized functions like food intake and digestion, were made possible by clusters of nerve cell bodies with many interconnections called **ganglia,** or **nuclei,** since they contain the nuclei of many neurons. Later, neural networks at the head end evolved into specialized structures that had increasingly precise control over other parts of the body and over the increasingly varied activities of the organism. This development toward increasing dominance by higher centers, with development of more specialized brain structures exercising this con-

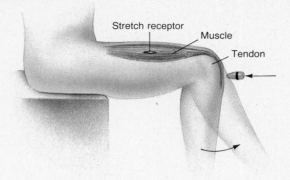

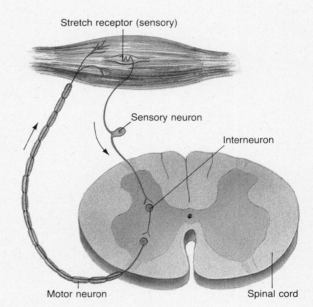

△ **Figure 3.10** *A Reflex Arc*

This is a simplified drawing of a reflex arc. Three kinds of neurons are represented here: (a) a sensory (afferent) neuron leading from a muscle cell: (b) an interneuron in the spinal cord, and (c) a motor neuron with its long myelinated axon extending to the same muscle. Actually, a stimulus would excite many afferent neurons, each of which would connect with large numbers of interneurons; many motor neurons would then carry messages back to the stimulated area.

trol, is called **encephalization** (*cephalus* means "head").

Because neural networks in humans are so complex, scientists trying to relate neural circuits to particular actions often study simple organisms such as invertebrates (animals without a backbone). A favorite has been the large sea snail *Aplysia*, because its relatively few neurons are large enough to be identified so that systems of neurons can be traced and "wiring diagrams" worked out for given types of behavior. For example, *Aplysia's* heart rate is controlled by only a few cells that excite it to pump and a few that inhibit it. These are "command cells," individual cells at a critical position to control other cells and thereby entire behavioral sequences. A neural circuit of only 70 cells is involved in *Aplysia's* reflex action of withdrawing its gill when its siphon is touched by a stimulus—a reflex necessary for its survival (see **Figure 3.11**).

▽ **Figure 3.11** *Gill Withdrawal Reflex in Aplysia*

Above are sketches of Aplysia *in the normal state and with its gill withdrawn. Below is a schematic diagram of the abdominal ganglion with its sensory and motor connections. The 24 sensory neurons and 30 peripheral motor neurons are each represented by a single line, but the 13 motor neurons and 3 interneurons in this network are shown. Two of the interneurons are excitatory; the third, inhibitory.*

Adapted from Kandel, 1976.

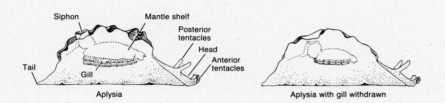

Aplysia

Aplysia with gill withdrawn

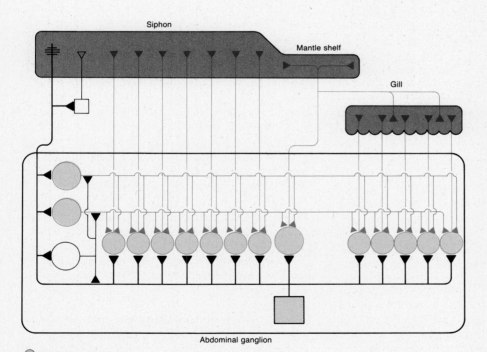

Abdominal ganglion

🔘 Motor neuron

🔘 Excitatory interneuron

⚪ Inhibitory interneuron

🔲 Sensory neurons (24 represented)

☐ Peripheral siphon motor neurons (30 represented)

Although *Aplysia* has invariant connections "hard-wired" into its nervous system, it is still capable of modifying its behavior through learning. One form of learning that it exhibits is **habituation,** a decrease in strength of responding when a stimulus that was originally new is presented repeatedly. Habituation is a primitive but widespread type of learning by which organisms learn to ignore stimuli that carry no new information. It frees them to attend to other stimulus events that are more meaningful. Any novel, unexpected, or threatening stimulus elicits an **orienting reaction,** a complex physiological and behavioral response that maximizes sensitivity to environmental input and prepares the body for emergency action, but this lasts only while new information is being received.

Tactile stimuli applied to the siphon of *Aplysia* elicit an orienting reaction and gill withdrawal at first. But with repeated stimulation, the gill-withdrawal response habituates: it becomes less and less until it is not made at all. It is clear that this lessened response is not due to fatigue, however, because if a noxious stimulus is now applied to another part of the body, there is strong gill withdrawal.

After an hour of no stimulation, the reflex starts to return and after a day of no stimulation recovery is complete. This type of habituation can be thought of as short-term memory and the recovery or loss of habituation as forgetting. When four repeated sessions of 10 stimuli each are administered, however, habituation is profound—the "memory" lasts for weeks.

When the mechanism for habituation was traced by neurobiologist Eric Kandel and his associates, they found that during habituation a smaller amount of neurotransmitter was being released at the synapse, due to the action of an interneuron (Kandel, 1979). Though some details are still to be filled in, this finding is important because it identifies a specific biochemical mechanism that explains an observed change in behavior.

With this background on the operation of the nervous system, neural and hormonal transmission, and neural networks, we are ready to go to the top and study how the brain performs its remarkable functions.

HOW DOES THE BRAIN CONTROL BEHAVIOR?

In the hierarchical organization of the human nervous system, the brain represents by far the highest level of complexity. It is in the brain where information about the external world and the organism's internal state is coordinated, where our actions are controlled, and where our higher mental processes take place. Here we will investigate the development and structure of the brain and the primary responsibilities of its different parts.

Development of the brain

The early stages of the development of all vertebrate embryos are quite similar: the primitive structure that eventually becomes the brain looks the same at first in a frog, rat, cat, or human embryo. The way the brain forms and separates into divisions is also the same across many species. But the higher the species, the larger and more complex the brain becomes and the more sophisticated functions it can perform.

The development of the nervous system in members of each species follows genetic instructions that result in the "hard wiring" of basic neural circuits. In the human brain, these instructions lead to a remarkably precise and efficient communication and computational system unmatched in many ways by any supercomputer. But heredity does not do it all. Stimulation and information from the environment are needed also to "fine tune" the brain structures for behaving appropriately in the individual's particular environmental niche. Let's see how this happens.

Primitive brain and neural structures. The first organ systems to become functional during the development of the human embryo are the cardiovascular and nervous systems. By the third week the heart begins to beat, and during the second month the human embryo responds to stroking by contracting muscles that move its neck. This simple avoidance reflex shows that some of the machinery of the nervous system is already in place and functioning at this early age.

Actually, the first neural structure begins to be formed during the second week after conception when a line of specialized cells grows rapidly, forming a *neural plate*. This swells as cells divide and soon curls to form the *neural tube* from which the whole nervous system will develop.

The lower end of the tube lengthens to become the spinal cord. It first develops circuits for responding (efferent tracts), then circuits for sensory input (afferent tracts). The first simple reflexes are direct excitatory connections between sensory and motor neurons; then, as development proceeds, inhibitory cells are formed. Interneurons develop that can carry signals between the two sides of the spinal cord and coordinate movements on the two sides of the body. Other interneurons form tracts that carry information up and down the spinal cord and into and out of the developing brain.

Meanwhile, by the fourth week after conception, a dramatic spurt of growth has created three "bumps" at the upper end of the neural tube. The lower one, the **hindbrain,** will differentiate into structures that will control basic life processes like breathing and heartbeat; the second one, the **midbrain,** will differentiate into reflex centers and structures that relay sensory and motor information to

and from higher brain centers. The **forebrain,** at the top, will differentiate into two parts. The lower one, the **diencephalon** ("between brain"), will control body temperature, hormonal release, autonomic nervous system functions, and primitive emotional and motivational processes (see **Figure 3.12**).

This much of the brain is sometimes called the "old brain"; we share its parts with other species though in somewhat different forms. Where we differ most is in the size and complexity of development of the upper part of the forebrain, the *telencephalon* (*tele* means "final"). In higher animals it proliferates to become the most prominent part of the brain— two hemispheres with increasingly convoluted, "wrinkled" surfaces. This vastly increased surface makes possible ever greater precision and variety in information processing (see **Figure 3.13**). It is this part of the brain that is associated with consciousness: however, consciousness cannot exist in the absence of some excitation of the forebrain via the activity of the lower divisions of the brain.

The lower control centers remain in the human brain and retain some control over the structures below them. The forebrain dominates the old brain but

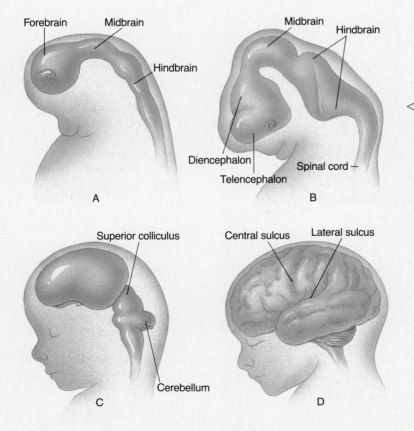

◁ Figure 3.12 *Fetal Brain Development*

The diagrams illustrate the development of the human brain from the third week after conception to birth. A, 3-week embryo; B, 6-week embryo; C, 11-week fetus; D, newborn infant.

▷ **Figure 3.13**

Cerebral development is increasingly more advanced in higher classes of vertebrates. In the frog (A), an amphibian, the cerebrum is relatively small while the hindbrain and optic lobes are quite prominent. In the alligator (B), an advanced reptile, the cerebral region is larger but the hindbrain is still relatively prominent. In a primitive mammal such as the shrew (C), the cerebrum is proportionately larger, but smooth. In the horse (D), a more advanced mammal, the cerebrum is still larger, and the convolutions of its surface further increase the cortical area.

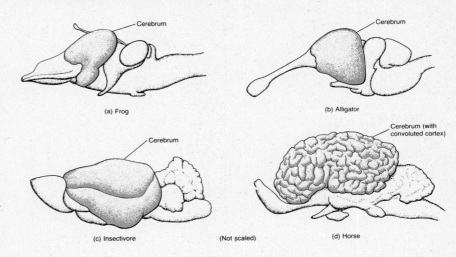

does not entirely rule it. The coupling of the higher centers to the old brain has been compared to "adding a jet engine to an old horse cart" (Jacob, 1977). No doubt some of our inconsistencies and contradictory impulses reflect this division of control.

The production and development of neurons.

The ability of the embryo to respond to stimulation so early is due partly to the incredible production of neurons in the prenatal brain—some 500,000 per minute at peak production! (Rosenzweig & Leiman, 1982). Many of these neurons migrate from their place of origin to specific destinations where they will function ever after. They may then differentiate into neurons that have unique appearances and capabilities characteristic of the region into which they settle. For example, the specialized cells in the retinas of the eyes started out in the brain.

Shortly after birth, three main changes in neurons account for the increasing size and weight of the maturing brain as well as its improving functions. One is extensive lengthening and branching of dendrites, accompanied by an increase in the size of the cell bodies that nourish them. *Synapses* are also formed in large numbers at this time, permitting more complex communication between neurons.

Second is the prolific spread of myelin tissue around some axons—a process called *myelinization*. (As we have seen, myelinated axons conduct signals more rapidly than others.) The myelin sheath is formed by glial cells, which have been developing since before birth but now burst forth in profusion. Glial calls develop from the same type of immature

cells as neurons; why a common initial tissue develops into these different kinds of cells is a mystery. Unlike neurons, glial cells are continually being added throughout the organism's life.

Critical periods and the role of experience.

The various parts of the brain and nervous system develop at different rates, and the period of most rapid biochemical change for a given structure is a *critical period,* a time of maximum sensitivity. Certain influences must be present then if development is to proceed normally, whereas abnormal influences do their greatest damage to the structure at this time. Both genetic and environmental influence exert their biggest effects during these critical periods.

Among the environmental factors that can prevent normal development of the brain are malnutrition, inadequate oxygen in circulating blood, infections, radiation, drugs, injuries, and inadequate stimulation. We will discuss only the first and last of these here.

Neural tissue needs amino acids from proteins. Diets deficient in protein prevent the normal development of certain brain structures. Getting insufficient protein during fetal development or the period of rapid neural growth after birth can permanently impair the brain. Nearly a half million preschool children worldwide are estimated to be suffering various degrees of malnutrition; survivors grow up with both physical and mental handicaps from which both they and their own children will suffer (Noback & Demarest, 1975; Wurtman, 1978).

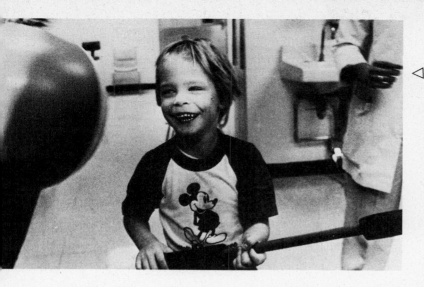

On January 15, 1984, 4-year-old Jimmy Tontlewicz was pulled from the icy waters of Lake Michigan, where he had been submerged for nearly 30 minutes after a sledding accident. Doctors feared that if Jimmy regained consciousness at all, lack of oxygen would have resulted in permanent brain damage. Miraculously, however, Jimmy demonstrated the remarkable recuperative capacity of the human brain. He is shown here playing with a bat and ball six weeks after his dramatic rescue. Jimmy returned to his home a few weeks later, but continued to undergo therapy.

Laboratory experiments have demonstrated that environmental stimulation—or lack of it—can permanently change brain chemistry, brain anatomy, and behavior (Gottlieb, 1976; Rosenzweig & Bennett, 1977).

In one study rats were reared in "enriched" or "impoverished" environments and their behavior and brain development compared. Those reared with toys and other young rats to interact with showed better learning performance than those reared in isolation in small, bare cages. In addition, their brains, when studied later, were found to have more dendritic branches, thicker cortical areas, and more glial cells (Cummins et al., 1977).

In another study it was demonstrated that normal development of the visual system did not occur if the animals were given markedly reduced visual stimulation at critical times. When a kitten's right eye was exposed only to *horizontal* lines during the critical period for the development of the visual system and the left eye only to *vertical* lines, then in adulthood the right eye did not respond to vertical lines but only to horizontal ones, while the left eye had the reverse defect (Hirsch & Spinelli, 1971).

According to a recent survey of research, sensory stimulation can play three roles in the development of the visual system. It can *start* development, channeling it in a particular direction, it can *vary* development by accelerating or retarding certain processes, and it can *maintain* development by providing adequate stimulation to genetically programmed circuits (Movshon & van Sluyters, 1981). Here is how nature and nurture work together to produce an optimally functioning brain (Rosenzweig, 1984).

It seems clear that neurons that are used during development survive and develop further, whereas unstimulated ones weaken and die. In some regions of the brain as many as half of the nerve cells die in early life. It is experience that determines which ones are needed: experience supplies the stimulation the cells require for establishing reliable connections or at least for preventing their untimely death. Fortunately for us, genetic instructions provide for the production of many more neurons and neural connections than experience will demonstrate a need for. Even with the great early loss of unused neurons, we retain such an ample supply that the brain can often compensate for damage to sizable portions of it later in life. Let's see now what the different parts of this amazing brain do.

Functional organization of the human brain

Many physiological psychologists regard the brain as essentially "*a mechanism for governing motor activity*. Its primary function is essentially the transforming of sensory patterns into patterns of motor coordination. . . . From the fishes to man there is apparent only a gradual refinement and elaboration of brain mechanisms with nowhere any radical alteration of the fundamental operating principles. . . ." (Sperry, 1952, p. 297). Yet the part of the process devoted to information processing between sensory input and motor output has been so vastly extended in the human brain that eventual action often takes second place to thought: thought, in all its variety and complexity, takes center stage.

95

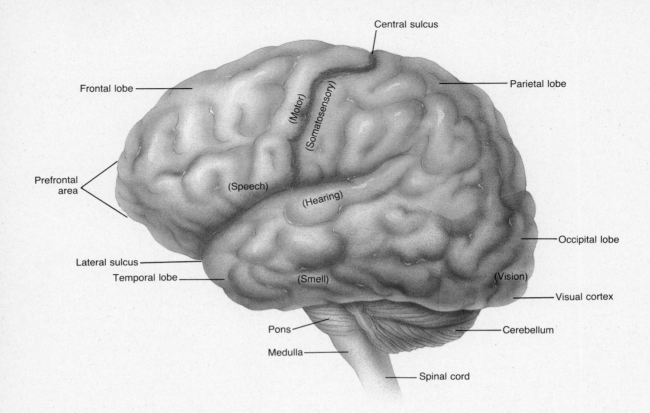

Central sulcus

Frontal lobe

Parietal lobe

(Motor)

(Somatosensory)

Prefrontal
area

(Speech)

(Hearing)

Occipital lobe

Lateral sulcus

Temporal lobe

(Smell)

(Vision)

Visual cortex

Pons

Cerebellum

Medulla

Spinal cord

Figure 3.14
The Human Brain

*Above is a drawing of an intact
brain, showing the left cerebral
hemisphere and some of the
lower brain centers. Note that the
cerebrum is divided into four
prominent lobes: temporal,
frontal, parietal, and occipital. The
primary functions of the various
areas are shown in parentheses.*

*In the lower view, the brain
has been cut through the middle
from front to back. Structures of
the forebrain, midbrain, and
hindbrain are shown, as is the
corpus callosum, which connects
the two hemispheres.*

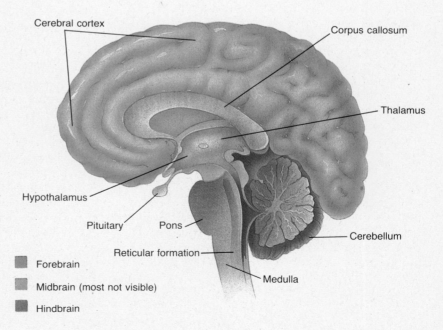

Cerebral cortex

Corpus callosum

Thalamus

Hypothalamus

Pituitary

Pons

Reticular formation

Cerebellum

Medulla

Forebrain

Midbrain (most not visible)

Hindbrain

Two views of the human brain are shown in **Figure 3.14.** As will be apparent, the upper part of the early forebrain has expanded over the top and sides of the old brain, increasing its outer surface even more by forming many folds and deep grooves. This upper part of the brain is called the **cerebrum** or "new brain." It is divided into two halves called the **cerebral hemispheres,** which are connected only by a white bundle of myelinated axons called the **corpus callosum** that carry messages between the two hemispheres. The outer layer of the cerebrum, the **cortex** (meaning "bark"), is gray; it is made up of the cell bodies and unmyelinated fibers of billions of neurons and is the part of the brain necessary for precise perception and conscious thought. (It is also called the **neocortex** to distinguish it from cortical tissue in other parts of the brain.) The inner part of the cerebrum is white; it is made up of countless myelinated fibers which pass through the old brain on their way to and from the other parts of the body. The control centers carried over from the old diencephalon (the earliest part of the forebrain to develop) also contain the "gray matter" of many cell nuclei. The spinal cord has remained a tube; it and several cavities *(ventricles)* in the brain that are connected with it are filled with *cerebrospinal fluid.* In this section we can only summarize what is known so far about the special responsibilities of the main parts of the brain.

Functions of the lower brain centers. In the adult human brains shown in **Figure 3.14,** we see what has happened to the "bumps" on the embryonic neural tube. The hindbrain, just above the spinal cord, has developed into several structures. Most prominent is the **cerebellum,** a wrinkled structure tucked under the back of the cerebrum which controls balance and motor coordination. In front of it is the **brain stem,** which contains structures involved in the control of basic life processes. One of these, the **pons,** is a connecting link to the cerebellum; another, the **medulla,** is responsible for controlling repetitive processes such as breathing and heartbeat. Running through these structures is the **reticular formation,** a long structure in the middle of the brain stem through which sensory messages pass on their way to higher centers of the brain. It acts as a general arousal system for the whole brain and is important in alertness and attention.

At the upper end of the old brain, forming a rim around the brain stem, is the **limbic system** (see Figure 3.15). This is a transition zone where old brain merges with neocortex; it contains centers for emotional behavior and basic motivational urges, such as copulation and pain avoidance. Aggressive behavior appears to have its own brain center, the **amygdala,** in the limbic system. Another part of the limbic system, the **hippocampus,** is involved in memory. Below the corpus callosum is the **thalamus,** a relay station for all incoming sensory information, and below it is an important control center, the **hypothalamus.** The hypothalamus regulates many vital processes such as eating, drinking, body temperature, and hormonal activity. We shall explore the role of the hypothalamus further in Chapter 8.

Localization of cortical functions. The cortex of the cerebral hemispheres is where the highest level of neural integration takes place. Its billions of neurons provide the mechanisms by which a series of "yes-no" electrochemical nerve impulses lead to our recognition of a Beethoven sonata or a friend's smile. Although ultimately the brain always works as a whole, and sole responsibility of one part for a particular function is rare or may not exist, we can identify certain parts of the cortex that have more responsibility than others for particular control and coordination functions. But even when a particular part is shown to be *essential* for a particular function we cannot say that part has total responsibility.

The outer part of the cerebral hemispheres is divided into lobes by a deep horizontal groove called the **lateral sulcus** and a vertical one called the **central sulcus.** Only about a fourth of the cortical area of the human cerebrum is devoted to sending messages to the muscles or receiving sensory input. These are called, respectively, *motor projection areas* and *sensory projection areas* and occur along the two deep grooves and at the back of the brain. The remaining three fourths of the cortex consists of *association areas* where sensory and motor messages are correlated and integrated. Such "higher" mental processes as analytical thinking are attributed largely to the frontal areas of the cortex (Goodman, 1978).

There are more than six hundred voluntary muscles in the human body; their action is controlled by the motor projection area, or **motor cortex,** located along the front of the central sulcus.

Muscles in the *lower* part of the body are controlled by neurons in the *top* part of the motor pro-

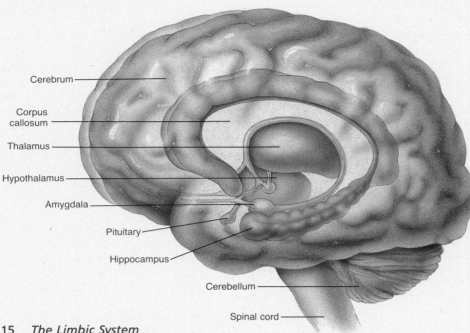

Cerebrum

Corpus callosum

Thalamus

Hypothalamus

Amygdala

Pituitary

Hippocampus

Cerebellum

Spinal cord

△ **Figure 3.15** *The Limbic System*

Here the surface of the cerebral hemisphere is shown as transparent, giving us a view of the limbic system structures deep within. The major components of the limbic system include the amygdala, hippocampus, thalamus, hypothalamus, and certain parts of the frontal and temporal lobes of the cortex.

jection area and vice versa, so that a sketch of the parts of the body controlled by each brain area (as in **Figure 3.16**) shows the body upside down. As you can see, the upper parts of the body can receive far more detailed instructions than the lower parts. In fact, the two largest motor projection areas are devoted to the fingers—especially the thumb—and to the muscles involved in speech, reflecting the importance of tools and talking in human activity. Messages from one side of the brain go to muscles on the *opposite* side of the body.

The sensory projection areas that receive messages from the various parts of the body are also called **somatosensory areas** (*soma,* as we have seen, means "body"). These are the areas associated with feelings of pain, temperature, touch, and body position. The primary somatosensory areas are in the parietal lobes, just across the central sulcus from the corresponding motor areas. Here, too, the body is represented upside down and most space is given to the lips, tongue, thumb, and index fingers—the parts of the body that provide the most important sensory input. Like the motor areas, the somatosensory areas communicate with the *opposite* side of the body.

Auditory information is processed in the **auditory cortex,** which is in the temporal lobes, just below the lateral sulcus. Different parts of the area appear to be more sensitive to different pitch ranges. Each auditory area of the cortex, the left and the right, receives input from both ears.

Visual input is processed at the back of the brain in the **visual cortex,** located in the occipital lobes. Here, the most space is devoted to input from the central part of the retinas of the eyes, the area from which the most detailed information comes.

The visual cortex of each hemisphere receives input from both eyes. Messages from the outer half of each retina remain in the same hemisphere, while those from the inner half of each retina cross over to the opposite hemisphere at a region called the **optic chiasma.** (A small part of the central part of each retina projects to both hemispheres.) Because the lenses in the eyes reverse the images, the *left* half of the visual field is projected onto the *right* side of both retinas and the visual cortex of the *right* hemisphere. Information from the right half of the visual field goes to the left hemisphere. Yet what we see is an unbroken, unified visual field. We will have more to say about visual processes in the next chapter.

Cerebral dominance. What do you conclude from the following three pieces of evidence? (a) Patients suffering strokes that paralyze the *right* side of their bodies often develop speech disturbances. (b) People with brain damage from an accident or stroke may have difficulty in writing, speaking, and understanding others—but only if the brain damage is on the *left* side. (c) Most people's left hemisphere is slightly larger than the right (Galaburda et al., 1978).

Though the two hemispheres of the brain are similar in many ways, both clinical and experimental evidence clearly indicate asymmetry: the two sides of

▽ | **Figure 3.16** *Primary Motor and Somatosensory Areas*

The primary motor and somatosensory areas of the cortex lie along the central sulcus: the motor area just in front of it, the somatosensory area just behind it. Corresponding parts of the body are represented by points roughly across the sulcus from each other, and representation is upside down; that is, the legs and feet are represented at the top and around the inner surface between the hemispheres, hands and arms below them, and the head at the bottom. The greater precision of sensitivity and control in head and hands than in other parts of the body is reflected in larger areas of representation on the cortex. In the case of both the primary motor and the primary somatosensory area, communication is with the opposite side of the body.

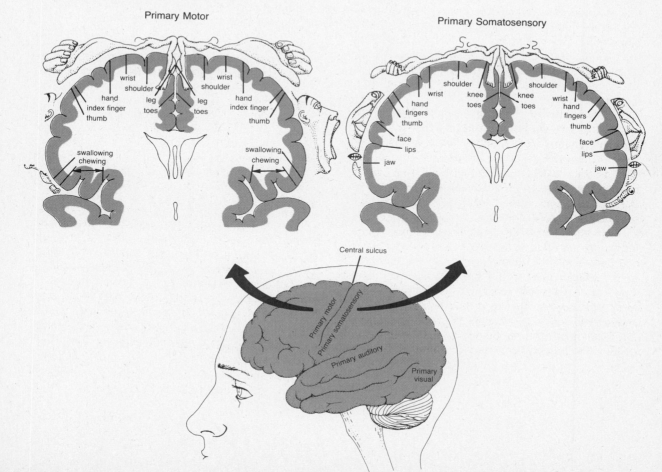

the brain differ in their anatomical, chemical, and electrical properties. This asymmetry can be attributed to the fact that the two sides of the brain have primary responsibility for different functions. This tendency for one cerebral hemisphere to play a more dominant role than the other in controlling particular functions is called **cerebral dominance.** The most notable example of such dominance is that language-related functions are usually controlled by the left side of the brain. This explains why the left hemisphere is usually larger and why damage to it may cause language disorders. It also explains why people suffering paralysis on the right side from a stroke may have speech problems: from the right-side paralysis we know that the damage was to the left side of the brain.

Researchers have now found that the left hemisphere dominates language functions in 95 percent of all right-handers. About 70 percent of left-handers also show left-brain dominance for language. The other 5 percent of right-handers and 15 percent of left-handers have speech controlled by the right hemisphere. For another 15 percent of left-handers, language functions occur in both sides of the brain (this is called *bilateral speech control*). Persons with right-brain dominance in language functions are at higher risk for developing disorders that interfere with language-related functions such as reading. Interestingly, males are more likely than females to be left-handed and also to have more speech-related learning disorders.

Patients with right-hemisphere damage are more likely to have *perceptual* and *attentional* problems, possibly including serious difficulties in spatial orientation. For example, they may feel lost in a previously familiar place or be unable to fit geometric shapes together. Patients with right-hemisphere damage in the parietal region may show a syndrome in which the patient totally ignores the left side of his or her body and left visual field—eating only what is on the right side of a plate of food, for example.

Many important discoveries about the contributions of each half of the brain have come from studying "split-brain" patients—people who have had the connection between their hemispheres severed to control epileptic seizures (see Springer & Deutsch, 1984). This operation has, in effect, left them with two separate brains in one head—and two conscious minds, which we will discuss in Chapter 6.

Much of our knowledge about brain asymmetries has come from observation of people who have suffered brain damage on one side or whose cerebral hemispheres could not communicate with each other. But hemispheric differences also exist in normal, healthy subjects. For example, with both men and women and both left-handers and right-handers, the rate of blood flow generally increases in the left hemisphere during verbal task performance and in the right hemisphere during performance of spatial tasks, suggesting greater activity in those parts of the brain for those tasks (Gur et al., 1982).

In general, studies have found the left side of the brain more important in controlling verbal activities and the right side more important in directing visual-spatial activities. One recent study suggests, however, that specialization may be more pronounced in men than it is in women (Inglis & Lawson, 1981).

Another important finding that comes from studies of subjects with normally functioning brains is the degree to which the two hemispheres make different contributions to the same function. For example, as **Table 3.2** shows, both hemispheres contribute to language and memory functions, to perceptual-cognitive functions, and to emotional functions, but their special aptitudes are evidently different.

This generalization is in keeping with the findings of a recent, methodologically sophisticated study. Subjects were given tasks requiring a series of split-second decisions and actions, while measurements were taken of the electrical activity of both hemispheres through brain-wave recordings. Brain-wave activity rapidly shifted back and forth laterally (from one side of the brain to the other), depending on the kind of judgment and response being made at the moment. This shifting lateralization of brain-wave activity was aptly termed "shadows of thought" (Gevins et al., 1983).

Focus on left-hemisphere speech control led to the mistaken belief that cerebral dominance would be found only in humans. But it is found in other species as well. For example, the development of a canary's songs is controlled by the left side of its brain. And rats handled frequently when young were found to have stored that early experience in the right hemisphere. As adults, they were less aggressive than those not given early handling. This effect

Table 3.2 *Specialization in the Cerebral Hemispheres*

	Left Hemisphere	Right Hemisphere
Language and Memory Functions	Controls spontaneous speaking, writing	Can direct repetitive but not spontaneous verbal utterances
	Directs formulation of replies to complex commands	Can direct response to simple commands
	Directs recognition of words	Directs recognition of faces
	Controls memory of words and numbers	Controls memory of shapes and music
		Guides drawing of geometric shapes
Perceptual and Cognitive Functions	Orchestrates sequences of movements	Functions in map interpretation
		Functions in mental rotation of images
Emotional functions	Is involved in feelings of anxiety	Controls emotional responsiveness
	Is responsible for negative emotions in response to unpleasant events	Is responsible for self-generated positive, expansive emotions

Both hemispheres are active in language and memory functions, in perceptual functions, and in emotional functions, but their contributions are different (adapted from Buchsbaum, 1980, and Tucker, 1981).

was eliminated in animals that had their right hemispheres removed. A growing body of research has led to the assertion that "It is now likely that no animal species, no matter how humble, lacks cerebral dominance" (Geschwind, cited in Marks, 1981).

While it has been possible to find brain regions that have special responsibilities in particular activities, relationships between specific brain structures and the complex behaviors we are most interested in—such as comprehension, creativity, and love—have yet to be identified. Much of what an organism does may have a primary control center somewhere in the brain but also involve widespread activity of the whole brain. The best metaphor for the brain may be not an electronic computer but a modern corporation. The success of the organization depends on many different groups, each performing a special task but always communicating with top management about the process and products of its activities. Top management's evaluations and integrations of these various reports then become the basis for directing ongoing and future corporate ventures.

HOW IS THE BRAIN STUDIED?

In describing *what* is known about the functions of various brain structures, we have skipped over questions about *how* that knowledge was learned. What methods are used to probe the secrets of the brain?

Autopsies have provided some of the information we have about how damage to brain structure from injury or disease contributes to mental or behavioral disorders. But the three basic techniques most used in studying neural activity in *living* brains have been: (a) stimulation, (b) lesions, and (c) the recording of electrical activity. This section reviews these three classical approaches, as well as a new technology that makes use of the chemical processes within the brain itself to get at the secrets of its workings.

Touching a sensitive nerve

We opened this chapter by describing surgeon Wilder Penfield's stimulation of the cortex of a surgical patient. Penfield's explorations of the surface of the cortex, together with subsequent studies, have made it possible to draw precise maps of cortical projection areas.

Stimulating the surface of the cortex, however, reveals relatively superficial information compared with what has been discovered by probing deeper into regions of the brain that are hidden from view. In the mid-1950s, Walter Hess pioneered in the development of a precise technology using electrical stimulation to probe the functions of the brain. Hess put electrodes deep into specific parts of the brain of a freely moving cat. By pressing a button, Hess could then send a small electrical current to the brain at the point of the electrode.

Hess carefully recorded the behavioral consequences of stimulating each of 4500 brain sites in nearly 500 cats. Electrical stimulation of certain regions of the limbic system led gentle cats to bristle with rage and hurl themselves upon a nearby object—which, in the early days, was sometimes the startled experimenter. Sleep, sexual arousal, anxiety, or terror could be provoked by the flick of the switch—and just as abruptly turned off. Sometimes complicated, stereotyped behavior patterns were turned on in the animals, as though the electricity were activating a prerecorded program. For example, cats have an unmistakable manner of stalking and capturing prey. This could be reliably produced, time after time, by stimulating a certain part of the limbic system (Hess & Akert, 1955).

Hess's deep stimulation electrode technique was like a beacon illuminating primitive brain regions for more detailed study by a host of other researchers.

Other investigators found that electrical stimulation deep inside the brains of rats would arouse them sexually and even result in a male's ejaculation without a female rat in view. Like addicts craving drugs, the rats would go to great lengths to manipulate an apparatus that would deliver a jolt of electricity to certain regions of their brains. James Olds, who pioneered this aspect of the research, called these areas the brain's "pleasure centers" (Olds & Milner, 1954; Olds, 1973).

Other areas of rats' brains appear to be punishing sites; still others, paradoxically, seem both pleasurable and painful. Researchers studying patients suffering from chronic pain or epilepsy have identified "pleasure centers" in the human brain (Heath, 1972).

Lesions are forever

The **lesion** technique involves careful destruction (lesioning) of particular brain areas by either surgically removing them, cutting connections to them, or destroying brain tissue using intense heat, cold, electricity, or laser beams. Lesioning is a valuable tool for revealing whether a brain region is essential for a particular physical or psychological function. Done in the laboratory and followed up by behavioral tests, it can produce known damage and findings more precise than what can be learned from lesions caused by disease, accidents, wars, and other "natural," nonexperimental causes. (see **Close-up** on p. 103.) Our conception of the brain has been radically changed as the results of laboratory experiments with animals have been repeatedly compared and coordinated with the growing body of clinical findings on human behavior changes following brain damage.

Usually stimulation and lesioning techniques are used in combination in the laboratory: if one increases a reaction, the other will generally decrease it. This is a double check on interpretations of a causal connection between the activity of the brain region and a particular behavior. Lesioning, like stimulation, has revealed the brain to be a highly differentiated, complex, and precisely organized master control organ.

Knowledge of brain functions gained from laboratory studies has been supplemented by observation of the effects of lesions used as a therapeutic technique. A type of lesion used widely with epileptic and violent psychotic patients in the 1940s was the *frontal lobotomy,* which involved severing the nerve fibers connecting the frontal lobes with other brain areas. Though seizures and violent reactions disappeared, so—often—did the individual's emotional tone, sense of self, and sense of the future. Because such lesions are irreversible, they are little used today.

"Reverse" lesioning studies have been carried out in observations of *recovery* from brain damage. Philip Teitelbaum (1977) has found that when a part of the brain is damaged, the behavior it has been controlling may disappear completely or "decompose" into a less complex, fragmentary form which sometimes makes it easier to study. Then, as recovery takes place, the behavioral elements may be "put back in place," becoming integrated again in much the same

The Curious Accident of Mr. Phineas Gage

The iron bar shown here is in the collection of the Museum of Harvard Medical School, a relic of a terrible accident. In September 1848, Phineas Gage, a twenty-five-year-old railroad worker in Vermont, was tamping a charge of black powder into a hole drilled deep into rock in preparation for blasting. The powder unexpectedly exploded, blowing the tamping iron, over three feet long and weighing thirteen pounds, through Gage's head and high into the air.

Incredibly, Gage regained consciousness and was taken by wagon to his hotel, where he was able to walk upstairs. T.M. Harlow, the physician who attended him, noted that the hole in Gage's skull was 2'' by 3½'' wide, with shreds of brain all around it. He cleaned and dressed the wound, but two days later Gage became delirious and remained near death for the next two weeks. The wound became seriously infected, but eventually healed. In a month Gage could get out of bed without help; in two months he could walk unassisted.

Gage lived on for over twelve years. Physical impairment was remarkably slight: he lost vision in his left eye and the left side of his face was partially paralyzed, but his posture, movement, and speech were all unimpaired. Yet psychologically he was a changed man, as this summary by Harlow makes clear:

"His physical health is good, and I am inclined to say that he has recovered. Has no pain in head, but says it has a queer feeling which he is not able to describe. Applied for his situation as foreman, but is undecided whether to work or travel. His contractors, who regarded him as the most efficient and capable foreman in their employ previous to his injury, considered the change in his mind so marked that they could not give him his place again. The equilibrium or balance, so to speak, between his intellectual faculties and animal propensities, seems to have been destroyed. He is fitful, irreverent, indulging at times in the grossest profanity (which was not previously his custom), manifesting but little deference for his fellows, impatient of restraint or advice when it conflicts with his desires, at times pertinaciously obstinate, yet capricious and vacillating, devising many plans of future operation, which are no sooner arranged than they are abandoned in turn for others appearing more feasible. A child in his intellectual capacity and manifestations, he has the animal passions of a strong man. Previous to his injury, though untrained in the schools, he possessed a well-balanced mind, and was looked upon by those who knew him as a shrewd, smart business man, very energetic and persistent in executing all his plans of operation. In this regard his mind was radically changed, so decidedly that his friends and acquaintances said he was 'no longer Gage' " (Bigelow, 1850, pp. 13–22).

Gage's case is one of the earliest documented examples of massive damage to the frontal regions of the brain, and it illustrates the great subtlety of the psychological symptoms that accompany such lesions. Indeed, it was Gage's family and friends, rather than his doctor, who noticed the changes in him. Gage's symptoms, such as "obstinacy" or "capriciousness," are hardly so remarkable that we would attribute them to brain damage in someone whose history we didn't know. Yet it is interesting to note that they represent the very kinds of antisocial behavior that prefrontal lobotomies are supposed to *prevent*.

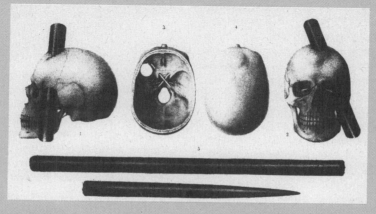

way they developed the first time in the young organism. Teitelbaum's research has shown that redevelopment of behavioral coordination in cats with hypothalamic damage and human adults with Parkinson's disease is similar to the development of normal infants, both human and animal.

Recording the activity of neurons

A third way to understand how the brain functions is to record its electrical activity. Three types of records can be made: (a) records of activity made within a cell (intracellular), (b) records of a cell's activity made from the outside (extracellular), and (c) records of the action of many neurons at once through measuring brain waves and evoked potentials.

The tool used in the first two techniques is a *microelectrode,* a tiny needle made of thin metal or hollow glass filled with a saline solution. When placed in or near a neuron, this device detects electrical impulses, which are then greatly amplified so that they can be displayed on a screen or stored in a computer.

For *intracellular recordings,* the tiny microelectrodes are placed *inside* individual neurons. Usually invertebrates, such as *Aplysia,* are used in this research because their neurons are relatively few in number and large enough to be identified. It is thus possible to record the graded potentials within simple nerve cells. Such recordings may help illuminate the fundamental mechanisms used to process information in the brains of higher animals.

In *extracellular recordings,* the microelectrode is positioned to reach beneath the surface of the cortex, but *outside* a neuron. In a typical study, the electrode is placed in the visual cortex of a cat which is anesthetized but whose brain is still actively receiving inputs from the eye. Different visual patterns are then displayed. A given neuron will respond with a burst of impulses when a certain stimulus—perhaps a line of a certain angle—is displayed, but remain inactive when any other pattern is presented. Researchers using this technique have been able to draw detailed maps of the stimulus "preferences" of different cells in the visual cortex.

Besides responding to stimulation, the brain constantly generates electrical energy. Its signals can be recorded on the *surface* of the scalp of a human subject as **electroencephalograms** (EEGs). The *brainwave patterns* thus recorded show characteristic forms, indicating whether someone is alert, relaxed, asleep, or dreaming. But they tell us little about any response to a stimulus.

The patterns of brain activity caused by specific stimuli are called **evoked potentials.** To record them, the specific brain signals are usually extracted from the background "noise" of ongoing spontaneous brain waves. The researcher does this by using computer analyses to average out all the electrical activity that is *unrelated* to the stimulus—exposing the evoked potential signal. The characteristics of this signal vary for different areas of the brain and for different stimuli and different mental processes (John et al., 1977).

The use of evoked potentials in studying brain processes is demonstrated by a study of reactions to unexpected events.

The stimuli were seven-word sentences, in some of which the last word was incongruous and hence unexpected. (Example: "He took a sip from the transmitter." As sentences were presented, one word at a time, the subject read them silently. Every time a word was presented that did not fit what might be expected in the context, a specific type of evoked potential appeared. Some part or parts of the brain must have been set to assess and respond to the new stimuli in terms of previously learned information (Kutas et al., 1980).

Each of these recording methods has good features and some drawbacks. If we compare neurons with people, then intracellular recording is like reading someone's thoughts, extracellular recording is like listening to someone talk, and the EEG is like listening to the roar of a crowd. The EEG may seem least useful of the three. However, it is the one most commonly used to study the brain activity of normal living human beings.

Looking at living brains

Researchers have recently developed new techniques for obtaining detailed pictures of the living brain at work. These pictures help locate diseased tissue but also show where various brain activities take place as normal individuals are exposed to various stimuli. The biggest advantage of this approach is that it can show what is happening in different regions of a living, thinking brain at the same time.

One of these powerful new techniques is **positron emission tomography (PET).** This technique is based on the fact that a sugar called glucose is the main source of energy for the brain. When brain cells are active, they increase their intake of glucose from the surrounding blood supply. In PET research, a radioactive substance similar to glucose is injected into the bloodstream. It, too, will be taken up by active neurons. Recording instruments outside the skull can detect the radioactivity emitted by this substance and keep track of the brain locations from which it came. A computer program can then be used to construct a dynamic, ongoing portrait of the brain, showing where neural activity is occurring.

You now have some answers by physiological psychologists to the general question, "What makes behavior work?" In addition, you can better appreciate how they study the complex relationships between physical structures, biochemical processes, and behavioral functions. As new technologies enable scientists to illuminate more of the darker, deeper recesses of the "black box" of the brain, we are witnessing a virtual explosion of knowledge about how the brain and nervous system influence our psychological development, daily actions, and disorders of functioning.

Wherever possible throughout our journey, we will seek greater understanding of the various processes of thought, feeling, and action by considering what is known about their neural substrate. Of course, many of our concerns cannot be reduced to this level, as when we ask, "How can a nuclear war be prevented?" But we will see that an ever increasing number of psychological problems are being probed at this molecular level of analysis—problems such as the brain mechanisms in memory, motivation, stress, emotion, and mental disorder.

Learning and remembering, pleasure and pain, attraction and repulsion—all these begin as sensory stimulus events that must be detected and processed in special ways if our lives are to have meaning and direction. The study of sensation and perception, which follows in the next two chapters, helps us understand how we make contact with the world outside our brains, extract information from it, and transform the information into plans for appropriate actions. We will continue in the chapter after that to focus on one of the most profound issues of human existence—the nature of consciousness and its alteration.

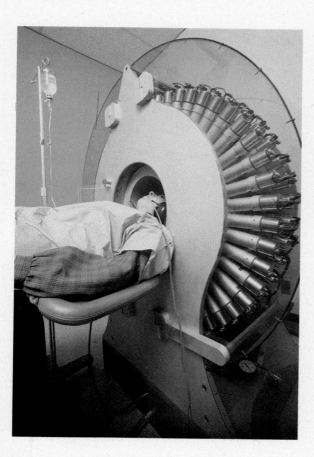

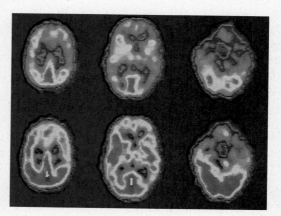

△ *On the left is a patient undergoing a PET scan; on the right are two sets of PET scans (red indicates the areas of highest activity). The top row shows metabolic activity in a musician's brain while he read the score of a Beethoven piano sonata: the greatest activity is in the visual cortex at the back of the brain. The lower row shows the brain activity of the same person as he read the score again while listening to the music. There is increased activity not only in the auditory area, but also in those associated with fine fingering movements.*

SUMMARY

■ Physiological psychology is the study of the relationship between behavior, including mental events, and body processes.

■ Historically mind and body were viewed dualistically, as separate entities. Today physiological psychologists view "mind" as an integrative capacity developed by the brain that frees the organism from control by sensory input.

■ Cell differentiation and specialization create a need for communication and integration within the organism. The nervous and endocrine systems meet this need, sending neural and hormonal messengers throughout the body.

■ The nervous system is made up of the central nervous system, which includes the brain and spinal cord, and the peripheral nervous system. The latter includes the somatic nervous system and the autonomic nervous system, which is divided into the sympathetic division (which functions as a "trouble shooter") and the parasympathetic division (which functions as a "housekeeper").

■ The endocrines are ductless glands controlled by neural and chemical signals. Their hormones regulate many biochemical processes and help arouse the body for action in emergencies.

■ Neurons are unique cells specialized to receive and transmit information to other cells. A neuron is made up of dendrites, a cell body or soma, and an axon that ends in terminal buttons. Sensory (afferent) neurons carry messages toward the central nervous system; motor (efferent) ones carry messages away to muscles and glands. The interneurons, which lie between them, make up the bulk of the neurons in the nervous system.

■ Nerve conduction is an electrochemical phenomenon. The inside of an inactive neuron has a negative electrical charge relative to the outside, creating a polarized state known as a *resting potential*. Changes in permeability of the membrane allow ions of certain chemicals to cross it and alter the electrical charge, depolarizing the membrane.

■ If stimulation exceeds a threshold of excitability, graded potentials (slow-spreading activity along the dendrite or cell body membrane) trigger an action potential (nerve impulse). This action potential occurs in the axon as successive sections of the membrane become permeable. Conduction is most rapid in myelinated neurons and always follows the law of forward conduction from the axon of one neuron to the dendrites or cell body of the next.

■ At a synapse, or junction of two neurons, electrical conduction becomes chemical conduction. Neurotransmitters are released from tiny vesicles in the presynaptic terminal button and travel across the gap to the receiving sites on the next neuron, inhibiting or initiating electrical activity in that neuron. Neurotransmitters may activate neuroregulators within the postsynaptic cell. These "second messengers" prolong the excitation and may be involved in learning and memory.

■ Any novel, unexpected stimulus elicits an orienting reaction that maximizes the organism's sensitivity to stimulation. With repetition of the stimulus there is a reduction in response called *habituation;* it is a primitive form of learning that frees the organism to attend to more informative input.

■ Neural networks are circuits of neurons that function as a system, permitting more complex information processing than is possible for individual cells.

■ Lower brain centers that control basic life processes have evolved similarly in humans and lower animals. The cerebral cortex, the outer layer of the brain, is where higher mental processes take place and is most highly developed in humans. About a fourth of its area is devoted to processing sensory and motor information; the rest involves more complex analysis and synthesis. Although the normal brain always functions as an integrated whole, researchers have identified primary centers for each of the senses, motivational behavior, and other complex processes such as aggression and hunger.

■ Hemispheric asymmetry is characteristic of all species though the two cerebral hemispheres are involved in different aspects of many of the same functions. In most humans the left hemisphere has dominance in verbal activity; the right hemisphere, in visual-spatial activities.

■ The three classical approaches to studying living brains have been the techniques of stimulation, lesioning (destroying tissue), and recording electrical activity. Brain-wave recordings (EEGs) are records of both ongoing spontaneous brain activity and evoked potentials (specific neural reactions to particular stimuli). Positron emission tomography (PET) is a powerful new technique for monitoring the active brain by use of radioactive particles.

Part Two

Perceptual Processes

Chapter Four
Sensation

Chapter Five
Perception

Chapter Six
The Nature of Consciousness

4

SENSATION

Written in collaboration with Stephen E. Palmer

SENSORY KNOWLEDGE OF THE WORLD
Reality and illusion
Sensation, perception, and classification

FROM PHYSICAL ENERGY TO MENTAL EVENTS
Psychophysics
Constructing psychophysical scales

THE VISUAL SYSTEM
The eye
Processing in the retina
Pathways to the brain

DIMENSIONS OF VISUAL EXPERIENCE
Color
Spatial properties
Time and motion

HEARING
The physics of sound
Psychological dimensions of sound
The physiology of hearing

OTHER SENSES
The chemical senses
The body senses
The pain sense

SUMMARY

Michael was a college student with a passion for photography. One evening, when he was trying out some new techniques for taking pictures outdoors in low light, he noticed something curious about the moon. It was full, and while it was low over the horizon, it looked very large and imposing, with bare trees silhouetted against it. It made a great picture. But as it rose higher in the sky, the moon seemed to get smaller.

Although Michael had casually noticed this change before, he had never observed it so carefully or wondered why. The *actual* size of the moon couldn't change, but its *apparent* size certainly did. "Perhaps it's further away when it's high in the sky so that it just *looks* smaller," he thought. But when he looked it up, he found out that the moon's orbit is almost perfectly circular, staying the same distance from the earth's surface at all times. Finally, he hit on what he thought must be the explanation: the earth's atmosphere must somehow *distort* the light coming from the moon, thereby making it *look* bigger on the horizon.

The next day he related his discovery to his girlfriend, Marsha. Rather than being impressed, as he had expected, she asked him how he knew that the moon's image had *actually* gotten any smaller at all. Michael replied that he knew it did because he had seen it "with his own two eyes." When that didn't seem to satisfy her, Michael decided to *prove* what he had seen by using his photographic series of the rising moon: the pictures would surely show the same distortion he had seen. But when he developed his pictures and measured the moon in them, he was surprised to see that the moon was *exactly the same size* in every one.

Marsha was not surprised. Indeed, she had predicted that outcome. She knew that the ap-parent change in the moon's size was not due to events out in the atmosphere, but to processes taking place in Michael's brain. Michael had just demonstrated a well-known psychological effect, called the "moon illusion," which she knew about from her introductory psychology course.

She explained that according to the best accepted theory, the moon looks bigger on the horizon because people tend to perceive the sky as "flattened," as suggested in the lower curve of the drawing, and thus perceive the moon to be closer at its zenith and farther away at the horizon. Actually, it is equally far away and equally large at all positions, but because people perceive the horizon moon as farther away, they see it as bigger, compensating for the additional perceived distance (Kaufman & Rock, 1962; Rock & Kaufman, 1962). Michael wasn't sure that this theory explained everything—for instance, he wondered *why* the moon seemed farther away at the horizon than overhead—but his experience had convinced him that seeing the world around him was far more complicated—and interesting—than he had thought. He decided he might even sign up for the introductory psychology course next term to learn more about the differences between reality and illusion.

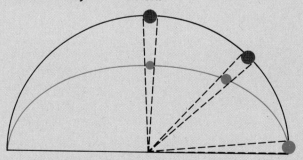

From "The Moon Illusion" by Lloyd Kaufman and Irvin Rock, *Scientific American*, July 1962. Copyright © 1962 by Scientific American, Inc. All rights reserved. Reprinted by permission.

Michael's experiences point out that our awareness of the physical world around us involves not a passive registration of an absolute and fixed reality, but an active *construction* derived from mental processing. Though *based* on the physical objects in the real world, our awareness must go considerably *beyond* the information presented to our sense organs. We look with our eyes, but "see" with our brains and understand what we see by mental activity.

The processes of sensing and perceiving objects in the environment are obviously not infallible—as Michael's story shows us—but they do work surprisingly well most of the time and usually without any real effort on our part. How does it all happen? How does an external object like the moon make itself known to our consciousness? Why does it appear dull white against the blue sky during the day and luminous at night? Why does it appear stationary against the sky when the night is clear (even though it is actually moving), yet seem to fly rapidly through a filmy cloud that moves past it? And, how do scientists study these processes, which are largely unconscious and unobservable? In this chapter and the next two, we will find out some of the answers to these and other questions about how we sense, perceive, and consciously experience the world we live in by seeing, hearing, tasting, smelling, and touching it.

SENSORY KNOWLEDGE OF THE WORLD

Ordinarily, our experience of external reality is relatively accurate and error-free. In fact, it *has* to be for us to survive. We need food to sustain us, shelter to protect us, interactions with other people to fulfill our social needs, and awareness of danger to keep us out of harm's way. To meet these needs, we must somehow get reliable information about the world we live in and travel through. All species have developed some kind of information-gathering apparatus. We humans lack the acute sensitivity to some signals that other species have perfected—such as the vision of hawks or the hearing of bats—but we have complex sensory organs and additional neural apparatus that enable us to process a wider range of much more complex sensory input.

Because our experiences of the world can usually be counted on, most of us—like Michael—come to accept the notion that "seeing is believing." What we "see with our own two eyes" we automatically interpret as existing out there in the physical structure of the external world. Actually, the relation between what we see and what exists to be seen is not so simple. Our brains actively transform and interpret the information they receive from all of our senses, vision included.

Reality and illusion

Consider some obvious sensory qualities like the length, slant, and color of lines. Simple as they seem, it is easy to demonstrate that what you see may not be what is actually there. In the photo on this page, for example, you know that the pencil is not really divided, although it appears to be. When your senses deceive you into experiencing a stimulus pattern in a manner that is demonstrably incorrect, it is called an **illusion**. In this case, your misinterpretation of the sensory stimulus is shared by most people in the same perceptual situation. This is not true in two other cases of distorted experience—hallucinations and delusions. *Hallucinations* are false perceptions that are produced by many conditions, among them certain mental disorders, brain diseases, intoxication from alcohol, and a variety of other drugs. *Delusions* are false beliefs that a person maintains despite contrary evidence of their irrationality; they arise from unconscious sources and appear to serve some personal need, such as to relieve guilt or bolster self-esteem.

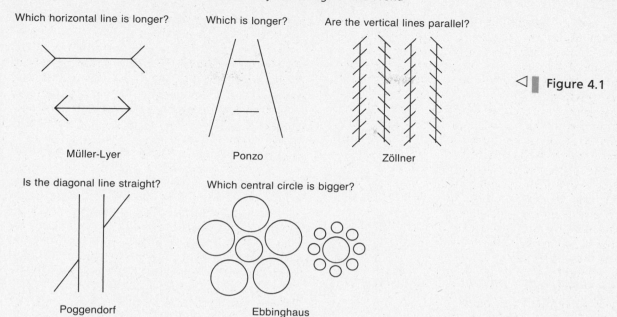

◁ Figure 4.1

Figure 4.1 shows several visual illusions, named after the psychologists who discovered them. First, look at the Müller-Lyer illusion. Which of the horizontal lines is longer? Now measure the lines. They are actually the same length. Somehow the presence of the "arrowheads" influences the way your visual system processes the information about the two central lines and the upper one appears to be longer. Just why this happens is controversial—but the fact that it happens clearly shows that you do not perceive the world just as it is. Check the other illusions with a ruler. You will see that these other patterns of lines lead to the same conclusion: *context* can distort the appearance of the elements within it, so that the sensory experiences you have do not *necessarily* correspond to physical reality.

Illusions also occur for other visual qualities, such as brightness. Look at the grid of squares, called the *Hermann grid,* in **Figure 4.2.** The gray spots you see at the intersections are *not* really there. You can prove this to yourself by noticing that when you try to look directly at one, it disappears!

Psychologists have discovered many such illusions, not only in vision but in other sensory modalities as well. They occur because, unlike Michael's camera, the central nervous system does not simply record events. Rather, there are complex processes for detecting, integrating, and interpreting information about the world in terms of what we already know and expect; thus what we see goes beyond the present physical stimulus properties. The fact that these processes usually occur effortlessly and without error does not mean that they are simple!

◁ Figure 4.2 *The Hermann Grid*

Sensation, perception, and classification

Many psychologists find it useful to divide the complicated process of coming to know the physical world into three kinds of processes, usually referred to as sensation, perception, and classification. **Sensation** refers to early processes that *analyze* physical energy in the world—such as light and sound waves—and *convert* it into neural activity that codes simple information about how the receptor organs are being stimulated. **Perception** refers to later processes that *organize* and *interpret* information in the sensory image as having been produced by the properties of objects in the external, three-dimensional world. **Classification** refers to still later processes in this sequence by which we *identify* and *label* perceptual objects as members of meaningful categories—like "cars" and "trees" and "people."

To make the distinctions among these three kinds of processes clearer, let's consider how they apply to your experiences in seeing the simple visual scene shown in **Figure 4.3**: a red block sitting on a piece of blue paper. At the *sensory* level of processing, the three-dimensional scene is registered as a two-dimensional image by your eye and *analyzed* according to the color and spatial properties of the five regions defined by the three different shades of red and the two different shades of blue. These aspects of your experiences are called "sensory" because they are concerned with properties of the image on your "sense" organs.

At the *perceptual* level of processing, these five patches of color are *organized* into just two external objects: a red one and a blue one. The three different shades of red are *interpreted* as the visible surfaces of a three-dimensional object whose color is

actually uniform. The images of the surfaces are darker or lighter because they are at different angles to the light source. Similarly, the two shades of blue are *interpreted* as coming from a uniformly colored flat surface, even though part of it seems darker because it lies in the shadow of the red object. These aspects of your experience are called "perceptual" because they are concerned with your "perception" of objects rather than simply sensations of color.

At the *classificatory* level of processing, both the colors and the shapes of the objects are categorized in terms of "kinds" of things you know about: the central object has a color you *identify* as "red" and a shape you *label* as a "block," while the other one is "blue" and "a piece of paper." These aspects of your experience are "classificatory" because they are concerned with *classes* of objects or properties. Notice that this process of classification finally produces the kind of description that we started with: "a red block sitting on a piece of blue paper."

The distinction between sensation and perception can also be applied to the illusions you just saw. The Hermann grid (Figure 4.2) can be explained in terms of sensory processes that transform—and in this case distort—the properties of the image in particular ways. The moon illusion, however, is clearly perceptual, since its explanation relies on interpreting the distance of an object in the three-dimensional world. Not all illusions are yet well enough understood to be categorized without controversy, however.

Although the term "perception" is often used in a broad sense to refer to all three processes together, the division into sensation, perception, and classification is useful in pointing up the parts of this complex process. Therefore, we will organize our discussion around this distinction, examining sensation in this chapter and perception and classification in the next one. We will be using "perception" in its narrower sense as going beyond sensory information in providing a meaningful awareness and knowledge of our world of objects, actors, and episodes.

Now let's examine what has been discovered about the ways in which the physical energy from the external world of stimulus events is translated into the physiological and psychological processes of sensation.

▽ ▊ **Figure 4.3**

FROM PHYSICAL ENERGY TO MENTAL EVENTS

At the heart of sensation lies a profound mystery: How do physical energies give rise to psychological experiences? Stimulus energy arrives at our eyes (or ears or other sensory receptors) as physical energy of some kind. There it is converted into electrochemical signals that the nervous system can transmit—still physical energy but coded by our nervous system so that when the signal reaches the cerebral cortex, we have a sensation of a particular color or sound. The study of sensation is the study of the translation from physical energy to mental process. Although the central mystery of this conversion remains, research has taught us a great deal about how and where it happens and what physical and psychological processes can affect it.

The field of sensory psychology has two main branches: sensory physiology and psychophysics. **Sensory physiology** is the study of how biological mechanisms convert physical events into neural events. Here the goal is to discover what happens at a neural level in the chain of events from physical energy to sensory experience. It concerns questions such as how electrochemical activity in the nervous system can give us sensations of different quality (red rather than green) or quantity (loud rather than soft).

We have already encountered some of the concepts and methods of sensory physiology in Chapter 3. Later parts of this chapter will discuss the physiological mechanisms of each sensory modality in turn. In the present section, we will concentrate on the other major area of sensory psychology, called *psychophysics.*

Psychophysics

How loud must a fire alarm at a factory be in order for workers to hear it over the din of the machinery? How bright does a warning light on a pilot's control panel have to be to appear twice as bright as the other lights? How loud can a motorcycle be before its driver should be cited for noise pollution?

These are practical questions about sensation that often arise in decisions about safety regulations, product design, and legal issues. To answer them, we must somehow be able to *measure* the intensity of sensory experiences—the brightness of lights, the loudness of sounds—by relating these psychological experiences to magnitudes of physical stimulation. This is the central task of **psychophysics,** which is the study of the correspondence between psychological experience and physical stimulation.

Psychophysical techniques are methods for measuring the strength of sensations experienced by an alert, normal organism in response to stimuli of different strengths. Whether the stimuli are for light, sound, taste, odor, or touch, the techniques are the same—determining thresholds and constructing psychophysical scales relating strength of sensation to strength of stimuli. Two kinds of thresholds can be measured—absolute thresholds and difference thresholds.

Absolute thresholds. What is the smallest, weakest stimulus energy that an organism can detect? How dim can a light be, for instance, and still be visible? How soft can a tone be and still be heard? These questions ask about the **absolute threshold** for different types of stimulation: the minimum amount of physical energy needed to produce a sensory experience reliably. According to the classical view of sensory thresholds, stimuli below the threshold amount produce no sensation; stimuli above it do.

Absolute thresholds are measured psychophysically by asking vigilant observers to perform a "detection" task, such as trying to see a dim light in a dark room, or trying to hear a soft sound in a quiet room. Over a series of many "trials," the stimulus is presented at varying intensities, and on each trial the observer indicates whether or not he or she was aware of it. If you've ever had your hearing evaluated, you were probably a "subject" in such a test.

The results of a study like this can be summarized in a **psychometric function:** a graph that plots the percentage of *detections* (on the vertical, or Y-axis) for each *stimulus intensity* (on the horizontal, or X-axis). A typical psychometric function is shown in **Figure 4.4.** For very dim lights, clearly below threshold, detection is at 0 percent; for bright lights, clearly above threshold, detection is at 100 percent. If there were a single, true absolute threshold, you would expect the transition from 0 to 100 percent detection

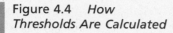

Figure 4.4 *How Thresholds Are Calculated*

Since there is no point at which a stimulus suddenly becomes clearly detectable, a person's absolute threshold is defined as the intensity at which the stimulus is detected half of the time over many trials.

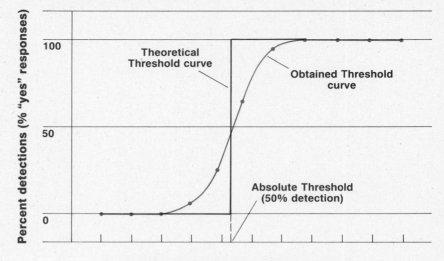

to be very sharp, occurring right at the point where the intensity reached the threshold. But this does not happen. Instead, the psychometric curve is almost always a smooth S-shaped curve, in which there is a region of transition from no detection to detection more and more of the time, finally reaching accurate detection all the time.

The usual practice is to define the threshold (somewhat arbitrarily) as the intensity level at which the psychometric function crosses the 50 percent detection level. This is an operational definition of a **threshold**: the stimulus level at which a sensory signal is detected half the time. Thresholds for different sense modalities can be measured in the same way, simply by changing the stimulus dimension. **Table 4.1** shows absolute threshold levels for several familiar natural stimuli.

Is there really such a thing as a specific absolute threshold at all? Some psychologists think not. The smooth transition found from not detecting to detecting weak stimuli implies a *gradual* rather than a sharp change from absence to presence of sensation. In addition, there seem to be circumstances under which people behave as though they have seen or heard something even when their detection performance has indicated a stimulus at or below the sensory threshold (Dixon, 1971)—a phenomenon called *subliminal perception*. Another problem for the classical concept of sensory thresholds is that "response bias" can affect threshold measurements.

Response bias. A **response bias** is a systematic tendency, due to nonsensory factors, for an observer to favor responding in a particular way. After all, someone could respond "yes" in a detection task for any number of reasons, such as wanting to be selected for a job requiring acute sensitivity. Response biases are most likely to arise in situations that have important consequences for the observer's life.

Why does someone's detection threshold become distorted by response bias? At least three sources

Table 4.1 *Approximate Thresholds of Familiar Events*

Sense modality	Detection threshold
Light	A candle flame seen at 30 miles on a dark clear night.
Sound	The tick of a watch under quiet conditions at twenty feet.
Taste	One teaspoon of sugar in 2 gallons of water.
Smell	One drop of perfume diffused into the entire volume of a 3 room apartment.
Touch	The wing of a bee falling on your cheek from a distance of 1 cm.

(From Galanter, 1962, p. 97)

have been identified: desire, expectation, and habit. When we want a particular outcome, we are more likely to give whatever response will achieve that desired objective. "I didn't see anything, Officer" is more likely if we want to avoid getting involved; "Yes, I'm sure he's the one, Sir" is a more probable response if we want to be in line for the reward.

Our expectations, or knowledge of stimulus probabilities may also influence our readiness to report a sensory event. The same weak blip on a sonar scope is more likely to be detected and reported as a submarine if we are on a cruiser during wartime than if we are on a freighter on Lake Michigan.

Finally, people develop habits of responding, individual differences in the tendency to be "yea sayers," who chronically answer "yes," or to be "nay sayers" or "don't knowers."

Researchers use the technique of *catch trials* to find out whether response biases are operating in sensory detection tasks. *No* stimulus is presented on a few of the trials, to "catch" the subject who has a tendency to respond, "yes." The threshold estimate of the real stimulus is then adjusted according to how often such "false alarms" occur.

The theory of signal detectability. A systematic approach to the problem of response bias has been developed in the **theory of signal detectability** (TSD). This theory is actually an alternative to the threshold approach in psychophysics. It replaces the theoretical concept of a single absolute threshold with two other ones: an initial *sensory process,* which reflects the strength of the stimulus, and a separate *decision process* later, which reflects the observer's response biases. This theory also replaces

the procedure for measuring thresholds with a different (and more complex) procedure that can measure both the sensory and decision processes at once.

The measurement procedure is actually just an extension of the idea of catch trials. The basic design is given in **Figure 4.5A**. A weak stimulus is presented on half the trials, called *signal trials;* no stimulus is presented on the other half, called *noise trials.* On each trial the subject responds by saying "yes" if the signal was present, "no" if it was not. As shown in Matrix A of the figure, each response is scored as hit, miss, false alarm, or correct rejection, depending on whether or not a signal was in fact presented and whether or not the observer responded that it was (Green & Swets, 1966).

An observer who is a "yea sayer" will give a high number of hits but also a high number of false alarms, as shown in Matrix B; one who is a "nay sayer" will give a lower number of hits but also a lower number of false alarms (Matrix C). By combining the percentages of hits and false alarms according to a particular mathematical formula (which will not concern us here) this procedure provides sepa-

▽ **Figure 4.5** *The Theory of Signal Detectability*

Matrix A shows the possible outcomes when a subject answers "yes" or "no" when asked if a target stimulus occurred on a given trial. Matrices B and C show typical responses of a "yea sayer" and a "nay sayer," respectively.

A

Matrix of possibilities

Stimulus Condition	Response Given	
	"Yes"	"No"
Signal On	Hit	Miss
Signal Off	False alarm	Correct rejection

B

	Responses of a "Yea sayer"	
	Yes Response	No Response
Signal On	92%	8%
Signal Off	46%	54%

$d' = 1.5$

C

	Responses of a "Nay sayer"	
	Yes Response	No Response
Signal On	40%	60%
Signal Off	4%	96%

$d' = 1.5$

rate measures: for *sensory discriminability* (called *d'*, pronounced "d-prime") and for *response bias* (called *beta*). This procedure makes it possible to find out whether two observers have the same sensitivity despite large differences in response bias.

According to the theory of signal detectability, any stimulus event (signal or noise) produces *some* neural activity in the sensory system—perhaps the firing of some set of neurons. In deciding whether a stimulus was present, the observer compares the sensory value in the neural system with some self-set internal *response criterion.* If the response of the sensory process exceeds that critical amount, the observer responds "yes"; if not, "no." Thus, the discrete "threshold" appears in the decision process instead of the sensory one.

The response criterion reflects the observer's permanent or temporary *strategy* for responding. By providing a way of separating sensory process from response bias, the theory of signal detectability allows the experimenter to identify and separate the roles of the sensory stimulus and the individual's criterion level, or response bias, in producing the response.

This approach has become the dominant one in modern psychophysics. Actually, it is a general model of decision making that can be used in contexts quite different from psychophysics. For example, suppose you are a doctor interpreting the results of a blood test from which you must judge whether the patient's kidneys are about to fail—and hence whether an operation should be performed. Here, too, there is an actual signal (the blood test), and the criterion question of what test level to accept as evidence that an operation is necessary.

If you don't operate and the kidneys fail (a miss), the patient dies; however, if you do operate and they wouldn't have failed (false alarm), you have wasted a lot of time and effort, not to mention the possibility that you might be sued for malpractice. Similar decision problems arise for determining a prisoner's parole, a mental patient's release, or a suicidal hot-line caller's need for emergency intervention.

Difference thresholds. Suppose you are a programmer inventing a new video game. You have decided to represent the number of friendly and enemy spaceships that have been destroyed by bars of different lengths: each time another ship is downed, the corresponding bar gets a little longer. You want the game players always to be able to tell which of the two bars is longer so they know who is winning, but you want the additions to the bar length to be as small as possible so that many spaceships can be represented. What you need here is a **difference threshold,** the smallest physical difference that will be recognized as a difference.

You would find it in pretty much the same way as you would an absolute threshold, except using a *pair* of stimuli on each trial and asking your subjects whether they were *different* (instead of just whether a stimulus was present). For this particular problem, you would show your subject two bars, on each trial, one of some standard length (call its length *l*) and one just a bit longer (of length *l* + Δ*l*, where Δ*l* indicates a small increase in length and is read "delta-*l*"). For each pair, the observer would say "same" or "different." After many such trials you would plot a psychometric function by graphing the percent of "different" responses on the vertical axis as a function of the actual differences in length (Δl) on the horizontal axis. The difference threshold is the length difference at which the curve crosses the 50 percent value—the difference at which the stimuli are recognized as different half of the time. This difference threshold value is also known as the **just noticeable difference** or *jnd.*

Now suppose you have performed this experiment with a standard bar length of 10 mm using increases of varying amounts and have found the difference threshold to be about 1 mm. So you know that a 10 mm bar will be detected as different from an 11 mm bar 50 percent of the time. Can you go ahead and design your video game display now?

Unfortunately, you're not through yet because the difference threshold is not the same for long bars as for short ones. With a standard bar of 20 mm, for instance, you would have had to add about 2 mm to get a just noticeable difference. For one of 40 mm you would need to add 4 mm, and so on. **Figure 4.6** shows some examples of jnds with bars of several lengths: they increase steadily with the length of the standard bar.

What remains the *same,* however, is the *ratio* of the size of the increase that produces a just noticeable difference (Δl) to the length of the standard bar (l). For example, 1 mm/10 mm = 0.1 and 2 mm/20 mm = 0.1. Ernst Weber discovered this constant relationship back in 1843 and found that it held for a wide range of stimulus dimensions. The only difference between stimulus dimensions was the particular *value* of this constant ratio. He summarized all his findings in a single equation, now called **Weber's law:**

$$\frac{\Delta l}{l} = k$$

where Δl is the size of the increase that produces a difference threshold or jnd, l is the intensity of the standard stimulus, and k is the constant ratio for the particular stimulus dimension (0.1 in our line-length example). Weber's law means, roughly, that the bigger or more intense the standard stimulus, the larger the increment you will need in order to get a just noticeable difference. Or, the smaller or weaker the standard stimulus, the less the increase needed before you detect a jnd. A few drops of water added to a test tube are more likely to be noticed than the same amount added to a jug. This is a very general property of all sensory systems. The bar length example is plotted in **Figure 4.6**. Work through it to be sure you understand what a jnd is, what Weber's law is, and how they are related.

Constructing psychophysical scales

You are already familiar with *physical* scales—such as the metric scale for lengths and the Fahrenheit scale for temperature, to name just two. Could such scales be used directly for measuring psychological sensations? When you think about it, Weber's law suggests that they could *not* because the *psychological difference* between 1 and 2 inches is much bigger than the psychological difference between 101 and 102 inches, whereas the *physical difference* is the same.

But what about a scale measuring *psychologically* meaningful units numerically in terms of corresponding units on a *physical* scale? Is there some way of finding *what stimulus differences are experienced as equal sensory intervals?*

One approach to constructing psychophysical scales is based on regarding just noticeable differences as psychologically equal intervals. After all, they are equal in the sense of being just noticeably different from neighboring stimuli, so why not just assume that jnds are the psychological units of sensation? Using our bar length example, the experience of 1 mm difference between 10 mm and 11 mm bars is taken as being *psychologically* the same as the 1.5 mm difference between bars of 15 and 16.5 mm and the 2 mm difference for bars 20 and 22 mm long. Together with Weber's law, this implies that equal increases in the physical intensity of the stim-

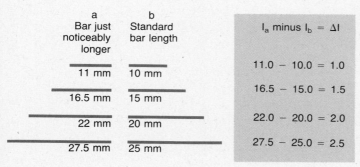

a Bar just noticeably longer	b Standard bar length	l_a minus l_b = Δl
11 mm	10 mm	11.0 − 10.0 = 1.0
16.5 mm	15 mm	16.5 − 15.0 = 1.5
22 mm	20 mm	22.0 − 20.0 = 2.0
27.5 mm	25 mm	27.5 − 25.0 = 2.5

◁ **Figure 4.6** *Just Noticeable Differences and Weber's Law*

The longer the standard bar, the longer the amount you must add (Δl) to see a just noticeable difference. The added amount of length that you detect on half of the trials is called the difference threshold. When you plot these increments against standard bars of increasing length, the proportion stays the same: the amount that must be added is always one-tenth of the standard length. This relationship is a linear one, producing a straight line on the graph.

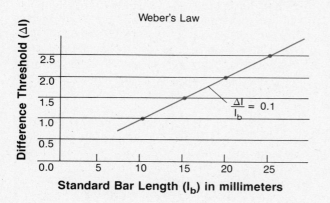

Weber's Law

▷ **Figure 4.7** *Two Psychophysical Scales*

According to Fechner's equation, based on just noticeable differences, sensation units first increase rapidly with equal increases in stimulus intensity but then increase more and more slowly. (Adding one candle to two increases the brightness you see much more than adding one candle to 100.)

But according to Stevens' equation, based on direct judgments of sensory magnitude, the psychophysical curve is different for different stimuli. For brightness, the curve is similar to Fechner's, but for a stimulus like electric shock, slight increases in physical intensity produce greater and greater sensations of pain. (From Stevens, 1961).

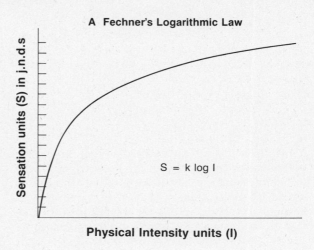

A Fechner's Logarithmic Law

Sensation units (S) in j.n.d.s

$S = k \log I$

Physical Intensity units (I)

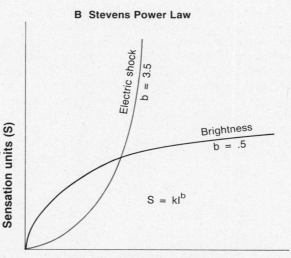

B Stevens Power Law

Sensation units (S)

Electric shock $b = 3.5$

Brightness $b = .5$

$S = kI^b$

Physical Intensity units (I)

ulus will produce sensations that rise rapidly at first and then more and more slowly, as shown in **Figure 4.7A.** This relationship was proposed by Gustav Fechner in 1860; it is expressed mathematically in an equation known as **Fechner's law:**

$$S = k \log I$$

where S is the magnitude of the sensory experience, I is the physical intensity, and k is a constant for the dimension being scaled. According to Fechner's law, a person's experience of sensory intensity increases arithmetically (2, 3, 4) as the stimulus intensity increases geometrically (2, 4, 8). Thus within limits *sensory experience* is proportional to the *logarithm of stimulus intensity*. This equation represents one form of mathematical relationship between psychology and physics—between sensory experience and physical reality.

A hundred years later, S. S. Stevens devised a different method of constructing psychophysical scales, and he obtained a different answer. He asked observers to scale their sensations *directly* into numbers, using a method called **magnitude estimation.** Observers were presented with an initial stimulus— say, a light of some intensity—and were told to as-

sign some value to it—say, 10. Then they were presented with another light at a different magnitude and told that if they perceived it as twice as bright, they should call it 20. If it were half as bright they should call it 5, and so on. When Stevens constructed psychological scales in this manner, he found that the results could be described by a *power function* whose equation is:

$$S = kI^b$$

where S is (again) the magnitude of the sensory experience, I is (again) the physical intensity of the stimulus, *k* is a constant (*not* Fechner's constant but a different one), and *b* is an exponent that varies for different sensory dimensions. **Figure 4.7B** shows psychophysical curves for brightness and electrical shock, where the exponents are very different. Doubling the physical intensity of a light less than doubles the sensation of brightness, which is qualitatively consistent with Fechner's law. As you might guess, however, doubling the magnitude of an electrical shock *more* than doubles its corresponding sensation. Fechner's law cannot predict such a result.

Stevens' approach has proved to be very useful because almost any psychological dimension can be readily scaled in this way. Psychologists have used magnitude estimation to construct psychological scales for everything from pitch and length to beauty, the seriousness of crimes, and the goodness of Swedish monarchs (Stevens, 1961, 1962).

Although similar equations express the relationships between stimuli and sensations in the various sensory modalities, each sense responds to a different kind of stimulus energy, provides us with different qualities of sensory experience, and does so through the operation of its own ingenious physiological mechanisms. In the remainder of this chapter, we will look at the physical stimuli, psychological experiences, and physiological mechanisms involved in vision, hearing, the chemical senses, the body senses, and finally, pain.

▽ ▌ **Figure 4.8**   *Structure of the Human Eye*

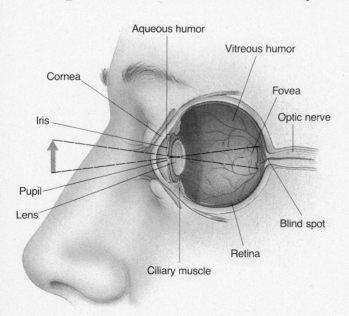

Aqueous humor
Vitreous humor
Cornea
Fovea
Optic nerve
Iris
Pupil
Lens
Blind spot
Retina
Ciliary muscle

THE VISUAL SYSTEM

Vision is the most complex, highly developed, and important sense for humans and most other mobile creatures because animals with good vision have an enormous evolutionary advantage. As predators, they can detect their prey from far away; as prey, they can detect and keep their distance from predators. Vision also enables us to be aware of changing features in the physical environment and to adapt our behavior accordingly. Finally, with the help of microscopes and telescopes, vision allows us to probe the secrets of nature in parts of it as small as a molecule and as large as a galaxy.

The eye

Since the eye is designed to detect light, let us follow a ray of light into an eye to see what happens (see **Figure 4.8**). First, light enters the **cornea,** a transparent bulge on the front of the eye that is filled with a clear liquid called the **aqueous humor.** Next, it passes through the **pupil,** an opening in the opaque **iris,** a muscular disk that surrounds the pupil and controls the amount of light entering the eye by contracting or relaxing. The iris also has the pigment that gives the eye its color.

Just behind the iris, light passes through the **lens,** a structure enclosed in a flexible membrane capsule which in most adults is clear, transparent, and convex. In older people, the lens becomes flattened, more opaque, and amber-tinted. The shape of the lens is controlled by **ciliary muscles** attached to its edge. Light then travels through the **vitreous humor,** a clear fluid that fills the central chamber of the eye, finally striking the **retina** on the back surface. At the retina, light can be absorbed by any of the 125 million light-sensitive receptors.

Each of the eye's components performs a critical role in the eye's sensory capabilities. The amount of light striking the retina is controlled by the iris and the pupil. When illumination is dim, the pupil dilates so that more light enters the eye. In bright light, the pupil constricts, allowing less light to enter. Interestingly, pupil size also changes in response to psychological factors. For instance, positive emotional reactions dilate the pupil, whereas negative ones constrict it. Pupil size also reflects mental effort, dilating when concentration is intense. All of this is involuntary and occurs without your knowledge.

Light entering the eye is useful only if it is focused on the retina in a reasonably clear image. For this to happen, light must be bent inward toward the center of the eye (see Figure 4.8). The curvature of the cornea does most of the job; the lens does the rest, reversing and inverting the light pattern as it does so. The lens is particularly important, however, because of its *variable focusing* ability for near and far objects. The ciliary muscles can change the thickness of the lens, and hence its optical properties, in a process called **accommodation.**

People who are *myopic* (nearsighted) cannot focus distant objects properly, while those who are *hyper-metropic* (farsighted) cannot focus nearby objects well. As people get older, the lens gradually loses its elasticity, so that it cannot become thick enough for close vision. After about age 45, the blur point—the closest point at which you can focus clearly—gets progressively farther away. When this happens, people who have never needed glasses before begin to need them for reading and other ''close work,'' whereas people who already wear glasses may need to switch to bifocals (glasses that have a near focus in the lower part and a far one in the upper part).

Processing in the retina

The most critical function of the eye is to convert the information about the world that is being carried by light waves into neural signals that the brain can process. This happens in the retina at the back of the eye, where integration of the input also begins (see **Figure 4.9**).

Rods and cones. The basic conversion from light energy to neural responses is performed in the retina by **photoreceptors**—receptor cells sensitive to light. There are two distinct types of these photoreceptors, called *rods* and *cones* because of their shapes. **Rods** are light-sensitive receptor cells concentrated in the periphery, or outer part, of the retina. They are most useful for seeing in dim illumination and do not produce sensations of color. **Cones** are receptor cells concentrated in the center of the retina, although there are some in the periphery too. They are responsible for our visual experience under most ''normal'' conditions of lighting and for *all* our experiences of color.

In the very center of the retina is a small region called the **fovea,** which contains nothing but densely packed cones. It is the area of your sharpest vision: both color and spatial detail are most accurately detected there.

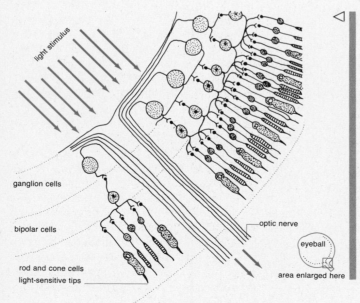

ganglion cells

bipolar cells

optic nerve

eyeball

rod and cone cells
light-sensitive tips

area enlarged here

◁ **Figure 4.9** *Retinal Pathways*

This is a stylized and greatly simplified diagram showing examples of the pathways that connect three of the layers of nerve cells in the retina. Incoming light passes through all these layers to reach the receptors, which are at the back of the eyeball and pointed away from the source of light. Note that the bipolar cells ''gather'' impulses from more than one receptor cell and send the results to several ganglion cells. Nerve impulses from the ganglion cells leave the eye via the optic nerve and travel to the next relay point.

Bipolar and ganglion cells.

The responses of many nearby receptors are gathered by bipolar and ganglion cells, also found in the retina. The **bipolar cells** are nerve cells that combine impulses from many receptors and send the results to ganglion cells. They have a single dendrite with branched endings and one axon and terminal button. Each **ganglion cell** then integrates the impulses from many bipolar cells into a single firing rate. The axons of the ganglion cells make up the **optic nerve,** which carries this information out of the eye and back toward the brain.

Peculiarities of retinal design.

Your eye seems to give you such clear and complete images that you would never suspect some of the peculiarities present in the design of the retina. To start, you would expect that the receptor cells would be in the *first* layer of the retina that the incoming light would reach. Wrong! Actually they are in the *last* layer, as shown in the figure (4.9). This means that light delivers its message to the receptors only *after* it has passed through several layers of cells. Luckily, these cells are fairly transparent, so that the optical quality of the image does not suffer as much as you might expect. However, the blood vessels in the retina also lie in front of the receptors, and they are not at all transparent. Normally, you do not see them because your brain adjusts by "filling in" the image where their shadows fall.

To see the blood vessels in your own eye, try the following exercise: Look at a white surface (a plain wall or blank piece of paper) with one eye closed and shine a pen flashlight into the *white* of the open eye at the *outside corner,* gently shaking the pen light up and down. You will be able to see the blood vessels clearly because their shadows will be in front of different receptors, to which the brain has not yet adjusted.

Another interesting curiosity in the anatomical design of the retina exists where the optic nerve leaves the eye. This region, called the *optic disk* or **blind spot** contains no receptor cells at all. Yet you do not experience blindness there, except under very special circumstances because: (a) the blind spots of the two eyes are so positioned that receptors in each eye register what is missed in the other, and (b) the brain "fills in" this region with appropriate sensory qualities just as it does for the shadows of the blood vessels.

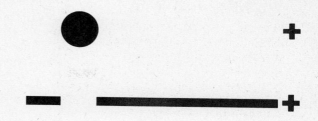

To find your blind spot, hold the book at arm's length, close your right eye, and fixate on the upper cross with your *left* eye as you bring the book slowly closer. When the black dot is in your blind spot, it will disappear. Yet you experience no gaping hole in your visual field; instead, your visual system fills in this area with the background whiteness of the surrounding area. So you "see" the whiteness, which isn't there, while failing to see the dot, which is.

To convince yourself that higher brain processes "fill in" the missing part of the visual field with appropriate information, close your right eye again and focus on the lower cross as you bring the book closer to you. This time, the gap in the line will disappear and be filled in with an illusory line that completes the broken one. At least in the blind spot, what you see isn't always what you get!

Pathways to the brain

At the back of the brain, in both cerebral hemispheres, is an area specialized for processing information coming from the eyes. To get there, nerve impulses leaving the eye travel back to the **optic chiasma,** named for its resemblance to the Greek letter χ (chi, pronounced "kye"). In humans, the axons in the optic nerve are divided into two bundles at the optic chiasma; those from the inner half of each eye cross over to the other side to continue their journey toward the back of the brain.

From the optic chiasma there are two separate pathways on each side. A small one goes to the **superior colliculus,** a cluster of nerve cell bodies in the brain stem. This is a primitive visual center that seems to do some processing of information about *where* things are in the world but not about *what* they are (Schneider, 1969). The other pathway, the major one, goes first to the **lateral geniculate nucleus** of the thalamus and then to the **visual cortex** at the back of the brain, as shown in **Figure 4.10.**

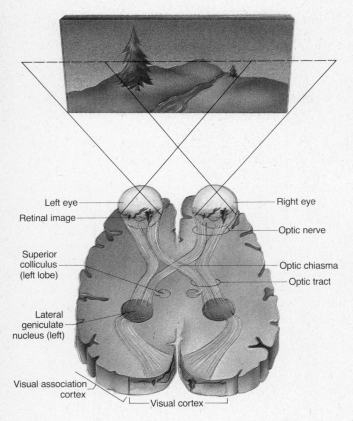

△ **Figure 4.10** *Pathways in the Human Visual System*

The diagram shows how light from the visual field projects onto the two retinas and the routes by which neural messages from there are sent to the two visual centers of each hemisphere (based on Frisby, 1980).

At the synapses in the lateral geniculate nucleus, influences from other brain regions, such as the reticular formation, are believed to interact with the impulses coming from the eyes before the latter are finally sent to the primary visual areas in the cortex. Cortical processing of information from the two eyes gives us our perception of color, depth, shape, and recognition of known patterns. Researchers now think that in humans only information that goes to the cortex ultimately becomes conscious.

DIMENSIONS OF VISUAL EXPERIENCE

One of the most remarkable features of the human visual system is that our experiences of form, color, position, depth, and other aspects of perceived objects are based on different kinds of processing of the *same* sensory information. How those transformations occur in the case of color, spatial properties, time, and motion is our next concern.

Color

Physical objects and beams of light seem to have the marvelous property of being colored. Despite appearances, however, the color does not exist in either the objects or the light. Rather, it is a psychological property of your sensory experience, created when your brain processes the information contained in light. Although the processes involved are fairly complex, color vision is one of the best understood aspects of our visual experience.

Wavelength of light: The stimulus for color. Any physicist will tell you that visible light is a kind of energy that is capable of being detected by our sensory receptors. In fact, the light we see is just a small portion of a physical dimension called the **electromagnetic spectrum.** This energy spectrum also includes X-rays, microwaves, radio waves, and TV waves, as shown in **Figure 4.11,** but we have no receptors that are sensitive to them. As a result, we cannot perceive them without the help of instruments—X-ray cameras, radios, and television sets—that convert them into something we *can* see or hear.

All electromagnetic energy comes in tiny, indivisible units called **photons.** The only physical property that distinguishes one photon from another is its **wavelength,** measured in units of distance of the wave-like propagation of a photon along its path. Wavelengths of visible light are measured in *nanometers* (billionths of a meter).

Photons with wavelengths ranging from about 400 to 700 nanometers are called *light;* they are the only ones that have any effect on your visual nervous system. As a result, any visible light can be completely described in terms of the number of photons it contains at wavelengths between 400 and 700 nanometers. For instance, "white" sunlight is the

(Figure labels)

Left eye
Retinal image
Superior colliculus (left lobe)
Lateral geniculate nucleus (left)
Visual association cortex
Visual cortex
Right eye
Optic nerve
Optic chiasma
Optic tract

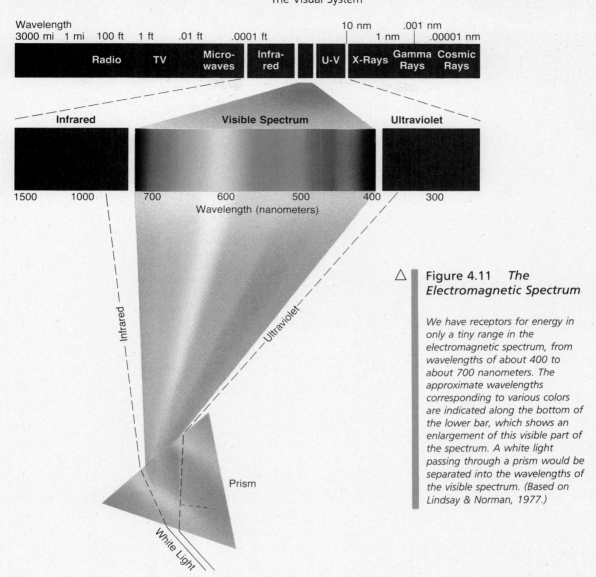

△ **Figure 4.11** *The Electromagnetic Spectrum*

We have receptors for energy in only a tiny range in the electromagnetic spectrum, from wavelengths of about 400 to about 700 nanometers. The approximate wavelengths corresponding to various colors are indicated along the bottom of the lower bar, which shows an enlargement of this visible part of the spectrum. A white light passing through a prism would be separated into the wavelengths of the visible spectrum. (Based on Lindsay & Norman, 1977.)

combination of all wavelengths of the visible spectrum in equal amounts. A prism separates sunlight into its component wavelengths, allowing you to experience a "rainbow" of different color sensations in response to the different wavelengths of light.

The important point here is that *light* is described physically in terms of *wavelengths,* not colors. Colors exist only in your experience.

Color space. To understand how you see colors from light of different wavelengths, we need to have a systematic way to describe different color experi-

ences. Psychologists do this by representing each color sensation as a position in *color space,* using a three-dimensional model for describing a color experience in terms of its *hue, saturation,* and *brightness.* These represent the three basic dimensions of our perception of light. All the sensations of color that people can experience are located within this space, forming the **color spindle** (or **color solid**) shown in **Figure 4.12.**

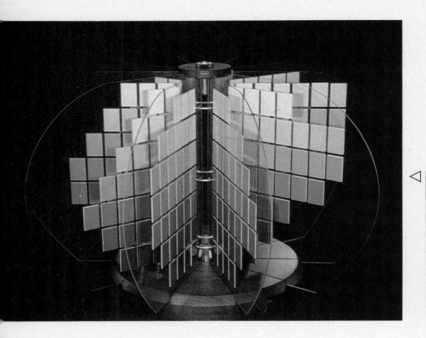

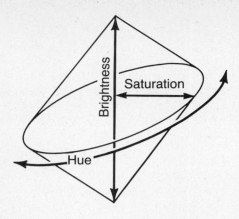

◁ **Figure 4.12** *The Color Spindle*

The color spindle (or color solid) shows each possible color sensation located somewhere within the three-dimensional color space whose dimensions are hue, saturation, and brightness, as shown in the schematic diagram. The values of a color experience along these three dimensions determine where it goes in color space; all color experiences together form the spindle shown here.

▽ **Figure 4.13** *The Color Circle*

The color circle shows the hues arranged in a circle, according to their perceived similarity. (The relation of this hue circle to the entire color spindle is shown in the schematic diagram.) Between the hues with shortest and longest wavelengths are the nonspectral hues, *which are not found on the electromagnetic spectrum but are created by mixing lights that are a part of the spectrum.* (Based on Rock, 1975.)

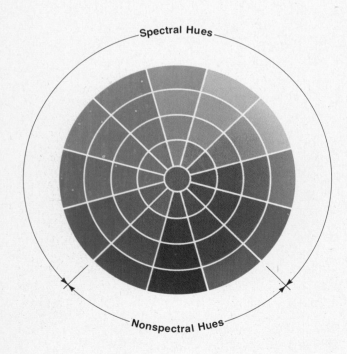

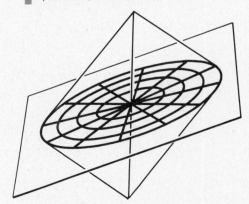

Hue is the dimension of color space that captures what you might call the "essential color" of a light. In "pure" lights that contain only one wavelength (like a laser beam) the psychological experience of *hue* corresponds directly to the physical dimension of the light's wavelength, as we saw in Figure 4.11. In color space, the hue sensations produced by different wavelengths of light lie along the outside of the **color circle,** which is just the slice through the color spindle shown in **Figure 4.13.** Here the shortest and longest wavelengths are shown as close together, reflecting the *psychological similarity* of violets and red.

Saturation is the psychological dimension that captures the "purity" and "vividness" of color sensations. In the color spindle, saturation is the distance outward from the central axis; the "pure" colors lying on the outer edge have the highest saturation, grays at the center have zero saturation, and the "muted," "muddy," and "pastel" colors with intermediate saturation lie in between, as shown in Figure 4.13.

Brightness is the dimension of color experience that captures the intensity of light. White has the most brightness, black the least. Brightness is the vertical dimension of color space with white at the top, black at the bottom, and all the grays in between. These "neutral" color sensations (sensations with no hue) lie along the vertical axis of the color spindle. All colors have some value on the brightness dimension—the brighter a color, the higher it is in the color spindle.

Figure 4.14 shows a vertical slice through the color spindle that illustrates how the saturation and brightness dimensions for a blue hue form a *color triangle.* The grays, from black to white, form a vertical strip along one side, representing the vertical axis of the spindle.

Complementary colors and afterimages. Complementary colors are colors opposite each other on the color circle (Figure 4.13). One interesting fact about complementary colors is that each hue gives

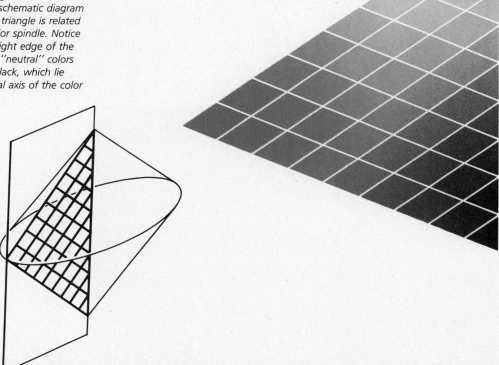

▷ **Figure 4.14** *The Color Triangle for Blue*

This triangle shows a variety of colors with the same hue that differ only in brightness and saturation. The schematic diagram shows how this triangle is related to the entire color spindle. Notice that along the right edge of the triangle are the "neutral" colors from white to black, which lie along the vertical axis of the color spindle.

its complementary hue as a color **afterimage**—an effect of a visual stimulus after that stimulus has ended. This means that you can find the complement for a given hue by staring at a highly saturated patch of it for at least 30 seconds while fixating on a dot in the center. When you then look at a white surface, the afterimage gives you the complementary hue.

For an especially dramatic example of color afterimages, stare at the dot in the center of the green, black and yellow flag **(Figure 4.15)** for at least 30 seconds, moving your eyes as little as possible. Then focus on a white sheet of paper until an image forms. Were you surprised? Do you understand why you saw the colors you did? Red is the complement of green, blue the complement of yellow, and white the complement of black.

Afterimages (or *aftereffects*) may be negative, as in this example, or positive. Negative afterimages are opposite or the reverse of the original experience and are more common and longer lasting. Positive afterimages are caused by a continuation of the receptor and neural processing following stimulation. They are rare and brief. An example is continuing to see the light of a flash bulb.

Color blindness. Not everyone sees colors the same way. In fact, about 8 percent of all males and about 0.3 percent of all females have some form of **color blindness** or *color weakness:* they cannot distinguish between some or all of the colors in the color solid.

To see whether you have a major color deficiency, look at **Figure 4.16.** If you see the numbers 5 and 26 in the pattern of dots, your color vision is proba-bly normal. If you see something else, you are probably at least partially color blind. (Try the test on others as well—especially anyone you know who is color blind—to find out what they see.)

Most color-blind people have trouble distinguishing red and green, especially at weak saturations. Rare are those who confuse yellows and blues—about one or two people per thousand. Rarest of all are those who see no color at all but only variations in brightness. Only about 500 cases of this total color blindness have ever been reported.

Theories of color vision. Now that we know something about the phenomena of color vision, let's examine how it happens at the neural level. What are the physiological mechanisms that enable us to see and distinguish colors? How do different wavelengths of light produce different color experiences?

The first scientific theory of color vision was proposed by Sir Thomas Young around 1800. He suggested that there were three types of color receptors in the normal human eye that produced psychologically "primary" color sensations—red, green, and blue. All other colors, he believed, were combinations of these three primaries. Young's theory was later refined and extended by Hermann von Helmholtz and came to be known as the Young-Helmholtz **trichromatic theory.**

Trichromatic theory was widely accepted for a long time because it provided a plausible explanation for how three kinds of receptors could produce all the color sensations most people have and how people could be color blind if they had only one or two kinds of receptors. But other facts and observations

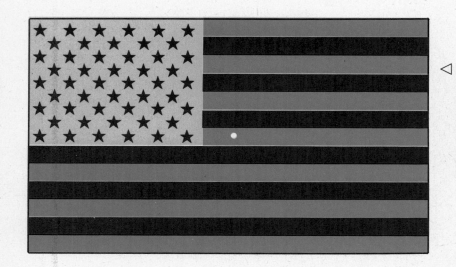

▷ Figure 4.15 *Color Afterimages*

Stare at the dot in the center of the green, black, and yellow flag for at least 30 seconds, then fixate on the center of a sheet of white paper or a blank wall.

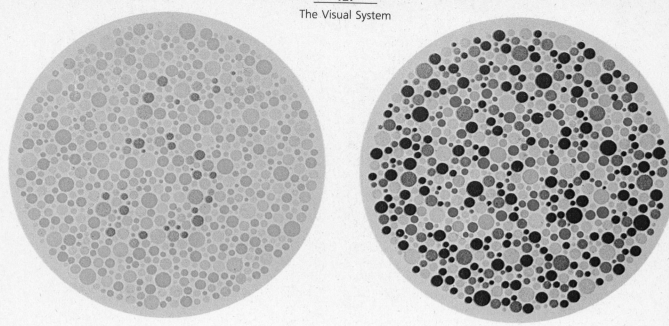

△ | **Figure 4.16** *Color-Blindness Tests*

What numbers do you see in these two patterns? People with normal color vision see 5 in the left one and 26 in the right one, but people with certain types of color blindness see something different. If you know people who are color blind, find out what they see. (Courtesy of Macmillan Science Co., Inc.).

were not as well explained. Why does adaptation to one color produce color afterimages that have the complementary hue? Why do color-blind people always fail to distinguish *pairs* of colors: red and green or blue and yellow?

Answers to these questions became the cornerstones for a second theory of color vision proposed by Ewald Hering in the late 1800s. According to his **opponent-process theory,** all color experiences arise from three underlying *systems,* each of which includes two "opponent" elements: red vs. green, blue vs. yellow, and black vs. white. Hering theorized that colors produced complementary afterimages because one element of the system became fatigued and thus increased the relative contribution of its opponent element. In his theory, types of color blindness came in pairs because the color system was actually built from pairs of opposites.

For many years scientists argued over which theory was correct. Eventually, it was realized that

they were not really in conflict, but described two different stages of processing, corresponding to successive physiological structures in the visual system (Hurvich & Jameson, 1957). We know now that there are indeed three types of cones, each of which is most sensitive to light at a different wavelength, and they work very much as predicted by the original Young-Helmholtz trichromatic theory. One type of cone responds most vigorously to *short* wavelengths of light (seen as blue), a second type to *medium* wavelengths (seen as green), and a third to *long* wavelengths (seen as red). These correspond to the three primary colors in the Young-Helmholtz theory. People who are color blind lack or are deficient in one or more of these three types of receptor cones.

The retinal ganglion cells then combine the outputs of these three cone types in different ways, working in accordance with Hering's opponent-process theory (R. De Valois & Jacobs, 1968). Some cells in this system are excited by light that produces sensations of red and are inhibited by light that produces sensations of green. Other cells in the system do the opposite: they are excited by light that looks green and are inhibited by light that looks red. Together, these two types of ganglion cells form the physiological basis of the red/green opponent-process system. Other ganglion cells make up the blue/yellow system and the black/white system, by combining the outputs of the three types of cones in different ways.

Spatial properties

Close your eyes, then get up and try to walk out of the room you are now in. Go ahead—try it. Now, what was it you missed most when you couldn't see? It probably wasn't color, but the lack of information about *space*. Your ability to identify objects and locate them in the three-dimensional environment requires sensory processes that detect *spatial properties* of the light patterns that fall on your retinas.

The light reaching your eye from different parts of the visual field must vary in color (hue, saturation, or brightness) if you are to detect any spatial properties at all. When uniform light is presented over the entire visual field (a homogeneous stimulus called a *Ganzfeld*—German for "whole field"), you see nothing but an undifferentiated fog. (You can see what this is like by cutting a Ping-Pong ball in half and taping the two halves over your eyes.)

Fortunately, almost all visual stimuli contain regions that differ in color or brightness, and these differences are what give you information about various spatial properties like shape, position, size, and orientation. But exactly how the visual system processes information from visual scenes to give the perception of spatial properties continues to be debated.

Investigators have assumed that the overall process of spatial perception involves several basic stages: first, complex patterns are analyzed into small subunits, with each cell in the visual pathway, from retina to visual cortex, responding only to selected aspects of a part of the pattern. Then the parts are synthesized back into a complex pattern in the brain. Little is known about the final synthesis stage, but we do know a fair amount about the early stages of analysis.

Early spatial processing. The cells at each level in the visual pathway respond to a particular part of the visual field. Each retinal ganglion cell integrates the information about light patterns coming from many receptor cells. The visual area that a given ganglion cell gets messages from via all these receptor cells is called its **receptive field.** Receptive fields of retinal ganglion cells are round and of two types: those in which stimulation in the center produces excitation and stimulation in the surrounding part produces inhibition, and the opposite organization with an inhibitory center and an excitatory surround (see **Figure 4.18** a and b).

Research in sensory physiology reveals that ganglion cells respond to the *differences* in stimulation coming from their center and the surround. They are most excited by *stimulus contrast;* those with "on" centers fire most strongly to a bright spot surrounded by a dark border, while those with "off" centers fire most vigorously to a dark spot surrounded by a light border. Uniform illumination causes the center and surround to cancel each other's activity: a cell is not as excited by uniform illumination as it is by a spot or bar of light.

Some cells remain "on" as long as a stimulus is present; they are called *X cells.* Others respond strongly at first, then rapidly weaken with continued stimulation—the *Y cells.* These cells are believed to project different kinds of information to the visual centers in the brain. The Y cells may be more involved in the analysis of overall visual form, while *X* cells may supply the fine detail necessary for a high degree of visual acuity (Sherman, 1979).

The center-surround receptive fields of cells in the retina have been used to explain some illusions of brightness, like the Hermann grid (see Figure 4.2). A receptive field whose excitatory center is located at an intersection will get twice as much inhibition from its surround as will a receptive field in other places between the black squares (see **Figure 4.17**). This

▽ **Figure 4.17**

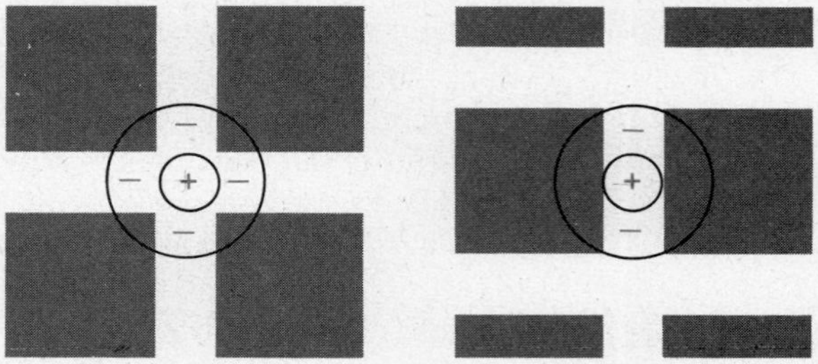

additional inhibition will cause the retinal ganglion cells responding to the intersections to fire much less strongly than the others, producing the illusion of blurry gray spots there. The spots disappear when you look directly at them because in the fovea there are no receptive fields large enough to include parts of the black squares.

The cells in the lateral geniculate nuclei have properties like those of the retinal ganglion cells. However, the cells in the visual cortex do not respond to stimuli that are effective at the lower levels of visual processing. David Hubel and Thorsten Wiesel pioneered the study of these cells in the early 1960s and later won a Nobel prize for this work. They recorded the firing rates from single cells in the visual cortex of cats in response to moving spots and bars in the visual field. Some cells responded to lines, others to edges; some responded to particular positions or orientations of a stimulus, others to particular shapes, still others to movement in a particular direction.

When Hubel and Wiesel mapped out the receptive fields of these cortical cells, they found both excitatory and inhibitory regions, as in the case of the retinal ganglion cells, but the receptive fields of the cortical cells were almost always *elongated* rather than round. As a result, these cells were strongly excited (or inhibited) by *bars* of light or by *edges* in their favorite orientation (Hubel & Wiesel, 1962, 1979). Because these cortical cells were simply and directly related to specific receptive fields, Hubel and Wiesel called them *simple cells.* Their output, in turn, is processed by other, even more complex types of cortical cells. (See **Figure 4.18**).

▽ | **Figure 4.18**   *Receptive Fields of Ganglion and Cortical Cells*

The receptive field of a cell is the area in the visual field *from which it receives stimulation. The receptive fields of the ganglion cells in the retina are circular (a, b); those of the simplest cells in the visual cortex are elongated in a particular orientation (c, d, e, f). In both cases the cell responding to the receptive field is* excited *by light in the regions marked by pluses (+), while it is* inhibited *by light in the regions marked by minuses (−).*

Recent studies have found that the elongated receptive fields of simple cortical cells are wider than first thought, responding not only to edges and bars but also to striped gratings in the same orientation (g, h), suggesting that they may be "spatial frequency analyzers" rather than simply "feature analyzers". This is currently a highly controversial issue.

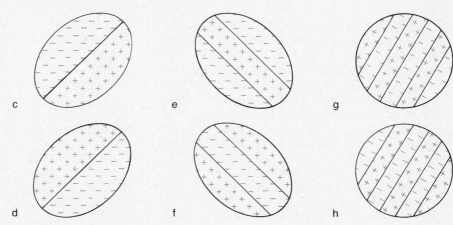

Retinal Receptive Fields
of Ganglion Cells

Retinal Receptive Fields of Cortical Cells

The feature-detection model. Based on this research, a hierarchical model of the visual system was proposed, in which cells at each of several levels were assumed to detect different features of the visual stimulus. This is called the **feature-detection model.** It suggests that individual feature-detector cells at each level successively analyze a visual pattern, each adding its input; all this information is then synthesized to form a total unit, enabling the viewer to recognize any known form.

This model of vision, based solely on feature-detection cells in the cortex, is less widely accepted currently because of theoretical and empirical challenges to it. It has been pointed out that recognizing just one object, like your grandmother, would require a huge number of cells and processing separate features in successive stages would take too long. It was also discovered that most cortical cells were even more sensitive to successive *bands of dark and light* than to simple bars of the same contrast. This research by Russell and Karen De Valois (1980) and their colleagues formed part of the argument for a competing model of how patterns and forms are perceived, called the *spatial-frequency model.*

The spatial-frequency model. The visual system detects variations in brightness over space, not just at one point where there is an edge that produces contrast in stimulation. The ability of the visual system to detect these differences over a broad area is studied by the use of patterns of alternating black and white stripes called *gratings.* Stripes of differing widths and contrast between dark and light are used. To the extent that an observer is able to distinguish the stripes from a uniform gray field, his or her visual system must be processing the spatial information in the brightness changes of the grating.

The number of dark-light cycles in a pattern over a given distance of visual space is called its **spatial frequency.** Spatial frequencies are thus greater with many narrow stripes than with fewer, wider ones across the same space. Studying pattern vision in terms of spatial frequencies allows researchers to use a more powerful mathematical analysis (called *Fourier analysis*) to quantify visual acuity and sensitivity (Campbell & Robeson, 1968).

Researchers now study spatial vision by measuring how well a subject can detect test patterns called *sine-wave gratings,* alternating light-dark stripes, as shown in **Figure 4.19.** This pattern is called a "sine-wave" grating because if a tiny light meter is moved across it, as shown in the line of dots along the grating's bottom edge in the figure, the meter measures

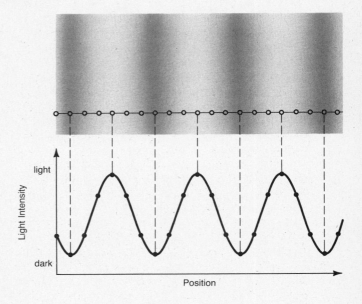

△ **Figure 4.19** *Spatial Frequency Gratings*

The light intensity of the black and white stripes in a grating pattern is shown as cycles in a wave pattern. Spatial frequency is measured from peak to peak, reflecting the width of the stripes. Contrast is measured by the height of the wave from peak to valley, reflecting the brightness difference between the stripes. (The length of these waves across visual space has no relation to the wavelength of the incoming photons of light discussed in the previous section on color vision.) (From Levine & Shefner, 1981.)

the amount of light coming from the bright and dark parts as a smooth curve—called a **sine wave.** The sine wave corresponding with this pattern is shown in the graph below the grating. Take a close look at this sine-wave curve because we will see it again a bit later when we discuss hearing.

Sine-wave gratings can vary not only in spatial frequency but also in contrast and orientation. Contrast refers to the brightness difference between the light and dark stripes, while orientation is the "tilt" of the stripes, the extent of deviation from a vertical position.

Observers can be presented with sine-wave gratings that vary in spacing, contrast, and orientation in order to determine the sensitivity of their visual system to different kinds of information. Doing so has revealed that it is difficult to perceive spatial frequencies that are either too fine (stripes too close together) or too coarse (stripes too wide). It is also possible to measure the amount of contrast necessary between the dark and light bars for each frequency of spacing to be perceived.

What interests psychologists most about people's ability to detect these sine-wave gratings is the possibility that the human visual system may actually analyze complex spatial patterns into something like a sum of many such gratings. With the inclusion of many gratings at many different spatial frequencies and many different orientations, very complex patterns can be constructed. For example, it can be demonstrated that any two-dimensional pattern—from an American flag to a photograph of Groucho Marx—can be analyzed mathematically as the sum of many, many sine-wave gratings. The low spatial frequencies are responsible for the overall shape of a pattern, as in the "blurry" picture of Groucho in **Figure 4.20;** the high spatial frequencies are responsible for the sharp edges and fine detail, as shown in the "outline" picture of Groucho.

Not only can visual stimuli be analyzed as spatial frequency patterns, but cortical cells can be shown to function in response to specific spatial frequencies (De Valois & De Valois, 1980). When an observer views a sine-wave grating of a particular spatial frequency for a minute or so, he or she will become less sensitive to that particular frequency but not to other frequencies higher or lower (Blakemore & Campbell, 1969).

The view that the visual system consists of cells that break down each complex stimulus into its spatial frequency components using a sine-wave analysis is surely revolutionary. However, there are many who continue to believe that the feature-detection model will prove to be the correct explanation of how we sense the spatial properties of visual stimuli.

Time and motion

The visual stimulation that gives us information about the world is constantly moving and changing over time as it falls on our retinas—and fortunately so. It turns out that changes in stimulation over time and space are essential for visual sensation to occur at all.

▽ **Figure 4.20** *High and Low Spatial Frequencies*

Detection of only the low spatial frequencies would give us the blurry view in B. Detection of only the high spatial frequencies would give us the outline view in C. Normal detection of all frequencies gives us the full view in A. (From Frisby, 1980.)

a

b

c

The effects of unchanging stimulation. After a period of unchanged stimulation visual receptor cells tend to lose their power to respond. This is called **sensory adaptation.** It is a phenomenon that occurs in other sensory modalities as well. After prolonged exposure, colors seem to lose their intensity and tend toward gray; warm water feels less warm after a time; an odor that is noticeable when you enter a room soon seems to disappear.

In Chapter 3, we saw that organisms *habituate*—stop making motor responses to stimuli that are no longer providing novel information (though the same muscles respond as strongly as ever to a new stimulus). Sensory adaptation may be another part of the organism's ability to ignore stimuli with reduced informational value, thereby freeing more processing capacity for attending to new stimuli that may have more significance.

A different type of adaptation—to darkness—results in an *increased* sensitivity to low levels of light. For example, you may have noticed that when you first go out of a brightly lit house on a dark, moonless night, you see very few stars. But then, as you stay and watch, the sky begins to fill with more and more stars. The reason for this is not that the stars get brighter, but that your eyes get more sensitive to the light that is already there. This process is called **dark adaptation;** the same process occurs when your eyes "adjust to the dark" in a movie theater or after you turn out the lights at night.

Psychologists have studied dark adaptation by measuring subjects' absolute thresholds for light after different lengths of time in the dark. Two distinct phases occur: the first ends when the curve levels off at an intermediate level of sensitivity after about 10 minutes; in the second, the curve continues downward, leveling off about 20 minutes later at a point of much greater sensitivity. Try to guess why the curve has these two parts before reading the caption for **Figure 4.21.**

Even with an unchanging scene, our eyes keep shifting slightly due to a continuous tremor of the eye muscles called *physiological nystagmus*. The result is that the stimulation for some cells keeps changing. Otherwise we would see nothing at all. This inability to see if stimulation does not change has been demonstrated by clever experiments using a tiny projector fastened to a contact lens as shown in **Figure 4.22.** It projects an image directly onto the subject's retina, and whenever the person's eye moves, the projected image moves with it. The result is that the image keeps falling on exactly the same receptor cells, and within a few seconds, this **stabilized image** disappears entirely: the retinal cells simply stop responding.

In our normal experience, the only natural image that ever stays completely stabilized—and therefore invisible due to adaptation—is the pattern of the blood vessels in the retina that lie in the path of the incoming light. In this case, as we have seen, the brain somehow fills in the missing parts of the picture.

Seeing continuity in discontinuous events. Two other ways the nervous system "fills in" missing details to give us a coherent continuing experience are shown in our ability to see a flickering light as continuous and to see rapid sequences of static "snapshots" as the same objects moving.

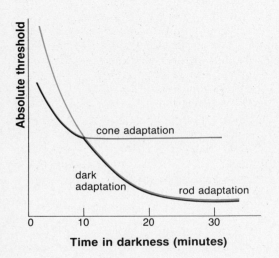

◁ ▎ Figure 4.21   *Dark Adaptation*

Changes in absolute threshold over a 30-minute period in darkness show this two-phase curve because rods and cones adapt at different rates and to different levels of sensitivity. Cone adaptation is rapid, but the threshold of cones never drops as far as the threshold for rods. When the cone adaptation curve is combined with the rod adaptation curve, the overall dark adaptation curve results.

Absolute threshold

cone adaptation

dark adaptation

rod adaptation

0   10   20   30

Time in darkness (minutes)

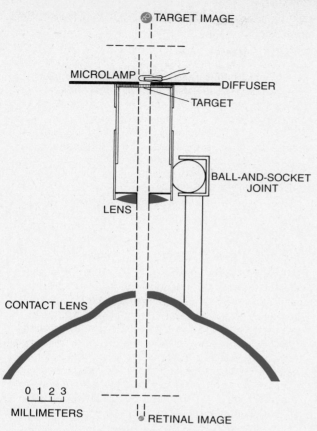

◁ ▌ **Figure 4.22** *Stabilized Image Device*

TARGET IMAGE

MICROLAMP

DIFFUSER

TARGET

BALL-AND-SOCKET JOINT

LENS

CONTACT LENS

0 1 2 3

MILLIMETERS

RETINAL IMAGE

When a light goes off and on several times per second, you see it as flickering. But if it alternates faster and faster, there comes a point when you no longer see any flicker and start to see the light as continually on. The point at which this happens depends on the brightness of the light as well as the on-off rate: brighter lights must be flickered more rapidly to be seen as continuous.

The frequency at which this happens is called the **critical flicker frequency.** The phenomenon of seeing the on-off light as continuously *on* is called **flicker fusion.** It occurs because receptors in the retina need time to convert light energy into neural responses when a light is turned on and time to *stop* responding when the light goes off. If the light is turned on and off faster than the receptors can start and stop firing, the neural response to one flash overlaps that to the next one. When you look at TV images, the "continuous" image you see is actually created by a series of separate light patterns pre-

sented so rapidly that you do not see the flicker.

As with the continuity seen in the fusion of flickering light, a succession of still images of an object in slightly different positions can be seen as continuity of the same object in motion if the static pictures are shown in quick enough succession. This is called **stroboscopic motion;** movies are a familiar example. Somehow the stationary frames are responded to as continuous motion by the visual system of the observer.

Detecting motion. Your visual system can detect only intermediate rates of continuous motion: you do not see very fast or very slow motion. If a light moves very slowly—as the moon does across the sky—you do not experience motion but only notice after a time that its position has changed. On the other hand, if the light moves too fast, you no longer see the spot at all but instead experience a solid, motionless bar of light.

The most common neural theory to explain perception of both real motion and stroboscopic motion is that the visual system contains *motion-detector neurons.* Recordings from single cells in the cortex of cats and monkeys have shown that there are indeed neurons sensitive to motion in a specific direction. As one would expect from the motion-detector hypothesis, some cells fire strongly when presented with a grating or bar moving in one direction and are inhibited strongly by motion in the opposite direction (Hubel & Wiesel, 1962).

If there are special motion-detector cells, there should be negative aftereffects following prolonged viewing of moving stimuli, much like the color afterimages you experienced after staring at the flag. There are indeed, and you can experience some motion aftereffects yourself by following the instructions in the **Close-up** on page 134.

Yet motion-detector cells cannot be the whole explanation for our perception of motion. As we will see in the next chapter, experiencing motion is not simply a sensory process but also a perceptual one, in which brain processes interpret and sometimes override the sensory information.

Sensory adaptation to motion produces negative after-effects comparable to those you saw with color, where you looked at the green, black, and yellow flag and later saw a red, white, and blue afterimage. When receptors for motion in one direction are fatigued, your visual system gives you sensations of motion in the opposite direction from unmoving stimuli.

A well-known example of this is the *waterfall illusion:* after staring at a waterfall for a time, people experience a *rising* motion when they look at stationary objects. The same thing occurs in the laboratory when a grating pattern is moved in one direction on a TV screen while the observer fixates on an unmoving point in the center of the screen. If the grating is stopped after a minute or more of adaptation, the observer sees the stripes as drifting steadily in the opposite direction.

To experience some striking motion aftereffects, cut out the spiral on the page just inside the back cover and place it on your turntable at 33⅓ rpm. in a well-lit room. (If you have a tall, automatic record-changing spindle, it is best to remove it.) Stare at the center of the spiral from directly above for 30 seconds or more while it turns; then quickly look away at a stationary object—some particularly good patterns to try are someone's face or the type of grid shown in Figure

4.2. If you can make your turntable stop very quickly, you can also use the spiral itself as a test pattern. Whatever you look at will seem to twist counterclockwise and contract in a rubberlike fashion.

When you have finished working with the spiral, take a rest for a few minutes. Otherwise, you may have trouble reading because the words will keep twisting. Once you are ready for more, turn the spiral over and try the same thing with the pattern of radial spokes. Its aftereffect will be counterclockwise rotation but without the simultaneous contraction of the spiral.

While you are adapting to it, however, look for another illusion that motion of this pattern can cause: the purely black and white pattern will give a strong sensation of yellow radial spokes along with the black and white ones. This phenomenon is called *subjective color.* At 45 rpm you will probably begin to see purple as well as yellow, while at 78 rpm (if your turntable has that speed) you can see a whole rainbow of different colors. These subjective color effects are still a mystery to psychologists as well as to you. (After you have been engrossed by looking at the colors for several minutes, don't forget to look at some patterned object afterward to see the dramatic motion aftereffect from all that adaptation!)

HEARING

Like vision, **audition** (hearing) provides us with reliable spatial information over extended distances. In fact, it may be even more important than vision for orienting toward distant events. We often hear things before we see them, particularly if they take place behind us or on the other side of opaque objects like walls. Although vision is better for identifying an object once it is in our field of view, we often see it at all only because we have used our ears to point our eyes in the right direction.

A second reason why hearing is so important for humans is its role in the understanding of spoken language; it is the principal sensory modality for human communication. People who lack the capacity to hear are excluded from much normal human in-

teraction and may suffer psychological problems associated with feelings of frustration, rejection, and isolation as a result. Blindness is obvious to others so they make adjustments for it; deafness often is not and sometimes goes unrecognized—even by the individual if the onset is gradual. Depression and paranoid disorders may accompany undetected loss of hearing (Post, 1980; Zimbardo et al., 1981).

The physics of sound

Clap your hands together. Whistle. Tap your pencil on the table. All these actions create sounds, but why? The reason is that they cause objects to vibrate. The vibrating object then transmits this vibrational energy to the surrounding medium, usually air, by pushing its molecules back and forth. These slight changes in air pressure spread outward from the vibrating object in sound waves traveling at a rate of about 1100 feet per second. Sound cannot be created in a true vacuum (like outer space) because there are no molecules for vibrating objects to move.

Air pressure changes—changes in the density of air molecules in space—travel in *waves,* as shown in **Figure 4.23.** These particular waves are called *sine waves;* they are similar to the ones we discussed in connection with spatial frequencies in vision. Sounds produced by a single sine wave are called **pure tones.**

A sine wave has two basic physical properties that determine how it sounds to us: its frequency and its amplitude. **Frequency** measures the number of cycles the wave completes in a given amount of time. One cycle, as indicated in Figure 4.23, is the left-to-right distance from a point in one wave to the same point in the next wave. Sound frequency is usually expressed in *cycles per second (cps)* or *Hertz (Hz).* The physical property of *frequency* determines the psychological property of *pitch:* high frequencies lead to experiences of high sounds, low frequencies to experiences of low ones.

Amplitude measures the physical property of *strength* of the sound wave, as shown in its peak-to-valley height. Amplitude is defined in units of sound pressure or energy. The amplitude of a tone determines its perceived *loudness:* sound waves with large amplitudes are experienced as loud; those with small amplitudes as soft.

A pure tone, such as one produced by a tuning fork, has only one frequency and one amplitude. Most sounds in the real world, however, are not pure tones but are produced by complex waves containing a combination of frequencies and amplitudes. The differing *qualities* of the sounds we hear (clarinet versus piano, for example) are due to these differing combinations of frequencies and amplitudes.

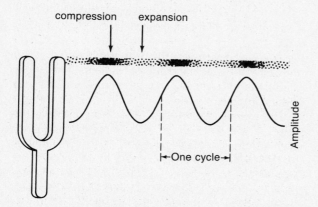

compression   expansion

|←One cycle→|

Amplitude

Psychological dimensions of sound

Three dimensions of the sounds we experience, then, are pitch, loudness, and quality. Though you already know a bit about what characteristics of sound waves produce these experiences, we need to take a closer look.

Pitch. Paralleling the physical dimension of sound frequency from low to high is the experience of low to high pitches. The full range of human sensitivity to pure tones extends from frequencies as low as 20 cycles per second to frequencies as high as 20,000 cycles per second. (Frequencies below 20 cycles per second may be experienced through touch, as vibrations rather than as sound.) Out of the full range of frequencies to which we are sensitive, the corresponding notes on a piano cover the interval only from about 30 cycles per second to 4000.

The psychophysical relationship between pitch and frequency is not a linear one: at the low end, increasing the frequency by just a few cycles per second raises the pitch quite noticeably, but at the high end, a much bigger increase is needed to hear the difference in pitch. To illustrate, the two lowest notes on a piano differ by only 1.6 cycles per second, whereas the two highest ones differ by 235 cycles per second—more than 140 times greater. This relationship between pitch and sound frequency is a case in which Fechner's logarithmic law holds.

Loudness. The human auditory system is sensitive to an enormous range of physical intensities. At absolute threshold, the auditory system is sensitive enough to hear the tick of a wristwatch at 20 feet. If it were much more sensitive, we would hear the blood flowing in our ears. At the other extreme, a jet airliner taking off from as far away as 100 yards is so loud that it is painful. In fact, the jet produces a sound wave with more than a *billion* times the energy of the ticking watch, in terms of physical units of sound pressure.

Because the range of hearing is so great, physical intensities are usually expressed in units called *decibels* (dB) that are logarithms of *ratios* rather than ab-

◁ ▌ **Figure 4.23** *Sound Waves*

Noise Pollution and Hearing Loss

The typical urban environment is a very noisy place. Street traffic, jackhammers, jet planes, and even standard household appliances like dishwashers, radios, and telephones all contribute to the high level of noise pollution in our lives. Most of us are so used to it that we hardly give it a second thought. Perhaps we should, though, because prolonged exposure to very intense sounds can produce permanent hearing loss.

How high the intensity must be to impair hearing depends to a large extent on how long the exposure lasts. A sudden explosion at 200 decibels can cause massive damage in a fraction of a second. However, routine exposure to sounds less than 100 decibels can also cause significant hearing loss. Hearing loss from loud sounds is called *stimulation deafness*. Most people report such hearing loss for up to several hours after listening to a rock concert in an enclosed area. Not surprisingly, then, more permanent hearing loss is an occupational hazard for rock musicians because they are exposed to such intense sound levels so frequently. It also occurs in many other occupations where people are exposed to loud noises for extended periods.

Stimulation deafness was studied in women who worked in a weaving mill where they were exposed to noises of 98 decibels for eight hours a day, five days a week. Hearing loss was measured by the rise in their absolute thresholds for sounds. For those who had worked in the mill for ten years or longer, the average absolute threshold was 35 decibels higher than for the new employees (Taylor et al., 1965).

With this much hearing loss you would not be able to hear people whispering just five feet away in a quiet room; you would just see their lips moving soundlessly.

The main damage caused by prolonged exposure to loud noise is to the sensitive hair cells that convert the motion of the basilar membrane into neural impulses (p. 138). When these hair cells are damaged, they do not regenerate, and they are so tiny and so inaccessible that surgery is out of the question. Damage to them is permanent.

Hearing loss due to loud noise is greatest in the high frequencies (at or above 4000 cycles per second). In fact, all people in our noisy society experience progressive loss of sensitivity to high frequencies with age. It is not known whether the loss as we get older is due partly to the aging process itself or entirely to the cumulative effect of a lifetime's exposure to environmental noise. In any case, it is a good idea to avoid even brief exposure to excessively loud noise or prolonged exposure to moderately loud noise. If you must be exposed, wear earplugs or some other protective device.

---

solute amounts. **Figure 4.24** shows the loudness of some representative natural sounds in decibel units, with the corresponding sound pressures shown for comparison. Notice that sounds louder than about 90 dB can produce hearing loss, depending on how long you are exposed to them. (See Close-up, above.)

Timbre. Quality, the third dimension of auditory sensation, is called **timbre** (pronounced "tamber"). The timbre of a sound reflects the complexity of the sound wave. **Figure 4.25** shows the complex waveforms that correspond to several familiar sounds. A complex sound can be analyzed as a sum of many different pure tones with different amplitudes and frequencies. The graph in the figure shows the **sound spectrum** for a piano playing middle C—a graph of all the frequencies actually present and their amplitudes.

In a complex tone such as this, the lowest frequency (here about 256 cycles per second) is responsible for the pitch we hear; it is called the *fundamental*. The higher frequencies are called *harmonics* or *overtones* and are simple multiples of the fundamental. The complete *sound* we hear is produced by the total effect of *all* the frequencies shown in the spectrum. If pure tones at these frequencies and intensities were all added together, the result would sound the same to us as middle C on a piano. Amazingly, the human ear actually analyzes complex waves into these component waves.

The sounds that we call "noise" do not have the clear, simple structure of a fundamental frequency plus harmonics. Noise contains many frequencies that are not systematically related to each other. For instance, the static noise you hear between radio stations contains energy at *all* audible frequencies; you hear it as having no pitch because it has no fundamental frequency.

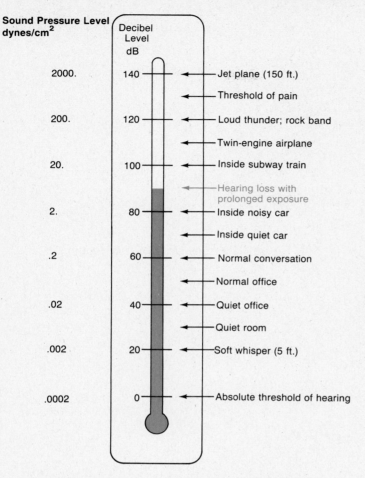

Sound Pressure Level dynes/cm^2

	Decibel Level dB	
2000.	140	Jet plane (150 ft.)
		Threshold of pain
200.	120	Loud thunder; rock band
		Twin-engine airplane
20.	100	Inside subway train
		Hearing loss with prolonged exposure
2.	80	Inside noisy car
		Inside quiet car
.2	60	Normal conversation
		Normal office
.02	40	Quiet office
		Quiet room
.002	20	Soft whisper (5 ft.)
.0002	0	Absolute threshold of hearing

△ **Figure 4.24** *Loudness of Familiar Sounds*

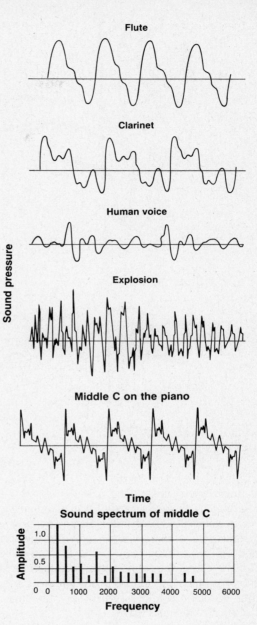

Flute

Clarinet

Human voice

Explosion

Middle C on the piano

Time

Sound spectrum of middle C

The physiology of hearing

Now that we know something about our psychological experiences of sound and how they correspond psychophysically to the stimulus, let's see how those experiences might arise from physiological activity in the auditory system. First we will look at the way the ear works; then we will consider some theories about how pitch experiences are coded in the auditory system.

△ Figure 4.25 *Waveforms of Familiar Sounds*

The complex waveforms of five familiar sounds are shown here. At the bottom is the sound spectrum for middle C on the piano. The basic wavelength is produced by the fundamental, in this case at 256 cycles. But the strings are also vibrating at several higher frequencies, which produce the jaggedness of the wave pattern. These additional frequencies are identified in the sound spectrum. (Adapted from Boring, Langfeld, & Weld, 1948, and Fletcher, 1929.)

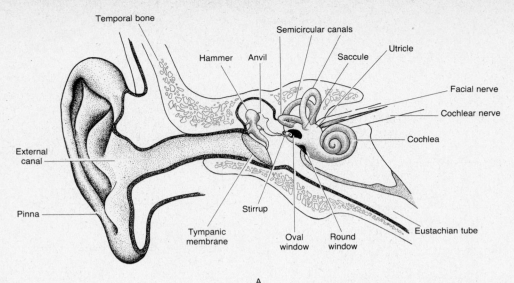

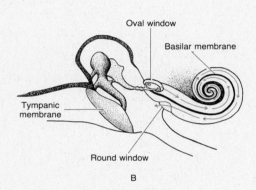

◁▌ **Figure 4.26**   *Structure of the Human Ear*

The auditory system. The first thing that must happen for us to hear a sound is that it must get into our ears (see **Figure 4.26**). Some sound enters the *external canal* directly and some after being reflected off the external ear, or *pinna*. At the inner end of the canal, the sound wave encounters a thin membrane called the *eardrum* or **tympanic membrane,** which is set into motion by the pressure variations of the sound wave.

The eardrum separates the outer ear from the *middle ear,* a chamber in the skull that contains three bones called the *hammer,* the *anvil,* and the *stirrup.* These bones form a mechanical chain that transmits and concentrates vibrations from the eardrum to the primary organ of hearing, the **cochlea,** which is located in the *inner ear.*

The cochlea is a complex and amazing organ. It is basically a fluid-filled, coiled tube with a membrane (called the **basilar membrane**) running down the middle along its length. Fluid inside the cochlea is set into wave motion when the footplate of the stirrup vibrates against the **oval window** at the base of the cochlea. This fluid wave travels down the length of the coiled tube, around the end, and back to the base on the other side of the basilar membrane, where it is absorbed by the **round window.** As the fluid moves, it causes the basilar membrane to move in a wave-like motion; this motion bends the tiny *hair cells* connected to it. These hair cells ultimately change the mechanical vibrations of the basilar membrane into neural activity by stimulating nerve endings as they bend.

Nerve impulses leave the cochlea in a bundle of fibers called the **auditory nerve.** These fibers synapse in the *cochlear nucleus* of the brain stem, from which about 60 percent of the input crosses to the opposite side of the brain, the rest remaining on the same side. Auditory signals pass through a series of other nuclei on their way to the **auditory cortex** in the temporal lobes of the cerebral hemispheres.

In cases of deafness, some part of this pathway is impaired and messages about pitch or loudness—or any sound at all—do not reach the brain. A remarkable device being developed to combat deafness is the "bionic ear." A removable microphone positioned behind the ear fits into an implanted plug that has wires leading into the cochlea. Messages picked up by the microphone are conveyed to a microprocessor (worn on the person's belt) which turns the sound waves into electrical signals. They are then transmitted to the plug and thence into the cochlea, which responds to the electrical signals and sends them on to the cortex. It is hoped that some people who do not benefit from hearing aids will eventually be helped by this new bionic ear, but much work must still be done to perfect it.

Theories of pitch perception. To explain how the auditory system converts sound waves into sensations of pitch, two quite distinct theories have been proposed: place theory and frequency theory.

Place theory was initially proposed by Hermann von Helmholtz in the 1800s and was later modified, elaborated, and tested by George von Békésy, who won a Nobel prize for this work in 1961. Place theory states that different frequencies produce most activation at particular locations along the basilar membrane, with the result that pitch can be coded by the place where greatest activation occurs. The basilar membrane responds to sounds by moving in a traveling wave, as shown in **Figure 4.27**. For high-

▷ **Figure 4.27** *Movement of the Basilar Membrane*

Part A shows how the sound wave moves the basilar membrane in a traveling wave. (For simplicity, the basilar membrane has been "unrolled" from its coiled shape and shown as a rectangle.) In Part B, the same motion is shown in three "snapshots". The curve labeled 1 depicts the basilar membrane in the position shown in A. Later positions of the membrane are shown by the lighter lines labeled 2 and 3. The dashed lines show the whole region taken up by the motion of the membrane—its "overall envelope" of motion. Part C shows the overall envelopes that result from tones of different frequencies. The lower the frequency, the farther away from the oval window is the place of greatest motion. (A from G. L. Rasmussen and W. F. Windle (Eds.), Neural mechanisms of the auditory and vestibular systems, 1960. Courtesy of Charles C. Thomas, Publisher, Springfield, Illinois. B and C based on Goldstein, 1980.)

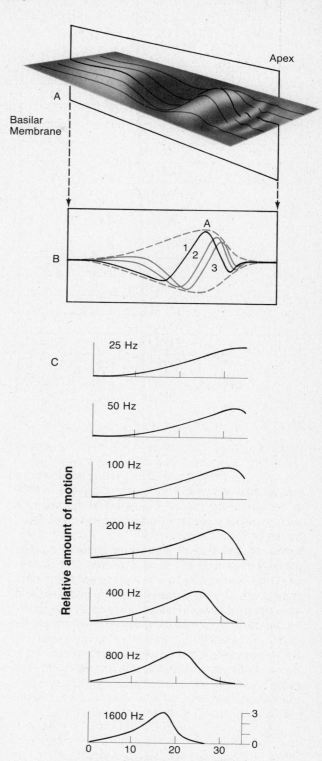

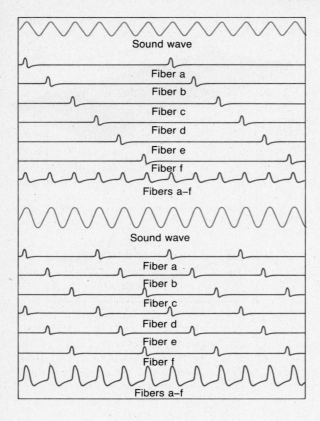

Sound wave

Fiber a

Fiber b

Fiber c

Fiber d

Fiber e

Fiber f

Fibers a–f

Sound wave

Fiber a

Fiber b

Fiber c

Fiber d

Fiber e

Fiber f

Fibers a–f

◁ **Figure 4.28** *The Volley Principle*

The combined firing of a group of cells (red curves) makes possible the coding of sound frequencies and amplitudes (blue curves) that would be beyond the firing capacity of a single cell. (From Wever, 1949.)

frequency tones, the wave motion of the basilar membrane is greatest at the base of the cochlea— the large end where the oval and round windows are located. For low-frequency tones, the wave motion of the basilar membrane is greatest at the opposite end. Thus the location of greatest movement *could* be the code for pitch.

The second theory, **frequency theory,** explains pitch by the *timing* of neural responses. Its hypothesis is that neurons fire only at a certain phase in each cycle of the sine wave, perhaps at the peaks, so that their firing rate would be determined by the tone's frequency. This rate of firing would be the code for pitch. An extension of frequency theory called the **volley principle** explains what might happen when the peaks in a sound wave come too rapidly for any single neuron to fire at each peak: as shown in **Figure 4.28** several neurons *as a group* could fire at the frequency of the stimulus tone (Wever, 1949).

As with the trichromatic and opponent-process theories of color vision, the place and frequency theories of pitch perception were long thought to be in direct conflict. More recently it has become clear that both are correct, with each working only for a portion of the audible frequency range. On the one hand, frequency mechanisms seem to account well for coding frequencies below about 5000 cycles per second; at higher frequencies neurons cannot fire quickly and precisely enough to code the signal well, even in volleys. On the other hand, place theory accounts well for our perception of pitch at frequencies *above* 1000 cycles per second: below that the motion of the basilar membrane is too broad to provide an adequate signal to the neural receptors. Between 1000 and 5000 cycles per second both mechanisms can operate.

So again, as in the case of the competing color theories, the two pitch theories have proven to be compatible after all. Each explains part of the puzzle best. A complex sensory task is divided between two systems, allowing greater precision in the resulting experience than either system could provide alone.

OTHER SENSES

Vision and hearing have been the most-studied senses because they are the most important to us. But we depend on many other senses too, in which different kinds of receptors enable us to code stimulus input for flavors, odors, pressure, gravity, and temperature. We use them every day in eating, sleeping, working, playing, and keeping out of harm's way. We will close our discussion of sensation with a brief analysis of the chemical senses, the body senses, and sensitivity to pain.

The chemical senses

We have two senses that respond to the *chemical* properties of substances: taste, or **gustation,** and smell, or **olfaction.** These senses presumably evolved together as a system for seeking and sampling food. Taste is the more ''immediate'' sense in that it operates only when a substance is in direct physical contact with the tongue and mouth. Smell is a ''distance'' sense for food—extracting chemical information from the air so that the organism can seek food in the right direction (Moncrieff, 1951).

Taste and smell work together closely when food is actually being eaten. In fact, the food you eat when you have a cold seems tasteless because the nasal passages are blocked so that you can't smell it. Hold your nose and try to tell the difference between pieces of apple and raw potato or between meats like beef, pork, and lamb. Without your sense of smell to help you, it isn't easy.

Taste. There are at least four primary taste qualities: sweet, sour, bitter, and saline (salty). These are thought to define your *taste space* (analogous to color space). In it the primary tastes are positioned at the corners of a prism, as shown in **Figure 4.29** and various taste combinations lie within its boundaries (Henning, 1916). There may also be a fifth primary taste, alkaline, but further research is needed to establish this with certainty (Shiffman & Erickson, 1971).

The receptors for taste are in the *taste buds,* sensory cells embedded in tiny structures called *papillae,* which are distributed in the mouth cavity, particularly on the upper side of the tongue, as shown in **Figure 4.30.** Sensitivity to sweetness is greatest at the tip of the tongue; to sourness on the edges; to bitterness, at the back. Sensitivity to saline (saltiness) is spread over the whole surface.

Single-cell recordings of taste receptors in rats show, however, that individual receptors do not fire just to stimuli producing one of the four primary tastes. Rather, tastes seem to be coded in terms of *relative* activity in the different types of receptors, each of which responds somewhat to *all* the taste stimuli. For instance, all receptors fire to both salt solutions and sweet solutions, but some fire more to one, and some fire more to the other (Pfaffman, 1959).

Smell. Evolutionarily important objects like food, predators, prey, and potential mates all emit organic molecules into the air. These molecules are physical stimuli for smell. They are important because they provide information about odor-producing objects *at a distance.* The significance of olfaction varies greatly across species. Dogs, rats, insects, and many other creatures for whom smell is central to survival have a far keener sense of smell than we do, and relatively

▽ **Figure 4.29** *Taste Space*

These four tastes—shown with the names of substances in which each taste predominates— are regarded as the primary ones. Although different parts of the tongue and mouth are more sensitive to one or another, individual taste receptors seem to respond to them all, but in varying proportions. (From Henning, 1916.)

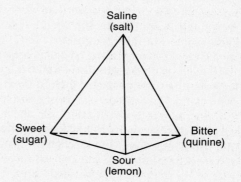

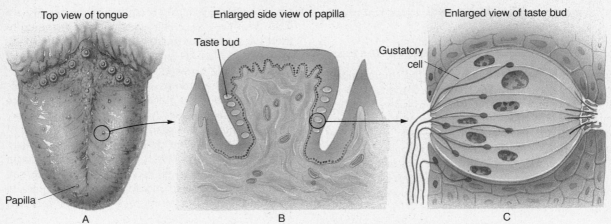

Top view of tongue   Enlarged side view of papilla   Enlarged view of taste bud

Taste bud

Gustatory cell

Papilla

A   B   C

△ **Figure 4.30** *Receptors for Taste*

Part A shows the distribution of papillae on the upper side of the tongue. Part B shows a single papilla enlarged so that the individual taste buds are visible; one of these taste buds is enlarged in Part C.

more of their brain area is devoted to smell than is true for us.

Members of some species communicate with each other by secreting and detecting chemical signals called **pheromones.** For instance, worker ants and bees use pheromone signals to let others know that they have found a food source (Marler & Hamilton, 1966). Pheromones are also used to indicate receptivity to sexual behavior, to mark out territory by urination, and to signal the presence of danger.

Humans seem to use the sense of smell primarily in conjunction with taste in seeking and sampling food. But there are some hints that humans may also secrete and sense sexual pheromones. Particularly suggestive is the fact that menstrual cycles of close friends in a women's dormitory have been shown to fall in synchrony (McClintock, 1971). It could be that this is due to nonconscious communication through pheromones. Another suggestive fact is that sex pheromones of other mammals are used extensively in perfumes which are bought and used by humans to attract members of the opposite sex.

Not much is known about the physiological mechanisms of smell. The odor-sensitive receptors are located deep in the nasal passages, making them very difficult to study. Their sensory signals are sent to the olfactory bulb of the brain, located just above the receptors and just below the frontal lobes of the cortex. One hypothesis about the mechanism for smell is the **stereochemical** (lock-and-key) **theory** (Amoore, 1965). It suggests that receptor sites in the odor-sensitive cells have distinctive sizes and shapes corresponding with those of the chemical molecules that stimulate them (as in the case of endorphins). This theory does not have wide acceptance, but no alternative theory has fared much better.

The body senses

To move around purposefully in our environment we need constant information about where our limbs and other body parts are in relation to each other and to objects in the environment. Without this knowledge, even our simplest actions would be hopelessly uncoordinated. In fact, we wouldn't even be able to sit or stand upright. The information we need to do these things comes from three senses that are grouped together by psychologists as "body senses": the *vestibular, kinesthetic,* and *cutaneous senses.*

The vestibular sense. The **vestibular sense** tells us how our bodies—especially our heads—are oriented in the world with respect to gravity. It also tells us when we are moving—or, more precisely, when the *direction* or *rate* of our motion is *changing.* The receptors for this information are tiny hairs in fluid-filled sacs and canals in the inner ear; these hairs are bent when the fluid moves and presses on them, as happens when we turn our head quickly or when a car or elevator we are in slows down or speeds up. The *saccule* and *utricle* shown in Figure 4.26 tell us about acceleration or deceleration; the three canals, called the **semicircular canals,** are at right angles to each other and thus can tell us about motion in any *direction.* For instance, they tell us how our head is moving when we turn, nod, or tilt it sideways.

The vestibular sense is also important in our ability to keep ourselves upright. People who lose their vestibular sense due to accident or disease are initially quite disoriented and prone to falling, especially if they are in the dark or if their eyes are closed so that they have no visual information about their position and motion. They may also suffer from vertigo (dizziness) for a while. However, most patients eventually compensate by greater reliance on visual information.

The kinesthetic sense. Whether we are standing erect, riding a bicycle, drawing a picture, removing a splinter with tweezers, or making love, our brains need to have accurate information about the current position and movement of our body parts relative to each other. The **kinesthetic sense** (also called *kinesthesis*) provides this information by giving us constant sensory feedback about what the body is doing during motor activities. Without it, we would be unable to coordinate most of the voluntary movements we make so effortlessly.

We have two potential sources of kinesthetic information. The first is from receptors that lie in the joints. These receptors respond to pressures that accompany different positions of the limbs and to pressure changes that accompany movements of the joints. Evidence suggests that these receptors in the joints provide the main source of information about position of the limbs relative to each other (Geldard, 1972). The second source of kinesthetic information is receptors in the muscles and tendons that hold bones together. These receptors respond to changes in tension that accompany shortening and lengthening of the muscles and tendons. They are involved in motor control and coordination but tell us little about *body position.*

The cutaneous senses. The skin is a remarkably versatile organ. In addition to protecting us against surface injury, holding in body fluids, and helping regulate body temperature, it contains nerve endings that produce sensations of pressure, warmth, and cold when they are stimulated by contact with external objects. Together these are called the **cutaneous senses** (skin senses). Their importance to an organism's survival is obvious.

The skin's sensitivity to pressure varies tremendously over the body. For example, we are ten times more accurate in sensing the position of stimulation on our fingertips than on our backs. This variation in sensitivity of different body regions is reflected in the density of nerve endings in these regions and also in the amount of sensory cortex devoted to them. In Chapter 3 we learned that our sensitivity is greatest where we need it most—on our faces, tongues, and hands to provide precise sensory feedback from these parts of the body for effective eating, speaking, and grasping. (See **Close-up,** p. 144.)

Two different types of cutaneous receptors seem to work together to tell us how hot or cold something is. Some evidence for this is that small spots on the skin tend to be sensitive just to cold or just to warmth, except that the cold receptors respond when stimulated by objects *either* below the temperature of the skin or well above it (Hensel, 1968).

Curiously, the sensation "hot" has no special receptors but seems to depend on the joint activity of the cold and warmth receptors. The most striking evidence for this is the thermal illusion illustrated in **Figure 4.31.** When two tubes, one cool and one warm, are intertwined as shown, the sensation from holding them is one of burning heat, even though neither of the tubes is really hot at all.

Constant stimulation by a cold or hot stimulus produces sensory adaptation: the receptors stop responding to the constant temperature. When you dive into cold water or step into a hot bath, the temperature is a shock at first, but soon feels much more comfortable.

The intermediate point at which you feel neither warmth nor cold is called **physiological zero.** Normally, this is about 90°, but it may shift temporarily as a result of sensory adaptation. Your adaptation to either warmth or coolness may become so complete that you are unaware of the temperature. That temperature has then become your new physiological zero, and new sensations of warmth or coolness will be felt relative to *it.*

Seeing with the Skin

Could blind people "see" if they were somehow provided with visual information in another sensory modality? This intriguing question led a team of scientists to develop a *visual substitution system* that converts visual images into vibrational patterns on the skin. The system consists of a television camera that records the visual image and a device that converts it into patterns of vibration. The pattern of vibrations is then applied to the subject's back, using a 20 × 20 array of vibrators, as shown in the drawing. Light regions in the image cause more vibration in the corresponding regions of the array and dark regions, less. With this system and some practice, blind people do indeed manage to "see" remarkably well.

In a series of tests, both blind and blindfolded subjects were soon able to discriminate among simple geometrical shapes like lines and curves in different orientations. Then they learned to identify twenty-five moderately complex, three-dimensional objects, such as a coffee cup, a telephone, and a stuffed animal. With still more practice they were able to "see" these objects in relative locations in space as well.

It also appears that active exploration of the environment by the viewer is critical for seeing with the skin, as it is for seeing with the eyes. If the TV camera is kept in a fixed place or moved by someone else, performance is much poorer than if the subject can move it while scanning the stimulation pattern (White et al., 1970).

It is still uncertain whether such a sensory substitution scheme can be developed into a useful prosthetic device for the blind. The vibrator apparatus is bulky, and the poor spatial discrimination ability of the skin on the back limits the amount of detail that the skin receptors can convey.

Another approach currently being investigated to provide "vision" for the blind is direct electrical stimulation of the brain, using an array of electrodes implanted in the visual cortex of blind volunteers. Applying current to one of the electrodes causes the observer to see a *phosphene:* a small, glowing spot at about arm's length. A pattern of stimulation causes a pattern of phosphenes (Dobelle, 1977). This cortical implant system has the advantage of being far more portable than the vibrator array. Many other problems must be overcome, however, before it will be possible to produce a really useful aid for the blind to "see" objects by stimulation of the skin or the brain.

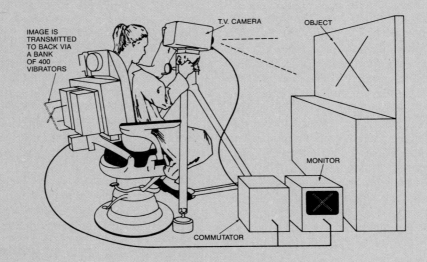

IMAGE IS TRANSMITTED TO BACK VIA A BANK OF 400 VIBRATORS

T.V. CAMERA

OBJECT

MONITOR

COMMUTATOR

You can demonstrate this dramatically in the following way: put your left hand in a bowl of cool water (about 70 degrees Fahrenheit) and your right hand in a separate bowl of warm water (about 100 degrees Fahrenheit). Allow each to adapt for several minutes until they reach physiological zero, where you no longer feel any temperature. Then put them both into a third bowl of water at an intermediate temperature (about 85 degrees Fahrenheit). The very same water will feel warm to your left hand and cool to your right hand. This happens because the receptors in each hand are responding to the *change* from their own physiological zero, not to the temperature of the water itself.

Once again, we see that our senses, though often accurate in telling us about the physical world, can be led astray by adaptation, context effects, and stimulus patterns arranged to yield illusions of reality.

▽ ▌ **Figure 4.31** *Heat Illusion Apparatus*

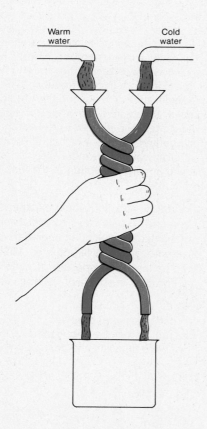

Warm water

Cold water

The pain sense

Pain is the body's response to noxious stimuli—those that are intense enough to cause tissue damage or threaten to do so. Simply put, pain is a hurt we feel, an experience of unpleasantness, tension, or suffering.

It is likely you have felt acute pain from a toothache, a headache, a burn, or a sports injury or home accident. For many millions of people, acute pain experiences do not pass but linger on as chronic pain, sometimes indefinitely, in the form of migraines, back pain, sciatica, arthritis, or cancer-related pain. About a third of Americans are estimated to suffer from persistent or recurring pain (Wallis, 1984).

Almost all animals are born with some type of *pain defense system* that triggers automatic withdrawal reflexes to certain stimulus events. When the stimulus intensity reaches threshold, organisms respond by *escaping*—if they can. In addition, they quickly learn to identify painful stimulus situations and *avoid* them whenever possible. There also seem to be brain-directed physiological defenses against pain.

You might think that it would be nice never to experience pain. Actually, such a condition would be deadly. Some people are born with a congenital insensitivity to pain; usually their bodies become scarred and their limbs deformed from injuries. In fact, because of their failure to notice and respond to tissue-damaging stimuli, they tend to die young (Manfredi et al., 1981). Their experience makes us aware that for the rest of us pain serves as an essential *signal:* it warns us of potential harm and thus helps us survive in hostile environments and cope with sickness and injury.

The sensory bases of pain. Despite the obvious significance of pain and much medical research to uncover the physiological processes involved, pain remains a scientific mystery. There are no specific receptors for pain such as exist for every other sense, no specific nerve fibers for sending only pain signals, and no specific form of stimulation for pain.

What has been discovered are powerful chemicals that are released at the point of intense stimulation (say, when you bang your elbow). They are stored in or near free nerve endings and sensitize the nerves to transmit impulses from the injured area toward the brain. Among these chemicals are a little understood substance called *P* (for pain), prostaglandins, and bradykinin. Aspirin and other popular drugs for pain relief work by inhibiting the production of prostaglandins.

The peripheral nerve signal is then transmitted to the spinal cord. From there it is relayed to the thalamus and thence to the cerebral cortex, where the location and intensity of the pain are identified, the significance evaluated, and action plans formulated.

Peripheral nerve fibers send pain signals to the central nervous system by two pathways—a fast-conducting set of nerve fibers that are covered with myelin, and slower, smaller nerve fibers without any myelin coating. These different types of nerve fibers appear to be responsible for the two distinct classes of pain experience we have. The fast-conducting, myelinated fibers carry pain signals described as "bright" or "pricking" sensations, with a fast onset and quick offset. Such pain is caused by specific stimulation, such as electric shock, and we can readily localize the area of the skin affected. The slower, unmyelinated nerve fibers produce "burning" or "dull" sensations; they start more slowly, are diffuse rather than specifically localized, and last longer. When myelinated nerve fibers in the periphery of the body are destroyed, as by poisoning or alcoholism, people can no longer experience the "pricking" pain, but only the "burning" pain.

One effect of these pain signals is to release **endorphins**—the brain's own morphine (see p. 89). Endorphins produce *analgesia* (pain reduction) by reducing sensitivity to pain stimuli. Endorphins appear to be responsible for the pain relief from stimulation by acupuncture needles, as well as from direct electrical stimulation of the brain stem (Hosobuchi, 1979). People who suffer from chronic pain that is not relieved by standard medical treatments have been found to have abnormally low concentrations of endorphins in their cerebrospinal fluid (Akil, 1978). Apparently the body has some mechanism besides endorphins for producing analgesia, but little is known about this yet (Lewis et al., 1980).

One theory about how pain may be modulated is *gate-control theory* (Melzack, 1973, 1980). The nervous system is assumed to be able to process only a limited amount of sensory information at any one time. If too much information is being sent through, certain cells in the spinal cord act as a gate, interrupting the pain signal so it does not get to the brain. Some of these other competing influences may come from rubbing the hurt area, from the emotional arousal of competition, or from the social situation. But the major influences controlling pain come from the brain.

Central processing of pain. The pain response is a very complex one because emotional reactions, context factors, and our interpretation of the situation—factors depending on central processes in the brain—can be as important as the physical stimuli in determining the pain we experience, and also in the relief of pain. In fact, the sensation of pain may not be directly related to the intensity of the noxious stimulus at all—or even to whether it is present or absent.

The importance of central processes in the experience of pain is shown in two extreme cases—one where there is *pain* with *no physical stimulus* for it, another where there is *no pain* with an *intensely painful stimulus*. Up to 10 percent of amputees report extreme or chronic pain in the limb that is no longer there—the *phantom limb phenomenon*. In contrast, some individuals taking part in religious rituals are able to block out pain while exposed to the intense stimulation of walking on beds of hot coals or having their bodies pierced with needles.

The *meaning* you attach to a particular experience can affect how much pain you feel.

In a classic study, men who were seriously wounded in battle were compared with men in civilian life who had received similar "wounds" with the same amounts of tissue damage in surgical operations. Only 25 percent of the soldiers wanted a narcotic for pain relief, while over 80 percent of the civilian men requested it. The difference in pain reaction was attributed to the significance of the wound for the two groups of men. For the soldiers, the wound was part of the expected context and may even have meant a ticket to safety, getting them out of battle. For the civilians, the surgical wound was more likely to be a disaster signal and a major disruption of the individual's life (Beecher, 1956).

Although pain is a private, individual experience, the way people respond to pain can become a habit learned from other people, such as members of one's family or ethnic group (Weisenberg, 1977). One early study compared the responses of patients from four ethnic groups in similarly painful situations.

When surgical patients were observed and interviewed, ethnic group membership generally predicted how they were handling the pain they were

◁ *"Fire walking" on beds of glowing coals is an ancient custom still practiced in Sri Lanka and many other parts of the world. Neither medical science nor anthropology has yet been able to account for the fact that its practitioners feel no pain and show no evidence of physical injury.*

experiencing. The Jewish and Italian patients emotionally exaggerated the intensity of their pain and felt free to cry out to elicit support from family members or hospital staff. By contrast, Irish and "Old American" patients (Anglo-Saxon Protestants from at least three generations of Americans) adopted a detached, matter-of-fact orientation and inhibited any public show of emotion. When their pain became intense, the Irish patients would withdraw, but they would moan or cry out only when they were alone (Zborowski, 1969).

This basic pattern of ethnic differences in response to pain was also found in a laboratory study of experimentally induced pain (via electric shock) to housewives from different cultural backgrounds (Sternbach & Tursky, 1965).

Another influence of learning on pain responses is seen in the differing effects of sympathy and attention versus withdrawal of attention on the part of family members. When pain complaints are followed by attention and social support, they become more frequent, whereas when they lead to withdrawal of attention and affection, they become less frequent.

In a study of 20 married patients, interviews were held with all the patients on the day of their admission to a pain-management program. Among other things, information was obtained about the patients'

perceptions of their spouses' typical response to their pain. During the study they reported their pain twice—once they believed their spouses were observing from behind a one-way mirror and once when a neutral individual, identified as a clerk, was the observer.

Those who thought their spouses were nonsolicitous reported lower pain levels, while those who perceived their spouses as relatively solicitous complained more when they believed their spouses were observing them than in the neutral observer condition (Block, 1980).

Not only can we learn pain responses if they are rewarded by other people, but we can *unlearn* them as well.

One clinic for chronic pain sufferers reported success using a three-part strategy: increasing the patient's activity level to ever more strenuous activities, giving analgesic "pain cocktails" randomly but never when pain was being reported, and training relatives not to respond positively to complaints of pain. Follow-ups showed that all patients made fewer pain complaints, were up and active for long periods, and showed greatly reduced dependence on medication. Almost all had returned to work (Fordyce, 1973).

Another demonstration of the importance of central activity in felt pain is shown in people's responses to various techniques for relieving pain. For example, hypnosis can be quite effective in relieving the experience of pain.

The intense pains women experience during labor and delivery of a baby have been reduced or even eliminated by hypnotic suggestions. One obstetrician successfully used hypnosis as the sole form of anesthesia in 814 out of 1000 deliveries, some of them requiring Caesarian operations (Hilgard & Hilgard, 1974). Hypnosis will be discussed in greater detail in Chapter 6.

People also may find relief from pain by taking a drug that they *expect* to be a "pain killer" when in fact the "drug" is a placebo, an inert substance with no medicinal value.

In a survey of 4681 patients treated with placebos for over twenty ailments or symptoms, including colds, epilepsy, and multiple sclerosis, successful results were achieved in 27 percent of the cases (Haas et al., 1959).

Another survey reported that headaches were relieved by placebos in 58 percent of 4588 cases. Overall, about one third of all patients treated with placebo in fifteen test series achieved positive results. Even pain from incurable organic illness was lessened. With cancer patients, 43 percent were relieved by injection of a placebo, as compared with 65 percent by injection or morphine (Beecher, 1959).

Believing that a particular treatment will lead to pain reduction is thus sufficient to bring about major psychological and perhaps physiological relief. It appears that belief, as well as perception of pain, can trigger the release of pain-killing endorphins in the brain. Recent evidence suggests that "positive placebo responders" may have higher concentrations of endorphins than do other people (Levine et al., 1978).

So, how you perceive your pain, what you communicate about it to others, and even how you respond to pain-relieving treatments may reveal more about your psychological state—about the kind of *inferences* you are making—than about the intensity of the pain stimulus. What you *perceive* may be different from, and even independent of, what you *sense*—a paradox that leads us to the topic of our next chapter: perception.

SUMMARY

■ Our perceptual systems do not simply record information about the external world but actively organize and interpret that information. Knowledge about perceptual illusions can give us clues to normal organizing processes.

■ At the sensory level of processing, physical energy is detected and transformed into neural energy and sensory experiences. At the perceptual level, brain processes organize sensations into coherent images and give us a perception of objects and patterns. At the level of classification, percepts of objects are recognized, identified, and categorized.

■ The field of sensory psychology includes sensory physiology, the study of how biological mechanisms convert physical events into neural and sensory ones, and psychophysics, the study of the correspondence between physical stimulation and sensory experience. Psychophysical techniques include attempts to discover absolute thresholds and difference thresholds and to construct psychophysical scales for measuring and comparing sensations.

■ The theory of signal detectability (TSD) challenges the assumption that there are absolute thresholds. Instead it holds that any stimulus produces *some* sensory response, and it overcomes the problems of response bias by providing separate measures for the sensory response and the decision criterion.

■ The smallest unit of difference between a standard stimulus and a comparison stimulus that can be perceived is called a just noticeable difference (jnd). This difference increases geometrically, maintaining the same ratio to the standard stimulus. This same relationship is found in different sensory modalities.

■ In the eye, light energy is converted to neural impulses by photoreceptors in the retina, the rods and cones. Ganglion cells in the retina integrate the input from several receptors; their axons form the optic nerves, which meet at the optic chiasma, where fibers from the inner halves of both retinas cross over to the opposite side of the brain. From the optic chiasma, a small pathway goes to the superior colliculus, where some information about the location of the stimulus object is processed. A large pathway goes by way of the lateral geniculate nucleus to the visual cortex, where information about color and detail is processed.

■ The stimulus for color is the wavelength of light, the visible portion of the electromagnetic spectrum. Color sensations differ in hue, saturation, and brightness. Current color-vision theory combines the Young-Helmholtz trichromatic theory (receptor processing) and the opponent-process theory (ganglion cell processing).

■ Cells in the retina as well as higher centers have receptive fields with an excitatory central area and an inhibitory surround, or the reverse.

■ Researchers disagree about whether spatial information is detected by feature-detector cells or analyzed as spatial frequency patterns. Detection of spatial frequencies is studied by use of sine-wave gratings with alternating black and white stripes of varying width and contrast.

■ Changes in stimulation over time and space are necessary for sensation to occur; unchanged stimulation leads to sensory adaptation. The brain's ability to give us sensations of continuity from discontinuous stimuli is shown in the phenomena of flicker fusion and stroboscopic motion.

■ Audition (hearing) is produced by sound waves that vary in frequency, amplitude, and complexity. Our sensations of sound vary in pitch, loudness, and timbre (quality). Sound waves are converted to neural events in the cochlea, where tiny hair cells are stimulated by the pressure changes in the moving fluid. Place theory accounts best for the coding of high frequencies; frequency theory accounts best for the coding of low frequencies.

■ Gustation (taste) is a chemical sense that works with olfaction (smell) in seeking and sampling food. Taste receptors are taste buds embedded in papillae, mostly in the tongue. They give us four primary taste qualities: sweet, sour, bitter, and salty.

■ Olfaction (smell) is accomplished by odor-sensitive cells deep in the nasal passages. Pheromones are chemical signals detected by smell that indicate sexual receptivity, mark territory, signal danger, and communicate other information in many species.

■ The vestibular sense gives us information about the direction and rate of bodily motion. The kinesthetic sense, through receptors in joints and muscles, gives information about the position of body parts and helps in motor coordination.

■ The cutaneous (skin) senses give sensations of pressure, warmth, and cold. Sensations of heat are produced by simultaneous stimulation of cold and warmth receptors.

■ Pain, the body's response to potentially harmful stimuli, has both physiological and psychological determinants. Pain signals release endorphins, which reduce feelings of pain. Emotional reactions, context factors, interpretations of the situation, and beliefs—factors dependent on brain processing—can be more important than the physical stimulus in both pain and pain relief.

5

PERCEPTION

Written in collaboration with Stephen E. Palmer

- **THE TASK OF PERCEPTION**
  Interpreting retinal images
  Evidence from ambiguous figures
  Theories of visual perception
- **PERCEPTUAL PROCESSES**
  Organizational processes
  Depth perception
  Perceptual constancies
- **CLASSIFICATION PROCESSES**
  "Bottom-up" and "top-down" processes
  Pattern recognition
  The influence of contexts and expectations
  The role of personal and social factors
- **SUMMARY**

Richard X. was a scientist who had considerable psychological training and experience in *introspection,* the process of carefully describing the contents of one's own conscious experience. His special skill enabled him to make a unique and valuable contribution to psychology when, tragically, he suffered brain damage that altered his visual experience of the world. Fortunately, the damage did not affect the centers of his brain responsible for speech, and he was able to describe his unusual visual experiences quite clearly.

In general terms, the brain damage seemed to have affected his ability to put sensory data together properly. For example, Richard reported that if he saw a complex object, such as a person, and there were several other people nearby in his visual field, he sometimes saw the different parts of the person as not belonging together as a single object. However, if the person then moved, so that all parts of him went in the same direction, Richard would see them as belonging together as one complete person. Without some common factor—like motion—to help "glue" things together, he tended to see a confusion of lots of separate objects, all of which were simultaneously present in his field of view, but which he did not experience as going together in the same way they would have before the neurological damage occurred.

In the example just mentioned, the common motion helped Richard put things together correctly, but he also described several cases in which things got put together *incorrectly* in ways that gave quite absurd results. One factor that often seemed responsible for this was common color: he reported that he frequently saw objects of the same color as belonging together, even if they were quite separated in space. For example, he might well have seen a lemon, banana, and canary in the kitchen as going together because they were all yellow. Richard also reported seeing different people in a crowd as belonging together simply because they were wearing the same color clothes. Less frequently he would see things as belonging together that had no obvious common factor. For instance, he recalled once seeing something that seemed to be one object but was really partly an automobile, partly a tree, and partly a man in a white shirt. Most of the time, however, things that a normal person would perceive to be parts of the same object would appear to him as quite different and unrelated.

Richard also had difficulty putting together sights and sounds from the same event. When someone spoke to him, he sometimes perceived it as two distinct events: a visual experience of a person whose mouth was moving plus a separate auditory experience of the spoken message. Both parts were meaningful to him, but he reported that on these occasions the mouth did not seem to belong to what he heard any more than if the voice in a movie had been dubbed with the wrong tape for the conversation. As you may be able to imagine, Richard's experiences of his environment during such episodes were disjointed, fragmented, and bizarre, quite unlike what he had been used to before his problems began. (Marcel, 1983).

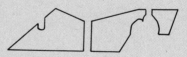

△ *Can you guess what these shapes represent? We're going to find out in this chapter how your visual system can interpret a set of images like this as a single object in the environment.*

There was nothing whatever wrong with Richard X.'s eyes or with his ability to analyze the properties of stimulus objects: he saw the parts and qualities of objects accurately. Rather, his problem lay in *perceptual synthesis:* putting the bits and pieces of sensory information together properly to form a unified, coherent perception of a single event.

Normally, processes in our brains fuse the sights, sounds, touches, tastes, and smells of objects into a unified experience of a single environment with all these characteristics. We are not consciously aware of how we accomplish this synthesis any more than we are aware of how we perform the sensory analysis that precedes it. But the case of Richard X. demonstrates that in normal perception neural processes *must* be synthesizing sensory information all the time. Were this not so, we would all constantly be having perceptually disjointed experiences like his.

How does sensory information get put together, both within any single sensory modality and across modalities? How do we identify objects as meaningful things that we know about? To what extent do you see things the way I do, and to what extent do our perceptions depend on who we are, what we know, and what we want? These are just a few of the questions about the psychology of perception that we will consider in the present chapter.

THE TASK OF PERCEPTION

Close your eyes, turn your head away from the book, and then open your eyes again. What do you see? Chances are, you perceive an environment composed of many familiar objects in a three-dimensional arrangement. This seems only natural, since you assume that you are only seeing what is there: the objects in the world are causing you to see what you see. Usually this assumption serves you so well that you do not question it.

But several things happen between the reflection of the light waves from whatever is out there and your perception of "familiar objects in three-dimensional space." Consider how three baseball umpires describe what they do. Since the outcome of a game may depend on whether they call "strike" or "ball," their decisions are very important.

The first umpire describes how he crouches in close behind the catcher, never takes his eye off the ball, and carefully follows its trajectory as it crosses the plate. "Then I simply call it as it is," he says. The second umpire is equally careful in monitoring the ball, batter, and plate, but he reports, "I call it as I see it." The third umpire says he doesn't get as involved as the others in all those preparations for seeing the situation as accurately as possible. He says, "The pitcher's ball is *nothing until I decide to call it something;* then it's a strike if I say it is."

The first umpire emphasizes the sensory aspects of perception, believing that his response is determined solely by "objective" properties of the stimulus. The second moves beyond that to reporting a perceptual experience, a *percept* in his consciousness. His statement implies that he might be wrong, that a percept can be veridical (accurate) or not. The third umpire adds another aspect of perceiving, the fact that we see things as belonging to categories ("balls" or "strikes" in this case). This process depends on knowledge and skill—and sometimes on what the observer *wants* to see.

Although each umpire is classifying a perceptual event as a "ball" or "strike," what is emphasized as most important corresponds to the three stages of the perceptual process outlined in Chapter 4—a *sensory* stage, in which information from stimulation of sensory organs is coded and analyzed; a *perceptual* stage, in which information is interpreted and syn-

▽ ▌ **Figure 5.1**

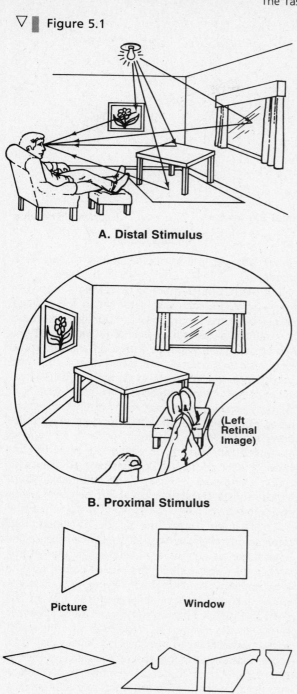

A. Distal Stimulus

B. Proximal Stimulus

(Left Retinal Image)

Picture

Window

Table top

Rug

C. Image shapes

thesized in terms of objects; and a *classification* stage, in which those objects are identified as belonging to familiar categories. The overall perceptual process goes beyond just receiving sensations: it makes sense out of them. From the constant, changing, often chaotic sensory signals, it extracts and organizes the aspects that are stable and orderly and relevant for us.

In this chapter we will be focusing on the second and third steps in this overall perceptual process. And though the term *perception* is often used to include the whole process, we will be using it here in its more restricted sense, as the second of the three stages, the stage in which sensory input is ordered and synthesized. First, in this section, we will look more closely at the important distinctions among the stages and at further evidence for them in ambiguous figures, and then we will summarize three of the theories that psychologists have proposed for explaining what is happening in this remarkable process of discovering what is "out there."

Interpreting retinal images

Let's suppose you are a man sitting in an easy chair with your feet up, looking at a portion of a room (**Figure 5.1A**). Light is reflected from the objects and some of it enters your eye, forming an image on your retina. This "eyeball's eye" view of the room as it would appear to your left eye is shown in **Figure 5.1B**. (The bump on the right is your nose, and the hands and feet at the bottom are your own.) How does this retinal image compare with the environment that produced it?

One very important difference is that the retinal image at the back of your eyeball is *two-dimensional* whereas the environment "out there" is *three-dimensional*. This produces many differences that you may not notice without looking carefully. For instance, compare the shapes of the physical objects out there in the world with the shapes of their corresponding retinal images (5.1C) The table, rug, window, and picture in the real-world scene are all rectangular, but only the image of the window actually produces a rectangle in your retinal image. The image of the picture is a trapezoid, that of the table top is an irregular four-sided figure, and the image of the rug is actually three separate regions with more than 20 different sides! How, then, do you manage to see all of these objects as simple, standard rectangles when your retinal images of them are so different?

Notice also that many parts of what you perceive in the room are not actually present in your retinal image at all. For instance, you perceive the vertical edge between the two walls as going all the way to the floor, but your retinal image of that edge stops at the table top. Similarly, in your retinal image parts of the rug are "hidden" behind the table, the stool, and your feet. Yet this does not keep you from perceiving the rug (correctly) as a single, unbroken rectangle. In fact, when you consider all the differences there are between the environmental objects and the images of them on your retina, you may be surprised that you can see the scene as well as you do (and not as Richard X. would see it).

The differences between a *physical object* in the world and its *optical image* on your retina are so profound and important that psychologists distinguish carefully between them as two different stimuli for perception. The physical object in the world is called the **distal stimulus;** the optical image on the retina is called the **proximal stimulus** (see **Figure 5.2**). These names are easier to remember if you consider that *distal* means "distant," or *far from the observer* and *proximal* means "proximate," or *next to the observer.*

The critical point of our discussion can now be restated more concisely: what you *perceive* corresponds to the *distal stimulus*—the "real" object in the environment—whereas the stimulus from which you must derive this information is the *proximal stimulus*—the image on the retina—which is often quite different. In fact, **perception** can be thought of as *the process of determining what the distal stimulus is from information contained in the proximal stimulus.*

The distinction between proximal and distal stimuli applies to all kinds of perception, not just to vision. Auditory images—the patterns of sound waves that enter our ears—are different from the physical objects that produce them. Even tactile images—the patterns of pressure and temperature that you feel on your skin as you actively explore objects with your hands—are not the same as the physical objects that cause them. In each case, perception involves processes that somehow use information in the proximal

▽ ▮ **Figure 5.2**

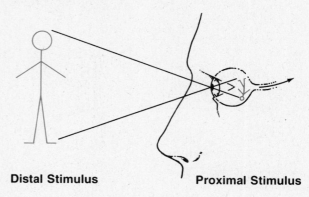

Distal Stimulus   **Proximal Stimulus**

stimulus to tell you about properties of the distal stimulus.

But there is much more to perceiving a scene like this living room than just determining the *physical properties* of the distal stimulus. You also see objects as instances of familiar, meaningful *types* or *categories* of objects: a window, a picture, a table, and a rug. Besides accurately perceiving the shapes and colors, you *interpret* them in terms of your past experience with similar objects. Classifying objects in this way allows you to treat many distinct objects as being essentially the same in important ways: windows are for looking through, pictures for looking at, tables for working or eating on, and rugs for walking, sitting, or lying on. This process of classification is also part of what you do automatically and almost constantly as you go about perceiving your environment.

To illustrate further the distinction among the three stages in perceiving, let's examine one of the objects in this scene—the picture hanging on the wall. In the *sensory stage,* this picture corresponds to a two-dimensional trapezoid in your retinal image, whose top and bottom sides converge toward the right and whose left and right sides are different in length. In the *perceptual stage,* you see this trapezoid as actually being a rectangle turned away from you in three-dimensional space. You perceive the top and bottom sides as actually parallel, but receding into the distance toward the right, and you perceive the left and right sides as actually equal in length. In the *classification stage*, you recognize this rectangular object as a member of the category "pictures," objects that are used to decorate walls of rooms.

Figure 5.3 is a flow chart illustrating this sequence of events. The processes that take information from one stage to the next are shown in the arrows between the boxes. The organization of our discussion in this chapter will follow this diagram.

We have already discussed the sensory stage in the previous chapter. Next we will discuss how processes of organization, depth perception, and constancy lead from sensation to perception. Finally, we will discuss the further process of pattern recognition that leads from perception to classification, plus the influences of other mental processes on classification.

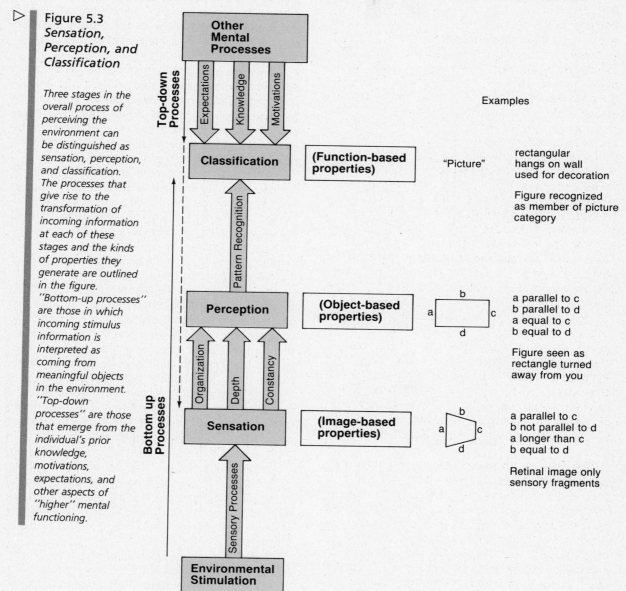

Figure 5.3
Sensation, Perception, and Classification

Three stages in the overall process of perceiving the environment can be distinguished as sensation, perception, and classification. The processes that give rise to the transformation of incoming information at each of these stages and the kinds of properties they generate are outlined in the figure. "Bottom-up processes" are those in which incoming stimulus information is interpreted as coming from meaningful objects in the environment. "Top-down processes" are those that emerge from the individual's prior knowledge, motivations, expectations, and other aspects of "higher" mental functioning.

▽ | Figure 5.4

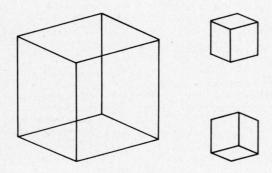

Vase or faces?

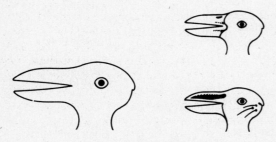

The Necker cube

Duck or rabbit?

Evidence from ambiguous figures

How do we know that interpretive processes take us from each stage to the next, as we are supposing here? The answer to this question is complex, but part of the evidence comes from what psychologists call *ambiguous figures:* stimulus patterns that can be seen in two or more distinct ways. Ambiguity is important for understanding perception because it shows that a *single image* at the sensory level can result in more than one *interpretation* at the perceptual and classification levels.

Sometimes ambiguity arises because the same image can be interpreted as two or more different *objects* in the environment; this produces ambiguity in the perception stage. At other times, ambiguity arises because the object you are perceiving can be interpreted as belonging to different *categories;* this produces ambiguity in the classification stage.

Figure 5.4 shows three examples of ambiguous figures, with unambiguous versions of each. Look at each one until you see the two alternative interpretations. Notice that once you have seen both of them, your perception flips back and forth between them as you look at the ambiguous figure. This perceptual *instability* of ambiguous figures is one of their most important characteristics.

The vase/face and the Necker cube are examples of ambiguity in the *perception* stage. You have two different perceptions of objects in space relative to you, the observer. The vase/faces can be seen as either a central white object on a black background or as two black objects with a white background between them. The Necker cube can be seen as a three-dimensional hollow cube either *below* you and angled to your left or *above* you and angled toward your right. In both cases the ambiguous alternatives are different physical arrangements of objects in three-dimensional space, both of which result from the same stimulus image—but not at the same time.

The duck/rabbit figure is an example of ambiguity in the *classification* stage. It is perceived as the same physical shape in both interpretations; the ambiguity arises in determining the *kind* of object it represents—a duck or a rabbit.

One of the most fundamental properties of normal human perception is its tendency to transform ambiguity and uncertainty about the environment into an unambiguous interpretation that we can act upon with confidence. Richard X. lacked this perceptual mechanism: damage to his brain prevented him from organizing separate sensory inputs into perceptual wholes that were meaningful interpretations of the world about him. In a world filled with variability and change, our perceptual system has the task of discovering invariance and stability.

Theories of visual perception

How does the visual system enable us to get meaningful knowledge about objects in a unified world? The problem of the many differences between the distal stimulus of the "real" object and the proximal stimulus of its retinal image has already been described. Two other major problems that the visual system must somehow overcome are: (a) how to convert millions of piecemeal bits of information from the individual receptors in two retinas into a single experience of a coherent environment, and (b) how to perceive a three-dimensional world when the sensory input on the retina is two-dimensional.

In this section we will look briefly at three perceptual theories about how the visual system solves these problems. Our discussion will center around three basic issues of concern to many psychologists: nativism versus empiricism, atomism versus holism, and organismic versus environmental explanations of behavior. The basic positions of the three theories are summarized in **Table 5.1**.

Structuralism. The earliest major theory of perception was known as **structuralism**. Its roots lay in philosophy, particularly in the writings of British empiricists such as Berkeley, Hume, and Locke. The structuralist view was that perception arises from a process in which basic "atoms of sensation" arouse memories of previous sensations that have been associated (linked together) in memory through repeated *experiences*. In the case of vision, the atoms of sensations were thought to be bits of color, sensed by photoreceptors in the retina. These highly local sensations were assumed to combine by simple "aggregation"—that is, just by being put together spatially as you would compose a mosaic of tiny bits of tile.

Structuralists also proposed that visual experiences aroused memories from other sensory modalities by simple association. Thus the memory of how a dog *looked* would be associated in memory with how it *sounded* and *smelled*. Perception was thought to occur by means of very rapid and unconscious neural processes that activated memories ac-

Table 5.1 *Theories of Visual Perception*

Theories	Nativism vs. Empiricism	Atomism vs. Holism	Organism vs. Environment
Structuralism	Empiricism	Atomism	Organism
Gestaltism	Nativism	Holism	Organism
Ecological Optics	Nativism	Holism	Environment

Three of the basic questions about which psychologists have made differing assumptions are: (a) nativism versus empiricism—whether we start life with innate ideas and abilities or with a "blank slate" on which experience writes everything we know; (b) atomism versus holism—whether organic wholes are built up as the sum of many parts or have characteristics not predictable from the parts separately, which at least partly determine the behavior of the parts; (c) organism versus environment—whether the causes of behavior are instincts, intentions, and ideas inside the organism or stimuli and pressures in the environment. The positions taken on each of these issues by the three theories of perception we are discussing are summarized in the chart; the most central concept for each theory is indicated in bold type.

quired earlier through experience with the world. According to the empiricist assumption of structuralism, the mind of a newborn baby was like a "blank slate," waiting for sensory experiences to etch knowledge about the world. As more and more was learned about the world through associations between many bits of experience, a person's perceptions became correspondingly richer, more accurate, and more complex.

Gestaltism. Historically, Gestalt psychology arose in Germany early in this century as a reaction against structuralism. The leaders of the movement—Kurt Koffka (1935), Wolfgang Köhler (1947), and Max Wertheimer (1923)—rejected the idea that perception was a mere combining of local sensations. In fact, *Gestalt* is a German word that means, roughly, "whole configuration," or form. The rallying cry of Gestaltists was, "The whole is *more* than the sum of its parts!" They pointed out that whole patterns have *emergent properties* that are not shared by any of the component pieces. This idea can be illustrated

Ambiguity in Art

The ambiguous figures that psychologists have developed, although interesting, are rather simple and prosaic. However, several prominent modern artists became fascinated with such figures because of the complex, dynamic visual experience they create in the viewer. For this reason, perceptual ambiguity has been used as the central artistic device in many works of art.

Shown here are three excellent examples. The first, by Victor Vasareley, produces depth reversals like the Necker cube. The corners of the surfaces can be seen either as coming out toward you or going away from you. The next, by M. C. Escher, is based on "figure/ground" reversals like the vase/faces. In "Sky and Water" Escher has created an ambiguous mosaic of inter-

by a line made up of many separate points (see **Figure 5.5**). Alone, each point has just two perceptual properties: its color and its position. But when many of them are arranged in a line, the line has additional properties such as length, orientation, and curvature that were not properties of any of its points separately. These properties *emerge* only from the whole configuration. Similarly, a musical work like Beethoven's Fifth Symphony is much more than a mere collection of notes. Its greatness lies in the emergent properties of its melodies and rich harmonies rather than in properties of the individual notes of which it is composed.

▷ ▌ **Figure 5.5**

Gestaltists, therefore, studied and theorized about the perception of whole figures. They were particularly interested in the way in which the structure of the whole visual field *organizes* the parts within it, a topic that we will discuss more fully in the next section.

In a further reaction against structuralism, Gestalt theorists rejected *empiricism* and accepted *nativism*

leaving fish and birds at the center where you tend to see the fish *or* the birds, but not both. Toward the top and bottom the figures become gradually less ambiguous. Notice that when you look at the unambiguous birds at the top, you tend to see birds rather than fish in the ambiguous center section, whereas when you look at the unambiguous fish at the bottom, you tend to see fish rather than birds in the center section. This demonstrates the influence of *context* on your perception, a topic we will discuss later in more detail.

The final example is "Slave Market with the Disappearing Bust of Voltaire" by Salvadore Dali. It is a

more complex sort of ambiguity in which a whole section of the picture must be radically reorganized and reinterpreted to allow perception of the "invisible" bust of Voltaire. The white sky under the lower arch is Voltaire's forehead and hair; the white portions of the two ladies' dresses are his cheeks, nose, and chin. If you have trouble seeing him, try looking from farther away. Squinting and taking off your glasses may also help. Once you have seen Voltaire in this picture, however, you will never be able to look at it without knowing that this French philosopher-writer is hiding there.

as the basis for perceptual organization: they believed that most organizational mechanisms were innate—"prewired" at birth in brain mechanisms and universal for the species, not learned from experience.

In trying to find a physiological mechanism to explain the organizing forces in perception, Köhler hypothesized that perception was determined by the operation of electrical fields in the brain. The development of EEGs as a means of recording electrical activity of the brain (discussed in Chapter 3) at first seemed to support this bold idea. However, later research showed that these electrical fields could be

disrupted in animals without affecting their perceptual abilities, contrary to Köhler's prediction (Lashley et al., 1951). Largely because of this failure, Gestalt theory became less influential, even though Köhler's idea about electrical fields was not the only way in which Gestalt organizing processes might occur in the brain. Many Gestalt principles of perceptual organization are still accepted, however.

Ecological Optics. The third theory of perception, called **Ecological Optics,** is primarily the work of one man, J. J. Gibson (1966, 1979). Gibson was

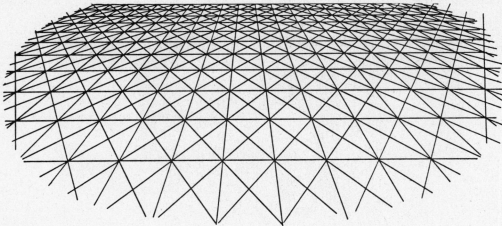

△ ▌ **Figure 5.6**

strongly influenced by the Gestalt movement, particularly by its emphasis on *wholes* and *nativism.* Gibson's reaction against structuralism went even further, however. Instead of trying to understand perception as resulting from the structure of the organism, he proposed that it could be better understood through an analysis of the immediately surrounding *environment (or ecology).* As one writer put it, Gibson's approach was "Ask not what's inside your head, but what your head's inside of" (Mace, 1977). In effect, Gibson's theory of Ecological Optics is concerned with *stimuli* for perception rather than the *mechanisms* by which we perceive. This approach was a radical departure from all previous theories.

Gibson's idea is really not as bizarre as it might seem at first. He began a program of research to discover what aspects of the *proximal* stimulus provide information about the *distal* stimulus. He contended that the *whole pattern* of proximal stimulation provided much more information about the distal stimulus than had been previously suspected. To take just one example, Gibson noticed that when a real-world surface of uniform texture (the distal stimulus) is slanted away from the observer in depth, its image on the retina (the proximal stimulus) is no longer uniform, but forms a **texture gradient**: the images of the uniform texture elements are smaller at greater distances because they are projected onto

smaller areas of the retina (see **Figure 5.6**). Many surfaces in the world have uniform textures that create texture gradients like this when we view them at a slant: grassy meadows, linoleum tile, textured ceilings, and wood grains on furniture. Gibson identified such texture gradients in the proximal stimulus as one source of information about the depth, slant, and size of objects in the environment—which are properties of the distal stimulus. He also showed that people could use texture gradients to perceive these properties in objects (J. J. Gibson, 1950).

Gibson's theory of Ecological Optics is also important because it emphasizes perceiving as *active exploration* of the environment. When the observer is moving in the world, the pattern of stimulation on the retina is constantly changing over time as well as space. Gibson stressed the richness of this "optical flow" in perceptual events. Much of the earlier work on perception was based on having subjects sit in one place while viewing simple, unmoving stimuli under highly restricted and artificial conditions. But Gibson and others argued that perceptual systems evolved in organisms on the move, seeking food, water, mates, and shelter in a complex and changing environment. The theory of Ecological Optics tried to specify what information about the environment is available to the eyes of a *moving* observer.

Each of these theories has produced important new ideas and discoveries. In the discussion that follows, we will take an eclectic position, noting the important contributions of all three theories along the way.

PERCEPTUAL PROCESSES

Vision is the most important and complex perceptual system in humans and most other mammals. In the present chapter almost all of our discussion is about vision, not because other perceptual systems are either uninteresting or unimportant, but because (a) vision has been more intensively studied than the other modalities, and (b) on the printed page it is easier to provide visual demonstrations than auditory or tactual ones. In the present section we will explore what is known about three kinds of processes that transform sensory information into perception of real-world objects: organization, depth perception, and constancy.

Organizational processes

Imagine how confusing the world would be if we were totally unable to put together and organize the information available from the output of our millions of retinal receptors. We would experience a kaleidoscope of disconnected bits of color moving and swirling before our eyes. (Even Richard X. was somewhat better off than this. He could put parts together, only sometimes he did it wrong.) The processes that put sensory information together to give us the perception of a coherent scene over the whole visual field are referred to collectively as processes of **perceptual organization**. We have seen that what the person experiences, as a result of the perceptual processing, is called a **percept**.

For example, your percept of the two-dimensional geometric design in **Figure 5.7** is probably three diagonal rows of figures, the first being composed of squares, the second of arrowheads, and the third of diamonds. Nothing seems remarkable about this until you analyze all the organizational processing that you must be performing to see the design in this way. The organizational processes we will be discussing in this section include region segregation, figure and ground, closure, grouping, figural goodness, reference frames, spatial and temporal integration, motion perception, and cross-modal integration.

Region segregation. First, consider your initial sensory response to Figure 5.7. Because your retina is composed of many separate receptors, your eye responds to this stimulus pattern with a mosaic of millions of independent neural responses coding the amount of light falling on tiny areas of your retina (see Figure 5.7B). The first task of perceptual organization is to determine which of these tiny areas belong with which others. In other words, the outputs of the separate receptors must be synthesized by being structured into larger regions that are internally uniform in their properties.

The primary information for this "region segregation" process comes from color and texture. An abrupt change in color (hue, saturation, or brightness) signifies the presence of an "edge" between two regions. Abrupt changes in texture likewise can mark edges between visibly different regions. Finding

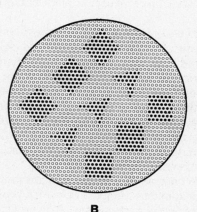

A

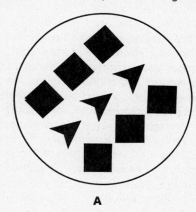

B

△ | Figure 5.7

these *edges* is the first step in organizational processing.

Many researchers now believe that the cells in the visual cortex discovered by Hubel and Wiesel, discussed in Chapter 4, are involved in these region-segregating processes (Marr, 1982). Some cells have elongated receptive fields that are ideally suited for detecting "edges" between regions that differ in color. Others have receptive fields that seem to detect little "bars" or "lines" such as occur in textures like grassy fields, wood grains, and woven fabrics. These cortical "line-detector" cells may be responsible for our ability to discriminate between regions that have different textures (Beck, 1972; Julesz, 1981).

Figure and ground. As a result of region segregation, the stimulus in our example has now been divided into thirteen regions: twelve small dark ones and a single large light one. You can now think of each of these regions as a unified entity, like thirteen separate pieces of glass in a stained-glass window. Another organizational process now divides the regions into *figures* and *ground. Figures* are seen as object-like regions; *ground* is the background against which the figures stand out. In our present example, you probably see the dark regions as figures and the light region as ground. However, you can also see this stimulus pattern differently by reversing figure and ground, much as you did with the ambiguous vase/faces drawing and the Escher work. To do this, try to see the white region as a large white sheet of paper that has nine holes cut in it, through which you can see a black background extending behind it.

In perceiving these two interpretations, notice that when you perceive a region as figure, the boundaries between light and dark are interpreted as edges or contours that *belong to the figure,* defining its shape. In contrast, the ground seems to extend *behind* these edges rather than stopping *at* them as it actually does in the stimulus. Such facts suggest that this aspect of perceptual organization is related to depth perception, a topic we will discuss in the next section.

The tendency to perceive a figure as being in front of a ground is very strong. In fact, you can even get this effect in a stimulus when the perceived figure doesn't actually exist! In **Figure 5.8** you perceive a solid white triangle against a ground containing

▽ ▌ **Figure 5.8**

three black circles and a black "X" on a white surface. Notice, however, that there are really just three solid black figures and four disconnected lines in the stimulus pattern. You see the illusory white triangle in front because the straight edges of the black shapes and the interruptions in the lines are aligned in a way that *suggests* a solid white triangle covering parts of whole black circles and a complete "X."

There seem to be three levels of figure/ground organization in this case: the top white triangle, the black circles and the "X" behind it, and the larger white surface behind everything else. Notice that perceptually you divide the white area in the stimulus into two different regions: the white triangle and the white ground. Where this division occurs, you perceive illusory *subjective contours* which, in fact, do not exist in the distal stimulus but only in your subjective experience.

Closure. Your perception of the white triangle in Figure 5.8 also demonstrates another powerful organizing process—that of **closure,** in which you tend to see incomplete figures as complete. Though the stimulus here gives you only the three angles, your perceptual system supplies the edges in between that make the figure a complete triangle. Likewise, in **Figure 5.9,** you have no trouble perceiving a horse.

Grouping. You also perceive the nine distinct figural regions of Figure 5.7A not as separate and independent items but rather, as grouped together into three distinct rows, each composed of three identical shapes along a diagonal line. How does your visual system accomplish this grouping, and what factors control it?

The problem of grouping was first studied extensively by Max Wertheimer, one of the founders of the Gestalt movement, with arrays of simple geometric figures. By varying a single factor and observing how it affected the way people perceived the structure of the array he was able to formulate a set of "laws of grouping." Several of these laws are illustrated in **Figure 5.10**.

In part A, there is an array of equally spaced circles that is ambiguous in its grouping: you can see it equally well as rows or columns of dots. However, when the spacing is changed slightly so that the horizontal distances between adjacent dots are less than the vertical distances (array B), you see the array unambiguously as organized into horizontal rows. When the spacing is instead changed so that the vertical distances are less (array C), you see the array as organized into vertical columns. These illustrate Wertheimer's **law of proximity:** all else being equal, the nearest (most "proximal") elements are grouped together.

By varying the color of the dots instead of their spacing, array D is generated. Although there is equal spacing between the dots, your visual system automatically organizes this stimulus into rows because of their *similar color.*

You see array E as organized into columns because of *similar size,* and array F as organized into

△ ▌ **Figure 5.9**

▽ ▌ **Figure 5.10**

Perceptual Grouping

A

B

C

D

E

F

G

rows because of *similar shape and orientation.* Shape similarity was the factor responsible for your seeing the figures in Figure 5.7 as grouped into diagonal rows from bottom left to top right.

These grouping effects (and more) can be summarized by the **law of similarity:** all else being equal, the most similar elements are seen as grouped together.

When elements in the visual field are moving, similarity of motion also produces a powerful group-

▽ ▌ Figure 5.11

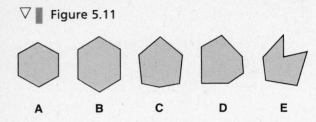

A   B   C   D   E

ing. The **law of common fate** states that elements moving in the same direction and at the same rate are seen as grouped together. If the dots in every other column of Figure 5.9G were moving upward, as indicated by the blurring, you would see the array grouped into columns because of their similarity in motion. You get this effect at a ballet when several dancers move in a pattern different from the others. Remember that Richard X. found that an object in his visual field became organized properly when it moved as a whole. His experience was evidence of the powerful organizing effect of common fate which, along with proximity, is subsumed under the law of similarity.

These effects show the principle we mentioned earlier, that perception depends on *emergent properties* of the configuration. The law of similarity operates only when two or more elements are simultaneously present in the visual field. The Gestaltists interpreted such results to mean that the *whole* stimulus pattern is somehow determining the organization of its own *parts*. They saw this as convincing evidence that the whole percept is *more than* and *different from* the mere collection of its parts. The strong argument was that perceiving the whole—the Gestalt—is itself more basic and takes place earlier in the process than the perception of its elements. This was a radical departure from structuralism, which stated that the whole had to be built up from sensations of smaller parts. The Gestalt demonstrations of perceptual grouping challenged and eventually superseded the structuralists' view of percepts as mere collections of sensory "atoms."

Figural goodness. Once a given region has been segregated and selected as a figure against a ground, with groupings among similar parts, the edges must be further organized into specific *shapes.* You might think that this would require simply perceiving all of the edges of a figure, but here again

the Gestaltists showed that visual organization is far more complex. If the whole shape were merely the sum of its edges, then all shapes having the same number of edges should be equally easy to perceive. But this is not true.

Organizational processes in shape perception are sensitive to something the Gestaltist called **figural goodness,** a concept which includes perceived simplicity, symmetry, and regularity. **Figure 5.11** shows several figures that exhibit a range in figural goodness even though they all have six sides. You will probably agree that A is the "best" figure and E the "worst," with the others falling in order between these two extremes.

Experiments have shown that "good" figures are more easily and accurately perceived, remembered, and described than "bad" ones (Garner, 1974). Such results suggest that shapes of "good" figures can be coded more rapidly and economically by the visual system than those of "bad" figures. In fact, the visual system sometimes tends to see a single "bad" figure as composed of two overlapping "good" ones (**Figure 5.12).** This example demonstrates that organizational processes provide the *best* and *simplest* interpretation that is consistent with sensory stimulation.

Reference frames. Higher levels of organization are achieved when the shapes of figures are perceived relative to **reference frames** established by the spatial and temporal context. The perceptual effects of reference frames are also demonstrated in Figure 5.7: if you saw one of the upper figures alone, it would look like a diamond, whereas one of the lower ones would look like a square (as shown in **Figure 5.13A**). But when you see these figures as parts of diagonal rows, the shapes reverse: the line composed of diamonds looks like a tilted column of

▽ ▌ Figure 5.12

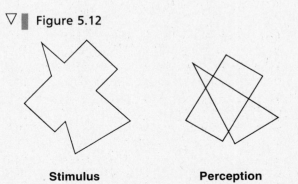

Stimulus   **Perception**

▽ **Figure 5.13**

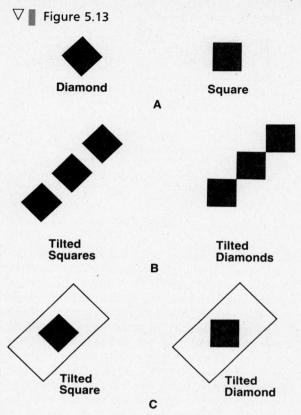

Diamond   **Square**

A

Tilted   **Tilted**
Squares   **Diamonds**

B

Tilted   **Tilted**
Square   **Diamond**

C

squares and the line composed of squares looks like a tilted column of *diamonds* (**Figure 5.13B**).

The shapes of the figures look different when they are in diagonal rows because the orientation of each figure is seen in relation to the reference frame established by the whole row (Palmer, 1983). In effect, you see the shapes of the figures as you would if the rows were vertical instead of diagonal. (Turn the book 45 degrees clockwise to see what this looks like. ↗)

There are other ways to establish a contextual reference frame that does the same thing. **Figure 5.13C** shows these same figures inside of rectangular frames tilted 45 degrees. If you cover the frames, the left figure looks like a diamond, the right one like a square. When you uncover them, the left one changes into a square, the right one into a diamond.

Spatial and temporal integration. Reference frames are just one example of the visual system's tendency to organize individual parts in relation to larger spatial contexts. In fact, even the whole visual field at any moment is seldom perceived as ending at the edges of our vision. Instead we perceive it as a restricted glimpse of a larger visual world extending in all directions to unseen areas of the environment.

You must be able to integrate your perceptions from these restricted glimpses of the world from one moment to the next. As you fixate on different parts of the same figure, what you see in your present fixation is somehow properly integrated with what you saw in the last one, which was properly integrated with the one before that, and so on. If this were not true, you would not perceive the same objects in successive views, but a hodge-podge of unrelated and overlapping shapes. It is quite possible that Richard X. had some problem integrating different fixations over time and that this was partially responsible for his disjointed perception.

The process of putting together visual information from one fixation to the next in both space and time is absolutely critical for useful perception. The world around you is so much larger than a single field of view that you could never know about the spatial layout of your surroundings without organizational processes that integrate the visual information from many eye fixations into a single continuing episode of related images (Hochberg, 1968).

Complex objects often require several eye fixations before you can build up a complete spatial interpretation even when they are small enough to fit into a single field of view. One interesting consequence of how you put together the information from different fixations is that you are able to perceive "impossible" objects. The triangle shown in **Figure 5.14** is such an object. Each fixation of corners and sides provides an interpretation that is con-

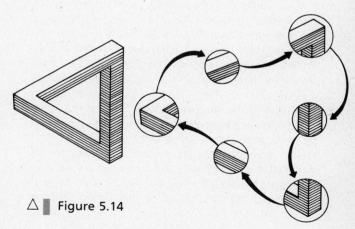

△ **Figure 5.14**

sistent with an object that seems to be a three-dimensional triangle. But when you try to integrate them into a coherent whole, the pieces just don't fit together properly.

Motion perception. Although most of the visible environment is usually stationary, certain kinds of objects are not. The ones that move tend to be particularly important, since they are likely to be potential predators, prey, enemies, mates, or dangerous objects. Perceiving an object that is in different places in successive scenes as being a single object in motion is therefore critical for survival.

It is tempting to think that all of our motion perception can be accounted for by "motion-detector" cells in our brains, as described in the last chapter. Unfortunately, motion perception is a far more complicated affair, requiring higher levels of perceptual organization in the brain to integrate and interpret the responses of different retinal cells over time. A few examples will show why.

If you sit in a darkened room and fixate on a stationary spot of light inside a lighted rectangle that is moving very slowly back and forth **(Figure 5.15A)**, you will perceive instead a *moving* dot going back and forth within a *stationary* rectangle. This illusion, called **induced motion,** occurs even when your eyes are quite still and fixated on the dot. In this case, your motion-detector cells would not be firing at all in response to the stationary dot but presumably *would* be firing in response to the moving lines of the rectangle. To see the *dot* as moving instead requires some higher level of perceptual organization in which the dot and its supposed motion are perceived within the *reference frame* provided by the rectangle.

There seems to be a strong tendency for the visual system to take a larger, surrounding figure as the reference frame for a smaller figure inside it. You have probably experienced induced motion many times without knowing it. The moon (which is nearly stationary) frequently looks as if it is moving through a cloud when, in fact, it is the cloud that is moving past the moon **(Figure 5.15B)**. The surrounding cloud *induces* perceived movement in the moon just as the rectangle does in the dot.

It is even possible for you to see motion in the visual field when actually it is *you* who are moving. Have you ever been in a train that started up very slowly, and seen the pillars on the station platform

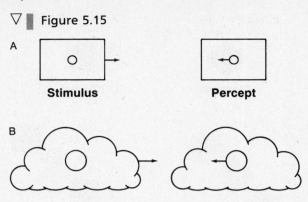

▽ ▌ **Figure 5.15**

A

Stimulus   Percept

B

or a stationary train next to you as moving backward instead?

Another movement illusion that demonstrates the existence of some higher-level organizing processes for motion perception is called *apparent motion* or the **phi phenomenon.** The simplest form of apparent motion occurs when two stationary spots of light in different positions in the visual field are turned on and off alternately at a rate of about 4 to 5 times per second. Even at this slow rate of alternation, it appears that a single light is moving back and forth between the two spots. This perception of motion occurs whether you fixate on one part of the field or allow your eyes to move back and forth with the apparently moving light. When you move your eyes back and forth, both spots of light stimulate the same retinal location, the fovea, so that there is no displacement on the retina for motion-detector cells to respond to (Rock & Ebenholtz, 1962). This perception of apparent motion must take place at some higher level, then, after information about eye movements has been integrated with information about positions of the stimuli.

Apparent motion is somewhat like stroboscopic motion, discussed in the last chapter, in which successive still pictures are perceived as objects in motion. The primary differences between the two are that apparent motion can take place over larger distances and longer time intervals than stroboscopic motion. It is also suspected that the neural mechanism for them are different, apparent motion occurring at a higher, more central level of the visual nervous system than stoboscopic motion.

Cross-modal integration. You do not perceive the world just by vision, of course. Think of all the different ways that you can experience the presence of friends without even seeing them at all: you can hear their voices or the familiar sound of their footsteps, you can smell the fragrance of a favorite scent, or you can touch their faces or bodies. Because the different senses are all informing you about the same objects and events in the world, there must be some final level of perceptual organization that brings together sensations from the different modalities. This cross-modal process, then, integrates them into a unified percept of the same object or event in a single environment—as, in fact, you experience it.

Cross-modal integration is particularly important when different sensory modalities get information about the *same properties* of the same objects. Take, for example, the information you get about the location of some object, say your roommate. You can usually hear and see his or her location; sometimes you can smell him or her too—for better or for worse. In fact, you usually get all these inputs simultaneously, so it is important to be able to put them together if your experience of the world is to be unified and consistent.

One way that psychologists study cross-modal perception is by creating conditions in which the information coming from two sensory sources *conflicts* in some way. When this occurs, one of two things can happen: either the discrepancy is perceived or it isn't. If it is, then this is good evidence that integration has been attempted but has failed. For instance, when the timing between a movie and its sound track is even slightly off, you perceive that it's not "in synch" almost immediately. Similarly, it is generally surprising to you when the sound of a distant event arrives later than its visual counterpart, as happens in a large baseball stadium when you *see* the batter hit the ball before you *hear* the sound of bat meeting ball. Both examples illustrate how sensitive you are to timing discrepancies between corresponding sights and sounds.

But in other cases you may be totally unaware of even large discrepancies between the inputs from two or more different sense modalities. This happens when one sense *dominates* the others so completely that you perceive only what is consistent with *its* in-put. In most cases that have been studied, it is vision that dominates the other senses, a phenomenon called **visual capture.** For instance, visual perception of location dominates auditory perception of location. A good ventriloquist can make the sound of his or her voice seem to come from the dummy because the dummy's mouth moves synchronously with the vocal sounds while the ventriloquist's does not.

Another example of visual capture is at work when you attend a drive-in movie. The sounds of the soundtrack come from a single loudspeaker hooked to the window of your car, rather than from the screen several hundred feet in front of you where you see the events happening. Even so, you perceive the sounds as coming from the mouth of the person who is speaking, the window that is shattering, or the door that is being slammed in the picture, not from the side speaker.

All the organizational processes we have discussed so far are required to explain how humans can see a unified world from the successive, partial, and unorganized patterns of stimulation that affect our sensory organs. Unlike Richard X., we are able to synthesize the many bits of sensory information we receive in such a way as to make sense of them. We know our brain does it very well, but we haven't yet learned how it does it.

Depth perception

All the examples discussed thus far have been two-dimensional patterns on flat surfaces. Everyday perceiving, however, involves objects in three-dimensional space. Perceiving all three spatial dimensions is absolutely vital if we are to be able to approach things we want, such as food and people we like, and avoid dangerous ones, like speeding cars. This requires having accurate information about depth (the distance from you to an object) as well as about its direction from you. Your ears can be used to help in determining the *direction* to an object, but they are not much help with *depth*.

Seeing how far away an object is may not seem to be much of a problem at first, but have you ever tried to figure out how the visual system might do it? The difficulty is that it has to be done using retinal images that have only two spatial dimensions—vertical and horizontal. There is no third dimension for depth.

To illustrate the problem of having a 2-D retina doing a 3-D job, consider the situation shown in **Figure 5.16**. When a spot of light stimulates the retina at the point labeled a, how do you know whether it came from position a_1 or a_2 in the environment? In fact, it could have come from *anywhere* along the line labeled A, because light from any point on that line projects onto the same retinal cell. Similarly, all points on line B project onto the single retinal point labeled b. To make matters worse, a straight line connecting any point on line A to any point on line B ($a_1 - b_2$ or $a_2 - b_1$, for example) would produce the same image on the retina. The net result of all these possibilities is that the image on your retina is ambiguous in depth: the same retinal image could have been produced by objects at many distances from you. For this reason, the same retinal image can be given many different perceptual interpretations.

The ambiguity of the Necker cube (Figure 5.4B) results from this ambiguity in depth. Another interesting example is shown in **Figure 5.17**. The "Ames chair" looks like a normal, solid chair when it is viewed with one eye from the one particular position at which all of its parts project onto the appropriate retinal locations. From other viewing positions, however, the "solid chair" is seen to be an illusion: it is just a suspended collection of disconnected sticks.

Fortunately, this illusion occurs only under these very unusual viewing conditions. Normally you would have both eyes open and would move your head while viewing it, giving you more than enough information to see the "chair" accurately as a mere collection of sticks at odd angles in depth. Still, the fact that you can be fooled under certain circumstances shows that depth perception requires an *interpreta-*

▷ **Figure 5.17**
The Ames Chair

tion of sensory input, and that this interpretation can be wrong. Your interpretation relies on many different information sources about distance (often called *depth cues*) some of which we will now examine more closely.

Binocular cues. Have you ever wondered why you have *two* eyes instead of just one? The second eye is more than just a spare; it provides some of the best, most compelling information about depth. Two sources of depth information that are *binocular* (from *bi* meaning "two" and *ocular* meaning "of the eyes") are *binocular disparity* and *convergence*.

Because the eyes are about two to three inches apart horizontally, they receive slightly different views of the world. To convince yourself of this, try the following experiment. First, close your left eye and use the right one to line up your two index fingers with some small object in the distance with one finger at arm's length, the other about a foot in front of your face. Now, keep your fingers stationary, close your right eye, and open the left one while continuing to fixate on the distant object. What happened to the position of your two fingers? The second eye does not see them lined up with the distant object, but off to the side, because it gets a slightly different view.

This displacement between the horizontal positions of corresponding images in your two eyes is called **binocular disparity**. It provides depth information because the *amount* of disparity depends on the relative distance of the objects from you. For in-

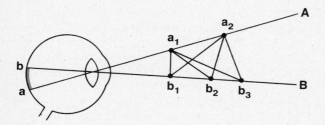

△ **Figure 5.16**
Depth Ambiguity

bit for the same image to fall on both foveas. You can actually see the eyes converge if you watch a friend focus first on a distant object and then on one a foot or so away.

Convergence information sent back to the brain from the eye muscles is useful for depth perception only up to about 10 feet, however. At greater distances the angular differences are too small to detect because the eyes are nearly parallel when you fixate on a distant object.

Motion cues. Fortunately not all information about depth depends on having two eyes. To convince yourself of this, close or cover one eye and look around. Although the world may not seem quite so compellingly three-dimensional as it did when you looked with both eyes, you still see a three-dimensional world. In fact, many people with just one eye get along very well indeed using only monocular (one-eyed) sources of depth information. Motion is among the best of these.

stance, when you switched eyes, the closer finger was displaced farther to the side than was the distant finger.

When you look at the world with both eyes open, most objects that you see are stimulating different positions on your two retinas, but you are not aware of this. The one you directly focus on projects onto the two foveas. Any others that happen to be at that same distance from you will also project onto corresponding retinal positions in the two eyes, but everything else will actually produce images at different places on the two retinas—because of binocular disparity. If the disparity between corresponding images in the two retinas is small enough, the visual system is able to "fuse" them into a perception of a single object *in depth*. However, if the images are too far apart, as when you "cross" your eyes, you actually see the double images.

When you stop to think about it, what your visual system does is pretty amazing: it takes two different retinal images, compares them for horizontal displacement of corresponding parts (binocular disparity), and produces a unitary perception of a single object in depth as a result. In effect, it *interprets* horizontal displacement between the two images as depth in the three-dimensional world.

Other binocular information about depth comes from **convergence**. The two eyes converge—turn inward—to some extent whenever they are fixated on an object (see **Figure 5.18**). When the object is very close—a finger a few inches in front of your face—the eyes must turn toward each other quite a

▽ **Figure 5.18**

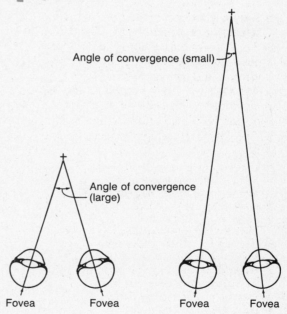

Angle of convergence (small)

Angle of convergence (large)

Fovea   Fovea   Fovea   Fovea

Motion Gradients

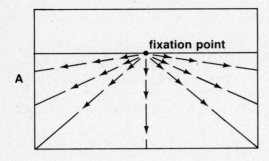

fixation point

A

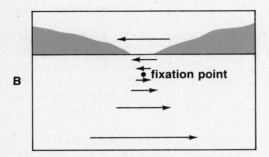

B

fixation point

△ **Figure 5.19**
Motion Gradients

When you are moving in a stationary environment, the speed and direction of motion of points in your retinal image depends on their distance in depth relative to the fixated point (which does not move). Direction of motion of these points is indicated by the direction of the arrows, and speed is indicated by the length of the arrows. Part A shows the motion gradient (or "optical flow") of the image as you look at the point toward which you are moving (like looking out the front window of your car as you drive toward the fixation point). Part B shows it as you look at right angles to the direction of motion (like looking out the side window). (From Gibson, 1950.)

To see how motion produces depth information, try the following demonstration. Close one eye, line up your two index fingers with some distant object as you did before, and then move your head to the side while fixating on the distant object and keeping your fingers still. As you move your head, you see both your fingers move, but the close finger moves farther and faster than the more distant one. The fixated object does not move at all. This source of information about depth is called **relative motion parallax.**

Motion parallax provides information about depth because, as you move, the relative distances of objects in the world determine the amount and direction of their relative motion in your retinal image of the scene. This relationship is illustrated in **Figure 5.19A** for motion along the line of sight toward the fixated object (as you look at the distant point toward which you are driving) and in **Figure 5.19B** for motion perpendicular to the line of sight (as you look out the side window).

Gibson's theory of Ecological Optics emphasized the importance of the overall pattern of motion parallax over the whole visual field. He called this information *motion perspective.* It is defined by *gradients* of motion parallax—systematic changes in motion parallax over extended portions of the visual field. They are represented in Figure 5.19 by the pattern of arrows indicating direction and speed of motion of various parts of the visual field.

You may have noticed that the way we demonstrated relative motion parallax with two fingers was very similar to the way we demonstrated binocular disparity. This is not accidental. Relative motion parallax and binocular disparity are very closely related sources of depth information. Both concern *differences* between spatially separated views of the same scene. However, relative motion parallax results from *many* slightly different spatial views of the world that occur *over time* (as the head is moved) and can occur even with one eye closed, whereas binocular disparity results from *two* slightly different views that occur *simultaneously* (one from each eye). For distant objects, motion parallax is the more powerful source of information about depth because we can move our heads over much greater distances than the two or three inches that separate our two eyes. For relatively close viewing, however, binocular disparity produces a far more compelling perception of depth.

▽▌ Figure 5.20

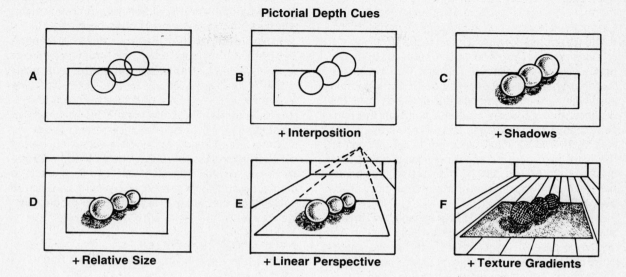

Pictorial Depth Cues

A

B   **+ Interposition**

C   **+ Shadows**

D   **+ Relative Size**

E   **+ Linear Perspective**

F   **+ Texture Gradients**

Pictorial cues. Further sources of information about depth are available even with just one eye and no motion of the head. These are called *pictorial* cues because they include the kinds of depth information found in pictures.

Some of the most important sources of pictorial information are present in **Figure 5.20**, which shows successive stages of adding depth cues to the drawing of three golf balls lying in the corner of a room on a rug. The first sketch is a simple outline drawing such as a young child might produce (Figure 5.20A). It looks like a two-dimensional pattern consisting of three circles intersecting each other and a rectangle, with a line above them. So far, there is no perception of depth.

The first depth cue added is *interposition* or *occlusion*. It arises when an opaque object blocks the light coming toward your eye from an object behind it so that only the front one is fully present in your retinal image. This gives you depth information because the occluded objects must be further away than the occluding one. In our picture, we begin to add pictorial depth by occluding the back edge of the rug behind all three balls and parts of the two farther balls behind the closer ones (Figure 5.20B). This results in the perception of three opaque, round objects, one be-

hind another, on a rectangular surface. Some limited impression of depth is already apparent. Also notice that you still "see" three *round* objects, even though the stimulus energy does not provide complete information for the roundness of the second and third ones. Your visual system "completes" these shapes behind the occluding objects, much as it completed the black disks behind the illusory triangle (Figure 5.8).

The fact that opaque surfaces block light produces additional depth information from *shadows*. Shadows provide important information about the three dimensional shape of objects and about the position of the light source (Figure 5.20C). In the present case, shadows make the three round objects really look like spheres for the first time and indicate that the light source is behind and to the right of them.

Three additional sources of pictorial information are all related to how light projects from a three-dimensional world onto a two-dimensional surface like the retina. A basic rule of light projection is that *objects of the same size that are at different distances project images of different sizes on the retina;* the closest one projects the largest image and the farthest one, the smallest image. This is called the *size/distance relation*.

The size/distance relation makes *relative size* a cue for depth perception. In our present example, making the closest ball (the one that occludes the others) the largest and the farthest one the smallest adds the appropriate relative size information to the picture and increases your impression of depth in this two-dimensional drawing (Figure 5.20D).

Linear perspective, too, is a depth cue that depends on the size/distance relation. It refers to the fact that when parallel lines (by definition separated everywhere by the same distance) recede into the distance, they converge toward a point on the horizon in your retinal image. This very important fact was discovered by Renaissance artists, who began to use it to paint depth compellingly for the first time around 1400 (Vasari, 1967). Prior to that time artists had used only information from interposition, shadows, and relative size.

In our present picture, linear perspective means that the side edges of the rug and floor, which are actually parallel to each other in the environment, must be shown as converging toward a point in the background. When the picture is drawn in this way, it provides the same linear perspective information as a "real" room and is therefore seen as having the third dimension of depth.

The last kind of pictorial depth cue that we will add to our picture comes from Gibson's *texture gradients,* mentioned earlier (p. 160). They too result from the size/distance relation, but as applied to textures of surfaces rather than to edges. The texture of a rug is actually uniform, but the size/distance relation requires that its texture elements be drawn smaller and smaller in the parts of the rug that are farther and farther away (Figure 5.20F). Similarly, the uniformly sized boards on the floor are drawn to show a texture gradient, and the identical little dimples on the surfaces of the golf balls form texture gradients on the balls. All these cues add significantly to the perceived depth and realism in the picture.

By now it should be clear that there is not just one source of depth information but many. Under normal viewing conditions, however, information from many different sources comes together in a single, coherent three-dimensional interpretation of the environment. *What you experience is depth "out there,"* not the different "cues" to depth that were in the proximal stimulus. In other words, you don't *perceive* double images, differential motion, occlusion, shadows, relative size, or convergence of parallel lines, even though all these things are constantly present in the patterns of light that enter your eyes (unless you are an art student especially sensitive to drawing perspective). Rather, your visual system *uses*

these sources of information "automatically," without your conscious awareness, to give you a perception of depth in the three-dimensional environment, and that is what you consciously experience.

It may even be true that your depth perception processes are at work when you don't consciously experience depth. This idea underlies the usual explanation of the Ponzo illusion (see p. 111). According to it, the upper line looks longer because you unconsciously interpret the converging sides according to linear perspective as parallel lines receding into the distance, like railroad tracks. This means that you unconsciously process the upper line as though it were farther away than the lower one and thus see it as longer because a farther object would have to be longer than the nearer one for both to produce retinal images of the same size.

Perceptual constancies

The goal of perception is to obtain information about the world around us, not about images on our sensory organs. We have already shown a number of ways in which the human visual system meets this goal by going beyond the information it is given directly. Another very important way it does so is by perceiving an unchanging world despite the constant changes that occur in the pattern of stimulation on the retina as the result of different viewing conditions.

Put this book down on the table, then move your head closer to it—just a few inches away—then move your head back to a normal reading distance. Although the book stimulated a much larger part of your retina when it was up close than when it was far away, you saw the book's size as constant.

Now set the book upright and try tilting your head clockwise. When you do this, the image of the book rotates counterclockwise on your retina, but you still perceive the book to be upright: its perceived orientation is *constant*. In general, then, you see the world as *invariant, constant,* and *stable* despite changes in the stimulation of your sensory receptors. This is a very general principle of perception—and a very useful ability to have.

Psychologists refer to this general phenomenon as *perceptual constancy.* Roughly speaking, it means that what you *perceive* is the properties of the *distal* stimuli, which are generally constant, rather than those of *proximal* stimuli, which change every time you move your eyes or head. Constancy generally holds over almost all visible properties, but here we will discuss only three cases in which it has been intensively studied: size, shape, and orientation.

Size and shape constancy. What determines your perception of the size of an object? Part of the answer must be that you perceive its actual size on the basis of the size of its retinal image. However, the demonstration with your book shows that the size of the retinal image depends on both the actual size of the book and its *distance* from the eye. Because of this relation between size and distance (the same one we discussed in the section on depth perception) the perceptual system must determine an object's actual size by *combining* information from the size of its retinal image with other information about how far away the object is located. As you now know, information about distance is available from the depth cues of binocular disparity, eye convergence, motion parallax, and other sources. Your visual system combines them with retinal information about image size to yield a perception of object size that usually corresponds with the actual size of the distal stimulus. **Size constancy** refers to this ability to perceive the true size of an object despite variations in the size of its retinal image.

The theory that size constancy was achieved from retinal size by taking distance into account was first proposed by Hermann von Helmholtz. The perceptual process that does this he called *unconscious inference.* It is a process of "inference" because the visual system must *figure out* (or "infer") the size of an object "out there" by combining several different kinds of information, sometimes including prior knowledge. It is "unconscious" because the observer is not *aware* of knowing the size/distance relation or of using it to perceive objective size. Unconscious inferences about the true sizes of objects seem to be made rapidly, automatically, and without conscious effort of any sort—a major achievement in our perceptual processing of information.

If the size of an object is perceived by taking distance cues into account, then we should be fooled about size whenever we are fooled about distance. One such illusion occurs in the "Ames room" shown in **Figure 5.21A.** Your six-foot-tall author looks like

▽ ▮ **Figure 5.21**

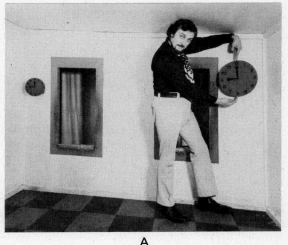

A

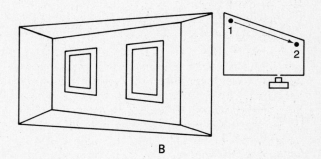

B

a midget in the left corner of this room but like a giant in the right corner. The reason for this illusion is that you perceive the room to be rectangular, with the two back corners equally distant from you. Thus you perceive my actual size as being consistent with the size of the images on your retina in both cases. The bigger image corresponds to a bigger person. In fact, however, I am *not* at the same distance because the Ames room, like the Ames chair, creates a clever illusion. It *looks* like a rectangular room, but it is actually made from nonrectangular surfaces at odd angles in depth and height (see **Figure 5.21B**). Any person on the right will make a larger retinal image because he or she is closer. But this larger image will be perceived as that of a larger person because the room—the reference frame—is seen as "normal" and the sizes of things inside are perceived relative to it.

Another way that the perceptual system can infer objective size is by using *prior knowledge* about the characteristic size of similarly shaped objects. For instance, once you recognize the shape of an object as that of a house, or a tree, or a dog you have a pretty good idea of how big it is, even without knowing its distance. Most of the time your perception would be correct. But, as movie directors are well aware, you can be fooled by miniature scenery constructed to scale, which can give you a perception of normally sized real objects. Children are similarly fooled by puppets and are delighted when the puppeteer suddenly pokes his or her head into the scene, looking like a giant.

When information about perceived distance and prior knowledge of sizes are in conflict, the distance information is more powerful, as was demonstrated by your perception of Figure 5.21. Even though you know that a man's size does not change as he walks across a room, you *still* see the same person as being vastly different in size in the two corners despite your knowledge that the room is not rectangular. The depth information that makes the room look rectangular simply overpowers your knowledge. This is a case in which what you perceive wins over what you know. In the final section of this chapter, we will see when the reverse holds true.

Sometimes shape information is not sufficient to produce accurate perception of size, especially when past experience does not give you a knowledge of what familiar objects look like at extreme distances. This happened to a Pygmy named Kenge who had lived all his life in dense tropical forests using sound cues rather than visual ones to guide his hunting. Kenge had occasion, one day, to travel across an open plain for the first time with an anthropologist named Colin Turnbull, who described Kenge's reactions as follows.

"Kenge looked over the plains and down to where a herd of about a hundred buffalo were grazing some miles away. He asked me what kind of *insects* they were, and I told him they were buffalo, twice as big as the forest buffalo known to him. He laughed loudly and told me not to tell such stupid stories, and asked me again what kind of insects they were. He then talked to himself, for want of more intelligent company, and tried to liken the buffalo to the various beetles and ants with which he was familiar.

"He was still doing this when we got into the car and drove down to where the animals were grazing. He watched them getting larger and larger, and though he was as courageous as any Pygmy, he moved over and sat close to me and muttered that it was witchcraft. . . . Finally, when he realized that they were real buffalo he was no longer afraid, but what puzzled him still was why they had been so small, and whether they *really* had been small and had so suddenly grown larger, or whether it had been some kind of trickery." (Turnbull, 1961, p. 305)

In this unfamiliar perceptual environment, Kenge first tried to fit his novel perceptions into a familiar context, by assuming the tiny, distant specks he saw were insects. With no previous experience of seeing buffalo at a distance, he had no basis for size constancy, and as the fast-moving car approached them and Kenge's retinal images got larger and larger, he had the frightening illusion of the animals as chang-

▽ ▌ **Figure 5.22**

ing in size. We can assume that with further experience he would have come to see them as Turnbull did.

Shape constancy is closely related to size constancy. You perceive an object's actual shape correctly even when it is slanted away from you, making the shape of the retinal image substantially different from that of the object itself. For instance, a circle tipped away from you projects an elliptical image onto your retina; a rectangle tipped away projects a trapezoidal image (**Figure 5.22**). Yet you usually perceive them accurately as a circle and a rectangle slanted away in space. When there is good depth information available from binocular disparity, motion parallax, or even pictorial cues, your visual system can determine an object's true shape simply by taking your distance from its different parts into account.

Orientation constancy. When you tilted your head to the side in viewing your book, the world did not seem to tilt, but only your own head. This perception was due to **orientation constancy**: the ability to perceive the actual orientation of objects in the world despite their orientation in your retinal image. This form of constancy, too, results from a process of unconscious inference. Information about the orientation of the object in the environment is inferred from the orientation of its retinal image by taking head tilt into account, which you know about largely through the *vestibular system* in your inner ear (as discussed in Chapter 4). By using its output together with retinal orientation, your visual system is usually able to give you a perception of the correct orientation of the object in the environment.

Actually, there are significant individual differences among people in reconciling these contradictory data: some rely more heavily on this internal vestibular information, others more heavily on visual information from the external environment (see Close-up on p. 176).

In familiar environments, prior knowledge provides additional information about objective orientation. You know from experience that certain things are horizontal (the surface of a body of water, the floor of a room), and others vertical (trees, walls, hanging objects). Once you recognize them from their shape, you know their probable orientation with respect to gravity. There is no guarantee that they are actually oriented in this way, however. When they aren't, your perception of orientation may suffer, as it did when you assumed that the floor of the Ames room was horizontal.

Perceptual constancy holds for many visual properties over a wide range of stimulus conditions. Under extreme conditions, however, it nearly always breaks down. For example, when you look at people from the top of a skyscraper, they look like ants even though you *know* what their sizes still are in reality.

The perception of constancy in the environment is one of our most important abilities. It is information about the *world* (the *distal* stimulus) that we must have for survival, not information about the retinal images (the *proximal* stimulus). It is critical that we perceive *constant* and *stable* properties of continuing objects in the world despite the enormous variations in the properties of the light patterns that stimulate our eyes. Without constancy, our eyes really wouldn't do us much good because we wouldn't be seeing *the world "out there,"* but only the images on the backs of our eyes. It might be said that the task of perception is to discover *invariant* properties of our environment despite the variations in our retinal impressions of them.

Field Dependence in Perception and Personality

Are you the sort of person who has a strong interpersonal orientation and is emotionally open, or do you prefer nonsocial situations in which you can keep your emotions pretty much to yourself? Strange as it may sound, psychologists have found that your answer to this kind of question could probably be predicted from your performance on *perceptual* tests related to orientation perception. A personality dimension called *field dependence* has been proposed which is thought to reflect a person's preference for depending on external versus internal sources of information in *both* perceptual and social situations (Witkin & Goodenough, 1977).

The primary test for field dependence in perception is judging when lines are vertical (aligned with gravity) in situations in which there is conflicting visual information. In one version, called the *rod-and-frame* test, subjects are shown a tilted rod inside a tilted frame with no other visual information. They are asked to adjust the tilt of the rod so that it is upright with respect to gravity (A). Some people are able to do this quite accurately despite the tilt of the frame (B). They are called "field independent" because they seem to rely almost exclusively on *internal* bodily information from their vestibular and kinesthetic systems to define "vertical" (see Chapter 4) and are able to ignore contradictory information from the visually tilted frame. Other

people, however, adjust the rod so that it is strongly tilted toward the orientation of the frame (C). They are called "field dependent" because they seem to *depend* more upon the *external* field information provided by the frame and less on internal information.

A number of studies have investigated the relation between "field dependence" in perceptual and social situations.

In one such study, subjects were asked by an interviewer to talk about a topic that interested them. In one condition, the interviewer kept silent during the subject's response; in the other, the same interviewer gave feedback ("umm hmm" or "yeah") during the response. Field-dependent subjects produced less verbal output in the silent condition than in the feedback condition, whereas field-independent subjects were not much affected by the interviewer's reactions. Later, in filling out a questionnaire, field-dependent subjects in the silent condition more often agreed with the statement, "I think I might have done a little better if the interviewer had told me at times just how I was doing," whereas field-independent subjects tended to agree with the statement, "I don't think it made much difference one way or the other that the interviewer didn't tell me how I was doing during the interview" (Gates, 1971).

CLASSIFICATION PROCESSES

You can think of all the perceptual processes described thus far as providing reasonably accurate knowledge about physical properties of the distal stimulus—the position, size, shape, texture, and color of three-dimensional objects in a three-dimensional environment. With just this knowledge and some basic motor skills, you would be able to walk around without bumping into objects, manipulate things that are small and light enough to move, and make accurate models of the objects that you perceive. But you would not know how the objects are used or how they relate to each other—or to you. It would be like visiting an alien planet where all the objects were new to you; you would not know

which ones to eat, which ones were dangerous, or which ones you would need to do all the things you do every day.

To get this information about the objects you perceive, you need to be able to *classify* them—that is, to identify or recognize them as members of meaningful categories that you know about from experience. Classification results in knowing that things are members of categories like dogs, chairs, books, people, and houses.

"Bottom-up" and "top-down" processes

Classifying objects implies matching what you see against your stored knowledge. The processes of bringing in and organizing information from the en-

**A Initial Position
of Rod and Frame test**

**B Field Independent
Person's Response**

**Field Dependent
Person's Response**

An interesting extension of this result to therapist-patient interactions is a finding based on analysis of therapy sessions transcripts. Therapists ask more specific questions and give more support in sessions with their field-dependent patients than in sessions with their field-independent patients (Witkin et al., 1977).

From many such studies, it has been concluded that people shown to be field-dependent in a perceptual test tend: (a) to make greater use of social feedback in ambiguous situations, (b) to be more attentive to social cues, (c) to be more interested in other people, (d) to be emotionally open, (e) to like social situations, and (f) to choose careers in welfare, humanitarian, and helping professions. *Field independent* people tend: (a) not to rely much on social feedback, (b) to be generally less sensitive to social cues, (c) to be more impersonal, (d) to keep their emotions to themselves, (e) to be less gregarious, and (f) to choose careers in mathematical, scientific, and analytic professions (Witkin & Goodenough, 1977).

The correspondence between people's social preferences and their behavior on the rod-and-frame test suggests that we each have our own unique "cognitive style" that determines how we seek, acquire, and evaluate information about all aspects of our environment, both physical and social (G. Klein, 1970).

vironment are often called *data-driven* or "bottom-up" processes because they are guided by the sensory information. Sensations of visual features and perceptions of organized objects are largely the result of "bottom-up" processes.

But even in these stages of perceiving there is some influence from higher centers in the brain. What you notice from the huge array of stimuli bombarding your senses is determined partly by what you need or want at that moment. And the *way* you organize the sensory data, especially ambiguous data, often shows the influence of your past experience. Processes that originate in the brain and influence the selection, organization, or interpretation of sensory data are called *hypothesis-driven* or "top-down" processes.

For a dramatic example of "top-down" processes at work, look at the two upside-down pictures of

British Prime Minister Margaret Thatcher in **Figure 5.23** before reading further. You can probably tell that one of them has been altered slightly around the eyes and mouth, but the two pictures look pretty much alike. Now turn the book upside down and look again. The same pictures look extraordinarily different now. One is still Margaret Thatcher, but the other is a ghoulish monster! Why did you not see that obvious difference before turning the book upside down?

Through the vast experience you have had in socially important tasks like identifying people and interpreting their emotional expressions, you have become enormously sensitive to subtle differences in the shapes and positions of eyes and mouths—but only when they are in or near their characteristic upright orientation. In this example, you see the very

△ ▌ Figure 5.23

same stimulus pattern as familiar or relatively unfamiliar just by changing its orientation. This demonstrates how greatly your experience with a kind of object can affect the way you perceive and classify it. (If you want to find out the exact orientation at which your experience with upright faces begins to affect your perception, rotate the face slowly from upside-down until you see it take on its grotesque expression.)

Classification—the third stage of perceiving—is a process in which memory, conceptual analysis, expectation, motivation, personality characteristics, and social experience are all brought to bear in comprehending what is being perceived. To *perception* it adds *conception*—mental activity. To *fact* it adds *meaning*. It is classification that gives our experiences continuity over time and across situations. In this section we will examine two theories of how we learn to recognize a pattern as something we know and then will look at examples of how expectations and personal motivation affect this stage of perceiving.

Pattern recognition

When you look around, you see familiar objects such as chairs, people, books, telephones, and houses. But how did you form these categories and how do you *recognize* or *identify* a pattern of visible stimulus properties as belonging to a particular category?

To make clearer the problems you must solve in making such an identification, we will consider a simpler example. How do you recognize a simple two-dimensional pattern like the capital letter *A?* This may seem like an easy task until you realize that there are lots of other shapes of *A*s that you would need to put into the same category (see **Figure 5.24**). Even this doesn't seem too hard until you realize that the same pattern-recognition process must also *exclude* all non-*A*s. These are the two horns of the pattern-recognition dilemma: all the category members must be included by the same rule that excludes all the nonmembers. Two different approaches to solving this problem are recognition by *critical features* and recognition by *prototypes*.

Critical features theories. The critical features approach to object classification suggests that every perceptual category is defined by a list of **critical features**—perceivable attributes that are necessary and sufficient conditions for membership in the category. Here the classification rule is that an object is a member of the category if, and only if, it has every feature on the list.

Two kinds of features are possible in such a list: *local parts* and *global properties*. For patterns like letters, "local parts" are things like the presence of component lines of various lengths and orientations, intersections between lines, and angles of various sizes. "Global properties" are attributes of the figure as a whole, such as symmetry, closedness, and connectedness.

Using features like these, we might try to define the category of "capital *A*s" by the list of critical features shown at the top of **Figure 5.25**. It seems like a pretty good definition until you try to use it to dis-

△ ▌ Figure 5.24

▽ ▌ **Figure 5.25**

1 horizontal line
2 diagonal lines
3 acute angles
2 obtuse angles
vertically symmetric
closed

2 horizontal lines
1 vertical line
1 diagonal line
3 right angles
1 acute angle
2 obtuse angles
asymmetric
closed
(yet clearly an A)

1 horizontal line
2 diagonal lines
3 acute angles
2 obtuse angles
vertically symmetric
closed
(yet clearly *not* an A)

criminate between unusual *A*s and certain kinds of non-*A*s. The lower sections show examples of both kinds of error: a real *A* that is excluded because its features do *not* match the list of critical features and a non-*A* that is included because its features do match. This is an unsolved problem with the critical features approach: in principle, it sounds as if it should work, but in practice, it is almost impossible to find a list of features that really does include all the "right" cases and exclude all the "wrong" ones.

Prototype theories. There is another problem with the critical features approach that suggests a different way of thinking about perceptual categories and classification. Look again at the capital *A*s shown in Figure 5.24. With identification by critical features, all of these examples should be *equally good A*s since they (presumably) all have the necessary and sufficient features needed for membership, whatever those may be. But that doesn't fit with most people's perceptions of these figures: some of them are *representative* examples of *A*s, others are odd in varying degrees, and a few are truly bizarre. How can some be better than others if they all have all the critical features?

What this argument suggests is that categories are structured around an *ideal* or *most representative instance*. This most representative example of a category is called the **prototype** (Rosch, 1973). It need not even be a real object, since there may be no actual capital *A* that is just like it, and, similarly, no actual dog that is just like your notion of the prototypical dog—the "doggiest" possible dog.

According to the prototype approach, an object is classified as a member of a category if it is *more similar* to the prototype of that category than it is to the prototype of any other category. From this point of view, capital *A*s are all patterns that are perceived to be more similar to the prototypical *A* than to the prototypical *B, C, D,* or whatever. Dogs are just those objects that look more like the prototypical dog than like the prototypical cat, bird, fish, or whatever.

But the prototype theory runs into problems too. The biggest one is illustrated by the fact that the third figure in Figure 5.25 looks more like an *A* than like any other letter, but it still is not an *A!* Some combination of these two theoretical approaches seems to be required, but the right one has yet to be found. What they agree on is that somehow we recognize objects by matching the perceptual information against stored knowledge. (We will find the same two approaches—and the same dilemmas—in Chapter 10, when we look at how our concepts and categories are formed in the first place.)

The influence of contexts and expectations

Have you ever had the experience of seeing someone you knew in a place where you didn't expect to see him or her, such as in the wrong city or the wrong social group? It takes much longer to recognize someone in such a situation, and sometimes you aren't even sure that it really *is* the person you know. The problem is not that he or she *looks* any different, but that the *context* is wrong: you didn't *expect* that person to be there then. The spatial and temporal context for recognizing an object provides an important source of information for classifying objects because once you have identified the context you have expectations about what other objects you are—and are not—likely to see nearby.

▽ **Figure 5.26**

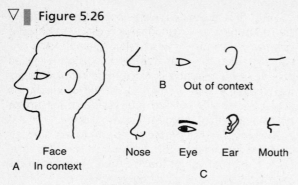

B   Out of context

Face   Nose   Eye   Ear   Mouth
A   In context
                            C

(From Explorations in Cognition by Donald A. Norman and David E. Rumelhart. Copyright © 1975 by W. H. Freeman and Company. Reprinted by permission.)

To illustrate how powerfully context can affect classification, consider the face shown in **Figure 5.26**. When the separate features are all shown together in the context of a head, each feature can be drawn very simply with minimal detail and still be recognized: the nose can be just a curve, the mouth no more than a line at the proper place. Out of this context, however, these same lines cease to be recognizable; substantially more accurate detail is needed before you would recognize what they are. With a stronger or more familiar context, you need less information to recognize an object within it (Palmer, 1975a).

Examples like these demonstrate that perceptual classification depends on your expectations as well as on the physical properties of the objects you see. These expectations are affected by both the spatial and the temporal contexts in which the perception takes place. They demonstrate an important principle: *object classification is a constructive, interpretive process.* Classification can arrive at different results depending on what you already know, where you are, and what else you see around you. Expectations from context are an important element in "top-down" processing.

Context is sometimes so powerful that the same object is classified in different ways when it appears in different contexts. Read the words below.

THE CAT

They say "THE CAT," right? Now look again at the middle letter of each word. Physically, they are ex-

actly the same; yet you perceived the first as an "H" and the second as an "A." Why? Clearly your perception was affected by what you know about words in English. The context provided by "T E" makes an "H" highly likely (and an "A" unlikely), whereas the reverse is true of the context of "C T" (Selfridge, 1955).

To explain contextual effects like these, it has been suggested that classification of perceptual data must depend on complex information structures in memory. Instead of storing information in memory in isolated bits, we organize our knowledge of the world into integrated packages, clusters of information that are called **schemas**. These are made up of information from different sources, organized around various topics, themes, and types. We have schemas about dating, college lectures, restaurants, good friends, and much more. Schemas may organize information according to objects, activities, people, or ideas that usually are found together or share some basic features.

Schemas not only are a source of factual knowledge in relevant situations but give us expectations. Once formed, they exert powerful influences on the way we classify the context and *predict* what objects are *likely* to be present in that context. We then use both these expectations and the sensory and perceptual information in classifying the objects in the visual field. All this happens very quickly, automatically, and unconsciously. We will have a more detailed look in later chapters at the influence of schemas in remembering and thinking.

Another aspect of this influence of context and expectation on your perception (and response) is called *set.* **Set** is a temporary readiness to perceive or react to a stimulus in a particular way. There are three types of set: perceptual, motor, and mental.

A *perceptual set* is a readiness to detect a particular stimulus. A new mother is perceptually set to hear the cries of her child. Often a perceptual set leads you to see an ambiguous stimulus as the one you are expecting, as in the case of your perception of THE CAT.

A *motor set* is readiness to make a quick, prepared response. A contestant in a 100-yard dash event is set to "come out of the blocks" as fast as possible at the sound of the starting gun. A *mental set* is a readiness to deal with a situation such as a problem-solving task or a game in a way determined by rules, instructions, or expectations from preceding cases. Examples of the way mental sets can prevent flexibility in problem-solving will be described in Chapter 10.

The role of personal and social factors

How we perceive and classify something can depend on more than even its physical properties and its context. It can also be affected by what we *want*.

Starting in the late 1940s, the "New Look" school of perception arose and raised the basic question, Where is the *perceiver* in perceptual theory? (Klein & Schlesinger, 1949). This approach attempted to integrate the ideas and methods of perceptual psychologists with conceptions of personality based on psychoanalytic theory and other person-centered approaches. Attempts were directed toward demonstrating that certain *organismic* variables (attributes of the perceiving organism) exerted consistent effects on perception.

One line of research was concerned with the effects of *need* on *thresholds* for perceptual recognition. A basic hypothesis around which this research was organized was that perception includes *psychological defenses* that protect the person from identifying stimuli that are unpleasant or anxiety-provoking. This view suggests a perceptual process called **perceptual defense.** It is similar to the process of *repression,* proposed by Freud, by which mental processes prevent painful perceptions from entering conscious awareness. (See **Close-up** on p. 182.)

Deprivation. Another series of studies showed the effects of motivation induced by hunger or personal and social motives in altering personal judgments and perceptions. For example, one experiment investigated the effects of food and water deprivation on word identification.

Some subjects went without food for 24 hours before the experiment, some for 10 hours, and some ate just beforehand. All subjects then tried to identify briefly flashed words, including words like *lemonade* and *munch,* that were related to their state of deprivation, and matched neutral words, like *serenade* and *hunch.* Both of the deprived groups perceived the need-related words at shorter exposures than did the nondeprived subjects, but there were *no* differences in the responses of the three groups to neutral words (see **Figure 5.27**). Evidently, the deprived subjects' more rapid processing of the food-related words was influenced by their motivational state (Wispé & Drambarean, 1953).

Being hungry is usually a temporary motivational state, but more permanent deprivation seems to affect perception, too.

In a classic experiment, children were asked to adjust the size of a circle of light to make it the same size as U.S. coins—a penny, a nickel, a dime, and a quarter. Children from poor families tended to judge the coins to be *larger* than they actually are, whereas children from wealthy families tended to judge them to be *smaller.* This effect was explained on the grounds that the poor children were much more highly motivated with respect to money than were the richer children (Bruner & Goodman, 1947).

Comparable effects were found when middle-class adults were hypnotized and given the suggestion that they were either "rich" or "poor" (see **Figure 5.28**). In this way, the researchers controlled for prior *experience* with coin sizes while varying only the subjects' *motivational level* (Ashley et al., 1951).

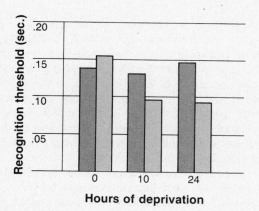

Hours of deprivation

△ **Figure 5.27**
Need-Related Responses

While words unrelated to food were recognized equally fast by all three groups, need-related words were recognized more readily by food-deprived than nondeprived groups. (Adapted from Wispé & Drambarean, 1953.)

Personality. A second line of research coming out of the "New Look" approach to perception studied consistent *differences between individuals* in their perceptual-cognitive organization of the *same situations.* Tests were developed for identifying people

Perceptual Defense

Do you ever look away or shut your eyes at particularly gruesome moments in a violent movie? If so, you are engaging in an overt, conscious form of *perceptual defense:* doing something to avoid perceiving an emotionally aversive event. Psychologists in the "New Look" movement in the 1940s suggested that something similar might happen covertly and unconsciously during perception as a defense against the experience of unpleasant, threatening, or taboo events.

To test the hypothesis of perceptual defense, psychologists performed experiments to see how much time it took for subjects to identify "threatening" words such as "BITCH" and "RAPED," versus emotionally "neutral" words like "HOUSE" and "TREE."

In one well-known study, words from two such lists were presented to subjects very briefly. The presentation time for each word started at .01 seconds and was gradually increased until the word was identified correctly. On the average, threatening words required longer exposures than did neutral ones (McGinnies, 1949).

This seemed to show that the visual system somehow tries to defend us against consciously perceiving emotionally threatening words. But such studies have often been criticized for possible flaws in their design. For example, in this case it was suggested that the differences between the thresholds for reading threatening and neutral words could be explained by differing amounts of use in the language. Threatening words tend to be words that are less often used than the neutral words. It might simply take longer to recognize seldom-used words. Later studies, however, corrected this problem by equating the two groups of words for usage—and generally continued to find evidence of perceptual defense.

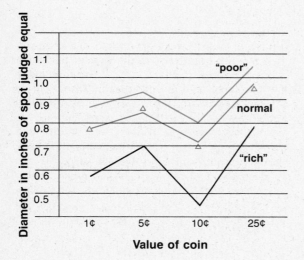

△ Figure 5.28

This figure shows the sizes of white spots judged to be equal in size to the four coins at the start of the experiment in the normal state and under "poor" and "rich" conditions when subjects were hypnotized. Triangles indicate the actual sizes of the coins. (From the American Journal of Psychology, 1951, 64, 564-72 by W. R. Ashley, et al. Reprinted by permission of the University of Illinois Press.)

who were *high* or *low* on a particular personality dimension that was hypothesized to be associated with a distinctive perceptual-conceptual strategy. Then those two types of individuals were given a variety of perceptual or cognitive tasks to see if their approaches were in fact characteristically different. In general, more effects of these personality variables were found on cognitive tasks (for example, memory) than on perceptual ones (see Wolitzky & Wachtel, 1973).

One personality dimension found to influence perception was *field dependence versus field independence,* already described in the Close-up on page 176. Besides the rod-and-frame test, this personality dimension shows up in tasks where subjects are asked to find simple geometric figures that are disguised by being embedded in a larger complex pattern. Field independent people do so easily: their perception tends to be more psychologically differentiated than that of people who are field dependent (Witkin et al., 1962).

Other researchers objected that the "defense" result might merely reflect a *response bias* against publicly *saying* objectionable words. Their argument was that the subjects might have actually identified the threatening words at the same exposure as the neutral ones, but suppressed their responses to the threatening words until they were absolutely sure of what had been presented. This is the same response bias problem that was discussed in the preceding chapter (p. 114). Subjects might use a stricter criterion for responding to the threatening words; as a result, they might seem to have a higher threshold for seeing them.

Studies testing this "response suppression" hypothesis, however, have generally shown that at least some of the difference in response to threatening and neutral words is, in fact, due to perceptual effects rather than to response bias (Broadbent & Gregory, 1967).

The concept of perceptual defense has also been criticized on purely logical grounds (Spence, 1967). How could a perceptual system defend itself against a threatening word unless it had *already identified* the word as threatening? This objection suggests that perceptual defense is inherently contradictory. This would be true if conscious perception were a single process that happens all at once, but as we have seen, it is a complex process that may have many stages prior to conscious experience. It is quite possible that an early unconscious stage may identify the word and its emotional tone. In this case, the identification that occurred in the early stage could indeed be kept from consciousness (Erdelyi, 1974).

Another personality dimension that produces consistent differences in perceptual tasks has been called *leveling versus sharpening.* Given a task with a sequence of gradually changing stimuli, sharpeners see the elements of each stimulus display as independent of what went before, exaggerate some, and tend to perceive them more accurately. Levelers, on the other hand, miss the subtle differences; their perceptions are dominated by the similarities, apparently because their perceptual processing is too much influenced by memory of what has gone before.

People who typically deal with threat by denying its potential significance or who avoid noticing or classifying it as a threat are termed *repressors.* At the opposite end of this continuum are *sensitizers,* who tend to be especially vigilant, perceiving subtle, disguised cues of potential approaching threats. This *repressor-sensitizer* continuum is related to a variety of cognitive-perceptual behaviors (Ericksen, 1966). For example, when shown very sexual pictures, repressors look very little and recall much less than sensitizers (Luborsky et al., 1965). Such differences probably arise from the ways the two groups use attentional processes: the sensitizers have developed a more active scanning and searching attention than the repressors.

Although many interesting findings have emerged from these attempts to "put the person back into perception," there is yet to be a comprehensive theory that integrates the complex network of processes involved in perception, cognition, and personality.

Social influence. One of the first demonstrations of the effects of social influence on perception involved a phenomenon known as the **autokinetic effect.** This effect occurs when a small, stationary light is observed for an extended period of time in an otherwise completely dark room. After several minutes, most people begin to see the light wander slowly away from its initial position. Why this occurs is not understood, but Muzafer Sherif showed that people's reports of the direction and extent of movement can be systematically biased by the *social context.*

Subjects observed the light for a time alone, reporting what they saw. Then they performed the same task with several other observers present (actually confederates of the experimenter) who consistently reported movement in a certain direction. Not only did the real subjects' judgments change to conform to those of the other "observers," but later, when they were alone again, they continued to report that the stationary light was moving in this direction (M. Sherif, 1935).

A deviant *minority* can influence perception too.

In another study, two confederates consistently called a green color "blue" during a color-naming task while the majority of the subjects named it correctly. But later, when they were tested alone, some of the subjects who had been in the accurate majority shifted their judgments of the boundary between blue and green toward blue (Moscovici, 1976).

These results indicate that both social majorities and minorities can influence perception and classification in other perceivers. Response bias (discussed in the preceding chapter) seems a plausible explanation for these findings, but the possibility of an actual change in experience is hard to rule out, especially where the subjects insist that what they reported was what they actually saw. In any case, the power of even a minority—or a persuasive leader—to change others' definitions of reality is very real.

There are many ways in which social variables may influence perception—from broad cultural influences which set basic, accepted social categories to attitudes that can function as "anchors" or standards for evaluating new inputs (Deregowski, 1980). It is not surprising that how an individual classifies objects and events in the environment can also be affected by the ways other similar people are seen to classify the same things. After all, we humans are social creatures who depend on interactions with others for many of our most significant experiences and much of our information. What each of us considers to be "reality" is determined in large part by common agreement—*consensual validation*—among members of the groups to which we belong. In the next chapter, we will see that even as private a process as our consciousness is, to some extent, influenced by the actual or symbolic presence of other people. Our final chapters on social psychology will give many examples of this powerful effect of social forces on individuals' thoughts, feelings, and actions.

The "top-down" effects of expectations, deprivation, personality, and social influence variables all highlight the same important fact—that perceptual experience in response to a stimulus event is a response of the *whole organism.* Besides the information provided when your sensory receptors are stimulated, your final perception depends on who you are, whom you are with, and what you expect, want, and value.

The interaction of "top-down" and "bottom-up" processes also means that perception is an act of constructing reality to fit one's assumptions about how it "probably is" or "should be." The perceiver becomes a *gambler,* willing to bet that the present input can be understood in terms of past knowledge and personal theories. But the perceiver is also a compulsive *interior decorator,* constantly rearranging what is there so things fit better and are more coherent, and rejecting incongruity and messiness in favor of clarity and consistency.

If perceiving were completely "bottom-up" processing, we would all be bound to the same mundane, concrete reality of the here and now. We could register experience but not profit from it on later occasions, nor would we see the world differently under different personal circumstances. If processing in perception were completely "top-down," however, we would each be lost in our own fantasy world of what we expect and hope to perceive. A proper balance between them achieves the basic goal of perception: to experience what is out there in the world in a way that maximally serves our needs as biological and social organisms moving about in a physical environment. In later chapters we will see how this same interaction of "bottom-up" and "top-down" processes affects attention, memory, and thinking.

SUMMARY

■ Perception is a constructive process of going beyond sensory stimulation to discover what objects exist in the world around us. The task of perception is to determine what the distal (external) stimulus is from the information contained in the proximal (sensory) stimulus.

■ Perceiving is a three-stage process consisting of a sensory stage, in which sensory information is coded and analyzed, a perceptual stage, in which information is organized and synthesized, and a classification stage, in which identification and categorization take place.

■ Ambiguity sometimes arises because the same sensory information may be organized into different percepts. It is also possible for the same percepts to be interpreted and classified differently.

■ According to the theory of structuralism, individual sensations are put together and combined with associations from past experience to create meaningful experiences. According to Gestalt theory, innate organizing processes in the brain give us whole figures that are "more than the sum of the parts." According to the theory of Ecological Optics, perception is an active exploration of the environment in which the proximal stimulus provides more information about the distal stimulus than was formerly realized.

■ Organizational processes provide the best and simplest percepts consistent with the sensory data. As a result of these processes, our percepts are segregated into regions and organized into figures that stand out against the ground. We tend to see incomplete figures as wholes, to group items by various kinds of similarity, to prefer "good" figures and see them more readily.

■ Perception of parts depends on the reference frame in which they occur. We tend to organize and interpret parts in relation to the spatial and temporal context in which we experience them. We also tend to see a reference frame as stationary and the parts within it as moving rather than the reverse, regardless of the sensory stimulus.

■ When different senses receive contradictory information, the visual information usually dominates in the perception that we experience.

■ In converting the two-dimensional information on the retina to a perception of three-dimensional space, the visual system gauges object size and distance in relation to each other: distance is interpreted on the basis of known size, and size on the basis of various distance cues. Distance cues include binocular disparity, convergence of the two eyes, relative motion parallax, and pictorial cues such as interposition, shadows, relative size, linear perspective, and texture gradients.

■ Despite the changing properties of retinal images, we tend to perceive objects as retaining the same size, shape, and orientation. Prior knowledge normally reinforces these and other constancies in perception; under extreme conditions, perceptual constancy may break down. Nevertheless, the study of perceptual constancies reveals that a major function of perception lies in discovering the stable, invariant properties of stimuli that may change in many ways.

■ Classification, the third stage of perceiving, is the stage in which perceived objects are identified and given meaning through "top-down" processes which may draw on memory, concept analysis, expectation, motivation, and personality characteristics.

■ The task of pattern recognition is to identify all instances of a category while excluding all non-instances. Critical features theories and prototype theories of pattern recognition have been proposed to account for how this process occurs, although neither is wholly satisfactory.

■ The context within which pattern recognition occurs provides expectations for the classification process. Expectations, schemas, and perceptual sets all may guide recognition of incomplete or ambiguous data in one direction rather than another that would be equally possible given the perceptual data. Personality characteristics, motives, and social influences all contribute to the meanings we see in perceptual data and may lead us to distort the information provided by the data.

6

THE NATURE OF CONSCIOUSNESS

■ THE PSYCHOLOGY OF CONSCIOUSNESS
Consciousness as an aid to survival
The changing scientific status of consciousness
Psychological studies of attention
Mental processing without consciousness
■ THE DUALITY OF CONSCIOUSNESS
Two minds in one brain?
Complementary orientations to the world?
■ EVERYDAY CHANGES IN CONSCIOUSNESS
Daydreaming and fantasy
Sleeping and dreaming
■ EXTENDED STATES OF CONSCIOUSNESS
Hallucinations
Hypnosis
Mind alteration with drugs
■ CONSCIOUSNESS: THE ORDINARY AND THE EXTRAORDINARY
■ SUMMARY

K aren wasn't worried about the operation because it was only "minor surgery" to remove an irritating cyst in her mouth. Nevertheless, the nurse insisted on medication to help her sleep better, so she'd be well rested for the operation.

"Go away, Doggie, can't you see that I have to study for my history exam? No time to play today. Look at all those books everywhere waiting for me to read. How am I ever going to read them all?" As Doggie barked, the books became iridescent, then began to melt, their liquid hues blending into a spectacular rainbow pond.

"Wow!" Karen heard herself saying as she awoke. She had been dreaming of the summer cottage where she had spent her childhood vacations. She had always wanted a dog but could never have one because of her allergies. But the history midterm was all too real, with a lot of cramming to squeeze in before next week. She slipped back into a deep sleep that was broken in the early morning by the attendants who wheeled her off to the operating room.

"100, 99, 98, 97 . . .," Karen counted as the anesthetic was being injected into her vein. Wildly oscillating, vibrating geometric patterns flashed before her. "92, 91, 9. . ." All dark, all sensation gone, awareness shut down.

Minutes into the operation, the surgeon exclaimed, "Why, this may not be a cyst at all . . . It may be cancer!" Fortunately, the biopsy proved the cyst was benign and the doctor's reaction just a false alarm. In the recovery room, the surgeon told the groggy, slightly nauseated Karen that she didn't have to worry: everything was fine.

But Karen had a difficult time falling asleep that night. She felt anxious. Tears rolled down her face, and she didn't know why. Maybe it was that history midterm, she thought. The next day Karen was depressed; attempts to restore her usual good spirits were unsuccessful. The depression worsened and Karen sought professional help.

Under hypnosis, a therapist asked Karen to lift her hand if she felt that something was disturbing her, even if she did not know what it was. Karen's hand soon rose. When the therapist suggested that she report what was disturbing her, she exclaimed, "The cyst may be cancerous!" After being able to express her fear openly and being reassured, Karen's depression lifted. Was it really possible that in her unconscious, anesthetized state some part of Karen's mind had been able to comprehend the surgeon's fearful message?

This possibility has been checked out in formal studies using both negative and positive messages. In cases where negative messages were given, ten patients were anesthetized. When recordings of their bodily functions indicated they had "lost consciousness," the anesthetist said in an urgent tone, *"Just a moment. I don't like the patient's colour. The lips are too blue, very blue. More oxygen please (pause). . . . Good, everything is fine now."*

Upon awakening, not one of the patients recalled anything that had happened while they were anesthetized. But after entering hypnosis and being given the suggestion to reexperience the operation, four of the ten were able to repeat practically verbatim the traumatic words used by the anesthetist. Four other patients displayed a severe degree of anxiety while reliving the operation even though they could not say why. And at a crucial moment, each of the four woke from the hypnosis and refused to participate further. The remaining two patients, though seemingly capable of reliving the operation under hypnosis, later said they had not heard anything (Levinson, 1967).

In the second case, recorded suggestions for quick recovery, given during general anesthesia, had positive effects. Patients who got those positive messages needed less postoperative pain-killing medication. They could even be released from the hospital two and a half days sooner than control-group patients, who had been exposed to either soothing music or silence during their anesthesia (Hutchins, 1961; Pearson, 1961).

Karen's case focuses our attention on the complex and fascinating manner in which human consciousness operates. Her ordinary state of alert, conscious awareness was altered in many ways—by drugs of different types, by sleeping and dreaming, by such "unconscious" impulses as the frustrated desire for a puppy and the fear of cancer, and by hypnosis. Less dramatically, but as significant her consciousness changed as the focus of her attention shifted from the present situation to past memories and to future events. Somehow she even took in information when she was not conscious.

What is consciousness and how can such a private event be studied scientifically? What role does attention play in the conscious processing of information? Would a person have *two* conscious minds if the two halves of the brain were separated? What are the different states of consciousness and how does a person pass from one to another? These are some of the questions we will be trying to answer in this chapter.

THE PSYCHOLOGY OF CONSCIOUSNESS

"A penny for your thoughts."

Before collecting, how can you be certain that they really are *your thoughts*? By what mental process did you separate *your* thoughts from *my* thoughts—some of which you also know and need to hang onto—at least until exam time?

Consciousness is the general term for *awareness*—including awareness of ourselves as distinct from other organisms and objects. Ordinary waking consciousness includes the stream of immediate experience comprising our perceptions, thoughts, feelings, and desires at any particular moment of awareness—along with our "commentary" on them and on our actions. Besides our awareness of some *content*—something we are analyzing or interpreting, including some sense of self—consciousness also includes the *state of being aware*.

What functions does consciousness serve? Or, put more simply, what does it do for us? How would we be different if we had never developed any consciousness, suddenly had it changed, or somehow lost it?

Consciousness as an aid to survival

Consciousness probably evolved because it increased individuals' chances of survival by enabling them to base intentional, voluntary actions on an optimal interpretation of "reality"—to make sense of sensory and perceptual information at a level that was useful for their purposes at a given time and place.

Consciousness helps us in three important ways to make sense of the "blooming, buzzing confusion" that assaults our sensory receptors. First it reduces the constant flow of stimulus energy by restricting what we notice. We "tune out" what is not relevant at the moment—it becomes "noise"—and focus on what is relevant—it becomes signal. Second, it enables us to segment the continuous flow of experience into *objects* (patterns in space) and *events* (patterns in time), following the laws of perceptual organization described in the last chapter. Thanks to our consciousness, we can pull out one thing at a time from life's endless conveyor belt of stimuli—to analyze it, interpret it, compare it to other things, and decide how to act on it (Marcel, 1983).

Third, it is our consciousness that enables us to draw on past memories in making the best sense we can of present input and planning appropriate actions. Instead of simply reacting to the present stimulus, we can recall similar events, acts, and outcomes from the past. We also analyze causes, imagine situations and alternatives not present at the time, plan future actions, and direct behavior toward consequences we want.

Consciousness is the process or property of mind that enables us to do these things. It is the ability to engage in an active, stable *construction of reality* through a selective analysis of ongoing objects and events in the context of our past experiences. Only in consciousness can the higher mental processes occur. Thus consciousness gives us a potential for flexible, appropriate response far beyond that of other species—a tremendous aid in survival (see Ornstein, 1975).

Because all humans have evolved with similar sensory and nervous systems, there are many similarities in their constructions of reality. People tend to agree on a common view of reality, especially on the meaning of objects and events that are related to survival. Other people affirm your interpretations, and you affirm theirs, increasing the confidence you both feel in your views. This agreement and mutual affirmation of views is called **consensual validation**, as we saw in Chapter 5. Similarities are greatest for those who have had a common cultural background of experience. What is perceived as dangerous, safe, nourishing, or desirable tends to be the same for most members of a society (Natsoulas, 1978).

But there are also important *differences* in people's consciousness, especially where they have lived in very different habitats and faced different survival tasks. And there are also some important variations among people within the same general cultural setting. Since consciousness is a *personal* construction of reality based on a limited selection from the flux of available stimulation, each of us will attend more to certain features than others. The uniqueness of your own personal consciousness persists over time and across situations and helps give unity and continuity to your sense of self. It is the center of the *unique personality* that differentiates you from every other individual in your universe (Buss, 1980).

But your personal world view is only one of the possible constructions of reality that you could be making. In fact, there are times when you give up your ordinary consciousness and construct other forms. For example, you do so every time you sleep and dream—or have daydreams and fantasies. It can also happen if the normal functioning of your sensory and nervous systems is altered by alcohol, psychoactive drugs, or brain surgery; by sensory deprivation or sensory overexcitement (overload); or by special procedures that occur in hypnosis or some mystical practices. Finally, a unique construction of reality—one that sacrifices consensual validation—is built up in the minds of those with severe mental disorders. In their hallucinations, they may respond to voices no one else hears, while in their phobias and delusions, they come to believe that harmless things and innocent people are threatening and dangerous.

Shakespeare points to the different perceptions and reactions created by *alternative* constructions of reality when he notes that: "The lunatic, the lover, and the poet, are of imagination all compact [similar]." Each develops a personal view of reality that is different from the normal, ordinary consciousness of those around them—those who act sane, are not carried away by the lover's blind passion, and are unwilling to suspend the mundane view of events for the poet's more creative interpretations.

In the next sections, we will briefly review the changing scientific status of the concept of consciousness, and the new research on the relationship between consciousness and attention.

"A penny for *my* thoughts?"

The changing scientific status of consciousness

Scientific psychology started out as the study of consciousness. About a hundred years ago, at Wilhelm Wundt's laboratory in Germany, subjects were reporting their personal mental states using the method of *introspection,* in the belief that this was the best method for getting at the contents of consciousness. A little later, under the direction of E. B. Titchener, one of Wundt's students, trained observers at Cornell University sipped lemonade and viewed precisely calibrated color patches while describing the sensations and emotions that accompanied these external events. Titchener's interest was not so much in the *contents* of consciousness as in the mind's ways of measuring sensations. At Harvard, William James, too, championed the importance of consciousness. He asserted: "Psychology [is] the description and explanation of 'consciousness' as such" (1890, p.1). Moreover, he regarded the idea that "all people unhesitatingly believe that they feel themselves thinking" to be "the most fundamental of all postulates in Psychology . . ." (1890, p.5).

But introspection by trained self-observers of laboratory-induced sensations was a sterile approach. It did not do justice to the richness of human thought, emotion, and behavior and, of course, did not provide access to subconscious or unconscious mental processes, as illustrated in Karen's case. Moreover, it excluded study of infants, retarded people, and those with mental disorders since they either could not verbalize their consciousness or could not do so in a trustworthy, acceptable way. As introspection was replaced by more objective research methods, a new psychology arose that also got rid of consciousness.

Objective behaviorism, as advanced by J. B. Watson, dismissed mind along with the then popular method of studying it. In his new view, outlined in *Psychology from the Standpoint of a Behaviorist* (1919), he warned readers that he was purposely doing "violence to the traditional" since his work had "no discussion of consciousness and no reference to such terms as sensation, perception, attention, will, image and the like. . . . I frankly don't know what they mean, nor do I believe anyone else can use them consistently" (p. viii). For many years thereafter, the field of psychology suffered an almost total "loss of consciousness" (see Webb, 1981).

Consciousness returned to psychology gradually, beginning in the 1950s as the cognitive revolution made inroads into all those areas of study in which research subjects had been treated solely as "behaving organisms." Computers replaced mazes for studying problem solving, comprehension of stories replaced rote memory of nonsense syllables, and researchers again studied mental processes as well as reinforced actions.

Contemporary psychology has found a comfortable place for consciousness by accepting the *"new dualism"* that we talked about in Chapter 1. (Galanter, 1979). It now studies mental events (mind) by studying their *consequences* in the control of human actions (body) (E. Hilgard, 1980). It has begun to use a "new introspection" in which research subjects report their thoughts out loud as they work on a task, or complete a questionnaire (Klinger, 1978). Researchers also use brain-wave patterns or brain scans of radioactive particles as indices of different types of human conscious activity, as noted in Chapter 3.

One interesting new method for sampling thoughts uses an electronic signal generator to send beeps to small earphones at randomly programmed intervals. Subjects wearing the earphones respond to these signals by jotting down the thought occurring at the instant the signal began, their ongoing activity, and the time of day. In this way, thought-records can be gathered over a number of days to assess what people tend to think about and what cognitive patterns emerge in their everyday lives (Hurlburt, 1979).

The "stream of consciousness" is once again flowing in psychology, thanks to the rise to prominence of this new cognitive orientation, but also to the emergence in the past few decades of more esoteric psychologies. The psychedelic drug scene of the 1960s provided abundant examples of "mind alteration" at work—and at play. A more liberalized view as to what is acceptable subject matter for a scientific psychology has also been growing over the last thirty years as its most reputable researchers have brought into the laboratory investigations of sleep and dreams (Dement, 1976), daydreaming (Singer, 1978), hypnosis (E. Hilgard, 1977), and the dual consciousness of patients with brains surgically split into "two minds" (Gazzaniga & LeDoux, 1978; Sperry, 1968).

Psychological studies of attention

One aspect of consciousness that is now of special interest to researchers is the concept of attention. **Attention** is defined as a state of focused awareness accompanied by sensory clearness and a central nervous system readiness to respond to stimulation. Attention can be thought of as the bridge over which some parts of the external world—the aspects selectively focused on—are brought into the subjective world of our consciousness so that we may regulate our own behavior (Carver & Scheier, 1981).

What we selectively attend to depends upon a number of external and internal factors. We attend to external stimuli that are intense, novel, changing, unexpected, or stand out as salient or special—a sign with moving parts, or a friend's face in a classroom of strangers. Our current physiological condition also can direct our attention, as when hunger makes us notice newspaper ads for food or restaurants. An activity we are engaged in can capture our attention, leading us to disregard stimuli that are not "task-relevant." Listening to a charismatic speaker, watching an exciting movie, reading an absorbing novel, playing a video game are some attention-restricting activities. Past experience, special interest, or expertise in a given area carries with it not just an expanded knowledge base, but a greater sensitivity to particular stimuli, events, and relationships—as revealed by Sherlock Holmes' detective work or the birdwatcher's spottings of rare birds that others do not see.

Attention as essential for consciousness. Attention has been the focus of research because of its importance for consciousness and thus for higher-level mental processing. Of all the things that happen around us of which we *could* be aware, we actually *become* aware—conscious—only of those on which we focus our attention.

Attention is like a spotlight that illuminates certain portions of our surroundings. When we focus our at-

tention on something and thus become conscious of it, we can begin to process it cognitively—converting sensory information to perceptions and memories, or developing ideas through analysis, judgment, reasoning, and imagination. When the spotlight of attention shifts to something else, conscious processing of the earlier material ceases and processing of the new content begins.

When we select something to attend to—because of its striking character or its relevance to some purpose or goal—we inevitably ignore many other possibilities. Only a small portion of the information constantly being taken in by our senses can be attended to. How does the mind deal with this overload of information?

Attention as a filter for sensory input. Credit for reawakening interest in attention as a subject for research goes to English researcher Donald Broadbent. In his book *Perception and Communication* (1958), Broadbent outlined a number of ideas that were novel and exciting to other researchers and provided an empirical basis for investigation of attention.

Broadbent's metaphor for the mind was a communication channel that actively processed and transmitted information. How much information this communication channel could process at any time was limited by the inability of attentional mechanisms to switch between different sources of input.

Imagine listening to a lecture as a couple of students on your left begin to share some gossip and a person on your right starts to tell a joke. What do you hear, notice, remember? You will probably stay tuned to the lecturer if the material is interesting or important for tomorrow's exam; your neighbors' conversations will be ignored as distracting "noise." But if the lecture is boring or irrelevant to your goals, and one of the conversations is about your best friend and the other concerns sex, chances are you'll try to attend to what the students are saying. But you will *not* be able to listen to all three sources of input simultaneously—or even two; you must selectively attend to only one at a time.

◁ *An unusual or unexpected sight is more likely to catch our attention than is one we routinely encounter.*

This phenomenon of attending to one of several ongoing conversations is called the "cocktail party effect," since that is the task a person often faces when surrounded by multiple conversations at a cocktail party. Broadbent and others have simulated the effect experimentally in the laboratory by the technique of **dichotic listening,** in which different messages are sent at the same time to the two ears by using earphones and separate tape-recorded inputs. A different story may be presented to each ear and the subject instructed to listen to one or the other. To increase selective listening, the subject may be further told to repeat the story aloud as it comes into the attended ear—that is, to "shadow" it while ignoring the other story.

It is not surprising that subjects do not remember information presented to the unattended ear. What *is* remarkable is that they do not even notice major changes in that input—for example if the tape is played backward or the language changes from English to German. But they do notice a change in pitch of the speaker's voice, as when it is switched from a male to a female speaker (Cherry, 1953). Gross physical features of the unattended message receive perceptual analysis, apparently below the level of consciousness, but the meaning does not get through into consciousness.

Broadbent conceived of attention as a *selective filter* which handled the large amount of sensory information constantly arriving by (a) *blocking out* most unwanted input while (b) *relaying* specific desired information—admitting it to consciousness. Such a filter would act a little like a tuning dial on a radio or TV, which lets us receive certain of the many available messages but not others. According to Broadbent's theory, the unattended, blocked-out information is sent to a "buffer" where it is held for a short while until either the filter is tuned to it and it gets processed or it is lost. (This "buffer" is roughly equivalent to the "sensory memory" of later theories of memory, to be described in Chapter 9.)

Broadbent demonstrated this delayed processing of previously blocked material by an ingenious procedure.

One set of three digits (say, 2–6–1) was presented through earphones to the left ear, and another (say 7–9–5) was presented simultaneously to the right ear. (See **Figure 6.1.**) Subjects were asked to report both. They were able to perform this *split-span task* by recalling all the input to one ear first and then the input to the other ear. Thus they said "261 795" rather than "2–7 6–9 1–5." (Broadbent, 1954).

Broadbent assumed that the subjects had tuned their selective filter first to the attended ear and then, after responding to that input, had switched the filter to the information being held in the buffer.

According to Broadbent's theory, the limited capacity of attention creates a "bottleneck" in the flow of information through the cognitive system. Filter theory postulates limits on early stages of perception caused by the fact that we can be conscious of only the single channel we are attending to at any one time. Other sensory information is being held briefly but not processed (Broadbent, 1971).

Attention as a matter of degree. Despite the influence of this theoretical approach to consciousness and attention, there were problems it couldn't handle. For example, in dichotic listening tasks, we *do* notice our own names or other personally relevant material arriving at the unattended ear. And when a story being listened to in one ear and shadowed is suddenly switched to the other ear and replaced by a new story in the first ear, subjects continue to report a few words from the original story (arriving now in the supposedly unattended ear) *if* they make more sense than the words in the new story (Treisman, 1960). This means that there must still be some analysis for meaning—and hence some attention—in the channel *not* being consciously attended to.

Much research has thus converged to support the conclusion that attention is not "all-or-none," as fil-

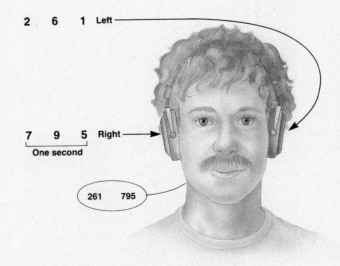

2   6   1   Left

7   9   5   Right

One second

261   795

(After Lachman et al., 1979).

△ ▐ Figure 6.1

ter theory postulated but rather a matter of degree. Evidently the supposedly ignored input gets some analysis too, though only partial and not conscious. That which is attended to in consciousness receives more processing over a longer time and thus is better remembered in general and in its many details (Norman, 1968).

Attention as a synthesizer of input and knowledge. A second modification in filter theory was necessary to include the finding from many experiments that past learning can influence responding, even without the person's conscious awareness. In one such study, subjects trained to respond physiologically to certain words gave those physiological responses even when the words were presented in the unattended ear and even though the subjects reported not being aware of hearing any of them (Von Wright et al., 1975). Such findings demonstrate that there must be some mechanism below the level of consciousness that monitors unattended input for *meaningful* information—which, in turn, implies that we must be drawing on information already stored in memory.

Ulric Neisser (1967) proposed a theory of attention that included both analysis guided by sensory input and analysis guided by one's already developed world view. (From Chapter 5 you will recognize the former as data-driven, "bottom-up" processing and the latter as hypothesis-driven, "top-down" processing.) According to Neisser's theory, people *construct* percepts by adding what they already know to the incoming environmental sensory input. Information that reaches consciousness has already been processed in this constructive fashion. Attended new information is synthesized with the already known—whether the latter is consciously attended to or not. In cases where we have either incomplete sensory information or excessive stimulation, we rely more on "top-down" processing—prior knowledge—to predict and construct what the object or event should be.

Attention as a limited processing capacity. While jogging with a friend, ask your friend to divide 86 by 14 or to tell you how many windows there are in his or her family home. Notice the effect of these mental activities on slowing down the running pace. When people do two things at once, attention focused on one task affects their performance of the other. In one view, attention is a *processing capacity* which is a *limited* resource that is used in different ways according to a person's needs, task demands, past history, and skill (Kahneman, 1973).

An ingenious study demonstrated the limited processing capacity of attention.

Subjects were asked to do two simple things: (a) respond by pressing a key with their *right* hand if a visual display (say, a letter *A*) matched one that had been presented a half second earlier, and (b) respond by pressing another key with their *left* hand whenever they heard a randomly presented tone. The matching task was preceded by a warning signal indicating that the first letter would appear one second later.

Before, during, and shortly after the warning signal, the subjects' reaction times to the randomly presented tone were fairly consistent, but when the tone was presented between the first and second letters, it was a different story. The subjects had "something on their minds" during these times, and reaction time to the tone was over half again as long. The researchers concluded that the mental preparation for one response required attentional processing that was then not available for the other response, as can be seen in **Figure 6.2** (Posner & Boies, 1971; see also Griffith, 1976).

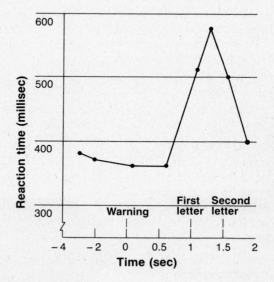

Figure 6.2

Reaction time to the randomly presented tone depended on whether the subjects were devoting attention to the matching task (Posner & Boies, 1971).

An analogy can be drawn between this view of attention and a city's power plant. Too much demand for power at the same time will cause a brownout, but that may be avoided if the available power is allocated flexibly according to anticipated demands. Mental processes too take power; if this power is overtaxed by too many demands, it will not be sufficient, but we can make our supply of attention go further by allocating it in flexible ways, giving more to difficult tasks, to certain well-learned rules like "Pay attention when someone yells 'Fire!'," or to conscious decisions.

Another way we make our supply of attention go further is by *routinizing* some of the things we do frequently to the point where they require little or no attention or mental effort to perform. If you drive a car, recall how much more attention driving took when you were learning to drive than it does now. Bike riding, dancing, and reading are other skills that take little conscious attention once they are mastered.

Could you learn to perform two complex cognitive tasks at once? Apparently so: after a great deal of practice, subjects in one study became able to read and take dictation simultaneously (Spelke et al., 1976).

Mental processing without consciousness

So you can't be conscious of something unless you attend to it. But the reverse is not true. You can attend to something—in the sense of processing it—at an unconscious level. Driving requires constant detection of and adaptation to stimulus conditions that you pay little or no conscious attention to. And recall our *Opening Case* of Karen's unconscious processing

of the surgeon's frightening message. Though our capacity for conscious processing of information is limited, there seems to be no limit to the amount of out-of-conscious, "underground" processing that can go on. (See **Close-up** on p. 195.)

Preattentive processing in perception. As we saw in the previous chapters, there is an initial, *preattentive stage* in the perceptual sequence, a purely sensory stage that occurs automatically and nonconsciously to register the stimulus features that are present. Not until the stages of *attentive processing* (which include perception and classification) are the sensory elements synthesized into a coherent and meaningful whole. If attention is diverted or overloaded, these "feature-integration" processes may fail to occur. When this happens the stimulus features are not properly organized and may be forgotten (Treisman & Gelade, 1980).

Although we tend to believe that we have a running awareness of what is going on in our minds, what we are aware of is only the top of the mind's iceberg. Often we attribute our reactions to a cause that in fact was not present. Or we try to explain a conclusion by reasoning backward to a plausible line of thought that could have accounted for it—but actually did not. The errors we make in assuming that these mental processes were conscious have been shown in a recent study.

After viewing a documentary film, students rated it on several dimensions, such as how interesting it was. For one experimental group the projector was out of focus, while a second experimental group had to contend with the distracting noise of a power saw outside. A control group had neither source of distraction. When asked if their ratings were affected by the noise or the poor focus, over 50 percent of the "noise" group reported that the noise lowered their ratings, and more than 25 percent of the "poor focus" group said that the poor focus did so. Actually, the ratings of all three groups were nearly identical. The distractions reported as being negative influences in fact had no effect on the subjects' ratings.

In other conditions, students failed to report (and were assumed to be unaware of) the influence of stimulus factors that *were* shown to have behavioral

◁ *Many of us are overly confident in our ability to attend to more than one thing at a time—even though our processing capacity is limited.*

Blindsight

"Blindsight" sounds like a contradiction in terms. But we know that the detailed processing of visual input that occurs in the visual cortex is only the final stage of the overall process of converting light waves to conscious vision. An earlier, nonconscious stage of processing—and the place in the brain where it may occur—is revealed in the story of Don.

When he was 14 years old, Don began to have severe, prolonged headaches. They were always preceded by visual experiences of a flashing oval light in his left visual field which was later replaced by a blank white region with colored fringes around it. Within fifteen minutes the headache would begin on the right side of his head, followed by vomiting, increased blindness in the left visual field, and up to two full days with no sleep. As he grew older, these attacks became increasingly frequent despite his doctors' attempts to treat them. Finally, at age 34, Don decided to undergo surgery in an attempt to correct the problem.

A neurosurgeon removed a small portion of his right occipital cortex. The surgery was successful in the sense that it permanently cured his headaches. Unfortunately, because the region that had been removed contained the primary sensory cortex for the left visual field, the surgery also left Don totally blind in the left half of his visual field—at least by all standard tests. For instance, when a bright spot of light was shown directly to the left of his fixation point, he was simply unaware of its presence.

On an informed hunch, however, a group of psychologists gave him this test, but asked him to "guess" where the spot of light might be located by pointing with his left index finger. The results were remarkable. Don was nearly as accurate at locating the spot in his "blind" left field as he was at locating spots in the right visual field which he saw clearly! Further experiments showed that he could also "guess" whether a line in his "blind" field was vertical or horizontal, and whether a figure presented there was an "X" or an "O." Yet throughout the tests Don was completely unaware of the presence of the spots, lines, or figures. He claimed he was merely "guessing." When he was shown video tapes of his testing, he was openly astonished to see himself pointing to lights he had not "seen" (Weiskrantz et al., 1974).

Don's "vision" of objects he was unaware of seeing has been aptly dubbed *blindsight*. Comparable results have since been found in several other patients with similar damage in the visual cortex (Perenin & Jeannerod, 1975). It is thought that blindsight may be made possible by the operation of the visual pathway that goes from the eye to the superior colliculus (see p. 122).

In humans, there seems to be no conscious awareness of visual objects in the absence of involvement of the visual cortex. However, we do know that animals can see, as evidenced by the fact that they can perform visual tasks in the absence of a visual cortex. The lower center evidently developed earlier evolutionally and still retains abilities that we more generously endowed humans have lost. But it appears that this lower structure still contributes information to us about *where* objects are—below the level of our consciousness.

effects on them, while reporting that stimuli affected their reactions which actually did *not* (Nisbett & Wilson, 1977, 1979).

So there is little evidence to support our belief in the direct introspective awareness of our complex mental processes. Our illusion of awareness is maintained for several reasons: (a) we confuse what we know with the processes by which we know it; (b) we rely on assumptions of plausible cause-effect relationships instead of true awareness of our "on-line" cognitive processes; and (c) we have inadequate feedback to disconfirm our false beliefs. Think about how you might prove that people are unaware of how their minds do what they do.

Nonconscious, subconscious, and unconscious processing. We have encountered several examples of the processing of information outside of consciousness that nevertheless influenced behavior, such as the studies of field dependence and perceptual defense in Chapter 5 and the man with "blindsight" described in the Close-up in this chapter.

Nonconscious processes involve information not represented in either consciousness or memory which nevertheless can influence fundamental bodily or mental activities. Two examples of nonconscious processes are the regulation of blood pressure, in which physiological information is detected and acted on without our awareness, and the basic perception of figure and ground, in which we are unaware of the organizing processes that give us this perception.

By contrast, **subconscious processes** involve material not currently in consciousness but retrievable from memory by special recall procedures. Karen's depression was the result of a subconscious process; once it was brought into her consciousness by hypnotic therapy, she could recognize it and deal with it appropriately.

The term *unconscious* is often used for all processes that are not conscious. In psychoanalytic theory, however, it has a special meaning, referring to processes that are kept out of consciousness to prevent anxiety. Such processes stem from the need to repress unpleasant memories and feelings. Freud described the **unconscious** as "any mental process the existence of which we are obliged to assume was active at a certain time, although [the person was] not aware of it at that time. We infer it from its effects" (1925). For example, unconscious motivation is inferred when a bright student's failures are seen as a way of punishing an overdemanding parent.

Freud assumed that in such cases the content of the real ideas or motives is *repressed*—put out of consciousness because it is too upsetting or threatening to deal with continually. But the feelings associated with it remain. One of Freud's contributions was in revealing the extent to which adult behavior is influenced by unconscious processes. His view challenged the comforting picture of humans as totally rational creatures. (These processes will be discussed in greater detail in later chapters.)

Our ability to process information outside of consciousness enables us to deal with far more information than we could handle if it all had to "stand in line" to go through conscious processing one item at a time. On the other hand, mental processing that does not receive our conscious attention can be maladaptive if we react "mindlessly" in a passive, nonquestioning way to situations that require new discriminations and new adaptations.

We expect mindless responses in animals driven by fixed action patterns, like the mother turkey responding to the cheep-cheep sounds (Ch. 1). But we more sophisticated organisms sometimes behave in similarly mindless ways. For example, the response of *compliance* (doing what someone else wants you to) can be elicited by the single stimulus word "because."

Students waiting in line to use a library copying machine were asked to comply with a request to go ahead of them by a person (the researcher) who said: "Excuse me, I have five pages. May I use the Xerox machine because I'm in a rush?" Ninety-four percent of the students complied, allowing the requester to skip ahead. When she made the same request without giving any reason, only 60 percent complied.

Was it the *reason* given, or the *"because"* that elicited the compliance? In a third condition, the request was changed to "because I have to make some copies" [not a reason]. Again, nearly all complied; in 93 percent of those who were essentially told, "do it because of nothing," a compliant response was triggered. The same result occurred when the researcher asked seated subway passengers to give up their seats simply "because" (Langer, 1978).

Processing information outside of consciousness simplifies our task but can extract a high price by limiting our awareness of the real present environment and its requirements. In such processing analytic reasoning and objective judgment do not occur. Only in consciousness are we able to mobilize our best and most uniquely human mental resources in working toward particular goals. Perhaps this is why, as Posner and Snyder (1974) have suggested, "Consciousness is reserved for special processing." To compare tasks that do and do not require consciousness, try the test in **Figure 6.3.**

PURPLE	BLUE	RED
GREEN	**YELLOW**	ORANGE
RED	BLACK	**BLUE**
ORANGE	**GREEN**	**BROWN**
BLUE	YELLOW	PURPLE

△ **Figure 6.3** *The Stroop Task*

1. *Time yourself as you read aloud all the words, ignoring the colors in which they are printed.*
2. *Then, time yourself as you read the colors, ignoring what the words say.*
The first task you could do quickly and effortlessly, with little or no thought; the second required your full conscious attention because you had to deal with cognitive interference (based on Stroop, 1935).

THE DUALITY OF CONSCIOUSNESS

When the philosopher Descartes distinguished mind from body, he decided that consciousness had to be located in the tiny pineal gland (see p. 75). It belonged there, he felt, because there was an "undeniable unity" of consciousness, and the pineal gland was the single organ he saw in a brain that consisted mostly of *pairs* of similar parts. The logic was good, but the facts were wrong. We know now that the part of the brain responsible for consciousness is the part most obviously divided into two parts—the two cerebral hemispheres.

Two minds in one brain?

In Chapter 3 we talked about the division of labor and dominance between the right and left halves of the "new brain"—the cerebral hemispheres. We deferred until the present chapter the intriguing question of whether each half might be able to act as a separate conscious mind if they were separated in some way. The chance to investigate this possibility has been provided by a procedure in which surgeons control severe epilepsy by severing the corpus callosum—the bundle of about 200 million association nerve fibers that normally links the two hemispheres. The goal of this surgery is to prevent the violent electrical rhythms that accompany epileptic seizures from crossing between the hemispheres (Wilson et al., 1977). The operation is usually successful and the patient's behavior thereafter appears normal.

The first split-brain operations on human patients were performed by William Van Wagener, a neurosurgeon, in the early 1940s (Van Wagener & Herren, 1940). Over a decade later, experimenters cut the corpus callosum in animals and then trained them in a visual discrimination task with one eye covered. When the eye patch was switched to the other eye, the animal took as long to learn the task as it had the first time. The second half of the brain had not learned anything from the experience given to the first half (Myers & Sperry, 1958). But the complex story of separate processing of information in each half of a split brain had just begun.

To test the capabilities of the separated hemispheres of epileptic patients, Roger Sperry (1968) and Michael Gazzaniga (1970) devised situations that could allow visual information to be presented separately to each hemisphere (as shown in **Figure 6.4**). Their findings have greatly extended those from the "natural experiments" mentioned in Chapter 3, in which stroke victims and other brain-damaged subjects were studied.

As in the earlier studies, the left hemisphere was superior to the right hemisphere in problems involving language or requiring logic and sequential or analytic processing of concepts. The left hemisphere could "talk back" to the researchers. The subjects could speak, write and calculate. Communication with the right hemisphere was achieved by confronting it with manual tasks involving identification or matching or assembly of objects—tasks that did not require the use of words.

◁ **Figure 6.4**

Coordination between eye and hand is normal if a split-brain patient uses the left hand to find and match an object that appears in the left visual field (both registered in the right hemisphere). However, when asked to use the right hand to match an object seen in the left visual field, the patient cannot do so because sensory messages from the right hand are going to the left cerebral hemisphere and there is no longer a connection between the two hemispheres. Here the cup is misperceived as matching the pear (Sperry, 1968).

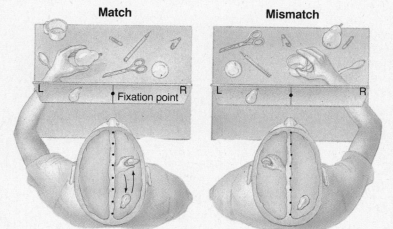

Match **Mismatch**

Fixation point

The right hemisphere turned out to be better than the left at solving problems involving spatial relationships and at recognition of patterns. But it could only add up to ten and was about at the level of a 2-year-old in the use and comprehension of word combinations.

The two hemispheres also seemed to have different "styles" for processing the same information. For example, on matching tasks, the left hemisphere seemed to match objects analytically and verbally, by similarity in *function*. The right hemisphere matched things that *looked alike* or *fitted together* to form a *whole pattern*. Thus, when shown pictures of a hat and a knife and fork, and asked to match the correct one with a picture of cake on a plate, the split-brain patient would report "You eat cake with a fork and knife"—when the images were presented only to the left hemisphere (via the right eye). But when the test stimuli were presented to the right hemisphere, the patient might perceive "hat" as going with the "cake" since the items were similar in shape (Levy & Trevarthen, 1976).

The intact brain functions as a whole with a vast, precise communication network integrating virtually all parts and functions. But when the hemispheres are disconnected, the result is two separate minds, a split brain with a double consciousness. Each hemisphere can respond independently and simultaneously when stimuli are presented separately to the two sides. When stimuli are presented to only one side, responding will be emotional or analytic, according to which hemisphere gets the task of interpreting the message. Lacking language competence, however, the visual-spatial skills of the disconnected human right hemisphere are limited, vastly inferior to the cognitive skills of a chimpanzee. It is not just language facility that the right hemisphere has failed to develop, but a range of mental processes necessary for comprehension and understanding of both external and internal events.

The dominance of the left hemisphere and the role of its language capability in aiding our construction of meaning is conveyed by researcher Michael Gazzaniga (1983):

"The emerging picture is that our cognitive system is not a unified network with a single purpose and train of thought. A more accurate metaphor is that our sense of subjective awareness arises out of our dominant left hemisphere's unrelenting need to explain actions taken from any one of a multitude of mental systems that dwell within us . . . . These systems coexist with the language system, are not necessarily in touch with the language processes prior to a behavior. Once actions are taken, the left, observing these behaviors, constructs a story as to the meaning, and this in turn becomes part of the language system's understanding of the person" (p. 535).

Two illustrative case studies of the different functioning of the two "minds" of split brains are presented in the Close-up on page 200.

Complementary orientations to the world?

From these and many other studies of hemisphere asymmetries, new views and speculations about human consciousness have emerged (Springer & Deutsch, 1984). Some psychologists have gone beyond the research findings to suggest that the two sides of the brain represent contrasting orientations to the world. In extreme versions of this hypothesis, the left brain is seen as the masculine, analytic, rational side of human nature; the right brain, as the feminine, sympathetic, nonrational aspect. A comparison of the differing modes attributed to the two hemispheres of the brain is outlined in **Table 6.1** on the yin and yang of experience. In Chinese philosophy the terms *yin* and *yang* refer to two forces or principles that are opposite but complementary. Yin represents the negative, passive, feminine side of human nature, while yang represents the positive, active, masculine, aspect. Their interaction is seen as determining the fate of individuals as well as that of the universe.

It has also been suggested that Western educational systems overemphasize abilities that favor dominance of the left hemisphere—verbal fluency, logical reasoning, and a future orientation, among others. By contrast, in societies influenced by Eastern religious practices, there is likely to be greater development of the intuition, holism, and timelessness characteristic of the right side of the brain (Ornstein, 1972).

Some researchers are developing techniques designed to boost the right hemisphere's role in our mental activities. They attempt to break down reliance on words, names, causal sequences, linear operations, and logical analysis, emphasizing instead organic, nonlinear reasoning to deal with wholes and patterns instead of isolated parts (Buzan, 1976; Edwards, 1979). Systematic evaluation research on the success of these right-hemisphere "enhancers" is needed before these interesting speculations can be accepted as educationally valuable or scientifically valid.

"EVERY ONCE IN A WHILE MY RIGHT BRAIN THROWS SOMETHING IN."

Table 6.1   *The Yin and Yang of Experience: A Comparison of Left-Mode and Right-Mode Characteristics*

L —MODE	R —MODE
Verbal: Using words to name, describe, define.	*Nonverbal:* Awareness of things, but minimal connection with words.
Analytic: Figuring things out step-by-step and part-by-part.	*Synthetic:* Putting things together to form wholes.
Symbolic: Using a symbol to *stand for* something. For example, the drawn form ◉ stands for *eye*, the sign + stands for the process of addition.	*Concrete:* Relating to things as they are, at the present moment.
Abstract: Taking out a small bit of information and using it to represent the whole thing.	*Analogic:* Seeing likenesses between things; understanding metaphoric relationships.
Temporal: Keeping track of time, sequencing one thing after another: Doing first things first, second things second, etc.	*Nontemporal:* Without a sense of time.
Rational: Drawing conclusions based on *reason* and *facts.*	*Nonrational:* Not requiring a basis of reason or facts; willingness to suspend judgment.
Digital: Using numbers as in counting.	*Spatial:* Seeing where things are in relation to other things, and how parts go together to form a whole.
Logical: Drawing conclusions based on logic: one thing following another in logical order—for example, a mathematical theorem or a well-stated argument.	*Intuitive:* Making leaps of insight, often based on incomplete patterns, hunches, feelings, or visual images.
Linear: Thinking in terms of linked ideas, one thought directly following another, often leading to a convergent conclusion.	*Holistic:* Seeing whole things all at once; perceiving the overall patterns and structures, often leading to divergent conclusions.

(From Edwards, 1979)

Now You See It, Now You Don't Know That You See It

Mrs. N. G., a California housewife recovered from split-brain surgery, sits in front of a screen that blocks her view of her hands and objects on the table. As she fixates on a point in the center of her visual field, a projector flashes pictures into one or the other eye. Her task is to report verbally what she was shown and then to match that image by touching the appropriate object among the set of those on the table.

A cup is flashed in the right half of her visual field—and thus to her left hemisphere. "Cup" she replies, and she quickly feels through the array with her right hand until she finds a cup. No problem. Next, a spoon is flashed in her left visual field—and thus to her right hemisphere. Mrs. N. G. reports seeing nothing. When asked to pick out the object that was flashed using her left hand (controlled by the right hemisphere), she says it's not possible. But after touching each one she holds up the spoon. "What a lucky guess," she exclaims with surprise. Time after time she picks the correct object although she insists she saw nothing and was totally unaware of the relationship between the image flashed (to the right hemisphere) and the object identified by touch. Often, her left hemisphere comes to the aid of the puzzled right side, constructing stories to help explain the responding of the silent, confused right hemisphere.

A different message sent to her right hemisphere evokes an emotional reaction. When a sexually suggestive picture of a nude is flashed to her right hemisphere, Mrs. N. G. says she sees only a flash of light. But she blushes and giggles. In trying to explain her "uncaused" embarrassment, Mrs. N. G. exclaims, "Oh, doctor, you have some machine!" Again we see evidence of processing of information below the level of consciousness, in this case by the language-poor right hemisphere.

Another split-brain patient, Paul is a boy of 15 who has partial representation of language functions in the right hemisphere. Left hemisphere damage at an early age had probably been compensated for by the "plasticity" of the brain in developing some language ability on the right side. He can answer what his right half-brain sees or hears by spelling out words with letter blocks from a Scrabble game.

For example, the first part of a question, ("Who . . .") is asked orally, thus being picked up by both ears and going to both hemispheres. The end of the question ("are you?") is then flashed in the left visual field, thus going only to the right hemisphere. In response to the input "Who (are you?)," received in this way, Paul arranges the blocks to form his name, "PAUL." He is able to spell his mood ("good"), his

EVERYDAY CHANGES IN CONSCIOUSNESS

Watch children stand on their heads or spin around in order to make themselves dizzy, and ask them why they do it. "So everything looks funny." "It feels weird." "To see things tumble around in my head." Answers like these underscore the assumption that "human beings are born with a drive to experience modes of awareness other than the normal waking one; from very young ages, children experiment with techniques to change consciousness" (Weil, 1977, p.37).

hobby ("car"), his favorite person ("Henry Wi Fuzi," for Henry Winkler, TV's Fonzi), tomorrow's day, and questions about his career goals ("automobile race[r]"). The researchers have concluded that Paul's right hemisphere possesses qualities of a conscious state: a sense of self, personal feelings, evaluations, future orientation, and goals.

Interestingly, when the *left* hemisphere is asked what is a desirable job for Paul, it answers, "Oh, be a draftsman." The fact that the two hemispheres do not always agree is seen as further evidence that the right side of the brain possesses conscious properties independent of the left. It seems to have a will of its own. For most of us, however, consciousness and self-awareness appear to be tied to the development of a verbal system, which we then use to represent symbolically what we perceive in both our inner and our outer worlds (Le Doux et al., 1977).

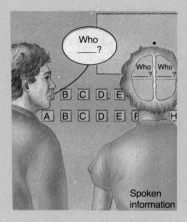
Spoken information

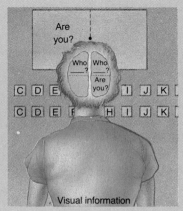
Visual information

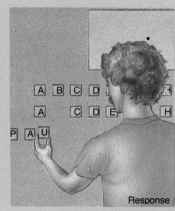
Response

(After Gazzaniga, 1980)

As they grow older, some people continue these "experiments" by taking drugs, including alcohol and caffeine, that alter their ordinary awareness. Some change their consciousness through prayer, meditation, or hypnosis. But we all do so every time we daydream, have fantasies, or slip from wakefulness into sleep and have nightdreams. Before we examine some of these mental states, we need to consider their general characteristics.

A useful orientation to these realities is provided by Charles Tart, a pioneering researcher in this area.

"An altered state of consciousness for a given individual is one in which he clearly feels a *qualitative* shift in his pattern of mental functioning; that is, he feels not just a *quantitative* shift (more or less alert, more or less visual imagery, sharper or duller, etc.) but also that some quality or qualities of his mental processes are *different*. Mental functions operate that do not operate at all ordinarily, perceptual qualities appear that have no normal counterparts, and so forth" (Tart, 1969, pp.1-2).

The use of the term *altered* has been criticized because it implies that there is one standard, desirable state of consciousness. Most researchers today prefer to speak of *alternate* or *extended* states of consciousness, since these words carry no implication of abnormality, or of superiority of the ordinary state. In this section we will look at everyday changes in consciousness that are familiar to us all because they are unavoidable and occur naturally. Then, in the next section, we will examine some more extreme forms of consciousness change that are brought about by external agents or particular physiological conditions. These alternate states of consciousness are similar in being qualitatively different from ordinary consciousness but vary in their degree of difference, duration, and other features.

Daydreaming and fantasy

How clearly can you imagine each of the following: (a) a full moon coming over the horizon; (b) inheriting a million dollars; (c) what you should have said to the teacher you disliked most in high school? Close your eyes and see.

These "pictures in the mind's eye" are the stuff of daydreams. **Daydreaming** is a mild form of consciousness alteration that involves a shift of attention away from responding to external stimulation toward responding to some internal stimulus. An operational definition of *daydreaming* is: "the report of thoughts that involve a shift of attention away from an immediately demanding task" [without, of course, any reference to current external factors] (Singer, 1975, p. 730).

Do you daydream, according to such definitions? You have plenty of company if you do.

In one sample of 240 respondents, ages 18 to 50, with some college education, 96 percent reported daydreaming daily. Young adults (ages 18 to 29) reported the most daydreaming; there was a significant decline with age (Singer & McCraven, 1961).

In general, research by Jerome Singer (1966, 1976) and others shows that daydreaming is a common human activity when people are alone and relaxed. Daydreaming is reported to occur most often in bed shortly before sleep, and least often upon awakening and during meals or sexual activity (unless the honeymoon is really over). Most people report that they enjoy daydreaming and are not embarrassed by it because they feel it is a normal function.

When we fantasize about what might be "if things were different," we are not necessarily escaping from life but may be confronting the mysteries of life with wonder and respect. Wishing and reality-testing activities seem to form the basic core of our daydreams. In fact, most daytime dreaming is concerned with practical, immediate concerns, especially future interpersonal behavior, rather than wild speculations. Next in frequency come daydreams dealing with sexual satisfaction, altruistic concerns, unusual good fortune (inheriting money), and likely future events (vacations).

In a survey of sexual fantasies, single Canadian women students between the ages of 18 and 47 were asked to check items that applied to them. The top six fantasies checked were: having intercourse with a husband or boyfriend (90 percent), being undressed by a man (79 percent), a previous sexual experience (78 percent), intercourse in an exotic place

◁ *Daydreaming is natural for people of all ages. It provides a means of transcending time and space. We can try out new roles, have our wishes fulfilled, travel to exciting places—all in a matter of moments. Only when such activity becomes more "real" and important than the world around us should we begin to worry.*

(72 percent), undressing a man (71 percent), oral sex (66 percent).

The older women and those involved in intimate relationships had the most active fantasy lives: only 2 percent of the women said they never had sexual fantasies. The main reasons given for indulging in fantasy were that it was a "pleasant pastime," to become aroused, to help in falling asleep, and to achieve orgasm (Pelletier & Herold, 1983).

Intense imaginative involvement with the constructions of one's consciousness comes easily for children and sometimes is a way to deal with difficult home situations, abusive parents, or loneliness. But it occurs for adults too when we "lose ourselves" in a dramatic performance or have an intense sense of the beauty of nature.

Daydreams are rarely as vivid and compelling as nightdreams, but people vary in the extent to which they are able to become imaginatively involved in the realities they create. These individual differences are thought to be enduring personality factors not usually assessed by standard psychological tests (Tellegen & Atkinson, 1974).

Sleeping and dreaming

We slip daily between states of consciousness as we move from waking to sleeping and then to dreaming. And in between being awake and asleep is a drowsy condition which is not sleep but another alternate state of consciousness.

Although keeping records of dreams has been a popular activity for ages (Calkins, 1893), such dream diaries offer no clues about the transformations of consciousness associated with sleeping. Before psychologists could study sleep, they had to find *external* indicators of the *internal* behavior of sleep that could be observed and measured.

The methodological breakthrough for the study of sleep came with the development of a technology to record brain-wave activity in the form of an electro-encephalogram (EEG). This provided an objective, ongoing measure of how brain activity varied when people were awake or asleep. In 1937, Loomis and his associates made the important discovery that brain waves change in form with the onset of sleep and show further systematic changes during the entire sleep period.

The next significant advance in sleep research occurred when it was found that bursts of rapid eye movement (REM) appeared at periodic intervals during sleep (Aserinsky & Kleitman, 1953). When these rapid eye movements were linked to the occurrence of dreaming, many investigators were excited by this new path into a previously hidden side of human activity (Dement & Kleitman, 1957). Since then our understanding of this nightly alteration of consciousness has been studied in sleep laboratories throughout the world.

The mystery of sleep. About a third of your life will be spent sleeping, no matter how much you might wish to extend the active, waking side of your life. Even when we spend totally relaxed, uneventful days on vacation, we still sleep a significant part of the time. It appears that humans have a need to sleep, but why we do is not known. The wonder of sleep is the universal restriction it forces upon all active creatures to spend so much time doing so little.

One reason we sleep each day can be found in the operation of our "biological clock." Even in an environment where all conditions are held constant (light, temperature, humidity, and noise) humans and animals will go to sleep about once every 24 hours. A regular 24-hour cycle also occurs for body temperature, urine production, secretion of certain hormones, and even our ability to memorize telephone numbers.

Any consistent pattern of cyclical body activities that lasts about 24 hours is called a *circadian cycle,* or **circadian rhythm** (*circadian* means "about a day"). The body's circadian rhythms are generated internally, but the "biological clock" can be set or reset by light and other stimuli. Predictable cycles with peaks and troughs for over a hundred physiological and performance variables have been identified, some with periods longer or shorter than 24 hours. One theory is that our daily cycle of best efficiency in the morning with a let-down in early afternoon is a holdover from the evolution of our species in a tropical climate (Thompson & Harsha, 1984).

Sleep is promoted when large amounts of the hormone *melatonin* are released from the pineal gland (Binkley, 1979). Light inhibits production of melatonin although the pineal gland will release some melatonin even in unchanging light conditions.

Melatonin is not the biological clock, however. Whatever and wherever the biological clock may be, it is based on processes that continue to work despite interference of all kinds. Animals born blind have nearly normal 24-hour circadian rhythms. Nor are these on-off cycles much disturbed by deprivation of food or water, by drugs, by periods of forced activity or inactivity, or even by removal of any of the hormonal organs (Richter, 1965).

How much someone sleeps is not correlated with activity during the day, but with certain personality variables. Individuals who slept longer than average, when compared to those who slept less than average, were found to be more nervous and worrisome and to be more artistic, creative, and nonconforming. Short-sleepers tended to be more energetic and extraverted (Hartmann, 1973). Whether sleep influences personality, or personality type affects sleep or a third process causes the two to be related cannot be determined from this correlational study.

The two most general answers to the question why we need to sleep, are *restoration* and *conservation.* Sleep enables the body to engage in restoration of its "housekeeping" functions such as digestion and waste product removal. It may also be a period of relative inactivity when neurotransmitters are synthesized to compensate for the quantities used in daily activities or when postsynaptic receptors are returned to their optimal level of sensitivity (Stern & Morgane, 1974). An evolutionary theory of the function of sleep suggests that it is a mechanism that evolved and survived natural selection because it enabled animals to conserve energy at times when there was no need to forage for food and mates, and no work to be done (Webb, 1974; Allison & Cicchetti, 1976; Cartwright, 1982).

Regardless of why we sleep, it is clear that sleep is divided into distinct stages during which different brain activities are taking place. EEGs taken during sleep show two general states of brain activity; *delta sleep,* in which the EEG pattern is slow and orderly, and *desynchronized* or *paradoxical sleep,* in which the EEG pattern resembles the erratic low-voltage pattern of the waking state, although we are very much asleep. Because bursts of rapid eye movement occur during such sleep, desynchronized sleep is usu-

ally called *REM sleep.* Persons awakened during REM sleep often report dreaming, while those awakened during non-REM sleep are much less likely to do so. The EEG pattern of non-REM sleep shows several distinctive wave patterns, as illustrated in **Figure 6.5.**

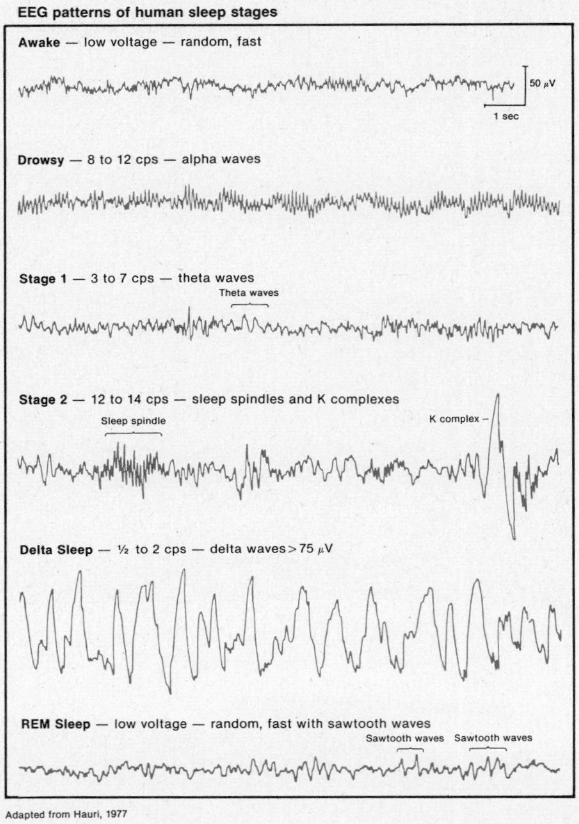

EEG patterns of human sleep stages

Awake — low voltage — random, fast

Drowsy — 8 to 12 cps — alpha waves

Stage 1 — 3 to 7 cps — theta waves
Theta waves

Stage 2 — 12 to 14 cps — sleep spindles and K complexes
Sleep spindle   K complex

Delta Sleep — ½ to 2 cps — delta waves > 75 μV

REM Sleep — low voltage — random, fast with sawtooth waves
Sawtooth waves   Sawtooth waves

Adapted from Hauri, 1977

△ **Figure 6.5   *EEG Patterns of Human Sleep Stages***

Between wakefulness and REM sleep, our brain waves change through several characteristic patterns that are not seen when we are awake. Stages 3 and 4 of non-REM sleep are so similar that some researchers merge them and simply call the whole phase "delta sleep" (adapted from Hauri, 1977).

The adult falling asleep passes through stages 1, 2, 3, and 4 in a cycle lasting approximately 90 minutes and then "emerges" into a period of REM sleep lasting about 10 minutes. A night of sleep usually consists of four to six such cycles. With each subsequent cycle, delta sleep gets shorter and the REM period lengthens. During the last cycle, REM sleep can last for 30 to 60 minutes. **Figure 6.6** shows a typical pattern.

Humans and most other animals exhibit regular sleep-wake cycles, orderly stages of sleep, and some standard ratio of REM to non-REM sleep. For humans, this changes with age. A baby will sleep 16 hours a day with perhaps half of it in REM sleep. By age 1, total sleep time decreases to about 13 hours, of which REM sleep constitutes only 25 to 30 percent. A young adult will sleep 7 to 8 hours with about 20 percent REM sleep; and the elderly sleep about 6 hours with about 15 percent REM sleep. The duration of delta sleep begins to drop at age 30 and by the time a person is 60 to 70 years old, delta sleep virtually disappears. The cyclic nature of the sleep-wake cycle has been associated with activity in specific areas of the brain and with the release of chemicals that influence sleeping and waking (Maugh, 1982). **Figure 6.7** shows these changing sleep patterns.

Deprivation of REM sleep needs to be made up specifically by longer than usual periods of REM sleep during one's next sleep or over several sleep episodes. It may even be that we need to sleep in order to get REM sleep—rather than simply to rest weary

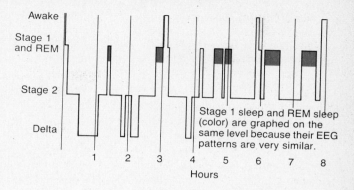

(Adapted from Hauri, 1977)

△ | *Figure 6.6   Typical Sleep Pattern of a Young Adult*

bodies and minds. A number of interesting, but not yet fully demonstrated, benefits have been attributed to REM sleep. For example, it is suggested by some that, in infancy, REM sleep is responsible for establishing the pathways between our nerves and muscles that enable us to move our eyes. REM sleep may also be establishing the functional structures in the brain, like those involving the learning of motor skills. It could be playing a role in the maintenance of mood and emotion. REM sleep may also be required for storing memories and fitting recent experiences into networks of previous beliefs or memories (see Dement, 1976; Cartwright, 1978).

▷ | **Figure 6.7   *Patterns of Human Sleep over a Lifetime***

The graph shows changes with age in total amounts of daily sleep, both REM and non-REM, and percentage of REM sleep. Note that the amount of REM sleep decreases considerably over the years, while non-REM diminishes less sharply (adapted from Roffwarg et al., 1966).

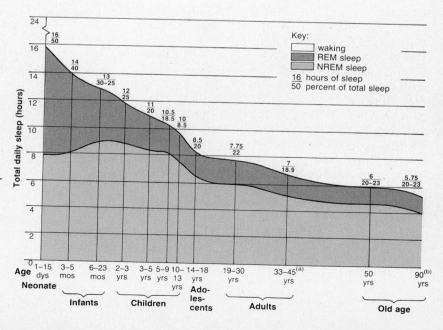

What causes dreams?

"Dreams offer a royal road to the mind when it is in a state governed by rules and principles quite different from those that apply during waking" (Hobson & McCarley, 1977).

Subjects aroused during REM sleep recall ongoing visual images that form a coherent drama, are vivid, and may be in color with sound. Despite bizarre or fantastic qualities of the plot, the unreal situation is accepted by the sleeper as "natural." Some dreaming also takes place during non-REM periods, but it is of a different quality. Dreaming associated with non-REM states is less likely to contain dramatic story content. It is full of specific thoughts but has minimal sensory imagery. The percentage of dreaming reported from REM and non-REM awakenings in ten studies and the definitions of dreaming they used are summarized in **Table 6.2.**

People occasionally report being aware that they are dreaming. The existence of these "lucid dreams" has recently been demonstrated by having subjects signal (by gestures) when they realized that they were dreaming. They were able to signal to the researchers during REM sleep that a lucid dream was taking place, without disturbing their sleep and with memory for the dream. It appears that lucid dreaming is a learnable skill (LaBerge, 1980; LaBerge et al., 1981).

One physiological explanation recently advanced proposes that dreams are the brain's attempt to form a coherent interpretation of essentially random bursts of ongoing cortical activity during REM sleep. The cortex retrieves memories that could be associated with the signals it is receiving from deep within the brain stem. Finding no logical connections in the stimulation, it makes illogical remote associations or fills the gaps with recent memories (Hobson & McCarley, 1977).

According to Freud (1900), however, dreams are much more than the brain's search for a good story to account for its electrical discharges. Freud saw dreams as symbolic expressions of unconscious wishes that have been carefully disguised by an internal "censor." In Freudian terms, what you remember and report of your dreams is only the *manifest* content. The real meaning of a dream is in its *latent* (hidden) content—unconscious impulses and wishes that have been denied overt gratification and appear in dreams in disguised forms. The manifest content is the acceptable version of the story; the latent content represents the socially or personally unacceptable version—but the true, "uncut" one. In sleep, the usually vigilant censor is relaxed, and by a variety of psychological processes, unacceptable unconscious material is transformed into an acceptable manifest story line and so slips by.

It is evident from Freud's writing in his classic *Interpretation of Dreams* (1900) that *his* mind was on sex. To him, dream symbols were largely sex symbols in varying states of undress.

"—All elongated objects, such as sticks, tree trunks and umbrellas (the opening of these last being comparable to an erection) may stand for the male organ—as well as all long, sharp weapons, such as knives, daggers and pikes. . . . —Boxes, cases, chests, cupboards and ovens represent the uterus, and also hollow objects, ships, and vessels of all kinds.

"—Rooms in dreams are usually women; if the various ways in and out of them are represented, this interpretation is scarcely open to doubt. . . . A dream of going through a suite of rooms is a brothel or harem dream. . . . —It is highly probable that all

Table 6.2 *Dreaming During REM and Non-REM Sleep*

Definition of Dreaming Used in Study	Percent Recalling REM Dreams	Percent Recalling Non-REM Dreams
"any item of specific content"	87	74
"visual, auditory, or kinesthetic imagery"	82	54
"a dream recalled in some detail"	69	34
self-definition by each subject	85	24
"specific content of mental experience"	86	23
"detailed dream description"	74	7
"coherent, fairly detailed description"	79	7
"any sensory imagery with . . . progression of the mental activity"	81	7
self-definition by each subject	60	3
self-definition by each subject	88	0

(Adapted from F. R. Freeman, Sleep Research: A Critical Review, 1972. Courtesy of Charles C. Thomas, Publisher, Springfield, Illinois)

complicated machinery and apparatus occurring in dreams stand for the genitals (and as a rule male ones). . . . Nor is there any doubt that all weapons and tools are used as symbols for the male organ: e.g., ploughs, hammers, rifles, revolvers, daggers, sabres, etc." (pp. 354-56)

According to Freud, the two main functions of dreams are to guard sleep and to serve as sources of wish fulfillment. They allow uninterrupted sleep by draining off psychic tensions created during the day and allow us to achieve the unconscious fulfillment of our wishes.

Dreams are real while they last.
Can we say more of Life?

Havelock Ellis

EXTENDED STATES OF CONSCIOUSNESS

It is one thing to have ordinary, waking consciousness undergo daily transformations as we daydream, sleep, or engage in nightdreaming and quite another matter to go beyond these familiar forms to extended states of consciousness. Examples of these less common "alternate" states of consciousness are seen in hallucinations and in the experiences associated with hypnosis and certain kinds of drugs.

Hallucinations

Hallucinations are vivid perceptions in the absence of objective stimulation. The images and sensations experienced are the products of the hallucinator's mind rather than the consequence of external stimuli but are often believed by the individual to be perceptions of reality.

Hallucinations can occur during states of high fever, epilepsy, and migraine headaches. They are also a characteristic of severe mental disorder, in which the patient gives up the conception of reality based on consensual validation and responds to private mental events as if they were representations of external sensory stimuli, believing in the reality of the voices heard or the figures seen.

Hallucinations have also been associated with heightened arousal states and religious ecstasies. In fact, in some cultures and circumstances, hallucinations are interpreted as mystical insights that confer special status on the visionary. So in different settings, the same vivid perception of direct contact with spiritual forces may be deprecated as a "hallucination" or honored as a "vision" or "revelation." It is thus important to recognize that evaluation of such mental states depends as much on the judgment of observers as on the content of the perceptual experience itself. On the other hand, some visions with religious content clearly represent states induced by mental disturbance, epilepsy, or migraines. For example, it is now believed that the visions recorded by the nun and mystic Hildegard of Bingen (1098-1180) can be accounted for as consistent patterns of visual imagery produced by migraines (Sacks, 1973).

◁ *This drawing by the mystic Hildegard of Bingen depicts a vision of a shower of brilliant stars, extinguished after its passage. It is typical of a migraine-induced hallucination.*

primitive ceremonies of numerous kinds, or moments of extreme emotion (whether the emotion be ecstatic love or unbearable grief).

But it also appears that the brain requires some minimal level of external stimulation. Some subjects, when kept in a special environment that minimizes all sensory stimulation, show a tendency to hallucinate. Sensory isolation "destructures the environment" and may force subjects to try to restore meaning and stable orientation to the situation. Hallucinations may be a way of reconstructing a reality in accordance with one's personality, past experiences, and the demands of the present experimental setting (Zubeck et al., 1961; see also Suedfeld, 1980, for positive effects of chosen reduced sensory stimulation).

Hypnosis

Hypnosis holds a strange fascination for most people. It seems that mere words spoken by the hypnotist can cause major changes in the behavior of the hypnotic subject. We feel uneasy about this apparent power of one person over another and about the vulnerability of the person so influenced. But is that view of their relationship accurate? What is hypnosis, what are its important features, and what are some of its valid psychological uses?

Hypnosis is a term derived from the name *Hypnos*, the Greek god of sleep. Sleep plays no part in hypnosis, though, except in the person's *appearance* of being in a deeply relaxed, sleeplike state, in some cases. But if the person actually falls asleep, there is no longer any responsiveness to hypnotic suggestions.

There are many different conceptions of what hypnosis is, along with a variety of definitions. For

Hallucinations may be induced by psychoactive drugs, such as LSD and peyote, as well as by the withdrawal of alcohol in severe cases of alcoholism (delirium tremens, "the DTs"). For the most part, however, these are not regarded as "true hallucinations" since they are direct effects of the drug on the brain rather than part of a new view of reality that the person is creating.

Instead of asking what turns hallucinations on, some psychologists wonder, "Why do we not hallucinate all the time?" They believe that the ability to hallucinate is always present in each of us, but normally is inhibited by ongoing interaction with sensory input, by our constant reality testing, and by feedback from the environment. When sensory input and feedback are lacking and there is no way to test our ideas against outer reality, there is indeed a tendency to hallucinate. Hallucinations are also fostered by heightened arousal, states of intense need, or inability to suppress threatening thoughts.

Many instances of altered states of consciousness are reported following such "overstimulating" experiences as mob riots, religious revival meetings, prolonged dancing (such as is done by "whirling" dervishes), extreme fright or panic, trance states during

our purposes, a broad definition of **hypnosis** presents it as an alternate state of awareness induced by a variety of techniques and characterized by the special ability of some people to respond to suggestions with changes in perception, memory, motivation, and sense of self-control (Orne, 1980). More simply, hypnosis is often equated with hypersuggestibility, a state of heightened responsiveness to another person's suggestions. Not only does the hypnotic subject follow these suggestions, but there is often the feeling that the behavior is emitted as if "by itself," without intention or any volitional effort on the part of the subject.

Hypnotic suggestibility. Most dramatic stage performances of hypnosis give the impression that the power of hypnosis should be credited to the skills of the hypnotist. Perhaps it is something in his or her "hypnotic gaze" that makes the commands so compelling. But this is a false conclusion. The real star of the show is the person who is hypnotized—not the hypnotist. The hypnotist is little more than a coach or experienced travel guide who shows the way.

The single most important factor in hypnosis is the participant's ability or "talent" to become hypnotized. **Hypnotizability** represents the degree to which an individual is responsive to standardized suggestions. There are wide individual differences in this susceptibility to hypnotic suggestions, varying from persons who are not at all responsive to any suggestion to persons who are totally responsive to virtually every suggestion. The highly hypnotizable person may respond to suggestions for changes in motor reactions (limbs rigid or flexible), for experiencing hallucinations and amnesia, and for becoming insensitive to powerful stimuli. Thus hypnotizing someone is a technique for changing the hypnotized person's representation of reality.

The "power" of hypnosis can be traced to the existence of this ability in certain people to respond to suggestion, along with the creation of an appropriate psychological environment. A hypnotizable person can be hypnotized by anyone he or she is willing to respond to, while someone unhypnotizable will not respond to the tactics of the most skilled hypnotist. It is also possible for some hypnotizable people to become self-hypnotized, to give and respond to their own suggestions. This phenomenon is called *autohypnosis* (hypnosis by one's self).

Hypnotic induction is primarily a matter of vivid imagination and openness to the suggestions of the hypnotist. It is not, as many people assume, a mysterious process by which one individual "gains power" over another.

Hypnosis usually begins with **hypnotic induction,** a preliminary set of activities that prepare the participant for this alternate state of awareness. Induction activities involve suggestions to imagine certain experiences, to visualize events and reactions. When practiced repeatedly, the hypnotic induction procedure acts as a learned signal to the subject to experience this special, out-of-the-ordinary state by minimizing distractions, concentrating on suggested stimuli, and believing that a special state of consciousness is about to happen.

The typical induction procedure uses suggestions for deep relaxation, but some people can become hypnotized by the use of an active, alert induction—even by imagining jogging or riding a bicycle. A child in the dentist's chair can be hypnotized while his or her attention is directed to vivid stories or to imagining exciting adventures of a favorite TV character. Meanwhile the dentist drills and fills cavities with no anesthesia, but the child feels no pain (Banyai & E. Hilgard, 1976).

The operational definition of hypnotizability is the number of items passed (experienced) on a standardized induction test. Some "easy" items—such as imagining an arm getting heavier—are passed by most people. More difficult ones—such as hallucinating a buzzing fly, or forgetting suggested events—are passed by only a few. **Figure 6.8** shows the percentage of college-age subjects who are at various levels of hypnotizability the first time they are given the hypnotic induction test.

This objective measure of hypnotizability is the most important single predictor of a person's responsiveness to a variety of hypnotic phenomena. For example, high scorers are more likely than low scorers to be able to relieve pain by hypnosis (experience hypnotic analgesia) and to respond to hypnotic suggestions to have *positive hallucinations* (see or hear something not objectively present) or *negative hallucinations* (not perceive something that is present).

Hypnotizability is a relatively stable attribute of a given individual. An adult's scores remain about the same when measured over a ten-year period (Morgan et al., 1974). Children tend to be more suggestible than adults, with hypnotic responsiveness peaking just before adolescence and declining thereafter. There is some evidence for genetic determinants of hypnotizability, in the fact that the scores of identical twins are more similar than are those of fraternal twins (Morgan et al., 1970).

Responsiveness to hypnotic suggestion can be slightly enhanced with intensive practice, as well as by sensory deprivation or drugs such as LSD or mescaline (Diamond, 1974; Sanders & Reyhen, 1969; Sjoberg & Hollister, 1965). But these procedures do not transform unsusceptible subjects into highly responsive ones.

Although hypnotizability is relatively stable, it is surprising to discover that it is not correlated with any personality trait, nor is it the same as gullibility, conformity, role playing, or reaction to the social demands of the situation (see Fromm & Shor, 1979). It is a unique "suscept-*ability*." It develops early in life along with the sense of being able to become *completely absorbed* in some ongoing experience. The hypnotizable person is one who is capable of deep involvement in the imaginative-feeling areas of experience, such as in reading novels or listening to music. Also associated with hypnotizability is a willingness to suspend ordinary reality testing temporarily and accept "as if" suggestions as though they were about reality (J. Hilgard, 1970, 1979).

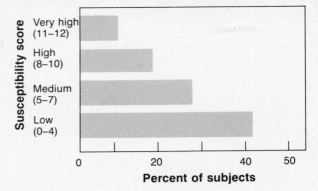

Figure 6.8 *Level of Hypnosis at First Induction*

The graph shows results for 533 subjects hypnotized for the first time. Hypnotizability was measured on the Stanford Hypnotic Susceptibility Scale, which consists of 12 items (based on E. Hilgard, 1965).

Research efforts to find physiological indicators of the state of hypnosis have not been successful, perhaps because of the many different mental and behavioral events that may be induced under hypnosis. It has been demonstrated however, that hypnotizability is associated with a preference for greater use of the functions of the right hemisphere of the brain relative to the more analytic left hemisphere (Gur & Gur, 1974).

Altered personal reality under hypnosis. It is necessary to maintain a scientific skepticism regarding the claims made for hypnosis, especially when the claims are based on individual case reports or research lacking proper control conditions (Barber, 1969). Still, there does exist a reliable body of empirical evidence bolstered by conservative expert opinion strongly suggesting that hypnosis can exert a powerful influence on many psychological and bodily functions (Bowers, 1976; E. Hilgard, 1968, 1973; Burrows & Dennerstein, 1980). Here we will single out only two especially intriguing phenomena that illustrate hypnotic changes in personal reality—"trance logic" and dissociation. In the following example of "trance logic," the investigator used a procedure known as *age regression,* in which the hypnotized subject is made to believe that he or she is at some particular earlier age.

A subject "who spoke only German at age six and who was age regressed to that time answered 'Nein' ['No'] when asked whether he understood English. . . . When this question was rephrased to him 10 times in English, he indicated each time in German that he was unable to comprehend English, explaining in childlike German such details as that his parents speak English in order that he not understand. While professing his inability to comprehend English, he continued responding appropriately in German to the hypnotist's complex English questions" (Orne, 1972, p. 427).

This person, while hypnotized, was showing "trance logic"; he could tolerate paradoxes instead of insisting that his experience make sense by ordinary logic. **Trance logic** is a characteristic feature of some highly hypnotizable subjects, who register information at one level of processing, but deny it at other levels. Information gets in, but then the person acts as if it is not there. It provides yet another example of our ability to process information below the level of consciousness.

Some highly suggestible individuals are especially responsive to stored information that is not directly accessible to their conscious awareness. While they are in the hypnotic trance state, they function at two levels of consciousness—a full but hypnotic consciousness of what they are experiencing, as suggested, and a concealed, out-of-consciousness awareness. Such subjects can sometimes reveal this hidden level of their consciousness if they are instructed to engage in "automatic writing." Here the person has no conscious volition or awareness of what he or she is writing, yet somehow the pen moves and meaningful words are written. "Automatic talking" can also occur. The person's concealed cognitive system reports on itself without the conscious system becoming aware of what is going on.

Ernest Hilgard has coined the term "hidden observer" to refer to the covert awareness of knowledge that is not acknowledged consciously. This phenomenon was first observed in hypnotic subjects who had reported feeling no pain when subjected to a painful stimulus and told they would feel nothing. When they were then told that a hidden part of them knew what was going on in their body and could report it accurately, the subjects processed the pain experience and reported pain as fully as those who had not been hypnotized (E. Hilgard, 1977).

The "double consciousness" revealed by this hidden observer research is shown further in these statements from college student subjects:

"The hidden observer and the hypnotized part are both *all of me,* but the hidden observer is more aware and reported honestly what was there. The hypnotized part of me just *wasn't aware* of the pain" (Knox et al., 1974, p. 845).

"In hypnosis I kept my mind and body separate, and my mind was wandering to other places—not aware of the pain in my arm. When the hidden observer was called up, the hypnotized part had to step back for a minute and let the hidden part tell the truth" (Knox et al., 1974, p. 846).

This *dissociation*—functioning of consciousness at different levels—may also occur in altered states of consciousness induced by religious ecstasy and drugs. These and other hypnotic phenomena not only are interesting in themselves, but point up the subtle operating characteristics and capabilities of a human mind that can function at conscious and nonconscious levels simultaneously.

Multiple personalities and hypnosis. One of the most dramatic forms of a radically altered consciousness occurs in people who develop multiple personalities. *Multiple personality* is a dissociative mental disorder in which two or more distinct personalities exist within the same individual. At any particular time one of these personalities is dominant in directing the individual's behavior. Although the original personality is unaware of the other personalities, they are conscious of it. Each of the emerging other personalities contrasts in some significant way with the "true" self, perhaps being outgoing if the person is shy, tough if weak, sexually assertive if fearful and sexually naive. Each personality has a unique identity, name, relationships, behavior patterns and even characteristic brain-wave activity. In some cases, dozens of different characters emerge to help the person deal with a difficult life situation. The emergence of these alternate personalities, each with its own consciousness is sudden, precipitated by stressful experiences.

Although multiple personality is usually dealt with only by clinical psychologists and psychiatrists concerned about treating these severely disturbed individuals, the study of multiple personality may help us understand the nature of consciousness. It reveals that a mind can be divided into separately functioning parts or selves by unconscious choice, as effectively as by a surgeon's scalpel. Studying these divisions can help us appreciate better the dissociative state that hypnosis can generate.

Hypnosis offers the most effective form of therapy for this disorder (and has been suspected by some of fostering its development). Hypnosis enables the patient to exhibit the multiple personalities, and then over time makes the original self aware of these subpersonalities, thus giving the person a means for integrating them into an effective single self. This approach has been popularized in books like *The Three Faces of Eve* (Thigpen & Cleckley, 1957) and *Sybil* (Schreiber, 1973).

Why should hypnosis work better than drug therapy or other therapeutic approaches? Perhaps it is because of the way in which the personality and consciousness of the patient became divided originally. Patients with multiple personality are typically women who were severely abused physically or sexually for extended periods during childhood by parents, relatives, or close friends. They may have been beaten or locked up by those who were supposed to love them, on whom they were so dependent that they could not fight back or run away. So they have fled symbolically through dissociation. They protect their vulnerable self by creating more hardy internal actors and actresses to help cope with the traumatic situation. Somehow these abused children create an alternate reality and enter it so fully that it comes to substitute for their actual reality. They seem to do so by a process similar to self-hypnosis. When it works to relieve the unbearable stress of the situation, they continue to cope in this way. **Table 6.3** outlines some of the functions that alternate personalities were found to serve in one study of female patients (Bliss, 1980).

In ongoing research at the National Institute of Mental Health in Bethesda, MD (Putnam, 1984) more than sixty patients have been studied to determine more precisely how different each of their alternate personalities really is and the extent to which they reflect the operation of extended states of consciousness. Some of the patients have personalities

Table 6.3 *Functions of alternate personalities*

Patient's Problem	*Personality's Task*
Emotional experiences	
Unhappiness	Be happy
Fear of crying	Cry for her
Guilty Feelings	Be guilty
Anger and rage	Experience anger
Unloving mother	A good, kind mother
Feel ugly	Be beautiful
Skills	
Feels stupid, incompetent, and untalented	Be an intellectual, a singer, artist, or writer
Unloved by mother	Be like mother, or like a sister who is preferred by mother
Mistreated	Be unafraid to retaliate for abuses
Want to escape, but afraid	Run away
Sexuality	
Inability to cope with heterosexuality, rape, sexual abuse	Handle sexuality to the point of promiscuity and prostitution
Homosexual impulses	Be a lesbian
Motivation	
Sense of inadequacy, inability, futility	Push her to achieve and excel

(Adapted from Bliss, 1980)

△ These paintings were made by Huichol Indians using yarn and beeswax on wood. They depict hallucinations induced by use of the drug peyote. The first is an eyes-open hallucination of a tree; the second depicts deer's heads rotating around the brightness of the fire god.

that speak and understand foreign languages the patient does not know, or have memories, emotions, or values that are alien to the patient. This research may tell us some of the ways in which divided consciousness can give birth to new minds in an imaginative, distressed person.

Mind alteration with drugs

Since ancient times, people everywhere have taken drugs that altered their perception of reality. There is archeological evidence for the uninterrupted use of *sophora* seed (called mescal bean) for over ten thousand years in the southwestern United States and Mexico. From the ninth millenium B.C. to the nineteenth century A.D., New World peoples smoked sophora to bring on ecstatic hallucinatory visions. Then sophora was replaced by the more benign peyote cactus, which is still used in the sacred rituals of many Indians.

In modern-day use, drugs are less associated with "sacred" communal rituals to reach new plateaus of mystical awareness than with attempts by individuals to feel mellow, cope with stress, tune out the unpleasantness of current realities, or tune in to alternate states of consciousness. This drug-induced alter-

ation in the functioning of mind and in the nature of consciousness was popularized in our era in the 1954 publication of *The Doors of Perception* by Aldous Huxley. Huxley took mescaline as a personal experiment to test the validity of poet William Blake's assertion in *The Marriage of Heaven and Hell* (1793):

"If the doors of perception were cleansed every thing would appear to man as it is, infinite.
"For man has closed himself up, till he sees all thro' narrow chinks of his concern."

The experience for Huxley was one that transcended his perception of ordinary reality, leading to new modes of thought, more mystical than rational. He described the final stage of giving up his ego within the mescaline experience as one where "there is an 'obscure knowledge' that All is in all—that All is actually each. This is as near, I take it, as a finite mind can ever come to 'perceiving everything that is happening everywhere in the universe.'"

In few societies has there been as extensive use of drugs or as much interest in drugs by such young users as there is in the United States today. Experimenting with drugs, which increased steadily among high-school students during the 1970s, had levelled off and has been declining since, according to annual surveys of 16,000 to 17,000 high school seniors (Johnston et al., 1982). But nearly two thirds of the current generation of American high-school seniors report having used an illicit drug. Males are more likely to use drugs than females, and to know more users (Brunswick, 1980).

A large-scale 1971 survey of over 8000 secondary-school students in New York State revealed that adolescents were much more likely to use marijuana if their friends did than if their friends did not. Of those who perceived all their friends to be users, 92 percent used marijuana themselves, as compared to only 7 percent of those who perceived none of their friends to be users.

As can be seen in **Figure 6.9,** the influence of best friends overwhelms that of parents. Marijuana use is related in a small way to parental drug use, but it does not make much difference if your parents do not use drugs if your best friend does—chances are that you will too. And, on the other hand, if your best friend does not use drugs, it does not make much difference if your parents do—chances are you will *not* (Kandel, 1973).

In this section, we will focus on the **psychoactive drugs**—those chemicals which affect mental processes and behavior by changing conscious aware-

ness of reality for a while. We will begin by considering what drug dependence is, then will compare the effects of several kinds of psychoactive drugs, and finally will see what *non*drug factors can increase or decrease their effects.

Dependence and addiction. In Chapter 3, the effects of drugs in blocking, enhancing, or prolonging activity at the synapses were described. Although a semi-permeable membrane called the *blood-brain barrier* surrounds the blood vessels in the central nervous system, generally protecting the brain from harmful substances, many psychoactive drugs can get through this membrane into the brain. Once there, they alter its communication system profoundly, affecting perception, memory, mood, and behavior.

But continued use of drugs lessens their effects. This condition is called **tolerance.** As tolerance develops, greater dosages are required to achieve the same effect. Hand in hand with tolerance goes **physiological dependence,** a process in which the body becomes adjusted to and dependent on the substance, in part because of depletion of neurotransmitters by the frequent presence of the drug. The tragic outcome of tolerance and dependence is **addiction,** the state of actually requiring the drug in one's body and suffering painful *withdrawal symp-*

▽ ▌ Figure 6.9   *Marijuana Use among Friends of Users*

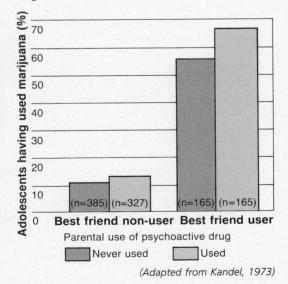

(Adapted from Kandel, 1973)

toms (shakes, sweats, nausea) if the drug is not present.

When an individual finds the use of a drug so desirable or pleasurable that a craving develops, with or without addiction, it is known as **psychological dependence.** Psychological dependence can occur with any drug (including the seemingly benign drugs caffeine and nicotine). The result of either physiological or psychological dependence is that the person's life-style comes to revolve around drug use so closely that his or her capacity to function can be restricted or even impaired. Also the expense involved in maintaining a drug habit of daily—and increasing—amounts of cocaine, heroin, amphetamines, or other drugs can drive the person to robbery, assault, prostitution or drug peddling to get money to buy drugs. What started as simple chemical activity of drugs at tiny synapses turns out to have enormous personal and social consequences.

Kinds of psychoactive drugs. Because of their differing effects on the central nervous system, psychoactive drugs are grouped into three general categories: depressants, stimulants, and hallucinogens. Let's briefly review how these different types of chemicals act to change the consciousness of users.

1. Depressants. Alcohol, opiates, and barbiturates are examples of *depressant drugs.* These drugs tend to depress ("slow down") the mental and physical activity of the body by inhibiting or decreasing the transmission of nerve impulses in the central nervous system.

Alcohol was apparently the first psychoactive substance used extensively by our ancestors. Under its influence some people become silly, boisterous, friendly, and talkative; others, abusive and violent; still others, quietly depressed. At small dosages, alcohol can produce relaxation and slightly improve speed of reaction in an adult. But the body can break down alcohol at only approximately one ounce per hour; greater amounts consumed in a short time period overtax the central nervous system. Driving fatalities and accidents occur six times more often with 0.10 percent alcohol in the bloodstream (resulting from 3 to 4 cocktails or 4 to 6 bottles of beer) than with half this amount. When the level of alcohol in the blood reaches 0.15 percent, there are gross negative effects on thinking, memory, and judgment

along with emotional instability and motor incoordination—a very altered consciousness.

Opiates have been used since ancient times for their pain-killing medicinal properties (Beecher, 1972). From the dried sap of the unripe seed capsule of the opium poppy come two well-known pain relievers—*codeine* and *morphine,* the latter named after Morpheus, the Greek god of dreams, because of

▽ *Alcohol is only one of the wide variety of drugs in daily use in our society. Cultural groups may differ in the forms of drug use they find acceptable, but the fact remains that we are a drug-using culture and the line between use and abuse is not always an easy one to draw.*

its ability to induce sleep. (It also depresses respiration, lowers blood pressure, and causes sexual impotence.) In the early 1900s a new drug was advertised as a cure for those few who suffered chronic morphine intoxication and as an agent to relieve withdrawal symptoms—*heroin.* As you can guess, it "relieved" the withdrawal symptoms because it provided a similar chemical substance, and heroin proved as addictive as its predecessors.

Heroin, also a derivative of opium, may be liquefied and injected into a vein. There is reported to be a sudden rush of warmth—which the majority of pain-free, nonaddicted individuals who experience it find very unpleasant. In contrast, the addict might describe it as a warm, intense feeling of well-being (euphoria), the closest thing to orgasm. The heroin abuser's actual sexual experiences typically involve decreased sexual appetite and performance. There is also subsequent drowsiness, lack of energy, and mental clouding (see Kaplan, 1983).

Barbiturates and other sedatives in low dosages can reduce anxiety, bring about feelings of calm, and reduce muscle tremors. Higher dosages bring about sleep but reduce the time spent in REM sleep. After the withdrawal of barbiturates given over prolonged periods, there are extended REM periods but they are punctuated by frightening nightmares. Overdoses of barbiturates lead to loss of all sensations and coma. More deaths are caused by overdoses of barbiturates, taken either accidentally or with suicidal intent, than by any other poison (Kolb, 1973). The combination of alcohol and barbiturates is particularly lethal.

2. Stimulants. Amphetamines, cocaine, and caffeine are examples of stimulant drugs. Stimulants increase the transmission of impulses in the central nervous system and tend to "speed up" the mental and physical activity of the body.

Amphetamines, or "speed," have differing effects on mental functioning depending on the dosage and the manner of use. Low dosages can promote feelings of alertness, and an increase of abilities, aiding activities that require extended concentration and alertness (Weiss & Laties, 1962). Regular use of oral amphetamines, however—to suppress appetite or to stay awake for very long periods of time—eventually leads to irritability, anxiety, and paranoid fears. When the desirable effects can no longer be maintained with oral

doses, the individual may begin to take higher doses intravenously (Goodman & Gilman, 1970).

Regular users of amphetamines are driven to persist and to increase their dosage and frequency of injection by the desire to reexperience the initial rush of pleasurable sensation and remain euphoric, as well as by the desire to avoid the fatigue and depression of the later phase of amphetamine reaction— "coming down" (Kramer, 1969). Although amphetamine addicts don't experience the same kind of withdrawal reactions (Holden, 1976), they are likely to become increasingly fearful, hostile, and agitated. The slogan "Speed kills" refers partly to the "death" of the personality, will, and psychological freedom of someone who is dependent upon this drug.

Modern psychopharmacology may have begun with Sigmund Freud's introduction of the drug *cocaine* (Pfefferbaum, 1977). His initial optimism that cocaine would relieve psychic distress was based on his personal use of this drug during his own depressions. In 1884 he wrote, "in my last severe depression, I took coca again and a small dose lifted me to the heights in a wonderful fashion" (Jones, 1953, p. 84). However, Freud's initial enthusiasm was soon tempered by the recognition that cocaine could be addicting and could cause a toxic psychosis.

In 1885, a new product called Coca-Cola appeared on the market. It had not only the stimulant properties of cocaine but an extract of the African kola nut which added caffeine. Of course, only the caffeine remains now.

The effects of cocaine are usually pleasant with small doses, becoming more unpleasant as the dosage increases. As with all stimulants, the general effects of cocaine are to increase blood pressure, respiration rate, and pulse and to decrease appetite. (Amphetamine-based diet pills are sold commercially to control weight by their appetite-reducing action.)

Caffeine and *nicotine* are both stimulants. As you may know from experience, two cups of strong coffee or tea administer enough caffeine to have a profound effect on heart, blood, and circulatory functions about ten minutes later—and to disturb your sleep if taken before retiring.

In higher concentrations than exist in cigarette tobacco, nicotine was the active ingredient used by certain native Indian shamans to attain mystical states or trances. Unlike modern users, however, the Indians believed that nicotine was addictive and chose when to be under its influence.

3. Hallucinogens. Consciousness is profoundly altered by a number of drugs that qualify as **hallucin-**

ogens, drugs that are capable of producing states of awareness in which visual, auditory, or other sensory hallucinations occur. Hallucinogens are also called *psychedelic* drugs (from the Greek *psyche* and *delos,* "mind manifesting").

By contrast with the individual use of hallucinogens in our society, use of these drugs in other cultures has often been a collective religious practice, associated with different basic views about reality. For example, among the Jivaro Indians of the Ecuadorian Amazon, sacred rituals relying on drugs are based on the belief that "normal waking life is simply a 'lie,' or illusion, while the true forces that determine daily events are supernatural and can only be manipulated with the aid of hallucinogenic drugs" (Harner, 1973, p. 16). In fact, in a survey of 488 societies covering every region of the world, 90 percent were found to engage in one or more institutionalized, culturally patterned forms of consciousness alteration—with or without drugs (Bourguignon, 1973).

Among the designated "true hallucinogens" are *lysergic acid diethylamide* (LSD), *lysergic acid amide* (from morning glory seeds), *psilocybin* (the "magic mushroom"), *diethyltryptamine,* and *mescaline* (from the peyote cactus). In addition to distorting perceptual experience, these drugs affect the flow of ideas and feelings, rendering them unstable and incoherent. Under the influence of hallucinogens bizarre perceptual distortions may occur. Time may seem to contract or expand, one's body image changes in strange ways, sensory stimulation may fuse in *synesthesias* (colors are "heard," and sounds "tasted"), and feelings of ecstasy may commingle with a sense of oneness with the universe (see **Close-up** on p. 218).

The effects of hallucinogenic drugs may last up to six hours and "flashbacks" may occur later. In extreme form, the symptoms may resemble or mimic signs of mental disorders.

LSD appears to prevent the release of the neurotransmitter serotonin, which is normally released in amounts that vary with the individual's activity level. As activity slows down, less serotonin is released; during sleep hardly any is discharged, and during REM sleep none is released. Under the influence of LSD, however, a nerve cell releases no serotonin even though the drug user is awake, alert, and fully conscious.

"This may provide an important insight into understanding hallucinations and perhaps, more generally,

other altered states of consciousness. In a given behavioral situation, an altered state of consciousness may occur when a key brain mechanism, such as the serotonin system, functions in a manner that is appropriate to a different behavioral situation" (Jacobs & Trulson, 1979, p. 403).

Despite their mind-altering effects, *marijuana* and *hashish* are actually sedatives. Marijuana is the most popular of all the illicit drugs. It is made from *cannabis sativa,* a hemp plant that was originally used to make rope.

More than in the case of most other drugs, the effects of marijuana depend on social and personal factors. Naive users often have to learn how to become "high" from observing veteran users. In large quantities, the effects may be more like those of the strong psychedelic drugs, distorting time sense and altering perception. The altered state produced by marijuana is more controllable and generally less intense, although very high doses may cause panic states and failure of judgment and coordination.

While marijuana decreases verbal, analytical reasoning, it has been shown to enhance performance on certain nonanalytical tests of a holistic-visual-spatial nature (Harshman et al., 1976). This finding is in line with earlier experiential reports that marijuana enhances nonverbal perception, depth perception, and the perception of meaning in stimuli that would be seen as meaningless lines or shapes by someone in an ordinary state of consciousness (Tart, 1971). From these descriptions, which cerebral hemisphere would seem to be most responsive to the effects of this mind-altering drug?

Psychological and social factors in drug effects.

The *psychoactive chemical agent* is only partly responsible for the changes in consciousness that the drug-taker experiences. Also important are the amount taken (the dose), the manner in which it is taken (smoked, swallowed, sniffed, or injected), the unique physiological properties of the individual (weight and metabolism), the person's *mental set,* (expectations of what the drug experience will be), and the *setting* or *context* of the drug experience (the whole physical, social, and cultural environment in which the drug is taken). The effects produced by a drug may be different from one person to the next, and the effects for the same individual may vary when the same amount of a drug is taken at different times or under different circumstances.

The interaction of psychological variables with, chemical factors was shown dramatically in a study of social drinking and behavior.

Characteristics of Alternate and Extended States of Consciousness

The following are some of the effects hallucinogenic drugs have in common, which are also found in reports of mystical states.

1. *Distortions of perceptual processes, time sense, and body image.* A common characteristic is distortion of many familiar perceptions, including those of the visual and auditory senses, as well as those of time and space. A sense of being separate from one's body, or of having portions of the body feel and/or look very different from usual, is often reported.

2. *Feelings of objectivity and ego-transcendence.* This is the sense that one is viewing the world with greater objectivity, more able to perceive phenomena as if they were independent of oneself and even of all human beings. One seems to be able to divorce oneself from personal needs and desires and see things as they "really" are, in some ultimate, impersonal sense. Sometimes this sense of objectivity is experienced as a loss of control, a feeling of being outside oneself—an experience that may be either positive or negative.

3. *Self-validating sense of truth.* The experience may be seen as more "real" or "true" than the perceptions of ordinary consciousness. Knowledge itself is experienced at an "intuitive" level: one believes one is "seeing" beyond appearances into essential qualities.

4. *Positive emotional quality.* Joy, ecstasy, reverence, peace, and overwhelming love are frequently reported when transcendent experiences are interpreted within a religious or philosophical framework. In the reports of Eastern mystics, the experience is less one of ecstasy than of a deep and profoundly restful peace in which the individual feels in harmony with all things.

5. *Paradoxicality.* Descriptions of alternate states of consciousness tend to seem contradictory and illogical when analyzed on logical, rational grounds. The polarities of life seem to be experienced simultaneously, to reach some resolution, and yet to remain separate.

6. *Ineffability.* Individuals frequently claim an inability to communicate their experience. The qualities seem so unique that no words seem appropriate. Often, too, the experience seems to contain so many paradoxical qualities that it makes no sense to describe it.

7. *Unity and fusion.* Distinctions and discontinuities may disappear between self and others; between past, present, and future; between animate and inanimate; between inner and outer reality; and between actual and potential. The separateness of self vanishes, the boundaries dissolve, and there is a fusion of self with what previously was nonself.

Other characteristics sometimes mentioned in various reports are feelings of rejuvenation; sudden, intense emotionality; extreme suggestibility; loss of control; and ideas that assume new significance and meaning (Ludwig, 1966; Nideffer, 1976).

A large group of students volunteered to participate in scientific research by drinking and responding to questionnaires in a social setting. They all knew that only half of them would be receiving alcohol in their "vodka and tonic." However, half of those who actually had vodka were told they *didn't* and half of those who did not were told that they *did.*

After a few drinks, it didn't matter whether their drink actually contained alcohol. Students who *thought* they were getting a "real" vodka and tonic behaved differently from those who *thought* they were drinking straight tonic, regardless of the actual content of their drinks. Those who were falsely led to believe they had alcohol acted as free, uninhibited, and happy, and displayed as much loss of motor control as did the group that had received alcohol and had been told so. Those who reported they felt no difference were all subjects who had been *told* that they had not received an alcoholic drink. Yet half of these subjects had actually had vodka and tonic (Marlatt, 1978). Believing "made it so," regardless of the physical reality.

This study brings us back to our starting point in this chapter, the question of how we can change our psychological reality by just "changing our minds"—without artificial mind-manipulating substances or external agents.

CONSCIOUSNESS: THE ORDINARY AND THE EXTRAORDINARY

It has been a long journey from experimental studies of attention as an essential process in ordinary consciousness to the psychedelic creation of an extraordinary reality. Is there an underlying conceptual unity that links together the enormous variety of topics and processes we have gathered under the broad banner of "consciousness"? Put differently, what do we now know about the nature of human consciousness from investigations of such diverse phenomena as split brains and multiple personalities, dreaming and hallucinating, psychoactive drugs, and mental processing without conscious awareness? Can we fit these seemingly isolated parts into a coherent framework?

The evolution of the human brain enabled those of our forebears to survive who could cope with a hostile environment even when their sensory and physical abilities were not adequate. They compensated for their relative lack of highly specialized sense receptors, or strength, or speed, or protective coloration, or limited, safe habitat by developing mental skills. Humans became capable of symbolic representation of the outer world and of their own possible actions—enabling them to remember, plan, predict, and anticipate (Craik, 1943). Instead of merely reacting to stimuli in the physical present, the complex human brain offered the option of imagining how what *was* could be transformed into what *might be.*

This was a tremendous new survival tool. Henceforth, the capacity to deal with objective reality in the here-and-now of present time was expanded by the capacity to bring back lessons from the past (memory) and to imagine alternative futures (foresight). But a brain that can deal with immediate *objective* realities and also not physically present *subjective* realities needs a mechanism to keep track of what is being focused on and of whether the source of the stimulation being processed is in objects and events outside or in its own internally generated thoughts and concepts.

If "mind" is the sum of the integrative mental activities that brain processes give rise to, then consciousness is the mind's *active construction of incoming information into a coherent, stable, organized pattern of symbols.* This construction is a way of making sense of a confusing world, of imposing order on and finding meaning in events that often seem chaotic and nonsensical (see Johnson-Laird, 1983).

We have seen that different states of consciousness can be experienced within the same stimulus environment, depending on how the information is processed and synthesized. Different constructions may result, at least in part, from different strategies for deploying attention. By selectively focusing on certain parts of the incoming information, we disregard other equally available input. Our constructions can also be affected by changes in physiological or psychological functioning (brain damage, drugs, sleep, and hypnosis, among others), as well as by social factors, by set and context, and by schemas, which organize our expectations. And finally, our constructions are affected by the ways we learn to protect ourselves from threatening realities. According to Freud's theory, we do so through unconscious processes and dreams. The constructions of multiple personalities also seem to have their origin in this effort to defend the integrity of the self.

Our language competence is another capacity that depends on facility in manipulating symbols and signs to stand for real things. Through scenarios and plots that we construct, our language ability helps us explain not only what stimulation means to us but what its causes and consequences are likely to be. We construct our realities in part by explaining how and why parts fit together. Language development and the development of consciousness may be seen as varying together in the development of each child as well as in the evolution of our species.

Usually the demand to be in touch with ongoing "urgent" events forces our attention to be little more than a shifting searchlight illuminating the task-relevant dimensions of our current experience. But we are aware that these reality-based constraints on our consciousness limit the range and depth of our experience and do not fulfill our potential. Though there are both constructive and self-defeating ways of doing so, perhaps we all long at times to reach beyond the confines of ordinary reality (see Targ & Harary, 1984). The ability and willingness to expand our consciousness is the mental equivalent of walking erect when it is easier to crawl, of seeking the uncertainty of freedom when it is safer to accept the security of the familiar.

In later chapters we will explore how a variety of cognitive processes operate to enable us to remember, sometimes forget, think, comprehend, solve problems, and make judgments. But first we need to study how we are changed by experience. How do we learn associations between stimulus events, discover the consequences of our actions, and come to predict significant events based on what we already know? Moreover, we will want to know what conditions in us and in the environment account for the energy and persistence of our efforts to behave in one way rather than another. These questions about learning and motivation will be examined in the next two chapters.

SUMMARY

■ Consciousness is a general term for awareness; it is made up of the whole stream of immediate experience, including the content of awareness and the state of being aware, with some sense of self. It enables us to restrict what we notice, segment the flow of experience, and deliberately use relevant memories. It is our sharpest tool for constructing a representation of reality.

■ Attention is a focused awareness. Only what is attended to becomes conscious; only in consciousness can higher mental processes be performed. Attention has been thought of as a selective filter, as occurring in degrees rather than all-or-none, as a mechanism that synthesizes "bottom-up" and "top-down" processing, and as a limited resource that can be somewhat extended by learning.

■ Preattentive processing of information occurs in the early parts of perceiving. Processing of information outside of consciousness may be nonconscious, subconscious, or unconscious.

■ When the two cerebral hemispheres are severed, the person with a "split brain" behaves in ways that suggest each hemisphere can function as an independent conscious mind. The right hemisphere is better at solving problems involving spatial relationships and pattern recognition and at matching objects by visual features. The left hemisphere is better in problems involving language, logic, and analysis, and at matching objects by function. It has been speculated that the two hemispheres represent contrasting orientations to the world.

■ Everyday changes in consciousness include daydreaming, fantasy, sleep, and nightdreaming. Extended, or alternate, states of consciousness include hallucinations, hypnotic states, and altered consciousness resulting from drugs.

■ Sleep occurs in several stages; rapid-eye-movement (REM) sleep, during which dreaming often occurs, alternates with non-REM sleep in cycles during the night. The sleep-waking cycle is only one of the body's internally generated circadian rhythms.

■ Explanations for dreaming range from the hypothesis that dreams are simply the brain's attempt to make sense of random cortical activity to Freud's theory that dreams provide a means for disguised expression of forbidden wishes while guarding the individual's sound sleep.

■ Hypnosis is a technique for changing the hypnotized person's representation of reality. Individuals differ in hypnotizability—the degree to which they respond to hypnotic suggestions. The hypnotized person may respond to suggestions for changes in motor reactions, for experiencing hallucinations or amnesia, or for being insensitive to powerful stimuli; hypnosis can even substitute for anesthesia in surgery.

■ Trance logic and the "hidden observer" phenomenon show that information of which the hypnotized person is unaware may still be processed below the level of consciousness. The phenomenon of multiple personality seems to be a more extreme example of the ability to keep two or more thought systems separated from each other below the level of consciousness.

■ Psychoactive drugs are chemicals that affect mental processes and behavior by changing awareness of reality for a time. They act by enhancing, blocking, or prolonging activity at synapses.

■ Continued use of many drugs leads to tolerance, in which a larger dosage is required to achieve the same effect, and can result in physiological or psychological dependence. With addiction, the body becomes dependent on the drug and withholding it leads to painful withdrawal symptoms.

■ Psychoactive drugs include depressants, stimulants, and hallucinogens. With some drugs, such as alcohol and marijuana, the effects may depend as much on psychological variables, such as expectations and the social setting, as on the chemical properties of the drug.

■ If "mind" is the sum of all the integrative mental activities that brain processes give rise to, then consciousness is the active construction of available information into a coherent pattern that imposes order and meaning on stimulus events. This construction is affected by the stimulus input but also by the different strategies of attention, physiological alterations, social factors, schemas, personal expectations, and emotional needs. Our impetus to experiment with and transcend ordinary consciousness may represent an attempt to go beyond current constraints on our consciousness to achieve a still fuller and more comprehensive construction of reality.

Part Three

Action Processes

Chapter Seven
Conditioning and Learning

Chapter Eight
Motivation and Emotion

7

CONDITIONING AND LEARNING

■ THE STUDY OF LEARNING
Philosophical assumptions
What is learning?

■ CLASSICAL CONDITIONING: LEARNING BASED ON SIGNALS
Pavlov's discovery
The classical conditioning paradigm
The anatomy of classical conditioning

■ OPERANT CONDITIONING: LEARNING ABOUT CONSEQUENCES
Thorndike and the law of effect
Skinner's experimental analysis of behavior
The operant conditioning paradigm
Properties of reinforcers
The mechanics of reinforcement

■ NEW DEVELOPMENTS IN LEARNING THEORY
Biological constraints on conditioning
Cognitive influences on conditioning
What is learned in conditioning?

■ SUMMARY

Have you ever had an experience with a hit-and-run shower? You step into a warm, soothing shower to unwind after a long, hard day. The comforting warmth of the water begins to relax you and makes you oblivious to almost everything. Suddenly, the water pressure drops and the water becomes scalding hot. Your relaxation is shattered. You are in pain. Just as quickly, the water returns to its previous delightful temperature. You continue your shower, though not quite able to regain your former contented state. But soon, the water pressure abruptly drops again. Bam! On comes the hot flow, accompanied by pain, muscle twitches, and anger on your part. You do not have to learn these reactions. The necessary connections are physiologically built in.

After being hit with scalding water several times—always after a drop in water pressure—you react physically and emotionally to the drop in water pressure—that is, you react *before* the scalding water hits. You have learned an *association between two environmental events:* the drop in water pressure and the following change in water temperature. And because the pressure change is a *signal* for the temperature change, it now evokes a physical and emotional response in you similar to the response caused by the hot water itself. You begin reacting even before the scalding water starts.

Meanwhile you have probably learned that shrieking in pain, cursing, and jumping up and down produce no relief from the scalding water, whereas getting out of the way does. If so, when the water pressure drops, you now move quickly to a safe corner, out of danger. You have learned a second kind of association—an *association between your behavior and its consequences.* You have learned which response, out of several you were making, was appropriate for avoiding this unpleasant event.

This shower scenario illustrates two of the most basic kinds of learning that psychologists study, the learning of associations between two stimuli and of associations between behavior and its results. In this chapter we will see several ways in which these two kinds of associations have been studied. In the last part of the chapter we will examine accumulating evidence that understanding even these apparently simple kinds of learning is not as simple as it may seem.

Before we immerse ourselves in the details of the learning process, it is well to step back and appreciate the broader significance of this phenomenon. Learning is the parent of adaptability. Because we can change how we act, think, and feel through our personal experiences, we are freed from the restraints of a rigidly determined genetic inheritance or from existing conditions in the environment. We have an enormous capacity for modifying both ourselves and our surroundings. This capacity can make our present lives richer and improve the quality of our future existence—or threaten our well-being and even our survival if we learn maladaptive ideas and actions.

THE STUDY OF LEARNING

To understand how psychologists have defined and studied learning, we first need some background on the basic assumptions that guide the questions they ask and the answers they look for.

Philosophical assumptions

Long before psychology existed as a discipline philosophers recognized learning as a source of knowledge and of much human action. From their reflections about why we do what we do and how we learn, two important doctrines emerged that have been important to psychology: the law of association and the principle of adaptive hedonism.

In brief, the **law of association** holds that we acquire knowledge through associating ideas—mental events that originate in sensory information from the environment. If two experiences occur in close sequence in time or space, a mental association will be formed between them. Seventeenth-century philosopher John Locke, whom we met in Chapter 2, was a prominent supporter of this view. It followed logically from his claim that our minds, at birth, are blank slates and that everything we know as adults has had to be learned.

The **principle of adaptive hedonism,** identified with Jeremy Bentham, emerged in the eighteenth century as an explanation of the basic source of human motivation. Bentham's principle was that individuals act in ways that provide pleasure and avoid doing what results in pain.

When psychology split off from its philosophical roots, it took along the doctrines of associationism and adaptive hedonism as basic assumptions. The studies of associative learning described in this chapter were based on them, though the focus has been on how organisms learn associations between stimuli or between stimuli and responses rather than on how people learn associations between ideas. As we will see, cognitive psychologists are now pointing again to the importance of ideas even in the learning of simple stimulus-response associations.

What is learning?

We can define **learning** as a process that results in a relatively permanent change in behavior or behavioral potential based on experience. Learning itself is an intervening variable; it is not observed directly but is inferred from changes in observable behavior. Let's look more closely at the three critical parts of the definition.

A change in behavior or behavioral potential. It is obvious that learning has taken place when you "teach an old dog new tricks" or demonstrate a new skill yourself, such as driving a car or earning a high score on a video game. Learning is apparent from improvements in your performance.

But often your performance doesn't show everything that you have learned. The test questions may be too specific, or you may do poorly because of test anxiety. When motivation is either very weak or very strong, performance may not be a good indicator of learning. Sometimes, too, you acquire general knowledge, such as an appreciation of modern art or an understanding of Eastern religions, that may not show up in particular changed actions. Here you have learned a potential for behavioral change because you have learned attitudes and values that can influence the kind of books you read and how you spend your leisure time.

The definition of *learning* therefore, includes the phrase "or behavioral potential" because often it is shown later that learning did take place even though it was not shown in performance at the time. Learning that does not show up until later—when the circumstances allow or elicit appropriate performance—is called **latent learning.** So although overt performance is used as an indicator of learning, the performance and the underlying learning cannot be assumed to be identical.

A relatively permanent change. To qualify as learned, a change in behavior or behavioral potential must be relatively permanent. Once you learn to swim, you will probably always be able to do so. But some changes in behavior are transitory. Your pupils dilate or contract as the brightness of light changes, and your normally smooth performance in driving may change temporarily because of fatigue or shifting attention. These are changes in behavior, and they are based on experience, but they do not last. So we cannot say learning has taken place.

On the other hand, some (or much) of your hard-earned learning, especially of ideas, is eventually forgotten or changed by what you learn later—hence the term "relatively permanent" in the definition. Learned changes last longer than the transient ones caused by fatigue, but not necessarily forever.

Based on experience. Experience means something that happens to us during our lifetime, usually involving interaction with our environment. Experience includes taking in information (and evaluating and transforming it) and making responses that affect the environment, as in practicing the skill of driving a car. Learning can take place only through experience. Psychologists are especially interested in discovering what aspects of behavior can be changed through experience and how such changes come about.

Some lasting changes in behavior require a combination of experience and maturational readiness. As we saw in Chapter 2, it is the timetable set by maturation that determines when an infant is ready to crawl, stand, walk, run, and be toilet trained: no amount of training or practice will produce those changed behaviors before the child has matured sufficiently. But when children are maturationally ready, then new experience can alter their behavioral potential and lead to new performance.

▷ Ivan Pavlov (1849–1936) and his staff are shown here with the apparatus used in his conditioning experiments. The dog was harnessed to the wooden frame; a tube conducted its saliva to a measuring device that recorded quantity and rate of salivation to stimuli.

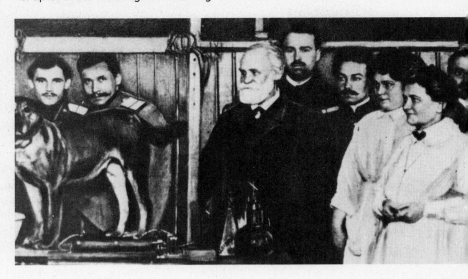

CLASSICAL CONDITIONING: LEARNING BASED ON SIGNALS

In the *Opening Case* that began our chapter, the first association you learned was between two stimulus events. The drop in water pressure—a harmless, neutral stimulus—acquired importance because it was a reliable signal for the occurrence of the painful stimulus—scalding water. When these stimulus events were paired repeatedly, reactions that at first had been aroused only by the hot water began to occur in response to the water pressure change as well. This kind of associative learning is called *classical conditioning.* **Classical conditioning** can be defined as a form of learning in which an organism learns a new association between two stimuli—a neutral one and one that already elicits a reflexive response. Following conditioning, the formerly neutral stimulus elicits a new response often similar to the original response.

Pavlov's discovery

Ivan Pavlov (1849–1936), a Russian physiologist, is credited with discovering the principles of classical conditioning. Pavlov won the 1904 Nobel Prize for his pioneering research on the role of saliva and gas-tric secretions in digestion. He had devised a technique for studying digestive processes in living animals by implanting tubes in their glands and digestive organs that diverted bodily secretions to containers outside the animal's body.

To start these secretions, Pavlov's assistants put food (meat powder) into the mouths of dogs. After this procedure had been repeated on a number of trials, Pavlov observed an interesting phenomenon. The secretions would start *before* food was in the dogs' mouths. They would start at the mere sight of the food and later at the sight of the assistant who brought the food or even the sound of the assistant's footsteps. Indeed, any stimulus the dog could perceive that regularly preceded presentation of the food came to evoke the same reaction as the food itself!

Pavlov quickly realized the significance of these ''psychic secretions'' as he called them. At the age of 50, he redirected his research toward the study of this form of learning (see Pavlov, 1928).

The behaviors Pavlov studied were reflexes. **Reflexes,** also called *respondent behaviors,* are unlearned responses, such as salivation, pupil contraction, knee jerk, and eye blinking, that are automatically called forth by specific stimuli which have biological relevance for the organism. They temporarily change the organism in some way that promotes biological adaptation to the environment. For example, salivation, the reflex studied by Pavlov, helps digestion of food; eye blinking protects the eye from foreign matter. With conditioning, Pavlov's animals learned to make reflexive responses to new stimuli that had no such biological relevance for them. (Classical conditioning is also often called *respondent conditioning* because it is these automatic respondent behaviors that are involved initially.)

The classical conditioning paradigm

Paradigm is an important term for you to know because it is used often in psychology, as well as in other contexts you will come across in your studies. A **paradigm** is a symbolic model or diagram that helps us understand the essential features of a process. It is a way of representing how basic events are related. A paradigm provides a structure for analyzing experimental data.

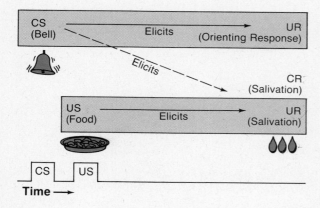

△ **Figure 7.1** *Classical Conditioning Paradigm*

Originally, the sound of a bell elicits only an orienting response; food elicits salivation. If the food is consistently presented immediately after the bell is rung, the bell will soon come to elicit salivation. Note that the solid arrows in the diagram indicate an unlearned (biologically determined) relationship between a stimulus and a response. The broken arrow symbolizes a learned (experientially determined) relationship.

The classical conditioning paradigm **(Figure 7.1)** reveals fundamental properties of associative learning, such as how organisms come to learn relationships between pairs of stimulus events. In classical conditioning a neutral stimulus is paired repeatedly with a biologically significant stimulus and acquires the power to elicit a behavioral response like the one originally triggered only by the biologically significant stimulus.

Initially, there exists a natural relationship between this stimulus and a reflex that it reliably elicits. Because learning has *not* been necessary for the relationship between them, this stimulus (e.g., meat powder) is called an **unconditioned stimulus** (US) and the reflex (e.g., salivation) is called an **unconditioned response** (UR). Before conditioning, a neutral stimulus, such as a bell, may elicit an **orienting response**—a general response of attention to the source of novel stimulation—but will not elicit the unconditioned response. The dog may prick up his ears but will not salivate. During conditioning, the neutral stimulus, the bell, and the unconditioned stimulus, the meat powder, are both presented a number of times in close proximity. After repeated pairings, the bell presented alone elicits salivation. This nonedible object has acquired some of the power to influence behavior that was originally limited to the food. Because learning has taken place, the initially neutral stimulus is now called the **conditioned stimulus** (CS) and the response to the conditioned stimulus alone is called the **conditioned response** (CR).

In the classical conditioning paradigm, neither stimulus is under the organism's control. Their presentation and timing are programmed by the environment, in this case by the experimenter. The response, too, occurs involuntarily.

The anatomy of classical conditioning

In continuing experimentation, many special aspects of conditioning have been studied by researchers since Pavlov's time. What stimulus situations help or hinder conditioning? What strengthens or weakens conditioned responses? How similar must a new neutral stimulus be to an unconditioned stimulus to call forth the same conditioned response? Here we will review what is known about these and other aspects of classical conditioning from years of research across many different animal species, stimulus features, and types of responses.

▷ ▌ Figure 7.2 *Four Temporal Patterns in Classical Conditioning*

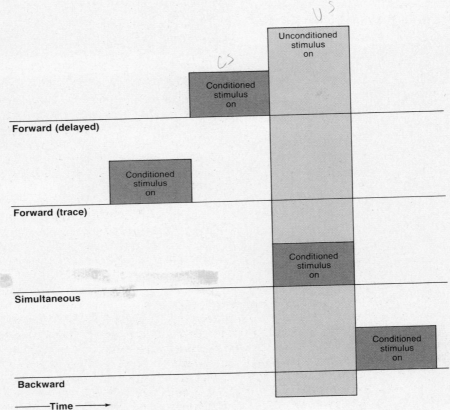

(Adapted from Tarpey, 1982)

Acquisition. In the acquisition stage of conditioning, as we have seen, repeated pairings of a neutral, to-be-conditioned stimulus with an unconditioned stimulus result in changes in behavior in response to the conditioned stimulus. Each time the two stimulus events are paired is called a **conditioning trial.** From these changes we *infer* the development of associations between the two stimuli.

In studying conditioning, the experimenter may vary several aspects of this basic situation, such as the number of trials the organism gets, the time interval between successive trials, the time interval between the two stimuli, and the intensity or quality of either or both stimuli. Variations in these and other aspects of the situation are the *independent variables* in conditioning studies. The three major *dependent variables* are (a) the strength of the conditioned response—its *amplitude* (how big it is); (b) how much time it takes before the response is made after the conditioned stimulus appears—its *latency* (how fast); and (c) how long the response continues to be elicited by the new stimulus in the absence of the unconditioned stimulus—its *persistence* (how durable).

In conditioning, as in telling a good joke, timing is critical for achieving the strongest reaction. The conditioned and unconditioned stimuli must be close enough in time—*contiguous* enough—to be perceived as being related.

Four patterns of onset and offset of the two stimuli have been studied, as shown in *Figure 7.2.* The most common is **forward conditioning,** in which the conditioned stimulus comes on first. There are two possible patterns in forward conditioning: **delayed forward conditioning,** in which the conditioned stimulus stays on until the unconditioned stimulus comes on, and **trace forward conditioning,** in which the conditioned stimulus does not stay on but presumably some form of its memory trace bridges the time gap between its offset and the onset of the unconditioned stimulus. In **simultaneous conditioning** the two stimuli are presented at the same time. Finally, in the case of **backward conditioning,** the conditioned stimulus comes on *after* the unconditioned one occurs.

Conditioning is usually better with a short interval between stimuli rather than a long one and best with forward conditioning procedures. For motor and skeletal responses such as an eye blink, about half a second is the best interval; for visceral responses such as heart rate and salivation, however, an interval of five to fifteen seconds works best. Conditioning is generally poor with the simultaneous procedure and worst with the backward procedure. Evidence of backward conditioning may appear after a few pairings but then disappear with extended training as the animal learns that the conditioned stimulus is followed by a period free of the unconditioned stimulus. In both these cases, conditioning is weak because the conditioned stimulus has no signal value regarding the onset of the important unconditioned stimulus.

Conditioning occurs most rapidly when the neutral stimulus stands out against the many other neutral stimuli that are in the background. A stimulus will be more readily noticed the more *intense* it is and the more it *contrasts* with the background. Either a strong, novel stimulus in an unfamiliar situation or a strong, familiar stimulus in a novel context leads to good conditioning (Kalat, 1974; Lubow et al., 1976). Long duration and a good record of predicting the unconditioned stimulus are also features that facilitate conditioning (Rescorla, 1972; Rescorla & Wagner, 1972).

Extinction and spontaneous recovery. When the unconditioned stimulus is no longer presented with the conditioned stimulus, a conditioned response to the conditioned stimulus becomes weaker and eventually stops occurring. This is called **extinction.** Returning to our *Opening Case,* if water pressure change stopped being followed by hotter water, you would eventually stop perceiving the water pressure drop as a signal for scalding sensations and would no longer respond to it.

An extinguished response is out of sight, behaviorally speaking, but not out of mind, cognitively speaking. After a rest period, it will reappear in a weak form when the conditioned stimulus is presented alone again. **Spontaneous recovery** is the name for this reappearance of an apparently extinguished conditioned response without any new pairings of the two stimuli. (See **Figure 7.3.**) With further acquisition training (further pairings of CS and US), the conditioned response gains strength more rapidly than it did initially. However, it is quickly weakened with further extinction training (CS and no US). But eliminating a conditioned response completely seems to be harder than acquiring it.

Stimulus generalization. Once a conditioned response has been acquired to a particular stimulus, similar stimuli may also evoke the response. If conditioning was to a high tone, a lower tone will also

▷ **Figure 7.3** *Extinction and Spontaneous Recovery*

Salivation in response to the conditioned stimulus increases during conditioning trials while it is being paired with the unconditioned stimulus. When the unconditioned stimulus is no longer presented, the response decreases to its original rate. It reappears after a rest period but then rapidly extinguishes again if not paired with the unconditioned stimulus.

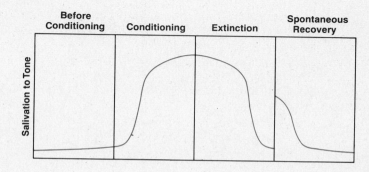

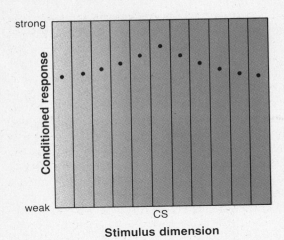

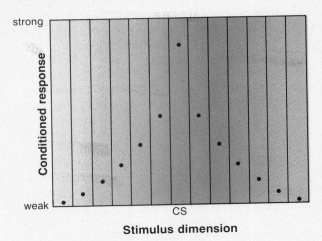

△ **Figure 7.4** *Stimulus Generalization Gradients*

After conditioning to one stimulus, indicated here as a medium green hue, the subject responds almost as strongly to similar hues, as shown in the flat generalization gradient on the left. When more different hues are presented, the subject responds weakly, leading to a steep generalization gradient, as shown on the right.

The experimenter could change the curve on the left to resemble the one on the right by discrimination training, in which the conditioned and unconditioned stimulus continued to be paired while the other stimuli were presented repeatedly alone without the unconditioned stimulus.

elicit the response. A child bitten by a big dog is likely to respond with fear even to small dogs. This automatic extension of conditioned responding to stimuli that have never been paired with the unconditioned stimulus is called **stimulus generalization.** The more similar the new stimulus is to the conditioned stimulus, the stronger the response will be. When response strength is measured for each of a series of increasingly dissimilar stimuli along a given dimension, as in *Figure 7.4,* a *gradient,* or slope, of generalization is found.

Since important stimuli rarely occur in exactly the same form every time in nature, stimulus generalization builds in a "similarity safety factor" by extending the range of learning beyond the original specific experience. A predator can make a different sound or

be seen from a different angle and still be recognized and responded to; in addition, new but comparable events can be recognized as having the same meaning or behavioral significance.

Stimulus discrimination. Though stimuli similar to the original conditioned stimulus may merit a similar response, the line must be drawn somewhere. **Stimulus discrimination** is a conditioning process in which the organism learns to respond *differently* to stimuli that are different from the conditioned stimulus on some dimension (differences in hue or in pitch, for example). The organism's perceptual discrimination between similar stimuli (tones of 1000, 1200, and 1500 cycles per second, for example) is sharpened with training in which only one of them (1200 cps, for example) is associated with the unconditioned stimulus, whereas the others are repeatedly presented *without* the unconditioned stimulus. This procedure provides the organism with "negative examples," examples of stimuli that should *not* be treated as similar.

Early in conditioning, stimuli similar to the neutral stimulus being used will elicit a similar response though not quite as strong. As discrimination training proceeds, the responses to the dissimilar stimuli weaken: the organism learns which events to treat as part of a class that are equivalent to the unconditioned stimulus and which to ignore.

For optimum adaptation, the initial perceptual tendency to generalize and respond to all somewhat similar stimuli needs to give way to discrimination between them, with response only to those that are in fact followed by the unconditioned stimulus. Ideally, then, conditioning is a process in which discrimination ultimately wins over generalization—but it is a balancing act between these two counteracting tendencies.

Appetitive and aversive conditioning. Pavlov's conditioning with the use of meat powder is an example of *appetitive conditioning*—conditioning in which the unconditioned stimulus is of positive value to the organism. The *Opening Case*, by contrast, involved unpleasant sensations to escape and avoid; it was an example of *aversive conditioning*—conditioning in which the unconditioned stimulus is of negative value to the organism. Laboratory studies of aversive conditioning have used unconditioned stimuli like electric shock and puffs of air to the eye that all members of a species find aversive.

For example, an electric shock to the leg is an unconditioned stimulus that elicits an unconditioned response of leg withdrawal or muscle flexing. Sounding a bell repeatedly before each electric shock to the leg of an animal constrained in a harness will soon condition the animal to twitch its muscle in response to the bell alone.

An important discovery from these studies has been that with aversive (also called *noxious*) stimuli, the organism learns not only a specific conditioned muscle response but a generalized fear reaction as well. The leg withdrawal is accompanied by reactions of the autonomic nervous system—changes in heart rate, respiration, and electrical resistance of the skin (the *galvanic skin response,* GSR, to be discussed in Chapter 13). The muscle response, too, may come to involve more than the limited area stimulated. All these changes become part of an overall conditioned fear response. Furthermore, when strong fear is involved, conditioning may take place after only one pairing of a neutral stimulus with the fear-arousing stimulus.

A classic early study of conditioned fear in a human being was that of John B. Watson and Rosalie Rayner with an infant named Albert. Watson and Rayner (1920) conditioned Albert to fear a white rat he had initially liked by pairing its appearance with an aversive unconditioned stimulus—a loud gong struck just behind the child. The boy's learned fear then generalized to other furry objects as described in the *Close-up* on pages 232–33.

In this early period of experimentation with conditioning, the careful attention to possible harmful effects that is characteristic of research with human subjects today was sometimes lacking. For better or for worse, Watson never had the opportunity to control a child's environment through conditioning over a long enough period of time to produce a doctor, lawyer, psychologist, or thief as he had boasted a behaviorist could do.

We know now that conditioned fear is very resistant to extinction. Even if the overt components of muscle reaction eventually disappear, the reactions of the autonomic nervous system continue, leaving the individual still vulnerable to arousal by the old signals. Conditioned fear reactions may persist for years, even when the original frightening stimulus is never again experienced.

> During World War II, the signal used to call sailors to battle stations aboard U.S. Navy ships was a gong sounding at the rate of 100 rings a minute. To personnel on board, it was associated with the sounds of guns and bombs; thus it became a conditioned stimulus for strong emotional arousal.
>
> Fifteen years after the war, a study was conducted comparing the emotional reactions of hospitalized navy and army veterans to a series of 20 different sound stimuli. Although none of the sounds were current signals for danger, the sound of the "call to battle stations" still produced strong emotional arousal in the navy veterans who had previously experienced that association. Their response to the former danger signal (as determined by galvanic-skin-response measures) was significantly more vigorous than that of the army veterans (Edwards & Acker, 1962).

We all carry around this kind of excess baggage of learned readiness to respond with fear, joy, or other emotions to old signals (often from our childhood) that are no longer appropriate or valid in our current situation.

Second-order conditioning. Following conditioning, the conditioned stimulus has acquired some of the power of the biologically significant unconditioned stimulus, as shown by the fact that it now

Little Albert and the White Rat

When John B. Watson and his colleague Rosalie Rayner set out to induce a conditioned fear in a robust, fearless infant named Albert, to study stimulus generalization, and then remove the conditioned fear, they were unsure of the outcome. They were hoping the experiment would demonstrate the superiority of the behaviorist belief that fears were learnable over the then-popular assumption that human fears were instinctive, built in. Let's review how it was possible for Albert to be transformed from a child who rarely cried into a "cry baby" fearful even of Santa Claus.

8 months, 26 days old: Tested for unlearned effects of loud noise (US) of steel bar being struck just behind him. Startle response (UR) was noted; infant jumped violently, fell forward, buried face in mattress, whimpered. Innate US-UR connection recorded.

9 months old: Presented Albert with the following animals and objects to play with or observe: a white rat, rabbit, dog, monkey, masks with and without hair, cotton wool, and burning newspapers. No negative response noted to any of these objects.

11 months, 3 days old: The white rat, which Albert had played with regularly for weeks, was selected to be the conditioned stimulus. When Albert reached for and touched his rodent playmate, the steel bar was struck. The loud noise startled Albert; he withdrew his hand and became distressed.

11 months, 10 days old: Conditioning trials were given in which the white rat (CS) was paired with the loud noise (US). When the rat was next presented alone, it had acquired the power to elicit the strong negative emotional response of fear (CR) of the former friend. Albert began to cry, turned, fell over, and crawled away with all his might.

11 months, 15 days old: Tests made for stimulus generalization. The fear response was *not elicited by a set of blocks,* but it did occur to all *furry* or *hairy* objects: a rabbit, dog, fur coat, cotton wool, human hair, and even a Santa Claus mask. Albert had apparently learned to fear "furriness."

Whether Albert developed into a Scrooge who hated Christmas with its furry reminders of Santa, we don't know. But we do know that the last phase of

elicits the response alone. In a sense, it has become a "surrogate" unconditioned stimulus: it can stand in for, and act like, the unconditioned stimulus. Can this conditioned stimulus be used to condition yet another stimulus to produce the same response? It can, for both appetitive and aversive responses. This process is called **second-order conditioning** (also called *higher-order conditioning*).

In Phase One of one study subjects were conditioned to respond to a light (CS_1) paired with food (US). In Phase Two they were exposed to pairing of a sound stimulus (CS_2) with the light (CS_1) without any presentation of the food. When tested with the sound stimulus alone, they gave the same conditioned response as had previously been elicited by the light (Holland & Rescorla, 1975). Later studies showed such second-order conditioning to be stronger when there was *perceptual similarity* between the two conditioned stimulus events (when both were tones, lights, colors, or patterns (Rescorla, 1980).

Second-order conditioning, like original conditioning, is fastest when the new stimulus (CS_2) is a reliable predictor of the original conditioned stimulus (CS_1) and better with a forward conditioning pattern than with a simultaneous or backward one (Leyland & Mackintosh, 1978). It vastly extends the domain of classical conditioning, since a biologically powerful stimulus is no longer required for conditioning to take place. Instead, respondent behaviors become potentially controllable by a limitless array of stimuli once they have been associated with other stimulus events whose power is *either* natural or acquired through learning. Second-order conditioning is an important process for understanding many types of complex human behaviors, both normal and abnormal.

With extended trials—during which pairing of the two conditioned stimuli is not accompanied by the unconditioned stimulus—the second-order conditioned response will usually become weaker. Eventually the response to both of the conditioned stimuli will extinguish.

the experiment—undoing the learned fear—was never conducted. The experimenters noted that "unfortunately, Albert was taken from the hospital the day the tests were made. Hence, the opportunity of building up an experimental technique by means of which we could remove the conditioned emotional response was denied us" (Watson & Rayner, 1920).

A few years later, an associate of Watson's, Mary Cover Jones (1924), was successful in using conditioning principles to remove conditioned fears in other youngsters (see Chapter 15). But her success does not absolve Watson and Rayner from ethical responsibility for having left a child with an unnecessary fear. The record shows that they had known a month earlier that he would be leaving the hospital.

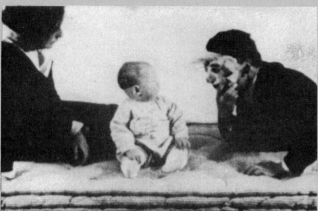

◁ *An actual photograph of Watson (in mask) and Rayner testing Albert for stimulus generalization.*

Though the classical conditioning paradigm was first developed in connection with animals, extensive studies with human subjects have demonstrated its importance in many everyday human reactions. For example, the whirring of the dentist's drill at a given frequency becomes a conditioned stimulus for the pain that the drilling causes. The unconditioned response to that pain is muscle twitching in the mouth area and a general response of tension and anxiety. After a while the sound elicits these reactions. However, if the dentist's drill changes to a very high frequency, then little or no conditioned responding may occur because of discrimination between the two sounds, even though the context is obviously unchanged.

Many of our attitudes have been formed without our awareness (Staats & Staats, 1958). Indeed, it is impossible to avoid developing conditioned emotional responses—to Momma, apple pie, the flag, and many other stimuli. Sometimes this conditioning is purposely arranged, as can be seen by the many advertisements that pair alluring stimulus properties such as popularity, prestige, or sexual satisfaction with products that have little or nothing to do with such pleasant experiences. To find out about an unexpected example of the practical effects of conditioning, see the *Close-up* on pages 234–35.

The ability of neutral stimuli to acquire the power to elicit strong responses automatically through conditioning makes us all vulnerable. Although there are some limitations on this process—to be discussed later—the tremendous implications of the ease with which conditioning takes place should not escape you. Virtually any stimulus you can perceive can be associated with almost any response so that you learn to value, desire, or fear the stimulus. (For notable exceptions, see the last section of this chapter on biological constraints.)

Conditioning the Body's Immune System

Every natural environment is filled with disease-bearing microorganisms, pollutants, and other substances that can damage the organism. To adapt to such environments, the body must protect itself from such assault. It does so through an immune system that develops antibodies capable of counterattack against these invaders.

The immunological system involves both a highly sensitive process for rapid detection of alien substances and a swift response process of releasing highly specific types of antibodies that can contain or destroy specific forms of invaders. Susceptibility to disease becomes greater when the immune system is not functioning adequately.

Until recently, it had been assumed that immunological reactions were automatic, biological processes that occurred without any intervention by the central nervous system. However, it now appears that this vital system is under psychological as well as biological control. This relationship has been demonstrated in studies in which immune responses of animals were suppressed by classical conditioning procedures.

Before we examine the procedure used to show this important finding, it is fascinating to note the curious result that pointed the researchers toward this issue. During a study of conditioned taste aversion, rats were given a distinctively flavored, sweet-tasting solution (CS) followed by a toxic drug (US) that induced illness. The rats quickly learned to avoid or reduce consumption of the sweet solution. However, when the amount of that CS consumed on the single conditioning trial was large, some of the conditioned animals died later in extinction trials, when they were presented with the CS but *no* toxic drug (Ader, 1981). What killed them?

It could not have been the toxic drug because its dosage had been too low to be lethal, and it had been

---

OPERANT CONDITIONING: LEARNING ABOUT CONSEQUENCES

In classical conditioning, you learn to *predict* something important in your environment. For example, you may learn that a certain look from your lover (CS) signals (enables you to predict) that you are about to be caressed (US). You then come to respond with arousal (CR) to that "look of love" even before you feel your lover's actual touch (UR). This learning is helpful as far as it goes, but wouldn't it be nice to learn how to get that look of love to occur in the first place? Just passively learning about signals that already exist or waiting around till they come is often not enough for most of us.

Learning how to *control* stimulus events, as well as predict them, means learning how to produce the consequences you want and how to minimize the ones you don't. In the *Opening Case,* you learned that jumping into the corner in the shower saved you from the scalding water that you knew was about to come. Similarly, you may learn that when you whisper "sweet nothings" in your sweetheart's ear, that look of love becomes more probable than when you shout, "Go ahead and kiss me!" Little Albert's efforts to get away from the rat, too, were an attempt to go beyond prediction to control—to reduce a perceived threat.

These responses are called **operant behaviors.** Through these behaviors the organism operates on the environment instead of simply reacting to something the environment does to it, as in the case of respondent behaviors. The effects it achieves—the consequences of the action—then determine the probability that the response will be repeated.

Conditioning of this kind—changing behavior by changing its consequences—is called **operant conditioning.** In operant conditioning the critical environmental stimuli thus come *after* the behavior and are obtained by the action of the learner. This contrasts with classical conditioning, in which the learner's behavior has no effect on consequences, the stimulus is presented before the response, and the same sequence of stimuli is presented whether or not any response is made.

Another way to look at the differences between these two types of basic learning is to contrast the *content* of the learning. In classical conditioning, the subject learns relationships between stimulus events,

given only once, during the earlier conditioning. But a search for clues turned up the fact that the drug used to produce vomiting, cyclophosphamide, also produces another effect—suppression of the activity of the immune system. Could the sweet CS solution have become a conditioned signal to suppress the immune system as the drug had no doubt done earlier? With the repeated exposure to this CS during extinction training, might the immune system then have been suppressed to the point that the animals became vulnerable to the disease-bearing substances in the laboratory environment?

To test this speculation, Robert Ader and Nathan Cohen (1981) conditioned animals with the same procedure (saccharine solution as the CS, plus toxic drug as the US) and later exposed them to saccharine alone. Three to six days earlier, they had been injected with an alien substance, red blood cells taken from sheep. The animals produced significantly fewer antibodies to combat this assault than did control animals for whom the saccharine solution was not a conditioned stimulus. These results and others from independent investigators support the hypothesis that the *learned association* of the conditioned stimulus (saccharine) with the immuno-suppressing drug enabled the conditioned stimulus alone to elicit suppression of the immune system. In this way, conditioning increased the organism's susceptibility to disease.

The implications of this research are considerable, both for extending our knowledge about how psychological and biological functions interact and for understanding and perhaps modifying the process by which organisms resist or become vulnerable to disease.

while in operant conditioning the subject learns relationships between overt responses and their stimulus consequences.

Two American psychologists—Edward L. Thorndike and B. F. Skinner—stand out as pioneers in the development of the principles of association between stimuli and responses. Let's examine the contributions of each.

Thorndike and the law of effect

At about the same time that Pavlov was inducing Russian dogs to salivate to the sound of a bell by classical conditioning, Edward L. Thorndike (1898) was watching American cats escape from solitary confinement. Thorndike's hungry cats had to discover how to operate a latch on each of a series of "puzzle boxes" in order to escape and get food (see **Figure 7.5**). He reported his observations and inferences about what kind of

learning was taking place in his subjects as follows:

"When put into the box the cat shows evident signs of discomfort and of an impulse to escape from confinement. It tries to squeeze through any opening; it claws and bites at the bars or wire; it thrusts its paws out through any opening and claws at everything it reaches; . . . It does not pay very much attention to the food outside (the reward for the hungry cat), but seems simply to strive instinctively to escape from confinement. The vigor with which it struggles is extraordinary. For eight or ten minutes it will claw and bite and squeeze incessantly. . . . Whether the impulse to struggle be due to an instinctive reaction to confinement or to an *association*, it is likely to succeed in letting the cat out of the box. The cat that is clawing all over the box in her impulsive struggle will probably claw the string or loop or button so as to open the door. And gradually all the other nonsuccessful impulses will be

E. L. Thorndike (1874–1949).

stamped out and the particular impulse leading to the successful act will be *stamped in* by the resulting pleasure, until, after many trials, the cat will, when put in the box, immediately claw the button or loop in a definite way'' (p. 13).

What did Thorndike's cats learn that was different from the learning of Pavlov's dogs? According to Thorndike's paradigm, learning was an association not between two stimuli but between stimuli in the situation and the response that the subject learned to make—a stimulus-response (S–R) connection. Thorndike believed that responses repeatedly followed by reward brought ''satisfaction,'' as a result of which they were strengthened, or ''stamped in,'' while nonrewarded responses were weakened, or ''stamped out.'' Thorndike's conditioning paradigm allowed the animal to respond freely, but only one of its responses would have a satisfying consequence.

You will recognize this as a psychological version of the philosophical concept of *adaptive hedonism* discussed earlier in this chapter: organisms tend to learn to do what feels good. Generally such behaviors are adaptive in aiding survival, but you can no doubt come up with a list of learned behaviors that feel good in the short run but are destructive over

time—smoking and taking addictive drugs being two obvious ones.

According to Thorndike, the learning of reinforced S–R connections occurs gradually and automatically in a mechanistic way as the animal experiences the consequences of its actions through blind trial and error. At the beginning, many stimuli are present that may be relevant and many responses are possible. Gradually, the animal discovers which ones lead to satisfaction and which ones do not. In Thorndike's view, the cats learned to get out of the puzzle boxes because they happened to make the correct responses, which then were influenced by what he called the ''law of effect.''

The **law of effect** asserts that only behavior which has the effect of producing a desired outcome is likely to be repeated. Put more formally, this basic law of learning states that the power of a stimulus to evoke a response is strengthened when the response is followed by a reward and weakened if the response is not followed by a reward. Little Albert learned two different types of response—a conditioned fear response at the sight of the white rat and a learned avoidance response. Often the two kinds of conditioning occur together.

Thorndike called this kind of learning **instrumental conditioning** because the subject's response was instrumental to (a means of) obtaining a reward. Later researchers changed the term to *operant conditioning* (and changed the experimental situation in certain ways, as we shall see), but the terms are still sometimes used interchangeably.

Thorndike believed that the principles he had discovered were also applicable to human learning. His ideas had a major impact on the educational psychology of his time—even though he believed that learning involved trial and error *without conscious thought.* (Some students may facetiously agree that their education consists of the transfer of a professor's notes to their notebook without the interference of conscious thought by either party.)

A whole generation of researchers used Thorndike's paradigm to study instrumental responses but used situations in which the responses were more specific and quantifiable than escape from puzzle boxes. The favorite research subjects became rats though many other species were also used. The most popular responses measured were speed of running to the goal box in a runway or maze and number of

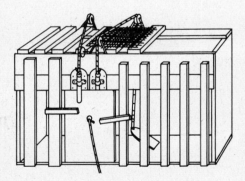

△ **Figure 7.5** *One of Thorndike's Puzzle Boxes*

Thorndike's cats were confined in boxes like this one and food was placed outside of the box. To get out, the animal had to loosen a bolt, bar, or loop in order to release a weight which would then pull the door open. (After Thorndike, 1898)

△ *Experimenters studying instrumental responses after Thorndike commonly used the situation of a rat running through a maze to a goal box.*

lever presses in a box in which lever pressing made a reward available or enabled the animal to escape from an aversive stimulus. By the 1950s there were over a thousand research reports a year on factors influencing lever pressing in rats. In most cases, the ultimate hope was that this basic research with simpler animals would shed more light on the mysteries of human learning.

Skinner's experimental analysis of behavior

Radical behaviorist B. F. Skinner has built on Thorndike's principles of instrumental learning but has gone far beyond them. He rejected Thorndike's interpretation that reinforcers changed subsequent responding because of the satisfaction the animal presumably felt. Skinner's biggest departure, in fact, was his assertion that *no* interpretation was even necessary. Whether an animal feels "satisfaction" is irrelevant: all that is needed is to analyze the observable actions of the organism and the environmental conditions and identify the predictable relationships among them. Only in this way, Skinner feels, can there be a true science of behavior.

Skinner was the first to use the term "operant."

Instead of studying complex actions with many components, like running through a maze that had to be learned, he preferred to study simple, already present, repetitive actions like the pecking response in pigeons, whose *rate* could be changed under different stimulus conditions. By systematically varying different stimuli, he could establish the *probability* of different rates of responding within the operant conditioning paradigm. His favorite research subject has been the pigeon.

Skinner calls his approach the "experimental analysis of behavior." In his words:

"A natural datum in a science of behavior is the probability that a given bit of behavior will occur at a given time. An experimental analysis deals with that probability in terms of frequency or rate of responding. . . . The task of an experimental analysis is to discover all the variables of which probability of response is a function" (1966, pp. 213, 214).

The **experimental analysis of behavior** means discovering, by systematic variation of stimulus conditions, all the ways that various kinds of experience affect the probability of responses. Skinner's analysis is experimental rather than theoretical because he refuses to make inferences about inner states or about

△ *A device for studying operant conditioning in the laboratory has been called a "Skinner box," after its inventor. It is a small cage for housing an animal and in which the experimenter is in control of the subject's physical environment. Though Skinner used rats as subjects, his favorite research animal has been the pigeon. In the Skinner box designed for use with pigeons, a pellet of food is delivered via the lower opening when the pigeon pecks a key.*

▽ B. F. Skinner at work building a scale model of a Skinner box.

rate of pecking, it must be contingent on the pecking response: it must occur regularly after that response but not after other responses, such as turning or moving away from the disk. Researchers can control behavior by arranging different patterns of timing and frequency of stimuli and making them available only after the desired response.

The approach of Skinner and his students seeks to understand the behavior of organisms in terms of the behavioral contingencies they have experienced in their environment. One of the goals of this approach is to show how the complex behaviors organisms learn can be understood to be the product of particular patterns of contingencies. Facts discovered in the laboratory are used to predict the consequences of particular patterns of responses and stimulus consequences in a wide variety of situations.

The operant conditioning paradigm

The paradigm for operant conditioning has three parts—operant behaviors, reinforcers, and discriminative stimuli. Let's see how these terms help us understand the process of operant conditioning.

Operants: emitted behaviors. Thorndike assumed that there must be stimuli in the situation initiating the instrumental behaviors he studied. Skinner does not. He assumes that responses already in the organism's repertoire are *emitted* spontaneously—that they are caused by internal conditions and regularly performed by the organism in the absence of specific, *eliciting* external stimuli. Pigeons peck, rats forage (search for food), babies cry and coo, some people gesture while talking, others stutter or say "like" and "you know" frequently. These emitted behaviors, as we have seen, are called *operant behaviors* (or *operants*) because they have an effect on the environment (getting food, being picked up or noticed, getting sympathy from others).

Operant behaviors, then, differ from the behaviors studied in classical conditioning in being emitted by the organism instead of elicited by an external stimulus, and in being repetitive, continuing responses rather than single, specific ones. And whereas classical conditioning involves involuntary responses like salivation, operant conditioning most often involves voluntary responses like pressing a lever, pecking a disk, or using the personal pronoun *I*.

any nonobservable bases for the behavioral relationships that he demonstrates in the laboratory. He formulates no theories about what is happening inside the organism. No intervening variables are assumed: inner conditions like "hunger" are defined operationally, in terms of operations the experimenter can carry out—for example, "deprivation of food for 24 hours." Approaching food and eating it can be observed and recorded; desire for food or pleasure at receiving it cannot. Therefore, such variables are never part of Skinner's descriptions.

A subtle shift has taken place—away from the earlier focus on instrumental learning. Instead, the emphasis is on discovering how to control existing behavior—make it more or less probable—by appropriate arrangement of environmental conditions.

Investigators can make responses more or less probable by setting up different behavioral contingencies. A **behavioral contingency** is a consistent relationship between a response and the stimulus conditions that follow it. Contingency between events is a central concept in operant conditioning. Such a relationship can increase or decrease the rate or probability of the response. For example, if a pigeon's disk-pecking response is usually followed by the presentation of grain, the rate of the pecking response will increase. But if the animal has been deprived of food, the grain will increase the rate of any response that it follows. For it to increase *only* the

Reinforcers and reinforcement. Reinforcers are significant events for the organism that can strongly influence subsequent responding. Reinforcers in operant conditioning correspond to the unconditioned stimulus in classical conditioning but with several key differences. Reinforcers come *after* the response instead of before it and are contingent upon the organism's making the desired response. The terms *reinforcer* and *reinforcement* are defined empirically—in terms of their effects.

If a stimulus *received* after a response increases the probability of that response occurring, it is called a **positive reinforcer**. The condition of receiving a positive reinforcer is called **positive reinforcement.** Getting grain following a pecking response is an example of positive reinforcement—for a pigeon, at least.

If a stimulus *not received* (avoided or terminated) after a response increases the probability of that response occurring, it is called a **negative reinforcer.** The condition of not receiving the aversive stimulus is called **negative reinforcement.** Escaping from the scalding water in our *Opening Case* was an instance of negative reinforcement. Both positive and negative reinforcement *increase* the probability or rate of the response that precedes them.

In general, positive reinforcement seems to work best when a new response or more of a present response is wanted. Negative reinforcement works better for getting people to avoid some undesirable response that they have been making frequently. It reinforces—and increases—the frequency of *not* making that response. For example, after several drinks in which alcohol is combined with a drug such as antabuse that produces vomiting, the drinker who cannot get alcohol without the drug will refuse it (Rachman & Teasdale, 1979). The hope is that the conditioned aversion will maintain the abstinence later when alcohol again becomes available without the drug. Whether it does so depends partly on what sources of reinforcement of drinking behavior there are in the individual's usual environment and what reinforcers are available for other responses, such as drinking nonalcoholic beverages.

In experimental research, **extinction** is a procedure in which reinforcement no longer follows the learned response. After repeated responding with no consequences, the behavior returns to the level it was before training, and the conditioned response is said to be *extinguished.*

Extinction training alone can be effective in getting rid of an unwanted response—but only if all reinforcers can really be withheld. This is difficult outside the laboratory, where many aspects of the person's environment may not be under the control of the would-be operant conditioner. In any case, extinction training to eliminate an undesired response is most effective when combined with positive reinforcement of the new response that *is* desired instead. Clowning in class to get attention is most likely to stop if the student finds that it doesn't work any more (extinction) and also discovers that other, more socially approved behaviors *do* bring attention (positive reinforcement).

Punishment is different from negative reinforcement. **Punishment** is the condition of receiving (instead of avoiding or escaping from) an aversive stimulus after a response; the general effect is to *decrease* the probability of that response. Touching a hot stove produces pain that punishes the preceding response; a child is less likely next time to reach out to touch the stove. Responses that are punished *immediately* tend to get *eliminated,* but if there is *any delay* between response and punishment, the response is only *suppressed.* When a formerly punished response no longer produces aversive consequences, it then increases in frequency to prepunishment levels. The complex effects of punishment are examined in the **Close-up** on page 240.

△ *The punishment of the resulting pain suffered when touching a hot flame is likely to decrease the probability that a child will do it again.*

The Psychology and Politics of Punishment

Throughout the ages many voices of authority have been raised in controversy over the benefits or ills of punishment. The Bible warns us, "He that spareth the rod hateth his own son" (Proverbs: 13–24). But critics argue that punishment is destructive. Does punishment build character or distort it? What has psychology to say on this question?

To change behavior, either extinction training or punishment may help get rid of the undesired response. Positive reinforcement of a substitute response at the same time will increase the probability that the new response will be repeated. But it is often difficult to follow this procedure because the current reinforcer of the undesired behavior may be obscure or not under the control of the person in authority. Thus many people simply turn to punishment to stop behavior they find objectionable. They do so because punishment stops most behaviors swiftly; also it may help relieve their frustration and give them a sense of control. Instead of a search for elusive reinforcers (or getting to understand the individual well enough to determine what will be reinforcing), they simply increase the intensity of some punishment until the response is suppressed.

But punishment can be counterproductive, causing negative side effects that may be more undesirable than the original behavior it was meant to stop. Punishment may (a) lead to *counteraggression* against the punisher or the institution; (b) encourage future use of physical abuse on the part of the person who is punished; (c) harm the self-image of the punished person; (d) create so much fear and terror that the undesirable behavior cannot be controlled by the person (as sometimes happens with toilet training); (e) isolate the person from peers who shun him or her as stigmatized by authority; and (f) cause serious physical injury (Bongiovanni, 1977).

Often the punishing agent is agitated and gets "carried away" during the process of administering the punishment. Studies of corporal punishment in schools reveal that it can be brutal and has included beating, paddling, kicking, forced eating of obnoxious substances, and public ridicule. The primary targets of corporal punishment are boys more than girls, minority children more than those of the dominant racial-ethnic group, and, surprisingly, children in grades one to four rather than older children (Hyman et al., 1977).

Psychological research has identified several conditions under which punishment is most likely to eliminate undesired behavior with a minimum of damage (adapted from Azrin & Holz, 1966; Park & Walters, 1967; Walters & Grusec, 1977):

1. *Alternative responses.* Availability of at least one alternative response that the individual can make which will *not* receive the punishing stimulus and which can be *positively* reinforced.
2. *Response specificity.* Clear explanation of what specific response is being punished and why.
3. *Timing and duration.* Swift, brief punishment immediately after the response occurs; delayed punishment *suppresses* but does not eliminate the response.
4. *Intensity.* For humane reasons, punishment only intense enough to stop the response.
5. *No escape.* No available unauthorized means of escape, avoidance, or distraction.
6. *No mixed messages.* No provision of positive reinforcement, such as displays of sympathy or extra attention, along with the punishment.
7. *Use of conditioned punishers.* Establishment of a physically harmless conditioned stimulus that can stand in for a physical, possibly harmful one (a child spanked in the corner later punished by simply having to *sit* in the corner).
8. *Use of "penalties."* Withdrawal of a positive stimulus (no TV instead of a spanking for a TV-watcher who hits a younger sibling).
9. *Restricted limits.* Limitation of punishment to the situation in which the undesirable response occurs, not letting it "spill over" to other settings and times.
10. *Limitation to specific responses, not general traits.* Care never to generalize from the specific undesirable response being punished (cheating on a test, tearing pages from library books) to general traits of the person being punished ("You're stupid," "a born criminal"). *Responses* may be undesirable, but *people* should never be made to feel that *they* are undesirable.

I'VE BEEN AN OPPRESSOR AND I'VE BEEN AN OPPRESSEE... AND, BELIEVE ME, BEING AN OPPRESSOR IS BEST!

Table 7.1 *Operant Conditioning Paradigm: Five Contingency Patterns*

	Discriminative Stimulus (S^D)	Emitted Response (R) $\longrightarrow$	Stimulus Consequence (S)
1. *Positive reinforcement:* A response in the presence of an effective signal (S^D) produces the desired consequence. This response increases.	Soft-drink machine	Put coin in slot	Get refreshing drink
2. *Negative reinforcement: escape.* An unpleasant situation is escaped from by an operant response. This escape response increases.	Heat	Fan oneself	Escape from heat
3. *Negative reinforcement: avoidance.* A stimulus signals the organism that an unpleasant event will occur soon. An appropriate response avoids its occurrence. This avoidance response increases.	Sound of firecracker fuse	Run for shelter	Avoid effects of explosion
4. *Extinction training:* A conditioned operant response is not followed by a reinforcer. It decreases in rate.	None or S$^\Delta$	Clowning behavior	No one notices
5. *Punishment:* A response is followed by an aversive stimulus. The response is eliminated or suppressed.	Attractive match box	Play with matches	Get burned or get caught and spanked

Operant researchers assume that any response that persists does so because there is some payoff for it—some reinforcement is continuing. Any behavior, they argue—even irrational or bizarre behavior—can be understood if one can discover what payoff is being obtained for it.

Once acquired, a response may be maintained by reinforcers different from those involved in the original conditioning. For example, symptoms of mental disorders are sometimes maintained because the person gets attention and sympathy and is excused from normal responsibilities. These "secondary gains" are the payoff that maintains the behavior.

Discriminative stimuli and stimulus control. We can learn not only what to do but when to do it. Organisms can learn *when* to make a previously successful response and *when not* to by learning to recognize advance signals that tell whether a payoff will or will not be available if the response is made. These relevant predictor signals are called **discriminative stimuli.**

For example, the experimenter may make food available only while a green light is present. Pecking a disk while the light is present will produce food, but the same pecking response while the light is red or absent will not. The stimulus that signals "reinforcer available"—in this case the green light—is called the *positive discriminative stimulus* (S^D) The "no rein-

forcer available" signal—in this case no light or a red light—is called the *negative discriminative stimulus* (S$^\Delta$, pronounced "ess delta").

A pigeon soon learns to distinguish between these two conditions, regularly pecking only when the green light is present. When this happens, its behavior is said to be under **stimulus control.**

The discriminative stimulus does not *cause* the behavior but is simply informational: it "sets the stage"—provides the occasion for the response to be made—but *does not elicit* it. The response is still an *emitted* one and still maintained by the payoff. But even though it remains an emitted response, the experimenter can now control when it will appear simply by presenting or not presenting the discriminative stimulus.

The concept of the discriminative stimulus completes the three-element paradigm of operant conditioning. This paradigm includes a preceding discriminating stimulus, which provides information about the availability of the payoff, an emitted response by the organism, and a stimulus consequence which follows and is contingent on the performance of the response. **Table 7.1** illustrates five variations in operant conditioning with different contingency patterns.

Because organisms are alert to discriminative stimuli that are signposts to reinforcers, they can be taught to make fine discriminations between many different stimulus events, such as patterns or hues. Selective reinforcement of S^D and not of S$^\Delta$ results in controlled responding to any stimuli the organism is capable of perceiving and distinguishing between. In fact, this procedure has been used as a diagnostic tool to determine whether an individual is *able* to perceive the difference between a pair of stimuli, such as similar tones, shapes, or odors, for example.

In human transactions, we often face the problem of determining whether a given social stimulus is really a discriminative stimulus. For example, a question by the teacher is usually an S^D for student responding—which, if correct, will be reinforced. Not so for *rhetorical questions,* however—questions asked only to stimulate thought and then be answered by the teacher. "What is the value of stimulus control?" the teacher asks . . . and answers, "Let me tell you of the many areas of our lives where we act because signals say 'go' or do not act because they say 'danger'." If you mistake such a rhetorical question for a real one and try to answer it, the teacher may show some form of disapproval instead of pleasure at your ready response.

In this case, to discriminate a "true question" (S^D) from a "pretend question" (S$^\Delta$), you have probably learned to look for subtle stimulus cues like voice inflection, eye contact with audience, length of pause after the question, and others. Can you think of situations where you have misread stimuli as being discriminative when they were not—and also situations where you missed an opportunity by not recognizing an action that was in fact intended as a discriminative stimulus—a signal for you to do something with or to another person?

Properties of reinforcers

The slogan of operant conditioning might be "all power to the reinforcers." These potent consequences of behavior, which can then change subsequent behavior, have a number of interesting and complex properties. They can start out as weak and become strong, can be learned rather than biologically determined, can be activities rather than objects. Yet in some situations even powerful reinforcers, as we shall see, may not be enough to change a dominant behavior pattern.

Primary and conditioned reinforcers. Biologically significant stimuli, called *unconditioned stimuli* in appetitive classical conditioning, are called **primary reinforcers** in operant conditioning, where their role is to *reinforce* a response rather than to *elicit* one. For example, food is an unconditioned stimulus in classical conditioning, and also a common primary reinforcer in operant conditioning. And just as neutral stimuli can become conditioned stimuli in classical conditioning, neutral stimuli associated with reinforcers can become **conditioned reinforcers** for operant responses and can come to serve as ends in themselves. In fact, much human behavior is influenced less by biologically significant reinforcers than by a wide variety of conditioned reinforcers. Money, grades, praise, smiles of approval, gold stars, and various kinds of status symbols are among the many potent conditioned reinforcers that influence much of our learning and behavior. The *Close-up* on page 243 examines the role of primary and conditioned reinforcers in drug addiction.

When a conditioned reinforcer controls a wide range of responses, it is said to be a *generalized* conditioned reinforcer. Money, for example, can be exchanged for many primary reinforcers. One survey showed a strong positive correlation between married men's incomes and sexual infidelity. The more money they made, the more likely they were to be involved in extramarital sexual affairs (Biracree, 1984). Money may become a reinforcer that maintains a high level of responding even when the person hoards it and never exchanges it for property or pleasures of mind or flesh.

Since virtually any stimulus can become a conditioned reinforcer by being paired with a primary reinforcer, inedible tokens can be used as conditioned reinforcers even with animal learners.

In an early study, chimps were trained to work and learn how to solve problems with edible raisins as their primary reinforcer. Then tokens were delivered along with the raisins. When only the tokens were presented, the chimps continued working for "money" which they could later deposit in a "chimp-o-mat" designed to exchange tokens for the valued raisins (Cowles, 1937).

Teachers and experimenters often find tokens and other conditioned reinforcers more effective and easier to use than primary reinforcers because: (a) few

Reinforcers in Drug Addiction

Both classical and operant conditioning appear to be contributing factors in the popularity of drugs that alter mood, arousal, and perception. Several aspects of conditioning influence the effects of these drugs.

An individual trying out a new drug may find that it produces a desired emotional state—perhaps euphoria, excitement, relaxation, or social rewards. These benefits serve as positive reinforcers.

After drugs have been taken for awhile, stopping can cause painful withdrawal symptoms. These function as punishment; escaping these aversive consequences provides negative reinforcement.

With repeated drug usage, *tolerance* may develop—decreased responsiveness to the drug. Higher dosage is needed to achieve the same effect—a problem for the drug user and a serious problem in medical treatment of chronic pain. Until recently, this increased tolerance was assumed to be due to physiological changes in the sensitivity of brain receptors (Snyder & Matthysse, 1975). But evidence is accumulating that a *learned* association is at least partly responsible.

Some time ago Pavlov (1927) and later his colleague Bykov (1959) pointed out that tolerance to opiates develops when the individual *anticipates* the pharmacological assault of the drug. Perhaps with advance notice—provided by the conditioned stimulus associated with the ritual of injection—the body somehow learns to protect itself by preventing the drug from having its usual effect.

Shephard Siegel (1977) reasoned that if anticipation leads to tolerance, then removing the anticipation through extinction training should lower the tolerance—increasing the power of the drug.

In one study, sensitivity of rats to a standard pain stimulus was reduced by morphine. Over six trials, however, tolerance developed and the original dose of morphine had little effect. At that point a randomly chosen half of the subjects, the *control group,* were given 12 days of rest without exposure to any drug administration. The other half, the *experimental group,* received 12 days of extinction training during which the drug injection procedure was given but no morphine—only a placebo.

On day 13, when both groups were again given the morphine injections, the control subjects showed the same level of tolerance as before: the morphine still had little effect in reducing their pain. For the experimental group, however, the tolerance had been lowered: once more the morphine reduced their pain. Since tolerance was reduced by the extinction training, Siegel reasoned that the tolerance must have developed originally, at least in part, from the learning of this association between the biological effect of the drug and the environmental signals from the original procedure.

Is drug tolerance just to the specific drug administration procedure or to the whole stimulus context in which the drug is customarily received? If it is the latter, then overdose and death might result even from a usually nonlethal dose if it were given in a new context.

In another study rats learned by classical conditioning training to expect heroin injections (US) in one setting (CS_1), but salt solution injections in a different setting (CS_2). All developed heroin tolerance in the first setting. Then, on the test day, all subjects got a larger-than-usual dose of heroin—nearly twice the previous amount. Half of them got it in the setting where heroin was expected; the other half got it in the setting where salt solutions had been given during conditioning.

More than twice as many subjects died when heroin was *not* expected (salt-solution setting) as when it *was* expected (usual heroin setting)—82 percent versus 31 percent. They even died more rapidly. The other group had valid expectations and were able to cope with this potentially dangerous situation (in as yet unknown ways). Those that died did not and were not (Siegel, 1979).

The same thing may happen with human addicts, too. Doses for which they have developed tolerance in a particular setting may be overdoses in a new setting where the stimuli are unfamiliar. This would occur because the new setting does not provide the conditioned cues necessary for eliciting the *learned* tolerance response to the drug. Without this protective reaction, the drug's effects will be more potent. And under such conditions, learning may be lethal.

△ Inedible tokens can be used as conditioned reinforcers with animals. In one study, chimps learned to deposit tokens in a "chimp-o-mat" and receive raisins in exchange.

talk. What would happen if getting a chance to run and shout were made contingent on a period of sitting still first? Would there be an increase in the sitting-still behavior?

In a classic study, this was just what happened. With a teacher who had unsuccessfully tried pleas, punishment, and a bit of screaming on her own part, it was planned that

". . . sitting quietly in a chair and looking at the blackboard would be intermittently followed by the sound of a bell, with the instruction, "run and scream." The Ss would then leap to their feet and run around screaming. At another signal, they would stop. . . ." At a later stage, Ss earned tokens for low probability behaviors which could later be used to "buy" the opportunity for high-probability activities. With this kind of procedure, control was virtually perfect after a few days" (Homme et al., 1963, p. 55).

The principle that a more preferred *activity* can be used to reinforce a less preferred one was formulated by David Premack (1965). He found that water-deprived rats learned to increase their running in an exercise wheel when running was followed by an opportunity to drink water, while non-thirsty but exercise-deprived rats would learn to increase their drinking when that response was followed by a chance to run. It means that a reinforcer need not be a substance from the environment but can be a valued activity. This **Premack principle** encourages parents and teachers to use reinforcers valued by the individual child. For a socially outgoing child, playing with friends can reinforce the less pleasant task of getting one's homework done first. For a shy bookworm, reading a new book can be used to reinforce the less preferred activity of playing with other children. Whatever one values can be used to reinforce and increase activities one does not currently value, with the possibility that they too will come to be valued.

This principle is enormously useful for self-management too. If you wish you could get your studying done but have trouble withstanding alluring distractions, try promising yourself a half-hour break to engage in an activity you really want to do—but only *after* you have put in a given period of study or read so many pages. If you do this on a regular basis, the sweet delights of the later pleasure will help the medicine of the concentrated study go down with increasing ease—assuming you really do keep your reinforcer dependent on doing the planned amount of studying first. Pleasure before study makes study a pain; pleasure after study makes study a gain.

primary reinforcers are under the teacher's control whereas almost any stimulus event that *is* under the control of the teacher can be used for a conditioned reinforcer; (b) conditioned reinforcers can be dispensed rapidly; (c) they are portable; and (d) their reinforcing effect may be more immediate since it depends only on the perception of receiving them and not on biological processing, as in the case of primary reinforcers (eating food).

In some mental hospitals, entire "token economies" have been set up based on this principle. Desired behavior is reinforced by the staff with tokens that can later be exchanged by the patients for a whole array of rewards and privileges of each individual's choice (Holden, 1978). These systems of reinforcement are especially effective in modifying the patients' behaviors regarding self-care, upkeep of their environment, and social interaction.

Preferred activities as positive reinforcers.
Positive reinforcers in the laboratory are usually substances—food or water, for example. But it is not only *things* that we value. For example, nursery-school children enjoy running and shouting—much more than sitting still and listening to someone else

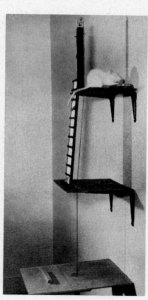

△ The operant technique of chaining can be used to teach a sequence of behaviors. Here a rat has learned to get to a top platform to obtain food by climbing a ladder to a lower platform, pulling a chain which raises the ladder to the highest platform, and then climbing the ladder to the top.

Shaping and chaining. A rat put in a maze will usually explore until it happens upon the goal box and discovers a tasty morsel in it; thereafter, the experimenter can change the rate of response by changing the reinforcement contingencies. But what if you want a boy to wear his glasses or an animal to do a new trick? How can you get the response to happen the first time so you can reinforce it? Here you could use the operant technique of **shaping,** which produces new behavior by reinforcing successive approximations of the final behavior desired. Following is an example of the use of shaping.

The patient was a 3-year-old boy who was hospitalized with a diagnosis of childhood schizophrenia. He lacked normal social and verbal behavior and was given to ungovernable tantrums and self-destructive actions. After having had a cataract operation, he refused to wear the glasses that were essential for the development of normal vision.

First the child was trained to expect a bit of candy or fruit at the clicking sound of a toy noisemaker. The sound soon became a conditioned reinforcer. Then training began with empty eyeglass frames. The child was reinforced (with the clicking sound) first for picking them up, then for holding them,

then for carrying them around. Slowly and by successive approximation, he was reinforced for bringing the frames closer to his eyes.

After a few weeks, he was putting the empty frames on his head at odd angles, and finally he was wearing them in the proper manner. With further training, the child learned to wear his glasses up to 12 hours a day (Wolf et al., 1964).

When shaping begins, any element of the target response is reinforced. Then, when this element is occurring regularly, only responses more like the desired response are reinforced. The standards are continually raised until eventually the desired action is being performed.

If you wanted to teach not just a single action, but a sequence of actions, you could add another technique called chaining. **Chaining** is the operant procedure in which many different responses in a sequence are reinforced until an effective chain of behaviors has been learned. As you might *not* expect, you start at the *end* of the sequence and work backwards.

You start by teaching the final response, and it is the only one that ever receives primary reinforcement. This final response then becomes a conditioned reinforcer for the response that has to occur just before it. In this way, other links are added to the behavior chain one at a time. Each one serves as a *discriminative stimulus* to the next response in line and a *conditioned reinforcer* for the one that comes before it in the sequence.

Shaping and chaining are essential parts of every animal trainer's program for teaching complex and unusual behaviors that are not likely to be emitted naturally. Dolphins leaping in tandem over a high wire and back-flipping while tossing a ball around have been trained using both of these operant conditioning techniques.

Unusual contingencies. Usually positive and negative reinforcement increase a desired response whereas punishment or extinction can eliminate an undesired response. But in rare cases, these contingencies do not work.

One such case is that in which mentally disturbed children repeatedly mutilate their bodies unless physically restrained. The behavior resists any kind of reinforcement. In such cases it has been found that if punishment is used temporarily to suppress the self-destructive behavior, the child will then begin to respond to positive reinforcers such as ice cream, cookies, M&Ms and praise. These reinforcers can then be used to shape desired new responses (Lovaas, 1977).

If punishment is clearly related to a prior response, it is said to be *response contingent.* Such punishment, as we have seen, typically suppresses the prior response. But what happens if punishment is *not* response contingent—has no relationship to one's actions? What is the consequence of getting punished no matter what you do? Apparently, this leads to another situation in which reinforcers will not work. This effect came to light in an extensive series of studies by Martin Seligman, Steven Maier, and their colleagues.

> In the original study, different groups of dogs went through a two-phase experiment. In Phase One, they received painful, unavoidable shocks which some dogs could escape by learning to press a switch. The others continued to receive the shock no matter what they did.
>
> In Phase Two, the next day, the dogs were put into a different apparatus, in which escape was possible simply by jumping over a small hurdle. A tone (conditioned stimulus) signaled that the shocks were about to start. The subjects that had learned to escape in the earlier situation quickly learned the new response, but the others rarely did so. Instead, they just sat there, crouching, passively getting shocked. This general response following noncontingent, inescapable shocks was termed **learned helplessness** (Seligman & Maier, 1967).

△ | *Through biofeedback training, individuals can learn to control nonconscious bodily processes. Blood pressure, muscle contractions, etc, are monitored and fed back to the subject by light or sound signals.*

The subjects' impaired performance seems to include three components—motivational deficits, emotional deficits, and cognitive deficits. The animals are slow to initiate actions that could improve the situation (a motivational effect). They are rigid, listless, apparently frightened, seeming to "give up" (an emotional effect). And they are poor learners in new situations where responding would be reinforced (a cognitive deficit). Even when they are shown how to escape by being dragged over to the safe side a few times, they do not learn to do so on their own (Maier & Seligman, 1976).

Parallels have been drawn between the deficits of learned helpless animals and depressed mental patients (Seligman, 1975). We will explore the usefulness of this analog of human depression in a later chapter. When applied to humans, other factors must be considered that influence a person's interpretation of why responding is ineffective and also determine how important a sense of control is to the individual (Abramson et al., 1978).

Biofeedback—amplifying weak contingencies. It was long assumed that such involuntary behavior as heart rate or blood pressure could not come under conscious control. Operant conditioners, however, have developed an ingenious technique by which subjects can learn to control nonconscious processes. Called **biofeedback training,** it is a procedure in which a subject is informed through visual or auditory displays about changes in bodily processes such as muscle contractions, brain waves, temperature, blood pressure, and others over which the individual usually has no control. These changes are monitored by recording devices and are amplified and fed back to the subject by variations in the intensity of the light or sound signal. This procedure has helped individuals to gain control over a variety of nonconscious biological processes.

In one especially creative application of biofeedback, children recovering from polio were helped to strengthen their atrophied muscles.

> Because their muscles were so weak, the children could not notice any effect when they tried to flex them and became discouraged about even trying. To give them reinforcing feedback, a psychologist first recorded the small amount of electrical activity in these weak muscles, then amplified it with a special apparatus, enough that it could light up an electric bulb. When the bulb was put behind a toy clown's face, the face lit up when the child flexed a muscle. This immediate, external feedback was so rewarding that the children gladly did their exercises—and increased their muscle control (cited in Stern and Ray, 1977, p. 36).

Often the most powerful reinforcers in a biofeedback paradigm are not tangible items, like money or candy, but the knowledge of success and the personal pride in knowing "I can do it." Biofeedback and other applications of the principles of conditioning in helping people modify their own behavior patterns will be presented more fully in later chapters.

The mechanics of reinforcement

Much research has centered on trying to identify the most effective amounts and distributions of reinforcers for controlling behavior.

The amount of reinforcement. In general, larger amounts of reinforcement are more effective. Two measures of learning show this relationship. The more the reward, the faster the rate of acquisition of a new response (improvement in performance) and the higher the upper level (terminal performance) achieved.

> This effect of bigger rewards in yielding better performance was clearly demonstrated in a study where hungry rats ran down an alleyway for food. Different rats received 1, 2, 5, 10, or 15 pellets of food in the goal box. The running speed of the rats down the alley varied directly with reward magnitude, each increase in reward improving performance. In the end, those who had been getting the largest reward were running more than twice as fast as those in the smallest reward condition (Roberts, 1969).

Interestingly, animals in the wild do not in fact always work hardest for the biggest reward. Instead, they balance the amount of effort or energy they lose in working for the reward against the size of the reward to be gained. They learn to achieve an *optimal* ratio of effort to reward magnitude—to get the best *relative* return for their investment of effort (Krebs, 1978). Bright students who settle for B grades that require 20 hours a week of study, passing up the chance for As that require 40 hours of work, are following this optimal effort-reward principle.

The distribution of reinforcement. If learning is a matter of associating events in memory, then the distribution of reinforcers in relation to responses will be important. How close must they be in time? Must a reinforcer be available every time? If not, what pattern will be most effective?

In classical conditioning, as we saw, short intervals between the two stimuli are best for forming most conditioned responses. Similarly, in operant conditioning, short intervals between response and reinforcement generate the best performance. With longer delays of reinforcement, learning is slower and may not occur at all. This makes sense because during a long time interval after the response, other kinds of responses or distracting stimuli may occur and the memory trace of the correct response may weaken as other responses are made. By the time the reinforcer finally comes, its contingent relationship to the particular earlier response may not be recognized and it may be enjoyed as "noncontingent good luck," unrelated to one's own actions.

Delayed-reward conditioning can be effective, but only if there are cues during the interval between response and reward to provide an information link between the present response and the eventual reward that is to come. For an animal subject, smells associated with food might serve as delayed-reward cues. For the student, verbal reminders of the future reward (e.g., a good job after graduation) can establish symbolic connections between present effort and the reinforcers that typically come long afterwards.

There is a legendary story that young B. F. Skinner was secluded in his laboratory over a long weekend with not enough of a food-reward supply for his hard-working pigeons. He economized by giving them a pellet after every two responses rather than after each one. From the pigeon's point of view, half

△ ▌ "FR 25! Pass it on!"

the time it responded, it got a reinforcer, and half the time it did not.

Under this condition of partial, or intermittent, reinforcement, the pigeons still acquired the operant response, although more slowly than usual. The surprise came during extinction training. When the reinforcer was omitted entirely, the animals trained under partial reinforcement continued to respond longer and more vigorously than pigeons who had gotten a payoff after every response. Half as many experiences of the response-reinforcer contingency had produced a more durable response!

Partial reinforcement effect is the name given to the behavioral principle that responses acquired under partial reinforcement are harder to extinguish than those acquired with continuous reinforcement. This effect has been found repeatedly in research across many different species (Bitterman, 1975). If you want someone to continue to respond in a particular way even when you are not around to provide reinforcement, be sure that you deliver your reinforcers on a partial schedule before you leave.

The discovery of the effectiveness of partial reinforcement led to extensive study of the effects of different **reinforcement schedules**—different patterns of delivering and withholding reinforcers (see **Figure 7.6**). Reinforcers were given either after a certain number of responses—called a "ratio schedule"—or after a specified interval of time regardless of the organism's rate of response—called an "interval schedule." In each case, there could be either a constant (fixed) pattern of reinforcement or an irregular (variable) one, making four types of schedules in all. It was found that each of these reinforcement schedules exerts a powerful and predictable effect on performance. Even when amount and kind of reinforcement are the same and deprivation is constant, performance will vary enormously according to the schedule on which reinforcers are given (see Ferster et al., 1975).

1. Fixed ratio schedule (FR). Here the organism receives a reward after making a fixed number of responses. With a fixed-ratio schedule of 25 (abbreviated as FR-25), the first 24 responses are unreinforced; reinforcement follows only every twenty-fifth response. The rate of responding is high with fixed-ratio schedules since a lot of work may be required (sometimes, hundreds of responses) before there is a single payoff. Such schedules do not encourage pigeons to count their pecks before they count their pay, but to put out a lot of pecks. With humans, fixed-ratio schedules operate when workers get paid once, only after making or selling a given total number of units, reaching a set quota.

2. Variable ratio schedule (VR). Here the number of responses required before a reward is delivered varies from one reward period to the next. A VR-10 schedule means that *on the average,* reinforcement would follow every tenth response. But it might come after only one, or not again until after twenty. Variable-ratio schedules keep the individual guessing when the payoff will come. They generate the highest rate of responding of any schedule. Gambling behavior is under the control of variable-ratio schedules. The response of dropping coins in a slot machine is maintained at a high, steady level by the payoff which comes after an unknown, variable number of coins has been deposited.

Variable ratio schedules resist extinction more than do fixed ratio schedules, especially when the variable ratio is large. A pigeon on a VR-110 schedule will respond with up to 12,000 pecks per hour and will continue responding for hours even with no reinforcement. Gamblers do likewise.

3. Fixed interval schedule (FI). Here a reward is given for the first response made after a fixed period of time has elapsed. On a FI-10 schedule, the subject, after getting a reinforcer, would have to wait ten seconds before another response would be reinforced. Other responses in between, before the time interval is over, are just wasted effort, they do not count toward reinforcement.

FI schedules reveal a typical but interesting curve with a "scalloped" form. After each reinforced response, the subject stops relevant responding for a time and does something else. As the time for the next payoff approaches, relevant responding begins again and increases sharply until the reinforcement occurs. Animals on fixed-interval schedules learn to discriminate the passage of time between rewards (Church et al., 1976). (You can now better appreci-

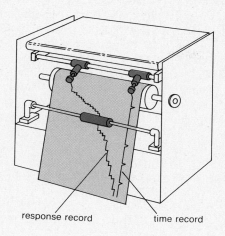

response record   time record

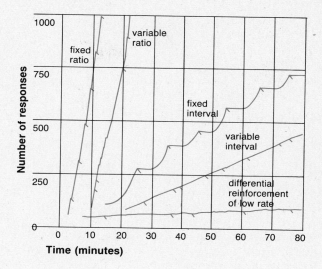

Time (minutes)

ate the wisdom in the advice: never buy a product made on Monday by workers paid on Friday.)

4. Variable interval schedule (VI). Here too reinforcement is given after a period of time has elapsed from the last reinforcement, but the interval varies. On a VI-10 schedule, reinforcers would be delivered for a response that was made ten seconds *on the average* after the last reinforced response. Thus there is sometimes a short wait, sometimes a long one between rewards. Nothing you can do will speed them up; your responses during these intervals have no consequences. No wonder this schedule generates a low, though stable rate of response.

Suppose your car-pool driver arrives to pick you up anywhere between 7:45 and 8:15 A.M. If it is cold outside, you will keep running to the window to see if the car is there yet. Your edgy, window-peeking behavior is under the control of a VI schedule. (Recommendation: get an FI driver.)

Extinction under variable interval schedules is gradual and much slower than under fixed interval schedules. Although there is a steady decline in responding without reinforcement, subjects trained with a high variable interval schedule continue to emit responses for a long time. In one such case, the pigeon pecked 18,000 times during the first 4 hours after reinforcement stopped and required 168 hours for extinction (Ferster & Skinner, 1957). This persistence of performance during extinction is one of the most powerful effects of partial reinforcement schedules.

△ **Figure 7.6** *Typical Curves for Different Reinforcement Schedules*

Operant responses are recorded on the moving paper of a cumulative recorder (left). The pen moves up each time a response is made; hatch marks indicate when reinforcers are presented. The more responses per time interval, the steeper the line.

Responding is fastest to the ratio schedules, slowest to the variable interval schedule, as shown in these idealized curves (right). The fixed-interval curve shows a "scallop" because the subject stops responding for a time after each reinforcement, then responds rapidly as the time for the next reinforcer approaches. The nearly flat curve shown is obtained by reinforcement of a low rate of responding. These records are characteristic whether the subject is a rat, a pigeon, or a child.

Figure redrawn from "Teaching Machines" by B. F. Skinner. Copyright © 1961 by Scientific American, Inc. All rights reserved.

NEW DEVELOPMENTS IN LEARNING THEORY

The bulk of research on animal learning has focused on *arbitrary* responses to stimuli that are conveniently available to the researcher in an artificial laboratory environment. This laboratory approach was adopted purposely by researchers who believed that the laws of learning they uncovered would be powerful general principles of behavior for all organisms and all learning.

> ". . . we arbitrarily choose almost any act from the animal's repertoire and reinforce it with food, water, or whatever else the animal will work to obtain. Although typically we teach a rat to press a bar or a pigeon to peck a key to obtain a pellet of food, we can readily train either to dance around the cage if we so choose. We usually use a light to signal the delivery of a pellet, but we can use a tone or a buzzer or any other stimulus the animal can detect. . . . The same act can be used for any reinforcement. . . . In effect, in any operant situation, the stimulus, the response, and the reinforcement are completely arbitrary and interchangeable. No one of them bears any biological built-in fixed connection to the others" (Teitelbaum, 1966, pp. 566–67).

The appealing simplicity of such a view has come under attack recently as psychologists have discovered certain *constraints* on this hoped-for generality of their findings. Some limits are imposed by the biological make-up of the organism and the environmental habitats particular species normally must adapt to. Other limits are imposed by cognitive processes, such as the subjects' interpretation of the situation, which we now know make conditioning less mechanical and more flexible than originally believed—and also make possible more complex kinds of learning than those envisioned in the simple classical and operant conditioning paradigms.

Biological constraints on conditioning

Over generations, organisms that have survived the particular challenges their species faced have passed on their genetic capacities to later members of the species. In order to fit a given ecological niche, each species must develop certain behavioral repertoires that aid survival. For instance, birds living on steep cliffs have to make nests that won't allow their eggs to roll out; those failing to do so fail to survive as a species. Some animals develop particular sense modalities, such as the vision of eagles and the hearing of bats; others develop special response capabilities, such as speed or strength. This, in turn, means that different species may have different capabilities for learning in a given situation. Some stimulus-response pairings may be more difficult to learn than others, depending on their relevance to survival for that species.

A **biological constraint on learning** is any limitation on capacity to learn that is caused by the inherited sensory, response, or cognitive capabilities of members of a given species. It is important to note that biological constraints challenge two assumptions of traditional learning theory: (a) the universal application of principles of conditioning to all species, and (b) the power of behavioral contingencies to result in learning even when the stimulus, response, or reinforcer is arbitrarily designated by the experimenter, trainer, or teacher.

Species-specific behavior. You have no doubt seen animals performing tricks on television, in the circus, or at zoos or fairs. Some play baseball or ping pong; others drive tiny race cars. For years, two psychologists, Keller and Marion Breland, have used conditioning techniques in training thousands of animals from many different species to perform a remarkable array of these learned behaviors. For some time, they had believed that general principles derived from laboratory research, using virtually any type of response or reward, could be directly applied to the control of animal behavior outside the laboratory—*until* some of their animals began to "misbehave."

For example, a raccoon was conditioned—after great difficulty—to pick up a coin and put it in a toy bank. The problem was that he would not let go of it until after he had held it a while in his little hands. Later, when he had two coins to be deposited, the conditioning broke down because he would not give them up at all. Instead he would rub them together, dip them into the container and then pull them back out again. (Raccoons often engage in rubbing and washing behaviors as part of the removal of the outer shell of a crayfish.) Likewise, when pigs were given the task of putting their hard-earned tokens into a large piggy bank, they instead would drop the coin, root (poke at) it along with their snouts, toss it up in the air, root it again, and so on. (Pigs root and shake as part of their food-getting repertoire.)

The Brelands' experience convinced them that even when animals have learned to make a conditioned response perfectly, the "learned behavior drifts toward instinctual behavior" over time. They termed this tendency **instinctual drift** (Breland & Breland, 1951, 1961). Animals tend increasingly to "do their own species thing" instead of doing what would get them food in the artificial situation.

The examples of animal "misbehavior" are not explainable by operant conditioning principles. They are understandable, however, if we add notions of biological constraints imposed by **species-specific** repertoires—unlearned behaviors common to all members of a given species. A pig can learn that a token is valuable by experiences in which the token is paired with food in a classical conditioning paradigm. But then the token is treated as if it were food—and the way pigs treat food is to root it about with their snouts. Doing so is incompatible with the operant conditioning task of putting the token in a piggy bank.

To demonstrate that operant conditioning principles hold even for pigs, what change might you suggest to the animal trainer? If the token were paired with a water reward for a thirsty pig, it would then not be rooted like food but deposited in the bank as a valuable commodity—dare we say, a liquid asset?

Coming prepared to learn. The Brelands' findings have highlighted a broader fact: learning is easier when the responses being learned are related to an animal's survival needs in its natural environment. Seligman (1970) has given the name *preparedness* to this predisposition to learn certain response-reinforcer relationships more easily than others.

For example, an experimenter can use a food reward to increase the digging response of hamsters but not to increase face-washing behavior. Why? Digging behavior is part of the hamster's repertoire of exploratory food-seeking behaviors. Face-washing is an activity done after, never before, meals. Trying to increase a post-meal response by making it a pre-meal response just won't work for hamsters (Shettleworth, 1972, 1975).

Besides these failures to learn "correct" *responses* (as arbitrarily defined by the experimenter), constraints on *stimulus* learning have also been found.

△ A species-specific repertoire for rabbits is to pull and tug at twigs and roots. Knowledge of that unlearned behavior allows a trainer to teach a rabbit to pull a lever that fires a cannon. The Brelands' research showed that an animal can be taught most easily by relating the learning to the animal's own natural tendencies.

For example, studies of *taste aversion* seem to violate usual principles of conditioning but make sense when viewed as part of a species' adaptiveness to its natural environment. In this case, a rat eats a food that is poisoned, and many hours later it becomes ill but survives. After only this one aversive experience and despite the long interval between tasting the food and illness, the rat learns to avoid the specific flavor of the poisoned food. Yet other stimuli present at the same time are not avoided later—only the taste stimuli. For example, when a flavor is followed by radiation-induced illness, rats will avoid that flavor in later trials, whereas a visual stimulus followed by the same radiation-induced illness is not avoided later. Yet rats easily learn to associate a visual signal with other kinds of dangerous events, such as shock (Garcia & Koelling, 1966). Even without conditioning, many animals show *bait shyness*, an unlearned reluctance to sample new food or food in a strange environment.

Of all the stimuli available to it, the animal seems to use the sensory cues that are most adaptive in its natural environment. Thus rats rely on taste cues for information about food while birds depend on visual cues.

> When rats and quail were both given blue salty water that made them ill and later were given a choice between salty water and blue water, the rats avoided the salty water while the quail avoided the blue water (Wilcoxon et al., 1971).
>
> In another study using rats as subjects, a bright stimulus was a better conditioned stimulus for danger than a dim or dark one, perhaps because darkness is associated with safety for rats in the wild (Welker & Wheatley, 1977).

Conditioning, then, depends not only on the pairing of any stimuli and responses, as was long thought, but also in part on how the organism is predisposed toward the particular features of the stimuli and responses to be associated. Paradoxically, acknowledging these biological constraints on conditioning is leading us to a richer, more comprehensive view of the learning process.

Cognitive influences on conditioning

Conditioning studies have revealed other cases in which conditioning did not take place where it "should have" or did take place where it would not have been predicted by early conditioning theories. In both cases the learner's perception and interpretation of events in the conditioning setting seem to change what was expected to be an automatic outcome of training. Three such "limiting" cases that we will discuss are blocking, sensory preconditioning, and observational learning.

Blocking. Even when a neutral stimulus and a powerful unconditioned stimulus are presented together, conditioning may not occur if another *conditioned* stimulus is already predicting the unconditioned stimulus. In a typical example, a conditioned response is established by pairing a tone with an unconditioned stimulus—a shock—in Phase One. In Phase Two, a compound stimulus—tone plus light—is paired repeatedly with the shock. According to traditional conditioning theory, the light should now become a conditioned stimulus, too. But this does not happen. The ability of the new stimulus to signal the unconditioned stimulus is not learned when it is presented *in a compound* with a stimulus that is already effective as a signal. This is called **blocking,** a phenomenon first studied by Leon Kamin (1969). Presumably there is no conditioning to the light because it provides no additional information beyond that already given by the tone. (See *Figure 7.7.*)

But this is a cognitive explanation. It postulates intervening processes of assessing the informational value of a stimulus, assessments which then influence learning. Kamin argues that conditioning occurs only when the powerful stimulus comes as a surprise to the organism. In this view, when an organism is surprised by a powerful stimulus, it scans its memory for a recent stimulus event that might be associated with it. If it finds such a stimulus, conditioning takes place. But once a conditioned stimulus is acting as a signal, another stimulus added to it will not motivate a memory search later because the unconditioned stimulus (e.g., the shock in the above example) has not been a surprise. So further conditioning will not occur.

You may be puzzled at this point. First of all, blocking might sound suspiciously like second-order conditioning (which we discussed on page 232) but with exactly the opposite results! That is not the case, however. The difference is in a key though subtle distinction: in second-order conditioning, the CS_2 is a *signal* for the CS_1, while in blocking the CS_2 occurs as a pair, in unison, with the CS_1 and has no *signal* value. A second puzzlement may present itself here, too. Earlier you were told that predictability of events was important, but now you are being told that surprise is also an important element. The apparent contradiction disappears when we consider *how* each is important. The power of surprise is that it promotes the initial learning about an important signal and its relation to a coming event of importance. This learned recognition of the signal then makes possible prediction of the event before it happens—a very useful ability. What the blocking studies show is that once the individual has come to expect the unconditioned stimulus on the basis of one dependable signal, it does not bother to learn about other stimuli that are also consistently present, presumably because their information is redundant. This is an economical use of the organism's mental ca-

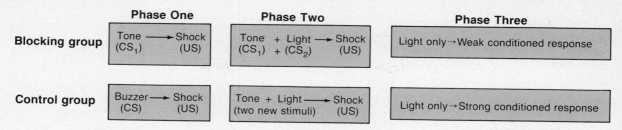

	Phase One	**Phase Two**	**Phase Three**
Blocking group	Tone ——→ Shock (CS₁) (US)	Tone + Light ——→ Shock (CS₁) + (CS₂) (US)	Light only→Weak conditioned response
Control group	Buzzer ——→ Shock (CS) (US)	Tone + Light ——→ Shock (two new stimuli) (US)	Light only→Strong conditioned response

△ Figure 7.7
The Blocking Paradigm

In Phase One, subjects of both groups learn a conditioned response—one to a tone and the other to a buzzer. In Phase Two, both groups are presented with tone plus light, followed by shock. The light provides no new information to the blocking group subjects and is ignored, but the control group subjects learn a new conditioned response to tone-plus-light. In Phase Three, when the light is presented alone, the blocking group subjects respond only weakly, showing that no association between light and shock was formed in Phase Two. The control group subjects, however, respond strongly, demonstrating the existence of the conditioned association.

pacity. The power of any particular stimulus to become a signal depends on what other stimuli are present that could serve as signals (Rudy & Wagner, 1975).

Sensory preconditioning. Another case where experimental findings seem to require a cognitive interpretation is one in which learning occurs where it would *not* be expected.

In a demonstration of this phenomenon, two neutral stimuli—such as a tone and a light—are paired in Phase One and elicit no overt response. No surprise so far: they have nothing of significance to predict. Then, in Phase Two, one of the stimuli (CS₁) is paired with a powerful unconditioned stimulus, such as shock, and a conditioned response develops. In Phase Three, the *other* stimulus, which has never

been paired with the powerful stimulus, is presented alone—and elicits the conditioned response. It, too, has become a conditioned stimulus (CS₂). Something must have been learned during Phase One, even though there was no way for it to be shown in performance at that time (Thompson, 1972).

This phenomenon is called **sensory preconditioning.** An association is learned between the sensory qualities of two paired stimuli prior to any pairing with an unconditioned stimulus. However, it is a "behaviorally silent," latent learning that does not show up till later (Dickinson, 1980).

At first glance, sensory preconditioning seems similar to second-order conditioning. But there is one big difference: the *reversal* of Phases One and Two. In second-order conditioning, a second neutral stimulus (CS₂) becomes a signal for an already conditioned stimulus (CS₁), acquiring thereby the power to elicit the conditioned response. The preconditioning effect is weaker, but still reveals that sensory stimuli are being associated with each other even prior to the role of either one as a predictor of significant events like food or shock. **Figure 7.8** compares the phenomena of blocking, sensory preconditioning, and second-order conditioning.

Learning from looking, not doing. Much social learning occurs in situations where learning would not be predicted by conditioning theory because the learner has made no active response and received no reinforcer. He or she has simply watched another person doing something—and getting reinforced or punished for it—and later demonstrated the ability to do exactly the same thing or to refrain from doing so. **Observational learning** is the name for learning based not on overt responding, but on watching others perform.

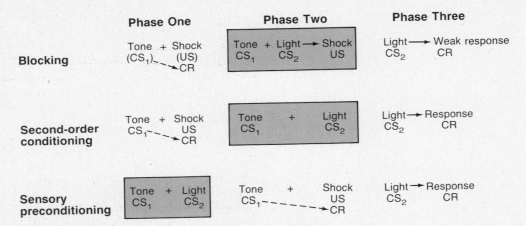

Figure 7.8 *Comparison of Blocking, Second-Order Conditioning, and Sensory Preconditioning*

The effect of pairing two neutral stimuli, such as a light and a tone, depends on what precedes, accompanies, and follows this pairing: (1) pairing with shock after conditioning to one → **blocking** *of the other; (2) pairing without shock after conditioning to one →* **second-order conditioning;** *(3) pairing without shock before conditioning to one →* **sensory preconditioning** *to the other.*

The classic demonstration of this kind of observational learning occurred in the laboratory of Albert Bandura. It involved children watching aggressive behavior. After watching adult models punching, hitting, and kicking a large plastic "BoBo" doll, these children later showed a greater frequency of the same behaviors than did children in control conditions who had not observed the aggressive models (Bandura, et al., 1963).

Subsequent studies showed that children could learn such behaviors from just watching film sequences of models, even cartoon characters. These studies also showed that people are more likely to imitate a model they see as somehow like themselves than a model seen as dissimilar. And they showed

that whether or not the model is seen to be rewarded for the behavior, the watcher will learn it just as well—but will be more likely to *perform* behavior that was seen to be rewarded. Finally, children learn not only situation-specific behaviors in this way but also general rules and behavioral strategies that are then generalized to situations different from the one in which the model was observed (Bandura, 1977a).

Learning must be taking place in all these cases even without a physical response or reinforcement. Children (and adults too) are able to learn associations, responses, and even rules just by watching someone else.

The capacity to learn from watching, as well as from doing, is extremely useful. It enables us to acquire large, integrated patterns of behavior without going through the tedious process of gradually eliminating wrong responses and building up the right ones through trial and error. It enables us to profit from the mistakes and successes of others. How to recognize snakes, mushrooms, or ivy that are poisonous or how to protect our eyes during a solar eclipse are examples of lessons better learned through observation than personal experience.

Through observation, we all learn many responses that we never make. Think of the varied contents of television shows you have watched in your life. Whether you use such learning depends on whether you see the likely consequences as being something you want, something you can get or "get away with," and something in line with your own values and self-image.

But there can be a tragic potential in learning through imitation, as was revealed in a news-service dispatch. Four Malaysian children, wearing Superman T-shirts, plunged to their deaths, apparently believing that they could fly like their hero (Reuters, 1982). And in another incident, a 12-year-old boy sexually assaulted a 10-year-old girl on a pool table while other children watched, in a reenactment of a barroom rape described in a trial shown on TV (Associated Press, 1984).

What is learned in conditioning?

In experimental studies of conditioning, the psychologist is interested in what factors affect learning and performance. The learning organism, typically, has no interest in the measurements the psychologist is making but copes the best it can with what may be a very artificial and constraining environment. It meets its needs by using a variety of resources and skills, including its ability to learn both associations between stimuli and associations between responses and their consequences. It also seems to learn much more.

Until recently, it was assumed that the individual played a passive role in conditioning, with associations formed and strengthened automatically by the reinforced pairing of stimulus events and behavior manipulated predictably by environmental events. What was learned was assumed to be fixed associa-

tions and specific responses. But evidence has been accumulating that what is learned is neither so automatic nor so specific as this. The examples of blocking and sensory preconditioning cited in the previous section, as well as the findings on observational learning, are indications that something important is happening between stimulus input and behavioral output.

Actions—and information. Earlier in the chapter a distinction was made between the covert process of learning and the overt behavior that reveals its occurrence. We have also seen several cases in which behavior did not accurately reflect what the learners ''knew.'' Organisms seem able to express or withhold what they know on different occasions and even to weigh likely payoffs against likely costs. They show a flexibility and appropriateness of responding that would not be possible if they had learned only specific responses and had only fixed associations with which to work.

The importance of cognitive processes in stimulus-response learning was demonstrated many years ago by psychologist Edward Tolman. He accepted the behaviorists' idea that psychologists must study observable behavior, but he created many situations in which mechanical, one-to-one associations between specific stimuli and responses could not explain the

◁ *Bandura demonstrated that children can learn aggressive behavior through observation. Children who watched an adult punch, hit, and kick a BoBo doll later demonstrated similar behaviors.*

behavior that was observed. Rather, Tolman (1948) claimed that what was being learned had to be something more like **cognitive maps,** inner representations of the learning situation as a whole, and *expectancies* about what the results of different actions would be, rather than merely specific paths that had led to goals in the past.

To show that animals, like humans, are capable of learning more than just a fixed response stamped in by being reinforced, Tolman and his students performed a series of studies on "place learning." They were able to demonstrate that when an original goal-path is blocked, the animal will take the shortest detour around the barrier even though that particular response was never previously reinforced (Tolman & Honzig, 1930). **Figure 7.9** shows the arrangement of one of these mazes. Rats seem to be reading their cognitive maps rather than blindly following habits elicited by particular stimuli in the setting.

Recent experiments on cognitive maps in rats, chimpanzees, and humans have confirmed Tolman's earlier findings (Menzel, 1978; Moar, 1980; Olton 1979). Organisms learn the general layout of their environment by exploring it even if they are not reinforced for learning particular paths. In fact, when foraging animals have found food in one spot, they are more likely to seek it elsewhere and *not* return to the same place for a while.

An amusing report of the importance of the cognitive factor of expectancy concerned an amiable monkey that had learned to make responses which brought it delicious treats, like a leaf of lettuce or a banana. It liked lettuce but much preferred bananas. One day it watched the experimenter place a banana under a container but did not see him secretly remove the banana and substitute a leaf of lettuce. When the monkey was given an opportunity to remove the container and discovered the lettuce, it threw a tantrum and even refused to touch the lettuce (Tinklepaugh, 1928).

Success is not so much the reward you get as how it compares with the reward you expected.

These findings, taken together, show that conditioning is neither blind nor mechanical. Besides the formation of an association between particular stimuli or between a response and a reinforcer, condi-

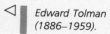
Edward Tolman (1886–1959).

tioning seems to include also the learning of expectancies, predictions, and evaluations of information—cognitive factors—and also learning about other aspects of the total stimulus context. Discriminative stimuli often provide us with these expectancies in real life, as in the operant conditioning laboratory. But when they are *not* present, we seem able to rely on cognitive maps or other mental representations of external reality to guide our behavior. And when reinforcers are used as incentives to induce behavior ("I'll give you ten dollars to mow the lawn") the expectancy as to whether the reinforcer is or is not forthcoming plus considerations of relative costs, and the value of the reinforcer to the individual (maybe a neighbor is offering more) can all be important factors in whether the response is made.

Associations—and generalizations. Learning rules from observing models and learning to be helpless after inescapable shock are but two examples in which both specific responses and more general reaction strategies were learned. In the observational learning studies, children learned particular behavior but also general rules and how to recognize when their rules were appropriate so that they could use them in situations with new elements. The helpless dogs learned to be passive and accept noncontingent shocks, and also learned a generalized inhibition against initiating action in new situations.

As we learn particular responses, we are also making generalizations—about situations like that, about our capability to meet life's requirements, about the other actors in the situation. We interpret, compare, contrast, give meaning to, and integrate the environmental challenges we meet and our responses to them. We reorganize ideas and pattern our actions differently. And we create symbols that go beyond anything we have experienced. From our encounters with the environment we learn particular associations—but much more, too.

Rote responses—and insight. Based on his experiments with cats, Thorndike believed that all learning depends on blind trial and error, in which correct responses are first made accidentally and then gradually "stamped in" by practice and reinforcement. His conclusion supported educational practices of the time, which emphasized rote prac-

tice and were not concerned with what learners might be perceiving and understanding.

A young German psychologist, Wolfgang Köhler, waiting out World War I on Tenerife Island off the coast of Africa, challenged this blind trial-and-error, associationist view of learning. He pointed out that although the cats could not have escaped by anything but trial and error, many puzzles in real life have meaningful internal relationships that provide clues as to what responses may be appropriate. Sometimes they require putting known facts together in new ways; sometimes they enable one to formulate hypotheses to test, or work out new theories to make sense of partial knowledge.

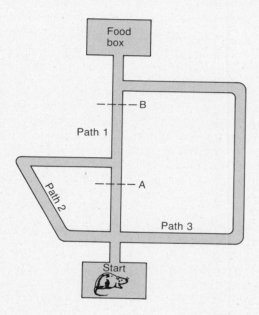

> Chimpanzees were handy on the island, so Köhler used them as subjects. He put them in enclosed areas where tasty morsels were in sight but out of reach—suspended high up or placed a few feet outside the enclosure—and watched what happened. Typically, his subjects would try unsuccessfully to reach the food directly and then would stop and survey the situation. After a period, often suddenly, they would try a new approach based on a novel way of using the objects at hand. They would drag a box under the fruit and climb onto it to reach the prize; later, when the fruit was hung higher, they reached it by piling boxes on top of each other. They would get food placed outside the enclosure by raking it in with a stick or—later—by using the short, accessible stick to rake in a longer stick that could do the job or even by fitting two sticks together (Köhler, 1925).

△ **Figure 7.9**

Example of a maze used to study place learning with rats. Subjects preferred Path 1 when it was open. With a block at A, they preferred Path 2. When a block was placed at B, the rats usually chose the longer Path 3, normally the least preferred one, as though they had a cognitive map and realized that Path 2 would be closed too. (Adapted from Tolman & Honzik, 1930)

Köhler concluded that whether an organism will solve a problem by gradual, blind trial and error or by **insight**—often sudden understanding of the relationships in the situation—will depend (a) on whether there are internal relationships in the problem that *can* be discovered, and (b) on whether they are within the mental capacity of the organism to grasp. Even if the latch in Thorndike's puzzle boxes had not been out of sight, the cats might not have had the ability to understand its mechanism by looking at it. Other research on problem solving will be presented in Chapter 10.

Conditioning in the laboratory provides little opportunity for subjects to make much use of their higher mental processes. But even there, the subject is clearly an active processor of information, scanning its environment for significant events, storing in memory many features encountered in its experi-

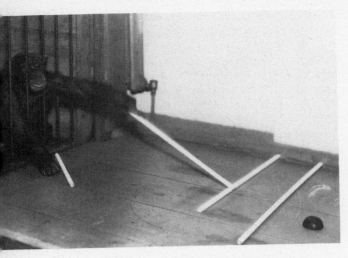

△ *A chimpanzee solving a problem by insight, an understanding of the relationships in the situation, in this case between the sticks and fruit. The chimp has learned to reach the fruit by using a shorter stick to rake in a longer stick that can in turn rake in the fruit.*

ence, integrating and organizing this stored information in useful ways, and drawing on appropriate parts of it in deciding on the best response in the current situation. In this cognitive view, changes in behavior are viewed as manifestations of mental processes, as public symptoms of private mental events.

In the past decade or so there has been a significant shift among psychologists toward this cognitive approach to learning. In subsequent chapters, we will see how it has guided our study of memory and thinking. But first we will turn to a consideration of the role of motivation in energizing and directing animals and humans to take action.

SUMMARY

■ Psychologists define learning as a relatively permanent change in behavior or behavioral potential based on experience. When psychology split off from philosophy, two assumptions it took along were that learning occurs through the association of ideas (law of association) and that all organisms are motivated to seek pleasure and avoid pain (principle of adaptive hedonism).

■ Two procedures for investigating learning widely adopted by psychologists are classical conditioning and operant conditioning. They provide means of experimentally studying associative learning.

■ Classical conditioning, developed by Pavlov, is a procedure for studying how organisms learn about relationships between events in their environment. In the classical conditioning paradigm, a biologically significant stimulus, called an unconditioned stimulus (US), elicits a reflex, called an unconditioned response (UR). A neutral stimulus that is then paired repeatedly with the unconditioned stimulus becomes a conditioned stimulus (CS), a stimulus capable of eliciting a similar response. This response is called a conditioned response (CR).

■ If, after training, the unconditioned stimulus is no longer presented with the conditioned stimulus, the conditioned response disappears. This is called extinction. After a rest period, however, conditioned responding partially returns when the conditioned stimulus is presented alone again. This is called spontaneous recovery.

■ Stimuli similar to the conditioned stimulus also elicit a conditioned response (stimulus generalization). If, however, they are never followed by the unconditioned stimulus, stimulus discrimination occurs: the organism stops responding to the irrelevant stimuli.

■ Instrumental conditioning procedures, developed by Thorndike, involve arranging relationships between a stimulus situation and responses to it that get reinforced. In this S–R approach, learning is instrumental to getting desired outcomes and the successful response is repeated.

■ The operant conditioning paradigm, developed by Skinner, is an arrangement for studying the effects of various reinforcement contingencies on emitted behaviors. Emitted behaviors are also called operants because they operate on—change—the environment. Partial, or intermittent, reinforcement leads to slower acquisition of a response but greater resistance to extinction later.

■ Both positive and negative reinforcement increase the rate of responding. Negative reinforcement is the condition of not receiving (or escaping) an aversive stimulus. In extinction training, reinforcement is withheld and response rate declines. Punishment involves receiving an aversive stimulus after a response; it may eliminate or temporarily suppress the response. The effects of punishment on learning and performance in humans are complex and depend on many variables.

■ Discriminative stimuli inform subjects when a particular reinforcement contingency is in effect. Responding is said to be under stimulus control when the response is made in the presence of a particular stimulus but not in its absence. The discriminative stimulus does not elicit the response but simply indicates that reinforcement will be available if the response is made.

■ Primary reinforcers are biologically important stimuli that function as reinforcers without learning. Conditioned reinforcers are learned; for humans they include money, praise, and symbols of status.

■ New responses may be learned by shaping or chaining procedures. A desired response may be shaped through successive reinforcement of closer approximations of the desired response. A chain of responses may be taught by making completion of each link a conditioned reinforcer for the response that comes before it and a discriminative stimulus for the next one in the chain.

■ Biofeedback training is a procedure in which an individual is given information about changes in body functions through visual or auditory signals and learns to control these inner changes.

■ Several kinds of research evidence that did not fit predictions of traditional conditioning theory have led to a broader understanding of the conditioning process by revealing biologically based constraints. The species-specific repertoires of different organisms, adaptive in their natural environments, make some response-reinforcement connections easier to learn than others; they may also prevent conditioning from occurring in artificial settings.

■ Cognitive influences on learning are shown in demonstrations of blocking and sensory preconditioning. Such influences are also apparent in subjects' ability to learn by observing models even though they make no response and receive no reinforcement themselves.

■ Current research on conditioning and learning reveals that organisms can do much more than learn specific responses and associations between concrete events. They can learn abstract, symbolic associations, general response patterns, rules, and an understanding of the meanings of relationships between stimuli and responses.

8

MOTIVATION AND EMOTION

■ UNDERSTANDING MOTIVATION
Why use motivational concepts?
Using motivational concepts in research

■ THEORETICAL PERSPECTIVES
Instincts as motivators
Drive theory and learning
Deficiency and growth motivation
Cognitions, expectations, and attributions

■ HUNGER AND EATING
The search for feeding regulators
A multiple-system approach

■ SEX AND SEXUALITY
Sexual arousal
Human sexuality

■ ACHIEVEMENT AND WORK
Achievement motivation
Work motivation
Motivation and the future

■ EMOTION
Are emotions innate or learned?
What starts an emotion?
Which is "primary"—thought or feeling?

■ SUMMARY

It was soon after Keith's seventeenth summer when he began to change. He had been second-string on the football team because he was "too easygoing." His girlfriend liked Keith's gentle manner, but was at times distressed because he was so slow getting turned on to her charms. That was before the changes began.

During team practice one day, Keith smashed through the blockers on an end run and nailed the halfback for a big loss—in fact, tackled him so hard that he broke his leg. A fight started when the burly center for the White Shirts cursed Keith for playing dirty. Keith knocked him out with a solid right hook. "Hey, what's gotten into Keith?" everyone was wondering. "Who cares?" was the coach's reaction. "The man is varsity material; he's got what it takes—he's all man!"

Off the playing field, Keith's life was changing in similarly dramatic ways. His girlfriend now called him "Tiger." Before, he could take sex or leave it; now it was an all-consuming passion. His appetite for food became enormous too. Keith seemed to be always hungry, eating, gaining weight, and growing steadily bigger.

He was encouraged to join the army to fight in the Vietnam War instead of in the town's bars. Once there, he became a legend of sorts. He volunteered to drive a high-explosive truck when no one else would. He would be fearless during enemy raids when everyone was justifiably afraid. Keith never felt particularly brave; he just didn't understand why the others were "so chicken."

In a society where the masculine traits of aggressiveness, sexuality, and fearless bravery are prized, big, bad Keith was a perfect "10." But something was wrong! Keith was having terrible headaches, which were coming on more frequently and more intensely.

Back home for his dad's funeral, Keith noticed a strange thing. He had really loved his father, but he was unable to experience the death emotionally. He felt only a cold emotion,

"as if" he were sad. The same was true in his relations with his girlfriend; his emotions lacked any feeling tone. They seemed to be flat, without highs or lows. But why? Why the sudden growth spurt, the raging appetite for food and sex, the aggressiveness, the loss of emotions? And why those blinding headaches?

Matters came to a head literally when Keith fainted from his headache pain. Fortunately the examining doctor recognized the unusual symptoms associated with the headaches—Keith had developed a brain tumor on his pituitary gland. He was suffering from a condition known as *acromegaly.* Over the past four years, since that seventeenth summer, as the tumor grew, so did the pressure on the pituitary, and so did Keith. Keith may have been a "superman" but he was not "his own man" at all. This big guy was at the mercy of a silent secretion coming from a tiny gland the size of a pea!

You will recall that the pituitary gland secretes a variety of chemicals, some of which control several of the endocrine glands, among them the adrenal glands (stress reactions of fight or flight), the testes (sexual behavior), and the thyroid (energy level). The pituitary also secretes a growth hormone. Together, these chemical reactions programmed Keith's desires, activities, and changes in body and mood. A variation in arousal is essential for experiencing appropriate emotional reactions, but he was too high, too "on" all the time to respond differently to making love or war, to the death of a parent or the attraction of a girlfriend.

The tumor was frozen surgically. As the headaches stopped, so did all of the other extreme effects of that powerful pituitary gland. Keith's appetite for food, sex, and aggression diminished. He became mild-mannered Clark Kent again—permanently.

But then Keith had to adjust to a new problem. He had lost his motivation to engage in any of the "masculine" activities that had become part of his life-style over the past four years. He was helped back to normal functioning by a combination of hormone therapy and supportive counseling. He was able to understand how he had become a victim of biological mechanisms that took away his personal control and distorted his motivation and emotional state. Keith has gone on to lead a healthy, well-adjusted life—happy to be an ordinary mortal, like most of the rest of us.*

For a different perspective on how motivational forces influence behavior, consider the case of Charles T.

Charles T. loved his work. He had started at the bottom on the assembly line in a TV factory and over the next twenty years had worked hard and well, moving steadily upward to become supervisor and, finally, chief personnel officer. He was entrusted with important decisions and became a valued troubleshooter. Charlie's executive status brought him special privileges, and the respect of his co-workers. "Mr. T." was a good boss and a fine man. He deserved all he got.

But one day he lost it all! His company went out of business, a victim of more efficient foreign competition. Sad, but not too bad, because Mr. T. was given the highest recommendation by the company's senior executives attesting to his intelligence, ability, and total company loyalty, and he was only forty-six years old at the time.

Armed with these glowing letters and an impressive resumé, Mr. T. began searching for the ideal replacement job. Interviewers were clearly impressed by the way he handled himself, but none called back. He was either "overqualified" or lacked experience for jobs requiring new high-technology skills. As his savings dwindled, Mr. T.'s usually cheerful disposition changed.

He was irritable for the first time anyone in his family could remember—and depressed. But he persisted in looking for work. He moved to Florida where many of his family lived and the cost of living was lower. Still no work.

One honest personnel officer finally told him why: "It's got nothing to do with your education, experience, references, whatever, Mr. T. The company doesn't want to hire older men, that's all."

Charlie was too old! He would show them, prove they were wrong, if only they'd give him a chance. They didn't. He grew resentful and bitter toward "them," and toward others less deserving who had jobs.

His once vibrant personality seemed to slowly drain out of him. He gave up looking for work. He had organized his life around his job. He had lived to work. But "when they take away your job, they. . . ." Charles T. was only fifty-one when he died of "natural causes" (Buczek, 1979).

---

*An actual case account of a former student of the author (with name changed).

The stories of Keith and Charlie introduce us to the complexity and range of human motivation and emotion. Keith's case forces us to acknowledge the role of physiological processes in regulating—and sometimes disrupting—our behavior. In Charlie's case we see the power of psychological and social processes in influencing our actions, feelings, and even life itself.

Why do we do what we do? What are the determinants of our actions? What internal and external forces stimulate passive organisms to become *actors?* These are the broad questions we try to answer in studying motivation.

After we consider different answers that psychologists have given to these questions—in the form of theories of motivation—we will examine in some detail three significant kinds of motivation: hunger, a primarily biologically based source of motivation; sex, which in humans mixes biology with psychology; and motivation for work and achievement, which clearly has a social-psychological basis. Unfortunately, it is not possible to include here many other kinds of motivation that play significant roles in our lives, such as thirst, affiliation, and religion, to name but a few. But we will ask questions about human emotions—the feeling side of motivation. Emotions color the quality of our lives—sometimes in rich tones, sometimes in dark hues.

UNDERSTANDING MOTIVATION

Motivation is the general term for the process of starting, directing, and maintaining physical and psychological activities. It is a broad concept that embraces all the internal mechanisms involved in (a) *preferences* for one activity over another, (b) *vigor* of responses, and (c) *persistence* of organized patterns of action toward relevant goals.

The word *motivation* comes from the Latin *movere*—"to move." Action is a fundamental property of living systems. Evolution favors organisms that can act on their own behalf to move toward and obtain what they need for survival and move away from or oppose what threatens them. For humans and other mobile creatures, life is a stream of action that includes general patterns as well as specific actions. Those psychologists whom you met in Chapter 7, studying learning in lower animals, were interested in the specific sources of motivation that led to the discrete responses that were being changed through learning. Other psychologists whom you will meet in subsequent chapters want to understand how broad motivational currents can shape a person's whole life-style.

No one has ever "seen" motivation, just as no one has ever "seen" learning. All we see are changes in behavior. To explain or justify these observed changes, we make inferences about underlying psychological and physiological processes—inferences that are formalized in the concept of motivation. Instead of trying to link each aspect of the behavior we see to particular preceding stimulus input, we postulate an overall *intervening variable* like hunger or sex or achievement, as shown in **Figure 8.1**.

The psychologist, like a detective, must use the available evidence from the stimulus conditions and the observable behavior to identify this basic internal variable—to establish the motive. The words we use to label the inner states that are part of this variable all share some implication of causal determination: *purpose, intention, goal-directed, need, want, drive, desire, motive.* Psychologists usually use the label **drive** to mean motivation for action that is assumed to be primarily biologically instigated, as in hunger. They often use **motive** to refer to psychologically and socially instigated motivation, which is generally

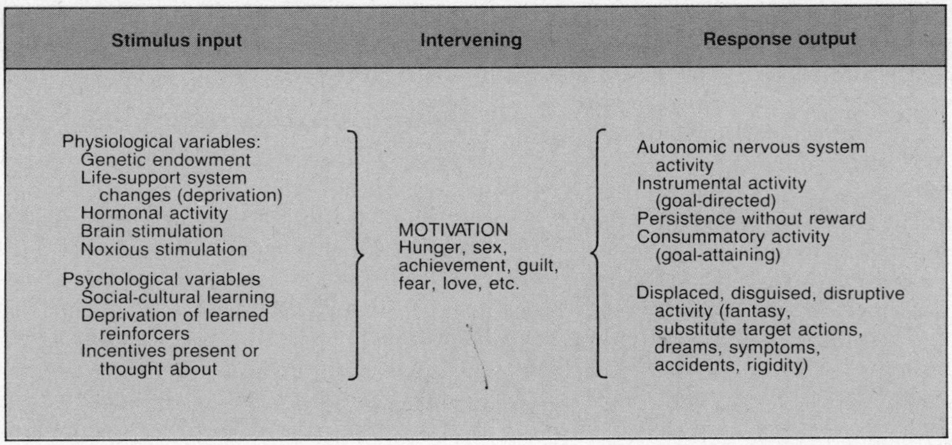

Stimulus input	Intervening	Response output

Physiological variables:
  Genetic endowment
  Life-support system
    changes (deprivation)
  Hormonal activity
  Brain stimulation
  Noxious stimulation
 	
Psychological variables
  Social-cultural learning
  Deprivation of learned
    reinforcers
  Incentives present or
    thought about
	MOTIVATION
	Hunger, sex,
	achievement, guilt,
	fear, love, etc.
		Autonomic nervous system
		    activity
		Instrumental activity
		    (goal-directed)
		Persistence without reward
		Consummatory activity
		    (goal-attaining)
		
		Displaced, disguised, disruptive
		    activity (fantasy,
		    substitute target actions,
		    dreams, symptoms,
		    accidents, rigidity)

△ **Figure 8.1** *Motivation as an Intervening Variable*

Since motivation is an intervening variable, only various kinds of stimulus input and response output can be observed. Any particular motivation, such as hunger, is assumed to be the result of a number of primary and acquired variables, such as those listed, and may lead to one or more of the kinds of response output shown. The function of the intervening variable is to link the input conditions to the output consequences.

assumed to be at least in part learned. A motive can be either conscious or nonconscious.

Psychologists vary in their usage of motivational concepts, however. Some, for example, prefer to use the term *need* only in connection with biological demands (the body's need for water). Others think *need* is appropriate in discussing psychological requirements also (the need for achievement).

Another important difference which generates heated argument among many psychologists is whether motivation is *teleological*—leading to purposeful action—or is just a general energizer of behavior without any implication that the organism is "striving toward a desired state."

One support for the teleological view came from those who accepted the doctrine of *hedonism,* which stated that organisms are motivated to seek pleasure and avoid pain. In Chapter 7 we saw that some psychologists studied learning as the behav-

ioral process that was started and maintained by such hedonistic forces within the organism. While radical behaviorists, such as Skinner, rejected all motivational concepts, other learning theorists, such as Clark Hull and Neal Miller, proposed a strong necessary link between motivation and learning. They argued that an unmotivated organism is passive, does not act, does not explore its environment, and therefore does not learn about the consequences of its responding. They proposed that responses that were followed by reinforcers (such as food) were learned because they reduced the motivation (hunger) presumed to have been responsible for the animal's responding in the first place. We are pairing learning and motivation in this section of our journey because of this historical association in psychology as the explanation for why organisms become active and why reinforcement is effective.

Before we look at some alternative theories of human motivation, let's consider first why many psychologists use motivational concepts to explain the behavior they study. We will then outline the kinds of behavioral indicators of motivation that researchers commonly use and the ways they manipulate motivational conditions.

Why use motivational concepts?

Despite the arguments of the radical behaviorists, other psychologists—and people generally—have found motivation a useful concept for several reasons. It helps to account for variability of behavior, to relate biological processes to behavior, to make outer behavior more intelligible, and to assign personal responsibility for actions.

To account for behavioral variability. Why might you do well on a task one day and poorly on the same task another day? Differing motivation could be one explanation. Likewise, when one child does very well at a competitive task and another child with the same ability and knowledge does very poorly, motivational differences seem a useful starting point in looking for explanations. Motivational explanations are used when the variations in people's performance in the *same* situation *cannot* be traced to differences in practice, reinforcement history, ability, skill, factors in the situation, or chance. More generally, then, if behavior never varied there would be no need for motivational concepts—or for psychology!

To relate biology to behavior. The concept of motivation reminds us that we, like Keith, are biological organisms. Besides reacting to external stimuli, we engage in behaviors that promote our survival and well-being, such as eating, sleeping, and keeping warm. Though we react to external stimulation in engaging in these behaviors, the external stimuli do not seem adequate to account for their universal occurrence in the species or the evident guidance of the behaviors by internal physiological processes.

The concept of motivation as an inner drive that determines behavior was introduced into psychology by Robert Woodworth (1918). He defined *drive* as energy released from the organism's store. This energy was nonspecific, blind as to direction. It was called forth by initiating stimuli and thereby made available for goal-directed activities. But other mechanisms, such as perceptual and learning processes, were thought to guide it in appropriate directions. According to Woodworth, drive is like the fuel in a vehicle, providing the energy of movement; other mechanisms determine when and where the vehicle goes, as well as the quality of the ride.

To infer private states from public acts

" 'Tis e'er the wont of simple folk to prize the deed and o'erlook the motive, and of learned folk to discount the deed and lay open the soul of the doer."

John Barth, *The Sot Weed Factor*

This novelist's words suggest two ways of responding to someone's behavior. We can take it at face value, or we can see the behavior as a symptom of an underlying emotional or motivational state. To the greeting "Good morning," do you respond "Good morning to you" or do you look for signs of what the person is really thinking or secretly feeling? Sigmund Freud's belief that all behavior has underlying causes, often unconscious, coupled with his idea that sex and aggression drive much of our behavior, has had a profound effect on psychologists' study of motivation as well as on popular views. Cognitive researchers are currently investigating the inferences that we make about inner determinants of outer behavior—and what makes them accurate or false (as we shall see in Chapters 10 and 16).

To assign responsibility for actions. The concept of personal responsibility is basic in law, religion, and ethics; personal responsibility, in turn, presupposes inner motivation and personal ability to control one's actions. People are judged less responsible for their actions when (a) they did not intend for the consequence to occur; (b) external forces were powerful enough to determine the behavior; or (c) the act was not under voluntary control because of the influence of drugs, alcohol, or intense emotion. Although these factors may be hard to sort out in a particular case, the concept of personal responsibility dissolves without the concept of motivation.

Using motivational concepts in research

Because motivation is an invisible, intervening variable, it is a slippery concept—and if we are not careful, a circular one. For example, we cannot say, "He ate because he was hungry," and then cite as evidence, "He must have been hungry because he ate." To be scientifically useful, the concept of motivation must be tied both to external behavioral indicators that can be measured and to observable operations that the researcher can perform. Only then can we start to look for consistent effects of motivation or for relationships between changes in stimulus conditions, assumed changes in the intervening variable of motivation, and changes in behavior.

For You, Baby, I'd Climb the Highest Mountain . . .

To assess the relative strengths of various drives, a group of psychologists at Columbia University in the late 1920s devised an *obstruction box* in which an electrified grid separated a motivated rat from something which it was assumed to want. The strength of a variety of drives (induced by deprivation) was pitted against a constant level of shock that the animal had to endure in order to reach food, water, a sexually responsive mate, or its own offspring. The behavioral index of drive strength was the number of times the animal would cross the "hot" grid in a given period of time. (It could also have been the highest level of

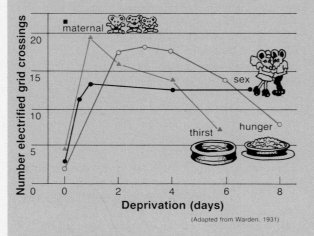

Deprivation (days)

(Adapted from Warden. 1931)

shock intensity that would be tolerated to reach the goal.) Typical of the data obtained with this method are the patterns reported in the figure at left.

The motivating effects of thirst (and hunger) were greatest after a short period of deprivation. Motivation declined when water or food deprivation became extreme. This is a pattern found with many kinds of motivation; it is called an *inverted-U function*. As motivation increases, the curve of performance first rises and later declines.

This curve was not found in two cases, however. With a little sex as a reward, sex-deprived rats kept running at a constant rate (after the first few hours). Mother rats endured the most suffering, running most often across the "hot" grid. This was interpreted as evidence for the existence of a powerful "maternal drive" in some animals.

You may be interested in another, incidental finding of these studies. Even without deprivation of any kind, the animals still crossed the grid a few times. Furthermore, even when there was nothing on the other side—except a chance to explore the novel environment—they crossed the barrier. In other research, when rats deprived of food or water were placed in a novel environment with plenty of opportunities to eat or drink, they explored instead. Only later did they begin to satisfy their hunger and thirst (Zimbardo & Montgomery, 1957). This behavior appears to be evidence of an exploratory drive that operates outside the constraints of homeostatic mechanisms.

Behavioral indicators of motivation. Among the many behaviors that have been taken as indicators of motivation and used to measure its strength are: (a) activity level, (b) rate of learning (with practice held constant), (c) final level of performance reached, (d) resistance of a response to extinction, (e) interference with ongoing activities, (f) preference for a particular goal or activity, and (g) consummatory behavior (for example, amount eaten or speed of eating). These are all *index variables:* they indicate the presence of motivation and something about its strength. Any one of them can be used in an operational definition of motivation because they all are external events that can be observed and measured. (For an example of persistence in overcoming barriers to reach a goal as an indicator of strength of motivation, see the **Close-up** above.)

With humans, motivation can be measured in additional ways. Researchers may ask participants to fill out questionnaires indicating personal evaluations of their needs, desires, anxieties, and so forth and use the test scores as indicators of strength of motivation. These test scores can then be correlated with other behavioral measures.

In one study using this approach, students' levels of anxiety were first measured on a standardized questionnaire and then all subjects experienced a conditioning situation. The unconditioned stimulus (US) was the aversive stimulus of a blast of air to the eye, eliciting an eye blink, and the conditioned stimulus (CS) was a tone or light paired with the blast of air.

Subjects who were high in anxiety (drive), as measured by the questionnaire, acquired the conditioned eyelid response faster than those whose anxiety was low (see **Figure 8.2**). The investigator reasoned that high anxiety increased the intensity and hence the aversive motivational value of the unconditioned stimulus, leading the high-anxiety subjects to respond more strongly than the low-anxiety subjects (Taylor, 1951).

Manipulating drives and motives. The study cited above, relating existing individual differences in anxiety level (from self-reports) to speed of conditioning, was a correlational study. But often researchers studying motivation want to see how changes in motivation will change behavior. This means using an experimental design, in which motivational conditions are manipulated to induce the motivational state or make it stronger or weaker. The two general classes of procedures used to induce or change drive states are *deprivation* and *stimulation.*

Deprivation for animal subjects may involve denial of access to needed substances, such as food, water, or specific substances like calcium or thiamine. Dep-

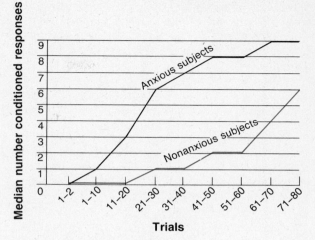

Figure 8.2 *Effect of Anxiety on Conditioning*

With successive blocks of trials, more anxious than nonanxious subjects showed conditioned responses. (Adapted from Taylor, 1951)

rivation for human subjects may involve withholding desired psychological conditions—perhaps the presence of other people. Social deprivation is assumed to be an aversive state that will motivate people to do something that will end it. This is one justification given for solitary confinement in prison as an extreme form of punishment.

Stimulation to trigger motives may involve giving aversive stimuli such as shocks, noise, heat, or cold, which lead to responses of avoidance or escape.

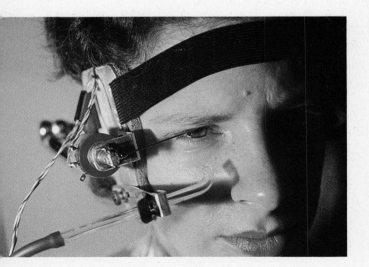

Eyelid conditioning is achieved through the use of this apparatus. A puff of air comes out of the tube toward the eye and is paired with a tone. A thin wire is attached to the eyelid so that any eyeblink is converted to an electrical signal that is then recorded.

Stimuli leading to affectively positive states may be investigated, as in the general stimulation that arouses the sex drive, or the self-stimulation of pleasure centers by electrical current through implanted electrodes (described in Chapter 3).

Barriers, unsolvable tasks, and competition are other stimulus conditions that researchers have used to induce drives in studies of motivation. Finally, motives may be aroused by the presentation of incentives—opportunities to gain something that is desired. For example, when prizes are shown to contestants prior to some performance, the purpose is to motivate the competitors. This is called *incentive motivation.*

Similarly, the presence of a novel environment may induce motivation to explore. Here it is believed that the external stimulus interacts with an internal predisposition toward certain actions that would not by itself lead to action. Across many species, exploration and curiosity have been shown to be among the most powerful motives (Butler & Harlow, 1954; Fowler, 1965).

THEORETICAL PERSPECTIVES

It will not surprise you to learn that there have been many attempts to explain what motivates behavior and how motivation works. These attempts differ in their explanations of how motivation originates, what processes occur, what role the environment plays, and the extent to which people's motives are aspects of their unique personalities or simply characteristic of the species. Some are general theories; others deal chiefly with animal or human motivation. Here we will look briefly at four theories of human motivation: instinct theory, drive theory, a theory of deficiency and growth motivation, and the theory that cognitions can be motivating.

Instincts as motivators

One of the earliest views on what motivates behavior is found in the notion of instincts. According to instinct theory, organisms are born with certain preprogrammed tendencies that are essential for their survival and provide the motivational force that directs behavior in appropriate channels. Some instinct theorists have seen this biological force as *mechanistic,* motivating behavior without purpose and beyond individual control. Others have adopted a conception of instincts that allows the organism choice in deciding upon different courses of action.

Animal instincts. All over the world, animals engage in regular cycles of activity that enable their species to survive. Salmon swim thousands of miles back to the exact stream where they were spawned, leaping up waterfalls till they come to the right spot, where the surviving males and females engage in ritualized courtship and mating. Fertilized eggs are deposited, the parents die, and in time their young swim downstream to live in the ocean until, a few years later, it is time for them to come back to complete their part in this continuing drama. Female green turtles living off the Brazilian coast regularly migrate 1400 miles to lay their eggs on a beach on Ascension Island where they were hatched, a target only five miles wide that they somehow locate in the open ocean.

◁ *Web building is an instinctive activity among spiders. The orb spider, shown here, spins different types of silk, a sticky kind that traps the prey, and a dry kind which allows the spider itself to walk safely.*

Similarly remarkable activities can be reported for most species of animals. Bears hibernate, bees communicate the location of food to other bees, army ants go on hunting expeditions, birds build nests, spiders spin webs—exactly as their parents and ancestors did before them.

These are all examples of **instincts,** unlearned behavior patterns that appear in the same form in every member of the species at a certain point in their development. Instinctive behaviors are also found in response to specific types of stimulation. Often they are elicited by combinations of internal secretions, such as hormones, and external stimulation, such as odor cues. Environmental cues that reliably evoke a specific response pattern in the members of a particular species are called **releasers.** (Do you remember the releaser that changed Tina's behavior toward her turkey chicks described in Chapter 1?) When the organism is at a given stage in its development, a behavior that is truly instinctive will appear "full blown" the first time that adequate stimuli are present. It will be performed adequately the first time, despite lack of previous opportunity to learn or practice it. Once released, it no longer depends on the external cue but is completed automatically.

Originally, instinct theorists were content to describe instincts in terms of mysterious inner forces that impelled certain activities to emerge. Today, instincts in animals are more often studied as **fixed action patterns** by ethologists (discussed in Chapter 1). **Ethology** is the observational study of animal be-

havior patterns that occur in animals' interactions with their natural environment (rather than in artificial laboratory settings). Ethologists study eliciting stimuli, environmental conditions, developmental stages, and specific response sequences in different animal species.

Human instincts. Early Christian theologians assumed that only animals were guided by instinct. They believed that God had given humans reason, free will, and thus responsibility for their actions and a chance to earn their way into heaven.

But in 1859 Charles Darwin presented evidence of a continuity of species from lower animals to humans, and ideas in psychology as well as in other fields began to change. William James, writing in 1890, stated his belief that humans rely on even more instincts than lower animals do to guide their behavior. Besides the biological instincts they share with animals, he described a host of human social instincts, such as sympathy, modesty, sociability, and love. For James, both human and animal instincts were purposive.

This view of instincts was extended by psychologist William McDougall. In 1908 he wrote: "The human mind has certain innate or inherited tendencies which are the essential springs or motive powers of all thought and action, whether individual or collective, and are the bases from which the character and will of individuals and of nations are gradually developed . . ." (p. 20). McDougall defined instincts as inherited dispositions that had three components: an *energizing* aspect, an *action* aspect, and *goal directedness.*

Sigmund Freud (1915) had a somewhat different view of instinct. Contrary to James and McDougall, Freud thought instincts had neither conscious purpose nor predetermined direction and that many means of satisfying them could be learned. He believed that instinctive urges exist to satisfy bodily needs and that they create a tension, or *psychic energy*. This tension drives us toward activities or objects that will bring satisfaction through reduction of the tension. Although they operate largely below the level of consciousness, instincts affect our conscious thoughts and feelings as well as our actions in many ways and frequently put us in conflict with society's demands. We are then motivated to reduce the tension caused by such conflicts.

The most fundamental aspect of human nature, according to Freud, is the conflict between the primal instincts of life and death. The *life instinct* (or *Eros*) functions to maintain life and to lead the individual to reproduce sexually. The *death instinct* (or *Thanatos*) is the negative force of nature that keeps even the noblest of creatures mortal through illness, aging, and finally death. In this view, all self-destructive behaviors are motivated by the death instinct turned inward, while aggression and vandalism result when it is turned outward.

By the 1920s, lists of over 10,000 human instincts were being compiled by psychologists (Bernard, 1924). Now humans were seen as better than animals because they had more instincts plus the power to reason and get to heaven too!

Challenges to instinct theory. At this same time, however, the notion of instincts as universal explanations for human behavior was beginning to suffer a slow death. Researchers were pointing out that instincts were not really explanations at all, not really universal, and not useful because they overemphasized fixed, inborn mechanisms whereas much behavior was clearly modifiable by learning. It became apparent that instincts were being postulated to explain every action. Even spitting, frowning, and studying psychology were supposedly motivated by instincts. But such explanations were *circular:* they did not really "explain," but only "named." Instead of postulating processes, mechanisms, or structures to account for observed behavior, instinct theorists merely provided convenient labels. Thus the "aggression instinct" was used to explain why people behaved aggressively, and aggressive behavior was taken as evidence for an instinct to aggress (Beach, 1955).

Meanwhile, cross-cultural anthropologists like Ruth Benedict (1959) and Margaret Mead (1939) had found enormous *differences* in behavior in different cultures. Behavior patterns that had been assumed to be universal expressions of "human nature" were now seen to be variable, reflecting specific cultural experiences and learned values.

But most damaging to the early instinct notions were the empirical demonstrations by the behaviorists that important behaviors are learned rather than inborn. Beginning with Watson, environmental determinants of actions and even of emotions were demonstrated, as we saw in the preceding chapter in the learned fear of little Albert. Freud's instinct doctrine fared better than McDougall's because it was part of his psychoanalytic theory, which included a basic conception of human nature; it also provided a therapeutic approach to mental disorders (to be discussed in Chapter 15). But for research psychologists, vague notions of inborn instincts were replaced by precise analyses of the environmental determinants of behavior. There is a general recognition today that the complexity that is the human-organism-in-action is usually influenced by the interaction of internal and external factors—by both what we are as biological organisms and what we can become through learning. The mechanism thought to be responsible for translating motivation into learning and learning back into motivated behavior was first described in *drive theory*.

Drive theory and learning

As you are watching television, you go to the refrigerator, get a cold drink, consume it, and feel better. According to drive theory, your drive—your motivation to find and consume a drink—is based on an internal biological need—namely thirst. But you go to the refrigerator and get something to drink instead of taking out a book to read because the refrigerator sequence has been reinforced previously by reduction of your thirst. In addition, because of regular past association of the sight of the refrigerator with thirst, merely seeing it can now motivate you to open it and search for a cool drink even when you are not thirsty. Similarly, the sight of soft drinks or beer on TV commercials can induce a drive to get something to drink even if you aren't thirsty.

This example outlines the main features of a theory of drive as proposed by Clark Hull (1943). Hull viewed motivation as necessary for learning to occur, and learning as essential for successful adaptation to the environment. Like Freud, Hull emphasized the role of *tension* in motivation and of *tension reduction* as a reinforcer. But unlike his psychoanalytic colleague, Hull believed that most human behavior was motivated less by innate forces (drives, or instinctual urges) and more by drives developed from experience.

The main elements of this drive theory approach, which were shared by many other behaviorists in the 1940s and 1950s, can be outlined as follows:

1. A biological need triggers a strong state of general arousal, or drive (D).
2. This nonspecific drive state energizes random activity.
3. When one of the random actions leads to a goal that reduces tension of the drive, the organism stops being randomly active.
4. The reinforcement (tension reduction) strengthens the association between the goal stimulus (S) and the successful response (R).

Using our previous example, having your thirst quenched after consuming a cold drink strengthens your association between the cold drink and the actions that produced it. In this way, over time, a learned *habit*, a learned association between stimulus and response ($_SH_R$), develops.

Drives can be induced by any intense internal stimulation (such as hunger or thirst) or by strong external stimuli (such as electric shock or noise). **Primary drives** are induced by internal biological needs and do not depend on learning. But just as neutral stimuli paired with reinforcers can acquire reinforcing power, so neutral stimuli paired with strong drives can acquire motivating power. The desire to possess money, for example, is a powerful acquired motivator for most of us. Drives acquired through conditioning are called **acquired drives** (also *secondary drives*). It was assumed by drive theorists that most psychological motives, such as seeking parental approval or desiring affiliation with other people, are secondary drives, acquired through learned association with some primary drive.

Fear as an acquired drive. Drive theorists studied fear not just as an emotional reaction to danger but as a powerful, acquired motivational state. In fact, they used it as a model to explain the supposed development and functioning of all psychological motives.

In the classic demonstration of fear as a learned drive, rats were shocked in one side of the two-compartment apparatus shown here. But they could escape the painful shock by jumping through the door between them to the other, safe side, and they soon learned to do so. Later, when the door was locked and they were put into the original compartment but *not* shocked, they still learned to escape to the other side by turning a wheel that opened the door (and later by pressing a lever that did so). The experimenter reasoned that learned fear was elicited by the external cues of the apparatus and motivated the animals to escape just as the shock itself had done. He also assumed that this learned fear provided the motivation necessary for learning the new responses (N. Miller, 1948).

Learned fear is an important acquired motivator because fear can so easily become associated with any situation in which pain or distress has been experienced and is very hard to extinguish. Learned fear is regarded as a drive because it energizes a wide variety of responses and leads to the learning of new behaviors that are reinforced through fear reduction. In some cases moderate levels of learned fear can motivate responses in humans that help them adjust to and prepare better for realistic impending threats, such as surgery (Janis, 1958; Leventhal, 1970).

Incentives and optimal arousal. Two challenges to drive theory came from research which showed (a) that organisms could become energized by environmental stimuli rather than only by inner conditions, and (b) that humans often act to increase tension rather than only to reduce it.

External stimuli often attract or repel us regardless of our inner state. The sight of a refrigerator, beverage ad on TV, or beautiful person, or the smell of certain foods, such as hot pizza, can arouse us to take appropriate actions even when we are not impelled from within by thirst, sex, or hunger drives. External stimuli such as these, which serve as anticipated rewards, are called **incentives.**

It seems clear that external cues that have been associated with reduction of a drive in the past (like refrigerators and cold drinks) can motivate behavior even when no drive exists. But research has demonstrated that even stimuli that have no biological utility can serve as incentives—for animals as well as hu-

△ Shown at top is a typical shuttlebox with two compartments, one lighted and the other dark. The floor of each compartment is a metal grid which can be electrified to produce a shock. The close-up view in the center shows the hatch between the compartments, which the rat can open by pressing the lever in the corner of the box. As shown at bottom, if the rat has been shocked in the lighted compartment, but not in the dark one, he soon learns to open the hatch and escape to the "safe" compartment as soon as he is placed in the lighted one, even in the absence of shock there.

mans. For example, saccharine, which does not satisfy hunger or have any biological value, will reinforce learning and performance for many organisms because of its sweet flavor (Sheffield, 1966; Sheffield & Roby, 1950).

Accordingly, in successors to Hull's drive theory, motivational arousal is seen as involving a relationship between environmental incentives that "pull" behavior and the inner psychological and physiological conditions that "push" behavior (Logan, 1960). More recent investigations have even revealed that "preparatory" responses (including secretion of saliva, gastric juices, pancreatic enzymes, and insulin) are induced by the sensory qualities of food (its sight, smell, taste). The intensity of these responses (called *cephalic* responses) is directly related to how palatable the food is seen to be—its incentive value, not its biological value (Powley, 1977).

According to drive theory, all activity is directed toward tension reduction. Such a theory has no explanation for the tension-arousing activities that people often choose (watching horror movies, going on roller-coaster rides, engaging in a protest hunger strike, for example). People also explore new environments, work on crossword puzzles "for their own sake," search for knowledge, and "stir up trouble."

From these and other observations, a theory of *optimal arousal* was developed according to which performance depends on both a preferred level of arousal and the complexity of the task (Hebb, 1955; Berlyne, 1960, 1967). There seems to be a general preference for moderately stimulating environments, neither too low (sensory deprivation) nor too high (aversive sensory overload).

There are individual differences in preferences for complex versus simple stimuli (Dorfman, 1965). You have probably noticed such differences in your friends' preferences for types of music, art, or leisure activities—and considered them just differences in "taste." There is some optimal level of arousal for each organism: when below it, stimulation is sought; when above it, stimulation is avoided.

But another factor enters in too. With experience, most events become less stimulating, thus motivating us to seek more exciting ones when the original thrill is gone (Zuckerman, 1979). As experience makes us "jaded," what used to arouse us may leave us indifferent or bored. To escape from boredom then becomes a new source of motivation.

"Ennui has made more gamblers than avarice, more drunkards than thirst, and perhaps as many suicides as despair."

C. C. Colton, *Lacon* (1820)

Deficiency and growth motivation

A theory of human motivation that explains both tension-reducing and tension-increasing actions is that of humanist psychologist, Abraham Maslow (1970), mentioned in Chapter 1. Maslow distinguished between **deficiency motivation**, in which individuals seek to restore their physical or psychological equilibrium, and **growth motivation**, in which individuals seek to go beyond what they have done and been in the past. Growth-motivated people may welcome uncertainty, an increase in tension, and even pain if they see it as a route toward greater fulfillment of their potential and a way to achieve their goals. Thus, for example, a martyr or revolutionary who voluntarily suffers for a religious or political cause may accept pain or humiliation as necessary in the attempt to change prevailing attitudes and institutions. Such a person suffers to achieve meaningful goals that fit with personal values.

Maslow's theory holds that we all have a **needs hierarchy,** as shown in **Figure 8.3** in which our in-born needs are arranged in a sequence of stages from most "primitive" to most "human." At the bottom of this hierarchy are the basic *biological needs,* such as hunger and thirst. When they are pressing,

other needs are put on "hold" and are unlikely to influence our actions. But when they are reasonably well satisfied, then the needs on the next level— *safety needs*—motivate us. When we are no longer concerned about danger, we become motivated by *attachment needs*—needs to belong, to affiliate with others, to love and be loved. If we are well fed and safe and feeling a sense of social belonging, we move up to *esteem needs.* These include the need to like oneself, to see oneself as competent and effective, and to be held in esteem by others.

At each level, Maslow argues, the need is inborn, not learned, although the way it is elicited and expressed is affected by the values learned in one's family and culture. Pathology may result when needs at any level are frustrated. Frustrated love needs, for example, can lead to hostility and perversions of sexuality.

As we move to the top of the hierarchy, we find the person who is nourished, safe, loved and loving, secure in a sense of a worthwhile self. Some people go beyond these basic human needs in the quest for fullest development of their potentials, or **self-actualization.** The self-actualizing person is self-aware, self-accepting, socially responsive, creative,

▷ **Figure 8.3** *Maslow's Hierarchy of Needs*

According to Maslow, needs at the lower levels of the hierarchy dominate the individual's motivation as long as they are unsatisfied. Once these are adequately satisfied, however, the higher needs occupy the individual's attention and effort. (After Maslow, 1970)

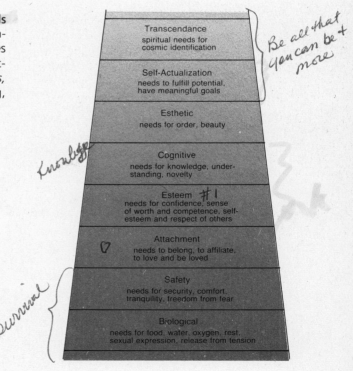

spontaneous, and open to novelty and challenge, among other positive attributes.

Maslow's hierarchy goes several steps further to include *needs for transcendence.* Such needs may lead to higher states of consciousness and a more "cosmic" vision of one's part in the universe. You probably recognize a similarity between this highest level of human striving and Kohlberg's top stage of moral development (see Chapter 2).

Maslow's theory has had more influence on therapy and education than on psychological research. For Maslow, as for his fellow humanistic psychologist, Carl Rogers (1959), the central motivational force for humans is the innate need to grow and actualize one's highest potentialities. Other psychologists have suggested that self-actualization motivation is essentially motivation to be open to new experiences, ideas, and feelings, to explore both our external and mental environments, and thus is a form of curiosity or stimulus motivation (Butler & Rice, 1963). Anxiety and guilt inhibit this motivation. In any case, becoming free from deficiency motivation allows the person to become more competent and fulfilled.

Such an "upbeat" approach was welcomed by many psychologists who had grown up on the earlier diet of negative motivational views, filled as they were with instincts, tension-reduction, unconscious urges, and other less than noble forces. "Accentuating the positive" in man and woman fit a new therapeutic conception of helping normal people toward greater "wellness," rather than just making disturbed people less so. Therapy to release and optimize each individual's human potential grew out of this motivational approach (an issue to be discussed in Chapter 15).

But some psychologists have resisted this theory of inherent goodness of individuals. They criticize this approach because (a) it lacks adequate experimental confirmation; (b) its concepts are vague, fuzzy, and not operationally defined; (c) the world is filled with too much violence, evil, and destructive behavior patterns for this goodness model to account for; and (d) environmental forces clearly exert strong influences on individual behavior, even overcoming the best intentions of "innately" good people (as we shall see in our later discussion in Chapter 17).

Cognitions, expectations, and attributions

Consider the *Wizard of Oz* as a psychological study of motivation. Dorothy and her three friends work hard to get to the Emerald City, overcoming barriers, persisting against all adversaries. They do so because they expect the Wizard to give them what they are missing. But the wise Wiz makes them aware that they, not he, always had the power to change their deficiencies to fulfilled wishes. For Dorothy, "home" can be a sense of security, of feeling comfortable with people she loves, wherever her heart is. The courage the Lion wants, the intelligence the Scarecrow longs for, and the emotions the Tin Man dreams of are each shown to be attributes they already possess if only they will think about them differently—not as things inside of them but as positive ways they are already relating to others. After all, did they not demonstrate those qualities on the journey to Oz—motivated itself by little more than an *expectation,* an idea about the future likelihood of getting something they wanted?

Cognitive approaches are currently being used by many psychologists to account for what motivates a variety of personal and social behaviors. They all share the Wizard's point of view, the concept that significant human motivation comes not from objective realities but from our interpretation of them. The reinforcing effect of a reward is lost if we don't believe it came because of our action. What we do now is often controlled by what we *think* caused our past successes and failures, what we *believe* is possible for us to do, and what we *anticipate* that the outcome of an action will be. Cognitive approaches to motivation put higher mental processes like these—rather than the arousal energy of drives, other biological mechanisms, or stimulus features—in charge of the acting self.

The importance of expectations in motivating behavior was developed in Julian Rotter's *social-learning theory* (1954) and extended in ways we shall see later in this chapter when we study achievement and work motivation. For Rotter, the probability that a person will engage in behavior X (studying for an exam instead of partying) is determined by his or her *expectation* of attaining a goal (getting a good grade) that follows that activity and the *personal value* of that goal to that person. This view about a future happening is based on the person's past reinforcement history which, in turn, has helped develop a locus of control orientation. A **locus of control orientation** is a belief about whether the outcomes of our actions are contingent on what *we* do (*internal control orientation*) or on events outside our personal control (*external control orientation*). One effect of a feeling of responsibility for outcomes (an internal control orientation) is shown in **Figure 8.4.**

A similar concept has been developed by Fritz Heider (1958) in terms of whether we attribute the outcome of our behavior (a poor grade, for example) to *dispositional* forces in us, such as lack of effort or insufficient intelligence, or to *situational* forces, such as an unfair test or a biased teacher. These attributions influence how we will behave; we are likely to try harder next time if we see our poor grade as due to our lack of effort, but may give up if we see it as resulting from injustice or lack of ability (Dweck, 1975). Attribution theory will be further discussed later in this chapter and in Chapter 16.

Now let's take a close look at a sampling of three very different motives that influence our lives—hunger, sex, and work and achievement motivation.

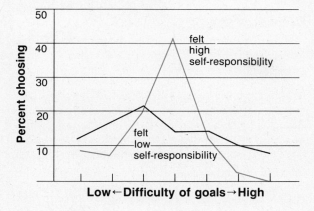

△ **Figure 8.4** *Goal Setting and Feelings of Responsibility*

Children 9 to 11 years old who felt responsible for both their successes and their failures set goals of intermediate difficulty. Those who did not feel that outcomes resulted from their own efforts showed no consistent pattern in goal setting: about as many set high goals as set low or intermediate ones. (Adapted from Meyer, 1968)

HUNGER AND EATING

The primary drives, such as hunger and thirst, represent nature's way of keeping its long-running show on the road even when there isn't time for everyone to learn how to play the part.

In Chapter 3 we saw that the body has many homeostatic mechanisms for maintaining internal conditions within the limits needed for the organism's well-being. Hunger motivation is one aspect of that general process. But in this case, mental and behavioral processes as well as physiological ones are required to maintain the balance. Automatic mechanisms cannot do the job because in order to survive, we need the energy stored in plants. This means that all our lives we must periodically seek out and consume plants and/or plant-eating animals. To maintain health, we need to take in regularly at least 22 different amino acids, a dozen vitamins, some minerals, and sufficient calories to meet our energy needs. The physiological and behavioral processes organized around hunger turn out to be enormously complex both for our species and across the range of differing species.

The search for feeding regulators

To regulate its food intake effectively, an organism must be able to (a) detect its internal food need; (b) initiate and organize eating behavior; (c) monitor the quantity and quality of the food eaten; and then (d) detect "enough" and stop eating. Researchers have tried to understand these processes by relating them either to peripheral mechanisms in different parts of the body, such as stomach contractions, or to central brain mechanisms, such as the functioning of the hypothalamus. But although hunger is probably the most studied drive, our understanding of it is still incomplete.

Hunger pangs as the basis for hunger. When you feel hungry where do those sensations come from? Does your stomach rumble and send out distress signals—pangs and cramps? A pioneering physiologist, Walter Cannon (1934), believed that these localized sensations of hunger from gastric activity were *the* basis for hunger. His basic view was that an empty stomach created disagreeable stimulation, "cramps," which triggered activity directed toward filling the stomach and turning off these disagreeable stimuli.

Cannon tested his hypothesis in an interesting experiment with a faithful student, A. L. Washburn.

The student trained himself to swallow an uninflated balloon attached to a rubber tube. The other end of the tube was attached to a recording device that would move with changes in air pressure. Cannon then inflated the balloon in Washburn's stomach; as his stomach contracted, air would be expelled from the balloon and deflect a recording pen (see photo).

When the student reported hunger pangs, the stomach was also severely contracted, the balloon deflated and a record made of this internal change. Cannon thought he had proved that stomach cramps were therefore responsible for feelings of hunger (Cannon & Washburn, 1912).

But Cannon had only established a *correlation, not a causal* connection. Although hunger pangs accompanied stomach contractions, maybe something else was causing both of these responses. (Remember our discussion in Chapter 1 of the dangers of misinterpreting correlations as causal relationships?)

Later research showed that stomach contractions are not even a necessary condition for hunger. Injections of sugar directly into the blood will stop the stomach contractions but not the hunger of an animal with an empty stomach. Human patients with their stomachs entirely removed still experience hunger pangs (Janowitz & Grossman, 1950), and rats with surgically removed stomachs still learn mazes when rewarded by food (Penick et al., 1963). So although those sensations originating in the stomach may play a role in our usual feelings of being hungry, they do not explain how the body detects its need for food.

Hypothalamic control of feeding: the dual hypothalamic theory of hunger. The hypothalamus is generally acknowledged to be the master control center for all homeostatic processes. Two parts of the hypothalamus were identified some years ago as possible control centers for feeding. Stimulation in the *lateral hypothalamus* excited feeding; stimulation in the *ventromedial hypothalamus* inhibited feeding. Not only did chemical or electrical stimulation to the "feeding center" excite feeding, but destruction of it caused the opposite effect: animals would not eat even if they had been deprived of food for a long time. Similarly with the "satiety center": stimulation of it caused animals to stop eating, whatever their need for food, while destruction of it led to gross overeating. These findings led to the **dual hypothalamic theory of hunger,** the theory that these two brain centers control the start and stopping of feeding (Stellar, 1954; Grossman, 1979).

Although this view was appealingly simple, it was challenged by the finding that nerve tracts passing through the hypothalamus from other brain centers are also playing a role. When these tracts are destroyed by damage to the hypothalamus, there are deficits in sensory and arousal functions related to eating behavior (Almli, 1978). A broader picture is clearly needed.

◁ *Shown here is the stomach-balloon apparatus like that used by Cannon and Washburn. Pressure on the balloon causes the stylus to move up and down on the revolving drum, producing a record of stomach activity.*

Lesions were made in this rat's ventromedial hypothalamus, following which the rat ate itself to the 1080 grams shown here—three or four times its normal weight.

A multiple-system approach

The current view is that the brain works in association with other systems, both biological and psychological, to gather information about the organism's energy requirements, nutritional state, acquired hungers, and food preferences, as well as social-cultural demands. It then sends signals out to neural, hormonal, organ, and muscle systems to initiate food seeking, eating, or inhibitory responses.

Table 8.1 summarizes the factors now believed to be involved in the complex regulation of hunger detection, feeding, and satiation. In general, the biological systems involved are responsive to the organism's energy needs and nutritional state. The psychological systems account for acquired food preferences and are responsive to social, emotional, and environmental stimuli that make both eating in general and specific foods in particular either desirable or aversive. Here we can only touch briefly on the features of each kind of factor.

Table 8.1   Factors in the Control of Feeding

Mechanisms Controlling Eating (integrated by lateral hypothalamus)	Mechanisms Controlling Not Eating (integrated by ventromedial hypothalamus)*
Factors of Biological Origin Nutritional deficiencies Low levels of blood glucose (sugar) High levels of fatty acids in the blood —both stimulate lateral hypothalamus Set point (level) of stored fats —when below critical set point, food seeking initiated *Factors of Psychological Origin* Specific hunger —learned preference for diets containing substances (salt, calcium, etc.) they lack Stress-induced eating Socially stimulated eating —family and cultural eating rituals, symbolically significant food *Factors of Mixed Origin* Sensory cues —sensory input to central nervous system elicits reflexes activating autonomic nervous system, preparing for digestion, metabolism, storage —palatability of food *maintains* eating by eliciting reflexes in brain that stimulate the lateral hypothalamus Anticipatory activities —eating that prevents depletion	*Factors of Biological Origin* Metabolic signals High levels of blood glucose Low levels of fatty acids Peripheral signals Full stomach, monitored by pressure detectors, stimulates ventromedial hypothalamus Taste cues from unpalatable foods induce rejection reflex Set point signals Level of stored body fat reaches critical set point of satiety, stimulating ventromedial hypothalamus *Factors of Psychological Origin* Fear Conditioned food aversions Conditioned satiety Cultural pressures toward slimness, dieting Mental disorders, such as anorexia *Includes short-term (stop eating) controls and long-term (suppression between meals) controls

To eat . . . Sugar and fat are the energy sources for metabolism. Evidently the two basic signals that initiate eating come from receptors that monitor the levels of sugar and fat in the blood.

According to the *glucostatic* theory of hunger (Mayer, 1955), when blood glucose is low or unavailable for metabolism, signals from liver cell receptors are sent to the lateral hypothalamus. The pancreas is then stimulated to release hormones that convert available glycogen in the liver into glucose, and the organism is motivated to seek and eat food. **Figure 8.5** shows the immediate effect of unavailability of glucose on increase in reported hunger in healthy adults (Thompson & Campbell, 1977).

In addition, during food deprivation, fat stored in body cells is released into the blood as a temporary energy source in the form of *free fatty acids.* According to the *lipostatic* theory of hunger, receptors that detect free fatty acid levels signal the lateral hypothalamus, which then stimulates the pituitary gland to release certain hormones and also stimulates the central nervous system to initiate eating responses (Kennedy, 1953).

With free access to food, adult animals and humans will maintain a stable body weight over their lifetime at a level consistent for the individual. An internal "scale" weighs the fat in your body and keeps the central nervous system informed. Whenever fats stored in specialized fat cells fall below a certain level, termed the *critical set point,* "eat signals" are sent out (Keesey & Powley, 1975). This internal set point exerts a major influence on how much you eat and how much you will weigh.

People programmed to be obese have more fat cells than those of normal weight, as a result of either genetic factors or overfeeding at critical periods in infancy. Beyond infancy, dieting or overeating changes the size of the fat cells but not their number. The number of fat cells a person has remains constant throughout life. This means that someone with a large number of fat cells who diets will lose weight and may become skinny but will still have the same critical set point and so will be a hungry, "latent fat" person (Nisbett, 1972).

Eating behaviors are also motivated by a variety of psychological influences. We all develop *specific hungers,* acquired through pairing of hunger with particular environmental stimuli. In addition, we develop specific hungers for essential substances such as calcium, salt, or vitamins if these substances are lacking in our diet. These hungers motivate selective eating. Animals avoid diets that have deficiencies, search for better ones, and develop a preference for a diet that has been associated with recovery from a deficiency-caused illness (Rozin & Kalat, 1971). Stressful stimulation also leads to overeating in both human and animal subjects (Antelman et al., 1976; Schachter et al., 1968).

My mother would respond to protests of "No more food, please! I'm not hungry!" with the rejoinder, "Anyone can eat when he's *hungry*—animals can do that. Eating my food when you're not hungry

◁ | **Figure 8.5** *Glucose Level and Felt Hunger*

Hunger ratings increase in well-fed males soon after an injection of the drug 2DG, which inhibits glucose in the blood. As food deprivation time gets longer, the control group (given saline injection) gradually begins to report more feelings of hunger, though not ever as high as the glucose-inhibited group. Eating lunch rapidly reduces hunger in both groups, though not as much in the glucose-inhibited group. Hormone release, metabolism, and several other processes are also affected by the glucose injections. (Adapted from Thompson & Campbell, 1977)

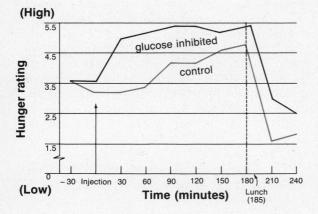

> *People who are obese have more fat cells than those of normal weight. This may be the result of genetic factors or of environmental ones such as overfeeding early in life. Dieting for such people may be difficult because the number of fat cells will remain the same even though they may shrink in size. When this happens, "eat signals" are sent out in order to bring the fat cells back up to their critical set point. Thus the obese person may be constantly hungry.*

shows that you love me!" Humans may eat (or fast) for the symbolic value of food as well as its nutritional value. Social and cultural factors determine when, how much, how fast, and what we eat.

Both biological and psychological factors influence our responses to the smell, taste, and appearance of foods. As we noted earlier, sensory input to the central nervous system elicits reflexes in the brain which activate the autonomic nervous system to secrete saliva, gastric juices, certain enzymes, and insulin—preparation for the digestion, metabolism, and storage of food (Powley, 1977). The body is thus ready to "put away" a meal properly after only one bite, one look, or one sniff. As signals of palatability, sensory cues have more influence on maintaining eating once begun than on initiating eating (Snowden, 1969).

Besides eating to *satisfy* hunger, we eat to *prevent* it. Observations of free-ranging animals in their native habitat suggest that they do what you probably do—eat *before* hunger sets in. Predators invest enormous energy in hunting for prey before hunger weakens them. Similarly, many species gather, store, and hoard food—"for later." Consider the motivations that go into the production, storage, and distribution of food in human societies. This eating *prevents depletion* instead of making up for a deficiency already present (Collier et al., 1972).

. . . or not to eat. Many of the mechanisms that stop eating are similar to those that start it but work through the ventromedial hypothalamus and rely on an opposite set of cues. We must also distinguish between *short-term inhibitors* (which terminate ongoing feeding) and *long-term inhibitors* (which suppress eating activities between meals).

High glucose levels and low free fatty acids in the blood are signals that the set point has been reached. But even before this nutritional information is processed by the brain, several peripheral cues are signaling "stop." Pressure detectors in the stomach signal distension while unpleasant taste cues can induce a *rejection reflex* (including vomiting).

Like eating, inhibition of eating is influenced by a host of emotional and learned psychological processes, some occurring during a meal, some between meals. Humans and animals do not eat when fearful. Animals do not eat much of a new food; they'll sample a bit, then wait for several hours before eating more—if no illness has developed. This protective "bait-shyness" reaction (see Chapter 7) keeps animals preferring "tried and true" diets and not trying new potentially harmful foods—unlike most of us.

Satiety, like hunger, can be conditioned if it is regularly paired with stimuli that usually occur at the end of the meal, such as someone's turning on the TV. And just as some cultural influences encourage eating as an important social ritual, others discourage it. Ultra-thin fashion models are portrayed as the ideal for women in our society, an ideal that becomes distorted in the self-destructive eating syndromes of young women who develop anorexia or bulimia. These disorders, which are being seen increasingly among college students, will be discussed in Chapter 14.

SEX AND SEXUALITY

While eating is essential to individual survival, sex is not. Some animals and humans remain celibate for a lifetime without apparent detriment to their daily functioning. However, survival of the species does depend on sex. The issue for evolutionary design was how to encourage animals to engage in the "altruistic" act of helping the species make it. This was not an easy problem, since the sexual act requires great energy consumption and subjects the individual to considerable stress. Nature's answer was to make sexual stimulation intensely pleasurable for the individual—a positive side effect of its more limited evolutionary purpose. A climactic orgasm serves as the ultimate reinforcer for all the time, effort, and work that go into the process of mating sperm with ova. So effective is this design that it has resulted in "altruism" above and beyond the call of nature.

There are a number of ways in which the sexual drive is unique:

- It is not essential to individual survival but only to species survival.
- Its arousal may be independent of deprivation.
- Arousal is as actively sought as reduction of tension.
- It will motivate an unusually wide variety of behaviors and psychological processes.
- It can be aroused by almost any conceivable stimulus—from genital touch to fleeting fantasy to conditioned fetish.
- Any stimulus associated with sexual arousal can become an acquired motivator, while any stimulus associated with sexual release can become a conditioned reinforcer.

Much of what is known about the physiology of sexual arousal and behavior comes from research on lower animals. In part, this is because of the long-standing taboo against a scientific study of sex in humans. (See the **Close-up** on p. 281.) Though Freud called attention to the importance of sexual motivation, research psychologists did not follow up on his ideas partly because sex did not fit well into the then-prevalent tension-reduction theory of motivation, according to which the motivated organism seeks to recover equilibrium—certainly not to increase tension! Fear and anxiety fit the model better

and so received more research attention (Brown, 1961). Here we will first consider some of what is known about the sex drive in animals and then turn our attention to human sexuality.

Sexual arousal

In species other than humans, sexual arousal is determined primarily by physiological processes. An animal becomes receptive to mating largely in response to the flow of hormones controlled by the pituitary gland and secreted from the *gonads,* the sex organs. In males these hormones are *androgens,* and they are continuously present in sufficient supply so that males are hormonally ready for mating at almost any time. But in the female of many species, the sex hormone, *estrogen,* is released according to regular time cycles of days or months (the estrus or "heat" cycle) or according to seasonal changes. Thus, the female is not always hormonally receptive to mating.

These hormones act on both the brain and genital tissue and often lead to a pattern of predictable, *stereotyped behavior* for all members of a species. If you've seen one pair of rats in their mating sequence, you've seen them all. The male rat chases the receptive female, she stops suddenly, raises her rear, and he enters her briefly, thrusts, and pulls out. She runs away, and the chase continues with ten to twenty of these brief intromissions before he ejaculates. Apes also couple only briefly, for about fifteen seconds, while for sables copulation lasts for as long as eight hours. Predators, such as lions, can afford to indulge in long, slow copulatory rituals. Their prey, such as antelope, copulate for only a few seconds, often on the run (Ford & Beach, 1951).

But even in animals, sexual arousal is not determined only by inner states and hormonal influences. Peripheral stimuli can sensitize or activate innate response patterns. In many species the sight and sound of ritualized display patterns by potential partners is a *necessary* condition for sexual response. Touch, taste, and smell can also serve as stimulants for sexual arousal. Some species, for example, secrete chemical signals, called **pheromones,** that attract suitors, sometimes from great distances. In many species, pheromones are emitted by the female when her fertility is optimal (and hormone level and

It's All Filth, Anyhow!

It's difficult for us, living in a time of open discussion and research on sexual matters to appreciate the extent of suppression of anything sexual that was common not so long ago. Several examples will illustrate what our ancestors had to put up with—from "knowledgeable experts."

William Alcott was a school teacher who, after becoming a physician, wrote extensively for the public about medical and moral topics. He condemned all forms of sexual "excess," especially "the destructive impulse" of masturbation. This "secret vice" leads to the following host of maladies, according to his observations and "evidence": (a) insanity (hospital records show that insanity from "solitary indulgence" is common); (b) idiocy; (c) epilepsy; (d) blindness (weakness of sight is one of the first symptoms); (e) paralysis ("not an uncommon punishment for this transgression"); and many more. All of this led the good doctor to wonder, quite reasonably—in his *The Young Man's Guide* of 1846—"is it not madness to expose ourselves to (these) attacks for the shortlived gratification of a moment?"

Over the decades, the list of horrible symptoms increased as each expert added some new ones he had "discovered." In warning parents of suspicious signs to look for in order to detect this secret vice, Dr. Harvey Kellogg, of Battle Creek, Michigan, listed over thirty *pages* worth in his popular little book. *Plain Facts About Sexual Life* (1877). Among them were defective development, sleeplessness, love of solitude, bashfulness, baldness, confusion of ideas, paralysis of lower extremities, pimples, big appetite, and nail biting—plus for girls, a "real wantonness" for the society of boys, and for boys, a "decided aversion to the society of girls."

Dr. Kellogg believed that a bland diet helped to suppress sexual desire. Have you ever eaten corn flakes? *Kellogg's* Corn Flakes? Made in Battle Creek, Michigan? Or maybe you've eaten the even blander "graham cracker," named for its originator, Dr. Sylvester Graham. He was a leading proponent of chastity to oppose sensuality which, he thought, forced noble human dignity to dissipate "energies in the low satisfaction of a brute!" (see Walters, 1974).

A final example of experts who viewed "sex as filth" has more serious implications for researchers. In 1899, Dr. Denslow Lewis presented a paper at the convention of the American Medical Association describing the physiology of sexual intercourse from a gynecological perspective. In it, he expressed the belief that the sexual act should be performed with satisfaction for both husband and wife and warned young husbands to acknowledge and respect their wives' rights. He even advocated early sex education.

Although it was customary to publish all presented papers, Dr. Lewis' paper was rejected. This subject, wrote a critic of the paper, "is attended with more or less filth and we besmirch ourselves by discussing it in public." Moreover, it was contended that the paper could not be sent in the mail because the AMA might be charged with sending obscene matter.

In the opinion of Dr. William Masters, one of the leading sex researchers of our time, the consequence of the suppression of this particularly accurate information was that it delayed investigation of the physiology and psychology of human sexual functions for many decades. Incidentally, Lewis' paper was eventually published by the AMA—in 1983.

---

sexual interest peak). These secretions are unconditioned stimuli for arousal and attraction in the male of the species. When captive male rhesus monkeys smell the odor of a sexually receptive female in an adjacent cage, they respond with a variety of sex-related physiological changes, including an increase in the size of their testes. In humans, though, reactions to sex-related odors are quite variable, determined more by *who* is giving off the smell than by any unlearned, irresistible, olfactory properties of the chemical communication. Indeed, we spend much time and effort washing away our natural scent and then splashing on animal or flowered perfume odors—to attract desirable others (see Hopson, 1979).

△ | *The male frigate bird displays itself sexually by inflating its chest.*

Human sexuality

In humans, sexuality is far more dependent on psychological factors and hence more variable than is the case with lower species. **Human sexuality** is described as including "the physical characteristics and capacities for specific sex behaviors, together with psychosexual learning, values, norms, and attitudes about these behaviors" (Chilman, 1979, p. 3). **Sexual arousal** in humans is the motivational state of excitement and tension brought about by physiological and cognitive reactions to erotic stimuli. *Erotic stimuli,* which may be physical or psychological, give rise to sexual excitement or feelings of passion. Sexual arousal induced by erotic stimuli is reduced by sexual activities that are satisfying, especially by achieving orgasm.

Scientific investigation of normal human sexual behavior was given the first important impetus by the work of Alfred Kinsey and his colleagues beginning in the 1940s (1948, 1953). They interviewed some 17,000 Americans about their sexual behavior and revealed—to a generally shocked American public—the extent to which certain behaviors, previously considered rare and even "abnormal," were actually quite widespread—or at least reported to be. But it was really William Masters and Virginia Johnson (1966, 1970, 1979) who broke down the traditional taboo. They legitimized the study of human sexuality by directly observing and recording under laboratory conditions the physiological patterns involved in ongoing human sexual performance.

The sexual response cycle. In order to study the human response to sexual stimulation directly, Masters and Johnson conducted controlled laboratory observations of thousands of males and females during tens of thousands of sexual response cycles of intercourse and masturbation. Their pioneering research on sexual arousal dispelled a number of myths and provided a useful model of the phases of human sexual response. Since their subjects were individuals and couples who volunteered for research on sexual stimulation, Masters and Johnson studied arousal and response only. They did *not* study the psychologically significant initial phase of sexual responding—that of *sexual desire,* the motivation to seek out or be available for sexual experience.

Masters and Johnson found that (a) men and women have similar sexual responses regardless of the source of arousal; (b) penis size is generally unrelated to any aspect of sexual performance; (c) although the sequence of phases of the sexual response cycle are similar in the two sexes, women are more variable, tending to respond more slowly but often remaining aroused longer; and (d) most women are able to have multiple orgasms, while men rarely do in a comparable time period.

Masters and Johnson found four phases in the human sexual response cycle: excitement, plateau, orgasm, and resolution (see **Figure 8.6**).

In the *excitement phase* (lasting from a few minutes to more than an hour) there are *vascular* (blood vessel) changes in the pelvic region. The penis becomes erect and the clitoris swells; blood and other fluids become congested in the testicles and vagina. Women may experience a "sex flush," a reddening of the body.

▽ | **Figure 8.6** *Phases of Human Sexual Response*

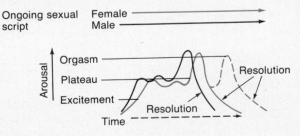

(Gagnon, 1977)

During the *plateau phase,* a maximum (though varying) level of arousal is reached. There is rapidly increased heartbeat, respiration, and blood pressure, increased glandular secretions, and both voluntary and involuntary muscle tension throughout the body. Vaginal lubrication increases and the breasts swell.

During the *orgasm phase,* both partners experience a very intense, very pleasurable sense of release from the sexual tension that has been building up. Orgasm is characterized by rhythmic contractions that occur approximately every eight-tenths of a second in the genital areas. Respiration and blood pressure reach very high levels in both men and women, and heart rate may double. In men, throbbing contractions lead to ejaculation, an "explosion" of semen. In women, orgasm may be achieved from effective stimulation of either the clitoris or the vaginal wall.

During the *resolution phase,* the body gradually returns to its normal preexcitement state, with both blood pressure and heartbeat slowing down. After one orgasm, most men enter a refractory period, lasting anywhere from a few minutes to several hours, during which no further orgasm is possible. Women, however, are capable of multiple orgasms in fairly rapid succession.

Touch, imagination and association. Although Masters and Johnson's research focused on the *physiology* of sexual responding, perhaps their most important discovery was the central significance of *psychological* processes in both arousal and satisfaction. They demonstrated conclusively that problems in sexual response often have psychological rather than physiological origins and can be changed through therapy. Of particular concern are the inability to complete the response cycle and achieve gratification, commonly called *impotence* in men and *frigidity* in women. Often the basis of the problem is a preoccupation with personal problems, fear of the consequences of sexual activity, or anxiety about the partner's evaluation of one's performance. However, poor nutrition, fatigue, stress, and excessive use of alcohol or drugs can also diminish sexual drive and performance.

Hormonal activity, so important in regulating sexual behavior among lower female mammals, has no known effect on sexual receptiveness or gratification in women. In males, the sex hormone testosterone (one of the androgens) is necessary for sexual arousal and performance. Testosterone levels become high enough only after puberty. Sexual stimulation and orgasm raise the level of this hormone but so do hostile or anxious mood states. Perhaps this similar reaction contributes to the association of sex with aggression reported by many men.

The sequence of sexual activities that may culminate in orgasm can be started by only one unconditioned stimulus but an endless variety of conditioned stimuli. The unconditioned stimulus is touch—stimulation of the genital areas. Touch in the form of genital caresses is a universal aspect of sexual foreplay in cultures throughout the world (Ford & Beach, 1951). But virtually any stimuli that become associated with genital touch and orgasm can become acquired motivators. This is true whether the stimuli are in the external environment or in one's memory or fantasy. Even the picture of a shoe can come to lead to sexual arousal in this way (Rachman, 1966). A nonsexual object that becomes capable of producing sexual arousal through conditioning is called a **fetish.** A fetish may become a psychological problem when it is *necessary* for arousal and/or objectionable to other people.

It has been suggested that sensations and fantasy during masturbation provide the primal setting for associating virtually any stimulus with pleasurable arousal (Storms, 1980, 1981). Inanimate objects, textures, sounds, visual images, odors—any tangible or imagined stimulus event—can come to elicit arousal through conditioned association. In this way, some people learn to become aroused *only* by those conditioned stimuli, such as the sight of high-heel shoes, young children, or even painful stimuli. Some of us learn culturally acceptable sexual orientations in this way, while others learn sexual deviations (to be discussed in Chapter 14).

In humans, sexuality can be less concerned with meeting physiological need than with satisfying cognitive desire. For most humans the goal of sexual activity is "the attainment of a cognitive state: the conscious perception of sexual satisfaction. This state depends on a combination of experiences originating in the experiencer's body and in that of the sexual partner" (Davidson, 1980, p. 227). Interpretations of experiences, the meaning of specific sexual events, sexual beliefs and values, and imagination and expectation all play a part in human sexual behavior and satisfaction (see Byrne, 1981). Even the subjective experience of orgasm, which has been compared by some to a profound altered state of consciousness (Davidson, 1980), usually depends not only on phys-

"Now, tell me. What's it like being a sex symbol?"

ical stimulation but also on interpersonal factors, such as being in a close, trusting relationship.

To promote a positive development of our own sexuality, we need to remember that sex is more than just a set of learned techniques, a performance of bodies in space, a giving or receiving of pleasurable physiological sensations. We need, as a very first step, to accept our own body and the responsibility for someone else's. We must want to give and be open to receive. We need to be willing to learn over time how best to give our gift and accept the gift of another.

It is not enough to know what to do physically. For many, the most satisfactory sex takes place within a loving, caring relationship between two people. If we want sex to reach its potential as a fulfilling human experience, we need to develop attitudes of trust and sharing. Sex strips us literally and figuratively of our protective garments. It lays bare our vulnerability. That is why sex can at the same time be so frightening if misused with power and hostility and so glorious if filled with assurances of mutual satisfaction, respect for the needs of one's partner, and love of his or her unique qualities.

Sexual scripts. Generalized sexual arousal can be channeled into different specific behaviors, depending on how the individual has learned to respond and think about sexual matters. **Sexual scripts** are socially learned programs of sexual responsiveness that include prescriptions, usually unspoken, of what to do, when, where, how, with whom or with what, and why (Gagnon, 1977). Different aspects of these scripts are assembled through social interaction over one's lifetime. The attitudes and values embodied in one's sexual script define one's general orientation to sexuality. Scripts of other types will be discussed in Chapter 10.

Scripts combine social norms, individual expectations, and preferred sequences of behavior from past learning. Your sexual scripts include not only scenarios of what you think is appropriate on your part but also your expectations for a sexual partner. Differing scripts can create problems of adjustment between partners when they are not discussed or synchronized (see **Figure 8.7**.)

For example, there is evidence that touch has different meanings for men and women.

Researchers questioned 40 male and 40 female undergraduates about the meaning they attach to touch, when applied to different parts of the anatomy by a friend. Quite different meanings were found between the sexes. For females, the more a touch was associated with sexual desire, the less it was considered to imply warmth, pleasantness, or friendliness. When a close male friend touches a woman in an area of her body that communicates sexual desire to her, then that is its only meaning to her. But for males, the same touch is interpreted as having a cluster of meanings: pleasantness, warmth, love, and sexual desire. Misunderstandings can arise when one person's "friendly touch" is perceived by the other as a "sexual advance" (Nguyen et al., 1975).

For most sexual actors within a given culture, socioeconomic class, gender, and educational level, sexual scripts include similar "stage directions." However, there are unique features in each individual's personal script, learned through his or her own history of sexual experience and thought. Because erotic stimuli can be intensely pleasurable while also often strongly prohibited by society and religion, we learn many different ways of responding to the variety of erotic stimuli we experience in this society. Here's where we really see the power of conditioned associations. Because any stimulus that has been associated with sexual arousal can become a potent elicitor of arousal later, there are enormous variations in the forms our human sexuality takes.

Even the apparent biologically based differences between men and women in the physiological pattern of sexual response, as catalogued by Masters and Johnson, may be influenced by social learning. Females are socialized not to acknowledge their sexuality, to act as passive sexual partners, to appear

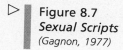

▷ **Figure 8.7**
Sexual Scripts
(Gagnon, 1977)

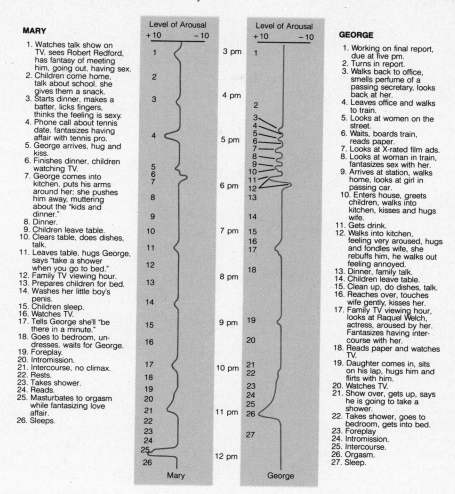

MARY

1. Watches talk show on TV. sees Robert Redford, has fantasy of meeting him, going out, having sex.
2. Children come home, talk about school. she gives them a snack.
3. Starts dinner, makes a batter. licks fingers, thinks the feeling is sexy.
4. Phone call about tennis date, fantasizes having affair with tennis pro.
5. George arrives, hug and kiss.
6. Finishes dinner, children watching TV.
7. George comes into kitchen, puts his arms around her: she pushes him away, muttering about the "kids and dinner."
8. Dinner.
9. Children leave table.
10. Clears table, does dishes, talk.
11. Leaves table, hugs George, says "take a shower when you go to bed."
12. Family TV viewing hour.
13. Prepares children for bed.
14. Washes her little boy's penis.
15. Children sleep.
16. Watches TV.
17. Tells George she'll "be there in a minute."
18. Goes to bedroom, undresses, waits for George.
19. Foreplay.
20. Intromission.
21. Intercourse, no climax.
22. Rests.
23. Takes shower.
24. Reads.
25. Masturbates to orgasm while fantasizing love affair.
26. Sleeps.

GEORGE

1. Working on final report, due at five pm.
2. Turns in report.
3. Walks back to office, smells perfume of a passing secretary, looks back at her.
4. Leaves office and walks to train.
5. Looks at women on the street.
6. Waits, boards train, reads paper.
7. Looks at X-rated film ads.
8. Looks at woman in train, fantasizes sex with her.
9. Arrives at station, walks home, looks at girl in passing car.
10. Enters house, greets children, walks into kitchen, kisses and hugs wife.
11. Gets drink.
12. Walks into kitchen, feeling very aroused, hugs and fondles wife, she rebuffs him, he walks out feeling annoyed.
13. Dinner, family talk.
14. Children leave table.
15. Clean up, do dishes, talk.
16. Reaches over, touches wife gently, kisses her.
17. Family TV viewing hour, looks at Raquel Welch, actress, aroused by her. Fantasizes having intercourse with her.
18. Reads paper and watches TV.
19. Daughter comes in, sits on his lap, hugs him and flirts with him.
20. Watches TV.
21. Show over, gets up, says he is going to take a shower.
22. Takes shower, goes to bedroom, gets into bed.
23. Foreplay.
24. Intromission.
25. Intercourse.
26. Orgasm.
27. Sleep.

alluring, yet sexually innocent, and to be responsible if "anything goes wrong." Little wonder, then, that they tend to be aroused more slowly than men. Males, by contrast, are socialized to think of sexual intercourse as validation of their masculine identity, as a performance to be evaluated, and as the prelude to orgasm. As such socialization practices change, differences between male and female sexual responsiveness diminish (P. Schwartz & Strom, 1978).

Social-class differences probably exert a more significant influence on sexual behavior than do gender differences within the same social class. Less educated women expect less from their mates in terms of frequency of intercourse and variety of sexual practices (Bell, 1974). But if their husbands begin to demand more "exotic" sexual practices they are more likely to feel guilty about "giving in" and to feel that their status as "good girls" is being endangered. Blue-collar couples seem to have more problems involving sexuality than do more affluent, better educated couples, although many couples in both groups report problems with sexual adjustment (Rubin, 1976).

Regardless of whether sex is a source of problems or pleasures, it remains an inescapable source of motivation in many aspects of our daily life. Plots of novels, plays, films, and soap operas revolve around sexual themes. Prostitution, pornography, the sale of birth-control products, and sexual advertising are major industries in many countries. It is understandable, then, that a study of introductory psychology students discovered that about 20 percent of the time that they were supposedly listening to the instructor, they were having sexual thoughts unrelated to the teacher's topic (Cameron et al., 1968). OK, now it's time to get back to work if you want to get ahead.

ACHIEVEMENT AND WORK

While many people work to live, some live to work. Their job becomes the primary source of their sense of self worth, their social network of friends, and their focus for scheduling time. It is also a source of pride, loyalty, and feelings of being part of a meaningful, stable enterprise. Losing one's job, as we saw in the case of Charlie T., can mean losing one's sense of self-worth and place in the social order. In this section we will look at research on achievement motivation and some theories and findings about employee motivation.

Achievement motivation

Not all societies value achievement to the extent that Americans do. There does not seem to be any universal motive to achieve. Yet for many people, the need to achieve clearly energizes and directs behavior. It also influences their perceptions of many situations and their interpretations of their own and others' behavior. For the past thirty years David McClelland and other psychologists have been investigating the conditions under which people develop a motive to achieve, and its impact on behavior. (The term *achievement* is used to mean both a need and a motive.)

The need for achievement. As early as 1938, Henry Murray had postulated a "need to achieve" which varied in strength in different people and influenced their tendency to approach success and evaluate their own performance. McClelland and his colleagues (1953) devised a way to measure the strength of this need and then looked for relationships between strength of achievement motivation in different societies, conditions that had fostered it, and its results in the work world.

To measure the strength of the need for achievement, he used his subjects' fantasies. Subjects were shown pictures and asked to make up stories about them—saying what was happening in the picture and what the probable outcome would be. Presumably, what they projected into the scene reflected their own values, interests, and motives. As McClelland put it, "If you want to find out what's on a person's mind, don't ask him, because he can't always tell you accurately. Study his fantasies and dreams. If you do this over a period of time, you will discover the themes to which his mind returns again and again. And these themes can be used to explain his actions . . ." (1971, p. 5). Clinical use of such projective pictures with people experiencing emotional problems will be described in Chapter 12.

From subjects' responses to a series of pictures like these, McClelland worked out measures of several human needs—needs for power, for affiliation, and for achievement. The *need for achievement* was designated as *n Ach*. For example, one picture used was of a boy holding a violin. **Figure 8.8** gives hy-

"I'll run through it again. First the exhilaration of a new work completed, followed by the excitement of approaching pub date. Reviews pouring in from everywhere while the bidding for the paperback rights soars to insane figures. An appearance on Merv Griffin or Dick Cavett, sandwiched in between like Engelbert Humperdinck and Juliet Prowse. Finally, a flood of letters from people to whom your name, yesterday unknown, now has the shimmer of national renown. Hit those keys!"
Drawing by Booth; © 1972, The New Yorker Magazine, Inc.

▷ **Figure 8.8**

Story Showing High *n Ach*	Story Showing Low *n Ach*
The boy has just finished his violin lesson. He's happy at the progress he is making and is beginning to believe that all his sacrifices will be worth it. To become a concert violinist he will have to forego playing with his buddies, cut out a lot of dates and partying, and practice everyday, 'no matter what.' Although he knows he could make more money by going into his father's business, the image of being a great violinist, of giving people joy with his music, counts more. He renews his personal commitment to do all it takes to make it —to give it his "best shot." "	The boy is holding his brother's violin wishing he could play it, but knowing that it isn't worth all the time and energy and money for lessons. He feels sorry for his brother who has to give up all the fun things in life to practice, practice, practice. It would be great to wake up one day and presto you're a top-notch musician, but it doesn't happen that way. The reality is boring practice, a no-fun youth, and a big possibility of not being anything more than just another guy who can play some musical instrument in a small-town band.

pothetical stories that subjects with high need for achievement and low need for achievement might have told. A great many studies in both laboratory and real-life settings have validated the usefulness of this measure. For example, persistence in working on an impossible task was greater for those with high *n Ach* when the task was announced as difficult rather than easy. Low *n Ach* subjects gave up sooner when they were led to believe the task was difficult but they persisted for the supposedly easy (actually impossible) task. In other research, high-scoring *n Ach* people were found to be more upwardly mobile than those with low scores; and sons who had high *n Ach* scores were more likely to advance above their father's occupational status than sons with low *n Ach* measures (see McClelland et al., 1976).

McClelland found that men with high levels of need for achievement tend to come from families that stress—and model—the importance of achievement striving. Young people who develop a high need to achieve tend to be relatively independent and more concerned with task success than with other people's feelings. It is the "sweet smell of success" that provides their major incentives in life, rather than the "familiar feel of friendship." In Chapter 2, we saw that this achievement orientation tends to be fostered for boys in our society in many subtle ways, while girls are encouraged to develop affiliative and emotionally expressive needs.

Even the economic growth of a society can be related to its encouragement of achievement motivation (often at the expense of social-emotional-community concerns). McClelland (1961, 1955) found that, in general, Protestant countries (in which achievement and independence tend to be twin virtues) were more economically advanced than Catholic countries. He found that men in these "achieving societies" were more often trained to be self-supporting earlier in life, thus to value autonomy as a success-seeking style.

Cultures socialize children to accept their preferred patterns of living through folk tales, school books, and formal education, among other "training devices." As mentioned in Chapter 1, an archival study found that the amount of achievement imagery in children's books read in one era was significantly correlated with several measures of economic achievement in the society a few decades later. Among the measures used were the number of patents issued and the amount of electric power produced (De Charms & Moeller, 1962).

A culture characterized as being highly achievement oriented is one that encourages assertiveness, ambition, and a willingness to take risks, and puts greater focus on the future than on the past or present. This complex of values is especially typical of English-speaking countries. There is some question whether this achievement orientation should be considered as a *universal* model for economic success for other societies or seen simply as a characteristic of English-speaking countries. Even the word "achievement" is not easy to translate into many languages other than English (see Hofstede, 1980; Barrett & Franke, 1971).

Trying to succeed versus trying not to fail. The need for achievement leads to performance motivation but not necessarily to a motive for success.

Some people work to achieve success, others to avoid failure—with very different results.

People who focus on attaining success tend to set more realistic goals and to choose tasks of intermediate difficulty. Those who are most concerned about avoiding failure tend to set more unrealistic goals (too low or too high in relation to their ability) and to choose tasks of low difficulty, where failure is least likely. But then if they succeed, their achievement is least satisfying (anyone could have done it under those circumstances). A fear of failure may also motivate a person to avoid achievement situations where failure looks possible or likely (see the **Close-up,** on p.289).

The theory of achievement motivation has been extended and refined over years of research and testing. The tendency to engage in achievement-oriented behaviors is now seen not as the simple result of a need for achievement but as a joint function of three major variables: (a) need for achievement *(n Ach);* (b) perceived probability of success; and (c) the incentive value to the individual of achieving success or avoiding failure (Atkinson & Raynor, 1974).

Interpretations regarding outcomes. People's motivation for achievement is further complicated by their attributions (interpretations) regarding why things turn out the way they do. Earlier (p. 275) the importance of a *locus of control orientation* was mentioned—our interpretation of whether the outcomes of our actions are the result of what *we* do (internal control orientation) or the result of *factors in the environment* (external control orientation). Another basic interpretation that we tend to make concerns *stability*—whether the situation is consistent or not. Four possible interpretations about the causes of outcomes follow from the combinations of these two dimensions, as shown in **Figure 8.9.**

For example, students may believe that a grade they get is primarily the result of internal factors, such as ability (a stable personality characteristic) or

effort (a changing personality characteristic). Or they may see it as caused primarily by external factors, such as the difficulty of the task (a stable situational problem) or luck (an unstable external feature).

Interpretations regarding the causes for a success or a failure also determine what emotion one feels about it.

Students were given short stories of successes and failures with a cause described for each one, and then were asked to report how strongly the character in the story would have experienced each of a list of emotional reactions. As expected, success was associated with "happy" and "satisfied" and failure with "upset" and "uncheerful." But other emotions were specific to the person's beliefs about why the success or failure occurred, as shown in **Table 8.2** (Weiner et al., 1978).

A person's explanation for success or failure also determines the amount of effort likely to be put in next time. For example, suppose Joan attributed her successes to skill and effort and her failures to bad luck, unfair tests, or external sources of discrimination. How would you expect her willingness to take risks to differ from that of Don who attributed his successes to luck, easy tests, and the hard work of teachers or coaches, and his failures to his personal qualities? Joan has "nothing to lose" by always taking a chance, while Don has "little to gain" by ever taking risks or even putting out effort.

Beliefs about *why* we have succeeded or failed, then, are important because they lead to (a) different interpretations of our past performance and general worth; (b) different emotions, goals, and effort in the present situation; and (c) different motivation in

▷ **Figure 8.9** *Attributions Regarding Causes*

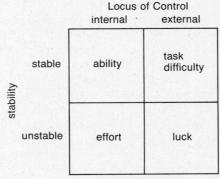

(Based on Weiner, 1980)

Who Has a Fear of Success?

It is reasonable for people to want to succeed and to want not to fail. But have you ever failed something "on purpose," when you knew you could have passed the test? Many men did so on military induction tests, trying to show by their failure that they were unfit to be drafted for military service during wartime. But there may be less obvious or even nonconscious ways that people avoid successes they could attain. Among the "mind-games" people go through to avoid success are thinking you don't really deserve it, haven't worked as hard as others to merit it, will be viewed negatively by others who will be envious or will make you feel "different." When these tactics become a person's general strategy for dealing with many life situations, we describe the person as being motivated by a *fear of success.*

Research interest in fear of success began with a doctoral dissertation by Matina Horner in 1969. Horner wondered about several facts. For women, *n Ach* scores did *not* predict performance. Not only have women failed to equal men's achievements in the modern occupational structure, but some women seem to back away from success when it appears within reach. Horner speculated that some women may have a *motive to avoid success* (MAS).

The initial research support for this concept came when she asked male and female college students to write stories in response to verbal cues. One of these cues for females was: "At the end of first-term finals, Anne finds herself at the top of her medical class." For males it was "John" who was at the top of his class. The stories were then scored for various themes. If they showed success leading to social rejection, fears, guilt, or denial, the stories were scored as revealing "fear of success."

The male stories tended to be filled with traditional Horatio Alger achievement themes, while nearly two-thirds of the women's stories expressed an "anxious awareness" that achievement reflecting intellectual competence or leadership potential was a desirable goal but incompatible with the also desirable goal of femininity (Horner, 1972).

This demonstration of dramatic gender differences stirred both academic researchers and the public (through popular media presentations). Literally hundreds of studies followed, attempting to mine the rich possibilities of this find (see Tresemer, 1977).

One series of studies compared women who did and did not have this hypothesized fear of success. Those who feared success were characterized as self-critical, low in self-esteem, externally controlled, ambivalent about professional and interpersonal goals, career-oriented (but aspiring to traditional female occupations). Those who did not fear success either had no conflict over stereotyped views of career vs. family or did not have goals that would conflict with the female stereotype (Patty, 1976).

Subsequent investigations have revealed that fear of success is *not* a women's motive that prevents them from performing adequately. Rather it reflects a concern about the negative consequences likely to accompany a woman's success in male-dominated occupations. When both men and women completed the Anne-stories, they were about equally likely to give fear of success themes, whereas neither sex showed as many such fears when they completed stories about John. This means that subjects in Horner's study were not necessarily *projecting* a fear of success that *they* felt but probably were just describing the reactions they expected for a character who was deviating from a traditional gender role pattern in our culture (Cherry & Deaux, 1975; Frieze et al., 1979).

But fear of success does exist and can be identified in elementary-school boys and girls. And men and women share not only this maladaptive motivation, but comparable thoughts, feelings, and behaviors. According to recent findings, "success-fearers" do perform poorly immediately after they have been successful, sabotaging their subsequent performance on similar tasks (but not dissimilar ones). Further, parents who are evaluative, critical, and controlling are most likely to have success-fearing children (Canavan-Gumpert et al., 1978). Attempts are being made to integrate fear-of-failure and fear-of-success orientations into a general (unisex) theory of achievement motivation (Jackaway & Teevan, 1976).

Table 8.2 *Emotional Reactions with Different Interpretations for Success and Failure*

Success attributed to:	*Led to:*
Ability	Confidence (competence)
Unstable effort	Activation, augmentation
Stable effort	Relaxation
Own personality	Self-enhancement
Other's effort, personality	Gratitude
Luck	Surprise
Failure attributed to:	*Led to:*
Ability	Incompetence
Effort (stable or unstable)	Guilt (shame)
Personality; intrinsic motivation	Resignation
Other's efforts, motivation, personality	Aggression
Luck	Surprise

(Adapted from Weiner, 1980)

the future—in turn, making future successes more likely or less so. When we attribute a failure to our low ability and a difficult task, we are likely to give up sooner, select simpler tasks, and lower our goals. But if we attribute our failure to bad luck or lack of effort, then we are likely to have higher motivation to try again for success (Fontaine, 1974; Rosenbaum, 1972; Valle & Frieze, 1976).

Changing students' explanations of their past failures can improve their level of performance. When school children were trained to attribute past failure to lack of effort rather than to lack of skill, they increased their effort on subsequent tasks—and had more success (Dweck, 1975).

When people acquire an internal control orientation that leads them to set goals and develop generally successful means of attaining them, they develop a sense of personal **self-efficacy.** This is a feeling that they have control over what happens to them. Perceived self-efficacy, in turn, influences the individual's thought patterns, performance, and emotional arousal: with higher perceived self-efficacy, performance is better and emotional arousal less. One's perception of self-efficacy also influences one's choice of coping patterns in response to stress as well as one's level of physiological arousal. By contrast, a feeling of *self-inefficacy* can lead to apathy, despondency, a sense of futility and a feeling that one is a victim of external forces (Bandura, 1977, 1982b).

Intrinsic and extrinsic motivation. Intrinsic motivation is motivation to engage in an activity for its own sake. Things that we do because we simply enjoy doing them—like playing video games, singing in the shower, or keeping a secret diary—are intrinsically motivated (see the **Close-up** on p. 291). But work, too, can be intrinsically motivated when the individual is deeply interested in the job to be done. It is intrinsic motivation that keeps one working late into the night just for the sake of solving a problem or doing the best possible job—even if no one but you knows it.

Extrinsic motivation is motivation to engage in an activity for some outside consequence rather than for its own sake. Gold stars, grades, and penalties for failure or misbehavior are testament to the belief that school children are extrinsically motivated and must be given external consequences if they are to learn. In extrinsic motivation, behavior is instrumental to obtaining something else, while in intrinsic motivation, behavior is carried out without a purpose beyond the immediate rewards of "doing it," consuming it for its pleasure. Taking vitamins is extrinsically motivated, eating cream puffs is intrinsically motivated.

What do you suppose would happen if extrinsic rewards were added for behavior that children were engaging in out of intrinsic motivation? A classroom study gave a clear answer.

Preschoolers were first observed during free play periods in their classrooms, where they could choose among many available activities without any im-

Close-up

Why are Video Games So Addicting?

Chris is a student whom teachers describe as "unmotivated." He is easily distracted while listening to lectures, has difficulty concentrating on reading assignments, and fails to show "focused discipline" when working on term papers. He is also not good at most sports because he seems to lack the necessary coordination.

But put Chris in front of a video game and he is as instantly transformed as Dr. Jekyll was when a strange drug turned him into Mr. Hyde. He becomes the prototype of the motivated organism—active, engaged; persistent, and totally absorbed in the task activity.

"World War III could be going on outside and it wouldn't matter at all to me once I am on a run and the adrenaline is flowing and I'm feeling this incredible 'rush'," said Chris during an interview. This youngster is not a weirdo, but just one of millions of the new electronic generation who have become addicted to video games.

There are many reasons for the appeal and psychological addiction of video games, the most important of which is that they are intrinsically motivating instructional environments. Students of these games learn how to play by trial and error at their own pace without verbal instruction by teachers or other adults. There are no external constraints to engage in the task nor tangible external rewards. Players work hard at learning how to be more efficient because the task is designed to be *fun*. The intrinsic reward is a perceived sense of control over what happens and of increasing competence that comes from discovering one has personal, skill-based control of desired outcomes (high scores).

△ *Playing video games is an intrinsically motivating activity.*

Four general features found to foster intrinsic motivation in this setting—as well as in educational settings—are challenge, control, curiosity, and fantasy. *Challenge* depends on tasks with clear performance criteria and an appropriate level of escalating difficulty. *Control* is provided by a responsive environment in which one's own actions determine the immediately displayed results and choices available, together with an opportunity to explore freely. *Curiosity* is aroused by novelty, complexity, surprise, and incongruity and abetted by constantly changing visual and auditory displays. *Fantasy* involves appeal to emotional needs of learners and encouragement of identification with imagined characters or contexts. In group settings, competition, cooperation, and social recognition can also enhance intrinsic motivation (Malone & Lepper, in press).

posed constraints. The amount of time they spent on drawing activities was recorded. Next, in a different setting within the school, children were asked to engage in a drawing activity. They were randomly assigned to one of three conditions. (1) *Expected reward*—children were shown tangible rewards they would receive for engaging in the activity of drawing. (2) *Unexpected reward control*—children were asked to draw but with no mention of any reward. However, after they drew their pictures, they got the same reward as those in the first group. They were

a control group to show that it is not just getting the reward, but the perceived contingency between activity and reward, that is crucial. (3) *No reward control*—children neither expected nor received a reward for engaging in the activity.

Two weeks later unobtrusive observations were made in these children's classrooms of the amount of free time spent in drawing activity—when they were "on their own." The results were strong and direct.

Those in the expected reward condition were spending *less* time on the target activity than were those in either of the other groups. In addition, they were less interested in the task than they had been during the initial observation period. Those in the other two conditions continued to show a high level of interest in the drawing task (Lepper et al., 1973). *Moral: a reward one day can take the former joy out of play.*

Evidently, extrinsic rewards in this case were superfluous. More important, they were actually detrimental. With a reward, the task itself is not enjoyed as much, and when the extrinsic rewards are withdrawn, it is less likely that the activity will be engaged in again (Lepper & Green, 1978; Lepper, 1981).

This *hidden* cost of rewards seems to be greatest where the rewards are (a) made obvious and given for activities with high intrinsic interest; and (b) provided for open-ended activities like problem solving and creative tasks, in which the performance plan is not well defined in advance. On the other hand, rewards may improve performance and not destroy intrinsic motivation when they are perceived as (a) conveying information about one's competence and progress and not as a means of control, and (b) given for well-learned activities that are part of a routine (Deci, 1975).

Albert Bandura (1981b) has found in extensive research that for those high in perceived self-efficacy, rewards seen as affirmation of competence and fulfillment of internal standards can increase one's interest in a task. He holds, however, that the major source of motivation comes not from external incentives but from self-incentives provided by the individual's own anticipatory thoughts about the likely costs and benefits of alternative actions. He points out that people also give themselves rewards through their thought processes (''Yeah, that's a good analysis'').

Work motivation

When a strike of public-transportation workers in New York City threatened to paralyze that great work center of millions of people, most of the workers, undaunted by the inconvenience, managed to get to their jobs. Even starting from miles away, they walked, jogged, biked, roller skated, and used any form of locomotion they could devise. But why?

The motivation to work energized their behavior, directed it, and led them to invent new solutions. This is one of the most potent and complex human motives, and there have been many attempts to explain it. Some answers have come from employers and some from *organizational psychologists* who study work motivation and the psychology of the workplace.

Theories of work motivation. Several familiar theories of work motivation are based on different views of human nature. Three that have influenced employers' treatment of their workers are (a) that workers are lazy and motivated only by money; (b) that workers are motivated primarily by social and emotional needs, with monetary incentives being less important; and (c) that people work to actualize their potentials and gain the pride of accomplishment. An illustration of the last type of motivation is given in the account of a developer of Apple Computer's MacIntosh Personal Computer:

◁ *People walking to work across the Brooklyn Bridge in New York during a transportation strike in 1980. People not only walked, but biked, roller skated, and chartered boats. Their motivation to work was so strong that they invented new solutions to overcome a major obstacle.*

"Steve said, well, if you get these done before midnight, we'll take you for pizza," and we stayed there . . . not because we wanted the pizza, but because we wanted to see that board working. And I think that none of our Mac PC boards ever had to have a wire run to fix something, which is pretty amazing. That's the attention to detail that you just can't get people to do for money. We do it for love . . . this is the most important thing in our lives . . . to make that great computer" (Lemmons, 1984).

One researcher, analyzing many different business organizations, found their policies based on one of two conflicting views, which he has summarized as Theory X and Theory Y. Theory X organizations believe that people dislike work and work only as hard as they have to to get security; they must be motivated by threats, coercion, or other external inducements. Theory Y organizations believe that people are basically creative and responsible and intrinsically motivated to do good work to the extent that the work is challenging (McGregor, 1960). A somewhat similar theory is Theory V, which asserts that the level of a worker's motivation depends on the extent to which effort on the job contributes to the attainment of his or her personal values, whatever they are. Ambitious people are those who have more personal values that work can serve (Locke, 1982).

According to still another theory, Theory Z, worker motivation, morale, and loyalty are highest when worker values and organization goals are meshed. Company policies that may do this include guaranteed lifetime employment, informal systems of social control, decision by group participation and consensus, emphasis on individual responsibility, and job rotation permitting workers to become generalists (Ouchi, 1981). Such policies have traditionally been characteristic of Japanese companies and are now being incorporated into some of the most successful American businesses in their "search for excellence" (Peters & Waterman, 1983).

The importance of setting goals. Considerable laboratory and field research supports the view that an intention to work toward an explicit goal is the primary motivating force in work behavior and task effort (Latham & Yukl, 1975; Steers & Porter, 1974). Specific, challenging goals lead to higher performance than either easy goals, no goals, or the vague goal of "do your best." Goals influence behavior by directing and focusing attention, mobilizing effort, increasing persistence, and encouraging the individual to work out appropriate strategies.

For an organizational goal to be an effective motivator in the workplace, however, the following conditions must be met: (a) it must be specific and challenging to the individual; (b) the worker must have adequate ability to achieve it; (c) feedback must be available about progress toward the goal; (d) tangible rewards must accompany goal (and subgoal) attainment; (e) the management must be supportive of worker needs and problems; and, perhaps most important, (f) the worker must accept the goal as a personal intention (Locke et al., 1981). Even in an organization where management sets group goals, a worker can still set his or her own personal goals and standards. "Happy workaholics" are found in this category of workers (Machlowitz, 1980). They are workers whose hard work becomes a vital extension of their personal identity.

Motivation and the future

Most theories of motivation focus on current stimuli and conditions that arouse and direct behavioral responses in the *present*. But they do not explain why you might persist in working hard even in a boring course, or tolerate unpleasant interactions for a good letter of recommendation. A major contribution of the research on motivation for achievement and work is its highlighting of the importance of a *future orientation* for the understanding of all human motivation. Many of the things we all do are for their *future* significance, not their present hedonic value (De Charms & Muir, 1978).

A future orientation toward achievement can intensify one's present tendency to put forth effort, but it does much more than that. A future orientation provides a *path* in which the stream of human action flows. It transforms a job into a career, an actor's lines into a plot. Human action is not a static sequence of specific behavioral acts bound by eliciting stimuli. Rather, it is a continuing series of episodes perceived by the actor as extending into the future. We want to know that to get to Oz we must "follow the yellow brick road," not just that we should "turn left at the scarecrow, then right. . . ." To understand human motivation, we need to understand what causes changes in the direction of the entire stream of action, not just what causes specific behaviors (Atkinson & Birch, 1970).

When Charles T.'s job was terminated, his future was suddenly deleted as well. With no picture of a future, helpless resignation and eventually stress-related death took over. It is apparent that human motivational theories need to take account of the temporal perspective of individuals and societies if they are to capture some of the subtle richness of human dynamics (see Gorman & Wessman, 1977). What may appear to be a lack of motivation or lack of cognitive planning ability may be better explained in terms of differences in people's time orientation. Someone who tends to focus more on the present or the past is likely to have difficulty conceiving future-oriented situations that require delay of gratification and planning, such as going to college. On the other hand, people who are excessively future oriented may not be as able to enjoy intrinsically motivated activities, such as sensory pleasures or intimate social relationships, or perhaps even to experience deep emotional feelings (Gonzalez & Zimbardo, 1985).

EMOTION

Keith's "superhuman" motivation (as expressed in his hunger, sexuality, and aggression) was created by the tumor, which triggered an excessive discharge of hormones into his body. But it also functioned to make Keith "subhuman" because it took away the feeling side of his motivation. He lost the ability to experience the human emotions of joy and sadness, pride and fear, love and grief. Since his constant level of high arousal did not change in response to changes in external events and activities, he had no way to correlate his internal feelings with the various happenings in his life. His experience highlights the extent to which we normally depend on our emotions to measure the impact that life events are having upon us.

Emotion and *motivation* have the same Latin origin referring to movement or activity. While the *motivated person* usually moves physically toward some goal or away from some aversive situation, the *emotional person* is "moved internally" by psychologically significant situations. This "moving experience" of emotion involves not only physiological reactions, but "stirred-up feelings" as well.

Aristotle was the first to distinguish between the *physiological* component of emotion, which he referred to as its "matter," and the *psychological* component, its "form or idea." Seventeenth- and eighteenth-century philosophers generally thought that the emotions were instinctive and nonrational, meant to be curbed by reason and intellect. Many common expressions still reflect this view: "I got so mad that I couldn't think straight"; or "In the heat of passion, I didn't realize what I was doing." Some psychologists have described emotion as an inner disturbance or disorientation resulting from suddenly being overwhelmed by an especially significant personal experience (Young, 1961).

Despite differences in definition and emphasis, there is a general consensus among contemporary psychologists that an **emotion** is a complex pattern of changes including physiological arousal, feelings, cognitive processes, and behavioral reactions made in response to a situation perceived by the individual to be personally significant in some way (Kleinginna & Kleinginna, 1981). The physiological arousal includes neural, visceral, and muscular changes; the feelings include both a general affective state (good-bad, positive-negative) and a specific feeling tone, such as joy or disgust. The cognitive processes may include interpretations, memories, and expectations; the behavioral reactions are both expressive (crying, smiling) and instrumental (screaming for help). Psychologists with different theoretical orientations tend to focus on one or another of these aspects.

But where do emotions originate? Are we born with them or are they learned?

Are emotions innate or learned?

Charles Darwin (1872) believed that emotional expressions are innate—the evolutionary remnants of previous adaptive behaviors. For example, he regarded our facial expression of anger as derived from the snarling behavior of an animal preparing for attack.

Robert Plutchik (1980) is a more recent proponent of emotions as innate. He has proposed that there are eight basic inborn emotions, made up of four pairs of opposites: joy and sadness, fear and anger, surprise and anticipation, and acceptance and disgust, as shown in **Figure 8.10**. All other emotions are assumed to be variations or derivatives of these eight. For example, love is a combination of joy and acceptance, awe of fear and surprise. Plutchik associates each primary emotion with an adaptive response. For instance, disgust is considered an evolutionary outgrowth of rejecting distasteful foods from the mouth, while joy is associated with reproductive activities.

Evidence that emotions are innate is provided by the fact that all infants show similar emotional expressions at birth or soon after. In addition, at least six emotional expressions—happiness, sadness, anger, fear, surprise, and disgust—are universally recognized across cultures. These emotions were even recognized in Caucasian faces by tribesmen from the

▽ ▌ Figure 8.10   *Dimensions of Emotion*

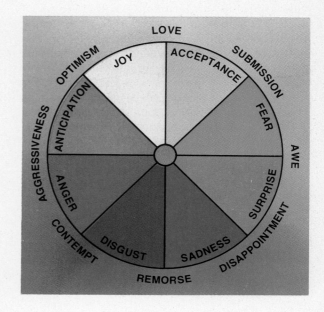

From "A Language for the Emotions" by Robert Plutchik reprinted by permission from Psychology Today, February 1980. Copyright © 1980 American Psychological Association.

New Guinea interior, who had rarely, if ever, seen Caucasians prior to the arrival of the psychologists who administered the tests (Ekman et al., 1969).

Some theorists, however, have pointed out that although some emotional *expressions* seem to be universal, there are cultural differences in the situations that *elicit* certain emotions and in **display rules,** the norms governing the public expression or display of emotions. These display rules define the social appropriateness of emotional expression and help regulate the who, when, where, what kind, how strong, and how long of emotional displays and may be quite subtle (Ekman, 1972; Averill, 1976).

▷ ▌ *Darwin believed that the human expression of anger is innate, derived from the snarling behavior of an animal preparing for an attack.*

For example, how long is it "acceptable" to grieve publicly for the loss of one's pet, one's close friend, one's parent? Is that time different from the appropriate duration of expressed delight over a straight-A set of end-term grades?

Recent analyses have taken the position that both innate and learned factors are involved in emotion. As with the ability to think and to use language, the child's emotional development seems to follow a genetically set timetable—*if* appropriate stimulation is available. Some of the developments in emotional response may be linked to specific anatomical changes in the brain (Konner, 1977). For example, smiling emerges in infants of all cultures when the necessary nerve pathways acquire their myelin sheaths, one or two months after birth. Similarly, the fairly universal occurrence in infants of fear of separation from their parents coincides with the development of neural tracts within the limbic system around the eighth month of life.

According to Izard (1982), the infant at birth is capable only of feeling a generalized positive state, a generalized negative state, and the emotions of interest and sadness. A few months later, joy and anger develop. By the time the infant is nine months old, shame and fear appear—emotions requiring a degree of self-awareness that the younger child is believed not to have. Emotional responses may continue to change throughout life, reflecting changes in both physiological and cognitive processes (Mandler, 1984). Many complex emotions involve the ability to empathize with someone else's feelings, an ability that young children must learn from social experience. And as memory and expectation develop, emotions can be triggered by thoughts as well as by a wider range of sensory stimuli.

What starts an emotion?

With physiological processes, feelings, cognitions, and behavioral reactions all parts of an emotion, what is the chain of events in an emotional response? What happens first, to get it all started? Here is where the liveliest disagreements have occurred in the psychological study of emotion.

Innate stimulus elicitors. Those who believed emotions were innate, like Darwin and later theorists, thought there must be "adequate stimuli" that would elicit each type of emotional reaction. But re-

search did not bear them out. If each of the emotions is initiated by its own stimuli, then it should be possible, when we see a person expressing an emotion, to identify the emotion and infer what kind of stimulus aroused it. The problem is that similar-appearing emotions occur in widely varying situations and observers cannot identify the emotion being experienced unless they know what situation the subject is facing (see Woodworth and Schlossberg, 1954).

In addition, an early study found that facial reactions in response to 17 emotional stimuli were impulsive and variable from one subject to the next, with no uniform relationships between stimuli and facial expressions. Only when the subjects were asked later to assume expressions appropriate to the different stimuli, as they recalled them, were their facial expressions "appropriate" to the stimuli, probably indicating an awareness of the appropriate display rules (Landis, 1924).

A stuck zipper, a rush-hour traffic jam, a conflict over an important decision, being ignored by a friend, and winning a lottery can all provoke emotional reactions in us. But the only thing they have in common is that they have a particular *meaning* for each of us—which has been learned. The concept of innate stimulus elicitors offers no explanation for most of the emotions we experience.

▽ *Can you tell from this man's facial expression what emotion he is probably experiencing?*

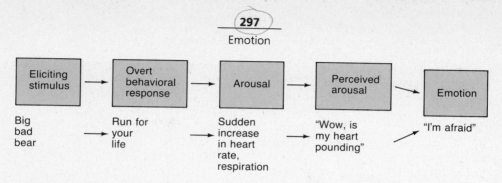

△ ▎ Figure 8.11   *Emotion Generation According to the James-Lange Theory*

Behavioral reactions. William James, in line with a Darwinian emphasis on survival mechanisms, saw emotions as instinctive responses to recurring survival situations—responses such as crying at a loss, striking out at an obstacle, or trembling at a threat. These instinctive reactions would be accompanied by visceral arousal. Different instinctive responses would then send different sensory and kinesthetic (motor) feedback to the brain—which, in turn would flood the person's consciousness and create the feeling of a specific emotion. As James put it, ". . . we feel sorry because we cry, angry because we strike, afraid because we tremble" (James, 1884). This was contrary to the commonsense view that we cry because we're sad or tremble because we're fearful. But it was taken seriously by psychologists and became known as the James-Lange theory of emotion (Carl Lange was a Danish scientist who presented similar ideas the same year as James). An outline of the proposed sequence of emotion generation in this theory is shown in **Figure 8.11.**

Subsequent research showed that animals continued to respond emotionally even if the afferent tracts of nerve fibers bringing in sensory impulses were surgically cut off (Cannon, 1929). Moreover, the same visceral reactions were found to occur in very different situations; palpitations of the heart accompany aerobic exercise, love making, or running away from danger—but clearly do not lead to the same emotions. Also, though rage and grief have different physiological components, many emotions cannot be distinguished physiologically.

A modern version of the theory of emotion as produced by behavioral responses is called the *facial feedback hypothesis:* smile and you will feel happy;

frown and you will feel upset (Izard, 1971; Tompkins, 1962). A recent study did find several different emotions *associated* with particular patterns of facial muscle movement (G. Schwartz et al., 1980), but the idea that facial expressions *cause* felt emotions has been questioned (Tourangeau and Ellsworth, 1979).

The best support for the role of facial feedback in creating emotions comes from a recent demonstration by Paul Ekman and his colleagues (1983, 1984).

After first analyzing facial expressions that were universal across many cultures, the researchers asked professional actors to move sets of facial muscles in ways that are characteristic of given emotions. (They were not asked to assume emotional expressions but just to move muscles.) At the same time, the actors' physiological reactions were monitored.

A distinct pattern of physiological changes accompanied some of the facial expressions. For those associated with anger, fear, and sadness, heart rate increased, while for those associated with happiness, surprise, and disgust, it decreased. In addition, skin temperature went up for anger (a "hot" emotion) and down for fear and sadness ("cold" emotions). In some cases, the actors also felt emotional states, but some merely felt "as if" emotions. The researchers hypothesize that the connections between facial-muscle emotional expressions, the motor cortex, and the hypothalamus are "hardwired," while interpretation of emotional experience depends on learning.

Central processes in emotion. Since there is little support for the role of critical innate stimuli or behavioral reactions in starting emotional experience, what about central processes within the organism? In Chapter 3 we spoke of the "new dualism" based on the recognition that both physiological and cognitive processes are valid objects of study—not as separate entities but as different levels of analysis of

△ *These are views of an actor carrying out commands to move sets of facial muscles. This sequence of muscle movements is associated with fear. Five physiological reactions were recorded while the actor was performing this task: heart rate, left-hand temperatures, right-hand temperatures, skin resistance, and muscle tension.*

functioning. In analyzing emotional reactions, we find both important. *Physiological systems* provide the machinery of response to internal and external stimuli by sending signals that activate or inhibit responding. *Cognitive systems* give meaning to our perceptions of stimulus situations as well as interpretations, labels, and evaluations to our reactions. Together, these central processes give emotions their substance, force, and distinctive quality.

Physiological reactions begin with the arousal of the brain as a whole by the *reticular activating system,* through which incoming sensory messages pass on their way to the brain (Lindsley, 1951; Zanchetti, 1967). As we saw in Chapter 3, this system functions as a nonspecific, general alarm system for the rest of the brain.

The influence of hormones on emotion has been shown in several kinds of studies. Hormone levels in the blood and urine rise during emotional states, whereas changes in emotional responding occur when hormones are administered and in diseases affecting the endocrine glands. Much research has also shown that perception of emotional stimuli is accompanied by release of hormones such as epinephrine and norepinephrine.

The *autonomic nervous system* also prepares the body for emotional responding by action of both its divisions; the balance between them depends on the quality and intensity of the arousing stimulation. With mild, unpleasant stimulation, the sympathetic division is more active; with mild, pleasant stimulation, the parasympathetic division is more active. But with more intense stimulation of either kind, both divisions are increasingly involved.

Integration of both the hormonal and the neural aspects of arousal is controlled by the *hypothalamus* and the *limbic system,* old-brain control systems for emotions and for patterns of attack, defense, and flight (see Chapter 3). Either lesioning or stimulation in various parts of the limbic system produces dramatic changes in emotional responding. Tame ani-

▽ *This man just missed a shot while playing ping pong. Now that you know the situation, do you have any different judgment about the emotion being expressed?*

mals may become killers; usual prey and predators may become peaceful companions.

In all complex emotions, the *neocortex* is involved through its internal neural networks and its connections with other parts of the body. The neocortex provides the associations, memories, and meanings that integrate psychological experience and biological response.

Situations with different meanings for the individual seem to induce different chemical responses. For example, human tears flow in sadness, happiness, anger, and sympathy, as well as in response to an irritating stimulus, but tears expressing sadness contain a greater concentration of protein than is found in tears shed in response to raw onions (Frey et al., 1981). For a comparison of sex differences in crying, see **Figure 8.12**.

Meaning implies a cognitive process of interpretation of the stimulus situation. Sensory experiences are thought to lead to emotion only when the stimuli are appraised by the individual as having personal significance. According to the cognitive view, cognitions precede and create emotional experiences, rather than being consequences of them. The constantly changing relationship between person and environment becomes a source of emotion when "central life agendas," such as survival, values, and goals, are engaged—but only as stimuli are recognized as being related to these values and goals. In the words of a leading proponent of this view, Richard Lazarus, ". . . emotional experience cannot be understood solely in terms of what happens in the person or in the brain, but grows out of ongoing transactions with the environment that are evaluated" (1984, p. 124).

Because of cognitive appraisal, what is "exciting" for me may be "boring" for you, or your "fun" may be my "fear." Cognitive activity also establishes *belief* in certain *causal* connections. I perceive my heart as racing *because* that attractive person is coming toward me. The cognitive processes in emotional responding may be conscious and deliberate, as in the search for a reason why your mood has suddenly changed. Or they may be rapid and nonconscious, as when you take a sudden dislike to someone you've just met "for no good reason."

The two-component theory of emotion. According to Stanley Schachter (1964), the experience of emotion is the joint effect of these two central processes—physiological arousal and cognitive appraisal, with both parts necessary for an emotion to occur. This has become known as the *two-component theory* of emotion.

In an ingeniously designed experiment, physiological arousal was manipulated for experimental subjects by disguised injections of epinephrine (arousing); control subjects received a placebo (nonarousing). The experimental subjects' cognitions about the cause of their arousal were manipulated by accurate information or misinformation about the connection between the arousal they felt and the earlier injection. The subjects then were given different social cues. Some spent time with another student (a confederate of the experimenter) who behaved emotionally in a euphoric manner. Others spent time with a confederate who behaved in an angry manner.

The researchers reported that subjects who did not have an appropriate explanation for their arousal felt happy if they had been with the euphoric confederate, angry if they had seen him act in an angry manner. Presumably, perception of the confederate's mood provided a relevant cognition for labeling their own unexplained arousal. This pattern of reported

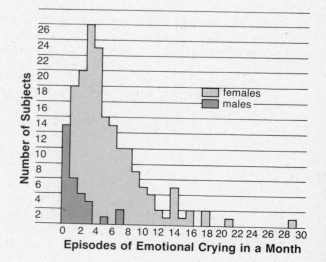

▽ **Figure 8.12** *Episodes of Emotional Crying*

In the first formal investigation of adult crying behavior, 45 male and 286 female subjects judged to be psychiatrically normal kept records of their emotional crying behavior during a month. Duration of episodes for both groups was about 6 minutes, and the most frequent stimuli for crying for both involved interpersonal relations and media presentations. A high proportion of both groups said they felt better after crying. (Frey et al., 1983)

emotions was not found for control groups, who either were not aroused or already had an appropriate explanation for their arousal (Schachter & Singer, 1962).

The experimenters' explanation was that the emotions reported by the experimental subjects were the result of physiological arousal that was affectively neutral plus cognitive appraisal. They reasoned that in most cases we can attribute our arousal to some obvious stimulus situation, as when we laugh at a good joke. However, when we experience arousal without a known source, as in this case, we will use cues from the immediate environment to interpret and label our arousal according to whatever emotion is appropriate to the social setting.

This research was important in drawing attention to the role of cognitive interpretations in emotional experience and in showing that independent components of emotion could be manipulated and studied in a laboratory setting. Better designed research has since challenged the two-component theory, however (see Maslach, 1979, and Reisenzein, 1983). It is not now believed that emotions necessarily follow from labeling unexplained arousal or even that physical arousal is a necessary condition for all emotional experience.

On the other hand, there has been evidence to support the notion that emotions can be readily misattributed to arousal states that are actually unrelated to that emotion.

In one study, male subjects who had just finished jogging were more attracted to a female (a confederate of the experimenter) than subjects who were not physically aroused. Similarly, subjects who had listened to an emotionally arousing tape recording were more attracted to the female confederate than those who heard an unarousing tape. The attraction occurred whether the tape involved positive arousal (a comedy routine) or negative arousal (a grisly description of a mob killing) (White et al., 1981). Apparently, physiological arousal caused by an exciting event or even just by physical exercise can be interpreted as sexual attraction or love depending on the social cues present at the time.

The finding that even negative arousal can be interpreted as feelings of love may explain some puzzling paradoxes of passion ("I love him and I hate him too"). It may also explain why parental interference may actually strengthen a couple's romantic feelings. Barriers force them to exert more effort to continue the relationship, and they interpret this effort as a sign of their love.

In recent years, cognitive appraisal of one's perceived arousal has been studied extensively both in laboratory situations and in usual life situations (see Leventhal et al., 1980, and Mandler, 1975). **Figure 8.13** shows two possible sequences of emotion generation, depending on whether there are recognized emotional eliciting stimuli in the environment or not.

Which is "primary"—thought or feeling?

The cognitive revolution is credited with replacing behaviorism's *actor* with a *thinker,* but one whose head is filled with "cold cognitions." According to the cognitive view, liking or disliking comes only after we have analyzed the situation cognitively. Feelings and preferences follow cognitions and inferences.

An alternate view is that feelings and preferences are not necessarily derived from thoughts but may be immediate reactions to stimuli, independent of cognitive analysis. We like this person and distrust that one, find her beautiful and him pretentious, enjoy chocolate and hate liver, are attracted to smiling faces and repulsed by frowns. These "gut reactions" give our experiences an immediate feeling tone that is part of their overall meaning and can be independent of our reasoning about them.

But don't you have to discriminate, recognize, and interpret what a stimulus is before you can feel anything about it? Not according to research by Robert Zajonc (pronounced "zy-onse").

In an extensive series of experiments, subjects were presented with a variety of stimuli, such as foreign words, Japanese characters, sets of numbers, and strange faces. The stimuli were exposed on a tachistoscope, which flashes them at exposure times below those necessary to recognize what the stimulus was. Subjects were still able to express a preference toward them without knowing why. Evidently, preference thresholds were lower than recognition thresholds. (See Chapter 4.)

Mere repeated exposure to given stimuli increased their attractiveness: those stimuli which were repeated most often produced the strongest liking. Yet this increased liking, too, was shown to occur independently of recognition (Zajonc, 1980).

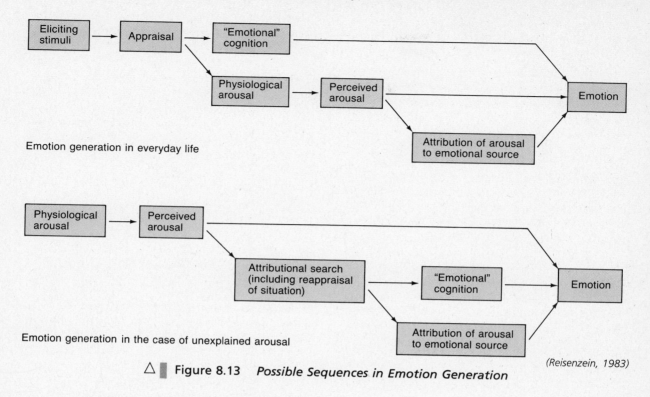

Emotion generation in everyday life

Emotion generation in the case of unexplained arousal

△ ▮ **Figure 8.13** *Possible Sequences in Emotion Generation*

(Reisenzein, 1983)

This line of research, though challenged by some investigators (Lazarus, 1984), forces us to consider the extent to which our reactions, including some emotions, are influenced by nonconscious and perhaps noncognitive factors (Zajonc, 1984).

One of the first psychologists to emphasize the pervasive role of immediate, unlearned affective reactions was Sylvan Tompkins (1962, 1981). He points out that infants respond with fear to loud sounds or difficulties in breathing with no need for cognitive appraisal or prior learning. They seem "prewired" to respond to certain stimuli, with an emotional response general enough to fit a wide range of circumstances. As adults, humans are excited by sex—and also by solving difficult problems. Tompkins, in fact, sees emotions as the primary motivating forces for human actions: they amplify our innate needs and acquired motives by providing a sense of urgency. It is emotions that endow any activity with a sense of importance and transform indifference to desire. In this view, without emotion, nothing matters; with emotion, anything can matter.

SUMMARY

▮ Motivation is a general term for the process of initiating, directing, and sustaining physical or psychological activities. It includes mechanisms involved in preferences, vigor of responses, and persistence of organized patterns of action toward relevant goals.

▮ Motivation is an intervening variable. It can be induced by physiological and/or psychological variables and may lead to physiological responses as well as conscious and nonconscious psychological ones.

▮ The strength of motivation is measured using index variables such as activity level, rate and amount of learning, resistance of a response to extinction, preferences, and consummatory behavior. Motivation has been manipulated in research by deprivation and by stimulation.

▮ According to instinct theory, motivation is mechanistic and inborn. Instinct theory as an explanation for human behavior was popular for a time but provided circular explanations and was replaced by behaviorism's emphasis on learning and environmental determinants of behavior. Contemporary psychologists view instincts as fixed action patterns, triggered by specific releaser stimuli without prior learning.

■ Drive theory related motivation to learning. According to drive theory, the tension of primary or secondary drives leads to action, including new responses. Successful responses, reinforced by tension reduction, are learned and retained. Learning is seen as requiring motivation, and motivation (tension reduction) as explaining learning.

■ Contrary to the assumptions of drive theory, organisms choose many activities that increase tension rather than reduce it, apparently preferring some optimal level of arousal rather than none at all.

■ Humanistic approaches to motivation postulate a hierarchy of innate human needs. Only as lower biological needs are met will the individual be motivated by higher psychological ones. In deficiency motivation, people seek to restore equilibrium; in growth motivation, they seek to go beyond present accomplishments to greater fulfillment of their potential—to become self-actualized.

■ Cognitive theorists are demonstrating the importance of our interpretations on motivation. What we believe about ourselves and the situation and expect the outcome of our action to be is as important as the external stimulus-based reality in determining the direction and strength of our motivation.

■ According to the dual hypothalamic theory of hunger, starting and stopping eating are both controlled by centers in the hypothalamus. Athough understanding is still incomplete, it is now recognized that many physical and psychological processes, both innate and learned, play a role in both eating and its inhibition. Food intake and body weight are regulated according to a ''set point,'' measured by the fat stored in specialized fat cells.

■ Sexual activity in lower animals is controlled hormonally and follows stereotyped, genetically determined patterns consistent for each species but widely variable among species.

■ In humans, sexual arousal, sexual behavior, and sexual satisfaction are quite variable and subject to learning. Though only touch is an unconditioned stimulus for sexual arousal, anything associated with sexual arousal through experience can become a conditioned stimulus for arousal. Most human sexual problems are the result of psychological rather than physiological factors.

■ We learn ''sexual scripts'' that guide our sexual behavior and our expectations of others. Discrepancies in partners' sexual scripts can lead to misunderstanding and frustration.

■ Achievement motivation is learned; it is central for many Americans but sometimes is more a motive not to fail than a motive to succeed. The need for achievement has been studied through people's fantasies in response to ambiguous pictures.

■ People's beliefs about whether they are responsible for outcomes and whether that condition is a stable one influence their interpretations of their successes or failures, their emotional reactions, and their subsequent motivation. With a perception of self-efficacy, performance and coping patterns are more effective.

■ Rewards given for activities we enjoy may lessen our intrinsic interest and motivation for that activity when the extrinsic rewards are no longer available.

■ Work motivation has been variously attributed to workers' desires for material rewards and security, avoidance of punishment or loss, social and emotional satisfactions, personal growth, identification with the purposes of the organization, and intrinsic interest in the task. Setting specific goals, accepted by workers, in a supportive organization, leads to higher performance than no goals or vague goals.

■ A future orientation provides a path in which the stream of action flows. To understand human motivation, we need to understand the direction of the entire stream of action rather than only specific actions.

■ An emotion is a complex pattern of changes including physiological arousal, feelings, cognitive processes, and behavioral reactions made in response to a situation perceived as personally significant.

■ Both innate and learned factors are involved in emotion. Research on children's emotional development and the universality of emotional expression across different cultures suggests an innate basis. But socially based display rules vary widely and most of the situations that arouse emotion in us do so through learning.

■ Theories of emotion have included: (a) the James-Lange theory, that behavioral reactions precede the other aspects of emotional response; (b) the two-component theory, that emotion results when unexplained physiological arousal is given meaning because of cues in the current social situation; (c) the theory that cognitive appraisal of a situation comes first, determining whether we will feel emotion and if so, which one; (d) the theory that affective preferences and feelings may precede cognitive appraisal or even recognition of a stimulus.

Part Four

Cognitive Processes

Chapter Nine
Remembering and Forgetting

Chapter Ten
Thinking and Communicating

9

REMEMBERING AND FORGETTING

■ WHAT IS MEMORY?
An information-processing view
Encoding, storage, and retrieval
Three memory systems

■ SENSORY MEMORY
Encoding for sensory memory
Storage: how much and how long?
Processing for transfer to short-term memory

■ SHORT-TERM MEMORY
Encoding in short-term memory
Storage in short-term memory
Processing in short-term memory
Retrieval from short-term memory

■ LONG-TERM MEMORY
Encoding for long-term memory
Storage in long-term memory
Retrieval from long-term memory
Two memories versus multiple levels

■ REMEMBERING AS A CONSTRUCTIVE PROCESS
Schemas
Eyewitness testimony

■ WHY DO WE FORGET?
Explanations of forgetting
The physical bases of forgetting—and remembering

■ SUMMARY

Nick A. is like most of us who tie a string around a finger, tack up a reminder on the door, or set our digital watch alarm when we need to remember something important. So it was not surprising to see Nick clutching the note he had scribbled earlier in case he forgot the question he wanted to ask his doctor. However, its message was rather surprising: "Ask Dr. S. if my memory is getting better." Nick suffers from a rare form of amnesia that makes him forget many events right after they happen.

Nick's partial amnesia is the result of a freak accident that occurred in 1960, when he was 22. A friend playfully thrust a miniature fencing foil toward him; it entered his nostril and severed a small area on the left side of his brain. Brain scans revealed no further damage.

Although Nick has good recall for events before 1960, he has been unable to establish new memories readily for events since that time. Because of this, he is not only isolated from much of his past (that from 1960 on) but also alienated from many events in the present. He cannot remember his dreams, or even if he has had any. Although he is friendly and polite and others seem to enjoy his company, he has no close friends. Typically, he recognizes someone he has met but cannot recall the person's name. He has stopped making dates because he forgets the appointed day, time, and place.

The simple, routine activities that we all take for granted pose serious, often insurmountable problems for Nick. After he reads a few paragraphs, he finds that the first sentences begin to slip from memory. Unless he looks away during television commercials and actively thinks about what he was just watching, he cannot remember the plot of the show. A phone call is enough to distract him from any ongoing activity, after which he usually starts something new. Cooking is a major challenge: "If I have two things on the stove, I can't remember how long each one is supposed to cook, or how long they've been on." Nick reports that, as a consequence, he ends up eating "a lot of cereal."

Nick's memory disorder raises many provocative questions about how memories are formed and experiences forgotten. Because Nick's case is a unique "natural experiment," psychologists and psychiatrists have been studying his behavior and his brain for some time. Their efforts are twofold: to help Nick overcome his problem and to discover more about the phenomena of human memory (Kaushall et al., 1981; Squire & Moore, 1979; Squire & Slater, 1978).

Since the accident, Nick has taken numerous psychological and medical tests in an effort to determine the extent of his injury. He scores "above average" in intelligence and "normal" on perceptual ability, language, and motor functions. However, he performs very poorly on memory tests in which he must associate words that are presented together repeatedly. His memory impairment is most severe for verbal material.

One thing Nick remembers quite well is that he has a memory problem. Yet he maintains a positive outlook and reveals a healthy, normal personality. His ability to function reasonably well and to remain optimistic despite his severe memory loss may be due to his having learned memory strategies that help him connect his past with the present. The primary way that Nick maintains a sense of his own past is by collecting things—mementos of trips, places, hobbies. These concrete, physical objects give him cues: having them in front of him, he can then "read" them in somewhat the way the rest of us "read" our stored memories.

Curiously, Nick's inability to recall recent events does not extend to remembering how to do things. For instance, he can remember how to mix, stir, and bake the ingredients in a recipe—but forgets what those ingredients are supposed to be. So he still has the capacity to store *procedural knowledge* (to remember *how*). But he has lost the ability to store facts about his environment—*declarative knowledge* (to remember *what*). Using his capacity to acquire new information when it is related to procedures or motor skills, he has worked out routines and stock stories to give the appearance of "remembering."

Nick's case is a fascinating one. Through it we recognize the powerful influence that an "ordinary" process like remembering has on our lives. Anything that interferes with the way our memory normally works not only changes how we think and behave, but also may alter our emotions and even change our personalities. Try to imagine what it would be like if suddenly you had no memory for your past, no memory of people you have known or things that have happened to you. Without such "anchors," what would happen to your sense of who you are?

The failure of memory for a prolonged period is called *amnesia*. Research on amnesiacs like Nick is but one way psychologists are trying to understand the complex mechanisms of memory. More often researchers study how people with normal, intact memories go about storing the enormous amount of information that they acquire, how they get it out of their memory when they need it, and also how they sometimes cannot find what they have stored away.

When someone cannot remember a past event, there is always a question as to whether the memory is truly lost or is simply not accessible. In this chapter you will find out that you have several different memory systems. You will learn how information gets into them and how later—hopefully—you retrieve it when you want it.

WHAT IS MEMORY?

Memory is the mental capacity to store and later recall or recognize events that were previously experienced. Where studies of conditioning focus on stimulus input and response output, studies of memory focus on what happens in between as the information is processed, stored, and later searched for. The associations formed between stimulus events and responses are themselves units of memory. An organism without a capacity for memory would not be able to profit from experience or training, to use associations for predicting what *will be* on the basis of what *was*.

The term *memory* also refers to what is retained—the total body of remembered experience as well as a specific experience that is recalled. The term *remembering* is used to mean either retaining experiences or bringing them back into awareness.

It quickly becomes apparent that memory is not like a photo album or documentary film, because memories are rarely exact copies of earlier experiences. What you remember is influenced by many factors, some operating at the time of the original event, others operating during storage, and still others operating at the time of recall. Even vivid memories may be distortions of what "really" happened in the past. They can be constructions or collages that blend past reality with expectation, fantasy, and social desirability. Memories can be affected by physical health, attention, emotion, prejudice, and many other conditions, as we shall see.

SYLVIA /Nicole Hollander

The collection of all your memories is the library of your personal history. Your memories form a living record of what you have heard, read, and experienced over the period of your life so far. But memories are much more. As you saw in Nick's case, where recent ones were missing, memories help you define yourself, connect your present thoughts and actions to the roots of your past, and prepare for a meaningful future.

An information-processing view

In earlier times, many psychologists were content to analyze behavior solely in terms of its relationship to stimulus inputs. It mattered little what activities were occurring in that "black box" of mind into which stimuli went and out of which responses came. Today psychologists studying remembering and other mental processes view the mind as an information-processing system and have adopted the computer as a useful metaphor. They find it helpful to talk about mental processes in the precise language of computer programming and functioning because it enables them to analyze the complex process of remembering into simpler subprocesses or *stages*. In this analysis, units of information are stored in our brains as memories in much the same way that bits of information are stored in the computer's "data bank."

Psychologists recognize that the human mind operates in more complex and subtle ways than any current computer, however. Digital computers process one thing at a time using transistors that respond to only two signals, 1 (on) and 0 (off), whereas brains use graded and changing signals and process many different kinds of information at the same time. And computers do not spontaneously modify or add to the information they are given to store. The trillions of variable-strength synapses in the brain permit processing far more complex than that provided by any computer so far (Sinclair, 1983). On the other hand, the brain's memory units are not as stable and unchanging as those of computer memory. The very act of recalling information changes it in some way. But borrowing from computer science has been enormously useful in helping researchers to formulate hypotheses about remembering and forgetting that can be tested experimentally.

Encoding, storage, and retrieval

Being able to recall an experience at some later time requires the operation of three mental processes: encoding, storage, and retrieval. **Encoding** is the translation of incoming stimulus energy into a unique neural code that your brain can process. **Storage** is the retention of encoded material over time. **Retrieval** is the recovery of the stored information at a later time. In other words, encoding and storage can be viewed as the processes that "establish" and "hold" a memory; retrieval is the process in "using" a memory—becoming conscious again of something you experienced in the past.

Encoding requires that you first attend to (notice) some selected stimulus event from the huge array nearly always available to you (though as we saw in Chapter 6, some preattentive processing occurs at a subconscious or preconscious level). Then you must identify the distinctive features of that experienced event. Both "bottom-up" and "top-down" processing will be involved here (see pp. 176–78).

Is the event a sound, a visual image, or a smell? If a sound, is it loud, soft, harsh, or what? Does it fit into some pattern with other sounds to form a name, a melody, a cry for help? Is it a sound you recognize as having heard before? During encoding you try to tag an experience with a variey of labels; some are specific and unique—"it's Adam Paisley,"—while others put the event into a general category or class—"it's a young student." This encoding process is usually so automatic and rapid that you are unaware of it.

Further encoding processes relate the new input to other things you already know or to goals or purposes for which it might later prove relevant. Retaining it will be better the more "links" you can establish and encode between this new item and what you already know. You remember relationships between single memories (of actors, actions, and consequences, for example) by forming *networks* of ideas that link together what you know. Memories with connections to other information are much more usable than isolated memory units.

Storage is a relatively more passive process in which the encoded information is retained over time. It involves neurophysiological changes in certain synapses and other as yet unknown biochemical modifications.

Minds, like libraries, must rely upon proper encoding and systematic storage to be useful. When you read "for fun," you make no special effort to organize the ideas for later retrieval. If you used that same process with information units in this text, making no effort to organize what you take in, you would be in trouble when test time came. Good encoding and storage organize information so that it will be easy to find when needed, thus anticipating the third process, retrieval.

Retrieval is the payoff for all your earlier effort. When it works, it enables you to gain access—sometimes in a split second—to information you stored earlier. Can you remember which comes before storage: decoding or encoding? The answer is simple to retrieve now, but will you still be able to retrieve "encoding" as swiftly and with as much confidence when you are tested on this chapter's contents days or weeks hence? Discovering *how* you are able to retrieve one specific bit of information from your memory storehouse filled with so much information is a challenge facing psychologists who want to know how memory works and how it can be improved.

We saw in Chapter 5 that perceptual processes can alter sensory information, and that past memories can sometimes distort perception. In this chapter we will see that there is an ongoing interplay between what we perceive and what we remember. The continuing interaction among encoding, storage, and retrieval is complex, and disturbances that occur during any one of them will affect what you can remember. The whole process is further complicated by the fact that encoding, storage, and retrieval processes take place in each of three basic memory systems.

For first-hand experience of some of the factors we will be discussing, give your personal answers to the questions that follow.

1. What is your social security number (and your best friend's)?
2. What was your first-grade teacher's name and eye color (and that of your current psychology instructor)?
3. Name the title, edition, and author of this textbook?
4. Can you form an image of this page when you close your eyes?
5. When did you *first* experience the emotion of guilt? (When was the *last* time you told your parents you loved them?)
6. Do you know the difference between iconic and echoic sensory information storage?
7. What is the significance of "Rosebud" to Citizen Kane (and "Watergate" to Richard Nixon)?
8. (Don't look back!) Citizen who?
9. Can you recall a complete dream you've had in the past week?
10. Were you a bit irritated the last time you had to answer a silly test such as this (so why did you do it?)

Was your recall quick and certain on some items, incomplete and vague on others? Were there some you didn't remember, but that you felt sure you either once knew or definitely never did? Were there some events that you had experienced but didn't remember because you didn't see them as significant at the time? Was your memory for negative emotional experiences similar to your ability to recall dates and places? Would questions phrased differently have helped you remember better? This experience of getting to know your own memory and retrieval mechanisms should help make concrete some of our more abstract discussions of types and processes of memory that follow.

Three memory systems

Although there is much that psychologists do not know about memory, they are fairly well agreed that there are three different memory systems within the overall system of remembering and recalling information: sensory memory, short-term memory, and long-term memory. **Sensory memory** preserves fleeting impressions of sensory stimuli—sights, sounds, smells, and textures—for only a second or two. **Short-term memory** includes recollections of what we have recently perceived; such limited information lasts only up to twenty seconds unless special attention is paid to it or it is reinstated by rehearsal. **Long-term memory** preserves information for retrieval at any later time—up to an entire lifetime. Information in long-term memory constitutes our knowledge about the world.

For examples of these three kinds of memories, imagine that as you are passing a movie theater, you notice a distinctive odor and hear loud sounds from inside (fleeting *sensory memories*). When you get home you decide to check the time of the next show. So you look up the theater's number and then dial the seven digits. Your *short-term memory* holds these digits for the brief period between looking up the number and dialing it, but you will probably have to look up the number again if the line is busy because your memory of the number will fade very soon unless you work at remembering it. Then, once you are given the show times, you will have to rely on your *long-term memory* to get you to the theater on time. It was your long-term memory that you relied on for most of the items on the memory test.

These three memory systems are also thought of as stages in the sequence of processing information. They differ not only in how much information they can hold and how long they can hold it, but also in how they process it. Memories that get into long-term storage have passed through the sensory and short-term stages first. In each stage, the information has been processed in ways that made it eligible for getting into the next one. Sense impressions become ideas or images; these, in turn, are organized into patterns that fit into existing networks in our long-term memory store.

It is important to keep in mind that memory is not a thing but a *process*. This is why *remembering* is perhaps a better term to use than *memory*. The three systems or stages in remembering are conceptual models of how psychologists believe that we process incoming information, retain, and use it. They are not believed to involve physically separate brain areas: rather, they seem to be functionally distinct subsystems within the overall system of remembering and recalling information. By finding out how information is processed in each subsystem, our hope is to understand why some conditions help us remember experiences, even "trivial" ones, while other conditions lead to the forgetting of even important experiences. **Figure 9.1** shows the hypothesized flow of information into and among these subsystems.

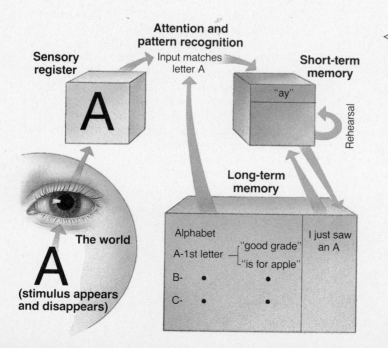

Figure 9.1 *A Model of the Human Memory System*

From Human Memory: Structures and Processes, *Second Edition by Roberta Klatsky. Copyright © 1975, 1980 by W. H. Freeman and Company. Reprinted by permission.*

SENSORY MEMORY

Sensory memories may be impressions from any of the senses. They are also sometimes called **sensory registers.** They are the first-stage components of most information-processing models of human memory. It is assumed that a register for each sense holds appropriate incoming stimulus information for a brief interval, and does so in a form that faithfully reproduces the original stimulus. This storage represents a primitive type of memory that occurs after sensation but *before* a stimulus is assigned to some category ("a bird") during pattern recognition. The form in which sensory memories are held is called *precategorical* since it takes place prior to the process of categorization (Crowder & Morton, 1969).

We know more about visual and auditory memories than the others. A visual memory is called an *icon* and lasts about half a second. An auditory memory is called an *echo* and lasts several seconds (Neisser, 1967). You can easily demonstrate the difference for yourself. When you turn off the radio, the sounds of the music tend to "echo" in your head for a while after the sound is gone. But if you pull down a window shade, the scene outside is gone almost at once.

Why should a memory system depend on the presence of icons and echos? What would happen if they did not occur? Without them, we could "see" and "hear" stimuli only while they were physically present. But recognition often takes more time than that. Sensory registers are essential for the task of holding input long enough to be recognized and passed on for further processing.

Encoding for sensory memory

To get into the sensory register, all that is needed is for the physical stimuli that impinge on your sensory receptors to be encoded into the biochemical processes that give rise to sensations and perceptions. Even at this stage there is selectivity, however, as we have seen in earlier chapters. Stimuli of vital importance to the organism take priority over others, as

when soldiers in battle who are focusing on detecting enemy gunners may be unaware of pain information. Through *sensory gating,* directed by processes in the brain, information in one sensory channel may be boosted while another is suppressed or disregarded.

Storage: how much and how long?

Though brief, your sensory storage capacity is large—as much as all your senses can process at one time. At first, researchers underestimated the amount that could actually be stored during this brief interval because of the reporting procedure they used. When subjects saw a visual display (such as that shown here) for a fraction of a second and then were asked to recall as many numbers as they could (*a whole-report procedure),* they could report only about 4 items. But was that the limit of their immediate memory span?

5	9	2
7	6	4
8	3	1

George Sperling was a young researcher who suspected that the number recalled might not be an accurate indication of the number that actually had gotten into the sensory memory. He devised an ingenious method—called the *partial-report procedure*—to test his hypothesis.

Sperling flashed the same arrays of numbers for the same amount of time (one tenth of a second) but now asked his subjects to report only one row, rather than the whole pattern. A signal of a high, medium, or low tone was sounded immediately *after* the presentation to indicate which row from the entire set the subjects were to report. He found that regardless of which row he asked for, the subjects' recall was nearly *perfect.* Sperling took this to indicate that all the items must have gotten into the sensory memory. When three rows of 4 items were flashed to other subjects, they were 76 percent accurate in their reports—again, about 9 items available for immediate recall (Sperling, 1960, 1963).

What happens if the identification signal is not immediate but slightly delayed? **Figure 9.2** shows that as the delay interval increases from zero to one second, the number of items reported declines steadily. Sperling's experiments demonstrate that immediate visual storage is quite accurate, but that the image or trace of the stimulus *decays* very rapidly.

Using Sperling's procedure, other researchers have shown that in auditory memory, too, more information is available than people can typically report (Darwin et al., 1972). Echoic memories may be necessary for processing many aspects of speech, such as intonation and emphasis.

Would we be better off if sensory memories lingered longer so that we would have more time to process them? Not really, because new information is constantly coming in and must be processed too. Old information must last just long enough to give us a sense of continuity but not long enough to interfere with new sensory impressions. As you read,

▽ **Figure 9.3** *Sequence of Events in Backward Masking*

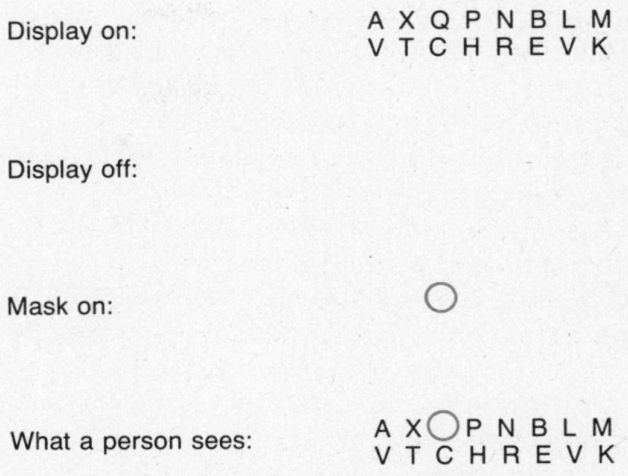

Display on:
      A X Q P N B L M
      V T C H R E V K

Display off:

Mask on:
      ○

What a person sees:
      A X ○ P N B L M
      V T C H R E V K

(Adapted from Averbach & Coriell, 1961)

the part you just attended to must be processed along the system, and drop out of sensory memory quickly so that your sensory system is able to register new information.

There is another way by which sensory registers get cleared of "old inputs" in addition to the rapid decay of stimulus traces. New inputs that are similar can *erase* iconic and echoic representations.

In one study two rows of letters were flashed briefly and 100 milliseconds later a circle was flashed where one of the letters had been. Normally, all the letters would have been seen 100 milliseconds after presentation. But instead of seeing all the letters with a circle around one of them, the subjects saw the two rows with the circle *instead of* that letter (Averbach & Coriell, 1961). **Figure 9.3** shows this sequence of events.

This phenomenon is known as *backward masking*. A stimulus following another of a similar kind erases or masks the preceding one, evidently because it interferes with the ongoing perceiving process.

But it is a race against the clock to complete pattern recognition and other coding before the sensory memory fades away. Most sensory inputs lose that race and fail to make it to either short-term memory or long-term memory.

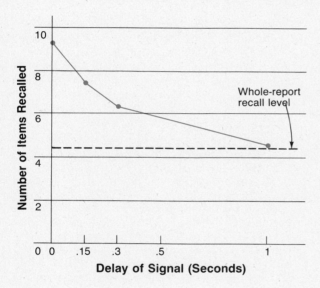

△ **Figure 9.2** *Recall by the Partial-Report Method*

The dots in the solid line show the average number of items recalled (for 4 subjects) by the partial-report method immediately following presentation and at three later times up to one second. For comparison, the number of items recalled from the 12 letters available by the whole-report method is shown by the dotted line. (Adapted from Sperling, 1960)

Processing for transfer to short-term memory

Though sensory gating has kept some stimulus input from being translated into sensations and perceptions, you still receive far more sensory information than you can remember—or could use if you did. Actually, only a tiny fraction of what you sense stays with you permanently, as you may have discovered in frustration when you tried to remember everything you saw and heard on a trip. What processes must take place before the sensory memories fade if they are to get into short-term memory—and thus have a chance of being remembered longer still?

The first requirement is that they be attended to. Of the vast range of sense impressions you experience and retain briefly in your sensory memory, only those that capture your attention become eligible for more lasting memory.

Selective attention—being aware of only part of the available sensory input—is a familiar experience for all of us. At a party we can participate intelligently in only one conversation at a time and manage to "tune out" the others going on around us. In a student dorm a half dozen stereos may be blasting away at once, but though all are detected by the receptors in our ears, we can select our own music—hear the stereo we want to hear. Then, if we get engaged in an animated conversation, we selectively attend to what is being said and the music recedes to the background of our attentional focus though it is as loud as ever. By selective attention, we choose the input that will be focused upon, and thus be remembered at least a little longer.

A fleeting sense impression becomes eligible for longer storage when pattern recognition occurs. As we saw in earlier chapters, the global process of taking in sensory input actually includes three parts: transformation of stimulus energy into sensory data (sensation), organization of data from individual receptors into patterns (perception), and "top-down" processes in which long-term memories help give meaning to the new information (classification). This third perceptual stage includes pattern recognition and incorporates influences from expectations or personal needs. Information has a better chance of getting into short-term memory and of having more attention focused on it if it is recognized as familiar or as something of value. **Figure 9.4** represents a special challenge to the pattern-recognition stage.

Three processes are assumed to occur during pattern recognition—analysis, comparison, and decision.

◁ **Figure 9.4**
What Is It?

In this drawing of an unfamiliar animal, a "hordograff," the parts are all familiar, yet they do not provide a whole recognizable as any known animal. (Courtesy of Stephen E. Palmer)

- In *analysis* the information in the sensory register is examined and perhaps broken down into its components.
- In *comparison* the analyzed information is matched against various memories stored in long-term memory, including memories for *contexts* in which the stimulus event has appeared in the past.
- In the *decision* process, the best matching code for the pattern is determined, leading to the final output of pattern recognition ("I got an *A*" rather than "I got a grade").

The interplay of the "bottom-up" data processing of the sensory registers and the "top-down" processing of stored items from long-term memory occurs virtually all the time swiftly and without conscious effort. It is usually an efficient interaction but can lead to distortions in what we remember, as we shall see.

The representation of information in some encoded form in storage is called a *memory code.* When there is no memory code already in long-term memory to match the stimulus with or relate it to, encoding for short-term memory is harder, takes longer, and is less likely to happen at all. This is why new information is easier to remember if you can relate it to something you already know. It may also be one reason why you probably have so few memories of your earliest years: you had very few memories already stored that could help you in encoding new experiences.

SHORT-TERM MEMORY

A stimulus that has been recognized is likely to be transferred to short-term memory, an intermediate memory process between the fleeting events of sensory memory and the more permanent storage of long-term memory. This memory-processing phase has a number of interesting characteristics that distinguish it from the other two stages.

Short-term memory has a very limited capacity, storing much *less* information than in either of the other stages. It also has a short duration of retention: what is stored is lost after about twenty seconds *unless* it is held in consciousness. But short-term memory is the only memory stage in which conscious processing of material takes place, and material held in it survives as long as it is held in conscious attention—far beyond the twenty-second limit possible without attention. This is why short-term memory is also called the *working memory:* material transferred to it from either sensory or long-term memory (both of them nonconscious) can be worked over, organized, thought about.

The working memory is part of our psychological present. It is what sets a context for new events and links separate episodes together into a continuing story. It is short-term memory that enables us to maintain and continually update our representation of the changing situation and to keep track of what topics are under discussion during a conversation.

Short-term memory gives a context for both comprehension and new perceptions. For example, suppose a waiter moves by your table carrying a tray of used dishes while you are deeply engaged in conversation with your date. A minute or so later, there is a crashing noise. You know it is not a falling tree or a car crash but interpret it immediately as most probably the crashing of dishes from that waiter's tray. Here short-term memory is using information from a recent event and also from long-term memory about what sounds different events make to help your interpretation of the new perception (Baddeley & Hitch, 1974).

Encoding in short-term memory

Information enters short-term memory as organized images and patterns that are usually recognized by the individual as familiar and meaningful. Verbal patterns that enter short-term memory usually seem to be held there in *acoustic* form—according to how they sound—even when they came through the individual's eyes rather than ears. We know this from research in which subjects are asked to recall lists of letters immediately after seeing them. Errors of recall tend to be confusions of letters that *sound* alike, rather than look alike. For example, the letter *D* is confused with similar sounding *T,* rather than with more similar looking *O* (Conrad, 1964).

You may be wondering how *deaf* people can manage if short-term memory uses acoustic encoding. Apparently the deaf use two alternatives to the acoustic coding most of us use. They rely on *visual encoding* (identifying letters, words, and sign-language symbols) and to a lesser extent *semantic encoding* (identifying the categories or classes to which visually observed events belong). This we deduce from the fact that the errors they make result from confusing items that are similar in appearance or in meaning instead of in sound (Belugi et al., 1975; Frumkin & Anisfeld, 1977). And even though hearing persons generally rely on acoustic encoding in their short-term memory stage, there is evidence that they too sometimes rely on visual and semantic encoding (Conrad, 1972).

Storage in short-term memory

The limited, brief storage capacity for short-term memory is called the **immediate memory span.** When the to-be-remembered items are unrelated, the capacity of short-term memory seems to be between five and nine "chunks" of information—about seven (plus or minus two) familiar things: letters, words, numbers, or almost any kind of meaningful item. Beyond this number as new items enter, earlier ones are displaced, like blocks on a surface big enough to hold only a given number: when the surface is full, putting a new block on pushes an old one off. For an account of George Miller's (1956) discovery of this "magical number seven," see the **Close-up** on page 314.

Even these seven items are not guaranteed to last for the twenty seconds that we *could* hold them, however. If we focus our attention on processing a few of them, the other ones may slip away.

The Magical Number Seven

". . . I have been persecuted by an integer. For seven years this number has followed me around, has entered in my most private data, and has assaulted me from the pages of our most public journals. . . . There is . . . a design behind it, some pattern governing its appearances" (Miller, 1956, p. 81).

So wrote psychologist George Miller about his persecution by the "magical number seven." Recall the power and glory of that special number:

The *seven* days of creation.
The *seven* ages of man.
The *seven* deadly sins.
The *seven* levels of hell.
The *seven* digits in phone numbers.
The *seven* wonders of the world.

The power of the number seven in human thinking knows no cultural bounds. When African tribal historians, for example, tell stories of their ancestors, they may be able to recite by heart 12,000-word tales, such as *The Mwindo Epic,* but they usually go back only *seven* generations. Anthropologists have noted that after tracing back their roots for seven generations, these oral historians usually say that the Primal Ancestor then "came from heaven" (D'Azevedo, 1962).

The special relevance of "seven" for our purposes is that human memory seems bound by that number. Read this list of random numbers once, cover them over, and write down as many as you can in the order they appear here.

8 1 7 3 6 4 9 4 2 8 5

correct _____

Processing in short-term memory

Luckily, there are two important ways through which the limited capacity of short-term storage can be increased so that more of the information there can be put into long-term memory. These are *chunking* and *rehearsal.* You already use them and now you'll discover why they help you.

Chunking. A chunk, as indicated above, is a meaningful unit of information. A chunk can be a single letter or number, a group of letters or other items, even a group of words or a sentence. For example, the sequence 1, 9, 8, 4 consists of four digits, which could be four chunks—about half of what your short-term memory can hold. But 1984 is only one chunk if you see the digits as making up the name of a year or the title of George Orwell's book—leaving you much more capacity for other chunks of information. **Chunking** is the process of taking single items and recoding them by grouping them on the basis of similarity or some organizing principle or combining them into larger patterns based on information stored in long-term memory.

How many chunks do you find in this sequence of 20 numbers: 19411914186518121776? You would answer "twenty" if you see them as unrelated digits but "five" if you group them as dates of major wars in United States history. In this case, it becomes easy for you to recall all the digits and in proper sequence after one quick glance, whereas it would be impossible for you to remember them all from a short exposure if you saw them as twenty unrelated items. Your memory span can always be greatly increased if you can discover how to organize information into chunks.

You can also structure incoming information according to its personal meaning to you (linking it to the ages of friends and relatives, for example). Or you can match new stimuli with various *codes* that have been stored in your long-term memory. Thus your memory for the sequence ERATVCIAFBIGMGEUSA will be better if you chunk it as ERA-TV-CIA-FBI-GM-GE-USA (Bower, 1972).

Even if you do not have appropriate rules, meanings, or codes to apply from your long-term memory, you still can use chunking. You can simply *group* the items in a rhythmical pattern or temporal group (181 pause, 379 pause, 256 pause, 460 pause . . . rather than 181379256460).

Now read this list of random letters, and perform the same memory test

J M R S O F L P T Z B

correct _____

If your short-term memory is like that of most others, you probably recalled about *seven* numbers and *seven* letters. Some people will recall five units, some as many as nine—that is, seven plus or minus two (7 ± 2). You will discover the same principle operating with recall of lists of random words or names (*seven* again!).

Miller's conclusion has been supported by much research validating the rule that the average capacity of short-term memory is about seven units of unrelated information. But units can vary in size, and some—like words made up of letters—actually contain several related parts. Realizing that a new concept was needed to describe the units of short-term memory, Miller dubbed them *chunks*.

Chunks vary in both size and complexity, and your chunks may differ from mine. Chunks are thus the personal currency of our memory banks. When memorizing numbers, you may store pairs of digits (35–46–21) while I may store triplets (354–621). Looking at a picture, I may chunk by location (grass with ball at bottom; tree with bird at top), while you may chunk by color (blue ball and blue bird; green grass and green tree). "A chunk is a mental refashioning of reality that each mind comes up with for itself" (Kanigel, 1981, p. 34).

But regardless of what is stored in any of your chunks or mine, there are only about *seven* chunks in action at any given time. How many? _____!

Rehearsal. The usefulness of repeating the digits of a telephone number to keep them in mind has already been mentioned. This is called **maintenance rehearsal.** The fate of unrehearsed information was demonstrated in an ingenious experiment.

Subjects heard three consonants read aloud—such as FCV—and had to recall them when given a signal after a variable interval of time ranging from 3 to 18 seconds. To prevent rehearsal, a *distractor task* was put between the stimulus input and the recall signal. (The subjects were given a 3-digit number and told to count backward from it by threes until the recall signal was presented.) Many different consonant sets were given and several short delays were used over a series of trials with a number of subjects.

As shown in **Figure 9.5**, recall deteriorated increasingly as the retention interval increased. After even 3 seconds there was considerable memory loss; by 18 seconds loss was nearly total. In the absence of opportunity to rehearse the information, the short-term memories faded rapidly with the passage of time (Peterson & Peterson, 1959).

In addition, there was probably interference from the competing information of the distractor task. Interference as a cause of forgetting will be discussed later in the chapter.

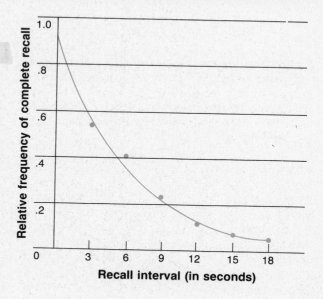

△ **Figure 9.5**   *Short-Term Recall Without Rehearsal*

When the interval between stimulus presentation and recall test was filled with a brief distracting task, the longer the interval, the poorer the recall. (Adapted from Peterson & Peterson, 1959)

Rehearsal keeps information in working memory and prevents competing inputs from pushing it out. But even information rehearsed verbatim does not necessarily get transferred to long-term memory. To make sure, you need to engage in **elaborative rehearsal,** a process in which the information is analyzed and related to already stored knowledge. This happens when you note that the telephone number 358-9211 can also be thought of as $3 + 5 = 8$ and $9 + 2 = 11$. This elaboration depends upon your having addition rules and summations stored in and transferred from long-term memory, but if you do, it helps give pattern and meaning to the otherwise unrelated and meaningless items. Similarly, you group the words in English sentences into chunks once you have learned the rules of syntax—how words can be arranged to form acceptable sentences. We will have more to say about elaborative rehearsal later when we discuss encoding for long-term memory.

The limited capacity of short-term memory is one of the fundamental and stable features of the human memory system. Yet we hear of "memory experts"—people who can remember long strings of numbers after a single presentation or multiply large numbers in their heads in a few seconds. Apparently part of their secret is in learning to shift information back and forth between short-term and long-term memory. To see how this skill might be developed, cognitive psychologist William Chase worked with a student, identified as S.F.

At the beginning, S.F. could repeat only the standard seven numbers in proper sequence, but after two and a half years of practice (an hour a day, two to five days a week), he could recall up to 80 digits or reproduce perfectly a matrix of 50 numbers—and do so more quickly than lifelong memory experts.

S.F. was neither coached nor given special training. He merely put in hundreds of hours' practice listening to random digits being read one per second and then recalling them in order. When he reported them correctly, another digit was added on the next trial; if he was incorrect, one digit was dropped on the next trial. After each trial S.F. gave a verbal report (a protocol) of his thought process.

S.F.'s protocols provided the key to his mental wizardry. Because he was a long-distance runner, S.F. noticed that many of the random numbers could be grouped into running times for different distances. For instance, he would recode the sequence: "3, 4, 9, 2, 5, 6, 1, 4, 9, 3, 5," as "three forty-nine point two, near record mile; fifty-six point fourteen, 10-mile time; nine thirty-five, slow 2 miles." Later S.F. also used ages, years of special events, and special numerical patterns to chunk the random digits. In this way he was able to use his long-term memory to convert long strings of random input into a smaller number of manageable and meaningful chunks (Chase & Ericsson, 1981; Ericsson & Chase, 1982).

Retrieval from short-term memory

You now know something about how you get 7 ± 2 chunks of information into your short-term memory. But how do you get them out? This is the problem of *retrieval.*

Retrieval from short-term memory has been studied experimentally by Saul Sternberg (1966, 1969). Although the task he used was quite simple, the results revealed in detail how items seem to be retrieved from short-term memory.

On each of many trials, subjects were given a *memory set* consisting of from one to six items—for instance, the digits 5, 2, 9, 4, 6. From trial to trial the list would vary in the digits shown and in length. After presenting each set, Sternberg immediately presented a single test "probe"—say 6—which the subject had to recognize as having been part of the memory set or not. Since the size of the set was less than the capacity of short-term memory (7 ± 2), subjects could easily perform the task without error.

The dependent variable was not accuracy but *speed of recognition.* How quickly could subjects press a "yes" button to indicate that they had seen the test item in the memory set or a "no" button to indicate they had not seen it? Reaction time was used here to find out what mental activities were occurring when short-term memory was being searched. Three components of the retrieval process were assumed to make up this reaction time: (a) the subject perceived and encoded the test stimulus—"it's a six"; (b) the test stimulus was then matched against the items in the stored memory set (5,2,9,4,6); and (c) a recognition response was made by pressing the "yes" button in this case, or the "no" button had the set been 5,2,9,4,7.

Sternberg believed that short-term memory might be scanned using any of three possible search strategies (see **Figure 9.6**):

1. *In parallel processing scanning* the entire stored set would be treated as a composite, and separate digits would be examined simultaneously, all "in

▷ **Figure 9.6 *Retrieval from Short-Term Memory***

Reaction time for retrieval from short-term memory increases with the length of the memory set and is the same for "no" and "yes" responses, as predicted for serial exhaustive processing. (Adapted from Sternberg, 1966)

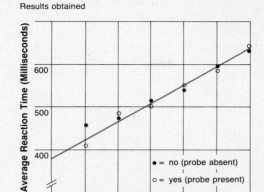

Results obtained

● = no (probe absent)
○ = yes (probe present)

Average Reaction Time (Milliseconds)

Number of Digits in Memory Set

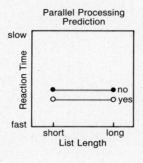

Parallel Processing Prediction

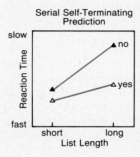

Serial Self-Terminating Prediction

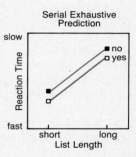

Serial Exhaustive Prediction

parallel." If this were what occurred, it would take no longer to search big sets than short ones, and reaction time would be the same.

2. *In serial self-terminating scanning* each digit would be examined in turn until the test probe digit was found; then the search would be terminated. With this process longer lists would require more search time than shorter ones. In addition, it would take more time for a "no" than for a "yes" because the subject would stop searching as soon as a match ("yes") was found, but would have to scan all the digits in the set before making a "no."

3. *In serial exhaustive scanning* the digits in the stored memory set would be scanned separately and the entire set would be examined before a "yes" or a "no" response was made. In this case, longer lists would have a slower reaction time, but "yes" and "no" responses would take equal time.

The results fit the memory scanning prediction of a serial exhaustive search. It took more time to recognize test stimuli from longer memory sets. But it took the same time to give a "yes" as a "no" response. Sternberg figured that it took about 400 milliseconds to encode the test stimulus, and then about 35 milliseconds more to compare it to each item in the memory set. This means that in a single second, a person could make about thirty such comparisons. With such fast scanning, we can afford the security of doing an exhaustive search before deciding what we really remember.

Although other researchers have offered a different interpretation (Townsend, 1972; Wingfield, 1973), Sternberg's work has been very influential in helping our understanding of retrieval from short-term memory. It not only showed how items were retrieved from short-term memory, but also how effectively reaction time could be used as a dependent measure to test theories about mental processes. Reaction time is now used very frequently as the dependent variable in studies of other cognitive processes, as we shall see in Chapter 10.

LONG-TERM MEMORY

A 95-year-old woman describes a family event that happened when she was 5 years old. She may even recall the expression on her mother's face, a twisted gold ribbon on a package, and how she felt. Somehow, despite all the activities and thoughts of the 90 intervening years, her brain has held those memories.

This is the miracle of our third memory system, long-term memory. It constitutes each person's total knowledge of the world and of the self. Long-term memory is the storehouse of all the experienced events, information, emotions, skills, words, categories, rules and judgments—and more—that have been transferred into it from sensory and short-term memories.

But this memory system enables you to do much more even than just retain a record of past events or thoughts. Material in long-term memory helps you deal with and store new information by "top-down" processing, as you have seen. It also makes it possible for you to solve new problems, reason, keep future appointments, and apply a variety of rules to manipulate abstract symbols—to think and even to create something you have never experienced.

Given how much information is stored in long-term memory, it is a marvel how accessible it is. You can often get the exact information you want in a split second. Who discovered classical conditioning? Name a play by Shakespeare. What was your happiest birthday? How often should you brush your teeth? The answers to these questions probably came effortlessly because of several special features of long-term memory: (a) words and concepts have been put into it (encoded) by their *meaning,* which has given them links to many other stored items; (b) the knowledge in your long-term memory is filed in a well-organized, orderly fashion (storage); and (c) many alternative cues are stored to help you extract exactly what you want from all that is there (retrieval).

Encoding for long-term memory

We have seen that short-term memory is a little like an office in-basket. Items are stored sequentially in a temporal order, by the order of their arrival. Long-term memory, by contrast, is more like a set of file cabinets or a library. Items are stored according to their meanings with perhaps many meanings for one item (corresponding to title, author, and subject in a card catalogue) and numerous cross references to related material. Thus in many cases there are a variety of possible ways to retrieve a particular item.

Meaningful organization. The importance of meaningful organization as the key to long-term storage is shown in the fact that we often remember the gist or sense of an idea rather than the actual sentence we heard. For example, if you hear the sentence, "Mary picked up the book," and later hear, "The book was picked up by Mary," you are likely to report that the second sentence was the one you heard earlier. The meaning was the same though the form was different. In fact, it is very hard to remember accurately something that makes no sense to you.

The reason that both chunking and elaborative rehearsal are helpful in preparing material for long-term storage is that they organize it and make it more meaningful. When you are not limited to the twenty seconds of short-term memory but can study material in front of you that you want to remember, there are several other things you can do to give the material organization or meaning or both.

For example, you may "make sense" of new information by putting it in a category you already have, transforming it into something familiar, or organizing it in some other way that is meaningful to you.

Suppose, for example, you are asked to learn the following list of words for later recall and are told that you may recall them in any order. (This task is called *free recall.*)

house	yellow
tree	green
bird	nest
dog	tiger
grass	tent
purple	shoe
horse	

How might you begin? You could first note that the list has 13 items and then see how many fit into different categories: animal—4; living places—4 if you include tree; colors—3; food—2. Or you could encode this input by grouping pairs together: tree–house; bird–nest; green–grass; horse–shoe; yellow–tiger, etc.

Older children (sixth-graders) recalled such lists better than younger ones because they were more likely to organize the items in some way, such as learning the items in pairs or grouping them by category. Most third-graders used only maintenance rehearsal—simply repeating the items. But when the younger children were taught how to look for ways to organize the items, their recall became as good as that of the older children (Ornstein & Naus, 1978).

The same material can usually be organized meaningfully in more than one way. Sometimes you encode by noticing the structure already in the material, such as the different levels of headings in this chapter. Other times you impose your own organization by outlining the main points and subpoints or fitting new items into a structure of knowledge you already have in that field. You may boil down several paragraphs into two main ideas with an example of each. You may make new distinctions in an old concept you already have stored, such as you have now done with *memory* as three stages in an overall system. Or you may add meaning or organization to new material by using personal experiences, references, or physically present reminders like a string around your finger or the mementos Nick used to help him remember.

△ **Figure 9.7**

The method of loci is a means of remembering the order of a list of names or objects by associating them with some sequence of places with which we are familiar.

Use of mnemonics. To help yourself remember, you can also draw on special strategies or devices called **mnemonics** (from the Greek word meaning "to remember"), which are ways of associating new information to be remembered with something familiar, previously encoded, and easily recalled. Among the mnemonics are natural language mediators, the method of loci, and visual imagery.

Natural language mediators are word meanings or spelling patterns already stored in long-term memory that can be associated with new information. For example, you might encode the paired nonsense syllables PAB—LOM by associating them with *pablum.* Or you might encode the word pair GIRL—STAGE as "The girl danced on the stage." You might remember more complex material or a list of words by making up a story to connect the parts. Associations that use rhyming can also help you remember. Even though the encoded item is then longer than the original one, your recall is better because you remember those mediators easily and they in turn lead you to the material you are looking for (Montague et al., 1966).

Another common mnemonic strategy is the *method of loci* (*locus* means "place"). To remember a list of names of people you are meeting, you might mentally put one in each room in your house in sequence; to remember them, you mentally go through the house and find the name associated with each spot.

Or you might remember a list of words like *mouse, car, melon,* and so on by associating them with the things you would see while walking around your living room. You might associate *mouse* with the *door,* possibly picturing the mouse opening the door for you. If a *couch* is next to the door, you might imagine a *car* resting on it, with its hazard lights blinking. (See **Figure 9.7**.)

Visual imagery is one of the most effective forms of encoding, perhaps because it gives you codes for both verbal and visual memories simultaneously (Paivio, 1968). Here you remember words by associating them with a visual image—the more vivid and distinctive the better. For example, if you wanted to remember the pair "CAT-BICYCLE," you might use an image of "a cat riding on a bicycle to deliver pizzas" (Bower, 1972). To test your own visual imagery, try the task in **Figure 9.8**.

Other mnemonic devices use organizational schemes or strategies that rely on word or sound associations or on putting the items into a pattern that is easy to remember. For example, a mnemonic for

▽ **Figure 9.8**

*How well do you know a penny?
See if you can draw what both
sides look like. For the answer,
check your loose change.*

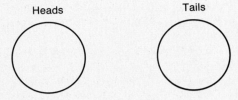

Heads   Tails

remembering the colors of the spectrum converts to a person's name, *Roy G. Biv* (red, orange, yellow, green, blue, indigo, violet). Similarly, the familiar "*Every good boy does fine*" is a mnemonic for remembering the musical notes on the treble clef: *E, G, B, D, F.*

You may have wondered how waiters and waitresses can remember many different orders when they do not write them down. Even after a delay of many minutes, they usually manage to set the right glass or plate in front of the right customer.

In a recent study of this phenomenon, 40 waitresses and 40 control subjects (college students) had to remember 7, 11, and 15 drink orders and later place them in front of the customers (actually dolls seated around tables).

When only 7 orders were taken, there was no difference between the two groups. But with 11 or 15 orders, the waitresses were significantly more accurate. In fact, some were 100 percent accurate with 15 orders. The waitresses reported that they worked to develop their memories by using mnemonic techniques that helped them associate each order visually with a particular face or specific location: "bourbon and soda poured over big eared brute first out of the chute" (first on her left). Interestingly, most of the waitresses reported that their memory was best on the busiest evenings. The investigator noted that motivation for performing this task well would be high since customer satisfaction and tips are strongly influenced by waitress accuracy (Bennett, 1983).

Encoding specificity. Your method of organizing material in the encoding stage directly affects not only how it is stored but, equally important, what

cues will work when you want to retrieve it. The close relationship among encoding, storage, and retrieval is called the **encoding specificity principle.** The better the match between your organization for encoding and the cues you are likely to be given later, the better your recall will be.

This means that it will be worth your while to study new material according to how you expect to have to retrieve it later. If you will get essay questions, look for and try to remember general information about abstract relationships, implications, and conceptual analysis because that is probably what you will be asked to retrieve. If you expect multiple-choice questions, you should pay more attention to specific, concrete, right-or-wrong factual details, comparisons, and distinctions when encoding.

The encoding specificity principle also means that when you are learning new material, you will be encoding details about the physical and psychological circumstances around you at the time—the context of the encoding. This learning too can provide additional retrieval cues *if* you are in similar circumstances when you try to retrieve the material you have studied. The power of such *context dependence* was demonstrated by the finding that divers who learned material under water remembered it better when tested under water, even when the material had nothing to do with water or diving (Baddeley, 1982). Context dependence is one reason why studying in a noisy environment may not help your retrieval when you will be tested in a quiet room.

State dependence is important too: retrieval will be better if there is no big change in your physical or psychological state between the time of learning and the time of retrieval. If you learned something when you were happy, it will be harder to remember it if you are sad than if you can reinstate the happy mood (Bower, 1981; Snyder & White, 1982; Teasdale et al., 1980).

Storage in long-term memory

Stored in your long-term memory is not only information you have taken in from outside in all its sensory diversity but also internally generated information such as creative thoughts, opinions, and values. How are all these kinds of information represented in storage?

Procedural and declarative knowledge. Do you remember how selective Nick's amnesia was? After his accident, he could store **procedural knowledge**—how to do things like brush his teeth or cook—but not some kinds of **declarative knowledge**—facts about events since his accident, how they were related, and what they meant. Cases like Nick's have led to the conclusion that procedural ("skill") knowledge and declarative ("fact") knowledge must somehow be stored differently.

Skill memories are memories of *actions* and are acquired by practice; they are often hard to learn but may be even harder to unlearn. They are not explicitly recalled except when being actually performed and are best performed *without* conscious thought. (Try to describe how to tie a shoelace or how to swim. Describing such a task is more difficult than just doing it.) Fact memories, by contrast, are memories of explicit *information;* they are recalled with conscious effort, along with the context in which they were learned. And though many facts persist in memory a long time, a great many are easily lost.

Procedural memory is thought to be a capacity of subcortical areas in the old brain, with the declarative memory system more recently evolved and built upon the primitive base. This difference may account for why both human and animal babies develop skill memories earlier than fact memories.

> Young monkeys were tested at different ages on both a skill acquisition task and a simple memory association task. They were as proficient as adults on the skill task at three months of age but could not do the other task until they were six months old and did not develop adult proficiency at it until they were almost two years old (Mishkin, 1982).

It looks as though we were workers who got things done before we became intellectuals who think about the dignity of labor.

Within memory for declarative knowledge there are two different types—episodic and semantic. This distinction was first proposed by Canadian psychologist Endel Tulving (1972). **Episodic memory** stores autobiographical information—an individual's own perceptual experiences along with some *temporal* coding (or "time tags") for when the event occurred and some coding for the *context*. Memories of your happiest birthday, or of your first love affair are part of your personal history and are stored in your episodic memory. Nick suffered from impaired episodic memory for events after his accident.

Successful recall of much of the factual information you have learned in college also involves epi-

sodic memory; many events, formulas, and concepts are stored in part according to a variety of personally relevant context features. For example, in trying to answer a particular test question you remember which course the material probably came from, whether you heard it during the lecture or read it in the text, whether you discussed it in a study group, and whether you put it in your notes. You may even have a mental image of what the relevant graph or figure was.

Ironically, every time you take anything *out* of your episodic memory storage, you also increase what is *in* there. You do so because you then remember and store your act of recalling it (when and where did you reply "Pavlov" and "Hamlet"?). Such additions often make what is there less accessible.

Semantic memory stores the basic *meaning* of words and concepts without reference to their time and place in your experience (though you may remember that too, in your episodic memory). It is more like an encyclopedia than an autobiography. The meaningful relationships in your semantic memory are organized around abstract and conceptual information. Your semantic memory includes "generic" facts (true for other people and independent of personal experience) about grammar, musical composition, or scientific principles, for examples. The formula $E = MC^2$ is stored in sematic memory. Nick's semantic memory for things learned before his accident was apparently unaffected by his accident.

Until quite recently, most research on long-term memory was concerned with only episodic memory for lists of *nonsense syllables* or pairs of unrelated stimuli. This research was based on the assumption that there was only one kind of remembering. By studying it in as "pure" a form as possible, uncontaminated by meanings in the stimulus materials, researchers hoped to find basic principles that could then be used to help understand more complex examples of remembering. (See the **Close-up** on p. 322.) The study of the memory of meaningful material was largely neglected until the 1950s when theorists began to use computers to simulate psychological processes in memory, language understanding, and comprehension of material read. Since then, it has become a major branch of memory research.

How is information represented in memory?

We know that information in long-term memory is stored in organized patterns, with networks of meaningfully related concepts and multiple connec-

Ebbinghaus and His Nonsense Syllables

The first significant study providing a truly quantitative measure of memory was published in 1885 by the German psychologist, Hermann Ebbinghaus. Ebbinghaus used "nonsense syllables"—meaningless three-letter units consisting of a vowel between two consonants, such as CEG or DAX. He used nonsense syllables, rather than meaningful three-letter words, because he hoped to obtain a "pure" measure of memory, one uncontaminated by previous learning or associations that the person might bring to the experimental memory task.

Herman Ebbinghaus (1850-1909).

Not only was Ebbinghaus the researcher; he was also his *own subject*. The task he used was called *serial learning,* and the method he used was rote learning. A list of nonsense syllables was presented one at a time and then repeated, in the same order, until he could recite all items in the correct order—the *criterion performance.*

Later, he would test himself to see how much he remembered. During the retention interval, he distracted himself from rehearsing the original list by learning other lists. Then, instead of trying to recall all the items on the original list, Ebbinghaus measured his memory by seeing how many trials it took him to *relearn* the original list. If he took fewer trials, it meant that he had *saved* information from his earlier learning.

For example, if Ebbinghaus took 12 trials to learn a list and 9 trials to relearn it several days later, his savings score for that elapsed time would be 25 percent (12–9 trials = 3 trials saved; 3 divided by 12 is 25 percent). This *savings method* for measuring retention is a very sensitive one, often showing evidence of some memory even when no items can be recalled at the start of the second learning period.

Using the savings method, Ebbinghaus examined how much memory was lost after different time inter-

vals. The curve he obtained is shown below. As you can see, he found a rapid initial loss, followed by a gradually slower decline. Ebbinghaus' curve is typical of results from experiments on rote memory of meaningless material.

Why did Ebbinghaus' memories fade so quickly? You might think that it was just due to the passage of time, but most of what we learn is remembered for far longer than Ebbinghaus' forgetting curve implies. It turns out that there are several reasons why Ebbinghaus forgot faster than usual.

One reason is that the materials he used—nonsense syllables—could not be tied to information already stored in his memory. Nor could they easily be chunked or rehearsed elaboratively. How can you image a CEG or a DAX when there are no such things? A second reason is *interference.* Because he learned so many lists of similar items, they began to get confused in his memory. If he had learned only one list, he probably would have remembered it a great deal longer.

Following Ebbinghaus' lead, the standard method of studying human verbal learning for many decades was to have subjects learn nonsense syllables. Besides avoiding the "complicating influence of meaning," such studies were in keeping with the interest in recording overt responses rather than investigating mental processes. Not until the focus changed to how information is processed did the study of memory shift to meaningful material.

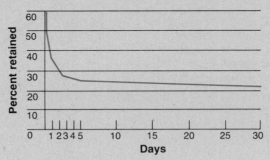

(After Ebbinghaus, 1885)

tions for many, perhaps all, chunks of knowledge. From the functional differences among procedural, episodic, and semantic memories we guess that there is probably some difference in the ways or places they are stored. Also one memory ability can be lost and another retained. We know that somehow there must also be representations of past sensory experiences (sights, sounds, smells, etc.), emotional experiences, experiences of movement (as in skill learning), and even episodes of interpersonal experiences—representations not only stored but stored with interconnections (Forgas, 1982). But we really know very little about how all the forms of experience that we remember are actually represented in long-term memory.

Researchers who study comprehension and memory of verbal material have hypothesized that the memory code is verbal—that people store representations of ideas in some type of linguistic code (see Clark & Clark, 1977). They use the term *proposition* to refer to the meaning unit in such a representation. Propositions consist of concepts and their interrelationships. "Don loves Joan who is pretty and lives in New York" is a sentence with three meaning units and hence three propositions: Don loves Joan; Joan lives in New York; Joan is pretty. Propositions are seen as "meaning atoms," the smallest abstract unit of knowledge.

According to some theorists, networks of such propositions form the structural building blocks of long-term memory. These semantic (meaning) networks enable us to locate stored information and alter or add to it (Anderson & Bower, 1973; Anderson, 1976).

Other investigators, however, believe that people use visual codes in addition to verbal ones for storing memories. This view of two forms of memory storage—in both verbal and visual codes—is called the **dual-code model of memory** (Begg & Paivio, 1969; Paivio, 1983). According to this view, sensory information and concrete sentences are more likely to be stored as images while abstract sentences are verbally coded. In one version of this dual code theory, images reside in a "visual buffer"—a spatial medium—where they can be worked on and transformed in various ways (e.g., rotated or scanned) by other cognitive processes (Kosslyn, 1983).

Much heated debate has surrounded the question of whether people use one memory code or two. In an attempt to reconcile the two positions, it has

been suggested that we may store *descriptions* of images rather than the images themselves (Pylyshyn, 1973) or that images may be stored as abstract codes from which the various features of the image can be recreated in somewhat the same way that a computer program creates visual images in video games (Anderson, 1978). We all know that the pictures we see on TV are not stored in the TV; memory storage of images could be analogous. In Chapter 10 we will consider the role of images in thinking.

Eidetic imagery. Evidence that literal images may be stored in memory is seen in the phenomenon of apparent "photographic memory," known technically as **eidetic imagery**. Research subjects who claim to have eidetic imagery report "seeing" the whole stimulus picture in front of their closed eyes as if they were experiencing it directly rather than scanning memory for traces of it. This skill is rare, found only in about 5 percent of children studied (Gray & Gummerman, 1975).

Instead of asking subjects to describe pictures they have been shown, researchers have developed a more demanding test for eidetic imagery. Two pictures are shown in succession, each meaningless by itself but together forming a composite that is meaningful. This superimposition method forces the subject to hold the two images in visual memory in enough detail so that they will fuse to form a single picture that is not predictable from either part alone. Using this method reduces the number of those who qualify as true "eidetikers," especially as the pictures become complex (Gummerman et al., 1972; Leask et al., 1969).

> One unusual case exists in the literature of a woman, Elizabeth, who appeared to have an amazing degree of eidetic imagery. She "passed" all the tests the researchers developed to challenge the existence of her "photographic memory." In the most stringent test, Elizabeth saw a special complex pattern of a million dots with one eye, then later (up to several hours) looked at another seemingly random dot array. She was able to fuse the earlier image with the currently perceived one to form a 3-D picture. Normally this can be accomplished only by looking at the two images at the same time with special 3-D glasses. Elizabeth must have had the ability to retain the first image in long-term memory and retrieve it on demand. There may be other people with her remarkable type of memory who have not yet been studied, but even this one rare case forces us to acknowledge the possibility of vivid visual memory storage (Stromeyer & Psotka, 1970).

Much remains to be learned about the structures and networks involved in memory storage and we will consider further evidence in the next chapter. It is clear, however, that the computer models of memory proposed so far are much simpler than the rich reality of personal memory.

Retrieval from long-term memory

Often an apparent failure of memory is actually a failure to get access to the stored information. A great deal of research has focused on the retrieval process and on the cues that are most effective for locating specific memories among the massive number being held in long-term storage.

The stimuli available to us as we search for a memory are called **retrieval cues.** They may be externally provided, as in items on a quiz (What memory principles do you associate with the research of Sternberg and Sperling?) or internally generated (Where have I met her before?). Just as only the cor-

rect call number will get us the library book we want, only a suitable key—retrieval cue—will unlock the particular stored memory we are after. Luckily, more than one key often works.

Aids to retrieval. The importance of encoding specificity has already been mentioned. Remembered material is much more accessible if it has been encoded in accordance with the retrieval cues that you have to work with. As we have seen, cues can be provided not only by the content of a test question but by the context and your state of mind. If these are the same during your memory search as during your earlier learning, you will have better access to what you learned.

Since organization helps you put information into storage, it is not surprising that cues based on *organization* can also help you get out what you know.

> In one study, subjects were given a list of words to memorize for free recall. The words were arranged by categories with each category name preceding the words, but category names were not mentioned: instructions were simply to memorize the words. During the recall test, half the subjects were given the category names as retrieval cues, while the other subjects were not given the category names but just asked to recall as many items as they could. Recall was much better for the subjects given the category names as retrieval cues.
>
> In the second recall test, however, where both groups were shown the category retrieval cues, they remembered equally well. The information had evidently been available in the long-term memory store of all the subjects all along but was just not as accessible without the retrieval cues to help locate the items (Tulving & Pearlstone, 1966).

Other research has shown that recall is aided whether the organization is imposed by the experimenter or generated by the subject (Mandler, 1972).

Even with good cues, not all stored content is equally accessible, as you know only too well. In the case of familiar, well-learned information, more aspects of it have been stored and connections with many different parts of the memory network have been established. So a number of cues can give you access to it, and you can get to a lot of information quickly by accessing any part of the network. On the other hand, in trying to find the one key that will unlock a less familiar memory, you may have to use special search strategies. (See the **Close-up** on p. 325.)

Don't Tell Me—It's on the Tip of My Tongue

1. What is the name of the waxy substance derived from sperm whales that is often used in perfumes?
2. What is the name of the small boats used in the harbors and rivers of China and Japan?
3. Do you know the name of the patronage bestowed on a person based on a family relationship, rather than on merit?

When these questions were asked of a large number of college students, there was one of three reactions: immediate recall of the correct word, failure to identify the word from the definition, or awareness of knowing the right word but not being able to recall it. This last reaction is a common phenomenon we all experience when a memory we are searching for is "on the tip of the tongue"—the TOT phenomenon (Brown & McNeil, 1966).

If these TOT words are really known and stored in memory, but are not available in the person's active-recall vocabulary, then it should be possible to demonstrate that many characteristics of the word can be retrieved through questioning. When asked to write down all the words they were thinking of as possible answers, subjects gave some words that were similar in *meaning* to the elusive TOT word, but more often they answered with words similar in *sound.* For the second question, they tended to answer "Siam," "Cheyenne," "Sarong," or "Saipan" more frequently than "junk" or "barge." They were also able to recall other details of the target word, such as its number of syllables and first letter.

You might want to demonstrate this phenomenon for yourself using your roommate or friends as subjects to see what they say while searching for *ambergris, sampan, nepotism,* and other words that might fall into the TOT category. From such research we learn that retrieval from memory storage is a complex process, rather than an all-or-none experience. And from our search experiences in such cases, we learn that our storage must include many aspects of the word, including sound, shape, and context, as well as meaning.

If you are asked whether a particular statement is true, you can answer most quickly if it involves a concept familiar to you. You also have more confidence in your answer. By contrast, where you must check less well-established memories, your retrieval processes will be slower, more conscious and intentional, and more uncertain because there are fewer possible routes to the material.

Methods of retrieval. You might assume that you either know something or don't, so that any method of testing what you know would give the same results. Not so. The two most used methods—recall and recognition—give quite different results.

Recall means reproducing the information to which you were previously exposed. A recall question might be, "What are the three memory systems?" **Recognition** means realizing that a certain stimulus event is one you have seen or heard before. A recognition question might be, "Which is the term for a visual sensory memory: (a) echo; (b) engram; (c) icon; (d) abstract code?" By giving you different retrieval cues to work with, these two methods call for different mental processes on your part.

In trying to identify a criminal, the police would be using the recall method if they asked the victim to describe from memory what distinguishing features the person had: "Did you notice anything unusual about the attacker?"

They could use the recognition method in one of two ways. With one technique, the victim might be shown photos from a file of criminal suspects, one at a time, and asked whether any of them was the attacker. The other technique would be to see if the victim could pick out a suspect in a police line-up from among several others known not to have committed the crime.

Both recall and recognition require a search using the cues given. Recall questions usually give you fewer cues to use than recognition questions and less specific ones. And even when both lead to a successful search, the next stage is different. For recognition, you need simply to match a remembered stimulus against a present perception; both are in

▽ ▮ Figure 9.9   *Flow Chart of Hypothesized Memory System*

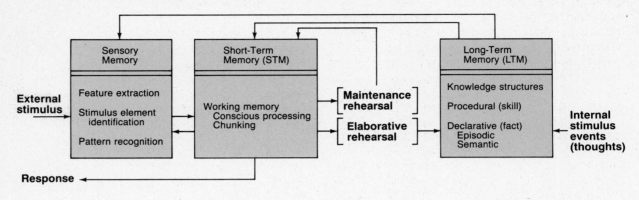

Storage:
   sensory
Capacity:
   large
Duration:
   brief (to 2 sec.)
Loss due to:
   time decay
   displacement (masking)

Storage:
   acoustic
   visual
   semantic
Capacity:
   small (7 + 2 chunks)
   increase by chunking
Duration:
   temporary (to 20 sec.)
   without rehearsal
Loss due to:
   time decay
   interference
   lack of rehearsal

Storage:
   semantic networks
   (organized, meaningful)
Capacity:
   unlimited
Duration:
   permanent
Loss due to:
   inadequate encoding
   time decay
   interference
   failure to consolidate
   motivated forgetting
   retrieval failure

your consciousness. But for recall, you must reconstruct from memory something that is not in the present environment and then describe it well enough that an observer can be sure from your words or drawings that it really is in your mind.

So it is hardly surprising that you can usually recognize far more than you can recall. It also explains why students find true-false or multiple-choice tests (recognition) easier than fill-in tests (recall) and why recognition tests usually lead to better test performance—though not necessarily higher grades.

Two memories versus multiple levels

The presentation so far has been based on a theory of qualitatively different systems for short- and long-term memory. Known as the **duplex theory,** it postulates a flow of information from temporary sensory and short-term memory to more lasting long-term memory (Atkinson & Shiffrin, 1968); its main features are summarized in **Figure 9.9.**

Although the duplex theory is now widely accepted, it has been challenged in recent years. Critics believe that there may be a single system of memory in which the only differentiation is in levels of processing: deeper processing results in better and longer memory because more analysis, interpretation, comparison, and elaboration take place. This view is called the **levels of processing theory** (Cermack & Craik, 1979; Craik & Lockhart, 1972).

Consider three levels at which the word *memory* can be processed: (a) *physical,* in terms of its appearance, the size and shape of the letters; (b) *acoustic,* involving the sound combinations that distinguish it from similar sounds (such as "memo"); and (c) *semantic,* according to its meaning (memory as a mental capacity or product of remembering). Levels-of-processing theorists claim that these processes differ in "depth." It takes least "mental work" to process input at a physical (visual) level, more at an acoustic level, and still more at a semantic level. Moreover, within any of these three types of processing, there can also be variations in level. It should now require "deeper" processing for you to complete the sentence "Memory means . . ." than it did before you started this chapter because the word is now linked to many new concepts and associations beyond just "what people remember."

This levels-of-processing view is important because of the emphasis it places on the varying depths at which information can be processed. However, it is unlikely to replace the duplex theory. The notion of separate memory structures is bolstered by several lines of evidence, including studies of amnesia, brain responses, and serial position effects. Let's briefly review this evidence.

Nick's case of amnesia reveals a person who retains long-term memory for events *prior* to his brain injury, and a short-term memory for events currently taking place, but no ability to transfer new information from short-term to long-term memory. Other amnesiacs too have shown more impairment of long-term than short-term memory, suggesting that there must be two memory systems (Milner, 1966; Wingfield & Byrnes, 1981).

A second source of support for a separate short-term memory system comes from a physiological study of brain responses during a test of recall. A unique brain waveform (a particular *evoked potential*) was found to be related to recall in a standard task that measured memory for very recent events, within the short-term memory period. The researchers interpreted this as evidence for a memory storage system that holds incoming information for a short time (Chapman et al., 1978). We will also see in a later section that different biochemical processes seem to operate in temporary versus permanent storage of memory.

The third type of evidence supporting a dual memory system comes from studies of the *serial position effect* in episodic memory. When trying to remember a list of similar items, we recall best those at the beginning and end of the list, as shown in **Figure 9.10**. Presumably, all items would have been processed at the same level in this case. The difference in retention could, however, be explained by two memory systems. At testing time, the items at the beginning of the list would be safely in long-term storage and those at the end would still be in short-

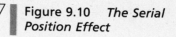
▽ **Figure 9.10** *The Serial Position Effect*

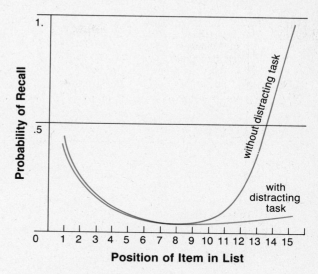

term memory. However, those in the middle would have neither advantage, and remembering them would be further hampered by interference from items before and after them.

This interpretation is further bolstered by the fact that when subjects are given a distracting task after exposure to the list but before the testing, the items in the last part of the list are recalled as poorly as those in the middle of the list, whereas early items are remembered as well as ever (Glanzer & Cunitz, 1966; Postman & Phillips, 1965).

This poorer memory for the middle position of any series—the serial position effect—is a general phenomenon that holds for different types of materials and different modes of presentation (Roediger & Crowder, 1976). For instance, in learning the alphabet, children make most errors on the middle letters (I to M). Most spelling errors also occur for letters in the middle of words. College students fail more exam items on material from the middle of a lecture than on material from the start or end of the lecture (Holen & Oaster, 1976; Jensen, 1962). So now you know what to devote some extra time and effort to—hit that middle! (You might also take note that this chapter is in about the middle of the book.)

REMEMBERING AS A CONSTRUCTIVE PROCESS

So far we have been talking as if we simply store and remember varying amounts of the information we receive. But sometimes what we "remember" is more than what we actually experienced or different from it in important ways. From laboratory studies of how people process and remember meaningful material, psychologists have been forced to a new conception of all remembering as a continuation of the active, *constructive* process of perception. According to this view, as we organize material to make it meaningful, we frequently add details to make it more complete or change it to make it fit better with other, already existing information in our personal memory store.

Adding new information to what we take in is a constructive process that happens when the given information seems incomplete and we proceed to fill in the rest to make a "good figure," as we saw in our study of perception of incomplete visual figures. In remembering, this process may involve putting material into a context that makes sense to us, or making inferences about events preceding the action experienced, unstated motives of the actors, or expected outcomes. For example, we see two friends parting and hear one say " . . . between 8 and 8:30." We may "remember" hearing them planning their next meeting though perhaps the time was related to something else entirely.

Changing information to make it conform to knowledge already in memory is a *distortion process.* When a new idea or experience is incompatible with our values, beliefs, or strongly felt emotions, it may be altered to be more consistent with our world view or self-concept. See **Figure 9.11** for the stimulus picture used in a classic study.

Subjects were shown this picture briefly and asked to describe it to someone who had not seen it, who in turn passed the information on to someone else, and so on. Before long, the razor, which was in the white man's hand in the original scene, was being described as being held by the black man (Allport & Postman, 1947).

Distortion can occur either at the encoding stage when the material is first processed or later at the retrieval stage, and perhaps even in between, during storage, as apparent inconsistencies and contradictions are dealt with. Usually we are quite unaware of such changes and confidently believe that our "memory" is an accurate record of what took place—surely not just a rumor transmission funnel (Spiro, 1977).

Schemas

The study of constructive processes is one of the most exciting new directions in memory research. Its focus is on how people organize, interpret, and retain meaningful input. Its most general principle is: *How and what you remember is determined by who you are and what you already know.*

Much of what we know seems to be stored as **schemas,** (or **schemata**), general conceptual frameworks or clusters of knowledge and preconceptions regarding certain objects, people, and situations and how they are related. Schemas give us expectations about what attributes we will find in future examples of various concepts and categories. For example, the term "registration day" probably conjures up a whole scene of noise, hassle, long lines, delay, and frustration. These features are all part of your schema for "registration day." To a political candidate, "registration day" will evoke quite a different schema.

Many of our constructions and distortions in remembering new information are the result of interpreting it in the light of expectations we have from existing schemas. Cues in the present input steer us to a particular schema and we proceed to fill in the rest of the picture from schema-relevant information.

The importance of schemas in helping us to organize and make sense of details—and remember them—has been shown in many studies (see Alba & Hasher, 1983).

In one study, a story read to the subjects included the following sentences: "Now three sturdy sisters sought proof. Forging along, sometimes through calm vastness, yet more often over turbulent peaks and valleys, days became weeks as many doubters spread fearful rumors about the edge."

Some subjects were given no title for this story, while others were told it was "Columbus Discovering America." The latter group recalled much more of the story, evidently because the title brought to mind a well-known schema (remember the Pinta, Nina, and Santa Maria?) that provided a meaningful con-

◁ **Figure 9.11**

Subjects were shown this picture in which the taller, better-dressed man is black and the man holding a razor is white. The fact that the scene became distorted as the subjects described it to others indicates that previously held beliefs can alter the processes of encoding and retrieval.

text for the ambiguously presented information (Dooling & Lachman, 1971).

In another study, some subjects read a story titled, "Watching a Peace March from the Fortieth Floor," while other subjects read the same story under the title, "A Space Trip to an Inhabited Planet." While most of the story was ambiguous enough to fit either title, one sentence fit only the space-trip title: "The landing was gentle, and luckily the atmosphere was such that no special suits had to be worn."

While more than half of those who were given the space-trip title remembered this sentence, only a few remembered it from the "peace-march" story. The titles seemed to have activated different schemas. For one schema the critical sentence fit, was interpreted as relevant, and was remembered; for the other it had no meaning and was lost or not retrievable (Bransford & Johnson, 1972).

We also have people-related schemas that can influence what we perceive and remember about people who are described to us (Cantor & Mischel, 1979b). For example, most of us have schemas for Republicans, cult leaders, environmentalists, and used-car salesmen. If a person we do not know is described as being a member of one of these categories, our schemas lead us to assume the presence of particular personality characteristics and also to have an emotional reaction favoring or disapproving the person.

On the other hand, when we hear several details about someone we do not know, we remember more of the details if we can relate them to an appropriate organizing schema.

Subjects were presented with a list of behaviors (ate lunch in the park, rented an apartment near work, etc.). Some of the subjects were told that this was a memory experiment and that they should try to remember as much of the information as possible. Other subjects were told that this was an experiment concerned with how people form impressions of others and that they should form an impression (or schema) of the person who had supposedly engaged in these behaviors.

After a short delay, all subjects were asked to recall as many of the behaviors as possible. The subjects who had processed the information in terms of a schema about a certain kind of person and thus in "more depth," remembered more than did those who tried to remember the same information as unrelated items on a list (Hamilton et al., 1980).

When we try to recall information that is not consistent with a schema we have formed about certain individuals, our memory may distort the input to make it more "schema-consistent." For example, if we are told that a couple are having a lot of disagreement during their courtship, but later are told that they are happily married, we are likely to forget about the earlier disagreement or else to be suspicious of their "happy" marriage. Either distortion permits a memory consistent with our schema. Where the same early information about disagreement is followed by a report of an *unhappy* outcome, we tend to remember the disagreement quite accurately (Spiro, 1977).

The same process is probably at work in the difficulty people have in learning and fairly representing an opponent's point of view. In political (and other) arguments both sides tend to remember the opposing viewpoint as oversimplified, less rational, and more extreme than their own, thereby achieving a more comfortable overall perspective of the problem and their relation to it.

Although the study of constructive processes in memory represents the "new look" in memory research, it was actually begun over fifty years ago by British psychologist Sir Frederick Bartlett and described in his classic book *Remembering* (1932). Bartlett's focus was on the kinds of construction that take place. His method was to observe how English undergraduates transmitted and remembered simple stories whose unfamiliar themes and wording were taken from another culture. His most famous story was "The War of the Ghosts," an American Indian tale, reproduced in **Figure 9.12** with a sample student narrative.

▽ **Figure 9.12** *Text from Bartlett's "War of the Ghosts" (1932) and a Sample Student Reproduction*

The War of the Ghosts

One night two young men from Egulac went down to the river to hunt seals, and while they were there it became foggy and calm. Then they heard war-cries, and they thought: "Maybe this is a war party." They escaped to the shore, and hid behind a log. Now canoes came up, and they heard the noise of paddles, and saw one canoe coming up to them. There were five men in the canoe, and they said:

"What do you think? We wish to take you along. We are going up the river to make war on the people."

One of the young men said: "I have no arrows."

"Arrows are in the canoe," they said.

"I will not go along. I might be killed. My relatives do not know where I have gone. But you," he said, turning to the other, "may go with them."

So one of the young men went, but the other returned home.

And the warriors went on up the river to a town on the other side of Kalama. The people came down to the water, and they began to fight, and many were killed. But presently the young man heard one of the warriors say: "Quick, let us go home: that Indian has been hit." Now he thought: "Oh, they are ghosts." He did not feel sick, but they said he had been shot.

So the canoes went back to Egulac, and the young man went ashore to his house, and made a fire. And he told everybody and said: "Behold I accompanied the ghosts, and we went to fight. Many of our fellows were killed, and many of those who attacked us were killed. They said I was hit, and I did not feel sick."

He told it all, and then he became quiet. When the sun rose he fell down. Something black came out of his mouth. His face became contorted. The people jumped up and cried.

He was dead.

Sample Reproduction

Two youths were standing by a river about to start seal-catching, when a boat appeared with five men in it. They were all armed for war.

The youths were at first frightened, but they were asked by the men to come and help them fight some enemies on the other bank. One youth said he could not come as his relations would be anxious about him; the other said he would go, and entered the boat.

In the evening he returned to his hut, and told his friends that he had been in a battle. A great many had been slain, and he had been wounded by an arrow; he had not felt any pain, he said. They told him that he must have been fighting in a battle of ghosts. Then he remembered that it had been queer and he became very excited.

In the morning, however, he became ill, and his friends gathered round; he fell down and his face became very pale. Then he writhed and shrieked and his friends were filled with terror. At last he became calm. Something hard and black came out of his mouth, and he lay contorted and dead.

a

b

Figure 9.13

A person who witnesses a car accident is likely to remember the accident as (a) less serious if the word hit *is used to describe it, and (b) more serious if the word* smashed *is used.*

Bartlett used two procedures to study how his subjects transformed this alien story into a coherent narrative that made sense to them.

In *serial reproduction,* one person would read the story and tell it from memory to a second person, who passed it on to a third, and so on. In *repeated reproduction,* the same person would read the story and retell it from memory over a number of repeated sessions (up to years apart). In both cases memory was very inaccurate—the "recalled" story that came out was often quite different from the story that went in. He found that constructive processes were intervening between input and output.

The original stories had evidently been unclear to the subjects because of a lack of understanding of the cultures represented. To get the stories to make more sense, the subjects unknowingly changed details to fit their own schemas. What came out of this process were coherent stories that were briefer, more clearly focused, and more understandable to the individuals—but not exactly what went into their memory system originally.

As demonstrated in the sample story, the distortions Bartlett found usually involved three kinds of constructive processes: (a) *leveling*—simplifying the story; (b) *sharpening*—highlighting and overemphasizing certain details; and (c) *assimilation*—changing the details to fit the subject's own background or knowledge better.

Eyewitness testimony

Juries tend to give much weight to the testimony of witnesses who were at the scene and report on what they saw "with their own eyes." But if memory is reconstructed to fit our schemas, how far should the memory of such witnesses be trusted?

The ease with which we can be misled into "remembering" information that was not present when we viewed a scene has been amply demonstrated in the laboratory research of Elizabeth Loftus (1979, 1984) and her colleagues. Bright college students with good memories have been misled into "recalling" that a *yield* sign was a *stop* sign, that a nonexistent barn was at the scene, that a green stop light was red,—and more.

The basic research design used in these studies typically involves two groups of people, both of whom view the same stimulus materials on film or slides. The experimental group later receive information designed to "contaminate" their memory, in the form of indirect suggestions that certain events were present or certain actions occurred. For example, they may hear another "witness" report something about a man's mustache when in fact the man had no mustache.

Evidence for the malleability of memory comes from comparing the recall of the original materials by these subjects with recall by the control subjects, who have been given no subsequent information. Although many subjects resist being misled, a significant proportion integrate the new information into their own memory representation and report the nonexistent mustache or other misinformation as part of what they saw.

Sometimes words are used in the questioning that suggest a particular interpretation. These words then function as misleading retrieval cues.

Subjects were shown a film in which a car accident occurred. Those who were later asked how fast the cars were going when they *smashed* into each other "remembered" the speed as about 25 percent faster than those who were asked how fast the cars were going when they *hit* each other (Loftus & Palmer, 1974). (See **Figure 9.13**.)

Such findings help explain the success of skillful lawyers in getting the responses they want from witnesses.

This line of research has practical, applied value and also contributes to basic knowledge (see Buckhout, 1980). Some courts of law are now recognizing the potential pitfalls of placing too much reliability on eyewitness testimony, while memory researchers are using this research paradigm to discover *how* memories are changed by subsequent information. Are they lost, suppressed, or blended? Researchers are also testing variables that extend or limit the general conclusion that "misleading mentions may make memories mucky" (see Bekerian & Bowers, 1983; McCloskey & Egeth, 1983).

Our capacity for constructive memory not only increases the problem of getting accurate eyewitness testimony but can shield us from some truths we do not want to accept. To the extent that it does so, we carry around a false picture of some aspects of reality. It makes bigots more bigoted because corrective information gets distorted and it makes all of us more likely to disregard new details in familiar contexts, where we remember what we expected.

Yet despite its faults, constructive memory is an enormously positive aspect of creative minds-at-work. More often than not, it helps us to make sense of our world by providing the right context in which to understand, interpret, remember, and act on minimal or fragmentary evidence. Without it, our memories would be little more than transcription services that would lose much of what transpired.

I don't mind being forgetful. The thing I hate is remembering that I forgot something.

WHY DO WE FORGET?

We all remember an enormous amount of material over long periods of time. College students can accurately recall many documented details surrounding the birth of a sibling sixteen years earlier when they were only three or four years old (Sheingold & Tenney, 1982). Conductor Arturo Toscanini, even at an advanced age, is reported to have known "by heart every note of every instrument of about 250 symphonic works and the words and music of about 100 operas"—plus many scores for other forms of music (Marek, 1975).

Knowledge in semantic memory is remembered even better than knowledge in episodic memory, regardless of the time interval since you experienced it. You will remember many basic things about psychology even if you forget your instructor's name and the details of taking the course. Within semantic knowledge, you will retain generalizations longer than details. For long-term retention, as for efficient encoding and retrieval, meaningful organization seems to be the key.

Yet even well-learned material may be lost over time. Why?

Explanations of forgetting

Forgetting can be understood in terms of several different theoretical perspectives. Each one states a viewpoint on what has happened to stored information when we cannot remember it:

1. *Decay*—it is lost over time, like the colors of a picture bleached by the sun.
2. *Interference*—it is blocked by similar inputs, as when multiple exposures of a negative interfere with the clarity of the original image.
3. *Retrieval failure*—it cannot be located, as when you can't find your car in a huge parking lot without knowing the appropriate section number.
4. *Motivated forgetting*—it is being hidden from consciousness for some personal reason, as when you forget the name of someone you don't like.

Let's look at each of these explanations in more detail.

Decay of memory traces. According to the first explanation, the primary problem is one of gradual *storage loss*. You remember what you wore yesterday better than what you wore last Wednesday and the details of today's lecture better than yesterday's.

Many memories clearly are lost or become "dim" or incomplete over time. On the other hand, to prove that decay is to blame for forgetting, we would have to prove that (a) no mental activity had occurred between original learning and the recall test that could have changed or interfered with the memories, and (b) they were in fact gone from the brain and not merely inaccessible for some reason. Although it seems plausible that decay is partly responsible for inability to remember things learned long ago, the only thing we can say with certainty is that decay is an important factor in sensory memory and in short-term memory when all maintenance rehearsal is prevented.

But some memories do *not* seem to become weaker. Recall that we mentioned that learned motor skills are retained for many years even with no practice. Once you learn to swim, you never forget how. In addition, trivia and irrelevant information, such as song titles and commercial jingles, seem to persist in memory.

Interference. We never learn anything in a vacuum; we are always having other experiences before and after we learn new material. Both our learning and our retention of new material are affected by interference from these other experiences. When the vocabulary list you learned yesterday interferes with your learning of today's list, the phenomenon is called **proactive interference** or PI (forward acting, earlier disrupts later). When studying today's list interferes with your memory for yesterday's list, the phenomenon is called **retroactive interference** or RI (backward acting, later disrupts earlier).

The greater the similarity between two sets of material to be learned, the greater the interference between them. Two vocabulary lists in the same foreign language would interfere with each other more than would a vocabulary list and a set of chemical formulas. Meaningless material is more vulnerable to interference than meaningful material, and the more difficult the distracting task, the more it will interfere with memory of material learned earlier.

Ebbinghaus, after learning dozens of lists of non-sense syllables, found himself forgetting about 65 percent of the new ones he was learning. Fifty years later, students at Northwestern University who learned Ebbinghaus' lists had the same experience. At first, they remembered much more. Then, after many trials with many lists, what they had learned earlier began to interfere proactively with their recall of current lists (Underwood, 1948, 1949).

Short-term memory seems most vulnerable to interference. Evidence from the studies of serial position effect, already mentioned, suggest that once material is consolidated in long-term memory, it is less subject to interference from later material.

Retrieval Failure. Often an apparent memory loss turns out to be only a failure of retrieval. A question worded a little differently will guide us to the information. Or a question requiring only recognition on our part will reveal knowledge that we could not get access to and reproduce by recall. Underwood's students who were having trouble recalling Ebbinghaus' lists often remembered better when retrieval cues were given. Some individuals can recall details under hypnosis for which they have no conscious memory at all; this is especially true of those with multiple personalities (discussed in Chapter 6). Penfield's studies (mentioned in Chapter 3) also revealed the retention of memories of which the individual had been unaware. And in cases of psychologically caused amnesia, the "forgotten" material is retained but blocked from retrieval, as can be shown when it is uncovered in psychotherapy.

In fact, research is even suggesting that some inability to remember events during infancy may be due to retrieval failure.

Three-month old babies learned to activate a mobile by kicking a foot to which a ribbon leading to the mobile was tied. But after eight days of no experience with the mobile, a test of retention showed no sign of memory for the previous learned response.

The experimenters then repeated the procedure except that this time they showed the infants the moving mobile the day before the test of retention. When the test was given, the learned response appeared as strong as ever, even when the test was as much as four weeks after the learning. The memory must have been present in the first part of the study but must simply not have been retrieved. The researchers hypothesized that much infant learning is kept alive by natural reinstatement of the retrieval cues in the child's ordinary environment. If this is true, it would provide a mechanism by which an in-

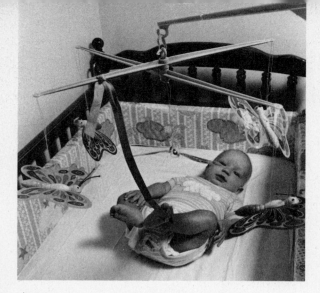

△ | *A baby's inability to remember what he or she has learned may be due to retrieval failure. This baby may learn to activate the mobile by kicking his foot, but he may not remember what he has learned a week later unless given a retrieval cue.*

fant's early experiences could continue to influence subsequent learning and behavior over an extended period (Rovee-Collier et al., 1980).

Even the best retrieval cues will not help if we did not store the material properly, just as a book not listed in the card catalogue is not retrievable in the library even if it is on a shelf somewhere. In any case, it seems clear that much of our failure to remember reflects poor encoding or inadequate retrieval cues rather than loss of the memory. Failure to call up a memory is never proof positive that the memory is not there.

Motivated forgetting. Sometimes we forget because we do not want to remember. We may push certain memories out of conscious awareness because they are too frightening, too painful, or too personally degrading. Rape victims, for example, sometimes cannot remember the details of their attack.

It was Sigmund Freud (1923) who first saw memory and forgetting as dynamic processes that enable the individual to maintain a sense of self-integrity. We all "forget" ideas we do not want to recognize as part of us, appointments we do not want to keep, names of people we do not like, and past events that threaten our basic sense of self or security. Freud gave the name **repression** to the mental process by which the person supposedly protects himself or herself from remembering unacceptable or painful information by pushing it out of consciousness. In Chapter 5 we reviewed experimental evidence for perceptual defense, in which painful or unpleasant information may be blocked out and hence neither perceived nor remembered.

Our motivational needs not only prevent retrieval of certain memories but can change the tone and content of memories that we do retrieve.

Research on childhood memories recalled by adults found that the most common emotion associated with the original experiences was *joy* (about 30 percent of the total). Next came *fear* (about 15 percent) followed by pleasure, anger, grief, and excitement. In general, unpleasant events were more often forgotten than pleasant events (Waldvogel, 1948).

Another study of early recollections revealed that many memories judged as traumatic by the researchers were selectively recoded by the subjects during recall as neutral or even pleasant. Evidently we can reconstruct our early childhood so that we remember the "good old days" not the way they were, but the way they "should have been" (Kihlstrom & Harackiewicz, 1982). Your parents are also likely to remember your childhood as more pleasant and less difficult than it really was (Robbins, 1963). (Try testing this idea with their recall of events you rate as positive or negative.)

The physical bases of forgetting— and remembering

Our analysis of how forgetting and remembering occur has been confined largely to an information-processing model of the encoding, storage, and retrieval of mental events at different stages of the memory system. But when we learn a new telephone number, learn to recognize a face, learn the contents of this chapter, or learn to avoid a dangerous stimulus, some lasting change is also occurring in the brain.

Physiological psychologists are beginning to identify the brain areas responsible for both laying down and losing memories. And at a more molecular level, researchers are searching for the biochemical mechanisms involved in memory formation and loss. One impetus to this new concern for finding out where memories are localized and how cells change when some brain region gives the command to "print that experience" has come from studying the losses of amnesiacs like Nick.

Amnesia and consolidation. Nick's amnesia was caused by an accident that destroyed a small part of his thalamus on the left side of his brain. This physical damage wiped out his ability to form new memories for facts but not memories for *images* (a right hemisphere function), for skills, or for facts learned before his accident. Nick's memory loss is similar to that of chronic alcoholic patients whose thalamus is also impaired. The thalamus is now considered to be essential for encoding new memories.

A comparison of Nick's amnesia with that of another well-studied research subject known as H.M. reveals some differences that point to two basically different kinds of memory failure. H.M.'s head injury as a child resulted in epileptic seizures which were surgically stopped by removal of most of two limbic system structures, the hippocampus and the nearby amygdala. His amnesia is more extensive than Nick's and differs in quality as well. For one thing, H.M. can learn new information but loses it very rapidly and cannot put a "time tag" on his new memories to mark when something occurred. He cannot fix the memory trace in the period following learning, while Nick's inability lies in creating memory traces at all. A second difference is that H.M. can't remember events that took place within a few years before his surgery, while Nick can recall events prior to his accident but cannot store new memories (Milner, 1966). H.M.'s amnesia is *retrograde* (backward-directed) *amnesia;* Nick's is *anterograde* (forward-directed) *amnesia.*

We now know that circuitry in the hippocampus is involved in "fixing" memories during some period of time following learning. This "fixing" process by which learned information is gradually transformed from a fragile, short-term memory to a durable, long-term memory code is called **consolidation** (Hebb, 1949). It is believed that the hippocampus helps make the connection between new and pre-existing information. The same memory loss as H.M.'s is seen in mentally disordered patients who receive electroconvulsive shocks in therapy. They lose recent memories. These shocks are believed to inactivate the hippocampus temporarily.

Memory consolidation begins immediately after a learning experience but may continue for years. H.M. lost only those memories that were not completely consolidated when his hippocampus was removed. Amnesia in such cases is now assumed to be a failure of memory storage, not of retrieval. The age of the memories at the time of brain tissue destruction determines whether they will be lost (if "too young" to be fully consolidated yet) or will be retrievable (if matured by consolidation).

Research on amnesia induced in rats by electroconvulsive shock indicates that consolidation of learned associations between stimuli (classical conditioning) depends on the hippocampus. Consolidation of learned associations between responses and consequences depends on cortical circuitry (Schneider, 1975). (For illustration of the structures of the brain mentioned here, see Chapter 3, p. 98.)

Biochemical mechanisms. Retrograde amnesia can also be caused by deep cooling of the body and by certain substances that inhibit protein synthesis. These amnesias can be overcome or weakened by later administration of a variety of drugs, among them strychnine, ether, amphetamine, and the hormone vasopressin (McGaugh & Herz, 1972). In fact, a team of researchers at the National Institute of Mental Health have found that vasopressin can enhance memory on a variety of tasks for both mentally disordered patients with cognitive impairments and normally functioning college students (Weingartner et al., 1981).

Our experiences have many effects on our mental and physical functioning: they provide sensory information, arouse the brain to thought and/or action, and release hormones. But only some of our experiences leave lasting impressions. Evidence is accumulating that one of the functions of hormones is to act as internal modulators of lasting memories (McGaugh, 1983). Several hormones released by stressful experiences have been shown to enhance retention, apparently by influencing brain processes that are responsible for memory storage. Some hormones (epinephrine, ACTH, and vasopressin) can either enhance or impair retention of learned experiences, under different conditions (Izquierdo et al., 1982). Hormones may prevent storage of an excessive amount of nonessential information or may block memory for painful and traumatic experiences, such as the pain of childbirth.

The specific biochemical mechanisms responsible for learning, memory, and forgetting are still a matter of speculation. Evidence seems to be pointing to a change in the properties of the membranes of some postsynaptic nerve cells as the mechanism for long-term storage. It appears that some synaptic connections can be permanently altered by repeated stimulation, while others continue to process new input in the same way, unchanged in any lasting way by experience (see Routtenberg, 1980).

The specific physical change that occurs in some cortical cells appears to take place at bumps, or spines, that stick out from the long-branching dendrites. In Chapter 3 (p. 95) we saw that animals reared in "enriched" environments learned and remembered better than animals reared in "impoverished" environments and were later found to have thicker cortical areas and more dendritic branches. They were also found to have a much greater number of these dendritic spines and to have synapses with a larger area of contact (Hubbard, 1975; Rosenzweig et al., 1972).

A current hypothesis suggests that when the dendritic spines change, they do so because the neurotransmitter that crosses the synaptic gap causes a calcium ion to enter the spine and activate a substance called *calpain.* Calpain works on the membrane to build up more receptors that act like "catchers' mitts," enabling the cell to catch new incoming messages more reliably (Lynch, 1984).

The new search for the engram. After a futile search for the place where memories are stored, psychologist Karl Lashley (1929, 1950) gave up, concluding that memories are not localized in any one spot in the brain but involve large parts of the brain. Lashley used the term **engram** for the hypothetical neurological change that he was looking for; current researchers use the term **memory trace** and think of it as a unit of information storage in the nervous system. In recent years, there has been growing evidence that Lashley did not look in the right places and did not realize that there are many different kinds of memory involving different brain circuits.

We distinguished earlier between skill and fact learning. The skill-learning center may be located in the basal ganglia striatum, a structure evolutionarily even more primitive than the limbic system. The limbic system (containing both the hippocampus and the amygdala) seems to be responsible for fact memories. It is also possible to show that there are at

◁ *Psychologist Richard Thompson has investigated where memories are stored in the brain. He has concluded, through research with rabbits, that the cerebellum is the likely site of storage for simple conditioned learning.*

least two distinct memory circuits in the limbic system, one for spatial memory, the other for emotional memory. The information that gives an image its geographical context involves signals from the visual cortex to the hippocampus, which then stimulates the thalamus to encode the memory. Emotional memories appear to work through the amygdala rather than the hippocampus (Mishkin, et al., in press).

Complex memories involve a number of sites in the cerebral cortex, but the memory for a simple conditioned response is now believed to be localized in the cerebellum. Richard Thompson and his research team have demonstrated that a lesion of only one cubic millimeter of cell tissue in the cerebellum of a rabbit causes permanent loss of a conditioned eyeblink to a tone that signals an air puff to one eye. The memory deficit is highly specific only to that learned association: the animal can still respond to the air puff, hear the tone, and learn the conditioned response in the other eye but cannot relearn the response in the first eye (McCormick et al., 1982).

The entire circuitry for learning and storing this simple conditioned response has been traced down to specific nuclei in and around the cerebellum. In more complex conditioning, as when there is a delay between the tone and the air puff, circuits in the hippocampus also become involved (McCormick & Thompson, 1984).

The discovery of exactly where and how learning and memory take place in the human nervous system will open exciting possibilities for aiding people with learning disabilities and memory impairments, such as those seen with the progressive deterioration of the brain in Alzheimer's disease. For Thompson and other researchers, the immediate goal is to understand how the brain works to produce a mind stocked with the valuable lessons provided by experience. "Without memory, there can be no mind. Memory is the essential brain substrate for all higher mental processes" (Thompson, 1984, p. 5).

A memory may be vulnerable to distortion and loss over time, and we could all improve the ways we commit information to memory. But to psychologists, memory is the "Queen of the Cognitive Sciences," and to poets, the very center of one's being.

I have a room whereinto no one enters
  Save I myself alone:
    There sits a blessed memory on a throne,
There my life centres; . . .

Christina Rossetti, "Memory"

SUMMARY

■ Remembering is studied by cognitive psychologists as a way of processing information. It is seen as a three-stage process in which information that arrives through our senses is encoded, stored, and later retrieved. Three separate memory systems have been proposed: sensory, short-term, and long-term memory.

■ In encoding for sensory memory, stimulus energy is changed to a neural code. Sensory memory has a large capacity but a very short duration. Attention and pattern recognition help sensory information to get into short-term memory.

■ Short-term memory has a limited capacity (7 ± 2 items) and lasts only twenty seconds without rehearsal. It is part of our psychological present and is also called the working memory. Material may be transferred to it from either sensory or long-term memory; only here can information be consciously processed.

■ Information entering short-term memory from sensory memory is usually encoded acoustically. Its capacity can be increased by chunking of isolated items into meaningful groups. Maintenance rehearsal extends the duration of material in short-term memory indefinitely; elaborative rehearsal prepares it for long-term storage.

■ Long-term memory constitutes the person's total knowledge of the world and of the self; it is unlimited in capacity. Meaningful organization is the key to encoding for long-term memory: the more familiar the material and the better the organization, the better the retention.

■ The more specifically material is encoded in terms of expected retrieval cues, the more efficient later retrieval will be. Similarity in context and mood between learning and retrieval also aids retrieval.

■ Procedural (skill) knowledge and declarative (fact) knowledge seem to be stored differently, as are the two kinds of declarative memories—episodic and semantic. Research on patients with amnesia (selective forgetting due to partial brain damage) reveals that one of these types of memories may be retained while another is lost. Declarative memory is evidently a more recently evolved capacity than procedural memory.

■ Investigators disagree about how many memory codes there are—whether only verbal, both verbal and visual, or some other combination or relationship.

■ There is also disagreement about whether there are actually three different memory systems (sensory, short-term, and long-term) or whether we simply process memories at different levels, i.e., use varying depths of processing.

■ Remembering is a constructive process and not simply a recording one. We remember what we want to and what we are prepared to remember. Schemas play a major role in constructive memory processes. Schemas are cognitive clusters built up from earlier experience which provide expectations and a context for interpreting new information and thus influence what is remembered. Information or misinformation provided during retrieval can bias our recall without our realizing it.

■ Explanations for forgetting include decay, interference, retrieval failure, and motivated forgetting. Each one is shown to play a role in some specific instances of forgetting.

■ The physical bases of remembering and forgetting are not yet known, though the brain circuits involved in different kinds of stored knowledge are being identified. Electroshock following learning interferes with the consolidation of new memories. A number of drugs are being discovered that can either facilitate or inhibit the establishment of new memories.

■ The specific biochemical mechanisms responsible for learning, remembering, and forgetting are still a matter of speculation. It appears that memory may involve lasting changes in the membranes of post-synaptic cells at some synapses. Specific neurotransmitters and hormones such as epinephrine may play an important role in fixing or "printing" memories. Active research is in progress to find the physical basis for memory traces.

10

THINKING AND COMMUNICATING

■ STUDYING THINKING
Cognition and the cognitive approach
Studying the unobservable

■ MENTAL STRUCTURES FOR THINKING
Concepts
Propositions
Schemas and scripts
Visual images and cognitive maps

■ KEYS TO COMPREHENSION
Integrating the unknown into the known
Revising mental structures and reducing discrepancy

■ MAKING DECISIONS AND JUDGMENTS
Utility and probability
Sources of error in decision making

■ SOLVING PROBLEMS
Well-defined and ill-defined problems
Understanding the problem
Finding the best search strategy: algorithms or heuristics?

■ IMPROVING COGNITIVE SKILLS
Acquiring and perfecting skills
Becoming an expert
Metacognitive knowledge

■ COMMUNICATING THOUGHTS
Verbal and nonverbal communication
The relation between language and thought
Criteria for "true" language
Is language uniquely human?

■ SUMMARY

Allow me to introduce you to a very exceptional creature, "Clever Hans." Hans was a remarkable horse who performed his intellectual feats in Germany around the turn of the century. He became a legend in his time because it appeared that he could read German, spell, comprehend complex questions, count, do mathematical operations—and that he possessed a remarkable memory.

Skeptical? So were the members of a scientific investigating commission who carefully checked out each of the claims of his trainer, Mr. von Osten, and those of many witnesses. However, they concluded that Hans was indeed clever-as-claimed, a "horse of a different color" who could think and reason about as well as most humans.

An animal who could perform higher mental processes that are assumed to be limited to humans challenges basic conceptions about the evolution of human intelligence. So, let us maintain our scientific skepticism a little longer while reviewing some of the observations reported by that Berlin Commission.

". . . The stately animal, a Russian trotting horse, stood like a docile pupil, managed not by the means of a whip, but by gentle encouragement and frequent reward of bread or carrots. He would answer correctly nearly all of the questions which were put to him in German. If he understood a question, he immediately indicated this by a nod of the head, if he failed to grasp its import, he communicated the fact by a shake of the head. We were told that the questioner had to confine himself to a certain vocabulary, but this was comparatively rich and the horse widened its scope daily without special instruction, but by simple contact with his environment. . . .

"Our intelligent horse was unable to speak, to be sure. His chief mode of expression was tapping with his right forefoot. A good deal was also expressed by means of movements of the head. Thus, 'yes' was expressed by a nod, 'no' by a deliberate movement from side to side; and 'upward,' 'downward,' 'right,' 'left,' were indicated by turning the head in these directions. . . .

"Let us turn now to some of his specific accomplishments. He had, apparently, completely mastered the cardinal numbers from 1 to 100 and the ordinals to 10, at least. Upon request he would count objects of all sorts, the persons present, even to distinctions of sex. Then hats, umbrellas, and eyeglasses. . . . Small numbers were given with a slow tapping of the right foot. With larger numbers he would increase his speed, and would often tap very rapidly right from the start. . ." (Pfungst, 1911, pp. 18–24).

So Clever Hans was tapping his way to stardom, until one day when someone noticed that he could not solve any of the problems posed to him when his trainer stood *behind* him. There were two other circumstances under which Hans had trouble: when the person asking a question did not know the answer, or when blinders covered Hans' eyes.

What was happening? Can *you* shut your eyes and figure it out? If you can, then you are able to think in ways that Hans could not.

The key to the puzzle is the evidence that Hans had to see the person who gave him the problem and that that person had to know the answer. It turned out that Hans had learned to respond to subtle visual cues unintentionally displayed by the questioners as to when to start tapping and when to stop, also when to nod "yes" or when to make a "no" motion. They expected him to think and reason and communicated their expectations nonverbally, without realizing it or intending to cheat. Hans surely was skilled at detecting these cues—and at learning the association between stopping his tapping and getting the carrot reward. But however good his horse sense, Hans never had "people sense"; he could tap all right, but he never really understood the lyrics. (For a fuller account of the Clever Hans phenomenon see Seboek & Rosenthal, 1981, and also Fernald, 1984.)

In order to figure out why Hans was not solving problems through the exercise of reason, you had to exercise yours. In doing so, you affirmed the greatest achievement of the human species—the ability to think abstract and complex thoughts.

In this chapter we will see how psychologists study thinking. We will look first at some of the ways objects and events are represented in thought and how these mental representations are used for understanding and responding to environmental challenges. Then we will look at some of the ways higher mental processes are used in making decisions and solving problems and how cognitive skills can be improved. Finally, we will inquire about the relationships between thoughts, as the silent contents of our private experience, and language, as the vehicle for their public expression, and at the question of whether only humans possess the gift of communicating by means of a grammar-based language.

STUDYING THINKING

Seventeenth-century philosopher René Descartes' classic statement, "Cogito, ergo sum" ("I think, therefore I am"), was a recognition that our sense of personal identity depends on an awareness of our own thought processes. It is thinking that turns our violations of moral codes into "guilt," our inappropriate or stupid deeds into "shame," and our accomplishments into "pride."

Only humans have the capacity to think about what was, is, will be, might be, and should be. Thinking provides the context for our perception, the purposes for our learning, and the meaning for our memories. Thinking interprets our existence. Humans are not only information processors but also information interpreters, ambiguity resolvers, event predictors. It is our thoughts in the inner universe of the mind that enable us to form an abstract working model of the outside world (see Hunt, 1982)—and then to use it to go about trying to improve what we don't like about that world.

Cognition and the cognitive approach

The study of thinking is the study of all the "higher mental processes." **Cognition** is a general term for all forms of knowing. These include attending, remembering, reasoning, imagining, anticipating, planning, deciding, problem solving, and communicating ideas. Cognition includes processes that mentally represent the world around us, such as classifying and interpreting; processes that we generate internally, as in dreams and fantasies; and the content of these processes, such as concepts, facts, and memories. The study of these higher mental processes and structures is called **cognitive psychology.** Cognitive psychologists investigate how people take in information, how they transform and manipulate it in various ways, and also how they store and retrieve it.

Besides the mental activities we normally associate with thinking, such as solving physics problems and making business judgments, psychologists who study cognition are also interested in many mental processes you may not have associated with *thinking.* Examples are the development of motor skills and the perceptual-cognitive process of pattern recognition by which you can tell that a blob of light waves out there is in fact your mother (our earlier concern in Chapters 4 and 5).

As we have seen, modern psychology has been shifting from its earlier emphasis on outer behavior and its external determinants to a concern for understanding the inner, private information processing that goes on out of sight but gives observed behavior its direction, meaning, and coherence. What early psychologists used to consider an inaccessible "black box" has become the primary focus of cognitive psychology, with new tools and strategies to open and explore its content and organization. The shift in focus began in the late 1950s with the convergence of an unlikely threesome of new research approaches involving computers, children, and communication.

1. Researchers Herbert Simon and Alan Newell used computers to simulate human problem solving, providing new ways of studying mental processes (Newell, Shaw, & Simon's "Elements of a Theory of Human Problem Solving," 1958).
2. Psychologist Jean Piaget was pioneering a successful way of inferring children's mental processes in understanding physical realities from observations of how they solved tasks and described events (Piaget's *The Construction of Reality in the Child,* 1954).
3. Linguistic researcher Noam Chomsky's studies of language showed that expression of ideas through language was not merely reinforced verbal behavior but part of a unique cognitive system for comprehension and production of symbols (Chomsky's *Syntactic Structures,* 1957).

These three new approaches to thought, coming at approximately the same time, boosted the scientific legitimacy of research on higher mental processes. Since then, the cognitive approach has gradually achieved a central position not only in the study of thinking but in many other areas of contemporary psychology as well (Mayer, 1981). Cognitive theory has become the guiding viewpoint in the psychology of the 1980s. We have already noted its importance in research on consciousness, learning, and memory and will see further evidence of the influence of cognitive processes in our study of stress, personality, therapy, and social psychology. In fact, an exciting new interdisciplinary field, **cognitive science,** has developed as a broad approach to studying the systems and processes that manipulate information. Cognitive science draws on the overlapping disciplines of cognitive psychology, linguistics, computer science, psychobiology, anthropology, and philosophy.

Studying the unobservable

If your thinking is an internal, private process that only you can experience, how can it ever be studied scientifically? Several general approaches and many specific methods have been tried, of which the most important will be reviewed briefly here: refinements on the method of introspection, observing subject's behavior, measuring reaction time, analyzing errors, recording eye and muscle movements, and comparing brain waves.

Introspection and think-aloud protocols. *Introspection,* as we saw in Chapter 1, was developed by pioneering psychologist Wilhelm Wundt in the late 1800s. It involved training people to analyze the contents of their own consciousness into component parts, such as sensations, images, and feelings. It yielded catalogues of these "elements" of consciousness but no clues about actual sequences of mental processes in life situations. And when the introspections of two people differed in the same situation, there was no empirical way to resolve the discrepancy.

A more serious problem with introspection becomes apparent when we realize that many or most of our mental processes are not even available for *our own* conscious inspection. As we saw in Chapter 6, an enormous amount of routine information processing occurs swiftly, almost automatically, *out of conscious awareness.* In the five seconds or so that it took you to read that last sentence, you identified the letters and words, retrieved the stored meaning of each of them, and hopefully comprehended the overall meaning of the sentence. You even began to store that unit of information away under different retrieval labels for ready access should it appear on a test. Do you know *how* you did *what* you just did so efficiently?

For an example of the method of introspection, try to introspect on your thoughts as you answer the following questions as quickly as possible. (The answers are in the footnote on page 344.)

a. What name of an animal begins with *I*?
b. What series of letters comes after BCZYMCDYXN? (Hint: the first subset ends at M.)

How did you find an answer for the first question? the second question? Could you follow your thoughts in both cases? If they were different, why?

Introspection can be used to supplement other methods, but it can never be a general technique for studying cognition. For that, we need a net broad enough to catch all the essentials of the events we are studying, and we must satisfy the basic requirement of any science—objective, repeatable measurements.

Recently, however, researchers have found a way to use introspection as an exploratory procedure to help map more precise research. During the actual process of working on a task, experimental subjects describe what they are doing and why. Their reports are called **think-aloud protocols.** Researchers use them to infer the mental strategies used and the ways knowledge is represented.

An example of the use of think-aloud protocols was cited in Chapter 9 in the report of a subject's ability to remember 80 digits. Another example was an investigation of how people plan everyday shopping trips.

Subjects were presented with a map of a city containing several stores and businesses. They were given several items to purchase and required to plan a day's shopping trip thinking aloud while they planned.

From the protocols, the researchers discovered that planning is not a logical, organized, hierarchical process. Instead, it is an opportunistic process: we follow many trains of thought simultaneously, jumping back and forth as we discover information that is relevant to one line of thought or another (Hayes-Roth & Hayes-Roth, 1979).

This jumping around is in sharp contrast to the models of planning that are built into robots or computerized decision aids in business. These set up planning in a very systematic manner with main points and subpoints recognized and treated in a logical fashion. Because the think-aloud protocols show how people actually do proceed instead of how a purely logical approach assumes they ought to behave, such protocols have been collected in a wide variety of studies. They have proven to be particularly useful in studies of the cognitive processes involved in problem solving.

To experience the think-aloud protocol method, solve this problem noting each of the steps you take in a "talk-aloud" protocol.

$$946$$
$$- 357$$

Now ask someone over 50 to do this subtraction and explain each step. You will probably hear something "strange" like, "You borrow 1 from the 4 and use it with the 6 to make 16. (16 − 7 is 9.) Then you pay back 1 to the 5, making it 6 and borrow another 1 from the 9 to put with the 4 to make 14. (14 − 6 is 8.) You pay it back to the 3, making it 4, and subtract 4 from 9 to get 5. Answer 589."

That's the way your author and other people of his generation learned it. Younger people learned the simpler method of just borrowing across the top and leaving the bottom numbers alone.

Behavioral observation. Many situations can be devised in which inferences about mental processes can be made from observation of various aspects of outer behavior. The principle here is to set up a situation in which alternate behaviors are possible which would reflect different mental processes. From the behavior that occurs, inferences are then made about what mental events must have taken place.

In one case, for example, the experimenter was interested in finding out at what age babies begin to supplement simple perceiving by using mental representations of external objects that are not currently present.

> Each of eighty babies, ranging in age from about three to nine months, was observed while watching an electric train move around a circular track. The train entered a tunnel, was out of sight for a few moments, then exited and continued its circular path. The first appearance of the moving train stopped the babies' previous, random behavior, whatever their age; they seemed "frozen" in their intense observation of it. Most of them then tracked it steadily until it went out of sight into the tunnel. But they continued to look at the tunnel entrance ("like cats at a mouse hole"), unaware of the exit at the other end.
>
> Over the course of a few successive runs, however, the older babies (especially those seven months and older) began to look more toward the exit as soon as the train vanished from view (as can be seen in the photo). From their shift in focus without any change in the stimulus, the experimenter inferred that a new mental process was taking place. The babies seemed to be using stored experiences to anticipate a not-yet-present event (Nelson, 1971, 1974).

> In a more recent study, researchers played a peekaboo game with 7-month-old infants. The children smiled less and raised their eyebrows more when the adult who appeared from behind a screen was different from the one they had watched going behind the screen. This behavioral finding suggests that the children had a mental representation of the first adult and thus were experiencing surprise when the adult's appearance was different (Parrott & Gleitman, 1984).

Measuring reaction time. The elapsed time between the presentation of some stimulus or signal and the subject's response to it is known as **reaction time.** It is one of the oldest methods used to infer mental processing. In the preceding chapter you saw how Sternberg (1969) used measurement of reaction time to infer that retrieval from short-term memory involved a serial exhaustive search of all items in a remembered list.

The reaction-time technique is also being used to assess the steps in understanding the meaning of words that we read.

> In one situation, a subject who is seated before a video screen sees pairs of words appear and must decide as quickly as possible if they belong to the same semantic (meaning) category. One button is pressed if they are judged "same," another if "different." For example, when the pair COW-TIGER appears, the subject responds "same," requiring about three fourths of a second to do so.
>
> After several pairs are responded to, the word BANANA appears alone on the screen, followed less than a second later by APPLE. This time, the subject's response—"same"—requires a fifth of a second *less* than before, when the word pairs were presented together (Hunt, 1982).

▷ *This seven-month-old baby intently waits for the toy train to reappear from the tunnel. Nelson noted that babies this age and older were able to quickly learn visual tracking and anticipation and inferred that they must be using stored experiences to do so.*

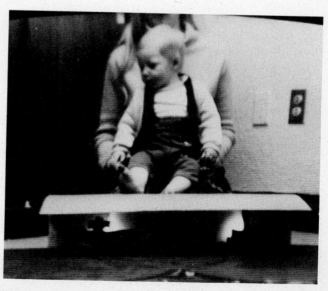

From this finding, the researcher concluded that one of the mental processes included in a subject's reaction time was looking up the meaning of each word in the "word dictionary" stored in long-term memory. When the first word of the pair was flashed early, its meaning must have been already retrieved before the second appeared, thus shortening the time required for deciding about their similarity. (For some background on the discovery and use of reaction time, see the **Close-up** on p. 345.)

Analyzing errors. When we come to a wrong conclusion, make an illogical inference, or remember something incorrectly, it is assumed that our errors probably are not random but reflect systematic properties of the thought processes involved. Analysis of thought errors can give us clues about these properties. This was the technique that revealed people's tendency to store *sounds* of letters in short-term memory rather than images of the visually presented letters, as mentioned in the preceding chapter. When trying to recall a short list of letters just displayed on a computer screen, subjects tended to make errors that confused letters which *sounded* alike such as F and S, rather than those that *looked* alike such as F and E (Conrad, 1964).

Sigmund Freud (1904/1914) pioneered in analyzing speech errors—slips of the tongue—to detect latent sexual or hostile impulses. For example, a person pretending to like you might say, "I'll never remember the first time I met you" (instead of "never forget"). Recently researchers have suggested that such slips may in fact be limited expressions (verbal-only performances) of intentions the speaker never did intend to carry out in overt action (Norman, 1981).

Slips of the tongue also provide evidence of how the human mind represents language structures. For example, an English-language speaker might exchange initial consonants ("tips of the slung" for "slips of the tongue") but never would say "stip the of tlung," which would violate several grammatical rules (Fromkin, 1980).

Recording eye and muscle movements. Much of our thinking depends on gathering information from the environment. One of the primary ways we do this is through our eyes. Monitoring how people move their eyes—what they look at in a picture and for how long—can provide a rich source of data about the ongoing thought processes.

A record of a reader's fixations also provides considerable insight into the cognitive processes that occur in comprehension of the content.

One study used these two similar sets of sentences:

I

It was dark and stormy the night the millionaire was murdered.
The killer left no clues for the police to follow.

II

It was dark and stormy the night the millionaire died.
The killer left no clues for the police to follow.

Researchers showed one sentence pair or the other to each subject and measured the time it took to read them. They found that the second pair took about a half second longer to read than the first. This might be expected because in the second pair the reader had to make an inference that "the killer" mentioned in the second sentence referred to the cause of death of the millionaire in the first sentence. No such inference was required in the first pair since the word *murder* implied that there was a killer involved.

In addition to this reaction-time analysis, the researchers examined each subject's eye movements while reading these sentences. They found that most of the extra time spent on the second pair was taken up in longer eye fixations on the word "killer" and also on the word "died." These eye-movement patterns supported the hypothesis that an inference was being made about the meaning of the word *killer* during the reading of the second pair of sentences, but not the first. The subjects' eye movements provided a "window" into the private thoughts of a mind-at-work (Just & Carpenter, 1981).

Mental processes are often accompanied by small movements of appropriate muscles. For example, during thoughts about "pounding with a hammer," there may be electrical activity in the arm muscles (*electromyograms,* or *EMG*) that can provide a measure of the invisible thinking. Or if you imagine "telling someone off," there may be patterns of muscle activity around your mouth and throat, similar to the overt responses that would actually express the thought—"Who do you think you are?"—(see Lang, 1979).

Answers to the questions on page 342 are (a) there aren't many animals whose names begin with *I*—two are ibis and impala; and (b) the next series of letters would be DEXWO.

Taking Time to Think

The relationship between reaction time and thought can best be appreciated if we examine it from a historical perspective. Reaction time studies fall roughly into four chronological periods:

1. In 1796 an assistant to the Astronomer Royal was fired from his post at the Greenwich Observatory because he consistently recorded the transit of a star about one second later than the Astronomer Royal himself. Not much scientific note was taken of this discrepancy until 1819, when the German astronomer Friedrich Bessel became interested in such "errors" of observation. He carefully compared his own reports of stellar transits with those of other astronomers, and found consistent differences. Bessel expressed these differences in the form of an equation. For example, the difference between the reports of Walbeck, another astronomer, and himself was:

W (Walbeck) − B (Bessel) = 1.041 sec.

This phenomenon of consistent discrepancies in observation was called the *personal equation.* The concept was one of the first instances of the systematic study of *individual differences* in behavior, a precursor of the concept of personality traits as an explanation for differences in reaction to the same situation.

2. Before 1850, scientists believed that impulses were conducted instantaneously along the nerves. However, in that year, Helmholtz demonstrated (a) that nerve conduction took time, and (b) that the time it took could be measured, as we saw in Chapter 3. Helmholtz administered a weak electric shock first to a man's toe and later to his thigh. The difference between the man's reaction times to these two stimuli was the measure of the speed of conduction in the sensory nerves. These experiments were the first true studies of reaction time ever to be done.

3. After Helmholtz had shown that there is an interval of time between a physical stimulus and a person's physiological response to it, scientists began to think that this might be a good measure of a person's mental processes. From the 1850s to about the 1930s, reaction time was studied under a variety of conditions, using different versions of a measuring device called the *chronoscope.* It was found that *simple reaction time,* the single response to a single stimulus is shorter than *discrimination reaction time,* in which different stimuli are presented and the subject responds only to a designated one. The longest time is taken by *choice reaction time,* in which there are several different stimuli and a different response must be made for each of them.

4. Adopting the principle that complex mental processes take more time than simple ones, present-day researchers are using reaction time in a number of research designs to infer the occurrence of various cognitive processes (as described in this chapter).

A large body of evidence suggests that covert oral responding occurs reliably in many situations. Both children and college students have been found to show physical activity in the mouth and throat while engaged in silent reading. Even dreams with a conversational content are accompanied by muscular activity in the dreamer's lips and throat (McGuigan, 1978).

Comparing brain waves. As we saw in Chapter 3, stimuli elicit electrical waves in the brain that can be measured at the scalp. Brain waves evoked by stimulus events are called **evoked potentials,** or *event-related potentials,* to distinguish them from the spontaneous electrical activity that is going on all the time in the living brain. At first, such a brain wave reflects properties of the stimulus, such as its intensity, but then it begins to reflect cognitive processes, such as evaluation. For example, the evoked potential is larger for unusual words or unexpected stimuli than for ordinary, expected ones, as when a subject processes the last word in a sentence like "He took a sip from the *computer*" (Donchin, 1975; Woods et al., 1980).

These precise measurements (and others being developed) are helping us understand the stages we go through in processing information. They can begin to resolve disputes about different conceptual models of what is happening inside that formerly mysterious "black box" of the mind. So mental processes are no longer as inaccessible to the scientist as they were when introspection was the only method available for studying mental activity.

MENTAL STRUCTURES FOR THINKING

In the last chapter we saw that remembering starts when "top-down" processing uses stored information to help us make sense of perceptual information coming to us from the outside world. It is as though we match our inner structures against the sensory input, enabling us to identify it as new or familiar, dangerous or desired, useful or irrelevant. This process of pattern recognition, however rudimentary, helps new input to get past the sensory register into short-term memory. Once there, further organizing processes may help us store it more permanently in long-term memory. Pattern recognition and the later organizational processing, in turn, are the first stages of our "higher mental processes"—the beginnings of what we call *thinking*. They go beyond the information supplied by the sensory input by using stored knowledge to interpret it (see Bruner, 1973).

As already indicated, our major task in storing information is to build an abstract working model of the outside world to use in our encounters with it. Some of the mental structures we seem to use in doing this, such as schemas, propositions, and abstract codes, were mentioned in the last chapter. Others include concepts, scripts, and cognitive maps. Actually, understanding of the forms of representation that we use remains fragmentary, often reflecting the hypotheses and research of particular psychologists who have started with different questions and definitions and used different methodologies. Thus schemas are associated with Bartlett, cognitive maps with Tolman, and so on.

There is ongoing controversy among investigators about a number of basic issues in cognitive psychology. It will be better data that will decide these issues. In this section we will look more closely at mental structures being investigated in current research on thinking.

Concepts

Imagine a world in which every object and every event looked new to you, unrelated to anything that had happened before. Getting burned yesterday would have taught you nothing about how to respond to a hot object today. In such a world of perpetual novelty, with no ways to classify information, you could not build on your experience one day for more effective behavior the next. Fortunately, you have the capacity to respond to stimuli not as unique, unrelated sensory events but as instances of categories that you have formed through your experiences. This ability to categorize individual experiences—to take the same action toward them or give them the same label—is regarded as one of the most basic abilities of living organisms (Mervis & Rosch, 1981). Recall from Chapter 2 that from the start infants are able to categorize objects in their environment—an apparently innate cognitive ability.

The categories we form are called **concepts**. Unlike memories, which are mental representations of specific happenings, concepts are mental representations of *kinds* of things. A concept may represent a kind of *object*, such as a ball; a kind of *event*, such as walking or talking; or a kind of *living organism*, such as a person or a horse. A concept can also represent a kind of *property*, such as red or large, or an

"'Dog, dog, pigeon, dog, . . .?' — You're a city kid, aren't you?"

abstraction, such as truth or love, or even a *relation,* such as smarter than, which tells us about a relative difference between two organisms but does not tell us about either of the individuals being compared (see E. Smith & Medin, 1981).

Critical features or prototypes? What do we store when we store a concept in memory? Do we store a definition, including the characteristics that a stimulus must have to be recognized as an instance of that concept? Or do we store a cluster of characteristics that *tend* to be found, with more typical examples of the concept having more of the characteristics?

In Chapter 5 we considered this same question in our discussion of what enables us to recognize a figure as a capital *A.* When we tried to define a capital *A* by listing critical features that all *As* must have, but that would exclude all non-*As,* we found that it did not work because certain unusual *As* did not qualify as *As* under our definition, whereas certain kinds of non-*As* did. Also, even among the examples of *As* that had all the required features, some looked like better, more representative *As* than others. This suggested that our categories may be structured around representative instances, or *prototypes,* rather than lists of necessary and sufficient features. But when we then tried to figure what were the most representative, most typical features of capital *As,* we again found that not all non-*As* were excluded. Some combination of these two theoretical approaches seemed to be required to explain how it is that we are in fact able to recognize all *As* and reject all non-*As.*

Since pattern recognition is a "top-down" process in which perceptual information is being matched against our stored concepts, we run into the same dilemma when we try to understand the basis on which we form those concepts in the first place. Though the question has not been resolved, it may be that the bases are somewhat different for different kinds of concepts. For example, concepts in science are often based on definitions of critical features: "Mammals are vertebrates that nurse their young." Here the boundaries between categories are clear and a list of critical features seems to work. Such concepts have also been called *logical concepts.*

But what about the concept *bird?* A dictionary definition is "a warm-blooded vertebrate with feathers and wings." Yet if you were asked to build a cage for a bird, you would probably visualize a robin-sized bird and construct a cage that would be far too small for an ostrich or a penguin—both of which are also birds. Your concept of bird seems to include something about *typicality*—the most typical member of the class—which goes beyond the list of features that qualifies creatures for birdhood.

Or consider the concept *game.* There is no single property that card games, video games, football games, Olympic games, and cooperative games all have in common. Nevertheless we regard them all as in some sense instances of our concept *game.* They share a "family resemblance" much as the members of a family do, where different children show somewhat different combinations of traits but can be recognized by outsiders as belonging to the same family.

Many—perhaps most—of our concepts in everyday life are like this. We can identify clusters of properties that different instances of the concept tend to share, but there may be no one property that *all* instances show. And we consider some instances as more representative of the concept—more typical of our mental prototype—than others. Such concepts are called *fuzzy concepts* because they have more poorly defined boundaries than concepts in science (Zadeh, 1965). They have also been called *natural concepts* or *probabilistic concepts.*

> Is a robin a bird? yes_____ no_____
> Is an ostrich a bird? yes_____ no_____

The psychological reality of typicality in categories is shown in the research finding that typical instances can be more quickly verified as members of a category than less representative ones. Reaction time in determining whether a robin is a bird is quicker in the example above because robins are more typical birds than ostriches are (Kintsch, 1981; Rosch et al., 1976).

Typicality, or representativeness, has practical implications too. Suppose you were given the job of designing direction signs for a zoo. If you put up a sign with a picture of a penguin, people would expect a penguin display. For the general bird house, you would do better to use a picture of a more typical bird.

Hierarchies and basic levels. Concepts are often organized in hierarchies. You have the broad category of *bird,* as well as several subcategories like *robins, ducks, ostriches,* and so forth. Your *bird* cat-egory, in turn, is a subcategory of a still larger cate-gory, *animals,* which is a subcategory of *living things.* These concepts and categories are arranged in a *hierarchy* of levels, from the most general and abstract at the top, to the most specific and concrete at the bottom. They are also linked to many other con-cepts; some birds are edible, some are endangered, some are state birds, etc.

There seems to be an *optimal* level in such hier-archies for how people categorize and think about objects. That level—called the *basic level*—is the one that can be accessed from memory most quickly and used most efficiently. For example, think about the chair at your desk. It belongs to three obvious levels in a conceptual hierarchy: furniture, chair, and desk chair. For most purposes, it would be optimal to think of it as a *chair.* The lower level category, *desk chair,* would provide more detail than you generally need, whereas a higher level category, *furniture,* would not usually be precise enough. So the basic level here would be *chair.* In spontaneously naming objects, you would probably call it a "chair" rather than either a "piece of furniture" or a "desk chair." And if you were shown a picture of it, your reaction time would be faster if you were asked to verify ("yes" or "no") that it was a chair than if you were asked to verify that it was a piece of furniture (see Rosch, 1978). It is now believed that dependence on basic levels of concepts is a fundamental aspect of thought.

Studying concept formation. When we form a new concept, we draw on two processes that were discussed in Chapter 7—generalization and discrimi-nation. We form a concept by developing a mental representation broad enough to include different in-stances of the concept, (generalization) but not so broad as to include noninstances (discrimination). Generalization identifies the "ball park"; discrimina-tion puts the fence around it. Both parts are essential if concepts are to guide our behavior appropriately.

Experimental studies of concept formation have tried to reproduce in the laboratory the processes we go through ordinarily in forming concepts.

In a typical study a researcher will present a series of cards containing colored geometric shapes or se-quences of numbers or letters in which several attri-butes can be varied, such as color, shape, and size. The experimenter decides what combination of these characteristics will define "the concept" (thus limit-ing the investigation to concepts based on critical features). As each display is presented, the subject is told whether it is or is not an instance of the con-cept. The subject's task is to discover the concept the experimenter has in mind.

To get a feel for this process, see if you can identify the concept below.

Display	Feedback
XXX	yes
xx	no
OO	no
ooo	no
OOO	yes
XX	no
xxx	no
XXX	yes
o	no
ooo	no
OOO	yes
xxx	no

▷ *International traffic signs show typical instances of basic level concepts that all drivers know regardless of the languages they speak.*

No U-turn   Gas station   Railroad crossing

To form the concept, you had to discover two things: (a) what features were and were not included in it; and (b) the rule for combining them. There were three possible features (letter, capital, number of elements), of which two—capital and number—turned out to be relevant. The rule was simply that both features must be present—the number three and capital. By the way, in trying to formulate a general rule on the basis of concrete examples, you were doing what scientists do when they work toward general conclusions and broad theories on the basis of specific observations.

Some rules are harder to discover than others. For example, it is hardest to discover a *conditional* rule—*if* it is red, *then* it must be square. *Disjunctive* rules are easier to learn—it is red *or* square but not both. Easiest to identify are *conjunctive* rules—it is *both* red *and* square (Bourne, 1967). Not surprisingly, the more rules or elements to be identified, the harder and slower the concept identification.

Most adult subjects in concept-formation experiments (about 90 percent) form a hypothesis about what the concept is and then test it on subsequent presentations, adapting or replacing it if it is disconfirmed (Levine, 1966). For example, after you discovered that XXX was an example of the concept but both xx and OO were not, you may have hypothesized that the concept was "three elements." But then, when ooo was said *not* to be an example, you had to try another hypothesis.

In some studies subjects are asked to try out their own patterns and are told whether each one is or is not an example of the concept the experimenter has in mind. Here subjects tend to have trouble using *disconfirming* evidence—knowledge that one of their patterns is *not* an instance of the concept. Instead of working back from there to locate the boundary of the concept, they try more patterns that they think may *confirm* a current hypothesis. This may lead them to overlook a simple solution and formulate an unnecessarily complex rule, as in the following case.

Subjects were given a series of numbers such as 2, 4, 6 and asked to discover what rule led to the series by trying out various sequences and being told each time whether their sequence did or did not follow the rule. One subject tried the following nine sequences:

1.	261	263	101	(−)	6.	41	43	67	(+)
2.	671	671	3	(−)	7.	51	53	161	(+)
3.	41	43	42	(−)	8.	42	43	45	(+)
4.	3	17	17	(−)	9.	67	43	45	(−)
5.	671	673	900	(+)					

On the basis of whether these sets are correct (+) or incorrect (−), can you formulate the rule? This subject came up with this consistent but unnecessarily intricate rule: "The rule is that the second number is random, and either the first number equals the second minus two and the third is random but greater than the second, *or* the third number equals the second plus two, and the first is random but less than the second." Actually, the experimenter's rule was simply "any series of numbers increasing in magnitude" (Wason, 1971). Go back and see if this rule fits all the evidence.

Here, because the subject was looking only for confirming evidence and because his roundabout rule led to correct sequences, he probably would never have discovered that the constraints he had established were unnecessary. The experimenter also found that subjects sometimes misperceived or rationalized feedback that contradicted a current hypothesis.

This finding of inadequate use of disconfirming evidence is especially interesting because it probably parallels much of our concept learning in real-life situations. In "testing" our hypotheses about people, including our positive or negative prejudices, we make the same mistake of overrelying on evidence that *confirms* our hypotheses, ignoring or denying equally available sources of *disconfirmation*. For example, in interviewing a stranger for a job—or for a roommate—we are more likely to ask questions that would elicit behavioral confirmations of the characteristics we *want* than questions that would yield answers revealing characteristics we *don't* want but are nevertheless true (Snyder & Swann, 1978).

In both concept formation tasks and forming impressions about people and their behavior, we tend to resist evidence that would challenge our beliefs and force some change in our hypotheses about the world. When that resistance to disconfirming evidence is extreme, *prejudice* is operating. When a false belief is maintained despite all contradictory evidence, a *delusion* has developed, which is a symptom of the mental disorder paranoia (Maher, 1966).

Propositions

In the last chapter we saw that verbal memories are believed by some to be stored in networks of propositions. A **proposition** is an abstract unit of meaning, an idea that expresses a relationship between concepts, objects, or events. It is the smallest unit of knowledge that makes an assertion (containing a subject and a predicate) which can be judged to be true or false. "People drink water." "Grandparents spoil grandchildren." These are simple examples of propositions.

Propositions are assumed to be represented in our minds in some *non*linguistic form, however. The same proposition (deep structure) can be expressed in different sentences (surface structures). For example, the meaning conveyed by the sentence "They drank water" is also conveyed by the sentences "They imbibed H_2O" and "Water was drunk by them."

Most of our complex thoughts can be broken down into a set of related propositions—some explicit, others only implied. For example, the sentence, "They drank water; the winners drank champagne; once again the poor were cheated," strings together several propositions and also implies propositions about chronic unfairness to the poor, such as discrimination on the part of the "haves" against the "have nots."

Evidence of the importance of propositions in our thought processes is found in the fact that it takes longer to understand the meaning of sentences containing more propositions even when the number of words in the sentences is the same (Kintsch, 1974). Researchers have also shown that when subjects are asked to remember a set of interrelated sentences, the more propositions there are related to a given concept, the longer it takes to recall any one of those propositions (Anderson & Bower, 1973).

Propositions help us capture and retain the essence of what we hear or read. They also enable us to make inferences rapidly. It is assumed that we locate, modify, or add to memories by making contact with networks of propositions stored in long-term memory.

Schemas and scripts

You are already familiar with the important concept of *schema* as a general cluster of stored knowledge that helps determine what we perceive and remember. Now we are ready to refocus on schemas as structures for *thinking.*

As we have seen, schemas include preconceptions and expectations about what attributes are typical for particular concepts or categories. New information, which is often incomplete or ambiguous, makes more sense when we can relate it to knowledge in our stored schemas. But going one step further, once we have assigned it to a particular schema, we then think about it and deal with it as if all the expected characteristics are present, whether or not they actually are.

For example, take the statement, "Tanya was upset to discover upon opening the basket that she'd forgotten the salt." Salt in the basket implies a picnic basket, which also suggests food on which salt might be put, such as hardboiled eggs. You automatically know what else could be there and equally important, what definitely is not: everything in the world larger than a picnic basket and all the things that would be inappropriate to take on a picnic—like a boa constrictor or your bronze-plated baby shoes. This body of information has been organized around your "picnic-basket schema." By relating the statement about Tanya to this preestablished schema, you understand the situation better because you can read in much more about what was happening than was contained in the statement itself.

According to researchers Rumelhart and Norman (1975), schemas are the primary units of meaning in the human information-processing system. In their view, the mind is a network of interrelated schemas, in which parts of schemas are themselves schemas. Schemas are clusters of knowledge and expectations and always have to do with general categories, whereas propositions are assertions and can relate specific *or* general items. We often derive specific propositions from our various schemas.

Scripts are clusters of knowledge about *sequences* of interrelated, specific events and actions that are expected to occur in a certain way in particular settings. Scripts are to procedural knowledge what schemas are to declarative knowledge. We have scripts for going to a restaurant, using the library, listening to a lecture, and visiting a sick friend.

Like scripts in plays, our mental scripts outline the "proper" sequence in which actions and reactions are expected to happen in given settings. When we follow our script in a given setting and other people follow a similar script, we all feel comfortable because we have comprehended the "meaning" of that situation in the same way and have the same expectations for each other (Schank & Abelson, 1977). But when others do not follow a script similar to ours, we are made uncomfortable by this "violation" of our script and may have difficulty understanding why the scene was "misplayed."

> Don arrived promptly at 8 PM for his first date with Joan. She invited him to meet her parents. He asked them if he could have her hand in marriage. They went to the church square dance. Afterwards they had a pizza and talked about their career plans after graduation.

You don't have to be prodded to recognize what part does not fit in this "first-date" script. But there are situations where misunderstandings, hurt feelings, or anger are caused by the fact that two people are operating from different scripts. As we saw in Chapter 8, men and women tend to have different sexual scripts regarding the meaning of touch. And sometimes we find ourselves in situations so different from our past experience that we have no script for them and must deal with them "fresh." Did you have any "unscripted" experiences when you first came to college? How did you feel while you were engaged in them? How did you try to understand them and decide what you should do?

Some scripts, such as being quiet in libraries, are controlled by aspects of the situation. These are said to be *situation-driven scripts*. Others are controlled by particular roles we are expected to play in society, such as parent, teacher, or counselor. These can be thought of as *role-driven scripts*.

Still other scripts are learned for informal situations where we have no traditional role to fulfill; they are *person-driven scripts*. These represent ways we have programmed ourselves to try to act consistently in different situations regardless of the different roles we are playing. They might be "honesty" scripts, "generosity" scripts, or "helpfulness" scripts, depending on our concept of ourselves. Person-driven scripts can be thought of as expressions of our personal style.

Visual images and cognitive maps

Do you think only in words or sometimes in pictures and spatial relationships? Although we may not actually store visual memories in visual form (see Chapter 9), we clearly are able to use imagery in our thinking. History is full of examples of famous discoveries made on the basis of mental imagery rather than the more typical propositional thought. For example, the discoverer of the chemical structure of benzene, F. A. Kekulé, often worked with mental images of dancing atoms, which he saw as hooking themselves into chains of molecules. His discovery of the benzene ring occurred in a dream in which a snake-like chain molecule suddenly grabbed its own tail, thus forming a ring—a new hypothesis about molecular structure.

Albert Einstein claimed to have thought entirely in terms of visual images, translating his findings into mathematical symbols and words only after the work of visually based discovery was finished. Michael Faraday, who discovered many properties of magnetism, knew little mathematics but worked by placing the supposed properties of magnetic fields in a visual image of relationships. (These and other historical examples have been chronicled by Roger Shepard, 1978.)

A NATION OF EINSTEINS

Many psychologists regard visual thought as a different mode of thought from verbal thought (Kosslyn, 1983; Paivio, 1983). Evidence of the psychological reality of mental images is provided in the following study showing their behavioral consequences.

Students were shown various examples of either the letter R or its mirror image after the figures had been rotated various amounts from 0 to 180 degrees (see **Figure 10.1**). As each figure appeared, they were to report whether it was a normal R or its mirror image. The time it took to make that decision was longer the more the figure had been rotated. This finding was interpreted as showing that the subjects were imaging the figure in their ''mind's eye'' and rotating the image into the upright position, before deciding whether the figure was an R or a mirror image. Such results support the idea that *thinking* processes using visual imagery are similar to the processes involved in visually *perceiving* real-world objects (see Shepard & Cooper, 1982).

It also appears that people scan their mental images of objects in much the same way they would scan the actual perceived objects.

In one study, subjects first memorized pictures of complex objects such as a motorboat (see **Figure 10.2**). Then they were asked to recall their visual im-

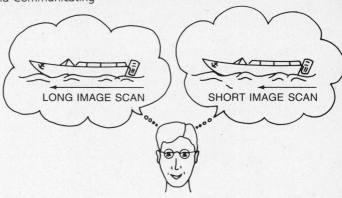

△ **Figure 10.2**

Subjects studied a picture of a boat and then were asked to look at the motor in their image of it. While doing so, they were asked whether the boat had (a) a windshield, or (b) an anchor. Their faster response to the closer windshield than to the more physically distant anchor was taken as evidence that they were scanning their visual images. (After Kosslyn, 1980)

age of the boat and focus on one spot, say the motor. When asked if the picture contained another object—a windshield or an anchor, for example (both were present)—it took longer to ''see'' the anchor at the other end of the boat than the windshield, which was only half as far from the motor. The researcher regarded the reaction-time difference as evidence of the times it took the subjects to scan the two physical distances in their mental images (Kosslyn, 1980).

▽ **Figure 10.1**

Subjects presented with these figures in random order were to say as quickly as possible whether each figure was a normal R or a mirror image. The more the figure was rotated from upright, the longer the reaction time. (After Shepard & Cooper, 1982)

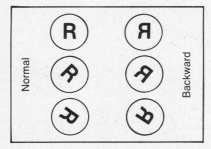

Many problems cannot be solved by visual imagery, however, as you will discover by trying to solve the problem below.

Take a large piece of typing paper. Fold it in half (now having two layers), fold it in half again (now having four layers) and continue folding it over on itself 50 times. It is true that it is impossible to fold an actual piece of paper 50 times. But for the sake of this problem, imagine that you can. About how thick would the 50-times folded paper be? Mark your estimate on the margin of this page (Adams, 1979).

If you are like most people, you visualized the piece of paper, imagined folding it over once, then twice, and then extrapolated the result of these foldings to 50 folds. But in all likelihood your estimate of the thickness was way off. The actual answer is about 50 million miles, about half the distance between the earth and the sun ($2^{50} \times .028$, the thickness of this paper). What happened was that you tried to solve the problem using *only* visual imagery. You know what paper looks like folded a few times. However, the effect of folding the paper 50 times, doubling the thickness each time, is so large that the problem has to be translated into mathematical symbols to be solved.

Visual thought adds complexity and richness to our thinking, however, as do the less studied forms of thought using our other senses of sound, taste, smell, and touch. It can also be very useful in solving types of problems in which the relationships can be grasped more clearly in diagram form than in words, as in the case of flow charts of procedures or models of how processes are related. The flow chart shown in **Figure 10.3,** proposed for the human information-processing system, puts verbal information into a visual form.

Visual thought is also useful for thinking about spatial or geographical relationships. A mental representation of physical space is called a *cognitive map.* E. C. Tolman's pioneering hypothesis about cognitive maps in learning was mentioned in Chapter 7. To explore some of your cognitive maps, try answering the questions below.

1. What is the most direct route from your psychology classroom to the bookstore? to your residence?
2. Which is farther north: Seattle or Montreal?
3. Which is farthest west: the entrance to the Panama Canal from the Atlantic Ocean (Caribbean side) or Pacific Ocean (Gulf of Panama side)?

To find the answers to these questions, you use a mental representation of the spatial environment as you have personally experienced it, remember it from a map you have seen, or reconstruct it from separate bits of information that you possess. Your cognitive maps help you move about effectively in order to get where you want to go; they also enable you to give

▷ **Figure 10.3** *The Human Information-Processing System*

This model of the human information-processing system incorporates the memory systems but emphasizes the directions of flow of information. It is shown here to illustrate spatial visualization of semantic material. (Farr, 1984)

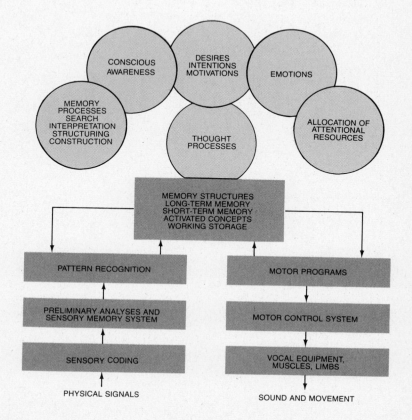

directions to someone else. By using cognitive maps you can get to the bathroom at home with your eyes closed, or to school even when your usual route is blocked (see Hart & Moore, 1973; Thorndyke & Hayes-Roth, 1978).

There has been a new interest among cognitive psychologists in the development of cognitive maps and spatial localization abilities in young children. Children improve with age both in creating cognitive maps from their experiences and in their ability to understand maps presented to them (Siegel et al., 1979).

One study found that 9-month-old infants could already use either external references or personal orientation in trying to locate objects that were hidden from their view. In an unfamiliar place, they depended upon their own bodies as a reference base. When an object was hidden under a cloth on their left side and they were then taken around to the other side of the table, they still searched for the object on their left. But when the same task was presented at home, the infants relied on stable external landmarks to guide their search correctly even when their own position was altered (Acredolo, 1977).

In another study, preschool children who had freely explored an unfamiliar place in search of a hidden object showed more accurate spatial localization than children who had been passively led through the space by an adult (Feldman & Acredolo, 1979).

But although we all seem to develop cognitive maps to help us navigate through the complex environments in which we live, they can sometimes lead us astray. Did you know that Seattle is farther north than Montreal? We are likely to miss on this because we think of Canada as being north of us and also don't realize how far the border drops south around the Great Lakes.

And did you realize that the Atlantic Ocean is actually more *westerly* than the Pacific Ocean at the Panama Canal entrances? Most of us are surprised at such information because our mental maps of Central America distort the sharp eastward curve of both coastlines to make them more vertical (B. Tversky, 1981). Similarly, on the mental maps of Parisians, the Seine River curves only gently through Paris instead of curving more sharply as it actually does. Thus some places that are on the Right Bank of the Seine are misjudged as being on the Left Bank by Parisians "who should know better" (Milgram & Jodelet, 1976). In addition, because nearby geography is so much more familiar to most of us than distant places, our cognitive maps of places far away become increasingly foreshortened.

PEWAUKEE

◁ *A native of Pewaukee, Wisconsin, might see the world a bit differently than a New Yorker or a San Franciscan since one's cognitive maps of distant geography are likely to be distorted.*

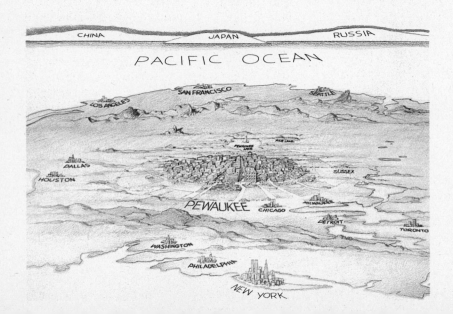

KEYS TO COMPREHENSION

Whatever forms they take, our various mental representations of our world, if accurate, enable us to deal more effectively with it. But humans also want to know for the sake of knowing. They want to understand the relationships and meanings of the reality with which they are interacting.

What does it mean to understand, or comprehend, something? According to educator-philosopher John Dewey, "To grasp the meaning of an event, thing, or situation is to see it in its relations to other things; to note how it operates or functions, what consequences follow from it; what causes it, what uses it can be put to" (1963, p. 135). All of these are aspects of comprehension.

When you say, "I don't understand that," you probably mean that you do not see the connection between what is being said and the context in which the word or idea is being used. When you say, "Now I see what you mean," there is a "click of comprehension" as the comforting cloak of familiarity wraps itself around a cognitive event that seemed novel or strange before.

We can draw together two generalizations about what must happen for us to experience that "click of comprehension." We can do this on the basis of what has already been said about "top-down" processes in perceiving and remembering and about the mental representations used in thinking. Comprehension of new information seems to occur through (a) integration of consistent new input into what we already know, and/or (b) overcoming discrepancy by changing a knowledge structure or by changing or ignoring the input. You will probably recognize that these two keys to comprehension are comparable to the processes of assimilation and accommodation discussed by Piaget in connection with young children's development of mental structures for dealing with the world (see Chapter 2).

Integrating the unknown into the known

What do these sentences mean to you?

The notes were sour because the seam was split.

The haystack was important because the cloth ripped.

In isolation, these sentences make little sense. In the first one it is not clear what notes are being referred to, or what the seam is, or how the two relate to each other to make the notes sour. In the second, there seems no relation between haystack and cloth. However, if you are given the words *bagpipes* and *parachute*, the sentences suddenly become understandable. The notes were sour because the seam in the bag of the bagpipes was split. If you were coming down in a torn parachute, the haystack could save your life.

The point is that the sentences were not comprehensible until you could somehow integrate them into what you already know. You needed cues to find the appropriate schemas to fit them into. But these cues were all you needed if you already knew what bagpipes and parachutes were.

This means that to be understandable, new input must contain not only the new information but something we know already. One notion for the strategy we use in understanding sentences is that we use the familiar part as a retrieval cue in our memory search for relevant matching information in our existing mental structures. As the new information is added to it, the mental structure is expanded and becomes more complex (Haviland & Clark, 1974).

This process of assimilating new input to some previous understanding occurs whether the previous information came in through personal experience, education, rumor, or some other of the many ways that we get information. The difficulty of understanding new input that *lacks* any familiar elements is shown in the humorous **Close-up** on page 356. By contrast, just one good cue can sometimes help you make sense of otherwise confusing input. The following passage was read by subjects in a study of comprehension:

"The procedure is actually quite simple. First you arrange things into different groups. Of course, one pile may be sufficient depending on how much there is to do. . . . . It is important not to overdo things.

Next Time I'll Say, "Nobody Called You"

A charming example of an attempt to assimilate strange new words and phrases into a working vocabulary and existing knowledge structures is evident in one of the old *Candid Camera* episodes (of Allen Funt). A boy, about six years old, is asked to answer the phone while a Mr. Smith goes out for a short while. Sure enough a phone message comes:

"I have an important message I'd like to give to Mr. Smith. Will you tell Mr. Smith that Mr. Terry called in reference to his special checking account, and it appears to be overdrawn?"

The boy dutifully keeps repeating it aloud to himself to keep it from fading out of his short-term memory. During the time of less than the minute that it takes for Mr. Smith to return, some of the variations that we can hear the child rehearsing are:

"Mr. Smith called and the notice will be tallyranted in the interdrawn."

"Mr. Smith called and the study will be telegraphy in the intercom."

"Mr. Smith called and the total will be granted in the intercom."

When Mr. Smith arrives for his message, the confused youngster delivers what he has reconstructed of that incomprehensible message:

"Mr. Terry called and the total will be granted in the intercom."

When asked to repeat it from the beginning, the child offers:

"Mr. Terry told me to tell you that the note will be called in the intergraning."

The complex structure of the original message is simplified into a grammatically correct form, but without knowing the meaning of the key words—"in reference to," "special checking account," "overdrawn,"— the child cannot understand what "it" is referring to. We may assume that "tallyranted" is a compound of "tell in reference," which certainly matches no prior sound or word in the boy's long-term memory store. So it is transformed into closer approximations to what he may already know: first, "will be telegraphy," and then, "total will be granted." Although "overdrawn," "interdrawn," "intercom" end up as the unfamiliar "intergraning," it may be his way of making sense out of "granted in the intercom," which surely is not what gets "tallyranted" in his account—or does it?

That is, it is better to do too few things at once than too many. In the short run, this may not seem important but complication can easily arise. A mistake can be expensive as well. At first, the whole procedure will seem complicated. Soon, however, it will become just another facet of life. It is difficult to foresee any end to the necessity for this in the immediate future, but then one can never tell. After the procedure is completed one arranges the materials into different groups again. Then they can be put into their appropriate places. Eventually they will be used once more and the whole cycle will then have to be repeated. However, that is part of life" (Bransford & Johnson, 1972, p. 722).

The subjects not given any title found the passage more incomprehensible and remembered it less well than those given the title "Washing Clothes." (Hear the *click* of comprehension?)

Comprehending, like perceiving and remembering, is a constructive and reconstructive process in which we draw on our existing mental structures to make the most sense we can out of new information. Once we interpret information as belonging to a particular schema, we may unwittingly change the information in our internal representation of it.

To see how this can occur, read the following passage.

Chief resident Jones adjusted his face mask while anxiously surveying a pale figure secured to the long gleaming table before him. One swift stroke of his small sharp instrument and a thin red line appeared. Then the eager young assistant carefully extended the opening as another aid pushed aside glistening surface fat so that the vital parts were laid bare. Everyone stared in horror at the ugly growth too large for removal. He now knew it was pointless to continue. (Stop. Without looking back, do the following exercise.)

Check off the words below that appeared in the story of resident Jones.

____patient, ____scalpel, ____blood,
____tumor, ____cancer, ____nurse,
____disease, ____surgery.

Most of the subjects in a study that used this passage identified a number of the words in the list as having been in the story, such as *patient, scalpel,* and *tumor.* None of them was. Interpreting the story as a medical one made it more understandable but then resulted in inaccurate recall (Lachman et al., 1979). Once they had related the story to their schema for hospital surgery, the subjects "remembered" labels from their schema that were not in what they had read. In this case drawing on a schema not only gave them an existing mental structure to tie the new material to but led them to change the information to make it more consistent with their expectations.

Revising mental structures and reducing discrepancy

We have trouble comprehending inconsistencies and parts that do not fit a pattern. When we encounter new information that does not readily fit into our mental structures or even contradicts them, we are uncomfortable. One way we reduce the discrepancy is by enlarging and changing our mental structures in appropriate ways to make a broader, more comprehensive understanding possible. This process of accommodation is one that begins in infancy and continues as long as we increase our knowledge and competence in any field. It is what is happening when a child is developing the concept of conservation or when a novice is becoming an expert.

But discrepancies between new information and existing mental structures can also be reduced by distortion or rejection of inconsistent elements, as when a friendly overture by someone you do not trust is written off as prompted by an ulterior motive. Other examples of distortion were cited in the last chapter in the studies by Alport and Postman and by Bartlett (pp. 328 and 330). Allport and Postman's subjects reduced the discrepancy in their perception of a white man holding a razor by "remembering" the razor as being in the black man's hand. Bartlett's British subjects changed the details in the American Indian stories in ways that made them more comprehensible. In both cases, the subjects avoided the discomfort of having to change their existing mental structures.

When new ideas are so different that the discrepancy cannot be overcome, they may simply be rejected as "nonsense" and ridiculed instead of being taken seriously, examined, and responded to in their own terms. This is what often happens when new ideas challenge traditional ways of thinking. The thinkers who propose them—whether in politics or in science—are likely to be labeled "foolish," "crazy," or "dangerous." Many of our "revolutionary" thinkers have met with initial rejection: Jesus (love thine enemy); Copernicus (the earth goes around the sun); Freud (the influence of unconscious processes); and Picasso (representation of reality in abstract, symbolic art forms).

When scientist Louis Pasteur said, "Chance favors the prepared mind," he meant a mind not only filled with relevant knowledge but also tolerant of novelty and ambiguity. But it is the exceptional case when new ideas force us to change our trusty old concepts, categories, and theories to more accurate and adaptive ones. Typically, we do so only after stubbornly hanging onto the old as long as possible (see Conant's *On Understanding Science,* 1958, and Kuhn's *The Structure of Scientific Revolution,* 1970).

MAKING DECISIONS AND JUDGMENTS

Making decisions is an essential part of our lives— from mundane and simple decisions like what brand of toothpaste to buy to significant and complex ones like what academic major, career, or mate to choose. Can psychology help us to understand the process— and do it better? Judgments and decisions will be discussed together here because they often occur as parts of the same mental activity; all decisions require judgments about alternatives, and all judgments require decisions about evidence.

Decision making is the process of choosing one option while rejecting others. The study of decision making, as carried out in economics, statistics, and game theory, focuses on the rules a decision maker *should* follow to achieve desired outcomes. This *normative* analysis treats the individual as an idealized decision maker who ensures the best outcome by abstracting all the available information and considering all of his or her relevant values. By contrast, when psychologists analyze decision making, they use a *descriptive* approach, identifying what people's beliefs and preferences actually are, not what they should be.

How *do* people go about judging alternatives and deciding to accept or reject them? How rational is most decision making? Why are good evidence and good arguments sometimes disregarded when decisions are being made?

Utility and probability

When making a decision among two or more alternatives, a person should weigh the desirability of each one on two scales: (a) its *utility*—how attractive that result would be if achieved; and (b) its *probability*—the likelihood that the choice would in fact bring about that outcome. For example, in deciding between graduate school in a field that interests you versus going into the family business, you might see the graduate-school option as training for work you would enjoy doing more and might ultimately get a better income from (high utility). But you might also see your chosen field as a crowded and competitive one in which you might not do as well (uncertain probability). You might see the family business option as less enjoyable (lower utility) but something

you could count on (higher probability). Most of the decisions we make involve estimates of utility and probability for each alternative.

A rational decision maker would assign a utility value to each potential outcome (perhaps on some scale, as from $+10$ to -10). These utility values would be multiplied by some figure representing the probability of each outcome and the results added up. The best choice would be clear, and the decision would be made accordingly. However, when we look at how people behave when estimating utilities and probabilities, most decisions about things that matter to us are not made so rationally.

Sources of error in decision making

Sometimes we make faulty decisions even when adequate facts are available because of nonrational psychological factors like wishful thinking or misinterpretation of utility and/or probability. In other cases, especially where we have incomplete information, we make faulty decisions because we rely on rules of thumb that give us a quick answer but an oversimplified view.

Nonrational factors. If we want something very much (high utility), we may underestimate the likelihood of negative outcomes and overestimate the likelihood of positive ones. This misjudgment of the probabilities seems to occur in many cases where teenagers become pregnant. Their decision not to use contraception is based in part on an underestimate of the risk despite what they "know" (Luker, 1975).

Groups can make the same kind of mistakes, even at the highest levels of political decision making. The decision to make the disastrous "Bay of Pigs" invasion of Cuba in 1960 was approved by President Kennedy after cabinet meetings in which contrary information was minimized or suppressed by those who were eager to undertake the invasion (Janis, 1972).

Other nonrational factors include (a) simplifying complex situations by not considering all the alternatives or all the relevant facts; (b) letting either optimism or negative preconceptions blind us to certain facts; and (c) making decisions under stress, which may disrupt both our search for relevant facts and our reasoning about them.

Risks, frames, and heuristics. An understanding of how people actually make decisions under conditions of uncertainty has been developed largely through the innovative theories and research of psychologists Daniel Kahneman and Amos Tversky (1984). They have shown that many of the decisions we make are biased by psychological factors other than a rational weighing of utility and probability.

For example, people have attitudes toward risks and values that they bring into most decision situations. Often decisions must be made without full knowledge of probable outcomes, such as whether one would get caught for cheating or whether one would get a raise for doing extra work. Under some conditions we are averse to taking risks, while at other times we choose risk over certainty.

Another way in which our decisions may be biased is through the misuse of heuristics, rules of thumb that help us make decisions when we do not have all the facts. For example, a common heuristic for deciding whether to trust a stranger is, "Don't trust someone who doesn't look you in the eye." We all develop heuristics for dealing with complex and uncertain situations; they help us make decisions quickly and with little effort but do not guarantee a good decision.

Two heuristics that have been extensively studied are those of *availability* and *representativeness.* Both are heuristics for estimating probabilities (A. Tversky & Kahneman, 1973, 1980).

People who tend to assume that their personal experience is a reliable sample of the general class of events they are talking about are using the *availability heuristic.* For example, crime victims may overestimate the extent of crime that occurs in their area because of their own experiences. For the same reason, those who are unemployed may judge the percentage of unemployed workers to be higher than do those who are employed. But estimating probabilities on the basis of what is available in one's own consciousness can lead to error if one's experience has *not* been typical.

The availability heuristic also operates to influence our judgments about causes of events. Anything that focuses our attention on a particular event or actor as a cause in one case increases its availability in our consciousness and leads us to overestimate its significance as a cause in other situations (McArthur & Post, 1977; Taylor & Fiske, 1978). Next time you hear someone justify a judgment in terms of "in my personal experience. . .," think about the availability bias that may be at work.

We use the *representativeness heuristic* when we assign someone to a category on the basis of a few characteristics that we think are representative of that category. This intuitive judgment is dominated by the specific features of the individual case while relevant statistical considerations are typically ignored.

Consider the following examples.

a. You have an 85% chance to win $100
b. You are assured a gain of $80.

Which do you choose? a____ b____

c. You have an 85% chance to lose $100
d. You are assured a loss of $80.

Which do you choose? c____ d____

Most people choose *b* over *a,* a risk-*aversive* preference for a sure gain over a probable large gain. They also choose *c* over *d,* a risk-*seeking* strategy, preferring a gamble over a sure loss.

But these preferences for or against risky choices can be changed by the way the problem is described, or framed.

What are your preferences in the following example, regarding a medical program to combat a new disease that is expected to kill 600 people?

a. Program A will save 200 lives.
b. Program B has a one-third probability of saving 600 people and a two-thirds probability that no one will be saved.

Which do you choose? Program A__ Program B__

c. If Program A' is adopted, 400 people will die.
d. If Program B' is adopted, there is a one-third probability that no one will die and a two-thirds probability that 600 people will die.

Which do you choose? Program A'__ Program B'__

In the original framing most subjects choose Program A over Program B, but when the choices are presented differently, the majority of the subjects prefer Program B' over Program A' though you should be able to show that the choices presented are actually the same (A. Tversky & Kahneman, 1981).

For an example of your use of the representativeness heuristic, answer the following question:

> The author has a friend who is a college professor. He is an excellent gardener, reads poetry, is shy, and is slight of build. Would you judge that he is probably in (a) Japanese studies or (b) psychology?

If you decided Japanese studies, you were matching the description with your stereotypes of representative people in the two fields. You probably did not take into consideration the much larger number of professors in psychology than in Japanese studies and thus the statistical probability that he was a psychologist. Neither did you consider the probability that as a psychologist, the author would be likely to have more friends in his own area of study (Nisbett & Ross, 1980). Actually, the friend just described is a psychology professor.

In one study, subjects were presented with a series of personality descriptions of individuals supposedly drawn at random from a list of 100 engineers and lawyers. They were to assign each description to one category or the other. Though they were told the proportion of the two groups, this information about statistical probability was disregarded. A given type of description was likely to be assigned to the "engineer" category if it was representative of a subject's engineers schema regardless of whether the engineers were said to be 30 percent of the group or 70 percent. The subjects relied only on representativeness in making their judgments and ignored the relevant probability data (Kahneman & A. Tversky, 1973).

Availability and representativeness are just two of the many heuristics that we all tend to use in making judgments about the world every day. The biased judgments resulting from these and other rules of thumb are like perceptual illusions in that they can systematically distort our view of reality and remain compelling even when we know the true state of affairs. Realizing their inaccuracy in special circumstances helps us become aware of the processes by which we are organizing and evaluating information all the time.

If we cannot assume that all people are rational beings all the time, we can say for certain that all people are heuristic beings. We store many complexity-reducing rules of thumb because they allow us to make quick, acceptable judgments almost all of the time. Often they are the best we could do, given the constraints and uncertainties of the situation, and they serve us well by guiding us down a simple, straight-and-narrow path in the countless judgments we must make daily. Problems arise, however, when the path in the real world curves or is wide. Trouble lies ahead when these mechanisms are overapplied or misapplied (see Kahneman, et al., 1982; Nisbett & Ross, 1980).

The power of the vivid example. Joseph Stalin is reputed to have said, "A single death of a Russian soldier is a tragedy; a million deaths is a statistic." Journalists exploit this error of emphasis whenever they present a national trend or social movement in terms of a few character sketches of specific individuals. We tend to give disproportionate weight to available information that is concrete and vividly presented, such as your uncle's complaint about the lemon of a car he got stuck with, and to undervalue abstract statistics, probabilities, or the annual repair records of that particular make of car.

This explains why a study showed that a *New Yorker* article profiling the problems of a single supposedly "typical" welfare case had more impact in changing the readers' attitudes toward welfare than did a presentation of essentially the same relevant data in summary form (Hamill et al., 1980). Research on the power of the vivid case study has led to the conclusion that the lay person is an "intuitive psychologist [who] is, perhaps, as often misled by overreliance upon his senses as he is dogged by adherence to prior theories" (Ross, 1978).

SOLVING PROBLEMS

What goes on four legs in the morning, on two legs at noon, and on three legs in the twilight?

In Greek mythology, this was the riddle posed by the evil Sphinx who held the people of ancient Thebes in tyranny until someone could solve it. Oedipus solved the riddle and delivered his people from bondage. To break the code, he had to translate two key elements that were being used in a special way.

"Morning," "noon," and "twilight" were meant to represent different periods in a human lifetime, not times of one day. The "legs" were hands and knees for a crawling baby, legs later on, and two legs and a cane in old age. The solution to the riddle was *man* (used generically).

Many problems are discrepancies between what you know and what you need to know. When you solve a problem, you reduce that discrepancy by finding how to get the missing information. To get into the spirit of problem solving yourself, try the problems in **Figure 10.4**. See **Figure 10.5** for the answers.

▽   **Figure 10.4**   *Can You Solve It?*

A. *Can you connect all the dots in the pattern by drawing four straight, connected lines?*

B. *A prankster has put 3 ping pong balls into a 6-foot long pipe that is standing vertically in the corner of the physics lab, fastened to the floor. How would you get the ping pong balls out?*

C. *The checkerboard shown has had 2 corner pieces cut out, leaving 62 squares. You have 31 dominoes, each of which covers exactly 2 checkerboard squares. Can you use them to cover the whole checkerboard? (From* How to Solve Problems: Elements of a Theory of Problems and Problem Solving *by Wayne A. Wickelgren. Copyright © 1974 by W. H. Freeman and Company. Reprinted by permission.)*

D. *You are in the situation depicted and given the task of tying 2 strings together. If you hold one, the other is out of reach. Can you do it?*

E. *You are given the objects shown. The task is to mount a lighted candle on the door. Can you do it?*

F. *You are given 3 "water-jar" problems. Using only the 3 containers (water supply is unlimited), can you obtain the exact amount specified in each case? (After Luchins, 1942)*

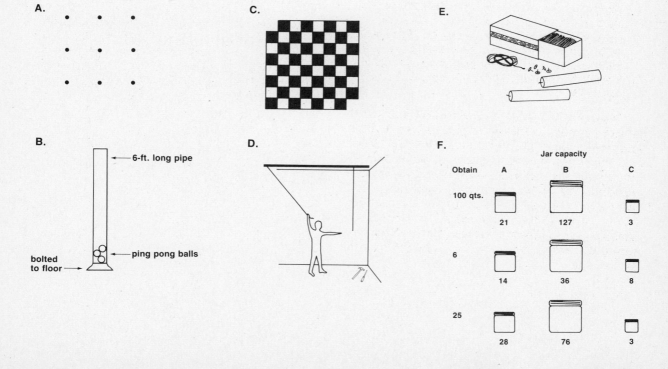

A.

B.
— 6-ft. long pipe

bolted to floor →   ← ping pong balls

C.

D.

E.

F.

Obtain	Jar capacity		
	A	B	C
100 qts.	21	127	3
6	14	36	8
25	28	76	3

In information-processing terms, a problem has three parts: (a) the *initial state*—the incomplete information you start with, perhaps corresponding with some unsatisfactory set of conditions in the world; (b) the *goal state*—the set of information or state of the world you hope to achieve; and (c) a set of *operations*—the steps you must take to move from the initial state to the goal state (Newell & Simon, 1972). Together, these three parts of a problem define what is called the *problem space*. You can think of solving a problem as being like searching for—and finding—a path through a maze (the problem space) that gets you from where you are (the initial state) to where you want to be (the goal state) by a series of turns (the allowable operations) that lead from each place in the maze to the next.

Well-defined and ill-defined problems

There is an important distinction between well-defined and ill-defined problems (Simon, 1973). A *well-defined* problem is like an algebra problem, in which the initial state, the goal state, and the operations are all clearly specified. Here the task is simply to discover how to use allowable known operations to get the answer. By contrast, an *ill-defined* problem is one in which the initial state, the goal state, and/or the operations may be unclear and vaguely specified. In some cases there may not even be a single correct solution. Designing a home, writing a novel, and curing cancer are examples of ill-defined problems. In such cases, the problem solver's major task is first to define exactly what the problem is—to make explicit where one is beginning, what an ideal solution would look like, and what possible means there are for getting there. Once that is done, the task becomes a well-defined problem which can be solved by finding a sequence of operations that will in fact achieve an acceptable solution.

As we know more, have more abilities, and understand better how to solve problems, problems that may still be ill-defined for others become more well-defined for us. The "I can't" lament of the three-year-old child facing the problem of carrying four liquid-filled glasses becomes the older child's confident solution: "Of course I can do it, it's a cinch! I'll use a tray."

▽ ▎ **Figure 10.5** *Answers to the Problems*

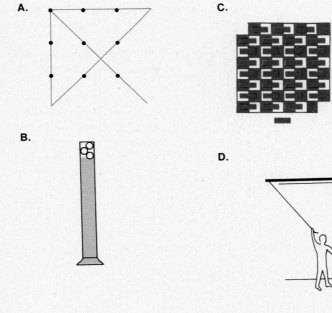

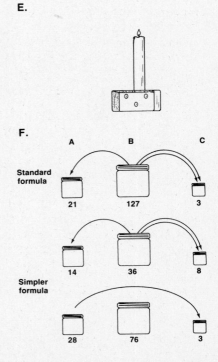

Designing a building is an example of an ill-defined problem. The architect must determine the initial state of the problem—what are the function or functions of the building, where will it be located, how many and what kind of people will it serve, etc.? One can then draw plans and build models—a set of operations—that will move toward the goal state of the completed building.

Understanding the problem

Setting up an *internal representation* of the problem space—specifying all the elements in it—is not automatic. Often it means finding the appropriate schema from analogous previous tasks or situations—but not being restricted by them when the new problem calls for something beyond your existing schemas—as you found out if you solved the problems on page 361. (See **Figure 10.5.**)

All these problems show the importance of an accurate internal representation of the problem space. To connect the nine dots, you have to realize that nothing in the instructions limited you to the area of the dots themselves. To get the ping pong balls out of the pipe, you can fill the pipe with water and the balls will float to the top. In the checkerboard problem, if you reason that any domino must cover both a white and a black space, then you know at once that with two white squares missing, you cannot cover the rest with thirty-one dominoes.

To connect the two strings, you need to see one of the tools as a weight rather than as an instrument. By tying one of them to the end of one string and setting it swinging, you can grasp the other string and catch the tool as it swings close to you. To mount the candle on the door, you can see the match box as a platform instead of a container, tack it to the door, and fasten the candle to it (if you drip

some wax on it from the lighted candle, the bottom of the candle will stick to it as the wax hardens). These last two problems show a phenomenon called **functional fixedness** (Duncker, 1945; Maier, 1931). Your schemas for these familiar objects include only their usual functions and put conceptual "blinders" on your perception of them—showing again the power of schemas in guiding perception.

Another kind of mental rigidity may have hampered your solution of the third water-jar problem. If you had discovered in the first two problems that Jar B minus Jar A minus twice Jar C gave you the answer, you probably tried the same formula for the third problem—and found it didn't work. Actually, a much simpler formula of simply filling Jar A and pouring off enough to fill Jar C would have left you with the right amount. But if you were using the other formula, you probably did not notice this simpler possibility. Your previous success with the other formula would have given you a *mental set* (*Einstellung* in German)—in this case a readiness to respond to new water-jar problems using the same procedure (Luchins, 1942).

Another restrictive mental set is seen in the tendency to take the "safe course" and stick with the "tried and true" instead of trying to see things with fresh eyes and find better ways of doing things. Sometimes this is simply habit, but sometimes it is motivated by fears of making a mistake or being criticized. Using the knowledge available to them, children are sometimes more creative problem solvers than adults because they are not constrained by existing mental sets or schemas and have not yet been socialized away from fantasy toward logical, linear forms of thought. (See Adams, 1979, and de Bono, 1970, for a fuller discussion of how you can learn to be a more creative problem solver.)

Finding the best search strategy: Algorithms or heuristics?

After the problem space is known, the problem is well-defined—but not yet solved! Solving the problem still requires using the operations to get from the initial state to the goal state. Using the problem-as-a-maze analogy, you must still decide on a strategy for "searching" through the maze for the right path.

One search strategy is an **algorithm,** a formal or rote procedure for solving problems by repetition, trying every possible combination until the right one is found. For example, to solve the problem of making a word out of the letters *OTRHS,* there would be 120 possible combinations that you could try on the way to the solution: *SHORT.* But for an eight-letter group such as *TERALBAY,* there would be 20,160 combinations. A search of all the combinations here would be long and tedious—but it would have the virtue of finding the solution.

Luckily, there is an alternative that most of us use to solve a great many problems every day. In problem solving as in making judgments, there are *heuristics,* informal rules of thumb that provide short-cuts. These are general strategies that have often worked in such situations in the past and may work in the present case. For example, in the word jumble *TERALBAY* a heuristic might be "Look for short words that could be made from some of the letters and then see if the other letters fit around them." Using such a strategy, you might generate the string *ABLY (tearably?),* or *ABLE (raytable?),* or *TRAY (latraybe?).* By using this search strategy, you would probably not need to try more than a few of the 20,160 possibilities before you came up with the solution: *BETRAYAL* (Bourne et al., 1979).

Using a heuristic does *not* guarantee that a solution will be found eventually; using an algorithm, tedious though it might be, does. But heuristics do work often enough that we use them and gradually learn which ones to depend on in which situations. One way experience teaches us to be better problem solvers is by teaching us when and how to use heuristics.

IMPROVING COGNITIVE SKILLS

When Charles Berlitz was a child, each member of his family spoke to him in a different language. By the time he was three years old, he spoke four languages; now, as an adult and founder of the Berlitz Schools for foreign languages, he speaks more than twenty-four. But this expertise hardly compares to the language prowess of his grandfather, who spoke fifty-eight languages!

If you have been struggling to acquire only one or two foreign languages, it is hard to imagine how anyone could become so skilled. Yet you have many cognitive skills—perhaps in reading, mathematics, or computer programming—that you take for granted but that may seem remarkable to others who are novices in those domains.

In the last chapter we distinguished between declarative knowledge ("knowing what") and procedural knowledge ("knowing how"). Cognitive skills are information-processing skills that involve procedural knowledge. Investigating cognitive skills is a new focus in psychology. Here we will look at three of the ways they are being studied: (a) through direct observation of skill learning; (b) through investigation of expertise, by comparing experts with novices and by constructing computer programs to simulate human problem solving; and (c) through investigation of people's awareness of what they do and don't know—their metacognitive knowledge.

Acquiring and perfecting skills

When you have reached the point of quick, error-free, effortless performance at a task, you are said to be *skilled.* Research on cognitive and motor skills indicates that you progress through a distinct series of phases, or stages—*if* you practice sufficiently and receive adequate feedback.

Steps in learning a skill. Investigators have identified three stages in skill learning, whether the skill is a motor or a cognitive one: (a) the knowledge stage, (b) the associational, active practice stage, and (c) the autonomous, or automatic, stage (Fitts & Posner, 1967). In the first stage you learn the facts of the task, including the sequence of steps to be taken. You build a mental structure of what must be done. For example, you memorize the location of the gear shift or the names and moves of each chess piece.

In the second stage, you begin to use this knowledge. Your declarative knowledge is changed into procedural knowledge as you go through the motions you have learned about. Errors of understanding are eliminated, associations among the parts of the sequence are built and strengthened, and separate elements become parts of larger units, as in the chunking we talked about in Chapter 9.

In the third stage you learn to produce the responses automatically, with little or no thought. As it becomes automatic, any skill requires less attention, is available on call, and does not interfere with other skills. Verbal mediation becomes unnecessary and the ability to verbalize what you are doing may even be lost. Eventually the skill becomes truly "mindless." For example, you drive, dance, read complex prose, carry on complex conversations, and much more without explicitly thinking about how you are doing so or what rules you are using so effectively. Once this happens, you can concentrate on higher level features of the activity, such as strategy, style, or interpretation.

Practice and feedback. The key ingredient that changes your first, slow, awkward, effortful attempts into smooth proficiency is practice. The effect of practice on improving skills is one of the most reliable effects found by psychologists—assuming that there is prompt, accurate, specific feedback to help you identify and eliminate errors.

In the early stages of learning a skill, performance improves rapidly. Later, improvement continues but usually at a slower and slower pace: it takes increasing amounts of practice to make comparable advances. Discovered long ago for motor skills, the same generalization has been found to apply to cognitive skills (Anderson, 1980). This relationship between practice and improvement, with less and less improvement for the same amounts of practice, is called a *power function*. Equal amounts of improvement for equal amounts of practice would be a *linear function*. The amazing thing is that no matter how good you are, more practice can always make you better still (see **Figure 10.6**).

Feedback serves three distinguishable functions: (a) it provides *information* both about the results of

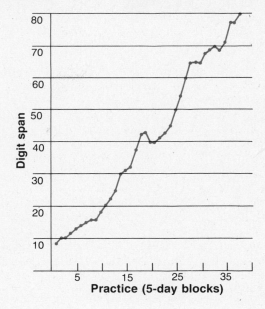

Figure 10.6 *Continuing Improvement with Practice*

This curve records the continuing improvement in memorizing strings of digits shown by S. F., the student described in Chapter 9. Digit span was defined as the length of sequence that he remembered correctly half of the time. Each day represented about an hour of practice. Starting with a digit span of about 7, S. F. was still improving when he had reached a digit span of 79. With continued practice, we would expect the curve to begin to level off, to resemble a power function. (From Ericsson et al., 1980, p. 1181)

a response and about its characteristics (temporal, spatial, directional, level of intensity, and so on); (b) it provides positive or negative *reinforcement*, depending on the adequacy of the response; and (c) it provides *motivation* to continue the task by helping to make the world and one's behavior predictable and potentially controllable.

In order for sensory feedback to act as an *informative signal* to guide physical actions so they will result in desired consequences, several conditions

Table 10.1 *Tips for Developing Cognitive Skills*

Principles for developing cognitive skills can be summarized as follows (Anderson, 1981, 1982).

1. *Space your practice.* In learning a new skill, regularly practice a short time each day, trying to complete a unit of study or one action pattern. One early study found that four hours a day of practice on Morse code netted as good results as seven hours a day (Bray, 1948).

2. *Master the subskills.* Many skills have component parts. Develop these to the point where they are automatic so you don't have to attend to them. Then start focusing on the higher level, overall skill.

3. *Internalize an ideal model.* Observe the correct performance of an expert role model so you can get a good picture of what you are trying to achieve. Then monitor your own performance noting explicitly how it compares with that of your model. This is what happens when children learn to play the violin by the Suzuki method: they listen to the music, become familiar with how it should sound, and then try to match their own performance to that model.

4. *Seek immediate feedback and use it immediately.* Get knowledge as quickly as you can about the quality of your performance—if possible while the feeling of your action is still in your working memory. Then try to use the feedback while *it* is still in your working memory. Skill at video games can be acquired quickly because of the immediate electronic feedback and opportunity to use it to alter responding.

must be met. The feedback must be strong enough and clear enough to be detected and responded to immediately, while noise in the form of external and internal distractions need to be minimized. Complex or weak feedback can be changed into a more usable form by being amplified or slowed down and separated into components as in a videotaped, slow-motion recording of a behavioral sequence such as a golf swing or tennis backhand. You then can become aware of just what you are doing in each part of the sequence.

Fullest use of feedback information also requires a clear image of the ideal, or goal, performance you are working toward, so that the *differences* you detect between current performance and desired performance can be very precise. Practice can then be directed toward the *criterion* of no difference at all.

For many kinds of cognitive and social skills, such as thinking, writing, or conversation, feedback comes in the form of social evaluation of the quality of your performance. Such feedback is often delayed, inconsistent, not reliable, or even not available unless requested, and the setting may be a public one, as in large high-school or college classes. If feedback is essential for developing adequate performance skills, then it is a responsibility of the performer to find means of getting appropriate feedback. For some tips on developing cognitive skills, see **Table 10.1**.

Becoming an expert

How does an expert differ from a novice in a given area, be he or she a research scientist, a physician, a chess master, a chef, or an expert in any other domain? Simply put, experts know more.

Interestingly, many experts can *show* you what they do but cannot *tell* you how they do it. It has become so automatic that they have difficulty becoming aware again of the steps in the process. Try verbalizing to a child how you tie your shoelaces, ride a bike, or understand a joke. Even experts in highly technical professions, such as cardiologists who can make an accurate diagnosis based on only a few bits of case history, probably cannot tell you how they know.

Even if experts cannot tell you what they are doing, you can get at it by comparing how experts and novices go about solving the same cognitive tasks. Another way expertise is being studied is by computer programs that act as "expert systems" in addressing problems usually thought to require human experts to solve. Let's examine both of these approaches: direct comparison of human experts and novices, and computer simulation of the expert performance of specialists.

Novice and experts. The most obvious difference between novices and experts is in the extensive knowledge about a narrow class of issues and problems that experts have built up through practice with feedback. Their expanded knowledge structures include: (a) efficient systems of rules, schemas, and scripts; (b) heuristic shortcuts for searching through a large amount of information and stored knowledge for a limited number of relevant possibilities; (c) capacity for both "top-down" and "bottom-up" processing at or close to the same time; (d) storage of a great deal of factual and procedural information as well as an overall perspective; and (e) the ability to bring general or commonsense knowledge to bear on technical or special domains of knowledge.

Cognitive psychologists have long been interested in the complex game of chess as a focus for understanding specialized information-processing skills (Binet, 1894; Chase & Simon, 1973). Chess masters and novices have been found to be similar on many dimensions—intelligence, memory, and the number of moves they consider before selecting the move to make. But they differ in their ability to recognize and remember possible patterns—differences in their ability to chunk information.

When chess masters were asked to examine a pattern of pieces on a board for five seconds, then reproduce it from memory, they could do so for patterns of about twenty pieces. Novice chess players could reconstruct patterns of only five pieces—which you will remember as the average amount stored in short-term memory. However, this difference held true only when the pieces were arranged in "legal" patterns—patterns that could occur in a chess game. When the pieces were in random "nonlegal" patterns, chess masters could reproduce only about five pieces—the same as the novices (de Groot, 1965).

This finding evidently reflects the fact that chess masters, after years of experience, have developed complex, comprehensive knowledge structures about legal chessboard configurations which have been stored as chunks. It has been estimated that a chess master knows about 50,000 of these patterns (Simon & Gilmartin, 1973).

Chess experts seem to have developed greater skill at interrelating visual information from the external world with patterns of positions stored in long-term memory networks (Chase & Simon, 1973).

Novices and a chess master were briefly shown chess pieces in various positions. As the number of spaces between the two pieces increased from one to four, it took novices longer to determine whether one designated piece could capture another. By contrast, the reaction times of the chess master were the same regardless of the distance; his visual imagery did not seem to involve distance coding (Milojkovic, 1982).

Studies of how people solve problems in physics and geometry reveal other ways in which experts and novices differ.

When asked to sort physics problems into categories according to their similarity, novices and experts differed in how they represented problems internally in thinking about them. Novices relied more on the surface information given in the description of the problem; experts classified the information according to their knowledge of physical laws and common principles. The experts saw underlying structures from previous analysis of many problems in that field (Chi et al., 1981).

These and other differences between experts and novices suggest that there is a good deal more to expertise than simple accumulation of facts. Research strongly supports the view that the expert's advantage comes from "his or her memory-storage structure—how richly the facts and procedures and relationships relevant to a domain are represented in the head. The expert has condensed or chunked many large blocks of basic information in a meaningful way so that he or she can quickly and successfully search for well-organized, well-encoded memories" (Farr, 1984).

Expert artificial intelligence. The second way expertise is being studied currently is by trying to develop computer programs that can make the kinds of judgments human experts make. Such "computer thought" is called **artificial intelligence (AI)**.

The basic method used to study the complex cognitive activity of humans is that of *simulation modeling*. Computer programs originally attempted to simulate or mimic the mental processes of persons dealing with information during particular activities, such as forming concepts or making decisions. Herb Simon won a Nobel Prize in 1978 for his work on decision making under conditions of uncertainty.

To program a computer to find "intelligent" solutions to intellectual problems, two basic ingredients are built in: a *knowledge base* and a *method of search,* consisting of certain heuristics, or rules of thumb. Factual knowledge is stored as a network of propositions; rules of thumb are stored in the form of "if-then" instructions: *If* this condition occurs, *then* do that. A program specifies efficient ways to search through the information stored in the computer's memory of data, facts, and associations in a sequence of steps that narrows all possible combinations and permutations into manageable proportions.

The range of problems that researchers in artificial intelligence are working on includes problems related to speech recognition, language understanding, image analysis, robotics (apparatus programmed to carry out motor functions), and consultation systems. When AI computer programs are designed to serve as consultants for decision making, they are called "expert systems." Each one addresses a specific problem area, such as diagnosis of internal medical symptoms, or geological exploration.

The most successful of these expert systems are *classification* programs. They are used in a limited, well-defined context to weigh and balance all the evidence in a given case and then to decide how it should be categorized.

The first step in constructing an expert system is to make overt and explicit the relevant knowledge that human specialists possess. It is very difficult to identify and then encode all this semiorganized and sometimes subconscious information. Often experts have difficulty in expressing what they know, and programmers have difficulty in faithfully capturing both major and subtle aspects of the expert's knowledge.

Expert systems face many other "cognitive pitfalls" even after the specialist's knowledge base is well represented. How should the system reason and make inferences—from goals backward to data or from data forward to conclusions? How can it recognize the limits of its knowledge and make "best guesses" in situations of uncertainty?

Three additional issues of concern to AI researchers are (a) how to integrate different domains of knowledge; (b) how to get the expert system to learn from experience; and (c) how to build some common sense into it.

For example, while a program like *Internist-1* may know a great deal about internal medicine, it has no stored information about anatomy, physiology, or the time course of disease processes. A still unanswered question is how much information *outside* of a specific domain of knowledge is essential for accurate decision making *in* that domain.

A present challenge is to enable expert systems to discover new rules and refine old ones. But surprisingly, the thing that expert systems and all applications of AI lack most is "common sense." For example, the computer's conclusion, based on integrating all data on a patient, might include "suffering menstrual distress"—even for a male patient.

> "What makes common sense reasoning so difficult is that you need to know so many facts about the world. How many facts? A million? . . ." (Feigenbaum, quoted in *Waldrop,* 1984, p. 804).

Despite these problems, expert systems are fast losing their novice status. *Internist-1* made the correct diagnosis in 25 cases that represented 43 different categories taken from a medical research journal. This score of 58 percent correct compares favorably with the 65 percent score obtained by the physicians who were caring for the patients, but was not as high as the score of 81 percent correct in diagnoses made by expert clinicians.

Another expert system, *Prospector,* is a mineral exploration consultation system that has made assessments which repeatedly agreed closely with those of expert geologists. *Mycin* is an expert system developed to aid physicians in the selection of antibiotics for patients with severe infections. In one evaluation of its recommendation decisions, expert evaluators preferred them to or found them as good as those made by five infectious disease experts who recommended therapy for the same patients. It is important to add that the evaluators made "blind" evaluations of the recommendations, not knowing who or what had made them (see Duda & Shortliffe, 1983).

The goal of expert systems is not to duplicate intelligent human behavior in all its aspects, but to go beyond what is presently known, or known incompletely. By discovering new ways to encode knowledge and use it more powerfully, these systems can help solve human problems across many different domains. In the process of doing this, AI expert systems may also help us to understand how to make human experts even better at what *they* do best and maybe even find some new short cuts that the rest of us can use. (For more details on this fascinating new area of application of cognitive psychology, see Feigenbaum & McCorduck, 1983; Gervarter, 1982; Shortliffe, 1983.)

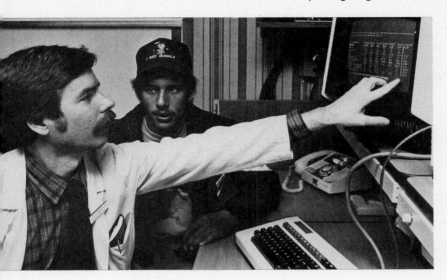

◁ *Medical doctors are using expert systems to help them make diagnoses. Here a cancer specialist consults with a patient using an AI program.*

Metacognitive knowledge

You are the quarterback. It is third down, with two yards to go for a first down. Your team is behind by one touchdown with only a minute left to play and forty yards to go for the touchdown. You notice the defense is prepared for your team to run to get the short yardage. A long pass would surprise the secondary defense and could mean a touchdown. However, your best receiver is tired—but so are the defenders. You know that your passing is generally less effective on long passes than short ones. How will you make your decision?

Here it is not enough to know the specifics of how to throw a football and how far it has to go to reach the receiver. You must also rely on what you know about yourself and the other people and about how the possible strategies are likely to work.

This means using your *metacognitive* knowledge relevant to this situation. **Metacognitive knowledge** is the awareness of what you know and of how well you are comprehending the current information. Metacognitive processes enable you to monitor your own mental activities—what you are learning and understanding in a given situation. They enable you to analyze what you need to know, predict the outcome of different strategies (and check the results later), and evaluate your progress. You use your metacognitive knowledge when you organize your study differently for a multiple-choice exam than for an essay exam, or when you decide which options to take on an essay exam and how much time to devote to each part, according to the points it is worth.

In dealing with a task, your metacognitive knowledge search leads you to (a) evaluate your own skills and your physical and mental state, as well as those of the other persons involved; (b) search your stored knowledge about various possible strategies and evaluate them; (c) decide how much knowledge you have and how much you still need; and (d) assess how much attention to pay to incoming information. These four variables of person, task knowledge, strategy, and sensitivity may act separately to influence your decisions; more often they *interact* (Brown & De Loache, 1978).

John Flavell (1979, 1981) is the pioneering theorist and researcher in this newly emerging area. He believes that a better understanding of how metacognitive knowledge develops and is used or misused will help greatly in teaching children and adults to gather information and evaluate the strategies they are using (see **Table 10.2**).

In an early study of metacognition, preschool and elementary-school children were asked to study a set of items until they were certain they could recall them perfectly when tested. Both groups of children studied the items for a while and were tested when they said, "ready." The older children usually *were* ready when they said they were and showed nearly perfect recall. The younger children usually *were not* ready and failed.

Table 10.2 *Metacognitive Knowledge and Skills*

Kind of metacognitive knowledge	Possible cognitive goals	Possible strategies	Self-monitoring during activity
Task knowledge	I think I'll write my term paper on topic A rather than topic B because the concepts in A are more familiar and will be easier to write about.	Since I'll have to explain this to my friends as well as just learn how to do it myself, I'd better figure out how to express it in words and what points to cover first.	I have the sudden sinking feeling that I can't possibly learn all this in time for tomorrow's test.
Person	I have more aptitude for the social sciences than for the physical sciences, so I'd better try for a B.A. in some social science.	I feel I understand this. However, since I know such feelings can be deceptive and since a correct understanding is very important in this instance, I'd better go over it again.	While listening to a talk I am reminded of how hard it is for me to follow orally given information, compared to most of my friends.
Strategy	I'd better try to persuade my husband to do A rather than B, because I can make a better case and more convincing appeal for A than for B.	I know I am likely to forget things like these unless I write them down, and I simply must remember these things. So I'll write them all down.	It just dawned on me how to find out if A really likes me: I'll ask B, who knows and likes both of us.
Sensitivity	When the message is a set of directions rather than, say, some casual remarks, my goal as listener will be to attain a complete and explicit understanding of the message rather than just the general gist.	Repeated failure to solve a problem using this approach means I should try another approach.	I suddenly realize that I'll need to remember what she is talking about now, as contrasted with what she was talking about earlier.

(Adapted from Flavell, 1981)

The difference in the test results was traced to the different *rehearsal strategies* the two groups of children had used. The younger ones *only looked* at the items, while the older children tested themselves by closing their eyes and rehearsing what they knew from memory, without the aid of perception. They were using a strategy that allowed a better cognitive appraisal of their own cognitive state. The younger children did not yet know how to monitor or check their own memory or level of comprehension, the difficulty of a problem, or what resources they had (Flavell et al., 1970).

The implications of research on metacognitive processes are profound. To become proficient, you need to go beyond learning knowledge and skills. You must become aware—and maintain a running awareness of—what you know and can do, where you are in a sequence, when procedures should be modified to meet the special requirements of this problem, and so on. These are all aspects of metacognitive knowledge. Children should be encouraged early to start dealing with a problem by analyzing what they already know about such problems, where they are deficient, and what a successful solution might look like. Then they need to be taught to keep monitoring their progress or lack of it, detecting confusion in themselves or in information sources, while being aware of when they need additional information or resources. Novices become experts—and learners become their own teachers—when they take charge of their own search for knowledge.

COMMUNICATING THOUGHTS

Imagine yourself among a group of people who are speaking a language foreign to you. They share their thoughts, plan actions, and express feelings; their use of language helps to bind them into a social community—and isolates you. You cannot comprehend what is being communicated, nor can you tell them what's on your mind. Without the ability to express your thoughts in words, you feel both ignorant and childlike. You can point to objects, and use some universally understood gestures like smiling or shaking your head, but that doesn't get you very far. You need language to communicate abstract concepts, such as "yesterday" or "democracy," to express what things mean to you, or to tell how you perceive relationships.

The acquisition of language by a child during the first years of life is considered by many to be the single greatest achievement of human intelligence. Ten linguistic experts working full time for ten years were unable to program a computer to use the English language as well as the average young child does (Moskowitz, 1978).

We looked at children's development of language in Chapter 2. In this section we are interested in some of the ways in which thoughts can be transmitted to other people, the relation between language and thought, and the question of whether only humans can use language.

Verbal and nonverbal communication

The central process in communication is converting private thoughts and feelings into symbols, signs, or words that others can recognize and convert back into ideas and feelings. Four communication systems carry our messages: natural language, artificial languages, visual communication, and nonverbal communication.

Natural language is an extremely complex cognitive skill and system for transmitting specific meanings through words, which can be spoken, written, signed or sung. *Artificial languages* include musical notation, math equations, and some computer programs that communicate specialized information concisely and with little ambiguity by using agreed-upon systems of symbols, signs, and formulas. Pictures and diagrams are means of *visual communication* that are used to convey ideas or feelings or both. *Nonverbal communication* includes body movements (postures, gestures, and use of physical space) as well as nonlinguistic characteristics of speech, such as voice tone, hesitation, and volume.

Later, in our study of social psychology, we will see how nonverbal communication is used to establish status and power relationships. Although natural language makes possible more precise cognitive communication, nonverbal elements account for a significant portion of the total message being conveyed when two people are interacting with each other (Mehrabian, 1971).

The relation between language and thought

Controversies about the relationship between language and thought have raged for many years. Both are vital to the human enterprise, but there have been difficulties in gathering evidence to support or refute the claims of one view or another. Here we will briefly review some of the principal views concerning language and thought.

Previous theories. Nearly two thousand years ago, Aristotle championed the view now held by most cognitive psychologists—that the processes and structures of thought determine the structure of language. In this analysis, language is seen as only a tool of thought, shaped to fit the requirements of the cognitive and communicative processes it serves. Language is one way people encode events and experiences that are important to remember.

But by the time psychologists began to study language, the idea that thought could have primacy over language was heresy. Thoughts could be allowed into a scientific view of human behavior only if they could be defined as overt responses of some kind. Behaviorist John B. Watson (1930) defined them as subvocal speech, a kind of "silent talk," asserting that thinking could not take place without movements of the vocal apparatus. He noted that people who use sign language to communicate have been observed to make signs during their sleep. By analogy, it seemed logical to expect that people who speak using their vocal cords would have to use the same muscles when they think.

In this case, a critical test of Watson's position was possible. It was conducted by a team of researchers, the senior member of which served as the experimental subject. He allowed himself to be temporarily paralyzed by a curare-like drug that prevented him from making any muscular movements at all (his breathing required a respirator). He found that he could indeed still think even though he could not move a muscle in his voice box (S. Smith et al., 1947). So Watson was wrong. Thought does not require any motor activity.

If thought is not the same thing as subvocal language, as Watson claimed, then perhaps thought is determined and shaped by the language that people use. This view, put forth by linguist B. L. Whorf (1956) was called *linguistic determinism*. Whorf argued that the languages developed by different cultural groups structure their world views in different ways. He cited as evidence the fact that Eskimos have many different words for *snow* while groups for whom snow is not so important have only one or a few. Similarly, some rice-eating cultural groups have nearly a hundred names for different kinds of rice, and there are thousands of words for camel in Arabic.

Although interesting, these examples are not unequivocal support for Whorf's hypothesis. Perhaps it is the other way around. Perhaps cultural needs first alter the way people think about their environment, in turn requiring a more precise vocabulary. Maybe it is the concepts that are important for which people then develop more terms and terms of greater precision; this could explain the differences from one culture to another.

There are many sources of support for a belief in the primacy of thought over language. Language is a relatively late invention on the evolutionary timetable, certainly coming long after prehistoric peoples were using thought to solve problems and even making cave drawings to represent what they believed was significant in their lives. Also, in declarative sentences there is a preferred word order the world over in the use of subjects, verbs, and objects. In 80 percent of the world's languages, the subject comes first, and the object is always last. This consistency in languages is assumed to reflect a basic property of human thought (Ultan, 1969).

Current approaches. Following Watson's lead, psychologists for many years continued to treat language as a performance—as conditionable behavior (Skinner, 1957). But by the 1950s linguists, led by Noam Chomsky (1957, 1975), were arguing forcefully that behaviorists missed the unique features of language by focusing on recurring aspects of small speech units such as words. For Chomsky, language could be understood only as a complex, abstract system governed by rules and built upon an innate capacity for language and linguistic competence. To him, the study of language should not be about what people *do* in learning words but about what they *know* about language structure, as evidenced by their competence in constructing meaningful sentences.

This challenge by linguists to the behavioristic psychologists' view of language was joined by the emerging band of psychologists who were becoming interested in studying information processing. These psychologists demonstrated the psychological reality of syntax and other covert features of language through studies such as the following.

Subjects memorized strings of pseudo words that meant nothing, ordinarily had zero frequency of appearing together, and were without any pattern of regularity.

In the first condition, the string was simply a list of nonsense words, such as: *haky deeb um flut recile pav tolfent dison*. In the second condition, articles (the, a) and suffixes (s, est, ed, ly) were randomly added to these nonsense words: *haky deebs the um flutest reciled pav a tolfently dison*. In a third condition, capital letters and periods were added, and the nonsense strings were constructed to resemble sentences: *A haky deebs reciled the dison tolfently um flutest pav.*

Although the word strings in the first condition were the shortest, they were the hardest to recall. Next hardest to recall were the words in the second condition. Best remembered were the word strings in the third condition (Epstein, 1961).

This result could be explained only by the differences in grammatical information in the three word strings.

A large body of research has provided other behavioral data in support of the view that people possess and act upon complex linguistic knowledge (e.g., G. Miller, 1962). But in recent years cognitive psychologists have diverged from their earlier allegiance to the strictly linguistic views of language. In the first place, they feel linguists have underrated the importance of semantic (meaning) factors. Many of the experimental findings have shown the operation of *nonlinguistic* factors, such as context, expectations, general knowledge, or focus of attention and not simply syntax or other grammatical features. Also, it was found that details of the syntactic structure or other grammatical features were forgotten much sooner than the semantic content. For example, given the sentence, "The ball that Bruce threw went to Joanne," subjects would remember the gist—that Bruce threw the ball to Joanne—better than the grammatical structure of the sentence. The interpreted, *deep* structure of sentences was thus shown to be partially independent of the literal, *surface* structure, indicating the importance of meaning (Slobin, 1979).

Cognitive psychologists have also rejected the linguists' notion of language and thought as independent systems, arguing for many interdependencies between language and thought. Much current research, in fact, is aimed at showing the convergence and interrelationships between concepts related to language and concepts related to long-term memory and comprehension (Clark & Clark, 1977).

Criteria for "true" language

Many animal species have communication systems. Dolphins whistle, birds call, bees dance, dogs bark. But do these qualify as "true" language? What are the criteria by which a communication system can be evaluated as a language system?

Although the thousands of modern human languages differ in many ways, they all share the following basic characteristics (taken from a longer list by Hockett, 1960):

1. *Specialization.* The chief purpose of a language is to communicate information to others. Other behaviors may also communicate a message without that being their primary purpose. For example, a panting dog communicates that it is hot, but the panting is a physiological mechanism designed to relieve the animal's discomfort. It is not done for the purpose of sending its master a message. The dog would still pant in the master's absence.

THE FAR SIDE/GARY LARSON

Hang him, you idiots. Hang him. String him up is a figure of speech

2. *Arbitrariness.* The combination of sounds selected to refer to something is arbitrary: there is no direct connection between the thing named and the features of the word chosen to name it. The color we call *green* is called *vert* in French, *zöld* in Hungarian. However, once a word is selected to stand for something, then all speakers of the language must agree to use it in the same way.

3. *Displacement.* Unlike the warning cries of animals sensing danger, language may be generated in the absence of any immediate controlling stimuli. Similarly, we use language to talk about things not in the here and now—about the past, the future, and even imagined realities.

4. *Productivity and novelty.* Language makes possible a virtually infinite number of utterances. Speakers of a language can produce novel phrases and sentences that they have never heard before.

5. *Iteration and recursion.* Iteration is the addition of words and phrases to sentences; recursion is the embedding of one language structure within another of the same kind. Both of these processes allow for infinite variability. Following are examples of iteration:

Iteration extends the meaning.

Iteration extends the meaning and adds complexity.

Iteration extends the meaning and adds complexity, and is a feature found only in human communication systems.

Both iteration and recursion are used in the popular children's story, *The House that Jack Built*.

Is language uniquely human?

It is obvious that only human language meets all five of these criteria for language. But does that mean that no other species has the *ability* to use language to express thoughts? Would it be possible to train members of another species, such as chimpanzees, to use a symbolic language system? Several researchers have been engaged in just such a venture for a number of years. This research requires an enormous investment of time, effort, patience, and ingenuity, but that has not deterred psychologists from attempting to teach apes to use language.

Early efforts aimed at getting apes to use spoken language met with little success (Hayes, 1951; Kellogg & Kellogg, 1933). But did these failures mean that apes could not handle the rules of the language, or only that the subjects did not have the vocal apparatus necessary for producing speech?

In the late 1960s, a different approach was tried that did not depend on the animal's vocal apparatus. Some investigators were able to teach apes, mostly chimps, to communicate using American Sign Language for the deaf (Fouts & Rigby, 1977; Gardner & Gardner, 1972). Others taught chimps to use plastic symbols as words, to combine them to communicate thoughts, and even to type messages on a keyboard console where each key represented one of their symbol words (Premack, 1976; Rumbaugh, 1977).

These animals learned to use hundreds of different signs or symbols, to combine them to form larger units, and to generalize a sign or symbol (for example, from "more tickling" to "more banana"). In addition, they used their words as we do—as symbols representing objects, in order to convey information to another individual.

The controversy seemed headed toward the conclusion that these animals are capable of true language until observation of a young chimp, named Nim Chimpsky (in honor of Noam Chomsky) suggested that it really wasn't so. Close videotape analysis of Nim's sign combinations led to the conclusion that Nim was merely producing a string of signs and not true sentences. Nim's utterances seemed to be largely imitations of his trainer's signs, along with signs that would elicit a quick response from the trainer (and a tasty reward). What was lacking was the essential characteristic of human language—*the spontaneous combination of words to form novel phrases or sentences that are understandable by others.* After years of intense training, neither Nim nor any of the other apes has been able to increase the length and complexity of the phrases they produce. The crux of the argument is that chimps do not learn to use word signs *creatively* to form new combinations of signs in a grammatically competent way (Terrace, 1979).

Other researchers are challenging these negative conclusions, however. Some claim that even if language training does not lead chimps to use language spontaneously, it does enhance their ability to perform certain abstract reasoning tasks (Premack, 1983). And the notion of true language as being "for humans only" is now being challenged by research with gorillas.

> For over a decade two gorillas, Koko and Michael, have been studied and coached in sign language by Francine Patterson (1981). Koko signs to herself and her dolls when she is alone, combines signs into new patterns, and uses language to express complex concepts, as when she refers to herself and signs "fine animal gorilla." The pair of gorillas also use sign language with each other. But will they teach their offspring to communicate with sign language without the help of their human teacher? That eagerly awaited test will come if and when these gorillas mate.

It is too soon to know how the dispute over the various species' capacity for language will be resolved. But it is interesting to note in concluding this chapter that the "Clever Hans" phenomenon with which we began our study of thought processes has been at work once again. Nim Chimpsky was also discovered to have been responding to prompting by the trainers who were reinforcing his use of symbols. Maybe higher levels of thinking and language are uniquely human, but we humans may still be fooled by a horse that taps in German or a chimp that signs for his supper.

△ *Above, a chimp signing "brush." At right, Koko, using her computer terminal, and trainer Francine Patterson. Koko's ability to communicate in sign language has been impressive. Some researchers believe that apes are capable of true language, but others feel that what appear to be language abilities are the result of subtle cues inadvertently given by the apes' trainers.*

SUMMARY

■ Cognition is a general term for all forms of knowing, including attending, remembering, reasoning, imagining, anticipating, planning, deciding, solving problems, and communicating ideas. Cognitive psychology is the study of these higher mental processes and of the mental structures that make them possible. Cognitive science is an interdisciplinary approach to studying systems that manipulate information.

■ Though thinking cannot be observed, it can be inferred from observation of several kinds of processes, such as reports of introspection, think-aloud protocols, adaptive behavior, reaction time, errors, eye and muscle movements, and brain waves.

■ The basic mental structures for thinking are concepts, which are mental representations of *kinds* of things rather than of specific examples. Our ability to form concepts enables us to react to new events as members of classes. We organize concepts in networks and hierarchies in our mental structures, but depend on basic levels in thinking and in recognizing stimuli.

■ In forming concepts, we develop mental representations broad enough to include different instances but narrow enough to exclude noninstances. In using hypotheses to identify concepts, people tend to underuse disconfirming evidence.

■ Most complex thought is believed to be based on networks of propositions. These, in turn, may be derived from networks of schemas and scripts, knowledge clusters about factual and procedural information, respectively. Schemas and scripts include expectations and thus influence perception, thought, and memory.

■ Visual images and cognitive maps are additional mental structures; they are used in thinking in which spatial relationships are important.

■ Comprehending new information is a process comparable to the interweaving of assimilation and accommodation in childhood: what is familiar is added to existing structures and what is unfamiliar or does not fit forces changes in the structures or is distorted or ignored.

■ In making decisions and judgments, we balance utility against probability. Irrational factors may lead to inaccurate weighing of these criteria. In conditions of uncertainty, we all use heuristics—short cuts—such as availability and representativeness. Vivid examples influence our judgments more than statistics.

■ In solving problems we must define the initial state, the goal state, and the operations that can get us from the first to the second—a difficult task in itself in ill-defined problems. Functional fixedness and other mental sets can hamper creative problem solving. Algorithms ensure an eventual solution if there is one, but are impractical in many cases. Heuristics can often reach the solution faster.

■ In skill development, declarative knowledge is gained, converted into procedural knowledge, and eventually made automatic. Both practice and adequate feedback are essential.

■ Experts, compared with novices, have more specific and general knowledge, have greater facility in using appropriate rules and strategies, and represent problems internally according to common principles rather than surface structure.

■ The thinking processes of experts in various fields are also being studied with computers. Computers are being programmed to carry out classification tasks formerly believed to require human experts, such as diagnosing disease. Current research is focused on how to supplement specialized knowledge with essential general knowledge, on how to build in the ability to learn from experience and on how to build some common sense into expert systems.

■ Metacognitive knowledge is the awareness of what we know and need to know and of how well we are comprehending information or dealing with a problem. Metacognitive skills can be learned and taught.

■ Humans communicate ideas through natural language, artificial languages, visual communication, and nonverbal means such as gestures. Nonverbal elements carry a large part of the message conveyed when two people interact.

■ Theories of the relation between thought and language have included a number of opposing claims: that language depends on thought, that thought depends on language, and that they are closely interrelated, with innate linguistic predispositions providing structural constraints but experience providing meaning and other nonlinguistic features. Cognitive psychologists are demonstrating close interrelationships between language and other cognitive processes.

■ Criteria for "true language" include use of speech symbols specifically for communication, an arbitrary relationship between objects and the symbols for them, use of the symbols independently of the stimulus situation, capacity for originality and a virtually infinite number of utterances, and iteration and recursion in sentence structure.

■ Chimpanzees and gorillas lack the vocal apparatus necessary for spoken language but can learn to use both tangible symbols and sign-language symbols for communication. Whether they can employ these symbols in true language is still a matter of debate.

Part Five

Personality Processes

Chapter Eleven
Understanding Human Personality

Chapter Twelve
Assessing Individual Differences

UNDERSTANDING HUMAN PERSONALITY

■ STUDYING PERSONALITY
Research strategies
Theories about personality

■ TYPE AND TRAIT THEORIES
Categorizing with types
Describing with traits
Criticisms of type and trait theories

■ PSYCHODYNAMIC THEORIES
Freudian psychoanalysis
Neo-Freudian theories
Criticisms of Freudian theory

■ HUMANISTIC THEORIES
A person-centered approach
Self theory
Criticisms of humanistic theories

■ LEARNING THEORIES
A strict behavioristic approach
Reconciling the analytic and behavioral approaches
Bandura's social learning theory
Criticism of learning theories

■ COGNITIVE THEORIES
Personal construct theory
Cognitive social learning theory
Criticisms of cognitive theories

■ COMPARING THEORIES

■ SUMMARY

Winn was a sophomore when he came to the attention of a team of psychologists studying personality. He was singled out not because of his "problem behavior" but rather because he was *happy!* His self-report on a standard psychological test indicated that he was generally more happy than other students and was rarely depressed. Also, people who observed his behavior rated him as very happy; and those who searched his past concluded that it was happy, too.

Winn's parents had provided a stable and conventional upbringing in a small midwestern city. The oldest of several sons, Winn described his parents as "wonderful, kind, and understanding." They were affectionate to each other, to their children, and to their extended families. They emphasized moral values, punished him when he got "too far out of line," and, like the teachers at the Sunday school he regularly attended, stressed "vices and virtues."

The conventionality and emphasis on control in Winn's upbringing were reflected in his being more cautious than impulsive, more rational than emotionally expressive. His fantasies were neither intense nor bizarre; rather, they were mature visions of a desirable future with a satisfying marriage and a large, happy family.

By college, Winn was tall, lean, and handsome, with an athlete's natural abilities. He was aware that most people liked and respected him, and he in turn tried to make others happy. In fact, making life happy and good for others was one of his strongly held personal values.

Winn enjoyed his work, thrived on competition, and was motivated by the need to be successful. But he reserved time from his studies for music, sports, and dating. By carefully allocating his time and resources, Winn was able to be an honors physics major, play in the college band, and enjoy an active social life.

Even the happiest of people have their ups and downs, and so did Winn. However, his lows were infrequent and usually reflected shifts from zestful, extremely happy days to somewhat less happy ones. During the period he was being studied, his lowest mood came when he developed a sudden, painful illness. His happiest days came when he was involved with other people.

The personality researchers wondered if Winn's happiness was just a facade that concealed a more troubled inner person. Their attempts to get at deeper issues with Winn provided a picture of a more complex person, but not really a more troubled one. From Winn's responses to psychological tests, the portrait emerged of someone able to be open and undefensive about being tender. His answers were generally conventional and unoriginal. However, there were indications of some deeper emotional areas of personality that he could not accept. He used intellectual defenses to distance himself from situations that aroused anger and erotic feelings.

His stories (told in response to standard test stimuli designed to reveal underlying conflicts and unconscious motives) were of nice children in a world of temptations. It was a world where giving in to temptation was evil and led to grief, while good was rewarded.

If there were flaws in the personality of this happy young man, they showed up only in a rather strong fear of disapproval and in a seeming barrier that existed between his rationally ordered existence and the impulsive side of his nature, which he rarely acknowledged. Despite these human frailties, the researchers who studied him concluded that Winn was what he appeared to be: a person of "genuine, consistent zest and happiness" (Ricks & Wessman, 1966).

From Winn's case we get a positive example of the psychological study of regularities in individual actions and characteristic features of people that make them recognizable. What is there about people that serves to identify them as distinctive from others in the same situation? It is not just that people look different or respond differently to a given stimulus. There also seems to be a subjective, private aspect of individuals that gives coherence and order to their behavior. Taken together, these special features, unique aspects, orderly and consistent properties of individuals are what we usually mean by personality.

If psychologists studied *you,* how might their portrait of your personality be similar to Winn's, and in what ways different? Most of us like to think of ourselves as unique, but if so, how so?

Up to this point in our psychological journey we have seen how scientific investigations focus on specific processes that are similar in all of us, such as nerve signal transmission, perception, conditioning, and decision making. We have also been aware that the goal in much of this research is to discover general laws of behavior that account for why different individuals in the same stimulus situation react alike.

In this chapter a different perspective on psychology is presented, one that studies the whole person as the sum of those separate processes of feelings, thoughts, and actions. We will begin by examining the major issues and strategies in the psychological study of personality. Then we will survey the major theories of personality, each of which attempts to provide the "best" or "right" approach to understanding human nature.

Interest in personality is obviously not limited to psychologists. Philosophers, theologians, dramatists, and novelists have long sought to understand how personality and character are formed, maintained, or transformed. The special province of the psychologist however, is the measurement of personality. The English scientist, Francis Galton began the first scientific study of how individuals differ only a few years after Wundt established his psychological laboratory. Galton staked out the claim for personality measurement when he wrote: "The character which shapes our conduct is a definite and durable 'something,' and therefore . . . it is reasonable to attempt to measure it" (1884, p. 179). The next chapter deals with assessment of individuals, especially their intelligence and personality. We will see that there are many ways in which Winn might have been studied in addition to the approach taken to reveal what he was "really like."

STUDYING PERSONALITY

In popular usage, the word *personality* is something akin to "attractiveness," "charm," or "charisma." "She may not be pretty, but she has a nice personality." "Be careful, he has a very forceful personality." Personality is a quality movie stars and those politicians we like have a lot of, while the rest of us must make do with less.

Even as a child, you had probably developed and put to use your own system of appraising personality. You tried to determine who in your class would be friend or foe; you worked out techniques for dealing with your parents or particular teachers, and you tried to understand your own strengths and weaknesses. Your judgments were, in fact, primitive personality assessments. They were based largely on intuition and limited observations; such naive judgments are often accurate, but also are open to many sources of error.

By now you have become a full-fledged personality theorist. Whether or not you are aware of it, you have a set of ideas about your own personality and about the personalities of others with whom you interact. Like the rest of us, you carry around an "implicit personality theory" that helps you explain and predict people's behavior, and maybe even control your own at times. We will see shortly how your theory differs from the formal theories of professional psychologists. But as we present different theories, be sensitive to where your implicit theory agrees or disagrees with, or never included aspects central to, formal personality theorists.

The field of *personality psychology* puts the "person" back into psychology by attempting to integrate all aspects of functioning of the individual person. This requires building upon the accumulated knowledge of all the areas of psychology we have studied so far plus that of social psychology, which includes interpersonal and group processes. Personality psychology also goes beyond an interest in the normally functioning individual. It provides the research and theoretical foundation for understanding personal problems and pathologies of body, mind and behavior (Chapters 13 and 14), as well as a basis for therapeutic approaches to change personality (Chapter 15).

Psychologists give a variety of definitions for personality, but common to all of them are concepts of *uniqueness* and *characteristic behavior*. Simply put, **personality** is what characterizes an individual. It includes the *unique psychological qualities of an individual that influence a variety of characteristic behavior patterns* (both overt and covert) *across different situations* and *over time* (see, too, **Table 11.1** for additional terms used in personality descriptions). Although it is not clear just how consistent individuals *really* are, most personality theorists do continue to expect considerable consistency. What makes people behave in characteristic ways as unique individuals is looked on as *the* issue to be studied.

Yet this does not mean that psychologists working in personality are not interested in finding general laws. As in other areas of psychology, many personality theorists believe that there are principles that can be applied to all human beings but think it is vital for theorists to account for *differences* among people too. As we will see, many theories have been developed that attempt to accomplish this dual aim. They try to explain the uniformities in behavior across people (the *nomothetic* approach) and also what makes people different from one another and unique (the *idiographic* approach).

Just what *does* characterize an individual? Without really thinking about it, we are able to recognize our friends, even if we have not seen them for some time. If we know people well enough, we are even able to recognize them from someone else's account of their behavior. ("Oh, that must have been Jim. He always does things like that.") How are we able to do it? The key would seem to lie in *consistency*. We are able to recognize individuals, and to characterize them to others, by the ways they are consistent—across different situations and over time. Even if they are consistently unpredictable, that is something we can say about them that distinguishes them from less mercurial folk.

But the matter is more complex. Try the following test. Think about two people who are important in your life—one you like and one you do not like. Is either one primarily "good" (strong, kind, understanding) or primarily "bad" (weak, cruel, inconsiderate)? Or does it depend on the circumstances? Now

Table 11.1 *Terms used in personality descriptions*

In descriptions of the elements that are significant within an individual's personality, the following concepts are often included:

Term	Definition	Example
Temperament	Biologically-based characteristic manner of reacting, evident at or soon after birth, notably in emotionality and activity level.	Some newborns are excitable and active; others in the same nursery (or from different cultures) show a calm and passive temperament.
Trait	A constant, persistent, and specific way of behaving that can be measured along a continuum and is used both to characterize individuals and to predict their future behavior.	A person who donates to charity, gives money to friends in need, and gives up time for a worthy cause could be said to be high on the trait of "generosity."
Type	A distinct category to which people showing a particular pattern of traits can be assigned.	"Type-A" people are prone to coronary problems because of their characteristic way of dealing with life challenges.
Disposition	A tendency or set, within an individual to react to a given situation in a characteristic way; synonymous with *trait* in discussions of dispositional vs. situational explanations of behavior.	A person who is ready with a smile, kind word, or sympathetic ear is said to have a "friendly disposition."
Character	Nearly the same as *personality* when used to refer to the individual's total pattern of regularly occurring behavior. When used in evaluation of the *quality* of someone's personality, implies judgment of the person's morals and values along with other attributes.	Letters of recommendation usually refer to the person's trustworthy or emotionally stable character.
Character types	Used in some theories to designate identifiable, adult patterns of behavior organized around certain themes and formed early in life.	Freud's oral and anal character types.
State	A subjective, consciously perceived set of feelings of a certain kind, accompanied by autonomic nervous system arousal, or by cognitive processes. A state is more transitory than a trait.	Not being prepared for an exam will induce a state of worrying; always being upset at exams is a sign of the trait of test anxiety.
Mood	An emotional state that may temporarily dominate one's outlook and appearance.	Success brings on euphoria, failure puts us in a depressed or irritable mood.
Habit	A learned mode of behaving that is relatively fixed and reliably occurs in certain situations.	A prize-fighter may have the *habit* of making the sign of the cross before each round.
Attitude	A learned tendency to evaluate classes of objects or people favorably or unfavorably based on one's beliefs and feelings.	Authoritarian people often hold prejudiced attitudes toward minority groups.
Values	Something the individual learns to believe is important, worthwhile to have; a value can be a principle to live by or something to achieve or maintain.	For authoritarian personality types, order and power are important values.

(Based on Corsini, 1977)

think about yourself and answer those two questions.

Most often, the results of this simple demonstration are to discover that we see other people we know well as quite consistently either good or bad irrespective of the situation, while we see ourselves as more influenced by circumstances and thus more variable. This paradox highlights our tendency to attribute consistency to the behavior of others and to formulate consistent patterns of responses and traits when we characterize others.

This tendency to perceive consistency in other people is an extension of a more general tendency to perceive consistency in all events, part of a general process of organizing our world in such a way as to make it coherent, orderly, and more readily predictable. Thus we must raise the question of whether the consistency we perceive in people, around which theories about personality traits are organized, actually exists in the people observed or only in the minds of the observers.

Over the years, personality theorists have differed markedly in how they have described this consistency and in the ways in which they have tried to account for it. In fact, as we shall see, many researchers today are finding that the notion of consistency in personality across different situations and over time may not be as simple as had been thought. When we study human behavior we observe *both* personal consistency and variability due to situational influences. Theories and research must indicate when and how life circumstances influence the personal characteristics people bring to those situations, as well as how personality affects reactions to those situations.

Research strategies

The main difference between popular, nonpsychological approaches to understanding personality and that of personality psychology is *research*. Instead of just thinking, reasoning, and having opinions about personality, scientific researchers study personality *empirically*. They collect data through direct observation of individuals. Their evidence and the procedures used to gather it are open to replication by other investigators in order to be verified, modified,

or rejected. This reliance on the scientific method (outlined in Chapter 1) is the hallmark of personality research that makes it different from the way casual "people-watchers" form their views about personality (Neale & Liebert, 1973).

Three major research strategies for collecting information about the nature of personality are: the case study approach, the correlational approach, and the experimental approach. They use different types of observations made under particular conditions of data collection. Each one provides a special type of evidence that helps in putting together a total portrait of the human personality.

The case study method. For getting a lot of information about a single individual, the case study method is ideal. In-depth *qualitative* descriptions of the behavior of one person are organized into a unique biography. The researcher may use a variety of techniques to discover what this person is like, such as interviews, psychological tests, behavioral observations, and writings or other products he or she has created.

You have already seen this method applied in our *Opening Case* of Winn, where the researchers tried to gather an array of information that would help clarify why he was so well adjusted. In this case, the different sources of data converged to yield a pattern of uniformity between his outer behavior and his internal, subjective state. In other uses, the case study method may reveal discrepancies between what the person appears to be like and the person's inner dynamics. This is more often true in case studies of *abnormal* personality, as we saw earlier in the research on multiple personalities (Chapter 6). Sigmund Freud used case studies of his patients and others he developed from written records as evidence for his hypotheses about psychopathology.

The case study approach is useful for investigating the personality of a single individual across many of his or her own natural environments. It provides a source of rich data on the complexity of personality from which new hypotheses may be derived. The obvious weaknesses in this approach are the *lack of control* over what is observed and how, and the difficulty in making comparisons or generalizations from one case to another.

Psychologists who use the case study method to study personality by identifying a person's unique characteristics follow an **idiographic approach**. In this approach, each trait is viewed as unique in each personality because it functions differently, depending on the overall pattern of traits. For example, if Jeremy is discriminating, compulsive, and demanding, while John is discriminating, careful, and sensitive, then "being discriminating" would be a quite different trait in the two personalities. When traits are averaged across people to get group scores or correlations, this uniqueness is lost.

The contrasting **nomothetic approach** assumes that there is an underlying basic structure to personality and that universal trait dimensions common to everyone provide this structure. In this view, individuals differ only *in the degree* to which they possess personality traits. Researchers using a nomothetic approach try to establish universal, lawful relationships between different aspects of personality functioning, such as traits, by means of the correlational method.

The correlational method. The correlational method is called for when a researcher wants to determine if there is a consistent relationship between two or more *behaviors* (or events) for a group of people that are observed under the same conditions. Pairs of observations (usually personality test scores) on each person in the sample are correlated. The question answered by such correlational data is whether and to what extent the variables co-occur.* For example, "Is high self-esteem related to willingness to take risks?" or "Is aggressiveness greater in those with a low tolerance for frustration?"

Correlational methods are widely used in personality research because they provide an economical way to get a considerable amount of precise data on large samples of individuals. We will see that it is the preferred method of personality researchers who

---

*Correlation was explained in Chapter 1 and is discussed further in the *Appendix,* "Understanding Research."

study traits. The weakness in this method is one we pointed up in Chapter 1: we do not know the *direction* of the relationship, which one caused the other, or indeed, if they are even *causally* related.

An excellent example of the correlational method (within a longitudinal study) is a recent investigation of the personality correlates of children's ability to delay gratification.

To study how personality variables relate to delay of gratification, researchers tested 116 children on two tasks and correlated these behavioral data with personality test ratings. The tasks assessed the child's ability to resist the temptation to play with an attractive, "forbidden" toy until the experimenter returned (6 minutes later), and also to wait for several minutes before opening a gift placed nearby. Aspects of each child's personality were rated by teachers on a special assessment measure (the Q-sort test) at four ages: when they were 3, 4, 7, and 11 years of age. Delay of gratification scores were correlated with the personality ratings at each age for girls and boys separately.

Girls who delayed gratification were consistently described as intelligent, resourceful, and competent. Girls who failed to delay were rated as sulky, whiney, easily offended, and likely to be victimized by other children and go to pieces under stress. By contrast, boys who delayed gratification were rated over the four periods as deliberate, attentive, reasonable, reserved, cooperative, and able to concentrate. The nondelaying boys tended to be described as aggressive, irritable, restless, and not self-controlled. In general, girls showed a greater degree of delay of gratification than boys (Funder et al., 1984).

The experimental method. When the experimental method is used in personality research, a causal relationship is sought between *stimulus* conditions and personality-relevant *behaviors.* The objective is to test a hypothesis about the causal effect of a manipulated condition on outcome behaviors. There is a trade-off when using this method; the gain in control of variables, along with precision and reliability of specific information gathered, comes at the expense of less breadth of information collected. Personality researchers who follow a learning or cognitive theoretical view tend to use the experimental method more than do proponents of other personality theories.

An interesting use of this method studied the effects of guilt arousal on feelings of depression.

Eighteen female undergraduates who were found on a depression inventory to be depressed were randomly assigned to three experimental conditions. In all conditions, stimuli were flashed so briefly on a tachistoscope that they were *subliminal* (below the level of conscious perception).

In the *guilt* condition, the stimuli were "Leaving Mom is wrong" and a picture of a frowning young woman turning away from an older one. In the *symbiotic reassurance* condition, the stimuli were "Mommy and I are one" and a picture of a younger and older woman next to each other with shoulders joined. The *control* condition presented the neutral sentence, "People are talking," with a picture of two women in conversation. A double-blind procedure was used to ensure that neither the experimenter nor the subject was aware of the manipulated conditions. The dependent measure was change in depression score from before to after exposure to these subliminal messages.

The results supported the hypothesis that exposure to stimuli likely to arouse guilt increased depression compared to the control group scores. However, the positive message did not have the effect of reducing depression. This study is one that supports a psychodynamic interpretation of some aspects of personality functioning (Dauber, 1984).

Theories about personality

Theories about personality are hypothetical statements about the structure and functioning of individual personality. They help us achieve two of the major goals of psychology: (a) *understanding* different aspects of personality—its origins, correlates, and consequences, and (b) *predicting* behavior based on knowing something about personality. Different theories make different predictions about how people will behave under certain conditions.

In the previous correlational example, the observed relationship between delay of gratification and personality ratings was explained by the theoretical construct of "ego control," the individual's general ability to contain or release impulses, feelings,

and desires. (In the *Appendix*, p. 641, we have another example of the theorized effects of too much ego control in shy sudden murderers). Theoretical constructs are unseen, intervening variables that tie together phenomena that a general theory identifies as significant, such as subliminal activation of guilt and depression.

Before we examine a number of major theoretical approaches in personality, it is well to ask why we need so many different (often competing) theories. The answer is like that given in Chapter 1 for the reason there are a variety of alternate general conceptual models. Different theorists approach the complexity of human nature and the functioning of mind and behavior from different starting points, using different levels of analysis, while seeing some variables and processes as more important than other investigators believe them to be. Some deal with specific traits and behaviors, while others deal with more general dispositions. Some are more concerned with what a person *is,* while others place more emphasis on how he or she has changed or may develop in the future. Some theories grew out of observations of people with psychological problems, while others are based on observations of normal people in normal circumstances. Thus, each theory approaches the subject at hand from a different orientation. Each can teach us something about personality, and together they can teach us even more.

The many current theoretical approaches to understanding personality can be grouped into five categories: type and trait theories, psychodynamic theories, humanistic theories, learning theories, and cognitive theories.

TYPE AND TRAIT THEORIES

Labeling and classifying the many personality characteristics we observe can help us organize the diversity of human behavior. But simplicity in the task is not guaranteed! One dictionary search found 18,000 adjectives in the English language which we use to describe personality traits.

Two of the oldest approaches to describing personality involve describing people as belonging to a limited number of types or as possessing particular traits that all people are assumed to have in varying degrees. Let's examine what each conception contributes to our understanding of personality.

Categorizing with types

Do you ever classify the people in your life according to their college class, academic major, sex, race, fraternity or sorority affiliation? Some personality theorists, too, classify people into separate groups according to their personality **types,** which are distinct patterns of personality characteristics. In a typological approach, people are assigned to categories on the basis of particular similarities. These categories do not overlap: if a person is assigned to one category—say according to a type of physique or occupation or sex—he or she is not in any other categories within that type. That is, personality types are all-or-none phenomena.

Most personality typologies are designed to specify a relationship between some simple, highly visible or easily determined characteristic and some behaviors that can be expected: if fat, then jolly; if an engineer, then conservative; if female, then sympathetic; and so it goes. You can appreciate why such systems have traditionally had much popular appeal.

One of the earliest type theories was proposed in the fifth century B.C. by Hippocrates. He theorized that the body contained four basic fluids or *humors,* each associated with a particular *temperament.* Each individual's personality depended on which one of these humors were predominant. Hippocrates' pairing of body humors with personality temperaments was:

"All right, I'm labeling you. Did it ever occur to you I wouldn't label you if you weren't such a type?"

- **Blood**—Sanguine temperament, cheerful and active
- **Phlegm**—Phlegmatic temperament, apathetic and sluggish
- **Black bile**—melancholy temperament, sad and brooding
- **Yellow bile**—choleric temperament, irascible and excitable

An interesting, popular type theory of personality was one advanced by an American physician, William Sheldon (1942). Sheldon sought to relate physique to temperament. He assigned people to categories based on their **somatotypes,** or body builds: *endomorphic* (fat, soft, round), *mesomorphic* (muscular, rectangular, strong), or *ectomorphic* (thin, long, fragile). The point of the typology was to specify relationships between these physiques (or constitutional types) and particular personality traits, activities, and preferences.

What would you expect a typical endomorph or a mesomorph to be like? You might guess that endomorphs would be relaxed, fond of eating, sociable, and gut-oriented. Mesomorphs would be physical people, filled with energy, courage, and assertive tendencies. Ectomorphs would be brainy, artistic, and introverted; they would think about life rather than consuming it or acting upon it (see **Figure 11.1**).

Though appealing in its simplicity, Sheldon's typology has proven to be of little value in predicting an individual's behavior from his or her somatotype—once the stereotypes that bias most people's expectations are eliminated (Tyler, 1965). In addition, people come in many different shapes, and many of us cannot be assigned readily to one of Sheldon's pure somatotypes.

Body Type
Temperament

Endomorphic
Soft & round

Relaxed, sociable,
& fond of eating

Mesomorphic
Muscular & strong

Energetic,
courageous,
& assertive

Ectomorphic
Thin and fragile

Brainy, artistic,
& introverted

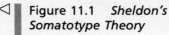

Figure 11.1 *Sheldon's Somatotype Theory*

Sheldon's (1942) theory of personality and body types is intriguing if unsubstantiated.

A more recent, better accepted type approach attempts to reduce the complexity of personality to a few major categories. H. J. Eysenck (1970, 1975), suggested that the two major dimensions of personality are *introversion-extraversion* and *stability-instability* (or *"neuroticism"*). Extraverts are sociable, outgoing, active, impulsive, "tough-minded" people. Introverts are their psychological opposites—"tender-minded," withdrawn, passive, cautious, and reflective.

Introverts are assumed to be born with a more sensitive, easily arousable autonomic nervous system than extraverts. (Incidentally, Eysenck spells it "extraversion"; others spell it "extroversion.") Eysenck's theory is based on a large amount of personality test data. Although the data show that people have many traits, the traits cluster into four categories that represent the smallest number of basic personality types according to this view. While most people fall at intermediate points within each of the four quadrants of Eysenck's personality circle (shown in the **Figure 11.2**), it is the extremes that distinguish the types. When a person is high on extraversion and also on instability, criminality is predicted as a possible life-style. Individuals diagnosed as *neurotic,* on the other hand, would be people who combine introversion with instability in this model.

Eysenck has studied how extraverts as a group differ from introverts in standard behavioral tests. One finding has been that introverts have lower thresholds for pain than extraverts. Introverts also learn faster than extraverts when unconditioned stimuli are weak or reinforcement is partial rather than continuous. Associations they learn in the presence of stimuli that create low levels of arousal are better recalled immediately than those learned when arousal is high. Extraverts perform better when they are more aroused, and also seem to need more external arousal to maintain their performance than do the self-stimulating introverts (Howarth & Eysenck, 1968).

Describing with traits

Psychologists who identify people as types assume that there are separate, *discontinuous* categories into which people fall. By contrast, psychologists who describe people in terms of traits typically assume the existence of underlying, continuous dimensions, such as intelligence or generosity, that everyone has to some degree. Traits are assumed to be qualities or attributes that people possess which influence behavior because they act as "generalized action tendencies." Knowing someone's traits ought to enable us to explain and perhaps predict better what he or

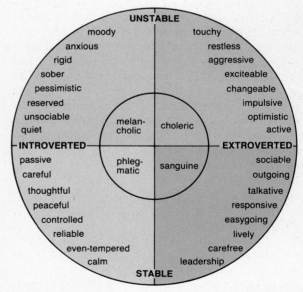

(From Eysenck, 1973, p. 191.)

Figure 11.2 *The Four Quadrants of Eysenck's Personality Circle*

she will do. Sometimes we can, but sometimes we can't for reasons to be discussed in this section.

Gordon Allport (1937, 1961, 1966) viewed traits as the building blocks of personality and the source of individual uniqueness. They produce consistencies in behavior because they are *enduring* attributes of the person and are *general* or broad in their scope. That is, they connect and unify a person's reactions to a variety of stimuli (see **Figure 11.3**).

Allport identified three kinds of traits. A *cardinal trait* is one around which a person organizes his or her life. For some it might involve power or achievement; for others, self-sacrifice for the good of others. Not all people develop cardinal traits. *Central traits* are traits we think of as major characteristics of a person, such as honesty or conscientiousness. *Secondary traits* are less important characteristics that are not central to our understanding of the individual's personality, such as particular attitudes, preferences, and style of behavior.

Gordon Allport (1897–1967)

According to Allport, these three kinds of traits form the structure of the personality—which, in turn, determines an individual's behavior. Allport saw *personality structures* rather than environmental conditions as the critical determiner of individual behavior. "The same fire that melts the butter hardens the egg," he said, as a way of showing that the same stimuli could have different effects on different individuals. Although he recognized *common* traits that were shared by individuals in a given culture, Allport was most interested in discovering the *unique traits* that made each person a singular entity. He argued for this view by stating that

"we must acknowledge the roughness and inadequacy of our universal dimensions. Thereby shall we enhance our own ability to understand, predict and control. By learning to handle the individuality of motives and the uniqueness of personality, we shall become better scientists, not worse" (Allport, 1960, p. 148).

Allport was the most influential of the ideographic trait theorists. He is identified as an idiographic trait theorist because he believed that each person has some unique, idiosyncratic traits as well as a unique combination of traits.

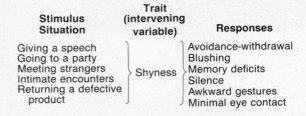

Stimulus Situation	Trait (intervening variable)	Responses
Giving a speech Going to a party Meeting strangers Intimate encounters Returning a defective product	Shyness	Avoidance-withdrawal Blushing Memory deficits Silence Awkward gestures Minimal eye contact

△ | **Figure 11.3**

Traits may act as intervening variables, relating sets of stimuli and responses that might seem at first glance to have little to do with each other.

An example of how Allport's trait approach is applied to understanding the personality of an individual follows.

Jenny was a mother whose life was "beset by frustration and defeat." She described much of her life in 301 letters she sent to a young couple over an 11-year period, starting when she was 58 years old and ending with her death. (The husband of the couple had been the college roommate of Jenny's son.) Each letter was read in sequence by 36 judges who then assigned 198 descriptive adjectives as illustrative of Jenny's personality. These adjectives were then reduced to a set of eight cardinal traits—such as aggressive, sentimental, possessive—by combining all adjectives that were similar. A second evaluation, based on statistical data, was done as a comparison against the impressionistic data of the judges. In this evaluation, key words in Jenny's letters were scored for the frequency with which they were paired with certain other words to form distinctive units of meaning. When these word pairs were statistically analyzed (by factor analysis), seven traits were found to characterize Jenny's personality—as expressed in her letters.

The descriptive and statistical data revealed a high degree of similarity and represented an instance in which a personality is *reconstructed* from available information when other kinds of data (from observations or personality tests) could not have been collected about the person (Allport, 1965, 1966).

Allport championed this idiographic research as the means to preserve a sense of the wholeness and uniqueness of each individual's personality. His approach requires intensive study of single individuals in a variety of their life contexts over time.

Criticisms of type and trait theories

Type and trait theories have been criticized as not being "real theories" in that they do not *explain* how behavior is caused, but merely identify and describe characteristics that are supposedly *correlated* with behavior. Furthermore, these theories offer no conception of the *development* of personality. Emphasis is on the *structure* of personality and its elements as they currently exist, with no corresponding concern for its origins or the dynamic relationships among the traits that together are assumed to form the whole personality.

We have seen that both kinds of theories represent a purely *dispositional* approach to the study of personality. As such, they rely heavily on self-reports of subjects from personality inventories and ignore the influences of situational variables. The subjective description a person gives in responding to test questions is assumed to be a direct measure of his or her traits, which in turn are seen as the basic components of personality. According to some critics (Tryon, 1979), there is a fallacy in making these test-trait-personality links. All we really can say scientifically is that the tests assess *performance* in a highly artificial situation, which may be influenced by aspects of the test situation and the person's response biases (e.g., to give socially desirable answers).

If a test-trait score is assumed to be an index of an underlying personality dimension, then it should predict that the personality disposition will be manifest in patterns of consistency in behavior across situations. At least it has to show up in how someone behaves in a given situation. The introvert, the generous woman, or the hostile man, as identified by test-trait scores, ought also to be similarly identifiable by their actions in certain settings. However, if only the personality test score is known, it is usually *not* possible to predict what someone will do in a given situation. To make matters worse, the correlations between scores on one personality test and those on other tests are low (Mischel, 1968; Rotter, 1954). Using personality traits as predictors, it does not appear possible to predict the behavior of even *most* of the people *most* of the time—much less the behavior of a particular individual.

Are people really consistent? The failure of the nomothetic trait-based approach to personality to predict relevant behavior in different situations has led in recent years to a basic challenge of the whole notion that personality-relevant behaviors are consistent. This challenge is based on a body of evidence such as the following:

> As we saw in Chapter 2, Hartshorne and May, in their classic *Studies in the Nature of Character* (1928, 1929), found little consistency among different measures of moral character, such as honesty and self-control, in a sample of over 10,000 schoolchildren. It was not possible to predict whether a child who cheated in class would cheat on take-home examinations or would lie or steal money. "Honesty" was therefore declared to be composed of *situation-specific habits* rather than a general trait.

◁ *Do people really possess traits such as "generosity"? Mischel and other theorists claim that most of our behavior is situation specific rather than trait related.*

"Punctuality" seems a good candidate for general trait status. Getting to class on time, keeping appointments promptly, not being late for the start of movies or church services ought to be components of a general personality trait of punctuality. Not so, according to the results of a study of over 300 college students (Dudycha, 1936). More than 15,000 observations were made of students' time of arrival to various college-related events. Punctuality in one situation was virtually *unrelated* to being on time in other situations.

In a third extensive study of consistency—of introversion and extraversion—counselors were trained to keep records on 51 boys. For three weeks they noted occurrences of behaviors related to nine personality traits (such as independence and gregariousness) in over 30 situations (cookouts, sports, and so forth). When the scores on any two behavioral items designed to measure the same trait were compared, the average correlation was very weak (Newcomb, 1929).

Columbia University psychologist Walter Mischel (1968) is one of the strongest critics of the concept of general personality traits. He surveyed a large body of literature on trait consistency across situations and was forced to conclude that the evidence for consistency was modest at best. The highest correlations he usually found in these studies were only about +.30, which means that only 60 percent of those who were in the better half on one measure would be predicted to be in the better half on the other measure. These low relationships mean that knowing a person's trait score provides little help in predicting his or her behavior, and that even *behavior* related to that trait in one situation offers little predictive value for behavior in other situations.

Mischel holds that *behavioral-situational specificity* is much more typical. You have probably had the experience of being very conscientious in one course for one teacher and just not caring in another course. Mischel would say that your apparent "inconsistency" was due to your ability to see the two situations as presenting different demands (Mischel, 1976).

Yet Mischel has not totally abandoned the concept of consistency in personality. He says, "No one seriously doubts that lives have coherence and that we perceive ourselves and others as relatively stable individuals who have substantial identity and continuity over time" (Mischel & Mischel, 1977, p. 335). Mischel argues that personality is better understood as having *temporal stability* (not changing over time) than as showing *cross-situational consistency* (consistency from one situation to another).

Even Allport believed that the low correlations found between traits and behavior proved only that people "are not consistent *in the same way,* not that they are inconsistent with *themselves*" (1937, p. 250). They may seem to behave inconsistently because the researcher's arbitrarily imposed general trait dimension is not relevant for them. For example, you may tell a lie to avoid hurting a friend's feelings, or cheat by giving test answers to someone in danger of flunking out. You may value honesty, but not interpret either of these acts as "dishonest."

Counterattacks to bolster trait theories. Some researchers have attempted to merge the idiographic and nomothetic trait approaches in order to counter Mischel's argument against consistency of traits across situations. For example, Daryl Bem has proposed using idiographic assessment methods within a nomothetic research paradigm: that is, use only people who define *themselves* as consistent on a particular general trait dimension, and then look at actual behaviors that are assumed to be related to that personality construct.

College student subjects were classified according to their responses to two questions: (a) How friendly are you? (on a seven-point scale) and (b) How much do you *vary* in friendliness from one situation to another? If their self-ratings of variability were above the average for students of their own sex with the same self-rating of friendliness, they were designated as *high in variability* (not consistent). If their ratings were below the average, they were called *low in variability* (consistent). Independent assessments of friendliness were obtained from each subject's father, mother, and a friend, as well as from behavioral observations of the subjects in a group discussion and with a solitary stranger.

Using *self-rated friendliness* as the only predictor variable was of little value in predicting either how others evaluated the subject's friendliness or how friendly the subject was in the test situations—a result in line with Mischel's findings. However, the subjects *self-reported variability* did relate highly to their consistency in friendliness across situations. Those who perceived themselves as *low in variability* (either generally friendly or generally not friendly) *did* show consistency across the different ratings and test situations. For the *high variability* subjects, on the other hand, the correlations between self-reported friendliness and the other measures of friendliness were low. In fact, among high variability subjects, self-evaluation of their own friendliness had *no* relationship to their spontaneous friendly behavior during a waiting period with a stranger (Bem & Allen, 1974).

Some trait theorists have welcomed the criticism by Mischel and other "situationists" because it has has forced them to explore the *interactions* between dispositional variables and situational variables, thereby leading to a richer portrait of personality (Magnusson & Endler, 1977). Others have contended that the resolution of the consistency paradox is to be found in better behavioral criteria and measurement procedures and in taking more measures over a larger number of situations. This, they feel, would increase reliability and hence generalizability (Epstein, 1979).

In our study of perception in Chapter 5, we saw that the attempt to impose stability and constancy on the variability of our experience is the hallmark of human perception. Could it be that our tendency to perceive consistency in personality is an extension of this general process of organizing our world to make it coherent, orderly, and more readily predictable? For additional viewpoints on this question, see the **Close-up** on page 392.

Regardless of how this controversy is resolved about the conditions under which personality trait scores predict behavior, we should not lose sight of a basic property of trait theories. They provide a *static* view of personality as a set of more or less enduring qualities. The emphasis is on an accurate description of the person's present personality without concern for how it might develop or how undesirable traits might be changed by therapy. The opposite of static is *dynamic;* a dynamic theory of personality emphasizes change, development, conflicting forces, and continual challenge of the environment. Let's see such a theory in action.

PSYCHODYNAMIC THEORIES

By the end of the nineteenth century, Charles Darwin had made the world aware of the common bonds that link human beings and animals. As we saw in Chapter 8, psychologists were quick to borrow Darwin's concept of "instinct" and transform it from its original use in accounting for stereotyped patterns of animal behavior to a concept representing the force underlying virtually all human actions. If a person went around hitting other people, it might be because of an inborn "instinct of pugnacity." If someone was miserly, it showed a "hoarding instinct." If psychologists had a new kind of behavior they wanted to explain, they had only to postulate a new instinct. But naming something is not the same as explaining it. Psychologists had a new term, "instinct," but not a better understanding of the psychological processes it was meant to describe. Clearly a more fruitful approach was needed. For many, this was provided in the work of Sigmund Freud.* He gave new meaning to the concept of human instincts, and in doing so, he revolutionized the very concept of human personality, as Darwin had done for the concept of human evolution. To Ernest Jones, Freud's biographer, Freud was " the Darwin of the mind" (1953).

Freudian psychoanalysis

Freud's theory of personality is a "grand theory" that boldly attempts to explain the origins and course of personality development, the nature of mind, the abnormal aspects of personality, and how personality can be changed by therapy. Here we will focus only on normal personality; Freud's other views will be treated at length in Chapters 14 and 15.

---

*Freud's ideas about the origins, development, and expression of both normal and abnormal personality are complex, numerous, and subtle. You have already met some of them in earlier chapters and can supplement the bare structure to be sketched here with your own reading of Freud's *Psychopathology of Everyday Life* (1904/1914), *Introductory Lectures on Psychoanalysis* (1923), and also Munroe's *Schools of Psychoanalytic Thought* (1955).

The Consistency Paradox

It seems to be "common sense" that people can be characterized according to dominant traits that they exhibit across different situations. We all know "gregarious" people, "shy" ones, "honest" ones, and so forth. There is also often considerable agreement among different people about the labels most appropriate for describing a particular individual.

Subjects rated themselves on a list of trait descriptions, and were also rated by their spouses. The two sets of ratings agreed fairly closely: if a subject saw him- or herself as possessing a certain trait, the spouse usually did too (McCrae, 1982).

From such evidence, we might assume that the reason we have impressions of people as consistent is simply that they do in fact have traits that are consistent. Yet, in general, efforts to predict a person's behavior, in a given situation from trait scores or from behavior in another situation have *not* been successful. Below are some of the reasons why we (and some personality theorists too) might "perceive" more consistency than actually occurs (adapted from Bem & Allen, 1974).

1. Each of us carries around an "implicit personality theory" which we use to connect the behaviors we see with the traits we infer and to predict other behaviors that we *don't* see. Our theories encourage us to fill in the gaps in what we actually see with what we think is probably there—what *ought* to be there according to our theory. In addition, there is *some* consistency (such as in intellectual ability or cognitive style), and this leads us to overgeneralize to other areas of personality (such as aggression or moral behavior) where consistency may not really be present.

2. We *underestimate* subtle forces in situations that may influence behavior. In doing so, we incorrectly attribute the causes of others' behavior to factors within them—to their traits or dispositions—factors we overestimate as enduring, stable determinants of their acts. We fail to account sufficiently for external pressures acting on the person toward conformity or social desirability, for example.

3. Often others will behave the way they think we want them to, thus exaggerating their apparent consistency in our eyes. They may act quite differently in the presence of other observers.

4. Most of us are free to choose the situations we enter, and we enter those we expect to feel comfortable in and able to handle. Those situations tend to be familiar ones, where the opportunities for new stimulation, conflict, or challenge are limited. In those situations our behavior tends to be restricted and thus

---

At the core of personality, according to psychoanalytic theory, are events within the person's mind, *intrapsychic events* that motivate behavior or are intentions to act. Often we are aware of these motivations (as when we study hard in order to achieve success). But some motivation also operates at an *unconscious* level (as when we do not study and fail a test that is important—to our demanding parents).

The *psychodynamic* nature of this approach comes from its emphasis on these inner wellsprings of behavior. For Freud, all behavior was motivated; every human action had a purpose and a cause that could be discovered by psychoanalyzing a person's thought associations, dreams, errors, and other behavioral clues. There is no room for chance events in psychoanalytic theory; all acts are determined by motives. The wish is parent to the deed; our actions emerge from what we really desire—even when they surprise us. Prominent among our desires, according to Freud, are sexual and aggressive wishes. Through both conscious and unconscious processes, these wishes affect our thoughts and behaviors.

The primary data for Freud's hypotheses about personality came from clinical observations and in-depth case studies of individual patients in therapy. Although this idiographic approach yields a rich harvest of ideas from which to formulate a complex theory, the theoretical ground is too soft for the heavy methodological equipment necessary to test a hypothesis scientifically. We shall return to the problem of validating Freud's ideas after we consider some of his fundamental concepts, his ideas on how personality is structured, and the roles of repression and psychological defenses.

does indeed tend to be consistent. It is no wonder that we act consistently in situations we have chosen for the sake of their constancy. When researchers put subjects in novel situations, they may do strange, personality-inconsistent things that they report are "not the real me." We will examine such studies in the social psychology chapters to come later.

5. Our judgments of others often come not from what we *observe* them doing but from what they *tell* us they do. Such self-reports are often biased and not accurate evidence of their behavior.

6. Our first impressions bias us strongly. Thereafter, we tend to interpret what we see as fitting in with and confirming our original view, which we assume was accurate. Once established, a belief needs little evidence to support it—but much to refute it—and prop up an illusion of consistency.

7. We tend to see consistency where it is not because we have come to equate consistency with goodness, reliability, and stability. As Mark Twain put it: "There are those who would misteach us that to stick in a rut is consistency—and a virtue, and that to climb out of the rut is inconsistency—and a vice" ("Consistency," 1923).

"All right, deep down it's a cry for psychiatric help—but at one level it's a stick-up."

tient's life. For instance, under hypnosis, a "blind" patient might recall witnessing her parents having intercourse when she was a small child. As an adult, her anticipation of her first sexual encounter might then have aroused powerful feelings associated with this earlier, disturbing episode. Her "blindness" might represent an attempt on her part to undo seeing the original event, and perhaps also to deny sexual feelings in herself. Her symptom would also have a secondary function *(secondary gain)*. By making her helpless and dependent, it would bring her attention, comfort, and sympathy from others.

Freud thus believed that symptoms, rather than being arbitrary, were related in a meaningful way to (and determined by) significant life events. He saw clinical observation and rational analysis as the keys that could unlock the secrets of both pathological and normal personality.

Fundamental concepts. Four concepts form the core of the psychodynamic approach: psychic determinism, early experience, drives and instincts, and unconscious processes.

1. Psychic determinism. In the late 1800s, cases of *hysteria* were recorded in Europe of bodily affliction for which no adequate physical explanation could be found. Those afflicted (mostly women) would experience impairments in bodily functioning—paralysis or blindness, for example—and yet they would have intact nervous systems and no obvious organic damage to their muscles or eyes. Freud, a neurologist, studied and attempted to treat the bizarre symptoms of this disorder.

Along with his colleague, Joseph Breuer, Freud observed that the particular physical symptom often seemed related to a prior forgotten event in the pa-

2. Early experience. Freud assumed a *continuity* of personality development from "womb to tomb," with all a person's past experiences contributing to the personality he or she shows today. But Freud believed that it is in infancy and early childhood that experience has its most profound impact on personality formation. This is especially true of the early stages of psychosexual development, which we discussed in Chapter 2 (see pp. 63–64). But as we saw,

Freud's theories were based on his adult patients' recollections and descriptions of their childhood experiences—*not* on direct observations of children. Nonetheless, his emphasis on early experience did much to make the scientific study of infant and child behavior respectable and fashionable.

3. Drives and instincts. His medical training as a neurologist led Freud to postulate a common biological basis for the mental abnormalities he observed in his patients. The source of motivation for human actions was ascribed to *psychic energy* found within each individual. How this energy is exchanged, transformed, and expressed is a central concern of psychoanalysis. Each of us is assumed to have inborn instincts or drives that are tension systems created by the organs of the body. These energy sources, when activated, can be expressed in many different ways. Although they are often referred to as instinctual urges, Freud's German term *Triebe* is closer to the concept of *drive* than to instinct (which is an inherited tendency to act in a characteristic way). One of Freud's contributions was in showing how the same drive, say that of sex, could be expressed directly through intercourse or masturbation, as well as indirectly through ''dirty'' jokes or creative art.

Freud originally postulated two basic drives. One he saw as involved with the *ego,* or *self-preservation* (hunger, thirst, and other physical needs of existence). The other he called *Eros;* it is related to *sexual urges* and involves preservation of the species.

Freud was more interested in the sexual urges, although some of his followers have given the ego drive an important place in personality, as we will see. Freud greatly expanded the notion of human sexual desires to include not only the urge for sexual union but also all other attempts to seek pleasure or to make physical contact with others. He used the term **libido** to describe the source of energy for sexual urges; he saw it as a psychic energy that drives us toward sensual pleasures of all types. Sexual urges demand immediate satisfaction, either through direct actions or through such indirect means as fantasies and dreams.

According to Freud, this broadly defined sexual drive does not arrive at puberty, but is already operating in infants. It is evident, he argued, in the pleasure infants derive from physical stimulation of the genitals and other sensitive, or *erogenous,* areas, such as the mouth and the anus. *Infantile sexuality* was a radical concept in Victorian times, when even adult sexuality was not mentioned in proper society.

Clinical observation of patients who had suffered traumatic experiences during World War I led Freud to add the concept of **Thanatos** (the death instinct) to his theory. Thanatos drives people toward aggressive and destructive behaviors. This primitive urge is part of the tendency for all living things to follow the law of entropy and return to an inorganic state.

In his dual theory of drives, Freud believed that both the sexual and aggressive drives were sources of motivation for virtually all behavior. We will discover (in Chapter 17) that pornography that depicts a hostile view of women stimulates both aggressive and sexual fantasies, as well as overt aggression (Donnerstein, 1983).

4. Unconscious processes. Though reaction was strong against the loss of innocence in the notion of infantile sexuality, it was even stronger in opposition to another of Freud's novel ideas—the unconscious. Other writers had pointed to such a process, but Freud put the concept of the unconscious determinants of human thought, feeling, and action on a very special pedestal. Behavior can be motivated by drives of which we are not aware. We may act without knowing why, or without direct access to the true cause of our actions. There is a *manifest* content to our behavior—what we say, do, and perceive—of which we are fully aware. But there is also a *latent* content that is concealed from us by unconscious processes. The *meaning* of neurotic (anxiety-based) symptoms, as well as of dreams and slips of the pen and tongue, are to be found at the unconscious level of thinking and information processing.

Consider the ''Freudian slip.'' According to Freud (as we saw in Chapter 10), impulses within us that we find unacceptable still strive for expression, even if inhibited, suppressed, or repressed. For example, ''forgetting'' a dentist appointment or being consistently late for dates with a particular person are not accidental but may be an instance of this striving to express the way we *really* feel. A host's greeting unwanted guests with ''I'm so sorry—oh, I mean glad you could come,'' may reveal his true feelings. When a faculty member at Oxford University asked the invited guests to raise their glasses in a toast to their ''dear queen,'' was another intention being expressed when it came out as ''Let us toast our queer dean''?

According to Freud, such slips are meaningful, the meaning being in the *unconscious intention.* Such

"errors" can be explained in terms of the final result produced, even though some other meaning was expected by the hearer or apparently intended by the speaker.

The concept of unconscious motivation adds a new dimension to personality by allowing for greater complexity of mental functioning than does a rational model. It is an elusive quality not readily captured in an objective personality test. The notion of an unconscious mind threatens those who want to believe they are in full command of their ship of mental state as it travels along.

The structure of personality. Freud accounted for personality differences by attributing them to the different ways in which people deal with their fundamental drives. To explain these differences, he pictured a continuing battle between two parts of the personality, the id and the superego, moderated by a third aspect of the self, the ego.

The **id** is conceived as the primitive, unconscious part of the personality, the storehouse of the fundamental drives. It operates irrationally. It acts on impulse and pushes for expression and immediate gratification "no matter what," without consideration of whether what is desired is realistically possible, socially desirable, or morally acceptable. The id is governed by the *pleasure principle*, the search for unregulated sexual, physical, and emotional pleasure.

The **superego** is the storehouse of an individual's values, including moral attitudes learned from society. The superego corresponds roughly to the **conscience**; it develops as a child *internalizes* the prohibitions of parents and other adults against socially undesirable actions. It is the inner voice of "oughts," and "should nots." The superego also includes the **ego ideal,** the individual's view of the kind of person he or she should strive to become. Thus the superego, society's representative in the individual, is often in conflict with the id, survival's representative. The id wants to do what feels good, while the superego, operating on the *morality principle,* insists on doing what is "right."

The **ego** is the reality-based aspect of the self that arbitrates the conflict between id impulses and superego demands. The ego represents the individual's personal view of physical and social reality, his or her conscious beliefs about what will lead to what and which things are possible. Part of the ego's job is to choose actions that will gratify id impulses without having undesirable consequences. The ego is governed by the *reality principle,* which puts reasonable choices before pleasurable demands. Thus, the ego would block an impulse to fly from the edge of a cliff and might substitute sky diving or a roller coaster ride instead.

When the id and the superego are in conflict, the ego arranges a compromise that at least partially satisfies both. But as id and superego pressures intensify, it becomes more difficult for the ego to work out optimal compromises.

Repression and ego defense. Sometimes the compromise involves "putting a lid on the id." Extreme desires of the id may have to be *repressed.* **Repression** is an important, uniquely Freudian concept that provides a psychological means through which strong conflicts created by id impulses are taken out of conscious awareness—pushed into the unconscious—and their overt expression controlled.

Table 11.2 *Summary chart of ego defense mechanisms*

Compensation	Covering up weakness by emphasizing desirable traits or making up for frustration in one area by gratification in another
Denial of reality	Protecting self from unpleasant reality by refusal to perceive it
Displacement	Discharging pent-up feelings, usually of hostility, on objects less dangerous than those which initially aroused the emotion
Emotional insulation	Withdrawing into passivity to protect self from being emotionally hurt
Fantasy	Gratifying frustrated desires in imaginary achievements ("daydreaming" is a common form)
Identification	Increasing feelings of worth by identifying self with another person or institution, often of illustrious standing
Introjection	Incorporating external values and standards into ego structure so individual is not at the mercy of them as external threats
Isolation	Cutting off emotional charge from hurtful situations or separating incompatible attitudes into logic-tight compartments (holding conflicting attitudes which are never thought of simultaneously or in relation to each other); also called *compartmentalization*
Projection	Placing blame for one's difficulties upon others, or attributing one's own "forbidden" desires to others
Rationalization	Attempting to prove that one's behavior is "rational" and justifiable and thus worthy of the approval of self and others
Reaction formation	Preventing dangerous desires from being expressed by endorsing opposing attitudes and types of behavior and using them as "barriers"
Regression	Retreating to earlier developmental level involving more childish responses and usually a lower level of aspiration
Repression	Pushing painful or dangerous thoughts out of consciousness, keeping them unconscious; this is considered to be *the most basic of the defense mechanisms*
Sublimation	Gratifying or working off frustrated sexual desires in substitutive nonsexual activities socially accepted by one's culture
Undoing	Atoning for, and thus counteracting unacceptable desires or acts

Repression is the most basic of the **ego defense mechanisms,** which are mental strategies the ego uses to defend itself from the conflicts experienced in the normal course of life.

These mechanisms are vital to an individual's psychological adaptation to conflicting demands from id, superego, and external reality. They are mental processes that enable the person to maintain a generally favorable self-image by utilizing a variety of mental tactics and strategies (as outlined in **Table 11.2**).

For example, if a child has strong feelings of hatred toward a parent—which, if acted out, would be dangerous—repression may take over. The hostile impulse is no longer consciously pressing for satisfaction or even recognized as existing. Though not seen or heard, however, repressed urges are not gone. They continue to play a role in personality functioning.

One of the more interesting aspects of repression is its effect on cognition and affect. The person is no longer consciously aware of the ideas that have been repressed, but continues to experience feelings associated with the repressed material. This "unexplained arousal" or "affect without appropriate cognitions" may find expression in a variety of disguised forms. For example, repressed hostility toward a parent might be expressed as general rebellion against authority. Or, repressed sexual urges might show up in someone's joining an antismut campaign to stamp out pornography—while being "forced" to carefully examine the offending material. The person may find some inaccurate explanation for the feelings and behavior or, lacking any rational explanation, acknowledge his or her "irrationality"—leading to further distress.

For Freud, **anxiety** is an intense emotional response caused by the preconscious recognition that a repressed conflict is about to emerge into consciousness. That is, anxiety is a danger signal: Repression is not working! Red alert! More defenses needed!

A second line of defense is then called into action in the form of one or more additional ego-defense mechanisms. For example, a mother who does not like her son and wants to be free of the responsibility to care for him might transform the unacceptable impulse to its opposite: "I don't hate my child, I love my child. See how I smother the dear little thing with love?" That would be an example of "reaction formation." Or she might use "projection" as an ego defense, seeing other people as wanting to limit her freedom, posing a threat to her child's life, or not concerned enough about proper care of their children. Or through "displacement," the rejecting mother might redirect hostile impulses away from her child and toward some person from a minority group.

> "From a psychoanalytic point of view, ego mechanisms of defense are mental processes that attempt to resolve conflicts among drive states, attacks, and external reality . . . they moderate levels of emotion produced by stress, they help keep awareness of certain drives at a minimal level, they provide time to help an individual deal with life traumas, and they help deal with unresolvable loss" (Plutchik et al., 1979, p. 229).

But useful as they are, they are self-deceptive and thus can get us into trouble.

According to Freudian theory, we all have some urges that are unacceptable in our society and thus all use these defense mechanisms to some extent. Overuse of them, however, constitutes *neurosis*. People who are neurotic spend so much of their energy deflecting, disguising, and rechanneling unacceptable urges to lessen their anxiety that they have little energy left over for productive living or satisfying relationships—for dealing with reality as it "is."

It is important to remember that sexuality and aggression were considered by Freud to be central aspects of the *normal* personality development. The pleasure derived from destroying someone's sand castle with one swift kick or defacing a building with graffiti, or smashing an automobile is indeed readily observable in normal children and adults. Nonetheless, Freud was rather pessimistic about the chances for escaping neurotic disorders. Perhaps because he grew up in the Victorian era, Freud believed that any society must teach its children that most expression of their basic drives is bad. Hence nearly everyone will have to be defending against such impulses nearly all the time. In Chapters 14 and 15 we will take a closer look at how a psychoanalytic perspective is used to explain and treat mental disorders.

△ | *Freud considered aggression to be drive-related behavior and a normal part of growing up.*

Neo-Freudian theories

Many of those who came after Freud kept his basic picture of personality as a battleground on which unconscious primal urges fight it out with social values. But many of Freud's intellectual descendants were also dissidents who made some major changes in the psychoanalytic tenets of personality. In general, these neo-Freudians have: (a) put greater emphasis on ego functions (such as ego defenses, development of the self, thinking, and mastery); (b) seen social variables (culture, family, and peers) as playing a greater role in shaping personality; (c) put less emphasis on the importance of general sexual urges, or libidinal energy; and (d) viewed personality development as extending beyond childhood to the entire lifespan.

In Chapter 2 we outlined the developmental theories of the neo-Freudian Erik Erikson. Two others, Harry Stack Sullivan and Margaret Mahler, will be discussed in Chapter 15.

Erich Fromm (1947) and Karen Horney (1939) were other followers who attempted to balance Freud's biological emphasis with more attention to social influence. But Freud's two most celebrated followers were Alfred Adler and Carl Jung, who operated on Freudian theory not with theoretical scalpels, but with conceptual swords.

△ Alfred Adler
(1870–1937)

Adler (1929) accepted the notion that personality is directed by unrecognized wishes: "Man knows more than he understands." But he rejected the significance of Eros and the pleasure principle. Adler believed that we all experience feelings of inferiority as helpless, dependent, small children and that our lives become dominated by the search for ways to overcome those feelings—*compensating* in such a way as to achieve feelings of adequacy or, more often, *overcompensating* in an attempt to become superior. Personality is structured around this underlying striving; the life-styles people develop are based on particular ways of overcoming their basic, pervasive feelings of inferiority. Personality conflict arises from incompatibility between external environmental pressures and internal strivings for adequacy rather than from competing urges within the person.

△ Carl Jung
(1875–1961)

Carl Jung (1959) expanded the conception of the unconscious. For him, the unconscious was not limited to the individual's unique life experiences but was filled with fundamental psychological truths shared by the whole of the human race. This **collective unconscious** predisposes us all to react to certain stimuli in the same way. It is responsible for our intuitive understanding of primitive myths, art forms, and symbols—which are the universal archetypes of existence. An **archetype** is a primitive symbolic representation of a particular experience or object. Each one is associated with an instinctive tendency to feel and think about that object or experience in a special way. Jung postulated many archetypes from history and mythology: the sun god, the hero, the earth mother. *Animus* is the male archetype that women experience, while *anima* is the female archetype that men experience. In reacting to someone of the opposite sex, then, we react to both their own particular characteristics and the male or female archetype. The archetype of the self is the *mandala* or magic circle; it symbolizes our striving for unity and wholeness (see Jung, 1973).

The healthy, integrated personality was seen by Jung as balancing opposing forces *within* the individual, such as masculine aggressiveness and feminine sensitivity. This view of personality as a constellation of competing internal forces in dynamic balance is called *analytic psychology.*

Jung, chosen by Freud as the "crown-prince" of the psychoanalytic movement, led a palace revolt by rejecting the primary importance of libido, so central to Freudian sexual theory. To the basic urges of sex and aggression he added two equally powerful unconscious instincts, the *need to create* and the *need to self-actualize.* Jung's views became central to the emergence of humanistic psychology in America.

> He looked at his own Soul with a Telescope. What seemed all irregular, he saw and showed to be beautiful Constellations; and he added to the Consciousness hidden worlds within worlds.
>
> Samuel Taylor Coleridge, *Notebooks*

△ The mandala, in Eastern cultures, traditionally represents the universe. Jung saw it as symbolic of the individual's striving for unity and wholeness.

Criticisms of Freudian theory

Critics of Freudian theory and its application to both normal personality and the treatment of neurosis through psychoanalysis have raised a number of objections. One criticism is that many psychoanalytic concepts are vague and not operationally defined. Thus much of the theory is difficult to evaluate scientifically because it is hard to make predictions that can be tested in controlled experiments. Because some of its central hypotheses cannot be disproved even in principle, its general theoretical status remains questionable. How can the concepts of libido, fixation, or repression be studied in any direct fashion? And how is it possible to predict whether an overly anxious person will use projection, denial, or reaction formation to defend a threatened ego?

One critic argues that Freud's psychodynamic concepts should always be thought of as actions and processes and not be *reified*—made into *things* or given life as *actors* (Shafer, 1976). That is, too often we talk about "the id in conflict with the superego" or say "the unconscious strives to . . ." as if id, superego, and "the unconscious" were agents that could do something—rather than explanatory concepts.

Another criticism of psychoanalytic theory is that it is good history but bad science. It is applied *retrospectively* to offer explanations *after* events have occurred; it does not reliably predict what will occur. Using psychoanalytic theory to understand personality typically involves historical reconstruction of the kind made famous by detective Sherlock Holmes—not scientific construction of probable actions and predictable outcomes. Its overemphasis on historical origins of current behavior directs attention away from current stimuli that may be inducing and maintaining the behavior. The theory neglects the person's expectations, goals, and future-based ideas.

Research that has attempted to isolate predictor variables derived from the theory is beset with problems of validity of the dependent measures of psychoanalytic constructs (Silverman, 1976). For example, one researcher predicted that women would hoard more pencils than men because pencils are phallic symbols and women allegedly have penis envy. He did in fact find more hoarding among female subjects (Johnson, 1966). But according to Freud's theory, hoarding is also a symptomatic response of someone with anal problems.

Even when the research is well-controlled, there is still a broad inductive leap from psychoanalytic constructs to measurable effects. For example, Freud assumed males experience *castration anxiety* because they imagine their fathers will retaliate against them for having sexual urges toward their mothers.

Researchers Sarnoff and Corwin (1959) reasoned that fear of death was a derivative of the repressed fear of castration. If so, they advanced the nonobvious prediction that becoming sexually aroused would increase one's fear of death—if the individual was high in castration anxiety. The Yale college students who served as subjects had their fear of death assessed on a self-report scale before and again after sexual arousal was experimentally manipulated. On the basis of their projective test responses, the subjects were divided into two groups high or low in castration anxiety. A month later each subject rated photos of women as part of an alleged study of esthetic judgments. Half of the students in each castration-anxiety group saw photos of nude women (high sexual arousal), while the others saw photos of clothed models (low sexual arousal). The fear-of-death scale was given again along with other measures. Only one group of subjects showed a significant increase in fear of death: males high in castration anxiety and in the high sexual arousal condition.

This provocative finding has not yet been independently replicated, nor have other measures and manipulations been used to extend the validity of the constructs involved. (Can you think of a non-Freudian explanation for an association between seeing nude photos and a greater concern for the shortness of life?)

Freud's theory developed from speculation based on clinical experience with people suffering from anxiety disorders and other problems of adjustment—people in whom something had gone wrong. Thus, another criticism is that it has little to say about *healthy* life-styles, which are not primarily defensive or defective. The theory offers a pessimistic view of human nature as developing out of conflicts, traumas, fixations, and anxieties. As such, it does not fully acknowledge the positive side of our existence or offer any information about healthy personalities striving for happiness and realization of their fullest potential.

There are probably no elements of Freud's theories that have not been strongly criticized. In fact, the ideas that have been most influential have also been most controversial.

HUMANISTIC THEORIES

Humanistic approaches to understanding personality are characterized by a concern for the integrity of the individual's personal, conscious experience and growth potential. Humanistic personality theorists, such as Carl Rogers and Abraham Maslow, have stressed a basic drive toward self-actualization as the organizer of all the diverse forces whose interplay continually creates what a person is.

In this view, the motivation for behavior comes from a person's unique biological and learned tendencies to develop and change in positive directions toward the goal of self-actualization. This innate striving toward self-fulfillment and the realization of one's unique potential is a constructive, guiding force that moves each person toward generally positive behaviors and the enhancement of the self.

Humanistic theories have also been described as being holistic, dispositional, phenomenological, and existential. And they are definitely optimistic about human nature.

They are *holistic* in the sense that they explain a person's separate acts always in terms of his or her entire personality. People are *not* seen as a collection of discrete traits, like different beans in a jar. Rather the metaphor for personality might be a balloon filled with a mixture of helium and other light gases. The balloon will soar naturally if let free and not held back by environmental constraints.

Humanistic theories are *dispositional* because they focus on innate qualities within the person that exert the major influence over the direction behavior will take. Situational inputs are more often seen as constraints and barriers, like the string that ties down the balloon. Once freed from negative situational conditions, the actualizing tendency should actively guide the person to choose life-enhancing situations. But humanistic theories are *not* dispositional in the same way as trait theories—which focus on enduring, stable characteristics—nor like the psychoanalytic view of childhood experiences that develop into restricting lifelong patterns. Humanistic dispositions fill the personality with a unitary tendency to become actualized that will find its natural expression in a healthy personality.

They are *phenomenological* because they emphasize the individual's frame of reference, the person's subjective view of reality—not the objective perspective of the observer analyzing that person. This view is also one of the "here and now," the present as perceived by the person. Past influences are important only to the extent that they have brought the person to the present situation.

Finally, humanistic theories have been described by theorists such as Rollo May (1975) as having an *existential* perspective. They focus on the person's conscious, higher mental processes that interpret current experiences and enable the person to meet or be overwhelmed by the everyday challenges of existence.

In this section we will briefly mention some of the special features of Carl Rogers' personality view and also the theory of self. Maslow's ideas have been outlined earlier in our study of human motivation (Chapter 8).

A person-centered approach

For Carl Rogers (1947, 1951, 1977), therapy is "client-centered" and personality theory is "person-centered." It is the private world of the individual—his or her *phenomenal field*—that must be understood. Rogers' advice is to listen to what people say about themselves. Attend to their concepts and to the significance they attach to their experiences.

As we have noted, at the core of this theoretical approach is the concept of **self-actualization,** a constant striving to realize one's inherent potential, to develop one's capacities and talents to the fullest. Experiences are evaluated positively and sought after when they are perceived to maintain or enhance the self. Those experiences which oppose the positive growth of the person are evaluated negatively and avoided.

Unfortunately, this drive at times comes into conflict with the need for approval or *conditional positive regard* from both the self and others. If important people in a child's environment express dismay at some things the child does without making it clear that their criticism applies to the *behavior* rather than to the *child,* he or she may begin to do only things that are "acceptable" to others.

It should be apparent why such an "upbeat" view of personality was a welcome treat for many psychologists who had been brought up on a diet of bitter-tasting Freudian medicine and its less wholesome—even if more tempting—morsels.

Self theory

Rogers also renewed psychological interest in the concept of the self. For humanistic psychologists the **self** is the irreducible unit out of which the coherence and stability of the personality emerge. The notion of a self is hardly new. "Know thyself" is an inscription carved on the shrine of the Delphic oracle in ancient Greece.

Within early psychology, the concern for analysis of the self found its strongest advocate in William James (1890). James identified three components of self-experience: the *material me* (the bodily self, along with physical objects one is surrounded by); the *social me* (one's awareness of his or her reputation in the eyes of others); and the *spiritual me* (the self that monitors private thoughts and feelings).

In Rogers' view the self or *self-concept* emerges as part of the actualizing tendency's process of enabling the child to *differentiate* between all that is within or part of him or her and all that is external. The *self* becomes a consistent, whole set of organized perceptions of the characteristics of "I" or "me" along with the relationships of that "I/me" to other people, and other aspects of life. The self-concept includes both what people perceive themselves to be, and their conception of what they would like to be ideally. *Consistency* in personality, according to Rogers, is between this *actual* and *ideal self* rather than between parts of personality, traits and actions, or past and present aspects of functioning.

There is a growing recognition among psychologists of the importance of the self-concept and the development of a person's sense of self for a full un-

△ *Humanistic psychologists have emphasized the importance of developing a sense of one's own identity. Here a first-grader constructs a likeness of himself while paper "classmates" look on.*

derstanding of human personality (Walsh & Vaughan, 1980; Wylie, 1968). A sense of **identity** includes the perception of one's self as distinct from other people and of other things as related to one's self or alien to one's self. It is central to our sense of a unique personality. A person's **self-esteem,** as a generalized evaluative attitude toward the self, influences both moods and behavior.

Although the concept of self has to do with individuals, the fullest development of self enables the individual to relate effectively to other people. Social psychologists have long acknowledged the powerful role that the self-concept plays in social situations. In a later chaper we will look at research on our efforts at *self-consistency* (trying to keep our attitudes consistent with what we do) and at *impression-management* (trying to control other people's evaluations of us).

401

What type of person are you? Tell me ten things about yourself. In each space below complete a statement beginning with the words "I am." Do this before you read further.

_____ 1. I am _____

_____ 2. I am _____

_____ 3. I am _____

_____ 4. I am _____

_____ 5. I am _____

_____ 6. I am _____

_____ 7. I am _____

_____ 8. I am _____

_____ 9. I am _____

_____10. I am _____

When you have completed your list, analyze your responses as follows (Kuhn & McPartland, 1954):

1. Put an *A* next to descriptions that refer to *physical characteristics* such as size, sex, race, and appearance. These should be statements that can be easily validated using a mirror, yardstick, scale, or other nonsocial measure.

2. Put a *B* next to references to your *social status,* such as mother, student, carpenter. This category contains descriptions that must be socially defined and validated.

3. Place a *C* next to descriptions of *abstract characteristics* that transcend particular situations, such as "I am friendly" and "I am a rock music fan." These will be comments that leave you free to vary your behavior across situations, but characterize you in terms of your personal style.

4. Finally, place a *D* next to statements that are very *vague and global,* such as "I am a person" or "I am at one with the universe."

Now add up the number of *A*'s, *B*'s, *C*'s, and *D*'s: Which category did you use most often? Which next, and least? Give the test to others and see how your self-portrait compares to theirs.

Me	Friend
_____A mode	_____A mode
_____B mode	_____B mode

Some of us have a conception of self that is bound to the evaluations of others and to situational characteristics. With this passive self-view, individuals focus on themselves as *objects* that stand out from the background only because others' evaluations distinguish them—or fail to. This seems to be the case for the extremely shy person. By contrast, an active conception of self—one in line with humanistic views—makes the self an *actor* or acting process that creates a unique figure against any background. It may also be that the conception of self we tend to use varies at different times in our lives, as can be seen in the **Close-up** above.

Criticisms of humanistic theories

It is difficult to criticize theories that are on the side of the angels. Who could possibly object to the importance of the self-concept, to fulfilling one's human potential, or to motives for growth? Behaviorists do. They criticize humanistic concepts for being fuzzy, without clear definitions. What exactly is self-actualization? Is it an inborn tendency or is it created by the cultural context? Humanistic theories also have difficulty accounting for the particular characteristics of individuals. They seem to be theories about human nature, about qualities we all share, more than theories about differences among people.

Behaviorists also claim that the general level at which such theories are formulated minimizes their research value. (An extensive bibliography of re-

_____C mode	_____C mode
_____D mode	_____D mode

In the 1950s, when people were asked to describe themselves as you did above, the majority of people gave responses in the *B* mode, describing themselves most in terms of their group memberships and their roles within society. Students of today tend to use the *C* mode most frequently, perhaps because the world is changing so rapidly that people no longer feel comfortable defining themselves in terms of their place in the social structure.

Louis Zurcher (1977) set out to determine whether differences in people's self-description were related to other characteristics. Comparing *B, C,* and *D* mode respondents he found that *B*-moders had the greatest sense of social belonging and social purpose. *D*-moders felt the most distant and detached from society and also had the greatest sense of autonomy and self-esteem. *C*-moders were characterized as having high levels of anxiety and experiencing life stress more intensely than the others.

It is theorized that we all experience all four modes at different stages of development. The *A* mode is predominant as children develop the sense of a physical self separate from others. The *B* mode comes as they learn and internalize social roles. But with adolescence comes a period of role confusion. As young adults, we choose among a large array of roles and may be forced into some roles unwillingly. It is almost inevitable that we begin to question who we really are. To cope with these times of questioning and change, a *C*-mode self-concept emerges, defining the self as stable across the different roles we play. But as we settle into a comfortable set of roles again, we realize that different roles require different types of behavior. Unless we shift back to a *B* mode at this point, the result can be anxiety and maladjustment.

This analysis of self suggests that shifts from *B* mode to *C* mode and back to *B* mode should be expected at different life periods. This view of self is different from other views of personality in that it emphasizes a *changing self* rather than a *stable self.* Indeed, Zurcher argues that an adaptive transformation would be for us to come to define stability itself in terms of change. Thus, the healthy self would be one that is capable of sliding between modes as required by the changing society we live in. Fixation at any particular mode would be maladaptive since it would inevitably lead to stress. Zurcher uses the term *mutable self* to describe this conception of self.

search using humanistic concepts [Roberts, 1973] suggests otherwise.) They go on to note that in emphasizing the role of the self as a source of experience and action, humanistic psychologists neglect the important environmental variables that also influence behavior.

Psychoanalytic theorists criticize the emphasis of humanistic theorists on present conscious experience. They argue that the power of the unconscious is not recognized in this approach. People who have unconscious conflicts and use defensive strategies for dealing with their conflicts cannot accurately describe themselves by simply looking at conscious processes.

Other criticisms of this general theory of personality are that it (a) ignores the person's unique history and influences from the past, as well as the developmental aspects of personality; (b) oversimplifies the complexity of personality by reducing it to the simplistic "given" of a self-actualizing tendency; (c) fails to predict how a specific individual will respond in a given situation; (d) makes the self a "take charge" little *homunculus,* a tiny mind with a personality that is not accountable to skeptical researchers. As some critics have concluded, "In the last analysis, explaining personality on the basis of hypothesized self-tendencies is reassuring doubletalk, not explanation" (Liebert & Spiegler, 1982, p. 411).

"And in the opposite corner, we have learning theory approaches weighing in heavy and tough . . ."

LEARNING THEORIES

In the heyday of football at the United States Military Academy at West Point, "Doc" Blanchard made yardage running straight ahead inside the opposing line, while Glenn Davis did so running around the end, on the outside. Their nicknames of "Mr. Inside" and "Mr. Outside" also seem to be apt characterizations of two of psychology's leading ball carriers, Carl Rogers and B. F. Skinner. We have seen that Rogers focuses his attention on what is going on inside the person. Skinner is the "Mr. Outside" of psychology. Other learning theorists, like Neal Miller, have tried to reconcile these views by showing how behavior is both internally generated and externally influenced by reinforcing contingencies. Albert Bandura borrows the empirical, research orientation of the behaviorists, adds in some self-concepts of the humanists, and mixes well to come up with a new social learning approach to personality.

A strict behavioristic approach

You will recall from our discussions in the learning chapter (Chapter 7) that the crux of a behavioristic approach is its focus on environmental contingencies (reinforcing circumstances) that control behavior. A strict behavioristic approach ignores what is "in" the person and denies that the "inside approach" has any psychological validity. From this perspective, behavior and personality are shaped primarily by the outside environment. Personality, then, is seen as the sum of overt and covert responses that are reliably elicited as a consequence of an individual's reinforcement history. People are different because they have had different histories of reinforcement.

When people seem to be acting differently in the same situation, behaviorists believe it is only because we are ignorant of the real stimuli controlling their behavior. That is, if they are behaving differently it is because they are actually responding to slightly different stimuli or their behavior is on different reinforcement schedules—not because of their different personalities.

For an operant psychologist, like Skinner, personality is studied as the set of a person's responses to the external environment. If you want to understand why a particular person does a particular thing, look to the situation—not to traits, states, dispositions, or similar "mental way stations." In support of this atheoretical view, Skinner has argued that

> "The practice of looking inside the organism for an explanation of behavior has tended to obscure the variables which are immediately available for a scientific analysis. These variables lie outside the organism, in its immediate environment and in its environmental history" (1953, p. 31).

Behaviorists are interested not in the *consistencies in behavior*—which led other theorists to propose enduring traits, instincts, or self-concepts—but in the *changes in behavior* as environmental conditions change. Their aim is to identify the external variables that can be shown to change responding. No mental states and no inferred dispositions are allowed—or needed—in their explanations of behavior.

Can you see why learning-behavioral approaches to personality are good for developing treatments to change personality—that is, to reduce undesirable behaviors and to increase desirable ones? It is also evident why they are not very satisfying for providing a view of how the environmental inputs and response outputs are organized and meaningfully integrated in a unique way by personality constructs (see **Close-up,** page 406, for more on the important dimensions on which environments differ.)

Reconciling the analytic and behavioral approaches

Is there a way to integrate some of the ideas in Freud's rich psychoanalytic theory with those in the more formal views based on learning principles? John Dollard and Neal Miller (1950) did so, using the behaviorist formulation of Clark Hull (1952) rather than Skinner's, because Hull allowed for concepts such as drive, inhibition, and habit, which Skinner had excluded.

Common to both Freudian and Hullian theory was the key role attributed to the motivating force of tension and the reinforcing (pleasurable) consequences of *tension reduction*. Both theorists conceived of the organism as acting in order to reduce "tension" produced by unsatisfied drives. Behavior that successfully reduces such tensions is repeated, eventually becoming a learned habit, reinforced by repeated tension-reduction. Another common ground is the emphasis of both theories on the importance of *early learning* in determining what an organism does later in life. Although the two theoretical systems use very different words to describe their conclusions, they come out with models of the human organism that have important parallels.

The central focus in Dollard and Miller's (1950) formulations is on the process of learning, or habit formation. They discuss four significant features of this process: drive, cue, response, and reinforcement (reward). *Drives* get the organism into action, *cues* suggest what behavior is appropriate (will lead to drive reduction), *response* is the behavior itself, and *reinforcement* strengthens the connection between cue and response by reducing the tension of drives.

A different type of reconciliation of a strict operant theory of behavior with personality approaches that stress aspects of the self comes from adding coverants to operants. A *coverant* is an "operant of the mind," a covert operant response that is influenced by the consequences it produces (Homme, 1965). Self-statements are thoughts we express to ourselves that are coverants. They may influence operants, as when the thought "he makes me angry" influences my aggressive action toward him. They may be influenced by operants, as when studying hard increases the probability you will think "I'm learning a lot and I enjoy this course." The third way coverants act is by influencing other coverants. One thought leads to another, as when you think "What a jerk I was for believing him" and other statements follow with greater probability—"I'm really gullible," "You can't trust men."

By adding a concern for these inner processes, learning theorists have widened the scope of the behavioristic view of human nature.

Bandura's social learning theory

A quite different approach to personality based on learning is found in the work of Albert Bandura of Stanford University. Through his theoretical writing and extensive research with children and adults, Bandura (1977a) has been an eloquent champion of a social learning approach to understanding personality that combines principles of learning with an emphasis on human interactions in social settings.

From a social learning perspective, human beings are neither driven by inner forces nor the helpless pawns of environmental influences.

In contrast to other behavioristic theories of learning, a social learning approach stresses the uniquely human cognitive processes that are involved in acquiring and maintaining patterns of

Albert Bandura
(1925–   )

behavior and, thus, personality. Because we can manipulate symbols and think about external events, we can foresee the possible consequences of our actions without having to actually experience them. Often we learn *vicariously* through observation of other people, in addition to learning from our own experience. Also, we can evaluate our own behavior (according to personal standards) and provide ourselves with reinforcements (such as self-approval or self-reproach). Thus we are capable of self-regulation, able to control our own actions, rather than being automatically controlled by external forces. Social learning theory thus rejects the environmental determinism of a strict behavioristic perspective. Instead, it points to a complex interaction of individual factors, behavior, and environmental stimuli. Each can influence or change the others, and the direction of change is rarely one-way; instead, it is *reciprocal*. Your behavior can be influenced by your attitudes, beliefs, or prior history of reinforcement, as well as by available stimuli in the environment. What you do can have an effect on the environment, and important aspects of your personality can be affected by the environment or by feedback from your behavior. In this *reciprocal determinism* (Bandura, 1981a), all the components are important in understanding human behavior, personality, and social ecology.

Perhaps the most important contribution of social learning theory is its focus on *observational learning* as the process by which one person observes the behavior of another person and changes merely by being exposed to that model's behavior. Through observational learning, children and adults acquire an enormous range of information about their social

The "Personality" of Situations

What do we mean by a "situation"? What are the important features of settings that cause people's behavior to change from one setting to another?

Many psychologists have studied this question by setting up laboratory experiments in which they manipulated particular conditions. Recently, some psychologists have approached the question from a different angle. They have tried to learn about the important features of real-life settings.

Rudolf Moos (1979) has been particularly influential in this kind of research on the ecology of behavior settings. In a series of studies conducted over a fifteen-year period, he has examined ten different kinds of real-life social settings, ranging from psychiatric treatment facilities to military basic training settings. The focus of the research has been twofold:

1. to examine the differences among various examples of the same type of setting—such as differences among inpatient wards;
2. to examine the differences and similarities among different types of settings—for example, to discover the characteristics needed to describe the "personalities" of treatment facilities as compared with the "personalities" of military training centers.

In all settings, he has found three basic domains to be important for describing the "personality" of the setting. These are: (a) the interpersonal relationship qualities; (b) the personal growth opportunities; and (c) the emphasis on system maintenance or change.

One setting which has been the focus of research by Moos is college student living groups. In that research, the University Residence Environment Scale (URES) was developed to measure each of the three basic domains. The subscales within each domain are shown in the table. Using this scale, Moos has studied over 10,000 students and residence staff, representing 229 living groups at 25 colleges and universities in 12 states. He has included diverse kinds of residence halls, such as student co-operatives, fraternities, freshman single-sex dorms, coed houses, and special graduate student housing.

Moos found that clear profiles emerged for different kinds of living groups. For example, women's living groups seemed to place special emphasis on emotional support and a formal, organized structure, whereas men's groups emphasized competition and a nonconformist stance. Mixed-sex groups combined many qualities of each of the others. They emphasized emotional support (like the women's groups) but also independence and competition (like the men's groups).

When Moos compared the changes that occurred during an academic year in women who lived in coed dorms and women living in single-sex dorms, he found that those in coed dorms were more likely to have lowered their career goals and increased their social activities. By contrast, women who had lived in women's dorms showed an increase in leadership and assertiveness and higher career goals.

Moos contends that these changes were the result of the different "personalities" of the living settings. Since coed groups emphasized community and nonacademic personal development, it was not surprising to find coed students more likely to pursue personal goals not related to a strong academic commitment.

But while the data are quite consistent with his explanations, they do not provide conclusive evidence that the setting actually had a major role in bringing about these changes. After all, students typically have considerable power to select their living environments. Students who choose to live in coed dorms may be

environment—what is appropriate and gets rewarded and what gets punished or ignored. In Chapter 7, this approach was presented as a challenge to traditional behavioristic theory because the individual does not have to *act* in order to learn. Skills, attitudes, and beliefs may be acquired simply by watching what others do and the consequences that follow. This means that a child can develop a gender identity and sex role on the basis of observational learning of how men and women behave in their culture and how the culture responds differently to them (S. Bem, 1984). Children may also learn "personality traits" of altruism (Staub, 1974) or ability to delay gratification through observation of models, whether "live" and physically present, or presented indirectly in "symbolic" form through books, movies, or TV. The effects of these models on children's willingness to delay gratification was demonstrated in an experiment with fourth- and fifth-graders.

Children's preferences for a high or low delay of reward were first assessed by giving them a series of 14 choices between small immediate rewards and larger delayed ones. The researchers wanted to show

Social environments of student living groups

Domain	Subscale	Description
Relationship	1. Involvement	Commitment to the house and residents; interaction and feeling of friendship in the house.
	2. Emotional support	Concern for others in the house; Providing aid for one another; open and honest communication.
Personal growth	3. Independence	Freedom and self-reliance versus socially proper and conformist behavior.
	4. Traditional social orientation	Dating, going to parties, etc.
	5. Competition	Competitive framework for activities.
	6. Academic achievement	Classroom and academic accomplishments and concerns.
	7. Intellectuality	Cultural, artistic, and other intellectual activities.
System maintenance and change	8. Order and organization	Formal structure, neatness, and organization.
	9. Student influence	Residents' role in formulating and enforcing policies.
	10. Innovation	Spontaneity and variety of behaviors and ideas.

(Adapted from Moos, 1979)

different from those who choose to live in single-sex groups. The setting, then, could be just a reflection of the student's prior attitudes, not a cause of them.

Thus, the question of what is cause and what is effect is hard to answer. Nonetheless, Moos's research is an interesting example of an attempt to look at the impact of natural settings. His results suggest that:

1. The dimensions of relationship, personal growth, and system maintenance or change are relevant in living settings of student groups, as they are in the other social settings he has studied.

2. Different kinds of living groups do seem to have "personalities," which can be described by the pattern of scores on the URES obtained by individuals living in them.

3. Changes that occur during an academic year in a student's attitudes and behavior seem to be in the directions emphasized by that student's living group.

that exposure to a person who modeled behavior *opposite* to the children's initial preference would modify their delay or immediate reward-seeking behavior. Children who initially found it difficult to delay were shown an adult model who consistently chose the postponed reward, while those who initially showed a high-delay preference saw an adult model who chose the immediate reward. The models also discussed their general philosophy toward aspects of life relevant to attitudes about delay of reward. Subjects were randomly assigned to one of three conditions: a live model, a symbolic model (in-

formation presented in written form), or no model present. They were then given a second test of their preferences in the absence of any model, and a third test a month later to see if any effects found immediately had generalized. The results in **Figure 11.4** indicate that modeling clearly alters delay preferences, that this effect remains over time, and that either type of model is equally effective in getting children to delay when they previously did not. However, live modeling is more effective than symbolic modeling in changing a "delayer" into an "impulsive

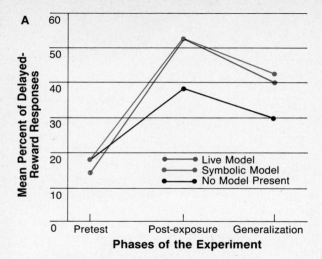

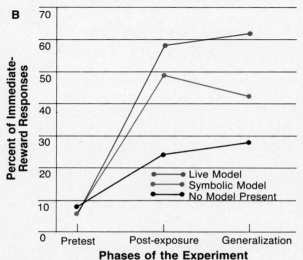

△ **Figure 11.4**

The first graph (A) shows the average change in responding of children who initially were low-delay responders, while the second graph (B) shows the average change for children who initially were high-delay responders. (After Bandura & Mischel, 1965, pp. 702–3).

hedonist" who opts for the bird in the hand and leaves the two in the bush for those who prefer to delay (Bandura & Mischel, 1965).

A more recent study of children's delay of gratification, showing its relation to personality variables, was described on page 384.

Bandura has recently (1977b, 1982b) begun to elaborate the concept of self-efficacy as a central part of social learning theory. As described briefly in Chapter 8, **self-efficacy** is a belief that one can perform adequately in a particular situation. A person's sense of capability influences his or her perception,

motivation, and performance in many ways. We don't even try to do things or take chances when we expect to be ineffectual. We avoid people and situations when we don't feel adequate to the performance they require. Even when we do in fact *have* the ability—and the desire—we may not take the required action, or persist in order to complete it successfully, if we *think* we lack what it takes.

Self-efficacy, as a sense of personal mastery, is not the same as an overall sense of self-confidence. Bandura believes that perceptions of one's abilities are best thought of as a host of *specific* evaluations; he feels that we should be careful not to oversimplify people's complex self-knowledge and self-evaluations into a simplistic single label like "self-esteem." However, a sense of self-efficacy can affect behavior in situations which differ from those in which it was generated, since, once established, positive expectations about one's efficacy can generalize to new situations (Bandura, 1977b).

Beyond our actual accomplishments, other sources of efficacy judgments include our observations of the performance of others; social and self-persuasion (others may convince us that we can do something, or we may convince ourselves); and monitoring of our emotional states as we think about or approach a task. For example, anxiety suggests low expectations of efficacy; excitement suggests expectations of success.

Besides influencing our choices of activities, tasks, situations, and companions, our self-efficacy judgments also influence how much effort we expend and how long we "hang in" when faced with difficulty. How vigorously and persistently a student pursues academic tasks depends more on his or her sense of self-efficacy than on actual ability. Expectations of success or failure can change in light of feedback from performance but are more likely to create the *predicted* feedback and thus to become self-fulfilling prophecies.

Expectations of failure—and a decision to stop trying—may, of course, be based on a perception of the situation as unresponsive, punishing, or unsupportive rather than on a perception of one's own inadequacy. Such expectations are called *outcome based* rather than *efficacy based* expectations. The person who believes that responding is useless because of low self-efficacy needs to develop competencies that will boost self-perception of efficacy. On the other hand, where a tendency to give up is based on outcome expectancies, then the environment and not the person may need to be changed so that reinforcements will in fact follow competent responding.

△ *A sense of self-efficacy can lead a determined individual to persevere in tasks that others might consider beyond their capabilities. This man clearly enjoys backpacking despite the fact that he is confined to a wheelchair.*

Criticisms of learning theories

Critics hold that some behavioristic approaches to personality have thrown out the baby's vibrant personality and kept the cold bath water. In placing such emphasis on environment, they have lost contact with the person. Is it stimulus variables or living people that personality is all about, they ask? If one insists that personality is built upon the learned repetition of previously reinforced responding, where is the origin of all *new* behavior—creative achievements, innovative ideas, inventions, and works of art? Other criticisms reject views of behavior that seem to deny choice and the freedom to reject and rise above one's past history of reinforcement. In addition, critics argue, much of the learning observed by behaviorists is performance that is reinforced because the organism is in a state of *deficiency motivation* (hungry, thirsty, so forth) and other kinds of action and reinforcements are not available. The full realization of human potential comes not from acting out of such appetitive motives but from people's aspirations toward joy, immortality, altruism, and love—motives that put us above "lower animals" and on the side of angels.

Some of these criticisms, leveled primarily against the radical behaviorism of Skinner, lose their force when confronted by the broader social learning theories. Increasingly, learning approaches are including cognitive processes along with behavioral ones, returning a mind to the body and perhaps even adding a unique personality "for good measure."

COGNITIVE THEORIES

Those who have proposed cognitive theories of personality point out that there are important individual differences in the way people think about and define any external situation. Cognitive theories stress the processes through which people turn their sensations and perceptions into organized impressions of reality. Like humanistic theories, they emphasize that individuals participate in creating their own personalities. People actively *choose* their own environments to a great extent. So even if the environment has an important impact on us, we are not just passive reactors. We weigh alternatives and select the settings in which we act and are acted upon.

Personal construct theory

George Kelly (1955) developed a theory of personality that places primary emphasis on each person's active, cognitive construction of his or her world. He argued strongly that no one is ever a victim of either past history or the present environment. Although events cannot be changed, all events are open to *alternative interpretations,* Kelly argued. People can always reconstruct their past, or define their present difficulties in different ways.

Kelly used science as a metaphor for this process. Scientists develop theories in order to *understand* the natural world and in order to *make predictions* about what will occur in the future under particular conditions. The test of a scientific theory is its utility—how well it explains and predicts. If a theory isn't working well, or if it is extended outside the set of events where it does work well, then a new, more useful theory can and should be developed.

Kelly argued that *all* people function like scientists. We want to be able to predict and explain the world around us, especially our interpersonal world. The theories we use to do so are called "personal constructs." Kelly defined a **personal construct** as a person's belief about how two things are alike and different from a third. For example, I might say that my uncle and my brother are alike because they are highly competitive, whereas my sister is different from them because she likes to "take a back seat" to others. In this case, I seem to be using a construct of "competitiveness versus giving in to others" to organize my perceptions of people around me. Other personal constructs might be based on attractiveness, or on how others can be exploited for one's personal gain.

Personal constructs are not just labels that an outsider applies after seeing what a person does, according to Kelly. They guide what we see when we look at the world and influence how we respond to it. Each person's belief system—set of personal constructs, in Kelly's terms—determines how he or she will think, feel, act, and define new situations. In other words, for Kelly, each person's total system of such personal constructs *is* that individual's "personality."

Construct systems are completely idiographic in Kelly's view: each person has a unique set of constructs. People differ in the content of their constructs, the number available, and the ways they are related. In order to understand other people, we have to try to see the world as they see it, through their construct system rather than our own.

Little research has come from Kelly's theory, largely because it places so much emphasis on the uniqueness of each person's personality. This approach has had more impact on clinicians, who can approach each case as an individual story, than on personality researchers, who are searching for general principles.

Cognitive social learning theory

Mischel has already been mentioned as one of those who has questioned the utility of traits for describing personality. As an alternative, Mischel proposes a cognitive theory of personality which also draws heavily on principles from social learning theory.

Like social learning theorists, Mischel places a great deal of emphasis on the influence of environmental variables on behavior. In his view, much of what we do and many of our beliefs and values are *not* best thought of as emerging properties of the self. Rather, he sees them as responses developed, maintained, or changed by our observation of influential models and by specific stimulus-response pairings in our own experience.

Dimensions of individual difference. Mischel also emphasizes the active role of the person in cognitively organizing his or her interactions with the environment (Mischel & Peake, 1982). (It is interesting to note that Kelly was Mischel's graduate advisor.)

How you respond to a specific environmental input, according to Mischel, depends on any or all of the following variables or processes:

- *Competencies*—what you know, what you can do, and your ability to generate certain cognitive and behavioral outcomes;
- *Encoding strategies*—the way you process incoming information, selectively attending, categorizing, and making associations to it;
- *Expectancies*—your anticipation of likely outcomes for given actions in particular situations;
- *Personal values*—the importance you attach to stimuli, events, people, and activities;
- *Self-regulatory systems and plans*—the rules you have developed for guiding your performance, setting goals, and evaluating your effectiveness.

What determines the nature of these variables for an individual? According to Mischel, they result from the individual's observations and interactions with other people and with inanimate aspects of the physical environment. When people respond differently to the same environmental input, it is because of differences in these person variables (Mischel, 1973).

Person versus environment. Mischel emphasizes the *adaptive flexibility* of human behavior. Although the person variables listed above are a continuing influence on our behavior, we also are able to adapt and change in response to the new demands of our environment. Mischel hypothesizes that, in general, person variables will have their greatest impact on behavior when cues in the situation are weak or ambiguous. When situations are strong and clear, there will be less individual variation in response. For example, in the dentist's waiting room, most of us tend to behave pretty much the same in response to the strong situational demands. At the beach, however, where many behaviors are appropriate, person variables will lead to large differences in behavior. A good deal of evidence in support of this view has been reported (Mischel 1979; Monson et al., 1982).

Criticisms of cognitive theories

One criticism leveled against cognitive theories is that they generally overlook emotion as an important component of personality. The variables emphasized

△ | *In many settings, situational cues outweigh person variables. Most "regulars" exhibit a similar pattern of behavior on commuter trains.*

(constructs, encoding strategies, and the like) are rational, information-processing variables. Emotions are reduced to the status of by-products of thoughts and behavior, rather than having independent importance. For those who feel that emotions are more central in the functioning of human personality, this is a serious flaw. Several new lines of research have demonstrated that emotions have an important effect on cognitive processes such as memory, reaction time, and decision making (Bower, 1981; Zajonc, 1980). Feelings may themselves be important determinants of cognitive content and structure, rather than just "cognitive coatings."

A second set of criticisms focuses on the vagueness of explanations of how personal constructs and competencies come about. This is particularly true of Kelly's theory—much less true of Mischel's. Although it is central to Kelly's view that people are free to change their constructs, it is unclear from his theory how constructs develop and what is needed for them to change. Moreover, an important theme in Kelly's personal construct theory is the prediction of future events, but the theory deals less with how someone anticipates his or her own behavior than it does with anticipating other people's behavior.

Despite these criticisms, cognitive personality theories have made major contributions to current thinking. For example, Kelly's theory has influenced a large number of cognitive therapists. Mischel's theoretical views have also had a great deal of influence on views of *when* person variables can be expected to be important and *when* situation variables probably will be. This may be a more useful perspective than controversy about *whether* person variables overall are more or less important than situational variables.

COMPARING THEORIES

A unified theory of personality that a majority of psychologists can endorse does not exist. Perhaps in the future such a theory may emerge, or maybe there will always be diverse theories, since different approaches start with different premises and explore different perspectives.

Several differences in basic assumptions have come up repeatedly as we have surveyed the various theories. It may be helpful to list the most important of these and to compare the emphasis given to them by the different approaches.

1. **Heredity versus environment**—nature or nurture, the importance of genetic and biological factors as compared with influences from the environment. Trait theories have been split on this issue; Freudian theory depends heavily on heredity; humanistic, learning, and cognitive theories all emphasize either environment as a determinant of behavior or interaction with the environment as a source of personality development and differences.

2. **Learning processes versus innate laws of behavior**—emphasis on *modifiability* versus a view of personality development as following an internal timetable. Here again, trait theories have been divided. Freudian theory has favored the inner determinant view—a pessimistic one—while an optimistic brand of innate striving is postulated by humanists.

3. **Emphasis on past, present, or future**—here trait theories emphasize past causes, whether innate or learned; Freudian theory emphasizes past events in early childhood; and learning theories emphasize past reinforcements. Humanistic theories tend to emphasize present phenomenal reality or future goals. Cognitive theories emphasize past and present, and the future if goal-setting is involved.

4. **Consciousness versus unconsciousness**—Freudian theory emphasizes unconscious processes; humanistic and cognitive theories emphasize conscious processes. Trait theories and learning theories, which are less concerned with mental processes, pay little attention to either consciousness or unconsciousness.

5. **Inner disposition versus outer situation**—as responsible for whatever consistency there is in a person's behavior over time. Learning theories emphasize situational factors; the others emphasize either dispositional factors or an interaction and joint contribution.

So each group of theories makes different contributions to our human "vehicle." Trait theories provide a catalog that describes the parts and structures. Psychodynamic theories add a powerful engine and the fuel to get the vehicle moving. Learning theories supply the steering wheel, directional signals, and other regulation equipment. Humanistic theories put a person in the driver's seat—a man or a woman who wants to travel to a unique place and enjoy the trip as much as the arrival at the destination. And cognitive theories add reminders to the driver that the way the trip is planned, organized, and remembered will differ according to the mental map he or she chooses for the journey.

Personality theories are, in part, attempts to explain how and why people differ. Another important activity for psychologists has been the *measurement* of differences among people. Different theories have different implications for *what* should be measured, *how* it should be measured, and *when* the information obtained justifies a decision to intervene in someone's life—to hire, fire, admit, reject, or treat the person being assessed. In the next chapter we take an in-depth look at the techniques and results of psychological assessment.

SUMMARY

■ Personality is what characterizes an individual—what is characteristic and unique about the person across different situations and over time. Personality theorists study the whole person as the sum of the separate processes of feelings, thoughts, and actions.

■ The focus of the idiographic approach is the organization of the unique person; that of the nomothetic approach is the uniformities across people, as well as the ways they vary on the same set of dimensions. Descriptions of consistency and even opinions of how much consistency there is have varied widely.

■ Personality can be studied through the case study method (intense study of one individual), the correlational method (what characteristics are related), and the experimental method (what conditions are causally related to characteristic behavior of individuals).

■ Some theorists, such as Sheldon and Eysenck, categorize people by all-or-none types, assumed to be related to particular characteristic behaviors. Others view traits as the building blocks of personality. Allport, an idiographic theorist, differentiated cardinal, central, and secondary traits.

■ Traits, as measured by personality tests, are poor predictors of behavior. Correlations between different behaviors assumed to reflect the same traits are low, though there is more temporal stability in behavior than cross-situational stability.

■ In his psychodynamic theory, Freud accepted Darwin's emphasis on instinctive biological energies as basic motivators and further proposed unconscious motivation as the key to behavior. Basic concepts of Freudian theory include psychic determinism in both behavior and some forms of illness; early experiences as key determinants of life-long personality; psychic energy from basic drives as giving power and direction to behavior; and powerful unconscious processes as determining behavior, feelings, dreams, and even slips of the tongue, often to the puzzlement of the individual.

■ Freud saw personality as made up of the id (guided by the pleasure principle), the superego (guided by learned social and moral restrictions), and the reconciling ego (guided by the reality principle). Unacceptable feelings and wishes are repressed; the individual develops various ego-defense mechanisms for lessening anxiety and bolstering self-esteem.

■ Neo-Freudians have put greater emphasis on ego functioning and social variables and less on sexual urges. They see personality development as a lifelong process. Adler thought each person developed a consisent life-style aimed at compensating or overcompensating for feelings of inferiority. Jung emphasized the notion of a collective unconscious, including archetypes (symbols of universal significance); he saw the needs to create and self-actualize as powerful unconscious instincts.

■ Freudian concepts are vague, not operationally defined, and difficult or impossible to test scientifically; they are applied retrospectively and do not predict a person's behavior or take into account his or her goals and ideas. Also, they are based on clinical experience with disturbed individuals and have little to say about healthy life-styles.

■ The focus of humanistic theories is on the growth potential of the individual. These theories are holistic, dispositional, phenomenological, existential, and optimistic. To understand an individual, one must understand his or her private world and self-concept. Some people see themselves more as objects; others, more as actors.

■ Humanistic theories are criticized for vagueness and oversimplification; for having little to say about individual differences; for neglect of environmental variables, unconscious influences, and the individual's past; and for inability to make predictions.

■ Strict behaviorists see personality as the sum of overt and covert responses that are reliably elicited as a consequence of the individual's reinforcement history. Different histories of reinforcement account for individual differences. Their interest is not in consistency in people's behavior but in how behavior changes when stimulus conditions change. Two behavioristic views that incorporate cognitive factors are the notion of coverants—operants of the mind—and Bandura's social learning theory, which includes the concepts of reciprocal determinism, observational learning, and self-efficacy.

■ Learning theories have been criticized for disregarding important characteristics of human organisms, for overemphasis on environmental determinants, and for being based on research with subjects in a state of deficiency motivation. But increasingly, approaches based on learning are taking into account cognitive processes as well as behavioral ones.

■ Cognitive theorists emphasize individual differences in perception and interpretation and the individual's creation of his or her own environment. According to Kelly's theory of personal constructs, all people, like scientists, construct the best picture they can of reality; personality is the person's total system of such constructs.

■ Mischel stresses the person's active role in cognitively organizing interactions with the environment in the light of his or her competencies, ways of processing information, expectancies, values, and self-imposed rules and plans. He sees person variables as having the greatest influence in weak or ambiguous situations, and situations as having greatest impact when they are strong and clear.

■ Cognitive theories are criticized for overemphasis on rational variables and neglect of emotion, and for vagueness about how personal constructs and competencies develop.

■ The various theories can be seen as varying in their assumptions about nature versus nurture; the modifiability of behavior; emphasis on past, present, or future; conscious versus unconscious; and the importance of inner dispositions versus outer situations in producing consistency in behavior.

12

ASSESSING INDIVIDUAL DIFFERENCES

■ WHAT IS ASSESSMENT?

■ METHODS OF ASSESSMENT
Basic features of formal assessment
Sources of information

■ ASSESSING INTELLIGENCE
Historical context
IQ tests
What is intelligence?
The use and misuse of IQ

■ ASSESSING PERSONALITY
Objective measures
Projective tests

■ ASSESSING CREATIVITY
What qualifies as creative?
Correlates of creativity

■ ASSESSMENT AND YOU
Vocational interests and aptitudes
Social strengths and weaknesses: Shyness
Political and ethical issues

■ SUMMARY

Little Maria loved her kindergarten class. There were such fun things to do and nice friends to play with that she often wished she could live in that clean, colorful school room and not have to go home to her rundown tenement apartment. But when most of her friends moved up to first grade, Maria and a few others were sent to a class for children who were "different." She couldn't be with her friends in the regular first grade because she had been assigned to the class for "retarded children."

That made her sad, and she was even more confused and upset later on when former classmates began calling her things like "dummy" and "retard." Soon she realized that she must indeed be different from them because a lot of the children in her new class were handicapped, or couldn't talk right. There weren't the same kinds of fun games to play, and everything seemed to take so long, to go so slowly.

Maria began to daydream to escape the boredom that was taking the joy out of her young life. So sometimes she was not prepared to hear the teacher's questions; she thought that the teacher too, must think she was a "dummy." She couldn't even enjoy the coloring book because the pictures were not printed clearly and the lines and letters were fuzzy. Because they were, she made silly mistakes when she had to read the numbers and words.

The following year, Maria was assigned again to the remedial class and might have gone through her entire public school education tracked in that class were it not for some special tests she took: not mental tests of what she knew and could do, but sensory tests of her vision and hearing. The test results clearly showed that Maria's academic problems were at least in part traceable to an undetected visual impairment—poor close vision but normal distant vision. In addition, she was somewhat hard of hearing.

The tester from this sensory assessment program arranged to have Maria's intelligence assessed using individually administered tests. She performed well above average! Maria had been misdiagnosed by teachers as "retarded" because her sensory impairments led to false impressions that she did not *understand* what she saw and heard.

On the basis of the new test data, Maria was given eyeglasses and eye muscle exercises to improve her vision. She was also seated in the front of the class, where she could hear the teacher better. But most important of all to her, she was sent along to the regular class, to be with some of her former good friends. She forgave them for the name-calling because they had made the same mistake that the teachers and even she had made. Maria went on to perform well academically and to enjoy school as a special place where people are concerned about helping others.

This special sensory testing program described above is called P.A.T.H.S. (Paramedical Approaches to Health Services) and is run by New York City Community School District 11; the original screening and help in arranging further testing is carried out by paramedical health interns. Similar programs are helping many children in other cities. The results of the assessment are used to gauge the child's ability to perform academically. They help correct mistaken judgments based on a teacher's limited—or in some cases, too readily prejudicial—observations. Those judgments may be confounded by undetected problems of a nonintellectual nature—in Maria's case, sensory problems; for other children, motivational or attentional problems. An untold number of children, like Maria, have been helped by such assessment procedures.

Psychological assessment of the attributes of individuals—measurement of intelligence, personality, creativity, and more—is a major contribution that psychology has made to society. It takes place in many educational and vocational settings. When a person's aptitudes, interests, attitudes, and personality are all taken into account, the chances of improving the "fit" of person to school or job are greatly increased. Assessment also helps the clinical psychologist detect problems in functioning that may require special counseling or treatment. Finally, researchers use assessment techniques to see if individuals have the characteristics predicted by their theories and to select individuals as subjects who have the particular characteristics most relevant for their research.

But there is much controversy about the use and misuse of test results and about some of the assumptions on which assessment is based. In this chapter we will examine what psychological assessment does, how it does it, and what problems it can help to correct—and create.

WHAT IS ASSESSMENT?

Psychological assessment is the use of specified testing procedures to evaluate the abilities, behaviors, and personal qualities of people. Assessment helps to better understand a person so that more informed decisions can be made about some current problems for future choices in the person's life (Maloney & Ward, 1976). It is often referred to as the measurement of *individual differences,* since the majority of assessment procedures describe individuals by specifying how they are different from or similar to other people—how many more test questions they can answer than other people their age, whether they seem more or less hypnotizable, or paranoid, whether their performance is more similar to that of a computer scientist or a creative artist, and so forth.

The development of formal tests and procedures for assessment is a relatively new enterprise in psychology. But long before Western psychology began devising tests to see how people "measured up," assessment techniques were commonplace in ancient China. In fact, China employed a sophisticated program of civil service testing over four thousand years ago, when officials were required to demonstrate their competence every third year at an oral examination. Two thousand years later, during the Han Dynasty, written civil service tests were used to assess competence in the areas of law, the military, agriculture, and geography. During the Ming Dynasty (1368–1644 A.D.), public officials were chosen on the basis of their performance at three stages of an objective selection procedure. Examinations were first given at the local level. The 4 percent who passed these tests had to endure nine days and nights of essay examinations on the classics. The 5 percent who passed the essay exams were allowed to complete a final set of tests conducted at the nation's capital.

China's selection procedures were observed and described by British diplomats and missionaries in the early 1800s. Modified versions of China's system were soon adopted by the British, and later by the Americans, for the selection of civil service personnel (Wiggins, 1973). While these early assessment techniques were used for purposes of job placement, assessment now takes place in a multitude of settings and is used for many different purposes. Tests to see how you are doing in school, how well you are likely to do later, what your strengths and weaknesses are, how well you would function in different settings— these are some of the varieties of aptitude and ability assessment you are likely to encounter.

The purposes of formal assessment are not really very different from most people's informal goals in "sizing up" others. Your parents probably wondered if you "had it in you" to "make it in college." If they predicted incorrectly it would be financially and emotionally costly. The *error* in such predictions, of course, can go in either of two directions: it is possible to predict failure (and withhold a college education) when the student would have been effective, or to estimate success (and support a college education) when the student is actually ineffective and flunks out. Similarly, of course, there are two kinds of accurate predictions: those in which success is predicted and achieved, and those in which failure is predicted and observed.

In many areas of our lives we also want to predict the future behavior of someone under circumstances that are largely unknown or uncertain. Your choice of a person to live with you as roommate or later as spouse and perhaps as parent of your children involves an important assessment prediction. So does choosing a career for yourself. While you are acting as assessor, you are also being assessed by others— potential dates, mates, employers, judges, superior officers, and others who are sizing up your qualifications.

Scientific psychology attempts to formalize the procedures by which predictions about individual behavior can be made with a minimum of error and a maximum of accuracy. Assessment begins with the measurement of a limited number of individual personality attributes and samples of behavior. From this narrow body of information about the person in the testing situation(s), predictions are made about his or her likely reactions at some future time in some other situation (not identical to the test situation).

Psychologists use assessment techniques to make sense of the incredible range of individual differences. They want to understand how different traits go together to form a unique personality. They are curious to discover ways of describing the diversity of individual behavior. By testing, classifying, and ca-

tegorizing individuals who share similar traits, psychologists can correlate behavioral differences with personality types. Part of such research is designed to test empirically the predictive value of different theories of personality looked at in the previous chapter.

Another aspect of the scientific concern for assessment has to do with learning about how people develop. At what ages do children develop which skills, attitudes, and ways of dealing with the world? How important are sex, race, intelligence and other human characteristics in predicting specific behavioral outcomes? The personality psychologist is interested in general answers to these and similar questions about relationships between the average behavioral tendency of people with certain characteristics. While the clinical psychologist's goal is to make predictions about the individual client, the research psychologist's goal is to discover consistencies and regularities in personality that translate to behavior in general. In all such testing, the goal is to find out more information that will further the development of psychology as a theoretical and applied science.

When assessment is used for an applied purpose (in contrast to the theoretical), the process begins with a *referral.* Someone asks a question about a particular individual and refers the person to a psychologist specially trained to make an assessment that might provide some answers. A judge may want to know if an admitted murderer is capable of understanding the consequences of his actions so that responsibility can be assigned to him or he can be judged insane. A teacher may wish to know why a child, like little Maria, has learning difficulties or shows behavior problems. Parents are often eager to know how intelligent their child really is, regardless of class grades. And clinical psychologists ask about a patient's status prior to treatment, as well as changes in status during or after treatment, in order to guide their therapeutic strategies (Korchin, 1976).

The referral questions asked influence the kinds of assessment that will be undertaken and the way the assessment conclusions will be phrased and interpreted. Depending on the theoretical orientation of the personality or clinical psychologist involved in the assessment, quite different views of the same person may emerge. Each may focus on something different while examining the same person or assessment data. "There is a psychoanalytic reality, a social-learning reality, an existential reality, and so on. The purpose of assessment is not to discover the true essence of the client but to describe that client in a useful way—a way that will lead to the solution of a problem" (Phares, 1984, p. 174).

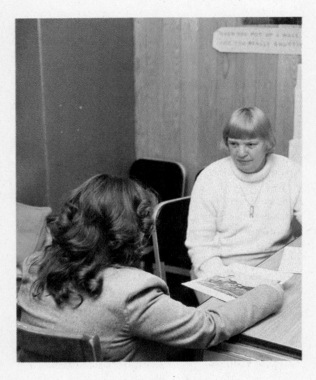

△ If a referral is due to a student's problem classroom behavior, the psychologist may, in addition to interviewing, also administer a battery of tests to determine if she has a learning disability.

METHODS OF ASSESSMENT

While there are clearly parallels between the informal assessment we all do of ourselves and other people and the more formal assessment carried out by professionals, there are important differences, too. As already noted, the methods of assessment used by psychologists are developed in more systematic ways, and they are used in a more organized manner for more carefully specified purposes. Indeed, that is what we mean when we call our everyday assessments "informal" and call those carried out in professional settings "formal."

We will first consider some of the characteristics that make professional assessments "formal." After discussing these requirements, we will inquire as to the sources of information psychologists use in making assessments. Here we will note that some of their techniques were derived from different *theoretical* perspectives of the kinds outlined in the previous chapter. However, there are also assessment techniques based on an *empirical* rather than theoretical foundation. That is, their construction was *not* guided by any theory of personality or intelligence or psychopathology. Instead, tests were developed on which different types of people responded differently, and thus they and others could be categorized on the basis of those performance differences.

Basic features of formal assessment

To be useful for classifying individuals or selecting those with particular qualities, an assessment procedure should meet three requirements. The assessment instrument, or test, should be (a) *reliable,* (b) *valid,* and, for most purposes, (c) *standardized.* If a test fails to meet these requirements, then we cannot be sure that a person's score on the test really indicates what it is supposed to, or that an assessment conclusion will be trustworthy.

Reliability. A test is **reliable** if it measures something consistently. If your bathroom scale gives you a different reading each time you step on it—sometimes higher, other times lower (even though you haven't eaten or changed your clothing, and little time has passed between "testings")—then your scale is not doing its job, and you don't believe the readings it gives. We would call it *unreliable* because we could not count on it to give consistent results.

One straightforward way of finding out how reliable tests are is to calculate their **test-retest reliability.** This is a measure of the correlation between the scores of the same people on the same test given on two different occasions. A perfectly reliable test would yield a correlation coefficient of $+1.00$. This would mean that the same exact pattern of scores would emerge both times; the same people would get the highest scores on each testing, and the same people would get the lowest scores on each testing. A totally unreliable test would result in a .00 correlation coefficient. That would mean there was no relationship between the first scores and the second set; someone who got the top score initially might get any score, even the lowest, the second time.

There are two other ways of assessing reliability. One is to administer alternate, *equivalent forms* of the test instead of giving exactly the same test twice. Doing so reduces effects of direct practice, memory, or the desire to appear consistent. The other is to measure the *internal consistency* of responses on a single test. For example, we can compare a person's score on the odd-numbered items of a test to that on the even-numbered items. A reliable test should yield the same score for each of its halves; it would then be said to have high internal consistency.

Correlation coefficients of reliability above .70 are found for the best psychological tests. By comparison, achievement tests constructed by classroom teachers generally range in reliability from as low as .30 up to only about .60. These correlations are for objective, true-false, and multiple-choice tests; you already know about the greater unreliability of essay-test scores.

Although a reliable test tends to give the same test scores when repeated, obtaining different test scores does not necessarily mean the test is unreliable. Sometimes the variable being measured actually changes. For example, if you took a test on theories of personality both before and after reading Chapter 11, you would (I hope!) do better the second time—because you would actually know more. In addition, many variables other than the one of primary interest may affect test scores. You may score differently on two different occasions because of changes in your mood, how tired you are, how hard you are trying, and so forth. If the test is designed to measure mood, fatigue, or motivation, then this change is just what we want. If not, then these variables will alter the desired test performance, say intelligence, to give a false picture of the person's ability.

Validity. If a test is reliable, we know it is doing a good job of measuring something. Of course, we also want to know what that "something" is. The **validity** of a test refers to whether it is measuring what the assessor intends it to measure. A valid test of intelligence tells us how intelligent people are and predicts performance in situations where intelligence is important. Scores on a valid intelligence test would not be affected by how experienced people are at taking tests. Scores on a valid measure of creativity would reflect actual creativity, not merely drawing ability, deviance, or a joyful mood.

To assess the **criterion validity** of a test, we compare peoples' scores on the test to their scores on some other standard, a *criterion,* theoretically associated with what was measured by the first test. Ideally, scores on the criterion directly reflect a personal characteristic or behavior theoretically related to, but not the same as, that assessed by the original test. For example, if a high-school test is designed to predict academic success in college, then college grades would be an appropriate criterion. If the correlation of test scores with subsequent college grades were high, then the test would be a valid predictor.

For many personal qualities of interest to psychologists, no ideal criterion exists. No single behavior or objective measure of performance can tell us how anxious, depressed, or aggressive a person is. Psychologists have theories about these more abstract variables, or *constructs*—ideas about what affects them, how they show up in behavior, and how they relate to other variables. **Construct validity** is the degree to which scores on a test based on the defined variable—the construct—correlate positively with scores of other tests, judges' ratings, behavioral measures or experimental results already considered valid indicators of the characteristic being measured (Cronbach & Meehl, 1955). So a new test of a construct such as "aggression" should correlate positively with existing tests of "aggression" that also assess that construct. For example, suppose you designed a test to measure aggressive tendencies in

"Then, as you can see, we give them some multiple-choice tests."

children. To assess its construct validity you might compare scores on the test to measures of how often the children fight with others, how many hostile comments they make, and how aggressive their teachers think they are.

Often problems of validity arise not because a test is defective, but because the criterion is poorly conceptualized or not well measured. If a criterion is not well-chosen and does not itself adequately represent that important "something" the psychologist is trying to test, then checking test scores against it can tell us little about how well the new test is serving its intended purpose.

For example, one admissions test in some medical schools consists of a stressful interview administered by a team of faculty. What criterion shall we use to judge the validity of the scores candidates earn on this type of interpersonal-evaluative stress analysis? Are they likely to be related to ability to handle the stresses medical students experience taking course examinations? Are they related to a physician's ability to make medical decisions under the stress of uncertain information? Both criteria are important, but at different stages of one's medical training. If the stress interview predicts *only* how well a student will cope with classroom stress and *not* how well he or she will handle "on-the-job stress" as a new doctor, is the test doing what it was intended to? Or is it valid if the interview leads to the rejection of students who are shy in socially threatening situations but would still make good physicians? To determine the validity of any test, we must first know what it is supposed to be measuring and then decide what observations will best reveal that characteristic. So it is essential to ask not only whether it's valid but also valid "for what purpose."

Standardization and norms. To be most useful, a measuring device should be **standardized**—administered to all persons in the same way under the same conditions. Standardization is a method that can establish **norms,** or statistical standards, so that an individual's score can be compared with those of others in a defined group.

Suppose you get a score of 68 on a test designed to reveal how depressed you are. What does that mean? Are you a little depressed, not at all depressed, about average, or what? You can find out by checking the test norms to see what the usual range of scores is and what the average is for students of your age and sex. You probably encountered test norms when you got your scores on aptitude tests (such as the SAT). The norms let you know how your scores compared to those of other students and helped you know how well you had done relative to that normative population.

Group norms are most useful for interpreting individual scores when the standardization group shares important qualities with those individuals (such as age, social class, and experience). When this is the case, the group norms provide a useful yardstick against which an individual's score can be interpreted.

But for norms to be meaningfully used to compare test performances, it is essential that everyone take the "same test." That sounds obvious, but it may not always occur in practice. Some people may be allowed more time than others, given clearer or fuller instructions, permitted to ask questions, or motivated to perform better by the tester's suggestions. For example, before administering a scale to assess children's degree of test anxiety, one teacher told her class, "We're going to have some fun with this new kind of question game this nice man will play with you." A teacher in another classroom prepared her class for the "same" assessment by cautioning, "This psychologist from Yale University is going to give you a test to see what you are thinking; I hope you will do well and show how good our class is!" Did the children's performance scores reflect only what the test was intended to measure?

Could you directly compare the scores of the children in these two classes on this "same test"? The answer is "no," because the way in which the test was administered was not standardized. When test procedures are not standardized by explicit instructions as to how to administer the test, or as to the way of scoring the results, it is difficult to interpret what a given test score means or how it relates to any comparison group.

Sources of information

Psychological assessment methods can be organized according to four techniques used to gather information about a person: interviews, life history and archival data, tests, and situational observations. They can also be classified according to who the information is coming from: the person being assessed or other people. If from the person, they are called *self-report measures;* if from others, *judges' ratings.*

Four assessment techniques. If you want a direct approach to learning about someone, ask him or her questions about values, beliefs, attitudes, behavior, and so forth in the form of an *interview.* Interviews may be unfocused, not structured, and the questions asked may only indirectly get at the information the interviewer wishes to elicit from the person. Or they may go the other extreme and be highly structured and quite direct in the relationship between the questions asked and the nature of the information being sought. In addition to interviewing the person in question, it is of course possible also to interview others who are able to report on him or her—friends, parents, or co-workers, for example.

A skillful interviewer is trained to be effective in five aspects of a *diagnostic interview* (one used to classify an individual into some ordered, organized categories). The interviewer must be able to: put the respondent at ease, know how to elicit the desired information, maintain control of the direction and pace of the interview, establish and maintain feelings of rapport, and finally bring the interview to a satis-factory conclusion. "Diagnostic interviewing has always been the clinician's personal, subjective effort to gain information and understanding and it remains the most important tool in clinical assessment and diagnosis" according to a recent—but disputed—appraisal of this form of assessment (Weins & Matarazzo, 1983, p. 327).

Interview data may be supplemented with secondary *life history* sources of information about the person taken from different types of available records. These may include school or military performances, written productions, medical data, photographs, or videotapes, especially those of different time periods and in relation to other people.

Psychological testing is the major method that is usually associated in most student's minds with assessment. Indeed the construction and use of tests, scales, and inventories to measure virtually all aspects of human functioning, such as intelligence, personality, and creativity, is a substantial activity for many psychologists.

We will see later in this chapter that tests may vary on a number of dimensions—general or specific, objective or subjective, verbal or nonverbal (performance), and others. A major virtue of tests over interviews is their *quantitative* characterizations of the individual along with the normative comparisons with others that are possible. We will also see that some psychological tests are based on, or derived from, particular personality theories that specify what is important to measure.

Situational observations can be used to assess behavior in real-life settings. The observer, rater, or judge observes the individual's behavioral patterns in one or more situations, such as work or leisure, at home or in school. The goal is to discover the determinants and consequences of various responses and habits of the individual. This general approach comes out of the tradition of experimental psychology, social learning theories of personality, and behavior modification therapies. Direct observations as an assessment technique has until recently taken a back seat to the preferred use of tests, which were more

 A skillful interviewer can elicit a wealth of information for the assessment process.

economical, less effortful, and provided normative data. However, situational observation is increasing in use across many areas of psychology and other social sciences. It is based on empirical investigations of what people say and do in a given context and what influences that behavior. Its practitioners are optimistic about its greater use in the next decade and its anticipated improvements in reliability, validity, comprehensiveness, and usefulness (Ciminero et al., 1977; Haynes, 1983).

Self-reports. *Self-report* measures, also called **self-inventories,** require respondents to answer questions or give information about themselves. They may be asked to tell what they like or dislike, whether they agree with certain statements, or how they feel in certain situations. For example, respondents might indicate which of the following they agree with more: "I live one day at a time, never planning far ahead," or "I enjoy setting goals and planning how to reach them as much as engaging in the activities themselves." Such measures are valuable because they tap the individual's own personal experience and feelings. They are convenient to give because trained interviewers are not needed, and they are generally easy to score.

The chief disadvantage of self-report measures is that people do not always give accurate responses on these inventories. We are not always in touch with our own feelings, we cannot remember all we have done or thought, and we may even intentionally lie in order to make ourselves look better. Despite this disadvantage, self-report measures are often very useful. This is especially true for those on which steps have been taken to spot response inaccuracies, be they intentional or not. In fact, many formal self-report measures are considered to be very objective, not because people's answers lack subjective bias (they don't!), but because of the standard ways in which the responses are handled—even to the point of being scored by a computer rather than a person. Several self-report inventories will be described in later sections of this chapter.

Judges' ratings. In psychological assessment, a judge's rating involves a systematic evaluation of some aspect of a person's behavior by another person, which in itself moves it into the observable, and therefore more readily objective, realm. For example

your teachers may be asked to rate your school performance and your interactions with peers ("Does Charlie work and play well with others?"); your parents may rate your cooperativeness as a young child; and your friends may give their impressions of your personality (see **Figure 12.1**).

A number of well-known assessment techniques involve ratings made by judges who do not know you personally. Often the judge is a psychologist, counselor, or trained interviewer. These judges may interact with you in a structured way, asking you to answer specific interview questions or to respond to specific test stimuli. Or their interaction with you may also be relatively unstructured and casual, or they may simply observe you without any interaction—either concealed or with your awareness. Afterwards, they may evaluate your responses on various dimensions. In some cases, they may base their evaluations on detailed guidelines provided by the developers of the assessment instrument. Sometimes the guidelines are less precise, allowing spontaneous reactions and informal impressions to play a greater role.

Can you think of any drawbacks that may result from the use of ratings made by interviewers or other judges? Some were covered briefly in our discussion of research foundations in Chapter 1 (see especially pp. 17–18). An important one to point up here is that the ratings you make of another person may tell more about *you,* or about your relationship with the person, than about the true characteristics of the person being rated. For example, if you like someone, you may tend to judge him or her favorably on nearly every dimension and be blind to the person's faults (a **"halo" effect**). Or, if a rater thinks most people in a certain category (blacks, Jews, Italians, women) have certain qualities, then that rater may "see" those qualities in any individual who happens to be in that category (a **"stereotype" effect**). These unwanted biases in ratings can be lessened if the rules for making ratings are clearly specified ("If he does X, then give him a 10"). And yet even trained observers can fall prey to bias.

Ratings are most reliable when they are of specific behaviors ("makes eye contact and smiles"); they become less reliable when the rating categories are general or vague ("is open to new experiences" or "is a sensitive person"). Focused behavior ratings allow less room for personal, and potentially biased, impressions. In addition, bias can be reduced by using more than one rater, which makes it possible to calculate the *interrater reliability.* That is, if two different raters independently make very similar judg-

CADET LEADERSHIP EVALUATION AND COUNSELING	CBT OR CFT	CLASS	REGULAR LETTER CO

CADET NAME (Last, First, MI) | POSITION HELD | LENGTH OF TIME IN POSITION

PART 1 – SUMMARY OF DUTIES ASSIGNED

PART 2 – EVALUATION SPECIFICS *(Be specific and elaborate on the following areas)*

Indicate by circling a number, your degree of agreement with items A through D below as being descriptive of the rated Cadet. Consider the listed definitions of each criteria in your rating (these same statements appear on the Officer's Evaluation Report). Elaborate in the comments section on any item you feel will assist in the development of the rated Cadet.

A. LEADERSHIP   LOW DEGREE (UNSATISFACTORY = 1) 1 2 3 4 5 HIGH DEGREE (OUTSTANDING = 5)

Sets and enforces high standards
Motivates, challenges, inspires and influences others
Is aware of and sensitive to others and their problems
Communicates in a clear, concise and understood manner
Manages and develops subordinates
Encourages initiative, responsibility, and resourcefulness

Comments:

B. PROFESSIONAL COMPETENCE   LOW DEGREE 1 2 3 4 5 HIGH DEGREE

Possesses capacity to acquire knowledge and grasp concepts
Displays sound judgment in making decisions
Demonstrates expertise in assigned tasks
Understands the temper of the times and is able to adjust accordingly
Exhibits insight and perceptivity in performance of duties

Comments:

C. INDIVIDUAL SELF-DISCIPLINE   LOW DEGREE 1 2 3 4 5 HIGH DEGREE

Possesses military bearing and is neat and well-groomed
Maintains appropriate level of physical fitness
Seeks self-improvement
Maintains high standards of personal conduct both on and off duty
Is adaptable in changing situations
Performs successfully under physical and mental stress

Comments:

D. PROFESSIONAL ORIENTATION   LOW DEGREE 1 2 3 4 5 HIGH DEGREE

Dedication and commitment to the goals and missions of the Army, the country, and USMA.
Persistence in mission accomplishment
Concern for the welfare of subordinates
Supports Equal Opportunity

Comments:

USMA FORM 1 MAY 78 **2–319** (Edition of 1 Apr 77 is obsolete)   ARMY-WP-SM-2740-78

◁ **Figure 12.1**

Pictured here is Page 1 of a rating scale used to assess cadets at The U.S. Military Academy at West Point. Page 2 concludes with comments on overall performance duty, strengths and weaknesses, and recommendations for improvement.

ments of the same individual, then we can feel more confident that the judgments accurately reflect that individual's characteristics, and not one judge's biases.

Judges' ratings based on samples of behavior that they observe directly and score on objective checklists are being used more and more to assess problem behaviors. Trained observers may visit a child's home, school, or play setting to try to record unobtrusively what the child is doing at selected fixed intervals, say every 30 seconds, or in response to a randomly generated signal. In this way, a *baseline rate* (an initial measure of frequency) of the problem behavior can be determined for temper tantrums, inattention, or social isolation, for example. Then, during and after a treatment program, the frequency of the behavior can also be measured and compared to the baseline measure in order to see if the treatment is having the desired effect. In this way better programs for treatment and for prevention of behavior problems are being designed (Haynes & Wilson, 1979).

MEN and WOMEN   by Calman

ASSESSING INTELLIGENCE

Intelligence is the capacity to profit from experience and to go beyond the given to the possible. It is in our intellectual development that we humans have been able to transcend our physical frailty and gain dominance over more powerful or numerous animals. No wonder, then, that intelligence is our most highly prized possession. But what is intelligence? What are its origins? How can it be assessed? What are its advantages?

The first major assessment endeavor by psychologists was an attempt to measure intelligence. The history of this endeavor illustrates some of the steps in the design of instruments for assessment, as well as some of the problems that may be encountered. The complexity of the task is reflected in the fact that while intelligence testing has been with us for many years, some of the problems still remain unsolved, and hot debate still rages about the meaning, measurement, and personal-societal implications of intelligence.

Is intelligence basically a single dimension on which people can be assessed in terms of how "smart" or "dumb" they are? Or should it be conceptualized not as a unitary attribute like a person's height, but as a collection of mental competencies analogous to athletic ability? In this section we will consider alternative views on this basic question of how to define and understand what intelligence is.

The way we think about intelligence and mental functioning influences how we try to assess it. Can the complexity and richness of human intelligence be quantified and reduced to a single score? Some psychologists believe so, while others argue that "assessment should depend on a picture, not a number"—a picture of how the different components of a person's intelligence interrelate (Hunt, 1984).

Even if we can measure intelligence and agree on a definition of it, what difference does it make to a person or a society? What practical consequences follow from assessing someone's intelligence, from discovering individual differences in intellectual functioning? Here we want to inquire not only whether intelligence tests are valid, but valid for what purpose and for what people. Many investigators believe that assessment of intellectual abilities is one of psychology's most significant contributions to society. In opposition are others who maintain that it has been, and continues to be, a systematic attempt by elitists to "measure" people so that desirable ones can be put in the right slots and the others rejected (Gould, 1981). Let's examine some of the evidence for such claims.

Historical context

A brief look at the history of intelligence testing will reveal how practical social and political concerns, measurement issues, and theory were entwined in the development of means of measuring intellectual differences among children and also among adults.

The initial impetus to discovering how to do so came from Europe, specifically France, with the educational objective of identifying children who were unable to learn in school. But intelligence testing soon became an "All-American" enterprise. At the beginning of the twentieth century, the United States was a nation in turmoil. The economic, social, and political order of the country was rapidly changing, and the vast impact of millions of new immigrants contributed to the confusion. At that time, "intelligence test results were used not only to differentiate between children experiencing academic problems, but also as a measuring stick to organize an entire society" (Hale, 1983, p. 373).

Binet's first intelligence test. The year 1905 marked the first published account of a workable intelligence test. Alfred Binet had responded to the call of the French Minister of Public Instruction to study the problem of how best to teach mentally retarded children in the public schools. Binet and his colleague, Theophile Simon, believed that before a program of instruction could be planned, it was necessary to develop a way of measuring the intelligence of the children they would be teaching.

Binet attempted to devise a test of intellectual performance that could be used as an objective way of classifying and separating retarded from normal school children (Sattler, 1982). This would have the virtue of reducing reliance on the more subjective, perhaps biased, evaluations of teachers.

Before seeing how Binet developed his first test, it is important to note four general features of his approach. First, he believed that these test scores were nothing more than a practical estimate of current performance differences, not a measure of innate intelligence. Second, these practical estimates should be used to identify children who needed special help in school because of learning disabilities. Third, since he emphasized the role of training and opportunity in influencing intelligence, Binet sought to identify areas of performance in which such children's abilities might be improved with special education. Finally, he began by using an *empirical* method of test construction rather than basing his test on a theoretical conception of what intelligence was.

Unlike Dr. Itard, who attempted to train the wild, retarded boy of Aveyron (see Chapter 2), Binet believed that it was first necessary to measure a child's intellectual ability before planning an instructional program. The key to his testing approach was *quantification* of intelligence test performance. Children at a given chronological age were given a number of problems or test items. These problems were chosen so that they could be scored objectively, were varied in nature, were not much influenced by differences in children's environments, and called for judgment and reasoning rather than mere rote memory (Binet & Simon, 1911).

Children of various ages were tested, and the average score obtained by normal children at each age was obtained. Then, an individual child's performance was compared to the average for those of his or her age. Test results were expressed in terms of the average age at which normal children achieved a particular score. This was called the **mental age (MA).** When a child's scores on various items of the test added up to the average score of a group of 5-year-olds, the child was said to have a *mental age* of 5, regardless of his or her actual **chronological age (CA).** "Retardation" was then defined operationally by Binet as a child's being two mental-age years behind his or her chronological age. As more children were tested longitudinally, it was found that those assessed as "retarded" at one age fell further behind the mental age of their birth cohorts as they grew older. So a child of 5 who performed at only the level of 3 year olds might, when he was 10, be comparable to 6 year olds. Although his *ratio* of mental age to chronological age would be constant (3/5 and 6/10), the total number of mental-age years of retardation would have increased from two to four.

Mental measurement in America. Nowhere did Binet's successful development of an intelligence test have a greater impact than in the United States. A unique combination of historical events and social-political forces made our country fertile ground for a virtual explosion of interest in assessing mental ability. Since that time the interest of psychologists in intellectual assessment has flourished into a mental measurement industry.

Among the contributing factors that made assessment of intelligence so important here were: (a) the enormous immigration of millions of people from Europe and Asia; (b) the emergence of a vast public school system along with a philosophy of education as the means to teach cultural values to these newcomers so they might rise above their lowly "station in life" through personal merit; and (c) the national emergency created by World War I that necessitated the formation of an efficient military in a short time (see Fass, 1980; Marks, 1976–77). Assessment was seen as a way of putting order into a chaotic society and an inexpensive, democratic means of separating those who could benefit from education or military leadership training from those who were not competent.

In 1917 when the United States declared war on Germany it was necessary to establish quickly a military force led by competent leaders. Drafting many immigrants who were not literate created a problem of determining who had the ability to profit from special training and who were mentally incompetent. The solution was to use tests that did not rely on verbal performance. Over 1.7 million recruits were evaluated with newly devised nonverbal, group-administered tests of mental ability. Incidentally, a group of famous psychologists designed these tests in only one month's time; they included Lewis Terman, Edward Thorndike, and Robert Yerkes (Marks, 1976–77). Two consequences of this large-scale testing program were (a) growing acceptance by the American public of the idea that intelligence tests could be used to differentiate people in terms of their leadership ability and other socially important characteristics, and (b) new attention, in the army report, given to alleged intellectual differences due to race and country of origin (Yerkes, 1921).

The first effect encouraged the widespread application of assessment methods in industry, the military, and schools. The second had the unfortunate effect of providing statistical evidence for prevailing prejudices against blacks and immigrants from southern Europe. Although the data were poorly collected and misinterpreted, they could have been used to show that environmental disadvantages robbed people of the chance to develop their intellectual abilities. Instead, they were used to support arguments of the inherited superiority of Anglo-Saxons and the intellectual inferiority of those alien "others." We shall return to this sore point.

IQ tests

Lewis Terman of Stanford University had been a public school administrator. Feeling that Binet's method for assessing intelligence was important, he adapted the questions for American schoolchildren, standardized administration of the test, and developed age-level norms by giving the test to thousands of children. In 1916 he published the Stanford Revision of the Binet Tests, commonly referred to as the *Stanford-Binet Intelligence Test* (Terman, 1916).

With his new test, Terman provided a foundation for the new concept of the **intelligence quotient, or IQ** (Stern, 1914). This was the ratio of mental age to chronological age (multiplied by 100 to eliminate decimals):

$$IQ = \frac{MA}{CA} \times 100$$

A child with a CA of 8 years whose test scores equaled those of 10-year-olds had an IQ of 125 (10/8 × 100), while a child of that age who performed at the level of 6-year-olds had an IQ of 75 (6/8 × 100). Individuals who performed at the mental age equivalent to their chronological age had IQs of 100, which was considered to be the average or "normal" IQ.

The new Stanford-Binet test soon became a standard instrument in clinical psychology, psychiatry, and educational counseling. At the same time, Terman's adoption of the IQ contributed to the development of a new conceptualization of the purpose and meaning of intelligence testing. Terman believed that intelligence is an inner quality, that it has a large hereditary component, and that IQ tests can measure this inner quality throughout the range of abilities that make up intelligence. The implicit message was that this IQ characterized something essential and unchanging about human intelligence.

△ *A psychologist administers a Stanford-Binet to a 4-year-old youngster. The task she is about to start involves tracing the shortest path to the end of a maze within a specified period of time.*

In line with these changes in the concept of intelligence, the next revision of the test (a) extended the upper limits of the scale to differentiate among adults of superior intelligence; and (b) extended the downward limits to assess the intelligence of children as young as two years (Terman & Merrill, 1937). Parallel test forms of high reliability were also designed so that people could be retested without having memory and practice effects influence their scores. Another revision of the Stanford-Binet intelligence test was made in 1960 to take account of vocabulary changes in our society over time (Terman & Merrill, 1960). For example, the word *Mars*, which was difficult for children in 1916 (equal in difficulty to *conscientious*), had by 1937 become as familiar as *skill*, and by 1961 was as easy as the everyday word *eyelash*. In 1972–73, there was a further revision, and the test norms were revamped to take account of the overall increase in test scores for the population; the norms were shifted up about 1/2 year per age level (Terman & Merrill, 1972).

IQ scores on this test are no longer derived by dividing chronological age into mental age. If you took the Stanford-Binet test now, you would receive 2 points for each of 6 questions you answered, within each mental age grouping (12 points per year). Then the tester would add up your points and check a table to compare your score with the average for your age. An IQ of 100 indicates that 50 percent of those your age earn lower scores. Scores between 90 and 110 are labeled as "normal," above

120 as "superior," and below 70 as evidence of "mental retardation" (see **Figure 12.2**).

It is important to remember that IQ scores, by themselves, do not tell how much children know or what they can do. A high-school student with an IQ of 100 would have knowledge and skills that a fourth grader with a higher IQ of 120 would not have. In addition, people labeled "retarded" on the basis of their IQ score vary considerably in what they are able to do and how much they can learn through instruction. It is also well here to recall the plight of little Maria from our *Opening Case;* there are many reasons why people's intelligence test scores can be lower than their actual ability. Even the latest version of the Stanford-Binet is based largely on the use of words or ability to think and communicate using written English. Children who have language impairments or come from non-English speaking homes would not get a fair estimate of their intellectual ability

David Wechsler, working at Bellevue Hospital in New York, provided a remedy for this problem of language dependence in the form of new intelligence tests that combined verbal subtests with performance subtests. Thus, in addition to an overall IQ score, separate estimates of verbal IQ and nonverbal IQ became possible.

The *verbal* sections of these instruments include tests of general information, comprehension, vocabulary, arithmetic, and digit span (repeating a series of digits after the examiner). The *performance* sections, which involve manipulation of materials with little or no verbal content, also have several parts. In the

block design test, for example, the subject tries to reproduce designs shown on cards by fitting together blocks with colored sides. In the picture arrangement test, the task is to arrange a series of pictures in the correct sequence so that a meaningful story is depicted. Other performance tests involve mazes, picture completion, and object assembly.

Today, for children from 2 through 15 years of age the assessment of intelligence on individually administered tests is made by the *Wechsler Intelligence Scale for Children-Revised,* or *WISC-R* (1974). For those ages 16 and over there is the *Wechsler Adult Intelligence Scale-Revised,* or *WAIS-R* (1981).

In addition to the individually given Stanford-Binet and Wechsler scales, many other tests have been developed that are given to groups, more easily scored, and more economical. More than a million Americans a year take some standard intelligence test. A proponent of such testing, Julian Stanley, argues for their value, especially that of the Stanford-Binet:

"Though 'IQ tests' are much maligned, especially because results from them can be misused greatly, the *Stanford-Binet Intelligence Scale* remains a psychometric marvel. No other instrument spans so well almost the entire range of mental ability from slow-learning preschoolers to brilliant adults. No other one mental test can provide the well-trained school or clinical psychologist with as valid a single IQ (1976, p. 668).

▽ **Figure 12.2**

Shown here is the distribution of IQ scores expected among a large sample of individuals. (From Matarazzo, 1972, p. 124)

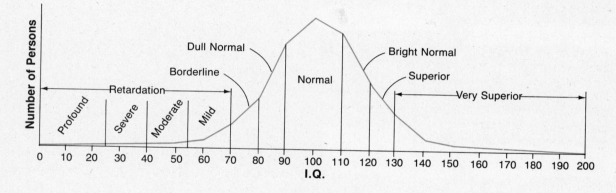

△ ▌ *Shown here are individuals performing an object assembly test on the WISC-R at left and the WAIS-R at right.*

What is intelligence?

In the area of intellectual assessment, psychologists have put the tests before the definition of what they are testing. There has been little agreement on what the concept of intelligence is or how to define it. Early attempts sought to link intelligence to a person's *social worth* by associating low intelligence with criminality and poverty (as in the infamous studies by Goddard of the Kallikak Family in 1914, and Dugdale's case study of the Jukes family in 1912). But no longer is intelligence linked with an individual's moral behavior.

An operational definition states "intelligence is what intelligence tests measure," while a somewhat less empirically based definition says it is "how well you do on an intelligence test." Today, however, at least some agreement has been reached. Both scientists and the general public see two kinds of abilities as central to intelligence—*verbal abilities* and *problem-solving abilities* (R. Sternberg, et al., 1981). Verbal abilities include verbal fluency, reading comprehension, conversational facility, and vocabulary. Problem-solving abilities include getting to the heart of a problem, approaching problems in optimal ways and making good decisions—those intellectual functions we discussed in Chapter 10.

We might say that underlying most conceptions of what intelligence consists of are three general classes of skills or abilities: (a) adapting to new situations and changing task demands, (b) learning or profiting optimally from experience or training, and (c) thinking abstractly using symbols and concepts (Phares, 1984).

It is also well for us to distinguish three concepts that are often measured by subtests of various intelligence tests and contribute to our general view of someone's intelligence.

"*Ability* is the currently available power to perform something and *aptitude* is the potential for performance after training. Both concepts have similarities with *achievement,* which is a measure of successful performance in the past" (Sundberg, 1977, p. 228).

Many theories of intelligence emerge from the theoretical models we have been considering throughout our journey, such as neurological-biological, learning, and developmental theories. In addition there are *psychometric* theories of intelligence based on inferences derived from special statistical analyses (called factor analysis) of intelligence test measurements. In some of these approaches general intelligence is identified as a general, central "*g-factor*" and many specific "*s-factors.*" The psychometric approaches to understanding intelligence that are of most current interest to psychologists are those of Raymond Cattell (1971) and J. P. Guilford (1967). However, rather than discuss them in more detail, we present in the **Close-up** on page 430 two very different views on intelligence that represent significant departures from previous conceptions of what it is and how it can best be studied.

The use and misuse of IQ

"What are IQ test scores good for? What is their predictive utility?" The answer is not as simple as one might expect. Making it even more complicated are emotionally colored claims from various groups. These include claims that IQ is a relatively fixed, inherited trait; that it can be used as an index of the genetic inferiority of certain groups; and that the tests are biased.

We will first outline what is currently known about the validity, stability and usefulness of IQ test scores. Then we will open the issue of the heritability of IQs, and finally review some of the concerns and evidence about misuse of IQ scores due to sources of bias.

Predicting school success and job status. IQ scores are valid for two types of prediction: academic success and the status of one's occupation. Grades in school are significantly correlated with intelligence test scores (Tyler, 1965; Wing & Wallach, 1971). This could simply mean that intelligence tests tap the same kind of performance as teachers require and to which they assign grades. It is also apparent that getting good grades is more than just having a big *g*-factor. To having "smarts," one must add motivation, positive parents' attitudes, and teacher's expectations—to name a few of the variables that contribute in unknown ways to school success or failure.

IQ also predicts the kind of job one will obtain. Occupational status is positively correlated with level of IQ, regardless of whether status is defined as income or prestige (Brody & Brody, 1976). But two limits on this relationship exist: (a) educational success may be the intervening state that determines the quality of the job one gets, so that IQ may really predict it only indirectly through its correlation with academic achievement, and (b) once in the profession, intelligence score differences do *not* discriminate among those who are eminent and those who are less successful (Matarazzo, 1972). Once on the job,

nonintellectual factors such as investment of energy, social skills, and work habits, play a more major role in one's success. And in a longitudinal study that compared early IQ with later adult success, the best predictor of a person's educational and occupational status as an adult was not childhood IQ, but the educational level of his or her father (McCall, 1977).

The predictive utility of IQ for even academic achievement can be affected by complex interactions with many factors. IQ scores will change over time with certain environmental changes, such as special education programs, change from a hostile or impoverished environment to a stimulating one, and increasing familiarization with mainstream cultural standards (Morris & Clarizio, 1977). IQ scores are also less stable the longer the time interval between testings. While there is relatively high reliability of IQ scores on repeated testing for *older* children as a group, IQ can still change substantially in individual cases. Inconstancies in IQ scores remind us that intelligence is not an inflexible entity, but one continually influenced by many variables.

Heredity versus environment. Is intelligence inherited, dependent on genes and biological background, as some claim, or is it developed as people learn how to adapt to the demands of their environment and specific cultural experiences, as others insist. This heated controversy is still being debated among psychologists on both scientific and political grounds (see Cattell, 1982; Jensen, 1973; Kamin, 1974).

Many early investigators approached the study of intelligence with a firm conviction that it was an innate, nonmodifiable potential, and thus an objective measure of the person. Around the 1930's the social climate began to change towards greater emphasis of environmental influences on behavior and intellectual performance. In this view it was not the bad seed but the bad soil that created a poor intellectual crop.

Today the most reasonable view is that of the *interaction* of heredity and environment in determining intelligence. Genes may set the intellectual limits for a *given* person behaving in a *given* environment. But even those limits can be changed by changing the environment in major ways (see Eysenck and Kamin, 1981; Gottesman, 1963). As we saw in Chapter 2, an interactive view suggests that there is a continuing interweaving between the two influences, with

Challenges to Traditional Views of Intelligence

Although the concept of IQ has come to be equated by the public with how smart a person "really is," and by some psychologists with a unitary trait of mind, Alfred Binet held a quite different view.

> ". . . intelligence is before all a process of knowing that is directed toward the external world, that works to reconstruct it in its entirety, by means of the little fragments that are given to us . . . comprehension, inventiveness, direction, and criticism: intelligence is contained in these four words" (Binet, 1911, pp. 117–18).

Two current approaches to understanding and assessing intelligence share aspects of Binet's early view. They focus on cognitive skills that have value to the thinking-acting person, and on multiple intelligences. Both offer provocative challenges to traditional notions of intelligence.

Earl Hunt (1983) a proponent of the first view, argues that the way to appreciate intelligence begins not by making a better IQ test, but with a theory of *cognitive processes* based on identification of important aspects of the mental performance. Three classes of cognitive performance identified as central to intellectual functioning are (a) a person's choice of how to internally (mentally) represent a problem; (b) his or her strategies for how to manipulate mental representations; and (c) the abilities necessary to execute whatever basic information-processing steps a strategy requires.

In this view, experimental researchers and cognitive theorists are invited to do something they have largely avoided: study *individual differences,* instead of only the averaged reactions of many people to the same experimental stimuli. Based on theoretical guidelines, tasks would be designed to tap individual differences in how problems are represented (using images or verbalization for example), how material is encoded, how information is transferred in one's working memory, and other aspects of information processing.

By studying intelligence in terms of the various mental activities we use in order to solve the problems and challenges posed by our environment and culture, several important consequences result. This approach encourages us to see the flexibility and adaptiveness of human thinking. It also encourages a different view of classification and selection. Rather than discriminating between those who *have* a given IQ and—get accepted—and those who are below that level—and get rejected—this view supports *diagnostic assessment* based on how to make the best use of each person's cognitive abilities and skills (Hunt, 1984).

Another new and different theory of intelligence has been proposed by Howard Gardner (1983). He identifies intelligence in terms of seven ways of viewing the world, each of which is equally important. The value of any of them is culturally determined, according to what is needed, useful, and prized by a given society. The seven intelligences are:

1. Linguistic ability;
2. Logical-mathematical ability;
3. Spatial ability—navigating in space, forming, transforming, and using mental images;
4. Musical ability—perceiving and creating pitch patterns;
5. Bodily-kinesthetic ability—skills of motor movement, coordination;
6. Interpersonal ability—understanding others;
7. Intrapersonal ability—understanding one's self, developing a sense of identity.

---

each factor's contribution at a given time helping determine what the other can achieve.

Many studies have found that the average IQ score of blacks in the United States is about 10 to 15 points below that of whites (Loehlin et al., 1975), though there is much overlapping of scores, and the differences within each group are very much greater than the differences between them. Confusion about the relative contribution of heredity to IQ scores and the implications for racial differences has stemmed from misunderstanding of the concept of **heritability.** Heritability is a statistical concept. It is an estimate of the relative contribution of genetic factors to the variability in scores that is found when a sample of individuals is tested; the *heritability ratio* is the ratio of the genetic part of the variability to

Gardner argues that Western society promotes the first two intelligences. Other societies promote different ones. For example, in the Caroline Island of Micronesia, sailors must navigate without maps among hundreds of islands using only their spatial intelligence and bodily-kinesthetic intelligence. Such abilities count more in that society than do those you call upon to write a term paper. In Bali, where artistic performance is part of everyday life, musical intelligence and bodily talents involved in coordination of fine dance steps are more highly valued. Interpersonal intelligence can be seen as central in societies where collective action and communal life are more important than in individualistic societies.

To assess these kinds of intelligence demands more than one paper-and-pencil test and simple quantified measures. Gardner's tests of intelligence require the testee to be observed and assessed in a variety of life situations as well as in the artificial samples of life depicted on traditional intelligence tests.

△ Howard Gardner sees intelligence as being evident in several different abilities that require more than one paper-and-pencil test to measure.

the total variability. (The total variability, in turn, is calculated from correlations between scores of pairs of individuals who vary in some systematic way—identical twins and fraternal twins, or children reared by their biological parents and children reared by adoptive parents, for example.)

The heritability ratio is calculated in various ways, but all are of necessity based on imprecise measures of the exact genetic influences that are operating and crude estimates rather than precise measures of the environmental influences. Furthermore, these estimates lump together prenatal influences, socioeconomic factors, parent-child interactions, and all other environmental influences that may be present. Thus, it is not surprising that estimates of heritability obtained by different researchers have ranged widely.

After a thorough analysis of the literature in the field, Philip Vernon (1979) has concluded, "It would seem that all the studies based on reasonably reliable data and fair-sized samples concur in indicating a substantial genetic variance of at least 60 percent underlying individual differences in phenotypical IQ [IQ scores]" (p. 198). Vernon goes on to say that 30 percent of the remaining variability is apparently due to environmental factors and 10 percent to genetic-environmental covariation (bright parents providing a better environment for bright children, for example). He believes it unlikely that general agreement on any precise figures will ever be reached because of the variety in techniques used and the inherent imprecision of the data used in the calculations. Critics go further, pointing out that overlapping between genetic and environmental influences is always present and invalidates any attempt to analyze their separate contributions (Layzer, 1974).

In any case, a heritability ratio is not the percent of the *trait* that is due to heredity but only the percent of the *variability* in a group of scores that can be attributed to hereditary influences. Heritability figures apply only to explanations of variability *within one population*. They do not apply to individuals or to differences between two populations. A problem arises when differences in IQ scores between racial groups are interpreted as being due to genetic dif-

ferences between the races on the basis of heritability estimates. Estimates of heritability obtained for explaining variability *within* one population cannot be used to explain differences *between two populations* (Gould, 1981; McKenzie, 1980).

An example should clarify the point of contention. Height is known to have high heritability—higher than IQ: the genes of fathers will strongly determine the heights of their sons. But suppose the average height of men is 5 feet 10 inches in an affluent culture but only 5 feet 6 inches in a culture with poor nutrition. Can we attribute the difference between them to different inherited height, or might nutrition be playing a substantial role? If we know they are both from the same racial group, we will suspect that the environment (nutrition) is the important factor. But if they are from different racial groups, we have no way of knowing whether heredity or diet is responsible for the differences in height that we see. Even if heritability of height is high in both groups— which it probably is—we cannot blame inherited genes for the shorter stature in the group with poor nutrition.

On the other hand, we have ample evidence that (a) intelligence test scores are substantially related to environmental variables associated with socioeconomic class, with higher social classes having higher IQ scores as shown in **Figure 12.3;** and (b) IQ scores of children who have experienced extreme deprivation can be raised by "enrichment" manipulations (Skeels, 1966) or by major changes in their lives (Heber, 1976). We saw some of this evidence in Chapter 2.

Perhaps the best way to summarize these and other relevant findings is to say that *both* heredity and environment affect intelligence. Furthermore, the level of each at any given time affects the degree to which the other can influence intellectual functioning.

△ The environmental contrasts are sharp in these two photos. At left is a photo of an allegedly "separate but equal" Tennessee schoolroom for black children in the 1950s. At right, parents of today urging their children on.

▽ **Figure 12.3**

Both these charts show evidence for the contribution of both heredity and environment to IQ scores. In (A), we see similar IQs for fathers and sons (influence of heredity), but the IQs of both fathers and sons were also related to social class level (influence of environment). In (B), we see that the closer the biological relationship, the more similar the IQs (influence of heredity), yet individuals with comparable heredity who were reared apart were more different than those reared together (influence of environment). (MZ stands for monozygotic, or identical, twins; DZ for dyzygotic, or fraternal, twins.)

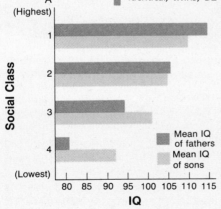

(A) (Adapted from Waller, 1971)

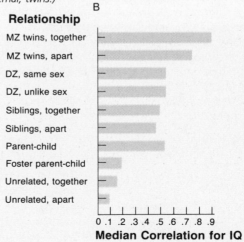

(B) (Adapted from Erlenmeyer-Kimling & Jarvik, 1963)

Sources of bias in intelligence testing. Low IQ test scores are used to assign children to EMR classes (Educable Mental Retardation) that are "stigmatizing" and "dead-ends" academically. Because a disproportionate number of minority children, especially blacks and Hispanics, are assigned to such classes, the use of such test practices was challenged as biased in a California court order (*Larry P*. v. *Wilson Riles,* 1979).

Intelligence tests are not "culture free," nor are school performance tests. Both reflect many variables, such as cultural values, history, language usage, general test-taking skills or "sophistication," the conditions of test administration, and the test-taker's expectations of being effective or ineffective (Anastasi, 1982).

There also are biases in the content of most intelligence tests that will influence a person's scores because of his or her cultural, class, or language background. For example, one IQ test asks what you should do if you find a stamped, addressed envelope. "Mail it" is scored as the only correct answer. If you were poor and said, "Check it out for money before mailing," that would be scored wrong. Intellectually wrong or morally wrong? Similarly, urban ghetto children might respond differently than those in the normative population to the IQ test item that asks what one should do if a same-sex, much younger child starts to fight with you.

Poverty can affect intellectual functioning in many ways. Poor prenatal health of the mother, poor nutrition of the child, a lack of books and other materials for verbal stimulation, a "survival orientation" that leaves little time or energy for parents to play with and intellectually stimulate their children—all of these can be detrimental to performance on tasks like those included in standard tests of IQ. In addition, there are differences between those who speak "standard English" at home and those who use dialects or "nonstandard English."

In a study designed to measure the effect of these language differences on IQ scores, the researchers enlisted the aid of black teachers and graduate students to translate the instructions of an IQ test into nonstandard English. The test they used was the *Boehm Test of Basic Concepts* (BTBC), an IQ test that asks children to mark pictures that match concepts of time, space, or quantity. Their subjects were 890 black children attending kindergarten, first, or second grade. The children were carefully divided into two groups so that the ages, sexes, and grade levels of those in one group would match those of the children in the other. In addition, the researchers

made sure that the children in the two groups had similar scores on other tests of intelligence.

Then, one group was given the standard English version of the Boehm; the other group was given the nonstandard English version. The results?

The children who took the nonstandard version scored significantly *higher* than those who took the same test with the standard instructions. What is surprising is that the nonstandard instructions did not *seem* to the researchers to be very different from the standard version. For example, the instructions on the standard version read *"behind the sofa,"* while the nonstandard version read *"in back of the couch."* Nevertheless, when these seemingly minor differences in language were added up over the entire test, they had a major effect on the phenotypic IQ score a child earned (Williams & Rivers, 1972).

Although individual test scores are certainly affected by such biases at some age levels, overall they have been shown to have a relatively small statistical effect (Lambert, 1981). The major issue is not how much test scores are lowered by content bias, but how much they can be raised by eliminating cultural disadvantages between groups in our society. It is likely that the term IQ soon will be dropped from the psychologist's vocabulary and maybe even from educational use. In its place will be terms that reflect intelligence as one's *current* level of functioning in academic or occupational settings rather than as a stamp of "mental worth." If so, the *conditions* that enhance or depress intellectual peformance can be studied and environments manipulated accordingly.

ASSESSING PERSONALITY

There is much more to understanding people than knowing how intelligent they are. Think of all the other ways in which you differ from your best friend or sibling; what qualities of people attract you to some and turn you off to others? Like you, psychologists wonder about what attributes characterize an individual, set one person apart as unique from others, or distinguish between people in one group and those in another (e.g., shy from non-shy or paranoid individuals from "normals"). Personality assessment is the traditional approach used to answer such questions.

Two assumptions basic to these attempts at understanding and describing human personality are that the causes of behavior are intrapsychic—within the person—and that personality is a reflection of stable traits or states. In order to describe and explain personality functioning, psychologists use tests specially designed to reveal what these personal traits are, how they fit together in particular individual cases, and the dimensions of personality on which individuals differ. This knowledge may be used in psychological research aimed at a better understanding of human functioning. More often it is used as part of the data on which recommendations are made for personnel selection and career choice, or for treatment of mental problems.

Objective measures

Objective tests of personality are self-report inventories on which individuals answer a series of questions about their thoughts, feelings, and actions. They may be administered either individually or, more economically, to large groups.

The scoring, like the administration, is relatively simple and follows objective rules. Some tests may be scored and even interpreted by computer programs. This means that objective tests do not require a skilled expert to interpret the results elicited by the test. The final score is usually a number along a single dimension (e.g., adjustment to maladjustment) or a set of scores on single traits (e.g., masculinity, dependency).

The first inventory that focused on *adjustment* problems was the *Woodworth Personal Data Sheet* in 1917. It asked questions such as, "Are you often frightened in the middle of the night?" (see DuBois,

1970). Today's *personality inventories* consist of a series of statements. When you fill one out, you read each statement and indicate whether or not it is true for you. On some inventories you are also asked how frequently each statement is true or how well each describes your behavior, thoughts, or feelings.

The most widely used objective personality test is the *Minnesota Multiphasic Personality Inventory*, known in brief as the MMPI (Dahlstrom et al., 1975). It is used in many clinical settings to aid in the diagnosis of patients and as a guide in their treatment. After reviewing its features and applications, we will briefly mention two other self-report inventories that are used widely with nonpatient populations—the *California Personality Inventory* (CPI), and the *Sixteen Personality Factor Questionnaire* (16PF).

The MMPI. The MMPI was developed by Starke Hathaway, a psychologist, and J. R. McKinley, a psychiatrist, at the University of Minnesota during the 1930s and first published in the 1940s (Hathaway & McKinley, 1940, 1943). Its basic purpose was to diagnose individuals according to a set of psychiatric labels. Scales were developed that were relevant to the kinds of problems patients showed in psychiatric settings. Norms were established for both psychiatric patients and normal subjects (visitors to the University of Minnesota hospital).

The MMPI scales were unlike other existing personality tests of the time because they were developed using an *empirical* scale strategy rather than the usual *intuitive* approach. Items were included on a scale only if they clearly distinguished between two groups, mental patients and a normal comparison group. Each item had to demonstrate its validity by being answered similarly by members within each group but differently between the two groups. The items were thus not selected on a rational, theoretical basis, or according to what the content seemed to mean to experts.

The test consists of 550 items, each answered simply "true" (for me), "false" (for me), or "cannot say." Individual item answers are grouped into categories that form several separate scales. Each item on a scale that is answered in the same direction as the clinical standardization group receives one point. The higher one's scale score, the more he or she is like the clinical group, and thus the less like the normal group. The more extreme the score, the less the likelihood that it was obtained by chance, which means it is probable the person is like what that scale is designed to measure.

Originally the *MMPI* had 10 *clinical* scales, such as depression, hysteria, and others outlined in **Table 12.1.**

In addition to these ten MMPI clinical scales, other scales have been developed for both research and special clinical purposes. These tap diverse aspects of personality—both personal problems and personal strengths. A unique feature of the *MMPI* is the inclusion of four scales to assess the validity of a person's responses. These *validity scales* check for dishonesty, carelessness, defensiveness, and evasiveness, any of which can bias a person's responses.

Table 12.1   *Simulated MMPI Items*

Clinical Scales	Simulated Items (Answered True)
Hypochondriasis (Hs). (Abnormal concern with bodily functions)	"At times I get strong cramps in my intestines."
Depression (D). (Pessimism, hopelessness, slowing of action and thought)	"I am often very tense on the job."
Conversion Hysteria (Hy). (Unconscious use of physical and mental problems to avoid conflicts or responsibility)	"Sometimes there is a feeling like something is pressing in on my head."
Psychopathic Deviate (Pd). (Disregard of social custom, shallow emotions, inability to profit from experience)	"I wish I could do over some of the things I have done."
Masculinity-Femininity (Mf). (Items differentiating between men and women)	"I used to like to do the dances in gym class."
Paranoia (Pa). (Abnormal suspiciousness, delusions of grandeur or persecution)	"It distresses me that people have the wrong ideas about me."
Psychasthenia (Pt). (Obsessions, compulsiveness, fears, guilt, indecisiveness)	"The things that run through my head sometimes are horrible."
Schizophrenia (Sc). (Bizarre, unusual thoughts or behavior, withdrawal, hallucinations, delusions)	"There are those out there who want to get me."
Hypomania (Ma). (Emotional excitement, flight of ideas, overactivity)	"Sometimes I think so fast I can't keep up."
Social Introversion (Si). (Shyness, disinterest in others, insecurity)	"I give up too easily when discussing things with others."

For example, some items are almost always answered in one direction (95 percent of all respondents say "True," or 95 percent say "False"). If someone were to answer many of these items with the *unlikely response,* it is possible that he or she would be answering randomly or untruthfully or could not read. The tester would have to check these possibilities before interpreting the rest of the profile. The pattern of the scores—which ones are highest, how they differ, and so on—forms the "MMPI profile" (see **Figure 12.4**). Individual profiles are compared to those common for particular groups, such as paranoid individuals, felons, and gamblers.

There are two general strategies for interpreting MMPI data: clinical and actuarial. In *clinical interpretation* an expert examines each of the scale scores, the features of the profiles (such as extremity and clustering of certain high scale scores), and adds personal experience about patients of each profile type to make inferences about the problems and traits of the person. When an *actuarial interpretation* is made, the psychologist (or computer) merely checks codebooks of empirically established characteristics that describe each profile class or code type. The interpretation is based solely on statistical baserates and norms without ever adding any subjective, expert evaluation or personal knowledge of the patient (see **Close-up** on p. 438).

The popularity of this objective assessment technique is seen in its current use in about 50 countries throughout the world, and in the fact that it has been the subject of over 8000 books and articles (Butcher & Finn, 1983). The MMPI has resisted criticism from both behaviorally oriented psychologists who propose behavioral assessment and situational observations as superior, and psychodynamically oriented clinicians who argue for the need to understand the origins of personal conflicts and the meaning people attribute to their problem behavior. The continued use of the MMPI is attributed to factors of reliability, good standardization, established validity, ease and economy of administration, and usefulness in making decisions about patients and psychopathology.

Nevertheless, other critics have objected to the widespread use of the MMPI and similar personality inventories in our society (see *APA*, 1965). They argue, with justification, that tests like the MMPI were designed to provide rather rough screening tools to

THE MINNESOTA REPORT   TM#   Page 1
for the Minnesota Multiphasic Personality Inventory : Adult System
By James N. Butcher, Ph.D.

Client No. : 22222222222   Gender : Female
Setting : Medical   Age : 44
Report Date : 18-JUL-84
PAS Code Number : 00011657 844 0004

PROFILE VALIDITY

This is a valid MMPI profile. The client was quite cooperative with the evaluation and appears to be willing to disclose personal information. There may be some tendency on the part of the client to be overly frank and to exaggerate her symptoms in an effort to obtain help. She may be open to the idea of psychological counseling if her clinical scale pattern reflects psychological symptoms in need of attention.

SYMPTOMATIC PATTERN

The client is exhibiting much somatic distress and may be experiencing a problem with her psychological adjustment. Her physical complaints are probably extreme, possibly reflecting a general lack of effectiveness in life. She is probably feeling quite tense and nervous, and may be feeling that she cannot get by without help for her physical problems. She is likely to be reporting a great deal of pain, and feels that others do not understand how sick she is feeling. She may be quite irritable and may become hostile if her symptoms are not given "proper" attention.

Many individuals with this profile have a history of psychophysiological disorders. They tend to overreact to minor problems with physical symptoms. Ulcers and gastrointestinal distress are common. The possibility of actual organic problems, therefore, should be carefully evaluated.

Her response content indicates that she is preoccupied with feeling guilty and unworthy, and feels that she deserves to be punished for wrongs she has committed. She feels regretful and unhappy about life, complains about having no zest for life, and seems plagued by anxiety and worry about the future. She has difficulty managing routine affairs, and the item content she endorsed suggests a poor memory, concentration problems, and an inability to make decisions. She appears to be immobilized and withdrawn and has no energy for life. According to her response content, there is a strong possibility that she has seriously contemplated suicide. A careful evaluation of this possibility is suggested. She views her physical health as failing and reports numerous somatic concerns. She feels that life is no longer worthwhile and that she is losing control of her thought processes.

INTERPERSONAL RELATIONS

She appears to be somewhat passive-dependent in relationships. She may manipulate others through her physical symptoms, and become hostile if sufficient attention is not paid to her complaints. Marital unhappiness is likely to be a factor in her present clinical picture. She is a rather

----
NOTE: This MMPI interpretation can serve as a useful source of hypotheses about clients. This report is based on objectively derived scale indexes and scale interpretations that have been developed in diverse groups of patients. The personality descriptions, inferences and recommendations contained herein need to be verified by other sources of clinical information since individual clients may not fully match the prototype. The information in this report should most appropriately be used by a trained, qualified test interpreter. The information contained in this report should be considered confidential.

MINNESOTA MULTIPHASIC PERSONALITY INVENTORY
Copyright THE UNIVERSITY OF MINNESOTA
1943, Renewed 1970. This Report 1982. All rights reserved.
Scored and Distributed Exclusively by NCS PROFESSIONAL ASSESSMENT SERVICES
Under License From The University of Minnesota

* "The Minnesota Report," "MMPI," and "Minnesota Multiphasic Personality Inventory" are trademarks owned by the University Press of the University of Minnesota.

Client No. : 22222222222   Report Date : 18-JUL-84   Page 2

introverted person who has some difficulties meeting other people. She is probably shy and may be uneasy and somewhat rigid and overcontrolled in social situations.

The content of this client's MMPI responses suggests the following additional information concerning her interpersonal relations. She feels intensely hostile and resentful of others, and would like to get back at them. She is competitive and uncooperative, tending to be very critical of others.

BEHAVIORAL STABILITY

There are likely to be long-standing personality problems predisposing her to develop physical symptoms under stress. Her present disorder could reflect, in part, an exaggerated response to environmental stress.

DIAGNOSTIC CONSIDERATIONS

Individuals with this profile type are often seen as neurotic, and may receive a diagnosis of Somatoform Disorder. Actual organic problems such as ulcers and hypertension might be part of the clinical picture. Some individuals with this profile have problems with abuse of pain medication or other prescription drugs. Her extremely high score on the MacAndrew Addiction Scale suggests great proneness to the development of an addictive disorder. Further evaluation of substance use or abuse problems is strongly recommended.

The content of her responses to the MMPI items suggests symptoms (convulsions, paralysis, clumsiness, and double vision) that are associated with neurological disorder. Vague pain symptoms, nausea, etc. that are found in neurotic conditions are also present, however. Further neurological evaluation would be needed to make a clear differentiation.

TREATMENT CONSIDERATIONS

She is likely to view her problems as physical and may not readily recognize the psychological factors involved. She tends to somatize problems rather than deal with them psychologically. She can also tolerate a high level of psychological conflict and therefore may not be motivated to change her behavior. She is not a very strong candidate for insight-oriented psychotherapy. Individuals with this profile often seek medical solutions to their psychological problems; however, they may respond to behaviorally oriented pain programs.

NCS Professional Assessment Services, P.O. Box 1416, Mpls, MN 55440

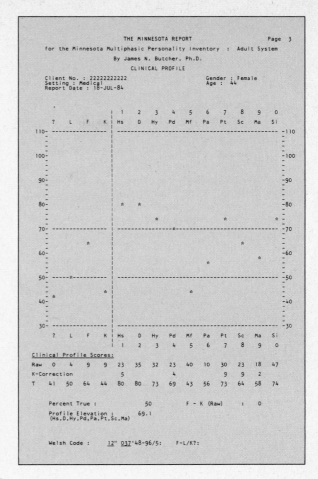

THE MINNESOTA REPORT   Page 3
for the Minnesota Multiphasic Personality Inventory : Adult System
By James N. Butcher, Ph.D.
CLINICAL PROFILE

Client No. : 22222222222   Gender : Female
Setting : Medical   Age : 44
Report Date : 18-JUL-84

Clinical Profile Scores:

	?	L	F	K	Hs	D	Hy	Pd	Mf	Pa	Pt	Sc	Ma	Si
Raw	0	4	9	9	23	35	32	23	40	10	30	23	18	47
K-Correction					5			4			9	9	2	
T	41	50	64	44	80	80	73	69	43	56	73	64	58	74

Percent True :   50   F - K (Raw)   : 0

Profile Elevation :   69.1
(Hs,D,Hy,Pd,Pa,Pt,Sc,Ma)

Welsh Code :   12" 037'48-96/5:   F-L/K?:

Figure 12.4   A Computerized Printout of an MMPI Profile

identify people who might need therapeutic counseling or who might be unable to perform certain job functions. But because of the way they were constructed, they should not be used as the sole source of information for making such decisions. Even a large battery of test items cannot possibly capture the full richness and complexity of anyone's personality. The test can only reveal the particular aspects of personality for which it has valid items.

On the positive side, tests like the MMPI have proven to be very useful in many contexts (Hedlund, 1977). As with intelligence testing, the problem does not seem to lie so much with the tests as with those who use them (or abuse them) for purposes the tests were not designed to serve.

Clinical versus Actuarial Prediction: When Statistics Speak Louder than Experts

On the basis of assessment information, predictions are made about some aspect of the lives of those who were tested—academic or job success, future maladjustment, homosexuality, marital conflict, criminal recidivism, parole violations, and more. The two methods of making these predictions rely either on expert clinical judgment or statistical procedures based on actuarial tables and probability formulas. Which do you suppose is better?

An early survey of the evidence on the relative efficiency of these types of prediction was conducted by Paul Meehl (1954). Its results surprised many psychologists. The statistical approach was equal or superior to the clinical approach. Subsequently made comparisons confirm this conclusion (Meehl, 1965; Sawyer, 1966).

How can a prediction of human behavior by a "cold-blooded" statistical formula be better than one based on the judgment of a sensitive, skilled clinician who knows about people "in the flesh?"

The picture is not as bleak for the human side of this controversy when we consider some of the *limits* on the comparisons made in the studies surveyed.

1. The "clinicians" were not the best experts available, but varied widely in experience and skill.
2. Their individual "hit rates" were lost because they were averaged over the entire sample, so those whose predictions might have been superior to the actuarial ones went unrecognized.
3. Most of the predictions were about specific outcomes, such as grades or vocational achievement, which usually do not concern clinicians.
4. The data the clinicians had to use was often derived from scales like the MMPI, designed for objective interpretation and not the kind of theoretically based data clinicians typically use.

These and other criticisms restrict the simple conclusion of the relative inferiority of clinical predictions. They force us instead to restate the question in terms of the conditions for which each approach can be expected to provide the best prediction (Holt, 1970).

The table below summarizes the occasions and conditions when each of the approaches is most valuable (adapted from Phares, 1984).

Clinical is best	*Statistical is best*
When no good tests are available.	When adequate norms on reliable, valid tests are available.
For information gathering.	For information combining.
Predicting rare, atypical cases.	Predicting average, typical instances.
If unforeseen conditions occur, making prediction idiosyncratic.	If predicted event is *not* affected by any special circumstances.
For global outcomes of patterns over time.	For specific, objective outcomes.
For the individual case studied by the expert.	For large, heterogeneous samples.
	When the sample being predicted is same or similar to normative one used to derive formula.
	Where human judgment is biased by fatigue, boredom, or prejudice.

Other objective inventories. The *California Personality Inventory* (CPI) is comparable to the MMPI in its empirical construction, the kinds of items used, and the use of special validity scales to assess test-taking attitudes (Gough, 1957).

The major difference is its purpose for assessing a variety of personality dimensions based on normal standardization groups and not psychiatric diagnosis based on patient groups. Its eighteen scales measure traits such as self-control, sociability, flexibility, responsibility, and self-acceptance. The CPI is used widely to predict job success among police, airline stewardesses, dentists, student teachers, and others (Gynther & Gynther, 1976).

The *Sixteen Personality Factor Questionnaire* (16PF), as developed by Raymond Cattell (1972), did not use the empirical criterion method of the MMPI and CPI. Instead, Cattell used the mathematical technique of factor analysis to reduce a large pool of 1800 test items to about 100 that were statistically organized into 16 clusters or factors. Each factor is thought to reflect a basic underlying personality trait. The 16PF is often used in vocational and personal counseling.

Behavior assessment. The MMPI and the inventories of Gough and Cattell have in common the premise that there are enduring qualities in a person that can be tapped by such instruments. A contrasting approach is that of **behavior assessment,** aimed at identifying specific current, observable behaviors that can be changed rather than stable, lasting characteristics in the person. Behavior assessment generally uses judges' ratings.

In the 1960s and 1970s, with the rise of the behavior therapies (to be discussed in Chapter 15), there arose a need for measuring typical current, very specific behavior patterns. It was assumed that problem behaviors were being maintained by conditions in the environment rather than conditions in the person and were specific to the situation; the best way to assess people seemed to be to observe directly how they behaved in the natural environments where the problem behavior occurred (Hartman et al., 1979).

Behavior assessment developed as a technique for measuring specific behaviors, such as tantrum behaviors or negative self-statements. Assessment is made of the rate or incidence of very specific problem behaviors before therapy starts, to provide a baseline, and then again after a period of therapy, to see whether the desired changes in behavior have occurred. Behavior assessment is now widely used and has had a remarkable record of usefulness and productivity (Haynes, 1983).

Projective tests

Have you ever looked at a cloud and "seen" a face or the shape of an animal? If you asked your friends to look, too, you may have discovered that they saw a nude reclining or a dragon or something else quite different. Psychologists rely on a similar phenomenon in their use of projective tests for personality assessment.

In **projective tests,** a person is given a series of stimuli that are purposely ambiguous, such as abstract patterns, incomplete pictures, and drawings that can be interpreted in several ways. The person may be asked to describe the patterns, finish the pictures, or tell stories about the drawings. Because the stimuli are vague, responses to them are determined partly by what the person being tested brings to the situation—namely, inner feelings, personal motives, and conflicts from prior life experiences. These idiosyncratic aspects of the person are projected, or "thrown outward," onto stimuli that permit various interpretations.

Projective tests were first used by psychoanalysts who hoped that such tests would reveal their patients' unconscious personality dynamics. For example, to uncover emotionally charged thoughts and fears, Carl Jung used a patient's *word associations* to a list of common words ("What is the first thing brought to mind by the word *house*?").

In addition to this technique of *associating* a verbal, auditory or visual stimulus to its personal meaning, four other projective techniques have been used to assess personality (Lindzey, 1961). They are techniques of: *construction*—making a story; *completion*—finishing a sequence of events in a story; *choice or ordering*—arranging materials in some order, ranking or choosing among alternatives; and *expressive*—acting or performing some role, or expressing the self through art.

Two of the more common projective tests are the Rorschach test and the Thematic Apperception Test (TAT).

The Rorschach. In the Rorschach test (developed by Swiss psychiatrist Hermann Rorschach in 1921), the ambiguous symmetrical stimuli are inkblots. Some are black and white, while some are colored (see **Figure 12.5**). The respondent is shown an inkblot and asked, "Tell me what you see, what it might be to you. There are no right or wrong answers."

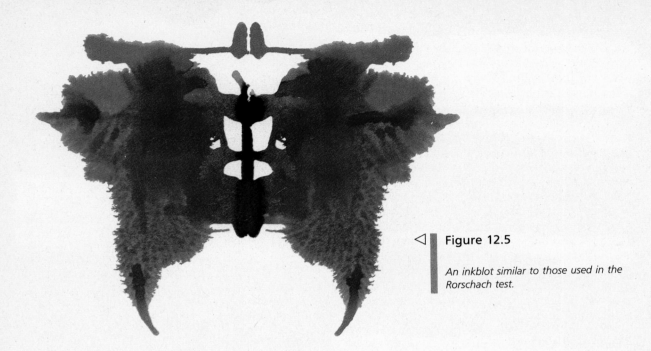

◁▌ Figure 12.5

An inkblot similar to those used in the Rorschach test.

The tester records verbatim what is said, the time to the first response, total time taken per card, and how the card is handled. Then in a second phase of *inquiry,* the tester is reminded of the previous responses and asked to elaborate on them: what prompted them, what location on the card they refer to, and so forth.

The responses are scored on three major dimensions: (a) *location* of the responses on the card, whole stimulus or part response, size of details; (b) *content* of the response in terms of the nature of the object and activities seen; and (c) *determinants,* which are the aspects of the card that prompted the response, such as its color or shading. Some scorers also note whether responses are original and unique or popular, conforming ones.

The problem begins when it comes to interpreting these scores into a coherent portrait of the individual's personality dynamics. It is a complex, highly subjective process that relies on clinical expertise and skilled intuition. Ideally, the tester uses these data as a source of hypotheses about the person that are then evaluated through other assessment procedures. Although the Rorschach has questionable reliability and validity, its use is recommended for getting at areas of information that people may resent or lie about in objective tests, such as sexual interests or aggressive fantasies (Levy & Orr, 1959).

The TAT. In the Thematic Apperception Test (developed by American psychologist Henry Murray, 1938), respondents are shown pictures of ambiguous scenes and asked to generate stories about them, describing what the people in the scenes are doing and thinking, what led up to each event, and how each situation will end (see **Figure 12.6**). The person administering the TAT evaluates the structure and content of the stories, as well as the behavior of the individual in telling them, in an attempt to discover some of the respondent's major concerns and personality characteristics. For example, the examiner might evaluate the person as "conscientious" if the stories concerned people who lived up to their obligations and were told in a serious, orderly way. The test can be used with clinical patients to reveal emotional problems or with normal individuals to reveal dominant needs, such as needs for power, affiliation, and achievement (McClelland, 1961). We studied the achievement motive in Chapter 8 and its assessment by the TAT.

The Rorschach, TAT, and other projective tests have been widely used, especially in clinical settings. In fact, more articles have been published about the Rorschach than about any other psychological test (Buros, 1974). However, projective tests have been subject to a number of criticisms. A basic problem with these tests is that the interpretation of responses is very *subjective* and depends largely upon the skill and experience of the examiner. The clinician using these techniques listens to (or reads) a person's responses, observes the manner in which they are given, and, based on a series of guidelines, tries to put together a theory about the person's underlying needs, traits, motives, and problems. Because of difficulties with reliability and validity, some researchers have claimed that projective techniques are *not* actually very effective for revealing personality dynamics (Buros, 1978). These tests are best used in conjunction with other assessment techniques, since decisions based solely on projective test data lack the authority that comes with reliable, valid tests.

▽ **Figure 12.6** *A Sample Card from the TAT Test*

ASSESSING CREATIVITY

Of those attributes that help define our humanity—language, tender emotions, a time sense, abstract reasoning—none is more mysterious or desired than the "creative urge."

Millions of years ago, our ancestors did something no other animal species has ever done. They took time out from the rigors of trying to survive in environments beset with physical dangers from cold, heat, famine, drought, and powerful predators to paint pictures on the walls of their cave homes. Some murals seem to represent their desires for a successful hunt for food; others reflect more mystical ways of winning over stronger predators and adversaries. At some point these expressions of inner needs and feelings became redirected toward art that was purely *decorative*. Human creativity was channeled to produce objects that were esthetically pleasing, whether or not they served any other function. In virtually every known civilization, homo sapiens has put this distinctive imprint on anything that could be shaped, colored, textured, twisted, or made to be something beyond what it was originally.

▽ *We humans put distinctive imprints on anything that can be shaped, colored, textured, twisted, or made to be something beyond what it was originally.*

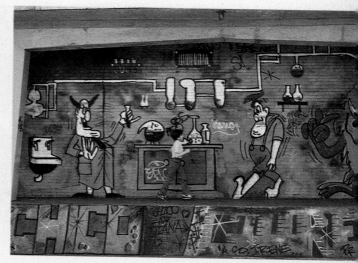

When we think of the creative person, great artists, inventors, scientists, and poets spring to mind—Michaelangelo, Ludwig van Beethoven, William Shakespeare, Albert Einstein, Marie Curie, Emily Dickinson. But ordinary, average people can be creative, even without public acclaim for their accomplishments. Let's look at the responses that a 10-year-old boy of average IQ gave to the question, "How many uses can you think of for a newspaper?" What can you infer about the boy's background from the variety of uses he comes up with for this ordinary object?

"You can read it, write on it, lay it down and paint a picture on it. If you didn't have covers, you could put it in your door for decoration, put it in the garbage can, put it on a chair if the chair is messy. If you have a puppy, you put newspaper in its box or put it in your back yard for the dog to play with. When you build something and you don't want anyone to see it, put newspaper around it. Put newspaper on the floor if you have no mattress, use it to pick up something hot, use it to stop bleeding, or to catch the drips from drying clothes. You can use a newspaper for curtains, put it in your shoe to cover what is hurting your foot, make a kite out of it, shade a light that is too bright. You can wrap fish in it, wipe windows, or wrap money in it and tape it [so it doesn't make noise]. You put washed shoes on newspaper, wipe eyeglasses with it, put it under a dripping sink, put a plant on it, make a paper bowl out of it, use it for a hat if it is raining, tie it on your feet for slippers. You can put it on the sand if you had no towel, use it for bases in baseball, make paper airplanes with it, use it as a dustpan when you sweep, ball it up for the cat to play with, wrap your hands in it if it is cold" (Ward et al., 1972).

In evaluating the many answers of this boy, you might say that he is very creative because he gave many responses that you would never have thought of. In fact, if you were to compare his answers to those of other 10-year-old children of average IQ, his performance might be even more impressive. But where does such an ability come from? Is it a general characteristic that he was born with, or is it something that he learned? If we look at this boy's answers again, we might guess that his *experience* has been an important factor. Clearly, the more often a person has had to use something in several ways, the more likely he or she is to think of other uses for it. Perhaps this child's responses would be considered less creative by other people with the same back-

ground. If so, this would imply that creativity is a relative quality that exists only when someone thinks it does. Many psychologists dispute such a viewpoint, however, and maintain that creativity can be reliably and objectively measured. (If you haven't guessed already, the 10-year-old boy with all the answers above came from a New York City ghetto.)

What qualifies as creative?

The most widely used definition of **creativity** is that it is the occurrence of uncommon or unusual, but appropriate, responses. This assumption underlies most of the tests that have been developed to measure creativity.

Although originality is usually taken for granted as a major factor in creativity, the importance of *appropriateness* is not always recognized. However, this is the criterion that distinguishes between creative and nonsensical acts. Solutions to a problem that are unique but totally worthless or irrelevant are not considered to be creative. But, of course, "appropriate," like "desirable," involves a value judgment that may vary with the judge's background, the culture, the era, and so forth.

Creativity has several facets. First, there is a perceptual element—*heightened sensitivity* to features of the world that other people do not usually notice. Creativity also involves *synthesis*—the ability to make connections that relate observations or ideas in novel, meaningful ways. Then, there is the ability to generate nonverbal images or special *internal representations* of a spatial or visual character. The creative *product* is the tangible "externalization" of these private images, whether in theories, inventions, or works of art (Shepard, 1978).

How can creative people be identified? What characteristics distinguish them from less creative people?

Was Pablo Picasso more creative than Sigmund Freud? Is jazz trumpeter Miles Davis as creative as dance choreographer Martha Graham? Is a Mozart sonata more creative than comedian Robin Williams' monologue? Comparative assessments like these are difficult to make in any objective way because they depend on both personal value judgments and social standards, and they mix creativity of different styles, types, and media. When psychologists assess creativ-

△ ▌ *Creativity plays a role in both sculpting and break-dancing.*

ity among "average" people, their goal is to determine how creative an individual is compared to a normative population of similar people.

As with intelligence, it is important to design *reliable* and *valid* measures of creativity. Unlike intelligence tests, however, creativity tests—by definition—cannot have one right answer. A common approach to measuring creativity has been to assess evidence of **divergent thinking**—the ability to come up with unusual but appropriate responses to standard questions like "How many uses can you think of for a newspaper?" In passing we should note that this is different from **convergent thinking**, in which one uses knowledge and logic to eliminate possibilities and reach the best solution to a problem. Most intelligence tests, with their well-defined problems and objectively best answers, focus primarily on convergent thinking.

One technique for assessing creativity was adapted from the projective methods originally developed for personality assessment. As we have mentioned, projective tests have had questionable utility for their original purpose. However, they have provided useful means for assessing creativity. For example, in inkblot tests, the average individual is apt to concentrate on simple, obvious features. The creative person is more likely to impose an elegant new order on the figure. Where the task is to complete a

drawing, the average individual is satisfied with a simple figure that "makes sense" while the creative individual produces a more complex and meaningful drawing (see **Figure 12.7**).

A different method of assessing creativity depends on behavior sampling and judge's ratings.

In a series of studies, college women were asked to make collages from pieces of lightweight paper or write Haiku poems. The products were then ranked—independent of their "technical goodness" or neatness or organization—for creativity by judges with some relevant expertise. This methodology has resulted in considerable agreement among the judges, thus increasing our confidence that it was actually creativity—and not some other quality—being assessed.

This research also suggests that creativity is influenced by the social context in which the creative task is performed. Subjects who had been told their products would be evaluated by experts were later judged lower in creativity than those subjects who had not been forewarned of the evaluation (Amabile, 1983).

Correlates of creativity

Are there other qualities that creative people typically have? In general, studies have shown that creative persons are distinguished more by their interests, at-

Common Responses
1. Smudges
2. Dark clouds

Uncommon Responses
1. Magnetized iron filings
2. A small boy and his mother hurrying along on a dark windy day, trying to get home before it rains

Common Responses
1. An African voodoo dancer
2. A cactus plant

Uncommon Responses
1. Mexican in sombrero running up a long hill to escape from rain clouds
2. A word written in Chinese

◁ **Figure 12.7**

Two tests based on the methods of projective testing and used to distinguish between creative and noncreative individuals are shown here. In the inkblot test, the individual must attribute order and meaning to vague configurations. The average individual is apt to concentrate on their simple, obvious features. The creative person is more likely to impose an elegant new order on the figure. In the drawing completion test, the average individual is satisfied with a simple figure that "makes sense" (above), while the creative individual produces a more complex and meaningful drawing (below).

Common Responses
1. An ape
2. Modern painting of a gorilla

Uncommon Responses
1. A baboon looking at itself in a hand mirror
2. Rodin's "The Thinker" shouting "Eureka!"

Common Response

Uncommon Response

titudes, and drives than by their intellectual abilities (Dellas & Gaier, 1970). The lack of a strong correlation between creativity and IQ may seem surprising, but research conducted so far has supported this conclusion (Barron & Harrington, 1981). For example, none of the many children with superior, "genius" level intelligence who were studied by Lewis Terman (described in Chapter 2) had produced any outstanding creative works when they were restudied forty years later (Terman & Oden, 1959). So it is possible for intelligence and creativity to function independently; knowing about the one tells us little about the other in any person. This lack of association again raises the issue about why so much emphasis is put on IQ and intellectual functioning in our society—and so little on finding ways to enhance creativity.

Other cognitive variables *do* seem characteristic of creative people, however. One of the most distinctive of these is a cognitive preference for *complexity*, as opposed to simplicity. This is revealed in a preference for drawings that are asymmetrical, dynamic, and even chaotic, rather than drawings that are regular, neat, and simple (see **Close-up** on p. 445).

Much creativity research has been concerned with the personality characteristics of creative individuals. The results have pointed to a group of characteristics that includes independence, intuitiveness, high energy, and self-acceptance (Barron & Harrington, 1981). Architects and research scientists were remarkably similar in these personality traits, despite the differences in the content of their professional work (Gough, 1961; MacKinnon, 1961). Writers displayed a similar pattern of traits, although they showed greater originality and an emphasis on fantasy (Barron, 1963; see also Koestler, 1964).

The Mad Artist/Crazy Genius Controversy

The popular view of the artist-as-mad and the creative genius-as-crazy has been around for a long time. As early as the first century A.D., the Roman philosopher Seneca wrote, ''There is no great genius without some touch of madness.''

There are indeed many examples of eminent creative people who have suffered serious psychological disorders. Most students are aware of the mental problems experienced by artist Vincent van Gogh, poets William Blake and Ezra Pound, and dancer Waslaw Nijinsky. The list of the mentally disturbed, based on various sources of evidence, includes many of the world's greatest creative artists and geniuses. Among them are Newton, Copernicus, Pascal, Darwin, Michelangelo, Beethoven, and Freud (see Karlsson, 1978; Prentky, 1980).

Such exemplars would seem to build a case for the popular association of creativity and madness, but what does the systematically collected research evidence tell us? Unfortunately, the data are mixed. Some research on creative people indicates that, as a group, they tend to have strong egos and constructive ways of handling problems (Cross et al., 1967). Hardly the seeds of madness there. But other research points to a similarity between schizophrenic individuals and creative people in their characteristic perceptual style. Both groups ''over-include'' loosely connected events and ideas, not excluding stimuli many ''normal'' people would judge as irrelevant (Hasenfus & Magaro, 1978).

Other analyses reveal that creative people commonly use thought processes that are intuitive, uncensored by socially acceptable ways of thinking. These directly experienced and expressed thoughts and feelings are called *primary process*. They are in contrast to those that are constrained by awareness of what is correct, desirable, or realistic, which are called *secondary process*. Loosening the inhibiting effects of secondary processes upon thinking can lead to original ideas and unusual associations that may then be *labeled* either as examples of creative genius or as deviant, strange thoughts characteristic of the mentally unbalanced (Becker, 1978). That decision rests in part on the values of the individual's society in assessing what is ''art,'' ''invention,'' or ''discovery''; what its tolerance is for the nontraditional; and what its definition is of mental disorder.

We may conclude from the available evidence that (a) there are some similarities between the thoughts and perceptual processes of creative and disturbed individuals; (b) many famous creative people have been mad; (c) we may think these cases are more common than they actually are because of their vividness and availability in our memories (recall the heuristic biases discussed in Chapter 10); and (d) most creative people appear to be normal or even superior on several dimensions of psychological health.

Finally, a different perspective on the genius-madness association comes from Ezra Pound: ''The concept of genius as akin to madness has been carefully fostered by the inferiority complex of the public'' (1934, p. 82).

ASSESSMENT AND YOU

Thus far we have presented some of the major features of assessment techniques and have discussed in detail certain approaches used for assessing intelligence, personality, and creativity. In this section, we briefly present two topics of particular interest to students. As a college student, you may be struggling with decisions related to what sort of job you would like to have when you finish school. The first part of this section deals with the role of assessment in vocational counseling. Beyond career decisions, if you are like most students, you are probably concerned about how well you get along with others and how you function in social situations. The second topic deals with shyness, a quality that many students view as a personal problem. Finally, we close the section by addressing some of the political and ethical issues posed by the widespread use of formal assessment procedures in our society today.

Vocational interests and aptitudes

Have you already decided what type of job you would like to have? Are you still undecided, or perhaps thinking of leaving a job you are already in? No matter how you answer, much assessment activity in this country is aimed at people like you. Many assessment instruments have been developed to help people learn what vocations best fit their personalities, values, interests, and skills—or, in some cases, to show them before it's too late that the career they have chosen may not be the wisest choice.

Assessing interests. Even if you do not yet know what jobs you might like best, you know you'd like to have a job that suits your interests. You'd like your job to involve activities you enjoy and to serve goals you consider worthwhile. However, you may be unsure about what your major interests and abilities are. Furthermore, you may have little idea of what people in many occupations actually do on the job, and may not really know how these job activities relate to your personal situation. A number of tests have been designed to help people identify their major interests and abilities and to suggest the best career directions for people with particular interest patterns.

Without question, the most widely used test for measuring vocational interests is the *Strong-Campbell Interest Inventory,* which was first constructed in 1927 by psychologist E. K. Strong. The test is based on an empirical approach similar to that used later for the MMPI. First, groups of men in different occupations answered items about activities they liked or disliked. Then the answers of those who were successful in particular occupations were compared with the answers of men in general. In this way, a set of items (norms) was determined that was representative of answers given by successful workers in each job category. Subsequent versions of the test have added norms relevant to women and to newer occupations. If you took this test, a vocational counselor could tell you what types of jobs are typically held by people with interests like yours. These are the jobs which are likely to appeal to you too.

Assessing abilities. Even if the characteristics of a job appeal to you, and it suits your personality and fits your values and interests, you are unlikely to be satisfied with it unless you can do it well. And, of course, your employer is unlikely to be satisfied with *you* if you are unable to do the job for which you were hired.

In order to recommend a career path for you, a vocational counselor will want to assess your abilities as well as your interests. Ability has two components, aptitude and achievement, as we noted in the earlier discussions of intelligence. *Aptitude tests* measure your potential for acquiring various skills—not necessarily how well you can perform tasks now, but how good you could be at them. *Achievement tests,* on the other hand, measure your current level of competence. Tests used to see how well you can speak a foreign language or how good you are at computer programming are examples of achievement tests. Tests have been developed for assessing aptitude and achievement in many domains. With knowledge of not only what you like to do, but also what you can do well, a counselor is in a good position to predict your "fit" for different jobs (see Anastasi, 1976; Sundberg & Matarazzo, 1979; Tyler, 1974).

Tests of ability are also used by companies seeking new employees. If you apply for a specific job, you may be asked to take tests involving the abilities required for that job. If the job involves typing, you may be given a timed typing test. If it involves hard physical labor, you may be given a test of strength. If managing other people will be an important part of the job, your tolerance for interpersonal stress and ability to assert yourself may be assessed. Here, again, the goal is to match people with the jobs for which they are best suited, and thus to increase the satisfaction of both employees and their employers.

Assessing jobs. The pay received for a job in an organization is usually determined by three primary factors: the nature and degree of *skill* required, the amount of *effort* demanded, and the extent of individual *responsibility* for decisions affecting company resources or personnel. Organizations invest much time and money in personnel selection to get the "right" person for positions at each level. They rely not only on assessment of applicants' characteristics, but also on a careful identification and analysis of the requirements of different jobs (Tenopyr & Oeltjen, 1982).

Job assessment is performed in many ways. Workers, supervisors, and specially trained job analysts are asked to provide information about what abilities are required for doing particular jobs. Subject-matter experts may rate the relevance of various kinds of knowledge, skills, and abilities. An inventory of requirements, including the tasks and duties the worker must perform, can then be prepared for each occupation. One such inventory that has been developed—the *Occupational Analysis Inventory*—provides information about a wide spectrum of occupations and can be very helpful to the job seeker (Pass & Cunningham, 1978).

Some companies are supplementing other assessment methods with *realistic job previews.* They show applicants what will be expected of them on the job through such means as films, tapes, employee checklists of most and least liked aspects of the job, and presentation of simulated "critical incidents" likely to arise in that job (Wanous, 1980). This gives applicants a clearer picture of what will be expected of them if they take the job and helps them decide how well the job fits their abilities and interests.

Finally, how well you do in a job often depends not only on *what you know* and *how hard you work,* but also on variables not directly related to the abilities needed to do the work. Among them might be your assertiveness, social skills, appearance, and general congruence or fit with the company's picture of its ideal supervisor, manager, or executive.

Social strengths and weaknesses: Shyness

Some of our unique personal characteristics become apparent only in social situations or when we are thinking about interacting with others. Shyness is a good example. It is impossible to define shyness without thinking of people in terms of the way they relate to and react to others—or fail to do so. Shyness can be a label that we apply to ourselves, or that others apply to us after observing our behavior in social settings.

Shy people are apprehensive about certain social situations. They try to avoid interacting with others and often behave inappropriately when with other people. Their shyness may be evident only in certain situations—when they are speaking to a large group or on a blind date, for example—or it may affect many facets of their lives. At the core of this state of social anxiety seem to be an excessive preoccupation with one's self and a fear that other people are evaluating one unfavorably (Pilkonis & Zimbardo, 1979). At a dance, for example, the effects of shyness might show up in any of four areas of individual functioning:

- *cognitive* ("Nobody will want to dance with me");
- *emotional* (feeling anxious and insecure);
- *physical* (blushing and sweating if asked to dance);
- *behavioral* (not looking at or smiling at others—and thus discouraging potential dancing partners).

The majority of people who say they are shy find their shyness undesirable. They wish that they could overcome its debilitating effects (see **Table 12.2**). And well they might, since the negative consequences of shyness can be great. Shy children judge themselves to be less attractive and less intelligent than others, are liked less by peers and by teachers, and are evaluated by teachers as less competent (see Zimbardo & Radl, 1982). As they get older, shyness may become associated with low self-esteem, being unpopular, feeling depressed, and being lonely (Buss, 1980; Cheek & Busch, 1981). Shyness can work against enjoying intimate experiences, becoming a leader, or being selected for jobs that require verbal fluency and assertiveness. Who is shy and how do we know about this often silent problem?

Table 12.2   *Inventory of Shyness Reactions*

Physiological Reactions	% Shy Students	Thoughts and Feelings	% Shy Students	Overt Behaviors	%Shy Students
Increased pulse	54%	Self-consciousness	85%	Silence	80%
Blushing	53%	Concern about impression management	67%	No eye contact	51%
Perspiration	49%			Avoidance of others	44%
Butterflies in stomach	48%	Concern for social evaluation	63%	Avoidance of action	42%
Heart pounding	48%	Negative self-evaluation	59%	Low speaking voice	40%
		Unpleasantness of situation	56%		

(Adapted from Zimbardo, Pilkonis, & Norwood, 1974)

Who is shy? Shyness is a common, pervasive problem that affects a large proportion of the population. About 40 percent of American college students, both men and women, describe themselves as "currently shy"—that is, they think of shyness as one of their traits or personal characteristics. Another 40 percent report that they used to be one of these "dispositionally shy" people but have outgrown it. In addition, about 15 percent are "situationally shy"; shyness is not perceived as an enduring trait *in* them, but a reaction elicited by unpleasant social situations (blind dates, giving speeches, dealing with authorities, and so forth). Shyness is reported with the same frequency among college males as it is for females, about two of every five perceive themselves to be chronically shy. As you might expect, even more young adolescents report being shy, especially among girls of junior-high-school age in our society. It is the rare person, then, who is not now and never has been dispositionally or situationally shy.

Public and private shyness. One of the surprising discoveries about shyness is the difference between public and private shyness. We tend to associate shyness with reticence about talking in public; the shy refrain from initiating conversation, or seem to be uncomfortable in social settings. Such shy people appear to be *introverted,* preferring solitary, intellectual activities to social ones. But some shy people are also *extraverts.* They experience social anxiety that is concealed from others while behaving publicly as if they were *not* shy. Somehow they are able to create a dual functioning self—the privately shy inner self and the publicly outgoing performing self.

These shy extraverts are often public figures and celebrities, such as Johnny Carson, Carol Burnett, Barbara Walters, and Michael Jackson, to name but a few. Their performance is not inhibited by shyness when they are in *control* of the situation, enacting a structured, well-released role in a familiar setting. Shyness intrudes however, when the situation changes to one that is unstructured, like a cocktail party, or where control is shared or not appropriate, as in intimate relationships. Other shy people find a tough offense is their best defense. They put people off by dominating conversations, being overly assertive and never allowing any give-and-take, sharing, or feedback. The result is the same as when the shy person simply withdraws—a weakened social relationship.

Assessing shyness. A variety of assessment techniques can be used to study this interesting and complex aspect of personal and social functioning. Each one has some advantages but also disadvantages, so a combination of approaches is best for revealing the breadth and depth of the construct of shyness.

Judges' ratings, taken from parents, teachers, and friends, are easy and inexpensive to gather. But they may be of limited value if the target person is not shy around them or in the situations in which they usually make their informal observations. Specific shyness *behavior ratings* may be made by assessing (a) the extent to which children are withdrawn from play with others in free-play situations, (Furman et al., 1979); (b) the percentage of time adults spend talking or how often they initiate a conversation; (c) how loud they talk, interrupt, or get interrupted in conversation, and how they use nonverbal gestures (Pilkonis, 1977; Zimbardo & Linsenmeier, 1983); and (d) how physically close other people are allowed to come, stand, or sit next to them (Carducci & Weber, 1979).

◁ *Many privately shy people find they are not inhibited by shyness when in a structured and familiar setting.*

On one hand, such assessment is time consuming, difficult to obtain, and the range of reactions used to index shyness is limited in any one study. On the plus side is the gain in precision of defining target behaviors, quantification, and interobserver reliability.

Objective personality scales have also been used by those who view shyness as a personality trait. Respondents are assigned to the shyness category, on the basis of their "yes/no" responses to a set of test items such as, "I find it difficult to talk with a person I have just met." Obviously such an approach is an efficient, economical way of gathering data on large groups of respondents that can be expressed as a single scale score. These shyness scale scores can then be readily correlated with scores on other scales in the same personality inventory or with scores the person gets on other tests. When this *criterion and construct validation* is used, shyness scores are found to be positively related to many other traits, among them: seclusiveness, lack of social poise, self-consciousness, submissiveness, inferiority, egocentricity, and embarrassment. It is also correlated negatively with self-esteem (Comrey, 1970; Saraf, 1980).

Criticism centers on reducing this complex aspect of human functioning to simple replies on a small number of items—as few as four statements on one test. A danger lies in the tendency to overgeneralize from such a small sample of narrowly focused responses to major conclusions about the respondent and the construct. For example, solely from the pattern of statistical correlations on his personality inventory, Cattell (1965) concluded that shyness was a personality factor that was largely inherited—as much as intelligence is—associated with strong parental discipline, and not modifiable by experience or therapy. Such conclusions are not supported by available evidence.

Because none of these assessment approaches allows the individual the opportunity to indicate what shyness means to him or her, or the ways in which it affects different aspects of personal and interpersonal life, a different assessment approach was developed to do so.

The *Stanford Shyness Survey* was designed to allow each respondent to define shyness in personal terms rather than on the basis of an expert's preconceived categories (Zimbardo, 1977). First, students answered open-ended questions such as: What kind

HERMAN

Have you got any books on how to overcome shyness?

of people and situations make you feel shy? How does shyness affect you? What are its consequences, positive and negative in your life? After analyzing the content of these answers from nearly a thousand subjects, *checklists* such as the following were prepared. "Which of the following situations elicits shyness in you? (check all applicable): _____ (1) meeting strangers, _____ (2) using the phone, _____ (3) giving a speech, _____ (4) being the center of attention in a large work group, _____ (5) one-to-one with an opposite sex person." (You might want to refer back to Table 1.1, Chapter 1, p. 13 for a summary of results of "What makes you shy?").

A battery of these easy-to-administer and score checklists were organized into a complete survey instrument that allows each person to give a direct self-report of shyness along many dimensions: perceived elicitors, accompanying reactions, personal consequences, frequency and severity of self-rated shyness, and others. The descriptive data given at the start of this section on the prevalence of shyness came from surveying thousands of respondents with this technique. The data correlate well with objective tests, judge's ratings, and behavioral measures.

Multiple objectives. This type of assessment approach was developed primarily as a research tool to help select subjects who varied in their shyness so they could be systematically observed in experiments. The kind of data it provides also aids in the theoretical exploration of the dynamics of shyness. However, from this body of personal information about shyness an applied goal can be served. It is possible to use this information as the basis for a treatment program to overcome or minimize the interfering effects of shyness. Understanding what elicits shyness and how shyness affects a very shy person allows a therapist to formulate strategies to (a) build social skills (if there are behavioral deficits), (b) boost self-esteem (if negative self-thoughts are frequent), and (c) manage anxiety (if physiological arousal gets excessive). Individual or group treatment may also stress cognitive reorganization (learning to think differently, to make new attributions about one's shyness and relationships to others). Finally, guided practice in actual social interactions which are shyness eliciting may be given in the person's usual life settings. All these methods have proved helpful. Less severely shy people even report having been helped by performing the exercises outlined in one of the shyness self-help books, but as yet there has been no study of the proven effectiveness of such shyness *bibliotherapy*.

Political and ethical issues

The primary goal of psychological assessment of individuals is to reduce errors of judgment that bias accurate assessment of people. This is achieved by replacing subjective judgments of teachers, physicians, employers, and other evaluators with more objective measures that have been carefully constructed and are open to critical evaluation. This is the goal that motivated Alfred Binet in his pioneering work. We also saw that process at work in the *Opening Case* of little Maria's trials and tribulations. It was hoped that testing would help democratize society and minimize decisions based on arbitrary criteria of sex, race, nationality, or physical appearance.

But despite these lofty goals, there is no area of psychology more enmeshed in controversy than that of assessment. Testing has become big business in the United States. It is a multimillion dollar industry including companies that develop tests, publish tests, analyze tests, and recommend courses of action based on these tests. These companies constitute a powerful group interested in maintaining and extending the use of testing.

Test scores already form the basis for major decisions about people's lives—in the absence of the less economical, more inefficient evaluation of the whole person "in the flesh." In addition, as we have become a nation of test-takers, our test scores have become *reified,* as "special, personal things." They are invested with an absolute significance that is no longer limited by relative comparisons with appropriate norms. People too often think of themselves as "*being* an IQ of 110," or "*being* a B student," as if the score were a label stamped on their forehead. Such labels may become barriers to advancement. For the person who is "negatively assessed" the scores may become self-imposed motivational limits that lower one's sense of self-efficacy and restrict the risks taken and challenges willing to be faced.

A related criticism is that the use of test scores and arbitrary cut-off points for determining school admissions, job placements, and so forth gives an illusion of scientific legitimacy to decisions that eliminate those considered "socially undesirable." Sometimes people are evaluated on the basis of tests whose norms may be inappropriate. We have already mentioned this problem with respect to IQ tests, and it occurs with personality assessment too.

For example, although MMPI norms were based solely on white mentally disturbed patients, MMPI scores are being used to make decisions about both black and white students, job seekers, and other groups. Blacks who do not show mental disorders on other assessment instruments have relatively high scores on the MMPI scales that measure nonconformity, alienation, and impulsivity. Are they more maladjusted than whites or might their scores change comparatively if they were based on norms developed for black test-takers (Gynther, 1981)? It is likely that the revision of the MMPI—now in progress—will clear up some of these questions. However, until that time comes, courts, parole offices, and other agencies will continue to use existing test scores, norms, and published manuals for test interpretation in order to decide the fate of some of those in their charge. It is easier to challenge another person's evaluation of your intelligence, personality, or psychopathology than to oppose the computerized print-out that describes the supposed "real you" in statistically objective terms. It is as if the test added a postscript, to the effect, "nothing personal, mind you, but this is just the way you are." Few people are willing to challenge the authoritative posture of test results even when such results may have an adverse impact on their lives.

Competency testing used in high schools, college-entrance examinations, job placement, and civil-service examinations is being challenged in the courts, and some states are passing laws to limit its use. The challenge comes from those who argue that the tests often do not provide accurate indices of what they are intended to measure. Even where they are valid, they have other objectionable features. For example, some say that personnel selection is too often a one-way fit of people to available jobs. Instead, perhaps some job descriptions might better be changed to fit the needs and abilities of the people.

Another problem of assessment is the pervasive assumption that intellectual abilities are inherited and the accompanying belief that those who do poorly on screening tests cannot learn to do better. This is an old issue that has centered around attempts to establish the degree to which IQ is influenced by nature versus nurture. Despite the obvious interaction of genetic endowment with learned experiences, advocates for both sides have attempted to minimize the contributions of the other type of input. Unfortunately, this difference in philosophy is not just a matter of personal opinion, but a difference that can influence public policy. Restrictive immigration laws, enforced sterilization programs, and resource cutbacks for educational enrichment programs (such as Head Start for minority children) have all been supported by those who believe mental abilities are inherited, unchangeable attributes—and opposed by those who believe in the importance of nurture in the realization of human potential. It is not an ivory-tower debate, but one in which the stakes are high—the basic understanding of our species—and the effects are widespread, influencing the quality of life for many in our society.

A final concern about the enterprise of traditional psychological assessment is its focus on locating traits, states, maladjustment, conflict, and pathology *within* the individual. This leads to thinking about "children as retarded" rather than about "educational systems that need to modify their programs so as to accommodate all their learners." It puts the spotlight on the deviant personality rather than on problems in the environment. Human assessors need to recognize that what people are now is a product of where they've been, where they think they are headed, and the current situation that is influencing their behavior. Such a view can help unite different assessment approaches as well as the social, behavioral, and dynamic approaches to understanding and dealing with personality, on which they are based.

The next chapter treats a different kind of assessment by asking about the impact of environmental stressors on our functioning. How can we determine the effects of stress on our behavior, emotions, thoughts, and physiological responses? In addition, we will discover how we can better manage the stress we are heir to and prevent those stresses waiting in the wings, all-too-ready to get into our act.

SUMMARY

■ The purpose of psychological assessment is to describe or classify individuals in ways that will be useful for prediction or treatment.

■ A useful assessment tool must be reliable and valid and must usually have been standardized. A reliable measure gives consistent results on different testings. A valid measure does in fact give a measure of the characteristic being tested. Standardization of a measuring device includes obtaining norms by giving it to a large number of people like those for whom it is intended and establishing uniform procedures for administering and scoring it.

■ Formal assessment is carried out through interviews, life history and archival data, tests, and situational observations. Self-report measures and judges' ratings are sources of assessment information that come from the individual or from others.

■ Self-report measures may suffer from intentional or unwitting biases and inaccuracies, but standardized procedures and quantification can enhance their usefulness.

■ Judges' ratings may be biased by the "halo" effect and the "stereotype" effect; their reliability is enhanced by multiple judges and judgments tied to specific, observable actions.

■ Objective, quantifiable intelligence testing began in France early in this century with the test prepared by Binet to identify and separate retarded from normal schoolchildren as a step in planning special training for the former. Scores were given in terms of mental ages.

■ In the United States, intelligence testing was seized on as a way to solve the practical problems of classifying draftees and determining which immigrants would profit from what kinds of education. Unfortunately, early results were misinterpreted by some as evidence of the inferiority of certain groups.

■ With the development of the Stanford revision of the Binet scale and the concept of the IQ, intelligence came to be seen as an inner, largely inherited, unchanging capacity.

■ Because the Stanford-Binet tests were standardized on white, English-speaking children, they often did not give accurate indications of the intelligence of non-English-speaking individuals. Tests developed by Wechsler, one for adults and one for children, provide separate scores for verbal and nonverbal items.

■ Though an operational definition of intelligence is simply "what intelligence tests measure," there is general agreement today that intelligence includes verbal abilities and problem-solving abilities. It is also regarded as involving adapting to new demands, learning from experience, and thinking abstractly.

■ *Ability* is defined as the currently available power to perform, *aptitude* as the potential for performance after training, *achievement* as the measure of success of performance.

■ According to psychometric theories of intelligence, intelligence consists of a general *g*-factor, and a number of specific *s*-factors.

■ IQ scores are valid for predicting academic success and the status of one's occupation. Once in a profession, factors other than intelligence are more important in determining success.

■ IQs of young children may change over time with several kinds of environmental change. IQs are relatively stable for older children, but individuals can show large changes.

■ The heritability of a trait is defined as the contribution of genetic factors to the variability in test scores on that trait *within* a given population. It does not apply to individuals or to differences in scores *between* populations. Both genetic and environmental factors contribute to the level of intelligence that an individual achieves, as does their interaction.

■ No test is entirely culture free. Content and manner of administration are inevitably more appropriate for some groups than others, and cultural differences in habits, motivation, family encouragement, and relevant past experience all affect a child's test scores.

■ Personality is assessed by both objective instruments and projective devices. The *Minnesota Multiphasic Personality Inventory* is a personality inventory that was developed to classify mental patients; it has several scales that were developed empirically to separate clinical populations from "normal" individuals. Responses can be scored and interpreted by a clinician or by computer.

■ The *California Personality Inventory,* too, was constructed empirically but was based on a "normal" standardization group; it measures 18 personality dimensions and is widely used in vocational counseling. The *16 Factor Personality Test* was developed by factor analysis and measures 16 factors thought to reflect basic personality traits.

■ Behavior assessment is a relatively new assessment approach in which specific behaviors are observed in a natural setting. It is used before and following behavior therapy and grows out of behaviorists' interest in behaviors that can be changed rather than enduring inner characteristics.

■ Projective tests are devices in which subjects are asked to respond to purposely incomplete or ambiguous stimuli of various kinds, which leave considerable room for the "projection" of fantasies, motivations, and thoughts by the individual. Two well-known projective tests are the *Rorschach* and the *Thematic Apperception Test.*

■ Most tests of creativity are designed to diagnose a person's ability to give unusual but appropriate responses. Creativity typically involves heightened sensitivity, synthesis of elements into new relationships, and the ability to translate private images into visible form. Projective devices, behavior sampling, and measures of divergent thinking have been used to test creativity. Creativity is not closely correlated with intelligence.

■ Vocational assessment includes an assessment of an individual's interests, aptitudes, and current level of achievement. The *Strong-Campbell Interest Inventory* compares the individual's interests with those of people successful in various occupations. The *Occupations Analysis Inventory* provides information about the requirements of various jobs.

■ Shyness is a common, pervasive problem and serious handicap. Both public and private shyness have been identified, as well as several aspects of shyness for which treatment programs have now been developed.

■ Assessment is prevalent in many areas of our lives but also has become highly controversial. Though often useful for prediction and as an indication of present performance level, test results should not be used to limit an individual's opportunities for development and change.

Part Six

Pathological Processes

Chapter Thirteen
Understanding and Managing Stress

Chapter Fourteen
Abnormal Psychology

Chapter Fifteen
Treating Psychopathologies

UNDERSTANDING AND MANAGING STRESS

■ THE CONCEPT OF STRESS
Meanings of "stress"
The role of cognitive appraisal

■ PHYSIOLOGICAL STRESS REACTIONS
Emergency reactions to external threats
The general adaptation syndrome
Stress and disease

■ PSYCHOLOGICAL STRESS REACTIONS
Behavioral patterns
Emotional aspects of the stress response
Cognitive effects of stress

■ SOURCES OF STRESS
Major life stressors
Life's little hassles
Catastrophic events
Chronic societal sources of stress

■ VULNERABILITY AND RESISTANCE
Common coping strategies
Supportiveness of the environment

■ MANAGING STRESS BETTER
Altering bodily reactions
Modifying cognitive strategies
Stress control and your mental health

■ SUMMARY

It started out like most school days for the big-city college teacher—only bleaker. He was late because he had overslept, having set the clock-radio alarm to 7:00 P.M. instead of 7:00 A.M. (a Freudian wishful fantasy, no doubt). But he was still tired. He hadn't slept well—had been worrying all night about his promotion decision, due to be handed down today by the senior faculty. If anyone ever deserved to be promoted he did—on sheer effort, devotion, and energy above and beyond the call of duty. But they might not see it that way.

He gulped down his coffee and bagel, checked to see if his socks were the same color, fly zipped, gathered lecture notes together, and raced down the four flights of stairs to head off another parking ticket. He had already been tagged for over $200 worth of them, and he was determined not to get stung again. But with alternate street parking from 8:00 A.M. and overcongested traffic, it was a Mission Impossible situation.

7:58 and counting. But where was his car? He couldn't remember where he had parked it last night because every night it was parked on a different street. He gambled on 71st—and lost. Running down 68th Street, he was just in time to see a policeman approaching his car. Too late; in an instant the ticket was issued and he owed the city another $15.00.

Outrage slowly turned to anger as he drove away. Nearly ran a pedestrian down at the corner (he deserved to be frightened for walking so slowly). They exchanged obscenities. In no time he was stuck in the morning rush traffic jam in the tunnel. Horns honking, exhaust fumes building up, tempers boiling.

Eleven minutes late to Psych 1, he begged departing students to return. Most did so resentfully. The lecture went badly; he couldn't concentrate or get his emotions under sufficient control. He felt guilty for having forced the class to stay and promised himself to give a dynamite lecture tomorrow to make up for today's disaster (but that would mean working late, and he was tired already).

During office hours, his research assistant told him she had to leave school to work full time because her father had died and she must support her family. She cried over the loss of her father and her education. He was distressed at the loss of his only reliable graduate assistant. He took some aspirin for the headache that got progressively worse during endless student counseling.

Afternoon mail a mixed bag. First letter told him his research article had been accepted for publication in a prestigious journal. Joy! Second letter told him he was overdrawn again at the bank—and it was ten days before payday. Wouldn't borrow from his kid brother again. Too humiliating. What could he sell? Began to feel overwhelmed. No way out. Depressed.

Finally invited into the Chairman's office. "We all respect the kind of work you've been doing. . . . *but (but! but!)* some people feel you need more time to mellow . . . too brash." Depressed: "I don't deserve it, I'm not any good." Angry: "They're all wrong." Result: more depressed; headache built up between his eyes.

Later in the day, he forgot to keep his appointment for a medical checkup on the headaches and chest pain he'd been having. Then he lost his temper with the secretary for not finishing the typing he had given her yesterday. She cried and he apologized. He decided to call it a day.

Stuck in the evening rush-hour traffic, as usual. But finally he got home—or, almost. He drove up 69th, down 70th, up 71st, down 72nd—in search of the elusive 10 x 4 feet of unoccupied asphalt in which to bury his car. The day ended like any other day—only much bleaker.

It is obvious from this all-too-real tale why stress has been called a "disease of civilization." The rapid pace of our lives, overcrowded living conditions, too many demands on our time, interferences with our personal ambitions, and the frustrating conditions of many jobs all contribute to the modern stress equation.

"Stress affects the lives of all people, everywhere. It is a cause of illness and accidents, producing stress in the victims and those who must care for them. Stress affects personality, modifying our perceptions, feelings, attitudes, and behavior, and it reaches beyond its immediate victims to affect the political, social, and work organizations whose activities they direct and carry out . . . . Growth and survival are very much related to . . . success in coping with stress" (Warshaw, 1979, p. 3).

Would we be better off without stress? That would be a life without challenge—no difficulties to surmount, no new fields to conquer, no reason to sharpen our wits or improve our abilities. How interesting would life be for you if you got everything you wanted with no effort? How would you have developed the skills you now have if no one had ever made any demands on you? With a stress-free life, how would you ever have had the satisfaction of knowing you could deal with complexity and control the events in your life?

Luckily, we have considerable control over how much stress we experience and how much it hurts us. In this chapter we will look at what psychologists mean by *stress*, how stress can affect us physically and psychologically, how common stressors in our society can affect our health, what factors can make us more vulnerable to stress—or less so—and how we can manage stress better.

Stress is an unavoidable part of living because every organism faces challenges from its environment and from its own needs. These challenges are "problems" it must solve if it is to survive and thrive. But researchers studying stress have sometimes reported findings that seemed contradictory because they were using different definitions of the term *stress*. Our first task is to make clear just what we will be meaning by the terms *stress* and *stressor*.

Meanings of "stress"

In this chapter we will be using the term **stress** to mean the pattern of specific and nonspecific responses an organism makes to stimulus events that disturb its equilibrium and tax or exceed its ability to cope. The stimulus events that do this include a large variety of external and internal conditions that collectively are called **stressors**. A stressor places a demand on the organism for some kind of adaptive response. The stress response is composed of a diverse combination of reactions on several levels, including physiological, behavioral, emotional, and cognitive changes.

The term *stress* is also used more broadly as a field of study. Thus many researchers use it to indicate a whole field of research, in which all aspects of the stress response are studied—the stressors that induce it, the individual's cognitive appraisal of the demand, and physiological, emotional, behavioral, and cognitive aspects of the stress response, including effective and ineffective coping strategies (see Monat & Lazarus, 1977).

The role of cognitive appraisal

Before the stress response begins, a demand on the organism (stressor) must be recognized on some level and evaluated. When the stressor is invading microbes, the body carries out the necessary recognition and evaluation and initiates appropriate countermeasures, all below the level of our consciousness. But even here the response is not a simple,

inevitable reaction to a stimulus but a carefully orchestrated, multifaceted response.

With stressors we can become aware of, **cognitive appraisal** plays a central role in defining the situation—what the demand is, how big a threat it is, what resources one has for meeting it, and what strategies are appropriate. Some stressors, such as bodily injury or finding one's house on fire are seen as threats by almost any one, but most of the stressors we are exposed to can be defined in various ways, depending on our overall life situation, the relation of this particular demand to our central goals, our competence for dealing with it, and our assessment of our competence. The situation that causes acute distress for me may be all in a day's work for you.

Cognitive appraisal is thus an intervening variable between the stimulus of the stressor and our response to it (see Neufeld, 1976). Our appraisal of the stressor and of our resources for meeting it can be as important as the actual stressor in determining our conscious experience, what coping strategies we will see as appropriate, and how successful we will be. If we define a stressor as too much for us to deal with, we create a self-fulfilling prophecy: we are indeed likely to fail even if objectively we are capable of dealing adequately with the demand. Even in the case of physical disease, doctors have long known that a patient's attitude can be as important as the physical condition in determining the course of the illness (see **Close-up,** p. 458).

Cognitive appraisal may even define a stressor as no threat at all but an interesting new challenge that will be fun to test oneself against. Here the experience may be one of exhilaration, of being "psyched up," with anticipation of achievement and increased self-esteem; such a positive reaction to a stressor has been called **eustress.** (*eu* means "good").

Richard Lazarus, a pioneer in recent stress research, has distinguished between two stages in our cognitive appraisal of demands made on us. He uses the term **primary appraisal** for the primary evaluation of the seriousness of the demand. It starts with the questions: "What's happening?" and "Is this thing good for me, stressful, or irrelevant?" If the answer is "stressful," the individual appraises the potential impact of the stressor by determining whether harm has occurred or is likely to and whether action is called for.

Once the person decides something must be done, **secondary appraisal** begins, in which the person evaluates what personal and social resources are available to deal with the stressful circumstance and what action is needed (Lazarus, 1966). Then, as coping responses are tried, appraisal continues and new responses are initiated if the first ones don't work and the stress persists. **Chronic stress** may be defined as a state of arousal, continuing over time, in which demands are perceived by the individual as greater than the inner and outer resources available for dealing with them (Powell & Eagleston, in press).

In the next two sections we will look at physiological and psychological aspects of the response to stressors that have been appraised as threats. In our society, such reactions are more often responses to psychological than physical stressors.

Voodoo Deaths

Captivating to the imagination are the sudden voodoo deaths described in anthropological reports. There are many documented cases in which healthy people who believed that they had transgressed sacred laws or had been the subject of a curse have died soon afterward.

The following is an account of behavior observed in one tribe when a man discovered that a bone was being pointed at him in a certain way by an enemy.

"He stands aghast, with his eyes staring at the treacherous pointer, and with his hands lifted as though to ward off the lethal medium, which he imagines is pouring into his body. His cheeks blanch and his eyes become glassy and the expression of his face becomes horribly distorted . . . . He attempts to shriek but usually the sound chokes in his throat, and all that one might see is froth at his mouth. His body begins to tremble and the muscles twist involuntarily. He sways backwards and falls to the ground, and after a short time appears to be in a swoon; but soon after he writhes as if in mortal agony, and, covering his face with his hands, begins to moan . . . . From this time onwards he sickens and frets, refusing to eat and keeping aloof from

the daily affairs of the tribe. Unless help is forthcoming in the shape of a countercharm . . . his death is only a matter of a comparatively short time" (Basedow, 1925, cited in Cannon, 1942, p. 172).

Other reports tell of healthy people succumbing to sudden death upon discovering that they have transgressed against the supernatural world by eating forbidden food. In one case, the expectation of death—and hence the death itself—was delayed until long after the fateful act.

A young traveler, visiting a friend, was served a dish containing fowl. He asked if it was wild hen, a delicacy banned for the young, and ate it only when assured that it was not. A few years later, the friend admitted laughingly that it had in fact been wild hen. The young man began to tremble and within twenty-four hours was dead (Pinkerton, 1814).

Reports such as these were thoroughly analyzed by the respected physiologist Walter Cannon (1942), who became convinced of the reality of the phenomenon

PHYSIOLOGICAL STRESS REACTIONS

We saw in Chapter 3 that the brain developed originally as a center for more efficient coordination of action. Efficiency meant flexibility of response to changing environmental requirements and also a quicker, often automatic response. One set of brain-controlled physiological stress responses occurs when the organism perceives an external threat (a predator, for example). Instant action and extra strength may be needed if the organism is to survive; a whole constellation of automatic mechanisms has evolved that meet this need. Another set of physiological stress reactions occurs when the danger is internal and the stability and integrity of the organism are threatened, as by invading microbes or other disease agents that upset the normal physiological processes.

In this section we will look at both emergency reactions to external threats and the syndrome that occurs in reaction to internal ones.

Emergency reactions to external threats

In the 1920s Walter Cannon, a Harvard University physiologist, outlined the first scientific description of the body's responses to stressors in an investigation of how animals and humans respond to danger. He found that a sequence of activity was triggered in the nerves and glands to prepare the body for combat and struggle—or for running away to safety. Cannon called this basic dual stress response the **"fight-or-flight" syndrome.**

though at the time such reports were generally greeted with scepticism by sophisticated westerners.

Two explanations for the "sudden death" phenomenon associated with extreme fright and feelings of hopelessness were advanced. According to Cannon's theory (1957), oversecretion of adrenalin could impair the capillary walls, allowing a passage of fluid to the surrounding tissues; the resulting reduction in the volume of the circulating blood could send the organism into a state of shock, leading to deterioration of the heart and nerve centers. Another researcher, who observed sudden death in wild rats placed under extreme, frightening stress, found that in this case overstimulation of the parasympathetic nervous system was responsible (Richter, 1957). More recently, an anthropologist studying Australian aborigines has found evidence that victims of sorcery may actually die from dehydration when family and friends withdraw all life-support systems, including water (Eastwell, 1984).

Today we not only recognize the reality of the close interdependence of psychological and physiological processes but are identifying the precise mechanisms by which emotions, attitudes, and beliefs can lead to physiological reactions that can become illness-inducing or life-threatening (see Lachman, 1983).

△ *Scientists have difficulty explaining the effectiveness of voodoo spells and curses.*

At the center of this primitive stress response is the brain's *hypothalamus,* which, as we have seen, is involved in a variety of emotional responses. The hypothalamus has sometimes been referred to as the "stress center" because of its twin functions in emergencies: (a) it controls the autonomic nervous system, and (b) it activates the pituitary gland.

Autonomic responses. The autonomic nervous system (described briefly in Chapter 3) regulates the activities of the body's organs. In conditions appraised as stressful, breathing becomes faster and fuller, heart rate increases, blood vessels constrict, and blood pressure rises. In addition to these internal changes, muscles open the passages of the throat and nose to allow more air into the lungs, while also producing facial expressions of strong emotion. Messages go to smooth muscles to stop certain bodily functions, such as digestion.

Another function of the autonomic nervous system during stress is to "get the adrenalin flowing." It signals the inner part of the adrenal glands, the adrenal medulla, to release two hormones, epinephrine and norepinephrine, which, in turn, signal a number of other organs to perform their specialized functions. The spleen releases more red blood corpuscles (to aid in clotting if there is an injury), while the bone marrow is stimulated to make more white corpuscles (to combat infection). The liver is stimulated to produce more sugar, which builds up body energy. It is believed that epinephrine (also called adrenalin) plays a more important role in fear reactions (and flight) while norepinephrine (also called noradrenalin) is more associated with rage reactions (and fight).

During stress the autonomic nervous system is also involved in the release of endorphins. In earlier chapters we saw that these brain opiates have the effect of reducing pain much as morphine does. Temporary reduction of sensitivity to pain during stress is called *stress-induced analgesia.*

Activation of this brain opiate system has been demonstrated by lessened sensitivity to pain in both human and animal subjects placed under stress.

> In one study human subjects were subjected to the stressful experience of a series of warnings that a painful, inescapable shock might soon be applied to a nerve. Each warning was followed by either a shock or a mild touch on the skin. The researcher also periodically measured the subject's reflex response to varying degrees of mild but painful stimulation.
>
> As the stressful situation continued, the threshold of the reflex response became higher. A higher level of shock was required to elicit the response. The threshold became lower again immediately following an injection of a chemical known to block the effect of brain opiates, whereas a placebo injection produced no change. The researcher concluded that stress-induced analgesia must have been produced by brain opiates as a result of the stressful situation (Willer et al., 1981).

Investigators are currently trying to find out what other kinds of stress reactions may be influenced by the brain's opiates.

Pituitary hormones. The pituitary gland responds to the signals from the hypothalamus by secreting two hormones vital to the stress reaction. The **thyrotrophic hormone (TTH)** stimulates the thyroid gland which, in turn, makes more energy available to the body. The **adrenocorticotrophic hormone (ACTH)** stimulates the outer part of the adrenal glands, the adrenal cortex, resulting in the release of a group of hormones called *steroids,* which are important in metabolic processes and in release of sugar into the blood from the liver. ACTH also signals various organs of the body to release about thirty other hormones, each of which plays a role in the body's adjustment to this "call to arms."

This same hormonal response occurs in response to both physical stressors, such as injury, pain, disease, and temperature extremes, and psychological stressors, such as anxiety, fear, and novelty (Selye, 1974). Because the hormones released by the action of ACTH occur so reliably when the individual is faced with a stressor, researchers use the concentration of these hormones in the blood as one measure of the intensity of the stress reaction.

It is obvious, then, that many bodily processes are activated by danger signals. Now let's consider their adaptive significance for people faced with two different stressful situations.

When a call comes into the firehouse, the firefighters respond with the physiological components of the stress response. Muscles tense, breathing speeds up, heart rate increases, adrenalin flows, and extra energy becomes available, and the firefighters become less sensitive to pain. They will need these responses in order to endure the physical strain of battling a potentially destructive, sometimes lethal, disaster. These built-in capacities to deal with stressors by mobilizing the body's active response systems have been valuable throughout the ages when there was a physical challenge to be met.

But now consider the person taking calls at the firehouse switchboard, or a person working on a crisis "hot line," taking calls from potentially suicidal strangers. These workers undergo the same physiological stress responses as a result of the psychological stressors they face. But for them this physiological response is not adaptive, because no physical activity is being demanded that might use the extra energy and strength. The office worker must instead try to stay calm, concentrate well on listening, and make

▽ *A volunteer worker on a suicide-prevention hotline may undergo the same physiological stress responses as a firefighter or other physically active rescue worker. In this case, however, the response is not adaptive because there is no demand for physical action.*

thoughtful decisions. Unfortunately, these skills are not enhanced by the stress response. So what developed in the species as an adaptive preparation for dealing with external danger is not the most adaptive pattern for dealing with many modern-day sources of stress. In fact, recurring or chronic arousal that is not dealt with by appropriate physical activity, may in time lead to malfunctioning.

The general adaptation syndrome

The first modern researcher to investigate the effects of continued severe stress on the body was a Hans Selye, a Canadian endocrinologist. While still in medical school, he asked a simple question. After his teacher had described the *differences* between five diseases in five patients under examination, Selye asked: "What is *similar* in all these cases of illness?"

In addition to knowing what specific symptoms different diseases produce, this 19-year-old medical student wanted to understand the basic condition of "being sick." For half a century, the curious mind of Hans Selye pioneered research at the University of Montreal directed toward finding out more about the *nonspecific stress response* that occurs in all long-continued physical

△ ▍ *Hans Selye (1907–1982)*

stress. His subjects were primarily experimental animals subjected to a wide range of physical stressors.

Selye studied stressors that threaten the physical functioning of the body rather than stressors like predators that require behavioral responses. According to Selye's theory of stress, there are many kinds of stressors (including all diseases and many other physical and psychological conditions), but all are alike in calling for adaptation by the organism to maintain or regain its integrity and well-being. (This is another aspect of homeostasis, mentioned in Chapter 8.) In addition to responses that are specific to the particular stressor (such as constriction of the blood vessels in response to cold), there is a characteristic pattern of *nonspecific* adaptational physiological mechanisms that occurs in response to continuing threat by almost any serious stressor. Selye called this pattern the **general adaptation syndrome**

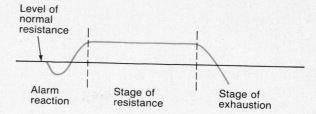

Level of
normal
resistance

Alarm
reaction

Stage of
resistance

Stage of
exhaustion

△ ▍ **Figure 13.1** *The General Adaptation Syndrome*

On exposure to a stressor, the body's resistance is diminished until the physiological changes of the alarm reaction bring it back up to the normal level. Then, if the stressor continues, the defensive changes "overshoot" in the stage of resistance and the bodily signs characteristic of the alarm reaction virtually disappear; resistance to that stressor rises above normal but is less to other stressors. Following prolonged exposure to the stressor, adaptation breaks down; in the stage of exhaustion, signs of the alarm reaction reappear, but now the stressor effects are irreversible, and the individual becomes ill and may die. (From Selye, 1956, p. 87).

(GAS). He found a characteristic sequence of three stages in this syndrome: an alarm reaction, a stage of resistance, and a stage of exhaustion (Selye, 1956). These stages are diagrammed in **Figure 13.1**.

The *alarm reaction* consists of the physiological changes by which the threatened organism immediately moves to restore its normal functioning. Whether the stressor is physical (such as inadequate food, loss of sleep, disease, bodily injury) or psychological (such as loss of love or personal security), the alarm reaction consists of the same general pattern of bodily and biochemical changes. This accounts for the fact that people suffering from different illnesses all seem to complain of such symptoms as headache, fever, fatigue, aching muscles and joints, loss of appetite, and a general feeling of being unwell. Unlike the emergency mobilization for behavioral action against an external danger, discussed in the preceding section, the alarm reaction mobilizes the body's defenses for restoration of inner balance.

If exposure to the stress-producing situation continues, the alarm reaction is followed by the *stage of resistance*, the second phase of the general adaptation syndrome. Here the organism appears to develop a resistance to the stressor. Even though the disturbing stimulation continues, the symptoms that occurred during the first stage disappear, and the physiological processes that had been disturbed during the alarm reaction appear to return to normal. This resistance to the stressor seems to be accomplished in large part through increased secretions from the anterior pituitary and the adrenal cortex (ACTH and *cortin,* respectively).

Although there is *greater* resistance to the original stressor during this second stage, however, there is *reduced* resistance to other stressors. Even a weak stressor may now produce a strong response if it comes when the body's resources are engaged in resisting an earlier, more potent stressor. Some people find they get irritated more easily when getting over a cold, for example. General resistance to disease is lost in this stage of resistance even though adaptation to the specific noxious agent is improved.

If exposure to the injurious stressor continues too long, a point is reached where the organism can no longer maintain its resistance. It then enters the third phase of Selye's general adaptation syndrome—the *stage of exhaustion.* The anterior pituitary and the adrenal cortex are unable to continue secreting their hormones at the increased rate. This means that the organism can no longer adapt to the chronic stress. Many of the symptoms of the alarm reaction now begin to reappear. If the stressor continues, death may occur.

When experimental animals died following prolonged exposure to stressors, Selye always found upon dissecting them that their adrenal glands were enlarged, their lymph nodes and the thymus (organs involved in immunity) shrunken, and their stomachs covered by bleeding ulcers. The long-continued stress had resulted in destruction of physical tissues of their bodies. In most real-life situations, of course, it is rare for stress not to be relieved before the stage of total exhaustion is reached.

The concept of the general adaptation syndrome has been exceptionally valuable in explaining disorders that had baffled physicians. Within this framework, many disorders can be viewed as the results of the physiological processes involved in the body's long-continued attempts to adapt to a dangerous stressor. The value of additional ACTH and cortisone in treating some of these diseases can also be understood: such treatment evidently helps the anterior pituitary and the adrenal cortex maintain the body's resistance to the stressor.

On the other hand, because Selye was a physician and because his research focused on reactions to physical stressors among experimental animals, such as the laboratory rat, his theory has had little to say about the importance of psychological aspects of stress in the case of human beings. In particular, Selye's critics believe he *overstated* the role of nonspecific, systemic factors in the production of stress-induced illness. And in work on animals, of course, there was no place for recognition of the importance of cognitive appraisal of threat in human stress reactions, where the perceived *meaning* of a situation determines which physiological reactions occur (see Lazarus, 1974; Mason, 1975). Selye himself came to examine similar concepts in his later writings (Selye, 1974). In any case, he is still recognized as the pioneering explorer of stress reactions; his insights and research have led to the creation of a whole new field of study.

Stress and disease

Selye's original theory emphasized that the stress response occurs as a reaction to various stressors, including illness. But the theory also shows how a long-continued stress reaction can itself lead to illness. In fact, stress is now believed to be a contributing factor in more than half of all cases of disease (Pelletier & Peper, 1977). For example, hypertension, a disease that increases the risk of heart attack and premature death, is a stress-related disease.

There are three ways in which stressors can be causal factors in illness. First, long-continued severe stress or chronic arousal resulting from perceived threat can in time lead to physiological malfunctioning and illness. Second, the complex physiological mechanisms of the general adaptation syndrome may fail to function appropriately and may themselves produce diseases. Third, the "wear and tear" on the body brought about by the continuing process of adaptation can result in eventual illness due to depletion of the organism's store of adaptation energy and cumulative damage to organ systems.

Psychosomatic disorders. In the case of the firehouse workers, we saw that emergency physiological arousal for dealing actively with perceived threat is not adaptive when action is not called for. This is true in the case of most psychological stressors, yet the physiological arousal is automatic and keeps occurring anyway whenever we are anxious or feel threatened or pressured. Continued severe stress or chronic arousal for action that is not taken can in time lead to physiological malfunctioning, such as high blood pressure, or even tissue damage, as in the case of gastric ulcers, which develop in some individuals who feel chronically threatened and hostile. **Psychosomatic** ("mind/body") **disorders**, also called *psychophysiologic disorders,* are physical disorders in which emotions and thought processes are believed to play a central role.

Psychosomatic disorders are often called **diseases of adaptation** because they have their roots in attempts to adapt to stressors. Stress-induced peptic ulcers or high blood pressure are classic examples of diseases of adaptation, although not all cases of these two disorders are induced by stress. Many disorders, including ulcers, high blood pressure, and skin problems, can have their origin in either physical or psychological factors or a combination of the two.

Traditional medicine long resisted the idea that organic diseases could have psychological causes. Acceptance of the revolutionary notion of psychogenic disease was supported by the publication in 1935 of Flanders Dunbar's classic work, *Emotions and Bodily Changes,* and a few years later by the reality of thousands of World War II soldiers debilitated by physiological symptoms resulting in large part from the psychological stressors of combat. Since that time, evidence from many research laboratories, medical clinics, and therapy settings has demonstrated that physiological and psychological systems are closely interwoven, neither one independent of the other. In today's laboratories the psychological antecedents of physical stress reactions are being studied scientifically and measured objectively (see **Close-up,** p. 464).

Wittkower and Dudek (1973) have identified five conditions that must be present for a disorder to be classified as psychosomatic:

1. The psychological sources of stress are present *before* any somatic symptoms appear.
2. The emotional arousal is unconscious or, if the person is aware of it, he or she feels powerless to change the situation that is causing it.
3. The activation of the autonomic nervous system by the stressor is chronic and long continued.
4. Defense mechanisms normally effective in adjusting to the stressful life situation have broken down, or ineffective defenses have been overused, increasing instead of lessening the stress.
5. There is some constitutional weakness in the organ system affected, due to heredity or previously experienced trauma.

In other words, these researchers believe that for a chronic psychological stressor to lead to a physical disorder, the person must have a constitutional vulnerability in a particular bodily system and an ineffective style of dealing with the stressful situation, and be either unaware of the chronic emotional arousal or convinced that there is no better way to cope with the difficult situation.

Stress-related symptoms of illness occur most often in disorders of four bodily systems—the nervous, respiratory, cardiovascular, and gastrointestinal systems. Psychological factors have also been clearly demonstrated in the development of some cases of ulcers, high blood pressure, colitis, migraine, low back pain, dermatitis, obesity, asthma, and other ailments. In fact, many major illnesses, including cancer, are now believed to be subject to influence by a variety of psychological factors.

Excessive or inappropriate body defenses. Other diseases of adaptation are diseases caused when the body overreacts or reacts inappropriately to foreign invaders or other stressors that may threaten its stability. Here defensive processes that normally are adaptive are used to excess or used unnecessarily.

If you get a sliver in your finger, the area will get red and swollen, pus will form, and the area will be warmer than the rest of the body. The local inflammatory response is part of the alarm reaction; it is a defensive reaction that barricades such irritants, preventing them from getting into the bloodstream. Inflammation is the typical first response of the body to many physical stressors.

How does the body know which "invaders" are potentially harmful? The answer is that the body does *not* always know, and sometimes it makes errors. Sometimes, in fact, it responds with local inflammation to stimuli that are actually benign. Allergic reactions are the clearest example of this response. Ragweed pollen has no direct harmful effects on the body; we are best off ignoring its presence. But for some people, ragweed pollen (or various other allergens) sets off an allergic response involving inflammation of nasal tissues and, often, a total-body general adaptation syndrome. Allergies are true diseases of adaptation: if the body did not evaluate the stressor as a danger and create an unnecessary stress response, there would be no disease.

Rheumatoid arthritis is another inflammatory disease of adaptation, although a far more complex one than an allergy. While the mechanisms of rheu-

Behavioral Medicine and Health Psychology

Two of the newest, most exciting areas of research on the puzzles of stress, its impact on human functioning, and ways to prevent its damaging effects are behavioral medicine and health psychology. Researchers in these areas are seeking to learn how mental and physical processes influence each other to cause illness, as well as how behavior and environments can be changed to promote health.

Behavioral medicine is an interdisciplinary field that integrates knowledge relevant to issues of disease and health from the behavioral and medical sciences (Miller, 1983). Research in this new field (formally established as recently as 1977) is focused on the attempt to identify the neurochemical mechanisms by which mental and emotional processes lead to disease. Answers are beginning to emerge from a synthesis of the precise, micro-level analysis of the biological sciences with the broader, molar perspective of psychological analysis of mind and body as a system influenced by both environmental forces and feedback from its own behavior.

As many as half of the deaths from the leading causes of death in the United States are estimated to be due ultimately to the patients' life-styles (Center for Disease Control, 1980). Among the life-style behaviors that lead to illness are smoking, alcohol and drug abuse, overeating, and Type-A behavior. As much as

80 percent of disease symptoms, including some cancers, are now believed to be of emotional rather than physical origin (Shapiro, 1978). Understanding the mechanisms by which subjective states and behavior patterns generate disease symptoms thus becomes essential if effective interventions are to be planned.

One focus of research in behavioral medicine is *psychoimmunology,* the study of how the immune system is affected by psychological processes. There is increasing evidence that this rapidly activated, acutely sensitive system functions as a "translating mechanism" by which life stress becomes a death-dealing disease. For example, the research by Judith Rodin cited in Chapter 1 (p. 14) is showing that feelings of loss of predictability and control in connection with highly stressful recent events, especially in older subjects, are correlated with decreases in specific types of cells that are known to kill foreign cells and regulate other immune responses, such as the production of antibodies. A smaller number of these cells would make the individual more susceptible to disease and less able to overcome it (Rodin 1983). This pioneering research may be the most powerful demonstration to date of the chain of events and mechanisms by which a person's interpretation of an environmental event (a mental process) alters internal functions at the biochemical level (a physiological process) to cause disease and even death.

---

matoid arthritis are not totally clear, it appears to be related to malfunctions in the body's production of adaptive stress-response hormones—in particular to an insufficient production of anti-inflammatory hormones. Flare-ups of rheumatoid arthritis can occur during periods of psychological stress. On the other hand, the use of artificial anti-inflammatory hormones (corticosteroids) can ease the symptoms of rheumatoid arthritis, and in some cases so can psychological treatment to increase coping abilities and stress management skills (Rogers et al., 1982).

Damage due to "wear and tear." As a result of his animal experiments, Selye came to believe that each of us has a limited reserve of energy which can be used to adapt to stressors, and that when it has been exhausted, we can no longer fight stressors and will be overcome by disease. This is why all organisms eventually reach the "stage of exhaustion"

in the general adaptation syndrome if the stressor is not removed. Although a person may lead an active, healthy life, successfully coping with specific stressors as they arise, each experience of stress uses up some adaptation energy. The thing to do, Selye argued, is to use our adaptation energy wisely, rather than squandering it by responding to events that might better be ignored.

Selye believed that aging itself is primarily the result of loss of "adaptation energy" and of damage to organ systems incurred during a lifetime of stress responses. He said, "Among all my autopsies (and I have performed well over one thousand), I have never seen a person who died of old age. In fact, *I do not think anyone has ever died of old age yet*" (Selye, 1976, p. 431).

Our bodies do not age at an even rate, according to some predetermined biological process. Rather, death occurs for each of us when our "weak link"

Health psychology is an even newer field of specialization. It is similar to behavioral medicine in its emphasis on relating behavioral knowledge to issues of disease and health but differs in two important ways. First, it is more exclusively based on the discipline of psychology, depending on psychological theories and psychological research in its approach to health issues rather than being an interdisciplinary field. Second, it has a broader focus on the whole health care system, rather than just the portion of the system encompassed by medicine. Whereas the traditional medical model is oriented toward pathology and medical expertise, health psychology is concerned with promoting and maintaining health and well-being also. In addition, health psychology looks beyond the practice of medicine by medical experts to see how a person's health is affected by other types of caregivers, by the person's own actions, and by social groups, organizations, and the environment (Stone et al., 1979).

Much research in health psychology deals with either the health behavior of the individual or processes in the health care system. Examples of its system-oriented research include studies of the dynamics of the doctor-patient relationship, the ecology of the treatment setting, and the stresses of careers in the health field, such as burnout. Research at the level of the individual may focus on any behavior that affects the person's well-being, whether favorably or unfavorably. Such "health behaviors" range from using a seat belt to failing to follow a doctor's recommendation or take a medication. (See also Weil, 1984).

Health psychologists try to understand the causes of health behaviors so as to be able to promote health more effectively. For example, smoking prevention programs with adolescents need to take account of adolescent motivations and the level of their cognitive problem-solving skills (Covington, 1981). Health psychologists also investigate questions such as what can be done to reduce the stressfulness of certain medical procedures and whether certain coping styles are related to better recovery.

Recent research on cancer patients by UCLA psychologist Shelley Taylor (1983) emphasizes the importance of belief, even belief not founded in reality. For example, a patient may believe that her breast cancer was caused by poor diet and may change her eating patterns to prevent a recurrence. Even though there is little evidence to support her belief in diet as the cause of her illness, her belief gives her a sense of control through a change in her behavior. Her belief—even if an illusion—protects her against the negative effects of the threat of recurrence and enables her to develop a healthier life-style enhanced by confidence and optimism.

gives out (assuming no special disease or accident). The "weak link" is determined partly by genetic vulnerability and partly by the stressors each of us has faced.

It is important to recognize that explanations of aging which focus on stress are far from complete. Aging is a complex process, and there are other hypotheses about its causes (see Timiras, 1978). There is also controversy about whether Selye's arguments adequately describe the ways in which stress affects aging. However, there is general agreement that long-continued, severe stress hastens aging, and that reductions in severe stress could contribute to a longer and healthier life span.

△ *How much older do you think former President Nixon is in the second photo than in the first?*
_____ years _____ months
For the correct answer, turn to p. 466.

PSYCHOLOGICAL STRESS REACTIONS

Our physiological stress reactions are automatic and predictable, built-in responses over which we normally have no conscious control. Not so our psychological reactions. They are learned and are heavily dependent on our perceptions and interpretations of the world and of our capacity for dealing with it. They include behavioral, emotional, and cognitive aspects.

Behavioral patterns

The experience of exposure to a stressor leads to a variety of behavioral changes depending on the severity of the stress experienced, the individual's characteristics, and the environmental possibilities.

Level of stress. The behavior of a person under stress depends in part on the level of stress experienced. Laboratory research on animals and humans, including observations of animals in their natural environments, and studies of patients in mental hospitals, has found a clear and consistent pattern in this regard.

Mild stress activates and intensifies biologically significant behaviors, such as eating, aggression, and sexual behavior. Mild stress makes the organism more alert; energies are focused and performance may improve. This finding is in keeping with earlier observations that the most efficient use of cues occurs at a moderate level of general arousal—better than at either lower or higher levels (Hebb, 1958).

Mild stress may lead to positive behavioral adjustments, such as becoming better informed, becoming vigilant to sources of threat, seeking protection and support from others, and learning better attitudes and coping skills. It may be that such positive behavioral reactions to mild stress occur only in response to certain kinds of stressors.

Continued unresolved stresses, such as those that beset the harried professor in our *Opening Case,* can accumulate to become more severe with time, caus-

Would you believe that only six months separate the two Nixons on page 465? The first photo was taken in January 1974, the second in June of the same year, shortly before the Watergate scandal forced his resignation.

ing maladaptive behavioral reactions such as increased irritability, poor concentration, lessened productivity, and chronic impatience. However, any of those stressors occurring only occasionally or seen as within the person's capacity to control cause no problem.

Moderately severe stress typically disrupts behavior, especially complex behavior requiring skilled coordination. Giving a speech or playing in a recital are familiar examples. Moderate stress may also produce repetitive, stereotyped actions, poorly tuned to environmental requirements. *Severe stress* inhibits and suppresses behavior and may lead to total immobility, as in the case of the dogs that learned helplessness after being shocked where no escape was possible (p. 246). It has been argued that immobility under severe stress may be a defensive reaction, representing "an attempt by the organism to reduce or eliminate the deleterious effects of stress . . . a form of self-therapy" (Antelman & Caggiula, 1980).

Stereotyped behaviors. When moderately severe stress continues, stereotyped actions may become a continuing pattern. Repetitive movements with no apparent goal, such as rocking, swaying, sucking, and pacing in circles have been observed in chimps reared in isolated confinement, as well as in autistic children (where the causal factors are less clear). These responses have mixed effects. They are *adaptive* in reducing a high level of stressor stimulation by lessening the individual's sensitivity to the environment. At the same time, they are *nonadaptive* in being rigid and inflexible and in persisting even when the environmental situation makes other responses more appropriate.

Overeating as a response to stress. In humans, overeating is a typical behavioral response of some people to everyday stress. As one unhappy and obese woman reported, "Sometimes I think I'm not hungry at all. It is that I am just unhappy in certain things—things that I cannot get. Food is the easiest thing to get that makes me feel nice and comfortable" (Bruch, 1973).

Aggression as a response to stress. Animal studies have found that aggressive behavior occurs in response to a variety of stressors, including isolation, overcrowding, morphine withdrawal, and electric shock. When pairs of animals are shocked in a laboratory cage from which they cannot escape, they begin fighting soon after the shock starts and stop when it ends. When only one animal is present, the same shock induces eating (Azrin, 1967).

In humans, aggressive behavior is often the result of frustration. **Frustration** is a state of the organism assumed to exist when goal-directed activity is blocked in some manner. Frustration is greatest when one has high goal motivation and is close to the goal and when progress is only partly blocked.

Frustration is both a response to a stressor and itself a stressor that activates behavior aimed at reducing the discomfort. What it leads to may be aggression. As we shall see in Chapter 17 an early hypothesis, the *frustration-aggression hypothesis*—assumed a regular relation, predicting that the greater the frustration, the greater would be the resulting aggression. (Dollard et al., 1939).

Sometimes aggression resulting from frustration is overt and directed toward removing (or destroying) the external source of frustration. However, this is not always possible or wise; hence the aggression may be *displaced* from the real target onto some substitute target that is not as threatening and cannot retaliate. We may pick on those who are smaller or weaker or on those who are social outcasts.

Displacement of aggression may also take the form of destruction of property associated with frustrating experiences, as in children's vandalism against their school. Or aggression may be turned inward in self-hatred, even suicide. Displacement of aggression, as discussed here, is similar to the ego-defense mechanism of displacement of hostility, but the focus here is on behavior undertaken in response to a stressor rather than on behavior undertaken to protect oneself against recognizing forbidden unconscious impulses.

Emotional aspects of the stress response

The stress response includes a variety of emotional reactions ranging from exhilaration, in the cases where the stressor is seen as an exciting, manageable challenge, to the far more common negative emotions of irritation, anger, anxiety, discouragement, and depression. Most stress is acutely uncomfortable, producing only negative emotions and efforts to lessen the discomfort in direct or indirect ways. In this section we will look at three emotional reactions and the stress situations often associated with them: depression, burnout, and posttraumatic stress disorder.

Depression. Life changes involving the loss or separation from friends and loved ones are frequent forerunners of depression. Being left behind when important others die or move away seems more likely to result in depression than a similar separation caused by one's own action (Paykel, 1973). Experiencing a cluster of stressful events is another predictor of emotional depression. We will examine the emotional reactions involved in depression when we review affective disorders in Chapter 14.

Burnout. Hour after hour, day after day, workers in health and social service professions must *care* about many clients or patients. In all too many cases, over time, they become increasingly unable to cope with the continuing emotional arousal caused by these encounters; eventually, "burnout" occurs. **Burnout** is a syndrome of emotional exhaustion, in which care givers lose their concern and emotional feeling for the people they are working to help and come to treat them in detached and even dehumanized ways.

Several social and situational factors affect the occurrence and level of burnout—and, by implication,

▷ *The mass murder of 21 innocent people in a McDonald's restaurant in July 1984 by a man who was distressed and angry after losing several jobs is a frightening instance of displacement of aggression.*

suggest ways of preventing or minimizing it. For example, the quality of the professional interaction is greatly affected by the *ratio of helpers to clients*—the number of people for whom the professional is providing care. The greater the number, the greater the cognitive, sensory, and emotional overload for the professional.

Another important factor is the *amount of direct contact with clients.* Longer work hours are correlated with more stress and negative staff attitudes *only* when they involve continuous direct contact with clients or patients. This is especially true when the nature of the contact is very difficult and upsetting (patients who are dying, clients who are physically or verbally abusive). The emotional strain of such prolonged contact can be eased by a work schedule that provides chances for the professional to withdraw from the high-stress situations temporarily.

The form of such withdrawals is important, however: they have positive results if they take the form of "time-outs" in which the professional chooses to perform some "nonpeople work" for a time while another staff member handles the client responsibilities. Withdrawal that leaves the clients uncared for is more likely to lead to feelings of guilt and of being trapped (Maslach, 1982).

Posttraumatic stress disorders. Rape victims, survivors of plane crashes, combat veterans, and others who have experienced extremely traumatic events may react emotionally with a **posttraumatic stress disorder.** This reaction is characterized by involuntary reexperiencing of the traumatic event(s)—especially the original feelings of shock, horror, and fear—in dreams or "flashbacks." In addition, victims experience an emotional numbing in relation to everyday events, associated with feelings of alienation from other people. Finally, the emotional pain of this reaction can result in an increase of various symptoms, such as sleep problems, guilt about surviving, difficulty in concentrating, and an exaggerated startle response (see **Close-up,** p. 469.)

▷ *Severe stress is often induced by the immediate situation for military personnel such as this U.S. Marine serving in Beirut. But equally damaging posttraumatic stress responses may occur months or even years later.*

The emotional responses of posttraumatic stress can occur immediately following the disaster in an acute form and subside over a period of several months or can persist, becoming a chronic syndrome often called the *residual stress pattern* (Silver & Wortman, 1980). In other cases, people may show no immediate reaction but may experience a full-blown posttraumatic stress disorder after a delay of months or even years. Clinicians are still discovering veterans of World War II and the Korean War who are displaying residual or delayed posttraumatic stress disorders (Dickman & Zeiss, 1982).

This delayed posttraumatic stress syndrome has been a special problem in the case of Vietnam veterans (Blank, 1982). The problems of many seemed to be made worse by feelings that they had been rejected by an unsympathetic American public and that they had been betrayed by their government and had spent important years of their lives in a wasted effort (Thienes-Hontos et al., 1982).

In a study of Vietnam veterans with combat experience, called the "Forgotten Warrior Project," John Wilson (1980), a psychologist at Cleveland State University found that:

1. Their suicide rate was 23 to 33 percent higher than the national average.
2. Of those who had been married when they left the United States, 38 percent were divorced within six months after returning.
3. The rate of hospitalization for alcoholism or drinking problems was high and increasing.
4. About half of them still had some emotional problems related to adjustment of civilian life.

The Aftershock of Rape

Two women who had been sexually assaulted on their college campus describe some of the enduring psychological dynamics generated by that extremely stressful episode.

Shock

Alice: I was in shock for a pretty long time. I could talk about the fact that I was a rape victim, but the emotions didn't start surfacing until a month later.

Beth: During the first two weeks there were people I had chosen to tell who were very, very supportive. But after two weeks, it was like, Okay, she's over it, we can go on now.' But the farther along you get, the more support you need, because as time passes, you become aware of your emotions and the need to deal with them.

Denial

Alice: There is a point where you deny it happened. You just completely bury it.

Beth: It's so unreal that you don't want to believe that it actually happened or that it can happen. Then you go through a long period of fear and anger.

Fear

Alice: I'm terrified of going jogging. [Alice had been jogging when she was raped.] I completely stopped any kind of physical activity after I was raped. I started it again this quarter. But every time I go jogging I have a perpetual fear. My pulse doubles. Of course I don't go jogging alone any more, but still the fear is there constantly.

Beth: I've experienced some really irrational thoughts. I was home at Christmas riding in the car with my Dad—my Dad!—and the guy who attacked me was about 21 years old—and yet I got really afraid all of a sudden of my Dad. It's just something you have to work out. There's not anything anybody can do.

Betrayal and loneliness

Alice: There's also a feeling of having all your friends betray you. I had a dream in which I was being assaulted outside my dorm. In the dream, everyone was looking out their windows—the faces were so clear—every one of my friends lined up against the windows watching. And there were even people two feet away from me. They all saw what was happening and none of them did anything. I woke up and had a feeling of extreme loneliness. Sometimes you just feel like there's nobody around.

Beth: I still feel very lonely [4 months later]. I didn't have any close friends when I got here. [Beth was raped at the start of her freshman year.] I felt betrayed by my family and friends from high school because they weren't here.

(Excerpted from the *Stanford Daily*, February 2, 1982, with permission. For a systematic analysis of psychological and social issues involved in rape, see Cann et al., 1981.)

Cognitive effects of stress

Once a stressor has been interpreted as threatening to one's well-being or self-esteem, a variety of intellectual functions may be adversely affected. In general, the greater the stress, the greater the reduction in cognitive efficiency and interference with flexible thinking.

Since attention is a limited resource, focusing on the threatening aspects of a situation and on one's anxiety and arousal reduces the amount of attention available for effective coping with the task at hand, and thereby lessening the threat. Thus one's attentional focus is narrowed both by the awareness of the threat to one's well-being and by the action of the autonomic nervous system in creating a state of arousal (Mandler, 1982). Memory is affected too, since short-term memory is limited by the amount of attention given to new input, and retrieval of past relevant memories depends on smooth operation of the use of appropriate retrieval cues. Similarly, stress may interfere with problem solving, judging, and decision making by narrowing perceptions of alternatives and by substituting stereotyped, rigid thinking for more creative responding (Janis, 1982).

A chronic feeling of threat can also be carried into ordinary situations, as happens when highly text-anxious students carry their anxiety into class discussions too. And finally, there is evidence that a high level of stress impairs children's intellectual development.

To test the hypothesis that stress affects competence and intelligence, researchers developed a stress index based on such variables as family problems and physical disorders. Stress indices were calculated for over 4000 7-year-old children, and each child's intelligence was tested. Some of the children were from middle-class white backgrounds, the others from lower-class black families.

For both groups, the higher the stress index, the lower was the child's IQ. This was particularly true of the black children, and also of children with eye problems. For all the children, visual discrimination was poorer as their stress index increased. Children who were held back a year or were assigned to special education classes also showed greater intellectual deficits.

The researchers concluded that the stress variables combined to influence the performances measured by the IQ test both in the immediate testing situation and also more generally, through interaction with other personal and social factors (Brown & Rosenbaum, 1983).

We saw in the Chapter 12 *Opening Case* of little Maria how her undiagnosed eye problem, aggravated by her stressful experience in first grade, led to performance that gave teachers a false picture of her ability.

The various elements of stress that we have been discussing are diagrammed in **Figure 13.2.** But what about the stressors that can lead to these responses? What are some of the expected—and unexpected— conditions that produce stress in our society? And how automatic is their effect: what makes us more vulnerable or less so, and are there ways we can cope with stress that lessen its damaging effects? These are questions we will be exploring in the next sections.

▽ | Figure 13.2   *A Model of Stress*

This chart summarizes the main relationships discussed in this chapter. Cognitive appraisal of the stress situation influences and is influenced by the stressor itself and the physical, social, and personal resources perceived by the person as available for dealing with it. The person, embodying a unique combination of physiological, psychological, and cultural characteristics, reacts to threat in various possible ways, including physiological, behavioral, emotional, and cognitive responses, some adaptive and some maladaptive or even lethal.

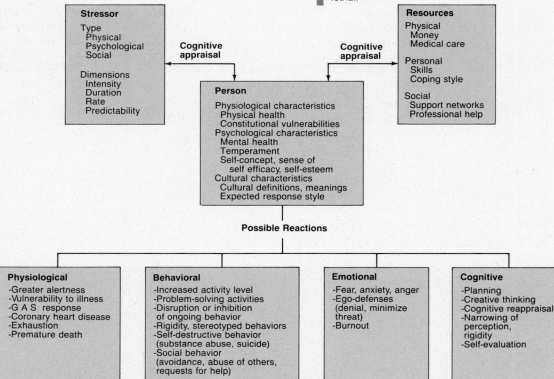

Stressor

Type
  Physical
  Psychological
  Social

Dimensions
  Intensity
  Duration
  Rate
  Predictability

Cognitive appraisal

Cognitive appraisal

Resources

Physical
  Money
  Medical care

Personal
  Skills
  Coping style

Social
  Support networks
  Professional help

Person

Physiological characteristics
  Physical health
  Constitutional vulnerabilities
Psychological characteristics
  Mental health
  Temperament
  Self-concept, sense of
    self efficacy, self-esteem
Cultural characteristics
  Cultural definitions, meanings
  Expected response style

Possible Reactions

Physiological
-Greater alertness
-Vulnerability to illness
-G A S response
-Coronary heart disease
-Exhaustion
-Premature death

Behavioral
-Increased activity level
-Problem-solving activities
-Disruption or inhibition
 of ongoing behavior
-Rigidity, stereotyped behaviors
-Self-destructive behavior
 (substance abuse, suicide)
-Social behavior
 (avoidance, abuse of others,
 requests for help)

Emotional
-Fear, anxiety, anger
-Ego-defenses
 (denial, minimize
 threat)
-Burnout

Cognitive
-Planning
-Creative thinking
-Cognitive reappraisal
-Narrowing of
 perception,
 rigidity
-Self-evaluation

SOURCES OF STRESS

Stress is a recurring problem. Naturally occurring changes are an unavoidable part of the lives of all of us. People close to us get sick, move away, die. We get a new job, leave home, start college, succeed, fail, begin a romance, get married, break up. In addition to the big life changes, there are also "life's little hassles"—such as frustrating traffic jams or a snoring roommate.

Also, unpredictable things keep happening. For some of us there will be traumatic experiences—the stress of natural disasters like earthquakes or floods or the unnatural disasters of war or violent abuse by others. And for some of us chronic societal problems will be an important source of stress. In this section we shall sample some of these contributors to the stress of our lives.

Major life stressors

Sudden changes in our life situation are at the core of stressful life events for many of us. They may make it harder for us to act effectively; sometimes they make us physically ill. Even events that we welcome may require major changes in our routines and adaptation to new requirements; this can be stressful.

The influence of major life changes on subsequent mental and physical health has been a source of considerable research. It started with the development of the Social Readjustment Rating Scale (SRRS), a simple scale for rating the degree of adjustment required by forty-three life changes that many people experience, including both pleasant and unpleasant changes (see **Table 13.1**). The scale was developed by having a large number of adults from all walks of life rate the amount of readjustment required for each change, as compared with marriage, which was arbitrarily assigned a value of 50 *life change units* (LCU). Researchers ask a subject to check off all the items that apply over a given past time period. They then calculate the total number of life change units the individual has undergone during that period, using it as a measure of the amount of stress the individual has experienced (Holmes & Rahe, 1967).

Many studies have found that life change intensity, as measured by this scale, rises significantly before the onset of an illness. Life stress has been related to sudden cardiac death, tuberculosis, multiple sclerosis, diabetes, complications of pregnancy and birth, chronic illness, and many minor physical problems. It is believed that life stress increases the person's overall susceptibility to illness (Holmes & Masuda, 1974). But illness is itself a major stressor. As expected, LCU values are also high during an illness and for some time thereafter (Rahe & Arthur, 1977).

An improvement in measuring the effects of life events is provided in the Life Experiences Survey (LES), which has two special features. First, it provides both positive and negative change scores, rather than negative only, as in the original scale. Second, its scores reflect individualized ratings of the impact or each event and its desirability to the person making the evaluation. For example, the death of a spouse who was not loved and left a big inheritance might be rated as quite desirable. Thus this scale goes beyond a mere count of remembered life change to measure the person's own perception (appraisal) of the personal significance of each change (Sarason et al., 1978).

One problem with studies relating stressful life events to subsequent illness is that they tend to be *retrospective*. That is, both the stress measures and the illness measures are obtained by looking back to recall prior events. This presents an opportunity for distortion in memory to bias the results. For example, subjects who are sick may be more likely to remember past stressors than subjects who are well. More recently, however, *prospective* (looking ahead) studies have had similar findings. Life change scores on the *LES* have been obtained, and negative scores have been found to be significantly correlated with physical symptoms reported six months *later* (Johnson & Sarason, 1979). The message again is clear—too many stressful life events are bad for your health.

Life's little hassles

Life is filled with low-level frustrations. Your pencil breaks during an exam, you get stuck in traffic, or you forget to set your alarm clock for an important appointment. To what extent do these minor irritations pile up to become stressors that play havoc with your health? The answer is: to a bigger extent than you might imagine.

Table 13.1 *The Social Readjustment Rating Scale*

Events	Scale of Impact	Events	Scale of Impact
Death of spouse	100	Son or daughter leaving home	29
Divorce	73	Trouble with in-laws	29
Marital separation	65	Outstanding personal achievement	28
Jail term	63	Spouse begins or stops work	26
Death of close family member	63	Begin or end school	26
Personal injury or illness	53	Change in living conditions	25
Marriage	50	Revision of personal habits	24
Fired at work	47	Trouble with boss	23
Marital reconciliation	45	Change in work hours or conditions	20
Retirement	45	Change in residence	20
Change in health of family member	44	Change in schools	20
Pregnancy	40	Change in recreation	19
Sex difficulties	39	Change in church activities	19
Gain in new family member	39	Change in social activities	18
Business readjustment	39	Taking out a mortgage or loan for a lesser purchase	17
Change in financial state	38		
Death of close friend	37	Change in sleeping habits	16
Change to different line of work	36	Change in number of family get-togethers	15
Change in number of arguments with spouse	35	Change in eating habits	15
Taking out a mortgage or loan for a major purchase	31	Vacation	13
		Christmas	12
Foreclosure of mortgage or loan	30	Violations of the law	11
Change in responsibilities at work	29		

(Holmes & Rahe, 1967)

A psychiatrist distributed one hundred questionnaires to the faithful waiting for the 7:12 A.M. "bullet" train from Long Island into Manhattan. From the forty-nine completed questionnaires returned, it was determined that these average commuters had just gulped down their breakfast in less than eleven minutes, if at all; were prepared to spend three hours each day in transit; and in ten years had logged about 7500 hours of rail time—assuming two-week vacations and no time off for illness. Two thirds of the commuters believed their family relations were impaired by their commuting. Fifty-nine percent experienced fatigue, 47 percent were filled with conscious anger, 28 percent were anxious, and others reported headaches, muscle pains, indigestion, and other symptoms of the long-term consequences of beating the rat race in the city by living in the country (Charatan, 1973).

In another study, when a group of 100 white, middle-class, middle-aged men and women kept track of their daily hassles over a one-year period (along with a record of major life changes and physical

▽ *Such "minor" daily frustrations as those we encounter driving to and from work can build up to the point where they interfere with our physical well-being.*

symptoms), a clear relationship emerged between hassles and health problems: the more frequent and intense the hassles people reported, the poorer was their health, both physical and mental (Lazarus, 1981).

This is only a correlational finding, however; the causal relationships are not clear.

Interpersonal conflicts, public humiliation, and threats to status or security are among the hassles that create acute psychological disturbance for many people. They can also affect physiological functioning.

In a study of 117 patients who had been admitted to a hospital for cardiac arrest and other heart malfunctions, it was found that 25—about a fifth—showed no structural heart disease but had experienced a sudden psychological disturbance within the 24 hours prior to their heart disturbance. Primarily the emotions of anger, fear, and emotional excitement had been aroused; in more than half of the cases, the stressful episode had happened only an hour before the onset of heart attack. One man had heart arrhythmias whenever his wife left the hospital after visiting him because he feared she would be attacked in the streets (Reich et al., 1981).

Again we see the close relationship between psychological and physiological processes.

Catastrophic events

Dining and dancing in a beautiful setting on a Friday evening sounds like a prescription for relieving the stress of a hard week of work. But it became instead a precription for a disaster, creating great stress, when two aerial walkways collapsed into the lobby of a hotel in Kansas City, Missouri, during a tea dance.

Immediately affected were the two thousand dancers and spectators, over three hundred of whom were killed or injured. Also experiencing stress were a thousand rescue workers, who worked more than ten hours just to get through the rubble to all the victims. Another five thousand people were less directly affected: workers at the hotel, personnel at hospitals in the area, and friends and families of victims (Gist & Stolz, 1982). No count could be made of those who were affected in the community and beyond, as people tried to deal with the senselessness of the event and the anxieties it created about the possibility of other such disasters elsewhere.

Research on the physical and psychological effects of catastrophic events has been prolific. However, it has followed a rather different research tradition from the one used in studies of personal stressors, and, there is no scale assessing the relative impact of different kinds of natural disasters.

Researchers have found that five stages occur predictably in people's responses to disasters:

Typically, there is a period of shock and even "psychic numbness," during which people cannot fully comprehend what has happened. The next phase involves what has been called "automatic action"; people try to respond to the disaster and may behave adaptively but with little awareness of their actions and poor later memory of the experience.

In the next stage, people often feel great accomplishment and even a positive sense of communal effort for a shared purpose. Also in this phase, people feel weary and are aware that they are using up their reserves of energy. During the next phase, they experience a letdown; their energy is depleted and the impact of the tragedy is finally comprehended and felt emotionally. An extended period of recovery follows, as people try to rebuild and to adapt to the changes brought about by the disaster (Cohen & Ahearn, 1980).

Knowledge of these typical stages in reactions in the past provides a model that is helpful in predicting people's reactions when disaster strikes, enabling rescue workers to anticipate and help victims deal with the problems that arise. Responses to such varied events as floods, tornadoes, airplane crashes, and factory explosions have all been shown to fit this model of disaster reactions.

The research leading to the development of this model also has helped to dispel the myth that at the onset of a disaster people will experience wild terror and engage in a mad, senseless rush to escape. In fact, such panic is rare: most people behave appropriately and rationally and deal as best they can with the situation (Chapman, 1962). In cases where mass panic does occur, three conditions are present: (a) people are aware of imminent danger; (b) they perceive that limited escape routes are available and will soon be blocked; and (c) there is no information about alternatives for dealing with the oncoming disaster.

Chronic societal sources of stress

What of environmental stressors that are part of the ongoing circumstances of life: overcrowding, economic recession, fear of nuclear war? What cumulative effect do such stressors have on us?

For today's children, the threat of nuclear war is a major source of stress. Studies of the nuclear fears of children since the mid 1960s have shown that children know and care about the threat of nuclear war and have a high degree of uncertainty about their own future. One of the early researchers, psychologist Sibyl Escalona, concluded, "The profound uncertainty about whether or not mankind has a foreseeable future exerts a corrosive and malignant influence upon important development processes in normal and well-functioning children." (Escalona, 1965). Although her survey did not refer to the bomb or nuclear war, 70 percent of the children sampled mentioned spontaneously that their future would include nuclear weapons and destructive war.

More recently psychiatrists William Beardslee and John Mack (1983) made a detailed analysis of the attitudes of 1000 students in several parts of the country. They found a general disquiet and uneasiness about the future, with many students deeply disturbed. Studies since have found a significant increase in the expression of fear, helplessness, and anger toward the adult generation, with many young people questioning whether it is worthwhile working hard to prepare for a future that they do not expect to have (Hanna, 1984; Yudkin, 1984).

Adults, too, are worried about nuclear disaster, but for many, problems of employment and and economic security are causes of more immediate anxiety. Many stress-related problems increase when the economy is in a downswing. Admission to mental hospitals, infant mortality, suicide, and deaths due to alcohol-related diseases and cardiovascular problems all increase (Brenner, 1976).

△ *Twentieth-century technology has brought new frustrations into the lives of many Americans. The threat of nuclear war looms large in the minds of children as well as adults throughout the country. And chemical contamination of the environment has forced the relocation of entire communities at the cost of great stress to individuals.*

In a recent study, unemployed men reported more symptoms, such as depression, anxiety, and worries about health than did those who were employed. Because these symptoms disappeared when they were subsequently reemployed, the researchers argued that the symptoms had been the results of being unemployed, rather than that more disturbed workers had been particularly likely to lose their jobs (Liem & Rayman, 1982).

The pollution of our environment creates stresses as well. The chemical miracles of our modern technology have led to unexpected contamination of whole areas where people have had to be evacuated, as at Love Canal, near Buffalo, and Times Beach, Missouri. In addition, class action suits have been brought against industries and government units on behalf of workers who believe their health problems are the result of exposure to toxic substances, such as asbestos and dioxin.

The malfunctioning and consequent release of radioactive steam at the Three Mile Island nuclear power plant in 1979 provided a dramatic example of an environmental stressor. Those living in the area experienced considerable stress from fears about the immediate and long-term health consequences. In addition, widespread stress was experienced by citizens in other parts of the country, worried about other possible nuclear accidents. One consequence of this nuclear accident was the Appeal Court's decision to recognize the *legal status* of psychological stress as a necessary part of the environmental impact survey that must be carried out before the plant could be reopened.

Such problems are not simply technological ones, but also political and psychological; thus better technology cannot solve them. This source of stress, as with the others considered in this section, arises out of our imperfect human capacity to solve all the problems of a complex society. Many modern day stressors will require solutions not at the individual level, but through cooperation within communities and even across nations.

VULNERABILITY AND RESISTANCE

No doubt you have observed that some people experience one stressful event after another and do not break down, while others are seriously upset by even low-level stress. This is because the effect of most stressors is not a direct one but is determined partly by other conditions. One of these we have already mentioned—our cognitive appraisal of the stressor and of our resources for dealing with it. This cognitive appraisal defines the situation for us, and it is our definition—rather than the stressor itself—that determines what we try to accomplish and what methods we see as appropriate. For example, the stressor of a threatened job loss may be appraised as a warning signal which, if met by more conscientious work and some apple-polishing, will probably go away. Or it may be appraised as a seal of doom, proving one to be a failure or proving the "system" to be unjust. Behavior undertaken after these appraisals will be very different.

So the variable of cognitive appraisal is the first of many **moderator variables**—varibles that *moderate* (change) the effect of a stressor. Another moderator variable in the case of the threatened job loss would be the presence or absence of unemployment compensation and other job opportunities. Still others would be the individual's financial and psychological resources and characteristic way of approaching difficult situations—whether with a chip on the shoulder or self-blame, for example. Moderator variables are all the conditions in the individual's functioning and in the situation that can change the effect of the stressor. Moderator variables help determine whether life stresses will have negative consequences and how negative the consequences will be. Here we will look at two classes of moderator variables—common coping strategies and supportive environments.

Common coping strategies

Coping means doing something about a situation that is seen as posing a problem. In this section we will concentrate primarily on techniques that many of us use naturally and habitually that we have learned without intentional analysis or planning.

When we turn later to the topic of managing stress, we will focus on some of the steps we can take deliberately to minimize stress and its damaging effects.

Dealing with problems or lessening discomfort. Coping strategies can be grouped into two main types, depending on whether the goal is to *deal with the problem* or to *lessen the discomfort of it*. Several subcategories of these two basic approaches are shown in **Table 13.2** (Lazarus, 1975).

The first main approach includes any strategy for dealing *directly* with the stressor, whether through overt action or through realistic problem-solving mental activities. We face up to the bully, or run away. Or we try to win him or her over with bribes or other incentives. Taking martial arts training or notifying the "proper authorities" are other approaches that may prevent the bully from continuing to be a threat.

In all these strategies, our focus is on the problem to be dealt with and on the agent that has induced the stress. The "call to action" is acknowledged, the situation and our resources for dealing with it are appraised, and a response is undertaken that we think is appropriate for removing or lessening the threat.

In the second approach, we do not look for ways of changing the stressful situation; instead we try to change our feelings and thoughts about it. This coping strategy is called *emotion regulation*. It is a palliative rather than a problem-solving strategy because it is aimed at relieving the emotional impact of stress to make us feel better, even though the threatening or harmful stressor is not changed.

Relying on this approach, a person may take alcohol or tranquilizers to take the threat out of a stressor—and it may work for a while. On occasion, haven't you dealt with an unpleasant event by using consciously planned distractions such as going to a movie, watching TV, or seeking out a friend for emotional support (rather than advice on how to deal with the stress)? Sometimes, we confront a feared demon in heroic fantasies by "whistling a happy tune" or with laughter (see **Close-up,** p. 477).

When people reported on how they would appraise a variety of stressful situations and what coping strategies they would use in each case, four general strategies were found: (a) changing the situation; (b) seeking more information before acting; (c) accepting it as it was, and (d) holding back from what one wanted to do. The first two are active strategies aimed at solving the problem; the last two are passive forms of self-restraint that can only change the discomfort (Folkman & Lazarus, 1980).

In other research, comparing depressed and nondepressed middle-aged people over a one-year period, it was found that those who were depressed were using appraisals and coping patterns that created problems and perpetuated their depression. They were just as likely as the nondepressed to feel that something *could* be done about the situations they faced and even to focus on problem solutions. But they diverged in their tendency to accentuate

Table 13.2 *Taxonomy of Coping Strategies*

Change stressor or one's relationship to it through direct actions and/or problem-solving activities.	Fight (destroy, remove, or weaken the threat)
	Flight (distance oneself from the threat)
	Seek options to fight or flight (negotiating, bargaining, compromising)
	Prevent future stress (act to increase one's resistance or decrease strength of anticipated stress).
Change self through "activities" that make one feel better but do not change the stressor.	Somatically focused activities (use of drugs, relaxation, biofeedback)
	Cognitively focused activities (planned distractions, fantasies, thoughts about oneself)
	Unconscious processes that distort reality and result in intrapsychic stress.

(Lazarus, 1975)

It's Not So Stressful When I Laugh

For decades the *Reader's Digest* has carried a feature of jokes entitled "Laughter, the Best Medicine." Is it? What is the relationship between laughter and stress? There are several lines of evidence to suggest that humor is used by children to handle stressful home life; that professional comedians and comedy writers tend to come from family backgrounds filled with tension, and that laughter may be good therapy for certain kinds of illness.

A longitudinal study examined the development of humor in young children during the first six years of their lives.

The elementary-school age children who laughed most were those who had been exposed to "tough and potentially hazardous situations" and whose mothers had withheld help in solving problems. In contrast, children who had been "babied" and protected from conflict had a less developed sense of humor (McGhee, 1979).

This finding supports the view of Freud (1905/1960) that humor may develop as a means of coping with stressful situations or anxiety-arousing circumstances.

Humor as a "coping mechanism" is revealed in two studies in which professional comedians and comedy writers were interviewed. Most professional humorists tended to be funny as children and continued this style of relating to people into adulthood (Fry & Allen, 1975). Their childhood typically showed a pattern of early stress and poor home adjustment. Their early lives were "marked by suffering, isolation, and feelings of deprivation. Humor offered a relief from their sufferings and a defense against inescapable panic and anxiety" (Janus, 1975, p. 174).

Carol Burnett, for example, had parents who were both alcoholics and fought frequently. She describes using humor as a way of gaining strength rather than "buckling under" in her tension-filled home. Humor created a playful state of mind for her as a child, deflected her attention away from its source onto the role of child-as-comedian, and dissipated some of the hostile feelings.

If a stressful childhood can promote the development of humor, maybe laughter can work to reduce adult stress. Norman Cousins, former editor of *The*

Saturday Review, used such reasoning to help himself recover from a serious illness. He was hospitalized for a rare disease of the connective tissue, which is crippling and from which he was told he would not recover. Working with a cooperative physician, he checked out of the hospital and into a hotel room where for several months he supplemented massive injections of ascorbic acid (vitamin C) with a steady diet of old Candid Camera films and other belly-laugh-inducing movies. He completely recovered from his "incurable illness."

Fifteen years later, a high-pressure schedule of travel, speaking, and deadlines led to a heart attack and a diagnosis of damaged heart muscle and congested coronary arteries. Cousins was able to avoid a by-pass operation by again confidently taking charge of his own recovery. Following a regimen of diet, gradually increasing exercise, writing, amateur photography, and *humor,* he was able to resume full-time work less than a year after his attack (Cousins, 1979, 1983).

△ ▮ *Norman Cousins*

the negative. They worried more about not being stronger, *wished* they could change themselves and/or the situation, kept putting off action pending more information, and spent more time seeking emotional support for their feelings of distress. What emerged was an indecisive coping style that was likely to promote a sense of personal inadequacy—which in turn was a source of more depression (Coyne et al., 1981).

The ego defense mechanisms discussed in Chapter 11 are familiar emotion-regulating approaches. Undertaken unconsciously to protect us from the pain of inner anxieties, they enable us to appraise the situation in less self-threatening ways. They lead to coping strategies that are essentially aimed at self-protection rather than at solving the problem.

Some executives who face high levels of life stress develop physical illnesses (even within a three-year period), while others in similar circumstances do not. Why the difference?

One investigation found that stress-resistant "hardy" executives differed from the vulnerable ones in their: (a) strong commitment to self; (b) attitude of vigorousness toward the environment; and (c) sense of internal locus of control. Those who did not become ill perceived that they controlled significant outcomes, whereas those who became ill tended to perceive external forces as being in control (Kobasa et al., 1982).

Differing responses to the same stressor by different people, then, are the rule rather than the exception, as a result of moderating personality variables. These personality variables include both learned coping styles and biological predispositions to respond in a certain way. Here we will look at an example of each.

The Type-A behavior pattern. Some years ago two medical researchers identified a style of coping with stress called the **Type-A behavior pattern** that puts one at risk for coronary heart disease. People who show this pattern are always in a hurry, unable to relax, and abrupt in their speech and gestures, frequently interrupting to finish what someone else is saying. They are highly competitive, insist on "going it alone," strive intensely for achievement, show a high level of drive and hostility, and engage in compulsive activity. Some of these characteristics are val-

ued in our society, but this is a very *dysfunctional* coping style. Type-A businessmen, for example, are stricken with coronary heart disease more than twice as often as men in the general population (Friedman & Rosenman, 1974; Jenkins, 1976). In fact, many studies, including comprehensive *prospective* studies, have shown that people manifesting the Type-A behavior pattern are at significantly greater risk for all forms of cardiovascular disease (Dembroski et al., 1978; Haynes & Feinleib, 1980).

Do the personalities of these Type-A people direct them toward competitive social and work environments, or does functioning in such settings promote the coronary-prone behavior pattern? The available evidence puts the blame on cultural and socioeconomic pressures for inducing this coping style. For example, the Type-A behavior pattern is much rarer in nonindustrial societies. One survey of this evidence concludes that it is the social pressures "related to the roles of men in our society that push them to develop the coronary-prone behavior pattern, and [that] this makes a major contribution to men's higher risk of coronary heart disease" (Waldron, 1976, p. 8). Unfortunately, Type-A behavior patterns are now being seen among college and high school students and even among children in grade school (Thoresen & Eagleston, 1983).

Men have been much more likely to develop the Type-A behavior pattern than women, evidently because the society has encouraged and reinforced those traits as essential for success in a competitive business enterprise. Alas, as more women enter top-level business positions, we are seeing more female Type-A behavior emerging, though twice as many Type-A men under fifty currently have coronary heart disease as do Type-A women of similar age. By contrast, among people who are clearly *not* Type-A, the chances of such disease are equally low in both sexes. Thus men and women who adopt a less competitive, less intense life-style have a better chance of avoiding coronary heart disease.

It has long been known that men, as a group, die younger than women in our society. An analysis of the causes of death that contribute most to this sex differential shows clearly that the responsible agent is *behavior*—not genetic factors. Biologist Ingrid Waldron (1976) concludes that "each of these causes of death is linked to behaviors which are encouraged or accepted more in males than in females: using guns, drinking alcohol, smoking, working at hazardous jobs, and seeming to be fearless. Thus, the behaviors of males in our society make a major contri-

△ *While Type-A behavior patterns have traditionally been seen in men, they are becoming more and more typical of women who are entering highly competitive career paths.*

bution to their elevated mortality'' (p. 2). The choice to live a high-pressured life has both behavioral and medical consequences.

The Gamma temperament. **Temperament** is a dispositional tendency, a biological endowment you are born with that does not change much over time. It influences your characteristic behavioral style and how emotionally responsive you tend to be. It is one determinant of your characteristic intensity, tempo, and energy level.

Temperament styles in youth have been shown to be related to incidence of major psychological and physical disorders later in life.

Over 1300 medical students from Johns Hopkins University (starting with classes in 1948) were studied over a thirty-year period. At the beginning they were given a battery of psychological tests and medical evaluations, and every year thereafter they submitted full medical reports. From the original testing, three subgroups were identified on the basis of characteristics of temperament:

Alphas: (Slow/Solid) Cautious, steady, self-reliant, slower to adapt, nonadventurous (about 20 percent of the group).

Betas: (Rapid/Facile) Lively, spontaneous, clever, flexible (about 30 percent of the group).

Gammas: (Irregular/Uneven) Often brilliant but confused, sometimes overcautious and sometimes impulsive, sometimes overly modest and sometimes tyrannical (about half the group).

Medical records showed that the moody Gammas fared the worst of the three types. During the thirty-year period, over three fourths of the Gammas suffered a serious illness, while only one fourth of the Alphas or Betas did. Gammas were the most likely to have major cancer (in contrast to skin cancer or other less serious forms) or blockage of heart functions. More of them also died prematurely (Betz & Thomas, 1979).

Such correlations between temperament and illness are possible because temperament is a powerful influence on one's most natural behavioral style. But because it is only *one* of the determinants of behavior, there is no reason for a ''natural'' Gamma to be trapped forever in an unproductive behavioral style.

Supportiveness of the environment

''Life in societies is the most powerful weapon in the struggle for life. . . . Thus it was that thousands of years before man appeared, association [of animals in social units] was preparing the way for human society'' (Chapin, 1913, p. 103).

We all cope with stress as individuals, but for a lifetime of effective coping and for the continued success of our species, it is necessary for us to band together with our family, friends, and neighbors (at home and throughout our small planet). *Isolation* can lead to inadequate coping, and is itself the cause of much stress. Much contemporary research points to the improvement in coping that can come from being part of a social support network and from living and working in a healthy environment.

Social support networks. Most critical life events involve a disruption of a social network, of the interpersonal relationship between the stressed individual and one or more important other people. To the extent that a person is socially isolated (not part of a supportive social network of family, friends, coworkers or neighbors) that person is ''at risk'' for a variety of adverse effects.

A large-scale study investigated the relation between death rate and the stress moderator variable of *absence of a social support system*.

Nearly seven thousand adults were surveyed in 1965 to determine their health and health-related behaviors, as well as other background factors and the extent of their social relationships. From this information a *social network index* was computed for each person, based on the number and importance of social contacts in the person's life. Mortality (death rate) data were then collected for a nine-year period on 96 percent of this original sample.

The social network index was significantly correlated with overall death rate and also with cause of death. For every age group and both sexes, there were more deaths among people who had few social contacts than among those with many connections. This effect was independent of their health status at the time of the initial survey and independent of their socioeconomic status. Furthermore, those who were socially isolated had been more likely to engage in poor health behaviors (smoking, drinking, overeating, irregular eating, inadequate sleep). But the extent of their social contacts still predicted their mortality over and above the effects of any or all of these poor health practices. In fact, most of the deaths occurred among those who lacked social and community ties. It is clear that lack of a social support system increases one's vulnerability to disease and death (Berkman, 1977; Berkman & Syme, 1979).

Other studies have found that both humans and animals with little social support are less able to cope with stressors (Nerem et al., 1980). Socially uncon- nected people engage in more maladaptive ways of thinking and behaving than do those who share their concerns with other people (Silberfeld, 1978). And *decreases* in social support in family and work environments are related to *increases* in psychological maladjustment. This negative relationship was found even when the researchers looked at groups who had had the same *initial* levels of support, maladjustment, and life change (Holohan & Moos, 1981).

By contrast, there is now a sizable body of evidence to support the conclusion that the moderator variable of social support makes people *less* vulnerable to stress. When people have friends they can talk to, seek advice from, and get sympathy from, they are better able to handle job stresses, unemployment, marital disruption, serious illness, and other catastrophes as well as their everyday problems of living (Pilisuk, 1982; Gottlieb, 1981).

Structure of the physical environment. The quality of the physical environment can add to stress or help reduce it, as well as influence the coping strategies people use. In a study of residential care programs for the elderly, more cohesive, supportive groups developed where the environment provided such simple amenities as lounges and seating arrangements that were well-grouped for conversation (Moos & Lemke, 1984).

Likewise, the physical structure of a college dormitory influences the social climate among the students.

In one study residents in dormitories with long corridors with many rooms along them had more difficulty developing a social support network than residents in dormitories with short corridors. The smaller areas helped define small friendship groups, while the extended areas created a greater sense of impersonality (Baum & Valins, 1979).

◁ *A social support network of caring individuals is an important part of a healthy environment.*

When the long-corridor students felt that their living conditions were crowded, they developed coping patterns for dealing with conflict situations that differed from the patterns developed by those living in short-corridor dormitories. On an experimental task in which it is possible either to cooperate or to compete, the short-corridor residents tended to be more cooperative. The long-corridor students tended to be either more competitive or more likely to withdraw (Baum et al., 1982).

In appraising your environment, you may define social and psychological dimensions that are more important to you than the physical dimension. These social and psychological dimensions can be critically important in increasing or decreasing stress. For example, your perception of freedom of choice to enter a particular environment or not to do so may determine whether your adaptation to it will be successful or will fail. As we saw in Chapter 1, women who chose to go into a retirement home lived longer, as a group, than those who entered feeling they had no choice (Ferrare, 1962).

Policies and programs in an institutional setting can also increase or decrease stress for the residents and hinder or help their attempts to cope. Residential programs for elders that encourage autonomy and group cohesiveness not only increase the residents' participation in community activities but reduce their need for health care services. Moreover, when they have minor tasks like watering plants and are allowed to make some personal decisions, the elderly come to have a greater sense of personal control in handling the stressors in their lives. The effect: lower mortality rates (Rodin, 1980).

These are only samples of the studies that are establishing strong links between the quality of our physical-social environments and our physical and mental health. For too many of us, the urban settings we live in are too noisy, too crowded, too fast-paced, too unpredictable—in short, too stressful (Glass & Singer, 1972). Like the harried professor in our *Opening Case,* we are constantly coping with a succession of frustrating, stressful events—too often in ways that increase our stress still further. We need to give more thought to changing our unhealthy, stress-inducing *environments,* as a complement to developing more effective and satisfying behavior patterns.

MANAGING STRESS BETTER

If living is inevitably stressful, and if too much stress can disrupt our lives and even kill us in the prime of life, we need to learn to manage stress effectively if we are to survive and thrive. We can learn to prevent and avoid some stressful episodes, to "inoculate" ourselves against the effects of stressors we can anticipate, and to cope better with whatever undesirable threats and harms come our way.

Because animals of the wild must adapt biologically to their environment, their mechanisms for coping are coded in their genes and limited by the slow timetable of evolutionary processes. Human beings have a tremendous potential for adapting not only biologically, over generations, but psychologically, within a lifetime—even within a short period of time if we decide we want to change.

In this final section of the chapter we will look at a collection of techniques that people can learn for reducing the amount of stress they experience and lessening its harmful effects. We will look at two approaches that involve altering physiological responding and two that involve modifying how we think about stressful situations. We will also look at some ways we can lessen stress by choosing environments and activities that make us less vulnerable and make damaging stress less likely.

Altering bodily reactions

"Stress equals tension" for many people. This often means tight muscles, high blood pressure, constricted blood vessels in the brain, and chronic oversecretion of hormones. Fortunately, many of these tension responses can be controlled by a variety of techniques—some ages old, some quite new.

Relaxation and meditation. Relaxation through meditation has ancient roots in many parts of the world. For centuries in Eastern cultures, ways to calm the mind and still the body's tensions have been practiced. Today Zen discipline and Yoga exercises from Japan and India are part of daily life for many people both there and, increasingly, in the West. In our own culture, a growing number of people have been attracted to workshops and therapy in relaxation training and to various forms of meditation.

Just as stress is the nonspecific response of the body to any demand made on it, there is growing evidence that complete relaxation is a potent anti-stress response. The *relaxation response* is a condition in which muscle tension, cortical activity, and heart rate and blood pressure all decrease and breathing slows. There is reduced electrical activity in the brain, and input to the central nervous system from the outside environment is lowered. In this low level of arousal, recuperation from stress can take place.

Four conditions are regarded as necessary for producing the relaxation response: (a) a quiet environment, (b) closed eyes, (c) a comfortable position, and (d) a repetitive mental device. The first three lower input to the nervous system, while the fourth lowers its internal stimulation (Benson, 1975).

Progressive relaxation is a technique that has been widely used in American psychotherapy. Designed by Edmund Jacobson (1970), the approach teaches people to alternately tense and relax their muscles. In this way they learn the experience of relaxation, and how to extend it to each specific muscle. After several months of daily practice with progressive relaxation, people are able to achieve deep levels of relaxation. The relaxation response can also be produced by hypnosis.

The beneficial effects of these relaxation training methods extend beyond the time when the person is actively practicing them. For example, in one study hypertensive patients who learned to lower their blood pressure by relaxing continued to have lower blood pressure when they were asleep (Agras et al., 1980). In Chapter 16 we will see how relaxation training is used in desensitization therapy.

The requirements of the relaxation response are met by most traditional and religious techniques of meditation and prayer. In addition to whatever spiritual function they may serve, such techniques directly ease physical and psychological stress.

A recent form of meditation *not* based on religious belief is called *Transcendental Meditation,* or TM. One simply sits comfortably with closed eyes, and engages in effortless mental repetition of a special sound for short periods of time (usually twenty minutes twice daily). The benefits claimed for TM by its advocates include improved learning performance; lessened anxiety, hostility, and aggression; and improved therapeutic progress among mental patients, prisoners, and drug abusers (Schwartz, 1974; Kanellakos & Ferguson, 1973).

△ ▍ *Meditation is a widely practiced stress-management technique.*

However, a recent, thorough review of published experimental evidence found *no* support for the conclusion that somatic arousal is lower in meditating subjects than in resting ones. Nor was there any support for the widely held belief that those who meditate have reduced somatic responses to stressful situations (Holmes, 1984). This seems to be an instance in which poorly controlled earlier research led to a false conclusion.

Biofeedback. As we saw in Chapter 10, feedback is essential in the learning of a new action. Feedback serves three functions: (a) *reinforcing,* providing negative or positive consequences for errors or correct responses; (b) *informational,* providing the knowledge needed for correcting errors; and (c) *motivational,* providing encouragement to continue the effort.

Biological feedback, or *biofeedback,* was described briefly in Chapter 7. Sophisticated recording devices and computers make it possible to provide this feedback by detecting small changes in a body process, amplifying them, and indicating they are present by means of a visual or auditory signal which is "on" whenever the change is occurring. Paradoxically, though the individual does not know how he or she does it, concentrating on the desired result in the presence of this signal produces change in the desired direction.

Biofeedback is being used for a variety of special applications, such as control of blood pressure, relaxation of forehead muscles (involved in tension headaches), and even overcoming extreme blushing. It is also being used for inducing nonspecific general relaxation.

For example, one way the body reacts to stress is through changes in the skin's electrical conductivity. This is the **galvanic skin response (GSR);** it is the basis of lie-detector tests and reflects emotional changes that are controlled by the sympathetic nervous system. It is measured by passing a small electrical current across the palm of the hand. When you are calm, your skin resistance is high; when you begin to tense up, your skin resistance decreases. When these small changes in resistance are transformed into sound and amplified, you can hear immediately how tense you are at a given moment. As you relax mentally, changes in sound tell you that your body is becoming less tense.

If you are wondering about the inexpensive do-it-yourself biofeedback devices now being marketed, it would be wise to exercise caution and skepticism. It is unlikely that the average person can alter bodily processes to any substantial degree using a cheap device and working without proper training. In addition, it is dangerous to rely solely on biofeedback technology to put your brain and body back into normal working condition without making any changes in your habits and life-style. We have all become too intolerant of pain and anxiety and too eager to reach for the quick and easy solution—even though we know intellectually that happiness is not going to come commercially prepackaged.

Modifying cognitive strategies

A powerful way of handling stress more adaptively is to change our evaluations of stressors and our self-defeating cognitions about how we are dealing with them.

Reappraising stressors. The close connection between cognitive appraisal and the degree of autonomic nervous system arousal has been demonstrated in studies where the cognitive appraisal was systematically varied.

When subjects watched an upsetting film showing vivid circumcision rites in a primitive tribe, they were *less* physiologically aroused when the film had a sound track that either *denied* the dangers or discussed them in an *intellectual,* detached way (Speisman et al., 1964).

In another study, subjects viewing a film of an industrial accident were less aroused if they were "emotionally inoculated" by being warned in advance that it was coming and given a chance to imagine the threatening scenes beforehand. As shown in **Figure 13.3** this cognitive preparation, which gave them an opportunity to rehearse mentally both the stressful episode and their coping responses to it, was more successful than relaxation training in lowering arousal (Folkins et al., 1968).

▽ | **Figure 13.3**

Stress induced by highly arousing films can be lowered to some extent by relaxation training. "Emotional inoculation" through cognitive rehearsal of the stressful scenes lowers the stress response even more. (Adapted from Folkins et al., 1968)

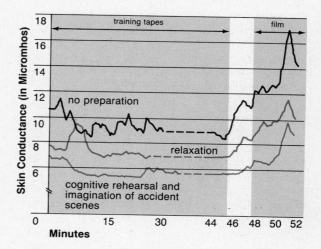

Learning to think differently about certain stressors, to relabel them, or to imagine them in a less threatening (perhaps even funny) context are forms of cognitive reappraisal that can reduce stress.

Encouraging results have been reported in an ongoing five-year program to change the cognitions and coping patterns in 1000 Type-A subjects who had suffered heart attacks. Treatment has included cognitive, behavioral, and social retraining as well as discussion of the biochemical consequences of anger, irritation, and impatience. Although not all subjects are showing clearcut changes in their stress-related behavior, the researchers report success in the most important measure—a lower rate of recurrence of heart attack than for control groups (Thoresen et al., 1981).

Restructuring cognitions. Another way of managing stress better is intentionally changing what we are telling ourselves about stress and about our handling of it. Such messages can lead to both cognitive restructuring and more effective coping. For example, depressed or insecure people often tell themselves that they are no good, that they'll do poorly, and—if something goes well—that it was a fluke.

Meichenbaum (1977) has proposed a three-phase process of intentionally changing this self-fulfilling cycle. In Phase 1, the person works to develop a greater awareness of his or her actual behavior, what instigates it, and what its results are. One of the best ways of doing this is to keep a daily log. By helping the person redefine his or her problems in terms of what causes and maintains them, this self-monitoring can increase the person's feelings of control.

In Phase 2, the individual begins to imagine and start new behaviors that are incompatible with the maladaptive, self-defeating behaviors—perhaps smiling at someone, offering a compliment, or acting assertively.

In Phase 3, after adaptive behaviors are being emitted, the person appraises their consequences, avoiding the former internal dialogue of put-downs. Instead of telling himself "I did it, I got the date, but she was probably so desperate she would have gone out with anyone," a man will say, "I got the date because I asked for it in an effective way and because she probably thinks I'm an interesting person."

In sum, this approach means initiating responses and self-statements that are incompatible with previous defeatist cognitions. The person realizes that he or she is changing and takes full credit for it—which promotes further successes.

Table 13.3 gives examples of the new kinds of self-statements that help at different stages in dealing with stressful situations. Such cognitive restructuring is an important part of many current therapy programs for overcoming maladaptive coping patterns, but individuals do not have to be in therapy to use these techniques.

▽ *All too often, the things we tell ourselves about our own behavior encourage us to "live in the past," as Cathy is doing here. But, as Meichenbaum points out, we can learn to send ourselves messages that will help us behave more effectively in the future.*

Table 13.3 *Examples of Coping Self-statements*

Preparation
I can develop a plan to deal with it.
Just think about what I can do about it. That's better than getting anxious.
No negative self-statements, just think rationally.

Confrontation
One step at a time; I can handle this situation.
This anxiety is what the doctor said I would feel; it's a reminder to use my coping exercises.
Relax; I'm in control. Take a slow deep breath. Ah, good.

Coping
When fear comes just pause.
Keep focus on the present; what is it I have to do?
Don't try to eliminate fear totally; just keep it manageable.
It's not the worst thing that can happen.
Just think about something else.

Self-reinforcement
It worked; I was able to do it.
It wasn't as bad as I expected.
I'm really pleased with the progress I'm making.

(Adapted from Meichenbaum, 1975)

Stress control and your mental health

The harried professor in our *Opening Case* experienced stress piled upon stress. But many choices he had made contributed to his stress level—to eat poorly, to live in an overcrowded, noisy city, to own a car, to work at a competitive job, to spend more than he earned. What choices are *you* making? Are they producing stresses that are damaging to your health and well-being?

Managing stress is not just something researchers study. Instead of waiting for stress or illness to come and then reacting to it, we need to set goals and structure our lives and life-styles in ways most likely to bring us what we really want. The following ideas are presented as guidelines to encourage you to adopt a more active role in taking charge of your own life and in creating a more positive psychological environment for yourself and others.

1. Look for the causes of your behavior in the current situation or in its relation to past situations, and *not* just in some defect in yourself. Understand the *context* of your behavior.

2. Compare your reactions, thoughts, and feelings with those of other comparable individuals in your current life environment to help gauge appropriateness and relevance of your responses.

3. Have several close friends with whom you can share feelings, joys, and worries. Work at developing, maintaining, and expanding your social support networks.

4. Don't be afraid to risk showing others that you want to be their friend or even to give and accept love. Don't let rejection deter you from trying again—after "cleaning up your act."

5. Never say bad things about yourself, especially never attribute to yourself irreversible, chronic, negative traits—such as "stupid," "ugly," "uncreative," "a failure." Look for sources of your unhappiness in elements that can be modified. Make your self-criticism constructive—what can you do differently next time to get what you want?

6. Always take full credit for your successes and happiness (and share your positive feeling with other people).

7. Keep an inventory of all the things that make you special and unique, those qualities you have to offer to others. For example, a shy person can offer a talkative person the gift of being an attentive listener. Know your sources of personal strength, and the coping resources available to you.

8. When you feel you are losing control over your emotions (hyperexcited or depressed), distance yourself from the situation you are in by: (a) physically leaving it; (b) role-playing the position of some other person in the situation or conflict; (c) projecting your imagination into the future to gain temporal perspective on what seems like an overwhelming problem here and now; or (d) talking to someone who is sympathetic.

9. Don't dwell on past misfortunes or sources of guilt, shame, and failure. The past is gone and only thinking about it keeps it alive in memory. Nothing you have said or done is new under the sun.

10. Remember that failure and disappointment are sometimes blessings in disguise, telling you that your goals are not right for you or saving you from bigger letdowns later on. Learn from every failure experience.

11. If you see someone you think is troubled, intervene in a concerned, gentle way to find out if anything is wrong and if you can help or get help. Often listening to a friend's troubles is all the therapy

needed, if it comes soon enough. Don't isolate the "stranger," be tolerant of deviance—but of course respect your own need for personal safety as well.

12. If you discover you cannot help yourself or the other person in distress, seek the counsel of a trained specialist in your student health department. In some cases a problem that appears to be a psychological one may really be physical, as with glandular conditions.

13. Assume that anyone could be helped by an opportunity to discuss his or her problems openly with a mental health specialist; therefore, if you do go to one, there is no need to feel stigmatized.

14. Develop long-range goals, think about what you want to be doing five, ten, twenty years from now and about alternative ways of getting there. Always try to enjoy the process of getting there too; "travel hopefully" and you will arrive eventually and more fulfilled.

15. Take time to relax, to meditate, to enjoy hobbies and activities that you can do alone and by means of which you can get in touch with yourself.

16. Think of yourself not as a passive object to which bad things just happen, but as an active agent who at any time can change the direction of your entire life. You are what you chose to be and you are seen by others in terms of what you choose to show them.

17. Remember that as long as there's life, there's hope for a better life, and as long as we care for one another, our lives will get better.

SUMMARY

■ Stress is the pattern of reactions an organism makes in response to stressors, stimulus events that tax its ability to cope.

■ Cognitive appraisal defines the demand: primary appraisal determines whether the demand is stressful, while secondary appraisal evaluates what personal and social resources are available and what action is called for. In chronic stress, demands over time are perceived as greater than resources.

■ Physiological stress reactions are automatic mechanisms facilitating swift emergency action. They are regulated by the hypothalamus and include many emergency body changes, carried out through the action of the autonomic nervous system and the pituitary gland. They lessen sensitivity to pain and provide extra energy for fight or flight. They are useful in combating physical stressors but can be maladaptive in response to psychological stressors, especially when stress is severe or chronic.

■ The general adaptation syndrome is a three-stage pattern of physiological defenses against continuing stressors that threaten internal well-being. Following the alarm reaction, there is a period of stabilization of a high level of physiological defense in a stage of resistance, until adaptive resources fail in the stage of exhaustion.

■ Psychosomatic diseases are physical diseases caused by chronic physiological stress reactions to perceived threat. Other diseases of adaptation occur when normal adaptive responses become excessive or are inappropriate to the situation. The "wear and tear" on the body brought about by continuing responses to stress is considered to be a factor in aging.

■ Psychological stress reactions include behavioral, emotional, and cognitive elements. Mild stress can enhance performance and even be experienced as pleasant (eustress). Moderate stress disrupts behavior and may lead to repetitive, stereotyped actions. Severe stress suppresses behavior. Behavioral stress reactions include overeating and aggression.

■ Emotional stress reactions include irritation, anger, depression, and burnout. Posttraumatic stress disorders are emotional stress reactions that follow acutely stressful experiences, sometimes occurring months or years after the experience and including many behavioral and physiological as well as emotional symptoms.

■ Cognitive stress reactions include a narrowing of attention; rigidity of thought; and interference with judgment, problem solving, and memory.

■ Psychological stressors are more common than physical stressors for most of us. Major life changes, even pleasant ones, can be stressful, as can the accumulation of everyday "hassles." Catastrophic events can be sources of severe stress, as can long-term environmental problems.

■ We do not react directly to a stressor but to our perception and interpretation of it; thus our cognitive appraisal is a moderator variable: it moderates (changes) the effect of the stressor. Other moderator variables are our inner and outer resources for dealing with the stressor and our attitudes and coping patterns. All these conditions help determine our vulnerability.

■ Two basic coping strategies for dealing with perceived threat are: (a) to deal with the problem itself in some way, and (b) to lessen the discomfort and anxiety we are feeling. The first leads to threat reduction and better coping skills; the second to greater anxiety, maladaptive defenses such as excessive drinking; dependence on others, overuse of ego defense mechanisms, and perhaps mental or physical illness.

■ Type-A behavior is a competitive, hard-driving, hostile coping style associated with high risk for coronary heart disease. Most common in men, it is now being seen more in women and even in adolescents and children.

■ Temperament is a factor in stress reactions: people diagnosed as showing Gamma temperament, characterized by unevenness, are three times as likely to have major illness as those described as slow/solid or rapid/facile.

■ Those most vulnerable to stress are individuals who lack a social support network and are in life situations in which they feel they have no control.

■ We can learn to manage stress better through (a) changing health-threatening physiological reactions (as in relaxation and biofeedback), (b) changing our cognitive strategies, and (c) choosing our life-style.

14

ABNORMAL PSYCHOLOGY

■ THE PROBLEM OF MENTAL DISORDERS

■ CLASSIFYING MENTAL DISORDERS
What is abnormal?
DSM-III

■ MAJOR TYPES OF MENTAL DISORDER
Personality disorders
Anxiety disorders
Somatoform disorders
Dissociative disorders
Psychosexual disorders
Affective disorders
Paranoid disorders
Schizophrenic disorders

■ UNDERSTANDING MENTAL DISORDERS
Major models of mental disorder
Using the models to make sense of schizophrenia
Making judgments about individuals

■ SUMMARY

Jane is a 63-year-old woman who has been married for forty years. Her husband, a very successful businessman, seems devoted to her. But Jane has been very upset for the last few years. She has trouble getting out of bed in the morning, and trouble getting to sleep at night. She has stopped doing any housework and sometimes doesn't even get dressed during the day. She feels guilty about this, but just "can't get going." Nothing seems interesting or pleasant to her, and lately, she doesn't even feel like eating. She has another problem, too: she can't leave the house alone. If her husband or a friend is with her, she is fine. But when alone, she worries constantly that she'll leave the gas on or water running and cause a terrible accident. She repeatedly checks the house to make sure that everything is turned off, but when it comes time to leave, she has become too anxious to walk out the door. If someone else is with her, she trusts their report that everything will be okay, but she can't trust herself.

Sam is a 20-year-old college student. Lately he has been feeling fantastic. He has so much energy that he almost never needs to sleep, and he is completely confident that he is the top student at his school. He is bothered that everyone else seems so slow; they don't seem to understand the brilliance of his monologues and no one seems able to keep up his pace. Sam has some exciting financial ideas and can't figure out why his friends aren't writing checks to get in on his schemes. He has been having problems lately with his bank, which is foolishly insisting that he not overdraw his account. They lack the visionary wisdom, he is sure, to comprehend his financial wizardry, but their nervous concerns shouldn't be allowed to hold him back. Sam's other problem is that he is failing several of his courses, but he knows that is only because his professors are too dull to appreciate his brilliant contributions and too rigid about expecting papers in on certain deadlines. Sam knows that he is just fine; his euphoria is not dimmed at all by the fact that his friends are withdrawing, his bank credit rating is sinking, and he is flunking out of school.

Ellen is a 28-year-old woman who has worked very hard to create a niche for herself in a highly competitive company. She lives in Los Angeles, far from her family and most of her friends. Ellen doesn't have time to make new friends, and besides, she's not sure if she can really trust any of the people she meets through her work. Ellen is ambitious and she's doing well, but at least once a week she experiences intense anxiety. Her heart pounds fast, she has trouble breathing, and she feels dizzy and unsteady. At the same time, she feels unreal, as if this couldn't really be happening. At these times, Ellen is terrified that she might be going crazy and worries about whether she might do something bizarre and uncontrollable during such an attack. The attacks usually occur on weekends, when she is alone and has no plans. Lately she worries a lot about what would happen if she ever had such an attack at work. What would people think? What would happen to her hard-won career?

What is happening to these people? In everyday language, such psychological problems might be referred to as "nervous breakdowns." Psychologists and other mental health workers, however, do not use this term, because it is too vague to be of any value. Psychologists want to examine and understand both the similarities and the differences between the psychological problems that afflict so many people in so many ways. One obvious reason to seek knowledge about these disorders of mind and behavior is to use it in the design of treatments to alleviate the problems. In the next chapter we will examine a number of therapeutic approaches that have been developed to treat or prevent these disorders.

Here our concern is to learn first what these disorders of thought, feeling, and action are. We want to know how they are diagnosed and classified by clinical psychologists and psychiatrists. Having surveyed a wide variety of the major categories of such disturbances, we will next try to understand how they come about, and to discover what variables and processes may be implicated in the development and maintenance of abnormal psychological functioning.

Psychopathology is the broad area of the study of mental disorders by medical or psychological specialists. **Clinical psychology** is the field that specalizes in the psychological treatment of individuals with mental disorders. Many students find the study of mental disorders and their treatment one of the most fascinating areas of psychology. Indeed, more psychology majors enter this field of psychology than any other. If you also find the topic of mental disorders especially interesting, then as you read through this chapter, try to discover what it is about it that is so intellectually appealing while at the same time being so personally distressing.

Before we look at the various forms that mental disorders take (and how the three *Opening Cases* relate to them), we need to put the phenomena in a broader prospective. Just how serious is the problem of mental disorder? And how do researchers and clinicians ever agree on consistent terms to use in diagnosing mental disorders that can show up in so many different symptoms yet be unique in any individual case?

THE PROBLEM OF MENTAL DISORDERS

Have you ever worried excessively, felt depressed and anxious without knowing why, been fearful of something you knew rationally could not harm you, felt someone was a threat to your well-being, believed you were not living up to your potential, thought about suicide as an escape, or abused alcohol and drugs to self-treat a psychological problem? It is the rare student who does not have more than one "yes" in reply to these questions.

As you might expect, the scope of this nation's problems with mental health and mental disorder is vast. It can be pervasive, touching the daily lives of many of us. It can be insidious, working its way into many situations that diminish our emotional and physical well-being. It can be devastating, destroying the effective functioning of individuals and their families, as well as creating an enormous financial burden through lost productivity and the high costs of prolonged treatment.

A **mental disorder** is defined "as a clinically significant behavioral or psychological syndrome or pattern that occurs in an individual and that is typically associated with either a painful symptom *(distress)* or impairment in one or more important areas of functioning *(disability)*" (DSM-III, 1980, p. 6).

How many people suffer from mental disorders? The dismal official picture of the extent of mental disorder in the United States can be seen in the figures in **Table 14.1.** Actually, these were only estimates based on populations that could be readily identified, such as patients in mental hospitals and other institutions, and clients in therapy. Such figures *underestimate* the true scope of the problem.

Many disturbed people are privately treated at home, while others have learned to conceal their disturbances and not act "crazy" in public. Still others act out their mental problems in ways that society does not judge as mentally disordered—perhaps joining "hate" groups, or engaging in socially acceptable forms of violence. Just as unemployment statistics do not include all those who are chronically unemployed and have stopped looking for work, so, too, statistics on mental disorder omit those who suffer in silence, living a marginal existence on the fringes of society.

For a fuller appreciation of how serious and extensive the problem of mental disorder is, we might

Table 14.1 *Estimates of Mental Disorders in the United States*

30 million Americans receive some kind of mental-health care at any one time
10 million people have a significant alcohol-related problem
8 million children need help for psychological disorders
6 million people are mentally retarded
2 million youth have specific learning disabilities
2 million people suffer profound depression
2 million Americans are or have been schizophrenic
1 million Americans have organic psychosis (toxic, neurological origin, or other brain diseases)
500,000 are addicted to heroin
200,000 child-abuse cases are reported annually
1 of every 10,000 children is autistic

(Based on the President's Commission on Mental Health, 1977)

include all those who attempt suicide or commit violent crimes. Finally, consider the many people you know who at some time in their lives become their own worst enemy by letting fears control their actions or allowing a distorted self-image to diminish their will to try something new, to improve, to succeed.

A tragic example of psychopathology-in-action is the case of Jim Backus, whom you probably know as the funny voice of Mr. Magoo.

Backus was a sociable humorist, a character comic in the TV series "Gilligan's Island," a writer, and a good golfer. He now is a recluse who refuses to see old friends, fears going into restaurants or working in front of a camera. He stopped writing and playing golf. An interviewer reported that: "The other day Backus sat in a chair in his home, a frightened, insecure man, contrasting tragically with the raucous, extroverted Backus of old, needing reassurance that he wasn't indeed, in the clutches of a life-threatening disease."

Backus suffered from an extreme case of hypochondria, believing he was afflicted with Parkinson's disease. Despite medical reassurances, his panic, depression, and fears got steadily worse. He told the interviewer: "I haven't been out of this house in almost six years. I was terrified when the doorbell rang. I'd run and hide. I'm trying to get over the acute panic right now as we talk. . . . Your mind can do this to you. You know it's doing it to you but you're powerless to stop it." With the help of his wife, Backus has written the story of this living nightmare in book entitled *Backus Strikes Back* (1984). The book in itself is a positive sign of his being able to get well again (adapted from Scott, 1984, p. 58).

Statistics about the prevalence of mental disorders are likely to reveal only the tip of the iceberg of abnormality. They underestimate the actual extent of the problem for the reasons noted above, those of exclusion of many types of disordered, antisocial, self-destructive behaviors, as well as from problems in defining and reporting cases of mental disorder. But statistics are just numbers; however large and impressive, they are always *impersonal*. Throughout this and the next chapter, as we talk about categories and processes and models, I would suggest you keep in mind also the *person*, someone like us, or like Jim Backus, who has lost control over thoughts, feelings, or actions.

◁ *Some individuals who join groups such as the Klu Klux Klan may be acting out their mental problems in ways that society does not judge formally as mentally disordered.*

CLASSIFYING MENTAL DISORDERS

Imagine you are a physician and a patient reports headaches, pains, dizziness, palpitations, weakness. You would likely examine a set of physical evidence from blood and urine tests, X-rays, and other sources in search of the organic basis of the problem. The pattern of these test results would help you diagnose the problem and begin to plan a treatment. But suppose all tests prove negative, and you find no physical evidence to support or justify the reported disturbances and debilitation. What would you do then? "Most physicians either send these patients away after telling them there is nothing wrong or prescribe a sedative, and then forget the whole matter or blame the patient by labeling him a 'crock'—medical slang for a neurotic complainer" (Pitts, 1969, p. 60). About 5 percent of the U.S. population are estimated to have anxiety symptoms—such as those in the example above—with no organic cause. That amounts to some 11 million Americans for this one type of psychopathology alone.

The evidence the clinical psychologist or psychiatrist must rely on to make a diagnosis is usually based on observations of what the person says and does—the patient's behavior and what others report about that behavior. The first general decision to be made is whether or not to label the behavior abnormal. Once it is determined that there is something wrong with the person's behavior or personality, the next decision becomes how to judge the specific ways in which the person is *abnormal*. This judgment results in a diagnosis or classification of the person as belonging to one or more established categories of mental disorder. So we need to know: What is abnormal, and also what is the system that professionals use to classify abnormality into specific categories?

～What is abnormal?

What are some of the conditions under which a person might be labeled as *abnormal?* The person is *suffering* and acts in ways that are *maladaptive,* that do not contribute to his or her well-being. The person's behavior is *irrational;* it does not seem to make sense or be comprehensible. The person behaves *unpredictably* from situation to situation or over time, as if there were a *loss of control.* In appearance or actions, the person is *unconventional,* deviating from commonly acceptable standards. At times, the person does things that are *morally unacceptable,* violating other standards of what is right and just to do. Finally, it is more likely that a person will be labeled abnormal if he or she creates *observer discomfort,* making others feel threatened or distressed (Rosenhan & Seligman, 1984).

It should be obvious that any one of these elements of abnormality could fit you or your friends at times. The problem is that none of them is a *necessary* condition that all cases of abnormality share. And none constitutes a *sufficient* condition that distinguishes all cases of abnormal behavior from normal variations in behavior. A solution has been to judge what is abnormal *not* as a difference in *kind* between two distinct types of people or acts, but as a difference in the *degree* to which it resembles a set of agreed upon criteria of abnormality.

A useful analogy is the "family resemblance" of children to parents; while never an exact fit, there is often a good match of enough elements between them to judge them as belonging together in the same family. So, too, with what is abnormal. We can

▷ *Though for some the hairdos of these teens may seem "unconventional" and create "observer discomfort," they do not necessarily constitute a picture of abnormality.*

use the concept of family resemblance in two ways, general and specific. First, we decide on the general resemblance of the person's characteristics to the family of characteristics we consider to be abnormal. Then more detailed family resemblance matches are made with the specific ways in which abnormal behavior is expressed.

DSM-III

Professionals who must make judgments of the specific categories of abnormality have developed a manual to help in making this classification. By classifying problems into useful categories they can design research studies to find out about the causes or the natural course of different kinds of psychological problems. They want to discover which problems might improve without treatment, which might lead to positive personal growth, which might become debilitating, chronic mental problems. And only with a good classification scheme can individuals be diagnosed reliably and studies be designed to determine what treatment programs are most helpful for different kinds of problems.

For all these reasons, mental health workers have sought to develop and agree on a common classification scheme for psychological problems that can then be used to *diagnose* the problem of any specific individual. The currently accepted scheme is one developed by the American Psychiatric Association and set forth in a diagnostic manual for clinicians and researchers. It classifies, defines, and describes over two hundred mental disorders. The complete name for this manual is the *Diagnostic and Statistical Manual of Mental Disorders, 3rd Edition* (1980), but it is known more simply as **DSM-III.** With its carefully developed diagnostic language, the DSM-III can identify clinical disorders more reliably and report them in a uniform way, making possible more precise evaluation studies of which treatments work best in which cases.

The attempt to classify disorders is complex and controversial. Any classification is influenced by the theory one holds about mental problems, and no one theoretical approach is shared by all workers in the field of mental health. It is unlikely, therefore, that any diagnostic scheme will ever be universally accepted, and DSM-III certainly has its critics (see, for example, Smith & Kraft, 1983). But it is clearly an improvement over earlier diagnostic approaches; no doubt it, too, will be modified in time by the new research evidence it is helping to generate.

DSM-III tries in particular to minimize former differences between the basic approaches of *psychiatry* (which emphasizes concepts of disease, illness, and a medical interpretation of mental disorders) and *psychology* (which emphasizes the causal role of anxiety and learning). It does so in the following ways:

- Behavior syndromes (patterns) rather than people are classified and described. (DSM-III never refers to "schizophrenics" but rather to "people who show schizophrenia.")
- Terminology acceptable to both psychologists and psychiatrists is used, such as "mental health professionals" or "clinicians" instead of "psychiatrists." Likewise, "mental disorder" is used instead of "mental illness."
- When the **etiology**—the *causes* or factors related to the development of a disorder—is not known, then only *descriptive* statements are made in DSM-III; theoretical statements about how the disturbances come about are avoided. This is important because, as we shall discuss later in this chapter, there is considerable disagreement about the causes of most mental disorders. The descriptive terms allow clinicians to develop a common language for *describing* problems, while leaving opportunity for disagreement and continued research about the best models for *explaining* and *treating* the problems.

For most of the DSM-III categories, the criteria were based on the *clinical judgments* of a panel of about 100 psychiatrists and psychologists. The *reliability* of these diagnostic categories was then established by having over 800 clinicians test them in field settings where they worked—to demonstrate that different judges would use the categories in the same way. However, the *validity* of these DSM-III categories—the extent to which the differentiations and descriptions accurately represent mental disorders—remains to be tested.

In this context, validity is a complex concept. One validity question of interest would be whether disorders thought to be unrelated might turn out to be better thought of as similar—and vice versa. For example, are all the subtypes of depression best thought of as variants of one basic kind of problem, or are there very different kinds of depression that have different causes and require different treatment? Validity studies are ongoing (Spitzer, 1981; Stangler & Printz, 1980), but determining the validity of all of DSM-III is clearly going to be a difficult task.

DSM-III does more than just put an individual into a category. It differs from earlier schemes in assessing an individual's symptoms in relation to three overall kinds of disorder (mental disorder, personality disorder, and organic disorder) and also according to the level of stress being faced and the individual's overall recent level of functioning. In fact, each individual can be evaluated on each of five dimensions, or *axes,* in a *multiaxial evaluation system* (see **Table 14.2**). The first three axes show what symptoms are present (often an individual may show both mental and physical symptoms, for example). The other two axes evaluate his or her life situation and best level of general functioning during the past year.

We turn now to a consideration of the major categories of mental disorders that are currently recognized by psychologists and psychiatrists. After describing the kinds of problems people experience, we will examine a number of attempts to explain these disorders and then see how these explanations can combine to give us a fuller understanding of one of the most complex mental disorders—schizophrenia.

MAJOR TYPES OF MENTAL DISORDER

Here we will discuss a few of the personality disorders listed on Axis II, which students are more likely to encounter in their everyday contacts. But our focus will be primarily on major mental disorders found on Axis I of the DSM-III classification, emphasizing those that are most prevalent and illustrative of the range of mental problems that humans can experience.

Three main categories must be excluded simply because of space limitations. The first is the set of *organic mental disorders.* These are the psychological or behavioral abnormalities associated with temporary or permanent brain damage or malfunction. They may be due to aging of the brain, disease, accidents, or excessive ingestion of substances such as alcohol, lead, and many types of pharmacological agents (such as barbiturates, amphetamines, and opiates, as discussed in Chapter 6).

The second category that we will not cover in this chapter is *substance-use disorders,* which includes both dependence on and abuse of alcohol and drugs. This category of disorders has taken on prominence as drug and alcohol use and abuse has become a growing problem. We discussed many of the issues surrounding the use of drugs in the broader context of states of consciousness (see Chapter 6).

Table 14.2 *The Five Axes of DSM-III*

Axis	Classification	Purpose
AXIS I	Clinical syndromes	Conditions considered ''mental disorders''
AXIS II	a) Personality disorders	Personality characteristics serious enough to be considered problems but not representing ''mental disorders''
	b) Specific developmental disorders	Developmental disorders in children in such specific skills as reading, language, and articulation that are unrelated to any mental disorder
AXIS III	Physical disorders	Physical problems relevant to understanding or managing the mental problems of the individual
AXIS IV	Severity of psychosocial stressors	Amount and degree of stress experienced by the individual in the preceding year
AXIS V	Highest level of adaptive functioning in past year	Highest level of functioning in three life areas (social, work, and leisure activity) during the past year

(Based on DSM-III, 1980)

The third diagnostic category to be omitted from our discussion here is the group of *disorders that typically arise in childhood or adolescence,* such as retardation, stuttering, or childhood behavior problems. To do these justice would require much more time and space than we have in this survey; should you be interested in pursuing this subject further, check your college catalog for courses focusing on behavior disorders of childhood and adolescence. One disorder from this category, however, which is particularly common in college women, is presented in the **Close-up** on page 496.

Our discussion in this section will focus on what the various disorders look like to observers and feel like to those afflicted. That is, we will focus here on description. In most cases, we will hold off on attempts at explanation until the second half of the chapter, by which time you will have a better idea of the range of disorders that are involved. Consideration of *treatment* and *prognosis* (outlook) for such problems will be the subject of the next chapter.

Personality disorders

Personality disorders consist of longstanding (chronic), inflexible, maladaptive patterns of perceiving, thinking, or behaving. They can seriously impair the individual's ability to function in social or work settings, or cause significant distress. In DSM-III, there are twelve types of personality disorders grouped into three broad clusters of behavior that is (a) "odd or eccentric"; (b) "dramatic, emotional, erratic"; or (c) "anxious or fearful." We will discuss three of the better known personality disorders below. *Narcissistic* and *antisocial personality disorders* are in the second cluster, and *compulsive personality disorder* is in the third cluster.

While we all know people who seem particularly impressed with themselves, specific criteria must be met before such a pattern constitutes **narcissistic personality disorder.** The person must have a grandiose sense of self-importance, preoccupation with fantasies of success or power, and a need for constant attention or admiration. Inappropriate re-

sponses to criticism or defeat also need to be present; this can be either apparent indifference to criticism or a marked overreaction to it. Finally, there must be impairment of interpersonal relationships, characterized by such things as feeling entitled to special favors with no reciprocal obligations, exploiting others to indulge oneself, relationships that vary between overevaluation and complete rejection, and lack of empathy for the feelings of others.

Some of these attributes may remind you of the *Opening Case* of Sam, the euphoric student. In some ways he sounds narcissistic, but other features of his problems don't fit—for example, his lack of need for sleep and his unvaryingly euphoric mood. Later we will come to a diagnostic category that fits Sam's behavior much better.

Individuals with **compulsive personality disorder** are task-oriented perfectionists, overly devoted to their work to the exclusion of pleasure. Individuals showing this disorder often display an inability to express warm and tender emotions, along with a stubborn insistence that others do things their way. They get preoccupied with rules, roles, trivia, while missing the big picture and ignoring the needs of others. Typically, they either avoid or postpone making decisions or completing projects; that is, they are often "all talk but little show." If this sounds like a classmate you know, it is more likely to be a male than a female, according to a recent survey of students seeking outpatient services in a large university clinic (Stangler & Printz, 1980).

People with **antisocial personality disorders** often create trouble for all of us. They start early in life disrupting class, getting into fights, running away from home, having promiscuous sexual experiences, never keeping their jobs. Their history of continuous and chronic antisocial actions typically includes vio-

▷ *People with antisocial personality disorder tend to develop a criminal life-style and wind up in jail.*

Starvation Is to Anorexia as Binging Is to Bulimia

When the desire to be thin becomes a compulsion, young women may develop a starvation syndrome termed **anorexia nervosa.** These victims of an uncontrollable choice to stop eating are typically bright teenage girls from affluent families. They tend to be energetic perfectionists, still bubbling over with energy even while wasting away. Not only do they lose considerable weight (at least 25 percent of original body weight), but they eventually become so weak that they are bedridden and must be fed intravenously to prevent death from starvation—when surrounded with plenty.

Other serious symptoms of this "relentless pursuit of thinness" (a "weight phobia") are: a collapse of the girl's circulation, absence of menstrual periods, depression, tiredness, inability to feel hungry, and abnormal preoccupation with herself. This serious psychiatric problem is thought to reflect disturbances in one's sense of autonomy and mastery over her body, along with disturbances in body image (Bruch, 1978). Popular singer Karen Carpenter was a recent victim of anorexia, dying in 1983 of cardiac arrest caused by metabolic imbalance and loss of essential proteins from severe weight loss.

The psychology of anorexia nervosa can include a history of being overdependent and resentful of parents, failure of an intense love affair or separation from a loved one, a history of self-punishment and excessive parental concern for food. It may also be that these girls resent having the secondary sex characteristics—breasts, hips, buttocks. Starving makes them disappear (Garfinkel et al., 1980).

A distinct subgroup among anoretic patients are bulimic women, who consume large amounts of food in a short period of time, frequently induce vomiting or who use laxatives—then binge, fast, and binge again. **Bulimia** is a disorder focused around food and eating, but it involves impulsive feasting rather than the compulsive fasting of anorexia nervosa. Nearly half the patients hospitalized for anorexia were found to have periodically resorted to bulimia (Casper et al., 1980).

The psychological profiles of fasting anoretic and bulimic patients, however, are dramatically different. The anoretic patient tends to be more introverted, denies hunger, and displays little overt distress. Females with bulimia tend to show more extroversion, impulsiveness, a high incidence of stealing, use of street drugs and alcohol, and greater anxiety, depression, guilt, self-mutilation, and suicide attempts. Frequently, mothers of bulimic women are obese.

Anorexia and bulimia are serious disorders that begin to show up in high school and college. They are problems requiring professional help as well as *your* personal concern. Notice when a classmate loses a great deal of weight in a short time and express your concern. An anoretic student of mine, who started with average weight and lost 40 pounds in three months, was upset that not one person in her dorm or any class had been concerned enough to notice and mention this abnormal weight loss to her. Their indifference or "civil inattention" only served to increase her depression and sense of worthlessness. ATTEND AND CARE.

---

lating the rights of others and refusing to accept social norms with respect to lawful behavior. They may break the law, develop a criminal life-style, and wind up in jail. In fact, approximately 80 percent of all criminals are diagnosed as antisocial personalities (Guze et al., 1969).

You were probably able to recognize many familiar qualities in the descriptions of these three personality disorders. Most of us have some human frailties that appear among these criteria. It is important, however, to remember that to be diagnosable, they

must be the predominant characteristics of a person. Few people meet *all* the criteria necessary for a formal diagnosis of personality disorder. This is also true of the more serious disorders we discuss next: some of the criteria may seem to apply to you or those you know (your "family resemblance"); others may sound very strange, or even bizarre. In any case, beware of the natural human tendency to apply labels or categories to people you may know, especially in

Anxiety disorders

You are probably familiar with the term *neurosis* (and its adjective *neurotic*). In earlier editions of the DSM, neurosis has been a formal diagnostic category; in the DSM-III, however, such is no longer the case. The reasoning underlying this change was that, over the years, the frequent use of neurosis as a label had so broadened its meaning that it had become virtually useless as a reliable or valid category. As such, disorders that used to be considered under the ''family name'' of neuroses are now further delineated into the categories of anxiety, somatoform, and dissociative disorders; and some are also included in the affective and psychosexual disorders. We shall look at each of these revised categories in turn. Notwithstanding, however, many people continue to feel that the term *neurosis* is a useful one, and, of course, research carried out prior to the DSM-III uses such categorization. You will no doubt come across it in your reading, and we will take a moment here to review it.

In traditional usage, **neurosis** has represented a mental disorder in which there are one or more symptoms related to ineffective attempts to deal with anxiety, such as a phobia or a compulsion. There is no clear-cut organic problem, no violation of basic social norms, and no loss of orientation to reality, but the individual shows a lifelong pattern of self-defeating and inadequate coping strategies aimed more at reducing anxiety than at solving life problems. By one means or another, the neurotic person proves to others that he or she is impotent in the face of a threatening world.

There is no clear dividing line between neurotic and normal individuals: the difference is one of degree. Neurotic symptoms are only rarely severe enough to require hospitalization, but they are distressing and the individual recognizes them as personally unacceptable and alien. (*Ego-dystonic* is a term used to describe this alien feeling, while *ego-syntonic* means ''acceptable to the self''). With that brief background, let us turn now to the anxiety disorders.

Anxiety problems are common in the United States. It is estimated that about 4 percent of the entire general population (over 8 million people) have at some time experienced the symptoms that psychiatric classification would term **anxiety disorders**.

△ *The man shown here is a tragic example of the dangerous effects of labeling. Born in a mental hospital to parents with mental problems, Jack Smith was assumed to be mentally retarded and received no formal schooling after age 12, in spite of the fact that he showed interest in learning. His early years were spent in a state orphanage, followed by 38 years in a mental hospital. In 1976, a Michigan judge declared that Mr. Smith was not mentally ill or dangerous, based on findings of a psychiatric evaluation. By that time, however, the 54-year-old man was considered ''so impaired that it would be unwise to put him out on the streets'' (New York Times, March 11, 1979, p. 26). Mr. Smith now lives in a nursing home.*

the case of the subject matter at hand. As you are no doubt aware, the labels of abnormal psychology can be very powerful and very damaging if abused. Any labeling here should be left to the professionals who are trained and licensed to use them to help individuals suffering from behavioral and mental problems. Any other use is name-calling, pure and simple. With that in mind, we shall turn now to some of the Axis I disorders, beginning with problems that are less serious and moving toward increasing levels of severity and more abnormal functioning.

All the anxiety disorders include physiological arousal (changes in heart rate, respiration, muscle tension, dizziness) along with the feelings of tension, tremor, shaking, and intense feelings of apprehension without knowing why. Such anxiety without any known cause is called **free-floating anxiety.** Having no idea why the reaction is occurring, the person becomes even more upset at the feeling of losing control—"for no good reason."

There are two major subcategories of anxiety disorders: *phobic disorders* and *anxiety states.* The latter is further subdivided into generalized anxiety disorder, panic disorder, obsessive-compulsive disorder, and posttraumatic stress disorder. Physiological arousal and free-floating anxiety occur in all of them, but there are differences in the person's experience of anxiety, in the situations in which it is felt, and in the particular symptoms that develop.

Phobic disorders. Fear is a rational reaction to an objective, identified external danger (such as a fire in one's home or being mugged on the street) and may involve flight or attack in self-defense. In contrast, a person with a **phobic disorder** recognizes that he or she is suffering from a persistent and irrational fear of some specific object, activity, or situation (the *phobic stimulus*) that causes a compelling desire to avoid it (the *phobic reaction*).

Sometimes, the phobic stimulus may not be the "real" or sufficient cause of the phobic disorder. For example, a bridge phobia might really represent a fear of increased responsibility. The phobic person may even know this but will still focus on the external stimulus—the bridge—that triggers the internal feelings of anxiety. At other times, a phobia is exactly what it appears to be—a bridge phobia may quite simply be a fear of bridges.

Many of us have irrational fears of spiders or snakes (or even multiple-choice tests). Such fears become phobic disorders only when they interfere with a person's life adjustment or cause significant distress.

> Edith is afraid of writing her name in public. She is terrified when placed in a situation where she might be asked to sign her name, and she gets the common anxiety symptoms: muscle tension, rapid heart rate, and apprehension. This phobia has far-reaching effects on her life. She can't go shopping if she would need to sign a check or credit card slip. She no longer can play golf, because she can't sign the golf register. She can't go to the bank unless all transactions are prepared ahead of time in her home. She can't sign her Diner's card at a restaurant, she can't sign any papers that require approval of a notary public, and she can't vote because she can't sign the voting register.

So even a very specific phobia can have wide impact on everyday life!

Almost any stimulus can come to generate a phobic avoidance reaction. The list below presents a few of the common phobias among the many hundreds in the clinical literature (Melville, 1977):

Phobia	Fear of
acrophobia	high places
agoraphobia	open spaces, public places
autophobia	oneself
claustrophobia	confined places
hypergiaphobia	responsibility
ideophobia	ideas
monophobia	being alone
nyctophobia	darkness
pathophobia	disease
social phobia	apearing in public
scopophobia	being stared at
xenophobia	the unknown
zoophobia	animals

Some phobias are much more common than others. We shall discuss two of them here: agoraphobia and social phobia.

The extreme fear of being in public places or open spaces from which one cannot escape is the essential feature of **agoraphobia.** It deprives agoraphobic individuals of their freedom; in extreme cases they literally become prisoners in their own homes. It is not possible for them to hold a job or carry on normal daily activities because their fears constrict contact with the outside world.

When the anticipation of a public appearance (speaking, writing, performing artistically, or eating in public) causes a persistent, irrational fear, a **social phobia** is operating. The person recognizes that the fear is excessive and unreasonable, yet feels compelled to avoid the phobic stimulus for fear of being humiliated or embarrassed by his or her unacceptable or inappropriate performance.

A vicious cycle may develop that supports a self-fulfilling prophecy. The person so fears the scrutiny and rejection of others who will judge his or her performance that enough anxiety is created to impair the performance—"see, I told you so, I was right to avoid trying to do that in the first place." Brilliant students with social phobias have been known to drop out of law school, for example, when they discovered that public oral performance was regularly expected of them.

Anxiety states. Because anxiety is the chief characteristic in *all* the anxiety disorders, it may seem strange for a subcategory to be named **anxiety states.** The diagnosis of this syndrome is made when anxiety attacks occur in the *absence* of specific phobias. We will review three major kinds of anxiety states: *generalized anxiety disorder, panic disorder,* and *obsessive-compulsive disorder.* The fourth disorder that fits in the category of anxiety states is *post-traumatic stress disorder,* which has already been reviewed in the last chapter.

1. Generalized anxiety disorder. When anxiety persists for at least a month and is generalized, without any of the specific symptoms of the other anxiety disorders, it is diagnosed as a **generalized anxiety disorder.** Here the anxiety itself is the principal problem. The way this anxiety is expressed varies from person to person. For a formal DSM-III diagnosis, symptoms must be from at least three of the following four categories:

1. *Motor tension* (jitters, trembling, tension, aches, fatigue, twitches, inability to relax);
2. *Autonomic hyperactivity* (heart pounding or racing, shallow breathing, sweating, dizziness, upset stomach, diarrhea, other signs of physiological overreaction);
3. *Apprehensive expectation* (continuous anxiety, worry, anticipation of some misfortune for self or others);
4. *Vigilance and scanning* (hyperattentiveness to environmental events and to one's own internal reactions, leading to distractibility, poor concentration, "edginess," and sleep difficulties).

Despite all this, the chronically anxious person continues to function with only mild impairment in his or her social life or job. But the constant physical and psychological drain takes a toll that may show up in greater susceptibility to many common illnesses, such as colds and flu, headaches, infections, and heart attacks.

2. Panic disorders. In **panic disorders,** there are episodes of full-blown anxiety and intense feelings of unpredictability, usually lasting only minutes, but recurring at least once a week, on the average. These panic attacks include the symptoms of autonomic hyperactivity, along with dizziness, faintness, choking or smothering sensations, and feelings of unreality, terror, and impending doom. These attacks occur at times other than during physical exertion or actual threats to one's life.

The following excerpts taken during a panic attack, will help you appreciate the panic being experienced:

"Uh, I'm not going to make it, I can't get help, I can't get anyone to understand the feeling . . . it's like a feeling that sweeps over from the top of my head to the tip of my toes. And I detest the feeling. I'm very frightened."

"It feels, I just get all, like hot through me, and shaky, and my heart just feels like it's pounding and breathing really really quick . . . . It feels like I'm going to die or something" (Muskin & Fyer, 1981, p. 81).

"Are you expecting a case of agoraphobia?"

Because of the random nature of these "hit and run" attacks, *anticipatory anxiety* develops as an added complication. The dread of the "next attack" and of being helpless and suddenly out of control often leads the person to avoid public places—yet fear being alone. You might recognize the beginnings of this pattern if you look back to the *Opening Case* of Ellen, who fits all the criteria for panic disorder.

3. Obsessive-compulsive disorders. Obsessions are thoughts, images, or impulses that recur or persist; they are unwanted invasions of consciousness, seem to be senseless or repugnant, and are unacceptable to the person. But they are difficult or impossible to ignore or suppress, though the person may try to resist them.

You probably have had some sort of mild obsessional experience, such as the intrusion of petty worries, "Did I really lock the door?" or "Did I turn off the oven?" or the persistence of a haunting melody you simply could not stop from running through your mind. Neurotic obsessive thoughts are much more compelling, cause much distress, and may interfere with the person's social or role functioning.

An obsessional *thought* might be "Am I the one who really killed John Lennon?" An obsessional *impulse* might be to expose one's genitals in class. An obsessional *image* might be the view of someone who disagrees with you being violently destroyed. A content analysis of the obsessions of 82 obsessional neurotics yielded 5 broad categories of obsessions, in the following order of frequency: (a) dirt and contamination, (b) aggression, (c) the orderliness of inanimate objects, (d) sex, and (e) religion (Akhtar et al., 1975).

Compulsions are repetitive acts carried out in stereotyped rituals that seem to follow certain rules: the person feels compelled to engage in these excessive or exaggerated behaviors. At least initially he or she resists carrying them out. But though they appear senseless to the compulsive person when he or she is calm, they provide a release of tension when anxiety is high. In addition, preoccupation with carrying out these minor ritualistic tasks often leaves the compulsive individual with no time or energy to carry out the impulsive action that is unconsciously being guarded against. In some cases, these compulsive rituals seem designed to undo guilt feelings for real or imagined sins; an example is repetitive hand washing—a kind of Lady Macbeth reaction.

Obsessions and compulsions may occur separately, but they go together so often, that they are considered two aspects of a single disorder. In one study of 150 hospitalized obsessional patients, nearly 70 percent had both obsessions and compulsions. Of the rest, most had only obsessions (Welner et al., 1976).

Compulsions can grow so out of proportion as to virtually enslave a person (Rachman & Hodgson, 1980). This had happened with Jane, the woman in the *Opening Case* who couldn't leave her house. She had both obsessive thoughts and compulsive rituals. You should notice, though, that Jane had another problem as well which was not an anxiety problem but involved fatigue, loss of interest, and sleep problems. This second syndrome is one we will discuss later.

▷ *After participating in the murder of King Duncan, Shakespeare's Lady Macbeth is depicted as experiencing a compulsive need to wash her hands, presumably to cleanse them of the blood of her victim.*

Somatoform disorders

When physical complaints suggest a physical disorder, but no organic problems are found, the reaction is assumed to reflect psychological conflicts. Such reactions are termed **somatoform disorders** (*soma* means "body").

A mild form of this process of turning a psychological reaction into a physical one can be seen in young children, who will point to a sudden bodily pain that justifies their crying when, in fact, they are emotionally distressed—rejected by a playmate or reprimanded by a parent, perhaps. In its neurotic form, such concern about health is a central preoccupation, with recurring and persisting complaints about illness and assorted pains. The person seeks medical attention frequently and may spend a great deal of money on unnecessary treatment and hospitalization, including surgery for suspected tumors. We will discuss briefly two forms of this transformation of mental problems into somatic complaints—hypochondriasis and conversion disorder.

Hypochondriasis. The preoccupation with bodily sensations as possible signs of a serious disease despite medical reassurance that all is well is called **hypochondriasis**. Individuals suffering from this disorder are often said to "enjoy poor health," for their greatest satisfaction seems to be in finding bodily symptoms that confirm their dire predictions. These supposed ailments not only prevent active engagement in life—with its risk of failure—but also may bring attention, sympathy, and service from others. For some, the choice may seem to be between "being ill" and "going crazy": Better to have a concrete physical ailment that is making you ill than a vague emotional problem for which you are somehow held personally responsible. Isn't it easier to get sympathy for a tumor in the brain than for free-floating anxiety in the mind? But, as we saw in the case of Jim Backus, the long-term consequences of hypochondriasis can be devastating.

Conversion disorder. In this extreme abnormal reaction, there is a loss of a specific sensory or motor function—the person suddenly goes blind or is paralyzed, for example—without any organic cause. This "conversion" of a working, healthy part of the body into a nonfunctional state is a **conversion disorder.**

Conversion symptoms are reinforced in two ways. The individual gets the "primary gain" of removal from a threatening situation in a way that keeps a serious internal conflict out of awareness. The symptom usually has a symbolic value that represents and is a partial solution to that emotional conflict. Thus, a soldier who sees a wounded buddy in need of help but is himself under heavy fire and feels unable to offer help may express his conflict as "blindness."

Conversion reactions—and other types of mental disorders too—also often achieve the "secondary gain" of extra sympathy and social support that might not otherwise be forthcoming. Such benefits, in turn, further reinforce the reactions and contribute to maintaining them. Interestingly, conversion reactions are more common in areas where the education level is low; they become rarer as the level of education increases. The disorder serves little purpose when one's symptoms violate generally available medical knowledge—and are then not "acceptable."

In a dramatic case of conversion disorder, a married, middle-aged salesman entered the hospital with what appeared to be recurring seizures that paralyzed half of his body while they were going on. Before his brain was to be operated upon, the staff made a routine psychological assessment. From the man's responses on several different tests, the consulting psychologist (Seymour Sarason of Yale University) detected a pattern that suggested a severe conflict over sexual identity. Sodium amytal was administered, and the patient was interviewed while under the influence of this so-called "truth serum." His seizures disappeared while he recounted a recent (his first) homosexual exploit with a sailor he had picked up while on a sales trip. He felt enormous guilt over what he considered a "sinful act," as well as anxiety and confusion over his "manhood." Psychotherapy, rather than surgery, alleviated the conversion symptoms and helped him deal directly with his emotional and sexual problems.

Dissociative disorders

Have you ever forgotten an appointment you really did not want to keep? Unpleasant, feared situations can be avoided by such convenient slips of memory. "Forgetting" keeps you away from a situation where your self-esteem or well-being might be threatened, but you cannot be blamed for not facing the situation—you just forgot. Carried to an extreme, this normal mechanism can result in a sudden, temporary alteration of consciousness in the form of a severe memory loss, loss of personal identity, or even the disturbed motor behavior of wandering away from home. There are the main features of the **dissociative disorders.**

It is important for us to see ourselves as basically in control of our behavior—including our emotions, thoughts, and actions. Essential to this perception of self-control is the sense of selfhood—the consistency of different aspects of the self and the continuity of our identity over time and place. Psychologists believe that in dissociated states, individuals escape from their conflicts by giving up this precious consistency and continuity—in a sense, disowning part of themselves. In Chapter 6, we discussed one dissociative disorder, *multiple personality,* in connection with our discussion of hypnosis (see pp. 211–12). Here we will discuss two others: *psychogenic amnesia* and *psychogenic fugue.*

Psychogenic amnesia. The sudden extensive inability to recall important personal material (not caused by neurological disorders) constitutes **psychogenic amnesia**—mentally caused blocking out of certain memories. Its most common form is *localized amnesia* in which all events during a given pe-

riod of time are forgotten, usually involving some traumatic experience. A rape victim, for example, may recall nothing from the time she was approached until she wandered into a police station. In *selective amnesia* only some of the traumatic events are forgotten. In the case above, the victim might remember what the rapist looked like but have no apparent memory of the details of the violent act itself.

Psychogenic fugue. Often an amnesic person who has given up an old identity may actually travel to some other place, either a completely new one or a familiar place that was emotionally supportive at some earlier time. This is called a **psychogenic fugue,** from the latin word meaning "to flee." Once in a new place, the person may assume a new identity and create a new life-style, dissociated psychologically, temporally, and geographically from his or her prior unacceptable life. Cases have been reported in which such persons were rediscovered several years after their disappearance. We do not know how many remain undiscovered and lead the rest of their lives as their "recycled" selves.

Psychosexual disorders

Through sexual experiences, we are attracted to others, share deep levels of intimacy, enjoy sensuous pleasure, and may discover romantic love. These

When found in a Florida park in September 1980, this woman was emaciated, incoherent, and near death. Dubbed "Jane Doe" by authorities, she was suffering from a rare form of psychogenic amnesia in which she had lost the memory of her name, her past, and her ability to read and write. Unable to unveil any concrete leads about her identity, Jane and her doctor appeared on the "Good Morning America" television show and appealed to relatives to step forward to identify Jane. The response was overwhelming, and authorities came to believe that Jane Doe was the daughter of a couple from Illinois, whose daughter had gone to Florida to open a boutique. Their last contact with their daughter had been a phone call in 1976. Despite the couple's certainty, Jane Doe was not able to remember her past and eventually returned to Florida.

benefits of sex are learned through experience, daily observations, literature, and the mass media. On the other hand, a contrary message is also being communicated: sex is dangerous. Sex can be a weapon by which people can reject, abuse, and violate us—or we can harm others. Society provides both powerful temptations *for* and strong deterrents *against* sexual impulses and actions—thereby making sex a conflict-filled experience for many people. Sexual taboos still prevent open discussion of things sexual in many families and in schools, allowing ignorance and false myths to go unchecked.

Psychosexual disorders center around problems of: *sexual inhibitions and dysfunctions, sexual deviations,* and *gender identity.*

Sexual inhibitions and dysfunctions. There are three stages of the normal sexual response cycle where *sexual inhibitions* may disturb one's sense of sexual pleasure, desire, or objective performance. Initial sexual desire may be inhibited, with the result that the person does not have any fantasies or thoughts about the pleasurable nature of sexual activity. During foreplay, sexual excitement may be inhibited. Finally, during the act of sex, problems can result in no orgasm or one that comes too soon or is delayed. When such inhibitions occur regularly in a setting appropriate for sexual activity, they are regarded as psychosexual disorders.

Sexual deviance. For other people, the sexual cycle presents no problem, but sexual arousal is possible only in the context of unusual sexual practices or when accompanied by bizarre imagery. Their deviation from the normal is in the thoughts or acts to which they are attracted.

"Para" means *beyond;* "philia" means *like* or *love.* To an individual with a **paraphilia** disorder, sexual excitement necessarily and involuntarily demands the presence of nonconventional sexual objects, sexual practices, or sexual circumstances. Pedophilia, fetishism, masochism, and sadism are some of the paraphilias. **Pedophilia** is a paraphilia that involves an adult's action or fantasy about sexual activity with young children. In **fetishism,** sexual excitement is achieved repeatedly with the aid of nonliving objects (fetishes). A fetish may be an article of clothing or other objects associated with someone with whom the individual had an intimate involvement (real or imagined).

Masochism and **sadism** both involve sexual excitement through the experience of personal suffering. Sexual masochists prefer arousal that comes from being humiliated, bound, or beaten. They are unable to achieve adequate sexual arousal without the fantasy or actuality of their own pain, abuse, and suffering (sometimes self-inflicted). Sexual sadists are all too willing to wield the whip against the masochist. They get sexual excitement from inflicting injury or humiliation on others—with or without their informed consent. When the disorder becomes severe, the sadist may rape, torture, or kill the victim. Not all rapists, however, are sexual sadists—only those whose motivation is to inflict suffering in order to become sexually excited.

How do paraphilias develop? One explanation suggests that they are due to an abnormal first sexual experience. Another suggests that the sexual deviance may arise due to *conditioning* based on an imagined sexual fantasy or a memory of early sexual arousal. A young man masturbates repeatedly, using the context of a fantasy or remembered contact as the arousal stimulus and the orgasm he achieves powerfully reinforces this activity. Over time, this imagined sexual stimulus becomes the only one capable of inducing sexual arousal. Thus a middle-aged pedophiliac person may have masturbated to the memory of his first prepubertal sexual encounter—but as he aged, his fantasy partners remained children. One's theory or knowledge about the origins of paraphilias has implications for treatment; in this case, reconditioning procedures would be seen as appropriate (Marquis, 1970; McGuire et al., 1965).

Gender identity disorder. Gender identity is the sense of being male or female. **Gender role** is the public expression of that identity; it includes all the ways one indicates to the world that he or she is male or female. When one's anatomical sex (possession of a penis or a vagina) is incongruent with one's sense of which sex he or she belongs to, the person is classified as having a **gender identity disorder.**

You should not confuse this rare disorder with the common problem many young people experience of feeling inadequate in meeting the expectations associated with their gender role (such as not being sufficiently virile or sexually attractive). The person with a gender identity disorder actually *feels* more like a member of the other sex. **Transsexuals** are people whose sense of discomfort and feelings of inappropriateness about their anatomic sex are so strong that they wish to be rid of their genitals and live as a member of the other sex.

Affective disorders

With the affective disorders, we first encounter cases severe enough and different enough from those that resemble the neurotic codes to be called *psychotic*. **Psychosis** is the general category for a number of severe mental disorders in which perception, thinking, and emotion are impaired. A person characterized as *psychotic* is one who is suffering from a major organic or psychological dysfunction that causes him or her to feel, think, and/or act in very deviant ways. These extremely abnormal reactions may cause the person to lose contact with reality, requiring intensive treatment and perhaps hospitalization.

Some psychotic conditions result from organic brain damage which makes it impossible for the person to meet the ordinary demands of life. The **functional psychoses** consist of three subgroups which are *not* attributable to brain damage though in some cases subtle biochemical abnormalities may be involved. They are the major affective disorders, paranoid states, and schizophrenia.

Affective disorders are disturbances of mood in which the person is either excessively depressed or excessively elated (manic), or in some cases both, in turn, without organic cause. The person's behavior is exaggerated and self-defeating, but he or she is not out of touch with reality. But in some cases the disorder is severe enough to be labeled *psychotic*.

During a **manic episode,** the mood is one of elation, expansiveness, or irritability. Accompanying this highly charged mood state (lasting for at least a week) are restless activity; a flight of ideas; pressure to talk fast, loud, and often; and an inflated, grandiose sense of self-esteem. Typically there is a decreased need for sleep, and the person is easily distractable. Caught up in this manic mood, the person shows unwarranted optimism, takes unnecessary risks, promises anything, and may give away everything. You may recognize that now we have defined a syndrome which almost exactly captures the problems of Sam, the young man described in the *Opening Cases.*

At the other extreme of the mood continuum, is the **depressive episode,** in which there is a loss of interest or pleasure in almost everything. This disturbance is usually coupled with feelings of sadness, discouragement, and dissatisfaction and usually oc-

curs with other symptoms, such as feelings of worthlessness or guilt, decreased energy, and suicidal thoughts, as shown in **Table 14.3.** Looking at these, you probably recognize Jane, the woman described earlier. We have already pointed out the obsessive-compulsive pattern she displayed; in addition, she was experiencing a major depression. It is not uncommon for people to meet the criteria for more than one of the problem categories in the DSM-III classification. Just as you can have the flu and a bladder infection at the same time, it is quite possible, especially in the milder forms of affective disorder, to be both abnormally depressed and anxious at the same time.

The more severely disturbed patients tend to show only a manic pattern or only a depressive one; or some alternate between manic and depressive periods, often in some regular cycle. With or without treatment, an episode typically runs its course (perhaps in a few weeks or months) and then subsides—but can recur later if not treated. Between episodes there are often long periods of normality.

Depression has been called the "common cold of psychopathology." Of all forms of pathology described in this chapter, it is the one most students are likely to have already experienced. We have all at one time or another been depressed at the loss of or separation from a loved one, at the failure to achieve a desired goal, or from chronic frustration and stress.

Table 14.3 *Characteristics of Pathological Depression*

Characteristic	Example
Dysphoric mood	Sad, blue, hopeless; loss of interest or pleasure in almost all usual activities
Appetite	Poor appetite; significant weight loss
Sleep	Insomnia *or* hypersomnia (sleeping too much)
Motor activity	Markedly slowed down (motor retardation) *or* agitated
Guilt	Feelings of worthlessness; self-reproach
Concentration	Diminished ability to think or concentrate; forgetfulness
Suicide	Recurrent thoughts of death; suicidal ideas or attempts

But this normal, "garden variety" depression is transitory and specific to the particular situation. In depressive disorders the symptoms are more intense, prolonged, recurrent, not bound to a particular situation or event—and disabling. In any given year, it is estimated that at least 5 percent of adults between 18 and 75 years of age may have serious depressive symptoms, and depression accounts for the majority of all mental hospital admissions. Unfortunately, this common illness is greatly overlooked in the United States today, with only a small percentage of the estimated over 10 million depressive individuals receiving treatment (Bielski & Friedel, 1977).

One current view of depression centers around the theme of negative cognitive distortions. Aaron Beck (1976) has argued that the depressed person shows three specific cognitive distortions, which he calls "the cognitive triad" of depression: a negative world view, a negative self-conception, and a negative appraisal of the future. (With the chronic "bad news" we all hear every day, some have questioned whether the negative picture depressive patients have is really all that unrealistic!)

Interesting findings regarding cognitive distortions in depressed and other patients emerged in a recent study comparing self-ratings and observer ratings of depressed patients with those of patients suffering from other disorders and also those of normal individuals.

As expected, the depressed group rated themselves less positively on social competencies than did either of the nondepressed groups. But unexpected results were found in the discrepancies between how patients rated themselves and how observers rated them. Judged by agreement with observer ratings, depressed patients were the *most realistic* in their self-perceptions, while the nondepressed controls distorted their self-perceptions in a *positive* direction. This "illusory glow" of perceived competence helped perpetuate positive self-attributions among the nondepressed and also made them likely to attend to and remember more positive than negative events (Lewinsohn et al., 1980).

The realistic, depressed person "sees it like it is"—if it is negative feedback.

Support for this intriguing new look at the cognitively "wiser but sadder" world of the depressed person comes from another study in which depressed and nondepressed students were confronted with a series of problems.

The problems varied in the degree of *contingency* between the performer's responding and the outcomes obtained—the extent to which the person's behavior actually influenced the outcomes. Nondepressed students selectively distorted the situation. They overestimated the degree of contingency when the outcomes were desired while underestimating it when the outcomes were not what they wanted—thus giving themselves more credit than they were due when things went well and less blame than they deserved for undesired results. In contrast, the depressed students gave accurate judgments of the degree of contingency that really existed between their responses and the outcomes in both cases (Alloy & Abramson, 1979).

◁ *Depression has been called the "common cold of psychopathology."*

Another study confirmed the first finding—nonde-pressed subjects took more credit than they were due for successes on an achievement test and less blame for failures, blaming them on "bad luck." But in this case the depressed subjects also showed distortion in both cases—in the *opposite direction,* attributing successes to just "luck," while attributing failures to their lack of ability (Barthe & Hammen, 1981).

Although some studies show depressed subjects to be more realistic on specific measures, it is important to realize that they are still experiencing a serious mood disturbance and are immobilized by the kind of learned helplessness that we discussed in Chapter 7 (Seligman, 1975). Some are so incapacitated that they must be hospitalized. Few would argue that the person who embraces suicide as the only escape from severe psychological pain is "wiser" or more realistic than others who can perceive less extreme alternatives for dealing with the problems that have led to the depression.

Suicide is typically preceded by a period of extreme depression. While most depressed people do not commit suicide, most suicidal patients are depressed. They commit suicide at a rate twenty-five times as high as nondepressed comparison groups (Flood & Seager, 1968; Schneidman, 1976). Among college students, suicide is the second most frequent cause of death. In the general population, some estimates of the number of suicidal deaths run as high as 100,000 per year. Since depression occurs more frequently in women, it is therefore not surprising that they *attempt* suicide about three times more often than do men. But men's attempts are more successful—they tend to use guns, while women use less potentially lethal means, such as an overdose of sleeping pills (Perlin, 1975).

Paranoid disorders

Paranoid disorders are among the more fascinating and frightening of all the forms of psychopathology. There is only one major symptom in a paranoid disorder: a persistent delusion. A **delusion** is a rigidly held belief that persists despite contradictory information about its content and lack of social support for its truth. Paranoid delusions typically consist of scenarios in which the individual is sure that some person or group of people is posing a serious personal threat.

There are four types of paranoid delusions.

1. *Delusions of persecution:* Individuals feel that they are constantly being spied on and plotted against and are in mortal danger of attack. Delusions of persecution may accompany delusions of grandeur—the individual is a great person but is continually being opposed by evil forces.
2. *Delusional jealousy:* Individuals become convinced—*without* due cause—that, for example, their mate is unfaithful. "Data" are contrived to fit the theory and prove the "truth" of the delusion.
3. *Delusions of grandeur:* Individuals believe they are some important or exalted being, such as a millionaire or a great inventor.
4. *Delusions of reference:* Individuals misconstrue chance happenings as being directly aimed at them. A paranoid individual who sees two people in earnest conversation immediately concludes that he or she is being talked about. Even lyrics in popular songs or words spoken by radio or TV actors are perceived as having some special message for the individual, often as exposing some personal secret.

In the early stages of a paranoid disorder, the ideas that make up the delusional belief often do not fit together well and even contain elements that are inconsistent. But over time, as the tale is retold and practiced, it becomes more coherent, logical, and systematized. The accusations seem more rational, and other people—especially strangers—may sympathize with the individual's plight or even offer support in this "struggle against the forces of evil." A paranoid disorder is classified as **paranoia** when the persecutory delusional system lasts for at least six months.

Another curious aspect of this disorder is the relatively high intelligence and economic level of the paranoid person compared to those suffering from all other psychological disorders. Paranoid individuals can usually function for some time without others realizing their need for treatment and hospitalization. Except for the highly specific delusion, there are often no other signs of pathology. The personality is intact; the person usually maintains a job and goes through daily functions without impairment. However, social and marital adjustment are typically poor, in part because people close to the individual are ei-

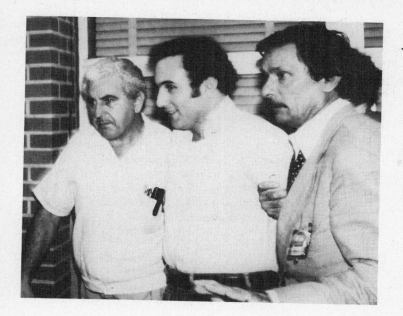

In August 1977, David Berkowitz (center) of New York City was arrested and later convicted of the "Son of Sam" murders. Two court-appointed psychiatrists had declared Berkowitz "paranoid," but he later claimed to have fabricated his paranoid symptoms "so as to find . . . justification for my criminal acts against society." He is currently serving a 30-year sentence.

ther the targets of the delusions or "safe" listeners who are forced to hear the sorry story constantly (Meisner, 1978).

Paranoid reactions are often precipitated by non-social external events that do, in fact, threaten the person's sense of self-esteem, security, and autonomy. These include threats to life (from disease, illness, major surgery, and war), impaired sensory functions, social isolation, senility, or abrupt change of status due to immigration, unemployment, or demotion (see **Close-up,** p. 508). Many of us react to such threats to our self-esteem by *introjecting* (internalizing) them, blaming ourselves, and feeling self-reproach. In paranoid disorders, by contrast, they are *externalized*: blame is turned outward onto external agents.

Paranoia can be frightening to the community when its suspiciousness turns into overt hostility and frequent law suits—or worse, when the paranoia is shared by several individuals. In this case, a persuasive paranoid person, such as a Charles Manson or cult leader, Jim Jones, may recruit other people into his campaign to rid the world of some threat embodied in people that fit a given category. When three or more share the delusion, it can become an ideology, protected by the free speech amendments of our constitution! In this way, bizarre social movements may arise.

Schizophrenic disorders

There is an underlying continuum between normal reactions and most other disorders; everyone knows what it is like to be depressed or anxious, even though most of us never experience these feelings at the degree of severity that constitutes a disorder. Schizophrenia seems to represent a qualitatively different experience. The schizophrenic person does not necessarily pass through a neurotic stage, nor do very disturbed neurotic individuals eventually become schizophrenic. In fact, whereas *anxiety* is often predominant in the disorders presented up to now, anxiety tends to be *absent* or at least peripheral in **schizophrenic disorders.** The neurotic individual seems to be "too much" in contact with his or her world (of guilt, frustration, fear, and rejection). In contrast, the schizophrenic individual's mind seems to have been "loosed from its mooring"—to be sailing off to a far-away world of its own.

Schizophrenia is a severe form of psychopathology in which the personality seems to disintegrate: perception is distorted, emotions are blunted, thoughts are bizarre, and language is strange. The person with a schizophrenic disorder is the one we conjure up when we think about "real" mental disorder, "madness," psychosis, or insanity.

Between two to three million living Americans at one time or another have suffered from this most mysterious and tragic mental disorder. Half of the beds in this nation's mental institutions are currently

Why Are You Whispering about Me?

"What is madness? To have erroneous perceptions and to reason correctly from them."
Voltaire, Philosophical Dictionary, 1974

Elderly people seem especially prone to paranoid thinking. It was originally thought that this could be traced to circulation disorders in brain functioning brought on by senility which, in turn, created the disordered thought processes of paranoia. However, it has recently been discovered that many older patients hospitalized for paranoia have had unrecognized hearing deficits (Cooper, 1976).

If people cannot hear well what other people are saying and do not realize that the problem is their own sensory impairment, there is a good likelihood that they will find a social cause for the problem. In trying to make sense of the unusual perceptual experience (people are moving their mouths in apparent conversation, but little sound is heard), the hearing-impaired person may reasonably assume they are whispering. If confronted with this accusation, the others deny it (because they aren't), but then they become "liars" (because the person sees what they are doing). In other scenarios, not recognizing one's hearing loss can result in perceived lack of respect on the part of others who are seen as "turning their back" on the person. Because the polite "goodbye" or the request to "please

wait while I check on it" is not heard, the older person reacts with anger—to the dismay and irritation of others.

Does this mean that paranoia may simply reflect perfectly rational cognitive processes in the service of explaining an unrecognized perceptual disorder—as Brendan Maher (1974) has hypothesized? The following study was designed to find out.

Normal, healthy male college students were induced to experience the perceptual disorder found in many older paranoid patients—namely, deafness without awareness. A hearing deficit was induced through hypnotic suggestion in these subjects, along with amnesia for its source. Each subject was brought to a social situation in a laboratory where he was to work on some tasks with two other students. They were actually confederates of the experimenter, who enacted a standard script of recalling a funny party where they had met. Several solitary and group tasks followed, during which the confederates spoke often to each other but only occasionally to the subject—creating the opportunity to feel excluded.

Across a variety of measures, these young subjects acted as if they were paranoid. They were suspicious, irritated, angry, and hostile (in their self-rat-

occupied by schizophrenic patients. Overall, it is estimated that 2 percent of the population will have an episode of schizophrenia during their lives. This estimate is much higher for college students (Koh & Peterson, 1974) and for the urban poor (Dohrenwend & Dohrenwend, 1974). The first occurrence of a schizophrenic episode more commonly occurs for men *before* they are age 25 and for women after that age but before they are 45 years old (Lewine et al., 1981).

Mark Vonnegut, son of novelist Kurt Vonnegut, was in his early twenties when the first symptoms of schizophrenia appeared. While pruning some fruit trees, he recalled hallucinating, distorting the reality that was there and creating a reality that wasn't:

"I began to wonder if I was hurting the trees and found myself apologizing. Each tree began to take on personality. I began to wonder if any of them liked me. I became completely absorbed in looking at each tree and began to notice that they were ever so slightly luminescent, shining with a soft inner light that played around the branches. And from out of nowhere came an incredibly wrinkled, irridescent face. Starting as a small point infinitely distant, it rushed forward, becoming infinitely huge. I could see nothing else. My heart had stopped. The moment stretched forever. I tried to make the face go away but it mocked me . . . I was holding my life in my hands and was powerless to stop it from dripping through my fingers. I tried to look the face in the eyes and realized I had left all familiar ground" (1975, p. 96).

ings and according to ratings by the confederates). On the MMPI and other personality tests designed to assess paranoia, they changed significantly toward paranoia from before to after this experience. They were significantly more paranoid on all assessment measures than either of two control groups, one in which subjects had been hypnotized to be temporarily deaf but with awareness of the deafness and its source, and the other in which subjects were given a different posthypnotic suggestion but with no hypnotically induced deafness (Zimbardo et al., 1981).

This finding lends support to the theory that a cognitive-social process underlies the development of paranoid delusions in some cases. It points to the importance of full medical checkups for older people (and others, too) before a psychiatric diagnosis is made of behavior that is apparently abnormal. For the elderly paranoid person found to be suffering from an undetected hearing disorder, the first recommended therapy consists of simply providing a hearing aid. It should also make us more aware of how easy it is to be unaware of the source of some personal perception of reality that differs from that of others—and thus use perfect logic to reason incorrectly from that false initial premise to a "crazy" conclusion.

During the next weeks, young Vonnegut's behavior went out of control more often and more extremely. He cried without reason. Terror would evaporate into periods of ectasy, with no corresponding change in his life situation. "There were times when I was scared, shaking, convulsing in excruciating pain and bottomless despair." For twelve days he ate nothing and did not sleep. While visiting friends in a small town, he stripped and ran naked down the street. Suicidal despair nearly ended his young, once promising life. In *Eden Express* (1975), Mark Vonnegut tells the story of his break with reality, its forms, and his eventual recovery after being hospitalized twice for "acute schizophrenia."

Some people do *not* recover from the acute episodes but instead go on to become chronically schizophrenic. Observing such chronic patients, one typically sees social withdrawal, eccentric behavior, illogical or incoherent speech, and seemingly inappropriate affect (mood and emotion). These patterns can go on and on, associated with impaired personal grooming and hygiene and a failure to follow social rules of appropriate behavior. Whether such people are internally experiencing the thoughts and feelings described by Mark Vonnegut, we cannot know—but their suffering is usually all too apparent.

In this final section on mental disorders, we shall examine the main types of schizophrenic reactions and the psychological processes that are distorted when a person is drawn into this "other reality."

Schizophrenic reaction types. Imagine all the things that possibly could go wrong with a person's mental life: with that view, welcome to the world of schizophrenia. *Thinking* becomes illogical; the normal associations among ideas are remote or without apparent pattern. *Language* may become incoherent—a "word salad" of unrelated words—or the individual may become mute. *Hallucinations* occur, involving imagined sights or sounds (usually voices) that are assumed to be real. The person may hear a voice that keeps a running commentary on his or her behavior, or may hear several voices in conversation.

Delusions are common; often the person believes that he or she is persecuted or a person of great importance. In other delusions, frequent themes are jealousy, bodily processes, religion, or death and destruction—for example, that one's brain is rotting away. Some delusions are absurd, without possible factual basis, such as the belief that one's thoughts are being broadcast, controlled, or taken away by alien forces.

Emotions may be flat or inappropriate to the situation. *Psychomotor behavior* may be disorganized (grimaces, strange mannerisms), or the posture may become rigid. Even when only some of these symptoms are present, there will certainly be deteriorated functioning in work, social relations, and self-care.

Reliably diagnosing schizophrenia has been a problem for workers trying to understand and treat this disorder. The DSM-III classification deals directly with this problem by using explicitly defined operational criteria, as shown in the chart of types in **Table 14.4,** and by narrowing the boundaries between types of disorders.

There is also a current trend toward viewing schizophrenia not as a single or unitary disorder but as a cluster of disorders and thus as a heterogeneous concept (Haier, 1980). In this thinking, clinical subtypes might be defined on the basis of biological, genetic, or neurophysiological variables rather than by "classic" symptoms, such as hallucinations and delusions. For example, when two groups of schizo-

Table 14.4 *Types of Schizophrenic Disorder*

Type	Description
DISORGANIZED TYPE (formerly Hebephrenia)	The person shows severe disorganization of emotional responding, language, and social behavior. Affect is blunted (no high or low degrees of emotion), inappropriate to an emotional stimulus, and often silly (giggling "at nothing"). Language is so incoherent, full of unusual words and incomplete sentences, that communication with others breaks down. Delusions are disorganized, not coherently structured around a theme. Mannerisms are unusual, odd, and childish, hypochondriacal complaints are frequent, and social withdrawal is extreme. This is a chronic disorder that rarely shows remission once it starts in adolescence.
CATATONIC TYPE	The person seems frozen in a stupor, with little or no reaction to anything in the environment, and is mute. Rigidity of posture occurs despite efforts at getting the person to move. Negativism is displayed in the form of motionless resistance to instructions. Posturing is inappropriate or bizarre positions are voluntarily assumed. Excitement sometimes alternates with the stupor; then motor activity is agitated, apparently purposeless, and not influenced by external stimuli.
PARANOID TYPE	The person's delusions are persecutory, grandiose, or of jealousy. Hallucinations occur that are filled with voices or images of people organized around themes of persecution or grandiosity. The paranoid patient's anger, unfocused anxiety, and argumentativeness can lead to violence. Gender identity confusion can lead to fear of homosexuality. But behavior is not grossly disorganized, nor is functioning impaired if the delusions are not acted out. Onset tends to be later in life than other schizophrenic subtypes.
UNDIFFERENTIATED TYPE	The person exhibits prominent delusions, hallucinations, incoherent speech, or grossly disorganized behavior that fit the criteria of more than one other type—or no clear type. This type is thus a hodge-podge of symptoms that do not clearly differentiate among various schizophrenic reactions.

(Based on DSM-III, 1980)

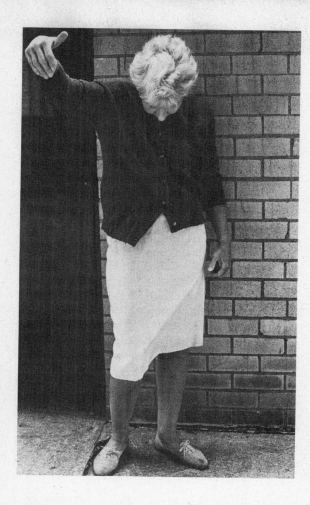

phrenic patients were compared—one with and the other without a family history of schizophrenia—the two groups were found to differ consistently in their brain waves in response to electrical stimulation although they were not distinguishable on the basis of clinical symptoms (Asarnow et al., 1978).

Schizophrenic process. A number of intriguing characteristics of the schizophrenic process are being discovered through controlled psychological research. Schizophrenic patients, as a group, exhibit a greater sensitivity to sensory stimuli than normal subjects. This hypersensitivity results in a "flooding" by external stimulation and great distractibility, making it difficult for the person to find constancy in the sensory environment. Disturbed thought patterns may thus be the consequence of an inability to give sustained selective attention to particular events or processes that are taking place.

In order to think, the person may attempt to shut out external stimulation, yet the attempt is not completely successful and the immediate stimulus situation keeps intruding. Not being able to filter out and ignore irrelevant stimuli results in a confusion of "signals" and "noise." Not surprisingly, schizophrenic patients show a loss of abstract thinking in favor of concrete thinking. Improved experimental studies of the biology and psychology of attention, comparing normal and schizophrenic individuals, are needed to enhance our understanding of how the world of schizophrenia becomes so different from ours (see Garmezy & Matthysse, 1977).

The schizophrenic patient's speech seems to be under the control of immediate stimuli. Distracted from complete expression of a simple train of thought by constantly changing sensory input and vivid inner reality, the schizophrenic speaker does not make sense to a listener. The incomprehensibility of schizophrenic speech is due, in part, to bizarre intrusions by thoughts that are irrelevant to the statement being uttered—intrusions that the person cannot suppress. Normal speaking requires that the speaker remember what has just been said (past), monitor where he or she is (present), and direct the spoken sentence toward some final goal (future). This coherence between past and present and future is not possible for the schizophrenic individual; thus he or she cannot maintain long interconnected strings of words.

It has been argued that bizarre schizophrenic speech is a particular brand of nonsense in which there is a deviation from normal whenever the person comes to a "vulnerable" word—one that has multiple meanings to the person. At that point, a personally relevant but semantically inappropriate word is used. For example, a patient may say "Doctor, I have pains in my chest and hope and wonder if my box is broken and heart is beaten." *Chest* is a vulnerable word; it can mean a respiratory cage or a container like a *hope* chest. *Wonder* could mean *Wonder Bread,* kept in a bread *box.* Similarly hearts *beat* and are *broken* (Maher, 1968). By carefully listening to schizophrenic speech, it is often possible for the clinician to decode the sense in what appears at first to be pure nonsense (Forest, 1976).

Psychotic patients often lump together "what is" and "what ought to be." Or they may dissociate effects from their causes, actions from thoughts, feelings from actions, conclusions from premises, or truth from evidence. It has been suggested that whereas most of us evaluate the reality of our inner world against criteria in the external world, psychotic individuals *reverse* this usual reality-testing procedure. Their inner experience is the criterion against which they test the validity of outer experience (Meyer & Ekstein, 1970). Theirs is a world in which thinking it makes it so. Thus, it may be that what appears to us as bizarre, inappropriate, and irrational behavior follows from the creation of a closed system that is self-validating and internally consistent.

UNDERSTANDING MENTAL DISORDERS

In examining the specific categories·of disorder, we have come from the vague popular conception of "nervous breakdown" to more precise descriptions of disorders that include aspects of cognitive, emotional, and behavioral functioning. But when the question is not *how* mental disorders afflict individuals, but instead *why* they do, then we find little agreement.

In this final section we shift our focus to examine a diversity of viewpoints that attempt to explain the "why" of mental illness. First, we will consider explanations that have been popular at different historical periods and in other cultures. Then we'll see how several current scientific models account for these phenomena and how together they can add to our understanding of the causes of schizophrenia—that most puzzling of all challenges to scientist, physician, and lay person. Finally, we will look briefly at the role of judgment in the decision that someone is mentally disordered and at the problem of public stigmatizing of the mentally ill in our society.

Major models of mental disorder

In every age, in every known society, there has been some explanation for mental disorders that was in accord with the dominant, accepted view of the causes of good and evil, health and sickness. In some instances, these models have begun by assuming that the disorder is not logically explicable. In other cases, the disorders have been seen not as unrelated events but as special cases of broader phenomena that are understood. Only in the last hundred years have we begun to have models based on scientific research, whose predictions could be checked by further research.

In earlier times, when religious views were very influential, abnormal behavior was assumed to be caused by *demonic possession,* the devil's take-over of someone's body and mind. During the Renaissance (about 1350–1630 A.D.) when intellectual and artistic enlightenment flourished, so did the Inquisition, which found untold thousands of people guilty of being bewitched—and sentenced them to death. One symptom of demonic possession was "sudden loss of reason'' (see **Close-up** on page 514 for a modern view of the causes of one's becoming ''bewitched'').

Culture and "madness." All cultures establish certain rules (norms) to be followed and roles to be enacted if people are to be considered normal and acceptable members of their society. Each culture also maintains more general belief systems about the forces that determine life and death, health and sickness, success and failure. This means that there is some *cultural relativity* in what is judged as ''mad'' or abnormal in different societies: what one sees as abnormal, another may see as appropriate (such as wearing your mother's skull around your neck to ward off evil spirits). It also means that some styles of mental disorder are more likely than others to be seen in a particular society (see Triandis & Draguns, 1980).

On the other hand, all known cultures consider people abnormal if they (a) exhibit unpredictable behavior or (b) do not communicate with others. Some symptoms of mental disorder appear to be *universal* manifestations of affliction and are regarded as pathological in all cultural settings. In such distinctly contrasting groups as the Eskimos of northwest Alaska and the Yorubas of rural tropical Nigeria, we find descriptions of a disorder in which beliefs, feelings, and actions are thought to come from the person's mind over which he or she has lost control. This pattern resembles what is diagnosed as schizophrenia in the United States (Murphy, 1976).

In many cultures—not only preliterate ones but ''developed'' ones too—folk beliefs about the causes of mental illness are part of a more general world view about unexpected personal disasters—sudden illness, infertility, crop failure, premature deaths of loved ones. These discontinuities in life's drama are attributed to the operation of ''evil magic.'' Unnatural effects are induced by supernatural influences through spells and hexes of one person on another who is envied or resented for some success. Thus some human enemy calls upon a malign agency to bring down the unsuspecting victim or a family member. This view is seen in witchcraft theories in West Africa, in sorcery among Cree Indians of Canada, in the voodoo practices of Haitians, and in the ''evil eye'' beliefs still common among most Mediterranean peoples (Wintrob, 1973).

△ The man wears the skull of his deceased mother to protect him from her ghost—perfectly ''normal'' behavior for members of his New Guinea tribe. An individual in our society who did the same thing would almost certainly be considered mentally disordered.

In many cultures, notably those of some African groups and of the southwestern U.S. Indians, mental disorder is seen not as something in the individual, but as part of an *ecological relationship:* it is a sign of *disharmony* in the relationship of members of the tribe to their earthly environment and spiritual reality. Treatment, in this view, consists of communal rituals that renew the vitality of the bonds among the afflicted individual, his or her society, and the natural habitat in which he or she lives (Nobles, 1972).

If these beliefs about mental disorder as disharmony in the person's social relationships seem ''quaint'' and unscientific, consider the fact that to the extent that an individual feels *isolated* from a meaningful social context or is not part of a social support network, he or she is in fact ''at risk'' for a

Salem Witchcraft: Possession, Mental Disorder, or Food Poisoning?

In the year 1692, the New England colony of Salem, Massachusetts, was swept by an outbreak of public hysteria that resulted in the execution of many people accused of witchcraft. Most of the "bewitched" were young women who had been behaving in strange ways that could not be readily explained. The victims suffered convulsions and reported sensations of being pinched, pricked, or bitten. Many became temporarily blind or deaf; others reported visions and sensations of flying through the air. Many reported feeling nauseated and weak; other physical problems also were experienced, such as swelling of the face.

When someone's behavior suddenly deviates from the normal, others always seek an explanation. For the people of Salem, who accepted without question the prevailing explanatory model of that time, the explanation was clear: the women were victims of witches in the community. To the modern mind, other explanations seem more reasonable. Some have argued that the women were probably suffering from conversion disorders, others that they may have been schizophrenic. These explanations share the assumption that the symptoms reflected some sort of mental disorder.

More recently, a new hypothesis has been proposed—that the "bewitched" were victims of poisoning from ergot fungus, which had contaminated their rye crop, the primary grain source at that time (Capo-

real, 1976). This hypothesis of a physical cause for the strange symptoms has been investigated by historian Mary Matossian (1982), who has traced court records, agricultural records, weather records, and medical literature to pull together a picture of how the outbreak could have occurred.

The weather preceding 1692 provided perfect, cool, damp conditions for the growth of the fungus. Young women are more susceptible to ergot poisoning, and all the households affected by the "witchcraft" symptoms were farming households on land which most favored the growth of ergot-infected rye. The symptoms of ergot poisoning closely fit the available behavioral records: convulsions, sensations of crawling or pinching on the skin, spasms of facial muscles and tongue, and so on. In addition, ergot is the source of lysergic acid diethylamide (LSD), a potent hallucinogen. Even cows grazing on land near the affected households also were reported to show similarly strange symptoms (for a critique of this hypothesis, see Spanos & Gottlieb, 1976).

We will probably never know for certain what happened in Salem in 1692; records are too limited to validate or refute the ergot hypothesis completely. But we know it was the only place and the only time in the United States where "witchcraft" broke out. We in the 1980's, looking back on our ancestors of almost 300

variety of pathological conditions, as you saw in the preceding chapter. Isolation plays a primary causal role in many cases of depression, suicide, mass murder, rape, child-abuse, paranoia, and psychotic states. *Social isolation is perhaps the best single predictor variable of most pathological reactions.*

Biological theories. In sharp contrast to the views that emphasize social and environmental factors in the development of mental disorders are the predominantly biological theories. Mental disorder, in these approaches, is a malfunctioning of the brain. It is generally agreed that the brain is a biochemical

organ whose elements are held in delicate balance and that a number of conditions can disrupt this balance, predisposing a person to mental disorder. But is a disruption of brain function always a causal factor in serious mental disorders? Some would say so.

One way abnormal brain functioning can be brought about is through faulty heredity. Some interpret schizophrenia as a hereditary disease because people genetically related to schizophrenic individuals have a greater likelihood of becoming affected than those with no schizophrenic relatives (Kessler, 1980). We will review some of this evidence a little later.

years ago, have very different models for explaining the bizarre behavior they observed. Our descendants in 2280 may look back on our explanations as equally naive and inappropriate, but they will undoubtedly share the need to find a satisfactory explanation when others behave in deviant, mystifying fashion.

△ ▌ *A scene from a Salem witch trial.*

In recent years, rapid advances in the field of neurobiology (biology of the brain) have linked certain mental disorders with specific abnormalities in biochemical processes (as we noted in Chapter 3). Biochemical interpretations of disorder have also been encouraged by studies showing the ways in which drugs can alter the normal reality of the mind, as well as by the proven success of chemical therapy in alleviating certain pathological symptoms (Bowers, 1980). In addition, mental disorders have been linked with severe malnutrition, brain injury, lead poisoning, oxygen deficiency, and pathology of the metabolic activity of brain cells.

According to the **medical model,** mental illness was the result of a disease of the nervous system. Patients so afflicted were to be treated by "curing the disease" rather than by merely working to eliminate the symptoms of strange behavior.

A medical model implies a view of the disturbed person as a passive victim of disease processes. It also minimizes the importance of environmental stress, personal conflict, maladaptive learning patterns, and distressed interpersonal relationships in the development of mental disorder. Current biological theories, however, are going beyond this to a much broader view of the subtle ways in which neurochemical processes can change our processing of information and our interactions with those around us.

Psychological approaches. Psychological models recognize that some mental disorders are *organic,* with a physical, biochemical basis, but focus instead on those disorders that are *functional,* apparently triggered by experience and learning and occurring in the absence of brain pathology. Within the overall psychological approach, different models have been developed with their own accounts of just how a normal person is transformed into one who functions abnormally. Of the many current psychological models of abnormality, we will outline three dominant ones—the psychodynamic, the behavioristic, and the cognitive models.

Freud's psychodynamic model. Sigmund Freud rejected what had been essentially static models of the suffering individual as a passive victim of either demons or disease. He proposed a more dynamic view in which the individual was seen as an active—though unknowing—agent in creating his or her mental anguish.

As we noted in earlier chapters, Freud thought that unconscious motivation and the repression of unacceptable impulses accounted for much that was abnormal. He developed psychoanalytic theory to the point where much apparently irrational and senseless neurotic behavior could be explained rationally by the theory. His ideas profoundly changed our basic conception of human nature, for he believed that neurotic disorders were simply an extension of "normal processes" that we all experience in psychic conflict and ego defense. In his classic work *The Psychopathology of Everyday Life,* written in 1904, Freud tried to demonstrate that at times all human beings experience distortions of thinking and feeling which are *similar in kind* to those of the emotionally disturbed neurotic individual—but just not so severe.

But Freud was a neurologist whose theory is really an extension of the medical model. His psychodynamic theory of neurosis assumes an inner core of psychic functioning that has been disturbed by inability to handle excessive inner conflict. From this disease core spring the manifest symptoms that we can observe (Freud, 1949). However, the patient is unaware of the connection between the symptoms and their underlying origin and thus perceives them as irrational.

Freud's plan envisioned a model of mental functioning that would ultimately integrate the biology of the brain with the psychology of the mind (Pribram & Gill, 1976). But Freud's vision also provided a foundation for a whole new psychological approach in which learning, thought processes, and social relationships play key roles.

Behavioristic models. Freudian notions gained ready acceptance among American clinical psychologists and psychiatrists. However, you will recall that American research psychology from the 1930s to the early 1970s was dominated by a behavioristic orientation. To those who insisted on observable responses as the only acceptable psychological data, psychodynamic processes were too vague to be useful. Recasting them in the language of behavioral learning theory was one step toward integrating some of the theoretical richness of Freud's concepts with an empirically based view of how people learn—maladaptive as well as adaptive behavior patterns (Dollard & Miller, 1950).

Current behavioral approaches to understanding maladaptive behaviors typically examine the inadequate coping strategies people use in solving their problems and life stresses. Often behavior is inhibited or ineffective not because the person is intellectually unaware of what to do, but because high levels of anxiety are causing rigidity or interfering with translation of plans into meaningful actions, or because the individual has learned self-defeating strategies. By discovering the environmental contingencies that maintain any undesirable, abnormal behavior, the investigator can recommend treatment for changing those aspects of the *situation.* The expectation is that doing so will then modify the person's behavior in desired ways (see Franks & Barbrack, 1983).

Cognitive models. Over the past decade, a cognitive view of human nature has replaced the strictly behavioristic view. It suggests that we should *not* expect to discover the origins of mental disorders in the objective reality of stimulus environments, reinforcers, and overt responses. Rather, what is important in disordered—as well as ordered—functioning is what we *perceive* or *think* about ourselves and about our relations to other people and to our environment. Among the cognitive variables that can guide—or misguide—our adaptive responding are our self-esteem, our perceived degree of control over important reinforcers, and our beliefs in our own efficacy to change how we act to cope with threatening events.

This newest approach to understanding mental disorders assumes that emotional upsets are caused not directly by events but by the mediating processes of our perceptions and interpretations of events. Psychological problems are seen as due largely to our distortions of reality in regard to the situation or ourselves, based on faulty reasoning, misattributions, or poor problem solving.

None of us can get past our perceptions and interpretations to see the world directly; we have only our perceptions to go by, bolstered by the context of conceptions and generalizations and meanings we have built up through our experiences so far. Sometimes our conceptions help us and sometimes they harm us; either way, they are our own personal way of dealing with the complexities and uncertainties of everyday life.

"Man creates his own gods to fill in gaps in his knowledge about a sometimes terrifying environment, creating at least an illusion of control which is presumably comforting. Perhaps the next best thing to being the master of one's fate is being deluded into thinking that he is" (Geer et al., 1970, pp. 737–38).

None of these broad models is adequate for a complete account of all mental disorders. Some fare well for certain disorders—such as the psychodynamic approach for understanding some anxiety disorders, or the learning approach for understanding phobias, or the cognitive approach for understanding depression. Similarly, some models are helpful in illuminating one facet of a disorder but do not offer an adequate causal analysis. When we come to the puzzle of schizophrenia, none of them seems adequate, yet several offer important contributions to our understanding.

Using the models to make sense of schizophrenia

"Despite thousands of scientific publications and innumerable psychiatric theories, no one is yet certain as to what is fundamental in the schizophrenic process" (Snyder, 1974, p. 73).

The same conclusion can be drawn about the etiology of this severe mental disorder. We do not yet know what causes a person to take the wrong path in life that can lead to the cul-de-sac of schizophrenia.

Different models point to quite different initial causes of schizophrenia, different pathways by which it develops, and different modes of treatment (as we shall see in the next chapter). Biologically oriented researchers look for problems with brain mechanisms caused by *inherited disorders* or *biochemical malfunctioning*. From a psychodynamic view, schizophrenia is a *regression to an infantile stage* of functioning caused by an inability to handle id/ego sexual impulses. This leads to an erosion of the boundaries between the internal ego and external reality. To a behaviorist, the origins of schizophrenia can be traced to *social reinforcements* for behaving abnormally. And the cognitive model emphasizes *attentional* and *perceptual problems*. Let's look further at the contributions several of these models can make to our understanding of how a person may become a patient with a schizophrenic disorder.

Genetic predisposition. It has long been known that schizophrenia tends to run in families (Bleuler, 1978; Kallmann, 1946); thus, the possibility of genetic transmission of some predisposition of schizophrenia is a likely causal candidate. Three independent lines of research—family studies, twin studies, and adoption studies—point to a common conclusion: persons "genetically at risk" for schizophrenia (related genetically to someone who has been schizophrenic) are more likely to become affected than those who are not (Kessler, 1980). A large body

 A new approach to understanding mental disorders is to view them as due, in part, to how the individual perceives and interprets events in everyday life.

of empirical research supports the notion that a *potential* for schizophrenia may be transmitted genetically (Gottesman & Shields, 1976).

For example, when both parents are schizophrenic, the schizophrenia risk of their offspring ranges from 35 to 50 percent. Where either parent is normal, the risk for the offspring drops sharply. It is greater with first-degree relatives (siblings and children), greater in families with many affected relatives, and greater where their schizophrenic reactions are severe (Hanson et al., 1977). In fact, for all close relatives of a diagnosed "index case" of schizophrenia, the risk factor may be as great as 46 times higher than the average risk for schizophrenia in the general population (see **Figure 14.1**).

Just "running in families" does not prove that the cause of a behavior is hereditary, however, because family members share the same environment as well as the same heredity. To separate the influence of heredity from that of learned components in schizophrenia, studies of twins and adopted children are used. Where one member of a pair of *identical twins* is schizophrenic, the chances that the other will also be affected are 4 to 5 times greater than among pairs of nonidentical twins, though in both cases the twins usually have shared the same general environments. Put technically, among monozygotic (identical) twins the **concordance rates** for schizophrenia (rates for cases in which both twins are affected) far exceed the concordance rates among dizygotic (fraternal) twins. Yet environmental factors also play a role, as shown by the fact that the concordance rates among identical twins are far from perfect: in many cases where one member of the pair develops schizophrenia, the other one never does.

The most compelling evidence for the role of genetic factors in the etiology of schizophrenia comes from adoption studies. When the offspring of a schizophrenic parent are reared by a normal parent in a foster home, they still have the same risk for the disorder as if they had been brought up by the biological parent (Heston, 1970; Rosenthal et al., 1975). In addition, adoptees who are schizophrenic have significantly more biological relatives with schizophrenic disorders than adoptive relatives with the disorder (Kety et al., 1975). Another study showed that adopted children of biologically normal parents raised by schizophrenic individuals were much less likely to be diagnosed later in life as schizophrenic than were children born of schizophrenic parents who were raised by normal, adoptive parents (Wender, 1972).

In some cases, a physiological—or medical—problem can affect the way a person is treated by others—which, in turn, can either minimize or exacerbate the person's problems. This means that even where physiological abnormalities are present, it can be useful to look also at the social context in which mental disorders occur.

A study of pairs of twins in which only one twin was schizophrenic found that those who became schizophrenic had been smaller or weaker at birth or been less healthy as young children. These fragile twins

▷ Figure 14.1 *Genetic Risk for Schizophrenic Disorder*

Out of a sample of 100 children of schizophrenic parents, from 10 to 50 percent will have the genetic structure that can lead to schizophrenia. Of these, about 5 percent will develop schizophrenia early and 5 percent later in life. It is important to note that as many as 40 percent of the high-risk subjects will not become schizophrenic. (Adapted from Hanson et al., 1977)

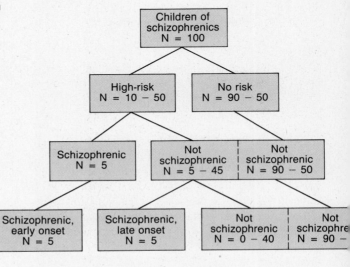

◁ *Pictured here celebrating their 51st birthday in 1981 are the Genain quadruplets. These four genetically identical women each experienced a schizophrenic disorder, which would seem to suggest a hereditary role in the development of schizophrenic disorder. But for each of the quads, the disorder was different in severity, duration, and outcome—facts that would seem to suggest an environmental role. For more on their fascinating story, see Rosenthal (1963).*

then had become the objects of intense worry and attention on the part of concerned adults. When these twins became older and faced adulthood, with its accompanying demands for autonomy and separation from parents and home, they were overwhelmed, and symptoms of schizophrenia appeared (Yahraes, 1975).

Here biology, social environment, and personal experiences had interacted to set the stage for a full-blown schizophrenic reaction.

Biochemical processes. "For every twisted thought there is a twisted molecule" is one assumption of a biochemical model of schizophrenia. Particular biochemical materials and processes in the brain are viewed as essential for the production—and reduction—of schizophrenic reactions. This viewpoint gained support in the 1950s with the development of new "miracle drugs" (the Phenothiazine tranquilizers) that altered certain schizophrenic disorders in dramatic ways.

The success of drug therapy has led medical researchers to search for the natural biochemical processes that influence the development or remission of schizophrenia. The most promising biochemical research today is focused on specific blood substances, neurotransmitters in the central nervous system, and opiate receptors in the brain.

Dopamine is one neurotransmitter that may be responsible for both the abnormalities in movement found in Parkinson's disease and the rigid catatonic postures and other motor symptoms seen in schizophrenia. The **dopamine hypothesis** holds that schizophrenia is associated with a relative excess of dopamine at specific receptor sites in the central nervous system (Carlsson, 1978). This view states that schizophrenic symptoms may be due to the relative increase in the activity of neurons that use dopamine as their neurotransmitter. Researchers are studying the relationships between drugs that alter the availability or reception of dopamine and changes in patterns of movement and other symptoms of schizophrenic disorders. Although the dopamine hypothesis is the most tenable one concerning the biochemical mechanisms for schizophrenia, the evidence is circumstantial and not yet compelling. There is also the possibility that dopamine availability may be one factor in the sequence of development of schizophrenia but not the elusive central factor.

A new candidate for a role in schizophrenia is the endorphins, the brain's opiates (described in Chapter 3). Endorphins may modulate those neurotransmitter systems that improve or worsen schizophrenic symptoms (Watson et al., 1979). Some researchers have argued for endorphin *excess,* others for endorphin *deficiency* as the cause of schizophrenia; at present, the issue is still unresolved. "Despite a great deal of progress in understanding what is happening, the brain is still a 'gray box' " (Marx, 1981, p. 1015).

It is unlikely that one biological "silver bullet" will ever be found that will explain the origins of the wide range of schizophrenic symptoms. But there is no question that increasingly refined methodology will clarify our understanding of the biochemical processes at work in schizophrenia.

Family interaction. If it is difficult to prove that a highly specific biological factor is a *sufficient* cause of schizophrenia, it is equally hard to prove that a vague general psychological one is a *necessary* condition. At best, what we can expect to discover is the relative contributions of each of a complex of variables that together produce a schizophrenic reaction pattern. Just as genetic factors can make an individual biologically vulnerable, so environmental factors (such as parental rejection or overprotection, excessive or inconsistent discipline, or extreme insecurity) can psychologically predispose some individuals to mental disorder. Studies of the family structure of schizophrenic patients, as well as of other features of their social context, reveal the extent to which functional psychosis may represent learned ways of attempting to cope with chronic stress and unresolvable conflicts (Liem, 1980).

One of the most reliable predictors of schizophrenic development is a pattern of *social isolation* during adolescence, in which the individual withdraws from interacting with others. This may be a consequence of feeling different or "abnormal" in some way, or of not having learned how to relate to other people in a positive and meaningful way, or both.

Sociologists, family therapists, and psychologists have all studied family role relationships in the development of schizophrenia; generally, these studies have been guided by psychodynamic theory (Lidz et al., 1965). Many such studies show that one of the most abnormal things about the backgrounds of schizophrenic children is the use of the child by unhappy parents in working out their own feelings of frustration and hostility. Often the child is cast in the role of "buffer" or mediator and made to feel responsible for the continuation or failure of the marriage.

Another finding has been that the basic *power structure* in families with children at risk for schizophrenia differs from that of families with low-risk children. For example, in the families of schizophrenic children (or children who later become schizophrenic), parents often tend to form coalitions that exclude the child. The schizophrenic patient's failure to differentiate between self and external world may also be traced to an early, intense *symbiotic attachment* between mother and child in which the two failed to differentiate themselves from each other, were highly dependent on one another, intruded in each other's lives, and had difficulty separating.

Studies of disordered family communication show less responsiveness and less interpersonal sensitivity in the speech patterns of families with a schizophrenic member than in normal families. In families with a disturbed offspring, the members do not listen to each other or spend as much time in information exchange as do normal families. Members of families with withdrawn adolescents are less able to predict each other's responses in a test situation (see Goldstein & Rodnick, 1975).

The disordered communication in these families can "drive the child crazy" by distorting his or her reality through concealing or denying the true meaning of an event, or by injecting a substitute meaning that is confusing (Wynne et al., 1979). **Double bind** is the term for a situation in which the child receives multiple messages from a parent that are contradictory and cannot all be met. The mother may complain that a son is not affectionate, yet reject his attempts to touch her. Torn between these different verbal and nonverbal meanings, between demands

◁ *All adolescents like some time to themselves, but if there is a pattern of social isolation, it could be a predictor of schizophrenic development.*

and feelings, the child's grip on reality testing may begin to slip. The result may be that the child will see his feelings, perceptions, and self-knowledge as unreliable indicators of the way things are "really like" (Bateson, et al., 1956).

These interesting studies of deviance in family communication styles have treated the family as a *closed system*. Current research is examining the family as a functional unit in a larger social context and thus influenced by many context factors, including resources available to the family, the state of the economy, extended family relationships, social class, occupations, and other "macro" variables (see Bronfenbrenner, 1977).

Cognitive processes. Among the hallmarks of schizophrenia are deficits in attention, thought, memory, and language, as we have seen. Some psychologists argue that instead of being consequences of schizophrenia these deficits may play a role in causing the disorder. "The crucial behavior, from which other indicators of schizophrenia may be deduced, lies in the extinction of attention to social stimuli to which 'normal' people respond" (Ullmann & Krasner, 1975, p. 375). Attentional deficits may involve not noticing important environmental or cultural cues that most people use to socially regulate or "normalize" their behavior. Or such deficits may lead the person to notice remote, irrelevant thought or word associations while thinking or talking, thereby confusing these distracting peripheral ideas and stimuli with the main points or central themes.

Schizophrenic thought disorder is in part due to an inability to focus or sustain attention on relevant task features. This impaired selective attention results in poor performance across a variety of perceptual and cognitive tasks (Garmezy, 1977; Place & Gilmore, 1980). What is the nature of this attentional disorder? Results of a recent neurophysiological study support the hypothesis that schizophrenic attentional deficits are due to the inability to control and maintain an effective selective processing strategy, rather than a general slowness of information processing or an absence of attentional selectivity.

On the basis of evoked brain potentials (see Chapter 3) measured during dichotic listening tasks that required attention to auditory signals in one or the other ear (or in both together), researchers found that schizophrenic subjects *can* focus their attention selectively to information in different ears, but only

under certain conditions. They perform well in the early stages of selecting one channel of information based on some physical stimulus characteristic (such as its pitch). But they are poor at processing information that requires a response to a stimulus target that has been detected. They also perform much worse than a normal comparison group of subjects where *divided attention* is required to select information coming into both ears at the same time. Thus, their disorder appears to be in the cognitive mechanism that controls the strategy for selectively attending to certain kinds of information (Baribeau-Braun et al., 1983).

It is clear that genetic predispositions, biochemical processes, family structure and communication, and cognitive-behavioral processes have all been demonstrated to play roles in at least some cases of schizophrenia. But their roles are interactive ones. No one of them alone explains schizophrenia in every case. Much of the mystery of schizophrenia remains.

Making judgments about individuals

Even with a carefully worked out classification system, the task of actually putting a person into the group called "mentally disordered" remains a matter for human judgment. All human judgments are subject to bias and error, and all judgments about a person are likely to have significance for both the judger and the person judged. How objective are these judgments likely to be and how does being called "mentally disordered" affect a person's self-image and interactions with other people?

The problem of objectivity. Who declares people to be mentally disordered, and how objective is the process? In our society today, we generally make such a decision on the basis of some combination of the following evidence: (a) they are under psychiatric care; (b) influential members of the community (teachers, judges, parents, spouses, priests) agree that the behavior represents a dangerous degree of maladjustment; (c) a psychiatrist or clinical psychologist diagnoses mental disturbance; (d) their test scores on psychological self-report inventories deviate by a specified extent from scores of a group designated as normal; (e) they declare themselves to be "mentally sick" either directly by applying this term to themselves or indirectly by expressing feelings such as unhappiness, anxiety, depression, hostility, or inadequacy extreme enough to be associated with emotional disturbance; (f) they behave publicly in ways dangerous to themselves (suicidal threats or gestures, inability to care for themselves, etc.) or to others (aggressive or homicidal impulses or gestures).

The decision to declare someone mentally disordered or *insane* (the legal term) is always a *judgment about behavior.* It is a judgment made by one or more people about the behavioral functioning of another individual—often one of less political power or socioeconomic status. Because psychiatric diagnoses are only *judgments* and are validated only by agreement with other judgments rather than by the kinds of objective, impersonal evidence used to validate medical diagnoses, they are susceptible to many sources of judgmental bias—bias based on expectation, status, gender, and other factors.

We have seen throughout our study of psychology that the *meaning* of behavior is jointly determined by its *content* and the *context* in which it occurs. The same act in different settings conveys very different meanings. A man kisses another man; it may mean a homosexual advance, ritual greeting (in France), or Mafia "kiss of death" (in Sicily). These are but a few of the meanings that this behavior can have depending on its context. Unfortunately, the diagnosis of a behavior as psychotic can also depend on where the behavior is seen: even professionals' judgments may be influenced by the context as well as the behavior being judged.

> In a classic study by David Rosenhan, eight sane people gained admission to different psychiatric hospitals by pretending to have a single symptom—hallucinations. All eight of these pseudopatients were diagnosed on admission as either "paranoid schizophrenic" or "manic-depressive."
>
> Once admitted, they behaved normally; but when a sane person is in an insane place, he or she is likely to be judged insane. The context of the mental hospital ward biased the diagnosis. The pseudopatients remained on the wards for almost three weeks, on the average, and not one was detected by staff as being sane. When they were finally released—with the help of spouses or colleagues—their discharge diagnosis was still "schizophrenia" but *"in remission"* (symptoms not active) (Rosenhan, 1973, 1975; see also criticisms by Fleischman, 1973; Lieberman, 1973).

This research challenged the former system of classification of mental disorders, but it also raises basic issues about the validity of people's judgments of "abnormality" in other people and how dependent such judgments may be on factors other than the person's behavior.

In the view of psychiatrist Thomas Szasz, in fact, clinical judgments are all there is. "Mental illness" does not even exist—it is a "myth" (1961, 1977). Szasz argues that the symptoms used as evidence of mental illness are merely medical labels that sanction professional intervention into what are social problems—people violating social norms. Once labeled, these people can then be treated either benignly or harshly for their problem "of being different" with no threat to our status quo. British psychiatrist R. D. Laing (1967) goes further yet—proposing that labeling people as mad often suppresses what is the creative, unique probing of reality by individuals who are questioning their social context.

Few clinicians would go this far. But the problem of the dependence on judgment when one person labels another "mentally disordered" remains a very real one.

> An outrageous example of the "medicalization of deviance" in the United States is found in an 1851 report in a medical journal on "The Diseases and Physical Peculiarities of the Negro Race." Its author, Samuel Cartwright, M.D., had been appointed by the Louisiana Medical Association to chair a committee to investigate the strange practices of Negro slaves. "Incontrovertible scientific evidence" was amassed to justify the accepted practice of slavery. In the course of doing so, several "diseases" previously unknown to the white race were discovered. One finding was that Negroes allegedly suffered from a sensory disease that made them insensitive "to pain when being punished" (thus no need to spare the whip).
>
> But the classic misuse of the medical model was the committee's invention of the new disease *drapetomania*—a mania to seek freedom—a mental illness that caused certain slaves to run away from their masters. Runaway slaves needed to be caught so that their illness could be properly treated (see Chorover, 1981)!

The problem of stigma. From a sociological point of view, the mentally disordered are people who are "deviant"—who deviate from the rest of us.

But "deviance" and "abnormality" are rarely used in a value-free statistical sense when other people's behavior is being judged. In practice, being "deviant" connotes moral inferiority and brings social rejection. In addition, the term *deviant* implies that the whole person "is different in kind from ordinary people and that there are no areas of his personality that are not afflicted by his 'problems'" (Scott, 1972, p. 14).

It has been proposed that each society defines itself negatively by pointing out what is *not*—rather than what *is*—appropriate, in this way setting boundaries on what is socially acceptable. Deviants, since they clarify these boundaries, serve to make the rest of the society feel more normal, healthy, moral, and law abiding—by contrast (Erickson, 1966). In any case, there is little doubt that in our society to be "mentally disordered" is to be publicly degraded and personally devalued. Society extracts costly penalties from those who deviate from its norms of what is right and "normal" (see **Figure 14.2**).

Those who are mentally disordered are stigmatized in ways that most physically ill people are not. *Stigma* means a mark or brand of disgrace; here it means a set of negative attitudes about a person that sets him or her apart as unacceptable (Clausen, 1981). Such negative attitudes toward the mentally disturbed come from many sources. Prominent among them are mass media portrayals of the mentally deranged as violent criminals, "sick jokes" that we hear and laugh at, family denial of the mental distress of one of its members, fear of loss of employment if others discover one is distressed or has received mental health care, and legal terminology that stresses mental incompetence (see Rabkin et al., 1980). The stigmatizing process not only marks the target as deviating from an acceptable norm but discredits the person as "flawed" (see E. Jones et al., 1984).

"For me, the stigma of mental illness was as devastating as the experience of hospitalization itself," writes a recovered patient. She describes her personal experience in vivid terms:

"Prior to being hospitalized for mental illness, I lived an enviable existence. Rewards, awards, and invitations filled my scrapbook. My diary tells of many occasions worth remembering . . . The crises of mental illness appeared as a nuclear explosion in my life. All that I had known and enjoyed previously was suddenly transformed, like some strange reverse process of nature, from a butterfly's beauty into a pupa's cocoon. There was a binding, confining quality to my life, in part chosen, in part imposed. Repeated rejections, the awkwardness of others around me, and my own discomfort and self-consciousness propelled me into solitary confinement.

"My recovery from mental illness and its aftermath involved a struggle—against my own body, which seemed without energy and stamina, and against a society that seemed reluctant to embrace me. It seemed that my greatest needs—to be wanted, needed, valued—were the very needs which others could not fulfill" (Houghton, 1980, pp. 7–8).

When it becomes difficult to continue usual interpersonal relations with the individual who is acting odd, upset, or "plain ornery," others begin to perceive him or her as unreliable, untrustworthy, a

▷ **Figure 14.2** *"Let the Punishment Fit the Crime"*

This figure illustrates a continuum of behaviors that are deemed increasingly unacceptable and are responded to with increasing severity. Basically, all these reactions are punishments for deviance; thus, behavior toward those who behave neurotically or psychotically can be seen to resemble that toward criminals and other antisocial deviants. (Adapted from Haas, 1965)

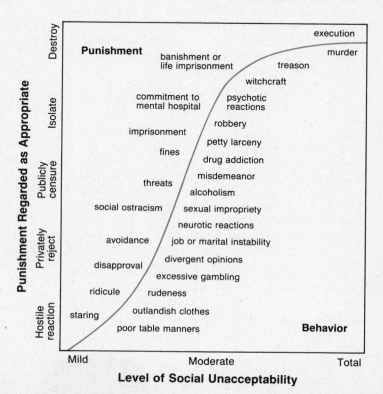

threat. They change the quality of their relationship so as to avoid and exclude the person. In response, the distressed person further isolates him- or herself, thereby being cut off from both social support and social checks on reality (Lemert, 1962).

Our negative attitudes toward the mentally disturbed bias our perceptions of and actions toward them and also influence their behavior toward us. A series of experiments conducted in laboratory and naturalistic settings demonstrates the unfavorable influences of the social situation on both the behavior of a person *perceived* to be a mental patient (even when not so) and that of the person making that judgment.

When one member of a pair of male college students was (falsely) led to believe the other had been a mental patient, he perceived the pseudo ex-patient to be inadequate, incompetent, and not likeable. And by making one of a pair of interacting males *falsely* believe *he* was perceived by the other as stigmatized, he behaved in ways that actually caused the other naive subject to reject him (Farina, 1980, Farina et al., 1971).

These findings suggest that friends and family may unwittingly contribute to the development of mental disorders, especially paranoid thinking.

There seem to be clear sex differences, too in the tendency to stigmatize those who are former mental patients, or believed to be. Men behave more harshly and are more rejecting than women. Women have been found to be more generous in their overall reactions to those who have been afflicted by mental disorder (Farina & Hagalauer, 1975).

Our growing understanding of mental disorder does more than enable society to reclaim its "familiar strangers." In making sense of mental disorder, we are forced to come to grips with basic conceptions of normality, reality, and social values. A mind loosed from its stable moorings does not just go on its solitary way; it bumps into other minds, sometimes challenging their stability. In discovering how to treat and prevent mental disorders, we not only help those unfortunates who are suffering but also expand our basic understanding of our own human nature. How do psychologists and psychiatrists intervene to "right" minds gone wrong, to modify behavior that doesn't work? We shall see in the next chapter.

SUMMARY

■ Psychopathology is the broad area of study of mental disorders by medical or psychological specialists. Clinical psychology is the field of psychology that specializes in the psychological treatment of individuals with mental disorders.

■ A mental disorder is a clinically significant behavioral or psychological pattern shown by an individual that is associated with distress and/or impairment of functioning.

■ Statistics about the incidence of mental disorders underestimate the actual extent of the problem, covering only those who are treated in public institutions and not including many types of antisocial and self-defeating behavior.

■ The judgment that a person is suffering from a mental disorder is made on the basis of several kinds of evidence, including suffering, behaving in maladaptive ways, irrationality, unpredictability, loss of control, moral unacceptability, or making other people uncomfortable.

■ A good classification scheme permits reliable diagnosis of individual cases and enables researchers to make studies of how particular problems develop, what can be expected, and what treatment programs will be most effective.

■ The currently used classification scheme, DSM-III, describes behavior syndromes instead of labeling individuals, uses terminology acceptable to both psychiatrists and psychologists, and uses only descriptive statements where causal factors are not known. DSM-III is a multiaxial system, with three axes for assessing symptoms and two for rating the stress situation and the individual's overall recent functioning.

■ Personality disorders are longstanding, inflexible, maladaptive patterns of perceiving, thinking, or behaving which seriously impair the individual's functioning or cause significant distress.

■ Most of the disorders formerly covered together in a category called *neurosis* are now delineated into anxiety, somatoform, and dissociative disorders, as well as some of the affective and psychosexual disorders.

■ Anxiety disorders affect millions of people in the U.S. They involve physiological arousal and free-floating anxiety—intense feelings of apprehension without any known cause. Two major subcategories are phobic disorder, characterized by a specific fear that the person recognizes is irrational, and four types of anxiety states, including generalized anxiety disorder, panic disorder, obsessive-compulsive disorder, and posttraumatic stress disorder.

■ Somatoform disorders include hypochondriasis and conversion disorder, in which there are physical symptoms in the absence of an organic basis sufficient to account for them. Dissociative disorders are patterns with extreme alterations of consciousness in the form of memory loss (psychogenic amnesia), sometimes accompanied by wandering away from home (psychogenic fugue), and loss of identity (multiple personality).

■ Psychosexual disorders center around problems of inhibition and dysfunction, deviance in expression, and gender identity. They reflect the conflictful temptations for and deterrents against sexual impulses and actions in our society.

■ Psychosis is a general category for a number of severe disorders in which perception, thinking, and emotion are so impaired that the person loses contact with reality, requiring intensive treatment and perhaps hospitalization. Some psychoses result from brain damage; others, known as *functional psychoses,* are not attributable to brain damage though in some cases biochemical abnormalities may be involved in addition to presumed psychological and social factors. The functional psychoses include the major affective disorders, paranoid states, and schizophrenia.

■ Affective disorders are disturbances of mood, with episodes of excessive elation or excessive depression or both, which may be severe enough to be called psychotic. Episodes tend to run their course with or without treatment but may recur.

■ A paranoid disorder centers around a false belief that persists despite contradictory information. The individual typically feels under serious threat of some kind.

■ Schizophrenic disorders are a group of psychotic disorders in which perception is distorted, emotions are blunted, thoughts are bizarre and fragmented, and language is strange and disjointed; hallucinations and delusions are common, and there may be grimaces and odd mannerisms. Schizophrenic patients as a group seem to be hypersensitive to external stimuli and highly distractible; coherence between past, present, and future is lost in thought and speech, though the individual may have created a closed, inner, self-validating system.

■ Widely differing views of mental disorders have been held, reflecting differing cultural and religious beliefs and world views. But certain symptoms, such as unpredictability and not communicating with others are seen as abnormal in all known cultures. In some cultures a mental disorder is seen as a breakdown not in the individual but in the individual's relation with the community and environment.

■ Biologically oriented theories have associated mental disorder with faulty heredity or brain malfunctioning or classified them as diseases of the nervous system. Psychological explanations have included psychodynamic models, such as Freud's that emphasize inner conflicts and defense mechanisms, behavioristic explanations based on learning through reinforcement, and cognitive models that emphasize the individual's perceptions and interpretations.

■ There is evidence for the importance of genetic predisposition, biochemical abnormalities, family interactions, and faulty cognitive processes in the development of mental disorder; several of these may contribute in a given case.

■ The decision that someone is mentally disordered is always based on someone's judgment and will depend on both the behavior being judged and the context in which it occurs, as well as on the beliefs of the observer. Too often a person identified as mentally disordered suffers stigma, which then distorts both that person's behavior and the subsequent behavior of others toward him or her.

15

THERAPIES FOR PERSONAL CHANGE

- **THE THERAPEUTIC CONTEXT**
  Overview of kinds of therapy
  Entering therapy
  Goals and settings
  Healers and therapists
- **HISTORICAL CONTEXT**
- **PSYCHODYNAMIC THERAPIES**
  Freudian psychoanalysis
  Beyond Freud
- **BEHAVIOR THERAPIES**
  Counterconditioning
  Contingency management
  Social learning therapy
  Generalization techniques
- **COGNITIVE THERAPIES**
  Cognitive behavior modification
  Changing false beliefs
- **EXISTENTIAL-HUMANISTIC THERAPIES**
  Group therapies
  Marital and family therapy
- **BIOMEDICAL THERAPIES**
  Psychosurgery and electroconvulsive therapy
  Chemotherapy
- **THERAPEUTIC EFFECTIVENESS**
- **PROMOTING MENTAL HEALTH**
- **SUMMARY**

Gary was a college freshman who sought treatment for a mental problem that was ruining his life. His case provides us with some interesting clues as to how a psychological disorder may develop and be treated successfully, if therapy begins early enough.

Like most people seeking professional treatment for a mental disorder, Gary came with *presenting symptoms.* These are the problem reactions that make one feel distressed and unable to function effectively in school, on the job, or in social settings.

Gary had three presenting symptoms, and they were all major. He appeared to be on his way to developing anorexia nervosa, sexual dysfunction, and also paranoid obsessional delusions. Any one of these problems was enough to occupy most of his attention, leaving little energy for schoolwork. The triad of problems— which all had begun about the same time—was simply overwhelming everything else in his life. Unless some remedy could be found soon, Gary knew he would have to drop out of college and maybe even be hospitalized.

It was fortunate that Gary came to see a therapist soon after his problems began. Most people wait months or years after their first abnormal symptoms appear before they seek treatment. Typically, the delay increases their suffering and makes more difficult the road to mental health.

After lengthy discussion with Gary, his therapist came up with an interpretation of his problems that could account for all three of the difficulties he was experiencing. The interpretation also suggested that a particular therapeutic approach would be most helpful. See how soon in this case you can detect where the analysis is headed.

Because Gary's symptoms were all of recent vintage, the therapist was able to get him to fix the onset of each one within approximately a week's time. Gary recalled:

"I started vomiting up most of the food I ate in the dorm cafeteria about mid-January. I just can't eat any more without feeling sick; been losing about 5 pounds a week. A little later, I noticed I couldn't maintain an erection when out on a heavy date, or when looking at sexy magazine photos. I couldn't study because I was weak, dizzy, and worried why these things were happening to *me.* But then an even worse punishment started happening. I had these thoughts, sometimes they were vivid images, of people I knew who were in bloody accidents or committing suicide—whenever they disagreed with me about anything. I can't shake these horrible thoughts and they keep occurring. I'm gonna flunk out—all these problems are causing me to mess up my studying. This has never happened to me, ever; you see, I'm a straight A student. I've always been 'perfect'—academically *perfect.* I need help with these emotional problems, or else I'm never going to graduate with honors."

What is cause and what is effect in Gary's problems and symptoms? Gary argues persuasively that the syndrome of symptoms is causing cognitive and emotional problems which, in turn, result in poor grades. But have you considered the *timing* of the onset of his symptoms, and the alternative reasons why this freshman might be getting poor grades at a major university even without any mental disorder to disrupt studying? Might it be possible that the poor grades were the cause and not the effect of the psychological problems? With Gary's permission, this alternative scenario was checked out with his teachers. The therapist discovered that Gary already knew he was running low grades in his courses *before* his first symptom appeared!

This "perfect" student had been confronted with the reality that he was only average when competing with classmates who were *all* high-school "hot shots." It was such a blow to his self-image to acknowledge an *ability deficiency* that he developed a set of psychological problems to justify and explain the sudden discontinuity he was experiencing as an "A student" who was getting just ordinary grades. He could not ask for help to make him smarter (nor was he yet aware of help available at his college to improve study habits and test-taking skills). But he could ask for psychological help for temporary emotional, motivational problems—and get some sympathy in the bargain.

The therapeutic help for Gary consisted of helping him to: (a) acknowledge the proper sequence of timing between poor grades and symptom onset; (b) become aware of the error he was making in thinking his average (not perfect) performance was due to psychological problems rather than to the higher level of college competition, as compared with that of his small-town high school; (c) admit that being "perfect" was a burden imposed by his parents' unrealistic expectations for him, as well as an impossibility for anyone to maintain in an imperfect world; (d) accept the reality that he was a good student who could graduate from a good school, and recognize that no one would ever ask him for his G.P.A. after graduation (he was planning to go into business); (e) seek assistance on his study and test-taking skills; and finally (f) enjoy the discovery that he could now learn for the sake of learning, not just for A grades. Once he could accept that, he would not have to be so grade-conscious; he would probably have more time to socialize and enjoy his college years.

In Gary's case, this brief therapy was extremely helpful. Gary's triad of symptoms vanished over the next few weeks and he did not develop any new symptoms. Four years later he received his B.A. degree and he now has a good job.

Such "miracle cures" are rare in psychology and psychiatry. It would not have been possible to pinpoint the crucial timing variable had Gary been treated much later—his memory would have been too vague as to when the symptoms started and the grades deteriorated. Still, various types of therapies have been successfully used to provide relief for distressed individuals. In this chapter we turn to the issue of how people suffering from one or another form of psychological distress can be helped. After exploring some historically important therapeutic approaches and approaches found in different cultures, we will investigate in detail several modern treatments for mental disorders. But first, let's get an overview of the main kinds of therapy and therapists and the contexts in which therapy occurs.

THE THERAPEUTIC CONTEXT

Therapy involves a helping relationship between people. Someone with a mental or medical problem is given help by someone who is designated by the society as a helper for that kind of problem. There are different types of therapy for mental disorders and many reasons why someone seeks help (and why others who need it do not). In addition, the purposes or goals of therapy are varied, as are the settings in which it occurs and the kinds of people who are the therapeutic helpers. But all therapies are *interventions* into a person's life, designed to change that person's functioning in some way.

Overview of kinds of therapy

Using a computer analogy, mental problems may occur either in the "hardware" of the defective human computer or in the "software" of the instructions that program its actions. Correspondingly, the two main kinds of therapy for mental disorders focus on one or the other. **Biomedical therapies** focus on changing the hardware—the mechanisms that run the central nervous system, endocrine system, or metabolism. They try to alter brain functioning by chemical or physical interventions, including surgery, electric shock, and drugs. Psychological therapies, collectively called **psychotherapy,** focus on changing the software—the faulty behaviors we have learned and the words, thoughts, interpretations, and feedback that direct our strategies for living.

The four major types of psychotherapy, in turn, are the psychodynamic, behavior, cognitive, and existential-humanistic therapies. The *psychodynamic* approach—more commonly called a *psychoanalytic* approach—views adult neurotic suffering as revealing the outer symptoms of inner, unresolved childhood traumas and conflicts. *Psychoanalysis* treats mental disorder with words. It is a "talking cure" in which the therapist helps the person develop insights about the relation between the overt symptoms and the unresolved hidden conflicts that presumably caused them.

Behavior therapies treat the behaviors themselves as the disturbance that must be modified. Disorders are viewed as learned behavior patterns rather than as the tip of an iceberg of mental disease. For the behavior therapist, changing the problem behavior corrects the disorder. This is done in many ways, including changing reinforcement contingencies for desirable and undesirable responding, extinguishing conditioned fear responses, and providing models of effective problem solving.

Cognitive therapies try to restructure the way a person thinks about him- or herself, as well as to alter the often distorted self-statements the person is making about the causes of the problem and the chances of alleviating it.

Therapies that have emerged from the *existential-humanistic* tradition emphasize the *values* of the patient. Existential-humanistic therapies are directed toward self-actualization, psychological growth, forming more meaningful interpersonal relationships, and enhancing freedom of choice. They tend to focus more on improving the functioning of essentially healthy people than on correcting the symptoms of seriously disturbed individuals.

We will look in some detail a little later at several kinds of biomedical intervention and at each of these four major kinds of psychotherapy.

Entering therapy

Why does anyone go into therapy? As with physical illness, it is not easy to specify what leads people to make a decision to seek professional help for their psychological problems. Optimally, we expect that people will enter therapy when their everyday functioning violates societal criteria of normality and/or their own sense of adequate adjustment. A person with a problem may seek therapy on his or her own initiative or may do so on the advice of others.

But many people who might benefit from therapy do not seek professional help. Sometimes it is inconvenient to do so. All of us put off doing some useful things that might involve a hassle or loss of time and

△ *There may be any number of reasons why a person does not seek help for psychological problems, including the fear of admitting you have a problem in the first place.*

of the stigma of admitting that you have a mental problem requiring help from a "stranger" seems to be more characteristic of older people, people in more conservative communities, and men. Second, some psychological problems themselves affect one's ability to make constructive life choices. The agoraphobic person finds it hard, even impossible, to leave home to seek therapy; a paranoid person will not trust mental health professionals or institutions. Third, in many communities, it is still much easier to get help from a medical doctor for physical health problems than it is to find a qualified, affordable mental health worker who has time to provide needed psychological help. Fourth, insurance plans may not defray the cost of outpatient psychotherapy.

People who do enter therapy are usually referred to as either "patients" or "clients." The term "patients" is more typically used by professionals who take a biomedical approach to the treatment of psychological problems or professionals who view problems as symptoms of underlying mental illnesses that must be treated by getting at underlying roots of the illness. Those who use the term "clients" are usually professionals who think of psychological disorders as "problems in living" (Szasz, 1961). We will try to use the preferred term for each approach as we present its views: *patient* for biomedical and psychoanalytic therapies and *client* for the other therapies.

Goals and settings

The therapeutic process can involve four tasks: (a) to reach a *diagnosis* about what is wrong, possibly putting a psychiatric label on the problem and classifying the disorder; (b) to propose a probable *etiology* (cause of the problem), identifying the probable origins of the disorder and the functions being served by the symptoms; (c) to make a *prognosis,* or estimate of the course the problem will take with and without any treatment; and finally, (d) to prescribe and carry out some form of *treatment,* therapeutic intervention designed to minimize or eliminate the troublesome symptoms and perhaps also their sources.

Despite the differences in theory, most therapeutic interventions have the same purpose—to reduce the patient's or client's suffering and increase his or

money. We do not get our car tuned as often as we should, or go for regular physical and dental checkups. In the case of mental disorder, if a person's behavior is judged dangerous to self or others, he or she can be involuntarily committed by a state court to a mental institution for treatment (see Wexler, 1976).

There are some special reasons—other than inconvenience—why people may not seek help for psychological problems. First, as discussed in the previous chapter, in many communities there is still some stigma associated with having psychological problems and being in therapy. Fear of therapy and

her sense of well-being, which usually means helping the person develop more effective means of coping with everyday demands and stresses. The goal is to replace psychological problems or inadequate functioning with improved psychological health and effective coping styles.

Healers and therapists

When psychological problems arise, most of us first seek out "informal counselors" who operate in more familiar settings. Many people turn to a family member, a close friend, a personal physician, a lawyer, or a favorite teacher for support, guidance, and counsel. Others get advice and a chance to "talk it out"

△ When psychological problems arise, many people seek help from "informal counselors," such as a teacher.

by opening up to the neighborhood bartender, beautician, cab driver, or someone else who is willing to listen. These informal therapists carry the bulk of the daily burden of relieving human suffering.

A survey of the therapists sought by American adults with "psychological problems" revealed that most people went for help to those outside the mental health establishment—42 percent going to their clergyman, 29 percent to their physician, and 11 percent to their lawyer. Fewer than a quarter sought out the services of a professional mental health worker (Gurin et al., 1960).

Although more people may seek out therapy now, usually it is only when the psychological problems become severe or persist after some form of informal therapy that a trained mental health professional is called upon—either a clinical psychologist or a psychiatrist.

Clinical psychologists have earned a Ph.D. degree in which their major graduate school training was in the assessment and treatment of psychological problems. In addition, they have completed a supervised internship in a clinical setting. They tend to have a broader background in psychology, assessment, and research than do psychiatrists. **Psychiatrists** have completed all medical school training for the M.D. degree and also have completed some postdoctoral specialty training in dealing with mental and emotional disorders. Their training lies more in the biomedical base of psychological problems, and only they can prescribe medications or convulsive therapy. **Psychoanalysts** are therapists with either an M.D. or a Ph.D. who have completed postgraduate training in an institute that offers specialized training in the Freudian approach to understanding and treating mental disorders.

From this general overview of the therapeutic context we shall proceed—first turning to the past to consider how therapy was delivered in earlier times, then returning to the present to examine the strategies and tactics involved in the major forms of contemporary therapy.

HISTORICAL CONTEXT

What kind of treatment might you have received in past centuries if you were suffering from psychological problems? It all depends on when and where.

Several events occurred in fourteenth century western Europe that dramatically affected the treatment of psychological problems—for the worse. Population increases—coupled with migration to big cities—created unemployment, poverty, and alienation in many countries. Special institutions arose to warehouse society's three main categories of misfits—the poor, the criminals, and the mentally disturbed. In 1403, St. Mary of Bethlehem, a London hospital for the poor, admitted its first patient with psychological problems. *Bedlam* (a corruption of Bethlehem) came to stand for the chaotic confusion of this place and the dehumanized treatment of people confined there. For the next three hundred years, patients were chained, tortured, and exhibited like animals in zoos for the amusement of the public, who paid admission to see the mad beasts perform their antics (Foucault, 1975).

△ In this famous engraving, artist William Hogarth depicted the conditions that existed in the London mental institution known as Bedlam in the 1730s. Two society women are viewing the inmates.

Meanwhile, in fifteenth-century Germany, mental disorders began to be labeled as witchcraft; the mad were assumed to be possessed by the devil who deprived them of reason. As the Inquisition and its "persecutory mania" spread throughout Europe, symptoms of mental disturbance were "cured" by some form of painful death.

Starting in eighteenth-century Europe, the view that people with psychological problems were just *sick* emerged. During this age of enlightenment and revolution, the French physician, Phillippe Pinel described the new concept of "mental illness." "The mentally ill," wrote Pinel in 1801, "far from being guilty people deserving of punishment are sick people whose miserable state deserves all the consideration that is due to suffering humanity. One should try with the most simple methods to restore their reason" (in Zilboorg & Henry, 1941, pp. 323–24).

In the United States, in the eighteenth century, psychologically disturbed citizens were physically removed from society and confined for their protection and that of the community—but given no treatment. But by mid-nineteenth century, when psychology was emerging as a respectable way of understanding human nature, a "cult of curability" swept the country. Insanity was thought to be related to the environmental stresses brought on by the turmoil of living in newly developing cities. When the confinement of the mentally ill assumed a new *rehabilitative* goal, the *asylum* became the central fixture of this social-political movement. The disturbed were confined to these asylums in the rural countryside, far from the stress of the city, not just for protection but to be treated (Rothman, 1971).

The idea that mental illness could be cured helped transform people's view of the disturbed. No longer were they seen as animal-like "madmen"; instead they were "sick patients" not personally responsible for their illness, deserving of the same quality of medical treatment and scientific analysis that society extends to the physically ill. Unfortunately, many of these asylums rapidly became overcrowded. The humane goal of rehabilitation soon became replaced by an emphasis on the *warehousing* of the mentally ill.

The disease view of psychological problems has contributed to the alliance of political institutions (enacting laws) with the mental health profession (attempting cures). This alliance is neither wholly positive nor wholly negative, but it is certainly important in the current systems by which both psycho-

therapy and biomedical therapy are delivered to disturbed people.

One of the founders of modern psychiatry, German psychiatrist J. C. Heinroth, helped provide the conceptual and moral justification for the disease view. Heinroth wrote in 1818 that madness was a complete loss of inner freedom or reason that deprived those afflicted of any ability to control their lives. Others who "know best" what is good for these patients must therefore care for them. Heinroth maintained that it was the duty of the state to cure mentally ill patients of the disease that forced them to be burdensome to society (cited in Szasz, 1979). From Heinroth's time to the present, "in this alliance between psychology and state, the state's protective power to confine the mentally ill has been transformed into a power of the state to treat, through its agent the mental health profession, the mental disorder thought to be the basis of the problem" (White & White, 1981, p. 954).

In reviewing these historical trends, it is important to note that so far we have presented only Western views. There has been movement from trying to exorcise demons to trying to cure sickness or other problems within an individual, but this shift seems less profound when contrasted with historical trends in other cultures.

The European and American world view emphasizes individuality, uniqueness, competition, independence, survival of the fittest, a mastery over nature, and personal responsibility for success and failure. Both demonology and the disease model are consistent with this emphasis, in regarding mental disorder as something that happens *inside* a person. But this view is not universally shared. In the African world view we see instead an emphasis on groupness, commonality, cooperation, interdependence, tribal survival, unity with nature, and collective responsibil-

ity (Nobles, 1976). It is *contrary* to the therapeutic practices in many non-European cultures to treat mentally ill individuals by removing them from society so that their personal ills may be cured by a medical expert.

Among the Navajo and in African cultures, healing is a matter that always takes place in a social context and involves the distressed person's beliefs, family, work, and life environment. Recently the African use of group support in therapy has been expanded into a procedure called "network therapy." The patient's entire network of relatives, co-workers, and friends becomes involved in the treatment (Lambo, 1978).

One therapeutic practice used in a number of healing ceremonies is dissociation of consciousness, induced in the distressed person or in the faith healer *(shaman)*. In the Western view, dissociation is itself a symptom of mental disorder to be prevented or corrected. But in other views, evil spirits are exorcised and good spirits communicated with as consciousness is altered. This use of ceremonial alteration of consciousness can be seen today among the cult of Puerto Rican *Espiritistas* in New York city, whose healing ceremonies involve communication with good spirits that are believed to exist outside the person's skin (Garrison, 1977).

Some of these views from other cultures have begun to work their way into Western practices. The social-interactive concept and the focus on the person *in a family context and a supportive community* have become particularly influential in our newer therapeutic approaches.

From this general background, we are ready to move to the central focus of the chapter—an analysis of the major forms of psychological and medical therapies.

Anna O. and the Talking Cure

Modern psychotherapy began in 1880 with the case of Fraulein Anna O. and her famous physician, Joseph Breuer. This bright, personable, attractive 21-year-old Viennese woman became incapacitated and developed a severe cough while nursing her ill father. When the physician began to treat her "nervous cough," he became aware of many more symptoms that seemed to have a psychological origin. Anna squinted, had double vision, and experienced paralyses, muscle contractions, and anesthesias (loss of sensitivity to pain stimuli).

Breuer told a young physician, Sigmund Freud, about this unusual patient. Together they coined the term *hysterical conversion* for the transformation of her blocked emotional impulses into physical symptoms (Breuer & Freud, 1895/1955). This case of Anna O. is the first detailed description of physical symptoms diagnosed as resulting from psychogenic causes—a hysterical illness. But it was Anna O. herself who devised her own treatment, with Breuer as therapist. She referred to the procedures as a "talking cure," or jokingly as "chimney sweeping."

In the context of hypnosis, Anna O. talked freely, giving full reign of her imagination ("free associations"). Once she was able to express herself in an open and direct fashion to her therapist, she no longer needed to use the indirect and disguised communication of physical symptoms. According to Breuer, her "complexes were disposed of by being given verbal expression during hypnosis."

Breuer and Freud's analysis of Anna O.'s disorder was in terms of internal psychodynamic forces (instincts and impulses). What they failed to acknowledge fully were the external social obstacles that limited the ambitions of all women for a professional career at that time and place. Some of her symptoms may have stemmed from repressed rage, while the intellectual and emotional involvement with her therapist helped break the monotony of her existence. After a year of nearly daily treatment, Breuer terminated the psychotherapy.

Anna O. went on to become a pioneer of social work, a leader in the struggle for women's rights, a

PSYCHODYNAMIC THERAPIES

Psychodynamic therapies assume that the patient's problems have been caused by the psychological tension between unconscious impulses and the constraints of his or her life situation. These therapies locate the core of the disturbance inside the disturbed person, accepting a general model of a disease core that shows up in symptoms. However, their emphasis is on ongoing, intense psychological processes rather than physical imbalances.

Freudian psychoanalysis

Psychoanalysis or **psychoanalytic therapy,** as developed by Freud, is the premier psychodynamic therapy. It is an intensive and prolonged technique for exploring unconscious motivations and conflicts in neurotic, anxiety-ridden individuals. As we saw in

our earlier discussion of Freudian theory, neurotic disorders are viewed as inabilities to resolve adequately the inner conflicts between the unconscious, irrational impulses of the *id* and the internalized social constraints imposed by the *superego*. As the individual progresses through the biologically determined stages from infancy to adulthood, according to Freudian theory, his or her particular psychological experiences at each stage determine whether there will be a fixation at an immature stage or progress to a more mature level of development. The goal of psychoanalysis is the establishment of intrapsychic harmony that expands one's awareness of the forces of the *id,* reduces overcompliance with the demands of the *superego,* and strengthens the role of the *ego.*

Of central importance to the therapist is understanding how the patient used the process of *repression* to handle conflicts by pushing unacceptable urges and feelings out of consciousness. Symptoms

playwright, and a housemother of an orphanage. Her true name was Bertha Pappenheim (Rosenbaum & Muroff, 1984).

The importance of Anna O.'s role in the development of modern psychotherapy is considerable.

"Before the invention of the talking cure, hypnosis was used mainly for suggestion and the physician was a doer. With the shift to catharsis, the physician became a listener. This step may seem trivial today, but in its time it was monumental. As a result of it, Breuer could state that his patient's life became known to him to an extent to which one person's life is seldom known to another. It also shifted the focus from biology to psychology. Instead of asking what caused the *disease* labeled hysteria, the physician now asked about the emotional antecedents of the disorder. Thus, Breuer's treatment of Anna O. started us on the road that would lead to definitive forms of psychotherapy. It led the way, too, to the giant steps taken by Breuer's young friend [Freud], who was so pro-foundly impressed when he heard about this remarkable case" (Hollender, 1980, p. 500).

In a provocative new view of Anna O.'s illness, E. M. Thornton (1984) casts doubt on the original diagnosis—even if the subsequent treatment did pave the way for the talking cure that was to become central in psychoanalytic therapy. A reasonably good alternative diagnosis is that her symptoms were those associated with *tuberculous meningitis,* which she might have contracted from her father who probably was dying from a form of tuberculosis himself. After Anna O. had terminated her treatment with Breuer, she entered a sanitorium from which she was later discharged relatively recovered from her illness. It is likely that many or all of her "hysterical conversion" reactions were of organic not psychological origin. On the other hand, she may still have experienced considerable suppressed rage and guilt over having to be her father's nurse for so long and not being given outlets for her considerable talents because of sexual discrimination.

are considered to be messages from the unconscious that something is wrong. Thus the psychoanalyst's task is to help the patient bring repressed thoughts to consciousness and gain insight into the relation between the current symptoms and the repressed conflicts from years gone by. In this psychodynamic view, therapy works and patients recover when they are "released from repression" established in early childhood (Munroe, 1955). Because a central goal of the therapist is to guide the patient toward discovering insights between present symptoms and past origins, psychodynamic therapies are often called **insight therapies.** Other therapies we will discuss do not have insight as a goal; rather they focus on the present, on behavior, or on giving direct advice.

The goals of psychoanalysis are ambitious. They involve not just the elimination of neurotic symptoms but a total personality reorganization. When psychoanalysis overcomes barriers to self-awareness and to freedom of thought and communication, the person can achieve more intimate human associations as well as more intellectual creativity. Because traditional psychoanalysis is an attempt to reconstruct long-standing repressed memories and then work through painful feelings to an effective resolution, it is a therapy that takes a long time (several years at least, with one to five sessions a week). It also requires introspective patients who are verbally fluent, highly motivated to remain in therapy, and willing and able to undergo considerable expense. Some of the newer forms of psychodynamic therapy are trying to deal with some of these drawbacks—especially attempting to make therapy briefer in total duration.

Psychoanalysts use several techniques for bringing repressed conflicts to consciousness and helping the patient resolve them. These include free association, analysis of resistance, dream analysis, and analysis of transference and countertransference (see **Close-up** p. 534).

Free association. The principal procedure used in psychoanalysis to probe the unconscious and release repressed material is called **free association**. The patient sits comfortably in a chair or lies in a relaxed position on a couch. Letting his or her mind wander freely, the patient gives a running account of thoughts, wishes, physical sensations, and mental images as they occur. Patients are encouraged to reveal every thought or feeling, no matter how personal, painful, or seemingly unimportant.

Freud maintained that free associations are *predetermined*, not random. The task of the analyst is to track the associations to their source and identify the significant patterns that lie beneath the surface of what is apparently "just words."

Throughout, the patient is encouraged to express strong feelings, usually toward authority figures, that have been repressed for fear of punishment or retaliation. Any such emotional release, by this or other processes, is termed **catharsis**.

Resistance. During the process of free association, the patient will at times show **resistance**—an inability or unwillingness to discuss certain ideas, desires, or experiences. Resistances prevent the return to consciousness of repressed material that is especially painful to recall. This material is often related to the individual's sexual life (which includes all things pleasurable) or to hostile, resentful feelings toward parents. Sometimes resistance is shown by the patient's coming late to therapy or "forgetting" it altogether. When the repressed material is finally brought into the open, the patient generally claims that it is too unimportant, too absurd, too irrelevant, or too unpleasant to be discussed.

The psychoanalyst attaches particular importance to subjects that the patient does *not* wish to discuss. Such resistances are conceived of as *barriers* between the unconscious and the conscious. The aim of psychoanalysis is to break down resistances and enable the patient to face these painful ideas, desires, and experiences. Breaking down resistances is a long and difficult process. It is considered to be essential, however, if the underlying problem is to be brought to consciousness where it can be resolved.

△ *The principal procedure used in psychoanalysis is free association, in which the patient gives a running account of thoughts, wishes, physical sensations, and mental images as they occur.*

Dream analysis. Psychoanalysts believe that dreams are an important source of information about the patient's unconscious motivation. When a person is asleep, the superego is presumably less on guard against the unacceptable impulses originating in the id, so a motive that cannot be expressed in waking life may find expression in a dream.

Some motives are so unacceptable to the conscious self that they cannot be revealed openly even in dreams but must be expressed in disguised or symbolic form. As we saw in Chapter 6, a dream has two kinds of content. The *manifest* (openly visible) content of the dream is what we remember and report upon awakening. Beneath this manifest content is the *latent* (hidden) content—the actual motives that are seeking expression but are so painful or unacceptable to us that we do not want to recognize their existence. The therapist attempts to uncover these hidden motives by studying the symbols that appear in the manifest content of dreams.

Consider the following dream and the therapist's analytic interpretation.

"'I am in a gym, performing various exercises, with some other men. They are arranged in a line, in which they perform the exercises. I try to join the line at the head, but am rejected; I then try for the second place, and am rejected again; I try one place after the other till coming to the end of the line, and am rejected from every one of them.'

"At first the dreamer has difficulty associating to the dream. The analyst points out that the dream seems to involve men only. The dreamer then realizes that the men in the dream were actually boys from his all-male Catholic primary school, a place dominated by 'oughts' and 'shoulds.' With this come unpleasant memories of the gym class, which the dreamer hated passionately. The only reason he attended was because he was forced to; had it been left up to him he would not have shown up at any of the classes. As an afterthought, he adds that his mother also thought that 'it was good for you.' The imagery of the dream is direct and clear—the dreamer is being rejected from the line; he does not belong there" (Kaufmann, 1979, p. 111).

However, the latent content of the dream may also involve ambivalence over homosexual feelings of seeing other boys naked before or after gym class. In addition, it may reflect inferiority feelings over his imagined small penis size—not being able to meet the requirements.

Transference and countertransference. During the course of the intensive therapy of psychoanalysis the patient usually develops an emotional reaction toward the therapist. Often the therapist is identified with a person who has been at the center of an emotional conflict in the past, most often a parent or a lover. This emotional reaction is called **transference**. The transference is called *positive transference* when the feelings attached to the therapist are those of love or admiration; *negative transference* is when the feelings consist of hostility or envy. Often the patient's attitude is *ambivalent,* including a mixture of positive and negative feelings.

The analyst's task in handling transference is a difficult and dangerous one because of the patient's emotional vulnerability. However, it is a crucial part of treatment. The therapist helps the patient to interpret the present transferred feelings by understanding their original source in earlier experiences and attitudes.

At the same time, personal feelings are also at work in the therapist's reactions to the patient. **Countertransference** may occur, in which the therapist comes to like or dislike the patient because of an unconscious perceived similarity of the patient to significant people in the therapist's life. In working through countertransference, the therapist may discover some unconscious dynamics of his or her own.

The therapist becomes a "living mirror" for the patient, and the patient, in turn, for the therapist. Failure by the therapist to recognize the operation of countertransference interferes with the effectiveness of therapy (Little, 1981).

Re-education. Freud characterized his approach to psychotherapy as a process of "re-education" (Freud, 1949). Such therapy, then and now, is designed to create new conditions in the relationship between therapist and patient that allow internal changes to occur. These changes represent improved mental functioning and better reality adjustment, as well as elimination of the sources of unconscious motivation that originally created the neurotic symptoms.

There are four ways in which the therapist-as-mentor re-educates the patient-as-pupil.

1. Within a safe and supporting environment, the therapist fills the role of a reasonable, accepting parent who cares for the patient.
2. The patient plays an active role in collaborating with the therapist to find solutions, insights, explanations, and new directions to his or her personal problems. But the therapist also sets clear limits on what the patient can do or expect in the therapy setting.
3. The therapist teaches delay of gratification, by which the patient learns to regulate frustration.
4. The therapist subtly tries to convince the patient to abandon nonproductive, ego-defensive maneuvers. Instead, a new and effective model of how to live a more satisfactory life is provided—in the form of the therapist's attitudes and values (Strupp, 1983).

Beyond Freud

Changes have been made in both psychoanalytic theory and practice by some of Freud's followers, who retain many of his basic ideas but modify one or another principle. In general, these neo-Freudians place more emphasis than Freud did on (a) the patient's *current* social environment (less on the past); (b) the continuing influence of life experiences (not just infantile fixations); (c) the role of social motivation and interpersonal relations of love (rather than on biological instincts and selfish concerns); (d) the significance of ego functioning and development of the self-concept (less on the conflict between *id* and *superego*); and (e) the possibility of using psychoanalytic therapy with psychotic disorders (not just neurotic ones).

To get a flavor of the more contemporary psychodynamic approaches of the neo-Freudians, we sample two of them in the work of Harry Stack Sullivan and Margaret Mahler.

△ *Harry Stack Sullivan (1892–1949).*

Sullivan supported the significance of social interaction. He felt that Freudian theory and therapy did not recognize the importance of interpersonal relationships or the patient's needs for acceptance, respect, and love. Mental disorders, he insisted, involve not only traumatic intrapsychic processes but troubled social relationships and even strong societal pressures. The young child needs to feel secure, to be treated by others with caring and tenderness. Anxiety and other mental ills arise out of insecurities in relations with parents and "significant others." In Sullivan's view, a self-system is built up to hold anxiety down to a tolerable level. This self-system is derived from the child's interpersonal experiences and is organized around conceptions of the self as the "good-me" (associated with the mother's tenderness), the "bad-me" (associated with the mother's tensions), and the "not-me" (a dissociated self that is unacceptable to the rest of the self).

Therapy based on this interpersonal view involves observing the *patient's feelings* about the *therapist's attitudes*. The therapeutic interview is seen as a social setting in which each party's feelings and attitudes are influenced by the other's. The patient is gently provoked to state his or her assumptions about the therapist's attitudes—and other assumptions as well. Misunderstandings are corrected without humiliation by use of various therapeutic tactics. Above all, the therapeutic situation, for Sullivan, was one where the therapist learned and taught *lovingly* (Sullivan, 1953; Wallach & Wallach, 1983).

Margaret Mahler was one of the first psychoanalysts to recognize and treat childhood schizophrenia. She traced the child's retreat from reality and fragmentation of ego to sources of disharmony in the mother-child relationship. The normal development of an autonomous ego requires a process of gradual separation of the mother and child, along with an emerging sense of *individuation,* a unique, stable identity. A child's development can be skewed toward mental disorder by pathology of the mother, a need on her part not to separate from her child, or a re-engulf-

△ *Margaret Mahler (b. 1897).*

ing of the separated child into an infantile dependency. Mahler also saw the mother's lack of "emotional availability" as a contributor to abnormal development.

To help such a child, the therapist must treat the disturbed parent-child relationship as well as the disturbed child. The therapist is sensitive to the conflict over separation-individuation and to the process by which the "dual unity" of mother and child needs to be differentiated into distinct selves. The therapy works through the phases of this process toward the goal of forming a stable sense of personal identity in the patient (Mahler, 1979).

Psychodynamic therapies continue to evolve with a varying emphasis placed on Freud's constructs. Although they have been widely criticized (as we shall see in a final section where different therapeutic approaches are evaluated), there is still considerable enthusiasm by supporters.

BEHAVIOR THERAPIES

Behavior therapies apply the principles of conditioning and reinforcement to modify undesirable behavior patterns associated with mental disorders. Fundamental to this orientation is a *rejection* of the medical model, and with it of assumptions about "mentally sick" people suffering from "mental illness." Behavior therapists argue that abnormal behaviors are acquired in the same way as normal behaviors: through a learning process. They assert that all pathological behavior, except where there is established organic causation, can be best understood and treated by focusing on the behavior itself, rather than by attempting to alter any underlying "disease core." The term *behavior* is used by contemporary behavior therapists to include all reactions that are influenced by learning variables—thoughts and feelings, as well as overt actions.

The therapies that have emerged from the theories of conditioning and learning are grounded in a pragmatic, empirical research tradition. The central task of all living organisms is seen as learning how to adapt to the demands of their current social and physical environment. It follows that when organisms have not learned how to cope effectively, their maladaptive reactions can be overcome by therapy based on principles of learning (or relearning). The unique aspect of this treatment is that it is directed toward a modification of *behavior,* rather than a cure of something within the individual.

Behavior modification is defined as "the attempt to apply learning and other experimentally derived psychological principles to problem behavior" (Bootzin, 1975). The terms *behavior therapy* and *behavior modification* are often used interchangeably. Both refer to the systematic use of principles of learning to increase the frequency of desired behaviors and/or decrease that of problem behaviors. The range of deviant behaviors and personal problems that typically are treated by behavior therapy is extensive, including fears, compulsions, depression, addictions, aggression, and delinquent behaviors.

The target behavior is not assumed to be a symptom of any underlying process. Change the problem behavior and the problem is changed, argue the behaviorists. Psychodynamic therapists predicted that treating only the outer behavior without confronting the true, inner problem would result in *symptom substitution*, the appearance of a new physical or psychological problem, but this has not happened. Research has shown that when pathological behaviors are eliminated by behavior therapy, new symptoms are *not* substituted, (Kazdin, 1982). "On the contrary, patients whose target symptoms improved often reported improvement in other, less important symptoms as well" (Sloane et al., 1975, p. 219).

The earliest recorded use of behavior therapy was carried out by Mary Cover Jones in 1924. She showed how fears learned through conditioning could be unlearned. Her subject was Peter, a three-year-old boy who was afraid of rabbits. The technique was simply to feed Peter at one end of a room while the rabbit was brought in at the other end. Over a series of sessions, the rabbit was gradually brought closer until finally all fear disappeared and Peter played freely with the rabbit. In essence, the procedure is identical to the technique of "systematic desensitization," which we will cover shortly.

△ ▌ *Mary Cover Jones*

Behavior therapies today are more sophisticated but still are based on classical conditioning or operant conditioning—or a combination of the two (see Chapter 7 if you need a refresher on these two types of conditioning). The development of neurotic fears and other undesirable emotional reactions is assumed to follow the paradigm of classical conditioning. Therapy to change these negative responses uses principles of *counterconditioning* to substitute a new response for the inadequate one. Operant conditioning principles are applied when the therapeutic task is to increase the frequency of desired actions or decrease undesired habits. *Contingency management* refers to the general treatment strategy of changing behavior by modifying (managing) its consequences. Special adaptations have also been developed for *social learning* and for getting new re-

Table 15.1 *Hierarchy of Anxiety-Producing Stimuli*

1. On the way to the university on the day of an examination.
2. In the process of answering an examination paper.
3. Before the unopened doors of the examination room.
4. Awaiting the distribution of examination papers.
5. The examination paper lies face down before her.
6. The night before an examination.
7. One day before an examination.
8. Two days before an examination.
9. Three days before an examination.
10. Four days before an examination.
11. Five days before an examination.
12. A week before an examination.
13. Two weeks before an examination.
14. A month before an examination.

(Adapted from Wolpe, 1973)

sponses learned in therapy to be *generalized* to life situations. Our information about behavior therapy is organized around these basic approaches to conditioning and learning.

Counterconditioning

Why does someone become anxious when faced with a harmless stimulus, such as a fly, a nonpoisonous snake, an open space, or a social contact? We know that *any* neutral stimulus may acquire the power to elicit strong conditioned reactions on the basis of prior association with an unconditioned stimulus. If the unconditioned stimulus has some special evolutionary significance to the individual, or is intense, physically painful, or emotionally traumatic, conditioning can occur with but a single pairing.

Strong emotional reactions that disrupt the person's life "for no good reason" are often conditioned responses that the person does not recognize as having been learned. To weaken the strength of negative learned associations, behavior therapists use the techniques of systematic desensitization, implosion, and aversive learning.

Systematic desensitization and implosion. It is difficult—but not impossible—to be both happy and sad, or relaxed and anxious, at the same time. This principle is applied in the **systematic desensitization** technique developed primarily by Joseph Wolpe (1958, 1973). Since anxiety is assumed to be a major cause of maladaptive avoidance, the client is taught to prevent the arousal of anxiety by relaxing.

Desensitization therapy involves three major steps. It begins by identifying the stimuli that provoke anxiety in the client and arranging them in a *hierarchy* ranked from weakest to strongest. For example, a student suffering from severe test anxiety constructed the hierarchy in **Table 15.1.** Note that she rated immediate anticipation of the examination as more stressful than taking the exam itself.

Second, the client is trained in a system of progressive deep-muscle relaxation. Relaxation training requires several sessions in which the client learns to distinguish between sensations of tension and relaxation and then "to let go of tension" in order to achieve a state of physical and mental relaxation.

Finally, the actual process of desensitization begins. The client, in a relaxed state, is told to imagine as vividly as possible the *weakest* anxiety stimulus on the list. If anxiety reactions occur, the client stops and concentrates on relaxing again. When the weakest stimulus can be visualized without discomfort, the client goes on to the next stronger one. Great care is taken not to arouse anxiety during this process of gradually approaching the "unthinkable" stimulus. If anxiety is evoked, the therapist terminates the imagery production, gets the client to relax again, and goes back to a weaker stimulus. After a number of sessions, the most distressing situations on the list can be imagined without anxiety—even situations that could not be faced originally.

As in other conditioning, stimulus generalization operates. Once anxiety to a particular stimulus is extinguished, there is a *generalization* of this effect to related stimuli. Thus desensitization works both directly, by replacing anxiety with a particular stimulus through relaxation, and indirectly, through generalization of anxiety reduction to similar stimuli.

Desensitization is ideally suited for treatment of specific phobic reactions. These "irrational" behaviors have been maintained (reinforced) by the relief experienced when the anxiety-producing stimuli were avoided or escaped. Desensitization has also been successfully applied to a diversity of other human problems, including such generalized fears as test anxiety, stage fright, impotence, and frigidity (Kazdin & Wilcoxin, 1976; Paul, 1969).

Another commonly used technique, *implosion,* uses an approach opposite to that of systematic desensitization. Instead of experiencing a gradual, step-by-step progression, the client is exposed at the start to the most frightening stimuli at the top of the anxiety hierarchy.

The rationale for this procedure begins with the recognition that neither anxiety nor the neurotic behavior will ever extinguish as long as the person is allowed to deny, avoid, or otherwise escape from experiencing the anxiety-arousing stimulus situations. The person must discover that contact with the stimulus does not actually have the anticipated negative effects (Stampfl & Levis, 1967).

One way to extinguish an irrational fear is to force the client to experience a full-blown anxiety reaction without suffering any harm. The therapeutic situation is arranged so that the frightening stimulus occurs in circumstances where the client cannot run away. The therapist *describes* an extremely frightening situation relating to the client's fear and urges the client to *imagine* being in it, experiencing it through all the senses as intensely as possible. In this way the client is *flooded* with a rapid exposure to anxiety-eliciting sensations.

Such imagining is assumed to cause an explosion of panic. Since this explosion is an inner one, the process is called *implosion;* hence the term *implosion therapy.* As this happens again and again and no harm is forthcoming, the stimulus loses its power to elicit anxiety. When anxiety no longer occurs, the maladaptive neurotic behavior previously used to avoid it disappears. Flooding has proven to be superior to systematic desensitization in the treatment of some behavior problems, such as agoraphobia. Treatment gains are shown to be enduring for most clients (Emmelkamp & Kuipers, 1979).

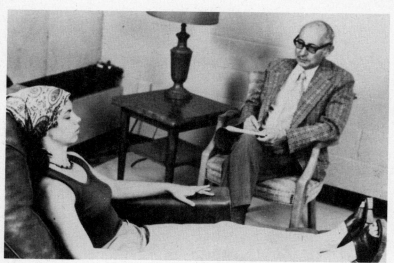

◁ *Psychiatrist Joseph Wolpe is shown here practicing systematic desensitization with a client. The client, in a relaxed state, is told to imagine as vividly as possible the weakest anxiety stimulus on her list. If anxiety occurs, she will stop and concentrate on relaxing again.*

Aversion therapy. Implosion and desensitization therapies help clients deal directly with stimuli they are avoiding that are not really harmful. But what might be done to help those who are *attracted* to stimuli that *are* harmful or illegal? Drug addiction, sexual perversions, and uncontrollable violence are human problems in which deviant behavior is elicited by "tempting stimuli." **Aversion therapy** uses counterconditioning procedures of aversive learning to pair these stimuli with strong noxious stimuli (such as electric shocks or nausea-producing drugs). In time, through conditioning, the same negative reactions are elicited by the conditioned tempting stimuli, and the person develops an aversion for them.

Why would anyone submit to such a therapy that is in effect a kind of torture? Usually people do so only under conditions where they realize that the long-term consequences of continuing their behavior pattern will destroy their health or ruin their lives. Or they may be coerced to do so involuntarily by institutional pressures, as has happened in some prison treatment programs.

Many critics are concerned that the painful procedures in aversion therapy give too much power to the therapist, can be more punitive than therapeutic, and are most likely to be used in situations where people have least freedom of choice over what is done to them. In recent years, use of aversive therapy in institutional rehabilitation programs has become more regulated by state laws and ethical guidelines for clinical treatment. In essence, the hope is that, under these restrictions, when used, it will be a therapy of choice rather than coercion.

"TODAY WE'LL TRY AVERSION-THERAPY. EVERY TIME YOU SAY SOMETHING STUPID, I'LL SPILL A BUCKET OF WATER ON YOUR HEAD."

Contingency management

The operant conditioning approach to developing desirable behavior is simple: find the reinforcer that will maintain a desired response, apply that reinforcer, contingent upon the response, and evaluate its effectiveness. This approach has been applied to modify behavior in the classroom, in mental hospitals, in homes for the aged, and in many other settings. Even patients who have been totally mute for many years but are physically capable of speech have been trained to speak by the use of operant techniques (Sherman, 1963). The two major techniques of contingency management in behavior therapy are *positive reinforcement* and specific *extinction strategies.*

Positive reinforcement strategies. When a response is followed immediately by a reward, the response will tend to be repeated and will increase in frequency over time. That central principle of operant learning becomes a therapeutic strategy when it is applied to modifying the frequency of emission of a "desirable" response.

Dramatic success has been obtained in the application of positive reinforcement procedures to the behavior problems of children with psychiatric disorders. Two examples of use of this method were cited in Chapter 7—the case of the little boy who would not wear his glasses and the use of chances to run and scream in a preschool as reinforcement for sitting still first.

Positive reinforcement procedures have been extended to many other settings and problems. In mental hospitals, **token economies** have been established in an attempt to reward positive behavior. In a token economy, patients are tangibly rewarded for socially constructive activities such as maintaining personal cleanliness, arriving on time for meals, and performing assigned tasks. Payment consists of tokens (such as poker chips) that may be used later to "purchase" such luxuries as more elegant dining facilities, increased television time, private sleeping accommodations, and weekend passes (Kazdin, 1980).

Hospital administrators have found that token economies can often be quite effective in eliciting desired behaviors, even on the part of rather severely disturbed patients. But the system works only when the "learners" have no other means of obtaining the

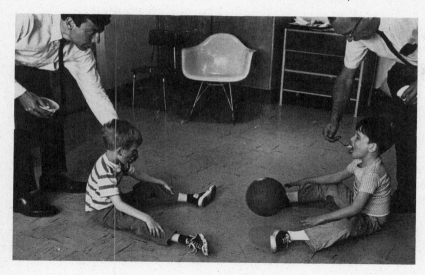

For playing ball with each other, these two autistic boys are receiving immediate positive reinforcement in the form of food.

things that the tokens will purchase. Some critics have argued that the result is that such a "materialist" system of behavior control gets used primarily with poor, deprived, institutionalized adults and children.

Behavior therapists have generally agreed with this criticism, but have wanted to maintain the obvious benefits of positive reinforcement systems. One resolution to the problem has been to involve individuals directly in their own contingency management. A **behavioral contract** is an explicit agreement (often in writing) that states what consequences will follow what behaviors. Such contracts are often required by behavior therapists working with clients on obesity or smoking problems. The contract may specify what the client is expected to do (client's obligations) and what in turn the client can expect from the therapist (therapist's obligations).

Behavioral contracting facilitates therapy by making both parties responsible for achieving the agreed-upon changes in behavior. Treatment goals are spelled out, as well as the specific rewards that are associated with meeting planned responsibilities and reaching desired subgoals. The therapeutic situation becomes more structured in terms of what each party can reasonably expect as appropriate content and acceptable interpersonal behavior. The person with less status and power (patient or child, for example) benefits from inclusion of a condition for

third-party arbitration of alleged contract violation (Nelson & Mowrey, 1976).

It is not reasonable to expect all individuals to be able to collaborate on behavioral contracts; hospitalized psychotic patients may not be able to understand the complicated steps and mutual commitments involved, for example. However, the idea of engaging the client or patient in a joint decision-making effort about how to use positive reinforcement to change behaviors is a step forward from the original institutional use of token economies. Some parents have found that contracts with their teenagers have brought more acceptable behavior while greatly improving the emotional climate of the home; reinforcements, in fact, often include more reasonable parental behaviors (Stuart, 1971).

Extinction strategies. Why do people continue to do something that causes pain and distress when they are capable of doing otherwise? The answer is that many forms of behavior have multiple consequences—some negative, some positive. Often subtle positive reinforcements keep the behavior going despite its obvious negative consequences. Children punished for misbehaving may continue to misbehave if punishment is the only form of personal attention they can earn.

Extinction is useful in therapy when neurotic behaviors have been maintained by unrecognized reinforcing circumstances. Those reinforcers are identified by a careful situational analysis, and then a program is arranged to withhold them in the presence of the undesirable response. When this approach is possible, the behavior becomes less frequent and is eventually extinguished.

Even psychotic behavior can be maintained and encouraged by unintentional reinforcement. It is standard procedure in many mental hospitals for the staff to ask patients frequently how they are feeling. This may suggest to the patients that the "appropriate" behavior is to be thinking and talking about one's feelings, unusual symptoms, hallucinations, and so on. In fact, the more bizarre the symptoms and verbalizations, the more attention the staff members may show in their efforts to understand the "dynamics" of the case.

Dramatic decreases in psychotic behavior sometimes have been observed when the staff was simply instructed to ignore the psychotic behavior and to give attention to the patients only when they were behaving normally (Ayllon & Michael, 1959). Just as positive reinforcement can increase the incidence of a behavior, the *lack* of desirable consequences can make it less likely to occur. With a "time-out from reinforcement" the target behavior stops being followed by its usual consequence—and should begin to extinguish.

We have not mentioned a most obvious, traditional form of behavior modification—"a good spanking for doing bad things." *Punishment* is not used by therapists because it is counterproductive to the long-term goal of all treatment programs, namely, the person's future self-regulation of behavior in his or her natural environment. Punishment "works" to stop ongoing behavior, suppressing it in the presence of the punishing agent. But it generates many negative side effects that are beneficial neither to the punished person nor to the interpersonal relationship with the punisher (as we noted in Chapter 7).

The only time punishment is called for in a treatment setting is in response to a patient's self-injurious behavior. But then it is used in combination with shaping of the appropriate behavior. This is the case with some autistic children who must be kept in restraints continuously because they bang their heads against the walls or crib. Electric shocks stop the self-destructive behavior, allow them to be free from "straightjackets" and able to be reinforced for new behaviors (Lovaas, 1977).

Social learning therapy

Behavior therapies have been given an expanded focus by social learning theorists who point out that humans learn—for better or worse—by observing the behavior of other people. Often we learn and apply rules for understanding new experiences not just through direct participation but also through symbolic means, such as watching other people's experiences in life, or in a movie or on TV. Social learning therapy is based on this kind of learning by observing others; it has been of special value in overcoming phobias and building social skills. We have noted in earlier chapters that this social learning approach was largely developed by Albert Bandura (1977a).

Imitation of models. Before desired responses can be reinforced, they must occur. Many new responses, especially complex ones, can be acquired more readily if the person can observe and imitate a person (model) who performs the desired behavior and is reinforced for doing so.

In treating a phobia of snakes, the therapist using this method will first demonstrate fearless approach behavior at a relatively minor level—perhaps approaching the snake's cage or touching the snake. The client is aided, through demonstration and supportive encouragement, to imitate the modeled behavior. Gradually the approach behaviors are shaped to the point where the client can pick the snake up and let it crawl freely over him or her. At no time is the client forced to perform any behavior. Resistance at any level is overcome by having the client return to a previously successful, less threatening approach behavior.

The remarkable power of this form of **participant modeling** can be seen in research comparing the participant modeling technique just described with symbolic modeling, desensitization, and a control condition (see **Figure 15.1**). In symbolic modeling therapy, subjects who had been trained in relaxation techniques watched film in which several models fearlessly handled snakes; the subjects could stop the film and relax themselves whenever a scene made them feel anxious. In the control condition, no therapeutic intervention was used. Participant modeling was clearly the most successful of these techniques. Snake phobia was eliminated in eleven of the twelve subjects in the participant modeling group (Bandura et al., 1970).

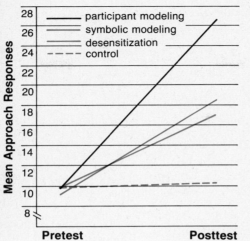

Figure 15.1

The subject shown in the photo first watched a model make a graduated series of snake-approach responses and then repeated them herself. She eventually was able to pick up the snake and let it crawl about on her. The graph compares the number of approach responses made by subjects before and after receiving participant modeling therapy with the behavior of those exposed to two other therapeutic techniques and a control group. (Adapted from Bandura, 1970)

Imitation of models has also been used to get autistic, mute children to talk. The children were first reinforced for making sounds resembling those of the model-therapist, then only for duplicating his words. Finally, reinforcement was contingent upon being more socially responsive (Lovaas, 1968).

Social skills training. A major therapeutic innovation encouraged by social learning therapists is training people with inadequate social skills to be more effective (Hersen & Bellack, 1976). Many difficulties arise for someone with a psychotic or neurotic disorder, or even just an everyday problem, simply because he or she is socially inhibited, inept, or unassertive. *Social skills* are sets of responses that enable a person to be effective when approaching or interacting with others. They include knowing *what* to say and do in given situations (content) in order to elicit a desired response (consequences), as well as *how* (style) and *when* (timing) to do so. One of the most common social skill problems is lack of assertiveness, inability to state one's own thoughts or wishes in a clear, direct, nonaggressive manner (Bower & Bower, 1976).

To overcome such a problem, many social learning therapists recommend **behavioral rehearsal**. This includes all the procedures used to establish and strengthen any basic skill, from personal hygiene to work habits to social interactions. It is accomplished through a combination of modeling, instruction, behavioral contracting, and repeated practice of what to say and do with specific feedback. Behavioral rehearsal procedures are being widely used in social skills training programs with many different populations.

One application of this approach modified abusive verbal outbursts in psychiatric patients. They were taught to handle interpersonal disagreements not by their usual strategies of avoidance, intimidation, or violence, but by learning to make appropriately assertive responses in those situations (Foy et al., 1975; Fredericksen et al., 1976).

It has been found that adult pathology has often been preceded by deficits in social skills in childhood (Oden & Asher, 1977). A considerable amount of research and therapy is currently directed at building competence in shy and withdrawn disturbed children (Conger & Keane, 1981; Zimbardo & Radl, 1981).

One study demonstrated that preschool-age children diagnosed as "social isolates" could be helped to become sociable in a short training period.

Twenty-four subjects were randomly assigned to one of three play conditions: with a same-age peer, with a peer 1 to 1½ years younger, or with no partner. The pairs were brought together for ten play sessions, each only 20 minutes long, over a period of about a month. Their classroom behavior before and after this treatment was recorded and revealed a strong effect of the intervention.

The opportunity to play with a younger playmate doubled the frequency with which the former social isolates interacted later on with other classmates—

Table 15.2 *Comparison of Psychoanalytic and Behavioristic Approaches to Psychotherapy*

Issue	Psychoanalysis	Behavior Therapy
Basic human nature	Biological instincts, primarily sexual and aggressive, press for immediate release, bringing people into conflict with social reality.	Like other animals, people are born only with the capacity for learning, which follows similar principles in all species.
Normal human development	Growth occurs through resolution of conflicts during successive stages. Through identification and internalization, mature ego controls and character structures emerge.	Adaptive behaviors are learned through reinforcement and imitation.
Nature of psychopathology	Pathology reflects inadequate conflict resolutions and fixations in earlier development, which leave overly strong impulses and/or weak controls. Symptoms are defensive responses to anxiety.	Problematic behavior derives from faulty learning of maladaptive behaviors. The "symptom" is the problem; there is no "underlying disease."
Goal of therapy	Attainment of psychosexual maturity, strengthened ego functions, reduced control by unconscious and repressed impulses.	Removal of "symptomatic" behavior by eliminating and replacing with adaptive behaviors.
Psychological realm emphasized	Motives and feelings, fantasies and cognitions.	Behavior and observable feelings and actions.
Time orientation	Oriented to discovering and interpreting past conflicts and repressed feelings, examining them in light of the present.	Little or no concern with early history or etiology. Present behavior is examined and treated.
Role of unconscious material	Primary in classical psychoanalysis, somewhat less emphasized by neo-Freudians.	No concern with unconscious processes or with subjective experience even in conscious realm.
Role of insight	Central; emerges in "corrective emotional experiences."	Irrelevant and/or unnecessary.
Role of therapist	A *detective*, searching out root conflicts and resistances; detached and neutral, to facilitate transference reactions.	A *trainer*, helping patient unlearn old behaviors and/or learn new ones. Control of reinforcement is important; interpersonal relation is minor.

(Adapted from Korchin, 1976)

bringing them up to the average level of the other children. Playing with a same-age peer also increased children's sociability, but not nearly so much. The researchers concluded that the one-on-one play situation had offered the shy children safe opportunities to be socially assertive. They were allowed to practice leadership skills that were likely to be approved by the nonthreatening, younger playmates (Furman et al., 1979).

In another study, social skills training with a group of hospitalized emotionally disturbed children changed both verbal and nonverbal components of their behavior in social settings. The children were taught to give appropriate verbal responses in various social situations (giving help or compliments, making requests). They were also taught to display appropriate affect (for example, to smile while giving a compliment) and to make eye contact and use proper body posture (face the person being talked to).

These improved social skills were generalized to "untreated" situations beyond those used in the training. The children also put them into practice on their own when on the ward. These good effects were found to be continuing even months later (Matson et al., 1980).

Generalization techniques

An issue of concern for behavior therapists is whether the new behavior patterns generated in the therapeutic setting will actually be used in the everyday situations faced by clients. This question is important for all therapies, and any measure of treatment effectiveness must include maintenance of long-term changes that go beyond the therapist's couch, the clinic, or the laboratory.

When essential aspects of the client's real-life setting are absent from the therapy program, behaviors that have been modified by therapy can be expected to deteriorate over time when therapy terminates. To prevent this loss, it is becoming common practice to build *generalization techniques* into the therapeutic procedure itself. These techniques attempt to *increase* the similarity of target behaviors, reinforcers, models, and stimulus demands between therapy and real-life settings.

For example, behaviors are taught that are likely to be reinforced naturally in the person's environment, such as showing courtesy or consideration. Rewards are given on a partial reinforcement schedule so their effect will be maintained when rewards are not always forthcoming in the real world. The dependence of token-economy patients on tangible token rewards is gradually *faded out* while social approval and more naturally occurring consequences are introduced. Opportunities are provided for patients to practice new behaviors under the supportive guidance of staff members during field trips away from the institution. Halfway houses also help to transfer new behaviors from the institution to the community setting (Fairweather et al., 1969; Orlando, 1981). Careful attention to ways of increasing the generalizability of treatment effects will enhance the long-term success of behavior therapy (Marks, 1981).

Before turning to cognitive therapies, take a few minutes to review the major differences between the two dominant psychotherapies—the psychoanalytical and the behavioral—as summarized in **Table 15.2.**

COGNITIVE THERAPIES

Cognitive therapies attempt to change problem feelings and behaviors by changing the way the client thinks about significant life experiences. Underlying this approach is the assumption that abnormal behavior patterns and emotional distress start with problems in *what* we think (cognitive content), and *how* we think (cognitive process).

Remember the case of Gary, the "nearly perfect student" in the *Opening Case?* Gary's problems were treated by changing the way he thought about himself, his expectations about academic performance, and the image he presented to others. He was given a brief exposure to a therapy designed to alter his current thoughts about these major problem areas in his life.

The increasing numbers of cognitive therapies focus on different types of cognitive processes and different methods for changing thoughts. The two major approaches are those that involve cognitive behavior modification (including "self-efficacy") and those that try to alter false belief systems (including "rational-emotive therapy" and cognitive therapy for depression).

Cognitive behavior modification

We are what we tell ourselves we can be, and we are guided by what we believe we ought to do. That is a starting assumption of **cognitive behavior modification.** Unacceptable behavior patterns are modified by changing the negative self-statements a person makes into constructive coping statements.

This therapeutic approach combines the cognitive emphasis on the importance of thoughts and attitudes in influencing motivation and responding with the focus of behaviorism on performance that is changed by modifying reinforcement contingencies.

You met Donald Meichenbaum's (1977) three-phase process for changing behavior patterns in Chapter 13. The sequence includes (a) *cognitive preparation* in which therapist and client discover how the client thinks about and expresses the problem for which therapy is sought; (b) *skill acquisition and rehearsal,* which involves learning new self-statements that are constructive, while minimizing the use of self-defeating ones (anxiety-eliciting or esteem reducing); and, finally, (c) *application and practice* of the new learning in actual situations starting in easy ones and graduating to those more difficult.

For example, for the negative self-statement "I was really boring at that party; they'll never ask me back" a more positive one is substituted. "Next time, if I want to appear interesting, I will plan some provocative opening lines, practice telling a good joke, and be responsive to the host's stories." Or someone "feeling overwhelmed" with a fear of tests could rehearse as follows:

1) "I've studied carefully and know enough of the information";
2) "I will take some deep breaths, pause, and be ready to do my best";
3) "I will focus on the present, attend only to the test materials";
4) "I will answer the questions I know first to increase my confidence";
5) "My fear may rise when I don't recall something, that's OK, I can manage it and use that energy to help me search my memory for the missing information";
6) "I can do (am doing) a good job on this test";
7) "It seems like a big deal now, but it will be over shortly and whatever happens will itself be just a memory when I look back on it in the future";
8) "I will reward myself for my studying and concentration with a movie tonight and two new albums if I do as well as I now think I will."

Building *expectations of being effective* increases the likelihood of behaving effectively. It is through setting attainable goals, being confident that one has realistic strategies for attaining them, and evaluating feedback realistically that people develop a sense of mastery and self-efficacy (Bandura et al., 1980).

Changing false beliefs

Cognitive behavior therapists emphasize the important role of thoughts, but still use many behavioral assumptions—such as the rewarding or punishing function of thoughts. Other cognitive therapists put less emphasis on behavioral processes. Their primary targets for change in psychotherapy are beliefs, attitudes, and habitual thought patterns, or "schemas."

These cognitive therapists argue that many psychological problems arise because of how we think about ourselves in relation to other people and events we face. Faulty thinking can be based on: (a) unreasonable attitudes ("Being perfect is the most important trait for a student to have"), (b) false premises ("If I do everything they want me to, then I'll be popular"), or (c) rigid rules that put behavior on "automatic pilot," so that prior patterns are repeated even when they have not worked ("I must obey authorities"). Emotional distress is seen as often caused by misunderstandings and by failing to distinguish between current reality and one's imagination (or expectations).

The cognitive therapist induces the patient to correct faulty patterns of thinking by applying more effective problem-solving techniques. Aaron Beck has successfully pioneered cognitive therapy for the problem of depression. He states the formula for treatment in simple form: "The therapist helps the patient to identify his warped thinking and to learn more realistic ways to formulate his experiences" (1976, p. 20). For example, depressed individuals may be instructed to write down negative thoughts about themselves, figure out why these self-criticisms are unjustified, and come up with more realistic (and less destructive) self-cognitions.

Beck believes that depression is maintained because depressed patients are unaware of the negative "automatic thoughts" that they habitually say to themselves. Examples are: "I will never be as good as my brother"; "Nobody would like me if they really knew me"; "I'm not smart enough to make it in this competitive school." The therapist then uses four tactics to change the cognitive foundation that supports the depression: (1) reality testing is conducted of the evidence the patient has for and against these automatic thoughts; (2) blame is reattributed to situational factors rather than to the patient's incompetence; (3) alternative solutions to the problem are openly discussed; and (4) basic assumptions are made explicit and challenged (such as Gary's that "In order to be accepted, I must be perfect") (Beck et al., 1979).

One of the earliest forms of cognitive therapy was the *rational-emotive therapy* developed by Albert Ellis (1962, 1977). It is a comprehensive system of personality change based on changing irrational beliefs that are causing undesirable, highly charged emotional reactions, such as severe anxiety. Clients may have core values *demanding* that they succeed and be approved, *insisting* that they be treated fairly, or *dictating* that the universe be more pleasant. The therapist teaches clients how to recognize the shoulds, oughts, and musts that are controlling their actions and preventing them from choosing the life they want.

△ *Albert Ellis (b. 1913).*

The therapist attempts to break through the client's "closed-mindedness" to show that an emotional reaction which follows some event is really due to beliefs about the event that the patient does not recognize. For example, failure to achieve orgasm during intercourse (event) is followed by the emotional reaction of depression and self-derogation. The belief that is causing the emotional reaction is likely to be "I am sexually inadequate and may be impotent, or frigid, because I failed to perform as expected." These (and other beliefs) are openly disputed through rational confrontation and examination of alternative reasons for the event, such as fatigue, too much alcohol, false notions of sexual "performance," or really not wanting to engage in intercourse at that time. This is followed by a variety of other techniques like those used in behavior modification, as well as humor and role-playing to replace dogmatic, irrational thinking with rational, situationally appropriate ideas.

Rational-emotive therapy aims at increasing the individual's sense of self-worth and the potential to be self-actualized by getting rid of the system of faulty beliefs that block personal growth. As such, it shares much with humanistic therapies, which we consider next.

EXISTENTIAL-HUMANISTIC THERAPIES

Among the primary symptoms for which many college students seek therapy are general dissatisfaction, feelings of alienation, and failure to achieve all they feel they should. Problems in everyday living, the lack of meaningful human relationships, and the absence of significant goals to strive for are thought of as "existential crises" by proponents of humanism and existentialism. These orientations have contributed to a therapy that addresses itself to basic problems of existence common to all human beings.

The humanistic movement has been called a "third force" in psychology because it grew out of a reaction to the pessimistic view of human nature offered by early psychoanalytic theory and the mechanistic view offered by early radical behaviorism. At the time the humanistic movement was forming in the United States, similar viewpoints, which came to be known collectively as *existentialism,* had already gained acceptance in Europe.

At the core of both humanistic and existential therapies is the concept of the whole person in the continual process of changing and of becoming. Although environment and heredity place certain restrictions on the process of becoming, we remain always free to choose what we will become by creating our own values and committing ourselves to them through our decisions. Along with this *freedom to choose;* however, comes the burden of responsibility. Since we are never fully aware of all the implications of our actions, we experience anxiety and despair. We also suffer from guilt over lost opportunities to achieve our full potential.

Psychotherapies that apply the principles of this general theory of human nature attempt to help clients define their own freedom, value their experiencing self and the richness of the present moment, cultivate their individuality, and discover ways of realizing their fullest potential (self-actualization). Of importance in the existential perspective is the current life situation as experienced by the individual (the person's phenomenological view).

The founder of existential psychotherapy in the United States is Rollo May (1969). He asserts the independence of the individual from seemingly deter-

△ *Rollo May
(b. 1909).*

ministic forces that compel the person to draw back from experiencing life fully. In his view, neurotic anxiety narrows one's existence by resigning the person to avoidance of the possibilities of living more fully. This form of *existential neurosis* comes not from repressed conflicts but from fearing and not meeting the challenges of life.

Client-centered therapy, as pioneered by Carl Rogers, is a clear example of the humanistic approach to treating people with problems. Promotion of the healthy psychological growth of the individual is its primary goal (Rogers, 1951). This approach postulates a basic tendency of human nature toward *self-actualization.* "It is the inherent tendency of the organism to develop all its capacities in ways which seem to maintain or enhance the organism" (Rogers, 1959, p. 196). When psychotherapy works, it releases the person's capacity toward self-actualization from restrictions imposed by feelings of lack of self-worth.

The therapeutic relationship itself is of primary importance in Rogers' person-centered therapy, depending on three qualities on the part of the helper-therapist: personal honesty, accurate empathy, and nonjudgmental caring. The therapist expresses *unconditional positive regard* for the client—a belief in the client's inherent goodness despite how the client acts. A consequence is the stripping away of the client's defenses that were erected to deal with criticism and rejection. The therapist is tuned in to his or her own feelings and thoughts and allows them to be transparent to the client. In addition to this genuineness, the therapist tries to experience the client's feelings. Such total empathy rests upon a caring for the client as a worthy, competent individual who is not to be evaluated or judged but to be assisted in discovering his or her individuality (Meador & Rogers, 1979).

Client-centered therapy strives to be *nondirective* by having the therapist merely facilitate the patient's search for self-awareness and self-acceptance, never to direct it. Unlike other therapies, in which the therapist interprets, gives answers, or instructs, here the therapist is a supportive listener who reflects, and at times restates, what the client is saying. Rogers believes that once freed to relate to others openly and to accept themselves, individuals have the potential to lead themselves to psychological health. This optimistic view has influenced many clinical practitioners (see Smith, 1982).

It should be apparent that the source of the "human potential movement" is to be found in the general perspective of the existential-humanistic therapies. The *human potential movement* encompasses all those practices and methods that release the potential of the average human being for greater levels of performance and greater richness of experience. Therapy for growth, personal enrichment, increased interpersonal sensitivity, and greater joy in sex is the modern offspring of the union of existential and humanistic views of human nature. Thus, therapy originally intended for the mentally disturbed has been extended to well, normal people who want to be more effective, productive, and happier human beings. This is one of the major changes in the direction of psychotherapy since the 1970s.

Group therapies

All the treatment approaches outlined thus far are primarily designed to be "one-on-one" relationships between a patient or client and a therapist. There are many reasons why therapy in groups has begun to flourish and may even be more effective than individual therapy in some cases. Among them are the fact that it (a) is less expensive to participants; (b) better utilizes limited mental health personnel; (c) is a less threatening power situation for many people; (d) allows powerful group processes to be used to influence individual maladaptive behavior, such as group consensus, commitment, and modeling; and (e) provides opportunity to observe and practice interpersonal skills.

The use of group processes as a medium for personal change is common to an extraordinarily diverse range of groups, with varied goals and philosophies. Recent estimates put the number of Americans who have participated in some form of encounter group for personal growth at over 5 million. Untold others participate in self-help groups (such as those for

◁ Group therapy can be designed to accommodate a variety of goals and philosophies.

weight reduction, alcoholism, or consciousness raising), and many are involved in more formal varieties of group psychotherapy that share some of the basic views of the humanist and existentialist approaches (Lieberman, 1977).

When group therapy is effective with certain kinds of problem behavior, what variables seem to account for its curative value? Some of the general variables would include:

■ feeling of belonging and acceptance;
■ opportunities to observe, imitate, and be socially rewarded;
■ experiencing the universality of human problems, weaknesses, and strengths;
■ recreating analogues to the primary family group which enables corrective emotional experiences to take place (Klein, 1983).

Two group therapy approaches that have developed special techniques now used by other therapists are gestalt therapy and transactional analysis. After we examine these techniques, we will see what is unique about new therapies for couples and families.

Gestalt therapy. **Gestalt therapy** focuses on ways to unite mind and body to make the person whole. Its goal of self-awareness is reached by learning to express pent-up feelings in the group and to recognize "unfinished business" from past conflicts that are carried into new relationships. Fritz Perls (1969),

its originator, asked participants to act out fantasies concerning conflicts and strong feelings and also to recreate their dreams, which were seen as repressed parts of personality. He said, "We have to *re-own* these projected, fragmented parts of our personality, and re-own the hidden potential that appears in the dream" (1967, p. 67).

Transactional analysis. In transactional analysis, as developed by Eric Berne (1972), group members are encouraged to describe the "games" they play in their interpersonal relationships and also to enact them. By doing so, they become aware of the habitual patterns of manipulation they impose on others.

One typical status manipulation is termed the "Why Don't You—Yes But" game of "one-up-manship." One person assumes a docile, low status role of soliciting advice from another person: "Why don't you try to find a solution to my problem?" Whatever the advice offered, the person counters with "Yes, but—you haven't considered . . ." all the things which make the advice worthless, or stupid. If the would-be helper continues to try to help, there is always another "yes, but," until the helper quits and the "victim" achieves victory and an illusory boost in status. Removing these deceptive strategies in therapy opens the possibility of achieving more honest, meaningful relationships to other people.

Marital and family therapy

Much group therapy involves strangers who come together periodically to form a temporary association from which they may benefit. However, some peoples' troubles come from their association with others they are familiar with—spouses and family members.

Couples counseling for marital problems seeks to clarify the communication patterns the partners typically use with each other and then to improve the quality of their interaction. By seeing the couple together, and often videotaping and playing back their interactions, the therapist can help them appreciate the verbal and nonverbal styles they use to dominate or control the other person. Each party may be taught how to reinforce desirable responding in the other and withdraw reinforcement for undesirable reactions. Or they may be taught nondirective listening skills to help the other person clarify and express feelings and ideas.

Couples therapy is more effective for resolving marital problems than is individual therapy for only one partner, and it has been shown to reduce marital crises and keep marriages intact (Cookerly, 1980; Gurman & Kniskern, 1978).

In **family therapy,** the client is also not an individual but a whole nuclear family, treated as members of a system of relationships. The family therapist works together with a troubled family to help them perceive *what* is happening *between* them that is creating problems for one or more of the members.

The focus is on altering the "spaces" between people and their relationships, rather than on changing processes within maladjusted individuals (Foley, 1979).

Family therapy can reduce tensions within the family and improve the functioning of individual members in the family. The therapist plays many roles, acting as an interpreter and clarifier of the interactions that are taking place in the therapy session, and as influence agent, mediator, and referee. A basic assumption most family therapists make is that the problems brought into therapy represent *situational* difficulties between people, problems of social interaction. These difficulties may develop over time as members are forced into or accept unsatisfying roles (Satir, 1967). Nonproductive communication patterns may be set up in response to natural transitions in the family system—loss of a job, a child's going to school, starting to date, getting married, having a new baby, and so forth.

In a *structured family therapy* approach, the family is seen as the system that is creating disturbances in the individuals rather than the other way around (Minuchin, 1974). The therapist focuses on how the family interacts in the present in order to understand its organizational structure, power hierarchy, channels of communication and who gives and gets blame for what goes wrong. As a consultant to an organization might do, the family therapist actively—but not always directly—tries to help the family "system" reorganize its structure and functioning to better meet the needs of its members and the demands imposed on it.

◁ *Couples therapy is more effective for resolving marital problems than is individual therapy for only one partner.*

BIOMEDICAL THERAPIES

The ecology of mind is held in delicate balance. It can be upset by mishaps in the workings of our genes, hormones, enzymes, metabolism, and other biochemical events. Behavior and affect (emotional tone) are end-products of brain mechanisms. When something goes wrong with the brain, we see the consequences in abnormal patterns of behavior and peculiar emotional reactions. Similarly, environmental, social, or behavioral disturbances can alter brain chemistry, as we know from the effects of certain kinds of pollution, drugs, and violence.

One approach to correcting these wrongs has been to change the functioning of the brains of disturbed people. This has been accomplished by means of surgically destroying specific areas in the brain or by administering electroshock to the brain of sufficient intensity to cause a temporary coma, and presumably disruption of the brain's own electrical activity. These approaches have been used less as our understanding of the biochemical bases of nervous system functioning has become more precise.

The newer interventions have been guided by research discoveries from many fields of neuroscience. The most dramatic modern therapeutic approach emerging from this research is *chemotherapy*—the use of drugs that alter mood and mental states—for a range of mental disorders. In addition, a growing awareness of the genetic involvement in certain kinds of mental disorder is likely to encourage applications of "genetic engineering" to make direct alterations in genes identified as causally linked to particular mental disorders (see **Close-up,** p. 554).

Psychosurgery and electroconvulsive therapy

Two of the most direct interventions for changing thought and mood disorders have involved cutting parts of the brain or subjecting the whole brain to intensive electrical stimulation.

The best-known form of psychosurgery is the **prefrontal lobotomy,** an operation that severs the nerve fibers connecting the frontal lobes of the brain with the thalamus, but removes no brain tissue. The procedure was developed by neurologist Egas Moniz, who won a Nobel Prize in 1949 for it. Prefrontal lo-

botomy soon became a popular "operation of last resort" in the United States and England because it could be performed quickly and simply in a physician's office.

The ideal candidates for a lobotomy were agitated schizophrenic patients, as well as patients who were compulsive and anxiety-ridden. The effects of neurosurgery were dramatic: a "new personality" emerged, one without intense emotional arousal and thus no longer overwhelmed by anxiety, guilt, or anger. In part, this positive effect occurred because the operation disconnected present functioning from memory for past traumas and conflicts and also from future concerns.

Unfortunately, the immediate benefits of psychosurgery in altering undesirable mood states and disrupting undesirable behavior patterns were offset by the most disheartening side effects. The lobotomized patient lost something—the unique flavor of the personality. Specifically, the psychological changes caused by the lobotomy were evident in the patient's inability to plan ahead, indifference to the opinions of others, childlike actions, and the intellectual and the emotional flatness of a person without a coherent sense of self. Because the effects of psychosurgery are permanent, its negative effects severe and common, and its positive results less certain, it is rarely used today.

Electroconvulsive therapy (ECT) is a "shock" treatment designed to produce upheaval in the central nervous system by the application of electric current to the patient's temples for a fraction of a second. The patient loses consciousness, has a convulsion similar to that in an epileptic seizure, and then falls into a comalike sleep state for some minutes. Following this coma, the patient tends to be more calm and more susceptible to psychotherapy. In the past, similar shocks to the nervous system were produced by other forms of convulsive therapy.

The effects of electroconvulsive therapy were initially hailed as "unparalleled" in the history of psychiatry. It has been especially effective in cases of severe depression. But no one knows why it works. It may be due to some aspect of the coma itself, to physiological changes in nervous system circuits, or even to a strong psychological reaction, such as determination to avoid another treatment or feeling sufficiently punished to get rid of guilt over an imagined wrong (Fink, 1979).

Close-up

Hopes for "Cures" Through Genetic Engineering

We know that heredity strongly influences susceptibility to schizophrenia. Research also has shown that heredity plays an important role in manic-depressive mental disorders. The incidence rate is less than 1 percent in the general population, but when one member of a set of identical twins has this disorder, the chances that the other twin does also are about 50 percent (Gottesman & Shields, 1972).

Genes work by altering enzymes or other proteins. When a person's genetic inheritance increases his or her susceptibility to psychotic behavior, part of the mechanism involved may be traced to the failure of one or more enzymes to carry out their normal biochemical functions in metabolism. Of the more than 100 diseases involving errors of metabolism, several dozen result in mental retardation.

In one kind of mental retardation, **phenylketonuria** (PKU), a recessive genetic defect is inherited (from both parents) in which a simple liver enzyme is missing (see Depue & Monroe, 1983). This enzyme is essential for breaking down the amino acid *phenylalanine* found in many foods. If a child with PKU eats foods with phenylalanine, the substance builds up in the blood, and brain damage results. "Prevention" of PKU damage includes early detection through routine urine and blood tests or when any of the manifest symptoms first appear (intellectual retardation, lack of pigmentation, musty odor, vomiting, convulsions). Then, basic treatment for individuals with PKU consists of avoiding foods with phenylalanine, such as lettuce or the artificial sweetener aspartame (Equal and Nutrasweet).

Recently, genetic researchers have discovered that another genetic defect is the direct cause of an even more destructive type of mental disorder called **Lesch-Nyhan syndrome** (see Vogel & Motulsky, 1982). Young people with this disorder become uncontrollably violent and mutilate themselves. Mental retardation follows, and the person dies prematurely. In families with a history of this syndrome, pregnant mothers can be tested (from samples of amniotic fluid) for the presence of the defective gene. After discussion with a genetics counselor, they then have the option of early abortion rather than bearing a child who will inevitably suffer this genetically controlled lethal disorder.

Biological disturbances due to metabolic disorders result in symptoms that are distinctly beyond the normal range in magnitude; thus, reliable diagnostic tests can be developed (Emery, 1979). By contrast, biological disturbances in the case of mental disorders like chronic schizophrenia are of low magnitude, more varied from one individual to another, and more variable over time. Recently, however, the role of MAO metabolism in schizophrenia has been deduced from the finding of reduced MAO activity in schizophrenic patients in many studies (Wyatt et al., 1980). The enzyme MAO (monamine oxidose) is known to influence the central nervous system by modulating the effects of certain transmitters, such as serotonin and norepinephrine.

While most metabolic disorders are outside of the central nervous system, most psychopathological disorders originate within it. The broader range of less distinctive symptoms in psychopathology may thus be attributed to the complex interplay of central-nervous-system processes involving neurotransmitters, corrective feedback circuits, and hormonal influences. In such a dynamic system, the alteration of any one component, as in the activity of an enzyme, may have only indirect effects of increasing the vulnerability of the entire system. This "biological biasing" effect will become greater when the individual is under intense or prolonged stress but not be substantial under nonstress conditions (Barchas et al., 1975).

Evidence for a physical cause of depression comes from a study that demonstrated an abnormally high number of receptor sites for the neurotransmitter acetylcholine among manic-depressive patients (Nadi et al., 1984). This indicates an oversensitivity to acetylcholine, which could lead to abnormal behavior. If this result is replicated, it could be possible to develop tests of vulnerability to manic-depression based on an index of acetylcholine receptor sites—and to begin preventive therapy in individuals who are at risk for the disorder.

As biomedical researchers discover more about inborn genetic errors in metabolic and psychopathological disorders and the pathways in the neurons system that they affect, new treatments can be developed. This suggests that certain mental disorders might be treated, or prevented, by alterations in the defective genetic material. There is reason to expect new breakthroughs in genetic engineering, whereby defective genes that control specific metabolic or neural functions will be identified and then "corrected" by innovative biogenetic techniques.

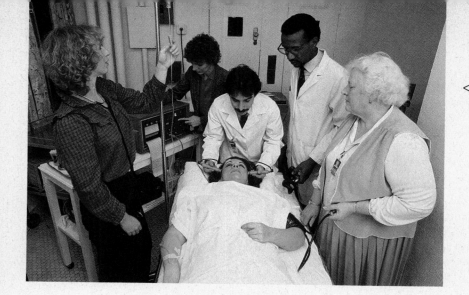

Methodologically sound evaluation studies indicate that electroconvulsive therapy also seems to have some beneficial effect with some types of schizophrenic patients, especially those with more recent onset of symptoms. But while it reduces some of the bizarre symptoms of schizophrenia, such as catatonic posturing, it does not change the problems of cognitive processing that seem central to schizophrenic pathology (Salzman, 1980).

There are many critics of this extreme form of biomedical therapy (see Breggin, 1979). An early review pointed to poorly conducted evaluation studies that lacked standardized procedures, diagnostic information on the types of patients, and reliable measures of patient response to treatment and used vague criteria for "improvement" and "cure." It found that immediate positive effects were not lasting: treated patients left the mental institution after short stays—but were soon readmitted. More serious, the patient's language and memory became impaired. Familiar knowledge—both declarative and procedural—was lost, damaging the self-esteem of a person who couldn't recall important information or perform routine tasks. In patients given extensive series of electroconvulsive treatments, signs of personality deterioration became apparent. The individual became dull, listless, and without concern for personal needs (Group for the Advancement of Psychiatry, 1950).

Even today, the debate continues between those who argue that it is the only effective treatment for some suicidally depressed patients and opponents who claim that it is used indiscriminately in understaffed, large state institutions, has permanently damaging effects to the brains of many patients, and is often used as a threat or punishment. In 1982, the citizens of Berkeley, California, voted to ban the use of electroconvulsive shock in any of their community mental health facilities. Though the action was later overturned on legal grounds, this does show that the public can organize an effective protest against an established form of treatment for mental disorders. In part, their opposition underscored a theme in Ken Kesey's novel, *One Flew Over the Cuckoo's Nest* (1962)—be wary of any "therapy" that might be a disguised form of suppressing dissent and making people easier for managers to manage.

Chemotherapy

In the history of the treatment of mental disorder, nothing has ever rivaled the "revolution" created by the discovery of drugs that could calm anxious patients, restore reality contact in withdrawn patients, and suppress hallucinations in psychotic patients. This new therapeutic era began in 1953–1954 with the introduction of tranquilizing drugs, notably *chlorpromazine* (American brand name, Thorazine) into mental hospital treatment programs.

Chemotherapy is the use of drugs to treat mental and behavioral disorders. The new scientific field of psychopharmacology gained almost instant recognition and status as a chemically based therapy for transforming patient behavior. Unruly, assaultive patients became cooperative, calm, and sociable. Those absorbed only in their delusions and hallucinations began to be responsive to the physical and social environment around them. No longer was there the need for staff to act as guards, putting patients in seclusion or straitjackets. Staff morale improved as rehabilitation became a reality that replaced mere custodial care of the mentally ill.

Another profound aspect of the chemotherapy revolution was its impact on the nation's mental hospital population. Over half a million Americans were living in mental institutions in 1955, for an average stay of several years—some for an entire lifetime. The steadily increasing numbers were stopped and reversed by the introduction of chlorpromazine and other drugs. By the early 1970s, it was estimated that less than half the country's mental patients actually resided in mental hospitals and that those who did were institutionalized for an average of only a few months.

In human terms, these statistics mean that, "since the introduction of these [antipsychotic] drugs, the 'snake pit' atmosphere of the back wards of mental hospitals, with walls and floors covered with human excrement, and filled twenty-four hours a day with terror-laden shrieking, essentially exist no more" (Snyder, 1974, p. 20).

Those who benefited most from psychopharmacology were younger patients who were suffering from acute rather than chronic psychoses and who had had recent, few, and short periods of institutionalization. Older, chronic patients who had been hospitalized for more than five years were not as much affected by chemotherapy, but still it reduced their hallucinations and delusions.

Three major categories of drugs are used today in chemotherapy programs: *antipsychotic, antianxiety,* and *antidepressant* compounds. As their names suggest, these drugs chemically alter specific brain functions that are responsible for psychotic symptoms, extreme anxiety, and depression, respectively.

Antipsychotic drugs. The psychotic symptoms of delusion, hallucinations, social withdrawal, and occasional agitation are altered by the **antipsychotic drugs.** Though each is chemically different, all the antipsychotic drugs have similar effects on particular aspects of brain functioning. Patients become calm

and tranquil, but remain alert. With many such patients, psychotherapy becomes possible for the first time.

Chlorpromazine is an antipsychotic drug that is derived from the compound *phenothiazine.* In our Prologue to *Psychology and Life,* Neal Miller outlined the steps in the discovery of this "wonder drug" and described its effective role in treatment of severe mental disorders.

One of the most remarkable antipsychotic drugs is a simple salt, the extract of a rock, which can influence the uniquely subtle property of mind that regulates our moods. *Lithium salt* is a chemical proven to be effective in the treatment of manic disorders. People who experience uncontrollable periods of hyperexcitement, during which their energy seems timeless and their behavior extravagant and flamboyant, are brought down from this state of manic excess by doses of lithium.

Seven or eight of every ten manic patients treated with lithium have a good chance to recover—even where other treatments have failed (N.I.M.H., 1977). Furthermore, regular maintenance doses of lithium can help break the cycle of recurring episodes of mania and/or depression. When used in this way, lithium regulates extreme mood swings; it also allows the person to be alert and creative (Ehrlich & Diamond, 1980). One negative side-effect of long-term administration of antipsychotic drugs is the development of an unusual disturbance of motor control, especially of the facial muscles, called **tardive dyskinesia.**

Antianxiety drugs. To cope with the "garden variety" of everyday hassles, untold millions of Americans "pop pills" that reduce tension and suppress anxiety. In general, these **antianxiety drugs** are tranquilizers that work by sedating the anxious person. The three classes of antianxiety compounds are *barbiturates, propanediols,* and *benzodiazepines.*

Barbiturates have a general relaxing effect but can be dangerous if taken in excess or in combination with alcohol. Propanediol drugs (such as Miltown and Equanil) reduce the tension that accompanies agitated anxiety. As tense muscles relax, the person experiences a general calming, soothing effect. Benzodiazepine drugs (Valium and Librium are two examples) are effective in reducing generalized fears and anxiety without affecting the person's ability to pay attention or process information.

Because these tranquilizers work so well, it is easy to become psychologically dependent on them or physically addicted to all three. When faced with a conflict or a source of emotional distress, many people are taking the mellow, low road of coping chemically rather than actively confronting the problem, trying to solve it, or accepting pain and grief as part of the human experience. In addition, there is considerable evidence that these drugs are physiologically addicting.

Antidepressant drugs. Depressed patients given **antidepressant drugs** often show significant improvement. The two basic antidepressants are the *tricyclics* and the *monoamine oxidase (MAO) inhibitors.* The tricyclics (such as Tofranil and Elavil) are the more widely used of the two because they are less toxic, do not require dietary restrictions, and seem to be more potent therapeutically.

In the case of many drugs, we know that patients taking them appear to get better, but we do not know why or how the drugs work. In the case of the antidepressants, however, the chemical and the physiological effects are better understood.

These drugs change the emotional state of a chronically depressed person (they are *not* appropriate for transient depression) by prolonging the action of two neurotransmitters, *serotonin* and *norepinephrine.* Affective disorders appear to be associated with a reduced availability of these chemicals at transmission points in the brain. Tricyclics increase their availability by preventing them from being reabsorbed so quickly by the neurons that release them. Thus, they keep circulating and are more available. MAO inhibitors produce the same effect through a different mechanism. Monoamine oxidase itself ordinarily alters serotonin and norepinephrine, thus stopping their effects on nerve receptors. MAO *inhibitors* allow these substances to remain in their effective states longer. Thus, both tricyclics and MAO inhibitors allow neurotransmitters that are in limited supply in the brains of depressed individuals to have greater impact on nerve transmission. As a consequence, these individuals feel—and act—less depressed.

THERAPEUTIC EFFECTIVENESS

"Do these therapies work?" That is *THE* question. The answer is not so easy to come by. You can begin to appreciate the difficulties by trying to formulate an answer to the comparable question, Does college education work? Are you asking about all people who enter college, those who complete it, or those who are motivated to make it work while exposed to it? Does it depend on which kind of college (or type of therapy) you're looking at, or on the particular teachers (therapists) involved? Do you want to know only to what extent the original goals are achieved (getting a B.A., or symptom relief), or are you interested in new goals added with experience but never attained once and for all (enjoying learning for its own sake, wanting to have an integrated, effective, personal style)? Should the effects of a college education be compared with those of other experiences requiring equal investments of time and money in order to decide if it was "worth it"? And finally, when should that decision be made, and by whom—at graduation or some years after, by you, parents, or teachers?

Parallel issues and problems plague any easy attempts to assess whether any given therapy is effective or is more effective than other forms of treatment. Certain factors seem related to the success of therapy, however, and some of these are listed in **Table 15.3.**

British psychologist Hans Eysenck created a furor some years ago (1952) by reporting a study showing that people receiving *no* therapy had just as high a cure rate as those receiving psychoanalysis or other forms of insight therapy. How could that be?

For unknown reasons, some percentage of mental patients improve without any professional intervention. This *spontaneous recovery* effect is the *baseline* against which the "cure rate" of therapies must be assessed. Simply put, doing something must be shown to lead to a significantly greater percentage of improved cases than doing nothing, or just letting time pass. As is often the case with physical ailments, many psychological problems improve because "time heals all (or a reasonable proportion of) wounds."

Placebo therapy must also be distinguished from substantive therapeutic effects if we are to deter-

Table 15.3 *Factors Affecting the Success of Psychotherapy*

	Positive (Success more likely)	Negative (Success less likely)
Disorder:	Neurotic, especially anxiety	Schizophrenic, paranoid
Pathology:	Short duration, not severe	Serious disturbance
Ego strength:	Strong, good	Weak, poor
Anxiety:	Not high	High
Defenses:	Adequate	Lacking
Patient's attitudes:	Motivated to change	Indifferent
	Realistic expectations for therapeutic change	Unrealistic expectations for change or none at all
Patient's activity in therapy:	Actively collaborates, involved, responsible for problem-solving	Passive, detached, makes therapist solely responsible
Therapeutic relationship:	Mutual liking and attraction	Unreciprocated attraction
Therapist characteristics:	Personally well adjusted, experienced	Poorly adjusted

No differences in outcome, or inconsistent findings, were found for these factors: age, sex, social class, and race of patient.

(Adapted, with permission, from the Annual Review of Psychology, *Volume 29, Copyright © 1978 by Annual Reviews, Inc.)*

mine whether client improvement results from specific clinical procedures or just from "being in therapy." Some psychologists believe that the patient's *belief* that therapy will help and the therapist's social influence in conveying this suggestion are key placebo ingredients in the success of any therapy (Fish, 1973).

While most psychotherapy researchers agree with Eysenck that it is important to show that psychotherapy is more effective than spontaneous recovery or client expectations, they criticized his findings because of many methodological problems in his study. And a later evaluation of about a hundred therapy outcome studies (of "reasonable" quality) found that psychotherapy *did* lead to greater improvement than spontaneous recovery in 80 percent of the cases (Meltzoff & Kornreich, 1970). Thus, it seems safe to conclude that the therapeutic experience itself is a useful one.

One of the well-controlled studies compared patients who had undergone psychoanalytic or behavior therapy with patients who had simply been on the "waiting list." It was found that both types of therapy were beneficial, with behavior therapy leading to the greatest overall improvement. The researchers also concluded that the improvement of patients in therapy was "not entirely due either to

spontaneous recovery or to the placebo effect of the nonspecific aspects of therapy, such as arousal of hope, expectation of help, and an initial cathartic interview" (Sloane et al., 1975, p. 224). Because of such findings, current researchers are less concerned with asking *whether* psychotherapy works than with asking *why* it works and whether any one treatment is most effective for any particular problem.

All the therapies presented in this chapter (and dozens more that we did not examine) have devoted defenders. What can be said about their comparative effectiveness? The answer, of course, is not simple.

In one exemplary attempt to find an answer, 375 controlled studies of therapy outcome were surveyed, using a sophisticated measure of relative improvement to calculate the degree of improvement for patients in each study for each kind of psychotherapy. Not all therapies were represented in their review; in particular, the current expansion of cognitive therapies is not reflected. Nevertheless, the survey provides a useful summary of relative effectiveness for most major psychotherapies, as shown in **Table 15.4** (Smith & Glass 1977).

In this survey the most effective approach was systematic desensitization. However, it is important to recognize that this approach is not suitable for the majority of clinical problems. It is particularly designed for anxiety problems, especially when there is a clear, known stimulus for the anxiety.

Relative improvement for behavioral therapies as a group was greater than for the three major nonbehavioral therapies. The difference was not large, however, and numerous factors make it difficult to know how confident we should be of that finding. For example, follow-up times were longer in the nonbehavioral studies, and therapist experience varied. Problems like these are common in conducting therapy outcome studies. Differences in the severity and types of patient difficulties, the kinds of outcome measures used, the fit between what the patient expects from therapy and the type of therapy offered, and a host of other crucial variables make the study of psychotherapy outcome a very complex business.

In a similar subsequent study, the same investigators found cognitive behavior modification to be the most effective (Smith et al., 1980). They are in agreement with Jerome Frank that no one theoretical approach can be considered clearly superior for all types of problems. As Frank had said, quoting from *Alice in Wonderland*, "*Everybody* has won, and *all* must have prizes" (1979).

But after distributing the prizes, many questions remain. Are some therapies clearly superior for some problems, but inferior for others? Are there underlying similarities across all psychotherapies that cause their effectiveness (despite differences in their "brand name" labels)? Are the human qualities of the therapist and the personal relationship between therapist and client more important than the theory that guides the technique (see Kazdin & Wilson, 1980, and Smith et al., 1980)?

Currently under way is the most ambitious test ever conducted of the effectiveness of different therapies for depression. As we have seen, depression is a serious problem in our society, with suicide a danger in many cases. Thus, clearer guidelines for the best therapy for it will be a great boon.

A 3-year test is being carried out by the National Institute for Mental Health at a cost of over $3 million and involving many institutions. Two psychotherapies—a cognitive therapy and a socially oriented psychodynamic therapy—are being compared with a drug treatment using a tricyclic depressant and a "placebo" drug control. Twenty-seven therapists have been trained in all these approaches and are being randomly assigned to administer a particular

Table 15.4 *Which Therapy Works Best?*

	Number of Studies Surveyed	Index of Average Relative Improvement
Traditional Psychodynamic	96	.59
Behavioral:		
Systematic desensitization	223	.91
Implosion	45	.64
Behavior Modification	132	.76
Cognitive Rational Emotive	35	.77
Existential-Humanistic:		
Client-centered	94	.63
Other Therapies		
Eclectic	70	.48
Gestalt	8	.26

(Adapted from Smith & Glass, 1977)

approach to a given patient. The 144 patients, who have been carefully screened to assure that they are comparable, are randomly assigned to one of the treatment groups. A comparison group of 36 patients are being "treated as usual" by experienced therapists with no special instructions. Outcome measures will include patient and therapist evaluations of relief from symptoms of depression and also an independent clinical evaluation of each case (Kolata, 1981).

While various therapists disagree with certain aspects of this clinical comparison study, the program of rigorous, systematic evaluations of what goes into and what comes out of the specific treatments is definitely welcome and can be expected to give us a new understanding of how depressed patients respond to different approaches.

It is important to recognize the limitations as well as the special contributions of any particular therapeutic approach in evaluating its effectiveness. Psychodynamic therapy typically is expensive, takes a long time, can only be conducted by a professional expert, and is geared toward patients with a relatively high level of verbal fluency, intelligence, and motivation to persist in therapy. Like all one-on-one, long-term treatments, it is not "cost effective" for the society, since the therapist is limited to treating only a small number of patients at any one time. Because the goals of psychodynamic therapy involve global changes in personality and adjustment, the criteria for evaluating its success are not precise and are difficult to assess.

Short-term therapy of a fixed duration, usually of 10 to 20 sessions, is becoming more popular for the practical and economic advantages it offers patients and society. Such brief therapy is better suited for acute than chronic problems, for crisis intervention, for modifying specific behaviors rather than general personality patterns. This symptom-oriented approach focuses on the present situation and not on past origins of the current problem. Brief therapy is not possible with traditional psychoanalytic therapy. However, brief approaches have been found to be useful in other therapies, especially behaviorally oriented ones and family or marital therapy with an existential-humanistic focus (Weakland et al., 1974).

Behavior therapies have, in addition to their economy of time and cost, the advantages of specifying concrete objectives that can be more readily assessed within rigorous experimental paradigms. They can also be administered by trained professionals and not just by specialists. However, while they work well for distinct types of behavior problems, such as phobias, they are not as suitable for broader classes of problems associated with motivation, mood, or thought disorders.

Cognitive approaches have supplemented the behavioral, but are not as useful where disturbed behavior is influenced by unconscious processes or where the individual's problem involves deficits in social or action skills that require practice and feedback.

Like the psychodynamic, existential-humanistic therapy works best for a selected group of verbal, intelligent, motivated individuals. The offshoots of this general approach into group therapies that each address a particular type of problem—such as interpersonal power or faulty communication patterns in married couples—has increased the practical utility of this usually abstract, indirect approach.

Biomedical therapies remain quite controversial, especially among many psychologists. They are seen as full of enormous promise, yet threatening with potential harm. We have seen that psychosurgery and ECT have equivocal success for certain types of extreme disorders but can also have highly undesirable side effects. Chemotherapy certainly has been a boon in the treatment of institutionalized mental patients, as well as outpatients with previously severe disorders. Among the hazards of long-term chemotherapy are (a) an overreliance on drug therapy in place of "human contact" therapies; (b) some serious physical side effects, including the syndrome of tardive dyskinesia; and (c) the development of a psychological dependence on drugs as a way to avoid developing adequate behavior patterns for coping with life's problems (Davison & Valins, 1969).

The problem of evaluating the effectiveness of chemotherapy is illustrated by the *revolving door phenomenon.* There is now a higher discharge rate from mental hospitals but an even higher return rate of mental patients.

Finally, much criticism has been leveled against the legal, political, and moral aspects of involuntarily committing people to mental hospitals and forcing them to have their brains cut, be subjected to electric shock, or be drugged. Recent court decisions have begun to address these sensitive issues and to increase the rights of patients to refuse treatment (see Bazelon, 1981; *Kaimovwits* v. *Michigan Department of Health,* 1973; *Rogers* v. *Okin,* 1979; White & White, 1981).

There is no question that biomedical interventions can change behavior and mental processes, both directly and indirectly—dramatically so in a short time in the case of some psychoses. To the extent that normal behavior and reactions depend on an intact brain and nervous system functioning smoothly, physical agents that restore or maintain such functioning will provide physical readiness for healthy adjustment. But to the extent that effective behavior depends also on learning in a social setting, one can expect that relearning and social interaction will also need to be part of therapy if new behavioral patterns are to be acquired. And if effective adjustment depends on a perception of one's own control over one's destiny, therapy must increase that perception of self-regulation and autonomy. Dependence on pills or other external physical agents is likely to work in the other direction.

For a practical guide to therapy, see the **Close-up** on page 561.

A Practical Guide to Therapy

Many of us have developed (or been taught) the feeling that we ought to be able to work out our own problems and not burden others with them. It somehow seems a sign of weakness to admit that we might need help. There is little doubt, however, that almost everyone sometimes experiences feelings of depression or loneliness or inability to cope. Numerous life experiences have the potential of inducing such personal crises. It is important to realize that everyone faces such crises at one time or another and that there is nothing wrong or unusual about reacting to them emotionally. Seeking help at such times may not be easy, but it is preferable to muddling through alone.

When our usual emotional supports, such as parents or close friends, are absent or unavailable, we should not hesitate to seek help from other sources. For most people, the duration of a crisis is usually short (from 4 to 6 weeks) and contains both the danger of increased psychological vulnerability and the opportunity for personal growth. The outcome seems to depend to a large degree on the availability of appropriate help and on one's own attitude and definition of the "problem."

In terms of prevention, however, it would make better sense to know about sources of help *before* they are needed. An interesting and worthwhile project would be to identify the various sources of psychological support available to you now. First of all, you should list the available sources of help outside the mental health profession, such as family, friends, teachers, clergy, "rap centers," and so on. Perhaps a visit to a local church or drop-in center would be instructive in indicating whether or not these places could be of help to you. You can simply explain that you are trying to identify sources of emotional support in the community (as a class project). Also, find out about the mental health facilities at your college as part of your growing knowledge of psychology in your life. Later on, if you need help or someone asks you for help, you will know where to go for it.

Most problems are in fact minor ones that go away in time and diminish in intensity as we look back on them. But the process of working them through helps us get in touch with ourselves and perhaps reduces the stressfulness of similar problems later. However, there are also cases of real distress in which perhaps you or a friend might become severely depressed, seriously contemplate suicide, or begin to develop paranoid feelings of persecution, hallucinations, or other signs of major psychological stress. For such problems you should go at once to an accredited professional therapist for help. Go early, before the symptoms themselves become problems (causing poor grades, disrupting friendships, etc.).

It is not unreasonable to talk ahead of time about the "therapeutic contract"—what you get for what you give. If you think it appropriate, you might want to explore the therapist's view of human nature and the causes of emotional and behavioral disturbance. Of course, feeling comfortable with the therapist and being able to develop feelings of trust are more important than knowing his or her philosophy. This can best be accomplished through sharing your problems and concerns and gauging the helpfulness of the response you get. Remember, though, that many therapists refrain from giving direct advice, seeking instead to help the client achieve his or her own resolution to the problem. You may judge for yourself whether or not this is what you need. Also, at first, the therapist must learn about you and your "problems," so in the early session(s), he or she may do more listening than advising or informing.

Therapy is an intimate social exchange in which you pay for a service. If you feel the service is not benefiting you, discuss this openly with the therapist; expose the possibility that failure of therapy represents the *therapist's failure* as well as your own. Discuss criteria for successful termination of therapy—when will the two of you know that you are "really" better? Also discuss the issue of terminating therapy if you are unsatisfied with it or think it has given you what you needed. This may itself be a positive step toward self-assertion. Professionals understand that no therapist relates well with everyone, and a good one will sometimes suggest that a client might do better with another therapist.

Two additional points should be mentioned. Even when terminating therapy that has "worked" for the problems that distressed you, you might still want to arrange for some future "booster sessions" with the therapist or therapy group should you feel they are needed. Finally, be willing to listen to others who may need your help. This course has not prepared you to be a therapist, but it should increase your sensitivity to other people's psychological concerns and your willingness to give up a little of your time and patience to reaffirm the human connection by being "there" when someone asks for your help.

PROMOTING MENTAL HEALTH

"Two friends were walking on a riverbank when a child swept by downstream in the current, screaming and drowning. One of the pair jumped in and rescued the kid. They had just resumed their stroll when another child appeared in the water, also struggling for air. The rescuer jumped in again and pulled the victim to safety. Soon a third drowning child came by. The still-dry friend began to trot up the riverbank. The rescuer yelled, 'Hey, where are you going? Here's another one.' The dry one replied, 'I'm going to get the bastard that's throwing them in'" (Wolman, 1975, p. 3).

The moral of this little story is clear: *preventing* a problem is the best solution. All traditional therapies have in common the focus on changing a person who is already distressed or disabled. They begin to do their work *after* the problem behaviors show up and *after* the suffering starts—too often *long* after, by which time the mental disorder has settled in.

The goal of *preventing* psychological problems is being put into practice by a number of community mental health centers under the general direction of the National Association for Mental Health. The first step towards this goal is the recognition that systematic efforts toward combating psychological problems can take place at any of three levels:

1. reducing the *severity* of existing disorders (using traditional therapies);
2. reducing *duration* of disorders by means by new programs for early identification and prompt treatment;
3. reducing the *incidence* of new cases among the unaffected, normal population that is potentially "at risk" for a particular disorder (Klein & Goldston, 1977).

The development of this three-stage model has signaled a "new look" in mental health care with major shifts in focus—in basic paradigms—in this field. The most important of these "paradigm shifts" are: (a) toward supplementing treatment with prevention; (b) toward going beyond a medical disease model to a public health model; (c) toward focusing on "at risk" situations, and away from "at risk" people; (d) toward looking for current precipitating factors in life settings rather than long-standing predisposing factors in people; (e) toward not just preventing problems but promoting positive mental health (see Albee & Joffe, 1977; Price et al., 1980).

Where the medical model is concerned with treating people who are afflicted, a **public health model** includes identifying and eliminating the sources of disease and illness that exist in the environment. In this approach, the affected individual is seen as the host or carrier—the end-product of an existing process of disease. Change the conditions that breed illness and there will be no need to change people later, with expensive, extensive treatments. The dramatic reduction of many contagious and infectious diseases, such as tuberculosis, smallpox, and malaria, has come about through this approach. With psychopathology, too, many sources of environmental or organizational stress can be identified; plans can then be made to alleviate them, thus reducing the number of people who will be exposed by them.

Some of our emotional problems undoubtedly stem from early life experiences, such as unresolved conflicts and inappropriate learning. Nevertheless, as we have seen, major sources of the stress we face are in the conditions under which we are living our daily lives. The newer approaches, directing attention toward *precipitating* factors in the person's current environment, deal in practical ways with changing *what is* rather than reinterpreting *what was*. They recognize that certain situations are likely to foster psychopathology—as when people are made to feel anonymous, rejected, isolated, or abused. They try to avoid psychopathology by involving people in learning how to avoid or change these kinds of situations.

We know that a large portion of the population suffers from debilitating fears and anxieties in response to a variety of situations. Prevention strategies could be developed for routinely training children and adults to cope more effectively with commonly experienced stressful situations (starting school, leaving home, marrying, bearing and rearing children, retiring, and so forth). Such training in coping skills could be administered by paraprofessionals in schools, via cable TV, or through other means of wide-scale delivery. This training could be provided at critical periods in adolescence and adulthood to prevent recurring interpersonal problems that are centered around issues such as heterosexual contact, public speaking, relating to authority, and being evaluated (Barrios & Shigetomi, 1980).

In one of the most encouraging examples of primary prevention of mental problems, children of mentally retarded mothers were "prevented" from also becoming retarded. Mentally retarded mothers tend to have children with subnormal intelligence. Low intelligence, in turn, is correlated with many disadvantages in vocational and social situations. Psychologist Rich Heber intervened in the lives of a group of mentally retarded mothers to try to break the negative cycle in which mental retardation not only limits many people to a life of poverty but condemns the next generation as well.

Half of a group of 40 mentally retarded mothers living in a large slum area were randomly assigned to a Prevention-intervention condition, while half were assigned to a Comparison-no intervention condition. The intervention included training the mothers to become literate and vocationally competent. Their children got early day care from the research staff, who also were generally involved in the home life of the mothers. This intervention lasted for about two years.

Outcome measures taken eight years later revealed: (1) no change in the IQ levels of the mothers; (2) more of the mothers in the Prevention group were working as compared with the Comparison group; they also made more money on their jobs, had more job stability, and had more verbal interactions with their children; (3) the average IQ of children in the Comparison group was 87, with a third of the children classified as "mentally retarded." However—and most remarkable—the average IQ of children in the Prevention group was 121, well above normal. Not a single one of these children was mentally retarded (Heber, 1978).

Although such a dramatic result needs to be independently replicated before it is accepted by the scientific community, this approach holds out much promise for profoundly influencing the lives of people society often writes off as "subnormal."

To prevent mental disorders is a complex and difficult task. It involves not only understanding the relevant causal factors, but overcoming individual and institutional resistance to change. A major reeducation effort is necessary to demonstrate the long-range utility of prevention and a community mental health approach to psychopathology and to justify the necessary expense in the face of other pressing problems demanding solutions.

An associated task facing professionals in the new fields of health psychology and behavioral medicine, as well as all of us, is how to foster the attitude that mental health should be promoted rather than mental illness treated or even prevented. We need to set our sights on [...] better, and on [...] stronger. Our m[...] extent that we h[...] self-efficacy. On[...] health philosophy[...] is to be, it is up t[...] enjoy my success,[...] continue to grow[...] unique individual[...] meaningful social [...] will examine the p[...]

SUMMARY

■ Therapies for psychological problems vary widely and include several quite different kinds of psychological therapies, as well as biomedical therapies. The goal of all of them is to replace psychological problems with improved psychological health and more effective coping styles.

■ Clinical psychologists have earned a Ph.D. degree specializing in assessment and treatment of psychological problems. Psychiatrists are medically trained professionals with expertise in mental and emotional diseases. Psychoanalysts are therapists with either an M.D. or a Ph.D. whose training is in the Freudian approach.

■ Treatment of those with mental disorders has changed with changes in attitude and understanding and has ranged from persecution to kindness to attempts at rehabilitation. Today in our society some disorders are attributed to physiological factors and treated medically, while others are recognized as psychological problems requiring psychological treatment.

■ Freudian psychoanalysis is an intensive, prolonged technique for exploring unconscious motivations and conflicts in neurotic, anxiety-ridden individuals. Its goal is to establish intrapsychic harmony among id, superego, and ego. Through free association, dream analysis, and analysis of resistances, the therapist seeks to uncover repressed conflicts; these are worked through in part in the handling of transference and countertransference.

...pies since Freud have put more ...ng life experiences, the current so-...social motivations, and the impor-...unctioning. Two neo-Freudians are Harry ...n, who emphasized interpersonal influences ...elf-system, and Margaret Mahler, an important ...butor to work on childhood schizophrenia.

■ Behavior therapies involve applications of principles of conditioning to the modification of specific behaviors. Counterconditioning is used in systematic desensitization and in aversion therapy; extinction is used in implosive therapy. Contingency management has been widely used in schools and other institutions to produce and maintain desired behavior through positive reinforcement and specific extinction strategies; token economies are often a part of contingency management and in some cases behavioral contracts are successful.

■ Social learning techniques include imitation of models and participant modeling, as well as specific social skills training, including behavioral rehearsal. Generalization techniques are ways of getting new knowledge applied beyond the therapy setting.

■ Cognitive therapies are aimed at changing problem feelings and behaviors by changing the individual's perceptions and thoughts. Cognitive behavior modification combines reinforcement of positive self-statements with new constructive actions; seeing one's successes and taking credit for them changes one's cognitions about oneself and creates expectations of effectiveness. Other cognitive therapies, such as rational-emotive therapy, focus on correcting faulty thought patterns.

■ Existential-humanistic therapies seek to replace feelings of dissatisfaction and alienation with commitment to positive values and willingness to take responsibility for one's life. Their focus is on psychological growth and self-actualization rather than the correction of deficiencies or disorders. This approach is at the center of the human potential movement.

■ Biomedical therapies include psychosurgery, now rarely used, and electroconvulsive therapy; the latter produces a period of calmness and greater susceptibility to therapy. It seems to have beneficial effects for severe depression and some kinds of schizophrenia (for reasons unknown), but the effects do not last, memory is impaired, and personality deterioration may develop.

■ Chemotherapy has revolutionized the treatment of mental patients and reversed the mounting numbers of the hospitalized. Today less than half as many mental patients must be hospitalized.

■ Antipsychotic drugs include chlorpromazine, helpful in treating schizophrenia, and lithium, which regulates manic swings. Antianxiety drugs are used by millions of Americans to reduce tension but may be addicting. Antidepressant drugs are effective with chronic, serious depression. But drugs do not cure mental problems, may have unwanted side effects, and may prevent more active attempts to develop better coping patterns.

■ Spontaneous recoveries and patients' beliefs that therapy will help them complicate attempts to assess the effectiveness of therapy. In general, studies indicate the therapeutic experience to be valuable. No one approach can be considered clearly superior for all types of problems. With more sophisticated evaluation studies, we can expect to learn more about the special benefits of particular therapies for particular problems.

■ Preventing a problem is the best solution. Three levels of prevention of mental disorders include reducing the rate of new cases, reducing the duration of disorders that occur through early recognition and prompt treatment, and reducing the severity of these disorders through therapy. Identification and elimination of environmental sources of problems is as important as looking for causes in individuals. The new focus is on changing *what is* rather than reinterpreting *what was*.

Part Seven

Social Processes

Chapter Sixteen
The Social Bases of Behavior

Chapter Seventeen
Exploring Social Issues

16

THE SOCIAL BASES OF BEHAVIOR

▪ THE APPROACH OF SOCIAL PSYCHOLOGY
The person in the social environment
The importance of social reality
Social applications

▪ SOCIAL PERCEPTION
Impression formation
Attribution

▪ ATTITUDES AND PERSUASION
The nature of attitudes
Persuasive communications

▪ INTERPERSONAL ATTRACTION
Reasons for affiliation
Liking
Loving

▪ GROUP PROCESSES
Group form and function
Group influence
Group leadership
Intergroup relations

▪ SUMMARY

I never imagined that a red shirt could qualify as a social event—until mine became one. For several days my identity and social class were bound up in the redness of my shirt. It was "me," and I wore it with pride. It made me feel special and dramatically different from all the other patients on my hospital ward. So why did I feel so relieved when I finally decided to surrender it and yield up my uniqueness?

It all started with a traffic accident. A group of faculty members was being driven from the uptown to the downtown campus when the university limousine crashed head-on into another car. Screams, crying, moaning, blood, silence. Compared to the broken bones of the other passengers and serious injuries to the driver, my mild concussion was hardly noticed. However, while waiting to be X-rayed, I passed out, lapsing into prolonged unconsciousness.

I awoke strapped into a hospital bed in the trauma ward of a local charity hospital. Intravenous fluid was being injected into my arm; my head throbbed and my neck ached. As my focus sharpened, the trauma ward looked like an old movie set for a prison camp film. It was physically deteriorated and filled with society's victims. They were mostly old alcoholics and derelicts who had been mugged for their last quarter, or who had fallen down a hole somewhere. They were the skid-row misfits you quickly pass by, hoping to avoid any eye contact so as not to feel guilt for their condition or fear for your safety.

Uniformed alike in their grubby green institutional pajamas, the trauma ward gang seemed like seaweed covering everything—except my red shirt and me. "Say, Red," said the nurse, "You're sure lucky. That other Italian, the driver, didn't pull through the operation. You're gonna be just fine once we get some hot soup and cold jello into you. But don't doze off! That's a bad sign for someone with a concussion. Stay awake, talk to the other guys."

Talk to *them?* What did we have in common? My red shirt said it all: I didn't belong there among the "greenies." I was not one of the boys, I was the man in the red shirt. I did not even have to proclaim that to the others. They immediately decoded the message of my red shirt. For days, no one talked to me; no one bothered me by insisting upon sharing a newspaper, extra sugar, or butter stolen from the kitchen cart. I was left totally alone. And my red shirt did it all for me, silently but certainly.

But after a few days, a curious impulse started rising in me—to take off the red shirt. "How silly can you get to keep on wearing a dirty old red shirt that never was a favorite anyway?" So, I took it off.

Only minutes after I had exchanged my red shirt for the community greens, all kinds of social activities erupted around my bed. The heavy silence was shattered, a newspaper was offered, someone came by to tell me a joke, another gave advice, there were concerns about my condition and requests for details of the fatal car crash. We played poker, made obscene comments about the staff and worse about the food. It felt good to laugh again and hear the burly leader of the "Trauma Tigers" exclaim: "I knew yuz was one of da bunch, you're a regular guy, after all." "Thanks, I'm glad we're gonna be buddies," I had replied, feeling the pride of having passed the friendship test and been accepted into their group, of being part of *our group.* The trauma ward was no longer traumatic for me—not home, but not so bad as it might look to an "outsider."

This is an actual example of social psychology in action. The basic question social psychologists attempt to answer is how one person's perceptions, thoughts, feelings, and actions are influenced by other people. **Social psychology** is that part of psychology which explores how individuals are affected by their social context. Its central focus is the study of **social influence**—the reciprocal influence of person and social situation. How are individuals changed by the social contexts in which they function, and how do they change those social contexts?

Social context is defined broadly as including not only the *presence* of other people both real and imagined, but also the *interactions* between them and the individual, the *setting* in which these interactions are taking place such as street corner or laboratory, the *kind of activities* that are occurring such as sharing or swearing, and the set of *unwritten rules and expectations* that are governing how people relate to each other—e.g., "Don't be the first one to help a stranger in distress" (C. Sherif, 1981).

With such a broad definition of *social context,* you will not be surprised to learn that many different processes are studied as part of social psychology. Some are processes that take place *within* a single person, such as my changing perceptions of the other patients in the trauma ward, my attitudes toward them before even meeting them, and my emerging need to affiliate with them. Some are processes that take place *between* people—first the mutual ignoring and then the enjoyed interchanges in the case of the trauma ward. Psychologists studying social processes that take place between people may study such questions as how friendships are formed, intimate relationships developed, and social status achieved. Finally, some of the processes studied in social psychology are *group* processes, such as the ways groups become cohesive, how they reward approved behaviors and punish "inappropriate," nonconforming acts. I was punished by being isolated as long as I was seen as an outsider, but welcomed warmly when I looked and acted like one of the gang.

We will begin this chapter by examining what is unique about the social psychological approach, as compared to other approaches in psychology and social science. Then we will look at samples of research and theory on each of the three kinds of social processes just described, processes within individuals, processes between interacting individuals, and processes at the group level. In the next, final chapter, we will broaden our perspective to consider a variety of contemporary social problems that the social psychological approach helps us to understand, such as violence and blind obedience to authority.

THE APPROACH OF SOCIAL PSYCHOLOGY

How much of what you do on any given day—what you think and how you feel—might be different if you had grown up as a solitary creature in a world without other people around you? Can you even contemplate such an existence? The social psychologist sees all humans as social beings whose development, functioning, and even sense of identity are shaped by their relationship to other people.

A basic theme that unifies the diverse array of research conducted by social psychologists is the importance of situation-centered explanations of human behavior. They seek to discover how events and experiences outside the person come to influence his or her behavior. This is in contrast with the traditionally more dominant theme in psychology—that human behavior is best understood by *person-centered* explanations, in which investigators attempt to look "inside" the person in order to understand how behavior is influenced by physiology, cognition, motivation, traits, or mental disorders. Although behavioral psychologists have stressed the importance of environmental stimuli in causing behavior, their research has generally used physical stimuli rather than social stimuli, and they have assumed a passive organism, *controlled* by these stimuli. Social psychologists stress the importance of both the situation and person variables.

Social psychology, then, studying how social contexts affect the cognitions, emotions, and actions of individuals, occupies a unique place in the study of human nature. It fills the niche between traditional psychology on one side and sociology and anthropology on the other. The latter disciplines study social institutions (like the family, church, or prison) as well as the broader influences of culture on people's orientations.

The person in the social environment

"No man is an island, entire of itself; every man is a piece of the continent." John Donne, Devotions.

Much research in psychology has focused on psychological processes in a social vacuum. Psychologists, despite their recognition of the importance of environmental stimuli have studied individuals as essentially autonomous beings, separate from the environment. Because most research in psychology has involved physical, tangible reinforcers, given or withheld by the experimenter for individual performance, typical experimental designs have provided little scope for the working of social influences or for differences in the subjects' interpretations of the situation.

The view that the individual is a significant unit of causality is a cornerstone in many areas of our lives. In religion, law, and psychiatry, the individual is held personally responsible—accountable—for sin, crime, and even mental health or illness. In most Western cultures, maturity is equated with becoming self-sufficient, not dependent on others. Success is seen as a matter of individual initiative, often the result of being unique enough and strong enough to stand apart from, or above, the rank and file.

These beliefs about the significance of the individual seem to go along with the rise of a capitalistic economic order, the tradition of romantic love, and the emphasis on character development in modern literature. But such beliefs are relatively new in history and characteristic of Western Anglo-American cultures, but not many African, Asian, or native American cultures.

Actually, a strong case can be made for the primary importance of the social group rather than the individual, even as the unit of evolution. Life in groups affords advantages for survival that the solitary individual lacks. The mutual protection and nurturance provided by group association allow more offspring to mature and reproduce. Group association also provides a medium for imitation through which the adaptive innovation of any one member can benefit all the rest, as we saw in the case of Imo's washing of sweet potatoes (Chapter 1). Recall also the findings, cited in Chapter 13, that one of the best defenses against life-threatening stress is being part of a social support network. Among the most important conclusions that psychology has advanced is that conditions of social isolation are associated with many forms of pathology, both physical and mental.

A basic assumption of social psychologists is that behavior is always a function of *person* variables *interacting* with *environmental* variables. They need to know about both the person and the social context if they are to understand, predict, and attempt to

control social phenomena. So they are studying the whole larger unit of person-in-social-environment. This is true whether they focus on social processes as *independent variables* (such as the effect of size of a majority opposing an individual), as *dependent variables* (such as the social behavior of complying with the group's standard or rule), or inner, *mediating variables* (such as an individual's interpretation of the social situation).

Social psychologists focus primarily on two aspects of any behavior setting: the stimuli operating at the time of the behavior and how the individual interprets the situation.

The situation. No description of social behavior is complete without a description of what was happening in the current situation when the behavior occurred. Who else was present, and what were they doing that might have influenced what took place? Social psychologists focus on stimuli operating in the present situation, with less emphasis on past causes.

For example, a prison guard who accuses a prisoner of an "unprovoked" assault against him is claiming that nothing in the situation influenced the prisoner's aggressive behavior. He is implying that the cause is to be found *within* the prisoner, in his aggressive personality. However, when we know the details of the setting in which the assault took place, a more probable external cause may become apparent. In one actual case, the guard had turned off the shower when the two-minute maximum shower time had elapsed even though the inmate was still all soaped up. When he refused the inmate's plea to turn the water back on long enough for rinsing off, the inmate attacked him. (Do you agree that the attack was unprovoked?)

You probably recognize a similarity between social psychology and operant conditioning in their insistence on making explicit the stimulus environment in which the behavior occurs. But the similarity ends there once phenomenology enters.

Personal interpretations. Person variables, for the social psychologist, include not only abilities or other personal characteristics of a person, as observed from the outside, but also the person's own subjective view of what is happening, known as the **phenomenological perspective.** How does the person perceive and define the situation and interpret his or her own actions and those of the other participants?

In the preceding example, the objective facts were that the guard turned off the shower after two minutes and the inmate attacked him. What were the perceptions of the two actors? In the prison guard's perspective, the inmate knew the two-minute shower rule and was violating it on purpose just to be hostile and show off to his buddies. In the inmate's phenomenology, his reasonable request for some rinse water was denied because the guard wanted to humiliate him publicly and demonstrate his *arbitrary power.*

Regardless of which view was accurate, each view was a *real* one because it had real consequences. Not only did it influence the immediate behavior and subsequent relationship of the two people involved, but the prisoner could have time added to his sentence, be sent to solitary confinement, or lose privileges if the guard's interpretation was accepted by the authorities.

It should also be apparent that one's subjective perspective of a social context can change over time, leading to different behavior and different relationships. This happened when I changed my red shirt for the group greens. Think about changes in your own phenomenology of what college represents from your first day on campus to now.

Read these two paragraphs, first A and then B, and ask a friend to read them in the *reverse* order—first B and then A. Compare your impressions of what Jim is really like. (Luchins, 1957.) This task is relevant to a study discussed on page 573.

A. Jim left the house to get some stationery. He walked out into the sun-filled street with two of his friends, basking in the sun as he walked. Jim entered the stationery store, which was full of people. Jim talked with an acquaintance while he waited for the clerk to catch his eye. On his way out, he stopped to chat with a school friend who was just coming into the store. Leaving the store, he walked toward school. On his way out he met the girl to whom he had been introduced the night before. They talked for a short while, and then Jim left for school.

B. After school Jim left the classroom alone. Leaving the school, he started on his long walk home. The street was brilliantly filled with sunshine. Jim walked down the street on the shady side. Coming down the street toward him, he saw the pretty girl whom he had met on the previous evening. Jim crossed the street and entered a candy store. The store was crowded with students, and he noticed a few familiar faces. Jim waited quietly until the counterman caught his eye and then gave his order. Taking his drink, he sat down at a side table. When he had finished his drink he went home.

The importance of social reality

In Chapter 1 we distinguished between objective descriptions of physical reality obtained through controlled observations, and subjective inferences we make about relationships between variables. Later (Chapter 4) we learned about the methods of psy-

chophysics in mapping psychological reactions to physical stimuli. For the social psychologist, the objective physical reality is less significant for understanding how and why people behave as they do than is the subjective social reality. Our interpretation of an unchanging situation can change as we come to "see" it as others do. Or the same situation may yield quite different interpretations by different perceivers. For example, for the physical reality of "a bright light moving rapidly across the sky," the social reality created for one group may be "an alien invasion"; for another, a "heavenly visitor." The first group may prepare to defend itself; the second may name a welcoming committee and prepare gifts. A more sophisticated society may have known that Haley's comet would appear at that time and have set up elaborate observing equipment.

All of us are constantly engaged in trying to construct an accurate view of the meanings that actions and situations have for the other people in our social groups. The attitudes, opinions, and beliefs held in common by members of a group form the basis of its social reality. The **social reality** is the phenomenological perspective of the group. When people share a common view of an event, activity, or person, their view becomes social reality by consensus. After I took off my red shirt, we "greenies" agreed about the staff and the food and other aspects of our social context. We shared the same social reality in choosing to look at the world from the same perspective.

Sometimes the shared social reality is a formal one, voted on or stated in a law or official action. It is part of the social reality of Americans that individuals have certain unalienable rights that our government can't take away or abridge. Our social reality with regard to women's abilities and rights is currently undergoing major change, as reflected in both legal decisions and informal interactions.

Most often social reality is an informal matter. It may come about by informal communication networks among peers, as when gossip is spread and reputations are ruined. You can imagine what the prison guard with the quick shower trigger told the other guards about "that trouble-maker"—or what the prisoner told other inmates about the "inhumane guard." Social reality is derived from the ways we account for ourselves and other people and events in our world through our everyday communications (Shotter, 1984).

Once people are set to see certain events occur or certain people act in specified ways, they will see what they are set to see and find confirming evi-

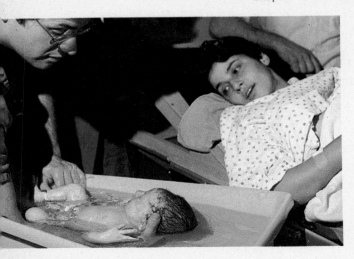

◁ ▌ These parents' expectations of
their newborn child will be
influenced by our society's
preconceived ideas about sex
differences.

that guard who is seen as exercising power so arbitrarily. A **self-fulfilling prophecy** occurs when a hypothesis about how someone will act exerts a subtle
influence on the person to act in the expected way
(see Merton, 1957).

Social applications

Before we begin our sampling of research and theory
on social processes, one other difference between
the approach of social psychology and that of other
areas should be noted. Many social psychologists are
strongly motivated by psychology's fifth goal—to improve the human condition. This concern is expressed in two major ways. First, the knowledge and
theories gained from laboratory experiments are
used to explain phenomena and remedy problems in
the real world (Deutsch & Hornstein, 1975).

Second, studies by social psychologists are often
carried out in natural settings, as close as possible to
where the processes of interest are occurring naturally. For example, during World War II, ordinary
meats were rationed and scarce, and it became important for housewives to use available and nutri-
tious—but unpopular—meats, such as heart and kidneys. Kurt Lewin conducted an attitude-change
experiment in a field setting with housewives as subjects. In this study, subjects who participated in
group discussion and made public decisions were far
more likely to change their food-buying habits than
were those who received the same information in a
lecture (Lewin, 1947). Lewin, a pioneer in modern
social psychology, believed that theory and research
must be integrated with practice if psychology is to
make its greatest contribution. "No action without
research, no research without action" was his dictum
(1948).

dence for their view of what is "true," regardless of
objective reality. In Chapter 2 we saw that parents
tend to have different expectations for and even perceptions of their sons and daughters.

> When parents of newborn infants (less than 24
> hours old) were asked to describe their babies, they
> gave very different ratings depending on the baby's
> sex. Compared to sons, daughters were rated as:
> softer, littler, weaker, more delicate, and more awk-
> ward—although there were no objective differences
> between the two groups in weight, length, or their
> general health index (Rubin et al., 1974).

> In a controlled experiment on this same phenom-
> enon, a group of parents all viewed a videotape of
> the same baby playing with a Jack-in-the-box toy.
> When the figure popped up, the baby was startled
> and cried a little, but showed mixed emotions as it
> continued to be curious about the toy. This behavior
> pattern was rated as revealing anger when the sub-
> jects had been told that the baby's name was David
> but as fear if they had been told that the baby's
> name was Diane (Condry & Condry, 1976).

These parents' preconceived ideas about what males
and females are like influenced (distorted) their perceptions of the physical reality—they saw it as it was
"supposed" to be, according to their schemas, not
as it really was.

Expectations of how someone will act can often
help *produce* that behavior. The guard will be less
friendly and more arbitrary around his "trouble-
maker," and the inmate will make more trouble for

SOCIAL PERCEPTION

In this section we will look at two social processes that take place *within individuals*—the process of forming impressions of people and the process of attributing causes to people's behavior. We will find that the same cognitive processes occur here as in other cases of perceiving, judging, and thinking. Social thinking differs from other thinking only in the content of the information being processed, not in the way the content is processed.

Impression formation

When you come in contact with another person, what do you see? Obviously you notice physical characteristics, such as the person's sex, skin color, height, hair color, clothing, and so forth. You also see behaviors, both verbal (what the person says) and nonverbal (how the person moves). See the **Close-up** on page 574.

But other people are not just observable objects in space, like trees and buildings. They are actors like us, with ideas and motives and abilities that we cannot see but try to infer from what we do see. In interacting with people, we are constantly making inferences and generalizations—constructing coherent pictures of what we think they are like inside. We need these pictures to be able to understand and predict their behavior. Equally important, the picture we create of a person determines how *we* will act and how we will feel about the person. Thus much research in social psychology has focused on the process by which we create our personal portraits of other people, and also how we construct self-portraits. Why do we make the particular inferences and generalizations about other people and ourselves that we do?

First impressions. Your parents and teachers probably taught you to try to "make a good first impression," whether you were out on a date or applying for a job. And they were right—first impressions *are* important. In fact, the first information we get about a person is often more influential than later information—a phenomenon known as the **primacy effect.**

Many studies have shown this influence of first impressions on later ideas of what someone is like. The two paragraphs on page 571 about Jim were taken from a classic study demonstrating this effect. Only 18 percent of those who had read paragraph *B* first rated Jim as friendly, as compared with 78 percent of those who had read paragraph *A* first (Luchins, 1957). Did you find the same difference?

Why should first impressions be so influential? One possibility is that we are most attentive when we are first learning about someone, so that the initial information is more clearly remembered. Another explanation is that a first impression provides a framework or central theme around which all subsequent information is organized. Information that is consistent with the first impression will be integrated with it, while discrepant information that does not fit well with our initial view may be distorted or even disregarded.

Social schemas. The categories and organizing principles that we use to make sense of the world around us have been conceptualized as *schemas,* as we saw in earlier chapters. Just as people use their existing schemas to interpret new information about

Our first impression of another person—and their first impression of us—may set the tone for the ensuing relationship.

Managing Impressions in Status Transactions

It is obvious that verbally fluent people tend to get listened to more than do quiet types. But you can be perceived as dominant and important without uttering a single word, just by controlling your "body language."

Social status is one's position, rank, or standing relative to other people in a given setting. Perceived social status is one of the most important factors in any social interaction in determining people's behavior toward each other (Schlenker, 1980). Typically, we disclose our social status to others without being aware of how we are doing it. Similarly, we respond to the *nonverbal communication* patterns of others without awareness of why we are dominating this person while deferring to that one.

In some cases, social status is pre-established by one's occupation or position of formal authority. Parents, judges, teachers, and doctors, for example, are in high-status positions relative to children, defendants, students, and patients. But suppose you enter a new group setting, as at a party, where people are not differentiated by their formal status. How does status information get transmitted informally?

Status transactions are forms of communication between people that establish their relative status, their

social power, and their territorial control. These transactions often involve moment-by-moment adjustments of each person's status. Watching them provides a fascinating study of social behavior, especially when the status differences are small.

You create a *high-status* impression when you convey a message of certainty, self-control, and authority. To do so: (a) you move slowly, smoothly, and purposefully; (b) your movements are *unitized,* so that related body parts move together as a unit of neck-shoulders or hand-wrist-arm; (c) your posture is erect and stable; (d) you make eye contact and coordinate it with your verbal delivery, not letting your eyes shift about; (e) you hold your head still while speaking; (f) your speech rate is even and measured, and your sentences are complete; and (g) you occupy more space by spreading out your arms and legs.

You create a *low-status* impression when you convey a sense of insecurity, of not being worth anyone's attention, of willingness to be submissive. This occurs when you fidget, fuss, move jerkily, touch your face and hair, shift position and eye contact frequently, hang onto objects in the room, stand with toes pointed in or occupy a restricted space, smile with teeth covering the bottom lip, speak breathlessly with

---

events, they also use schemas to interpret new information about people.

One type of schema involves the belief that certain personality traits are related to each other. For example, if we think that friendliness "goes with" generosity, we automatically assume that a person we see being friendly will be generous—even if we have not observed any actual generosity on his or her part. This informal set of beliefs about what traits are associated with each other is known as an im-plicit personality theory (Schneider, 1973). Each of us has such a theory of our own which we use in our evaluations of other people. But such assumptions are rarely tested to see if they are correct. Our subjective view of what "ought to be" can lead us to make inferences that go beyond the available information.

When subjects saw a silent videotape of a woman being interviewed, their judgment of her personality was strongly influenced by the supposed topic of the interview. Some subjects were told that the topic had been sex, while others were told it had been politics. Only those who believed the woman had been discussing sex judged her to have been anxious throughout the interview and to be an "anxiety-prone" individual in general (Snyder & Frankel, 1976).

As we saw in Chapter 10, another sort of schema, known as a **prototype,** is an abstract representation of the traits that characterize a particular personality type (Cantor & Mischel, 1979a). In other words, it is the standard or supposed "typical example" against which we match the person we are evaluating. For example, a prototype for extraversion might include such traits as outgoing, talkative, assertive, a party-goer, and so on. If we judge a person as matching

a hesitant little "er" before each sentence, giggle or laugh after a statement, and overqualify each statement—"at least it seems that way to me . . . sometimes . . . but I could be wrong."

These differences in behavioral style help create different cognitive structures in the other person's mind by which evaluative judgments are then made. Those seen as high in status are seen also as more competent and more intelligent. What they have to say then gets listened to and has a greater potential impact.

A study systematically varied the behavioral style of a person role-playing a juror in a personal-injury lawsuit. This juror argued an extremely deviant position on how much money should be awarded in the case. Subjects watched a videotape in which the juror gave his arguments, but his behavioral style was low status (deferential) in one version and high status (deference-demanding) in another. The juror was most successful in influencing the monetary judgments of the subjects when displaying high-status behaviors and least influential in the low-status role. This social-influence effect occurred even though the arguments used were identical in the two conditions. Even if the juror was described as having a high-status occupation, he was influential only if he displayed high-status behaviors (Lee & Ofshe, 1981).

Status transactions are also an essential feature in all drama, according to director and author Keith Johnstone (1979). Audience attention is held when the status of the actors is being figured out and when a status is being modified. In comedy, we laugh at the actor's mistake only if he or she loses status and we don't have sympathy for the individual. According to Johnstone, the function of comedians is to lower status—their own or other people's. In tragedy, a high-status person is ousted from society, but does not crumble into a low-status posture. It is pathetic when that happens. Sacrifices can be made only by high-status people. We want to see low-status people as happy being in their place.

Since all the world's a stage, try acting out some status transaction games with your friends. Start with some of the high- or low-status behaviors outlined above and notice how they influence the other person's reactions and your own subsequent behavior and feelings.

that prototype, we are likely to remember information about them that fits with the prototype, but to forget information that does not. Furthermore, we may even "remember" information that, while fitting the prototype, never actually occurred.

In one study, subjects read a long story about the life of a woman named Betty K. Subsequently, some of the subjects were told that Betty K. was homosexual, others were told she was heterosexual, and a third group were told nothing about her sexual orientation. All of the subjects were then asked to recall as many details of Betty K.'s life story as they could. Subjects who thought she was homosexual had better memory for information that would fit a prototype of homosexuality, while subjects who thought she was heterosexual had better memory for information that would fit a prototype for heterosexuality.

In addition, their recall errors were consistent with their prototypes—if they thought she was homosexual, they "remembered" information that had not appeared in the story but that fit a homosexuality prototype. In contrast, the control group showed no such biased patterns of recall (Snyder & Uranowitz, 1978).

Schemas about members of an identifiable group are called **stereotypes,** (see Hamilton, 1981). You may have stereotypes of college professors, or sorority members, or football players. Stereotypes usually include a cluster of characteristics that members of the group are assumed to have, such as intelligence, liberality, and absent-mindedness in the case of professors. If these generalizatons are fairly accurate, they help by making the process of social perception easier and more orderly. But when they are inaccurate or inflexible, they can produce biased judgments, because then we overlook a person's unique characteristics.

Stereotypes can include positively valued characteristics, or negatively valued ones, or both. However, the term "stereotype" often has a negative connotation in popular usage because it refers to biased, over-simplified views about another ethnic, racial, or religious group, which are used as a basis for rejection of its members. As such, stereotypes have been seen as a central cognitive mechanism in the development and maintenance of prejudice.

Attribution

A student is doing badly in school. Why? A woman sitting next to you in the theater is crying. Why? A policeman is hitting someone with his night stick. Why? In all these cases you begin with a knowledge of the behavior (the outcome) and proceed from there to try to understand what it means. In doing so, you engage in the process of making attributions. An **attribution,** as we saw in Chapter 8, is an inference about the causes of an action. For example, you could attribute the student's failure to lack of motivation or to poor teaching. The woman's crying might be due to an emotional scene in the movie, or it could be a personal problem that is bothering her. The policeman's abuse might be attributed to a dislike of all youthful radicals or it could be perceived as a natural response to an armed attacker.

The study of how we go about forming such attributions about causes has become one of the central areas of investigation in social psychology (Heider, 1944; Jones & Davis, 1965; Kelley, 1967). The attributions we make have immediate and tangible results for how we feel about the person and what we decide our own behavior should be. This is where thinking really does make it so. The way people define others' motivations creates social reality. Soldiers flee from an advancing enemy. Is their action a "strategic retreat" or a "cowardly escape"? A coach pushes his team to its physical limits. Is he doing it to build character and discipline or to enjoy exerting arbitrary power over younger minds?

Like personality characteristics, causes cannot be seen. All our attributions of cause are inferences based on our interpretations of what we observe. (See **Figure 16.1**) How do we make the inferences we do about causes of behavior?

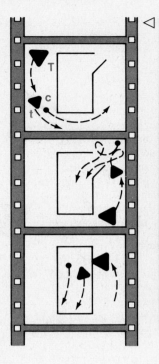

Figure 16.1

These geometric figures were stimuli in a convincing demonstration of the fact that we infer rather than observe personal characteristics and causes. When subjects were shown a film in which the geometrical forms simply moved in and out of the large rectangle at different speeds and in different patterns, they attributed underlying "motivations" to the "characters." They often "saw" the triangles as two males fighting over a female (the circle). The large triangle was "seen" as being aggressive, the small triangle as being heroic, and the circle as being timid. In the sequence shown here, most observers reported seeing T chase t and c into the house and close the door (Heider & Simmel, 1944).

Social judgment rules. In causal attribution, as in impression formation, we depend on our knowledge and belief structures from past experience to help us make sense of the present social event. We often follow certain rules of thumb that give us good answers in many cases but can also mislead us.

One such rule is the **covariation principle** (Kelley, 1967). We attribute an event to those causal conditions that vary with it—that are present when the event occurs and are absent when the event fails to occur. In a physical case, an allergist tries to determine the cause of an allergic reaction (rash, respiratory problems) by exposing the patient to a variety of possible allergy-inducing substances. The substance that is present when a positive reaction occurs and absent when there is no allergic reaction is assumed to be the cause. In a psychological case, a man under the influence of alcohol is arrested for spouse abuse. To what extent is alcohol abuse the cause of his violent behavior? Applying the covariation rule would help answer that question. Alcohol is judged responsible if he abuses his wife when he has been drinking heavily but not when he is sober.

The general question we are often trying to answer is whether an individual's action is due to personal characteristics or to situational pressures. If a person does a favor for his boss, is it because he has a kind, altruistic personality or is it because he is hoping to get a raise? When we make an attribution to personal characteristics, we often make a **correspondent inference:** we infer that the behavior is caused by some corresponding properties of the person. For example, if someone does a brave deed, it must be because he or she possesses the traits of bravery and courage (Jones & Davis, 1965).

However, we tend to discount personal, dispositional factors—judge them as unimportant—if there are ample factors in the situation to account for the behavior. For example, if a mother lies to save the life of her child, we attribute her behavior to the special situation rather than to a trait of dishonesty on her part. Likewise, if there are good reasons in the situation for the person to be kind (a hostess is supposed to be kind), then we are less likely to see the action as due to kindness inherent in the person.

On the other hand, we discount factors in the situation if the individual's characteristics were sufficiently prominent to predict the action. Thus a well-known coach will get credit for his team's victory even when the opposition "gave the game away." In both kinds of situations we are following the *discounting rule*—considering particular causes as less likely to the extent that other plausible causes are present.

Dispositional versus situational factors. In trying to decide whether an action should be attributed to the person or to the situation, we tend to consider at least two criteria: consensus and distinctiveness (Kelley, 1967). The **consensus criterion** is whether most other people would say or do the same thing in that situation. If so (high consensus), then we are less likely to attribute the act to the person's unique qualities. But if others would *not* engage in this behavior (low consensus), then we are more likely to assume that there is something special about the individual that caused him or her to act like this. The **distinctiveness criterion** is whether the act is unusual and atypical for that person. If so (high distinctiveness), then we infer that some situational factor must be responsible since the person would rarely do it. But if the individual does it often (low distinctiveness), then we tend to make a personal attribution.

Let's consider an example. You ask your friend Bob whether the social psychology lecturer is good, since you are considering signing up for her course.

Bob says, "She's awesome, really good; I enjoy the lectures and never miss a class." Should you sign up? Before you do, try applying the two criteria:

1. *Consensus*—What do other people say about her? Do lots of students think she is great, or is Bob alone in his opinion?
2. *Distinctiveness*—Is it unusual for Bob to be so enthusiastic about a teacher, or does he give rave reviews about everyone?

You compile your evidence: Others agree, and Bob rarely praises a teacher so much. Consensus and distinctiveness are both high, so you conclude that Bob's evaluation conveys information about the situation rather than about some dispositional aspect of Bob.

Biases and errors in attribution. Despite their attempts to make accurate attributions, most people have certain biases that can result in errors of judgment. An **attributional bias** is a persistent tendency to prefer one type of explanation over the other. Attributional biases are very common and are based on the kinds of errors we discussed in Chapter 9 in connection with judgments of how frequent or probable some event is. They include judgments distorted by the ready availability in memory of certain types of information, unjustified assumptions about how representative some observation or event really is, and also judgments distorted by our expectations and theories (Nisbett & Ross, 1980). Two of the most common attributional biases have been termed the *fundamental attribution error* and the *actor-observer bias.*

1. The fundamental attribution error. Suppose we observe someone giving money to charity and try to infer whether the act was caused by personal factors (generosity, guilt) or situational factors (seeing someone else donate, or pressure from peers to contribute). Often we have limited information about either the person or the situation, and therefore should reserve judgment about which is the more important causal factor. But typically we do not. Instead, most of us show a general tendency to over-attribute to the person inner qualities that are congruent with his or her observed behavior. At the same time we tend to minimize or ignore potential sources of influence that come from the situation. For example, a worker who has several accidents is seen as "accident-prone" or "unlucky" rather than as someone who works in an unsafe environment.

People tend to emphasize personal causes at the expense of powerful situational factors to such an extent that this phenomenon has been termed the **fundamental attribution error** (Ross, 1977; Jones, 1979). This tendency for observers to underestimate the impact of situational (context) factors and overestimate the influence of dispositional (personal) factors has been found in many studies.

> Subjects listened to a speech either for or against racial segregation. Even though they knew that the speaker had been told which side to take and had had no choice, the subjects still inferred that the speaker endorsed the position taken in the speech. This was true even when the speaker spoke in a monotone and read a prepared speech (Jones & Harris, 1967; Jones, 1979). Here the situational factors were adequate to account for the behavior, but the subjects ignored them and inferred that the person was responsible.

Some possible reasons for the fundamental attribution error are summarized in **Table 16.1.**

According to a different analysis, the attribution that is made can be influenced by the question that is asked. For example, if the subject listens to a speech and is asked to infer the speaker's "true attitude," the "central unit" in the inference process becomes speech-and-speaker. On the other hand, if the subject is asked, "How effective was the speech in convincing others, then the central unit is speech-and-situation-factors. According to this hypothesis, dispositional attributions are more likely to occur when the question creates an action-actor unit, whereas situational attributions will be more likely when the question creates an action-situation unit (Quattrone, 1982).

The fundamental attribution error can affect our lives in major ways. When judges, teachers, counselors, or employers attribute our failures or mistakes to inadequacies in us, they try to change *us,* ignoring possible causal factors in the situation. Too often, the fundamental attribution error leads people to blame the poor for their poverty, rape victims for inviting rape attacks, and lonely people for their aloneness (see Ryan, 1976).

Table 16.1 *Reasons for the Fundamental Attribution Error*

Information: Social realities in the situation (norms, power relationships) may be unknown to the observer.

Ideology: People tend to accept the doctrine of personal responsibility for one's actions.

Perception: To observers, actors are figures that stand out against the background of the situation.

Language: Western languages have many more terms for describing personality than for describing situations.

A poignant example of the power of this error in action can be seen in the case of a Director of Student Health who reported that over 500 students a year seek psychiatric aid for problems related to loneliness. Each one is treated for his or her "personal problem." "Suppose," he was asked, "all 500 came to the clinic the same day. Then what would you do?" He answered, "I'd call up some of the Deans and residential advisors to see what was wrong out there [in the situation]" (Dorosin, 1980).

So it appears that one reason people are being treated by various helping professions for dispositional problems is simply that they appear one at a time as individuals. Only when their symptoms are seen as a collective problem are situational explanations entertained and attempts made to change the social contexts rather than the people.

2. The actor-observer bias. Our general susceptibility to the fundamental attribution error of seeing causes in the person is greater when we judge other people's behavior than when we judge our own. As *observers* of others, we attribute their behavior to personal traits, but as *actors,* we attribute our own behavior to situational causes—a tendency known as the **actor-observer bias** (Jones & Nisbett, 1972). Consider the act of a student failing an exam. The professor (observer of this act) sees it as due to the student's lack of motivation or intelligence (personal factors), while the student (actor) is more likely to see it as due to an excessive course load or picky test questions (situational factors). Similarly, if the professor delivers a poor lecture, the student (observer of this act) might attribute it to the professor's lack of expertise on the topic (personal factor), while the

Table 16.2 Reasons for the Actor-Observer Bias

Information: Actors are aware of situational factors that influence them but can only infer such feelings of influence in others.

Self-knowledge: Actors know their past, what's typical or uncharacteristic for them but can observe someone else only in the present situation.

Perception: Actors are looking outward and thus see the situation but not themselves. They tend to see the effects of others on them more than their effects on others.

professor (actor) opts for the situational explanation of too little time to do justice to the material. Some possible reasons for actor-observer bias are summarized in **Table 16.2.**

Interestingly, this discrepancy between actors' and observers' judgments can change depending on perceptual focus.

When both actors and observers were instructed to focus on particular aspects of the situation, both gave situational explanations. When they were instructed to focus on aspects of the person, however, both shifted toward inferring personal characteristics as causes. Evidently, they *both* perceived the actor's characteristics as causal to the extent that the actor was prominent in their perception, but they saw the situation as causal to the extent that *it* was the more prominent perceptual feature (Storms, 1973; Taylor & Fiske, 1978).

An important principle emerges from this research: any distinctive feature of a person that leads him or her to get a disproportionate share of attention will also result in greater attribution of credit for positive outcomes—or blame for negative outcomes. For example, being the only black in a group of whites (or vice versa), or the only woman in a male environment, will increase the "solo" person's perceptual prominence, or salience. Observers will then exaggerate that person's perceived responsibility for the outcome, whether positive or negative. Compared to the same behavior observed in a mixed group a solo "obnoxious" person in a group will be judged as even more obnoxious, whereas a solo "nice" person will be seen as even nicer (Taylor, 1982).

3. Other attributional biases. There are many other attributional biases, three of which will be mentioned briefly. There seems to be a general *positivity bias,* or "Pollyanna" principle. Most of us tend to make positive evaluations of others (even strangers), to judge pleasant events as more likely than unpleasant ones, to anticipate positive interpersonal relationships, and even to use more pleasant words in free-association tasks. We seem cognitively biased to perceive "warm as the norm" (Matlin & Stang, 1978). On the other hand, under special circumstances, as when we are insecure about ourselves and our status, we may show a general *negativity bias.*

Students evaluating another student's intelligence and written work were more critical when their own status was low relative to the audience who would read their evaluations. However, students whose own status was higher did not show this negative bias in their evaluations of the other person (Amabile & Glazebook, 1981).

Many of us have a *self-serving bias*—a tendency to distort our phenomenological perspective in ways that help us maintain a good self-image. For example, we may take personal credit for successes but blame failures on bad luck or other situational factors. This bias is also demonstrated in *egocentric recall,* in which we keep in mind more of the good things *we* contributed (to a team project or conversation) than did someone else. This distorted recall biases our perception of who is responsible for various acts and outcomes.

Married couples were asked to indicate which activities were performed primarily by one of them and to recall specific examples of what each person had contributed to the activity. Each spouse believed that she or he had contributed more to the joint activities, and credited many more specific examples to self than to spouse, thereby taking more credit for being the responsible party. Their supposedly common social reality did not exist due to egocentric bias (Ross & Socoly, 1979).

To the extent that our attributions not only give us explanations of past and present deeds but influence our predictions of the future, they help determine our own individual phenomenology and the group's social reality. They influence what we think about ourselves and others, and hence what we decide is appropriate behavior for us in a variety of situations.

ATTITUDES AND PERSUASION

Long before cognitively oriented psychologists emphasized the important functions of schemas, social psychologists studied another inferred mental process, social attitudes. **Attitudes** are predispositions to react in a particular way. They are learned judgments about what actions are appropriate toward certain types of people or issues. Although an individual's attitudes are relatively *stable* attributes, they are considered more modifiable than personality traits (Allport, 1968).

While social psychologists attempt to understand how attitudes are formed and changed, hosts of would-be persuaders are interested in attitude change for the more practical reason of social control. Parents, teachers, employers, politicians, advertisers, and many others expend much effort at trying to influence our attitudes in order to change our behavior. They want us to think, feel, and be inclined to act in certain directions rather than others. George Orwell's novel *1984* made us aware of obvious government attempts at attitude change that were so extreme and coercive as to be labeled "mind control." But Big Brother comes packaged in many forms; often we are least aware of the most powerful (Schrag, 1978). **Persuasion** is human communication designed by one source to influence other people by modifying their attitudes, or one or more of the components that make up an attitude.

In this section, we will explore the nature of attitudes along with some principles and strategies of persuasion. Though attitudes are intra-individual processes, they link people to their social world of people, activities, and issues—as well as to all those who are active in helping to form or change their attitudes.

The nature of attitudes

Attitudes are based on four components: (a) *beliefs,* which are judgments about what is true or about relationships that are probable; (b) *values,* which are judgments about what is important, beautiful, desirable, etc.; (c) *affects,* which are feelings of attraction or repulsion, and (d) *behavior dispositions,* which are predispositions toward action (Bem, 1970; Fishbein & Ajzen, 1975).

A person's attitudes help determine what the person will notice, value, remember, and act upon. A social setting that might be positively valued by a college student might be perceived as dangerous and threatening by an elderly person who has developed a negative attitude about exposure to novel, dimly lit places with a lot of people and loud music. Attitudes offer justifications (reasons) for our feelings, give emotional meaning to our beliefs, and provide purposes for our actions.

To make these abstract distinctions concrete, try rating your attitude toward the Equal Rights Amendment (ERA), a proposed constitutional amendment aimed at eliminating economic and political discrimination based on sex? First reply by indicating how much in favor or against it you feel (affective evaluation).

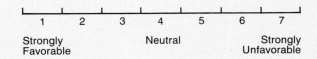

| 1 | 2 | 3 | 4 | 5 | 6 | 7 |

Strongly Favorable   Neutral   Strongly Unfavorable

Then list your beliefs about the issue as a set of propositions about the ERA, such as: "The ERA is long overdue in a democratic country that claims equality of all its citizens," or "The ERA will disrupt family life by encouraging women to work." You will find that many of your values are involved, such as the place and worth of women relative to men.

Based on your affect, beliefs, and values, what action will you take? Will you donate money or time to a campaign in favor of or opposing the ERA? Will you argue publicly for or against it, or support political candidates who would?

Your specific attitude about the ERA may be part of a more general attitude about women's liberation. So too your attitude toward "safe and sane" highway driving speeds may be part of a general attitude about energy conservation, or a general attitude about individual freedom from government restriction.

When an attitude is a *generalized* predisposition, it may exert control over many specific behaviors. By changing such a central attitude, we are likely to produce changes in a variety of specific actions. Changing attitudes toward energy conservation can result in slower driving, less use of heat and tap wa-

ter, more recycling, and litter pick-up (Stern & Aronson, 1984). Research has indeed found that knowing a person's general environmental attitude predicts a wide pattern of behaviors toward the environment (Weigel & Newman, 1976). Where the attitude-behavior link is strong, then we can also expect that attitude change will lead to behavior change.

The attitude-behavior link. The seemingly obvious assumption of consistency between attitudes and behavior has *not* been confirmed by research (Wicker, 1969). What people believe and feel about a lot of things often differs from how they behave toward them. Is there a strong relationship between your attitude toward the ERA and what you have done to support or oppose it? If not, what might account for the discrepancy? Researchers who are reluctant to abandon the theory that attitudes predict behavior have proposed a number of explanations for the low correlation between the two (Rokeach, 1968; Kleinke, 1984).

The most general reason for the discrepancy comes under the heading of *situational contexts*. When there is a difference between the situation in which an attitude is measured and that in which behavior is assessed, discrepancies can be expected. In one study, people who said they would not serve customers of a differing ethnic group (attitude) actually did so when "real-live" people of that group showed up (behavior), perhaps because the actual people differed from the abstract conceptions (La Piere, 1934). Or the context may function to con-

strain someone from acting on his or her private attitude. It would be difficult to donate to a cause if your friends were ridiculing it, or to express anger at an offensive joke if your boss expected you to laugh at it. Situations like these have strong *demand characteristics* that determine the behavior of most people in that setting regardless of their personal attitudes or other attributes.

In these cases we learn about the power of those situational forces from the fact that the individual's attitudes are *not* reflected in his or her behavior. On the other hand, an attitude *is* likely to predict behavior when the attitude includes a specific behavioral intention (Fishbein & Ajzen, 1975), when both attitude and behavior are very specific (Ajzen & Fishbein, 1977), and when the attitude is based on first-hand experience.

Knowing a heavy smoker who dies from cancer is more likely to affect one's smoking behavior than reading statistics about the effects of smoking on cancer (Fazio & Zanna, 1981).

A field study was conducted on the Cornell University campus after a housing shortage had forced some of the incoming freshmen to sleep on cots in the dorm lounges. All freshmen were asked about their attitudes toward the housing crisis and were then given an opportunity to take some related actions (such as signing a petition or joining a committee of dorm residents). While all of the respondents expressed the same attitude about the crisis, those who had had more direct experience with it (were actually sleeping in a lounge) showed a greater consistency between their expressed attitude and their subsequent behavioral attempts to alleviate the problem (Regan & Fazio, 1977).

Apparently, direct experience with an attitude object produces an attitude that is more vivid, better defined, and held with greater confidence. If you really know what your position is, you will be more likely to act in ways consistent with it.

The behavior-attitude connection. Have you ever done something that did not really fit your beliefs or was contrary to your values or feelings? Perhaps you can recall such an incident done as a favor or to make a good impression, maybe for some anticipated reward or to avoid punishment. What happens to private attitudes in the face of the undeniable behavioral evidence of such public deeds? One answer was given ages ago by Hebrew scholars who taught: "Do not ask people to believe before they pray. Get them to pray first and soon they will come to believe." This advice has proven to be psychologically justified. There is a strong link between public behavior and subsequent attitudes: *the act alters the attitude*. It does so when a special motivational state, called cognitive dissonance, is aroused.

Cognitive dissonance is the term and general theory developed by Leon Festinger (1957) to account for the state of conflict someone experiences after making a decision, taking an action, or being exposed to information that contradicts prior beliefs, feelings, or values. It is assumed that when cognitions about one's behavior and relevant attitudes are discrepant, one experiences distress and is then motivated to reduce it. Dissonance-reducing activities modify this unpleasant state and achieve consonance among one's cognitions.

For example, suppose the two dissonant cognitions are some self-knowledge ("I smoke") and a belief about smoking ("Smoking causes lung cancer"). To reduce the dissonance involved one could: *change one's belief* ("The evidence that smoking causes lung cancer is not very convincing"); *change one's behavior* (stop smoking); *reevaluate the behavior* ("I don't smoke very much"); or *add new cognitions* ("I smoke low-tar cigarettes") that make the inconsistency less serious. (The latter works until you learn that smoking low-tar cigarettes has been found *not* to lower cancer risk.)

Cognitive dissonance produces a motivation to make discrepant behavior seem more rational, following "naturally" and logically from one's attitude. If you can't deny that you took an action, you may assert that it was actually in keeping with your attitudes. "I did it because I like it—I've always liked it—sort of." The attitude change is then internalized in order to make acceptable what otherwise appears to be "irrational behavior"—doing something you don't believe in when you had the choice to do otherwise and no obvious external pressure forced you to take the action you did. Hundreds of experiments and field studies have shown the power of cognitive dissonance to change attitudes (Wicklund & Brehm, 1976).

In the classic dissonance experiment, lying for a small rather than large reward was shown to change attitudes toward the object of the lie.

Subjects participated in a very dull task and were then asked (as a favor to the experimenter) to lie to another subject by saying that the task had been fun and interesting. Half the subjects were paid $20 to tell the lie, while the others were paid only $1. The first group saw the $20 payment as sufficient external justification for lying. But the second group saw the $1 payment as an inadequate reason for telling the lie, so members of the second group were left with two dissonant cognitions: "The task was dull" and "I chose to tell another student it was fun and interesting even though I had no good reason for doing so." To reduce their dissonance, these subjects changed their evaluation of the task. They later expressed the belief that "It really was fun and interesting—I might like to do it again." In comparison, the subjects who lied for $20 did not change their evaluation of the dull task—it was still a bore, even though they had lied "for the money" (Festinger & Carlsmith, 1959).

On the basis of much research using this dissonance paradigm, a basic principle of social influence has emerged. Attitude change following dissonant public compliance is greatest when: (a) the behavioral commitment is elicited with *minimal justification*, the least amount of pressure necessary to get the compliance, and (b) the person's "illusion of free choice" to behave differently is emphasized. Under these circumstances, the individual engages in self-persuasion, becoming his or her own most convincing persuader. (See D. Bem, 1968, for an alternate interpretation of dissonance phenomena in terms of the actor's self-perception of behavior in a particular context.)

Persuasive communications

Aristotle, in his philosophical analysis of *rhetoric,* distinguished three factors that made a communication persuasive: *ethos* (communicator characteristics); *logos* (message features), and *pathos* (emotional nature of the audience). Rhetoric, as the study of persuasion, was considered by the Greeks to be a vital tool of democracy. It was the instrument with which a common citizen might influence others by the force of argument, as opposed to the power of rank and noble birth. The scientific study of communication effectiveness has followed Aristotle's lead by investigation *who* says *what* to *whom* with *what* effect (Lasswell, 1948). But the first systematic large-scale program of persuasion was carried out not by researchers but by a practitioner—Adolf Hitler. This Nazi dictator established a ministry of propaganda whose function was to produce materials that would modify the attitudes of enemy forces against resistance and turn the German people against the Jews. This was the first wide-scale use of film as a tool of persuasion: powerful images and symbols were used to evoke strong emotions such as fear, disgust, and resignation.

A little later, the United States developed its own "psychological warfare" program, to build up nationwide patriotic support for entering the war with films on "why we fight," and to bolster the morale of our armed forces. And social psychologists began to study the impact of these mass communications on attitude change in general. After the war, Carl Hovland created the first center for research on attitude change at Yale University (Hovland et al., 1949). For the next few decades, attitude and change was one of the major topics in social psychology (Hovland et al., 1953; McGuire, 1972).

Typical of this laboratory-based study of persuasion was the investigation of the credibility of the message source as a factor in attitude change. Credible communicators are perceived as being high in expertise about the topic and/or trustworthy. A given communication is more effective if it appears to come from a highly credible source, as compared with one of lower credibility (Hovland & Weiss, 1951). Source credibility has been shown to affect attitude change even when a position very different from that of the subjects is being advocated.

In one study students first ranked their preferences for nine stanzas from obscure modern poems. Then they read an essay expressing a different opinion of a stanza that they had ranked next to the bottom (poor quality). One group were told that the essay had been written by T. S. Eliot, a highly credible source. For another group, the source was allegedly Agnes Stearns, a college student who was studying to become a high school English teacher, a mildly credible source.

Three degrees of discrepancy between the subjects' original judgments and the new opinion were presented: Some of the subjects were told that the poem was the best example of a certain poetic style (extreme discrepancy). Others were told either that that stanza was "superior to all but two of the others" (moderate discrepancy) or that it was "just average" (mild discrepancy).

As you can see in **Figure 16.2,** the more credible communicator was more persuasive—produced more attitude change—at every level of discrepancy even though the content of the messages from the two sources was identical (Aronson et al., 1963).

◁ *This beer-hall coaster is part of Hitler's propaganda campaign to turn the Germans against the Jews. It reads, "Who buys from the Jews is a traitor."*

▷ **Figure 16.2**
Communicator Credibility

The graph shows both predicted and actual effects of communication from two sources, varying in three degrees of discrepancy from the subjects' original opinions. When the less credible source advocated an extremely discrepant view, there was an even greater difference in relative persuasive power (Aronson et al., 1963).

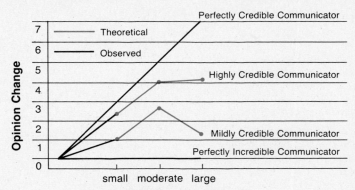

Over time, however, credible communications lose some of the persuasive impact that they added initially to a given message. This weakening of communicator credibility effects over a period of time is known as the *sleeper effect.* Later on, subjects are less likely to associate the message with the source from which it came and may even forget what the source was. In addition, they may critically evaluate the message and argue against it, which they did not do earlier because of the prestige effect of the credible source. So over time the message from the highly credible communicator has *less* impact on attitudes while that from the less credible source comes to have more impact than it did originally (Gillig & Greenwald, 1974).

Often persuasion works not only through formal written communications and speeches, but in a more informal fashion that does not rely as much on cognitive evaluation of new information. We may be persuaded to change our attitudes or modify our behavior by emotional appeals used in advertising. Or we may be influenced unknowingly by the subtle manipulation of the situational context, which can make us feel guilty, important, insecure, or grateful (Cialdini, 1984).

Sometimes a minimal communication in the form of a request for a small favor can result later in a surprisingly big consequence.

When homeowners were asked to allow a big, ugly public service billboard reading "Drive Carefully" to be installed on their front lawns, most (83 percent) refused. But a second group consented—76 percent agreed to this extreme request. Why the difference?

Two weeks earlier those in the second group had agreed to a small request—either to put a three-inch square sign reading "Be a Safe Driver" in their windows or to sign a petition "to keep California beautiful," which most did readily. Two weeks later, when a different person came to their door with the big request for the "Drive Carefully" billboard installation—unrelated to the earlier commitment—they were more receptive to the request than the control group, who had made no earlier commitment (Freedman & Fraser, 1966).

Apparently getting involved in taking a public action however small and trivial may create this "foot-in-the-door" phenomenon. We become vulnerable to big requests that we would have ordinarily rejected before the small commitment changed our self-image. In this study the subjects now saw themselves as "civic minded," but the persuader may design any other image into the persuasion attempt. We are persuadable not because we are naive or gullible but because we are social beings who are generally responsive to and attracted to other people—our next topic.

INTERPERSONAL ATTRACTION

Does "absence make the heart grow fonder," or is it "out of sight, out of mind"? Do "birds of a feather flock together," or does "familiarity breed contempt"? Was Shakespeare right when he wrote, "They do not love that do not show their love," or when he wrote, "Love looks not with the eyes, but with the mind"? There seem to be quotations, folk wisdom, and down-home good sense to handle all outcomes—so long as you select the one that suits the occasion and conveniently ignore its contradiction.

Early psychologists attributed social attraction to a supposed "gregarious instinct"—until it was demonstrated that individuals (animal or human) with no early experience of being with their kind did not show this supposedly universal sociability. Since then, psychologists have been trying to distill the flowery verse and common sense beliefs about sociability, liking, and loving into testable hypotheses.

In this section we will learn what social psychological research tells us about the situational variables involved in social relationships that become increasingly intense as we go from affiliation to friendship to love.

Reasons for affiliation

Gregarious instinct or no, human beings are clearly social animals, choosing overwhelmingly to live with or near other people and to spend time with them. The survival value of group life was mentioned earlier. But what motivates us to seek the company of others, rather than choose a solitary existence? And when we choose to affiliate, what factors determine our choice of companions?

Interacting with other people satisfies some of our most important psychological needs. The importance of other people in *consensual validation,* in which we affirm each other's constructions of reality, was mentioned in Chapter 6. Several other benefits are: *attention* (recognition of our existence, needs, unique identity); *soothing* (relief from hurt, pain, disappointment); *praise* (rewards for successful efforts); *stimu-*lation (competition, constructive feedback, teaching); *sharing* (cooperative activities and accomplishments); *affection* (giving and receiving trust, touch, and tenderness); and *social comparison* (a measuring stick for evaluating ourselves against other people) (Buss, 1980). The importance of all but the last is probably obvious to you.

Affiliating for social comparison. According to **social comparison theory,** a great value of affiliating with other people is that it enables us to evaluate our own strengths and weaknesses, resources, and biases. Especially when there is no clear physical or objective standard of correctness for us to use, other people become our subjective yardsticks, against which we assess ourselves (Festinger, 1954). Is this how other people feel? Do other people think the same way I do? Am I normal? How much better can they do this task that I can?

Such comparisons can be useful when we compare ourselves with people who are fairly similar to us in ability. If we want to know how good we are at tennis, we don't compare ourselves with champions like John McEnroe or Martina Navratilova—or with our 7-year-old cousin—but with acquaintances who have had a similar amount of experience. When we use other people to gauge the correctness of our ideas or behavior, there is no inherent reason to assume they are more correct than we, but we often tend to do so, doubting our own judgment, especially if the others have higher status than we do.

Research has shown that people who are fearful of something that may happen to them in a novel situation prefer being with someone else, even a total stranger, to being alone (Schachter, 1959). Why should fear produce this desire for company? One possibility is that people can get some more information about what is likely to happen. Or perhaps they think that being with someone else will distract them and take their mind off their fear. Or, as predicted by social comparison theory, they may want to find out how other people are feeling to determine the appropriateness of their own reactions.

These alternative explanations were tested in an experiment in which fear was induced in college students. They were led to expect that they would be undergoing a series of painful electric shocks after a short "waiting period." During this period the subjects had a choice of waiting alone or waiting with another person. Half of the subjects were told that the other person was also waiting to go through the shock procedure; half were told that the other person had already completed it.

The fearful subjects chose to affiliate with the person who was also about to undergo the shock procedure, and was thus experiencing an emotional state similar to theirs. This finding supports the social comparison interpretation. Had subjects wanted more information about the shocks, they would have affiliated with the person who had already completed the procedure and knew what would happen. And had they simply wanted somebody to distract them, they would have shown no difference in their preference—either person would do. Apparently, misery does not love just *any* sort of company. Rather, *misery loves miserable company* (Zimbardo & Formica, 1963).

There is also a general social phenomenon in which people who are feeling frustrated or anxious or have suffered a misfortune look for others who are worse off—a downward type of comparison. It seems comforting to compare their own bad situation with the "disaster" faced by someone even less fortunate (Wills, 1981).

Being alone. To say that people are social animals does not mean that they *always* want to socialize. Often you seek a quiet situation with no one to disturb you for carrying out activities that require a great deal of thought and attention. Or you may seek solitude for periods of personal thought and reflection, to sort out what's happening in your life, gain new insights, be creative, meditate, or pray. In such cases, being alone can serve the positive functions of personal growth, healing, and renewal (Suedfeld, 1980).

Sometimes, however, the choice to be alone may have a negative basis. If we are worried that people will not like us or will laugh at us, then we will avoid contact with them. If we think that social comparison may reveal something unpleasant or upsetting about our reactions, we may avoid it by choosing to be alone.

In a variation of the affiliation experiment described above, some subjects were led to feel fearful while others were made to feel anxious. Fear was aroused by the expectation of painful electric shock; anxiety was aroused by an experimental manipulation designed to stimulate a repressed conflict over needs for oral gratification. College student subjects were led to expect that they would have to suck on a variety of infantile objects (nipples and pacifiers) as part

of a study of the sensory physiology of the mouth and tongue. Although they were to engage in this harmless task by themselves, many became anxious but did not attribute their arousal to the situational demands.

As in the earlier research, the fearful subjects chose to wait with someone else. The anxious subjects, however, more often chose to wait alone (see **Figure 16.3**). Puzzled about their emotional arousal, they avoided the opportunity for social comparison. Isolation gave them time to try to figure out their unusual reaction and also prevented the others from noticing their presumably atypical and maybe inappropriate, reaction (Sarnoff & Zimbardo, 1961).

Although there are times when we choose to be alone, sometimes isolation is imposed on us against our will. Society recognizes the powerful need humans have for affiliation and punishes some prisoners by isolating them from human contact in solitary confinement.

A more common type of negative experience of being alone is simple loneliness. **Loneliness** is the perception of being unable to achieve the level of affiliation that we would like. Two types of loneliness have been identified. One is *social isolation,* which occurs when we feel cut off from a social support

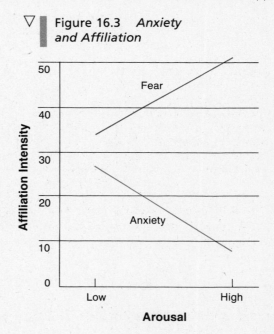

▽ ▌ Figure 16.3 *Anxiety and Affiliation*

network of family and friends that we are used to. This happens to most of us as children when we move away from our "old neighborhood" or later when we leave home for college, a job, or even marriage. We feel like strangers in an alien land—until we can establish new sources of social contact.

A second type of loneliness is *emotional isolation,* in which we feel the absence of a close, intimate relationship with another person. Even though surrounded by many acquaintances, people will feel lonely without emotionally meaningful connections (Weiss, 1973). Students who drop out of college after their freshman year decorate their dorm rooms with many items showing their close ties to their life at home. Those who do not drop out decorate their rooms with more items related to their new environment (Brown, 1984).

The way in which we interpret our state of loneliness affects our feelings and shapes our subsequent interactions with other people. Those who focus on the situation ("People are too busy to be friendly") are more likely to keep trying than those who blame their loneliness on their own personal inadequacies ("I'm ugly and stupid"). The latter tend to use ineffective strategies, leading to pessimism, depression, and more loneliness (Peplau et al., 1982).

Most college freshmen feel lonely during the first weeks of the term, but usually new social contacts develop and loneliness decreases over the year. Not so for the new students who are shy: their initial loneliness does not go away as they grow more familiar with the new environment. Even by the end of the school year they are still more lonely than their non-shy peers. The shy freshmen tend to have lower self-esteem and to blame their loneliness on their own social undesirability. They are then less ready to risk failure by putting out the effort needed to meet others and make friends (Cheek & Busch, 1981).

The most constructive way of viewing one's loneliness is to see it as an event or experience that you have control over and can change by your actions. (See **Table 16.3.**)

Liking

We all need to like and be liked in return. But why do we like some people more than others? Basically, it seems to depend on how rewarding the relationship is—which, in turn, is determined by several factors.

Table 16.3 *Causal Attributions for Loneliness*

| Stability | Locus of Control | |
	Internal	External
Stable	I am lonely because I'm unlovable; I'll never really be worth loving. It's depressing; I feel empty. I sit around at night alone, getting stoned, eating, and diverting myself with TV. (ABILITY)	The people around here are cold and impersonal; none of them share my interests or live up to my expectations. I'm sick of this place and don't intend to stay here much longer. (TASK DIFFICULTY)
Unstable	I'm lonely now, but won't be for long. I'll stop devoting so much time to work and go out and meet some new people. I'll start by calling the man I met at Ken's party. (EFFORT)	My lover and I have split up. That's the way relationships go these days; some of them work and some of them don't. Next time, maybe I'll be more fortunate. (LUCK)

One's loneliness, like one's success or failure, can be attributed to internal or external causes and seen as a continuing (stable) state of affairs or a changeable (unstable) one. Self-blame or waiting for your luck to change are counterproductive and will color your loneliness blue. Which attribution is most likely to be associated with production of behavior designed to reduce loneliness? (From Shaver & Rubinstein, 1980.)

Factors fostering friendship. In general, we like people whose attitudes, values, and beliefs are similar to ours. *Similarity* is rewarding because it makes the relationship more pleasant and harmonious. We have more to share and are less likely to have upsetting encounters. We also gain a sense of personal validation, since a similar person makes us feel that our attitudes are indeed the right ones.

Sometimes we may be attracted to a person with attributes that complement our own. *Complementary* traits enable us to broaden our perspective and learn new ways of behaving. The quiet person may find an assertive friend more appealing than someone who is similarly quiet and withdrawn. Overall, however, similarity is a more important factor in who we like than is complementarity.

Another ingredient in our liking someone is *reciprocal liking*—the perception that the other person likes us and is genuinely interested in us. We look for evidence that people are attracted to us and that we are special to them.

A number of studies have demonstrated that we tend to like *physically attractive* people more than unattractive ones. The rewards associated with beauty appear to derive from the stereotype that "what is beautiful is good." We think beautiful people are more desirable as friends and perceive them as more intelligent, more successful, more pleasant, and happier than other people—even when there is no objective basis for these judgments. We even perceive children to have different personality and behavioral characteristics depending on whether they are physically attractive. Children themselves react the same way: they like physically attractive children best (Dion, 1972).

Other things being equal, we tend to like people who live closer to us *(proximity)*. Perhaps you have noticed that students in adjacent dorm rooms are likely to become friends, or that the most popular students have rooms near such social crossroads as the lounge or the hall bathroom. But why are we more attracted to people whose paths cross often with ours? Familiarity may be one answer. According to research on the **mere exposure effect,** repeated exposure to the same stimulus produces greater attraction toward that stimulus (Zajonc, 1968). Since we are exposed more often to people who are in closer proximity, we come to like them more. (For a summary of the qualities judged most important for friendship, see the **Close-up** on page 589.)

Theories of liking. As researchers have learned more about all the factors that affect liking, they have tried to pull them together into a comprehensive theory. The concept of rewards is a key element in any such model. Indeed, some researchers have proposed a *reinforcement theory* of attraction, arguing that we like people who reward us and dislike people who punish or fail to reward us (Byrne, 1971).

This reinforcement principle is incorporated and developed further in **social exchange theory** (Kelley & Thibaut, 1978). This approach conceives of social interaction in economic terms as exchanges between people, which have both benefits and costs. Whenever two people interact, they each size up the costs and benefits to themselves. In general, if the benefits outweigh the costs, they will feel attracted to the other person and will continue in the relationship. However, this cost-benefit ratio is also evaluated in terms of the *comparison level* of other possibilities. If the individual has been in other relationships where the overall gains were greater, then he or she will be dissatisfied with the present relationship (even if its benefits do outweigh its costs). On the other hand, a person may remain in a relationship with an unfavorable cost-benefit ratio because the available alternatives are seen as even less rewarding.

Building on these reinforcement and exchange principles, another model of liking has been developed. **Equity theory** deals with the *ratio* of inputs to outcomes for both participants in a relationship. An equitable relationship is defined as one in which the participants' outcomes are proportional to their inputs. If you put a lot into a relationship (your costs), you should get a lot out of it (your benefits); but if you contribute very little, you should only get a little in return. Note that the outcomes to the part-

◁ *We tend to form friendships with people who are similar to ourselves, who are physically attractive, and who appear to like us.*

Ten Friendship Ingredients

What are the qualities you feel are most important in a friend? In a survey of the opinions of over 40,000 readers of *Psychology Today* magazine (Parlee, 1979) the most prized qualities of a friend were loyalty and the ability to keep confidences (not spread secrets). Warmth, affection, and the feeling that the other person was supportive were also important. The top ten ingredients of friendship and the percentage of respondents who rated each as "important" or "very important" are listed here. How does your list compare with these norms? Would the ingredients change if you were judging qualities of a potential life partner?

Top Ten Friendship Qualities	
	Percent
1. Keep confidences	89
2. Loyalty	88
3. Warmth, affection	82
4. Supportiveness	76
5. Frankness	75
6. Sense of humor	74
7. Willing to make time for me	62
8. Independence	61
9. Good conversationalist	59
10. Intelligence	57

From *Psychology Today,* October 1979, Reader Survey of about 40,000 respondents, self-selected, primarily white, single, female, college-educated, students and professional occupations.

ners are evaluated *relative* to what each invested, not in absolute terms according to how much each gained from the relationship.

According to equity theory, people feel happiest and are most attracted to their partner in equitable relationships, whereas inequitable relationships cause distress. We will get upset if we think we are getting *less* from the relationship than we are putting into it. This may seem obvious, but equity theory also makes the surprising prediction that we will be dissatisfied if we are getting *more* than we deserve, since this is also an instance of inequity. When a relationship is perceived as inequitable by one or both partners, attempts will be made to restore equity. Restoration of equity can take two forms: actual and psychological. People can make actual changes in their inputs or outcomes (such as reducing the number of gifts they give to someone who is providing little affection). Or, they can distort reality and convince themselves that they really *are* getting a good outcome (such as reinterpreting hostile criticism as an expression of concerned frankness).

Another theoretical contribution to our understanding of attraction concerns the *pattern* or sequence of rewards we get from someone, rather than their absolute number. According to a pure reinforcement perspective, you would like a person who always said nice things about you better than one who said some nice things and some bad things.

However, research has shown that when comments are in a *gain* pattern (negative comments first, nice ones later), you will like that person more than one who has been consistently favorable. Conversely, when the feedback is in a *loss* pattern (first positive, then negative), you will like that person even less than someone who consistently says negative things about you. These results have led to the hypothesis of a **gain-loss principle of attraction**: your feeling of attraction towards someone is influenced more by the direction of *change*, than by the level of his or her evaluation of you (Aronson, 1969).

Loving

Given the importance of love in promoting happiness and making the world go 'round, it may seem surprising that psychologists have only recently begun systematic research on this topic. Partly this was because of the popular belief that to study love scientifically would strip it of its romance and wonder. This view was publicly stated by Senator William Proxmire in criticizing the National Science Foundation for using taxpayers' money to fund research on romantic attraction:

I believe that 200 million other Americans want to leave some things in life a mystery, and right at the top of things we don't want to know is why a man falls in love with a woman and vice versa. . . . Here, if anywhere, Alexander Pope was right when he observed, ''if ignorance is bliss, 'tis folly to be wise'' (1975)

Another reason for the relative scarcity of research on love even today is the difficulty in defining it. One of the important questions has centered on the distinction between love and liking: is the difference a *quantitative* one, with love simply a more intense form of liking? Or is there a qualitative difference between liking and loving, making the two experiences different in kind? Most researchers have argued for the qualitative position, pending further evidence.

One attempt to study both love and liking involved the development of scales to measure these two concepts. The Love Scale included three components: affiliative and dependent needs, predisposition to help, and exclusiveness and absorption. The Liking Scale had items assessing variables such as perceived similarity, maturity, adjustment, and intelligence. The two scales were filled out by 182 dating couples at the University of Michigan. Results indicated that dating partners both liked and loved each other more than they liked or loved their friends. Women tended to express a greater liking for their dates than did men and were also more loving and liking toward friends of the same sex.

The researcher was also curious to know if a couple's scores on the love scale were related to their actual behavior toward one another.

To see if their behavior showed the absorption with each other that their scores indicated, he unobtrusively watched couples who were sitting alone waiting for the experiment to begin. He found that couples who had high scores on the love scale were indeed more likely to gaze into each others' eyes than couples with low love scores. And on a questionnaire about their relationship filled out six months later, those with high love scores were more likely to report that their relationship had made progress toward permanence (Rubin, 1973).

▷ *The course of long-term romantic relationships usually moves from passionate absorption in the other person to a deep, long-lasting affection.*

Romantic passion. Poets, songwriters, and lovers the world over have long celebrated the intoxicating and ecstatic experience of falling in love. This is the ''many-splendored thing,'' the peak experience in which the love-struck person is ruled more by the heart than by the head. The term ''falling'' conveys the abrupt and often precarious nature of the experience. Suddenly, one's life changes dramatically as the result of an encounter with another person. ''Falling'' in love is also somewhat brief and impermanent—after one falls in love, one either shifts to the state of ''being'' in love or else ''falls out'' of love. Falling in love seems to be reserved exclusively for romantic passion, as opposed to other forms of love (for example, one does not ''fall in love'' with one's child or friend). This may be due to the presence of physiological arousal and sexual excitement in passionate love.

Passionate (or romantic) love has been defined as a state of intense absorption in another, accompanied by a state of strong physiological arousal (Walster & Walster, 1978). In Chapter 8 we discussed the importance of love for the fullest and most satisfying sexuality. We also saw that any physiological arousal—even from physical exercise or unpleasant events could be interpreted as romantic attraction (White et al., 1981). These findings help to explain the frequent feelings of both love and hate at the same time and the cases where the pain and suffering caused by jealousy lead people to conclude that they must truly be in love. Striving hard to overcome barriers can have the same effect, as happens when parents object, or when people fall in love with someone who is unattainable or who spurns and rejects them. In any case, misattributing general arousal to romantic attraction may be a more common initiator of the cognition that we are "in love" than most of us realize.

Companionate love. What are the factors that maintain a relationship over time? Are they different, perhaps, from those that start the relationship in the first place? Apparently the answer is "Yes." As relationships grow and mature, their dynamics change and new elements take on special significance.

▽ **Figure 16.4   *Three Possible Courses of Involvement in Human Relationships***

Long-lasting loving relationships develop over time with increasing mutual self-disclosure and trust. The graphs show three courses such relationships can take as time goes on (adapted from Levinger, 1980).

As opposed to the intense and often short-term nature of passionate love, the love that is involved in a long-lasting commitment has been termed **companionate love**. It is defined as the affection we feel for those with whom our lives are deeply intertwined (Berscheid & Walster, 1978). By "intertwining" we usually mean that the two people have a great deal of mutual impact upon each other. Such close relationships are characterized by interactions that are frequent, strong, varied, and take place over a long time (Berscheid & Peplau, 1983).

The development of a close relationship occurs in stages and can follow several different paths (see **Figure 16.4**). It begins with mutual attraction between the two people and then moves into efforts to build the relationship. In the period of continuation, the relationship can become unstable and full of conflict, stable but static and unchanging, or stable and increasingly satisfying. For some relationships, the next stage is one of deterioration, but all relationships eventually end—in either separation or death (Levinger, 1980).

What is the process by which two people move from a superficial acquaintance to a close relationship? According to one theory, intimacy develops as a result of mutual *self-disclosure*, in which each person reveals personal and private information about him- or herself to the other (Altman & Taylor, 1973). Initially, the information that is disclosed is rather limited and nonrevealing, but over time more private thoughts and feelings are shared. Revealing intimate information about oneself can be a risky thing to do, so when someone shares such information with us, we infer that he or she likes and trusts us. And, as noted earlier in this chapter, we like those who like us. Consequently, we are likely to reciprocate with intimate disclosures about ourselves, and so the relationship will deepen and continue.

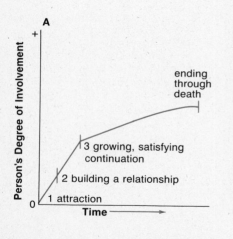
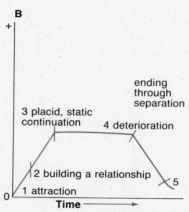
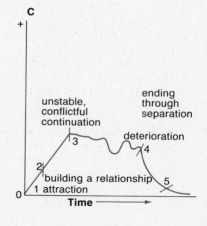

GROUP PROCESSES

A **group** is defined as two or more persons who are engaged in interaction such that each influences and is influenced by the other(s). A group becomes a *team* when the contributions of two or more individuals are coordinated for the good of successfully accomplishing a common objective or mission (Emurian et al., 1984). Throughout your life you can expect to belong to many different groups and be a member of various teams. This collective participation will exert powerful influences on your perceptions, feelings, and actions—often even more influence than your own personal attitudes.

> *"Success, recognition, and conformity are the bywords of the modern world where everyone seems to crave the anesthetizing security of being identified with the majority." Martin Luther King, Jr.,* Strength to Love, 1963

In this section we will look at how groups form and function, how group influence develops, what role leaders play, and some basic processes that develop in relationships between groups.

Group form and function

Groups usually have a particular structure, leader, and communication network. Often there is a common goal that unites the members, implies coopera-tive effort, and also produces identification with the group and the potential for considerable social influence.

Reasons for joining a group. Why do we choose to become part of a group? At the most basic level, it is to satisfy our personal needs. We may be seeking fun and excitement, or emotional comfort and companionship, or status. The group may provide an opportunity to acquire information, learn new skills, gain prestige, earn a living, or achieve other goals. Different individuals may have different reasons for joining the same group: one student joins a drama club to learn how to act, another to meet some nonconventional people. The motives that bring a person into a group are important because they will influence how much he or she "invests" in it—and also how vulnerable he or she will be to its pressures.

Group structure and roles. As you watch a sports team in action, you can see clearly that each member has a specific position to play. Each position is characterized by a certain set of behavior and is related in various ways to all of the other positions. Certain communication patterns are also apparent. In baseball, for example, the catcher will signal the pitcher about what type of pitch to throw; coaches will signal the fielders where to position themselves or will signal the batters when to try to hit and when to wait. Although some outcomes depend only on individual performance, many others depend on a highly coordinated effort among team members. This can be seen in the baton pass from one relay runner to the next, or where one player assists an-

◁ *Membership on the U.S. Olympic women's basketball team has welded these young women and their coach into a closeknit unit. Here they celebrate winning the gold medal in the 1984 summer games.*

other to score a goal by passing the basketball or hockey puck rather than shooting it.

This pattern of functional relationships among the various positions group members play constitutes the *group structure*. In most groups the rules and relationships are not as well defined as they are in a team sport, but they are a central part of all groups. The rules about who does what and when shape the interaction among the group members and provide expectations about what each person is supposed to do.

Such expectations develop in any group setting. Professors are expected to lecture, answer questions, and give exams, while students are expected to listen, ask questions, and take exams. A **role** is a socially defined pattern of behavior that is expected of a person who has a certain function in the group. Some of these role behaviors (such as the formal duties of the club treasurer) are explicit requirements, while others (such as who is expected to make the coffee before the meeting) may be based on implicit assumptions.

Often the various roles within a group are interlocking and are defined with reference to each other: boss-secretary, coach-athlete, minister-parishioner, prisoner-guard. Knowing what is expected from the person in each role—one's own and the other's—oils the machinery of social interaction.

Roles are largely independent of the particular individuals who occupy them. The expected behaviors are the same, regardless of the personal characteristics of the role-player. A judge is expected to be fair and impartial even when the decision is contrary to his or her personal values.

Although we *know* that these expectations guide the person's behavior, we sometimes are not sensitive to the constraints that accompany a role and thus misinterpret role-directed behavior as reflecting a person's own traits or choices. We tend not to recognize it as due to a "role-driven script" and assume that the person is acting out a "person-driven script" (see Chapter 10).

Pairs of students played the roles of questioner and contestant in a "college bowl" quiz game. The questioner had to think of ten difficult questions to ask the contestant, the contestant had to try to answer them, and the questioner then had to indicate whether the contestant's answers were correct. Both

the students and the audience knew that students had been *randomly* assigned to one role or the other. Nevertheless, the audience consistently judged the questioners to be smarter than the contestants. Even the contestants thought that a person who asked difficult questions was more knowledgeable than the person who could not answer them.

In making these judgments, they were all failing to take account of the inherent advantage of the questioner role and disadvantage of the contestant role. The questioner could choose any question for which he or she knew the answer, but the contestant had no choice of what material would be covered. So even though the questioners were actually no smarter than the contestants, their performance was more impressive because their *role* allowed them to control the situation to their advantage. Nevertheless, everyone attributed the more impressive performance of the questioners to greater knowledge (Ross et al., 1977).

This is another variation of the fundamental attribution error, in which causes of behavior are attributed to the person instead of to the situation. In this case, we fail to discount the influence of the arbitrarily assigned roles in determining the apparent expertise of the people playing each role.

Group influence

Have you ever done anything in a group that you would not ordinarily do by yourself? Have you ever been at a football rally, rock concert, fraternity or sorority initiation, beach party, or *The Rocky Horror Picture Show*, where usual standards of civilized decorum were suspended? Or were you ever not your "real self" in the presence of a date's parents, on a job interview, or with strangers in an elevator? If so, you are aware of some of the ways in which behavior is influenced when individuals are in group settings.

The power of other people to influence us is more common and more subtle than we generally realize. Here we shall first consider how the mere presence of others can have a facilitating effect on our individual performance. Next we examine how a group's standards or norms exert pressure on its members to conform or be rejected. Finally, we ask the "revolutionary" question, how can a minority change the views of the group majority?

◁ *The presence of others often facilitates performance whether or not the situation is a competitive one.*

Social facilitation. The first study of the impact that the *mere presence* of others has on individual behavior was published in 1897. It has the historical significance of being the first social psychological experiment.

The researcher, an avid bicyclist, had noticed that bicycle racers had faster times when they were racing with other people than when they were racing against a clock. To determine whether this effect held true for other activities, he had children perform the task of winding fishing reels. Sure enough: the children performed faster when another child was present in the room than when they were alone (Triplett, 1897).

This result was not due simply to competition, because other studies found that it occurred when the individual performed in front of an audience. It also occurred in a *co-acting group*—a group of people engaged in the same behavior but not interacting with each other, as in a case where several people are playing carnival games side-by-side but separately. This improvement of individual performance brought about by the mere presence of other people is called **social facilitation.**

The social facilitation effect turns out not to be as straightforward as it had seemed at first, however. Subsequent researchers have found that sometimes the presence of others *interferes* with performance, rather than facilitating it. Standing up before an audience, for example, may cause stage fright rather than a stellar performance. One explanation for these apparently contradictory findings is that the presence of other people has the general effect of increasing the individual's level of arousal, or drive. This high drive will facilitate performance when the person is engaging in behavior that is well-learned. But, if the responses are relatively new and not well-learned, then the increased drive can be disruptive, making the individual tense and interfering with optimal performance (Zajonc, 1976).

The social facilitation (and interference) effect demonstrates the power of even the most minimally social situation—the mere presence of other people. Most groups, however, involve more dynamic and direct interactions among their members. What sort of influence do these groups have on the individual?

Social norms. Besides the expectations regarding role behaviors, mentioned above, groups develop many expectations for all their members regarding appropriate behavior and attitudes. These group expectations are called **norms.** In some instances group norms are clear and explicit standards that function almost like laws.

Often, however, expectations of what members should or should not do in order to be "socially acceptable" are not spelled out. Rather, they serve as informal, covert regulators of behavior. New members become aware of their operation only gradually by observing two phenomena: uniformities in the behavior of all or most other members and the negative consequences of behaving "undesirably"—in nonnormative ways. We see these unwritten norms in action when codes of dress are subtly enforced to make everyone in the group look alike, whether in a group of businessmen, a gang of bikers, a fan club, or almost any type of permanent group.

Norms serve several indispensable functions. Awareness of the norms operating in a given group situation helps orient and regulate social interaction. Each participant can anticipate how others will enter the situation (for example, what they will wear) and what they are likely to say and do, as well as what behavior on his or her own part will be expected and approved. Some *tolerance for deviating* from the standard is also part of the norm—wide in some cases, narrow in others. Members usually can estimate how far they can go before experiencing the coercive power of the group in the form of the three deadly R's: ridicule, repression, and rejection.

For example, the extent to which students ask questions and volunteer information in class varies in different colleges. This happens in part because of peer pressure that makes student talking *unacceptable* if the prohibitive norm is to be "cool" or to let the teacher work for his or her salary, or *acceptable* if there is a competitive norm of talking to show how much you know or how incompetent the teacher is. A teacher unaware of the class norm will be confused by failure to stimulate class discussions or to suppress excessive participation, as the case may be. Similarly, an eager student not sensitive to the no-talk norm runs the danger of rejection by classmates unless he or she succumbs to the standard of silence.

Adhering to the norms of a group is the first step in establishing *identification* with it. Such identifica-tion allows the individual to have the feeling of sharing in whatever prestige and power the group possesses. The social control carried out by group norms influences us almost from birth as part of the socialization process discussed in Chapter 2.

We also learn from observation that norms operate even in certain situations where social interaction is limited and brief. For example, in elevators everyone is supposed to face front, not talk too loudly, and not maintain eye contact with strangers. In waiting lines, it is "not right" to push ahead out of one's place. It is improper to blow one's nose except into a handkerchief. And so on. However, it is also apparent that social norms are culture-bound: what is proper in one society is often unacceptable behavior in another. How close people stand when in conversation (closer for Latinos than Anglos) and whether you can "drop in" on a neighbor unannounced are guided by culturally determined norms. Many of the difficulties Americans face when they travel abroad stem from failure to appreciate that different norms are operating in what seem to be comparable situations.

Norms emerge in a new group through two processes: *diffusion* and *crystallization*. When people first enter a group, they bring with them their own expectations, previously acquired through other group memberships and life experiences. These various expectations are diffused and spread throughout the group as the members communicate with each other. But as people talk and carry out activities together, their expectations begin to converge or crystallize into a common perspective.

The classic experiment that demonstrated norm crystallization was cited in Chapter 5. It involved having subjects judge the amount of movement of a

▽ *Many types of groups exert subtle pressures toward conformity in dress.*

Creating Nazis in a High-School History Class

The development of norms and the power of roles to transform reality were clearly demonstrated by a California high-school history teacher. Ron Jones was leading a sophomore history class discussion on Nazi Germany when he decided that he had to modify his medium in order to make the message more meaningful. Like many of us, Jones' students could not comprehend how much a social-political movement could develop. The students refused to believe that the average citizen could have been ignorant of or indifferent to the suffering the Nazis were imposing on so many other German citizens.

The teacher told the class they would simulate some aspects of the German experience in order to experience some of the process by which groups develop power. Despite this forewarning, the role-playing "experiment" that took place over the next five days became a serious matter for the students and a shock for the teacher. Simulation and reality merged as these high-school students created a totalitarian system of beliefs and coercive control much like that fashioned by Hitler.

First there were new classroom rules. Rigid seating postures were imposed—and accepted. All answers were limited to three words or less. When no one challenged this and other arbitrary rules, the classroom atmosphere began to change. The more verbal students lost their positions of prominence as the less verbal took over. The next day the classroom movement was given a title, "The Third Wave," and a hand salute was introduced. Slogans were shouted out in unison. "Strength through discipline," "Strength through community," "Strength through action." Students made banners that were hung about the school, recruited new members, set up a system of spies and body guards.

The original core of twenty students swelled to 100 eager Third Wavers. Membership cards were issued. Some of the brightest students were ordered out of class. The new in-group were delighted and abused their "former" classmates as they were taken away.

This experimental learning demonstration had gone too far, and the teacher thought of an impressive way

light that was actually stationary but appeared to move when viewed in the darkness with no reference points—the *autokinetic effect.* Originally, the subjects' judgments varied widely, but when they made their judgments in a group, their estimates converged; a group norm developed which individual subjects then followed later even when they made judgments alone (Sherif, 1935).

Once norms are established in a group, they tend to perpetuate themselves. Current group members exert social pressure on incoming members to adhere to the norms, and they, in turn, put pressure on successive newcomers. Thus, norms can be transmitted from one generation of group members to the next, and can continue to influence people's behavior long after the original group which created the norm no longer exists (Insko et al., 1980).

Group norms have a strong impact on an individual's behavior as long as the member values that group. But if the person comes to value and identify with a new group, then he or she will change to follow the norms of the new group. The norms of

families and of teenage peer groups are often discrepant in our society. The strong need of young people to have the social and emotional support of their peers can lead to much pain as adolescents feel the need to follow new norms that may not be comfortable for them, while parents are bewildered and distressed at these new "alien" influences on their children. We saw in Chapter 6 the potent effect of friends in initiating teenagers into smoking marijuana. The formal or informal groups from which we derive our attitudes and standards of what is acceptable and appropriate and to which we refer for information, direction, and support for our life-style are called **reference groups.**

Often the process of coming under the influence of group norms is so gradual over an extended time period and so subtle that the individual does not perceive what is happening. But it is the rare cucumber who can emerge from the vinegar vat as anything but a pickle. Some insights into this process of be-to end it. He confided to his followers that they were part of a nationwide movement to discover students who were willing to fight for political change. They were "a *select* group of young people *chosen* to help in this cause," he told them. A rally was scheduled for the next day at which a national presidential candidate was supposed to announce on TV the formation of a Third Wave Youth program. Over 200 students filled the high-school auditorium in eager anticipation of this announcement. Banners were hung by exhilarated Third Wave members wearing white-shirted uniforms with homemade armbands. While muscular students stood guard at the door, friends of the teacher posing as reporters and photographers circulated among the mass of true believers. The TV was turned on and everyone waited—and waited—for the announcement. Instead, Ron Jones projected a film of a Nazi rally; the history of Germany's Third Reich appeared in ghostly images. "Everyone must accept the blame—no one can claim that they didn't in some way take part." That was the final message of the film—and of the classroom simulation.

Well, almost. The teacher then got up and explained the reason for the simulation and what he had learned from it, concluding with a prediction that, "You won't admit to participating in this madness . . . being manipulated . . . a follower . . . you will keep this day and this rally a secret." Amazingly, no one ever mentioned it again until ten years later when a former student met Jones on the street. The student gave the Third Wave salute, the teacher saluted back automatically. Ron Jones decided then that he had to write this important story and share it with others by showing it on TV (Jones, 1978).

It is only comparatively recent that German textbooks have broken silence and begun to analyze the Hitler era. But Japanese textbooks have begun to whitewash the militaristic era of Japan in the 1930's and 1940's, and American history books rarely mention the detention of over 100,000 American citizens of Japanese ancestry in *our* concentration camps during World War II.

coming the kind of person valued by the group are provided by a classic study conducted in a small New England college for women.

The prevailing norm at Bennington College was one of political and economic liberalism. On the other hand, most of the women had come from conservative homes and brought conservative attitudes with them. The question studied was what impact this "liberal atmosphere" would have on the attitudes of individual students.

The conservatism of the freshman class steadily declined as they progressed through college. By their senior year most students had been "converted" to a clearly liberal position. This seemed to be due both to faculty and upper-class social approval for expression of liberal views and to the greater availability of politically oriented information in the college community.

The students who had *resisted* this pervasive norm and retained their conservatism fell into two categories. Some, part of a small, close-knit group, simply had been unaware of the conflict between their conservatism and the prevailing campus attitudes. Others had maintained strong ties with their conservative families and continued to conform to the family standards (Newcomb, 1943).

Twenty years later, the marks of the Bennington experience were still evident. Most women who had left as liberals were still liberals; those who had resisted had remained conservatives. For the most part, both had married men with values like their own, thus creating a supportive home environment. Of those who left college as liberals but married conservative men, a high proportion had returned to their freshman-year conservatism (Newcomb, 1963).

Group norms, then, have the power to produce fundamental changes in our attitudes and behavior. In fact, the more we rely on social rewards from a group for our sense of self-worth and legitimacy, the greater will be the social pressure that it can bring to bear on us. For a fascinating demonstration of how norms can develop and take a frightening stranglehold on reality, see the **Close-up** above.

Conformity versus independence. In the norm crystallization experiment described earlier, in which the subjects' individual judgments of perceived motion became more like the group norm, the group's influence on the subject's judgment may not have seemed very relevant to real-life situations. After all, the perception of motion was an illusion in the first place, and the situation was so ambiguous that there was no physical reality on which the individual could depend. But later research showed convincingly that group norms can sway the judgments of individuals even when the stimuli being judged are very clear and can be perceived very accurately.

Ironically, this investigation by Solomon Asch (1955) began as an attempt to show that under conditions where physical reality was clear, individuals would *not* be swayed by social reality. Instead, it has become the classic illustration of *conformity*. **Conformity** is the tendency for people to adopt the behavior and opinions of other group members.

Groups of seven to nine male college students were shown cards with three lines of differing lengths and were asked to indicate which of the three lines was the same length as a line on a standard card (see **Figure 16.5A**). The lines were different enough that mistakes would ordinarily be made less than 1 percent of the time. In the experiment, however, all but one of the members of each group were confederates of the researcher, who were unanimous in the incorrect answers they gave on twelve of the eighteen trials. For example, they might all report that line *1* in the figure was the same length as line *A*. When it finally became the turn of the real subject to judge the lines, he yielded to the majority's wrong judgments in 37 percent of the trials.

This figure is misleading, however, for individual differences were marked. Of the 123 subjects, about 30 percent nearly always yielded, while another 25 percent never did so. But all who yielded underestimated the influence of the social pressure and the frequency of their conformity; some even claimed that they really had seen the lines as the same.

Next, the design of the experiment was changed slightly to investigate the effects of the size of the opposing majority. Pitted against just one person giving an incorrect judgment, the subject exhibited some uneasiness but did not conform. But when as many as 3 opposed him, errors rose to 32 percent. In contrast, when one other person *agreed* with the subject's perception, the effects of the majority were weakened: errors decreased to one fourth of what they had been with no agreeing partner. Significantly, this effect of a supportive "deviant" lasted even after the partner left (Asch, 1955). See **Figure 16.5B**.

Numerous studies of conformity have confirmed these results. The power of the group majority depends on its unanimity. Once it is broken—in any way—the rate of conformity drops dramatically. A person is also more likely to conform when: (a) the judgment task is difficult or ambiguous; (b) the group is a highly cohesive one to which the individual feels attracted; (c) the group members are perceived as competent, and the person feels incompetent; and (d) the person's responses are made known to others in the group.

Not all conformity is the same psychologically, however, because outward conformity may or may not mean personal acceptance of that position. One theoretical analysis distinguishes between three types of conformity: compliance, identification, and internalization. *Compliance* occurs when people conform in their outward behavior in order to avoid punishment or rejection by the group. Here, public conformity is not accompanied by private acceptance. *Identification* occurs when a person conforms because he or she wants to be like the group members or the leader. Here the person is not concerned about correctness but simply lets the group make the decision: "My country right or wrong." *Internalization* occurs when a person's conformity is based on the belief that the group is actually correct. For both internalization and identification, public conformity *is* accompanied by private acceptance—although the reasons for that acceptance differ (Kelman, 1961). We saw earlier that under dissonance-arousing conditions, conditions in which a person acts publicly in a way that is inconsistent with his or her beliefs, the beliefs may then change to become more consistent with the behavior.

Minority influence and nonconformity. Given the power of the majority to control resources and reinforcements, it is not surprising to observe the extent of conformity that exists at all levels of our society. What is remarkable is how anyone escapes this group domination, or how anything new—counternormative—ever comes about. How do revolutions against the status quo emerge? Are there any con-

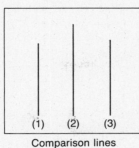

Standard line

Comparison lines

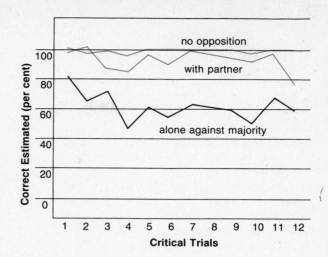

Figure 16.5

The concern of the dissenting subject is evident as he leans forward to check his judgment. In general, subjects found this a very disturbing situation. The graph compares the average number of correct judgments under normal circumstances with those made under social pressure both with and without a supporting partner.

ditions under which a small minority can turn the majority around and create new norms?

An example in which this occurred was cited in Chapter 5 in which slides of color were being judged. Here a third of the subjects followed the lead of the minority, who consistently said "green" whenever a blue slide appeared (Moscovici & Faucheux, 1972).

Researchers have also studied minority influence in the context of simulated jury deliberations, where a disagreeing minority prevented unanimous acceptance of the majority point of view. The minority group was never well liked, and its persuasiveness, when it occurred, was not immediate but appeared only gradually over time. The minority was most influential when it took a consistent position and seemed confident in doing so. Eventually, the power of the many may be undercut by the conviction of the few (Nemeth, 1979).

These findings show that conflict between the group and the individual does not have to be destructive of the person's integrity. Rather, such conflict is an essential precondition of innovations that can lead to positive social change. Individuals are constantly engaged in a two-way exchange with society. They adapt to its norms, roles, and status prescriptions but also can act upon it to reshape those norms (Moscovici, 1976).

In studies of both majority and minority influence, individuals are being persuaded to adopt other people's positions. But what about those times when the person simply chooses to be different from the group and *not* conform? Interestingly, there has been far less research on why people deviate from a group than why they go along with it.

Nonconformity can take several forms. *Anticonformity* involves taking a position that opposes that of the group majority on principle. *Whatever* the group does or says, right or wrong, the anticonforming individual will do just the opposite. Thus anticonformity is totally dependent on the group position—always differing from it. Young people trying to demonstrate freedom from family influence sometimes practice anticonformity. In contrast, *independence* involves responses that are made without regard to the group's position. Over time, the individual may agree with the group on some occasions and deviate from it on others. In either case the decision is determined not by what the group norm is, but by personal preference.

Being different from the group can be a negative experience. People may think there is something wrong with someone who is different, and the person may feel isolated and rejected by the group. But being unique and unusual also has positive value since one's self-concept and sense of personal identity are linked to the ways in which one is a distinctive social being and not just part of the mass of society. Researchers have found that most people strive for a moderate degree of uniqueness—they do not want to be either too similar to others or too different from them—but somewhere in between (Snyder & Fromkin, 1980).

Group leadership

The power of the whole group is invested in the person who is elevated to a position of leadership. What determines who will emerge from the body of the faceless group to become its head, guide its direction, and often give it a unique identity? And what style of leadership is most effective for successful group functioning? For centuries political and social analysts have puzzled over the ingredients that go into the recipe for leadership. Now it is the turn of psychologists.

▷ *Is leadership a function of the person or of the situation? Social psychologists are finding that the answer lies somewhere in between.*

Leader characteristics. Are great leaders born with special traits that give them charisma, a special emotional appeal that pushes them into positions of leadership? Or do great leaders emerge because of particular societal demands of the moment that happen to "put them on the spot"? Questions such as these focus our attention on two approaches to studying leadership: the *trait approach* and the *interaction approach*.

The trait approach assumes that leaders possess special personalities. Researchers following this approach try to identify the set of personal traits that

leaders possess and followers lack. But despite an extensive search, such universal leadership traits have proved to be very elusive.

For example, it has been thought that leaders ought to have a special talent for public speaking. Some research has confirmed this idea by showing that the *most talkative* person in a group is likely to be chosen as its leader (Bavelas et al., 1965). However, if the talkativeness consists of negative comments about the group and its activities, then the person will not be chosen as leader (Morris & Hackman, 1969). So talkativeness, in and of itself, is not necessarily a leadership trait.

Actually, it is little wonder that no standard set of traits characteristic of all leaders has been found. Could we possibly expect the same traits to be needed in leaders of, say, a Board of Deacons, a football team, and a criminal organization? It seems obvious that an effective leader must possess whatever resources are needed by the particular group in order to reach its goals at that time. These needed resources will be somewhat different for every situation. This is basically the assumption of the interaction approach. It holds that effective leadership depends neither on personality characteristics nor on situational factors alone, but on an optimal *combination* of leader personality and situational demands.

For example, one personality dimension on which people differ is the extent to which they endorse the manipulative interpersonal tactics advocated by Machiavelli in *The Prince* (1532). At one end of the continuum are "high Machs," who have *relative* standards of behavior ("Never tell anyone the real reason you did something, unless it's useful to do so"; "The most important thing in life is winning"). At the other extreme are low Machs, with *absolute* standards ("Honesty is always the best policy"; "If something is morally right, compromise is out of the question"). Essentially, the Machiavellian philosophy is one of pragmatism: "If it works, use it."

Are high Machs more likely to be good leaders? The answer is "yes"—in some situations. High Machs do not lose their cool, and are therefore more likely to be successful than low Machs if the situation is an emotionally arousing one, or involves face-to-face negotiation (Christie & Geis, 1970). Also, in unstructured situations, where there are no clear-cut procedures but a lot of room for improvisation, high Machs are effective and more likely to be chosen as the leader of the group (Okanes & Stinson, 1974). On the other hand, in situations needing a careful, logical, ethical approach, with sensitivity to the feelings of others, high Machs would be expected to make poor leaders.

So the same traits can make a good or poor leader depending on what the situation requires. It would appear that the interactionist approach can explain successful leadership better than the trait approach.

Leader behavior. Instead of trying to find out what kind of people leaders *are,* social psychologists have been more interested in what leaders *do.* What styles of leadership behavior are there, and what effects do they have on group functioning?

Early analyses focused on two major dimensions of leadership behavior: consideration of members and structure initiation. *Consideration* of members is the extent to which the leader displays warmth, trust, and respect toward other group members and encourages them to express their ideas and feelings. *Structure initiation* refers to the leader's ability to get the group moving toward its goal by organizing the work and setting performance standards (Halpin & Winer, 1952).

Some researchers have argued that these dimensions actually reflect separate leadership requirements in any group that are often met by two people rather than one. The *task leader* will be the one who initiates structure, trying to get the group's job done as efficiently as possible. Task leaders tend to focus on goals and the instrumental activities the group needs to engage in to achieve them. They are future-oriented toward group products. The *social-emotional leader* will be the one concerned with creating and maintaining a good psychological climate within the group; he or she will be considerate of the personal needs, problems, and uniqueness of individual members. The social-emotional leader is more focused on group processes taking place at the present time (Bales, 1958).

Leaders are less influenced by other group members than are highly ranked group members who are not leaders. Researchers examined acceptance of conformity pressures among cliques of boys living in a school for delinquents. They studied the relative tendency to conform to a group consensus judgment by group members who were the highest-ranked, second-ranked, and last-ranked in cliques of four or five boys (based on their prior social preference scores).

The boys saw lights flashed on a screen that were a given distance apart, and had to judge that distance. But unknown to them the person in the last position, who was the real subject of the experiment, saw a different set of lights. While the rest of the group saw lights flashed at only about 12 inches apart, the subject saw flashes that were about 48 inches apart. Each one announced his judgment aloud, the subject being the last to report.

All conformed to some extent. The leader conformed *least,* whereas the person next most highly valued (but not enough to be made the leader) conformed *most* (Harvey & Consalvi, 1960).

What is the impact of leadership style on the group? Are people happier or more productive with one type of leader than another? The classic experiment on this issue was conducted in 1939, when the influence of Hitler's autocratic domination in Germany was frightening people who believed that democratic leadership was not only more desirable, but more effective. At that time, some were even proposing that the best leaders were those who were nondirective, who provided resources when requested to do so but left all initiative to the group—a *laissez-faire* style of leadership.

To assess the effects of these three different leadership styles, Kurt Lewin and his colleagues created experimental groups in a laboratory setting, gave them different types of leaders, and then observed the groups in action.

The subjects were four five-member groups of 10 year-old boys who met after school to engage in hobby activities. Four men were trained in each of three leadership styles. An *autocratic* leader was to make all decisions and work assignments but not participate in the group activity. A *democratic* leader was to encourage and assist group decision-making and planning. Finally, a *laissez-faire* leader was to allow complete freedom for the group with a minimum of leader participation. At the end of each six-week period, each leader was transferred to a different group, at which time he also changed his leadership style. Thus, all groups experienced each leadership style under a different person, so that the leadership style was independent of the leader's personality.

The following generalizations emerged from this experiment:

1. A laissez-faire atmosphere is not the same as a democratic atmosphere. Less work—and poorer work—was done by the laissez-faire groups.

△ These photos from Lewin's classic study show the three leadership styles in action. The autocratic leader directs the work, the democratic leader works with the boys, and the laissez-faire leader remains aloof.

2. Democracy can be efficient. Although the quantity of work done in autocratic groups was somewhat higher, work motivation and interest were stronger in the democratic groups. Originality was greater under democracy.

3. Autocracy can create much hostility and aggression. The autocratic groups showed as much as thirty times more hostility, more demands for attention, more destruction of their own property, and more scapegoating behavior, using weaker individuals as targets.

4. Autocracy can create discontent that may not appear on the surface. More discontent was expressed in autocracy than in democracy, and four boys dropped out during autocratic periods. Nineteen of the twenty boys preferred their democratic leader to either of the other leader types.

5. Autocracy encourages dependence and less individuality. There was more submissive or dependent behavior in autocratic groups, and conversation was less varied, more confined to the immediate situation.

6. Democracy promotes more group-mindedness and friendliness. Mutual praise, friendly remarks, and overall playfulness were more frequent in democratic groups, and there was more readiness to share group property.

7. Leadership style is more influential than the leader's personality. The same man, no matter what his own traits, had a markedly different impact when he employed one leadership style as opposed to another (Lewin et al., 1939).

More recent research shows that the same leader behavior may be evaluated quite differently by different followers as a result of their own backgrounds, standards, expectations, and beliefs (Loye, 1977). Sadly, this means that the demagogue who can convince people that he or she is wise and concerned about ordinary people's problems may gain a more devoted following than someone who actually has more ability and concern for people's well-being as well as more ability to deal with problems the group faces.

It is also possible for a leader to get a commitment from a group by offering whatever the group seems to need or respond to. Then, once the members become loyal, dedicated followers, the leader may become increasingly controlling and demand ever more obedience to his absolute authority.

Such a pattern was seen in the transformation of the Reverend Jim Jones, pastor of a California religious congregation known as the People's Temple. Initially, he was a generous, social-emotional spiritual leader who was able to attract several thousand followers. Over time, he changed dramatically to become punitive, escalating his demands for group members' contributions of money, free labor, and unquestioned acceptance of his arbitrary rules. He was able to persuade his loyal church members to burn their Bibles, disown their religion, embrace Communism and leave their homes in the United States for life in a jungle compound in Guyana. Finally, he demonstrated the most awesome destructive power a leader may exert—at his suggestion on a November day in 1978, 912 men, women and children committed suicide by taking poison or had it forced upon them. It is worth noting the quotation from the philosopher Santayana that was hung as a banner above Jones' throne-like chair, "Those who do not remember the past are condemned to repeat it" (see Reiterman & Jacobs, 1983).

Intergroup relations

Some social psychologists are interested in social influence *between* groups rather than within them. They are concerned with the dynamics of intergroup relations, competition and cooperation, and conflict resolution.

When one group of people is differentiated from another, members of both groups develop a "we-feeling" about their own group, the **in-group**, and a "they-feeling" about the others, the **out-group**. Not only are distinctions made between "us" and "them," but there is a clear bias toward evaluating "us" as better (Brewer, 1979). This bias in favor of one's own group is called an *in-group bias*. It takes surprisingly little to produce it.

In a series of experiments, subjects were randomly divided into two groups: a "blue" and a "green" group. The groups were given blue or green pens and wrote on blue or green paper; they were addressed by the experimenter in terms of their group color. Even though these color categories had no intrinsic psychological significance and assignment to the groups was completely arbitrary, subjects gave a more positive evaluation of their own group than of the other. Furthermore, this in-group bias appeared even *before* the group members began to work together (Rabbie, 1981).

Apparently merely categorizing people into different groups under totally arbitrary pretexts is sufficient to cause a change in attitudes, so that people begin to favor their own "in-group" as superior and be hostile toward the "out-group," which is perceived to be inferior (Allen & Wilder, 1975; Rabbie & Wilkins, 1971). Furthermore, anything that leads to a perception of a "we-they" dichotomy then induces the members of each group to try to *increase* the extent and significance of the perceived difference, however trivial (Wilder, 1978).

An arbitrary assignment into a group labeled "inferior" can make children perform below their usual level, while average children led to believe they are in the "superior" group come to act more in keeping with their designated group category. A powerful demonstration of this effect was devised in a remarkable experiment by a third-grade class teacher, Jane Elliott, who wanted her pupils from an all-white, rural community to experience what prejudice and discrimination feel like to the victimized outgroup members.

> One day she arbitrarily designated brown-eyed children as "superior" to the "inferior" blue-eyed children. The superior, allegedly more intelligent "brown-eyes" were given special privileges, while the inferior "blue-eyes" had to obey rules that enforced their second-class status.
>
> The blue-eyed children immediately began to do more poorly on their lessons and became depressed, sullen, and angry. They described themselves as "sad," "bad," "stupid," "dull," and "mean." One boy said he felt like a "vegetable." Of the brown-eyed superiors, the teacher reported, "What had been marvelously cooperative, thoughtful children became nasty, vicious, discriminating little third-graders . . . it was ghastly."
>
> To show how arbitrary and irrational intergroup prejudice and its rationalizations are, Mrs. Elliott told the class on the next school day that she had been wrong, that it was really the blue-eyed children who were superior and the brown-eyed ones who were inferior. The brown-eyes now switched from their previously "happy," "good," "sweet," "nice," self-labels to derogatory ones similar to those used the day before by the blue-eyes. Their academic performance deteriorated, while that of the new ruling class improved. Old friendship patterns between children temporarily dissolved and were replaced with hostility until the experiment was called off (Elliott, 1977).

This experience of being in a disadvantaged out-group can have the positive effect of enabling people to develop greater empathy for members of groups that are discriminated against in society. In a replication of Mrs. Elliott's study, psychologists found that weeks later the children who had participated held less prejudiced beliefs than did a comparison group without this experience (Weiner & Wright, 1973).

The ease with which people can divide their social world into "us" and "them" and their immediate preference for the in-group have many important consequences for their behavior towards other people. They may be more sociable and helpful to someone who is "one of us" even if that individual is a stranger. Conversely, they may be more ready to act in negative ways towards any member of an out-group. There is also a general tendency to perceive one's own groups as being quite *variable* in their attributes whereas out-groups are seen in stereotypic ways, with all members perceived as being pretty much alike. This is true regardless of how much exposure we have to the out-groups and despite contrary experience with individual members of out-groups—of the other sex, college, occupation, race, or any other out-group category (Quattrone, 1985; Park & Rothbart, 1982).

Given the prevalence of this favoritism for the in-group, we can expect that there will often be a great deal of rivalry and competition between groups and sometimes mutual hostility and overt aggression. Is this inevitable? What factors aggravate conflict between groups and what factors would promote cooperation instead? Some answers are provided in a classic study by social psychologist Muzafer Sherif at his Robber's Cave summer camp for boys, as described in the **Close-up** on page 605.

Clearly this study with boys has implications for reducing the bitterness between antagonistic adult groups within our own society as well as between national groups. The task is to discover superordinate goals that will be perceived by these groups as in their best interest but achievable only through cooperation with each other. What might some superordinate goals be for labor and management? For Russians and Americans? For Arabs and Israelis?

This dual potential of groups—either to bring out the best in people or to create some of the worst crimes against humanity—will be one of our major concerns in the next chapter, as we examine several social issues, problems, and potential solutions.

The Rattlers vs. The Eagles

In a summer camp, friction was generated between two groups of boys and was later overcome as the groups worked toward common goals. In the beginning, the experimenters assigned the groups to different bunkhouses and kept them separate for daily group activities. By the end of this part of the experiment, the two groups had acquired definite group structures, including leaders, names (Rattlers and Eagles), private signals, and other identification symbols.

Next, rivalry between the groups was stimulated by a series of competitive events. As predicted, this both increased in-group solidarity and produced unfavorable stereotypes of the out-group and its members. After losing a tug-of-war, The Eagles burned the Rattlers' flag. The Rattlers retaliated, and a series of bunkhouse raids ensued, accompanied by name calling, fist fights, and other expressions of hostility. During the conflict, a physically daring leader emerged to replace the less aggressive boy who had led the "peacetime" Eagles. In this way relations with other groups can cause changes within a group and the emergence of new leaders.

An attempt was then made to break down the hostility and induce the two groups to cooperate with each other. First, the rival groups were brought into close contact in pleasant activities—such as eating and shooting off firecrackers. The groups refused to intermingle, however, and the activities merely provided them with further opportunities for expressions of hostility. Intergroup contact did not in itself decrease tension.

Situations were then contrived to bring about interaction of the groups to achieve *superordinate goals*—that is, important goals that required the combined efforts of both groups. The most striking episode in this period was one in which the tug-of-war rope, formerly the central object in a most antagonistic situation, served as a tool. On an overnight trip, a truck that was to bring their food "stalled," and the boys hit upon the idea of using the rope to pull the vehicle. After looping the rope through the bumper, the two groups pulled on different ends, but the next day, when the truck "stalled" again, members of the two groups intermingled on the two lines, eliminating group divisions. The camp's water supply also developed a "problem" that the groups worked together to solve.

Further evidence of the change in the boys' attitudes was obtained from friendship choices made at the end of the period of intense competition and again at the close of the experiment. Rattler's choices of Eagles as friends went up from 6 to 36 percent of their total friendship choices. Eagles' choices of Rattlers went up from 8 to 23 percent. The boys were also asked to rate each other on six characteristics designed to reveal the presence of stereotyped images. During the period of antagonism, Eagles received few favorable ratings from Rattlers, and Rattlers few from Eagles, but at the close of the experiment there was no significant difference in the ratings of in-group and out-group.members (Sherif et al., 1961; Sherif & Sherif, 1979).

SUMMARY

■ The central focus of social psychology is the study of social influence. Psychologists study this influence within individuals, in interactions between people, and in groups and intergroup relations.

■ In social psychological research the individual (or group) in the current social context is the unit of study rather than only the organisms or only the stimulus situation. Social processes are studied as independent variables, dependent variables, and intervening variables.

■ Social reality is created out of the phenomenological perspective of the participants in a situation. The shared social reality may be formally or informally defined. The social reality provides powerful schemas that shape a person's perceptions, expectations, and behavior, and create self-fulfilling prophecies.

■ A much-studied social process *within* individuals is social perception—how we form impressions of other people and explain their behavior. First impressions are more influential than later information. Our schemas about people include implicit personality theories and prototypes of various personality "types" by which we try to categorize people.

■ In attributing causes to people's behavior, we tend to follow the covariation principle, use correspondent inferences, and discount situational factors if there were personality factors adequate to account for the behavior (and vice versa). We use the consensus and distinctiveness criteria in judging whether an action was caused by factors in the individual or in the situation.

■ Common errors in attribution of causes are the fundamental attribution error and the actor-observer bias. Many people also show a positivity or negativity bias and a self-serving bias.

■ Attitudes are learned predispositions to react in a particular way to certain stimuli. They include beliefs, values, affects, and behavioral dispositions. Attitudes help determine what a person will notice, value, remember, and act upon. An attitude is most likely to predict behavior when it includes a specific behavioral intention, when both attitude and behavior are very specific, and when the attitude is based on first-hand experience.

■ When one is induced to act in a way contrary to one's attitude "for no good reason," cognitive dissonance is experienced; this dissonance is uncomfortable and may be reduced by a change in the attitude to make it more consistent with the behavior.

■ Systematic study of attitude change began following Hitler's massive and successful use of propaganda. Such studies investigated the role of the source of a message, features of the message itself, and audience characteristics in producing attitude change.

■ Emotional appeals and subtle manipulation of the situation can also produce attitude changes, as can the "foot-in-the-door technique" that changes one's self-image, thereby making one more susceptible to persuasion.

■ Affiliation with others provides opportunities for consensual validation, praise, stimulation, sharing affection, and social comparison, giving us a measuring stick for evaluating ourselves against others. People who are fearful in a novel situation often prefer to be with others, whereas those who are anxious and do not know why may avoid affiliation.

■ Loneliness may involve social isolation or emotional isolation or both. Lonely people who blame the situation for their loneliness are more likely to try to change it than those who blame their own inadequacies.

■ Liking depends on how mutually rewarding the relationship is; this, in turn, is influenced by similarity, presence of complementary traits, reciprocity, physical attractiveness, and proximity. Theories of liking include reinforcement theory, social exchange theory, equity theory, and the gain-loss principle, according to which attraction is influenced by the direction of change in rewards received.

■ Though there has been little research on love, one means of studying loving has involved a Love Scale. It has successfully predicted continuation and progress in the loving relationships of dating couples by tapping satisfaction of affiliative and dependence needs, predisposition to help, exclusiveness, and absorption with each other.

■ Our group memberships may influence our perceptions, feelings, and actions even more than our attitudes. Groups usually have a structure, leader, communication network, set of rules, and common goal; all these help to induce a sense of identification with the group on the part of the members and provide the potential for social influence.

■ Group influence occurs through the mere presence of other people but most strongly through group norms that members are expected to follow. Those who identify strongly with a group come to share its attitudes and values.

■ Pressure toward conformity is felt strongly by those who depend on the group for meeting their personal needs. Conformity may represent only external compliance, uncritical identification with the group position, or internalization of the group position. Under some conditions, a consistent, confident, deviant minority can change the position of the majority.

■ Leader characteristics vary, depending on the qualities needed at a given time and place. Separate leaders may meet the group's task and social-emotional needs. Though productivity may be high under autocratic leadership, dissatisfaction and hostility are greater; democratic leadership can be both efficient and satisfying; laissez-faire leadership is neither efficient nor satisfying.

■ When two groups are differentiated from each other, members of both develop "we-feelings" toward the in-group and "they-feelings" toward the out-group. These feelings are accompanied by a conviction of their own superiority and efforts to accentuate the perceived differences.

■ Rivalry increases these "we" and "they" distinctions and may lead to hostility and intergroup aggression. Working toward a superordinate goal of importance to all can lessen these antagonisms.

17

EXPLORING SOCIAL ISSUES

■ HUMAN POTENTIAL AND SOCIAL INFLUENCE
  The puzzle of human nature
  Individuation and deindividuation
■ DEHUMANIZED RELATIONSHIPS
  The functions of dehumanization
  Dehumanization techniques
■ OBEDIENCE TO AUTHORITY
  Milgram's obedience paradigm
  Authority systems, disobedience, and you
■ HUMAN AGGRESSION AND VIOLENCE
  Aggression as inborn
  Physiological bases of aggression
  The frustration-aggression hypothesis
  Aggression as provoked readiness
  Aggression as socially learned
  The violence of pornography
■ PSYCHOLOGY BEYOND THE INDIVIDUAL
  Social dilemmas
  Areas of application
■ SUMMARY
■ A POSTSCRIPT: PSYCHOLOGY AND YOU

Tommy Whitlow liked to relax on Sundays, doing nothing more serious or intellectual than to watch a ball game on TV. But his serenity was shattered one Sunday morning by a screeching siren as the city police arrived to arrest him at his home. They swept through the college town rounding up nine students in a surprise mass arrest. Each was charged with a felony, warned of his constitutional rights, searched, handcuffed, and carted off to the police station for booking. After fingerprinting and paperwork were completed, each prisoner was blindfolded and transported to the "Stanford County Prison." Here he was stripped naked and issued a smock-type uniform with his I.D. number on front and back. At this point, Tommy lost his name and became only Prisoner 647.

Orders were shouted at Prisoner 647, and he was pushed around by the guards if he didn't comply quickly enough. The guards all wore khaki uniforms. They, too, were not identified by name, and their anonymity was furthered by reflector sunglasses, which made eye contact with them impossible. Most of the youthful prisoners sat on cots in their barren cells, dazed and shocked by the unexpected events that had transformed their lives so suddenly. Just what kind of prison was this? Prisoner 647 and the others soon found out.

The guards insisted that their prisoners blindly obey all institutional rules, without question or hesitation. Failure to do so would lead to the loss of a privilege. At first, privi-leges were opportunities to read, write, or talk to other inmates. Later, however, the slightest disobedience was punished by loss of the "privilege" of eating, sleeping, or washing. Punishment also included menial, mindless work, such as cleaning toilets with bare hands, doing push-ups, and spending time in solitary confinement.

Every guard Prisoner 647 encountered engaged in abusive, authoritarian behavior at some time. Many appeared to enjoy the elevated status that accompanied putting on the guard uniforms, which transformed their routine, everyday existence into one where they had virtually total control over other people. The guards were always devising new strategies for making prisoners feel worthless, depriving them not only of basic freedoms, but even of a sense of humanity and individuality.

Less than thirty-six hours after the mass arrest, one of the prisoners began to cry uncontrollably. He also experienced fits of rage, disorganized thinking, and severe depression. Three more prisoners developed similar symptoms on successive days. A fifth prisoner developed a psychosomatic rash over his entire body when the Parole Board rejected his appeal.

After lights were out, Prisoner 647 tried hard to remember what Tommy was like before becoming a prisoner. He also tried to imagine what his tormentors did before they became guards. He reminded himself that he was a college student who had answered an ad to be a subject in a two-week-long experiment on prison life. He had volunteered in order to

make some money and to have some fun doing something unusual.

The guards were college students, too. In fact, everyone in that strange prison had been selected from a large pool of volunteers because he was a normally healthy, average, middle class college student! On the basis of extensive personality tests and clinical interviews, they had all been judged to be law-abiding, emotionally stable, physically healthy, and "normal-average." This was not a prison run by the state, but a mock prison experiment run by psychologists.

Assignment of the participants to the condition of "guard" or "prisoner" had been *randomly determined* by the flip of a coin. The assignment to these roles was the independent variable. At the start of the study, then, there were no measurable differences between the mock "guards" and the "prisoners."

The experimenters ended the planned two-week simulation study after just six days, because of the dramatic emotional and behavioral effects it was creating. (Those prisoners who seemed especially distressed had been released even sooner.) Students who were pacifists had become sadistic when they played the role of guard, while psychologically stable students had behaved pathologically as prisoners confined in this total environment. The power of this simulated prison situation had become strong enough to create a new *social reality*—it

was a real prison in the minds of the jailers and the captives.

Tommy Whitlow said later that he wouldn't want to go through it again but valued the experience because he learned so much about himself and about human nature. He and the other students were so basically healthy that they readily bounced back once away from that powerful situation and follow-ups revealed no lasting negative effects. But guards and prisoners alike had learned an important lesson: never underestimate the power of an evil situation to overwhelm the personalities and good upbringing of even the best and brightest among us (Zimbardo, 1975; Haney & Zimbardo, 1977; replicated in Australia by Lovibond et al., 1979).

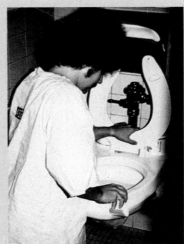 

What is the nature of human nature? Are we molded in the image of a Jesus or Buddha as loving, caring beings? Or are we really self-centered animals, driven to inflict suffering on others without any compassion? Does society curb our instinctively evil nature or is society the corrupting force that perverts our basic goodness?

In this final stage of our journey through the realm of psychology, we will consider some of these "big" questions. Our focus will be on the bonds between individuals and society, on how the social-psychological processes described in the last chapter can operate in life situations to pull us upward toward divinity or draw us downward toward destruction. Some of the themes in the story of Tommy's imprisonment that we will look at include the loss of individuality, dehumanization, obedience to authority, and human aggression.

We will end the chapter with a look at new areas of interest for the social psychologist, including the relationship between people and their physical environment. We will see why ecological issues are often "people problems" that need people-centered solutions if we are to improve our livable space on this planet.

HUMAN POTENTIAL AND SOCIAL INFLUENCE

Perhaps the most basic question in psychology is "What is the nature of human nature?" How are we to understand what people are all about, what they are capable of doing, being, or becoming? Add to these concerns that of the influence of society on the individual: is it beneficial or harmful? Are we programmed by our past, which we bring to new situations or controlled by the social context of the present?

In this section, we begin with such broad questions, continue the theme of the previous chapter about the power of situations on behavior, then focus on research that reveals some of the consequences of being made to feel special and distinctive by other people—or just a faceless creature in an anonymous setting.

The puzzle of human nature

According to some views, people do not "go wrong," but basically *are* wrong. In other words, people are evil by nature and will naturally hurt one another and engage in destructive acts—unless strong forces are present to restrain them. Among the most negative views of human nature, the following from Jonathan Swift's *Gulliver's Travels*, stands out as especially severe:

> "[The historical account of humans is a] heap of conspiracies, rebellions, murders, massacres, revolutions, banishments, the very worst effects that avarice, faction, hypocrisy, perfidiousness, cruelty, rage, madness, hatred, envy, lust, malice, and ambition could produce. . . . I cannot but conclude the bulk of your natives to be the most pernicious race of little odious vermin that nature ever suffered to crawl upon the surface of the earth."

But if we are basically so evil, then how can it be that we often do good? Why do we sometimes care for one another, form friendships, and act in ways that seem to benefit all involved? One answer (strongly stated by philosopher Thomas Hobbes) is that although we are naturally driven by base desires, appetites, and impulses, the proper education

Table 17.1 *Ways We Can Go Wrong: Perverting Perfection*

Attribute	Enables Us to	But Can Also Lead Us to
Memory	Profit from past mistakes Develop and use complex concepts Relate present to past Distinguish novel events from previously experienced ones	Carry grudges, suffer from former conflicts and past traumatic events Lose spontaneity of behavior because of commitments and obligations Feel excessive remorse or sense of loss
Time sense	Develop a history and sense of continuous self Relate present behavior to the future Distinguish between transience and permanence	Fear change, live in the past, feel guilt Dread an unknown future, become anxious Experience disappointments from unfulfilled expectations Concentrate on past or future, ignoring the present
Ability to associate elements and infer unseen events	Create, imagine events not experienced Generalize from partial data Construct theories, hypotheses	Form negative, crippling associations Misperceive self or others, develop stereotypic and delusional thinking
Perception of choice	Not be stimulus bound, be independent See ourselves as responsible agents Hope, build for future	Experience conflicts, indecision Suffer from inability to act when action is necessary
Responsibility, self-evaluation	Take pride in accomplishments Delay gratification, undertake difficult or unpopular tasks Be concerned about effects of our actions on others	Feel inadequate Feel guilt for not living up to standards or for letting someone down Feel constrained by obligations
Competence motivation	Do work well, set high standards Gain benefits of hard work Advance technologically, use resources to meet our needs	Fear failure, suffer feelings of inadequacy Be anxious about tests of our ability Work for self-aggrandizement, to be "number one," to beat others down
Ability to use language and other symbols	Communicate with others, present and absent, for information, comfort, pleasure, planning, social control	Circulate and be prey to rumors and falsehoods; conceal true feelings Mistake the symbol for the reality
Susceptibility to social influence	Follow group standards Learn and transmit values Cooperate; establish community	Overconform, sacrifice integrity Reject innovation and stifle creativity in ourselves and others
Love	Experience tender emotions Nurture growth and independence of others Support, encourage, comfort others Feel wanted and special	Become jealous, vengeful Possessively limit another person's freedom Become depressed and suicidal from loss of love

can transform us into responsible law-abiding human beings. Then, firm and well-meaning authorities can control our behavior.

Standing in opposition to this view of natural depravity is the idea that people are basically good, but that we are the victims of corrupting social forces. As we saw in Chapter 2, this theme was developed by the philosopher Jean Jacques Rousseau, who envisioned human beings as noble, primitive savages diminished by contact with society. To recapture and preserve their essential goodness, then, individuals must escape from civilization. For Americans, Henry Thoreau's isolated cabin at Walden Pond, Massachu-

setts, has become a symbol of breaking the bonds of dependence on social convention and a community-controlled life-style by returning to the solitary "natural life."

Where do *you* stand in this argument? Are we born good and corrupted by an evil society, or born evil and redeemed by a good society? Or is it that some people are basically good, while others are basically bad? Before casting your ballot, consider an alternative perspective. Maybe each of us has the capacity to be a saint *or* a sinner, altruistic *or* selfish, gentle *or* cruel, dominant *or* submissive. Perhaps human nature is a *capacity for learning,* for adapting, for constantly changing. Perhaps each person is born with that capacity and can learn many possible realities and alternative ways of being.

Human potentials for good and evil. The preceding chapters have documented the complex development and supreme refinement of human capacities that have resulted from untold millions of years of evolution, growth, and adaptation. We have become the rulers of this planet, controlling other animals and the physical matter of the earth for our survival, comfort, and happiness. This reign is currently being extended to life beneath the oceans as well as to outer space. We have reached this position because of our capacity for learning new relationships, for remembering old ones, for reasoning, inventing, and planning new action strategies. We have developed both natural and computer languages to manipulate symbols and transmit thoughts and information to others. Our perceptual, cognitive, and motor skills allow us to see, reflect, and act in countless intricate ways to avoid pain, gain pleasure, and change our surroundings to suit ourselves.

But each of these unique attributes can also become cancerous. Implanted in the very potential for perfectibility are the seeds of perversion and breakdown. A partial catalog of human traits and attributes and their possible positive and negative consequences is given in **Table 17.1.**

Which way they develop is influenced by the interaction of the psychological processes with processes at economic, political, historical, and cultural levels. As we develop and throughout our lives, cultural and social forces make certain options more available to us than others, certain potentialities more likely to be expressed. Equally important, though our past has shaped us, we can change at any moment as a result of a chance encounter or immersion in a new, powerful social reality (see Bandura, 1982a).

The power of the social situation. The situations in which we live and move determine the roles available to us. They also help define the social meaning that each role will have. Thus situations can be powerful agencies for changing us—or keeping us from changing.

In the simulated prison experiment, the guards were different from the prisoners in virtually every observable way—at the end of the study. Yet just a week before, they had been very similar. Chance, in the form of random assignment, decided their roles, and these roles created status and power difference which, in turn, led to all the other differences in how they thought, felt, and acted. See **Figure 17.1.**

No one taught them how to play their roles. We have to assume that each of the students had the capacity to become either a prisoner or a guard by calling upon stored knowledge structures about

Figure 17.1

This interaction profile shows guard and prisoner behavior across 25 occasions over 6 days in the simulated prison environment.

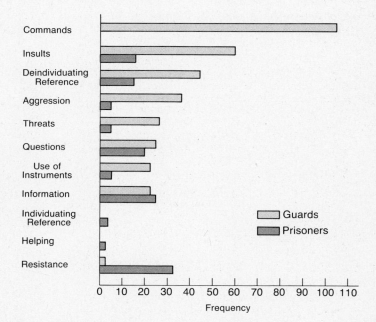

those roles. Without ever visiting a real prison or speaking with prison staff or inmates, we have all learned these roles (Banuazizi & Movahedi, 1975).

In our schemas and scripts, a guard limits the freedom of prisoners in order to manage their behavior more easily. This task is aided by the use of coercive rules. Prisoners can only *react* to the structure created by others. Rebellion or compliance are their primary options; the first gets punished, while the second takes away their sense of autonomy and dignity. The student participants had already experienced such power differences in many previous interactions: parent-child; teacher-student; doctor-patient; boss-worker; traditional male-female. They merely refined and intensified their script for this particular setting.

In real-life settings, the influence of the situation does not stop with creating roles and inducing role-consistent behavior. The participants then go on to justify or explain the status differences by discovering or inventing reasons why the master *deserves* top billing. Similarly, the person at the bottom is presumed to be there because of personal inferiority; the poor are blamed for passivity, slaves for stupidity, the unemployed for lack of ambition.

Too often, we limit our own freedom by sticking with the traditional roles we found operating in our groups and simply learned to play. Yet our human nature gives us the potential for learning new roles and expanding our repertoire in almost any direction. We need to seek out those situations that will help us change in ways we want to change, while avoiding or altering situations that can change us in destructive ways.

Individuation and deindividuation

"Sure, this robe of mine doth change my disposition."

Shakespeare, *The Winter's Tale*

A clear demonstration of the fact that the same individuals have the potential for both prosocial and antisocial behavior, depending on the social setting, has been provided by research on the effects of individuation and deindividuation. **Individuation** is the psychological state and the process in which a person is differentiated from the other people in a

given social context. The individual stands out and is unique and identifiable both to others and in his or her own perceptions (Snyder & Fromkin, 1980; Ziller, 1964). For example, we are individuated when we are called by name, when our special features or contributions are recognized, and when our actions are rewarded by others. Individuation acts to inhibit socially undesirable behaviors and to promote norm-appropriate acts (Ickes et al., 1978).

Other research has found that the extent to which people will *individuate* themselves, by behaving in distinctive ways, is a function of the potential rewards and punishments in the environment. If there is the possibility of a positive outcome (acclaim, prizes, recognition), then people will try to call attention to themselves and their unique characteristics. However, if negative consequences are anticipated (ridicule, attack, a burdensome assignment), then people will try to melt into the crowd and *not* look different from the rest of the group (Maslach, 1974). Recall how you and your elementary-school classmates acted when the teacher asked an easy question ("Call on me!") versus a hard one ("I want to be invisible").

The sense of distinctiveness associated with being individuated can have negative as well as positive consequences. Those perceived as "different" are more likely to be rejected, avoided, or mistreated (Freedman & Doob, 1968; Goffman, 1963). On the other hand, the different person in a group is more

▽ *Children are eager to be singled out as individuals when they are confident that the outcome of such recognition will be positive.*

salient, and if competent will be judged to be more influential (S. E. Taylor et al., 1979). The individuated person becomes so not merely in the perception of others, but also as a result of greater self-awareness, of an attentional focus on the self (Duval & Wicklund, 1972). When people focus on their self-concept, they tend to perceive it in terms of its distinctive and peculiar characteristics that make it "information rich" and thus differentiated from others in their social environment (McGuire et al., 1978).

> When students were identified as being high or low in their willingness to be individuated (on a self-report scale), a number of reactions were found to be correlated with this difference. Those willing to be individuated are more likely to have high self-esteem, and not to be shy. They have more distinctive possessions (e.g., a special kind of car) and unique nicknames, make controversial statements, and are more likely to look directly into someone's eyes while talking to them. In addition, their attempts at being distinctive extend to hairstyle, clothes, signature, and even the way they introduce themselves (Maslach et al., in press).

Deindividuation, by contrast, is the term for a subjective state and the process in which the person does not feel differentiated from others. In this state there is reduced self-awareness and lessened concern for social evaluation. This state can be induced by conditions in which the person feels anonymous or without responsibility, by conditions in which the person is immersed in the immediate present and does not think about the past or future; and by conditions in which sensory overload, drugs, strong emotions, or physical activity overwhelm rational, cognitive processing.

The term *deindividuation* was first used by Leon Festinger and his colleagues (1952) as a label for the process by which being anonymous in a group weakens feelings of social responsibility and fear of punishment. They theorized that when a person cannot be identified or judged by others, emotions and impulses that are usually held in check are more likely to be expressed. "You don't know who I am and I don't care who you are." Such perceived anonymity in a group setting interferes with identifying and remembering who said what. Since this early research, several studies have investigated the effects of deliberately created anonymity (Prentice-Dunn & Rogers, 1982; Singer et al., 1965).

The effects of anonymity. In one series of studies some of the subjects were made anonymous while others were clearly individuated and the amount of aggressive behavior of both groups was observed. Here, as in the prison study, the subjects were all the same at the start; any differences in aggressiveness would be the result of the difference in induced anonymity rather than existing personality differences.

Anonymity was created by having women tested in groups of four wear baggy lab coats and hoods that covered their faces. In addition, they sat in a darkened room and were never referred to by name. In other groups the women wore name tags, were frequently called by name, and saw the faces of the others in their group. All subjects were led to believe that they would be giving electrical shocks to each of two volunteer students as part of a supposed study of their empathy and the volunteers' ability to perform under stress.

The subjects listened to a taped interview with each "victim" before watching her twist, squirm, and jump in reaction to each "shock" they gave her (actually, she was a confederate who received no shock). In one condition the victim was portrayed in the interview as obnoxious, prejudiced, and "bitchy"; in the other, as sweet, warm, and altruistic.

▽ | *Hooded subjects observe through a one-way mirror as the experimenter apparently connects their "victim" to the shock generator.*

As predicted, the anonymous subjects shocked the victims more (twice as long) than did the identifiable subjects. Furthermore, the aggression by the anonymous subjects did not vary as a function of the characteristics of the victim: they shocked the victim more and more over time, regardless of whether she had been portrayed as nice or as obnoxious. In contrast, the identifiable subjects *did* shock the "nice" victim less over time although they also shocked the "obnoxious" victim more (Zimbardo, 1970).

Subsequent research supports the basic conclusion of this study. Conditions that foster anonymity lead people to act aggressively or to behave in other antisocial ways when they are given the opportunity to do so. College student subjects were more likely to cheat or steal from the researcher's office when they were treated as anonymous "guinea pigs" than when they were treated humanely as individuals (Kiernan & Kaplan, 1971). A field study of over 1300 Halloween trick-or-treaters had similar findings.

Costumed children were more likely to steal extra candies and money when their identities were not revealed than when they had been previously asked to identify themselves to the adult host. In addition, children in groups and thus deindividuated were more than twice as likely to transgress as those who were alone (Diener et al., 1976).

Anonymity increases aggression even when the aggressor must thereby give up tangible rewards.

In one experiment eight children were invited to a Halloween party where they were allowed to play aggressive or nonaggressive games in which they could win tokens. They were told that these tokens could be exchanged for attractive toys at an auction held at the end of the party. Playing the aggressive games involved physical competition (pushing and shoving) and took more time, thus earning fewer tokens. The aggressive and nonaggressive games were similar in content. For example, a child could compete with another to retrieve a single bean bag from a tunnel, or could be timed while retrieving it alone.

At first, the children played these games in their normal street clothes with name tags (condition A); then they were dressed in Halloween costumes that made them appear anonymous (condition B); finally, they were unmasked and wore their regular clothing again (condition A). As you can see in **Figure 17.2,** the children were more aggressive when they were

▽ Figure 17.2 *Aggression vs. Rewards*

The effects of simply being made anonymous are dramatic. Aggression was much higher in the anonymous condition despite the fact that the children earned far fewer tokens when they chose the aggressive games. (Based on Fraser, 1974.)

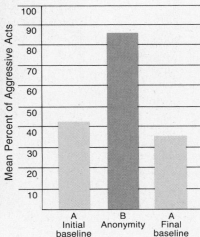

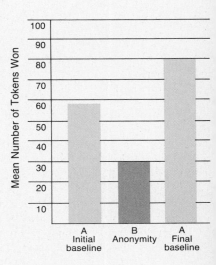

anonymous than when they were identifiable. They chose more aggressive games when they were anonymous even though it cost them valuable tokens to do so. It appears that there were intrinsic awards associated with being deindividuated and acting aggressively that were more powerful than the desire to earn tokens. The within-subjects, A-B-A design used in this study provided a powerful demonstration of the effect of the anonymity manipulation in altering behavior with the personalities and other attributes of the subjects held constant (Fraser, 1974).

The link between anonymity and aggression has been demonstrated in vastly different social settings. In some societies men prepare for war by putting on masks or painting their bodies. In other societies, there is no such process of changing one's appearance prior to becoming a warrior. Which of the two social groups do you predict would exhibit most aggression in combat?

To answer this question, data from twenty-three different cultures were examined. The striking results can be seen in **Table 17.2**. Of the fifteen societies in which warriors changed their appearance, twelve were high on the index of "killing, torturing, or mutilating the enemy," while only one of the eight with unchanged appearance were so aggressive (Watson, 1973).

Does deindividuation always bring out the worst side of human nature, as these studies seem to suggest? Not necessarily. Conditions that minimize self awareness and concern for social evaluation lower the threshold for expressing other ordinarily inhibited behaviors too.

Research subjects brought into a dark room to spend an hour with a group of strangers of both sexes behaved differently from others in a lighted room. Those in the anonymous setting talked more about personally significant things, and were more openly affectionate, touching and hugging others. The darkness provided an opportunity to "liberate" feelings of intimacy that are often suppressed in usual situations (Gergen et al., 1973).

Societal implications of deindividuation. In the life of a community there is a major social problem whenever social-economic-political conditions make people feel anonymous and threatened—and hence deindividuated. If they are outside the social reward structure, they may use aggression to get personal recognition and compensate for the anonymity and powerlessness they feel.

Table 17.2   A Cross-Cultural Study of Anonymity and Aggression

	Painted face	Unpainted face	Total
High Aggression	12	1	13
Low Aggression	3	7	10
Total	15	8	23

(Based on Watson, 1973)

A new social problem facing our society is the emergence of a permanent underclass. The *underclass* are the long-term poor, who are cut off from the rest of society because they lack education, employable skills, and personality traits regarded as desirable by others in the society. Many of the underclass youth have been described as "hostile," "passive," "alienated from the mainstream values," and "rebellious against authority." Without jobs, education, or a stable family structure, they never learn to cooperate with others, be on time, take orders, plan activities, or resist temptations. The criminals in this group commit a disproportionate amount of violent crime (Auletta, 1981; Myrdal 1971).

These young people are taking part in an "unnatural" social experiment in which they have been assigned by birth to the deindividuation treatment. We know only too well from the weak versions of such treatments in our psychology laboratories what the negative outcomes will be if this social experiment is not terminated soon. The tragedy is compounded by the fact that there is reason to believe they would have the capability for constructive, responsible behavior under conditions of high individuation and available rewards for prosocial behavior.

DEHUMANIZED RELATIONSHIPS

Would you ever deliberately humiliate, embarrass, or degrade another person? Can you imagine turning down a poor family's request for food or clothing if you could authorize it just by signing your name? Is it conceivable that you would ever decide that certain groups were unfit and order their extermination? What would it take to make *you* kill another person?

These and other antisocial behaviors become possible for normal, morally upright, and idealistic people under conditions in which they stop perceiving others as having the same feelings, thoughts, and purposes in life that they do. Such a psychological erasure of human qualities is called **dehumanization.** Dehumanization is a particular type of psychic defense mechanism used to protect the person from painful or overwhelming emotions in dealng with others. It leads to misperceiving certain other people as "subhuman" (animal-like), or as "nonhuman" objects.

When one is not responding to the human qualities of other persons, the golden rule may become "Do unto others as you would." The genocide of millions of people by governments and their military agents throughout the world has been carried out with the same efficiency as occurs daily at animal slaughterhouses—by the simple expedient of perceiving these fellow human beings as inferior forms of animal life.

In a laboratory experiment on dehumanization, college student subjects were led to believe that researchers were studying the effects of punishment on decision making. They supervised the work of a group of male students and had the option of punishing them with electric shock whenever inadequate decisions were made. Some of the subjects overheard the experimenter describe the students as perceptive and understanding. Other subjects overheard a dehumanizing characterization of the students as an animalistic, rotten bunch. Control subjects received neither positive nor negative descriptions of the potential victims.

Subjects who thought of their "victims" in dehumanized terms chose much higher levels of shock as punishment. (No shock was actually delivered.) They also felt less personal responsibility for the consequences of their punitive actions. Subjects given a humanized description of the victims showed *less* aggression against them than did the controls (see **Figure 17.3**). Finally, even the way the subjects justified their decision to administer the shocks differed depending on whether their victims had been dehumanized or humanized (Bandura et al., 1975).

The functions of dehumanization

Dehumanization may be: (a) socially imposed, (b) imposed in self-defense, (c) imposed deliberately for self-gratification, or (d) rationalized as the necessary means toward some noble end.

Socially imposed dehumanization. Dehumanization can occur in various work situations. Some jobs encourage workers to dehumanize other people

▷ **Figure 17.3**

"Overheard" cues that humanized or dehumanized performers affected the intensity of shocks that subjects administered to them. Shock victims who were described in humanized terms were shocked less than the neutral control group, while the dehumanized subjects categorized as "animals" were shocked the most—and increasingly so over the ten trials. (Adapted from Bandura et al., 1975.)

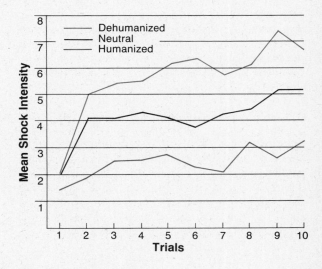

▷ *Jobs that require the seemingly endless repetition of one small portion of a task often lead to dehumanization and feelings of alienation.*

because large numbers of people have to be "processed" efficiently—college students during registration, subway commuters during rush hour, prisoners or mental patients during mealtime. Administrators of institutions often become concerned with minimizing disruptions and "managing the flow." Once the number of individuals requiring a given service becomes too great, they stop being seen or treated as individuals. After three days in which staff members at a mental hospital were confined on a ward in the role of mental patients, one staff-member-turned-patient said, "I used to look at patients as if they were a bunch of animals: I never knew what they were going through before" (Orlando, 1973).

In other cases, the jobs themselves dehumanize the worker by allowing no expression of personal feelings or unique abilities. Examples are assembly-line jobs that are repetitive, boring, and tedious. Workers feel no meaningful relationship to the product of their labors—and are, in fact, being gradually replaced by a new breed of workers who never complain about dehumanized work settings: industrial robots.

Dehumanization in self-defense. Individuals in many health and service professions work in situations that ordinarily arouse intense emotional feelings, elicit painful empathy, and/or involve "taboo" behaviors, such as invasion of privacy or violation of the human body. Dehumanizing their patients or clients may help them to handle such jobs. Treating people as "cases" in an objective, detached way enables them to perform necessary interviews and op-

erations with minimal emotional involvement. This self-protective "detachment" can become extreme, however.

Sometimes dehumanization is the result of emotional "burnout," as described in Chapter 13. Here the psychological stress and strain of a job become so severe that the person loses all human feeling for the people being served. They may become just "case loads" to social workers, "dockets" to lawyers, "crocks" to physicians—and burdens to all care givers who have "burned out."

Dehumanization for self-gratification. Sometimes others are used solely for one's own gain, or for entertainment, with no concern given to their feelings or thoughts. Men for whom sexual intercourse is only a self-gratifying experience—with a woman simply the means—show this dehumanization when they label her "a piece," "a cow," or "a good lay." The depths to which our insensitivity to others can go are revealed in the following reports:

In Chicago, a gas station was robbed and the two attendants were tied up. When a customer arrived, the attendants called out for help. Instead of helping them, the customer helped himself to a free tank of gas and two cartons of cigarettes and drove off. This scene was repeated in one form or another by nearly one hundred drivers over the next two hours, before someone finally called the police (United Press International, December 13, 1975).

In New York, a young man on his way to a job interview was mugged and most of his clothes were taken. Then, he was mugged again by others and stripped of his pants. A jeering mob chased him naked through Times Square, throwing bottles and laughing. Frightened, he ran into the subway for safety but was electrocuted when he hit the tracks, Then, with the entertainment over, the crowd left (*Washington Post,* July 2, 1981).

Dehumanization as a means to an end. At many times in history people have viewed a particular group as obstacles to the achievement of their goals. By perceiving such people in a dehumanized manner as "the enemy," "the masses," "a threat to national security," or "inferior," it becomes easier to take action against them in the name of some great cause, such as peace, liberty, or "God's will." Their suffering, injury, or destruction is then justified as a means toward a "noble" end. Many examples of such dehumanization come to mind, including the dropping of the atomic bomb on the residents of Hiroshima in order to "bring peace," the mass killing of Jews by the Nazis because "they are unfit," and the denial of medical treatment to black men afflicted with syphilis (the control group in a controversial study in Tuskegee, Alabama) in order to "study the course of the disease."

The ease with which people can be induced to adopt a dehumanized view of others was demonstrated in a study with college students.

The researcher brought together a large group of students and introduced a "professor" who asked for their assistance in a project "designed to eliminate the mentally and emotionally unfit." The idea was convincingly presented as high-minded and scientifically sound, beneficial for humanity, and actually even a kindness to those who would be eliminated. The students themselves were praised as being intelligent and educated, with high ethical values. In case they had any lingering misgivings, they were assured that careful research would be carried out before any actions were taken. A questionnaire was then administered to the students. The startling degree of acceptance of the proposed "final solution" is shown in **Table 17.3**. The students agreed that some people were not fit to survive and should be eliminated as painlessly as possible (Mansson, 1972). In a later replication of this study, a surprising 29 percent even supported the suggested measures when applied to their own families (Carlson & Wood, 1974).

This study of the "final solution" shows how little effort might be necessary to translate these "artifi-

---

Table 17.3   *Student Opinions Concerning the "Final Solution"*

1. Do you agree that there will always be people who are more fit in terms of survival than others?	*Agree*	90%
	Disagree	10%
2. If such killing is judged necessary, should the person or persons who make the decisions also carry out the act of killing?	*Yes*	57%
	No	43%
3. Would it work better if one person were responsible for the killing and another person carried out the act?	*Yes*	79%
	No	21%
4. Would it be better if several people pressed the button but only one button would be causing death? This way anonymity would be preserved and no one would know who actually did the killing.	*Yes*	64%
	No	36%
5. What would you judge to be the best and most efficient method of inducing death?	*Electrocution*	1%
	Painless poison	9%
	Painless drugs	89%
6. If you were required by law to assist, would you prefer to:		
(a) *be the one who assists in the decisions?*		85%
(b) *be the one who assists with the killing?*		8%
(c) *assist with both the decision and the killing?*		1%
No answer		6%
7. Most people agree that in matters of life and death extreme caution is required. Most people also agree that under extreme circumstances, it is entirely just to eliminate those judged dangerous to the general welfare. Do you agree?	*Yes*	91%
	No	5%
	Undecided	4%

(Adapted from Mansson, 1972)

cial" experimental findings into the same nightmare of reality that occurred in Germany in World War II—and in other places and other times both before and since then.

Dehumanization techniques

What are the models or strategies that people use to achieve dehumanization and emotional detachment? Very little research has been done on this question, but there appear to be several techniques that do the job. One of these is *relabeling*. The labels or terms used to describe people can make them appear more object-like and less human. Usually these terms are derogatory ones, such as "gook," "queer," or "hippie." Substituting verbs with less emotional meaning can have the same effect—to "waste" an enemy instead of to "kill." A recent news report revealed that "the State Department has decided to strike the word 'killing' from its human rights reports. It would be more precise, the government says, to say 'unlawful or arbitrary deprivation of life.'" (*San Francisco Examiner and Chronicle,* February 19, 1984). Similarly, it becomes easier to steal from the college bookstore if it is relabeled as "ripping off the establishment" or even "liberating" the merchandise.

A related technique of dehumanization is *intellectualization*. By dealing with the abstract qualities of other people (rather than their more human ones), the individual can "objectify" the situation and react in a less emotional way. "Rational" analyses of civil defense plans and detailed estimates of the number of survivors of a nuclear war help American and Soviet strategists avoid thinking about the human meaning of what they are talking about (Schell, 1982).

Perceiving that others in the same situation feel as we do or are doing the same thing can lessen our feelings of responsibility so that we may have fewer qualms about engaging in a particular behavior. Joking and laughing with others about what is happening also reduces our tension and anxiety. The "sick" humor of medical students dissecting cadavers may well serve this purpose.

The cataloging and analyzing of social pathologies involving deindividuation and dehumanization are depressing to write about and to read about. Our attitude in doing so should go beyond scientific detachment to a sense of personal concern and urgency—to understand how these processes work so that we may begin to resist or oppose them.

OBEDIENCE TO AUTHORITY

The two-sided aspect of human nature is also evident when we examine our relationships to authority figures. Sometimes we wisely follow the sensible guidance and good counsel of just authority. But other times we passively obey the unreasonable orders of just authority or the destructive suggestions of unjust authority. As author C. P. Snow reminds us,

> "When you think of the long and gloomy history of man, you will find more hideous crimes have been committed in the name of obedience than have been committed in the name of rebellion" (1961, p. 3).

What made Adolf Eichmann and other Nazis willing and able to send millions of Jews to the gas chambers? Did some character defect lead them to carry out orders blindly, even if the orders violated their own values and beliefs? Was the same personality distortion responsible for the mass slaughter of hundreds of Palestinians in refugee camps by Lebanese Christian troops in 1982? And how can we best explain the mass suicide-murders of the members of the Peoples Temple who engaged in the ultimate act of obedience? As we noted in the preceding chapter, hundreds willingly took their children's lives and their own because their leader, Reverend Jim Jones, told them to—to avoid being executed by the U.S. soldiers he imagined were about to invade their jungle compound in Jonestown, Guyana.

Here we are asking again the question raised in earlier chapters about dispositional versus situational causes of behavior. If we blame the individuals who did these terrible things, we are making the *fundamental attribution error* by underestimating the possible influence of the social situation while overestimating dispositional influences. Doing so is comforting because it creates a psychological distance between *us* ("good" people) and *them* ("bad" people). It also takes society and social conditions "off the hook" as contributors to the problem. The alternative is to acknowledge that *we* might be capable of these terrible actions.

How about *you?* Could *you* imagine being part of a company of American soldiers who massacred innocent women, children, and elderly citizens in the Vietnamese village of My Lai (Hersh, 1971; Opton, 1970, 1973)? Are there any conditions under which *you* would blindly obey an order from your religious leader to give poison to your family and then commit suicide? Would you obey a command to electrocute a stranger? Your answers—as mine used to be—are all most likely, *"No!* What kind of person do you think I am?" But after reading this next section, you may be more willing to answer, "Maybe. I don't know for sure." Depending on the power of the social forces operating to distort your moral judgment and weaken your will to resist, might even you do what other human beings have done in that situation, however horrible and alien to your way of thinking when you're outside that setting?

Milgram's obedience paradigm

To separate the variables of personality and situation, which are always entangled in natural settings, we need a controlled experiment. Social psychologist Stanley Milgram (1965, 1974) devised an effective and dramatic paradigm for demonstrating the power of situational forces to induce obedience to authority in people like you and me. We'll take a close look at the procedures and processes involved in his studies because they tell us some things about human nature that you may find personally relevant and socially significant.

Milgram's first experiments were conducted using Yale college students as paid volunteers. In later variations, Milgram put his "obedience laboratory" out in the community. He set up a storefront research unit in Bridgeport, Connecticut, recruiting through newspaper ads a broad cross section of the population varying widely in age, occupation, and education.

The basic experimental paradigm involved having subjects deliver a series of what they thought were extremely painful electric shocks to another subject. They did so not because they were sadistic, but because they were participating in a worthwhile cause—or so they believed. In their *role* as "teacher" they were to punish errors made by a "learner." They were led to believe that the purpose of the study was to discover how punishment affects memory so that learning and memory could be improved through the proper balance of reward and punishment. The major *rule* they were told to follow was to increase the level of shock by a certain amount each time the learner made an error. The experimenter acted as the legitimate *authority* figure: he

presented the rules, arranged for the assignment of roles (by a rigged drawing of lots), and ordered the "teacher" to do his job whenever he hesitated or dissented.

The *dependent variable* was the final level of shock the "teacher" gave before refusing to continue to obey the authority. The initial study was simply a demonstration of the phenomenon of obedience; there was *no* manipulation of an independent variable. Later versions did study the effect of varying factors such as the physical distance between the authority and "teacher," and also between "teacher" and "learner." Milgram used no formal control of comparison group in this study—as was also true of the Stanford Prison Study. In both these demonstrations, the comparison group is *you* and other "observers" with a belief about how they would behave under such circumstances.

The study was staged to make the subject think that by following orders, by being obedient, he was causing pain and suffering and perhaps even killing an innocent person. The "learner" was a pleasant, mild-mannered man about fifty years old who mentioned something about a heart condition, but was willing to go along with the procedure. He was strapped into an "electric chair" in the next room and communicated with the "teacher" via an intercom. His task was to memorize pairs of words, giving the second word in a pair when he heard the first one. The "learner" soon ran into difficulty and began making many errors.

The "teacher" punished each error by pressing a switch on a shock generator. The thirty switches were marked in 15-volt units from slight shock (15 volts) on up to Danger: Severe Shock XXX (450 volts). The teacher had been given a sample shock of about 75 volts to feel how much pain it caused.

The protests of the victim rose with the shock level being administered. At 75 volts, he began to moan and grunt; at 150 volts he demanded to be released from the experiment; at 180 volts he cried out that he could not stand the pain any longer. At 300 volts he insisted that he would no longer take part in the experiment and must be freed. He yelled out about his heart condition and screamed. If the subject hesitated or protested against delivering the next shock, the experimenter told him, "Teacher, you have no other choice; you must go on! Your job is to punish the learner's mistakes."

◁ *The experimenter instructs the "teacher" in the use of the shock generator. How would you behave if you were in the subject's place?*

room, the "teacher" was ordered to keep shocking him more and more strongly. But did he? Did they? Would you? (Stop! Before reading further, think about what your response would have been, then answer the questions below.)

As you might imagine, the situation was not an enjoyable one for the subjects. Most subjects complained and protested. They insisted they could not go on with their job. That the experimental situation produced considerable conflict in the subjects is readily apparent from their protests:

"180 volts delivered: 'He can't stand it! I'm not going to kill that man in there! You hear him hollering? He's hollering. He can't stand it. What if something happens to him? . . . I mean who is going to take the responsibility if anything happens to that gentleman?' (The experimenter accepts responsibility.) 'All right.'

"195 volts delivered: 'You see he's hollering. Hear that. Gee, I don't know.' (The experimenter says: 'The experiment requires that you go on.')—'I know it does, sir, but I mean—huh—he don't know what he's in for. He's up to 195 volts.' . . .

"240 volts delivered: 'Aw, no. You mean I've got to keep going up with that scale? No sir, I'm not going to kill that man! I'm not going to give him 450 volts!'" (1965, p. 67).

When the "learner" stopped responding, some subjects called out to him to respond, urging him to get the answer right so they would not have to continue shocking him, all the while protesting loudly to the experimenter. But the experimenter insisted that the "teacher" must go on. Rules are rules! So even when there was only silence from the "learner's"

How far do you think the average subject in Milgram's experiment actually went in administering the shocks? Suppose for a moment that you were the subject-teacher. How far up the scale would you go? Which of the thirty levels of shock would be the absolute limit beyond which you would refuse to continue? Indicate your estimates below.

1. The average subject probably stopped at _____ volts.
2. I would refuse to shock the other person beyond voltage level (circle one number):

0	15	30	45	60
75	90	105	120	135
150	165	180	195	210
225	240	255	270	285
300	315	330	345	360
375	390	405	420	435
450				

To shock or not to shock? When forty psychiatrists were asked to predict the performance of subjects in this experiment, they estimated that most would not go beyond 150 volts. In their professional opinion, fewer than 4 percent of the subjects would still be obedient at 300 volts and only about 0.1 percent would go all the way up to 450 volts. The psychiatrists presumed that only those few individuals who were *abnormal* in some way would blindly obey orders to harm another person in an experiment. How close are your predictions to theirs?

In fact, these professionals were quite wrong. They fell into the trap of the fundamental attribution error—overestimating the role of personality while being unaware of the power of the situation. The *majority* of the subjects obeyed! Nearly two thirds went all the way up to 450 volts. They followed orders, delivering the maximum punishment possible. No subject who got within five switches of the end ever refused to go all the way. By then, their resistance was broken; they had resolved their own conflict—and just tried to get it over with as quickly as possible. They *dissented* verbally, but they did not *disobey*.

Through later research we know that this obedience effect becomes even *stronger* when: (a) the "victim" is more physically remote; (b) the subject is under direct surveillance by the authority; and (c) the subject acts as an *intermediary* assisting another person who actually delivers the shock.

Attributions for blind obedience. Maybe the personalities of the obedient majority were different from those of the rebellious minority? Personality tests administered to the subjects did *not* reveal any traits that differentiated those who obeyed from those who refused or any psychological disturbance or abnormality in the obedient "punishers."

Maybe the subjects did not really believe the "cover story" of the experiment? Perhaps they figured out that the "victim" was really a confederate of the experimenter whose protests were tape recorded. Maybe they just "went along for the ride." To test this possibility, other researchers replicated the conceptual design of Milgram's study while making the effects more vivid and direct.

College students were asked to train a puppy on a discrimination task by punishing it with increasing levels of shock whenever it made an error. They could see it jumping around on an electrified grid when they pressed a switch. Actually, the puppy received only a low level of shock—just enough to make it squeal. The students dissented and complained. They said they were upset, they did not want to do it. Some even cried.

At a given point, an odorless, colorless anesthetic was secretly released into the puppy's enclosed chamber. The dog wobbled and finally fell asleep.

The subjects thought they had killed that cuddly puppy. But the experimenter reminded them of the rule: failure to respond is a punishable error; they must continue to give shocks.

Would anyone really do so?

Three fourths of all students did. They delivered the maximum shock. Every one of the female subjects proved to be totally obedient despite their tearful dissent (Sheridan & King, 1972).

Maybe subjects who knew they were in a "scientific experiment" were obeying out of a "higher" need to help science. In real life then, people would not obey an authority whose orders put someone's life in danger. Or would they? A team of psychiatrists and nurses performed the following field study to test the power of obedience in a real-life hospital setting.

A nurse (the subject) receives a call from a staff doctor whom she has not met. He tells her to administer some medication to a patient so that it can take effect by the time he arrives. He'll sign the drug order after he gets to the ward. He orders a dose of 20 milligrams of a drug called Astroten.

The label on the container of Astroten states that 5 milligrams is the usual dose and warns that the maximum dose is 10 milligrams. Would a nurse actually administer an excessive dose of a drug on the basis of a telephone call from an unfamiliar person? To do so is to go contrary to standard medical practice.

When this dilemma was *described* to twelve nurses, ten *said* they would disobey. When actually in the situation, however, almost every nurse obeyed! Twenty-one of twenty-two had started to pour the medication (actually a harmless substance) before a physician researcher stopped them (Hofling et al., 1966).

Like the prison study, this obedience research challenges the myth that evil lurks in the minds of evil people—the *Them* who are different dispositionally from the *Us* who would never do such things. The purpose in recounting these findings is not to diminish human nature but to make clear the human potential for frailty in the face of strong social forces in the situation, even for normal, well-meaning individuals.

Four conditions can be distinguished that lead to blind obedience to authority in violation of one's self-image and moral values:

1. Obedience is nurtured by the presence of a *legitimate authority* whom we trust and see as a valid representative of society, or who controls significant reinforcers. We feel freer to act when an authority assumes responsibility for the consequences of our action. Identification with a strong authority may also help us overcome feelings of personal weakness and insignificance.

2. Obedience is nurtured by the establishment of a *role relationship* in which we are subordinated to another person. In this role we do not feel as responsible for our behavior since we are not spontaneously initiating it, but merely carrying out orders. But other research has shown that if subjects see other people defy commands and refuse to accept their roles, then the majority of subjects *disobey* (Rosenhan, 1969).

3. Obedience is nurtured by the presence of *social norms* that specify socially acceptable behaviors. These norms come to govern and constrain what is perceived as possible and appropriate, and people feel embarrassed and apologetic about not conforming to what is expected. One subject in the original Milgram study said to the experimenter, "*I don't mean to be rude, sir,* but shouldn't we look in on him? He has a heart condition and may be dying." It is important to note that even among the hardy band of disobedient subjects, not one spontaneously got up to check on the "victim," even after having quit the experiment.

4. Obedience is nurtured by the *redefinition of evil as good.* Those who engage in evil deeds rarely if ever see them as evil. Instead, the deed is seen as not only reasonable but necessary. Here again is the paradox of human perfection—the same mind that can comprehend the most profound philosophical and metaphysical truths can distort and redefine reality in ways that eliminate inconsistency and maintain self-esteem. The prison guards were "keeping order." Milgram's subjects were being "concerned teachers." The Inquisition and seventeenth-century witch burnings were defined as "saving souls." Maintaining a nuclear arsenal that we are committed to use in case of nuclear attack is justified today in terms of "national security" and "preservation of our way of life." The physicians who assist jailors in the torture of political prisoners in many countries define their behavior as "doing their duty to their government" (Amnesty International, 1983). To appreciate how it is possible to attribute the most horrible deeds to noble causes, consider Hitler's statement:

"Thus, if we review all the causes of the German collapse, the final and decisive one is seen to be the failure to realize the racial problem and, more especially, the Jewish menace. . . . Thus do I now believe that I must act in the sense of the Almighty creator: by fighting against the Jews, I am doing the Lord's work" (Hitler, 1933, p. 25).

Authority systems, disobedience, and you

Milgram's subjects did not learn obedience to authority in the psychology laboratory. The research described here merely demonstrates the extent to which we all have been taught "the obedience lesson" in many socializing environments: "Do as you're told and there won't be any trouble." "Sit still and don't complain." "Don't talk back."

Obedience must exist at some optimal level in society if the best interests of all are to be met. The danger arises when we let the values prescribed by the situation replace our individual values.

Authority relations do not always involve only a leader and a follower. *Authority systems* emerge when people transfer or delegate the rights over their actions to agents of the primary authority or to an organization. An authority system exists when we pledge allegiance to a nation-state and thereby to all its government officials, or when we are employed by a corporation with its hierarchy of authorities.

Consider the statements made by the bombardier who released the first atomic bomb over Hiroshima. He was not told what his "pay load" was, but from the special preparations he "put two and two together and figured it was radioactive." "I'd flown so many missions by then that it was mostly a job to do." The power of authority systems over individuals as well as the naive belief in dispositional control even when faced with overwhelming evidence of situational control is loud and clear in the bombardier's self-analysis 25 years later:

Send Your Child to Disobedience School

Sarah McCarthy, a former public school teacher, believes that Milgram's results reflect the intense training for uncritical obedience that takes place daily in our schools, churches, and throughout society. Her concern is not, as is so often the case, with getting Johnny to be more compliant, but rather with why Johnny can't disobey when disobedience is called for.

"Along with worrying about the S.A.T. scores and whether or not Johnny can read, we must begin to question seriously whether Johnny is capable of disobedience . . . . We must stop equating sanity with conformity, eccentricity with craziness, and normalcy with number. We must get in touch with our own liberating ludicrousness, and practice being harmlessly deviant. . . .

"It seems that the best armor is the rational mind. We must insist that all authorities account for themselves, and we need to be as wary of false prophets as we are of false advertising. Leaders, political and spiritual, must be subjected to intense scrutiny, and we must insist that their thought processes and proclamations measure up to reasonable standards of rational thought. Above all, we must become skilled in activating our inner resources toward rebellion and disobedience, when this seems reasonable. . . .

" . . . Little notice is taken of the legions of overly obedient children in the schools; yet, for every overly disobedient child, there are probably twenty who are obeying too much. There is little motivation to encourage the unsqueaky wheels to develop as noisy, creative, independent thinkers who may become bold enough to disagree. Conceivably, we could administer modified Milgram obedience tests in the schools which detect hyperobedience, just as we test for intelligence, visual function, vocational attributes and tuberculosis. When a child is found to be too obedient, the schools should mobilize against this psychological crippler with the zeal by which they would react to an epidemic of smallpox. In alcoholism and other mental disturbances, the first major step toward a reversal of the pathology is recognition of the severity of the problem. Obedience should be added to the list of emotional disturbances requiring therapy. Disobedience schools should be at least as common as military schools and reform schools" (McCarthy, 1979, p. 34).

This same theme was echoed in recent congressional testimony by an F.B.I. agent working on cases of sexual molestation of children (of which nearly 75,000 were reported in a one-year period). This investigator called for education programs that teach children "they have the right to say no" to adults. On the basis of his experience, children become more vulnerable to adult child molesters because they have overlearned the lesson of blindly obeying authority figures (United Press, 4/12/84).

How does all this apply to you? What can you, as an adult, do to resist being obedient to unjust authority or to unjust demands of just authority? These suggestions may help:

"I don't believe in everything we do, but if I'm in the military, I've got to support the government. I may not agree, but if ordered I'll sure do it. I think everyone has enough sense never to use the bomb again" (*Newsweek*, August 10, 1970).

Are *you* that certain no one will ever order *you* to press THE button, and would you or wouldn't you press it?

What are your alternatives when you are in an authority system you consider unjust or when a just authority asks you to do something you consider wrong? You have five options (Fireman et al., 1978): (a) *comply*—carry out the orders; (b) *evade*—avoid confrontation with the authority by giving the appearance of complying but secretly not doing so; (c) *dissent*—publicly express doubts and disapproval but follow the order; (d) *resist or disobey*—openly refuse to follow orders by breaking out of role constraints

1. Don't let others define the situation for you without your questioning the premises, methods, and ends. For example, why was the "teacher" even necessary in the Milgram study; why couldn't the experimenter give the shocks if the true purpose was to study learning and not the "teacher's" reaction?
2. Be sensitive to small, initial, trivial steps that can escalate into big commitments; don't let the little foot in the door.
3. Separate the message from the communicator's characteristics so that you will evaluate what is said without the biasing influence of the age, position, sex, dress, title of the authority.
4. Remember you are not the role you play in various life dramas; be prepared to step out of it and evaluate what you are doing from other perspectives, especially that of a critic.
5. Be able to admit you made a mistake, were wrong, so you do not have to continue to do the unacceptable deed just to be consistent.
6. When in doubt, never make action-decisions in the influence situation; don't sign on the dotted line, take a time out to reflect and to check with independent sources.
7. Remember the fundamental attribution error and reverse it in order to better evaluate how you might be operating a mental vehicle under the influence of social control intoxicants (see also Andersen & Zimbardo, 1980; Sabini & Silver, 1983).

altogether; (e) *struggle*—mobilize resources to challenge the injustice even beyond your personal encounter—by asking "higher authorities" to intervene, or by organizing other people to take some form of collective rebellion. For a further look at how to resist obedience to unjust authority, see the **Close-up** above.

HUMAN AGGRESSION AND VIOLENCE

Aggression can be defined as physical or verbal behavior with the intent to injure or destroy. We have daily reminders of its prevalance in our society and world. Each year in the United States, about 6 percent of the nation's households have at least one member who is the victim of a violent crime—that is about five million people (U.S. Department of Justice Bulletin, June 1983). We get a frightening reminder of our own vulnerability with the daily diet of violent lead stories in the morning papers and in the evening TV news. Yet, paradoxically, Americans as a nation seem to be fascinated by violence as evidenced by the popularity of violent themes in cartoons, movies, and on TV. **Violence** is aggression in its most extreme and socially unacceptable form. It may be directed against people or property and usually is an expression of hostility and rage.

Research evidence on aggression has been drawn from a wide variety of sources, including physiological studies, clinical observations, and studies of aggressive interactions in both the laboratory and the "real world." In this section we will review several theories that have been proposed to account for aggressiveness: aggression as an inborn part of human nature or caused by physiological mechanisms, aggression as a response to frustration, aggression as simply an impulsive response to external stimuli, and aggression as socially learned.

Aggression as inborn

In his famous essay "Leviathan," Hobbes argued that people are naturally selfish, brutal, and cruel toward other people. He expressed this concept by the phrase *Homo homini lupus*—"Man is [like] a wolf to [his fellow] man." Although the wolf is unjustly maligned by this phrase (wolves are actually quite gentle with others of their own species), it expresses a common belief that human beings are instinctively aggressive animals. Freud thought so, and so do others who believe in the "animal instinct" side of human nature.

Freud's death instinct and catharsis. As we have seen, Freud believed that from the moment of birth a person possesses two opposing instincts: a life instinct *(Eros),* which provides energy for growth and survival, and a death instinct *(Thanatos),* which works toward the individual's self-destruction. He believed that the death instinct is often redirected outward against the external world in the form of aggression toward others.

According to Freud, energy for the death instinct is constantly being generated within the body. Freud visualized this energy as being like water accumulating in a reservoir. If it is not released in small amounts and in socially acceptable ways, it will accumulate and eventually spill over in some extreme and socially unacceptable form.

One safe way of draining off this energy is **catharsis** (a Greek word meaning purification or cleansing). In catharsis, emotions are expressed in their full intensity through crying, words, symbolic means, or other direct acts. Aristotle first used this concept to explain the way in which good drama first builds up and then purges feelings of intense emotion in the audience. As we saw in Chapter 15, catharsis is an important part of psychoanalytic therapy.

Some experimental support for Freud's hypothesis of aggressive energy and catharsis is found in a study by Robert Sears (1961).

Male children high in aggressiveness at age 5 were also high at age 12, some still overtly and antisocially. The others, however, showed low *antisocial* aggression, but high *prosocial* aggression (aggression for socially acceptable purposes, such as law enforcement or punishing others for rule-breaking). This second group also showed more *self-aggression* than did the boys who were still highly antisocial aggressors. Furthermore, the prosocial aggressors were more anxious and fearful of antisocial aggression than the antisocial aggressors.

Sears interpreted his findings as indicating that the same inner aggressive energy was simply finding different forms of expression.

In spite of some supporting evidence, however, Freud's theory has been criticized by psychologists for failing to specify any factors that could be used to *predict* either the occurrence of aggression or the direction or form it will take. It has a lovely literary, after-the-fact, descriptive quality but little scientific utility for predicting or controlling behavior. Indeed, in his later writings Freud himself abandoned reliance on this death instinct, although others have continued to incorporate some version of it into their conception of human nature.

The aggressive instinct. Another theory stressing the innateness of aggression is that of ethologist Konrad Lorenz (1966). On the basis of studies of animals, Lorenz argues that aggression is a spontaneous, innate readiness to fight, which is critical for an organism's survival. In most species, however, aggressiveness between individuals rarely involves actual injury or death because one animal will eventually "signal" appeasement or submission. According to Lorenz, human beings have somehow lost this pacification strategy for inhibiting aggression while retaining the instinct to aggress, and thus have become killers of their own kind.

Ardrey (1966) goes beyond Lorenz to argue that aggression results from **territoriality,** which is an innate drive to gain and defend property—the "territorial imperative." Animals of some species mark off their living area by various means, such as urination. Other members of the species then respond to these territorial markers by withdrawing from the area. If they do not, they risk aggressive confrontation with the owner.

Evidence for this instinct-based theory is not clearcut. Not all species display territorial behavior (Crook, 1973). And animals' responses to "appeasement gestures" are in fact quite variable, much as with humans (Barnett, 1967). Moreover, many instances of within-species killing among animals have been observed (E. Wilson, 1973). While territorial issues may well be the reason for some human conflicts, there is no need to assume that all aggression derives from an innate drive rather than from learned needs for power and security.

Physiological bases of aggression

In the summer of 1966, Charles Whitman killed his wife and mother, and then climbed to the top of a tower at the University of Texas. Armed with a high-powered hunting rifle equipped with a telescopic sight, he shot thirty-eight people, killing fourteen, before he himself was gunned down. A postmortem examination of Whitman's brain revealed a malignant tumor the size of a walnut in the area of the amygdala (Sweet et al., 1969).

The *amygdala* (part of the limbic system) was mentioned in Chapter 3 as being involved in aggressive behavior. Recall also the pattern of aggressive behavior in Keith (Chapter 8), whose pituitary tumor activated a hormonal imbalance. Brain disease of the limbic system or temporal lobe has sometimes been found in persons exhibiting a *dyscontrol syndrome,* characterized by senseless brutality, pathological intoxication, sexual assault, or repeated serious automobile accidents.

In both humans and animals, males appear to be more aggressive than females—a fact apparently due in part to the early influence of sex hormones on the brain. Female animals that have been injected with male sex hormones often display increased aggressive behavior (Edwards, 1971).

Some years ago, progestins (steroid hormones) were given to many women to prevent miscarriages. It turned out that both males and females exposed as fetuses to small amounts of these hormones showed a significantly higher potential for physical aggression than their unexposed siblings (see **Figure 17.4**). About ten million people in our country, alive today, were exposed to these drugs during the critical period of their development (Reinisch, 1981).

Although hormones have a direct influence on behavior in animals, they appear to work indirectly with humans, in whom personality factors are added to the behavioral tendencies. In humans the relationship between any physiological factors and aggression is far more complex than in other species because of the greater importance of learning and experience in the direction and control of human behavior (Moyer, 1976).

Researchers are discovering a number of different neurotransmitters that play a role in the expression of aggression. For example, intermale aggression in animals is higher when their level of catecholamines is high, but it is lower when serotonin level is high. The physiological regulation of aggression clearly involves a complex interaction of neurochemical and neuroendocrine systems (Whalen & Simon, 1984).

The frustration-aggression hypothesis

Almost twenty years after Freud proposed the existence of a death instinct, a group of academic psychologists at Yale University formally presented an alternative view of aggression called the *frustration-aggression hypothesis* (Dollard et al., 1939). Their hypothesis was that aggression was a drive acquired in response to frustration. **Frustration** was defined as the natural and inevitable condition that exists when an ongoing response toward a goal is blocked. The greater the present and accumulated frustration, the stronger the resulting aggressive response.

It soon became obvious, however, that not every act of aggression is preceded by frustration and that not every frustration results in aggression. The original frustration-aggression hypothesis was revised to state that every frustration produces an *instigation* to aggression, but that this instigation may be too weak to elicit actual aggressive behavior (N. Miller, 1941). These theorists agreed with Freud that the aggressive drive would increase if not expressed (if frustration continued). However, they saw the origin of aggressive behavior in *external* factors (accumulated frustrating situations), rather than in an aggressive "in-

▷ **Figure 17.4**

This bar graph shows the effect of exposure to progestins during fetal life for both males and females, and also the characteristically higher aggression scores for males both with and without this exposure. (Adapted from Reinisch, 1981.)

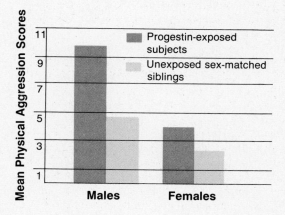

stinct.'' Recently, it has been recognized that the person's *perception* of how aversive the frustration is also helps to determine what response is made (Berkowitz, 1982).

When frustration occurs, the first and strongest aggressive impulse is toward the source of the frustration. If a child wants a piece of candy, but is prevented from having it by the parent, the child is most strongly motivated to be aggressive toward the parent. But because of the threat of punishment, such aggression may be inhibited and instead displaced onto a safer target, perhaps a younger sibling or the family pet. Other favorite targets of displaced aggression are minorities, children, and women, who are already in vulnerable positions and thus are not likely to retaliate. Displacing anger and aggression onto members of less powerful groups who are not responsible for the aggressor's frustration is called **scapegoating**.

According to the frustration-aggression hypothesis, the less similar the target is to the source of frustration, the weaker is the displaced aggression and the less complete the cathartic effect. Some research has suggested, however, that displaced aggression can be as strong as aggression directed at the source of frustration, and that it can reduce subsequent tendencies toward aggressive behavior (Konečni & Doob, 1972). Frustration is most likely to lead to aggression when aggressing has *instrumental value* in modifying the frustration (Buss, 1971).

Aggression as provoked readiness

A revision of the frustration-aggression hypothesis proposes an interaction between emotional states and environmental cues. Leonard Berkowitz (1982) maintains that frustration creates a *readiness* for aggressive acts, as does being previously reinforced for acting aggressively. But whether this readiness gets translated into overt aggression depends on the presence of a second factor—stimulus cues in the environment that are associated with aggression. For example, the presence of a weapon appears to serve as a *cue* that has been previously associated with the emotion of anger.

Berkowitz believes that much aggression is not planned or anticipated, but erupts impulsively in response to provocative environmental stimuli. Aggres-

sion may also be stimulated by events or conditions in the environment that arouse intense sexual or hostile emotions or that have aggressive elements (seeing a prize-fight, war movie, or international soccer match).

Interpersonal violence is rarely a case of one person acting aggressively and the other being totally passive. More typically, both people are involved in an escalating interaction.

One analysis of 344 arrest reports found that in the cases where violent incidents occurred, *both* parties were reacting to what they perceived as threats against their integrity and self-esteem. Often the encounter began with an officer's request for information or identification or an order to ''move on,'' ''break it up.'' In 60 percent of the episodes, the civilian reacted negatively to the officer's approach and failed to cooperate, perceiving the request as unwarranted or discourteous or as an expression of personal hostility. The officer viewed this uncooperativeness as irrational, disrespectful, and perhaps concealing criminal activity. A chain of events was then set off in which both parties contributed to the spiraling potential for violence (Toch, 1969).

Aggression as socially learned

Another answer to the ''why'' of aggression is that it is learned just like many other kinds of behavior, through experience with rewards, punishments, models, and social norms. Albert Bandura (1973) is the leading proponent of this view of the socially learned basis of human aggression.

Consequences, learned or anticipated. According to social learning theory, any kind of aversive experience (not only frustration) produces a general state of emotional arousal. This arousal can then lead to a number of different behaviors, depending on the individual's prior learning history. People whose aggression has been rewarded in the past may become aggressive; others may withdraw, turn to others for help, or engage in constructive problem solving, depending on what has worked for them in the past.

Aggression, like other responses, can also occur in the absence of emotional arousal if the individual feels that it will lead to some desired outcome (as when a child hits a younger one in order to get a toy). But boys who have been reinforced for aggres-

△ | *Children in wartorn countries such as Lebanon are surrounded from a very early age by models of aggression.*

sive responses in one situation tend to respond aggressively in other situations even when no rewards are provided (Horton, 1970).

Models and norms. Aggression can also be learned by watching others behaving aggressively. As we saw in Chapter 7, nursery-school children who watched adults or filmed models hitting, kicking, and punching a large inflated balloon doll later performed these actions themselves (Bandura et al., 1963).

In a subsequent study, children performed fewer imitative aggressive acts when they saw the model being punished. Later, however, when the experimenter offered each child a prize for doing just what the model had done, all the children readily performed the actions they had seen. Evidently the aggressive act had been learned plus the knowledge that such acts were inappropriate in the original situation. When the payoff was changed, the act was performed (Bandura, 1965).

Other research has shown that children who are emotionally aroused (as when they are participating in competitive games) are more likely to imitate a model's behavior whether the model is displaying aggressive or nonaggressive behavior (Christy et al., 1971).

The social group and broader culture too can encourage violent behavior. If the person's community or reference groups provide aggressive models and give approval and prestige for violent acts, individuals—especially young ones—are likely to feel under pressure to conform to the aggressive norm.

These same pressures may affect aggression indirectly through group pressure to use alcohol or other drugs. A study using American students as subjects found opposite effects for alcohol and marijuana.

Research on the relationship of alcohol and marijuana to aggression (shocks delivered in a competition against a partner) revealed that the two substances had opposite effects. As the dose of alcohol was increased (from .5 to 1.5 ounces per 40 pounds of body weight) the amount of aggression more than doubled. But larger doses of marijuana decreased the amount of shock administered to the other person (Taylor et al., 1976). See **Figure 17.5.**

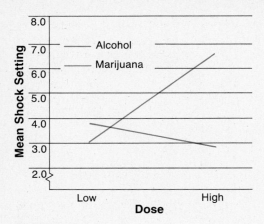

△ **Figure 17.5**

Mean shock setting as a function of high and low doses of alcohol and marijuana. Increasing the amount of alcohol in the system leads to greater aggression in the laboratory setting, while marijuana tends to have the opposite effect. (Adapted from S. P. Taylor et al., 1976.)

Does catharsis reduce aggression? Freud predicted that *catharsis*—expression of aggressive impulses by talking, actions, or vicariously experiencing others acting out aggressive impulses—would lessen aggressiveness by releasing pent-up energy safely. Social learning theory makes the opposite prediction: that expressing aggressive impulses or watching aggressiveness in others will *increase* the probability of future aggression. Which view does research support?

Support for the social learning hypothesis comes from studies which show that aggression increases after exposure to aggressive models. In addition, studies have demonstrated that expressing aggressive feelings in a permissive setting maintains the feelings at their original level, instead of reducing them.

Subjects were exposed to an anger-arousing antagonist; then half of them were allowed to express their anger and hostility to a sympathetic interviewer. The other subjects did not have such an interview but merely sat for a while. Later, subjects who had experienced the cathartic interview disliked the antagonist even more (rather than less) and remained more physiologically aroused than the control subjects (Kahn, 1966).

These results suggest that therapies encouraging the person to express or act out aggressive feelings for cathartic purposes may have an effect opposite to that intended.

Such findings seem to run counter to the common-sense notion that it is good to "let off steam" and "get it all off one's chest." It may help us to understand this contradiction if we make a distinction between *expressing emotional feelings* and *acting aggressively or watching aggressive actions*. Giving vent to your feelings (as in crying, laughing, or talking to others) may make you feel better or relieve your anxiety. However, *expressing aggression* against your enemy, verbally or in overt action, directly or vicariously, is *not* likely to reduce your tendency toward aggression. Learning how to negotiate conflicts verbally, however, can reduce the need for physical aggression against others.

TV violence: Catharsis or release? Anyone who watches television in the United States is very likely to see both drama and comedy episodes in which people are killed or injured in a wide variety of ingenious ways, cartoons with lovable but sadistic characters, and news programs with on-the-spot coverage of wars, assassinations, riots, and "crime in the streets." If children engage in aggressive actions after watching aggressive models for a few minutes in the laboratory, what do they learn from their extended consumption of violence on TV? Given their estimated viewing time of between twenty and forty-five hours per week, their view of social reality becomes a very negative one, according to one documented analysis (Gerbner, 1981).

From portrayals of violence on TV children learn that violence is frequent, rewarded, thought to be justified, clean, fun, imaginative, and more appropriate for males than females. They also come to exaggerate the real threat of violence in their daily lives—which, in turn, makes them fearful and suspicious of strangers. A national survey of American children between the ages of 7 and 11 indicates that the heavy TV viewers report more fears than the light viewers "that somebody bad might get into your house" or that "when you go outside somebody might hurt you" (Peterson & Zill, 1981).

Well-designed psychological studies suggest a clear link between seeing and doing.

One large-scale, ten-year, longitudinal study of children showed that preferences for violent TV programs in the third grade were correlated significantly with aggressive behavior in the thirteenth grade. The reverse was not true: children's early aggressiveness was not related to a later preference for watching violent TV (Eron et al., 1972).

Although there have been some studies claiming that media violence is cathartic and decreases children's tendencies toward overt aggression, major methodological flaws have reduced their credibility. Better controlled research has supported the opposite conclusion: boys who view movie violence become *more* aggressive than boys who are similar in other ways but see nonviolent films (Parke et al., 1977).

Not only are children more prone to act aggressively after viewing violence, but they become more tolerant of aggressive behavior in others. They are less likely to take responsible action and intervene, for example, in a fight between two younger children (Drabman & Thomas, 1974). Similar effects have been found in studies of the results of television viewing among adults (Gorney, 1976).

U.S. Surgeon General Everett Koop has interpreted the body of available research as providing a strong link between viewing television violence and the epidemic of violent behavior in our country. He argues further that a nation's political and social health is endangered "whenever any of our citizens feel unjustly threatened and withdraw in fear from casual human contact" (United Press, quoted in *San Francisco Chronicle,* February 6, 1984, p. 39).

Seeing violence routinely, often combined with humor, also has a "psychic numbing" effect, a dulling of both sensitivity to and moral outrage at real-life violence. One of the strongest counterforces to aggression is being part of a community that cares about others who are being victimized. Anything that reduces this concern and compassion indirectly contributes to violence.

The violence of pornography

The number of reported forcible rapes in the United States nearly doubled in the last decade. In 1982 nearly 78,000 women were raped—about one every seven minutes (*Statistical Abstracts,* 1984). This social problem has many causes, but some researchers believe that exposure to pornography contributes to the violence of men against women. *Erotic* films are explicit portrayals of passionate love and sexual activities. By contrast, *pornographic* films present images of violence and dehumanization as sexual entertainment. What is the evidence social psychologists have collected that popular pornography is implicated in aggressive reactions toward women?

The typical research paradigm involves college students viewing films with content that is either neutral, nonaggressive-erotic, or aggressive-erotic. Afterwards they are given an opportunity to engage in aggressive behavior and to report their feelings

and beliefs about rape and other issues (e.g., Malamuth & Donnerstein, 1982; Donnerstein, 1983).

Several consistent patterns of results emerge from such experiments. First, men are sexually aroused by aggressive-erotic films, become more accepting of rape myths such as ("women really want to be sexually dominated"), and even admit to the greater possibility of committing rape themselves. In addition, viewing sexual violence can increase the amount of aggression subsequently displayed toward women. Men paired with a male partner administered a somewhat higher level of shock after either the erotic or the aggressive-erotic film than after a neutral film. However, those paired with a female partner administered no higher shock after the non-aggressive-erotic film but a very much higher level of shock following the aggressive-erotic one, as shown in **Figure 17.6** (Donnerstein, 1980).

Despite this and other accumulating evidence that pornography fosters both general downgrading of women and specific tendencies toward violence against them, the right to exhibit such propaganda is a constitutionally guaranteed freedom in our country. Therein lies a major social and political problem—beyond the scope of psychologists except through their continued concern for documenting the destructive mental and behavioral effects of pornography.

▽ **Figure 17.6** *Pornography and Aggression*

Aggression was higher following aggressive-erotic films than following either neutral or nonaggressive-erotic films but only by men against women, not against other men. (Adapted from Donnerstein, 1980.)

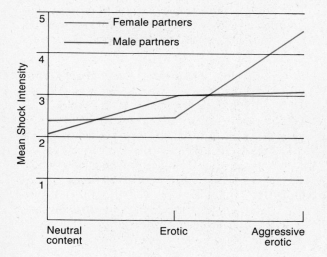

PSYCHOLOGY BEYOND THE INDIVIDUAL

The social problems presented in this chapter and the suggestions for dealing with them move us a long way beyond the traditional view of psychology as the study of individual actions and mental processes. We become aware of the person as but one level in a complex system that includes social groups, institutions, cultural values, historical circumstances, political and economic realities, and specific situational forces. Modern social psychologists have expanded the domain of their inquiry to include this broader network of interacting elements. Many new areas of application have opened up to both the curious investigator and the social change agent (see Fisher, 1982).

Psychological knowledge is being put to use in many different areas, holding the potential for enriching all concerned. In addition, this expansion of psychology's relevance to life problems provides greater opportunities and challenges to psychologists just beginning their professional careers (perhaps *you* in the near future?)

Among the new liaisons are: psychology and law; psychology and education; psychology and health care; psychology and politics (international relations, terrorism, conflict, public policy); psychology and the consumer; psychology and business; and a field of growing importance, the union of psychology and environmental issues. In this final phase of our journey, we will briefly examine a selection of these areas of application (see Oskamp, 1984). But first, let's consider the general problem of social dilemmas.

Social dilemmas

Social dilemmas are defined as choice situations with two properties: (a) the immediate social payoff to each person is higher for defecting from the social good than it is for cooperating, and (b) all individuals would be better off in the long run if they all cooperated than if some or all defect (Dawes, 1980).

Our interdependence on each other and on our shared environment becomes evident when we consider several social dilemmas facing us. Modern technology (industrial and medical) has wiped out many of the traditional checks on energy use, pollution, and population growth. We are using energy faster than it can be replenished, polluting the land, sea, and air, and overpopulating the earth. Many believe we are approaching the limits of the "carrying capacity" of "spaceship earth" (Hardin, 1976). Yet new global burdens are added daily because in most places it is to the apparent advantage of *each individual* to use more energy, to pollute more, and to have as many children as possible.

Turning down your thermostat makes you cold and saves only a small amount of energy. Not driving during a smog alert is an inconvenience to you and your car's exhaust makes only a minor contribution to pollution. Voluntarily restraining your demands for a wage increase you deserve has little effect on inflation but is a big sacrifice to you. For poor parents in many parts of the world, having many children helps ensure that some will survive to adulthood and provide security for their old age. It is obvious that what is best for each individual in the short run is worst for them collectively.

Tragedies and traps. A classic example of such a social dilemma was described by Garrett Hardin (1968). He drew an analogy between the problems of herdsmen sharing a common pasture and the problems involved in sharing our earth's limited resources. Each herdsman gains by adding one more animal to his herd and the loss to the land seems minimal. So each rational herdsman adds to his herd, but soon the common area is overgrazed. The result is the *tragedy of the commons.* "Each man is locked into a system that compels him to increase his herd without limit—in a world that is limited. Ruin is the destination toward which all men rush, each pursuing his own best interest in a society that believes in the freedom of the commons" (Hardin, 1968, p. 1244). The tragedy of the commons is an example of a *social trap,* a situation in which either choice will bring unacceptable results.

Our society offers many other examples of social traps. The use of pesticides and nitrates in farming increases crop yields but endangers nearby water supplies; communities that become economically dependent on the larger yields find that they must choose between economic collapse and serious health problems. Neither choice is acceptable. In a similar way, asbestos and X-rays have solved some problems but created others. In the arms race, too,

△ | *The demands of an industrialized society are often in conflict with our children's need for a healthful and pollution-free environment.*

building more powerful nuclear weapons can have the immediate effect of making us feel safer. But the long-term threat of nuclear war increases as both sides develop more and bigger weapons of destruction and neither one dares stop.

Survival of the cooperators. What can you do when you find yourself in a social dilemma? Is there any solution? Laboratory studies are not encouraging.

In one ingenious study where an overfishing situation was simulated, the researcher explained carefully just what the "sustainable yield" was—how fast the pool would be replenished with more "fish." In addition, subjects were permitted to discuss the situation as they "fished." Yet in every case they took from the supply too fast and it ran out (Brechner et al., 1975).

As a victim in a social trap, it would appear that your only hope is to remove yourself from it or else work to restructure it and change the choices it offers. Sometimes you *can* remove yourself by moving away or changing to a new job. Many individuals are trying to lessen their own dependence on oil and other nonrenewable resources by adopting a simpler life style. But society as a whole has found no such escape.

Three ways that restructuring of a situation could come about have been identified:

1. In situations like overfishing, where people are dependent on limited resources, they can sometimes agree to be bound by quotas and can set up mechanisms for enforcing the decisions they make together. Binding decisions and enforceability are needed if the choice of taking too much is to be eliminated. However, reaching such an agreement becomes more difficult as total available resources fall below the amount needed by individuals or nations.

2. In traps like the arms race, it may take a third party or a superordinate power to change the ground rules and set up a new system that offers the security nations are seeking but not achieving through armaments. As long as nations have no better means of defense, they are unlikely to agree voluntarily to give up their armies or their freedom to arm.

3. Some restructuring also occurs in the normal course of events. Systems try to maintain their equilibrium and resist change, but are always vulnerable to change resulting from shifts either in their component parts or in their environments. For example, the discovery of new chemicals or new farming methods or a shift in economic relationships could give farmers new choices (see Platt, 1973).

Research using dilemma games (where the strategy which seems best for each player at the time actually results in loss for all) suggests two possibilities for resolving social dilemmas in noncoercive ways.

1. *Change the payoffs* to encourage cooperation. This can be accomplished by rewarding altruistic behavior, encouraging people to follow social norms, and appealing to the need to obey dictates of conscience.

2. *Increase knowledge.* Better understanding of the situation and the potential payoffs may yield greater cooperation. If so, then increasing the salience and availability of that information should be beneficial for the group. Two of the techniques for doing this are: (a) increasing communication among participants (especially if participants expect everyone to follow through on agreements made), and (b) publicly disclosing acts of both defection and cooperation (Dawes, 1980).

The substance of these strategies may be found in three tried and tested ingredients—*knowledge* of the situation and the consequences, a personal sense of *morality,* and *trust* in the shared good sense of one's neighbors. But there also needs to be some assurance that cooperation will be rewarded. And psychologists need to contribute more of what they have learned from experimental studies of judgment and decision making to develop procedures for helping people make these socially relevant decisions (Pitz & Sachs, 1984).

Areas of application

Three areas in which psychological knowledge is now being applied to the study of social problems are psychology and law, psychology and education, and environmental psychology.

Psychology and law. Psychologists are applying their knowledge to—and learning much that is new from—the areas of law and criminal justice. How are people *socialized* to become law-abiding or law-breaking citizens? When a suspect is caught, what social-psychological aspects of the *judicial process* lead toward a decision of guilt or innocence? Eyewitness identification, police interrogation, plea bargaining, jury selection, and decision-making are but some of the aspects of the judicial process that are of interest to psychologists (Ellsworth & Getman, 1981; Konečni & Ebbesen, 1982). The penal system, deal-

▽ *The prison system is one of many social problem areas in which psychologists are becoming increasingly involved.*

ing with those convicted of crimes, raises additional psychological questions (Haney, 1980). Should the purpose of imprisonment be rehabilitation or punishment? How should the prison system be structured to accomplish either of these aims best? Justice may be better served by developing a sound interface between psychology and law (see Monahan & Loftus, 1982; Toch, 1979).

Psychology and education. Much that occurs in the educational process involves the psychology of the classroom. Peer interactions, teacher-student relationships, and the expectations of both teachers and students affect how much learning takes place as well as how students feel about the learning process. The student as learner responds to the ecology of the classroom, to pressures toward competition, to curriculum design, to educational technology, and to the school's organizational goals and strategies. So psychology's contributions to education should go well beyond a concern for simply reinforcing correct responding and improving basic skills (see Glaser, 1984).

One of the new discoveries that can be carried into the classroom is the finding that different principles seem to apply to five different kinds of learning outcomes: intellectual skills (procedural knowledge), verbal information (declarative knowledge), cognitive strategies, motor skills, and attitudes (Gagné, 1984). The next step is to carry out systematic studies of the procedures that can best foster these five kinds of outcomes in natural settings. Another current focus of research is how the new technologies represented by microcomputers and the instant feedback of videogames can be incorporated into the instructional process (Malone & Lepper, in press).

Psychologists are well aware of the importance of the classroom climate for educating the whole person; social, cognitive, and developmental psychologists are all working on ways to develop better classroom climates (Bar-Tal & Saxe, 1978). Too often, the school environment fosters interpersonal competition and provides a breeding ground for envy, jealousy, hostility, and self-derogation.

Elliot Aronson and his colleagues (1978) reasoned that by creating conditions in which students must depend on one another for learning the required material, teachers would be able to overcome some of the unnecessary conflicts that often exist in classrooms.

Working with fifth-graders, they developed a "jigsaw" technique for promoting cooperation in which each pupil is given part of the total material to master and then share with other group members. Performance is evaluated on the basis of the overall group presentation. Thus every member's contribution is essential and valued. Pupils are made to feel like team workers rather than competitors, and those in desegregated settings discover the advantages of sharing knowledge (and friendship) with "equal and interdependent" peers—regardless of race, creed, or sex.

This method of changing classroom climate has been put into practice in a number of schools. Positive results have been found for improved student and teacher morale as well as for a better level of academic performance. In addition, interracial conflict has decreased in classes where jig-sawing united formerly hostile students in a "common fate" (Gonzales, 1983).

Another school problem for which psychologists are contributing solutions is that of vandalism. Hundreds of millions of dollars are spent annually to repair the damage done to our schools by "vandals." Efforts aimed at identifying and punishing these elusive destroyers of public property have not lessened the problem.

Working on the assumption that school vandalism is a symptom of student dissatisfaction with the school, a team of psychologists set out to transform those negative feelings into positive ones. They trained teachers in 18 different schools to use praise and positive reinforcement for appropriate behavior in place of their ordinarily more frequent use of punishment and ridicule for unacceptable behavior. As the teachers began to accentuate the positive, the students started to eliminate the negative. Hitting, throwing objects, not paying attention and not doing assigned projects declined. Teachers were happier and so were more students. This improved atmosphere carried over into other classrooms where the teachers had not received special reinforcement training. But what effect did all these good vibrations have on vandalism? Over a three year period, school costs due to vandalism decreased by 75 percent (Mayer et al., 1983).

Environmental psychology. Systematic study of the effects of the larger environment on behavior (as opposed to specific stimuli) began in the 1950s with studies of behavior in psychiatric wards, where different physical arrangements seemed to produce different behavior on the part of the patients. Such studies have led to the new field of *environmental psychology* (Proshansky, 1976). Environmental psychologists study the relationships between psychological processes and physical environments, both natural and humanmade.

Environmental psychologists use an *ecological approach* to study how people and environments affect each other. The ecological approach emphasizes the reciprocity and mutual influence in the organism-environment relationship. Organism and environment influence each other, and both keep changing as a result. We see a circular pattern; humans change the natural environment and create physical and social structures. These, in turn, confine, direct, and change us, encouraging certain behaviors, while discouraging or preventing others, often in unanticipated ways.

Environmental psychology is oriented not so much toward past determinants as toward the future that is being created. This means, in turn, that it has to be concerned with *values.* Some environments are more nourishing for us than others, and some uses of the environment, as we have discovered, are destructive. This new psychology is concerned with identifying what makes environments supportive and what human behaviors will create those environments—while not trespassing on the health of the ecosystem that makes life possible in the first place (see Russell & Ward, 1982).

There is ample evidence of the influence of physical design on psychological activities and processes. Different physical arrangements have been studied in hospital settings, work places, homes, and whole cities. Different moods, self-images, and overt behaviors are consistently found to be related to these physical differences.

The way space is partitioned can help bring people together or isolate them. The type of windows in an apartment house can encourage residents to look out at activities on their streets and "keep an eye on the neighborhood" or, if they are small and high, can cut off such "people watching." An architect can design space to appeal to snobbery, to invite informality, or to induce confusion (Altman, 1976).

Can we make our cities more livable? What features of the environment encourage vandalism and crime? Does crowding cause physical and social pathology? What is the impact of uncontrollable levels of noise in the workplace or the home? Can psychological knowledge contribute to energy-conservation programs? These are among the intriguing questions being studied by environmental psychologists. By reformulating massive social issues into smaller, less overwhelming problems, social psychologists are beginning to get small wins that can add up to big victories (Weick, 1984).

There are a host of other examples we might cite of psychology for the good of people and society—going all the way from new approaches to controlling hypertension to antilitter research projects and citizen training in crime prevention through re-creating a sense of community values. Some psychologists are at work trying to elevate the level of moral functioning of prison guards and inmates, while others are studying the elements that will contribute to a sense of perceived control among otherwise hopeless institutionalized people. Some are trying to discover means of overcoming feelings of shyness and loneliness, while their colleagues strive to uncover the basis for lasting commitments and affectional bonds. This is a psychology quite different from that envisioned by Wilhelm Wundt in his little brass-instrument laboratory in Leipzig a hundred years ago. But we are witnessing a curious merger of the scientific search for knowledge, regularity, and order and the humanistic quest for understanding, acceptance, and personal fulfillment. There is no reason why modern psychology cannot do both.

SUMMARY

■ The same perceptual, cognitive, motor, and other potentials that enable us to create, solve problems, and relate constructively to each other also enable us to destroy and cause pain to ourselves and others. We all have potentials for both prosocial and antisocial behavior.

■ Aggression and other antisocial behavior increase under conditions of deindividuation and anonymity. Deindividuation lowers an individual's inhibitions against both antisocial behavior and emotional expression. Social groups that suffer long-lasting feelings of deindividuation become alienated from the mainstream of the society and a danger to themselves and the society.

■ Dehumanization may be socially imposed by those in political or economic power, or it may be imposed by individuals or groups in self-defense, for self-gratification, or as a means to an end. It is made easier by intellectualization and relabeling.

■ We tend to believe that atrocities are the work of evil people, failing to realize the power of the social situation and the strength of our habit of obedience. Milgram's research demonstrated that most people will obey a recognized authority despite the belief that they are causing suffering and perhaps death to another person; they may dissent, but most will not disobey.

■ Obedience is fostered by the presence of a trusted authority, a relationship in which one is in a subordinate position, the presence of social norms supporting it, and redefinition of the evil acts as good. Five possible responses to unjust orders are compliance, evasion, dissent, resistance, or struggle to change the injustice.

■ Among those who have seen aggression as inborn have been Freud, who saw it as instinctive, with catharsis as necessary to release pent-up aggressive feelings; and ethologists, who argue that the territoriality observed in animals is the basis for human aggression. Physiological psychologists cite the effects of tumors and other brain events in producing aggressive behavior.

■ Aggression has also been seen as a natural response to frustration, though in some cases practical realities prevent overt aggression or lead to displacement of the aggression onto other targets that cannot retaliate. Cues in the situation, combined with an inner readiness to be aggressive, have been seen by some as playing an important role.

■ Aggressive behavior may be learned through reinforcement, social norms, or imitation of the aggressive behavior of others. Though catharsis—expression of emotional feelings—may lessen such feelings, expressing aggressive impulses or watching aggressive behavior in others increases the probability of future aggression.

■ From watching violence on TV, children develop a negative view of social reality, seeing violence as acceptable, exaggerating the threat of violence in their own lives, and becoming more fearful and less likely to intervene to stop violence by others.

■ There is evidence that pornography, which combines sexual and aggressive themes, contributes to violence against women.

■ Social dilemmas are choice situations in which the course that will bring immediate benefits to the individual will bring loss or disaster to the whole society in the longer run. One such social dilemma is the tragedy of the commons. Social dilemmas can be resolved only by a restructuring of the situation to make available and reward other options.

■ Applications of psychology are occurring in many fields today. Among these are research and use of psychological principles in many aspects of the legal system; work in the educational system in improving teaching methods and climates for learning, and studies of how people and environments affect each other. Social psychologists have always emphasized the importance of applying knowledge to improve the human condition.

A POSTSCRIPT: PSYCHOLOGY AND YOU

Well, you've come a long way on this journey that has introduced you to the field of psychology. A lot of words have passed between us. Now is the time to reflect upon what in all this study of human nature is of significance to *you*.

You will soon be given your final examination to test your memory for definitions, facts, concepts, experiments, and extensions of the information contained in this book. After the examination, will you do a "memory dump"? Will you erase that information base so you'll have room for new input from your next courses? I hope not. I'd like to believe instead that you have come to appreciate that behind all the fancy definitions, abstract concepts, and fascinating little experiments is—*YOU*. Psychology is the study of how *you* think, how *you* feel, and how *you* act. What motivates you to do what you do? Why do you hold the attitudes and values you do? What makes you become depressed? On what are your decisions and attributions based—and biased? Can you change a troublesome aspect of your life-style? How can you best relate to other people?

Psychology can help answer these questions, though that may require giving it another chance. Read some more; there is a sizeable reference list at the back of this book for you to consult. Take some more psychology courses. Which topics did you find most interesting? If you liked a particular chapter best, you can probably take a whole course that expands upon it. While you're at it, why not consider the possibility of taking a minor or co-major in psychology? Psychology complements virtually every field of knowledge and every career, including art, business, medicine, education, law, architecture, psychiatry, and politics.

If you are really turned on about the prospect of becoming a professional psychologist, and would like to be able to design and conduct original research, treat patients, counsel clients, administer tests, or teach psychology to others, you should seek advice from the psychology department at your school. Someone there can tell you about the advantages and procedures for majoring in psychology. Whatever the state of the economy, there are always good positions available to the creative, curious, thinker, and the energetic contributor to knowledge.

Psychology has been a constant source of joy to me during the thirty years since I first declared my major at Brooklyn College. The more I learned in graduate school at Yale under the guidance of teachers like Neal Miller, whom you met at the start of our journey here, the more and better questions I was able to ask. Since then my students have been helping me to come up with some of the answers we've shared with you in *Psychology and Life*.

Psychology poses intriguing challenges and returns enormous rewards, both intellectual and emotional, to those who accept them. What could be more exciting and satisfying than discovering the neural basis of memory, how to treat schizophrenia or depression, to cope with stress, to reduce violence, to promote health, to find out how to help people love their neighbors and to like themselves? These challenges await *you*—if you choose to continue on the next phase of your journey into more advanced levels of psychology.

Playwright Tom Stoppard reminds us that "Every exit is an entry somewhere else." In exiting from *Psychology and Life,* I hope you will enter on a new journey better prepared for life because of what you have learned here and better able to put new life into the psychology everywhere that makes up the essence of human nature.

UNDERSTANDING RESEARCH

- DESIGNING A RESEARCH PROJECT
- PROVIDING ETHICAL SAFEGUARDS
- ANALYZING THE DATA
  Descriptive statistics
  Inferential statistics
- REPORTING RESEARCH FINDINGS

Prior to Valentine's Day, 1977, Fred Cowan of New Rochelle, New York, was described by relatives and acquaintances as a "nice, quiet man," a "gentle man who loved children," and a "real pussycat." But on that day, Cowan strolled into work toting a semiautomatic rifle and shot four co-workers, a policeman, and, finally, himself. In subsequent interviews, people who had known Cowan expressed shock and amazement at what he had done. One neighbor said that Cowan "belonged to the best family on the block." The principal of his parochial elementary school reported that Cowan had received grades of "A" in courtesy, cooperation, and religion. And yet, this quiet, courteous man who, according to a co-worker, "never talked to anybody and was someone you could push around," ended the only truly violent day in his life with six senseless murders.

News items like this lead us—laypeople and research psychologists alike—to wonder about the meaning and causes of human behavior. How could a seemingly gentle man like Fred Cowan so lose control of himself that he could go on such a violent rampage? How can it be that the first aggressive crime he ever commited was mass murder? The behavior of Dan W. in Chapter 1 raised the same questions. What kind of person can become a sudden murderer?

To help shed light on this phenomenon, a group of researchers at Stanford University conducted a psychological study. They had a hunch that sudden murderers would have personalities quite different from those of other murderers, and they hoped to point the way to a better understanding of people like Fred Cowan by learning what some of the differences are.

The researchers hypothesized that sudden murderers as a group have been typically shy, nonaggressive people who kept passions and impulses in check. For most of their lives, they suffered many silent injuries—seldom, if ever, expressing anger no matter how angry they really felt. On the outside, they appeared unbothered, but on the inside they may have been fighting to control a furious rage. Then, something explodes. At the slightest provocation—or with no apparent provocation at all—they release the stifled violence that has been building up for so long.

To test this idea about sudden murderers, the researchers obtained permission to administer psychological questionnaires to a group of prison inmates who were serving time for murder. Nineteen inmates (all male) agreed to participate in the study. Some had committed a series of crimes, while others had no criminal record prior to their first, sudden murder. All participants filled out three different questionnaires. The first was the Stanford Shyness Survey. The most important item on this questionnaire asks if the subject is a shy person; the answer is a simple yes or no.

The second questionnaire was the Bem Sex-Role Inventory (BSRI), which presents a list of adjectives, such as "aggressive" and "affectionate," and asks the subject to indicate how well each adjective describes him or her. One third of the adjectives on this scale are typically thought of as "masculine"; one third as "feminine," one third as neutral (Bem, 1974, 1981).

The third questionnaire was the Minnesota Multiphasic Personality Inventory (MMPI), which is designed to measure many different aspects of personality (see Chapter 12). The researchers at Stanford were most interested in the "Ego-Overcontrol" section, which measures the degree to which a person acts out or controls impulses. It was predicted that, compared to murderers with a prior criminal record, sudden murderers (a) would more often describe themselves as shy on the shyness survey; (b) would check more feminine traits than masculine ones on the sex-role scale; and (c) would be higher in "ego-overcontrol," as measured by the personality inventory.

Each of these predicted results was found. Among the general American population, 40 percent describe themselves as shy, but 8 out of 10 of the sudden murderers (80 percent) described themselves as shy, while only 1 in 9 of the habitual criminal murderers (11 percent) did so. On the sex-role scale, 70 percent of the sudden murderers showed up as more feminine than masculine, while only 22 percent of the habitual criminals said that the feminine adjectives described them more accurately than the masculine ones. Finally, sudden murderers were higher in overcontrol of impulses than were habitual criminal murderers (Lee et al., 1977).

But what do these results really mean? Clearly we cannot predict that every shy, feminine, nonimpulsive man will some day go on a killing spree. Can we say that any person with a "clean" criminal record who suddenly commits a murder is probably shy, feminine, and overcontrolled? Can we even draw meaningful conclusions about the particular subjects in this one study? How clear-cut were the results? How confident can we be that the same contrasts would be found if we studied murderers in another prison? These important questions are typical of the ones that can be asked about the findings of almost any psychological study. This section will help you understand better how psychologists use the scientific method to answer such questions.

DESIGNING A RESEARCH PROJECT

As you saw in Chapter 1, the scientific method is a collection of general procedures that scientists follow in gathering and interpreting their observations. (If you read Chapter 1 a long time ago, you may want to do a quick run-through of pages 11–22, in which some basic concepts and terms related to research were discussed.)

The first step in designing a research project is to choose an idea and formulate a hypothesis that you want to test. The idea for the study of sudden murderers came from thinking about such puzzling occurrences as the Cowan murders. Other ideas come from informal observation of the ordinary behavior of people we encounter in our personal lives, as we notice ways in which people differ and wonder what might account for their differences. Often psychologists get their research ideas from the results of other studies. They may be intrigued by unexpected findings, contradictory conclusions, or unexplained relationships that have been found. Theories are also an important source of research ideas.

Initially, most ideas for research are rather general. However, in order to be carefully tested, a general idea must be transformed into one or more specific hypotheses. For example, one hypothesis in the Sudden Murderers study was that sudden murderers are more shy than murderers who have committed many crimes. A hypothesis suggested by your own observations of shy and not-shy people might be that shy people are less self-confident than not-shy ones.

Before a hypothesis can be formally tested, the concepts involved must be carefully defined. You may have noticed in our Sudden Murderers example that we talked not only about broad, general concepts like "shyness" but also about an operational definition—"saying *yes* or *no* on the shyness questionnaire."

After researchers have carefully specified how they will measure some variable, they must still be concerned about the measure's validity and reliability. As we learned in Chapters 1 and 12, a measurement technique is considered valid if it really measures what it is supposed to measure, and reliable if subjects end up with about the same score each time the measurement is made.

The next step in research design is to choose a method to test your hypothesis. For example, the Sudden Murderers study used the method of psychological tests. Other methods range from naturalistic observations to controlled experiments, as described in Chapter 1. Each method has its advantages and disadvantages. Naturalistic observation and field experiments are often more trouble to conduct than laboratory experiments. But because people may behave more naturally in the "real world" than in a psychology laboratory, the results of field studies are often seen as more meaningful. On the other hand, there are so many factors that could influence a person's behavior in the real world that a laboratory study, which deals with just a few factors, may provide a clearer basis for drawing conclusions. No single method is perfect, or best for studying every problem.

After selecting a method, the researcher must choose a situation or context in which to conduct the study. The first part of this choice is whether the study is to be carried out in the laboratory or the field. Then additional details must be worked out. Investigators who want to conduct field research within some organization or institution (such as a prison) must often explain their plans and obtain permission from both the authorities (e.g., the prison superintendent) and the potential participants (e.g., the prisoners) before proceeding with the study. Researchers planning to do an experiment must come up with a context (either in the field or in a laboratory) in which they can both vary the independent variable and measure the dependent variable.

After deciding which method to use and where to carry out the study, the researcher must identify the **population** to be studied (e.g., adult males, college students, white rats) and must then choose a smaller **sample** from that population for actual observation. Not only is it usually impossible to observe the entire population you are interested in, but often it is unnecessary. If a sample is chosen correctly, and if the study is designed and carried out properly, not much more information would be gained by observing the whole population than by observing the small, representative sample. For example, public opinion polls are able to predict national voting trends quite accurately using samples of a few thousand voters when, in fact, there are tens of millions of voters in the population.

Choice of the sample, like assignment of individuals to different treatment groups, must be done randomly if you are to get a representative sample of the larger group. Ideally, the sample should be selected in such a way that each member of the population has an equal chance of being chosen. A sample picked in this way is called a **random sample.** However, a random sample is not always easily obtained. Psychologists interested in "all college students" or "adults in general" must usually settle for studying students at their own university, people living nearby, or people in a conveniently located organization or institution. They feel that the greater accessibility of these subjects outweighs the possible dangers of using a nonrandom sample. However, we must be careful in generalizing the results of such studies to predictions about the behavior of the larger population.

PROVIDING ETHICAL SAFEGUARDS

Whenever a researcher conducts a study, it is important that he or she protects the subjects' physical and psychological well-being. Most psychology experiments carry little risk to the subjects, especially where participants are merely asked to perform routine tasks. But experiments that study subjects' emotional reactions, self-images, or attitudes could potentially be upsetting or somehow psychologically disturbing.

Subjects should be assured in advance that they may leave the experiment at any time they wish. At the end of the experiment, they should be given a careful **debriefing,** in which the researcher explains the hypotheses and purposes of the study and makes sure that they do not leave the experiment feeling confused or upset or embarrassed. If it was necessary to mislead the subjects during any stage of the research, the experimenter should carefully explain the reasons for this deception. For instance, a researcher who was studying the effect of self-expectations on performance might intentionally lead some subjects to believe that they would do poorly on a test (while leading others to believe they would do well). After the experiment, the researcher should explain why it was necessary to make the subjects feel this way (temporarily) in order to test the hypothesis. The researcher should also reassure the subjects that these expectations had nothing to do with their actual abilities, but were solely a function of random assignment. That is, a subject who expected to perform poorly had been led to think so *not* because he or she was really incompetent but simply because, by chance, the researcher had assigned that person to the "poor expectation" experimental condition. In addition, subjects should be reassured that all responses and records of behavior will be kept strictly confidential.

Because of growing concern about the ethics of experimentation, most universities and research institutes now have a committee that reviews all proposals for psychological research before allowing the work to begin. Generally, if the review committee feels that an experiment involves some potential risk to subjects, the proposal will be approved only if the benefits of the research (to the subjects themselves and/or to scientific knowledge in general) outweigh those risks. In potentially "risky" experiments, the review committee may impose constraints, insist on monitoring initial demonstrations of the procedure, or deny approval (Steininger et al., 1984).

ANALYZING THE DATA

After all the subjects have participated in a study, the researcher can begin to examine their responses on all dependent measures, looking for differences between the groups. These behavioral outcomes form the data of the study. Data analysis can involve many different procedures, some of them surprisingly simple and straightforward. In the next section we will lead you through a step-by-step analysis of some of the data from the Sudden Murderers study (see **Table 1**). For most researchers in psychology, analyzing the data is an exciting step. They can now find out if their results will contribute to a better understanding of a particular aspect of behavior, or if they have to go "back to the drawing board" and redesign their research.

Table 1   *Raw Data from the Sudden Murderers Study*

Inmate #	Shyness[a]	BSRI Femininity	– Masculinity	= Difference[b]	MMPI Ego-overcontrol[c]
		Group 1—Sudden Murderers			
1	yes	97	92	+5	17
2	no	99	100	−1	17
3	yes	78	74	+4	13
4	yes	103	42	+61	17
5	yes	99	80	+19	13
6	yes	101	60	+41	19
7	no	78	107	−29	14
8	yes	84	61	+23	9
9	yes	109	122	−13	11
10	yes	101	96	+5	14
		Group 2—Habitual Criminal Murderers			
11	no	100	112	−12	15
12	no	104	118	−14	11
13	yes	74	107	−33	14
14	no	101	109	−8	10
15	no	98	105	−7	16
16	no	99	96	+3	11
17	no	66	83	−17	6
18	no	85	79	+6	9
19	no	91	101	−10	12

(Lee et al., 1977)
[a]*Each subject's response to the question. "Do you consider yourself to be a shy person?" is listed.*
[b]*Each subject was asked to indicate how much each "feminine" adjective was true of himself by using a seven-point scale (1 = "never or almost never true"; 7 = "always or almost always true"). The femininity score is the sum of those ratings for all twenty feminine adjectives. The masculinity score is similarly calculated. The difference score is calculated by subtracting the masculinity score from the femininity score.*
[c]*The "ego-overcontrol" subscale of the MMPI is scored so that the higher a subject's score, the more ego-overcontrol the subject exhibits.*

If you have looked ahead through the next few pages, and if you are like many other students, you may have been "turned off" by the sight of numbers and equations. Your apprehension is understandable. In fact, many psychological researchers began their careers as dyed-in-the-wool math haters. So try to keep this thought in mind: You do not need to be "good in math" to be able to understand the concepts we will be discussing. You just need the courage to see mathematical symbols for what they are—a shorthand way of representing simple ideas and arithmetic operations.

The "raw data" obtained from the nineteen inmates in the Sudden Murderers investigation are listed in the table. The raw data are the actual scores or other measures obtained. As you can see, there were ten inmates in the Sudden Murderers group and nine in the Habitual Criminal Murderers group. When first glancing at these data, any researcher would feel what you probably feel—confusion. What do all these scores mean? Do the two groups of murderers differ from one another on these various personality measures? It's difficult to say. To help them make sense of the data they collect and draw meaningful conclusions, psychologists rely on a mathematical tool called *statistics*. Statistics can be used to describe sets of scores, to describe relationships among variables, and to compare data collected from different groups of subjects.

Descriptive statistics

Instead of trying to keep in mind all the scores obtained by subjects, psychologists rely on special techniques for summarizing their data and getting special indices of *what scores are most typical* for each group and *how typical they really are*—whether the scores for each group are spread out or clustered closely together.

Frequency distributions. The shyness data are easy to summarize. Of the 19 scores, there are 9 yes and 10 no responses, with almost all the yes responses in Group 1 and almost all the no responses in Group 2. For the MMPI overcontrol scale, the scores range from 6 to 19 and it is harder to get a feel for how the groups compare by just looking at the numbers.

Now let's look at the BSRI sex-role scores, which show the inmates' ratings of feminine and masculine adjectives as characteristic of them. These scores

range from +61 down to −33. Of the 19 scores, 9 are positive and 10 negative. This means that 9 of the murderers described themselves as more feminine, 10 as more masculine.

To get a clearer picture of how these scores are distributed, we can draw up **frequency distributions**—summaries of how frequent the various scores are. The first step in preparing a frequency distribution for a set of numerical data is to *rank order* the scores from highest to lowest. The rank ordering for the sex-role scores is shown in **Table 2**.

The second step is to put these rank-ordered scores into a smaller number of categories, called *intervals*. For this example, ten categories were used, with each category covering ten possible scores.

The third step is to construct a frequency distribution table, listing the intervals from highest to lowest and noting the *frequencies*—the number of scores you got that fell within each interval. Our frequency distribution shows us that most of the BSRI difference scores are between −20 and +9 (see **Table 3**). For the most part, the inmates' difference

Table 2 *Rank Ordering of BSRI Sex-Role Difference Scores*

Highest +61	
+41	−7
+23	−8
+19	−10
+6	−12
+5	−13
+5	−14
+4	−17
+3	−29
−1	−33 Lowest

Table 3 *Frequency Distribution of BSRI Sex-Role Difference Scores*

Category	Frequency
+60 to +69	1
+50 to +59	0
+40 to +49	1
+30 to +39	0
+20 to +29	1
+10 to +19	1
0 to +9	5
−10 to −1	4
−20 to −11	4
−30 to −21	1
−40 to −31	1

▷ **Figure 1** *Bar Graph for Comparing Shyness of Two Groups of Murderers*

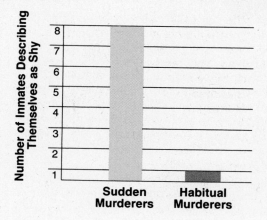

scores did not deviate much from zero—that is, they were not strongly positive or strongly negative.

Distributions are often easier to understand when they are displayed in pictorial form—that is, in a graph. The simplest type of graph is a *bar graph*. We can use a bar graph to illustrate how many more sudden murderers than habitual criminal murderers described themselves as shy (see **Figure 1**). For more complex data, such as the sex-role scores, we can use a *histogram*. A histogram is similar to a bar graph except that the bars touch each other and the categories are intervals—number categories instead of the name categories used in the bar graph. A histogram is a graph that gives a visual picture of how many scores in a distribution are in each interval. The histogram shown here gives the sex-role difference scores (see **Figure 2**). It is even easier to see from the histogram than from the frequency distribution that most scores cluster between −20 and +9 and that there are only a few extremely positive scores.

Central tendency. What we have done so far has given us a general picture of how the scores are *distributed*. Tables and graphs like these increase our general understanding of research results, but often we want to know more, such as which single score is most typical of the group as a whole. This is es-

pecially the case when we want to compare two groups. In this case, it is much easier to compare their typical scores than their entire distributions. A single, *representative* score that can be used to indicate the general level of scores obtained by a group of subjects is called a *measure of central tendency*. (It is in the *center* of the distribution, and other scores tend to cluster around it.) Actually, psychologists use three different measures of central tendency: the *mode*, the *median*, and the *mean*.

The **mode** is that score which occurs more often than any other. For the measure of shyness, the modal response of the sudden murderers was yes: 8 out of 10 said they were shy. Among habitual criminal murderers, the modal response was no. The BSRI sex-role scores for the sudden murderers have a

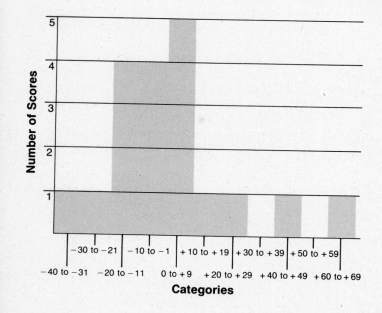

◁ **Figure 2** *Histogram of BSRI Sex-Role Scores*

mode of +5. Can you figure out what the mode of their MMPI overcontrol scores is? The answer is 17; three of the sudden murderers had that score, more than had any other score.

The mode is the easiest index of central tendency to determine, but it is often the least useful. You can see one reason for this if you notice that only one MMPI overcontrol score lies above the mode of 17, while six lie below it. Although 17 is the score obtained most often, it may not fit your idea of "typical" or "central."

The **median** is more clearly a central score; it separates the upper half of the scores in a distribution from the lower half. The number of scores larger than the median is the same as the number which are smaller. If you will rank order the BSRI difference scores of only the sudden murderers on a separate piece of paper, you will see that the median score is +5 (the same as the mode). Four scores are higher than +5 and four scores are lower. Similarly, the median MMPI overcontrol score for these subjects is 15, with four scores below it and four above it.

The median is not affected by extreme scores. For example, even if the highest BSRI difference score had been +129 instead of +61, the median value would still have been +5. That score would still separate the upper half of the data from the lower half.

The **mean** is what most people think of when they hear the word "average." It is also the statistic most often used to describe a set of data. To calculate the mean, you simply add up all of the scores in a distribution and divide by the total number of scores. The operation is summarized by the following formula:

$$M = \frac{\Sigma X}{N}$$

In this formula, M stands for the mean, X stands for each individual score, and the symbol Σ (the Greek letter "sigma," used as a summation sign) means "sum all." N, the number you divide the sum of all the scores by, is the total number of scores—how many scores there are. So the mean of the sex-role difference scores obtained by the sudden murderers would be calculated as follows:

$$M = \frac{\Sigma X}{N} = \frac{115}{10} = 11.5$$

Try to calculate their mean MMPI overcontrol scores yourself. You should come up with a mean of 14.4.

Unlike the median, the mean *is* affected by the precise values of all scores in the distribution. Changing the value of an extreme score *does* change the value of the mean. For example, if the BSRI difference score of inmate #4 were +101 instead of +61, the mean for the whole group would increase from 11.5 to 15.5.

Variability. In addition to knowing which score is most representative of the distribution as a whole, it is useful to know *how* representative that measure of central tendency really is. We want to know whether most of the other scores are fairly close to it or if they are widely spread out. *Measures of variability* tell us how close together the scores in a distribution are.

Can you see why measures of variability are important? An example may help. Suppose you are a teacher of young children. It is the beginning of the school year, and you will be teaching reading to a group of 30 second-graders. Knowing that the average child in the class can now read a first-grade reading book, but not more difficult books, will help you in planning your lessons. You could plan better, however, if you knew how *similar* the reading abilities of the 30 children are. Are they all at about the same level (little variability)? If so, then you can plan a fairly standard second-grade lesson for them. But what if several can read advanced material, while others can barely read at all (high variability)? Here the mean is not so representative and you will have to plan a variety of lessons to meet the children's differing needs.

The simplest measure of variability is the **range.** The range is the difference between the highest and the lowest values in the distribution. For the sudden murderers' BSRI difference scores, the range is 90 (+61 minus −29). The range of their MMPI overcontrol scores is 10 (19 minus 9). To compute the range, you need know only two of the scores—the highest and the lowest. This is what makes the range so simple to compute, but it is also the reason why psychologists prefer other measures of variability— more sensitive measures that take into account *all* the scores in a distribution, not just the extremes. One widely used measure is the **standard deviation.**

The standard deviation is a measure of variability that indicates the *average* difference between the scores and their mean. To figure out the standard deviation of a distribution, therefore, you need to know the mean of the distribution and the individual scores. The standard deviation is called *SD*, and the formula for calculating it is:

$$SD = \sqrt{\frac{\Sigma(X - M)^2}{N}}$$

This formula is a bit more complicated than the one used to calculate the mean, but the arithmetic is just as easy. As before, X is a symbol for the individual scores and *M* represents the mean. The total number of scores is represented by N, and Σ is the summation sign. The phrase (X − M) means "individual score minus the mean" and is commonly called the *deviation score.* The mean is subtracted from each score, and each resulting deviation score is squared (to get rid of negative values). Then you calculate the mean of *those:* you add the squared deviations and divide the sum by how many there are (N).

The symbol $\sqrt{}$ tells you to take the square root of the enclosed value to offset the previous squaring. The standard deviation of the MMPI overcontrol scores of the sudden murderers is calculated in **Table 4**. Recall that the mean of these scores is 14.4. This, then, is the value that must be subtracted from each score to obtain the corresponding deviation score.

The standard deviation tells us how variable a set of scores is. The larger the standard deviation, the more spread out the scores are. The standard deviation of the BSRI difference scores for the sudden murderers is 24.59, but it is only 10.73 for the habitual criminals. This shows that there was less variability in the habitual criminals group. Their scores clustered more closely about their mean than did those of the sudden murderers. When the standard deviation is small, then the mean is a good representative of the entire distribution. When the standard deviation is large, many individual scores are probably very different from the mean, and the mean is less "typical."

Correlation. Another useful statistic is the **correlation coefficient,** which indicates the degree of relationship between two variables (such as height and

Table 4 *Calculation of Standard Deviation of Sudden Murderers' Ego-Overcontrol Scores*

Score (X)	Deviation (score minus mean) (X − M)	Deviations Squared (score minus mean)^2 (X − M)^2
17	2.6	6.76
17	2.6	6.76
13	−1.4	1.96
17	2.6	6.76
13	−1.4	1.96
19	4.6	21.16
14	−.4	.16
9	−5.4	29.16
11	−3.4	11.56
14	−.4	.16
		$86.40 = \Sigma(X - M)^2$

Standard deviation = SD = $\sqrt{\dfrac{\Sigma(X - M)^2}{N}}$ =

$$\sqrt{\frac{86.40}{10}} = \sqrt{8.64} = 2.94$$

weight, or BSRI score and MMPI score). It tells us the extent to which scores on one measure are associated with scores on the other. If people with high scores on one variable tend to have high scores on the other variable too, then the correlation coefficient will be "positive" (greater than zero). If, however, most people with high scores on one variable tend to have *low* scores on the other variable, then the correlation will be "negative" (less than zero). If there is *no* consistent relationship between the scores, the correlation will be close to zero.

Correlation coefficients range from + 1 (perfect positive correlation) through zero to − 1 (perfect negative correlation). The further a coefficient is from zero, in *either* direction, the more closely related the two variables are, positively or negatively.

For example, among school-age children the correlation between height and weight is positive since taller children generally weigh more. The correlation between shyness and number of friends is negative since those who are *more* shy tend to have *fewer* friends. The correlation between grades and height would be about zero since these two variables are not related.

In addition to letting us know if two variables are related, the correlation coefficient enables us to make predictions. The taller children will tend to weigh more. But some children are very skinny and some shy children do have many friends. The higher the correlation, either positive or negative, the better predictions we can make about scores on one measure if we know scores on the other. (There are mathematical formulas that specify just how much predictions should be made.)

In the Sudden Murderers study, the correlation between the BSRI sex-role scores and the MMPI overcontrol scores turns out to be $+.35$. This means that the sex-role scores and the overcontrol scores are positively correlated: in general, more feminine subjects also tend to be higher in overcontrol. However, the correlation is rather low, compared to the highest possible value, $+1.00$, so we know that there are many exceptions to this relationship. If we also measured the self-esteem of these inmates and found a correlation of $-.68$ between sex-role scores and self-esteem, it would mean that there was a negative correlation: the more feminine male subjects tended to be *lower* in self-esteem. But it would still be a stronger relationship than the relationship between the sex-role scores and the overcontrol scores, since $-.68$ is farther from zero than $+.35$.

There are two more things you should keep in mind when interpreting a correlation coefficient. First, the most common techniques for calculating this index are designed to detect *linear* relationships between variables—that is, tendencies for one variable to keep increasing (or keep decreasing) as the other increases. If you plotted people's scores on a graph in which one variable was measured along the horizontal axis and the other along the vertical axis, you would find the points tending to cluster around

a line going from the lower left corner to the upper right one for a positive correlation or from upper left to lower right for a negative one. But in both cases, they would form a more or less straight line.

But sometimes when two variables are related, the relationship is a nonlinear one, as shown in **Figure 3** on stress and quality of performance. Here performance is better with moderate stress than with either low or high stress. Although stress and quality of performance are closely related in a fairly simple way, the linear correlation between them would be low because quality of performance does not either consistently rise or consistently fall as experienced stress increases.

Second, recall the discussion in Chapter 1 about the distinction between correlation and causation. A high correlation between two sets of scores shows an association and permits prediction but does *not* show the cause for the association. Even a perfect correlation does not necessarily imply causation.

Inferential statistics

So far, we have used a number of descriptive statistics to describe the data from the Sudden Murderers study; this has helped to give us an idea of the overall pattern of results. However, some basic questions remain unanswered. Recall that researchers begin with hypotheses. For the Sudden Murderers study,

▷ **Figure 3** *Linear and Nonlinear Relationships Between Two Variables*

The solid line shows the curvilinear (inverted-U) relationship found between level of arousal and performance: performance is better at moderate levels of arousal than at either very low or very high levels. The dotted lines show the directions that either a positive linear or negative linear relation would produce, the kind of curve found when there is a linear correlation between the two variables.

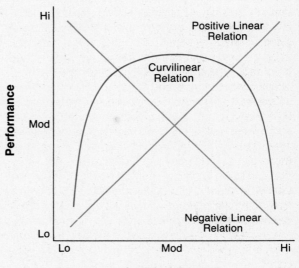

the researchers hypothesized that sudden murderers would be more shy, more overcontrolled, and more feminine than habitual criminal murderers. Our descriptive statistics let us compare average responses and variability in the two groups, and it looks as though there are some differences between them. But how do we know if the differences are large enough to be meaningful? Are they reliable? If we did this study again with other sudden murderers and other habitual criminal murderers, would we expect to find the same pattern of results or could these results have been due to chance? If we could somehow measure the entire population we are interested in—*all* sudden murderers and *all* habitual criminal murderers—would their means and standard deviations be the same as the ones we found for these samples, giving us the same differences between the two groups? Inferential statistics are used to answer these kinds of questions; they tell us what inferences we *can* make from our samples and what conclusions we can legitimately draw from our data.

Statistical significance. If the mean scores for two samples are different, why can't we assume that this reflects a true, underlying difference between these two groups? The primary reason is that any difference we get could simply be due to chance, rather than being a real difference.

A simple example illustrates the point. Suppose everyone in your class took a quiz and then the professor randomly selected 30 of the quiz scores, divided them randomly into two groups of 15, and calculated the mean score for each group. The two mean scores would probably be slightly different. By chance alone, somewhat more high scorers would be in one group than in the other. Thus, the difference between the two groups would be a chance one, not a real one. Now suppose the professor was doing an experiment and randomly varied the color of the paper on which quiz questions were printed. Half the quizzes were printed on white paper and half on pink paper, and the professor compared the mean score of 15 students using white paper to the mean score of 15 students using pink. Once again, these would probably differ, and this difference would most likely be due to chance. However, if the size of the obtained difference is larger than the difference which would result by chance alone, then the professor would feel confident that the difference is a real one and was actually related to paper color.

There are several statistical techniques for computing the likelihood that a research finding is due to chance. (We will review one of these, the *t*-test, a little later on). As we saw in Chapter 1, a difference is generally said to be *statistically significant* if the chances of finding a difference that large are at least less than 5 in 100 ($p < .05$).

The normal curve. In most cases the technique for determining how likely it is that a difference is due to chance depends on special properties of a distribution called the **normal curve**. When data on some variable (height, IQ, or femininity, for example) are collected from a large number of subjects, the numbers obtained often fit a curve roughly like that shown in **Figure 4**. Notice that the curve is symmetrical (the left half is a mirror image of the right side) and bell-shaped—high in the middle, where most scores are, and lower the farther you get from the mean. This is called a *normal curve*, or *normal distribution*. (When scores cluster toward one end instead of around the middle, it is called a *skewed distribution*.)

In a normal curve, the median is the same as the mean, and a certain percentage of the scores can be predicted to fall under different sections of the curve. In the curve shown here, IQ scores on the 1937 Stanford-Binet test have been plotted; these scores had a mean of 100 and a standard deviation of 16. If you indicate standard deviations as distances from the mean along the baseline, you find that a little over 68 percent of all the scores were between the mean of 100 and one standard deviation above and below it—between IQs of 84 and 116. Between the first and second standard deviations above and below the mean (IQs between 68 and 84 and between 116 and 132), roughly another 27 percent of the scores are found. Less than 5 percent of the scores fall in the third standard deviation above and below the mean, and *very* few beyond that—only about a quarter of a percent. These are characteristic percentages for all normal curves.

A normal curve is also obtained when you collect a series of measurements whose differences are due only to chance. If you flip a coin ten times in a row and record the number of heads and tails, you will probably get five of each—most of the time. If you kept flipping the coin for a hundred sets of ten tosses, you probably would get a few sets with all

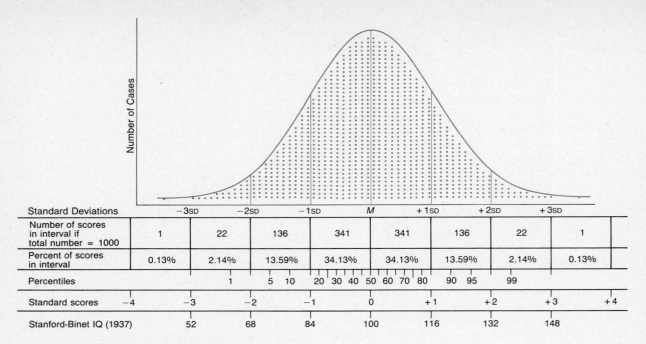

Standard Deviations	−3SD	−2SD	−1SD	M	+1SD	+2SD	+3SD	
Number of scores in interval if total number = 1000	1	22	136	341	341	136	22	1
Percent of scores in interval	0.13%	2.14%	13.59%	34.13%	34.13%	13.59%	2.14%	0.13%
Percentiles		1	5 10	20 30 40 50 60 70 80	90 95	99		
Standard scores	−4	−3	−2	−1	0	+1	+2	+3	+4
Stanford-Binet IQ (1937)		52	68	84	100	116	132	148	

△ | **Figure 4** *The Normal Curve*

The figure shows the distribution of scores that would be expected if 1000 randomly selected persons were measured on IQ or some other continuous trait. Each dot represents an individual's score. The baseline, or horizontal axis, *shows the amounts of whatever is being measured; the* vertical axis *shows how many individuals have each amount of the trait, as represented by their scores. Usually only the resulting curve at the top is shown, since this indicates the frequency with which each measure has occurred. Actual curves only approximate this hypothetical one, but come remarkably close to it with very large samples.*

This curve is very useful to psychologists because they know that in a large, randomly selected group, a consistent percentage of the cases will fall in a given segment of the distribution. For example, if the trait is one that is distributed normally, about 68 percent will fall in the middle third of the range of scores, between one standard deviation below and one standard deviation above the mean. Most of the scores in a distribution fall within three standard deviations above the mean and three standard deviations below it (but usually a few scores in an actual distribution will be lower and a few higher).

The distance of the standard deviation from the mean can be indicated along the baseline of the curve, as is done here. Since the standard deviations are equally spaced along the distributions, they are convenient dividing points for classification.

heads or no heads, but more sets where the number lay between these extremes, with the most typical outcome being about half each way. If you made a graph of your hundred tosses, you would probably get one that closely fit the normal curve.

In the pink-and-white-paper-for-quizzes example, if *only* chance is operating and both groups are from the same population (no difference), then the means of pink and white samples should be fairly close most of the time. From the percentages of scores found in different parts of the normal distribution, you know that less than a third of the pink means should be more than a standard deviation above or

below the real white mean. The chances of getting a pink mean more than three standard deviations above or below most of your white means would be very small. If you *did* get a difference that great, you would begin to think there might be a real difference after all, though you would still have to make further computations taking into account the size of your samples and the variability of the scores.

Statistical tests. There are many different types of tests for gauging statistical significance. The one used in a particular case depends upon the design of the study, the form of the data, and the size of the groups. Here we will give you only a brief overview of one of the most common tests, the *t-test,* which may be used when the investigator wants to know if the difference between the means of two small groups is a statistically significant one. It is based on the fact that if pairs of samples are repeatedly selected from one population, their means will be normally distributed. It provides a formula for calculating a statistic called *t.*

With smaller groups and more variable scores, larger differences between means are more likely to occur, even when the samples are drawn from the same population. So the *t* statistic is calculated using information about the two group means, about the number of subjects in each group, and about the variability of the scores. After calculating the value of *t* for a set of data, the researcher then looks up that value in a statistical table to find out the likelihood of getting a value that large, or even larger, by chance. If the likelihood is less than 5 in 100, then the difference that was found is said to be statistically significant.

We can use a *t*-test to see if the mean BSRI sex-role difference score of the sudden murderers is significantly different from that of the habitual criminal murderers. If we carry out the appropriate calculations and check the resulting *t* value against the values in the appropriate table, we discover that there is a very slim chance, less than 5 in 100 ($p < .05$) of obtaining such a large *t* value if no true difference exists. The difference is, therefore, statistically significant, and we can feel confident in saying that there is a real difference between the two groups. The sudden murderers *did* rate themselves as more feminine than did the habitual criminal murderers. On the other hand, the difference between the two groups of murderers in MMPI overcontrol scores turns out *not* to be statistically significant, so we must be more cautious in talking about this difference. There is a *trend* in the predicted direction: the difference is one that would occur by chance only 10 times in 100, but that is not within the standard 5-in-100 range. (The difference in shyness, analyzed using another statistical test, *is* significant.) So by using inferential statistics, we are able to answer some of the basic questions with which we began—and we are closer to understanding the psychology of people who suddenly change from their mild-mannered, shy style to become mass murderers.

REPORTING RESEARCH FINDINGS

If a statistically significant difference between groups has been found, the researchers may want to write up their findings for publication. Their report should include a detailed description of both the experimental procedure and the data analysis. This is particularly important because two major goals of publication are to add to the existing body of knowledge and to give other, independent researchers the opportunity to repeat, or *replicate,* the study. Even a statistically significant result will need to be obtained more than once before it is accepted as probably being valid.

After a research report has been written, it is submitted to a professional journal. Other psychologists knowledgeable about the topic review it to decide whether it is good enough to be published. Most research that is submitted for publication—after going through all the stages and procedures outlined here—is rejected. The standards must be rigorous because a study that is flawed or a conclusion that is not valid can lead to a lot of wasted energy if other researchers try to reproduce it.

There is also the danger that a researcher reading the published results of an investigation may simply accept the report at face value and base new research on it. In addition, people who hear about a conclusion may accept it and base personal decisions on it without waiting to hear about the results of attempted replications. So even though the results of all research should be viewed with some skepticism, those who decide which results will be made public still have a special obligation to be sure that the studies they choose for publication have been carried out carefully and do not suffer from biases and other problems.

From start to finish, the enterprise of psychological research is fascinating and complex. It combines sensitivity to people and their environment, creativity in generating original hypotheses, and a commitment to rigorous methodology in order to come up with a valuable discovery about human nature. If you understand how it works, you can understand and better evaluate the answers that psychologists (and many others) give to questions about human behavior. Perhaps you can even begin to tackle some of the unanswered questions yourself. Unlocking the mysteries of the human mind is an enormous challenge, a quest in need of talented, imaginative researchers. Why not you?

GLOSSARY

REFERENCES

ACKNOWLEDGMENTS

NAME INDEX

SUBJECT INDEX

GLOSSARY

A

Absolute threshold. The minimum amount of physical energy needed to reliably produce a sensory experience. (p. 113)

Accommodation. A process of restructuring or modifying cognitive structures so that new information can fit more easily into them. (p. 51)

Achievement tests. Standardized tests designed to measure an individual's current level of competence in a certain area. (p. 446)

Acquired drives. Learned motivational states. (p. 271)

Action potential. A nerve impulse activated in an axon when the graded potential that reaches the axon is above a certain threshold. (p. 85)

Actor-observer bias. The tendency of actors in a situation to attribute the causes of their own behavior to situational influences while observers tend to attribute the same actions to dispositional influences. (p. 578)

Addiction. A physical state in which the body requires the presence of a certain drug and withdrawal symptoms occur if the drug is not present. (p. 214)

Adrenocorticotrophic hormone (ACTH). A pituitary hormone which stimulates the adrenal cortex to release hormones important in metabolic processes and in physiological reactions to prolonged stress. (p. 460)

Affect. Emotion or mood state. (p. 46)

Affective disorders. Disorders in which the primary symptoms are associated with mood disturbances such as excessive depression, excessive elation, or both. (p. 504)

Afterimage. A visual sensation occurring after a stimulus has ended. (p. 126)

Age regression. A technique used during hypnosis in which the hypnotized individual receives suggestions that he or she is "returning" to an earlier period in life. (p. 211)

Aggression. Physical or verbal behavior with the intent to injure or destroy. (p. 627)

Agoraphobia. A type of phobia in which there is a fear of being in public places or away from familiar surroundings. (p. 498)

Algorithm. A rote procedure for solving problems in which every possible solution is tried; guaranteed to lead to a correct solution eventually if there is one. (p. 364)

All-or-none principle. Property of axon firing in which a uniform action potential is generated when a threshold has been reached, and no nerve impulse is generated when it has not been reached. (p. 85)

Amoral. Lacking in understanding of people's responsibilities to each other; neither moral nor immoral. (p. 62)

Amplitude. The physical property of strength of a sound wave, as measured by its peak-to-valley height. (p. 135)

Amygdala. Portion of the limbic system; brain center for aggression. (p. 97)

Analgesia. Pain reduction. (p. 145)

Anal stage. Second of Freud's psychosexual developmental stages; during this stage (approximately 2 years of age) gratification comes primarily from the elimination process. (p. 64)

Analytic psychology. Jung's view of personality as a constellation of competing internal forces in dynamic balance. (p. 398)

Androgens. Male hormones secreted in males by the gonads and related to male sexual behavior. (p. 350)

Animistic approach. The belief that behavior is brought about by a spirit within the person. (p. 74)

Anterograde amnesia. A type of amnesia in which there is a loss of the ability to form memories for newly presented facts. (p. 335)

Anxiety. The experience of apprehension, tension, and dread without an awareness of an appropriate causal determinant. (p. 497)

Anxiety states. Neurotic disorders in which anxiety occurs in the absence of specific phobias. (p. 499)

Apparent motion. A movement illusion in which one or more stationary lights going on and off in succession are perceived as a single moving light; also called the *phi phenomenon*. (p. 166)

Appetitive conditioning. Classical conditioning procedures in which the unconditioned stimulus is of positive value to the organism. (p. 231)

Applied research. Research undertaken with the explicit goal of finding solutions to practical problems. (p. 10)

Aptitude tests. Tests designed to measure an individual's potential for acquiring various skills. (p. 446)

Archetype. In Jungian personality theory, a universal, inherited, primitive, symbolic representation of a particular experience or object; part of the collective unconscious. (p. 398)

Archival research. A research method in which the investigator uses previously published findings or data already existing in documents, books, or cultural artifacts in order to determine the relationship between certain variables. (p. 16)

Artificial intelligence. "Computer thought"; computer programs that can make the kinds of judgments humans make. (p. 367)

Assimilation. A process whereby new cognitive elements are fitted; the new elements may be modified to fit more easily. (p. 51)

Association areas. Areas of the cerebral cortex encompassing three-fourths of the cortex where sensory and motor messages are correlated and integrated. (p. 97)

Attachment. A close emotional relationship between the child and the regular caregiver; inferred from behaviors that elicit and maintain nearness between the two. (p. 55)

Attention. A state of focused awareness accompanied by sensory clearness and a central nervous system readiness to response. (p. 190)

Attitude. A learned, relatively stable tendency to respond to people, concepts, and events in an evaluative way. (p. 580)

Attribution. An inference made about the causes of an action. (p. 576)

Attributional bias. A persistent tendency to prefer one type of causal explanation for behavior over another. (p. 577)

Attribution theory. A cognitive approach that is influential in understanding individual and social behavior which emphasizes inferences about the causes of behavior. (p. 275; p. 576)

Audition. The sensation of hearing. (p. 134)

Auditory cortex. Area of the temporal lobes of the cerebral hemisphere which receives and processes auditory signals. (p. 98; p. 139)

Auditory nerve. The nerve that carries impulses from the cochlea to the cochlear nucleus of the brain. (p. 138)

Authoritarian parenting. A style of parenting characterized by restrictive control without warmth or open parent-child dialogue; to be distinguished from *authoritative parenting* in which firm parental control is combined with warmth, open communication, and shared decisions. (p. 59)

Authoritative parenting. See *authoritarian parenting*.

Authority system. A social system that emerges when people transfer or delegate the rights over their actions to agents of the primary authority or to an organization. (p. 625)

Autohypnosis. The practice of inducing a hypnotic state in oneself. (p. 209)

Autokinetic effect. A visual illusion in which a stationary point of light in a dark room appears to slowly move from its initial position. (p. 183)

Autonomic nervous system. The part of the peripheral nervous system that governs activities not normally under voluntary control, such as processes of bodily maintenance. (p. 79)

Availability heuristic. A heuristic for estimating probabilities, based on dependence on one's personal experience. (p. 359)

Aversion therapy. A type of behavioral therapy used for individuals attracted to harmful stimuli in which procedures of aversive learning are used to pair the presently attractive substance with other noxious stimuli in order to elicit a negative reaction in the presence of the target substance. (p. 542)

Aversive conditioning. Classical conditioning procedures in which the unconditioned stimulus is of negative value to the organism. (p. 231)

Axon. Extended fiber of a neuron in which nerve impulses occur; transmits signals from the soma to the terminal buttons. (p. 83)

B

Backward masking. A phenomenon in which a sensory stimulus presented within a certain time interval after another similar stimulus has already been presented erases or masks the perception or processing of the first stimulus. (p. 311)

Barbituates. A group of drugs classified as depressants and used in low doses to reduce anxiety, and in higher doses for sleep induction. (p. 216)

Bar graph. A pictorial representation of the frequency with which observations fall within certain categories of a variable. (p. 647)

Basic level. The optimal level of categorization for thinking about an object; it is the level that can be accessed from memory most quickly and used most efficiently. (p. 348)

Basic research. Research undertaken to study a phenomenon or processes for accurate and comprehensive knowledge initially without regard to later practical applications. (p. 10)

Basilar membrane. A membrane in the cochlea which, when set into motion, stimulates hair cells which produce the neural effects of auditory stimulation. (p. 138)

Behavioral medicine. An interdisciplinary field that integrates knowledge from the behavior and medical sciences relevant to issues of disease and health. (p. 464)

Behavior assessment. A method of personality assessment in which specific, current, observable behaviors are identified and rated by judges to yield a personality profile. (p. 439)

Behavior genetics. A field of research that attempts to identify genetic components in behavioral traits. (p. 40)

Behaviorism. A scientific approach formulated by John B. Watson that views measurable or observable behavior as the only acceptable content for the science of psychology. (p. 25)

Behavioristic model. A psychological model that is primarily concerned with visible behavior and its relationships to environmental stimulation. Behaviorally oriented investigators attempt to understand how particular environmental stimuli control certain kinds of behavior. (p. 24)

Behavior modification. A behavioral psychotherapeutic approach that involves the use of operant and classical conditioning procedures to eliminate unwanted responses and reinforce desired ones. (p. 539)

Bias. An unwanted systematic source of error in scientific results and conclusions due to factors not related to the variables being studied or measured. (p. 17)

Binocular disparity. The displacement between the horizontal positions of corresponding images in the two eyes. (p. 168)

Biofeedback training. A procedure by which an individual acquires voluntary control over nonconscious biological processes by receiving information about successful changes. (p. 247)

Biomedical therapies. The group of therapies used to treat psychological disorders that focus on changing biological or physical mechanisms that may be associated with specific disorders. (p. 529)

Bipolar cells. Nerve cells that combine impulses from many receptors and send the results to ganglion cells. (p. 121)

Blind spot. Region of the retina which contains no photoreceptor cells because it is the place where the optic nerve leaves the eye. (p. 121)

Blocking. A phenomenon in which the ability of a new stimulus to signal an unconditioned stimulus is not learned when it is presented simultaneously with a stimulus that is already effective as a signal. (p. 252)

Blood-brain barrier. A semi-permeable membrane that keeps foreign substances in the bloodstream from flowing into the brain. (p. 214)

Brain stem. Hindbrain structure in front of the cerebellum which contains the reticular formation and structures involved in the control of basic life processes. (p. 96)

Brightness. The dimension of color space that captures the intensity of light. (p. 123)

Burnout. A syndrome of emotional exhaustion in which an individual loses concern and emotional feeling due to continuing emotional arousal and stress. (p. 467)

C

Cardinal trait. A trait around which a person organizes his or her life. (p. 388)

Case studies. Extensive biographies of selected individuals; many kinds of data may be collected from a variety of sources. (p. 16)

Castration anxiety. A type of anxiety assumed by Freud to arise from a male child's fear of punishment for sexual interest in the female parent. (p. 399)

Catch trial. Trial on which no stimulus is presented, a technique used to determine whether response biases are operating in sensory detection tasks. (p. 114)

Catharsis. The process and beneficial effect of expressing strongly felt, but usually inhibited, emotions. (p. 628)

Cause-and-effect relationship. A directional correlational relationship between two variables in which changes in one variable are assumed to lead to systematic and consistent changes in the other. (p. 20)

Central nervous system. The part of the nervous system consisting of the brain and spinal cord. (p. 79)

Central sulcus. A vertical groove that serves to divide the cerebral hemispheres into lobes. (p. 97)

Central trait. A major characteristic of a person that is assumed to be basic to an understanding of the individual. (p. 388)

Centrism. A thought pattern common during the beginning of the preoperational stage of cognitive development; characterized by the inability of a child to take more than one perceptual factor into account at the same time. (p. 53)

Cerebellum. A structure under the back of the cerebrum which controls balance and motor coordination. (p. 96)

Cerebral dominance. The tendency for one cerebral hemisphere to play a more dominant role than the other in controlling particular functions. (p. 99)

Cerebral hemispheres. The two halves of the cerebrum, connected by the corpus callosum. (p. 97)

Cerebrum. The upper part if the brain; covered by the cerebral cortex, the outer surface of folds and deep grooves. (p. 97)

Chaining. An operant procedure in which many different responses in a sequence are reinforced until an effective chain of behaviors has been learned. (p. 245)

Chromosomes. Large molecules consisting of double strands of DNA and proteins, which contain the genes responsible for hereditary traits. Every human cell contains 46 chromosomes except the germ cells which contain only 23. (p. 40)

Chronic stress. A state of arousal, continuing over time, in which demands are perceived by the individual as greater than the inner and outer resources available for dealing with them. (p. 457)

Chunk. A meaningful unit of information. (p. 314)

Chunking. The process of taking single items of information and recoding them by grouping on the basis of similarity or some other organizing principle. (p. 314)

Circadian rhythm. The consistent pattern of cyclical body activities that lasts approximately 24 hours and is determined by an internal "biological clock." (p. 203)

Classical conditioning. A form of learning in which behavior (conditioned response) comes to be elicited by a stimulus (conditioned stimulus) that has acquired its power through an association with a biologically significant stimulus (unconditioned stimulus). Also called *Pavlovian* or *respondent* conditioning. (p. 226)

Classification. Processes which identify and label perceptual objects as members of meaningful categories (e.g., "cars," "trees," or "people"). (p. 112)

Clinical psychologist. An individual who has earned a doctorate in psychology and whose training is in the assessment and treatment of psychological problems; unlike a psychiatrist, a psychologist cannot prescribe medications or physical treatments. (p. 531)

Clinical psychology. The field of psychology specializing in the research and treatment of psychological abnormality. (p. 490)

Closure. A perceptual organizing process as a result of which one tends to see incomplete figures as complete. (p. 162)

Cochlea. A fluid-filled organ in the inner ear that is the primary organ of hearing. (p. 138)

Cognition. The processes of knowing, including attending, remembering, reasoning, etc.; also the content of these processes, such as concepts and memories. (p. 340)

Cognitive development. The development of processes of knowing including imagining, perceiving, reasoning, and problem solving. (p. 50)

Cognitive dissonance theory. A tension-reduction theory about the motivating effects of discrepant or incongruous cognitions, and about the ways individuals attempt to reduce this tension. (p. 582)

Cognitive map. A mental representation of physical space. (p. 353)

Cognitive model. A psychological model that emphasizes and studies the mental processes that intervene between stimulus input and overt responses. (p. 25)

Cognitive psychology. The study of the higher mental processes and structures. (p. 340)

Cognitive science. An interdisciplinary field, a broad approach to studying systems and processes which manipulate information. (p. 341)

Cognitive therapies. Psychotherapeutic treatments that attempt to change problem feelings and behaviors by changing the way the client thinks about or perceives significant life experiences. (p. 547)

Cohort. A group of individuals defined as similar in some way (e.g., a birth cohort, individuals born the same year). (p. 37)

Collective unconscious. In Jungian personality theory, that part of an individual's unconscious which is inherited, evolutionarily developed, and common to all members of the species. (p. 398)

Color blindness. An inability to distinguish between some or all of the colors in the color solid. (p. 126)

Color space. A three-dimensional model for describing color experience in terms of hue, saturation, and brightness. (p. 123)

Companionate love. The affection felt for those with whom one's life is deeply intertwined. (p. 591)

Complementary colors. Colors opposite each other on the color circle. (p. 125)

Compliance. Conforming one's outward behavior to that of others in order to avoid punishment or rejection by members of a valued group. (p. 598)

Compulsion. An undesired repetitive act carried out in stereotypic, ritualistic fashion and one which the individual feels compelled to act out. (p. 500)

Concepts. Mental representations of kinds or categories of things; formed through experience with the world. (p. 346)

Concordance rate. The extent to which both members of a set of twins share a particular characteristic or trait used in assessing heritability. (p. 518)

Concrete operational stage. Third of Piaget's cognitive developmental stages (from 7–11 years); characterized by understanding of conservation and readiness for other mental operations involving concrete objects. (p. 53)

Conditioned response. In classical conditioning, a response elicited by some previously neutral stimulus. Occurs as a result of pairing the neutral stimulus with an unconditioned stimulus. (p. 227)

Conditioned stimulus. In classical conditioning, the previously neutral stimulus which comes to elicit a conditioned response. (p. 227)

Cones. Photoreceptors concentrated in the center of the retina which are responsible for visual experience under normal viewing conditions and for all experiences of color. (p. 120)

Conformity. The tendency for people to adopt the behavior, attitudes, and values of other members of a reference group. (p. 598)

Consciousness. The state of awareness of internal events and of the external environment. (p. 188)

Consensual validation. Mutual affirmation of views of reality. (p. 189)

Consensus criterion. A criterion used when deciding if an action should be attributed to situational or dispositional factors that involves deciding if most people would have behaved in a similar or dissimilar fashion in the same situation. (p. 577)

Conservation. The understanding that physical properties do not change when nothing is added or taken away, even though appearances may change. (p. 53)

Consolidation. The process by which learned information is gradually transformed from a fragile short-term memory to a more durable, long-term memory code. (p. 335)

Constancy. The ability to retain an unchanging percept of an object despite variations in the retinal image. (p. 172)

Constitutional factors. Basic physical and psychological characteristics; shaped by genetic and early environmental influences and remain fairly consistent throughout a person's life. (p. 43)

Construct validity. The degree to which scores on a test based on the defined variable correlate with scores of other tests, judges' ratings, or experimental results already considered valid indicators of the characteristic being measured. (p. 419)

Continuity. A theoretical view in developmental psychology which holds that development is essentially continuous and occurs through the accumulation of quantitative changes in behaviors. (p. 38)

Control group. The group of subjects in a controlled experiment who share all of the characteristics and procedures of the experimental group except exposure to the independent variable which is being studied. (p. 14)

Controlled experiment. A research method in which observations are made of specific behaviors under systematically varied conditions. (p. 13)

Controlled procedures. Consistent procedures for giving instructions, scoring responses, and for holding all other variables constant except for those being systematically varied. (p. 15)

Convergent thinking. An aspect of creativity in which one uses knowledge and logic to eliminate possibilities and reach the best solution to a problem. (p. 443)

Conversion disorder. A type of psychological disorder in which there is a loss of a specific sensory or motor function in the absence of any physiological or organic cause. (p. 501)

Coping strategies. Means of dealing with a situation perceived to be threatening. (p. 475)

Cornea. A transparent bulge at the front of the eye filled within a clear liquid, the aqueous humor. (p. 119)

Corpus callosum. A bundle of myelinated axons that connects the two cerebral hemispheres. (p. 97)

Correlation. A measure of the degree to which two variables are related or co-vary systematically. (p. 20)

Correspondent inference. A postulated social judgment rule stating that inferences about the causes of a person's behavior often explain the behavior in terms of personal characteristics of the individual. (p. 577)

Countertransference. The process in which the psychoanalyst develops personal feelings about the client because of perceived similarity of the client to significant people in the therapist's life. (p. 537)

Covariation principle. A postulated social judgment rule regarding how inferences about the cause of an event are often made in relation to the conditions that vary with the event. (p. 576)

Coverant. A covert operant response that is influenced by the consequences it produces. (p. 405)

Covert behaviors. The unseen psychological processes such as thoughts, images, or feelings, or physiological reactions that can not be directly observed. (p. 8)

Creativity. The uninhibited, imaginative thought processes involved in the act of creating; the occurrence of uncommon or unusual, but appropriate, responses to situations. (p. 442)

Criterion validity. The degree to which test scores indicate a result on a specific measure that is consistent with some other criterion of the characteristic being assessed. (p. 419)

Critical period. A sensitive time during development when the organism is optimally ready to acquire a particular behavior if the proper stimuli and experiences occur. (p. 38)

Critical set point. A particular level of fats stored in specialized fat cells; when fats fall below this level, "eat signals" are sent out. (p. 278)

Cross-cultural research. Research designed to discover whether some behavior found in one culture also occurs in other cultures. (p. 16)

Cross-model integration. Perceptual organization which brings together information from different sensory modalities to form a unified percept of an object. (p. 167)

Cross-sectional design. A research method in which groups of subjects of different chronological ages are observed and compared. (p. 36)

Cutaneous senses. The skin senses, which produce sensations of pressure, warmth, and cold. (p. 143)

Cytoplasm. Substance in the cell in which most of a cell's biochemical reactions take place, and in which metabolism occurs. (p. 77)

D

Dark adaptation. A process in which the eyes get more sensitive to light under conditions of low illumination. (p. 132)

Daydreaming. A mild form of consciousness alteration in which attention is temporarily shifted away from response to external stimulation toward responding to an internal stimulus. (p. 202)

Debriefing. A procedure carried out at the conclusion of an experiment in which the experimenter provides subjects with an explanation of the hypotheses and purposes of the study. (p. 644)

Decentration. The ability to take into account two or more physical dimensions at the same time. (p. 53)

Defense mechanism. A Freudian concept referring to a mental strategy (conscious or unconscious) used by the ego to defend itself from the conflicts experienced in the normal course of life. (p. 396)

Deficiency motivation. Motivation in which individuals seek to restore physical or psychological equilibrium. (p. 273)

Dehumanization. A type of defense mechanism in which the human qualities and values of other people are psychologically erased or cancelled. (p. 618)

Deindividuation The subjective state and the process in which the person does not feel differentiated from others. (p. 615)

Delta sleep. A stage during the sleep cycle in which electrical brain activity is characterized by large, slow waves. (p. 204)

Delusions. False beliefs maintained despite contrary evidence and lack of social support; they may arise from unconscious sources, and appear to serve personal needs, such as relieving guilt or bolstering self-esteem. (p. 110; p. 506)

Demand characteristics. Contextual factors that exert a strong influence over a person's behavior in a particular situation, regardless of personal attitudes or other attributes. (p. 581)

Demonic possession. Archaic conception of the causes of mental illness based on the belief that physical sickness and mental aberrations were caused by the "possession' of the individual's body by demons or evil spirits. (p. 512)

Dendrites. Branched fibers of a neuron which receive incoming signals. (p. 83)

Dependence. A process in which the body or mind becomes adjusted to and dependent on the ingestion of a certain substance. (p. 214)

Dependent variable. The response whose form or amount is expected to vary with changes in the independent variable. (p. 14)

Depressants. A group of drugs including alcohol, barbituates, and opiates which slow down mental and physical activities by reducing or inhibiting the transmission of nerve impulses in the central nervous system. (p. 215)

Depression. A type of affective disorder characterized by an emotional state of dejection, feelings of worthlessness, apprehension, and lessened participation in most physical activities. (p. 504)

Depressive episodes. Recurrent periods characterized by a loss of interest or pleasure in most activities. (p. 504)

Developmental age. The chronological age at which most children show a particular level of physical or mental development. (p. 38)

Developmental psychology. A branch of psychology that is concerned with the interaction between physical and psychological processes and stages of growth from conception across the life span. (p. 34)

Developmental stage. A period during which physical, mental, or behavioral functioning is different from times before and after it. (p. 38)

Diagnosis. A label and the process by which a clinician comes to apply that label to summarize the set of characteristics associated with a particular psychological disturbance. (p. 530)

Dichotic listening. An experimental technique in which a different auditory stimulus is simultaneously sent to each ear. (p. 192)

Diencephalon. The lower part of the forebrain; controls body temperature, hormonal release, autonomic nervous system functions, and primitive emotional and motivational processes. (p. 93)

Difference threshold. The smallest physical difference between two stimuli that will be recognized as a difference; also known as the *just noticeable difference.* (p. 116)

Discontinuity. A theoretical view in developmental psychology which holds that development is discontinuous, qualitatively different behaviors at different life periods. (p. 38)

Discounting rule. The tendency for people to consider certain causes as less likely explanations of behavior to the extent that other plausible causes are present. (p. 577)

Discriminative stimuli. Stimuli which act as predictors of reinforcement signaling when a particular behavior will result in positive reinforcement. (p. 241)

Diseases of adaptation. Diseases that have their roots in attempts to adapt to stressors. (p. 462)

Display rules. Social norms governing the public expression or display of emotions. (p. 295)

Dispositional theories. Those personality theories that focus on innate qualities within the person as the main force influencing behavior. (p. 400)

Dissociative disorder. A type of psychological reaction in which the individual experiences a sudden, temporary alteration of consciousness in the form of a severe memory loss or loss of personal identity. (p. 502)

Distal stimulus. The object in the environment, the source of stimulation, as contrasted with the *proximal stimulus*. (p. 154)

Distinctiveness criterion. A criterion used when deciding if an action should be attributed to situational or dispositional factors that involves determining if an action is unusual and atypical for a particular person. (p. 577)

Divergent thinking. An aspect of creativity characterized by the ability to produce unusual, but appropriate responses to standard questions. (p. 443)

Dominant genes. Genes that are expressed in the individual's development. (p. 40)

Dopamine hypothesis. A theory proposing a relationship between many of the symptoms associated with schizophrenia and a relative excess of the neurotransmitter, dopamine, at specific receptor sites in the central nervous system. (p. 519)

Double bind. A situation hypothesized to contribute to schizophrenic reactions, in which the child receives multiple messages from a parent that are contradictory and cannot be met. (p. 520)

Drapetomania. A "mental disorder" defined during slavery times as a mania to seek freedom that caused certain slaves to run away; it is an extreme example of the medicalization of deviance. (p. 523)

Dream analysis. The psychoanalytic technique involving the interpretation of dreams in order to gain insight into the person's unconscious motives or conflicts. (p. 536)

Drive. Term used to describe motivation that is biologically instigated. (p. 263)

DSM-III. The current diagnostic and statistical manual of the American Psychiatric Association that classifies, defines, and describes over two hundred mental disorders. (p. 493)

Dual code model of memory. A theoretical view regarding the nature of the coding system in memory which proposes that both visual and verbal codes are used to store information in memory as opposed to only verbal codes. (p. 323)

Dual hypothalamic theory of hunger. The theory that the lateral hypothalamus and ventromedial hypothalamus control the start and stopping of feeding. (p. 276)

Dualism. The belief that the mechanistic body and brain act separately from the spiritual soul and ephemeral mind. (p. 75)

Duplex theory of memory. A theory regarding the structure of the memory system that postulates qualitatively different systems for short- and long-term memory. (p. 326)

Dynamic unconscious. Unconscious forces which can affect the operation of conscious levels of personality function. (p. 395)

Dyscontrol syndrome. A state in which an individual displays little control over violent or aggressive impulses sometimes resulting in senseless brutality, sexual assault, or repeated serious automobile accidents; associated with brain disease. (p. 629)

E

Echo. An auditory memory lasting several seconds. (p. 310)

Ecological Optics. A theory of perception that emphasizes the richness of the stimulus information and the perceiver as an active explorer of the environment. (p. 160)

Ectomorph. A somatotype characterized by a body build that is thin, long, and fragile in appearance. (p. 386)

EEGs. Records of electrical signals from the brain recorded at the scalp. (p. 104)

Ego. In Freudian theory, that aspect of the personality involved in self-preservation activities and in directing instinctual drives and urges into appropriate channels. (p. 394)

Egocentrism. An aspect of centrism that refers to the preoperational child's difficulty in imagining a scene from someone else's perspective. (p. 53)

Ego ideal. In Freudian theory, the individual's view of the kind of person he or she should strive to become. (p. 395)

Eidectic imagery. An uncommon memory phenomenon in which a few individuals seem to be able to store detailed whole images of scenes or complex patterns for a relatively long period of time. (p. 323)

Elaborative rehearsal. Repetition of incoming information in which the new information is analyzed and related to already stored knowledge. (p. 315)

Electromagnetic spectrum. An energy spectrum which includes X-rays, microwaves, radio waves, TV waves, and visible light waves. (p. 122)

Emotion. A complex pattern of changes, including physiological arousal, feelings, cognitive processes, and behavioral reactions, made in response to a situation perceived to be personally significant. (p. 294)

Empirical evidence. Evidence obtained through the careful observation of perceivable events or phenomena. (p. 11)

Empiricism. The scientific method of relying on verifiable, factual information such as observation, sensory experience, or experimentation. (p. 33)

Encephalization. The evolutionary development characterized by increasing dominance by higher neural centers. (p. 90)

Encoding. Conversion of information into a code capable of being conveyed in a communication channel. (p. 307)

Encoding specificity principle. The principle referring to the close relationship between encoding, storage, and retrieval of information in which subsequent retrieval of information is enhanced if cues received at the time of recall are consistent with those present at the time of encoding. (p. 320)

Endocrine system. A glandular system transferring information between cells in different parts of the body by way of hormonal messengers. (p. 78)

Endomorph. A somatotype characterized by a body build that is full, round, or soft in appearance. (p. 386)

Environmental psychology. A branch of psychology which primarily studies the relationships between psychological processes and physical environments, both natural and humanmade. (p. 637)

Episodic memory. That component of long-term memory which stores autobiographical information in conjunction with some type of coding designating a time frame for past occurrences. (p. 321)

Equity theory. A model addressing factors influencing attraction and satisfaction within social relationships which postulates that equitable relationships are those in which the participants' outcomes are proportional to their inputs. (p. 588)

Eros. A concept of Freudian theory referring to the life instinct which provides energy for growth and survival. (p. 628)

Erotic stimuli. Physical or psychological stimuli which give rise to sexual excitement or feelings of passion. (p. 282)

Estrogen. A female hormone essential to triggering the release of eggs from the ovaries. (p. 82)

Ethology. The observational study of animal behavior patterns in an animal's natural environment. (p. 336)

Etiology. The causes or factors related to the development of a disorder. (p. 493)

Eustress. A positive reaction to a stressor defined as a challenge rather than a threat. (p. 457)

Evaluation research. A type of research in psychology that focuses on an evaluation of whether a particular social program or type of therapy achieves previously specified goals and whether it is cost effective. (p. 16)

Evoked potentials. The patterns of brain activity caused by specific stimuli. (p. 104)

Excitation. Stimulation that increases the activity or "firing rate" of a nerve cell. (p. 77)

Existentialism. A philosophy which emphasizes the individual's responsibility and potentiality for existence fully through choice. (p. 400)

Experimental group. The group of subjects in a controlled experiment for whom the independent variable or treatment variables are systematically altered. (p. 14)

Extinction. In conditioning, the weakening of a conditioned association in the absence of a reinforcer or unconditioned stimulus. (p. 229)

Extrinsic motivation. Motivation to engage in an activity for some outside consequence. (p. 290)

F

Facial feedback hypothesis. The hypothesis that physiological changes accompany the facial expressions characteristic of various emotions. (p. 294)

Feature-detection model. The theory that cells at different levels in the visual system detect different features of the stimulus. (p. 130)

Fechner's law. The assertion that the strength of a sensation is proportional to the logarithm of physical stimulus intensity. (p. 118)

Fetish. A nonsexual object that becomes capable of producing sexual arousal through conditioning. (p. 283)

Fetus. The name given to the developing embryo eight weeks after conception until birth. (p. 42)

Fight-or-flight syndrome. The sequence of internal activities triggered when an organism is faced with a threat; prepares the body for combat and struggle or for running away to safety. (p. 458)

Figure. Object-like regions of the visual field. (p. 162)

Fixation. According to Freudian theory, arrested psychosexual development in which the child does not progress to the next stage because of excessive frustration or overgratification during the current stage. (p. 64)

Fixed action pattern. An unlearned response released by a specific environmental event or object. (p. 3)

Fixed interval schedule. In operant conditioning, a schedule whereby reinforcement is delivered for the first response made after a fixed amount of time has elapsed. (p. 248)

Fixed ratio schedule. In operant conditioning, a schedule in which reinforcement is delivered only after a fixed number of responses. (p. 248)

Forebrain. The anterior portion of the brain, containing the diencephalon and telencephalon. (p. 93)

Formal operational stage. Fourth of Piaget's cognitive developmental stages; characterized by abstract thinking and conceptualization. (p. 53)

Fovea. Area of the retina which contains densely packed cones and forms the point of sharpest vision. (p. 120)

Free-floating anxiety. Anxiety not focused on any particular agent, or not associated with any known cause. (p. 498)

Frequency. The number of cycles a wave completes in a given amount of time. (p. 135)

Frequency distribution. An array of individual scores arranged in order from highest to lowest. (p. 646)

Frequency theory. The theory that neural firing rate is determined by a tone's frequency. (p. 140)

Frustration. A state of an organism assumed to exist when goal-directed activity is blocked in some manner. (p. 467)

Functional fixedness. An inhibition in perceiving a new use for an object previously associated with some other purpose; adversely affects problem-solving and creativity. (p. 363)

Functional psychoses. A group of psychotic disorders not attributable to brain damage or organic factors including affective disorders, paranoid states, and the schizophrenias. (p. 504)

Function words. Words like "the," "and," or "of" which help express relationships between other words. (p. 48)

Fundamental attribution error. The dual tendency of observers to underestimate the impact of situational factors on an actor's behavior and to overestimate the influence of dispositional factors. (p. 578)

G

Ganglion cells. Cells which integrate impulses from many bipolar cells into a single firing rate. (p. 121)

Gender. A psychological phenomenon; refers to learned sex-related behaviors and attitudes of males and females. (p. 60)

Gender identity. One's sense of "maleness" or "femaleness." Gender identity usually includes an awareness and acceptance of one's biological sex. (p. 60, p. 503)

Gender identity disorder. A type of psychosexual disorder in which a person's gender identity is incongruent with his or her anatomical sex. (p. 503)

Gender role. The set of behaviors and attitudes defined by society that are associated with being male or female, and expressed publicly by the individual. (p. 60, p. 503)

General adaptation syndrome. A pattern of nonspecific adaptational physiological mechanisms that occurs in response to continuing threat by almost any serious stressor. (p. 461)

Generalized anxiety disorder. A disorder in which the individual experiences anxiety that persists for at least one month and is not focused on a specific object or situation. (p. 499)

Genes. Ultramicroscopic areas of DNA within the chromosome; the basic unit of hereditary transmission. (p. 40)

Genital stage. Fifth and final stage of psychosexual development proposed by Freud (from puberty throughout adulthood); during this period the individual moves from autoeroticism to gaining sexual gratification from others and also learns socially appropriate channels for the expression of sexual impulses. (p. 64)

Genotype. The genetic constitution of an organism; many genes are not expressed in the individual's development. (p. 400)

Germ cells. In humans, the spermatozoa in the male and the ova in the female; the cells which carry and transmit the genetic information of the parents to the offspring. (p. 40)

Gestaltism. A theoretical approach to perception emphasizing whole configurations and emergent properties. (p. 157)

Glial cells. Cells which hold neurons close together and facilitate neural transmission by forming a sheath that insulates the axons of some neurons thereby speeding conduction of electrochemical impulses. (p. 84)

Glucostatic theory. The theory that when blood glucose is low or unavailable for metabolism, signals are sent to the lateral hypothalamus which result in motivation to seek and eat food. (p. 278)

Graded potential. Spreading activity along a dendrite or cell body membrane produced by stimulation from another neuron. (p. 85)

Ground. Background areas of the visual field, against which figures stand out. (p. 162)

Group. Two or more persons who are engaged in interaction such that each influences and is influenced by the other(s). (p. 592)

Grouping. A perceptual organizing process through which one tends to see independent items as grouped together; such grouping follows the laws of proximity, common fate, and similarity. (p. 163)

Growth motivation. Motivation in which individuals seek to develop themselves beyond what they have been and done in the past. (p. 273)

Gustation. The sensation of taste. (p. 141)

H

Habituation. A decrease in strength of responding when a stimulus is presented repeatedly. (p. 92)

Hallucinations. False sensory perceptions produced by a variety of conditions such as mental disorders, brain diseases, or intoxication from various drugs. (p. 110)

Hallucinogens. The group of psychoactive drugs that are capable of producing altered states of awareness in which visual, auditory, or other sensory hallucinations occur. (p. 216)

Halo effect. A bias in which an observer judges a liked person favorably on most or all dimensions. (p. 422)

Health psychology. A field in psychology that focuses on the application of psychological theories and research to health issues and health care. (p. 465)

Heritability. A statistical concept estimating the relative contribution of genetic factors to the variability in intelligence test scores that is found when a sample of individuals is tested. (p. 430)

Heritability ratio. The ratio of the estimated genetic part of the variability in intelligence test scores to the total variability. (p. 430)

Hertz. A unit of sound frequency expressed in cycles per second. (p. 135)

Heuristics. Cognitive strategies, or "rules of thumb," often used as shortcuts in solving complex inferential tasks. (p. 359)

Hidden observer. A term referring to the part of the self which maintains an intellectual awareness of and contact with reality even under altered states of awareness such as hypnosis. (p. 211)

Hindbrain. The posterior portion of the brain; controls basic life processes like breathing and heartrate. (p. 93)

Hippocampus. Part of the limbic system involved in memory. (p. 97)

Holistic approach. A theoretical approach in which separate actions are explained in terms of the person's entire personality. (p. 399)

Homeostasis. Constancy or equilibrium of the internal conditions of the body; the tendency of organisms to maintain equilibrium and resist change. (p. 81)

Hormones. Substances secreted into the bloodstream from specialized cells located in various glands; are carried in the blood until they attach themselves to the surface of a target tissue. (p. 78)

Hue. The dimension of color space that corresponds to the light's wavelength. (p. 157)

Humanistic model. A psychological model that emphasizes the individual's phenomenal world and inherent capacity for making rational choices and developing to maximum potential. (p. 26)

Hypnosis. An altered state of awareness induced by a variety of techniques and characterized by deep relaxation, susceptibility to suggestions, and changes in perception, memory, motivation, and self-control. (p. 209)

Hypnotic induction. A preliminary set of activities that precedes and prepares the participant for the altered awareness state of hypnosis. (p. 209)

Hypnotizability. The degree to which an individual is responsive to standardized hypnotic suggestions. (p. 209)

Hypochondriasis. A pathological condition characterized by a preoccupation with bodily sensations as possible signs of a serious disease despite medical reassurance. (p. 501)

Hypothalamus. A structure below the thalamus that regulates processes such as eating, drinking, body temperature, and hormonal activity. (p. 97)

Hypothesis. A tentative and testable explanation of the relationship between two (or more) events or variables; often stated as a prediction that a certain outcome will result from specific conditions. (p. 9)

Hysteria. A type of disorder common during the late 1800's in which impairments in physical functioning occurred in the absence of apparent organic disorder. (p. 393)

Hysterical amnesia. A type of motivated forgetting of certain stored information associated with anxiety-provoking experiences. (p. 334)

I

Icon. A visual memory lasting about half a second. (p. 310)

Identification. A cognitive process whereby one person adopts the point of view of another person or group as one's own. (p. 598)

Identity. Sense of self; includes the perception of one's self as distinct from other people and of other things as related to one's self or alien to one's self. (p. 401)

Idiographic approach. A methodological approach to the study of personality processes in which emphasis is placed on understanding the unique aspects of each individual's personality rather than common dimensions on which all individuals can be measured. (p. 384)

Immediate memory span. Refers to the limited, brief storage capacity of short-term memory that seems to be between five and nine chunks of information. (p. 313)

Implicit personality theory. The set of informal beliefs that a person holds regarding what personality traits are associated with or related to each other. (p. 574)

Implosion. A behavioral therapeutic technique that exposes a client to stimuli previously rated as most anxiety-provoking by the client in an attempt to extinguish the anxiety associated with the particular stimuli. (p. 541)

Imprinting. A primitive form of learning in which the infant animal physically follows and forms an attachment to the first moving object it sees and/or hears. (p. 56)

Incentive motivation. Motivation aroused by external stimuli. (p. 271)

Independent variable. In a controlled experiment, the stimulus that when varied is expected to change some behavior (the dependent variable). (p. 13)

Index variable. A variable that is itself not causal but is a manifest sign of an underlying causal variable. (p. 38)

Individuation. The psychological state in which a person is differentiated from other people in a given social context. (p. 614)

Induced motion. An illusion in which a stationary point of light within a moving reference frame is seen as moving, with the reference frame perceived as stationary. (p. 166)

Infancy period. In humans, the period from birth to 18 months, from the Latin word for "incapable of speech." (p. 44)

In-group bias. A tendency for one to more positively evaluate groups of which one is a member. (p. 603)

Inhibition. Stimulation that decreases activity or the "firing rate" of a nerve cell. (p. 77)

Insight. A phenomenon in problem solving tasks in which learning results from an understanding of relationships (often sudden) rather than from blind trial and error. (p. 257)

Instinct. An unlearned behavior pattern that appears in the same form in every member of the species at a certain point in its development. (p. 269)

Instinctual drift. The tendency for learned behavior to drift towards instinctual behavior over time. (p. 251)

Instrumental conditioning. See *Operant conditioning.*

Intellectualization. A defense mechanism that reduces anxiety by turning the threatening situation into an abstract problem or by explaining it in such a way as to reduce the threat. (p. 621)

Intelligence. The global capacity to profit from experience and to go beyond given information about the environment. (p. 423)

Intelligence quotient. An index of intelligence derived from sources on standardized intelligence tests; obtained by dividing the individual's mental age by chronological age and then multiplying by 100. (p. 426)

Interaction. The joint effect of two independent variables on a behavior that could not have been predicted from the separate effect of each on the dependent measure. (p. 22)

Interneurons. Neurons providing communication between other neurons; make up the bulk of nerve cells in the brain. (p. 83)

Interposition. A depth cue present when one object blocks off the view of part of another object; also known as *occlusion.* (p. 209)

Intervening variable. A condition or event whose existence is inferred in order to explain a link between some observable input and a measurable response output. (p. 8)

Interview. A face-to-face conversation between a researcher and a respondent for the purpose of gathering detailed information about the respondent. (p. 12)

Intrinsic motivation. Motivation to engage in an activity for its own sake. (p. 290)

Introspection. A method of gathering data in which trained subjects report their current conscious experience as accurately as possible. (p. 25)

Introversion-extraversion. A personality dimension that describes people by the degree to which they need other people as sources of rewards and cues to appropriate behaviors. (p. 387)

Ions. Electrically charged particles that flow through the membrane of a cell, changing its polarity and thereby its capacity to conduct electrochemical signals. (p. 83)

Iris. A muscular disk that surrounds the pupil and expands and contracts to control the amount of light entering the eye. (p. 119)

J

Just noticeable difference. See *Difference threshold.*

K

Kinesthetic sense. The sense concerned with bodily position and movement of the body parts relative to each other. (p. 143)

L

Latency stage. Fourth of Freud's psychosexual developmental stages (from age 6 to puberty); during this stage satisfaction is gained primarily through the exploration and development of skills and interests and exploration of the environment. (p. 64)

Latent content. In Freudian dream analysis, the hidden, actual content of a dream. (p. 207)

Latent learning. Associations learned from experience and observation in which there is no change in behavior at the time. (p. 225)

Lateral geniculate nucleus. Relay point in the thalamus through which impulses pass when going from the eye to the occipital cortex. (p. 122)

Lateral sulcus. A deep horizontal groove that serves to divide the cerebral hemispheres into lobes. (p. 96)

Law of common fate. Law of grouping which states that elements moving in the same direction at the same rate are grouped together. (p. 164)

Law of effect. A basic law of learning which states that the power of a stimulus to evoke a response is strengthened when the response is followed by a reward and weakened if the response is not followed by a reward. (p. 236)

Law of forward conduction. The principle stating that neurons transmit information in only one direction (from the axon of one neuron to the dendrites or soma of the next). (p. 83)

Law of proximity. Law of grouping which states that the nearest, or "most proximal," elements are grouped together. (p. 163)

Law of similarity. Law of grouping which states that the most similar elements are grouped together. (p. 163)

Law of the specific energy of nerves. The principle that all nerve impulses are virtually identical, and that the quality of sensory experience is determined by the type of receptor that is stimulated. (p. 76)

Leadership. Capacity possessed by individuals who exert more influence than other members on a group; may be directed toward task performance or social-emotional processes within the group. (p. 601)

Learned helplessness. The general pattern of nonresponding in the presence of noxious stimuli which often follows after an organism has previously experienced noncontingent, inescapable aversive stimuli. (p. 246)

Learning. A process that results in a relatively permanent change in behavior or behavioral potential based on experience. (p. 225)

Legitimate authority. One seen as a valid representative of society, authorized to demand compliance. (p. 625)

Lens. A structure behind the iris through which light travels before reaching the central chamber of the eye. (p. 119)

Lesion. The careful destruction of a particular brain area by surgical removal, the cutting of connections, or the destruction of brain tissue. (p. 102)

Levels of processing theory. A theory regarding the structure and characteristics of the memory system that postulates a single system of memory in which the only differentiation is in the levels of processing applied to incoming information. (p. 326)

Libido. In Freudian theory, the psychic energy that drives individuals toward sensual pleasures of all types, including sexual. (p. 394)

Limbic system. Area at the upper end of the old brain which contains centers for emotional behavior and basic motivational urges. (p. 97)

Linear perspective. A depth cue depending on the fact that parallel lines converge to a point on the horizon as they recede into distance. (p. 172)

Lipostatic theory. The theory that receptors detect free fatty acids released during food deprivation and signal the lateral hypothalamus, resulting in motivation to eat. (p. 278)

Locus of control. A generalized belief about whether the outcomes of our actions are caused by what we do or by events outside our control. (p. 275)

Loneliness. The perception of being unable to achieve the level of affiliation that one would desire. (p. 586)

Longitudinal study. A method of scientific investigation in which selected measurements and observations of the same individuals are taken repeatedly over time. (p. 16)

Long-term memory. Those memory processes associated with the preservation of information for retrieval at any later time and theoretically, having the characteristic of unlimited capacity. (p. 309)

Lysergic acid diethylamide (LSD). A hallucinogenic drug capable of producing vivid imagery, hallucinations, disorganized thought processes, and symptoms of mental disorders. (p. 217)

M

Magnitude estimation. A method of constructing psychophysical scales by having observers scale their sensations directly into numbers. (p. 118)

Mandala. The assumed archetype of the self appearing as a circle and symbolizing the striving for unity and wholeness. (p. 398)

Manic episode. A psychotic reaction characterized by a recurring period of extreme elation, unbounded euphoria without sufficient reason, and grandiose thoughts or feelings about personal abilities. (p. 504)

Manifest content. In Freudian dream analysis, the surface content of a dream that is remembered; assumed to mask the real meaning of a dream. (p. 207)

Masochism. A type of psychosexual disorder involving sexual excitement derived from the experience of personal suffering. (p. 503)

Maturation. Continuing influence of heredity during development and later life; important in age-related physical and behavioral changes characteristic of the species. (p. 41)

Mean. The most commonly used measure of central tendency of a distribution; the average value for a group of scores. (p. 648)

Mechanistic approach. The belief that complex behavior can be reduced to its underlying physical basis. (p. 75)

Median. A measure of central tendency of a distribution; the score within a group of observations for which half of the remaining scores have values less than and half have values greater than this number. (p. 648)

Medical model. A paradigm used to approach the study of psychological disorders which defines and studies psychological abnormality in a way analogous to that used to study and treat physical illness. (p. 515)

Medulla. Area of the brain stem responsible for controlling repetitive processes such as breathing and heartbeat. (p. 97)

Memory. The mental capacity to store and later recognize or recall events that were previously experienced. (p. 306)

Mental disorder. A clinically significant behavioral or psychological syndrome or pattern that occurs in an individual and that is typically associated with either a distressing symptom or impairment in one or more important areas of functioning. (p. 490)

Mental operation. The mental manipulation of information; depends on concepts of objects rather than direct perceptual information. (p. 53)

Mental set. A tendency to respond to a new problem in the manner used on a previous problem. (p. 363)

Mere exposure effect. The ability of repeated exposures to the same stimulus to produce greater attraction towards that stimulus, a preference that develops without necessarily being aware of the cognitions involved. (p. 588)

Mesomorph. A somatotype characterized by a body build that is muscular, rectangular, and strong. (p. 386)

Metabolism. The breakdown of nutrients into body energy. (p. 77)

Metacognitive knowledge. The awareness of what you know and how well you are comprehending a situation. (p. 369)

Microelectrode. A tiny needle filled with a saline solution used in the recording of electrical activity in the brain. (p. 104)

Micro level of analysis. A level of analysis in which fine-grained, small units of behavior are studied. (p. 22)

Midbrain. The portion of the brain containing reflex centers and structures that relay sensory and motor information to and from higher brain centers. (p. 93)

Mnemonics. Special strategies or devices used during the encoding of new information that use already familiar items to enhance subsequent access to the information in memory. (p. 319)

Mode. A measure of central tendency of a distribution; the score occurring most frequently among the observations. (p. 647)

Model. A conceptual framework which provides a simplified way of thinking about the basic components in a field of knowledge. (p. 23)

Moderator variables. Conditions in a situation and in an individual's functioning that can change the effect of a stressor. (p. 475)

Molar level of analysis. A level of analysis in which the behavior of the whole functioning organism in a complex environment is the focus of study. (p. 22)

Molecular level of analysis. A level of analysis in which precisely defined units of behavior are the focus, but the units are somewhat larger than at the micro level. (p. 22)

Monism. The view that mind and brain are aspects of a single reality. (p. 76)

Morality. A system of beliefs and values which ensure that individuals will act to keep their obligations to others in the society and will behave in ways that do not interfere with the rights and interests of others. (p. 62)

Motivation. General term for the process of starting, directing, and maintaining physical and psychological activities; includes mechanisms involved in preferences for one activity over another, and the vigor and persistence of responses. (p. 263)

Motive. Term used to refer to psychologically and socially instigated motivation, assumed to be at least in part learned. (p. 263)

Motor cortex. See *Motor projection area.*

Motor neurons. Neurons that carry messages from the central nervous system to the muscles or glands. (p. 83)

Motor projection area. Area of the cerebral cortex located along the front of the central sulcus, devoted to sending messages to the muscles; also known as the *motor cortex.* (p. 97)

Multiple personality. A dissociative disorder in which different aspects of the personality function independently of one another, creating the appearance of two or more distinct personalities within the same individual. (p. 211)

Myelin sheath. A covering that insulates some axons, speeding the conduction of nerve impulses. (p. 86)

Myopia. A visual disorder in which one can not properly focus distant objects. (p. 120)

N

Nativism. A philosophical view proposed by Jean Rousseau emphasizing the role of innate, hereditary factors in human development and in the acquisition of knowledge. (p. 33)

Naturalistic observation. Observation of naturally occurring behaviors with no attempt to change or interfere with them; data collection without laboratory controls or the manipulation of variables. (p. 12)

Nature-nurture controversy. A debate in psychology concerning the relative importance of heredity (nature) and learning or experience (nurture) in determining development and behavior. (p. 43)

Need's hierarchy. Sequence of from most "primitive" to most "human." (p. 273)

Negative reinforcement. The condition following a response, of not receiving or escaping an aversive stimulus, increases the probability of the response. (p. 239)

Neocortex. The outer layer of the cerebrum, necessary for precise perception and conscious thought. (p. 97)

Neonate. The newborn infant; in humans from birth to one month old. (p. 44)

Nervous system. Network of cells specialized for rapid communication by electrical transmission within cells and chemical messengers between adjacent cells. (p. 78)

Neuron. A nerve cell specialized to provide rapid communication within and between adjacent cells. (p. 78)

Neuroregulators. "Second messengers," chemicals activated by both neurotransmitters and hormones which work inside receiving cells, amplifying the effect of the transmitter or hormone, changing the electrical potential of the membrane, and altering the internal biochemistry of the cell. (p. 88)

Neurosis. A mental disorder in which there are one or more symptoms related to ineffective attempts to deal with anxiety. (p. 497)

Neurotransmitters. Chemical messengers released from neurons which cross the synapse and interact with receptors on the postsynaptic cell membrane. (p. 86)

Nodes of Ranvier. Tiny breaks along the myelin sheath that covers an axon. Nerve impulses skip from one node to the next. (p. 86)

Nomothetic approach. A methodological approach to the study of personality processes in which emphasis is placed on identifying universal trait dimensions or lawful relationships between different aspects of personality functioning. (p. 384)

Nonconscious processes. Processes involving information that is not represented in either consciousness or memory, such as the organization of incoming stimuli into figure and ground. (p. 195)

Normal curve. A symmetrical distribution where, in the ideal case, the mean, median, and mode have the same value. (p. 652)

Normative investigations. Research efforts designed to describe what is characteristic of a specific age or developmental stage. (p. 35)

Norms. Standards based on measurements of a large group of people; used for comparing the score of an individual with those of others within a well-defined group. (p. 35)

Nucleus. Area of the cell that contains DNA and directs activities in the cytoplasm through the production of nucleic acids. (p. 77)

O

Object permanence. Recognition that objects exist independently of the individual's action or awareness. (p. 52)

Observational learning. The process by which an individual learns new responses by watching the behavior of another. (p. 405)

Obsession. A persistent and unwanted thought, image, or impulse that is difficult to ignore or suppress. (p. 500)

Occlusion. See *Interposition*.

Olfaction. The sensation of smell. (p. 141)

Operant conditioning. A procedure in which the probability or ratio of a response is changed by a change in its consequences. Also known as *instrumental conditioning*. (p. 236)

Operational definition. A definition of a variable or condition in terms of the specific operations the investigator uses to determine its presence. (p. 17)

Opiates. A group of drugs derived from the opium poppy and classified as depressants. (p. 215)

Opponent process theory. The theory that all color experiences arise from three systems, each of which include two "opponent" elements: red vs. green, blue vs. yellow, and black vs. white. (p. 127)

Optic chiasma. Region of the brain at which messages from the inner half of each retina cross over to the opposite hemisphere. (p. 99)

Optic nerve. The axons of the ganglion cells, which carry information from the eye back toward the brain. (p. 121)

Oral stage. First and most primitive of Freud's psychosexual developmental stages, during which the mouth region is the primary source of gratification from nourishment, stimulation, and making contact with the environment. (p. 64)

Organismic variables. Attributes of the perceiving organism which may influence perception. (p. 181)

Orienting reaction. A physiological and behavioral response that maximizes sensitivity to environmental input and prepares the body for emergency action. (p. 92)

Orienting response. A general response of attention to the source of novel stimulation. (p. 227)

Overregulation. A grammatical error usually appearing during early language development in which rules of the language are applied too widely, resulting in incorrect linguistic forms. (p. 48)

Overt behaviors. Responses that are visible to an observer. (p. 8)

P

Pain. The body's response to noxious stimuli that are intense enough to cause, or threaten to cause, tissue damage. (p. 144)

Panic disorder. An anxiety disorder in which the individual experiences recurrent episodes of intense anxiety and feelings of unpredictability that usually last for a few minutes and include symptoms of autonomic hyperactivity. (p. 499)

Paradigm. A symbolic model in research that represents the essential features of a process being investigated. (p. 227)

Paranoid disorders. A group of psychotic disorders characterized by well-developed, systematized, intricate delusions. (p. 506)

Paraphilia. A type of psychosexual disorder in which sexual excitement necessarily and involuntarily demands the presence of nonconventional sexual objects, practices, or circumstances. (p. 503)

Paraplegic. An individual with paralysis of the legs and/or trunk resulting from spinal cord injury. (p. 79)

Parasympathetic division. The division of the autonomic nervous system that deals with internal monitoring and regulation of various bodily functions. (p. 79)

Partial reinforcement effect. The behavioral principle that responses acquired under intermittent reinforcement are more difficult to extinguish than those acquired with continuous reinforcement. (p. 248)

Partial-report technique. An experimental technique used in memory studies in which subjects presented with a pattern containing several individual stimuli are subsequently asked to recall just a portion of the pattern instead of all the information presented. (p. 310)

Pedophilia. A paraphilia that involves an adult's action with or fantasy about sexual activity with young children. (p. 503)

Percept. What the perceiver experiences. (p. 161)

Perception. Processes that organize information in the sensory image and interpret it as having been produced by properties of objects in the external, three-dimensional world. (p. 112)

Perceptual defense. A hypothesized perceptual process which protects the person from identifying stimuli that are unpleasant or anxiety provoking. (p. 181)

Peripheral nervous system. The part of the nervous system outside of the central nervous system. (p. 79)

Personal construct. In Kelly's theory, a person's interpretation of reality, his or her beliefs about how two things are similar to each other and different from a third. (p. 409)

Personality. The unique psychological qualities of an individual that influence a variety of characteristic behavior patterns (both overt and covert) across different situations and over time. (p. 381)

Personality disorder. A chronic, inflexible, maladaptive pattern of perceiving, thinking, and behaving that seriously impairs the individual's ability to function in social or other settings. (p. 495)

Personality inventory. A self-report questionnaire used for personality assessment that includes a series of items about personal thoughts, feelings, and behaviors. (p. 435)

Personality psychology. A field of psychology in which all aspects of normal and abnormal functioning of an individual are studied by the use of an integrative approach; the whole person is the unit of observation. (p. 381)

Persuasion. Systematic attempts to influence another person's thoughts, feelings, or actions by means of communicative arguments. (p. 580)

Phallic stage. Third of Freud's psychosexual developmental stages (from 3–5 years); during this stage satisfaction is gained primarily through genital manipulation and exploration. According to Freud, there is a strong attraction for the opposite-sex parent during this stage. (p. 64)

Phantom limb phenomenon. Extreme or chronic pain in a limb that has been amputated. (p. 146)

Phenomenological approach. An approach in personality psychology which attempts to understand a person by understanding his or her view of reality. (p. 400)

Phenomenology. A person's own subjective view and interpretation of a situation or environment. (p. 570)

Phenotype. The observable set of characteristics of an organism resulting from the interaction of genotype and the environment. (p. 40)

Pheromones. Chemical signals released by organisms to communicate with other members of the species. (p. 142)

Phi phenomenon. See *apparent motion*.

Phobic disorder. A neurotic pattern of behavior in which anxiety is associated with some specific external environmental object or situation. (p. 498)

Photon. A single, indivisible unit of electromagnetic energy. (p. 122)

Photoreceptors. Receptor cells in the retina which are sensitive to light. (p. 120)

Physiological psychology. The branch of psychology that studies the physical and chemical factors or processes involved in behavior. (p. 74)

Physiological zero. An intermediate temperature point at which one feels neither warmth nor cold. (p. 144)

Pineal gland. A centrally located area of the brain considered by Descartes to be the one spot at which the soul and body interact; now thought to be involved in regulation of certain fundamental behavior cycles. (p. 82)

Pitch. The sound quality of "highness" or "lowness," primarily dependent upon the frequency of the sound wave. (p. 135)

Pituitary gland. A gland located in the brain that secretes a variety of hormones which influence growth and the secretion of other hormones by other glands. (p. 82)

Place theory. The theory that different frequencies produce maximum activation at different locations along the basilar membrane, with the result that pitch can be coded by the place where activation occurs. (p. 139)

Pleasure principle. In Freudian theory, that principle which guides the functioning of the id and is characterized by the search for unregulated sexual, physical, and emotional pleasure. (p. 395)

Polarity. The electrical state (positive or negative) of the membrane of a cell. (p. 83)

Polygenic. A human characteristic dependent on a combination of several genes. (p. 40)

Population. The total group or universe of possible observations from which samples are drawn to study. (p. 644)

Pornography. Materials presenting images of violence and dehumanization for sexual entertainment. (p. 633)

Positive reinforcement. The condition of receiving a stimulus, following a response, that increases the rate or probability of the response. (p. 239)

Positron emission tomography. A technique for obtaining detailed pictures of activity in the living brain; involves injecting a radioactive substance which is taken up by the active neurons. (p. 105)

Posttraumatic stress disorder. A reaction in which the individual involuntarily reexperiences the emotional, cognitive, and behavioral aspects of a past trauma. (p. 468)

Preattentive stage. The initial sensory stage in the perceptual sequence of processing external information in which features of environmental stimuli are automatically registered without conscious awareness. (p. 194)

Prenatal. The period of development prior to birth. (p. 42)

Preoperational stage. Second of Piaget's stages of cognitive development (from 2–7 years); characterized by centrism, discovery of qualitative identity, and increasing use of symbols but continued dependence on appearances. (p. 52)

Preparedness. The learning principle that stimulus-reinforcer relationships are easier to learn when they are related to the organism's survival in the natural environment. (p. 251)

Primary appraisal. A term used in stress research referring to the first stage in the cognitive appraisal of a potentially stressful situation in which the individual evaluates the seriousness of a demand or potentially stressful situation. (p. 457)

Primary drives. Motivational state induced by biological needs and not dependent on learning. (p. 271)

Proactive interference. A memory phenomenon in which information previously stored interferes with the learning of new, but similar information. (p. 333)

Probability. The likelihood that an outcome will occur. (p. 358)

Prognosis. An estimate of the course that a problem will take with or without some type of intervention or treatment. (p. 530)

Progressive relaxation. A technique often used by clinicians which calls for the individual to alternatively tense and relax muscles as a way of learning the experience of relaxation. (p. 482)

Projective test. A method of personality assessment in which an individual is presented with a standardized set of ambiguous, abstract stimuli and asked to interpret the meaning of the stimuli; responses are assumed to reveal inner feelings, motives, and conflicts. (p. 439)

Proposition. An abstract unit of meaning that expresses a relationship between concepts, objects, or events. (p. 350)

Prototype. The most representative example of a category. (p. 179; p. 347)

Proximal stimulus. The image on the retina, as contrasted with the *distal stimulus.* (p. 154)

Psychiatrist. An individual who has completed all medical school training for the M.D. degree and also has completed some postdoctoral specialty training in dealing with mental and emotional disorders; a psychiatrist may prescribe medications for the treatment of psychological disorders. (p. 531)

Psychic energy. In Freudian theory, the primary source of motivation for human actions and the dynamic force behind all behavior. (p. 394)

Psychoactive drugs. Chemicals which affect mental processes and behavior by changing conscious awareness of reality. (p. 214)

Psychoanalyst. An individual who has earned either a Ph.D. or an M.D. and has completed postgraduate training in an institute that offers specialized training in the Freudian approach to understanding and treatment of mental disorders. (p. 531)

Psychodynamic model. A psychological model in which behavior is explained in terms of past experiences and motivational forces. Actions are viewed as stemming from inherited instincts, biological drives, and attempts to resolve conflicts between personal needs and social requirements. (p. 24)

Psychogenic amnesia. A type of amnesia not caused by any physical damage or neurological disorder in which there occurs a sudden inability to recall important personal information and is precipitated by psychological distress. (p. 502)

Psychogenic fugue. An amnesic state during which the individual travels to a new place and assumes a new identity and lifestyle. (p. 502)

Psychoimmunology. The study of how the immune system is affected by psychological processes. (p. 464)

Psychological assessment. The use of specified procedures to evaluate the abilities, behaviors, and personal qualities of people. (p. 416)

Psychological test. A measuring instrument used to assess an individual's standing relative to others on some mental or behavioral characteristic. (p. 13)

Psychology. The scientific study of the behavior and mental processes of organisms. (p. 6)

Psychometric function. A graph that plots the percentage of detections of a stimulus (on the vertical axis) for each stimulus intensity (on the horizontal axis). (p. 113)

Psychopathology. The study of mental or emotional disorders by medical or psychological specialists; also the general term for psychological abnormalities. (p. 490)

Psychophysics. The study of the correspondence between psychological experience and physical stimulation. (p. 113)

Psychophysiological model. A paradigm based on the assumption that the functioning of an organism is best explained in terms of the biological or physical structures and processes that make it work. (p. 23)

Psychosexual disorders. A group of psychological disorders including problems of sexual inhibitions and dysfunctions, sexual deviations, and gender identity. (p. 503)

Psychosexual stages. Stages of sexual development in the child proposed by Freud which involve successive ways of satisfying instinctual biological urges through stimulation of different areas of the body: the mouth, anus, and the genitals. (p. 64)

Psychosis. A severe mental disorder in which a person experiences impairments in reality-testing as manifested through thought, emotional, or perceptual difficulties. (p. 504)

Psychosocial stages. Successive developmental stages proposed by Erik Erikson that focus on the individual's orientation towards the self and others; these stages incorporate both sexual and social aspects of a person's development and social conflicts that arise from the interaction between an individual and the social environment. (p. 64)

Psychosomatic disorder. A physical disorder aggravated by or primarily attributable to prolonged emotional stress or other psychological causes. (p. 460)

Psychotherapy. The group of therapies used to treat psychological disorders that focus on changing faulty behaviors, thoughts, perceptions, and emotions that may be associated with specific disorders. (p. 529)

Punishment. The condition of receiving an aversive stimulus, which decreases the probability of the preceding response. (p. 239)

Pupil. An opening in the iris that allows light to enter the eye. (p. 119)

Pure tone. A sound produced by a single sine wave. (p. 135)

R

Random assignment. Assignment of subjects to either the experimental or control groups by a chance procedure so that each subject has an equal chance of being placed in either group. (p. 15)

Random sample. A group of individuals selected from the population in such a way that every member has the same likelihood of being selected as another. (p. 644)

Reaction time. The elapsed time between a stimulus presentation and a designated response; used as a measure of the time required for mental processes. (p. 76; p. 343)

Recall. A method of retrieval in which the individual is required to reproduce the information previously presented. (p. 325)

Receptive field. The visual area from which a given ganglion cell receives messages. (p. 128)

Recessive genes. Genes that are expressed in an individual's development only when paired with a similar gene. (p. 40)

Reciprocal determinism. A concept of Bandura's social learning theory referring to the notion that a complex reciprocal interaction exists between factors of the individual, behavior, and environmental stimuli, with each of these components affecting the others. (p. 405)

Recognition. A method of retrieval in which the individual is required to identify present stimuli as having been experienced before. (p. 325)

Redundancy. Duplication in a cellular system, providing a "margin of safety" guaranteeing that a specific job will get done even if some cells are damaged. (p. 77)

Reference frames. Spatial or temporal context. (p. 164)

Reference groups. The formal or informal groups from which one derives attitudes and standards of what is acceptable and appropriate and to which one refers for information, direction, and support for life-style. (p. 596)

Reflex arc. Neural circuit including nerve pathways carrying incoming sensory information and pathways carrying outgoing motor signals. (p. 77)

Rehearsal. Active repetition of information in order to enhance subsequent access to it. (p. 315)

Reinforcement schedule. In operant conditioning, the pattern of delivering and withholding reinforcement. (p. 248)

Reinforcers. Stimuli occurring after a response that change its rate or probability. (p. 238)

Relabeling. A strategy used to achieve dehumanization that involves the use of terms which make certain individuals appear less human-like and more object-like. (p. 621)

Relative motion parallax. A source of information about depth in which the relative distances of objects from the viewer determine the amount and direction of their relative motion in the retinal image. (p. 170)

Releaser. An environmental cue that evokes a specific response pattern in every member of a species. (p. 269)

Reliability. The degree to which individuals earn the same relative scores each time they are measured. (p. 16)

REM sleep. A stage during the sleep cycle in which electrical brain activity is characterized by erratic, low-voltage patterns similar to those observed during the waking state and during which there are bursts of rapid eye movements. Also known as *paradoxical sleep*. (p. 204)

Replication. Repetition of an experiment under similar conditions in order to see if the same results will be obtained. Usually conducted by an independent investigator. (p. 11)

Representative heuristic. A heuristic through which something is assigned to a category on the basis of a few characteristics regarded as representative of the category. (p. 359)

Repression. In Freudian theory, a defense mechanism by which painful or guilt-producing thoughts, feelings, or memories are excluded from conscious awareness. (p. 395)

Response. Any behavior of organisms in reaction to a stimulus. (p. 8)

Response bias. A systematic tendency, due to nonsensory factors, for an observer to favor responding in a particular way. (p. 114)

Resting potential. Neuronal state in which there is a negative electrical charge inside the neuron and a positive charge outside it; in such a situation, the neuron is ready to fire instantly when stimulated. (p. 84)

Reticular formation. A long structure in the middle of the brain stem through which sensory messages pass on their way to higher centers of the brain. (p. 97)

Retina. The layer at the back of the eye which contains photoreceptors. (p. 119)

Retrieval. The recovery of stored information from memory at a later time. (p. 307)

Retrieval cues. Internally or externally generated stimuli available to help with the retrieval of a memory. (p. 324)

Retroactive information. A memory phenomenon in which the learning of new information interferes with the memory of a previously stored similar item. (p. 333)

Retrograde amnesia. A type of amnesia in which there is loss of memory for events experienced prior to the event that precipitated the amnesia. (p. 335)

Reuptake. A process in which a neurotransmitter is taken back into the terminal buttons from which it was released. (p. 86)

Rods. Photoreceptors which are concentrated in the periphery of the retina, are most active for seeing in dim illumination, and do not produce sensations of color. (p. 120)

Role. A socially defined pattern of behavior that is expected of a person who has a certain function within a group or setting. (p. 593)

Role confusion. A difficulty particularly apparent during adolescence in which a person tries to fulfill conflicting social roles. (p. 66)

Romantic love. A state of intense absorption in another person, usually accompanied by a state of strong, physiological arousal. (p. 591)

S

Sadism. A type of psychosexual disorder involving sexual excitement derived from inflicting pain, suffering, or humiliation on others. (p. 503)

Sample. A specific group representative of a defined population upon which observations or measurements are taken. (p. 644)

Saturation. The dimension of color space that captures the "purity" and "vividness" of color sensations. (p. 123)

Scapegoat. A target other than the original source of frustration onto which aggression is displaced. (p. 630)

Schema. An integrated cluster of knowledge organized around a topic; includes expectations. (p. 180)

Scheme. A term first used by Piaget to denote a cognitive structure that relates means to ends; guides sensorimotor sequences such as sucking with little or no "thought." (p. 51)

Schizophrenic disorders. A group of psychotic disorders characterized by the breakdown of integrated personality functioning, withdrawal from reality, emotional distortions, and disturbed thought processes. (p. 507)

Scientific method. A set of attitudes and procedures for gathering and interpreting objective information in such a way as to minimize sources of error and yield dependable generalizations. (p. 11)

Script. A cluster of knowledge about a sequence of interrelated specific events and actions that are expected to occur in a certain way in particular settings. (p. 350)

Secondary appraisal. A term used in stress research referring to the second stage in the cognitive appraisal of a potentially stressful situation in which the individual evaluates what personal and social resources are available to deal with the stressful circumstance and determines what action is needed. (p. 457)

Secondary gain. Attention, comfort, and sympathy received as a result of incapacitating or handicapping physical symptoms. (p. 393)

Secondary trait. A characteristic of a person that is not crucial to an understanding of the individual but nevertheless provides some information about enduring qualities of the person. (p. 388)

Second-order conditioning. A classical conditioning procedure in which a neutral stimulus is paired with a conditioned stimulus rather than an unconditioned stimulus. Also called *higher-order conditioning.* (p. 232)

Selective attention. Refers to the ability to be aware of only part of the available sensory input. (p. 312)

Self-actualization. A concept in personality psychology referring to a person's constant striving to realize one's potential and to develop inherent talents and capabilities; many humanistic psychologists see the need for self-actualization as the most basic human need. (p. 274; p. 400)

Self-concept. The individual's awareness of his or her continuing identity as a person. (p. 401)

Self-efficacy. A belief that one can perform adequately. (p. 408)

Self-esteem. A generalized evaluative attitude towards the self that influences both moods and behavior. (p. 401)

Self-fulfilling prophecy. The notion that a hypothesis or expectation about how someone will act exerts a subtle influence on the person to act in the expected way, or for the perceiver to "see" what is expected. (p. 572)

Self-report method. An often used research technique in which a personality assessment is achieved through respondents' answers to a series of questions. (p. 422)

Semantic memory. That aspect of long-term memory which stores the basic meaning of words and concepts. (p. 321)

Semicircular canals. Fluid-filled canals in the inner ear which provide vestibular sense information. (p. 142)

Sensation. Processes that analyze physical energy in the world (e.g., light and sound waves) and convert it into neural activity that codes simple information about how the receptor organs are being stimulated. (p. 112)

Sensorimotor stage. First of Piaget's stages of cognitive development (from about 0–2 years); characterized by improvement and coordination of sensorimotor sequences, object permanence, and the beginning of internal symbolic representation. (p. 52)

Sensory adaptation. A phenomenon in which visual receptor cells lose their power to respond after a period of unchanged stimulation. (p. 132)

Sensory discriminability. A measure of an observer's sensitivity on a perceptual judgment task. (p. 116)

Sensory gating. A brain-directed process in which information in one sensory channel may be enhanced while information in another is suppressed or disregarded. (p. 310)

Sensory memory. Those memory processes involved in the momentary preservation of fleeting impressions of sensory stimuli. Also called *sensory register.* (p. 309)

Sensory neurons. Neurons that carry messages from the cells in the periphery toward the central nervous system. (p. 83)

Sensory physiology. The study of how biological mechanisms convert physical events into neural events. (p. 113)

Sensory preconditioning. The learning of an association between two paired stimuli prior to any pairing of either one with an unconditioned stimulus. (p. 253)

Sensory projection areas. Areas of the cerebral cortex devoted to receiving sensory input, located in the parietal and occipital lobes. (p. 98)

Sensory register. See *Sensory memory.*

Sequential design. A research approach in which a group of subjects spanning a small age range are grouped according to year of birth and are observed repeatedly over several years. This design combines some features of both the cross-sectional and longitudinal approaches. (p. 37)

Serial position effect. A characteristic of retrieval in which the recall of beginning and end items on a list is better than memory for items appearing in the middle. (p. 327)

Sex. The biologically based characteristics that distinguish males from females. (p. 60)

Sexual arousal. The motivational state of excitement and tension brought about by physiological and cognitive reactions to erotic stimuli. (p. 282)

Sexual scripts. Socially learned programs of sexual responsiveness. (p. 284)

Shaping. The operant learning technique in which a new behavior is produced by reinforcing successive approximations of the final behavior desired. (p. 245)

Short-term memory. Those memory processes associated with the preservation of events or experiences recently perceived; short-term memory is of limited capacity and stores information for only a short length of time without rehearsal. (p. 309)

Shyness. An apprehensiveness about certain social situations due to excessive preoccupation with being critically evaluated, resulting in a variety of behavioral, physical, cognitive, and emotional reactions. (p. 447)

Significant difference. A difference between groups or conditions that meets a conventional criterion of probability that it was not due to chance. (p. 19)

Sine-wave gratings. Patterns of alternating black and white stripes used to study visual systems. (p. 130)

Social comparison theory. A theory postulating a need for individuals to seek out and make subjective comparisons with certain other people in order to assess their own ability, opinions, and emotions. (p. 585)

Social context. The part of the total environment that includes other people, both real and imagined, interactions, the setting in which the interactions take place, and unwritten rules and expectations that govern how people relate to each other. (p. 568)

Social dilemma. A choice situation characterized by a social payoff that is higher for each individual for defecting from the social good than it is for cooperating but would be highest for all if all cooperated. (p. 634)

Social exchange theory. A hypothesis about social interaction that conceives of social interactions in economic terms as exchanges between people which have both benefits and costs. (p. 588)

Social facilitation. The facilitating effect that the presence of other people sometimes has on individual performance. (p. 594)

Socialization. The lifelong process whereby an individual's behavioral patterns, values, standards, skills, attitudes, and motives are shaped to conform to those regarded as desirable in a particular society. (p. 55)

Social norms. Expectations that a group has for its members regarding attitudes and behavior that are evaluated as acceptable and appropriate. (p. 594)

Social phobia. A type of phobia in which the individual experiences an irrational fear of speaking, writing, performing artistically, or eating in public. (p. 498)

Social psychology. The branch of psychology that studies the effect of social variables on individual behavior, attitudes, perceptions, and motives; it also studies group and inter-group phenomena. (p. 568)

Social reality. The phenomenological perspective and norms of the group which define reality for its members. (p. 571)

Social status. One's position, rank, or standing relative to other people in a given setting. (p. 574)

Social trap. A situation in which some social action has an immediate rewarding consequence but a long-term negative outcome. (p. 635)

Soma. The cell body of a neuron; contains the nucleus and cytoplasm of the cell. (p. 83)

Somatic nervous system. The part of the peripheral nervous system which controls the skeletal muscles of the body. (p. 79)

Somatoform disorders. A group of disorders characterized by bodily (somatic) complaints in the absence of any known organic problems and assumed to reflect psychological conflicts. (p. 501)

Somatosensory area. Area of the parietal lobes that receives sensory input from various body areas. (p. 98)

Somatotype. A descriptive category which classifies a person on the basis of a few salient physical characteristics with the hope of relating these to personality characteristics. (p. 384)

Sound spectrum. A graph of all the frequencies, with their amplitudes, present in a sound. (p. 136)

Spatial frequency. The number of dark-light cycles in a pattern over a given distance of visual space. (p. 130)

Spatial-frequency model. The theory that the visual system analyzes complex stimuli into spatial frequencies. (p. 130)

Spinal cord. The nerve tract in the spinal column between the brain and the peripheral nervous system. (p. 79)

Split-span task. Experimental task requiring recall of simultaneous input to the two ears. (p. 192)

Spontaneous recovery. The reappearance of an extinguished conditioned response after a rest period. (p. 229)

Stabilized image. An image that falls on exactly the same visual receptor cells for a period of time; the image disappears because the cells stop responding. (p. 132)

Standard deviation. A measure of the variability of scores in a distribution indicating the average difference between scores and their mean. (p. 649)

Standardization. Uniform procedures for treating each participant or for recording data. In test construction, includes giving the test to a large number of representative individuals to establish norms. (p. 17)

Standardized measuring device. A measuring device that has been administered to a large group of subjects representative of the group for which it is intended thus yielding statistical standards or norms by which to compare an individual's score. (p. 420)

Stanford-Binet intelligence test. The most widely used children's intelligence test; a version of the Binet written intelligence test in which subjects are tested individually using age-level subtests. (p. 426)

State-dependent learning. A characteristic of the memory system in which retrieval is relatively better if the psychological or physical state present at the time of learning is similar to that present at the time of retrieval. (p. 320)

Statistical variability. A measure of how widely scores in a distribution vary from each other. (p. 648)

Status transaction. A form of communication between people that establishes their relative status or social power. (p. 574)

Stereochemical theory. A theory of smell which suggests that receptor sites in odor-sensitive cells have distinctive sizes and shapes corresponding to those of the chemical molecules which stimulate them. (p. 142)

Stereotype effect. A bias sometimes occurring in judges' ratings or observations of an individual where judges' beliefs about the qualities that most people have who belong to a certain category influence the perception of an observed individual who belongs to that particular category. (p. 422)

Stimulants. Drugs that increase the transmission of impulses in the central nervous system and tend to speed up mental and physical activity. (p. 216)

Stimulus. An environmental condition that elicits a response from an organism. (p. 8)

Stimulus control. Control of the occurrence of a response by means of a dependable signal (i.e., a discriminative stimulus) indicating a reinforcer is available. (p. 241)

Stimulus discrimination. A conditioning process in which the organism learns to respond differently to stimuli that are different from the conditioned stimulus on some dimension. (p. 230)

Stimulus generalization. The automatic extension of conditioned responding to similar stimuli that have never been paired with the unconditioned stimulus. (p. 230)

Storage. The retention of encoded material over time involving neurophysiological changes in certain synapses. (p. 307)

Stress. The pattern of specific and nonspecific responses an organism makes to stimulus events that disturb its equilibrium and tax or exceed its ability to cope. (p. 456)

Stress-induced analgesia. The temporary reduction of sensitivity to pain during stress; achieved through the release of endorphins. (p. 460)

Stressors. Internal or external events or stimuli that induce stress. (p. 456)

Stroboscopic motion. A phenomenon in which a series of still images shown in rapid succession are seen as a continuous view of the object in motion. (p. 133)

Structuralism. The theory that perception arises from a process in which basic "atoms of sensation" arouse memories of previous sensations that have been associated through repeated experiences. (p. 157)

Subconscious processes. Mental processes involving material not currently in consciousness but retrievable by special recall procedures. (p. 196)

Superego. In Freudian theory, that aspect of personality representing the internalization of society's values, standards, and morals; the inner conscience. (p. 62)

Survey. A method of gathering information from a large number of people; self-report information is gathered in response to a list of questions that follow a fixed format. (p. 12)

Sympathetic division. The division of the autonomic nervous system that deals with emergency responding. (p. 79)

Synapse. The gap between one neuron and the next; it is filled with a fluid that does not permit electrical activity to pass across. (p. 86)

T

Tabula rasa. Term associated with the philosophical view proposed by John Locke that at birth individuals are born with a "blank slate" and that all knowledge comes from experience. (p. 33)

Taste buds. The receptors for taste, located primarily on the upper side of the tongue. (p. 141)

Telegraphic speech. The speech pattern of a normal child 2–3 years of age that consists of short, simple sentences with many nouns and verbs but lacks tense endings, plurals, and function words. (p. 48)

Telencephalon. The upper part of the forebrain; associated with consciousness. (p. 93)

Teleology. The view that an immaterial, purposeful mind gives behavior its direction by acting on a passive, mechanistic brain. (p. 75)

Temperament. A dispositional tendency; a stable biological endowment present at birth that influences characteristic behavioral style and general emotional responsiveness. (p. 479).

Tension reduction. The reinforcing state which follows from the reduction of unpleasant sensations which occur as a result of unsatisfied drives. (p. 404)

Territoriality. An innate drive to gain and defend property. (p. 628)

Testosterone. A male hormone secreted by the testes; responsible for sex-linked characteristics such as facial hair and deep voice. (p. 82)

Test-retest reliability. A measure of the correlation between the scores of the same people on the same test given on two different occasions. (p. 419)

Texture grandient. Change in apparent texture when a uniform textured surface is slanted away from the observer. (p. 160)

Thalamus. Structure below the corpus callosum that serves as a relay station for all incoming sensory information. (p. 97)

Thanatos. In Freudian theory, the death instinct, assumed to drive people towards aggressive and destructive behavior. (p. 394)

Thematic Apperception test (TAT). A type of projective test in which pictures of ambiguous scenes are presented to an individual who is encouraged to generate stories about the stimuli. (p. 440)

Theory. A set of interrelated principles that are used to explain or predict behavior. (p. 19)

Theory of signal detectibility. A theory that all perceptual judgments combine sensory and decision-making processes. (p. 115)

Think-aloud protocols. Reports of mental processes and strategies made by experimental subjects while working on a task. (p. 342)

Threshold. The minimum stimulus level at which a sensory signal is detected half the time. (p. 114)

Thyrotrophic hormone (TTH). A hormone released from the pituitary gland which stimulates the thyroid gland to make more energy available to the body during a stress reaction. (p. 460)

Timbre. A dimension of auditory sensation which reflects the complexity of the sound wave. (p. 136)

Token economy. A technique of positive reinforcement in which individuals are rewarded for socially constructive behaviors by tokens which may later be exchanged for privileges. (p. 244)

Tolerance. Lessened effect of a drug following continued use. (p. 214)

Trance logic. Denial at one level of information processing occurring at another level. (p. 211)

Transference. The process by which a person in psychoanalysis attaches to the therapist feelings formerly held towards some significant person who figured in a past emotional conflict. (p. 537)

Transsexual. An individual who has undergone a variety of psysiological and/or surgical treatments to alleviate a gender identity disorder by changing one's anatomical sex. (p. 503)

Trichromatic theory. The theory that there are three types of color receptors that produce the psychologically "primary" color sensations: red, green, and blue. (p. 126)

Two-component theory. The theory that emotion is the joint effect of two central processes: physiological arousal and cognitive appraisal. (p. 370)

Tympanic membrane. A thin membrane in the ear set into motion by the pressure variations of sound waves; also known as the eardrum. (p. 138)

Type-A behavior pattern. Competitive, compulsive, and hostile behaviors characteristic of a particular style of coping with stress; assumed to increase the risk of coronary heart disease. (p. 478)

U

Unconditioned response. In classical conditioning, the response which is elicited by an unconditioned stimulus without prior training or learning. (p. 227)

Unconditioned stimulus. In classical conditioning, the stimulus which elicits the unconditioned response and the presentation of which acts as reinforcement. (p. 227)

Unconscious processes. In Freudian theory, mental processes that are not directly observable or subject to verification by self-report, but whose existence is inferred from effects on observable behaviors. (p. 196)

Underclass. A term referring to the long-term poor who are isolated from the rest of society because they lack education, employable skills, and personality traits regarded as desirable by others in the society. (p. 617)

Utility. A measure of the attractiveness of a potential outcome. (p. 358)

V

Validity. The extent to which a test measures what it was intended to measure. (p. 16)

Variable. A factor that varies in amount or kind. (p. 12)

Variable interval schedule. In operant conditioning, a schedule in which reinforcement is delivered after differing lengths of time, regardless of the number of correct responses that have occurred. (p. 249)

Variable ratio schedule. In operant conditioning, a schedule in which reinforcement is given after a changing number of responses. (p. 248)

Vestibular sense The sense that tells us how our bodies are oriented in the world with respect to gravity. (p. 142)

Violence. The expression of hostility and rage directed against people or property. (p. 627)

Visual capture. A phenomenon in which vision dominates the other sensory modalities, such that you perceive only what is consistent with visual input. (p. 167)

Visual cortex. Area at the back of the brain, in the occipital lobes, where visual information is processed. (p. 98)

Volley principle. An extension of frequency theory which proposes that when peaks in a sound wave come too frequently for a single neuron to fire at each peak, several neurons as a group could fire at the frequency of the stimulus tone. (p. 140)

W

Wavelength. A physical property of waves measured in units of distance along the wave-like propagation; wavelength is the only property that distinguishes one photon from another. (p. 122)

Weber's law. The assertion that the size of a difference theshold is proportional to the intensity of the standard stimulus. (p. 117)

Whole-report procedure. An experimental technique used in memory studies in which subjects presented with a pattern containing several stimuli are subsequently asked to recall as many of the individual stimuli as possible. (p. 310)

Withdrawal symptoms. Painful physical symptoms experienced when the level of a drug to which physical addiction has occurred is decreased or eliminated. (p. 214)

Word association. A technique of personality assessment to which an individual's responses to a list of common words are used to try and identify unconscious personality dynamics. (p. 439)

REFERENCES

A

Abramson, L. Y., Seligman, M. E. P., & Teasdale, J. D. (1978). Learned helplessness in humans: Critique and reformulation. *Journal of Abnormal Psychology, 87,* 49–74.

Acredolo, L. P. (1977). Laboratory versus home: The effect of environment on the 9-month-old infant's choice of spatial reference system. *Developmental Psychology, 15,* 666–667.

Adams, J. L. (1979). *Conceptual blockbusting* (2nd Ed.). New York: Norton.

Ader, R. (1981). A historical account of conditioned immunobiologic responses. In R. Ader (Ed.), *Psychoneuroimmunology.* New York: Academic Press.

Ader, R., & Cohen, N. (1981). Conditioned immunopharmacological responses. In R. Ader (Ed.), Psychoneuroimmunology (pp. 281–319). New York: Academic Press.

Adler, A. (1929). *The practice and theory of individual psychology.* New York: Harcourt, Brace & World.

Agras, W. S., Taylor, C. B., & Kraemer, H. C., Allen, R. A., & Schneider, J. A. (1980). Relaxation training: Twenty-four-hour blood pressure changes. *Archives of General Psychiatry, 37,* 859–863.

Ajzen, I., & Fishbein, M. (1977). Attitude-behavior relations: A theoretical analysis and review of empirical research. *Psychological Bulletin, 84,* 888–918.

Akhtar, S., Wig, N. H., Verma, V. K., Pershod, D., & Verma, S. K. (1975). A phenomenological analysis of symptoms in obsessive-compulsive neurosis. *British Journal of Psychiatry, 127,* 342–348.

Akil, H. (1978). Endorphins, beta-LPH and ACTH: Biochemical pharmacological and anatomical studies. *Advances in Biochemical Psychopharmacology, 18,* 125–139.

Alba, J. W., & Hasher, L. (1983). Is memory schematic? *Psychological Bulletin, 93,* 203–231.

Albee, G. W., & Joffee, J. M. (Eds.). (1977). *Primary prevention of psychopathology: Vol. I. Issues.* Hanover, NH: University Press of New England.

Albuquerque, E. X., Aguayo, L. G., Warnick, R. K., Ickowicz, R. K., & Blaustein, M. P. (1983, June). Interactions of phencyclidine with ion channels of nerve and muscle: behavioral implications. *Federation Proceedings, 42* (9), 2584–2589.

Alcott, W. A. (1846). *The young man's guide,* (16th ed.) Boston: T. R. Marvin.

Allen, V. L., & Wilder, D. A. (1975). Categorization, belief, similarity, and intergroup competition. *Journal of Personality and Social Psychology, 32,* 971–977.

Allison, T., & Cicchetti, D. (1976). Sleep in mammals: Ecological and constitutional correlates. *Science, 194,* 732–734.

Alloy, L. B., & Abramson, L. Y. (1979). Judgment of contingency in depressed and nondepressed students: Sadder but wiser? *Journal of Experimental Psychology: General, 108,* 441–485.

Allport, G. W. (1937). *Personality: A psychological interpretation.* New York: Holt, Rinehart & Winston.

Allport, G. W. (1960). *Personality and social encounter.* Berkeley, CA: Beacon Press.

Allport, G. W. (1961). *Pattern and growth in personality.* New York: Holt, Rinehart & Winston.

Allport, G. W. (1965). *Letters from Jenny.* New York: Harcourt, Brace, & World.

Allport, G. W. (1966). Traits revisited. *American Psychologist, 21,* 1–10.

Allport, G. W. (1968). The historical background of modern social psychology. In G. Lindzey & E. Aronson (Eds.), *The handbook of social psychology* (2nd ed.). Reading, MA: Addison-Wesley.

Allport, G. W., & Postman, L. J. (1947). *The psychology of rumor.* New York: Holt, Rinehart & Winston.

Almli, C. R. (1978). The ontogeny of feeding and drinking behavior: Effects of early brain damage. *Neuroscience and Behavioral Reviews, 2,* 281–300.

Altman, I. A. (1976). Environmental psychology and social psychology, *Personality and Social Psychology Bulletin, 2,* 96–113.

Altman, I. & Taylor, D. (1973). *Social penetration: The development of interpersonal relationships.* New York: Holt, Rinehart & Winston.

Amabile, T. M. (1983). *The social psychology of creativity.* New York: Springer-Verlag.

Amabile, T. M., & Glazebook, A. H. (1981). A negativity bias in interpersonal evaluation. *Journal of Experimental Social Psychology, 18,* 1–22.

American Psychological Association. (1965). Special issue: Testing and public policy. *American Psychologist, 20,* 857–993.

Amoore, J. E. (1965). Psychophysics of odor. *Cold Springs Harbor symposia in quantitative biology, 30,* 623–637.

Amnesty International. (1983). *Chile: Evidence of torture.* London: Amnesty International Publications.

Anastasi, A. (1976). *Psychological testing* (4th ed.). New York: Macmillan.

Anastasi, A. (1982). *Psychological testing* (5th ed.). New York: Macmillan.

Andersen, S. M., & Zimbardo, P. G. (1980, November) Resisting mind control. *U.S.A. Today,* 44–47.

Anderson, J. R. (1976). *Language, memory, and thought.* Hillsdale, NJ: Erlbaum.

Anderson, J. R. (1978). Arguments concerning representations for mental imagery. *Psychological Review, 85,* 249–277.

Anderson, J. R. (1980). *Cognitive psychology and its implications.* San Francisco: Freeman.

Anderson, J. R. (Ed.). (1981). *Cognitive skills and their acquisition.* Hillsdale, NJ: Erlbaum.

Anderson, J. R. (1982). Acquisition of cognitive skill. *Psychological Review, 89,* 369–406.

Anderson, J. R., & Bower, G. H. (1973). *Human associative memory.* Washington, DC: Winston & Sons.

Antelman, S. M., & Caggiula, A. R. (1980). Stress-induced behavior: Chemotherapy without drugs. In J. M. Davidson & R. J. Davidson (Eds.), *The psychobiology of consciousness* (pp. 65–104). New York: Plenum.

Antelman, S. M., Rowland, N. E., & Fisher, A. E. (1976). Stimulation bound ingestive behavior: A view from the tail. *Physiology and Behavior, 17,* 743–748.

Ardrey, R. (1966). *The territorial imperative.* New York: Atheneum.

Arlow, J. A. (1979). Psychoanalysis. In R. J. Corsini (Ed.), *Current Psychotherapies* (pp. 1–43)., (2nd ed.) Itasca, IL: Peacock.

Aronson, E. (1969). Some antecedents of interpersonal attraction. In W. J. Arnold & D. Levine (Eds.), *Nebraska symposium on motivation.* Lincoln, NB: University of Nebraska Press.

Aronson, E., Blaney, N., Stephan, C., Sikes, J., & Snapp, M. (1978). *The jigsaw classroom.* Beverly Hills, CA: Sage.

Aronson, E., Turner, J. A., & Carlsmith, J. M. (1963). *Journal of Abnormal and Social Psychology, 67,* 31–36.

Asarnow, R. F., Cromwell, R. L., & Rennick, P. M. (1978). Cognitive and evoked response measures of information processing in schizophrenics with and without a family history of schizophrenia. *The Journal of Nervous and Mental Disease, 166,* 719–730.

Asch, S. E. (1955). Opinions and social pressure. *Scientific American, 193*(5), 31–35.

Aserinsky, E., & Kleitman, N. (1953). Regularly occurring periods of eye mobility and concomitant phenomena during sleep. *Science, 118,* 273–274.

Ashley, W. R., Harper, R. S., & Runyon, D. L. (1951). The perceived size of coins in normal and hypnotically induced economic states. *American Journal of Psychology, 64,* 564–572.

Atkinson, J. W., & Birch, D. (1970). *The dynamics of action.* New York: Wiley.

Atkinson, J. W., & Raynor, J. O. (1974). *Motivation and achievement.* Washington DC: Winston.

Atkinson, R. C., & Shiffrin, R. M. (1968). Human memory: A proposed system and its control processes. In K. W. Spence & J. T. Spence (Eds.), *The psychology of learning and motivation: Advances in research and theory* (Vol. 2). New York: Academic Press.

Auletta, K. (1981, November). The underclass. *New Yorker,* Nov. 9, 16, 23.

Averbach, I., & Coriell, A. S. (1961). Short-term memory in vision. *Bell System Technical Journal, 40,* 309–328.

Averill, J. R. (1976). Emotion and anxiety: Sociocultural, biological, and psychological determinants. In M. Zuckerman & C. D. Spielberger (Eds.), *Emotion and anxiety: New concepts, methods and applications* (pp. 87–130). Hillsdale NJ: Erlbaum.

Ayllon, T., & Michael, J. (1959). The psychiatric nurse as a behavioral engineer. *Journal of the Experimental Analysis of Behavior, 2,* 323–334.

Azrin, N. H. (1967). Pain and aggression. *Psychology Today, 1,* 27–33.

Azrin, N. H., & Holz, W. C. (1966). Punishment. In W. K. Honig (Ed.), *Operant behavior* (pp. 380–447). New York: Appleton-Century-Crofts.

B

Bach-y-Rita, P., Collins, C. C., Saunders, F. A., White, B., & Scadden, L. (1969). *Nature, 221,* 963–964.

Backus, J., & Backus, H. (1984). *Backus strikes back.* Briarcliff Manor: Stein and Day.

Baddeley, A. D. (1982). *Your memory, a user's guide.* New York: Macmillan.

Baddeley, A. D., & Hitch, G. (1974). Working memory. In G. H. Bower (Ed.), *The psychology of learning and motivation* (Vol. 8). New York: Academic Press.

Bales, R. F. 1958. Task roles and social roles in problem-solving groups. In E. E. Maccoby, T. M. Newcomb, & E. L. Hartley (Eds.), *Readings in social psychology* (3rd ed.). New York: Holt, Rinehart & Winston.

Baltes, P. B., Reese, H. W., & Lipsitt, L. P. (1980). Life-span developmental psychology. In M. Rosenzweig & L. Porter (Eds.), *Annual Review of Psychology.* Palo Alto, CA: Annual Reviews Press.

Bandura, A. (1965). Influence of models' reinforcement contingencies on the acquisition of imitative responses. *Journal of Personality and Social Psychology, 1,* 589–595.

Bandura, A. (1970). Modeling therapy. In W. S. Sahakian (Ed.), *Psychopathology today: Experimentation, theory, and research.* Itasca, IL: Peacock.

Bandura, A. (1973). *Aggression: A social learning analysis.* Englewood Cliffs, NJ: Prentice-Hall.

Bandura, A. (1977a). *Social learning theory.* Englewood Cliffs, New Jersey: Prentice-Hall.

Bandura, A. (1977b). Self-efficacy. *Psychological Review, 84,* 191–215.

Bandura, A. (1981a). In search of pure unidirectional determinants. *Behavior Therapy, 12,* 30–40.

Bandura, A. (1981b). Self-referent thought: A developmental analysis of self-efficacy. In J. H. Flavell & L. Ross (Eds.), *Social cognitive development: Frontiers and possible futures.* Cambridge, England: Cambridge University Press.

Bandura, A. (1982a). The psychology of chance encounters and life paths. *American Psychologist, 37,* 747–755.

Bandura, A. (1982b). Self-efficacy mechanism in human agency. *American Psychologist, 37,* 122–147.

Bandura, A., Adams, N. E., Hardy, A. B., & Howells, G. N. (1980). Tests of the generality of self-efficacy theory. *Cognitive Therapy and Research, 4,* 39–66.

Bandura, A., & Mischel, W. (1965). Modification of self-imposed delay of reward through exposure to live and symbolic models. *Journal of Personality and Social Psychology, 2,* 698–705.

Bandura, A., Ross, D., & Ross, S. A. (1963). Imitation of film-mediated aggressive models. *Journal of Abnormal and Social Psychology, 66,* 3–11.

Bandura, A., & Schunk, D. H. (1981). Cultivating competence, self-efficacy, and intrinsic interest through proximal self-motivation. *Journal of Personality and Social Psychology, 41,* 586–598.

Bandura, A., Underwood, B., & Fromson, M. E. (1975). Disinhibition of aggression through diffusion of responsibility and dehumanization of victims. *Journal of Research in Personality, 9,* 253–269.

Banuazizi, A., & Movahedi, S. (1975). Interpersonal dynamics in a simulated prison: A methodological analysis. *American Psychologist, 30,* 152–160.

Banyai, E. I., & Hilgard, E. R. (1976). Comparison of active-alert hypnotic induction with traditional relaxation induction. *Journal of Abnormal Psychology, 85,* 218–224.

Barber, T. X. (1969). *Hypnosis: A scientific approach.* New York: Van Nostrand.

Barchas, J. D., Ciaranello, R. D., Kessler, S., & Hamburg, D. A. (1975). Genetic aspects of catecholamine synthesis. In R. R. F. Eve, D. Rosenthal, & H. Brill (Eds.), *Genetic research in psychiatry* (pp. 27–62). Baltimore: Johns Hopkins University Press.

Baribeau-Braun, J., Dicton, T. W., Gosselin, J. Y. (1983). *Schizophrenia: A neurophysiological evaluation of abnormal information processing. Science, 219,* 874–876.

Barnett, S. A. (1967). Attack and defense in animal societies. In C. D. Clemente & D. B. Lindsley (Eds.), *Aggression and defense.* Los Angeles: University of California Press.

Barrett, G. V., & Franke, R. H. (1971). *Psychological motivation and the economic growth of nations.* Rochester, NY: Management Research Center, University of Rochester.

Barrios, B. A., & Shigetomi, C. C. (1980). Coping skills training: Potential for prevention of fears and anxieties. *Behavior Therapy, 11,* 431–439.

Barron, F. X. (1963). *Creativity and psychological growth: Origins of personal vitality and creative freedom.* Princeton, NJ: Van Nostrand.

Barron, F., & Harrington, D. M. (1981). Creativity, intelligence, and personality, *Annual Review of Psychology, 32,* 439–476.

Bar-Tal, D., & Saxe, L., (Eds.). (1978). *Social psychology of education: Theory and research.* Washington, DC: Hemisphere.

Barthe, D. G., & Hammen, C. L. (1981). The attributional model of depression: A naturalistic extension. *Personality & Social Psychology Bulletin, 7*(1), 53–58.

Bartlett, F. C. (1932). *Remembering: A study in experimental and social psychology.* Cambridge, England: Cambridge University Press.

Bateson, G., Jackson, D. D., Haley, J., & Weakland, J. H. (1956). Toward a theory of schizophrenia. *Behavioral Science, 1,* 251–264.

Baum, A., Calesnick, L. E., Davis, G. E., & Gatchel, R. J. (1982). Individual differences in coping with crowding: Stimulus screening and social overload. *Journal of Personality and Social Psychology, 43,* 821–830.

Baum, A., & Valins, S. (1979). Architectural mediation of residential density and control: Crowding and the regulation of social contact. In L. Berkowitz (Ed.), *Advances in experimental social psychology* (Vol. 12). New York: Academic Press.

Baumrind, D. (1967). Child care practices anteceding three patterns of preschool behavior. *Genetic Psychology Monographs, 75,* 43–88.

Baumrind, D. (1973). The development of instrumental competence through socialization. In A. Pick (Ed.), *Minnesota Symposium in Child Development* (Vol. 7). Minneapolis: University of Minnesota Press, 1973.

Baumrind, D. (1984, March). *Family socialization and developmental competence project (FSP).* Paper presented for the Program in Social Ecology, University of California, Irvine.

Bavelas, A., Hastorf, A. H., Gross, A. E., & Kite, W. R. (1965). Experiments on the alteration of group structure. *Journal of Experimental and Social Psychology, 1,* 55–70.

Bayley, N. (1956). Individual patterns of development. *Child Development, 27,* 45–74.

Bayley, N. (1969). *Bayley Scales of Infant Development.* New York: The Psychological Corporation.

Bazelon, D. C. (1981). The judiciary: What role in health improvement? *Science, 211,* 792–793.

Beach, F. A. (1955). The descent of instinct. *Psychological Review, 62,* 401–410.

Beardslee, W., & Mack, J. E. (1982, Spring). The impact on children and adolescents of nuclear developments. In *Psychosocial aspects of nuclear developments.* Task Force Report #20. Washington, DC: American Psychiatric Association.

Beardslee, W. R., & Mack, J. E. (1983). Adolescents and the threat of nuclear war: The evolution of a perspective. *Yale Journal of Biological Medicine, 56*(2), 79–91.

Beck, J. (1972). Similarity groupings and peripheral discriminability under uncertainty. *American Journal of Psychology, 85,* 1–20.

Beck, A. T. (1976). *Cognitive therapy and emotional disorders.* New York: International Universities Press.

Beck, A. T., Rush, A. J., Shaw, B. F., & Emery, G. (1979). *Cognitive therapy of depression.* New York: Guilford Press.

Beck, R. C. (1983). *Motivation* (2nd ed.). Englewood Cliffs, NJ: Prentice-Hall.

Becker, G. (1978).*The mad genius controversy: A study in the sociology of deviance.* Beverly Hills, CA: Sage.

Beecher, E. (1972). *Licit and illicit drugs.* Boston: Little Brown.

Beecher, H.K. (1956). Relationship of significance of wound to the pain experienced. *Journal of the American Medical Association, 161,* 1609–1613.

Beecher, H. K. (1959). Generalization from pain of various types and diverse origins. *Science, 130,* 267–268.

Begg, I., & Paivio, A. V. (1969). Concreteness and imagery in sentence meaning. *Journal of Verbal Learning and Behavior, 8,* 821–827.

Bekerian, D. A., & Bowers, J. M. (1983). Eyewitness testimony: Were we misled? *Journal of Experimental Psychology: Learning, Memory, and Cognition, 9,* 139–145.

Békésy, G. von (1960). *Experiments in hearing.* New York: McGraw-Hill.

Békésy, G. von. (1961). Concerning the fundamental component of periodic pulse patterns and modulated vibrations observed in the cochlear model with nerve supply. *Journal of the Acoustical Society of America, 33,* 888–896.

Bell, R. R. (1974). Female sexual satisfaction as related to levels of education. In L. Gross (Ed.), *Sexual behavior* (pp. 3–11). Flushing, NY: Spectrum.

Bellugi, U., Klima, E. S., & Siple, P. A. (1975). Remembering in signs. *Cognition, 3,* 93–125.

Belluzzi, J. D., Stein, L. (1977). Enkaphalin may mediate euphoria and drive-reduction reward. *Nature, 266,* 556–558.

Bem, D. J. (1968). Self-perception: An alternative interpretation of cognitive dissonance phenomena. *Psychological Review, 74,* 182–200.

Bem, D. J. (1970). *Beliefs, attitudes, and human affairs.* Belmont, CA: Brooks/Cole.

Bem, D. J. (1972). Self-perception theory. *Advances in Experimental Social Psychology, 6,* 2–62.

Bem, D. J., & Allen, A. (1974). On predicting some of the people some of the time: The search for cross-situational consistencies in behavior. *Psychological Review, 81*(6), 506–520.

Bem, S. L. (1974). The measurement of psychological androgyny. *Journal of Consulting and Clinical Psychology, 42,* 155–162.

Bem, S. L. (1981). *The Bem Sex Role Inventory: Professional manual.* Palo Alto, CA: Consulting Psychology Press.

Bem, S. L. (1984). Androgyny and gender schema theory: A conceptual and empirical integration. In T. B. Sonderegger (Ed.), *Nebraska Symposium on Motivation, 1984: The Psychology of Gender.* Lincoln, NB: University of Nebraska Press.

Benedict, R. (1959). *Patterns of culture.* Boston: Houghton Mifflin.

Bengtson, V. L., & Haber, D. A. (1975). Sociological approaches to aging. In D. S. Woodruff & J. E. Birren (Eds.), *Aging: Scientific perspectives and social issues.* New York: Van Nostrand.

Bennett, H. L. (1983). Remembering drink orders: The memory skills of cocktail waitresses. *Human Learning, 2,* 157–169.

Benson, H. (1975). *The relaxation response.* New York: Morrow.

Berkman, L.F. (1977, October). Psychosocial resources, health behavior, and mortality: A nine-year follow-up study. Paper presented at the American Public Health Association Annual Meeting. Washington, DC.

Berkman, L. F., & Syme, S. L. (1979). Social networks, host resistance, and mortality: A nine-year follow-up study of Alameda County residents. *American Journal of Epidemiology, 109,* 186–204.

Berkowitz, L. (1982). Aversive conditions as stimuli to aggression. In *Advances in Experimental Social Psychology, 15,* 249–288.

Berlyne, D. E. (1960). *Conflict, arousal, and curiosity.* New York: McGraw-Hill.

Berlyne, D. E. (1967). Reinforcement and arousal. In D. Levine (Ed.), *Nebraska Symposium on Motivation, 1966.* Lincoln, NB: University of Nebraska Press.

Bernard, L. L. (1924). *Instinct.* New York: Holt, Rinehart & Winston.

Berne, E. (1972). *What do you say after you say hello?* New York: Grove Press.

Berscheid, E. & Peplau, L. A. (1983). The emerging science of relationships. In H. H. Kelley, E. Berscheid, A. Christensen, J. Harvey, T. Huston, G. Levinger, E. McClintock, L. A. Peplau, & D. R. Peterson, *Close relationships.* San Francisco, CA: Freeman.

Berscheid, E., & Walster, E. H. (1978). *Interpersonal attraction* (2nd ed.). Reading, MA: Addison-Wesley.

Betz, B. J., & Thomas, C. B. (1979). Individual temperament as a predictor of health or premature disease. *The Johns Hopkins Medical Journal, 144* 81–89.

Bielski, R. J., & Friedel, R. O. (1977). Subtypes of depression, diagnosis and medical management. *Western Journal of Medicine, 126,* 347–352.

Bigelow, H. J. (1850). Dr. Harlow's case of recovery from the passage of an iron bar through the head. *American Journal of Medical Science, 20,* 13–22.

Binet, A. (1894). *Psychologie des grandes càlculateurs et joueurs d'echecs.* Paris: Hachette.

Binet, A. (1911). Les idées modernes sur les enfants. Paris: Flammarion.

Binkley, S. (1979). A timekeeping enzyme in the pineal gland. *Scientific American, 204*(4), 66–71.

Biracree, T. (1984). "How you rate: Men" and "How you rate: Women." New York: Dell.

Bitterman, M. E. (1975). The comparative analysis of learning. *Science, 188,* 699–709.

Bjorklund, F. F., & Zeman, B. R. (1982). Children's organization and metamemory awareness in their recall of familiar information. *Child Development, 53,* 799–810.

Blakemore, C., & Campbell, F. W. (1969). On the existence of neurons in the human visual system selectively sensitive to the orientation and size of retinal images. *Journal of Physiology, 203,* 237–260.

Blank, A. A., Jr. (1982). Stresses of war: The example of Vietnam. In L. Goldberger & S. Breznitz (Eds.), *Handbook of stress* (pp. 631–643). New York: Free Press/Macmillan.

Blaustein, M., & Albuquerque, E. (1983). Schizophrenic clues in angel dust (discovery of PCP nerve pathway). *Science News, 123,* 107.

Bleuler, M. (1978). The long-term course of schizophrenic psychoses. In L. C. Wynne, R. L. Cromwell, & S. Mattysse (Eds.), *The nature of schizophrenia: New approaches to research and treatment* (pp. 631–636). New York: Wiley.

Bliss, E. L. (1980). Multiple personalities: A report of 14 cases with implications for schizophrenia and hysteria. *Archives of General Psychiatry, 37,* 1388–1397.

Block, A. (1980). An investigation of the response of the spouse to chronic pain behavior. *Pain, 9,* 243-252.

Block, J. H. (1983). Differential premises arising from differential socialization of the sexes: Some conjectures. *Child Development, 54,* 1335–1354.

Block, J. H., Block, J., & Harrington, D. (1975). *Sex role typing and instrumental behavior: A developmental study.* Paper presented at the meeting of the Society for Research in Child Development.

Bolles, R. C., & Faneslow, M. S. (1982). Endorphins and behavior. *Annual Review of Psychology, 33,* 87–101.

Bongiovanni, A. (1977). *A review of research on the effects of punishment in the schools.* Paper presented at the Conference on Child Abuse. Children's Hospital National Medical Center, Washington, DC.

Bootzin, R. R. (1975). *Behavior modification and therapy: An introduction.* Cambridge, MA: Winthrop.

Boring, E. G. (1950). *A history of experimental psychology* (2nd ed.). New York: Appleton-Century-Crofts.

Boring, E. G., Langfeld, H. S., & Weld, H. P. (1948). *Foundations of psychology.* New York: Wiley.

Borke, H. (1975). Piaget's mountains revisited: Changes in the egocentric landscape. *Developmental Psychology, 11,* 240–243.

Botvin, G. J., & Murray, F. B. (1975). The efficacy of peer modeling and social conflict in the acquisition of conservation. *Child Development, 46,* 796–799.

Bourne, L. E., Jr. (1967). Learning and utilization of conceptual rules. In B. Kleinmutz (Ed.), *Concepts and the structure of memory.* New York: Wiley.

Bourne, L. E., Dominowski, R. L., & Loftus, E. F. (1979). *Cognitive processes.* Englewood Cliffs, NJ: Prentice-Hall.

Bower, G. H. (1972). A selective review of organizational factors in memory. In E. Tulving & W. Donaldson (Eds.), *Organization of memory.* New York: Academic Press.

Bower, G. H. (1981). Mood and memory. *American Psychologist, 36,* 129–148.

Bower, S. A., Bower, G. H. (1976). *Asserting yourself.* Reading, MA: Addison-Wesley.

Bowers, K. S. (1976). *Hypnosis for the seriously curious.* New York: Norton.

Bowers, M. B., Jr. (1980). Biochemical processes in schizophrenia: An update. In S. J. Keith & L. R. Mosher (Eds.), *Special Report: Schizophrenia, 1980.* Washington, DC: U.S. Government Printing Office.

Bowlby, J. (1969). *Attachment and loss: Vol. 1 Attachment.* New York: Basic Books.

Brackbill, Y. (1979). Developmental psychology. In. M. E. Meyer (Ed.), *Foundation of Contemporary Psychology* (pp. 468–487). New York: Oxford University Press.

Bransford, J. D., & Johnson, M. K. (1972). Contextual prerequisites for understanding: Some investigations of comprehension and recall. *Journal of Verbal Learning and Verbal Behavior, 11,* 717–721.

Bransford, J. D., & Johnson, M. K. (1973) Considerations of some problems of comprehension. In W. G. Chase (Ed.), *Visual information processing.* New York: Academic Press.

Brantigan, L. O., Brantigan, T. S., & Joseph, N. (1982). Effect of beta blockade and beta stimulation on stage fright. *American Journal of Medicine, 72,* 88–94.

Brasel, J. A., & Blizzard, R. M. (1974). The influence of the endocrine glands upon growth and development. In R. H. Williams (Ed.), *Textbook of endocrinology.* Philadelphia: Saunders.

Bray, C. W. (1948). *Psychology and military proficiency.* Princeton: Princeton University Press.

Brechner, K. C., Boyce, J., Cass, R. A., & Schroeder, D. A. (1975, September). *Social traps: Introduction and initial experiments.* Paper presented at annual meeting of the American Psychological Association.

Breggin, P. R. (1979). *Electroshock: Its brain disabling effects.* New York: Springer.

Breland, K., & Breland, M. (1951). A field of applied animal psychology. *American Psychologist, 6,* 202–204.

Breland, K., & Breland, M. (1961). A misbehavior of organisms. *American Psychologist, 16,* 681–684.

Brenner, M. H. (1976). *Estimating the social costs of national economic policy: Implications for mental and physical health and criminal violence.* Report prepared for the joint Economic Committee of Congress. Washington, DC: U.S. Government Printing Office.

Breuer, J., & Freud, S. (1955). Studies on hysteria. In J. Strachey (Ed. and Trans.), *The standard edition of the complete psychological works of Sigmund Freud* (Vol. 2). London: Hogarth Press. (Original work published 1895)

Brewer, M. B. (1979). In-group bias in the minimal intergroup situation: A cognitive-motivational analysis. *Psychological Bulletin, 86,* 307–324.

Brim, O. G., & Kagan, J. (1980). *Constancy and change in human development.* Cambridge, MA: Harvard University Press.

Broadbent, D. E. (1954). The role of auditory localization in attention and memory span. *Journal of Experimental Psychology, 47,* 191–196.

Broadbent, D. E. (1958). *Perception and communication.* London: Pergamon Press.

Broadbent, D. E. (1971). *Decision and stress.* New York: Academic Press.

Broadbent, D. E., & Gregory, M. (1967). Perception of emotionally toned words. *Nature, 215,* 581–584.

Brody, E. B., & Brody, N. (1976). *Intelligence: Nature, determinants, and consequences.* New York: Academic Press.

Bronfenbrenner, U. (1977). Toward an experimental ecology of human development. *American Psychologist, 32,* 513–531.

Brown, A. L., & De Loache, J. L. (1978). Skills, plans, and self-regulation. In R. S. Siegler (Ed.), *Children's thinking: What develops?* (pp. 3–35). Hillsdale, NJ: Erlbaum, 1978.

Brown, B., & Rosenbaum, L. (1983, May). *Stress effects on IQ.* Paper presented at the meeting of the American Association for the Advancement of Science, Detroit.

Brown, J. S. (1961). *The motivation of behavior.* New York: McGraw-Hill.

Brown, R. W., & McNeil, D. (1966). The "tip-of-the-tongue" phenomenon. *Journal of Verbal Learning and Verbal Behavior, 5,* 325–337.

Bruch, H. (1973). *Eating disorders: Obesity, anorexia nervosa and the person within.* New York: Basic Books.

Bruch, H. (1978). The golden cage: *The enigma of anorexia nervosa.* Cambridge, MA: Harvard University Press.

Bruner, J. S. (1973). *Beyond the information given.* New York: Norton.

Bruner, J. S., & Goodman, C. C. (1947). Value and need as organizing factors in perception. *Journal of Abnormal and Social Psychology, 42,* 33–44.

Bruner, J. S., Goodnow, J., & Austin, G. A. (1956). *A study of thinking,* New York: Wiley.

Bruner, J. S., Olver, R. R., & Greenfield, P. M. (1966). *Studies in cognitive growth.* New York: Wiley.

Brunswick, A. F. (1980). Smoking and health: A report of the Surgeon General. Washington, DC: U.S. Department of Health, Education & Welfare.

Buchsbaum, M. S. (1980). The two brains. In *1981 Yearbook* of sciences and the future (pp. 138–153). Chicago: Encyclopedia Britannica.

Buckhout, R. (1980). Nearly 2,000 witnesses can be wrong. *Bulletin of the Psychonomic Society, 16,* 307–310.

Buczek, R. (1979, July 30). Too old to be hired—so he just died. *Chicago Sun-Times.*

Bullock, T. H., Orkand, R., & Grinnell, A. (1977). *Introduction to the nervous system.* San Francisco: Freeman.

Buros, O. K. (Ed.). (1974). *Tests in print: II.* Highland Park, NJ: Gryphon Press.

Buros, O. K. (Ed.) (1978). *The eighth mental measurements yearbook.* Highland Park, NJ: Gryphon Press.

Burrows, G. D., & Dennerstein, L. (Eds.), *Handbook of hypnosis and psychosomatic medicine.* New York: Elsevier/North Holland Biomedical Press.

Buss, A. H. (1971). Aggression pays. In J. L. Singer (Ed.), *The control of aggression and violence.* New York: Academic Press.

Buss, A. H. (1980). *Self-consciousness and social anxiety.* San Francisco: Freeman.

Bussey, K., & Maughan, B. (1982). Gender differences in moral reasoning. *Journal of Personality and Social Psychology, 42,* 701–706.

Butcher, J. N., & Finn, S. (1983). Objective personality assessment in clinical settings. In M. H. Jersen, A. E. Kazdin, & A. S. Bellock (Eds.), *The clinical psychology handbook* (329–344). New York: Pergamon.

Butler, M. J., & Rice, L. N. (1963). Audience, self-actualization, and drive theory. In J. M. Wepman & R. W. Heine (Eds.), *Concepts of personality* (pp. 79–110). Chicago: Aldine.

Butler, R. A., & Harlow, H. F. (1954). Persistence of visual exploration in monkeys. *Journal of Comparative and Physiological Psychology, 47,* 258–263.

Buzan, T. (1976). *Use both sides of your brain.* New York: Dutton, 1976.

Bykov, K. M. (1957). *The cerebral cortex and the internal organs.* New York: Academic Press.

Byrne, D. (1965). Repression-Sensitization as dimension of personality. In B. Maitner, (Ed.), *Progress in experimental personality research.* New York: Academic Press.

Byrne, D. (1971). *The attraction paradigm.* New York: Academic Press.

Byrne, D. (1981, August). *Predicting human sexual behavior.* G. Stanley Hall Lecture, presented at the meeting of the American Psychological Association, Los Angeles.

C

Cairns, R. B., & Valsinger, J. (1984). Child psychology. *Annual Review of Psychology, 35,* 553–577.

Calkins, M. W. (1893). Statistics of dreams. *American Journal of Psychology, 5,* 311–343.

Cameron, P., Frank, R., Lifter, M. & Morrissey, P. (1968, September). Cognitive functionings of college students in a general psychology class. Paper presented at the meeting of the American Psychological Association, San Francisco.

Campbell, F. W., & Robeson, J. G. (1968). Application of Fourier analysis to the visibility of gratings. *Journal of Physiology, 197,* 551–566.

Canavan-Gumpert, D., Garner, K., & Gumpert, P. (1978). *The success-fearing personality.* Lexington, MA: D. C. Heath.

Cann, A., Calhoun, L. G., Selby, J. W., King, H. E. (Eds.). (1981). Rape. *Journal of Social Issues, 37* (whole no. 4).

Cannon, W. B. (1929). *Bodily changes in pain, hunger, fear and rage* (2nd ed.). New York: Appleton-Century-Crofts.

Cannon, W. B. (1934). Hunger and thirst: In C. Murchison (Ed.), *A handbook of general experimental psychology.* Worcester, MA: Clark University Press, 1934.

Cannon, W. B. (1942). "Voodoo" death. *American Anthropologist, 44,* 169–181.

Cannon, W. B. (1957). "Voodoo" death. *Psychosomatic Medicine, 19,* 182–190.

Cannon, W. B., & Washburn, A. L. (1912). An explanation of hunger. *American Journal of Physiology, 29,* 441–454.

Cantor, N., & Mischel, W. (1979a). Prototypes in person perception. In L. Berkowitz (Ed.), *Advances in experimental social psychology* (Vol. 12). New York: Academic Press.

Cantor, N., & Mischel, W. (1979b). Traits as prototypes: Effects on recognition memory. *Journal of Personality and Social Psychology, 35,* 38–48.

Caplan, G. (1969, November). A psychiatrist's casebook. *McCall's,* p. 65.

Caporeal, L. R. (1976). Ergotism: The satan loosed in Salem? *Science, 192,* 21–26.

Carducci, B. J., & Weber, A. W. (1979). Shyness as a determinant of interpersonal distance. *Psychological Reports, 44,* 1075–1078.

Carlson, J. G., & Wood, R. D. (1974). *Need the final solution be justified?* Unpublished manuscript. University of Hawaii.

Carlson, J. S., & Fullner, D. W. (1959). *College norms.* Eugene, Oregon: University of Oregon Counseling Center.

Carlsson, A. (1978). Antipsychotic drugs, neurotransmitters, and schizophrenia, *American Journal of Psychiatry, 135,* 164–173.

Carmichael, L. (1926). The development of behavior in vertebrates experimentally removed from the influence of external stimulation. *Psychological Review, 33,* 51–58.

Carmichael, L. (1970). The onset and early development of behavior. In P. H. Mussen (Ed.), *Carmichael's Manual of Child Psychology* (Vol. 1, 3rd edition). New York: Wiley.

Carpenter, G. C. (1973). Differential response to mother and stranger within the first month of life. *Bulletin of the British Psychological Society, 16,* 138.

Cartwright, R. D. (1978). *A primer on sleep and dreaming.* Reading, MA: Addison-Wesley.

Cartwright, R. D. (1982). The shape of dreams. *1983 Yearbook of science and the future.* Chicago: Encyclopedia Britannica, Inc.

Cartwright, S. (1851, May). The diseases and physical peculiarities of the negro race. *New Orleans Medical and Surgical Journal.*

Carver, C. S., & Scheier, M. F. (1981). *Attention and self-regulation: A control theory approach to human behavior.* New York: Springer-Verlag.

Casper, C., Eckert, E. D., Halmi, K. A., Goldberg, S. C., & Davis, J. M. (1980). Bulimia: Its incidence and clinical importance in patients with anorexia nervosa. *Archives of General Psychiatry, 37,* 1030–1035.

Cattell, R. B. (1965). *The scientific analysis of personality.* Baltimore: Penguin.

Cattell, R. B. (1971). *Abilities: Their structure and growth.* Boston: Houghton Mifflin.

Cattell, R. B. (1972). The 16 PF and basic personality structure: A reply to Eysenck. *Journal of Behavioral Science, 1,* 169–187.

Cattell, R. B. (1982). *The inheritance of personality and ability: Research methods and findings.* New York: Academic Press.

Catterall, W. A. (1984). The molecular basis of neuronal excitability. *Science, 223,* 653–661.

Center for Disease Control (1980). *Ten leading causes of death in the United States, 1977.* Washington DC: U.S. Government Printing Office.

Cermak, L. S., & Craik, F. I. M. (1979). *Levels of processing in human memory.* Hillsdale, NJ: Erlbaum.

Chapin, S. F. (1913). *Introduction to the study of social evolution.* New York: Century.

Chapman, D. W. (1962). A brief introduction to contemporary disaster research. In G. W. Baker & D. W. Chapman (Eds.), *Man and society in disaster* (pp. 3–22). New York: Basic Books.

Chapman, L. J., & Chapman, J. P. (1969). Illusory correlation as an obstacle to the use of valid psychodiagnostic signs. *Journal of Abnormal Psychology, 74,* 271–280.

Chapman, R. M., McCrary, J. W., & Chapman, J. A. (1978). Short-term memory: The "storage" component of human brain responses predicts recall. *Science, 202,* 1211–1213.

Charatan, F. (1973, Spring). Personal communication to the author.

Chase, W. G., & Ericsson, K. A. (1981). Skilled memory. In J. R. Anderson (Ed.), *Cognitive skills and their acquisition.* Hillsdale, NJ: Erlbaum.

Chase, W. G., & Simon, H. A. (1973). Perception in chess. In W. G. Chase (Ed.), *Visual information processing* (pp. 215–281). New York: Academic Press.

Cheek, J. M., & Busch, C. M. (1981). The influence of shyness on loneliness in a new situation. *Personality and Social Psychology Bulletin, 7,* 572–577.

Cherry, E. C. (1953). Some experiments on the recognition of speech, with one and with two ears. *Journal of the Acoustical Society of America, 25,* 975–979.

Cherry, F., & Deaux, K. (1975, May). *Fear of success vs. fear of gender inconsistent behavior: A sex similarity.* Paper presented at the meeting of the Midwestern Psychological Association, Chicago.

Chi, M. T. H., Feltovich, P. J., & Glaser, R. (1981). Categorization and representation of physics problems by experts and novices. *Cognitive Science, 5,* 121–152.

Chilman, C. S. (Ed.) (1979). *Adolescent sexuality in a changing American society: Social and psychological perspectives* (Dhew Publications No. 79-1426). Washington, DC: National Institute of Health.

Chomsky, N. (1957). *Syntactic Structures.* The Hague: Mouton.

Chomsky, N. (1965). *Aspects of a theory of syntax.* Cambridge, MA: MIT Press.

Chomsky, N. (1975). *Reflections on language,* New York: Pantheon Books.

Chorover, S. (1981, June). *Organizational recruitment in "open" and "closed" social systems: A neuropsychological perspective.* Conference paper presented at the Center for the Study of New Religious Movements, Berkeley, California.

Christie, R., & Geis, F. L. (Eds.). (1970). *Studies in Machiavellianism.* New York: Academic Press.

Christy, P. R., Gelfand, D. M., & Hartman, D. P. (1971). Effects of competition-induced frustration on two classes of modeled behavior. *Developmental Psychology, 5,* 104–111.

Church, R. M., Getty, D. J., & Lerner, N. D. (1976). Duration discrimination by rats. *Journal of Experimental Psychology: Animal Behavior Processes, 2,* 303–312.

Cialdini, R. B. (1984). *Influence: How and why people agree to things.* New York: Morrow.

Ciminero, A. R., Calhoun, K. S., & Adams, H. E. (Eds.). (1977). *Handbook of behavioral assessment.* New York: Wiley.

Clark, E. V. (1973). What's in a word? On the child's acquisition of semantics in his first language. In T. E. Moore (Ed.), *Cognitive development and the acquisition of language.* New York: Academic Press.

Clark, E. V., Hecht, B. F. (1983). Comprehension, production, and language acquisition. *Annual Review of Psychology, 34,* 325–349.

Clark, H. H., & Clark E. V. (1977). *Psychology and language: An introduction to psycholinguistics.* New York: Harcourt Brace Jovanovich.

Clarke-Stewart, K. A. (1973). Interactions between mothers and their young children: Characteristics and consequences. *Monograph of the Society of Research n Child Development, 38* (6–7, serial no. 153).

Clarke-Stewart, K. A. (1978). Recasting the lone stranger. In J. Glick & K. A. Clarke-Stewart (Eds.), *The development of social understanding.* New York: Gardner Press.

Clausen, J. A. (1981). Stigma and mental disorder: Phenomena and mental terminology. *Psychiatry, 44,* 287–296.

Clausen, T. (1968). Perspectives on childhood socialization. In J. A. Clausen (Ed.), *Socialization and society.* Boston: Little Brown.

Cohen, L. B., & Gelber, E. R. (1975). Infant visual memory. In L. Cohen & P. Salapatek (Eds.), *Infant perception: From sensation to cognition: Vol. 1. Basic visual processes* (pp. 347–403). New York: Academic Press.

Cohen, L. B. & Strauss, M. S. (1979). Concept acquisition in the human infant. *Child Development, 50,* 419–424.

Cohen, R. E., & Ahearn, F. L., Jr. (1980). *Handbook for mental health care of disaster victims.* Baltimore, MD: Johns Hopkins University Press.

Collier, G., Hirsch, E., & Hamlin, P. (1972). The ecological determinants of reinforcement. *Physiology and Behavior, 9,* 705–716.

Comrey, A. L. (1970). *Manual for the Comrey Personality Scales.* San Diego: Educational and Psychological Measurement.

Conant, J. B. (1958). *On understanding science: An historical approach.* New York: New Amsterdam Library.

Condry, J., & Condry, S. (1976). Sex differences: A study in the eye of the beholder. *Child Development, 47,* 812–819.

Conger, J. C., & Keane, S. P. (1981). Social skills intervention in the treatment of isolated or withdrawn children. *Psychological Bulletin, 90,* 478–495.

Conrad, R. (1964). Acoustic confusions in immediate memory, *British Journal of Psychology, 55,* 75–84.

Conrad, R. (1972). Short-term memory in the deaf: A test for speech coding. *British Journal of Psychology, 63,* 173–180.

Cookerly, J. R. (1980). Does marital therapy do any lasting good? *Journal of Marital and Family Therapy, 6,* 393–397.

Cooper, A. F. (1976). Deafness and psychiatric illness. *British Journal of Psychiatry, 129,* 216–226.

Coopersmith, S. (1967). *The antecedents of self-esteem.* San Francisco: Freeman.

Coren, S., Porac, C., & Ward, L. M. (1978). *Sensation and perception.* New York: Academic Press.

Corsini, R. J. (1977). *Current theories of personality.* Itasca, IL: Peacock.

Cousins, N. (1979). *The anatomy of an illness as perceived by a patient: Reflections on healing and rejuvenation.* New York: Norton.

Cousins, N. (1983). The healing heart. New York: Norton.

Covington, M. V. (1981). Strategies for smoking prevention and resistance among young adolescents. *Journal of Early Adolescence, 1,* 349–356.

Cowles, J. T. (1937). Food tokens as incentives for learning by chimpanzees. *Comparative Psychology Monographs, 14,* 1–96.

Coyne, J. C., Aldwin, C., & Lazarus, R. S. (1981). Depression and coping in stressful episodes. *Journal of Abnormal Psychology, 90,* 439–447.

Craik, F. I. M., & Lockhart, R. S. (1972). Levels of processing: A framework for memory research. *Journal of Verbal Learning and Verbal Behavior, 11,* 671–684.

Craik, K. (1943). *The nature of explanation.* Cambridge, England: Cambridge University Press.

Crick, F. H. C. (1979, September). Thinking about the brain. *Scientific American, 241,* 219–232.

Cronbach, L. J., & Meehl, P. E. (1955). Construct validity in psychological tests. *Psychological Bulletin, 52,* 281–302.

Crook, J. H. (1973). The nature and function of territorial aggression. In M. F. A. Montague (Ed.), *Man and aggression* (2nd ed.). New York: Oxford University Press.

Cross, P. G., Cattell, R. B., & Butcher, H. J. (1967). The personality patterns of creative artists. *British Journal of Educational Psychology, 37,* 292–299.

Crossman, E. R. F. W. (1959). A theory of the acquisition of speed-skill. *Ergonomics, 2,* 153–156.

Crowder, R. G., & Morton, J. (1969). Precategorical acoustic storage (PAS). *Perception and Psychophysics, 8,* 815–820.

Cummins, R. A., Livesey, P. J., & Evans, J. G. M. (1977). A developmental theory of environmental enrichment. *Science, 197,* 692–694.

Curtis, S. (1977). Genie: A psycholinguistic study of a modern day 'wild child.' *Perspectives in neurolinguistics and psycholinguistics.* New York: Academic Press.

D

Dahlstrom, W. G., Welsh, H. G., & Dahlstrom, L. E. (1975). *An MMPI handbook, Vol. I: Clinical interpretation.* Minnesota: University of Minnesota Press.

Darwin, C. (1872). *The expression of the emotions in man and animals.* London: Murray.

Darwin, C. J., Turvey, M. T., & Crowder, R. G. (1972). The auditory analogue of the Sperling partial report procedure: Evidence for brief auditory stage. *Cognitive Psychology, 3,* 255–267.

Dauber, R. B. (1984). Subliminal psychodynamic activation in depression: On the role of autonomy issues in depressed college women. *Journal of Abnormal Psychology, 93,* 9–18.

Davidson, J. M. (1980). The psychobiology of sexual experience. In J. M. Davidson & R. J. Davidson (Eds.), *The psychobiology of consciousness* (pp. 271–331). New York: Plenum.

Davison, G. C., & Valins, S. (1969). Maintenance of self-attributed and drug-attributed behavior change. *Journal of Personality and Social Behavior, 11,* 25–33.

Dawes, R. M. (1980). Social dilemmas. *Annual Review of Psychology, 31,* 169–193.

D'Azevedo, W. L. (1962). Uses of the past in Gola discourse. *Journal of African History, 3,* 11–34.

de Bono, F. (1970). *Lateral thinking.* New York: Harper.

De Charms, R., & Moeller, G. (1962). Values expressed in American children's readers: 1800–1950. *Journal of Abnormal and Social Psychology, 64,* 136–142.

De Charms, R. C., & Muir, M. S. (1978). Motivation: Social approaches. *Annual Review of Psychology, 29,* 91–113.

Deci, E. L. (1975). *Intrinsic motivation,* New York: Plenum.

De Fries, J. C. & Decker, S. N. (1982). Genetic aspects of reading disability: The Colorado family reading study. In P. G. Aaron & H. Malatesha (Eds.), *Reading disorders: Varieties and treatments* (pp. 255–279). New York: Academic Press.

DeGroot, A. D. (1965). *Thought and choice in chess.* The Hague: Mouton.

Dellas, M., & Gaier, E. L. (1970). Identification of creativity: The individual. *Psychological Bulletin, 73,* 55–73.

Dembroski, T. M., Weiss, S. M., Shields, J. L., et al. (1978). *Coronary-prone behavior.* New York: Springer-Verlag.

Dement, W. C. (1976). *Some watch while some must sleep.* San Francisco: San Francisco Book Co.

Dement, W. C., & Kleitman, N. (1957). Cyclic variations in EEG during sleep and their relations to eye movement, body mobility and dreaming. *Electroencephalography and Clinical Neurophysiology, 9,* 673–690.

Depue, R. A., & Monroe, S. M. (1983). Psychopathology research. In M. Hersen, A. E. Kazdin, & A. S. Bellack (Eds.), *The clinical psychology handbook* (pp. 239–264). New York: Pergamon Press.

Deregowski, J. B. (1980). *Illusions, patterns and pictures: A cross-cultural perspective* (pp. 966–977). London: Academic Press.

Descartes, R. (1911). Traitées de l'homme. In E. S. Haldane & G. T. Ross (Trans.), *The philosophical works of Descartes.* New York: Dover. (Original work published 1642).

Descartes, R. (1951). The passions of the soul. In E. S. Haldane & G. T. Ross (Trans.), *The philosophical works of Descartes.* New York: Dover. (Original work published 1646). *Des Moines Register* (1982, January 24).

Deutsch, M., & Hornstein, H. A. (1975). *Applying social psychology.* Hillsdale, NJ: Erlbaum.

DeValois, R. L., & DeValois, K. K. (1980). Spatial vision. *Annual Review of Psychology, 80.*

DeValois, R. L., & Jacobs, G. H. (1968). Primate color vision. *Science, 162,* 533–540.

DeVries, R. (1969). Constancy of generic identity in the years three to six. *Society for Research in Child Development Monographs, 34*(3, Serial No. 127).

Dewey, J. (1963). How we think. In R. M. Hutchins & M. J. Adler (Eds.), *Gateway to the great books* (Vol. 10). Chicago: Encyclopedia Britannica, Inc.

Diamond, M. J. (1974). Modification of hypnotizability: A review. *Psychological Bulletin, 81,* 180–198.

Dickinson, A. (1980). *Contemporary animal learning theory.* Cambridge, England: Cambridge University Press.

Dickman, H. & Zeiss, R. A. (1982). *Incidents and correlates of posttraumatic stress disorder among ex Prisoners of War of World War II.* Manuscript in progress. Palo Alto, CA: Veterans Administration.

Diener, E., Fraser, S. C., Beaman, A. L., & Kelem, R. T. (1976). Effects of deindividuation variables on stealing among Halloween trick-or-treaters. *Journal of Personality and Social Psychology, 33,* 178–183.

Dion, K. L., Berscheid, E., & Walster, E. (1972). What is beautiful is good. *Journal of Personality and Social Psychology, 24,* 285–290.

Dixon, N. F. (1971). *Subliminal perception: The nature of a controversy.* London: McGraw Hill.

Dobelle, W. H. (1977). Current status of research on providing sight to the blind by electrical stimulation of the brain. *Journal of Visual Impairment and Blindness, 71,* 290–297.

Dohrenwend, B. P., & Dohrenwend, B. S. (1974). Social and cultural influences on psychopathology. *Annual Review of Psychology, 25,* 417–452.

Dohrenwend, B. S., & Dohrenwend, B. P. (1981). *Stressful life events and their contexts.* New York: Wiley.

Dollard, J., Doob, L. W., Miller, N., Mower, O. H., & Sears, R. R. (1939). *Frustration and aggression.* New Haven: Yale University Press.

Dollard, J., & Miller, N. E. (1950). *Personality and psychotherapy.* New York: McGraw-Hill.

Donchin, E. (1975). On evoked potentials, cognition, and memory. *Science, 190,* 1004–1005.

Donnerstein, E. (1980). Aggressive-Erotica and violence against women. *Journal of Personality and Social Psychology, 39,* 269–277.

Donnerstein, E. (1982). Erotica and human aggression. In R. G. Green & E. Donnerstein (Eds.), *Aggression: Theoretical and empirical reviews: Vol. 1.* New York: Academic Press.

Donnerstein, E. (1983). Erotica and human aggression. In R. G. Green & E. Donnerstein (Eds.), *Aggression: Theoretical and empirical reviews: Vol. 2. Issues in research.* New York: Academic Press.

Dooling, D. J., & Lachman, R. (1971). Effects of comprehension on retention of prose. *Journal of Experimental Psychology, 88,* 216–222.

Dorfman, D. D. (1965). Esthetic preference as a function of pattern information. *Psychonomic Science, 3,* 85–86.

Dorosin, D. (1980). Personal communication to author.

Drabman, R. S., & Thomas, M. H. (1974). Does media violence increase children's tolerance of real-life aggression? *Developmental Psychology, 10,* 418–421.

DSM-III. (1980). *Diagnostic and statistical manual of mental disorders* (3rd ed.). Washington, DC: American Psychiatric Association.

DuBois, P. H. (1970). *A history of psychological testing.* Boston: Allyn and Bacon.

Duda, R. O., & Shortliffe, E. H. (1983). Expert systems research. *Science, 220,* 261–268.

Dudycha, G. J. (1936). An objective study of punctuality in relation to personality and achievement. *Archives of Psychology, 204,* 1–53.

Dugdale, R. L. (1912). *The Jukes* (4th ed.). New York: Putnam's Sons.

Dunbar, F. (1935). *Emotions and bodily changes.* New York: Columbia University Press.

Duncker, K. (1945). On problem solving. *Psychological Monographs, 58,* No. 270.

Duval, S., & Wicklund, R. A. (1972). *A theory of objective self awareness.* New York: Academic Press.

Dweck, C. S. (1975). The role of expectations and attributions in the alleviation of learned helplessness. *Journal of Personality and Social Psychology, 31,* 674–685.

E

Eastwell, H. D. (1984). Death watch in East Arnhem, Australia. *American Anthropologists, 86,* 119–121.

Ebbinghaus, H. (1913). *Memory.* New York: Columbia University, (Original work published 1885, Liepzig: Altenberg).

Edwards, A. E., & Acker, L. E. (1962). A demonstration of the long-term retention of a conditioned galvanic skin response. *Psychosomatic Medicine, 24,* 459–463.

Edwards, B. (1979). *Drawing on the right side of the brain.* Los Angeles: J. P. Tarcher.

Edwards, D. A. (1971). Neonatal administration of androstenedione, testosterone, or testosterone propionate: Effects on ovulation, sexual receptivity, and aggressive behavior in female mice. *Physiological Behavior, 6,* 223–228.

Ehrlich, B. E., & Diamond, J. M. (1980). Lithium, membranes, and manic-depressive illness. *Journal of Membrane Biology, 52,* 187–200.

Eimas, P. D., Siqueland, E. R., Jusczyk, P., & Vigorito, J. (1971). Speech perception in infants. *Science, 171,* 303–306.

Ekman, P. (1972). Universal and cultural differences in facial expressions of emotion. In J. Cole (Ed.), *Nebraska Symposium on Motivation,* Lincoln, NB: University of Nebraska Press.

Ekman, P. (1984). Expression and the nature of emotion. In K. R. Scherer, & P. Ekman, (Eds.), *Approaches to emotion.* Hillsdale, NJ: Erlbaum.

Ekman, P., Levenson, R., & Friesen, W. V. (1983). Autonomic nervous system activity distinguishes among emotions. *Science, 221,* 1208–1210.

Ekman, P., Sorenson, E. R., & Friesen, W. V. (1969). Pancultural elements in facial displays in emotion. *Science, 164,* 86–88.

Elliott, J. (1977). The power and pathology of prejudice. In P. G. Zimbardo & F. L. Ruch, *Psychology and life* (9th ed., Diamond Printing). Glenview, IL: Scott, Foresman.

Ellis, A. (1962). *Reason and emotion in psychotherapy.* New York: Lyle Stuart.

Ellis, A. (1977). The treatment of a psychopath with rational therapy. In S. J. Morse & R. I. Watson (Eds.), *Psychotherapies: A comparative casebook.* New York, Holt, Rinehart & Winston.

Ellsworth, P. C., & Getman J. (1981). Social science in legal decision making. In Social Science Research Council (Ed.), *Handbook of law and social science.* New York: Sage.

Emery, A. E. A. (1979). *Elements of medical genetics* (5th ed.). New York: Churchill Livingstone.

Emmelkamp, P. M. G., & Kuipers, A. (1979). Agoraphobia: A follow-up study four years after treatment. *British Journal of Psychology, 134,* 352–355.

Emurian, H. H., Brady, J. V., Ray, R. L., Meyerhoff, J. L., & Mougey, E. H. (1984). Experimental analysis of team performance. *Naval Research Reviews* (Office of Naval Research), *36,* 3–19.

Epstein, S. (1979). The stability of behavior: 1. On predicting most of the people much of the time. *Journal of Personality and Social Psychology, 37,* 1097–1126.

Epstein, W. (1961). The influence of syntactical structure on learning. *American Journal of Psychology, 74,* 80–85.

Erdelyi, M. H. (1974). A new look at the New Look: Perceptual defense and vigilance. *Psychological Review, 81,* 1–25.

Ericksen, C. W. (1966). Cognitive responses to internally cued anxiety. In C. D. Spielberger (Ed.), *Anxiety and behavior.* New York: Academic Press.

Ericsson, K. A., Chase, W. G., & Falcoon, S. (1980, June). Acquisition of a memory skill. *Science, 208,* 1181–1183.

Ericsson, K. A., & Chase, W. G. (1982). Exceptional memory. *American Scientist, 70,* 607–615.

Erikson, E. H. (1963). *Childhood and society* (2nd ed.). New York: Norton.

Erlenmeyer-Kimling, L., & Jarvik, L. F. (1963). Genetics and intelligence: A review. *Science, 142,* 1477–1478.

Eron, L. D., Huesmann, L. R., Lefkowitz, M. M., & Walder, L. O. (1972). Does television violence cause agression? *American Psychologist, 27,* 253–263.

Escalona, S. (1965). Children and the threat of nuclear war. *Behavioral Science and Human Survival.* California: Science and Behavior Books.

Eysenck, H. J. (1952). The effects of psychotherapy: An evaluation. *Journal of Consulting Psychology, 16,* 319–324.

Eysenck, H. J. (1966). *The effects of psychotherapy.* New York: International Sciences Press.

Eysenck, H. J. (1970). *The structure of human personality* (3rd ed.). London: Methuen.

Eysenck, H. J. (1973). *The inequality of man.* London: Temple Smith.

Eysenck, H. J. (1975). *The inequality of man.* San Diego: Educational and Industrial Testing Service.

Eysenck, H. J., & Kamin, L. (1981). *The intelligence controversy: H. J. Eysenck vs. Leon Kamin.* New York: Wiley-Interscience.

F

Fagot, B. I. (1974). Sex differences in toddlers' behavior and parental reaction. *Developmental Psychology, 16,* 459–465.

Fagot, B. I. (1978). The influence of sex of child on parental reactions to toddler children. *Child Development, 49,* 459–465.

Fairweather, G. W., Sanders, D. H., Maynard, R. F., & Cresler, D. L. (1969). *Community life for the mentally ill: Alternative to institutional care.* Chicago: Aldine.

Farina, A. (1980). Social attitudes and beliefs and their role in mental disorders. In J. G. Rabkin, L. Gelb, & J. B. Lazar (Eds.), *Attitudes toward the mentally ill: Research perspectives* (pp. 35–37). Rockville, Md.: National Institute of Mental Health.

Farina, A., Gliha, D., Boudreau, L. A., Allen, J. G., & Sherman, M. (1971). Mental illness and the impact of believing others know about it. *Journal of Abnormal Psychology, 77,* 1–5.

Farina, A., & Hagalauer, H. D. (1975). Sex and mental illness: The generosity of females. *Journal of Consulting and Clinical Psychology, 43,* 122.

Farr, M. J. (1984). Cognitive psychology. *Naval Research Reviews, 36,* 33–36.

Fass, P. S. (1980). The IQ: A cultural and historical framework. *American Journal of Education, 88,* 431–458.

Fazio, R. H., & Zanna, M. P. (1981). Direct experience and attitude-behavior consistency. In L. Berkowitz (Ed.), *Advances in experimental social psychology* (Vol. 14). New York: Academic Press.

Fechner, G. T. (1860). *Elemente der psychophysik.* Germany: Breitkopf und Hartel.

Feigenbaum, E. A., & McCorduck, P. (1983). *The fifth generation.* Reading, MA: Addison-Wesley.

Feldman, A., & Acredolo, L. P. (1979). The effect of active versus passive exploration on memory for spatial localization in children. *Child Development, 50,* 689–704.

Fernald, D. (1984). *The Hans legacy.* Hillsdale, NJ: Erlbaum.

Ferrare, N. A. (1962). *Institutionalization and attitude change in an aged population.* Unpublished doctoral dissertation, Western Reserve University.

Ferster, C. B., Culbertson, S., & Perrott Boren, M. C. (1975). *Behavior principles* (2nd ed.). Englewood Cliffs, NJ: Prentice-Hall.

Ferster, C. B., & Skinner, B. F. (1957). *Schedules of reinforcement.* New York: Appleton-Century Crofts.

Festinger, L. (1954). A theory of social comparison processes. *Human Relations, 7,* 117–140.

Festinger, L. (1957). *A theory of cognitive dissonance.* Stanford, CA: Stanford University Press.

Festinger, L., & Carlsmith, J. M. (1959). Cognitive consequences of forced compliance. *Journal of Abnormal and Social Psychology, 58,* 203–211.

Festinger, L., Pepitone, A., & Newcomb, T. (1952). Some consequences of deindividuation in a group. *Journal of Abnormal Social Psychology, 47,* 382–389.

Fink, M. (1979). *Convulsive therapy: Theory and practice.* New York: Raven Press.

Fireman, B., Gamson, W. A., Rytina, S., & Taylor, B. (1978). Encounters with unjust authority. In L. Kriesberg (Ed.), *Research in social movements, conflicts, and change* (Vol. II). Greenwich, CN: Jai Press.

Fish, J. M. (1973). *Placebo therapy.* San Francisco: Jossey-Bass.

Fishbein, M., & Ajzen, I. (1975). *Belief, attitude, intention, and behavior: An introduction to theory and research.* Reading, MA: Addison-Wesley.

Fisher, A. E. (1967). Chemical stimulation of the brain. In *Psychobiology: The biological bases of behavior.* San Francisco: Freeman.

Fisher, R. J. (1982). *Social psychology: An applied approach.* New York: St. Marten's Press.

Fitts, P. M., & Posner, M. (1967). *Human performance.* Belmont, CA.: Brooks, Cole.

Flavell, J. H. (1977). *Cognitive development.* Englewood Cliffs, NJ: Prentice-Hall.

Flavell, J. H. (1979). Metacognition and cognitive monitoring. *American Psychologist, 34,* 906–911.

Flavell, J. H. (1981). Cognitive monitoring. In W. P. Dickson (Ed.), *Children's oral communication skills* (pp. 35–60). New York: Academic Press.

Flavell, J. H., Friedricks, A. G., & Hoyt, J. D. (1970). Developmental changes in memorization processes. *Cognitive Psychology, 1,* 324–340.

Fleischman, P. R. (1973, April 27). Letter to *Science* concerning ''On being sane in insane places.'' *Science, 180,* p. 356.

Fletcher, H. (1929). *Speech and Hearing.* New York: Van Nostrand.

Floderus-Myrhed, B., Pedersen, N., & Rasmussen, I. (1980). Assessment of heritability for personality, based on a short form of the Eysenck Personality Inventory: A study of 12,898 twin pairs. *Behavior Genetics, 10,* 507–520.

Flood, R. A., & Seager, C. P. (1968). A retrospective examination of psychiatric case records of patients who subsequently committed suicide. *British Journal of Psychiatry, 114,* 433–450.

Foley, V. D. (1979). Family therapy. In R. J. Corsini (Ed.), *Current Psychotherapies* (pp. 460–469). (2nd ed.). Itasca, IL: Peacock.

Folkins, D. H., Lawson, K. D., Opton, E. M., Jr., & Lazarus, R. S. (1968). Desensitization and the experimental reduction of threat. *Journal of Abnormal Psychology, 73,* 100–113.

Folkman, S., & Lazarus, R. S. (1980). An analysis of coping in a middle-aged community sample. *Journal of Health and Social Behavior, 20,* 219–239.

Fontaine, G. (1974). Social comparison and some determinants of expected personal control and expected performance in a novel situation. *Journal of Personality and Social Psychology, 29,* 487–496.

Ford, C. S., & Beach, F. A. (1951). *Patterns of sexual behavior.* New York: Harper & Row.

Fordyce, W. E. (1973). An operant conditioning method for managing chronic pain. *Postgraduate Medicine, 53,* 123–128.

Forest, D. V. (1976). Nonsense and sense in schizophrenic language. *Schizophrenia Bulletin, 2,* 286–381.

Forgas, J. P. (1982). Episodic cognition: Internal representation of interaction routines. In L. Berkowitz (Ed.), *Advances in Experimental Social Psychology* (Vol. 5). New York: Academic Press.

Foucault, M. (1975). *The birth of the clinic.* New York: Vintage Books.

Fouts, R. S., & Rigby, R. L. (1977). Man-chimpanzee communication. In T. A. Seboek (Ed.), *How animals communicate.* Bloomington: University of Indiana Press.

Fowler, H. (1965). *Curiosity and exploratory behavior.* New York: Macmillan.

Fox, M. W. (1974). *Concepts in ethology: Animal and human behavior.* Minneapolis: University of Minnesota Press.

Foy, D. W., Eisler, R. M., Pinkston, S. (1975). Modeled assertion in a case of explosive rages. *Journal of Behavioral Therapy and Experimental Psychiatry, 6,* 135–137.

Frank, J. D. (1978). *Persuasion and healing* (2nd ed.). Baltimore: Johns Hopkins University Press.

Frank, J. D. (1979). The present status of outcome studies. *Journal of Consulting and Clinical Psychology, 47,* 310–316.

Franks, C. M., & Barbrack, C. R. (1983). Behavior therapy with adults: An integrative perspective. In M. Hersen, A. E. Kazdin, & A. S. Bellack (Eds.), *The clinical psychology handbook* (pp. 507–523). New York: Pergamon Press.

Fraser, S. C. (1974). *Deindividuation: Effects of anonymity on aggression in children.* Unpublished mimeograph report. University of Southern California.

Frederiksen, L. W., Jenkins, J. O., Foy, D. W., & Eisler, R. M. (1976). Social-skills training to modify abusive verbal outbursts in adults. *Journal of Applied Behavior Analysis. 9,* 117–125.

Freedman, J. L., & Doob, A. N. (1968). *Deviancy: The psychology of being different.* New York: Academic Press.

Freedman, J. L., & Fraser, S. C., (1966). Compliance without pressure: The foot-in-the-door technique. *Journal of Personality and Social Psychology, 4,* 195–202.

Freeman, F. R. (1972). *Sleep research: A critical review.* Springfield, IL: Charles C. Thomas.

Freud, S. (1900). *The interpretation of dreams.* In J. Strachey (Ed. and Trans.), *The standard edition of the complete psychological works of Sigmund Freud* (Vol. 5). London: Hogarth Press.

Freud, S. (1914). *The psychopathology everyday life.* New York: Macmillan. (Original work published 1904)

Freud, S. (1915). Instincts and their vicissitudes. In S. Freud, *The collected papers.* New York: Collier.

Freud, S. (1923). *Introductory lectures on psycho-analysis.* J. Riviera (Trans.). London: Allen & Unwin.

Freud, S. (1925). The unconscious. In S. Freud, *The collected papers* (Vol. 4) London: Hogarth.

Freud, S. (1949). *A general introduction to psychoanalysis.* New York: Penguin Books.

Freud, S. (1960). *Jokes and their relation to the unconscious.* New York: Norton. (Original work published 1905)

Freud, S. (1974). Screen memories. In J. Strachey (Ed. and Trans.), *The standard edition of the complete psychological works of Sigmund Freud)* (Vol. 3). London: Hogarth Press. (Original work published 1899)

Freud, S. (1976). Totem and taboo. In J. Strachey (Ed. and Trans.), *The standard edition of the complete psychological works of Sigmund Freud.* (Vol. 13). London: Hogarth Press. (Original work published 1913)

Freud, S. (1976). Three essays on the theory of sexuality. In J. Strachey (Ed. and Trans.), *The standard edition of the complete psychological works of Sigmund Freud.* (Vol. 7). London: Hogarth Press. (Original work published 1905)

Frey, W. H. II., De Sota-Johnson, D., & Hoffman, C. (1981). Effect of stimulus on the chemical composition of human tears. *American Journal of Opthalmology, 92,* 559–567.

Frey, W. H. II, Hoffman-Ahern, C., Johnson, R. A., Lydden, D. T., & Tuason, V. B. (1983, September). Crying behavior in the human adult. *Integrative Psychiatry, 1,* 94–98.

Friedman, M., & Rosenman, R. F. (1974). *Type A behavior and your heart.* New York: Knopf.

Frieze, I., Fisher, J. Hanusa, B., McHugh, M., & Valle, V. (1979). Attributions of success and failure in internal and external barriers to achievement in women. In J. Sherman & F. Denmark (Eds.), *Psychology of women: Future of research.* New York: Psychological Dimensions.

Frisby, J. P. (1980). *Seeing.* Oxford: Oxford University Press.

Fromkin, V. A. (Ed.). (1980). *Errors in linguistic performance: Slips of the tongue, pen, and hand.* New York: Academic Press.

Fromm, E. (1947). *Man for himself.* New York: Holt, Rinehart & Winston.

Fromm, E. & Shor, R. E. (Eds.) (1979). *Hypnosis: Developments in research and new perspectives* (2nd ed.). New York: Aldine.

Frumkin, B., & Anisfeld, M. (1977). Semantic and surface codes in the memory of deaf children. *Cognitive Psychology, 9,* 475–493.

Fry, W. F., & Allen, M. (1975). *Make 'em laugh.* Palo Alto: Science and Behavior Books.

Fuller, J. L. (1982). Psychology and genetics: A happy marriage? *Canadian Psychology, 23*, 11–21.

Funder, D. C., Block, J. H., & Block, J. (1984). Delay of gratification: Some longitudinal personality correlates. *Journal of Personality and Social Psychology, 44*, 1198–1213.

Furman, W., Rahe, D., & Hartup, W. W. (1979). Rehabilitation of socially withdrawn preschool children through mixed-aged and same-sex socialization. *Child Development, 50*, 915–922.

G

Gagné, R. M. (1984). Learning outcomes and their effects: Useful categories of human performance. *American Psychologist, 39*, 377–385.

Gagnon, J. H. (1977). *Human sexualities.* Glenview, IL: Scott, Foresman.

Galaburda, A. M., LeMay, M., Kemper, T. L., & Geschwind, N. (1978). Right-left asymmetries in the brain. *Science, 199*, 852–856.

Galanter, E. (1962). Contemporary psychophysics. In R. Brown et al., (Eds.), *New directions in psychology.* New York: Holt, Rinehart & Winston.

Galanter, E. (1979, May). *Psychophysics and the new dualism.* Paper presented at the meeting of the American Association for the Advancement of Science, Houston, Texas.

Gallagher, J. M., & Reid, D. K. (1981). *The learning theory of Piaget and Inhelder.* Monterey, CA: Brooks/Cole.

Galton, F. (1884). Measurement of character. *Fortnightly Review, 42*, 179–185.

Garcia, J., & Koelling, R. A. (1966). The relation of cue to consequence in avoidance learning. *Psychonomic Science, 4*, 123–124.

Garcia, J., McGowan, B. K., & Green, K. F. (1972). Biological constraints on conditioning. In A. Black & W. F. Prokasky (Eds.), *Classical conditioning: II.* New York: Appleton-Century-Crofts.

Gardner, B. T., & Gardner, R. A. (1972). Two-way communication with an infant chimpanzee. In A. M. Schrier & F. Stollnitz (Eds.), *Behavior of nonhuman primates* (Vol. 4). New York: Academic Press.

Gardner, H. (1983). *Frames of mind.* New York: Basic Books.

Gardner, L. I. (1972). Deprivation dwarfism. *Scientific American, 227*(7), 76–82.

Gardner, R., & Gardner, B. T. (1969). Teaching sign language to the chimpanzee. *Science, 165*, 644–672.

Garfinkel, P. E., Moldofsky, H., & Garner, D. M. (1980). The heterogeniety of anorexia nervosa. *Archives of General Psychiatry, 37*, 1036–1040.

Garmezy, N. (1974). Children at risk: The search for the antecedents of schizophrenia: Part II. *Schizophrenia Bulletin, 1*(9). 55–125.

Garmezy, N. (1977). The psychology and psychopathology of Allen Head. *Schizophrenia Bulletin, 3*, 360–369.

Garmezy, N., & Matthysse S. (Eds.). (1977). Special issue on the psychology and psychopathology of attention. *Schizophrenic Bulletin, 3*(3).

Garner, W. R. (1974). *The processing of information and structure.* Potomac, Maryland: Lawrence Erlbaum Associates.

Garnett, E. S., Firnau, G., & Nahmias, C. (1983, September). Dopamine visualized in the basal ganglia of living man. *Nature, 305*, 137–138.

Garrison, V. (1977). The "Puerto Rican syndrome" in psychiatry and Espiritismo. In V. Crapanzano & V. Garrison (Eds.), *Case studies in spirit possession.* New York: Wiley Interscience.

Gates, D. W. (1971). Verbal conditioning, transfer, and operant level "speech style" as functions of cognitive style. (Doctoral dissertation, City University of New York, 1971). *Dissertation Abstracts International, 32*, 3634B. (University Microfilms No. 71–30,719).

Gazzaniga, M. (1980). *Psychology.* New York: Harper and Row.

Gazzaniga, M. S. (1983). Right hemisphere language following brain bisection: A 20-year perspective. *American Psychologist, 38*, 525–537.

Gazzaniga, M. S., & LeDoux, J. E. (1978). *The integrated mind.* New York: Plenum.

Geer, J. H., Davidson, G. C., & Gatchel, R. I. (1970). Reduction of stress in humans through nonveridical perceived control of aversive stimulation. *Journal of Personality and Social Psychology, 16*, 731–738.

Geldard, F. A. (1972). *The human senses* (2nd ed.). New York: John Wiley.

Gerbner, G. (1981, April). Television: The American school child's national curriculum day in and day out. *PTA Today*, pp. 3–5.

Gergen, K. J., Gergen, M. M., & Barton, W. (1973, October). Deviance in the dark. *Psychology Today*, pp. 129–130.

Gevarter, W. B. (1982, May). *An overview of artificial intelligence and robotics: Vol. 3. Exput systems.* (NBSIR 82–2505). Washington, DC: National Bureau of Standards.

Gevins, A. S., Shaffer, R. E., Doyle, J. C., Cutillo, B. A., Tannehill, R. S., & Bressler, S. L. (1983). Shadows of thought: Shifting lateralization of human brain electrical potential patterns during brief visuomotor task. *Science, 220*, 97–99.

Gibson, E. J. & Walk, R. D. (1960). The "visual cliff." *Scientific American, 202*(4) 67–71.

Gibson, J. J. (1950). *The perception of the visual world.* New York: Houghton-Mifflin.

Gibson, J. J. (1966). *The senses considered as perceptual systems.* New York: Houghton-Mifflin.

Gibson, J. J. (1979). *An ecological approach to visual perception.* New York: Houghton-Mifflin.

Gillig, P. M., & Greenwald, A. G. (1974). Is it time to lay the sleeper effect to rest? *Journal of Personality and Social Psychology, 29*, 132–139.

Gilligan, C. (1977). In a different voice: Women's conception of self and morality. *Harvard Educational Review, 47*, 481–517.

Gilligan, C. (1982). *In a different voice: Psychological theory and women's development.* Cambridge, MA: Harvard University Press.

Gist, R., & Stolz, S. B. (1982). Mental health promotion and the media: Community response to the Kansas City hotel disaster. *American Psychologist, 37*, 1136–1139.

Glanzer, M., & Cunitz, A. R. (1966). Two storage mechanisms in free recall. *Journal of Verbal Learning and Verbal Behavior, 5*, 351–360.

Glaser, R. (1984). Education and thinking: The role of knowledge. *American Psychologist, 39*, 93–104.

Glass, D. C., & Singer, J. E. (1972). *Urban stress: Experiments on noise and social stressors.* New York: Academic Press.

Glassman, R. B. (1983). Free will has a neural substrate: Critique of Joseph F. Rychlak's *Discovering free will and personal responsibility. Zygon, 18*, 67–82.

Glucksberg, S., & Danks, J. H. (1975). *Experimental Psycholinguistics.* Hillsdale, NJ: Erlbaum.

Goddard, H. H. (1914). *The Kallikak Family, a study of the heredity of feeble-mindedness.* New York: Macmillan.

Goffman, E. (1963). *Stigma.* Englewood Cliffs, NJ: Prentice-Hall.

Goldstein, E. B. (1980). *Sensation and perception.* Belmont, CA: Wadsworth.

Goldstein, M., & Rodnick, E. H. (1975). The family's contribution to the etiology of schizophrenia: Current status. *Schizophrenia Bulletin, 14*, 48–63.

Gomes-Schwartz, B., Hadley, S. W., & Strupp, H. H. Individual psychotherapy and behavior therapy. *Annual Review of Psychology, 1978, 29*, 435–471.

Gonzalez, A., & Zimbardo, P. G. (1985, March). Time in Perspective. *Psychology Today*, pp. 20–26.

Goochee, C., Rasband, W., & Sokoloff, L. (1980). Computerized densitometry and color coding of (14C) deoxyglucose autoradiographs. *Annals of Neurology, 7*(4).

Goodman, D. A. (1978). Learning from lobotomy. *Human Behavior, 7* (1), 44–49.

Goodman, L. S., & Gilman, A. (1970). *The pharmacological basis of therapeutics* (4th ed.). New York: Macmillan.

Gorman, B. S., & Wessman, A. E. (1977). *The personal experience of time.* New York: Plenum.

Gorney, R. (1976, September). Paper presented at annual meeting of the American Psychiatric Association.

Gottesman, I. I. (1963). Genetic aspects of intelligent behavior. In N. Ellis (Ed.), *Handbook of mental deficiency: Psychological theory and research.* New York: McGraw-Hill.

Gottesman, I. I., & Shields, J. (1972). *Schizophrenia and genetics: A twin study vantage point.* New York: Academic Press.

Gottesman, I. I., & Shields, J. (1976). A critical review of recent adoption, twin, and family studies of schizophrenia: Behavioral genetics perspective. *Schizophrenia Bulletin, 2,* 360–401.

Gottlieb, G. (1976). The roles of experience in the development of behavior and the nervous system. In G. Gottlieb (Ed.), *Studies on the development of behavior and the nervous system* (Vol. 3). *Neural and behavioral specificity.* New York: Academic Press.

Gottlieb, B. H., (Ed.). (1981) *Social networks and social support.* Beverly Hills, CA: Sage.

Gough, H. G. (1957). *California Psychological Inventory Manual.* Palo Alto, CA: Consulting Psychology Press.

Gough, H. G. (1961). Techniques for identifying the creative research scientist. In *Conference on the creative person.* Berkeley, CA: University of California, Institute of Personality Assessment & Research.

Gould, S. J. (1981). *The mismeasure of man.* New York: Norton.

Gray, C. R., & Gummerman, K. (1975). The enigmatic eidetic image: A critical examination of methods, data, and theories. *Psychological Bulletin, 82,* 383–407.

Green, D. M., & Swets, J. A. (1966). *Signal detection theory and psychophysics.* New York: Wiley.

Griffith, D. (1976). The attentional demands of mnemonic control processes. *Memory and Cognition, 4,* 103–108.

Grossman, S. P. (1979). The biology of motivation. *Annual Review of Psychology, 30,* 209–242.

Group for the Advancement of Psychiatry (1950). *Revised Electro-Shock Therapy Report: Special Volume: Report No. 15,* 1–3.

Guilford, J. P. (1967). *Crystalized intelligences: The nature of human intelligence.* New York: McGraw-Hill.

Gummerman, K., Gray, C. R., & Wilson, J. M. (1972). An attempt to assess eidetic imagery objectively. *Psychonomic Science, 28,* 115–118.

Gur, R. C., & Gur, R. E. (1974). Handedness, sex and eyedness as moderating variables in the relation between hypnotic susceptibility and functional brain asymmetry. *Journal of Abnormal Psychology, 83,* 635–643.

Gur, R. C., Gur, R. E., Obrist, W. D., Hungerbuhler, J. P., & Younken, D. (1982). Sex and handedness differences in cerebral blood flow during rest and cognitive activity. *Science, 217,* 659–661.

Gurin, G., Veroff, J., & Feld, S. (1960). *Americans view their mental health.* New York: Basic Books.

Gurman, A. S., & Kniskern, D. P. (1978). Research in marital and family therapy. Progress, perspective, and prospect. In S. L. Garfield & A. E. Bergan (Eds.), *Handbook of psychotherapy and behavior change* (pp. 817–904). New York: Wiley.

Guze, S., Goodwin, D., Crane, J. (1969). Criminality and psychiatric disorders. *Archives of General Psychiatry, 20,* 583–591.

Gynther, M. D. (1981). Is the *MMPI* an appropriate assessment device for blacks? *Journal of Black Psychology, 7,* 67–75.

Gynther, M. D., & Gynther, R. A. (1976). Personality inventories. In I. B. Weiner (Ed.), *Clinical methods in psychology.* New York: Wiley-Interscience.

H

Haas, H., Fink, H., & Hartfelder, G. (1959). *Das placeboproblem.* Fortschoritte der Arzneimittleforschung, 1959, 1, 279–454. Translated in *Psychopharmacology Service Center Bulletin, 2*(8) 1–65. U.S. Department of Health, Education and Welfare, Public Health Service.

Haas, K. (1965). *Understanding ourselves and others.* Englewood Cliffs, NJ: Prentice-Hall.

Habot, T. B., & Libow, L. S. (1980). The interrelationship of mental and physical status and its assessment in the older adult: Mind-body interaction. In J. E. Birren & R. B. Sloane (Eds.), *Handbook of mental health and aging* (pp. 701–716). Englewood Cliffs, NJ: Prentice-Hall.

Haier, R. J. (1980). The diagnosis of schizophrenia: A review of recent developments. In S. J. Keith & L. R. Mosher (Eds.), *Special report: Schizophrenia, 1980.* Washington DC: U. S. Government Printing Office, 2–13.

Hale, R. L. (1983). Intellectual assessment. In M. Hersen, A. E. Kazdin, & A. S. Bellack (Eds.), *The clinical psychology handbook* pp. 345–376, New York: Pergamon.

Halliday, M. (1975). *Learning how to mean.* London: E. Arnold.

Halpin, A., & Winer, B. (1952). *The leadership behavior of the airplane commander.* Ohio State University Research Foundation.

Hamill, R., Wilson, T. D., & Nisbett, R. E. (1978). *Ignoring sample bias: Inferences about populations from atypical cases.* Unpublished manuscript, University of Michigan, Ann Arbor.

Hamilton, D.L. (Ed.) (1981). *Cognitive processes in stereotyping and intergroup behavior.* Hillsdale, NJ: Erlbaum.

Hamilton, D. L., Katz, L. B., & Leirer, V. O. (1980). Memory for persons. *Journal of Personality and Social Psychology, 39,* 1050–1063.

Haney, C. (1980). Psychology and legal change: On the limits of factual jurisprudence. *Law and Human Behavior, 4,* 147–199.

Haney, C., & Zimbardo, P. G. (1977). The socialization into criminality: On becoming a prisoner and a guard. In J. L. Tapp & F. L. Levine (Eds.), *Law, justice and the individual in society: Psychological and legal issues* (pp. 198–223). New York: Holt, Rinehart & Winston.

Hanna, S. D. (1984). *The psychosocial impact of the nuclear threat on children.* Unpublished manuscript. (Available from Physicians for Social Responsibility, 639 Massachusetts Ave., Cambridge, MA 02139)

Hanson, D., Gottesman, I., & Meehl, P. (1977). Genetic theories and the validation of psychiatric diagnosis: Implications for the study of children of schizophrenics. *Journal of Abnormal Psychology, 86,* 575–588.

Hardin, G. R. (1968). The tragedy of the commons. *Science, 162,* 1243–1248.

Hardin, G. R. (1976). Carrying capacity as an ethical concept. *Soundings: Interdisciplinary Journal, 59,* 121–137.

Harlow, H. F. (1965). Sexual behavior in the rhesus monkey. In F. Beach (Ed.), *Sex and behavior.* New York: Wiley.

Harlow, H. F., & Harlow, M. K. (1966). Learning to love. *American Scientist, 54,* 244–272.

Harlow, H. F., & Zimmerman, R. R. (1958). The development of affectional responses in infant monkeys. *Proceedings of the American Philosophical Society, 102,* 501–509.

Harner, M. J. (1973). The sound of rushing water. In M. J. Harner (Ed.), *Hallucinogens and shamanism.* Oxford: Oxford University Press. 15–27.

Harshman, R. A. Crawford, H. J., & Hecht, E. (1976). Marijuana, cognitive style, and lateralized hemispheric functions. In S. Cohen & R. C. Stillman (Eds.), *The therapeutic potential of marijuana.* New York: Plenum. 205–254.

Hart, R. A., & Moore, G. I. (1973). The development of spatial cognition: A review in R. M. Downs & D. Stea (Eds.), *Image and environment.* Chicago: Aldine.

Hartmann, D. P., Roper, B. L. & Bradford, D. (1979). Some relationships between behavioral and traditional assessment. *Journal of Behavioral Assessment, 1,* 3–21.

Hartmann, E. L. (1973). *The functions of sleep.* New Haven: Yale University Press.

Hartshorne, H., & May, M. A. (1928). *Studies in the Nature of Character: Vol. 1, Studies in deceit.* New York: Macmillan.

Hartshorne, H., & May, M. A. (1929). *Studies in the nature of character: Vol. 2, Studies in service and self-control.* New York: Macmillan.

Harvey, O. J., & Consalvi, C. (1960). Status and conformity in informal groups. *Journal of Abnormal and Social Psychology, 60,* 182–187.

Hasenfus, N., & Magaro, P. (1976). Creativity and schizophrenia: An equality of empirical constructs. *British Journal of Psychiatry, 129,* 346–349.

Hathaway, S. R., & McKinley, J. C. (1940). A multiphasic personality schedule (Minnesota): I Construction of the schedule. *Journal of Psychology, 10,* 249–254.

Hathaway, S. R., & McKinley, J. C. (1943). *The Minnesota Multiphasic Personality Schedule.* Minneapolis: University of Minnesota Press.

Hauri, P. (1977). *The sleep disorders.* Kalamazoo, MI: Upjohn.

Haviland, S. E., & Clark, H. H. (1974). What's new? Acquiring new information as a process in comprehension. *Journal of Verbal Learning and Verbal Behavior, 13,* 512–521.

Hayes, C. *The ape in our house.* New York: Harper, 1951.

Hayes-Roth, B., & Hayes-Roth, F. (1979). A cognitive model of planning. *Cognitive Science, 3,* 275–310.

Haynes, S. G., & Feinleib, M. (1980). Women, work, and coronary heart disease: Prospective findings from the Framingham Heart Study. *American Journal of Public Health, 70,* 133–141.

Haynes, S. N. (1983). Behavioral assessment. In M. Hersen, A. E. Kazdin, & A. S. Bellack (Eds.), *The clinical psychology Handbook* (pp. 397–425). New York: Pergamon.

Haynes, S. N., & Wilson, C. C. (1979). *Behavioral assessment: Recent advances in methods and concepts.* San Francisco: Jossey-Bass.

Heath, R. G. (1972). Pleasure and brain activity in man. *Journal of Nervous and Mental Diseases, 154,* 3–18.

Hebb, D. O. (1949). *The organization of behavior: A neuropsychological theory.* New York: Wiley.

Hebb, D. O. (1955). Drives and the CNS (conceptual nervous system). *Psychological Review, 62,* 243–254.

Hebb, D. O. (1958). *A textbook of psychology.* Philadelphia: Saunders.

Hebb, D. (1974). What is psychology about? *American Psychologist, 29,* 71–79.

Heber, R. (1976, June). *Sociocultural mental retardation: A longitudinal study.* Paper presented at the Vermont Conference on the Primary Prevention of Psychopathology.

Heber, F. R. (1978). Sociocultural mental retardation: A longitudinal study. In D. Forgays (Ed.), *Primary prevention of psychopathology: Vol. III. Environmental influences* Hanover, NH: University Press of New England.

Hedlund, J. L. (1977). MMPI clinical scale correlated. *Journal of Consulting and Clinical Psychology, 45,* 739–750.

Heider, F. (1958). *The psychology of interpersonal relationships.* New York: Wiley.

Heider, F., & Simmel, M. (1944). An experimental study of apparent behavior. *American Journal of Psychology, 57,* 243–259.

Heider, R. (1944). Social perception and phenomenal causality. *Psychological Review, 51,* 358–374.

Helmholtz, H. von. (1962). [Treatise on physiological optics] (Vol. 3). (Original work published 1866) (J. P. Southall, Ed. and Trans.) New York: Dover Press.

Henderson, N. D. (1980). Effects of early experience upon the behavior of animals: The second twenty-five years of research. In E. C. Simmel (Ed.), *Early experiences and early behavior: Implications for social development* (pp. 39–77). New York: Academic Press.

Henning, H. (1916). Die Qualitatenreihe des Gesmachs. *Z. Psychol., 74,* 203–219.

Hensel, H. (1968). Electrophysiology of cutaneous thermoreceptors. In D. R. Kenshalo (Ed.), *The skin senses* (pp. 384–399). Springfield, IL: Thomas.

Hering, E. (1861–1864). *Beitrage zur physiologie.* Leipzig: W. Engelmann.

Hersen, M., & Bellack, A. J. (1976). Assessment of social skills. In A. R. Ciminero, K. R. Calhoun, & H. E. Adams (Eds.), *Handbook of behavioral assessment* (pp. 509–554). New York: Wiley.

Hersh, S. M. (1971). *My Lai 4: A report on the massacre and its aftermath.* New York: Random House.

Hess, W., & Akert, K. (1955). Experimental data on the role of hypothalamus in the mechanism of emotional behavior. *Archives of Neurological Psychiatry, 73,* 127–129.

Heston, L. L. (1970). The genetics of schizophrenia and schizoid disease. *Science, 112,* 249–256.

Hetherington, E. M., & Parke, R. D. (1975). *Child psychology: A contemporary viewpoint.* New York: McGraw-Hill.

Hilgard, E. R. (1965). *Hypnotic susceptibility.* New York: Harcourt Brace Jovanovich.

Hilgard, E. R. (1968). *The experience of hypnosis.* New York: Harcourt Brace Jovanovich.

Hilgard, E. R. (1973). The domain of hypnosis with some comments on alternative paradigms. *American Psychologist, 28,* 972–982.

Hilgard, E. R. (1977). *Divided consciousness: Multiple controls in human thought and action.* New York: Wiley.

Hilgard, E. R. (1980). Consciousness in contemporary psychology. In M. Rosenzweig & L. Porter (Eds.), *Annual review of Psychology.*

Hilgard, E. R., & Hilgard, J. R. (1974). Hypnosis in the control of pain. *The Stanford Magazine,* Spring-Summer 58–62.

Hilgard, J. R. (1979). *Personality and hypnosis: A study of imaginative involvement* (2nd ed.). Chicago: University of Chicago Press.

Hirsch, H. V. B., & Spinelli, D. N. (1971). Modification of the distribution of receptive field orientation in cats by selective visual exposure during development. *Experimental Brain Research, 13,* 509–527.

Hitler, A. (1933). *Mein Kampf.* Cambridge, MA: Riverside.

Hobson, J. A., & McCarley, R. W. (1977). The brain as a dream state generator: An activation-synthesis hypothesis of the dream process. *American Journal of Psychiatry, 134,* 1335–1348.

Hochberg, J. (1968). In the mind's eye. In R. N. Haber (Ed.), *Contemporary theory and research in visual perception.* New York: Holt, Rinehart, & Winston.

Hochberg, J. (1971). Perception: II. Space and movement. In J. W. Kling & L. A. Riggs (Eds.), *Experimental psychology* (pp. 475–550). New York: Holt, Rinehart, & Winston.

Hockett, C. F. (1960). The origin of speech. *Scientific American, 203,* 89–96.

Hofer, M. (1981). *The roots of human behavior: An introduction to the psychobiology of early development.* San Francisco: Freeman.

Hofling, C.K., Brotzman, E., Dalrymple, S., Graves N., & Pierce, C. M. (1966). An experimental study in nurse-physician relationships. *Journal of Nervous and Mental Disease, 143* (2), 171–180.

Hofstede, G. (1980). *Culture's consequences: International differences in work-related values.* Beverly Hills, CA: Sage.

Holahan, C. J., & Moos, R. (1981). Social support and psychological distress: A longitudinal analysis. *Journal of Abnormal Psychology, 90,* 365–370.

Holden, C. (1978). *Patuxent:* Controversial prison clings to belief in rehabilitation. *Science, 199,* 665–668.

Holen, M. C., & Oaster, T. R. (1976). Serial position and isolation effects in a classroom lecture simulation. *Journal of Educational Psychology, 68,* 293–296.

Holland, P. C., & Rescorla, R. A. (1975). Second-order conditioning with food unconditioned stimulus. *Journal of Comparative and Physiological Psychology, 88,* 459–467.

Hollender, M. H. (1980). The case of Anna O.: A reformulation. *American Journal of Psychiatry, 137,* 797–800.

Holmes, D. S. (1984). Meditation and somatic arousal reduction. *American Psychologist, 39,* 1–100.

Holmes, T. H. (1970). Short-term intrusions into the life-style routine. *Journal of Psychosomatic Research, 14,* 121–132.

Holmes, T. H. & Masuda, M. (1974). Life change and stress susceptibility. In B. S. Dohrenwend & B. P. Dohrenwend, (Eds.), *Stressful life events: Their nature and effects* (pp. 45–72). New York: Wiley.

Holmes, T. H., & Rahe, R. H. (1967). The social readjustment rating scale. *Journal of Psychosomatic Research, 11* (2), 213–218.

Holstein, C. B. (1978). Irreversible, stepwise sequence in the development of moral judgment: a longitudinal study of males and females. *Child Development, 47,* 51–61.

Holt, R. R. (1970). Yet another look at clinical and statistical prediction: Or is clinical psychology worthwhile? *American Psychologist, 25,* 337–349.

Homme, L. E. (1965). Control of coverants, the operants of mind. *Psychological Record, 15,* 501–511.

Homme, L. E., de Baca, P. C., Devine, J. V., Steinhorst, R., & Rickert, E. J. (1963). Use of the Premack principle in controlling the behavior of nursery school children. *Journal of the Experimental Analysis of Behavior, 6,* 544.

Honzik, M. P. (1984). Life-span development. *Annual Review of Psychology, 35,* 309–331.

Hopson, J. L. (1979). *Scent signals: The silent language of sex.* New York: Morrow.

Horner, M. S. (1969). Sex differences in achievement motivation and performance in competitive and noncompetitive situations (Doctoral dissertation, University of Michigan, 1968). *Dissertation Abstracts International, 30,* 407B.

Horner, M. S. (1972). Human motivation. In *Psychology Today: An introduction* (pp. 369–385). (2nd ed.). Del Mar, CA: CRM Books.

Horney, K. (1939). *New ways in psychoanalyses.* New York: Norton.

Horton, L. E. (1970). Generalization of aggressive behavior in adolescent delinquent boys. *Journal of Applied Behavior Analysis, 3,* 205–211.

Hosobuchi, Y., Rossier, J., Bloom, F. E., & Guillemin, R. (1979). Stimulation of human periaqueductal gray for pain relief increases immunoreactive B-endorphin in ventricular fluid. *Science, 203,* 279–281.

Houghton, J. (1980). One personal experience: Before and after mental illness. In J. G. Rabkin, L. Gelb, & J. B. Lazar (Eds.), *Attitudes toward the mentally ill: Research perspectives* (pp. 7–14). Rockville, MD: National Institute of Mental Health.

Hovland, C. I., Janis, I. L., & Kelley, H. H. (1953). *Communication and persuasion.* New Haven: Yale University Press.

Hovland, C., Lumsdain, A., & Sheffield, F. (1949). *Experiments on mass communication.* Princeton, NJ: Princeton University Press.

Hovland, C., & Weiss, W. (1951). The influence of source credibility on communication effectiveness. *Public Opinion Quarterly, 15,* 635–650.

Howarth, E., & Eysenck, H. J. (1968). Extraversion, arousal, and paired associate recall. *Journal of Experimental Research in Personality, 3,* 114–116.

Hubbard, J. L. (1975). *The biological basis of mental activity.* Reading, MA: Addison-Wesley.

Hubel, D. H. (1979). The brain. *Scientific American, 241(9),* 45–53.

Hubel, D. H., & Wiesel, T. N. (1962). Receptive fields, binocular interaction, and functional architecture in the cat's visual cortex. *Journal of Physiology (London), 160,* 106–154.

Hubel, D. H., & Wiesel, T. N. (1979). Brain mechanisms of vision. *Scientific American, 241(9),* 150–168.

Hughes, J., Smith, T. W., Kosterlitz, H. W., Fotergill, L. A., Morgan, B. A., & Morris, H. R. (1975). Identification of two related pentapeptides from the brain with potent opiate antagonist activity. *Nature, 258,* 577–579.

Hull, C. L. (1943). *Principles of behavior: An introduction to behavior theory.* New York: Appleton-Century-Crofts.

Hull, C. L. (1952). *A behavior system: An introduction to behavior theory concerning the individual organism.* New Haven: Yale University Press.

Humphrey, T. (1970). The development of human fetal activity and its relation to postnatal behavior. In H. W. Reese & L. P. Lipsitt (Eds.), *Advance in Child Development and Behavior* (Vol. 5). New York: Academic Press.

Hunt, E. (1983). On the nature of intelligence. *Science, 219,* 141–146.

Hunt, E. (1984). Intelligence and mental competence. *Naval Research Reviews, 36,* 37–42.

Hunt, M. (1982). *The universe within: A new science explores the human mind.* New York: Simon & Schuster.

Hurlburt, R. T. (1979). Random sampling of cognitions and behavior. *Journal of Research in Personality, 13,* 103–111.

Hurvich, L. M., & Jameson, D. (1957). An opponent process theory of color vision. *Psychological Review, 64,* 384–404.

Hyman, I. A., McDowell, E., & Raines, B. (1977). Corporal punishment and alternatives in the schools: An overview of theoretical and practical issues. In J. H. Wise (Ed.), *Proceedings: Conference on corporal punishment in the schools* (pp. 1–18). Washington, DC: National Institute of Education.

I

Ickes, W., Layden, M. A., & Barnes, R. D. (1978). Objective self-awareness and individuation: An empirical link. *Journal of Personality, 46,* 146–161.

Inglis, J., & Lawson, J. S. (1981). Sex differences in the effects of unilateral brain damage on intelligence. *Science, 212,* 693–695.

Insko, C. A., Thibaut, J. W., Moehle, D., Wilson, M., Diamond, W. D., Gilmore, R., Solomon, M. R., & Lipsitz, A. (1980). Social evolution and the emergence of leadership. *Journal of Personality and Social Psychology, 39,* 431–448.

Itani, J. (1961). The society of Japanese monkeys. *Japan Quarterly, 8(4),* 421–430.

Itard, J. M. G. (1962). *The wild boy of Aveyron.* (G. & M. Humphrey, Trans.). New York: Appleton-Century-Crofts.

Iversen, L. L. (1979). The chemistry of the brain. *Scientific American, 241(9),* 134–149.

Izard, C. (1971). *The face of emotion.* New York: Appleton-Century-Crofts.

Izard, C. E. (Ed.). (1982). *Measuring emotions in infants and children.* New York: Cambridge University Press.

Izquierdo, I., Dias, R. D., Perry, M. L., Souza, D. O., Elisaretsky, E., & Carrascao, M. A. (1982). A physiological amnestic mechanism mediated by endogenous opiod peptides, and its possible role in learning. In C. Ajmone Marson & H. Matthies (Eds.), *Neuronal plasticity and memory formation* (pp. 89–113). New York: Raven.

J

Jackaway, R., & Teevan, R. (1976). Fear of failure and fear of success: Two dimensions of the same motive. *Sex Roles, 2,* 283–294.

Jacob, F. (1977). Evolution and tinkering. *Science, 196,* 161–166.

Jacobs, B. L., & Trulson, M. E. Mechanisms of action of L.S.D. *American Scientist. 1979, 67,* 396–404.

Jacobson, E. (1970). *Modern treatment of tense patients.* Springfield, IL: C. C. Thomas.

James, W. (1884). What is an emotion? *Mind, 9,* 188–205.

James, W. (1980). *The principles of psychology* (2 vols.). New York: Holt, Rinehart & Winston.

Janis, I. L. (1958). *Psychological stress.* New York: Wiley.

Janis, I. L. (1972). *Victims of groupthink: A psychological study of foreign-policy decisions and fiascoes.* Boston: Houghton Mifflin.

Janis, I. L. (1982). Decisionmaking under stress. In L. Goldberger & S. Breznitz (Eds.), *Handbook of stress* (pp. 69–87). New York: Free Press.

Janowitz, H. D., & Grossman, M. I. (1950). Hunger and appetite: Some definitions and concepts. *Journal of The Mount Sinai Hospital, 16,* 231–240.

Janus, S. S. (1975). The great comedians: Personality and other factors. *American Journal of Psychoanalysis, 3,* 169–174.

Jenkins, C. D. (1976), April 29 and May 6). Recent evidence supporting psychologic and social risk factors for coronary disease. *New England Journal of Medicine, 294,* 987–994 and 1033–1038.

Jenkins, H. M., and Moore, B. A. (1973). The form of the auto-shaped response with food or water reinforcers. *Journal of the Experimental Analysis of Behavior, 20*, 163–181.

Jenni, D. A., & Jenni, M. A. (1976). Carrying behavior in humans: Analysis of sex differences. *Science, 194*, 859–860.

Jensen, A. R. (1962). Spelling errors and the serial position effect. *Journal of Educational Psychology, 53*, 105–109.

Jensen, A. R. (1973). *Educability and group differences.* New York: Harper & Row.

John, E. R., et al. (1977). Neurometrics. *Science, 196*, 1393–1410.

Johnson, G. B. (1966). Penis envy or pencil hoarding? *Psychological Reports, 19*, 758.

Johnson, J. H., & Sarason, I. B. (1979). Recent developments in research on life stress. In V. Hamilton & D. M. Warburton (Eds.), *Human stress and cognition: An information processing approach* (pp. 205–233). Chichester, England: Wiley.

Johnson, T. D., & Gottlieb, G. (1981, October). Visual preferences of imprinted ducklings are altered by the maternal call. *Journal of Comparative and Physiological Psychology, 95(5)*, 665–675.

Johnson-Laird, Philip (1983). *Mental models.* Cambridge, England: Cambridge University Press.

Johnston, L. D., Bachman, J. G., & O'Malley, P. M. (1982). Student drug use, attitudes and beliefs: National trends 1975–1982. Rockville, MD: National Institute on Drug Abuse.

Johnstone, K. (1979). *Impro: Improvisation and theatre.* New York: Theatre Arts Books.

Jones, E. (1953). *The life and works of Sigmund Freud.* New York: Basic Books.

Jones, E. E. (1979). The rocky road from acts to dispositions. *American Psychologist, 34*, 107–117.

Jones, E. E., & Davis, K. E. (1965). From acts to dispositions: The attribution process in person perception. In L. Berkowitz (Ed.), *Advances in experimental social psychology* (Vol. 2). New York: Academic Press.

Jones, E. E., Farina, A., Hastorf, A. H., Markus, H., Miller, D. T., & Scott, R. A. (1984). *Social stigma: The psychology of marked relationships.* New York: Freeman.

Jones, E. E., & Harris, V. A. (1967). The attribution of attitudes. *Journal of Experimental Psychology, 3*, 1–24.

Jones, E. E., & Nisbett, R. E. (1972). The actor and the observer: Divergent perceptions on the causes of behavior. In E. E. Jones et al. (Eds.), *Attribution: Perceiving the causes of behavior.* Morristown, NJ: General Learning Press.

Jones, M. C. (1924). A laboratory study of fear: The case of Peter. *Pedagogical Seminary and Journal of Genetic Psychology, 31*, 308–315.

Jones, R. (1978). The third wave. In A. Pines & C. Maslach (Eds.), *Experiencing social psychology.* New York: Knopf.

Julesz, B. (1981). Textons, the elements of texture perception and their interaction. *Nature, 290*, 91–97.

Jung, C. G. (1933). *Psychological types.* New York: Harcourt, Brace & World.

Jung, C. G. (1955). *Synchronicity: An acausal connections principle.* New York: Bollinger Foundation.

Jung, C. G. (1959). The concept of the collective unconscious. In *The archetypes and the collective unconscious, collected works.* Vol. 9, Part 1, pp. 54–74. Princeton: Princeton University Press. (Original work published 1936)

Jung, C. G. (1973). *Memories, dreams, reflections* (Rev. ed). A. Jaffe (Ed.). New York: Pantheon Books.

Just, H. A., & Carpenter, P. A. (1981). Cognitive processes in reading: Models based on reader's eye fixations. In C. A. Prefetti, & A. M. Lesgold (Eds.), *Interactive processes and reading.* Hillsdale, NJ: Erlbaum.

K

Kagan, J., & Klein, R. E. (1973). Cross-cultural perspectives on early development. *American Psychologist, 28*, 947–961.

Kahn, M. (1966). The physiology of catharsis. *Journal of Personality and Social Psychology, 3*, 278–286.

Kahneman, S. (1973). *Attention and effort.* Englewood Cliffs, NJ: Prentice-Hall.

Kahneman, D., Slovic, P., & Tversky, A. (Eds.). (1982). Judgment under uncertainty: Heuristics and biases. Cambridge, MA: Cambridge University Press.

Kahneman, D., & Tversky, A. (1973). On the psychology of prediction. *Psychological Review, 80*, 237–251.

Kahneman, D., & Tversky, A. (1984). Choices, values, and frames. *American Psychologist, 39*, 341–350.

Kalat, J. W. (1974). Taste salience depends on novelty, not concentration in taste-aversion learning in the rat. *Journal of Comparative and Physiological Psychology, 86*, 47–50.

Kalat, J. W. (1984). *Biological Psychology.* (2nd ed.). Belmont, CA: Wadsworth.

Kallmann, F. J. (1946). The genetic theory of schizophrenia: An analysis of 691 schizophrenic index families. *American Journal of Psychiatry, 103*, 309–322.

Kamin, L. J. (1969). Predictability, surprise, attention, and conditioning. In B. A. Campbell & R. M. Church (Eds.), *Classical conditioning: A symposium.* New York: Appleton-Century-Crofts.

Kamin, L. J. (1974). *The science and politics of IQ.* Potomac, MD: Erlbaum.

Kandel, D. (1973). Adolescent marijuana use: Role of parents and peers. *Science, 181*, 1067–1070.

Kandel, E. R. (1976). *The cellular basis of behavior.* San Francisco: Freeman.

Kandel, E. R. (1979). Cellular insights into behavior and learning. *The Harvey Lectures,* Series 73, pp. 29–92.

Kanellakos, D. P., & Ferguson, P. (1973, spring). *The psychobiology of transcendental meditation.* Los Angeles: Maharishi International University.

Kanigel, R. (1981). Storing yesterday. *Johns Hopkins Magazine, 32*, 27–34.

Kaplan, J. (1983). *The hardest drug: Heroin and public policy.* Chicago: University of Chicago Press.

Karlsson, J. L. (1978). *Inheritance of creative intelligence.* Chicago: Nelson-Hall.

Kaufman, L., & Rock, I. (1962). The moon illusion. *Scientific American, 207* (7), 120–130.

Kaufmann, Y. (1979). Analytical psychotherapy. In R. J. Corsini and Contributors (Eds.), *Current psychotherapies* (pp. 95–113). (2nd ed.). Itasca, IL: Peacock.

Kaushall, P. I., Zetin, M., & Squire, L. R. (1981, June). A psychological study of chronic, circumscribed amnesia: Detailed report of a noted case. *Journal of Nervous and Mental Disorders, 169*, 383–389.

Kaye, H. (1967). Infant sucking behavior and its modification. In L. P. Lipsitt & C. C. Spiker (Eds.), *Advances in child development and behavior* (Vol. 3). New York: Academic Press.

Kazdin, A. E. (1980). *Behavior modification in applied settings.* (2nd ed). Homewood, IL: Dorsey.

Kazdin, A. E., & Wilcoxin, L. A. (1976). Systematic desensitization and nonspecific treatment effects: A methodological evaluation., *Psychological Bulletin, 83*, 729–758.

Kazdin, A. E., & Wilson, G. T. (1980). *Evaluation of behavior therapy: Issues, evidence, and research strategies.* Lincoln, NB: University of Nebraska Press.

Keesey, R. E., & Powley, T. L. (1975). Hypothalamic regulation of body weight. *American Scientist, 63*, 558–565.

Keith-Lucas, T., & Guttman, N. (1975). Robust single-trial delayed backward conditioning. *Journal of Comparative and Physiological Psychology, 88*, 468–476.

Kelley, H. H. (1967). Attribution theory in social psychology. In D. Levine (Ed.), *Nebraska symposium on motivation.* (Vol. 15). Lincoln, NB: University of Nebraska Press.

Kelley, H. H., & Thibaut, J. W. (1978). *Interpersonal relations: A theory of interdependence.* New York: Wiley-Interscience.

Kellogg, J. H. (1877). *Plain facts about sexual life*. Battle Creek, MI: Office of the Health Reformer.

Kellogg, W. N., & Kellogg, L. A. (1933). *The ape and the child*. New York: McGraw-Hill.

Kelly, G. A. (1955). *The psychology of personal constructs*. (2 vols.) New York: Norton.

Kelman, H. (1961). Processes of opinion change. *The Public Opinion Quarterly, 25*, 57–78.

Kennedy, G. C. (1953). The role of depot fat in the hypothalamic control of food intake in the rat. *Proceedings of the Royal Society* (Series B), *140*, 578–592.

Kesey, K. (1962). *One flew over the cuckoo's nest*. New York: Viking Press.

Kessler, S. (1980). The genetics of schizophrenia: A review. In S. J. Keith & L. R. Mosher (Eds.), *Special Report: Schizophrenia, 1980* (pp. 14–26). Washington, DC: U.S. Government Printing Office.

Kety, S. (1979). Disorders of the human brain. *Scientific American, 241*, 202–214.

Kety, S. S., Rosenthal, D., Wender, P. H., Schulsinger, F., & Jacobsen, B. (1975). Mental illness in the biological and adoptive families of adopted individuals who have become schizophrenic: A preliminary report based on psychiatric interviews. In R. R. Fieve, D. Rosenthal, & H. Brill (Eds.), *Genetic Research in Psychiatry* (pp. 147–165). Baltimore: The Johns Hopkins University Press.

Kiernan, R. J., & Kaplan, R. M. (1971, April). *Deindividuation, anonymity, and pilfering*. Paper presented at the Western Psychological Association meeting, San Francisco.

Kihlstrom, J. F., & Harackiewicz, J. M. (1982). The earliest recollection: A new survey. *Journal of Personality, 50*, 134–148.

Kinsey, A. C., Martin, C. E., & Pomeroy, W. B. (1948). *Sexual behavior in the human male*. Philadelphia: Saunders.

Kinsey, A. C., Pomeroy, W. B., Martin, C. E., & Gebhard, R. H. (1953). *Sexual behavior in the human female*. Philadelphia: Saunders.

Kintsch, W. (1974). *The representation of meaning in memory*. Hillsdale, NJ: Erlbaum.

Kintsch, W. (1981). Semantic memory: A tutorial. In R. S. Nickerson (Ed.), *Attention and Performance: Vol. VIII*. Hillsdale, NJ: Erlbaum.

Klatsky, R. L. (1980). *Human memory: Structures and processes* (2nd ed.). San Francisco: Freeman.

Klein, D. C., & Goldston, S. E. (Eds.). *Primary prevention: An idea whose time has come*. Washington, DC: U. S. Government Printing Office.

Klein, G. (1970). *Perception, motives, and personality*. New York: Knopf.

Klein, G. S., & Schlesinger, H. J. (1949). Where is the perceiver in perceptual theory? *Journal of Personality, 18*, 32–47.

Klein, R. H. (1983). Group treatment approaches. In M. Hersen, A. E. Kazdin, & A. S. Bellack (Eds.), *The clinical psychology handbook*. New York: Pergamon Press.

Kleinginna, P. R., & Kleinginna, A. M. (1981). A categorized list of motivation definitions with a suggestion for a consensual definition. *Motivation and Emotion, 5*, 263–291.

Kleinke, C. L. (1984). Two models for conceptualizing the attitude-behavior relationship. *Human Relations, 37*, 333–350.

Klinger, E. (1978). Modes of normal conscious flow. In K. S. Pope & J. L. Singer (Eds.), *The stream of consciousness: Scientific investigations into the flow of human experience* (pp. 226–258). New York: Plenum.

Knox, V. J., Morgan, A. H., & Hilgard, E. R. (1974). Pain and suffering in ischemia: The paradox of hypnotically suggested anesthesia as contradicted by reports from the "hidden observer." *Archives of General Psychiatry, 30*, 840–847.

Kobasa, S. C., Maddi, S. R., & Kahn, S. (1982). Hardiness and health: A prospective study. *Journal of Personality and Social Psychology, 42*, 168–177.

Kobre, K. R., & Lipsitt, L. P. (1972). A negative contrast effect in newborns. *Journal of Experimental Child Psychology, 2*, 81–91.

Koestler, A. (1964). *The act of creation*. London: Hutchinson.

Koffka, K. (1935). *Principles of Gestalt psychology*. New York: Harcourt Brace.

Koh, S. O., & Peterson, R. A. (1974). A perceptual memory for numerousness in "nonpsychotic schizophrenics." *Journal of Abnormal Psychology, 83*, 215–226.

Kohlberg, L. (1964). Development of moral character and moral ideology. In M. L. Hoffman & L. W. Hoffman (Eds.), *Review of child development research* (Vol. 1). New York: Russell Sage Foundation.

Kohlberg, L. (1967). Moral and religious education and the public schools: A developmental view. In T. Sizer (Ed.), *Religion and public education*. Boston: Houghton Mifflin.

Kohlberg, L. (1973). Continuities in childhood and adult moral development revisited. In P. B. Baltes & K. W. Schaie (Eds.), *Lifespan Developmental Psychology: Personality and Socialization*. New York: Academic Press.

Köhler, W. (1925). *The mentality of apes*. New York: Harcourt Brace Jovanovich.

Kohler, W. (1947). *Gestalt psychology*. New York: Liveright.

Kolata, G. B. (1981). Clinical trial of psychotherapies is under way. *Science, 212*, 432–433.

Kolb, L. C. (1973). *Modern clinical psychiatry*. Philadelphia: Saunders.

Konečni, V. J., & Doob, A. N. (1972). Catharsis through displacement of aggression. *Journal of Personality and Social Psychology, 23*, 379–387.

Konečni, V. J., & Ebbesen, E. B. (Eds.). (1982). *The criminal justice system: A social psychological analysis*. San Francisco: Freeman.

Konner, M. J. (1977). Research reported in Greenberg, J. The brain and emotions. *Science News, 112*, 74–75.

Korchin, S. J. (1976). *Modern clinical psychology*. New York: Basic Books.

Kosecoff, J. B., & Fink, A. (1982). *Evaluation basics: A practitioner's manual*. Beverly Hills, CA: Sage Publications.

Kosslyn, S. M. (1980). *Image and mind*. Cambridge, MA: Harvard University Press.

Kosslyn, S. M. (1983). *Ghosts in the mind's machine: Creating and using images in the brain*. New York: Norton.

Kramer, J. C. (1969). Introduction to amphetamine abuse. *Journal of Psychedelic Drugs, 2*, 1–16.

Krebs, J. R. (1978). Optimal foraging: Decision rules for predators. In J. R. Krebs & N. B. Davies (Eds.), *Behavioral ecology on evolutionary approach*. Oxford: Blackwell Scientific Publishers.

Kubler-Ross, E. (1969). *On Death and Dying*. Toronto: Macmillan.

Kuffler, S. W., & Nicholls, J. G. (1976). *From neuron to brain*. Sunderland, MA: Sinauer Associates.

Kuhn, M. H., & McPartland, T. S. (1954). An empirical investigation of self attitudes. *American Sociological Review, 19*, 68–76.

Kuhn, T. S. (1970). *The structure of scientific revolutions* (2nd Ed.). Chicago: University of Chicago Press.

Kutas, M., & Hillyard, S. A. (1980). Reading senseless sentences: Brain potentials reflect semantic incongruity. *Science, 207*, 203–205.

L

LaBerge, S. P. (1980). Lucid dreaming as a learnable skill. *Perceptual and Motor Skills, 51*, 1039–1042.

LaBerge, S. P., Nagel, L. E., Dement, W. C., Zarcone, V. P., Jr. (1981). Evidence for lucid dreaming during REM sleep. *Sleep Research, 10*, 148.

Lachman, R., Lachman, J. L. & Butterfield, E. C. (1979). *Cognitive psychology and information processing: An introduction*. Hillsdale, NJ: Erlbaum.

Lachman, S. J. (1983). A physiological interpretation of voodoo illness and voodoo death. *Omega, 13*(4), 345–360.

Laing, R. D. (1967, February 3). Schizophrenic split. *Time*, p. 56.

Lambert, N. M. (1981). Psychological evidence in Larry P. versus Wilson Riles. *American Psychologist, 36*, 937–952.

Lambo, T.A. (1978). Psychotherapy in Africa. *Human Nature, 1* (3), 32–39.

Landis, C. (1924). Studies of emotional reactions: II. General behavior and facial expressions. *Journal of Comparative Psychology, 4*, 447–509.

Lane, H. (1976). *The wild boy of Aveyron*. Cambridge, MA: Harvard University Press.

Lang, P. J. (1979). A bio-informational theory of emotional imagery. *Psychophysiology, 16*, 495–512.

Langer, E. (1978). Rethinking the role of thought in social interaction. In J. H. Harvey, W. J. Ickes, & R. F. Kidd (Eds.), *New directions in attribution research* (Vol. 2, pp. 35–38). Hillsdale, NJ: Erlbaum.

LaPiere, R. (1934). Attitudes versus actions. *Social Forces, 13*, 230–237.

Lashley, K. S. (1929). *Brain mechanisms and intelligence*. Chicago: University of Chicago Press.

Lashley, K. S. (1950). In search of the engram. In *Physiological mechanisms in animal behavior: Symposium of the Society for Experimental Biology*. New York: Academic Press.

Lashley, K. S., Chow, K. L., & Semmes, J. (1951). An examination of the electrical field theory of cerebral integration. *Psychological Review, 58*, 123–136.

Lasswell, H. D. (1948). The structure and function of communication in society. In L. Bryson (Ed.), *Communication of ideas*. New York: Harper.

Latham, G. P., & Yukl, G. A. (1975). A review of research on the application of goal setting in organizations. *Academic Management Journal, 18*, 824–845.

Layzer, D. (1974). Heritability analyses of IQ scores: Science or numerology? *Science, 183*, 1259–1266.

Lazarus, R. S. (1966). *Psychological stress and the coping process*. New York: McGraw-Hill.

Lazarus, R. S. (1974). Psychological stress and coping in adaptation and illness. *International Journal of Psychiatry in Medicine, 5*, 321–333.

Lazarus, R. S. (1975). A cognitively oriented psychologist looks at biofeedback. *American Psychologist, 30*, 553–561.

Lazarus, R. S. (1981, July). Little hassles can be hazardous to your health. *Psychology Today*, pp. 58–62.

Lazarus, R. S. (1984). On the primacy of cognition. *American Psychologist, 39*, 124–129.

Leask, J., Haber, R. N., & Haber, R. B. (1969). Eidetic imagery in children: II. Longitudinal and experimental results. *Psychonomic Monograph Supplements, 3* (3, Whole No. 35).

Le Doux, J. E., Wilson, D. H., & Gazzaniga, M. S. (1977). A divided mind: Observations on the conscious properties of the separated hemispheres. *Annals of Neurology, 2*, 417–421.

Lee, M. T., & Ofshe, R. (1981). The impact of behavioral style and status characteristics on social influence: A test of two competing theories. *Social Psychology Quarterly, 44*, 73–82.

Lee, M., Zimbardo, P., & Bertholf, M. (1977, November). Shy murderers. *Psychology Today*, pp. 68–70, 76, 148.

Leiderman, P. H. (1977). *Culture in infancy: Variations in the human experience*. New York: Academic Press.

Leiderman, P. H. (1981). Human mother to infant social bonding: Is there a sensitive phase? In G. Barlow, K. Immelmann, M. Main & L. Petrinovich (Eds.), *Ethology and child development*. London: Cambridge University Press.

Lemert, E. M. (1962). Paranoia and the dynamics of exclusion. *Sociometry, 25*, 2–20.

Lemmons, P. (1984, February). An interview: The Macintosh design team. *BYTE, 9*(2), 80.

Lempers, J. S., Flavell, E. R., & Flavell, J. H. (1977). The development in very young children of tacit knowledge concerning visual perception. *Genetic Psychology Monographs, 95*, 3–53.

Lenneberg, E. H. (1969). On explaining language. *Science, 164*, 635–643.

Lepper, M. R. (1981). Intrinsic and extrinsic motivation in children: Detrimental effects of superfluous social controls. In U. A. Collins (Ed.), *Aspects of the development of competence: The Minnesota Symposium on Child Psychology* (Vol. 14, pp. 155–214). Hillsdale, NJ: Erlbaum, 1981.

Lepper, M. R., & Greene, D. (Eds.). (1978). *The hidden costs of reward*. Hillsdale, NJ: Erlbaum.

Lepper, M. R. Greene, D., & Nisbett, R. E. (1973). Undermining children's intrinsic interest with extrinsic reward: A test of the overjustification hypothesis. *Journal of Personality and Social Psychology, 28*(1), 129–137.

Leventhal, H. (1970). Findings and theory in the study of fear communications. In L. Berkowitz (Ed.), *Advances in experimental social psychology* (Vol. 5 pp. 120–186). New York: Academic Press.

Leventhal, H., Meyer, D. L., & Nerenz, D. (1980). The common sense representation of illness danger. In S. Rochman (Ed.), *Medical Psychology* (Vol. 2). New York: Pergamon.

Levine, J. D., et al. (1978, August). Paper presented at the World Congress on Pain, Montreal.

Levine, M. (1966). Hypothesis behavior by humans during discrimination learning. *Journal of Experimental Psychology, 71*, 331–336.

Levinger, G. (1980). Toward the analysis of close relationships. *Journal of Experimental Social Psychology, 16*, 510–544.

Levinson, B. W. (1967). States of awareness during general anesthesia. In J. Lassner (Ed.), *Hypnosis and psychosomatic medicine* (pp. 200–207). New York: Springer-Verlag.

Levinson, D. L. (1978). The seasons of a man's life. New York: Knopf.

Levy, J., & Trevarthen, C. (1976). Metacontrol of hemispheric function in human split brain patients. *Journal of Experimental Psychology: Human perception and performance, 2*, 299–312.

Levy, L. H., & Orr, T. B. (1959). The social psychology of Rorschach validity research. *Journal of Abnormal and Social Psychology, 58*, 79–83.

Lewin, K. (1947). Group decision and social change. In T. N. Newcomb & E. L. Hartley (Eds.), *Readings in social psychology*. New York: Holt, Rinehart & Winston.

Lewin, K. (1948). *Resolving social conflicts*. New York: Harper.

Lewin, K., Lippitt, R., & White, R. K. (1939). Patterns of aggressive behavior in experimentally created social climates. *Journal of Social Psychology, 10*, 271–299.

Lewine, R. R., Strauss, J. S., & Gift, T. E. (1981). Sex differences in age at first hospital admission for schizophrenia: Fact or artifact? *American Journal of Psychiatry, 138*, 440–444.

Lewinsohn, P. M., & Amenson, C. S. (1978). Some relations between pleasant and unpleasant mood-related events and depression. *Journal of Abnormal Psychology, 87*, 644–654.

Lewinsohn, P. M., Mischel, W., Chaplin, W., & Barton, R. (1980). Social competence and depression: The role of illusory self-perceptions. *Journal of Abnormal Psychology, 89*, 203–212.

Lewis, C. (1981). The effects of parental firm control: A reinterpretation of findings. *Psychological Bulletin, 90*, 547–563.

Lewis, J. W., Cannon, J. T., & Liebeskind, J. C. (1980). Opiod and nonopiod mechanisms of stress analgesia. *Science, 208*, 623–625.

Leyland, C. M., and Mackintosh, N. J. (1978). Blocking of first and second-order autoshaping in pigeons. *Animal learning and Behavior, 6*, 391–394.

Lidz, T., Fleck, S., & Cornelison, A. R. (1965). *Schizophrenia and the family*. New York: International University Press.

Lieberman, L. R. (1973, April 3). Letter to *Science* concerning "On being sane in insane places." *Science, 179*.

Lieberman, M. A. (1977). Problems in integrating traditional group therapies with new forms. *International Journal of Group Psychotherapy, 27*, 19–32.

Liebert, R. M., & Spiegler, M. D. (1982). *Personality: Strategies and issues*. Homewood, IL: Dorsey Press.

Liem, J. H. (1980). Family studies of schizophrenia: An update and commentary. In S. J. Keith & L. R. Mosher (Eds.), *Special Report: Schizophrenia, 1980* (pp. 82–108). Washington, DC: U. S. Government Printing Office.

Liem, R., & Rayman, P. (1982). Health and social costs of unemployment: Research and policy considerations. *American Psychologist, 37,* 1116–1123.

Lifton, P. (1983). *Personality and morality: An empirical and theoretical examination of personality development, moral reasoning, and moral behavior.* Unpublished dissertation, University of California, Berkeley.

Lindsay, P. H., & Norman, D. A. (1977). *Human information processing* (2nd edition). New York: Academic Press.

Lindsley, D. B. (1951). Emotion. In S. S. Stevens (Ed.), *Handbook of experimental psychology.* New York: Wiley.

Lindzey, G. (1961). *Projective techniques and cross-cultural research.* New York: Appleton-Century-Crofts.

Lipsitt, L. P., & Reese, H. W. (1979). *Child Development.* Glenview, IL: Scott, Foresman.

Lipsitt, L. P., Reilly, B., Butcher, M. G., & Greenwood, M. M. (1976). The stability and interrelationships of newborn sucking and heart rate. *Developmental Psychobiology, 9,* 305–310.

Little, M. I. (1981). *Transference neurosis and transference psychosis.* New York: Jason Aronson.

Locke, E. A. (1982). *A new look at work motivation: Theory V.* Technical Report GS-12. Office of Naval Research, Arlington, VA.

Locke, E. A., Shaw, K. N., Saari, L. M., & Latham, G. P. (1981). Goal setting and task performance: 1969–1980. *Psychological Bulletin, 90,* 125–152.

Loehlin, J. C., Lindzey, G., & Spuhler, J. N. (1975). *Race differences in intelligence.* San Francisco: Freeman.

Loevinger, J., & Knoll, E. (1983). Personality: Stages, traits, and the self. *Annual Review of Psychology, 34,* 195–222.

Loftus, E. F. (1979). *Eyewitness testimony.* Cambridge, MA: Harvard University Press.

Loftus, E. F. (1984). The eyewitness on trial. In B. D. Sales & A. Alwork (Eds.), *With liberty and justice for all.* Englewood Cliffs, NJ: Prentice-Hall.

Loftus, E. F., & Palmer, J. P. (1974). Reconstruction of automobile destruction: An example of the interaction between language and memory. *Journal of Verbal Learning and Verbal Behavior, 13,* 585–589.

Logan, F. A. (1960). *Incentive.* New Haven, CT: Yale University Press.

Loomis, A. L., Harvey, E. N., & Hobart, G. A. (1937). Cerebral status during sleep as studied by human brain potentials. *Journal of Experimental Psychology, 21,* 127–144.

Lorenz, K. (1937). Imprinting. *The AUK, 54,* 245–273.

Lorenz, K. (1966). *On aggression.* New York: Harcourt Brace Jovanovich.

Lovaas, O. I. (1968). Learning theory approach to the treatment of childhood schizophrenia. In *California Mental Health Research Symposium: No. 2 Behavior theory and therapy.* Sacramento, CA: Department of Mental Hygiene.

Lovaas, O. I. (1977). *The autistic child: Language development through behavior modification.* New York: Halsted Press.

Lovibond, S. H., Adams, M., & Adams, W. G. (1979). The effects of three experimental prison environments on the behaviors of nonconflict volunteer subjects. *Australian Psychologist, 14,* 273–285.

Loye, D. (1977). *The leadership passion: A psychology of ideology.* San Francisco: Jossey-Bass.

Luborsky, L., Blinder, B., & Schimek, J. G. (1965). Cooking, recalling and GSR as a function of defense. *Journal of Abnormal Psychology, 70,* 270–280.

Lubow, R. E., Rifkin, B., & Alex, M. (1976). The context effect: The relationship between stimulus preexposure and environmental preexposure determines subsequent learning. *Journal of Experimental Psychology: Animal Behavior Processes, 2,* 38–47.

Luchins, A. S. (1942). Mechanization in problem solving. *Psychological Monographs, 54,* No. 248.

Luchins, A. S. (1957). Primacy-recency in impression formation. In C. I. Hovland (Ed.), *The order of presentation in persuasion* (pp. 34–35). New Haven, CT. Yale University Press.

Luker, K. C. (1975). *Taking chances: Abortion and the decision not to contracept.* Berkeley: University of California Press.

Lynch, G. (1984, April). A magical memory tour. *Psychology Today,* pp. 70–76.

M

Maccoby, E. E., & Martin, J. A. (1983). Socialization in the context of the family: Parent-child interaction. In E. M. Hetherington (Ed.), *Manual of Child Psychology. Vol. 4. Social Development.* N.Y.: John Wiley & Sons.

Mace, W. M. (1977). James J. Gibson's strategy for perceiving: Ask not what's inside your head, but what your head's inside of. In R. Shaw & J. Bransford (Eds.), *Perceiving, acting, and knowing.* Hillsdale, NJ: Erlbaum.

Machlowitz, M. (1980). *Workaholics: Living with them, working with them.* Reading, MA: Addison-Wesley.

MacKinnon, D. W. (1961). The study of creativity and creativity in architects. In *Conference on the creative person.* Berkeley: University of California, Institute of Personality Assessment and Research.

Magnusson, D., & Endler, N. S. (1977). Interactional psychology: Present status and future prospects. In D. Magnusson, & N. S. Endler (Eds.), *Personality at the crossroads: Current issues in interactional psychology.* Hillsdale, NJ: Erlbaum.

Maher, B. A. (1966). *Principles of psychopathology: An experimental approach.* New York: McGraw-Hill.

Maher, B. A. (1968, November). The shattered language of schizophrenia. *Psychology Today,* pp. 30ff.

Maher, B. A. (1974). Delusional thinking and cognitive disorder. In M. London & R. E. Nisbett (Eds.), *Thought and feeling: Cognitive alteration of feeling states.* Chicago: Aldine.

Mahler, M. S. (1979). *The selected papers of Margaret S. Mahler* (2 vols). New York: Jason Aronson.

Maier, N. R. F. (1931). Reasoning in humans: II. The solution of a problem and its appearance in consciousness. *Journal of Comparative Psychology, 12,* 181–194.

Maier, S. F., & Seligman, M. E. P. (1976). Learned helplessness: Theory and evidence. *Journal of Experimental Psychology, 105,* 3–46.

Malamuth, N. E., & Donnerstein, E. (1982). The effects of aggressive-pornographic mass media stimuli. *Advances in Experimental Social Psychology, 15,* 103–136.

Malone, T. W., & Lepper, M. R. (in press). Making learning fun: A taxonomy of intrinsic motivations for learning. In R. E. Snow & M. J. Farr (Eds.), *Aptitude, learning, and instruction: III. Cognitive and affective process analysis.* Hillsdale, NJ: Erlbaum.

Maloney, M. P., & Ward, M. P. (1976). *Psychological assessment: A conceptual approach.* New York: Academic Press.

Mandler, G. (1972). Organization and recognition. In E. Tulving & W. Donaldson (Eds.), *Organization of memory.* New York: Academic Press.

Mandler, G. (1975). *Mind and emotion.* New York: Wiley.

Mandler, G. (1982). Stress and thought processes. In L. Goldberger & S. Breznitz (Eds.), *Handbook of stress* (pp. 88-104). New York: Free Press/Macmillan.

Mandler, G. (1984). Mind and body: The psychology of emotion and stress. New York: Norton.

Manfredi, M., Bini, G., Cruccu, G., Accornero, N., Beradelli, A., & Medolago, L. (1981). Congenital absence of pain. *Archives of Neurology, 38,* 507–511.

Mansson, H. H. (1972). Justifying the final solution. *Omega, 3,* 79–87.

Marcel, A. J. (1983). Conscious and unconscious perception: An approach to the relation between phenomenal experience and perceptual processes. *Cognitive Psychology, 15,* 238–300.

Marek, G. R. (1975). *Toscanini.* London: Vision Press.

Marks, I. (1981). *Cure and care of neuroses: Theory and practice of behavioral psychotherapy.* New York: Wiley.

Marks, R. (1976–77). Providing for individual differences: A history of the intelligence testing movement in North America. *Interchange, 1,* 3–16.

Marlatt, G. A. (1978). Behavioral assessment of social drinking and alcoholism. In G. A. Marlatt & P. E. Nathan (Eds.), *Behavioral approaches to alcoholism.* New Brunswick, NJ: Rutger's Center for Alcohol Studies.

Marler, P. R., & Hamilton, W. J. (1966). *Mechanisms of animal behavior*. New York: Wiley.

Marquis, J. N. (1970). Orgasmic reconditioning: Changing sexual object choice through controlling masturbation fantasies. *Journal of Behavior Therapy and Experimental Psychiatry, 1*, 263–271.

Marr, D. (1982). *Vision*. San Francisco: Freeman.

Martin, J. A. (1981). A longitudinal study of the consequences of early mother-infant interaction: A microanalytic approach. *Monographs of the Society for Research in Child Development, 46* (203, serial no. 190).

Marx, J. L. (1981). Brain opiates in mental illness. *Science, 214*, 1013–1015.

Maslach, C. (1974). Social and personal bases of individuation. *Journal of Personality and Social Psychology, 29*, 411–425.

Maslach, C. (1979). Negative emotional biasing of unexplained arousal. *Journal of Personality and Social Psychology, 37*, 953–969.

Maslach, C. (1982). *Burnout: The cost of caring*. Englewood Cliffs, N.J.: Prentice-Hall.

Maslach, C., Stapp, J., & Santee, R. T. (in press). Individuation: Conceptual analysis and assessment. *Journal of Personality and Social Psychology*.

Maslow, A. H. (1970). *Motivation and personality* (rev. ed.). New York: Harper & Row.

Mason, J. W. (1975). An historical view of the stress field: Parts 1 & 2. *Journal of Human Stress, 1*, 6–12 and 22–36.

Mason, W. A., & Kenney, M. D. (1974). Reduction of filial attachments in Rhesus monkeys: Dogs as mother surrogates. *Science, 183*, 1209–1211.

Masters, John C. (1981). Developmental psychology. *Annual Review of Psychology, 32*, 117–151.

Masters, W. H., & Johnson, V. E. (1966). *Human sexual response*. Boston: Little, Brown.

Masters, W. H., & Johnson, V. E. (1970). *Human Sexual Inadequacy*. Boston: Little, Brown.

Masters, W. H., & Johnson, V. E. (1979). *Homosexuality in perspective*. Boston: Little, Brown.

Matarazzo, J. D. (1972). *Wechsler's measurement and appraisal of adult intelligence* (5th ed.). Baltimore: Williams & Wilkins.

Matlin, M., & Stang, D. (1978). *The Pollyanna principle*. Cambridge, MA: Schenkman.

Matossian, M. (1982). Ergot and the Salem witchcraft affair. *American Scientist, 70*, 355–357.

Matson, J. L., Esveldt-Dawson, K., Andrasik, F., Ollendick, T. H., Petti, T., & Hersen, M. (1980). Direct, observational, and generalization effects of social skills training with emotionally disturbed children. *Behavior Therapy, 11*, 522–531.

Maugh, T. H. (1982). Sleep-promoting factor isolated. *Science, 216*, 1400.

May, R. (1969). *Love and will*. New York: Norton.

Mayer, G. R., Butterworth, T., Nafpaktitis, M., & Sulzer-Azaroff, B. (1983). Preventing school vandalism and improving discipline: A three-year study. *Journal of Applied Behavior Analysis, 16*, 355–369.

Mayer, J. (1955). Regulation of energy intake and body weight: The glucostatic theory and lipostatic hypothesis. *Annals of the New York Academy of Sciences, 63*, 15–43.

Mayer, R. E. (1981). *The promise of cognitive psychology*. San Francisco: Freeman.

McArthur, L., & Post, D. (1977). Figural emphasis and person perception. *Journal of Experimental Social Psychology, 13*(6), 520–535.

McCall, R. B. (1977). Childhood IQs as predictors of adult education and occupational status. *Science, 197*, 483–485.

McCarthy, S. J. (1979, September). Why Johnny can't disobey. *The Humanist*, 30–33.

McClelland, D. C. (1955). Some social consequences of achievement motivation. In M. R. Jones (Ed.), *Nebraska symposium on motivation* (Vol. 3). Lincoln, NB: University of Nebraska Press.

McClelland, D. C. (1961). *The achieving society*. Princeton, NJ: Van Nostrand.

McClelland, D. C. (1971). *Motivational trends in society*. Morristown, NJ: General Learning Press.

McClelland, D. C. (1980). Motive dispositions: The merits of operant and respondent measures. In L. Wheeler (Ed.), *Review of Personality and Social Psychology*, (Vol. 1, pp. 10–41). Beverly Hills, CA: Sage.

McClelland, D. C., Atkinson, J. W., Clark, R. A. & Lowell, L. (1953). *The achievement motive*. New York: Appleton-Century-Crofts.

McClelland, D. C., Atkinson, J. W., Clark, R. A., & Lowell, E. L. (1976). *The achievement motive* (2nd ed.). New York: Irvington.

McClintok, M. K. (1971). Menstrual synchrony and suppression. *Nature, 229*, 244–245.

McCloskey, M., & Egeth, H. E. (1983). Eyewitness identification: What can a psychologist tell a jury? *American Psychologist, 38*, 550–563.

McCormick, D. A., Clark, G. A., Lavond, D. G., & Thompson, R. F. (1982). Initial localization of the memory trace for a basic form of learning. *Proceedings National Academy of Sciences, 79*, 2731–2735.

McCormick, D. A., & Thompson, R. F. (1984). Cerebellum: Essential involvement in the classically conditioned eyelid response. *Science, 223*, 296–299.

McCrae, R. R. (1982). Consensual validation of personality traits: Evidence from self-reports and ratings. *Journal of Personality and Social Psychology, 43*, 293–303.

McDougall, W. (1908). *An introduction to social psychology*. London: Methuen.

McGaugh, J. L. (1983). Hormonal influences on memory. *Annual Review of Psychology, 34*, 297–323.

McGaugh, J. L., & Herz, M. J. (1972). *Memory consolidation*. San Francisco: Albion.

McGhee, P. E. (1979). *Humor: Its origin and development*. San Francisco: Freeman.

McGinnies, E. (1949). Emotionality and perceptual defense. *Psychological Review, 56*, 244–251.

McGregor, D. (1960). *The human side of enterprise*. New York: McGraw-Hill.

McGuigan, F. J. (1978). *Cognitive psychophysiology: Principles of covert behavior*. Englewood Cliffs, NJ: Prentice-Hall.

McGuire, R. J., Carlise, J. M., & Young, B. G. (1965). Sexual deviations as conditioned behavior: A hypothesis. *Behavioral Research and Theory, 12*, 185–190.

McGuire, W. J. (1972). Attitude change: The information-processing paradigm. In C. G. McClintock (Ed.), *Experimental social psychology*. New York: Holt, Rinehart & Winston.

McGuire, W. J., McGuire, C. V., Child, P., & Fujioka, T. A. (1978). Salience of ethnicity in the spontaneous self-concept as a function of one's ethnic distinctiveness in the social environment. *Journal of Personality and Social Psychology, 36*, 511–520.

McKenzie, B. (1980). Hypothesized genetic racial differences in IQ: A criticism of three lines of evidence. *Behavior Genetics, 10*, 225–234.

McLearn, G. E., & De Fries, J. C. (1973). *Introduction to behavioral genetics*. San Francisco: Freeman.

Mead, M. (1939). *From the South Seas: Studies of adolescence and sex in primitive societies*. New York: Morrow.

Meador, B. D., & Rogers, C. R. (1979). Person-centered therapy, In R. J. Corsini (Ed.), *Current Psychotherapies* (pp. 131–184). (2nd ed). Itasca, IL: Peacock.

Meehl, P. E. (1954). *Clinical versus statistical prediction*. Minneapolis: University of Minnesota Press.

Meehl, P. E. (1965). Seer over sign: The first good example. *Journal of Experimental Research in Personality, 1*, 27–32.

Mehrabian, A. (1971). *Silent messages*. Belmont, CA: Wadsworth.

Meichenbaum, D. (1975). A self-instructional approach to stress management: A proposal for stress innoculating training. In D. C. Spielberger and I. G. Sarason, (Eds.), *Stress and anxiety* (pp. 237–263). (Vol. I). New York: Wiley.

Meichenbaum, D. (1977). *Cognitive-behavior modification: An integrative approach*. New York: Plenum.

Meisner, W. W. (1978). *The paranoid process*. New York: Jason Aronson.

Meltzoff, J., & Kornreich, M. (1970). *Research in psychotherapy*. New York: Atherton.

Melville, J. (1977). *Phobias and obsessions.* New York: Penguin Books.

Melzack, R. (1973). *The puzzle of pain.* New York: Basic Books.

Melzack, R. (1980). Psychological aspects of pain. In J. J. Bonica (Ed.), *Pain.* New York: Raven.

Menzel, E. M. (1978). Cognitive mapping in chimpanzees. In S. H. Hulse, H. Fowler, & W. K. Honzig (Eds.), *Cognitive processes in animal behavior* (pp. 375–422). Hillsdale, NJ: Erlbaum.

Merton, R. K. (1957). *Social theory and social structures.* New York: Free Press.

Mervis, C. B., & Rosch, E. (1981). Categorization of natural objects. In M. R. Rosenzweig & L. W. Porter (Eds.), *Annual Review of Psychology, 32,* 89–115.

Meyer, M. M., & Ekstein, R., (1970). The psychotic pursuit of reality. *Journal of Contemporary Psychotherapy, 3,* 3–12.

Meyer, W. U. (1968). In H. Heckhausen, Achievement motive research, *Nebraska symposium on motivation.* Lincoln: University of Nebraska Press.

Milgram, S. (1965). Some conditions of obedience and disobedience to authority. *Human Relations, 18,* 56–76.

Milgram, S. (1974). *Obedience to authority.* New York: Harper & Row.

Milgram, S., & Jodelet, D. (1976). Psychological maps of Paris. In H. M. Proshansky, W. H. Ittleson, & L. G. Rivlin. (Eds.), *Environmental psychology.* New York: Holt, Rinehart, & Winston.

Miller, G. A. (1956). The magic number seven plus or minus two: Some limits on our capacity for processing information. *Psychological Review, 63,* 81–97.

Miller, G. A. (1962). Some psychological studies of grammar. *American Psychologist, 17,* 748–762.

Miller, N. E. (1941). The frustration-aggression hypothesis. *Psychological Review, 48,* 337–342.

Miller, N. E. (1948). Fear as an acquired drive. *Journal of Experimental Psychology, 38,* 89–101.

Miller, N. E. (1951). Learnable drives and rewards. In S. S. Stevens (Ed.), *Handbook of experimental psychology* (pp. 435–472). New York: Wiley.

Miller, N. E. (1983). Behavioral medicine: Symbiosis between laboratory and clinic. *Annual Review of Psychology, 34,* 1–31.

Milner, B. (1966). Amnesia following operation on the temporal lobes. In C. W. Whitty & O. L. Zangwill (Eds.), *Amnesia* (pp. 109–133). London: Butterworth.

Milner, B. (1970). Memory and the medial temporal regions of the brain. In K. H. Pribram & D. E. Broadbent (Eds.), *Biology of memory.* New York: Academic Press.

Milojkovic, J. D. (1982). Chess imagery in novice and master. *Journal of Mental Imagery, 6,* 125–144.

Minuchin, S. (1974). *Families and family therapy.* Cambridge, MA: Harvard University Press.

Mischel, W. (1968). *Personality and assessment,* New York: Wiley.

Mischel, W. (1973). Toward a cognitive social learning reconceptualization of personality. *Psychological Review, 80,* 252–283.

Mischel, W. (1976). *Introduction to personality* (2nd ed.). New York: Holt, Rinehart & Winston.

Mischel, W. (1979). On the interface of cognition and personality: Beyond the person-situation debate. *American Psychologist, 34,* 740–754.

Mischel, W., & Mischel, H. N. (1977). *Essentials of Psychology.* New York: Random House.

Mischel, W., & Peake, P. (1982). Beyond déja vu in the search for cross-situational consistency. *Psychological Review. 89*(6), 730–755.

Mishkin, M. (1978). Memory in monkeys severely impaired by combined but not separate removal of amygdala and hippocampus. *Nature, 273,* 297–298.

Mishkin, M. (1982). A memory system in the monkey. *Philosophical Transactions of the Royal Society of London, 298,* 85–95.

Mishkin, M., Malamut, B., & Backevalier, J. (in press). Memories and habits: Two neural systems. In J. L. McGaugh, G. Lynch, & N. M. Weinberger (Eds.), *The neurobiology of learning and memory.* New York: Guilford Press.

Moar, I. (1980). The nature and acquisition of cognitive maps. In D. Cantor & T. Lee (Eds.), *Proceedings of the international conference on environmental psychology.* London: Architectural Press.

Monat, A., & Lazarus, R. S. (1977). *Stress and coping: An anthology.* New York: Columbia University Press.

Moncrieff, R. W. (1951). *The chemical senses.* London: Leonard Hill.

Moniz, E. (1973). Prefrontal leucotomy in the treatment of mental disorders. *American Journal of Psychiatry, 93,* 1379–1385.

Monahan, J., & Loftus, E. F. (1982). The psychology of law. *Annual Review of Psychology, 33,* 441–475.

Monson, T. C., Hesley, J. W., & Chernick, L. (1982). Specifying when personality traits can and cannot predict behavior: An alternative to abandoning the attempt to predict single-act criteria. *Journal of Personality and Social Psychology, 43,* 385–399.

Montague, W. E., Adams, J. A., & Kiess, H. O. (1966). Forgetting and natural language mediation. *Journal of Experimental Psychology, 72,* 829–833.

Moos, R. (1976). *The human context: environmental determinants of behavior.* New York: Wiley.

Moos, R. (1979). *Evaluating educational environments.* San Francisco: Jossey-Bass.

Moos R. (in press). Creating healthy human contexts: Environmental and individual strategies. In J. Rosen & L. Solomon (Eds.), *Prevention in health psychology.* Hanover, NH: University of New England Press.

Moos, R. & Lemke, S. (1984). Supportive residential settings for older people. In I. Altman, M. P. Lawton, & J. F. Wohlwill (Eds.), *Elderly people and the environment* (pp. 159–190). New York: Plenum.

Morgan, A. H., Hilgard, E. R., & Davert, E. C. The heritability of hypnotic susceptibility of twins: A preliminary report. *Behavior Genetics,* 1970, 1, 213–224.

Morgan, A. H., Johnson, D. L., & Hilgard, E. R. The stability of hypnotic susceptibility: A longitudinal study. *International Journal of Clinical and Experimental Hypnosis,* 1974, 22, 249–257.

Morris, C., & Hackman, J. (1969). Behavioral correlates of perceived leadership. *Journal of Personality and Social Psychology, 13,* 350–361.

Morris, J. J., & Clarizio, S. (1977). Improvement in IQ of high risk, disadvantaged preschool children enrolled in a developmental program. *Psychological Reports, 41,* 1, 111–1, 114.

Moscovici, S. (1976). *Social influence and social change.* New York: Academic Press.

Moscovici, S., & Faucheux, C. (1972). Social influence, conformity bias, and the study of active minorities. In L. Berkowitz (Ed.), *Advances in experimental social psychology* (Vol. 6). New York: Academic Press.

Moskowitz, B. A. (1978). The acquisition of language. *Scientific American, 239* (11), 92–108.

Movshon, J. A., & van Sluyters, R. C. (1981). Visual neural development. *Annual Review of Psychology, 32,* 477–522.

Moyer, K. E. (1976). *The psychobiology of aggression.* New York: Harper & Row.

Munroe, R. L. (1955). *Schools of Psychoanalytic thought.* New York: Dryden.

Murphy, J. M. (1976). Psychiatric labeling in cross cultural perspective. *Science, 191,* 1019–1028.

Murray, H. A. (1938). *Explorations in personality.* New York: Oxford University Press.

Muskin, P. R., & Fyer, A. J. (1981). Treatment of panic disorder. *Journal of Clinical Psychopharmacology. 1,* 81–90.

Mussen, P. H., Honzik, M. P., & Eichorn, D. H. (1982). Early adult antecedents of life satisfaction at age 70. *Journal of Gerontology, 37,* 316–322.

Myers, R. E., & Sperry, R. W. (1958). Interhemispheric communication through the corpus callosum: Mnemonic carry-over between the hemispheres. *Archives of Neurology and Psychiatry, 80,* 298–303.

Myrdal, G. (1971). *The challenge of world poverty.* New York: Random House.

References

N

Nadi, S. N., Nurnberger, J. I., & Gershon, E. S. (1984). Muscarinic cholinergic receptors on skin fibroblasts in familial affective disorder. *New England Journal of Medicine, 311*(4), 225–230.

Nathanson, J. A., & Greengard, P. (1977). "Second messengers" in the brain. *Scientific American, 237,* 108–119.

National Institute of Mental Health (1977). *Lithium and the treatment of mood disorders.* DHEW Publication No. (ADM) 77–73. Washington, DC: U.S. Government Printing Office.

Natsoulas, T. (1978, October). Consciousness. *American Psychologist, 33*(10), 906–914.

Nauta, W. J. H., & Feirtag, M. (1979). The organization of the brain. *Scientific American, 241*(9), 88–111.

Neale, J. M., & Liebert, R. M. (1973). *Science and behavior* (2nd ed.). Englewood Cliffs, NJ: Prentice-Hall.

Neisser, U. (1967). *Cognitive psychology.* New York: Appleton-Century-Crofts.

Nelson, K. E. (1971). Accommodation of visual tracking patterns in human infants to object movement patterns. *Journal of Experimental Child Psychology, 16,* 180–196.

Nelson, K. E. (1974). Short-term progress toward one component of object permanence. *Merrill-Palmer Quarterly, 20,* 3–8.

Nelson, K. E. (1979). The role of language in infant development. In M. H. Bornstein & W. Kessen (Eds.), *Psychological development from infancy* (pp. 307–338). Hillsdale, NJ: Erlbaum.

Nelson, Z. P., & Mowrey, D. D. (1976). Contracting in crisis intervention. *Community Mental Health Journal, 12,* 37–43.

Nemeth, C. (1979). The role of an active minority in intergroup relations. In W. Austin & S. Worchel (Eds.), *The social psychology of intergroup relations.* Monterey, CA: Brooks/Cole.

Nerem, R. M., Levesque, M. J., & Cornhill, J. F. (1980). Social environment as a factor in diet-induced arteriosclerosis. *Science, 208,* 1475–1476.

Nesselroade, J. R., & Baltes, P. B. (1974). Adolescent personality development and historical change: 1970–1972. *Monographs of the Society for Research in Child Development, 39.*

Neufeld, R. W. J. (1976). Evidence of stress as a function of experimentally altered appraisal of stimulus, aversiveness and coping adequacy. *Journal of Personality and Social Psychology, 33,* 632–646.

Neugarten, B. L. (1976). *The psychology of aging: An overview.* Master lectures on developmental psychology. Washington, DC: American Psychological Association.

Newcomb, T. M. (1929). *The consistency of certain extrovert-introvert behavior traits in 50 problem boys.* New York: Columbia University, Contributions to Education, No. 382.

Newcomb, T. M. (1943). *Personality and social change.* New York: Holt.

Newcomb, T. M. (1963). Persistence and regression of changed attitudes: Long-range studies. *Journal of Social Issues, 19,* 3–4.

Newell, A., Shaw, J. C., & Simon, H. A. (1958). Elements of a theory of human problem solving. *Psychological Review, 65,* 152–166.

Newell, A., & Simon, H. A. (1972). *Human problem solving.* Englewood Cliffs, NJ: Prentice-Hall.

Nguyen, T., Heslin, R., & Nguyen, M. L. (1975). The meanings of touch: Sex differences. *Journal of Communication, 25,* 92–103.

Nisbett, R. E. (1972). Hunger, obesity and the ventromedial hypothalamus. *Psychological Review, 79,* 433–453.

Nisbett, R.E., & Ross, L. (1980). *Human inference: Strategies and shortcomings of social judgment.* Englewood Cliffs, NJ: Prentice-Hall.

Nisbett, R. E., & Wilson, T. D. (1977). Telling more than we can know: verbal reports on mental processes. *Psychological Review, 84,* 231–259.

Noback, C. R., & Demarest, R. J. (1975). *The human nervous system* (2nd ed.). New York: McGraw Hill.

Nobles, W. W. (1972). African psychology: Foundations for black psychology. In R. L. Jones (Ed.), *Black psychology.* New York: Harper & Row.

Nobles, W. W. (1976). Black people in white insanity: An issue for black community mental health. *Journal of Afro-American Issues, 4,* 21–27.

Norman, D. A. (1968). Toward a theory of memory and attention. *Psychological Review, 1968, 75,* 522–536.

Norman, D. A. (1981). Categorization of action slips. *Psychological Review, 88,* 1–15.

Noyes, R. (1982). Beta-blocking drugs and anxiety. *Psychosomatics, 23,* 155–169.

O

Oden, S., & Asher, S. R. (1977). Coaching children in social skills for friendship making. *Child Development, 48,* 495–506.

Okanes, M., & Stinson, J. (1974). Machiavellianism and emergent leadership in a management simulation. *Psychological Reports, 35,* 255–259.

Olds, J. (1973). Commentary on positive reinforcement produced by electrical stimulation of septal areas and other regions of rat brain. In E. S. Valenstein (Ed.) *Brain stimulation and motivation: Research and commentary.* Glenview, IL: Scott, Foresman.

Olds, J., & Milner, P. (1954). Positive reinforcement produced by electrical stimulation of septal area and other regions of the rat brain. *Journal of Comparative and Physiological Psychology, 47,* 419–427.

Olton, D. S. (1979). Mazes, mazes, and memory. *American Psychologist, 34,* 583–596.

Opton, E. M. (1970). Lessons of My Lai. In N. Sanford & C. Comstock (Eds.), *Sanctions for evil* San Francisco: Jossey-Bass.

Opton, E. M., Jr. (1973). "It never happened and besides they deserved it." In W. E. Henry & N. Sanford (Eds.), *Sanctions for evil* (pp. 49–70). San Francisco: Jossey-Bass.

Orlando, N. J. (1973). The mock ward: A study in simulation. In O. Milton & R. G. Wahler (Eds.), *Behavior disorders: Perspectives and trends.* Philadelphia: Lippincott.

Orlando, N. J. (1981). Mental patient as therapeutic agent—self-change, power, and caring. *Psychotherapy: Theory, Research and Practice, 7,* 58–62.

Orne, M. T. (1972). On the simulating subject as a quasi-control group in hypnosis research: What, why, and how? In E. Fromm & R. E. Shor (Eds.), *Hypnosis: Research developments and perspectives* (pp. 399–443). Chicago: Aldine.

Orne, M. T. (1980). Hypnotic control of pain: Toward a clarification of the different psychological processes involved. In J. J. Bonica (Ed.), *Pain* (pp. 155–172). New York: Raven Press.

Ornstein, P. A., & Naus, M. J. (1978). Rehearsal processes in children's memory. In P. A. Ornstein (Ed.), *Memory development in children.* Hillsdale, NJ: Erlbaum.

Ornstein, R. E. (1972). *The psychology of consciousness.* San Francisco: Freeman.

Ornstein, R. E. (1975). *The psychology of consciousness.* New York: Penguin Books.

Oskamp, S. (1984). *Applied Social Psychology.* Englewood Cliffs, NJ: Prentice-Hall.

Ouchi, W. (1981). *Theory Z: How American business can meet the Japanese challenge.* Reading, MA: Addison-Wesley.

P

Paivio, A. (1983). The empirical case for dual coding. In J. C. Yuille (Ed.), *Imagery, memory and cognition* (pp. 307–332). Hillsdale, NJ: Erlbaum.

Palmer, S. E. (1975a). The effects of contextual scenes on the identification of objects. *Memory and Cognition, 3,* 519–526.

Palmer, S. E. (1975b). Visual perception and world knowledge. In D. A. Norman, D. E. Rumelhart, & the LNR Research Group, *Explorations in cognition.* San Francisco: W. H. Freeman.

Palmer, S. E. (1984). The psychology of perceptual organization: A transformational approach. In A. Rosenfeld & J. Beck (Eds.), *Human and machine vision*. New York: Academic Press.

Palmonari, A., & Ricci Bitti, P. (1981). Il dispacco dalla famiglia: la situazione italiana. *Psicologia Contemporanea, 47,* 26–27.

Park, B., & Rothbart, M. (1982). Perception of out-group homogeneity and levels of social categorization: Memory for the subordinate attributes of in-group and out-group members. *Journal of Personality and Social Psychology, 42,* 1051–1068.

Park, R. D., & Walters, R. H. (1967). Some factors influencing the efficacy of punishment training for inducing response inhibition. *Monographs of the Society for Research in Child Development, 32* (1. Whole No. 109).

Parke, R. D., Berkowitz, L., Leyens, J. P., West, S. G., & Sebastian, R. J. (1977). Some effects of violent and nonviolent movies on the behavior of juvenile delinquents. In L. Berkowitz (Ed.), *Advances in experimental social psychology* (Vol. 10). New York: Academic Press.

Parke, R. D., & Sawin, D. B. (1976). The father's role in infancy. *Family Coordinator, 25,* 265–371.

Parlee, M. B. (1979, October). The friendship bond. *Psychology Today, 13,* 43–45.

Parrott, J., & Gleitman, H. (1984, April). *The joy of peekaboo: Appearance or reappearance?* Paper presented at the meeting of the Eastern Psychological Association, Baltimore, MD.

Pass, J. J., & Cunningham, J. W. (1978). Occupational clusters based on systematically derived work dimensions: Final Report. *Journal of Supplemental Abstract Service.* Catalogue of selected documents. Psychology (Vol. 8, pp. 22–23).

Patterson, F. (1981). *The education of Koko.* New York: Holt, Rinehart, & Winston.

Patty, R. A. (1976). Motive to avoid success and instructional set. *Sex Roles, 2,* 81–83.

Paul, G. L. (1969). Outcome of systematic desensitization: II. Controlled investigations of individual treatment technique variations, and current status. In C. M. Franks (Ed.), *Behavior therapy: Appraisal and status.* New York: McGraw-Hill.

Pavlov, I. P. (1927). *Conditioned reflexes.* (G. V. Anrep, Trans.). London: Oxford University Press.

Pavlov, I. P. (1928). *Lectures on conditioned reflexes: Twenty-five years of objective study of higher nervous activity (behavior of animals).* (Vol. 1). (W. H. Gantt, Trans.). New York: International Publishers.

Paykel, E. S. (1973). Life events and acute depression. In J.P. Scott & E. C. Senay (Eds.), *Separation and depression* (pp. 215–236). Washington: American Association for the Advancement of Science.

Pelletier, L., & Herold, E. (1983, May). *A study of sexual fantasies among young single females.* Paper presented at the meeting of the World Congress of Sexuality, Washington, DC.

Pelletier, K. R., & Peper, E. (1977). Developing a biofeedback model: Alpha EEG feedback as a means for main control. *The International Journal of Clinical and Experimental Hypnosis, 25,* 361–371.

Penfield, W. (1958). *The excitable cortex in conscious man.* Liverpool: Liverpool University Press.

Penfield, W., & Baldwin, M. (1952). Temporal lobe seizures and the technique of subtotal lobectomy. *Annals of Surgery, 136,* 625–634.

Penfield, W. & Rasmussen, T. (1950). *The cerebral cortex of man.* New York: Macmillan.

Penick, S., Smith, G., Wienske, K., & Hinkle, L. (1963). An experimental evaluation of the relationship between hunger and gastric motility. *American Journal of Physiology, 205,* 421–434.

Penrose, L. S., & Penrose, R. (1958). Impossible objects: A special type of visual illusion. *British Journal of Psychology, 49.*

Peplau, L. A., Miceli, M., & Morasch, B. (1982). Loneliness and self-evaluation. In L. A. Peplau & D. Perlman (Eds.), *Loneliness.* New York: Wiley.

Perenin, M. T., & Jeannerod, M. (1975). Residual vision in cortically blind hemifields. *Neuropsychologia, 13,* 1–7.

Perlin, S. (Ed.). 1975). *A handbook for the study of suicide.* New York: Oxford University Press.

Perls, F. S. (1967). Group vs. individual therapy. *ECT: A review of general semantics, 34,* 306–312.

Perls, F. S. (1969). *Gestalt therapy verbatim.* Lafayette, CA: Real People Press.

Peters, T. J., & Waterman, R. H., Jr. (1983). *In search of excellence: Lessons from America's best-run companies.* New York: Warner.

Peterson, J. L., & Zill, N. (1981). Television viewing in the United States and children's intellectual, social, and emotional development *Television and Children, 2,* 21–28.

Peterson, L. R., & Peterson, M. J. (1959). Short-term retention of individual verbal items. *Journal of Experimental Psychology, 58,* 193–198.

Petter, G. (1968). *Problemi psicologici della preadolescenza e del adolescenza.* Firenze: Nuova Italia.

Pfaffman, C. (1959). The sense of taste In J. Field (Ed.), *Handbook of physiology: Section 1. Neurophysiology* (Vol. 1). Washington, DC: American Physiological Society.

Pfefferbaum, A. (1977). Psychotherapy and psychopharmacology. In J. D. Barchas, P. A. Berger, R. D. Ciacanello, & G. R. Elliott (Eds.), *Psychopharmacology: From theory to practice* (pp. 481–492). New York: Oxford University Press.

Pfungst, O. (1911). *Clever Hans (the horse of Mr. Von Osten).* R. Rosenthal (Trans.). New York: Holt, Rinehart & Winston.

Phares, E. J. (1984). *Clinical psychology: Concepts, methods, and professionals* (Rev. ed.). Homewood, IL: Dorsey.

Piaget, J. (1954). *The construction of reality in the child.* New York: Basic Books.

Piaget, J. (1960). *The Moral judgment of the child.* New York: Free Press.

Piaget, J. (1977). *The development of thought: Equilibrium of cognitive structures.* New York: Viking Press.

Piaget, J., & Inhelder, B. (1967). *The child's conception of space.* New York: Norton.

Pierrel, R., & Sherman, J. G. (1963, February) Train your pet the Barnabus way. *Brown Alumni Monthly,* pp. 8–14.

Pilisuk, M. (1982). Delivery of social support: The social innoculation. *American Journal of Orthopsychiatry, 52,* 20–36.

Pilkonis, P. A. (1977). The behavioral consequences of shyness. *Journal of Personality, 45,* 596–611.

Pilkonis, P. A., & Zimbardo, P. G. (1979). The personal and social dynamics of shyness. In C. E. Izard (Ed.), *Emotions in personality and psychopathology* (pp. 133–160). New York: Plenum.

Pines, M. (1983, November). Can a rock walk? *Psychology Today,* pp. 46–54.

Pinkerton, J. (Ed.). (1814). *A general collection of the best and most interesting voyages and travels in all parts of the world, 1808–1814.* London: Longman, Hurst, Rees, & Orne.

Pitts, F. N. (1969). The biochemistry of anxiety. *Scientific American, 220*(2), 69–75.

Pitz, G. F., & Sachs, N. J. (1984). Judgment and decision: Theory and application. *Annual Review of Psychology, 35,* 139–163.

Place, E. J. S., & Gilmore, G. C. (1980). Perceptual organization in schizophrenia. *Journal of Abnormal Psychology, 89,* 409–418.

Platt, J. (1973). Social traps. *American Psychologist, 28,* 641–651.

Plutchik, R. (1980). *Emotion: A psychoevolutionary synthesis.* New York: Harper & Row.

Plutchik, R., Kellerman, H., & Conte, H. Q. (1979). A structural theory of ego defenses and emotions. In C. Izard, (Ed.), *Emotions and psychopathology* (pp. 229–257). New York: Plenum.

Posner, J. K. (1982). The development of mathematical knowledge in two West African societies. *Child Development, 53,* 200–208.

Posner, M. I., & Boies, S. J. (1971). Components of attention. *Psychological Review, 78,* 391–408.

Posner, M. I., & Snyder, C. R. R. (1974). Attention and cognitive control. In R. L. Solso (Ed.), *Information processing and cognition: The Loyola Symposium* (pp. 55–88). Potomac, MD: Erlbaum.

Post, F. (1980). Paranoid, schizophrenic-like, and schizophrenic states in the aged. In J. E. Birren & R. B. Stone (Eds.), *Handbook of mental health and aging* (pp. 591–615). Englewood Cliffs, NJ: Prentice-Hall.

Postman, L. & Phillips, L. (1965). Short-term temporal changes in free recall. *Quarterly Journal of Experimental Psychology, 17,* 132–138.

Pound, E. (1934). *The ABC of reading.* New York: New Directions Publishing Co.

Powell, L. H., & Eagleston, J. R. (in press). The assessment of chronic stress in college students. In E. M. Altmaier (Ed.), *New directions in student services—Helping students manage stress.* San Francisco: Jossey-Bass.

Powers, W. T. (1973). Feedback: Beyond behaviorism. *Science, 17,* 351–356.

Powley, T. L. (1977). The ventromedial hypothalamic syndrome, satiety, and a cephalic phase hypothesis. *Psychological Review, 84,* 89–126.

Premack, D. (1965). Reinforcement theory. In D. Levine (Ed.), *Nebraska symposium on motivation* (pp. 123–180). Lincoln: University of Nebraska Press.

Premack, D. (1976). *Intelligence in ape and man.* Hillsdale, NJ: Erlbaum.

Premack, D. (1983). The codes of man and beasts. *The Behavioral and Brain Sciences, 6,*125–167.

Prentice-Dunn, S., & Rogers, R. W. (1982). Effects of public and private self-awareness on deindividuation and aggression. *Journal of Personality and Social Psychology, 42,* 503–513.

Prentky, R. A. (1980). *Creativity and psychopathology.* New York: Praeger.

President's Commission on Mental Health. (1977, September 1). Preliminary Report to the President.

Pribram, K. H., & Gill, M. M. (1976). *Freud's "Project" reassessed.* New York: Basic Books.

Price, R. H., Ketterer, R. F., Bader, B. C., & Monahan, J. (Eds.). (1980). *Prevention in mental health: Research, policy, and practice: Vol. 1.* Beverly Hills, CA: Sage.

Prince, G. (1973). *The practice of creativity.* New York: Collier.

Pritchard, R. M. (1961, June). Stabilized images on the retina. *Scientific American, 204,* (6) 72–78.

Proshansky, H. M. (1976). Environmental psychology and the real world. *American Psychologist, 31,* 303–310.

Proxmire, W. (1975). Quote on the National Science Foundation.

Putman, F. W. (1984, March). The psychophysiologic investigation of multiple personality disorder. (Symposium on Multiple Personality). *The Psychiatric Clinics of North America, 7*(1), 31–40.

Putoff, H. E., Targ, R., & May, E. E. (1979, July). *Experimental PSI research: Implications for physics.* SRI International Report.

Pylyshyn, Z. W. (1973). What the mind's eye tells the mind's brain: A critique of mental imagery. *Psychological Bulletin, 80,* 1–24.

Q

Quattrone, G. A. (1982). Overattribution and unit formation: When behavior engulfs the person. *Journal of Personality and Social Psychology, 42,* 593–607.

Quattrone, G. A. (in press). On the perception of a group's variability. In S. Worchel & W. G. Austin (Eds.), *The social psychology of intergroup relations* (rev. ed.). Chicago: Nelson Hall.

R

Rabbie, J. M. (1981). The effects of intergroup competition and cooperation on intra- and intergroup relationships. In J. Grzelak & V. Derlega (Eds.), *Living with other people: Theory and research on cooperation and helping.* New York: Academic Press.

Rabbie, J. M., & Wilkens, G. (1971). Intergroup competition and its effect on intragroup and intergroup relations. *European Journal of Psychology, 1,* 215–234.

Rabkin, J. G., Gelb, L., & Lazar, J. B. (1980). (Eds.), *Attitudes toward the mentally ill: Research perspectives.* (Report of an NIMH workshop), Rockville, MD: National Institute of Mental Health.

Rachman, S. (1966). Sexual fetishism: An experimental analogue. *Psychological Record, 16,* 293–296.

Rachman, S. & Hodgson, R. (1980). *Obsessions and compulsions.* Englewood Cliffs, NJ: Prentice-Hall.

Rachman, S. J., & Teasdale, J. (1979). Aversion therapy: An appraisal. In C. M. Franks (Ed.), *Behavior therapy: Appraisal and status* (pp. 279–320). New York: McGraw-Hill.

Rahe, R. H., & Arthur, R. J. (1977). Life-change patterns surrounding illness experience. In A. Monat & R. S. Lazarus, (Eds.), *Stress and coping* (pp. 36–44). New York: Columbia University Press.

Regan, D. T., & Fazio, R. (1977). On the consistency between attitudes and behavior: Look to the method of attitude formation. *Journal of Experimental Social Psychology, 13,* 28–45.

Reich, P., DeSilva, R. A., Lown, B., & Murawski, B. J. (1981). Acute psychological disturbances preceding life-threatening ventricular arrhythmias. *Journal of the American Medical Association, 246,* 233–235.

Reinisch, J. M. (1981). Prenatal exposure to synthetic progestions increases potential for aggression in humans. *Science, 211,* 1171–1173.

Reisenzein, R. (1983). The Schachter theory of emotion: Two decades later. *Psychological Bulletin, 94,* 239–264.

Reiterman, T., & Jacobs, J. (1983). Raven: *The untold story of Jim Jones and his people.* New York: Dutton.

Rescorla, R. A. (1972). Information variables in Pavlovian conditioning. In G. Bower (Ed.), *The psychology of learning and motivation.* (Vol. 6). New York: Academic Press.

Rescorla, R. A. (1980). *Pavlovian second-order conditioning: Studies in associative learning.* Hillsdale, NJ: Erlbaum.

Rescorla, R. A., & Wagner, A. R. (1972). A theory of Pavlovian conditioning: Variations in the effectiveness of reinforcement and nonreinforcement. In A. H. Black & W. F. Prokasy (Eds.), *Classical conditioning: II. Current research and theory* (pp. 64–94). New York: Appleton-Century-Crofts.

Reuters (1982, January 1). *Tiny superman fans making fatal dives.* Kota Kinabalu, Malaysia.

Richter, C. P. (1957). On the phenomenon of sudden death in animals and man. *Psychosomatic Medicine, 19,* 191–198.

Richter, C. P. (1965). *Biological clocks in medicine and psychiatry.* Springfield, IL: C. C. Thomas.

Richter, C. P. (1968). Psychopathology of periodic behavior in animals and man. In J. Zubin & H. F. Hunt (Eds.), *Comparative Psychopathology* (pp. 205–227). New York: Grune & Stratton.

Richter, C. P. (1975). Deep hypothermia and its effect on the 24-hour clock of rats and hamsters. *Johns Hopkins Medical Journal, 136,* 1–10.

Ricks, D. F., & Wessman, A. E.: (1966, spring). Winn: A case study of a happy man. *Humanistic Psychology, 6,* 2–16.

Robbins, L. C. (1963). The accuracy of parental recall of aspects of child development and of child rearing practices. *Journal of Abnormal and Social Psychology, 66,* 261–270.

Roberts, T. B. (1973). Maslow's human motivation needs hierarchy: A bibliography. *Research in Education.* ERIC document ED-069-591.

Roberts, W. A. (1969). Resistance to extinction following partial and consistent reinforcement with varying magnitudes of reward. *Journal of Comparative Physiological Psychology, 67,* 395–400.

Robinson, T. E., Becker, J. B., & Presty, S. K. (1982). Long-term facilitation of amphetamine-induced rotational behavior and striatal dopamine release produced by a single exposure to amphetamine: Sex differences. *Brain Research, 253,* 231–241.

Rock, I. (1975). *An introduction to perception.* New York: Macmillan.

Rock, I., & Ebenholtz, S. (1962). Stroboscopic movement based on change of phenomenal rather than retinal location. *American Journal of Psychology, 75,* 193–207.

Rodin, J. (1980). Managing the stress of aging: The role of control and coping. In S. Levine & H. Ursin (Eds.), *Coping and health* (pp. 191–202). New York: Plenum.

Rodin, J. (1983, April). Updated report on relationship between immunologic measures and psychosocial variables. Paper presented at the meeting of the Western Psychological Association, San Francisco.

Roediger, H. L., & Crowder, R. G. (1976). A serial position effect in recall of United States presidents. *Bulletin of the Psychonomic Society, 8,* 275–278.

Rogers, C. R. (1947). Some observations on the organization of personality. *American Psychologist, 2,* 358–368.

Rogers, C. R. (1951). *Client-centered therapy: Its current practice, implications and theory.* Boston: Houghton-Mifflin.

Rogers, C. R. (1959). A theory of therapy, personality, and interpersonal relationships, as developed in the client-centered framework. In S. Koch (Ed.), *Psychology: A study of a science* (Vol. 3). New York: McGraw-Hill.

Rogers, C. R. (1977). *On personal power: Inner strength and its revolutionary impact.* New York: Delacorte.

Rogers, M. P., Liang, M. H., & Partridge, A. J. (1982). Psychological care of adults with rheumatoid arthritis. *Annals of Internal Medicine, 96,* 344–348.

Rogoff, B. (1982). Integrating context and cognitive development. In M. E. Lamb & A. L. Brown (Eds.) *Advances in developmental psychology.* Hillsdale, NJ: Erlbaum.

Rokeach, M. (1968). *Beliefs, attitudes and values.* San Francisco: Jossey-Bass.

Rorschach, H. (1942). *Psychodiagnostics: A diagnostic test based on perception.* New York: Grune & Stratton.

Rosch, E. H. (1973). Natural categories. *Cognitive Psychology, 4,* 328–350.

Rosch, E. (1978). Principles of categorization. In E. Rosch & B. B. Lloyd (Eds.), *Cognition and Categorization* (pp. 27–48). Hillsdale, NJ: Erlbaum.

Rosch, E. H., Mervis, C. B., Gray, W. D., Johnson, D. M., & Boyes-Braem, P. (1976). Basic objects in natural categories. *Cognitive Psychology, 8,* 382–439.

Rose, R. J., Miller, J. Z., Dumont-Driscall, M., & Evans, M. M. (1979). Twin-family studies of perceptual speed ability. *Behavior Genetics, 9,* 71–86.

Rose, S. (1973). *The conscious brain.* New York: Knopf.

Rosen, H. (1980). *The development of socio-moral knowledge.* New York: Columbia University Press.

Rosenbaum, M., & Muroff, M. (Eds.) (1984). *Fourteen contemporary reinterpretations.* New York: Free Press.

Rosenbaum, R. M. (1972). *A dimensional analysis of the perceived causes of success and failure.* Unpublished doctoral dissertation. University of California, Los Angeles.

Rosenhan, D. (1969). Some origins of concern for others. In P. Mussen, J. Langer, & M. Covington (Eds.), *Trends and issues in developmental psychology.* New York: Holt, Rinehart & Winston.

Rosenhan, D. L. (1973). On being sane in insane places. *Science, 179,* 250–258.

Rosenhan, D. L. (1975). The contextual nature of psychiatric diagnoses. *Journal of Abnormal Psychology, 84,* 462–474.

Rosenhan, D. L., & Seligman, M. E. P. (1984). *Abnormal psychology.* New York: Norton.

Rosenthal, D. (Ed.). (1963). *The Genain Quadruplets.* New York: Basic Books.

Rosenthal, D., Wender, P. H., Kety, S. S., Schulsinger, F., Weiner, J., & Rieder, R. (1975). Parent-child relationships and psychopathological disorder in the child. *Archives of General Psychiatry, 32,* 466–476.

Rosenthal, R. (1966). *Experimenter effects in behavioral research.* New York: Appleton-Century-Crofts.

Rosenthal, R., & Jacobson, L. F. (1968). Teacher expectations for the disadvantaged. *Scientific American, 218*(4), 19–23.

Rosenzweig, M. R. (1984). Experience, memory, and the brain. *American Psychologist, 39,* 365–376.

Rosenzweig, M. R., & Bennett, E. L. (1977). Effects of environmental enrichment or impoverishment on learning and on brain values in rodents. In A. Oliverio (Ed.), *Genetics, environment, and intelligence.* Amsterdam: Elsevieri North Holland.

Rosenzweig, M. R., Bennett, E. L., & Diamond, M. C. (1972). Brain changes in response to experience. Scientific American, 226(2), 22–29.

Rosenzweig, M. R., & Lieman, A. L. (1982). *Physiological psychology.* Lexington, MA: Heath.

Ross, L. (1977). The intuitive psychologist and his shortcomings. In L. Berkowitz (Ed.), *Advances in experimental social psychology* (Vol. 10). New York: Academic Press.

Ross, L. (1978). Some afterthoughts on the intuitive psychologist. In L. Berkowitz (Ed.), *Cognitive theories in social psychology.* New York: Academic Press.

Ross, L., Amabile, T., & Steinmetz, J. (1977). Social roles, social control and biases in the social perception process. *Journal of Personality and Social Psychology, 37,* 485–494.

Ross, M., & Socoly, F. (1979). Egocentric biases in availability and attribution. *Journal of Personality and Social Psychology, 37,* 322–336.

Rothman, D. J. (1971). *The discovery of the asylum: Social order and disorder in the new republic.* Boston: Little, Brown.

Rotter, J. B. (1954). *Social learning and clinical psychology.* Englewood Cliffs, NJ: Prentice-Hall.

Routtenberg, A. (1980). Redundancy in the nervous system as substrate for consciousness. In J. M. Davidson & R. V. Davidson (Eds.), *The psychology of consciousness* (pp. 105–127). New York: Plenum Press.

Rovee-Collier, C. K., Sullivan, M. W., Enright, M., Lucas, D., & Fagen, J. W. (1980). Reactivation of infant memory. *Science, 208,* 1159–1161.

Rozin, P. (1976). The evolution of intelligence and access to the cognitive unconscious. In J. M. Sprague & A. A. Epstein (Eds.), *Progress in psychobiology and physiological psychology* (pp. 245–280). New York: Academic Press.

Rozin, P., & Kalat, J. W. (1971). Specific hungers and poison avoidance as adaptive specializations of learning. *Psychological Review, 78,* 459–486.

Rubin, J. Z., Provenzano, F. J., & Luria, Z. (1974). The eye of the beholder: Parents' views on sex of newborns. *American Journal of Orthopsychiatry, 44,* 512–519.

Rubin, L. B. (1976, October). The marriage bed. *Psychology Today,* pp. 44–50, 91–92.

Rubin, Z. (1973). *Liking and loving.* New York: Holt, Rinehart & Winston.

Rudy, J. W., & Wagner, A. R. (1975). Stimulus selection in associative learning. In W. K. Estes (Ed.), *Handbook of learning and cognition,* (Vol. 2). Hillsdale, NJ: Erlbaum.

Rumbaugh, D. M. (Ed.). (1977). *Language learning by a chimpanzee: The Lana project.* New York: Academic Press.

Rumelhart, D. E., & Norman, D. A. (1975). *Explorations in cognition.* San Francisco: Freeman.

Russell, J. A., & Ward, L. M. (1982). Environmental psychology. *Annual Review of Psychology, 33,* 651–688.

Ryan, W. (1976). *Blaming the victim* (rev. ed.). New York: Vintage Books.

Rychlak, J. (1979). *Discovering free will and personal responsibility.* New York: Oxford University Press.

S

Sabini, J., & Silver, M. (1982). *Moralities of everyday life.* New York: Oxford University Press.

Sacks, O. (1973). *Migraine: Evolution of a common disorder.* Berkeley: University of California Press.

Saegert, S., & Hart, R. (1976). The development of sex differences in the environmental competence of children. In P. Burnett (Ed.), *Women in society.* Chicago: Maarouta.

Salzman, C. (1980). The use of ECT in the treatment of schizophrenia. *American Journal of Psychiatry, 137,* 1032–1041.

Sanders, C. B., & Cicchetti, N. (1982). *School Health Manual.* New York: Board of Education of the City of New York, District Eleven. [Of special interest is Project P.E.G.—Prevention in Early Grades and Paramedical approaches to Health Services.]

Sanders, R. S., & Reyhen, J. (1969). Sensory deprivation and the enhancement of hypnotic susceptibility. *Journal of Abnormal Psychology, 74,* 375–381.

Saraf, K. (1980). Shyness: Body and self-catharses. (Doctoral dissertation, California School of Professional Psychology, Fresno, 1980). *Dissentation Abstracts International, 41*(10), 3902B.

Sarason, I. G., Johnson, J. H., & Siegel, J. M. (1978). Assessing the impact of life changes: Development of the Life Experiences Survey. *Journal of Consulting and Clinical Psychology, 46,* 932–946.

Sarnoff, I., & Corwin, S. M. (1959). Castration anxiety and the fear of death. *Journal of Personality, 27,* 374–385.

Sarnoff, I., & Zimbardo, P. G. (1961). Anxiety, fear, and social affiliation. *Journal of Abnormal and Social Psychology, 62,* 356–363.

Satir, V. (1967). *Conjoint family therapy.* (rev. ed.). Palo Alto: Science and Behavior Books.

Sattler, J. M. (1982). *Assessment of children's intelligence and special abilities.* Boston: Allyn & Bacon.

Sawyer, J. (1966). Measurement *and* prediction, clinical *and* statistical. *Psychological Bulletin, 66,* 178–200.

Scammon, R. E. (1930). The measurement of the body in childhood. In J. A. Harris, C. M. Jackson, D. G. Patterson, and R. E. Scammon (Eds.), *The measurement of man.* Minneapolis: University of Minnesota Press.

Schachter, S. (1959). *The psychology of affiliation.* Stanford: Stanford University Press.

Schachter, S. (1964). The interaction of cognitive and physiological determinants of emotional state. In L. Berkowitz (Ed.), *Advances in experimental social psychology* (Vol. 1, pp. 49–80). New York: Academic Press.

Schachter, S. (1971). *Emotion, obesity and crime.* New York: Academic Press.

Schachter, S., Goldman, R., Gordon, A. (1968). The effects of fear, food deprivation, and obesity on eating. *Journal of Personality and Social Psychology, 10,* 91–97.

Schachter, S., & Singer, J. (1962). Cognitive, social and physiological determinants of emotional state. *Psychological Review, 69,* 379–399.

Schaie, K. W. (1980). Intelligence and problem solving. In J. E. Birren & R. B. Sloan, (Eds.), *Handbook of mental health and aging* (pp. 262–284). Englewood Cliffs, NJ: Prentice-Hall.

Schank, R. C., & Abelson, R. (1977). *Scripts, plans, goals and understanding.* Hillsdale, NJ: Erlbaum.

Schell, J. (1982). *The fate of the earth.* New York: Knopf.

Schiffman, S. S., & Erickson, R. P. (1971). A theoretical review: A psychophysical model for gustatory quality. *Physiology and Behavior, 7,* 617–633.

Schlenker, B. R. (1980). *Impression management: The self-concept, social identity, and interpersonal relations.* Monterey, CA: Brooks/Cole.

Schneider, A. (1975). Two faces of memory consolidation: Storage of instrumental and classical conditioning. In D. Deutsch & J. A. Deutsch, (Eds.), *Short-term memory* (pp. 340–354). New York: Academic Press.

Schneider, D. J. (1973). Implicit personality theory: A review. *Psychological Bulletin, 79,* 294–309.

Schneider, G. E. (1969). Two visual systems. *Science, 163,* 895–902.

Schneider, W. (1984). Developmental trends in the meta-memory-memory behavior relationship. In D. L. Forrest-Pressley, G. E. Mackinnon, & P. G. Waller (Eds.), *Metacognition, cognition, and human performance.* New York: Academic Press.

Schneidman, E. S. (Ed), (1976). *Deaths of Man.* New York: Quadrangle.

Schrag, P. (1978). *Mind control.* New York: Delta.

Schreiber, F., (1973). *Sybil.* New York: Warner Books.

Schwartz, G. E. (1974, April). The facts on transcendental meditation: Part II. TM relaxes some people and makes them feel good. *Psychology Today,* pp. 39–44.

Schwartz, G. E., Brown, S. L., & Ahern, G. L. (1980). Facial muscle patterning and subjective experience during affective imagery: Sex differences. *Psychophysiology, 17,* 75–82.

Schwartz, P., & Strom, D. (1978). The social psychology of female sexuality. In J. Sherman & F. L. Denmark (Eds.), *Psychology of women: Future directions of research* (pp. 149–177). New York: Psychological Dimensions.

Scott, J. P. (1963). The process of primary socialization in canine and human infants. *Monograph of the Society for Research in Child Development, 28,* 1–47.

Scott, J. P., Stewart, J. M., & De Ghett V. J. (1974). Critical periods in the organization of systems. *Developmental Psychobiology, 7,* 489–513.

Scott, R. A. (1972). A proposed framework for analyzing deviance as a property of social order. In R. A. Scott & J. D. Douglas (Eds.), *Theoretical perspectives on deviance.* New York: Basic Books.

Scott, V. (1984, June 13). A six-year nightmare for Jim Backus [United Press]. *San Francisco Chronicle,* p. 58.

Sears, P., & Barbee, A. H. (1977). Career and life situations among Terman's gifted women. In J. C. Stanley, W. C. George, & C. H. Solano (Eds.), *The gifted and the creative: A fifty-year perspective* (pp. 28–65). Baltimore, MD: Johns Hopkins University Press.

Sears, R. R. (1961). Relation of early socialization experiences to aggression in middle childhood. *Journal of Abnormal and Social Psychology. 63,* 466–92.

Sears, R. R. (1977). Sources of life satisfactions of the Terman gifted men. *American Psychologist, 32,* 119–128.

Sebeok, T. A., & Rosenthal, R. (1981). The clever Hans phenomenon. *Annals of the New York Academy of Sciences,* Whole Vol. 364.

Selfridge, O. G. (1955). Pattern recognition and modern computers. *Proceedings of the Western Joint Computer Conference,* New York: Institute of Electrical and Electronics Engineers.

Seligman, M. E. P. (1970). On the generality of the laws of learning. *Psychological Review, 77,* 406–419.

Seligman, M. E. P. (1975). *Helplessness: On depression, development, and death.* San Francisco: Freeman.

Seligman, M. E. P., & Maier, S. F. (1967). Failure to escape traumatic shock. *Journal of Experimental Psychology, 74,* 1–9.

Selman, R. (1980). *The growth of interpersonal understanding.* New York: Academic Press.

Selye, H. (1956). *The stress of life.* New York: McGraw-Hill.

Selye, H. (1974). *Stress without distress.* New York: New American Library.

Selye, H. (1976). *Street in health and disease.* Woburn, MA: Butterworth.

Shafer, R. (1976). *A new language for psychoanalysis.* New Haven: Yale University Press.

Shapiro, A. K. (1978). Placebo effects in medical and psychological therapies. In S. L. Garfield & A. E. Bergen (Eds.), *Handbook of psychotherapy and behavioral change: An empirical analysis* (pp. 369–410). (2nd ed.) New York: Wiley.

Shaver, P., & Rubinstein, C. (1980). Childhood attachment experience and adult loneliness. In L. Wheeler (Ed.), *Review of personality and social psychology: 1.* Beverly Hills, CA: Sage.

Sheehy, G. (1976). *Passages: Predictable crises of adult life.* New York: Dutton.

Sheffield, F. D. (1966). New evidence on the drive-induction theory of reinforcement. In R. N. Haber (Ed.), *Current research in motivation* (pp. 111–122). New York: Holt.

Sheffield, F. D., & Roby, T. B. (1950). Reward value of a non-nutritive sweet taste. *Journal of Comparative and Physiological Psychology, 43,* 471–481.

Sheingold, K. & Tenney, Y. J. (1982). Memory for a salient childhood event. In U. Neisser (Ed.), *Memory observed.* San Francisco: Freeman.

Sheldon, W. (1942). *The varieties of temperament: A psychology of constitutional differences.* New York: Harper.

Shepard, R. N. (1978). Externalization of mental images and the act of creation. In B. S. Randhawa & W. E. Coffman (Eds.), *Visual learning, thinking, and communicating.* New York: Academic Press.

Shepard, R. N., & Cooper, L. A. (1982). *Mental images and their transformations.* Cambridge, MA: MIT Press.

Sheridan, C. L., & King, R. G. (1972). Obedience to authority with an authentic victim. *Proceedings of the 80th Annual Convention, American Psychological Association, Part I, 7,* 165–166.

Sherif, C. W. (1981, August). *Social and psychological bases of social psychology.* The G. Stanley Hall Lecture on social psychology, presented at the annual convention of the American Psychological Association, Los Angeles.

Sherif, M. (1935). A study of some social factors in perception. *Archives of Psychology. 27*(187).

Sherif, M., Harvey, O. J., White, B. J., Hood, W. E., & Sherif, C. W. (1961). *Intergroup conflict and cooperation: The Robber's Cave experiment.* Norman: University of Oklahoma Press.

Sherif, M., & Sherif, C. W. (1979). Research on intergroup relations. In W. G. Austin & S. Worchel (Eds.), *The social psychology of intergroup relations* (pp. 7–18). Monterey, CA: Brooks/Cole.

Sherman, J. A. (1963). Reinstatement of verbal behavior in a psychotic by reinforcement methods. *Journal of Speech and Hearing Disorders, 28,* 398–401.

Sherman, S. M. (1979). The functional significance of x and y cells in normal and visually deprived cats. *Trends in Neuroscience, 2,* 192–195.

Sherrington, C. S. (1906). *The integrative action of the nervous system.* New York: Scribner, 1906 (2nd ed. New Haven: Yale University Press, 1947).

Sherrod, K., Vietze, P., & Friedman, S. (1978). *Infancy.* Monterey, CA: Brooks/Cole.

Shettleworth, S. J. (1972). Constraints on learning. In D. S. Lehrman, R. A. Hinde, & E. Shaw (Eds.), *Advances in the study of behavior* (Vol. 4, pp. 1–62). New York: Academic Press.

Shettleworth, S. J. (1975). Reinforcement and the organization of behavior in golden hamsters: hunger, environment and food reinforcement. *Journal of Experimental Psychology: Animal Behavior Processes, 1,* 56–87.

Shirley, M. M. (1931). *The first two years.* Minneapolis: University of Minnesota Press.

Shortliffe, E. H. (1983). Medical consultation systems: Designing for doctors. In M. S. Sime & M. J. Coombs (Eds.), *Designing for human computer communication* (pp. 209–238). London: Academic Press.

Shotter, J. (1984). *Social accountability and selfhood.* Oxford: Blackwell.

Siegel, A. W., Allen, G. W., & Kirasic, K. C. (1979). Children's ability to make bidirectional distance comparisons: The advantage of thinking ahead. *Developmental Psychology, 15,* 656–665.

Siegel, S. (1977). Morphine tolerance acquisition as an associative process. *Journal of Experimental Psychology: Animal behavior processes, 3,* 1–13.

Siegel, S. (1979). The role of conditioning in drug tolerance and addiction. In J. D. Keehn (Ed.), *Psychopathology in animals: Research and clinical applications* (pp. 143–167). New York: Academic Press.

Silberfeld, M. (1978). Psychological symptoms and social supports. *Social Psychiatry, 13,* 11–17.

Silver, R., & Wortman, E. (1980). Coping with undesirable life events. In J. Garber & M. E. P. Seligman (Eds.), *Human helplessness: Theory and application.* New York: Academic Press.

Silverman, L. H. (1976). Psychoanalytic theory: "The reports of my death are greatly exaggerated." *American Psychologist, 31,* 621–637.

Simmel, E. C. (1980). *Early experiences and early behavior: Implications for social development.* New York: Academic Press.

Simon, H. A. (1973). The structure of ill-structured problems. *Artificial Intelligence, 4,* 181–202.

Simon, H. A., & Gilmartin, K. (1973). A simulation of memory for chess positions. *Cognitive Psychology, 5,* 29–46.

Sinclair, J. D. (1983, December). The hardware of the brain. *Psychology Today,* pp. 8, 11, 12.

Singer, J. E., Brush, C., & Lublin, S. C. (1965). Some aspects of deindividuation: Identification and conformity. *Journal of Experimental Social Psychology, 1,* 356–378.

Singer, J. L. (1966). *Daydreaming: An introduction to the experimental study of inner experience.* New York: Random House.

Singer, J. L. (1975). Navigating the stream of consciousness: Research in daydreaming and related inner experience. *American Psychologist, 30,* 727–739.

Singer, J. L. (1976). Fantasy: The foundation of serenity. *Psychology Today,* pp. 32 ff.

Singer, J. L. (1978). Experimental studies of daydreaming and the stream of thought. In K. S. Pope & J. L. Singer (Eds.), *The stream of consciousness: Scientific investigations into the flow of human experience* (pp. 187–223). New York: Plenum.

Singer, J. L., & McCraven, V. J. (1961). Some characteristics of adult daydreaming. *Journal of Psychology, 51,* 151–164.

Sjoberg, B. M., & Hollister, L. F. (1965). The effects of psychotomimetic drugs on primary suggestibility. *Psychopharmacologia, 8,* 251–262.

Skeels, H. M. (1966). Adult status of children with contrasting early life experiences. *Monographs of the Society for Research in Child Development, 31*(3).

Skinner, B. F. (1953). *Science and human behavior.* New York: Macmillan.

Skinner, B. F. (1957). *Verbal Behavior.* New York: Appleton-Century-Crofts.

Skinner, B. F. (1966). What is the experimental analysis of behavior? *Journal of the Experimental Analysis of Behavior, 9,* 213–18.

Sloane, R. B., Staples, F. R., Cristol, A. H., Yorkston, N. J., & Whipple, K. (1975). *Psychotherapy versus behavior therapy.* Cambridge, MA: Harvard University Press.

Slobin, D. (1979). *Psycholinguistics,* (2nd ed.). Glenview, IL: Scott, Foresman.

Smith, D. (1982). Trends in counseling and psychotherapy. *American Psychologist, 37,* 802–809.

Smith, D., & Kraft, W. A. (1983). DSM-III: Do psychologists really want an alternative? *American Psychologist, 38,* 777–785.

Smith, E. E., & Medin, D. L. (1981). *Cognitive Science Series: 4. Categories and concepts.* Cambridge, MA: Harvard University Press.

Smith, M. L., & Glass, G. V. (1977). Meta-analysis of psychotherapy outcome studies. *American Psychologist, 32,* 752–760.

Smith, M. L., Glass, G. V., & Miller, T. I. (1980). *The benefits of psychotherapy.* Baltimore, MD: Johns Hopkins University Press.

Smith, S. M., Brown, H. O., Toman, J. E. P. & Goodman, L. S. (1947). The lack of cerebral effects of d-tubercurarine. *Anesthesiology, 8,* 1–14.

Snow, C. P. (1961, January 7). In the name of obedience. *Nation, 192*(1), 3.

Snowden, C. T. (1969). Motivation, regulation and the control of meal parameters with oral and intragastric feeding. *Journal of Comparative and Physiological Psychology, 69,* 91–100.

Snyder, C. R., & Fromkin, H. L. (1980). *Uniqueness: The human pursuit of difference.* New York: Plenum.

Snyder, M., & Frankel, A. (1976). Observer bias:. A stringent test of behavior engulfing the field. *Journal of Personality and Social Psychology, 34,* 857–864.

Snyder, M., & Swann, W. B., Jr. (1978). Behavioral confirmation in social interaction: From social perception to social reality. *Journal of Experimental Social Psychology, 14,* 148–162.

Snyder, M., & Uranowitz, S. W. (1978). Reconstructing the past: Some cognitive consequences of person perception. *Journal of Personality and Social Psychology, 36,* 941–950.

Snyder, M., & White, P. (1982). Moods and memories: Elation, depression, and the remembering of the events of one's life. *Journal of Personality, 50,* 149–167.

Snyder, S. H. (1974). Catecholamines as mediators of drug effects in schizophrenia. In F. O. Schmitt & F. G. Worden (Eds.), *The neurosciences: Third study program* (pp. 721–732). Cambridge, MA: MIT Press.

Snyder, S. H., & Childers, S. R. (1979). Opiate receptors and opioid peptides. *Annual Review of Neurosciences, 2,* 35–64.

Snyder, S. H., & Mattysse, S. (1975). *Opiate receptor mechanisms.* Cambridge, MA: MIT Press.

Social Science Research Council. (1984, March). *ITEMS, 38,* 18–20.

Spanos, N. P., & Gottlieb, J. (1976). Ergotism and the Salem village witch trials. *Science, 194,* 1390–1394.

Speisman, J. C., Lazarus, R. S., Mordkoff, A. M., & Davison, L. A. (1964). The experimental reduction of stress based on ego-defense theory. *Journal of Abnormal and Social Psychology, 68,* 367–380.

Spelke, E., Hirst, W., & Neisser, U. (1976). Skills of divided attention. *Cognition, 4,* 215–230.

Spence, D. P. (1967). Subliminal perception and perceptual defense: Two sides of a single problem. *Behavioral Science, 12,* 183–193.

Sperling, G. (1960). The information available in brief visual presentations. *Psychological Monographs, 74,* 1–29.

Sperling, G. (1963). A model for visual memory tasks. *Human Factors, 5,* 19–31.

Sperry, R. W. (1952). Neurology and the mind-brain problem. *American Scientist, 40,* 291–312.

Sperry, R. W. (1968). Mental unity following surgical disconnection of the cerebral hemispheres. *The Harvey Lectures,* Series 62. New York: Academic Press.

Spiro, R. J. (1977). Remembering information from text: The "state of schema" approach. In R. C. Atkinson, R. J. Spiro, & W. E. Montague (Eds.), *Schooling and the acquisition of knowledge.* Hillsdale, NJ: Erlbaum.

Spitz, R. A., & Wolf, K. (1946). Anaclitic depression. *Psychoanalytic Study of Children, 2,* 313–342.

Spitzer, R. (1981, October). Nonmedical myths and the DSM-III. *APA Monitor.*

Springer, S. P., & Deutsch, G. (1984). *Left brain, right brain* (2nd ed.). San Francisco: Freeman.

Squire, L. R. (1975). Short-term memory as a biological entity. In D. Deutsch and J. A. Deutsch (Eds.), *Short-term memory* (pp. 1–40). New York: Academic Press.

Squire, L. R., & Moore, R. Y. (1979). Dorsal thalamic lesion in a noted case of human memory. *Annals of Neurology, 6,* 503–506.

Squire, L. R., & Slater, P. C. (1978). Anterograde and retrograde memory impairment in chronic amnesia. *Neuropsychologia, 16,* 313–322.

Staats, A. W., & Staats, C. K. (1958). Attitudes established by classical conditioning. *Journal of Abnormal and Social Psychology, 57,* 37–40.

Stampfl, T. G., & Levis, D. J. (1967). Essentials of implosive therapy: A learning theory-based psychodynamic behavioral therapy. *Journal of Abnormal Psychology, 72,* 496–503.

Stanford Daily (1982, February 2). *181*(2), pp. 1, 3, 5.

Stangler, R. S., & Printz, A. M. (1980). DSM-III: Psychiatric diagnosis in a University population. *American Journal of Psychiatry, 137,* 937–940.

Stanley, J. (1976). The study of the very bright. *Science, 192,* 668–669.

Stapp, J., & Fulcher, R. (1981). The employment of APA members. *American Psychologist, 36,* 1263–1314.

Steers, R. M., & Porter, L. W. (1974). The role of task-goal attributes in employee performance. *Psychological Bulletin, 81,* 434–452.

Steininger, M., Newell, J. D., & Garcia, L. T. (1984). *Ethical Issues in Psychology.* Homewood, IL: Dorsey.

Stellar, E. (1954). The physiology of motivation. *Psychological Review, 61,* 5–22.

Stenback, A. (1980). Depression and suicidal behavior. In J. E. Birren & R. B. Sloane (Eds.), *Handbook of mental health and aging* (pp. 616–652). Englewood Cliffs, NJ: Prentice-Hall.

Stern, P., & Aronson, E. (Eds.). (1984). *Energy use: The human dimension.* New York: Freeman.

Stern, R. M., & Ray, W. J. (1977). *Biofeedback.* Chicago: Dow Jones-Irwin.

Stern, W. (1914). The psychological methods of testing intelligence. *Educational Psychology Monographs* (No. 13).

Stern, W. C., & Morgane, P. S. (1974). Theoretical view of REM sleep function: Maintenance of catecholomine systems in the central nervous system. *Behavioral Biology, 11,* 1–32.

Sternbach, R. A., & Tursky, B. (1965). Ethnic differences among housewives in psychophysical and skin potential responses to electric shock. *Psychophysiology, 1,* 241–246.

Sternberg, R. J., Conway, B. E., Ketron, J. L., & Bernstein, M. (1981). People's conceptions of intelligence. *Journal of Personality and Social Psychology, 41,* 37–55.

Sternberg, S. (1966). High-speed scanning in human memory. *Science, 153,* 652–654.

Sternberg, S. (1969). Memory-scanning: Mental processes revealed by reaction time experiments. *American Scientist, 57,* 421–457.

Stevens, C. F. (1979). The neuron. *Scientific American, 241*(9), 54–65.

Stevens, S. S. (1960). The psychology of sensory function. *American Scientist, 48,* 226–253.

Stevens, S. S. (1961). To honor Fechner and repeal his law. *Science, 133,* 80–86.

Stevens, S. S. (1962). The surprising simplicity of sensory metrics. *American Psychologist, 17,* 29–39.

Stone, G. C., Cohen, F., & Adler, N. (1979). *Health psychology—A handbook.* San Francisco: Jossey-Bass.

Storms, M. (1973). Videotape and the attribution process: Reversing actors' and observers' points of view. *Journal of Personality and Social Psychology, 27,* 165–175.

Storms, M. D. (1980). Theories of sexual orientation. *Journal of Personality and Social Psychology, 38,* 783–792.

Storms, M. D. (1981). A theory of erotic orientation development. *Psychological Review, 88,* 340–353.

Straub, E. (1974). Helping a distressed person: Social, personality, and stimulus determinants. In L. Berkowitz (Ed.), *Advances in experimental and social psychology (Vol. 7).* New York: Academic Press.

Stromeyer, D. F., & Psotka, J. (1970). The detailed texture of eidetic images. *Nature, 225,* 346–349.

Strong, E. K. (1927). Differentiation of certified public accountants from other occupational groups. *Journal of Educational Psychology, 18,* 227–238.

Stroop, J. R. (1935). Studies of interference in serial verbal reactions. *Journal of Experimental Psychology, 18,* 643–662.

Strupp, H. H. (1983). Psychoanalytic psychotherapy. In M. Hersen, A. E. Kazdin & A. S. Bellock (Eds.), *The clinical psychology handbook* (pp. 471–488). New York: Pergamon Press.

Stuart, R. B. (1971). Behavioral contracting with families of delinquents. *Journal of Behavior Therapy and Experimental Psychiatry, 2,* 1–11.

Suedfeld, P. (1980). *Restricted environmental stimulation: Research and clinical applications.* New York: Wiley.

Sullivan, H. S. (1953). *The interpersonal theory of psychiatry.* New York: Norton.

Sundberg, N. D. (1977). *Assessment of persons.* Englewood Cliffs, NJ: Prentice-Hall.

Sundberg, N. D., & Matarazzo, J. D. (1979). Psychological assessment of individuals. In M. E. Meyer (Ed.), *Foundations of contemporary psychology* (pp. 580–617). New York: Oxford University Press.

Swazey, J. P. (1974). *Chlorpromazine in psychiatry: A study of therapeutic innovation,* Cambridge, MA: MIT Press.

Sweet, W. H., Ervin, F., & Mark, V. H. (1969). The relationship of violent behavior to focal cerebral disease. In S. Garattini & E. Sigg (Eds.), *Aggressive behavior.* New York: Wiley.

Szasz, T. S. (1961). *The myth of mental illness.* New York: Harper & Row.

Szasz, T. S. (1977). *The manufacture of models.* New York: Dell.

Szasz, T. S. (1979). *The myth of psychotherapy.* Garden City, NY: Doubleday.

T

Tajfel, H. (1957). Value and the perceptual judgment of magnitude. *Psychological Review, 18,* 32–47.

Targ, R., & Harary, K. (1984). *The mind race: Understanding and using psychic abilities.* New York: Villard Books.

Tarpy, R. M. (1982). *Principles of animal learning and motivation.* Glenview, IL: Scott, Foresman.

Tart, C. T. (1969). *Altered states of consciousness.* New York: Wiley.

Tart, C. T. (1971). *On being stoned: A psychological investigation of marijuana intoxication.* Palo Alto, CA: Science and Behavior Books.

Taylor, J. A. (1951). The relationship of anxiety to the conditioned eyelid response. *Journal of Experimental Psychology, 41,* 81–92.

Taylor, S. E. (1982). The availability bias in social perception and interaction. In D. Kahneman, P. Slovic, & A. Tversky (Eds.), *Judgment under uncertainty: Heuristics and biases* (pp. 190–200). Cambridge, England: Cambridge University Press.

Taylor, S. E. (1983). Adjustment to threatening events: A theory of cognitive adaptation. *American Psychologist, 38,* 1161–1173.

Taylor, S. E., Crocker, J., Fiske, S. T., Sprinzen, M., & Winkler, J. D. (1979). The generalizability of salience effects. *Journal of Personality and Social Psychology, 39.*

Taylor, S. E., & Fiske, S. T. (1978). Salience, attention, and attribution: Top of the head phenomena. In L. Berkowitz (Ed.), *Advances in experimental social psychology* (Vol. 11). New York: Academic Press.

Taylor, S. P., Vardaris, R. M., Rawtich, A. B., Gammon, C. B., Cranston, J. W., & Lubetkin, A. I. (1976). The effects of alcohol and delta-9-tetrahydrocannabinol on human physical aggression. *Aggressive Behavior, 2,* 153–161.

Taylor, W., Pearson, J., Mair, A., & Burns, W. (1965). Study of noise and hearing in jute weaving. *Journal of the Acoustical Society of America, 38,* 113–120.

Teasdale, J. D., Taylor, R., & Fogarty, S. J. (1980). Effects of induced elation-depression on the accessibility of memories of happy and unhappy experiences. *Behavioral Research and Therapy, 18,* 339–346.

Teitelbaum, P. (1966). The use of operant methods in the assessment and control of motivational states. In W. K. Honig (Ed.), *Operant behavior.* New York: Appleton-Century-Crofts.

Teitelbaum, P. (1977). The physiological analysis of motivated behavior. In P. Zimbardo & F. L. Ruch, *Psychology and Life* (9th ed., Diamond Printing). Glenview, IL: Scott, Foresman.

Tellegen, A., & Atkinson, S. (1974). Openness to absorbing and self-altering experiences ("absorption"), a trait related to hypnosis. *Journal of Abnormal Psychology, 83,* 268–277.

Tenopyr, M. L., & Oeltjen, P. D. (1982). Personnel selection and classification. *Annual Review of Psychology, 33,* 581–618.

Terman, L. M. (1916). *The measurement of intelligence.* Boston: Houghton Mifflin.

Terman, L. M. (1925). *Genetic studies of genius: Vol 1. Mental and physical traits of a thousand gifted children.* Stanford, CA: Stanford University Press.

Terman, L. M., & Merrill, M. A. (1937). *Measuring intelligence.* Boston: Houghton Mifflin.

Terman, L. M., & Merrill, M. A. (1960). *The Stanford-Binet intelligence scale.* Boston: Houghton Mifflin.

Terman, L. M., & Merrill, M. A. (1972). *Stanford-Binet intelligence scale—manual for the third revision, Form L-M.* Boston: Houghton Mifflin.

Terman, L. M., & Oden, M. H. (1947). The gifted child grows up. *Genetic studies of genius:* Vol. 4. Stanford, CA: Stanford University Press.

Terman, L. M., & Oden, M. H. (1959). The gifted group at mid-life. *Genetic studies of genius: Vol. 5.* Stanford, CA: Stanford University Press.

Terrace, H. (1979). *Nim: a chimpanzee who learned sign language.* New York: Knopf.

Thienes-Hontos, P., Watson, C. G., & Kucala, T. (1982). Stress-Disorder symptoms in Vietnam and Korean War veterans. *Journal of Consulting and Clinical Psychology, 50,* 558–561.

Thigpen, C. H., & Cleckley, H. A. (1957). *Three faces of Eve.* New York: McGraw-Hill.

Thompson, D. A., & Campbell, R. G. (1977). Hunger in humans induced by 2-Deoxy-D-Glucose: Glucoprivic control of taste preference and food intake. *Science, 198,* 1065–1068.

Thompson, M. J., & Harsha, D. W. (1984, January). Our rhythms still follow the African sun. *Psychology Today,* pp. 50–54.

Thompson, R. F. (1972). Sensory preconditioning. In R. F. Thompson & J. F. Voss (Eds.), *Topics in learning and performance.* New York: Academic Press.

Thompson, R. F. (1975). *Introduction to physiological psychology.* New York: Harper & Row.

Thompson, R. F. (1984, February 4). Searching for memories: Where and how are they stored in your brain? *Stanford Daily.*

Thompson, P. (1980). Margaret Thatcher: A new illusion. *Perception, 9,* 483–484.

Thoresen, C. E., & Eagleston, J. R. (1983). Chronic stress in children and adolescents (pp. 48–56). *Theory into Practice, 22* (Special edition: Coping with stress).

Thoresen, C. E., Telch, M. J., & Eagleston, J. R. (1981). Approaches to altering the Type A behavior pattern. *Psychosomatics, 22,* 472–479.

Thorndike, E. L. (1898). Animal intelligence. *Psychological Review Monograph Supplement, 2* (4, Whole No. 8).

Thorndyke, P. W., & Hayes-Roth, B. (1979). *Spatial knowledge acquisition from maps and navigation.* Paper presented at the Psychonomic Society meetings, San Antonio, Texas.

Thornton, E. M. (1984). *The Freudian fallacy: An alternative view of Freudian theory.* New York: The Dial Press/Doubleday

Timiras, P. S. (1978). Biological perspectives on aging. *American Scientist, 66,* 605–613.

Tinklepaugh, O. L. (1928). An experimental study of representational factors in monkeys. *Journal of Comparative Psychology, 8,* 197–236.

Toch, H. (1969). *Violent men.* Chicago: Aldine.

Toch, H. (Ed.). (1979). *Psychology of crime and criminal justice.* New York: Holt, Rinehart & Winston.

Tolman, E. C. (1948). Cognitive maps in rats and men. *Psychological Review, 55,* 189–208.

Tolman, E. C., & Honzik, C. H. (1930). "Insight" in rats. *University of Calif. Publications in Psychology, 4,* 215–232.

Tompkins, S. (1962). *Affect, imagery, consciousness* (Vol. 1). New York: Springer.

Tompkins, S. (1981). The quest for primary motives: Biography and autobiography of an idea. *Journal of Personality and Social Psychology, 41,* 306–329.

Tonndorf, J. (1960). Shearing motion in scala media of cochlear models. *Journal of the Acoustical Society of America, 32,* 238–244.

Tourangeau, R., & Ellsworth, P. C. (1979). The role of facial response in the experience of emotion. *Journal of Personality and Social Psychology, 37,* 1519–1531.

Townsend, J. T. (1972). Some results concerning the identifiability of parallel and serial processes. *British Journal of Mathematical and Statistical Psychology, 25,* 168–199.

Treisman, A. M. (1960). Contextual cues in selective listening. *Quarterly Journal of Experimental Psychology, 12,* 242–248.

Treisman, A. M., & Gelade, G. A. (1980). Feature-integration theory of attention. *Cognitive Psychology, 12,* 97–136.

Tresemer, D. W. (1977). *Fear of success.* New York: Plenum.

Triandis, H. C., & Draguns, J. G. (Eds.) (1980). *Handbook of cross-culture psychology* (Vol. 6). *Psychopathology.* Boston: Allyn and Bacon.

Triandis, H. C., & Heron, A. (Eds.) (1981). *Handbook of cross-cultural psychology: Volume 4. Developmental.* Boston: Allyn & Bacon.

Triplett, N. (1897). The dynamagenic factors in pacemaking and competition. *American Journal of Psychology, 9,* 507–533.

Tronick, E., Als, H., & Brazelton, T. B. (1980). Moradic Phases: A structural description analysis of infant-mother face to face interaction. *Merrill-Palmer Quarterly, 26,* 3–24.

Tryon, W. W. (1979). The test-trait fallacy. *American Psychologist, 34,* 402–406.

Tucker, O. M. (1981). Lateral brain functions, emotion, and conceptualization. *Psychological Bulletin, 89,* 19–46.

Tulving, E. (1972). Episodic and semantic memory. In E. Tulving & W. Donaldson (Eds.), *Organization of memory.* New York: Academic Press.

Tulving, E., & Pearlstone, Z. (1966). Availability versus accessibility of information in memory for words. *Journal of Verbal Learning and Verbal Behavior, 5,* 381–391.

Tversky, A., & Kahneman, D. (1973). Availability: A heuristic for judging frequency and probability. *Cognitive Psychology, 5,* 207–232.

Tversky, A., & Kahneman, D. (1980). Causal schemata in judgments under uncertainty. In M. Fishbein (Ed.), *Progress in social psychology.* Hillsdale, NJ: Erlbaum.

Tversky, A., & Kahneman, D. (1981). The framing of decisions and the rationality of choice. *Science, 211,* 453–458.

Tversky, B. (1981). Distortions in memory for maps. *Cognitive Psychology, 13,* 407–433.

Twain, M. (S. L. Clemens) (1923). *Mark Twain's speeches.* New York: Harper & Row.

Tyler, L. E. (1965). *The psychology of human differences.* (3rd ed.) New York: Appleton-Century-Crofts.

Tyler, L. E. (1974). *Individual differences.* Englewood Cliffs, NJ: Prentice-Hall.

U

Ullmann, L. P., & Krasner, L. (1975). *Psychological approach to abnormal behavior* (2nd ed.). Englewood Cliffs, NJ: Prentice-Hall.

Ultan, R. (1969). Some general characteristics of interrogative systems. *Working papers in language universals* (Stanford: Stanford University Press), *1,* 41–63.

Underwood, B. J. (1948). Retroactive and proactive inhibition after five and forty-eight hours. *Journal of Experimental Psychology, 38,* 28–38.

Underwood, B. J. (1949). Proactive inhibition as a function of time and degree of prior learning. *Journal of Experimental Psychology, 39,* 24–34.

United Press International. (1975, December 13).

United Press International (1984, April 12). Testimony on child molesting. (Press Release, Washington, DC: (Senate Judiciary Subcommittee Hearings on Child Molesting).

"U. S. Women Today" (1983). *New York Times* Poll taken Nov. 11–20, 1983, reported in *International Herald Tribune.*

V

Vaillant, G. E. (1977). *Adaptation to life.* Boston: Little, Brown.

Valle, V. A., & Frieze, I. H. (1976). Stability of causal attributions as a mediator in changing expectations for success. *Journal of Personality and Social Psychology, 33,* 579–587.

Van Riper, C. (1970). Historical approaches. In J. G. Sheehan (Ed.), *Stuttering: Research and therapy.* New York: Harper & Row.

Van Wagener, W., & Herren, R. (1940). Surgical division of commissural pathways in the corpus callosum. *Archives of Neurology and Psychiatry, 44,* 740–759.

Vasari, G. (1967). *Lives of the most eminent painters.* New York: Heritage.

Vaughan, E. (1977). Misconceptions about psychology among introductory psychology students. *Teaching of Psychology, 4,* 138–141.

Vernon, P. E. (1979). *Intelligence: Heredity and environment.* San Francisco: Freeman.

Vinsel, A., Brown, B. B., Altman, I. Foss, C. (1980). Primary regulations, territorial displays, and effectiveness of individual functioning. *Journal of Personality and Social Psychology, 39,* 1104–1115.

Vogel, F., & Motulsky, A. G. (1982). *Human genetics.* New York: Springer-Verlag.

von Hofsten, C., & Lindhagen, K. (1979). Observations on the development of reaching for moving objects. *Journal of Child Psychology, 28,* 158–173.

Vonnegut, M. (1975). *The Eden express.* New York: Bantam.

Von Wright, J. M., Anderson, K. & Stenham, U. (1975). Generalization of conditioned GSRs in dichotic listening. In P. M. A. Rabbit & S. Dornic (Eds.), *Attention and performance* (pp. 194–204). New York: Academic Press.

W

Waldron, I. (1976, March). Why do women live longer than men? *Journal of Human Stress,* 2–13.

Waldrop, M. M. (1984). Artificial intelligence (I): Into the world (Research news). *Science, 223,* 802–805.

Waldvogel, S. (1948). The frequency and affective character of childhood memories. *Psychological monographs, 62* (Whole No. 291).

Wallach, M. A., & Wallach, L. (1983). *Psychology's sanction for selfishness.* San Francisco: Freeman.

Waller, J. H. (1971). Achievement and social mobility: Relationships among IQ score, education, and occupation in two generations. *Social Biology, 18,* 252–259.

Wallis, C. (1984, June 11). Unlocking pain's secrets. *Time,* pp. 58–66.

Walsh, R. N., & Vaughan, F. (Eds.). (1980). *Beyond ego: Transpersonal dimensions in psychology.* Los Angeles: Tarcher.

Walster, E., & Walster, G. W. (1978). *A new look at love.* Reading, MA: Addison-Wesley.

Walster, E., Walster, G. W., & Berscheid, E. (1977). *Equity: Theory and research.* Boston: Allyn & Bacon.

Walters, C. C., & Grusec, J. E. (1977). *Punishment.* San Francisco: Freeman.

Walters, R. G. (1974). *Primers for prudery: Sexual advice to Victorian America.* Englewood Cliffs, NJ: Prentice-Hall.

Wanous, J. P. (1980). *Organizational entry: Recruitment, selection, and socialization of newcomers.* Reading, MA: Addison-Wesley.

Ward, W. C., Kogan, N., & Pankove, E. (1972). Incentive effects in children's creativity. *Child Development, 43*(2), 669–676.

Warden, C. J. (1931). *Animal motivation: Experimental studies on the albino rat.* New York: Columbia University Press.

Warshaw, L. (1979). *Managing stress.* Reading, MA: Addison-Wesley.

Wason, P. C. (1971). Problem solving and reasoning. *British Medical Bulletin, 27*(3), 206–210.

Watson, J. B. (1919). *Psychology from the standpoint of a behaviorist.* Philadelphia: Lippincott.

Watson, J. B. (1930). *Behaviorism.* New York: Norton.

Watson, J. B., & Rayner, R. (1920). Conditioned emotional reactions. *Journal of Experimental Psychology, 3,* 1–14.

Watson, R. I., Jr. (1973). Investigation into deindividuation using a cross-cultural survey technique. *Journal of Personality and Social Psychology, 25,* 342–345.

Watson, S. J., Akil, H., Berger, P. A., & Barchas, J. D. (1979). Some observations on the opiate peptides in schizophrenia. *Archives of General Psychiatry, 36,* 35–41.

Weakland, J. H., Fish, R., Watzlawick, P., & Bodin, A. M. (1974). Brief therapy: Focused problem resolution. *Family Process, 13,* 141–168.

Webb, W. B. (1974). Sleep as an adaptive response. *Perceptual and motor skills, 38,* 1023–1027.

Webb, W. B. (1981). The return of consciousness. In L. T. Benjamin, Jr. (Ed.), *The G. Stanley Hall Lecture Series.* Vol. 1. Washington, DC: American Psychological Association, *100,* 133–152.

Weber, E. H. (1834). *De pulsu, resorptione, auditu et tactu: Annotationes anatomical et physiological.* Leipzig: Koehler.

Wechsler, D. (1974). *Wechsler intelligence scale for children—Revised.* New York: Psychological Corp.

Wechsler, D. (1981). *Manual for the Wechsler Adult Intelligence Scale. Revised.* New York: Psychological Corp.

Weick, K. E. (1984). Small wins: Redefining the scale of social problems. *American Psychologist, 39,* 40–49.

Weigel, R. H., & Newman, L. S. (1976). Increasing attitude-behavior correspondence by broadening the scope of the behavioral measure. *Journal of Personality and Social Psychology, 33,* 793–802.

Weil, A. T. (1977). The marriage of the sun and the moon. In N. E. Zinberg (Ed.), *Alternate states of consciousness* (pp. 37–52). New York: Free Press.

Weil, A. T. (1984). *Health and healing.* Boston: Houghton Mifflin.

Weiner, B. (1980). *Human motivation.* New York: Holt, Rinehart & Winston.

Weiner, B., Russell, D., & Lerman, D. (1978). Affective consequences of causal ascriptions. In J. H. Harvey, W. J. Ickes, & R. F. Kidd (Eds.), *New directions in attribution research* (Vol. 2). Hillsdale, NJ: Erlbaum.

Weiner, M. J., & Wright, F. E. (1973). Effects of undergoing arbitrary discrimination upon subsequent attitudes toward a minority group. *Journal of Applied Social Psychology, 3,* 94–102.

Weingartner, H., Gold, P., Ballenger, J. C., Smallberg, S. A., Summers, R., Rubinow, D. R., Post, R. M., & Goodwin, F. K. (1981). Effects of vasopressin on human memory functions. *Science, 211,* 601–603.

Weins, A. N., & Matarazzo, J. D. (1983). Diagnostic interviewing. In M. Hersen, A. E. Kazdin, & A. S. Bellack (Eds.), *The clinical psychology handbook.* (pp. 309–328). New York: Pergamon.

Weisenberg, M. (1977). Cultural and racial reactions to pain. In M. Weisenberg (Ed.). *The control of pain.* New York: Psychological Dimensions.

Weiskrantz, L., Warington, E. K., Sanders, M. D., & Marshall, J. (1974). Visual capacity in the hemianopic field following a restricted occipital ablation. *Brain, 97,* 709–728.

Weiss, B., & Laties, V. G. (1962). Enhancement of human performance by caffeine and amphetamines. *Pharmacological Review, 14,* 1–27.

Weiss, M. (1984). *Double play: The San Francisco City Hall killings.* Reading, MA: Addison-Wesley.

Weiss, R. S. (1973). *Loneliness: The experience of emotional and social isolation.* Cambridge, MA: M.I.T. Press.

Welker, R. L., & Wheatley, K. L. (1977). Differential acquisition of conditioned suppression in rats with increased and decreased luminance levels as CS + S. *Learning and Motivation, 8,* 247–262.

Welner, A., Reish, T., Robbins, I., Fishman, R., & van Doren, T. (1976). Obsessive-compulsive neurosis. *Comprehensive Psychiatry, 17,* 527–539.

Wender, P. H. (1972). Adopted children and their families in the evaluation of nature-nurture interactions in the schizophrenic disorders. *Annual Review of Medicine, 23,* 255–372.

Werner, E. E., & Smith, R. S. (1982). *Vulnerable but invincible: A longitudinal study of resilient children and youth.* New York: McGraw-Hill.

Wertheimer, Max. (1923). Untersuchungen zur lehre von der gestalt, II. *Psychologische Forschung, 4,* 301–350.

Wever, E. G. (1949). *Theory of hearing.* New York: Wiley.

Whalen, R., & Simon, N. G. (1984). Biological motivation. *Annual Review of Psychology, 35,* 257–276.

White, B. W., Saunders, F. A. Scadden, L., Bach-Y-Rita, P., & Collins, C. C. (1970). Seeing with the skin. *Perception & Psychophysics, 7*(1), 23–27.

White, G. L., Fishbein, S., & Rutstein, J. (1981). Passionate love and the misattribution of arousal. *Journal of Personality and Social Psychology, 41,* 56–62.

White, M. D., & White, C. A. (1981). Involuntarily committed patients' constitutional right to refuse treatment. *American Psychologist, 36,* 953–962.

Whorf, B. L. (1956). *Language, thought, and reality.* Cambridge, MA: MIT Press.

Wickelgren, W. A. (1974). *How to solve problems.* San Francisco: Freeman.

Wicker, A. W. (1969). Attitudes versus actions: The relationship of verbal and overt behavioral responses to attitude objects. *Journal of Social Issues, 25*(4), 41–78.

Wicklund, R. A., & Brehm, J. W. (1976). *Perspectives on cognitive dissonance* Hillsdale, NJ: Erlbaum.

Wiggins, J. S. (1973). *Personality and prediction: Principles of personality assessment.* Reading MA: Addison-Wesley.

Wilcoxon, H. G., Dragoin, W. B., & Kral, P. A. (1971). Illness-induced aversions in rat and quail: relative salience of visual and gustatory cues. *Science, 171,* 826–828.

Wilder, D. A. (1978). Reduction of intergroup discrimination through individuation of the out-group. *Journal of Personality and Social Psychology, 36,* 1361–1374.

Willer, J. C., Dehen, H., & Cambier, J. (1981). Stress-induced analgesia in humans: Endogenous opioids and naloxone-reversible depression of pain reflexes. *Science, 212,* 689–691.

Williams, J. H. (1983). *The psychology of women* (2nd ed.). New York: Norton.

Williams, R. L., & Rivers, L. W. (1972, September). *The use of standard and nonstandard English in testing black children.* Paper presented at the meeting of the American Psychological Association, Honolulu, HI.

Wills, T. A. (1981). Downward comparison principles in social psychology. *Psychological Bulletin, 90,* 245–271.

Wilson, E. D., Reeves, A., & Culver, C. (1977). Cerebral commissurotomy for control of intractable seizures. *Neurology, 27,* 708–715.

Wilson, E. O. (1973). The natural history of lions. *Science, 179,* 466–467.

Wilson, J. P. (1980). Conflict, stress, and growth: The effects of war on the psychosocial development of Vietnam veterans. In C. R. Figley & S. Leventman (Eds.), *Strangers at home: Vietnam veterans since the war* (pp. 123–165). New York: Praeger.

Wing, C. W., & Wallach, M. A. (1971). *College admissions and the psychology of talent.* New York: Holt, Rinehart & Winston.

Wingfield, A. (1973). Effects of serial position and set size in auditory recognition memory. *Memory and Cognition, 1,* 53–55.

Wingfield, A., & Byrnes, D. L. (1981). *The psychology of human memory.* New York: Academic Press.

Wintrob, R. M. (1973). The influence of others: Witchcraft and rootwork as explanations of behavior disturbances. *Journal of Nervous and Mental Diseases, 156,* 318–326.

Wispe, L. G., & Drambarean, N. C. (1953). Physiological need, word frequency, and visual duration threshold. *Journal of Experimental Psychology, 46,* 25–31.

Witkin, H. A., Dyk, R. B., Faterson, H. F., Goodenough, D. R., & Karp, S. A. (1962). *Psychological differentiation.* New York: Wiley.

Witkin, H. A., & Goodenough, D. R. (1977). Field dependence and interpersonal behavior. *Psychological Bulletin, 84,* 661–689.

Witkin, H. A., Moore, C. A., Goodenough, D. R., & Cox, P. W. (1977). Field-dependent and field-independent cognitive styles and their educational implications. *Review of Educational Research, 47,* 1–64.

Wittkower, E. D., & Dudek, S. Z. (1973). Psychosomatic medicine: The mind-body-society interaction. In B. B. Wolman (Ed.), *Handbook of general psychology.* Englewood Cliffs, NJ: Prentice-Hall. 242–272.

Wohlwill, J. F. (1962). From perception to inference: A dimension of cognitive development. In W. Kessen & C. Kuhlman (Eds.), *Thought in the young child. Monographs of the Society for Research in Child Development, 27,* 87–112.

Wolf, M., Risley, T., & Mees, H. (1964). Application of operant conditioning procedures to the behavior problems of an autistic child. *Behavior Research and Therapy, 1,* 305–312.

Wolitzky, D. L., & Wachtel, P. L. (1973). Personality and perception. In B. J. Wolman (Ed.), *Handbook of general psychology* (pp. 826–857). Englewood Cliffs, NJ: Prentice-Hall.

Wolman, C. (1975). Therapy and capitalism. *Issues in Radical Therapy. 3*(1).

Wolpe, J. (1958). *Psychotherapy by reciprocal inhibition.* Stanford: Stanford University Press.

Wolpe, J. (1973). *The practice of behavior therapy* (2nd ed). New York: Pergamon.

Woods, D. L., Hillyard, S. A., Courchesne, E., Galambos, R. (1980). Electrophysiological signs of split-second decision-making. *Science, 207,* 655-657.

Woodworth, R. S. (1918). *Dynamic psychology.* New York; Columbia University Press.

Woodworth, R. S., & Schlossberg, H. (1954). *Experimental psychology* (rev. ed.). New York: Holt.

Woolridge, D. E. (1963). *The machinery of the brain.* New York: McGraw Hill.

Wurtman, R. J. (1978, April 6). Food for thought. *The Sciences,* p. 9. (N.Y. Academy of Sciences)

Wurtman, R. J. (1979). The effects of light on the human body. In R. Silver & H. H. Feder (Eds.), *Hormones and reproductive behavior* (pp. 1–13). San Francisco: Freeman.

Wurtman, R. J. (1982. Nutrients that modify brain functions. *Scientific American, 246(4),* 50–59.

Wurtz, R. H., Goldberg, M. E., & Robinson, D. L. (1982, June). Brain mechanisms of visual attention. *Scientific American, 246*(6), 124–135.

Wyatt, R. J., Potkin, S. G., Bridge, T. P., Phelps, B. H., & Wise, C. D. (1980). Monamine oxidose in schizophrenia: An overview. *Schizophrenia Bulletin, 6,* 199–207.

Wylie, R. C. (1968). The present stated self theory. In E. F. Birgatta & W. W. Lamabert (Eds.), *Handbook of personality theory and research.* Chicago: Rand McNally.

Wynne, L. C., Roohey, M. L., & Doane, J. (1979). Family studies. In L. Bellak (Ed.), *The schizophenic syndrome.* New York: Basic Books.

Y

Yahraes, H. (1975). *Research in the service of mental health: Summary report of the research task force of the National Institutes of Mental Health.* (V-5) Washington, DC: U.S. Government Printing Office.

Yarrow, L. (1975). *Infant and environment: Early cognitive and motivational development.* New York: Halsted.

Yerkes, R. M. (1921). Psychological examining in the United States Army. In R. M. Yerkes (Ed.), *Memoirs of the National Academy of Sciences, 15.* Washington, DC: U.S. Government Printing Office.

Young, P. T. (1961). *Motivation and emotion.* New York: Wiley.

Young, T. (1807). On the theory of light and colours. In *Lectures in natural philosophy* (Vol. 2, pp. 613–632). London: William Savage.

Yudkin, M. (1984, April). When kids think the unthinkable. *Psychology Today,* pp. 18–20, 24–25.

Z

Zadeh, L. A. (1965). Fuzzy sets. *Information Control, 8,* 338–353.

Zajonc, R. B. (1965). Social facilitation. *Science, 149,* 269-274.

Zajonc, R. B. (1968). Attitudinal effects of mere exposure. *Journal of Personality and Social Psychology, Monograph Supplement, 9* (2, Pt. 2), 1–27.

Zajonc, R. B. (1976). Family configuration and intelligence, *Science, 192,* 227–236.

Zajonc, R. B. (1980). Feeling and thinking: Preferences need no inferences. *American Psychologist, 35,* 151–175.

Zajonc, R. B. (1984). On the primacy of affect. *American Psychologist, 39,* 117–129.

Zanchetti, A. (1967). Subcortical and cortical mechanisms in arousal and emotional behavior. In G. C. Quarton, T. Melnechuk, & F. O. Schmitt (Eds.), *The neurosciences: A study program.* New York: Rockefeller University Press.

Zborowski, M. (1969). *People in pain.* San Francisco: Jossey-Bass.

Zilboorg, G., & Henry, G. W. (1941). *A history of medial psychology.* New York: Norton.

Ziller, R. C. (1964). Individuation and socialization. *Human Relations, 17,* 341–360.

Zimbardo, P. G. (1970). The human choice: Individuation, reason, and order versus deindividuation, impulse, and chaos. In W. J. Arnold & D. Levine (Eds.), *Nebraska Symposium on Motivation, 1969.* Lincoln, NB: University of Nebraska Press.

Zimbardo, P. G. (1975). On transforming experimental research into advocacy for social change. In M. Deutsch & H. Hornstein (Eds.), *Applying social psychology: Implications for research, practice and training.* Hillsdale, NJ: Erlbaum.

Zimbardo, P. G. (1977). *Shyness, what it is, what to do about it.* Reading, MA: Addison-Wesley.

Zimbardo, P. G., Andersen, S. M., & Kabat, L. G. (1981). Induced hearing deficit generates experimental paranoia. *Science, 212,* 1529–1531.

Zimbardo, P. G., & Formica, R. (1963) Emotional comparison and self-esteem as determinants of affiliation. *Journal of Personality, 31,* 141–162.

Zimbardo, P. G., & Linsenmeier, J. A. W. (1983). *The influences of personal, social and systems factors on team problem solving.* (Office of Naval Research Technical Report Z-83-01), Stanford: Stanford University.

Zimbardo, P. G., & Montgomery, K. D. (1957). The relative strengths of consummatory responses in hunger, thirst, and exploratory drive. *Journal of Comparative and Physiological Psychology, 50,* 504–508.

Zimbardo, P. G., Pilkonis, P. A., & Norwood, R. M. (1974, November). The silent prison of shyness. Office of Naval Research Technical Report Z-17. Stanford, CA: Stanford University.

Zimbardo, P. G., and Radl, S. (1981). *The shy child.* New York: McGraw-Hill.

Zubeck, J. P., Pushkar, D., Sansom, W., & Gowing, J. (1961). Perceptual changes after prolonged sensory isolation (darkness and silence). *Canadian Journal of Psychology, 15,* 83–100.

Zuckerman, M. (1979). Sensation seeking and risk taking. In C. E. Izard (Ed.), *Emotions in personality and psychopathology* New York: Plenum.

Zurcher, L. A. (1977). *The mutable self: A self-concept for social change.* Beverly Hills, CA: Sage.

ACKNOWLEDGMENTS

Credits for photographs, illustrations, and quoted material not given on page where they appear are listed below. To all, the author and publisher wish to express their appreciation.

Photo Credits

Cover photo: Michael Goss/Scott, Foresman. With the cooperation of the Evanston Historical Society.

Chapter 1

4 (top) Kojo Tanaka; (bottom) Wide World
6 (both) The Bettmann Archive
8 Marcia Weinstein
10 Sidney Harris
12 Marcia Weinstein
13 Richard Wood/The Picture Cube
18 Sidney Harris
19 Sidney Harris
23 Ira Wyman/Sygma
24 UPI/The Bettmann Archive
25 UPI/The Bettmann Archive
26 (left) Keystone Press Agency
26 (top right, bottom right) The Bettmann Archive

Chapter 2

33 (both) Bibliothèque Nationale, Paris
38 From Niklaas Hartsoeker, *Essai de Dioptrique*. Paris, 1694.
42 Carlo Bevilacqua/CEDRI
43 (both) William Vandivert
44 Scott, Foresman
45 Eric Kroll/Taurus
50 Wide World
52 Elizabeth Crews
53 (all) Marcia Weinstein
56 Thomas McAvoy, LIFE Magazine © 1955 Time Inc.
58 Harlow Primate Laboratory, University of Wisconsin
59 Harlow Primate Laboratory, University of Wisconsin
60 Scott, Foresman
61 Elizabeth Crews
64 © Jane Zich—1983. This cartoon originally published in the APA *Monitor*, April 1983.
66 Peter Vandermark/Stock, Boston
69 Abigail Heyman/Archive
70 Elizabeth Crews

Chapter 3

73 From *The Excitable Cortex in Conscious Man* by Wilder Penfield, Liverpool University Press, 1958 (2nd impression 1967).
75 The Bettmann Archive
79 Figure 3.1. Prepared by Rufus B. Weaver, M.D., 1888. Courtesy of Dr. Peter S. Amenta, Professor and Chairman, Department of Anatomy, School of Medicine, Hahnemann University
95 Wide World
103 From *American Journal of the Medical Sciences,* Vol. 20, 1850
105 (left) Dan McCoy/Rainbow; (right) Brookhaven National Laboratory and State University of New York, Stony Brook

Chapter 4

110 Scott, Foresman
124 Figure 4.12. Courtesy of Munsell Color, Baltimore, Maryland
127 Figure 4.16. Macmillan Science Co., Inc.
131 Figure 4.20. The Kobal Collection. From Frisby, J., *Seeing: Illusion, Brain, and Mind.* Oxford University Press, 1980.
147 Marcia Weinstein

Chapter 5

158 (left) "Gestalt Bleue," 1969 by Victor Vasarely. Courtesy of the artist; (right) © Beeldrecht, Amsterdam/VAGA, New York, Collection of C.V.S. Roosevelt, Washington, D.C.
159 The Salvador Dali Museum, St. Petersburg, Florida
168-169 Figure 5.17. Courtesy of Dr. F. P. Kilpatrick, from Kilpatrick, F. P. (ed.) *Explorations in Transactional Psychology.* New York University Press, 1961.
173 Figure 5.21. Photos by Alan Ross
178 Figure 5.23. From Thompson, *Perception,* 1980, Vol. 9, pages 483-484. With apologies to Mrs. Thatcher. Reproduced by permission of Pion Ltd., London.

Chapter 6

191 © 1984 Brent Jones
194 J. Berndt/The Picture Cube
199 Sidney Harris
200 Bonnie Griffith/The Picture Cube
202 John Running/Stock, Boston
207 H. Schwadron in *Psychology Today*
208 From *Scivius* by St. Hildegard of Bingen, c. 1170
209 Randa Bishop/DPI
213 (both) Collection of Ronald K. Siegel
214 Marcia Weinstein
215 (top) Abigail Heyman/Archive; (bottom) P. Chock/Stock, Boston

Acknowledgments

Chapter 7

226 The Bettmann Archive
233 Courtesy of Dr. Ben Harris, from Watson's 1919 film *Experimental Investigation of Babies*
235 The Bettmann Archive
237 (left) Courtesy of University of Chicago; (right) Courtesy of GenRad, Inc./Grason-Stadler Division
238 Joe McNally/Wheeler Pictures
239 Scott, Foresman
240 Malcolm Hancock
244 Yerkes Regional Primate Research Center of Emory University
245 (all) Courtesy of Dr. Loh Seng Tsai
246 Owen Franken/Stock, Boston
248 Courtesy of Dr. Warren R. Street, Central Washington State College/Reprinted by permission of APA *Monitor*
251 Animal Behavior Enterprises, Hot Springs, Arkansas
255 Courtesy of Dr. Albert Bandura
256 Courtesy of the Department of Psychology, University of California, Berkeley
258 Yerkes Regional Primate Research Center of Emory University

Chapter 8

267 Courtesy of Dr. Philip G. Zimbardo
269 Robert P. Carr
272 (all) Courtesy of Dr. Philip G. Zimbardo
276 John Sanderson
277 Courtesy of Dr. Neal E. Miller
279 © 1984 Brent Jones
282 Wolfgang Kaehler
284 © 1983, Punch Publs. Ltd. Reprinted with permission, Los Angeles Times Syndicate.
291 Mario J. Ruiz/Picture Group
292 Leslie Wong/Contact
295 (left) From *The Expression of the Emotions in Man and Animals* by Charles Darwin, London, 1904; (right) Wide World
296 Bohdan Hrynewych/Stock, Boston
298 (top) Photograph of actor Tom Harrison by Paul Ekman © 1983; (bottom) Bohdan Hrynewych/Stock, Boston

Chapter 9

306 © 1984 by Nicole Hollander
322 The Bettmann Archive
323 Sidney Harris
329 Fig. 9.11. Cartoon from *Transactions of the New York Academy of Sciences*, Vol. 8, No. 2, Fig. 1, p. 66, G. W. Allport and L. J. Postman. Copyright The New York Academy of Sciences, 1945. Reprinted by permission.
332 GUINDON by Richard Guindon. © 1982 Los Angeles Times Syndicate. Courtesy of News America Syndicate.
334 Scott, Foresman
336 Charles Painter/Stanford University News and Publications Service

Chapter 10

341 Malcolm Hancock
343 Courtesy of Dr. Keith Nelson
346 Cristina Miles Gavin for Scott, Foresman
351 Sidney Harris
354 Courtesy of Quad/Graphics, Inc., Pewaukee, Wisconsin
363 Rick Browne/Picture Group
369 Charles Painter/Stanford University News and Publications Service
373 Reprinted by permission of Chronicle Features, San Francisco
375 (left) Paul Fusco/Magnum; (right) Dr. Ronald H. Cohn/The Gorilla Foundation

Chapter 11

386 William Hamilton
388 Courtesy of Harvard University News Office
389 Scott, Foresman
393 © Punch/Rothco
395 Cristina Miles Gavin for Scott, Foresman
397 Michael Weisbrot/Stock, Boston
398 (top left) Wide World; (bottom left) The Bettmann Archive; (right) Collection of The Newark Museum
401 Elizabeth Crews
405 Courtesy of Dr. Albert Bandura
409 Kevin Horan/Picture Group
411 Scott, Foresman

Chapter 12

418 Scott, Foresman
420 Sidney Harris
421 Scott, Foresman
423 By permission of News America Syndicate
426 Scott, Foresman
428 (both) The Psychological Corporation
431 Rick Friedman/Black Star
432 Jacques M. Chenet/*Newsweek*
433 (left) Edward Clark, LIFE Magazine © 1949 Time Inc.; (right) Terry Parke/Gamma-Liaison
441 (left) Figure 12.6. Reprinted by permission of the publishers from Henry A. Murray, THEMATIC APPERCEPTION TEST, Cambridge, Mass.: Harvard University Press, Copyright © 1943 by the President and Fellows of Harvard College, © 1971 by Henry A. Murray; (right) Martha Cooper
443 (left) Elizabeth Crews; (right) Martha Cooper
444 Figure 12.7 Courtesy of Dr. Frank Barron
448 Marcia Weinstein

Chapter 13

459 Jerry Gordon/Archive
460 Paul Fortin/Stock, Boston
461 © Laszlo
465 (left) Ken Regan/Camera 5; (right) Frank Fisher/Gamma-Liaison
467 Manuel Ceniceras/Sygma
468 Eli Reed/Magnum
472 Arthur Grace/Stock, Boston
474 (top) Peter Silva/Picture Group; (bottom) Fred Ward/Black Star
477 Steve Schapiro/Sygma
479 © Joel Gordon 1983
480 Cary Wolinsky/Stock, Boston
482 Joel Gordon/DPI

Chapter 14

491 Leo de Wys
492 Marcia Weinstein
495 Rhoda Sidney/Leo de Wys
497 Tom Damman/NYT Pictures
499 © 1984 Punch/Rothco
500 Culver Pictures
502 Susan Greenwood/Gamma-Liaison
505 Jim McNee/Tom Stack & Assoc.
507 UPI/The Bettmann Archive
511 Elinor S. Beckwith/Taurus
513 Photograph by John Scofield, © 1962 National Geographic Society
515 Library of Congress
517 Owen Franken/Stock, Boston
519 NIMH
520 Scott, Foresman

Chapter 15

530 Ann Hagan Griffiths/Omni-Photo Communications
531 Scott, Foresman
532 The Trustees of Sir John Soane's Museum
533 Bulloz
536 Larry Smith/DPI
538 (left) William Alanson White Psychiatric Foundation; (right) Courtesy of Dr. Margaret S. Mahler
539 G. Paul Bishop
540 Table 15.1. Photograph by John Running/Stock, Boston
541 Courtesy of Dr. Joseph Wolpe
542 Sidney Harris
543 Allan Grant
545 Figure 15.1. Photograph courtesy of Dr. Philip G. Zimbardo
549 UPI/The Bettmann Archive
550 Courtesy of Dr. Rollo May
551 Bohdan Hrynewych/Stock, Boston
552 Ann Chwatsky/Leo de Wys
555 Andy Freeberg

Chapter 16

570 Elizabeth Crews
572 Diane M. Lowe/Stock, Boston
573 Frank Siteman/Taurus
581 Jean-Claude Lejeune
583 Wiener Library, London
588 Jean-Claude Lejeune
590 (top) Lenore Weber/Taurus; (bottom) Elizabeth Crews
592 Steven E. Sutton/Duomo
594 Jean-Claude Lejeune
595 (left) Rick Smolan/Stock, Boston; (right) Michael O'Brien/Archive
599 Figure 16.5. Photograph by William Vandivert
600 (top) British Information Services, New York; (bottom) Bob Adelman
602 (all) Courtesy of Dr. Ronald Lippitt
605 (all) From *An Outline of Social Psychology*, revised edition by Muzafer Sherif and Carolyn W. Sherif. Copyright 1948, 1956 by Harper & Row Publishers, Inc.

Chapter 17

609 (all) Courtesy of Dr. Philip G. Zimbardo
610 (all) Courtesy of Dr. Philip G. Zimbardo
614 Scott, Foresman
615 Courtesy of Dr. Philip G. Zimbardo
616 Figure 17.2. Photograph courtesy of Dr. Philip G. Zimbardo
619 Charles Harbutt/Archive
623 Courtesy of Dr. Philip G. Zimbardo
631 (left) Yaghodzadeh/Sygma; (right) G. Rancinan/Sygma
633 Reprinted by permission: Tribune Media Services, Inc.
635 Scott, Foresman
636 Betsy Cole/The Picture Cube

Appendix
643 Sidney Harris

Literary, Figures, and Tables

Chapter 1

7 From "Misconceptions about Psychology among Introductory Psychology Students." *Teaching Psychology*, 1977, 4, 138-141. Copyright © 1977 by Division Two of the American Psychological Association. Excerpt reprinted by permission.
10, 11 Figures 1.1A & 1.1B. Data from "The Employment of APA Members" by Joy Stapp and Robert Fulcher, *American Psychologist*, November 1981. Copyright © 1981 by the American Psychological Association, Inc. Reprinted by permission of the authors.
13 Table 1.1. From Philip G. Zimbardo, *Shyness: What It Is, What to Do About It.* Copyright © 1977, Addison-Wesley, Reading, Mass. Reprinted by permission.

Chapter 2

36 Table 2.1. From *Child Development* by L. P. Lipsitt and H. W. Reese, p. 18. © 1979 Scott, Foresman and Company.
37 Figure 2.1. From "Adolescent Personality Development and Historical Change: 1970-1972" by J. R. Nesselroade and P. B. Baltes, *Monographs of the Society for Research in Child Development*, 1974, 39 (1, Whole No. 154). © The Society for Research in Child Development, Inc. Reprinted by permission.
42 Figure 2.3. From *The First Two Years* by Mary M. Shirley, by permission of University of Minnesota Press.
44 Figure from "Carrying Behavior in Humans: Analysis of Sex Differences" by D. A. Jenni and M. A. Jenni, *Science*, November 19, 1976, Vol. 194, pp. 859-860. Copyright © 1976 by the American Association for the Advancement of Science. Reprinted by permission of the American Association for the Advancement of Science and the authors.
55 Table 2.4. *From Perspectives on Childhood Socialization* by J. Clausen. Copyright © 1968 by Little, Brown and Company. Reprinted by permission of the author.
68 Table from *Adaptation to Life* by George Vaillant. Copyright © 1977 by George E. Vaillant. By permission of Little, Brown and Company.

Chapter 3

87 Table 3.1. From "Some Synaptic Transmitters and Transmitter Candidates" from *Physiological Psychology* by Mark Rosenzweig and A. L. Leiman. Copyright © 1982 by D. C. Heath and Company. Adapted by permission.

91 Figure 3.11. From "Local, Reflex, and Central Commands Controlling Fill and Siphon Movements in Aplysia" by I. Kupfermann, et al., *Journal of Neurophysiology*, Vol. 37, pp. 996-1019. Copyright © 1974 by American Physiological Society. Reprinted by permission of the publisher.

93 Figure 3.12. From "Development of Human Brain 3 Weeks to Birth, Lateral View," *Introduction to Physiological Psychology* by Richard F. Thompson, Harper & Row, Publishers, 1975, adapted from figures 203 and 206 in *Human Embryology*, second edition by Bradley M. Patten, McGraw-Hill Book Company, 1953.

101 Table 3.2. Adapted from *1981 Yearbook of Science and the Future*, Copyright © 1980 by Encyclopaedia Brittanica, Inc. Used by permission.

Chapter 4

114 Table 4.1. From *New Directions in Psychology* by Roger Brown, et al. Copyright © 1962 by Holt, Rinehart and Winston, Inc. Reprinted by permission of the author.

118 Figure 4.7B. From *Sensory Communication* by W. A. Rosenblith. Copyright © 1961 by The Massachusetts Institute of Technology. Reprinted by permission.

122 Figure 4.10. Adapted from *Seeing: Illusion, Brain and Mind* by John P. Frisby. Copyright © 1979 by John P. Frisby. Reprinted by permission of Oxford University Press.

130 Figure 4.19. From Fundamentals of *Sensation and Perception* by Michael W. Levine and Jeremy M. Shefner. Copyright © 1981 by Random House, Inc. Reprinted by permission of Random House, Inc.

137 Figure 4.25 (top). From *The Science of Musical Sound* by D. C. Miller, Macmillan Company 1926. Reprinted by permission of Case Western Reserve University.

139 Figure 4.27 B & C, From *Experiments in Hearing* by Georg von Békésy, translated and edited by E. G. Wever. Copyright © 1960 by the McGraw-Hill Book Company, Inc. Adapted by permission.

140 Figure 4.28. From *Theory of Hearing* by Ernest Glen Wever. Copyright 1949 by John Wiley & Sons, Inc. Reprinted by permission of John Wiley & Sons, Inc.

144 Figure redrawn from "Seeing with the Skin" by Benjamin White, et al., *Perception and Psychophysics*, 1970, Vol. 7 (1). Copyright © 1970 by Psychonomic Journals, Inc. Reprinted by permission.

Chapter 5

160 Figure 5.6. James J. Gibson: *The Perception of the Visual World.* Copyright 1950, renewed 1977 by Houghton Mifflin Company. Used with permission.

165 Figure 5.14. From "Impossible Objects: A Special Type of Visual Illusion" by L. S. Penrose and R. Penrose, *The British Journal of Psychology*, Vol. 49, 1958. Reprinted by permission of The British Psychological Society.

169 Figure 5.18. From *Sensation and Perception* by Stanley Coren, et al. Copyright © 1979 by Academic Press, Inc. Reprinted by permission of the publisher and the authors.

170 Figure 5.19A & B. Adapted from James J. Gibson: *The Perception of the Visual World.* Copyright 1950, renewed 1977 Houghton Mifflin Company. Adapted with permission.

Chapter 6

192 Figure 6.1. From *Cognitive Psychology and Information Processing: An Introduction* by Roy Lachman, Janet L. Lachman and Earl C. Butterfield. Copyright © 1979 by Lawrence Erlbaum Associates, Inc. and the authors.

193 Figure 6.2. From "Components of Attention" by M. I. Posner and S. J. Boies, *Psychological Review*, 1971, 78. Copyright © 1971 by the American Psychological Association, Inc. Reprinted by permission of the publisher and the authors.

197 Figure 6.4. From R. W. Sperry from The Harvey Lectures, Series 62, 1968. New York: Academic Press, Inc. Reprinted by permission.

199 Table 6.1. From *Drawing on the Right Side of the Brain* by Betty Edwards. Copyright © 1979 by Betty Edwards. Reprinted by permission of J. P. Tarcher, Inc., Houghton Mifflin Company and Souvenir Press.

201 Figure from *Psychology* by Michael S. Gazzaniga. Copyright © 1980 by Michael S. Gazzaniga. Reprinted by permission of Harper & Row, Publishers, Inc

204 Figure 6.5. From *The Sleep Disorders* by Peter Hauri. Copyright © 1977 The Upjohn Company. Reprinted by permission from Scope® Publications, The Upjohn Company and the author.

205 Figure 6.6. From *The Sleep Disorders* by Peter Hauri. Copyright © 1977 The Upjohn Company. Reprinted by permission from Scope® Publications, The Upjohn Company and the author.

205 Figure 6.7. From "Ontogenetic Development of the Human Sleep-Dream Cycle" by H. P. Roffwarg, et al., *Science,* April 1966, 152 (9), pp. 604-619. Copyright © 1966 by the American Association for the Advancement of Science. Reprinted by permission of the American Association for the Advancement of Science.

210 Figure 6.8. Based on Ernest R. Hilgard, *Hypnotic Susceptibility.* Copyright © 1965 by Harcourt Brace Jovanovich, Inc. Reprinted by permission of the publisher.

212 Table 6.3. Functions of Personalities from "Multiple Personalities" by Eugene L. Bliss, M.D., *Archives of General Psychiatry*, Vol. 37, December 1980, p. 1390. Copyright © 1980, American Medical Association. Adapted by permission of the American Medical Association and the author.

214 Figure 6.9. Kandel, D. "Adolescent Marijuana Use: Role of Parents and Peers," *Science*, Vol. 181, pp. 1067-1070, Fig. 1. September 14, 1973. Copyright © 1973 by the American Association for the Advancement of Science. Reprinted by permission of the Association and the author.

Chapter 7

228 Fig 7.2. From *Principles of Animal Learning and Motivation* by R. M. Tarpy, p. 51. © 1982 Scott, Foresman.

257 Fig 7.9. From "Degrees of Hunger, Reward and Non-reward, and Maze Learning in Rats" by E. C. Tolman and C. H. Honzik, *University of California Publications in Psychology*, Vol. 4, No. 16, December 1930. Reprinted by permission.

Chapter 8

266 From Warden, C. J. *Animal Motivation: Experimental Studies on the Albino Rat,* 1931. Reprinted by permission of Columbia University Press.

275 Figure 8.4. From W. U. Meyer, page 127 in H. Heckhausen, "Achievement Motive Research," from *Nebraska Symposium on Motivation,* 1968, W. J. Arnold (Ed.). Copyright © 1968 by University of Nebraska Press. Reprinted by permission of University of Nebraska Press.

278 Figure 8.5. From "Hunger in Humans Induced by 2-Deoxy-D-Glucose: Glucoprivic Control of Taste Preference and Food Intake," Thompson, D. A. and Campbell, R. G., *Science,* December 9, 1977, Vol. 198, pp. 1065-1067, Fig. 2. Reprinted by permission.

282 Figure 8.6. From *Human Sexualities* by J. H. Gagnon, p. 207. © 1977 Scott, Foresman and Company.

285 Figure 8.7. From *Human Sexualities* by J. H. Gagnon, p. 121. © 1977 Scott, Foresman and Company.

288 Figure 8.9. Adapted from *Human Motivation* by Bernard Weiner. Copyright © 1980 by Holt, Rinehart and Winston. Reprinted by permission of CBS College Publishing.

290 Table 8.2. Adapted from *Human Motivation* by Bernard Weiner. Copyright © 1980 by Holt, Rinehart and Winston. Reprinted by permission of CBS College Publishing.

299 Figure 8.12. Reprinted by permission of the publisher and the author from "Crying Behavior in the Human Adult" by William H. Frey, II, Ph.D., et al., *Integrative Psychiatry,* September/October 1983. Copyright © 1983 by Elsevier Science Publishing Co., Inc.

301 Figure 8.13. From "The Schachter Theory of Emotion: Two Decades Later" by Rainer Reisenzein, *Psychological Bulletin,* 1983, Vol. 94, No. 2. Copyright © 1983 by the American Psychological Association, Inc. Reprinted by permission of the publisher and the author.

Chapter 9

311 Figure 9.2. From "The Information Available in Brief Visual Presentations" by George Sperling, *Psychological Monographs: General and Applied,* Vol. 174, No. 11, Whole No. 498, 1960. Copyright © 1960 by the American Psychological Association, Inc. Adapted by permission of the publisher and the author.

311 Figure 9.3. Adapted from "Short-Term Memory in Vision" by E. Averbach and A. S. Coriell, *The Bell System Technical Journal,* January 1961. Reprinted by permission.

315 Figure 9.5. From "Short-Term Retention of Individual Verbal Items" by Lloyd R. Peterson and Margaret Jean Peterson, *Journal of Experimental Psychology,* September 1959, Vol. 58, No. 3. Copyright © 1959 by the American Psychological Association, Inc. Reprinted by permission of the publisher and the authors.

317 Figure 9.6. From "High Speed Scanning in Human Memory," Sternberg, S., *Science,* Vol. 153, pp. 652-654, Fig. 1, August 5, 1966. Reprinted by permission.

330 Figure 9.12. From *Remembering: A Study in Experimental and Social Psychology* by F. C. Bartlett. Reprinted by permission of Cambridge University Press.

352 Figure 10.1. From *Mental Images and Their Transformations* by Roger N. Shepard and Lynn A. Cooper. Copyright © 1982 by The Massachusetts Institute of Technology. Reprinted by permission.

352 Figure 10.2. Adapted from "Scanning Visual Images: Some Structural Implications" by Stephen Michael Kosslyn, *Perception and Psychophysics* 1973, Vol. 14, No. 1, 90-94. Copyright © 1973 by The Psychonomic Society, Inc. Reprinted by permission.

Chapter 10

353 Figure 10.3. From "Cognitive Psychology" by M. J. Farr, *Naval Research Reviews,* One/1984 Vol. XXXVI. Reprinted by permission.

355-356 Excerpt from "Contextual Prerequisites for Understanding: Some Investigations of Comprehension and Recall" by John D. Bransford and Marcia K. Johnson, *Journal of Verbal Learning and Verbal Behavior,* 11, 717-726 (1972). Copyright © 1972 by Academic Press, Inc. Reprinted by permission of the publisher and the authors.

356 Excerpts from a Candid Camera episode reprinted by permission of Allen Funt.

365 Figure 10.6. From "Acquisition of a Memory Skill," K. Anders Ericsson, et al., *Science,* Vol. 208, p. 1181, Fig. 1, 6, June 1980. Copyright © 1980 American Association for the Advancement of Science. Reprinted by permission of the American Association for the Advancement of Science and the author.

370 Table 10.2. From *Children's Oral Communication Skills,* edited by W. Patrick Dickson. Copyright © 1981 the Board of Regents of the University of Wisconsin System. Reprinted by permission.

Chapter 11

382 Table 11.1. Reproduced by permission of the publisher, F. E. Peacock Publishers, Inc., Itasca, Illinois. From Raymond J. Corsini, *Current Personality Theories.* Copyright © 1977, pp. 2 and 3.

387 Figure 11.2. From *The Inequality of Man* by H. J. Eysenck. Copyright © 1973 Hans J. Eysenck. Reprinted by permission of Maurice Temple Smith Ltd.

407 Table from *Evaluating Educational Environments* by Rudolf H. Moos. Copyright © 1979 by Jossey-Bass, Inc., Publishers. Adapted by permission of the publisher.

408 Figure 11.4A & B. From "Self-Imposed Delay of Reward" by Albert Bandura and Walter Mischel, *Journal of Personality and Social Psychology,* November 1965, Vol. 2, No. 5. Copyright © 1965 by the American Psychological Association, Inc. Reprinted by permission of the publisher and the authors.

Chapter 12

423 Figure 12.1. Courtesy the Department of Behavioral Sciences and Leadership, United States Military Academy, West Point.

427 Figure 12.2. From *Wechsler's Measurement and Appraisal of Adult Intelligence* by J. D. Matarazzo. Copyright © 1972 by Oxford University Press, Inc. Reprinted by permission.

433 Figure 12.3A. From "Achievement and Social Mobility: Relationships among IQ Score, Education, and Occupation in Two Generations" by Jerome H. Waller, *Social Biology,* Vol. 18, September 1971, No. 3. Copyright © 1971 by The American Eugenics Society, Inc. Figure 12.3B. From "Genetics and Intelligence: A Review" by L. Erlenmeyer-Kimling and L. F. Jarvik, *Science,* December 13, 1963, Vol. 142, No. 3598. Copyright © 1963 by the American Association for the Advancement of Science. Adapted by permission of the American Association for the Advancement of Science and the authors.

436 Table 12.1. From *Minnesota Multiphasic Personality Inventory.* Copyright The University of Minnesota 1943, renewed 1970. Reprinted by permission of the University of Minnesota Press.

437 Figure 12.4A, B, & C. From *Minnesota Multiphasic Personality Inventory.* Copyright The University of Minnesota 1943, renewed 1970. Reprinted by permission of the University of Minnesota Press.

438 Table based on material from pp. 350-351 from *Clinical Psychology: Concepts, Methods, and Profession,* Rev. Ed. by E. Jerry Phares. (The Dorsey Press, Homewood, Illinois © 1984). Reprinted by permission.

447 Table 12.2. From Zimbardo, P. G., Pilkonis, P. A., and Norwood, R. M. "The Silent Prison of Shyness." The Office of Naval Research Technical Report Z-17, November 1974. Stanford, Cal.: Stanford University Press. Reprinted by permission of Philip G. Zimbardo.

Chapter 13

461 Figure 13.1. From *Stress Without Distress* by Hans Selye, M.D., J. B. Lippincott Company. Copyright © 1974 by Hans Selye, M.D. Reprinted by permission of Harper & Row, Publishers, Inc.

469 Excerpts from "The Aftershock of Rape," *The Stanford Daily,* February 2, 1982. Reprinted by permission.

472 Table 13.1. "The Social Readjustment Rating Scale" reprinted with permission from Journal of Psychosometic Research 11: 213-218, 1967, T. H. Holmes and R. H. Rahe, Copyright © 1967, Pergamon Press, Inc. and T. H. Holmes.

483 Figure 13.3. From "Desensitization and the Experimental Reduction of Threat" by Carlyle H. Folkins, et al., *Journal of Abnormal Psychology,* 1968, 73. Copyright © 1968 by the American Psychological Association, Inc. Reprinted by permission of the publisher and the authors.

485 Table 13.3. From D. Meichenbaum. "A Self-Instructional Approach to Stress Management: A Proposal for Stress Innoculating Training." In D. C. Spielberger and I. G. Sarason, (Eds.), *Stress and Anxiety,* Vol. 1. New York: Wiley, 1975, 237-263. Copyright © 1975 by Hemisphere Publishing Corporation. Reprinted by permission.

Chapter 14

490 Excerpt from *Diagnostic and Statistical Manual of Mental Disorders* (Third Edition). Copyright © 1980, The American Psychiatric Association. Reprinted by permission.

491 Excerpt from "A Six-Year Nightmare for Jim Backus" by Vernon Scott. Reprinted with permission of United Press International, Inc.

494 Table 14.2. From *Diagnostic and Statistical Manual of Mental Disorders* (Third Edition). Copyright © 1980, The American Psychiatric Association. Reprinted by permission.

499 Material based on *Diagnostic and Statistical Manual of Mental Disorders* (Third Edition). Copyright © 1980, The American Psychiatric Association. Reprinted by permission.

510 Table 14.4. From *Diagnostic and Statistical Manual of Mental Disorders* (Third Edition). Copyright © 1980, The American Psychiatric Association. Reprinted by permission.

518 Figure 14.1. From "Genetic Theories and the Validation of Psychiatric Diagnosis: Implications for the Study of Children of Schizophrenics" by Daniel R. Hanson, et al., *Journal of Abnormal Psychology,* 1977, 86. Copyright © 1977 by the American Psychological Association, Inc. Reprinted by permission of the publisher and the authors.

523 Figure 14.2. From Haas, K. "Let the Punishment Fit the Crime." *Understanding Ourselves and Others,* 1965. Reprinted by permission of Prentice-Hall, Inc. Englewood Cliffs, New Jersey.

Chapter 15

535 Excerpt from "The Case of Anna O.: A Reformulation" by Marc H. Hollender, M. D., *The American Journal of Psychiatry,* vol. 137:7, p. 800, 1980. Copyright © 1980, the American Psychiatric Association.

536-537 Excerpt from Yoram Kaufmann, "Analytical Psychotherapy." Reproduced by permission of the publisher, F. E. Peacock Publishers, Inc., Itasca, Illinois. From Raymond J. Corsini and Contributors, *Current Psychotherapies.* Copyright © 1979, p. 111.

540 Table 15.1. From J. Wolpe, *The Practice of Behavior Therapy* (2nd ed.). United Kingdom (and New York): Pergamon Press, 1973.

546 Table 15.2. Adapted from *Modern Clinical Psychology: Principles of Intervention in the Clinic and Community* by Sheldon J. Korchin. Copyright © 1976 by Sheldon J. Korchin. Reprinted by permission of Basic Books, Inc., Publishers.

559 Table 15.4. From "Meta-Analysis of Psychotherapy Outcome Studies" by Mary Lee Smith and Gene V. Glass, *American Psychologist,* Vol. 32, September 1977, No. 9. Copyright © 1977 by the American Psychological Association, Inc. Adapted by permission of the publisher and the authors.

Chapter 16

571 Excerpt from "Primacy-Recency in Impression Formation" by A. S. Luchins, *The Order of Presentation in Persuasion,* C. I. Hovland (Ed.). Copyright © 1957 Yale University Press, Inc. Reprinted by permission.

576 Figure 16.1. From "An Experimental Study of Apparent Behavior" by F. Heider and M. Simmel, *American Journal of Psychology,* Vol. 57, 1944, pp. 564-572. Reprinted by permission of the University of Illinois Press.

584 Figure 16.2. From "Communicator Credibility and Communication Discrepancy as Determinants of Opinion Change" by Eliot Aronson, Judith A. Turner and J. Merrill Carlsmith, *Journal of Abnormal and Social Psychology,* 1963, Vol. 67, No. 1. Copyright © 1963 by the American Psychological Association, Inc. Reprinted by permission of the publisher and the authors.

587 Table 16.3. From *Review of Personality and Social Psychology:* 1 by E. Wheeler, Ed. Copyright © 1980 by Sage Publications, Inc. Reprinted by permission.

589 Table from "The Friendship Bond" by Mary Brown Parlee and the Editors of *Psychology Today,* October 1979. Copyright © 1979 American Psychological Association. Reprinted by permission.

591 Figure 16.4. From "Toward Analysis of Close Relationships" by George Levinger, *Journal of Experimental Social Psychology,* 16, 510-544, 1980. Copyright © 1980 by Academic Press, Inc. Adapted by permission of the publisher and the author.

Chapter 17

618 Figure 17.3. From "Disinhibition of Aggression Through Diffusion of Responsibility and Dehumanization of Victims" by Albert Bandura, et al., *Journal of Research in Personality,* 1975, 9, pp. 253-269. Copyright © 1975 by Academic Press, Inc. Reprinted by permission of the publisher and the author.

620 Table 17.3. Mansson, H. H. From "Justifying the Final Solution," *Omega,* 1972, *3*(2), 79-87. Copyright © 1972, Baywood Publishing Company, Inc. Reprinted by permission.

626 Excerpt from "Why Johnny Can't Disobey" by Sarah J. McCarthy, *The Humanist,* September/October 1979. Copyright © 1979 by The Humanist. Reprinted by permission.

629 Figure 17.5. From "Prenatal Exposure to Synthetic Progestins Increases Potential for Aggression in Humans" by June M. Reinisch, *Science,* Vol. 211, 13, March 1981, pp. 1171-1173. Copyright © 1981 American Association for the Advancement of Science. Reprinted by permission of the American Association for the Advancement of Science and the author.

632 Figure 17.6. From "The Effects of Alcohol and Delta-9-Tetrahydrocannabinol on Human Physical Aggression" by Stuart P. Taylor, et al., *Aggressive Behavior,* Volume 2, pages 153-161. Copyright © 1976 Alan R. Liss, Inc. Adapted by permission.

634 Figure 17.7. From "Aggressive Erotica and Violence Against Women" by Edward Donnerstein, *Journal of Personality and Social Psychology,* August 1980, Vol. 39, No. 2. Copyright © 1980 by the American Psychological Association, Inc. Adapted by permission of the publisher and the author.

NAME INDEX

A

Abelson, R., 351
Abramson, L. Y., 246, 505
Accornero, N., 145
Acker, L. E., 231
Acredolo, L. P., 354
Adams, H. E., 422
Adams, J. A., 319
Adams, J. L., 352, 363
Adams, M., 610
Adams, N. E., 548
Adams, W. G., 610
Ader, R., 234–235
Adler, A., 397, 398, 413
Adler, N., 465
Agras, W. S., 482
Aguayo, L. G., 88
Ahearn, F. L., 473
Ajzen, I., 580, 581
Akert, K., 102
Akhtar, S., 500
Akil, H., 146, 519
Alba, J. W., 328
Albee, G. W., 562
Albuquerque, E. X., 88
Alcott, W. A., 281
Aldwin, C., 478
Alex, M., 229
Allen, A., 390–391
Allen, G. W., 354
Allen, J. G., 524
Allen, M., 477
Allen, R. A., 482
Allen, V. L., 604
Allison, T., 204
Alloy, L. B., 505
Allport, G. W., 328, 357, 388,
    390, 412, 580
Almli, C. R., 276
Als, H., 45
Altman, I., 587, 591, 638
Amabile, T. M., 443, 579, 593
Amoore, J. E., 142
Anastasi, A., 434
Andersen, S. M., 134, 509, 627
Anderson, J. R., 323, 350, 365,
    366
Anderson, K., 193
Andrasik, F., 546–547
Anisfeld, M., 313
Antelman, S. M., 278, 466
Ardrey, R., 628
Aristotle, 74, 371, 583, 628
Aronson, E., 581, 583, 584, 589,
    637
Arthur, R. J., 471
Asarnow, R. F., 511

Asch, S. E., 598
Aserinsky, E., 203
Asher, S. R., 545
Atkinson, J. W., 286, 288, 293
Atkinson, R. C., 326
Atkinson, S., 203
Averbach, I., 311
Averill, J. R., 295
Ayllon, T., 544
Azrin, N. H., 240, 467

B

Bachman, J. G., 214
Bach-y-Rita, P., 144
Backus, J., 491, 501
Baddeley, A. D., 313, 320
Bader, B. C., 562
Baldwin, M., 73
Bales, R. F., 601
Ballenger, J. C., 335
Baltes, P. B., 35, 37
Bandura, A., 26, 254, 290, 292,
    404, 405, 406–408, 413, 544,
    548, 613, 618, 630, 631
Banuazizi, A., 614
Banyai, E. I., 209
Barbee, A. H., 37, 70
Barber, T. X., 210
Barbrack, C. R., 516
Barchas, J. D., 519, 554
Baribeau-Braun, J., 521
Barnes, R. D., 614
Barnett, S. A., 628
Barrett, G. V., 287
Barrios, B. A., 562
Barron, F. X., 444
Bar-Tal, D., 637
Barth, J., 265
Barthe, D. G., 506
Bartlett, F. C., 330–331, 346,
    357
Barton, R., 505
Barton, W., 617
Basedow, H., 458
Bateson, G., 521
Baum, A., 480, 481
Baumrind, D., 58, 59
Bavelas, A., 601
Bayley, N., 35, 42
Bazelon, D. C., 560
Beach, F., 270, 280, 283
Beaman, A. L., 616
Beardslee, W. R., 474
Beck, A. T., 505, 548

Beck, J., 162
Becker, G., 445
Becker, J. B., 88
Beecher, E., 213
Beecher, H. K., 146, 148, 215
Begg, I., 323
Bekarian, D. A., 332
Bell, R. R., 285
Bellack, A. J., 545
Belugi, U., 313
Bem, D. J., 390–391, 580, 582
Bem, S. L., 406, 642
Benedict, R., 270
Bennett, E. L., 95, 336
Bennett, H. L., 320
Benson, H., 482
Bentham, J., 224
Beradelli, A., 145
Berger, P. A., 519
Berkman, L. F., 480
Berkowitz, D., 507
Berkowitz, L., 630, 633
Berlitz, C., 364
Berlyne, D. E., 272
Bernard, L. L., 270
Berne, E., 551
Bernstein, M., 428
Berscheid, E., 588, 591
Bertholf, M., 642
Bessel, F., 345
Betz, B. J., 479
Bielski, R. J., 505
Bigelow, H. J., 103
Binet, A., 367, 424–425, 430,
    450
Bini, G., 145
Binkley, S., 203
Biracree, T., 242
Birch, D., 293
Bitterman, M. E., 248
Bjorklund, F. A., 54
Blake, W., 213, 445
Blakemore, C. S., 131
Blanchard, D., 404
Blaney, N., 637
Blank, A. A., Jr., 468
Blaustein, M. P., 88
Bleuler, M., 517
Blinder, B., 183
Bliss, E. L., 212
Blizzard, R. M., 82
Block, A., 147
Block, J., 61, 384
Block, J. H., 61, 384
Bloom, F. E., 146

Bodin, A. M., 560
Boies, S. J., 193
Bolles, R. C., 89
Bongiovanni, A., 240
Bootzin, R. R., 539
Boring, E. G., 76, 137
Borke, H., 52, 54
Botvin, G. J., 54
Boudreau, L. A., 524
Bourguignon, E., 217
Bourne, L. E., 364
Bourne, L. E., Jr., 349
Bower, G. H., 314, 319, 320,
    323, 350, 411, 545
Bower, S. A., 545
Bowers, J. M., 332
Bowers, K. S., 210
Bowers, M. B., Jr., 515
Bowlby, J., 56
Boyce, J., 635
Boyes-Bream, P., 347
Brackbill, Y., 56
Bradford, D., 439
Brady, J. V., 592
Bransford, J. D., 329, 356
Brantigan, L. O., 80
Brantigan, T. S., 80
Brasel, J. A., 82
Bray, C. W., 366
Brazelton, T. B., 45
Brechner, K. C., 635
Breggin, P. R., 555
Brehm, J. W., 582
Breland, K., 250–251
Breland, M., 250–251
Brenner, M. H., 474
Bressler, S. L., 100
Breuer, J., 393, 534–535
Brewer, M. B., 603
Bridge, T. P., 554
Brim, O. G., 66
Broadbent, D. E., 183, 190, 192
Brody, E. B., 429
Brody, N., 429
Bronfenbrenner, U., 521
Brotzman, E., 624
Brown, A. L., 369
Brown, B., 470
Brown, B. B., 587
Brown, H. O., 372
Brown, J. S., 280
Brown, R. W., 325
Bruch, H., 466, 496
Bruner, J. S., 53, 181, 182, 346
Brunswick, A. F., 214
Brush, C., 615
Buchsbaum, M. S., 101
Buckhout, R., 331, 332
Buczek, R., 262

Bullock, T. H., 85
Burnett, C., 477
Burns, W., 136
Buros, O. K., 440, 441
Burrows, G. D., 210
Busch, C. M., 447, 587
Buss, A. H., 189, 447, 585, 630
Bussey, K., 62–63
Butcher, H. J., 445
Butcher, J. N., 436
Butcher, M. J., 45
Butler, M. J., 274
Butler, R. A., 268
Butterfield, E. C., 357
Butterworth, T., 637
Buzan, T., 199
Bykov, K. M., 243
Byrne, D., 283, 588
Byrnes, D. L., 327

C

Caggiula, A. R., 466
Cairns, R. B., 38
Calesnick, L. E., 481
Calhoun, K. S., 422
Calhoun, L. G., 469
Calkins, M. W., 203
Cambier, J., 460
Cameron, P., 285
Campbell, F. W., 130, 131
Campbell, R. G., 278
Canavan-Gumpert, D., 289
Cann, A., 469
Cannon, J. T., 146
Cannon, W. B., 275–276, 297, 458–459
Cantor, N., 329, 574
Caplan, G. A., 57
Caporeal, L. R., 514
Carducci, B. J., 448
Carlsmith, J. M., 582, 583, 584
Carlson, J. G., 620
Carlsson, A., 519
Carmichael, L., 38, 42
Carpenter, G. C., 45
Carpenter, K., 496
Carpenter, P. A., 344
Carrascao, M. A., 335
Cartwright, R. D., 204, 205
Cartwright, S., 522
Carver, C. S., 190
Casper, C., 496
Cass, R. A., 635
Cattell, R. B., 428, 429, 439, 445, 449
Catterall, W. A., 85
Cermack, L. S., 326
Chapin, S. F., 479
Chaplin, W., 505
Chapman, D. W., 473

Chapman, J. A., 327
Chapman, R. M., 327
Charatan, F., 472
Chase, W. G., 316, 365, 367
Cheek, J. M., 447, 587
Chernick, L., 410
Cherry, E. C., 192
Chi, M. T. H., 367
Child, P., 615
Childers, S. R., 89
Chilman, C. S., 282
Chomsky, N., 49–50, 341, 372, 374
Chorover, S., 522
Chow, K. L., 159
Christie, R., 601
Christy, P. R., 631
Church, R. M., 248
Cialdini, R. B., 584
Ciaranello, R. D., 554
Cicchetti, D., 204
Ciminero, A. R., 422
Clarizio, S., 429
Clark, E. V., 49, 323, 373
Clark, G. A., 336
Clark, H. H., 323, 355, 373
Clark, R. A., 286
Clarke-Stewart, K. A., 35, 57
Clausen, J. A., 523
Clausen, T., 55
Cleckley, H. A., 212
Cohen, F., 465
Cohen, L. B., 45, 48
Cohen, N., 235
Cohen, R. E., 473
Coleridge, S. T., 398
Collier, G., 279
Collins, C. C., 144
Colton, C. C., 272
Comrey, A. L., 449
Conant, J. B., 19, 357
Condry, J., 572
Condry, S., 572
Conger, J. C., 545
Conrad, R., 313, 344
Consalvi, C., 601–602
Conte, H. Q., 397
Conway, B. E., 428
Cookerly, J. R., 552
Cooper, A. F., 508
Cooper, L. A., 352
Coopersmith, S., 59–60
Coriell, A. S., 311
Cornelison, A. R., 520
Cornhill, J. F., 480
Corsini, R. J., 382
Corwin, S. M., 399
Courchesne, E., 345
Cousins, N., 477
Covington, M. V., 465
Cowan, F., 641, 643
Cowles, J. T., 242
Cox, P. W., 177
Coyne, J. C., 478
Craik, F. I. M., 326
Craik, K., 219
Crane, J., 496
Cranston, J. W., 631, 632
Crawford, H. J., 217

Cressler, D. L., 547
Crick, F., 74
Cristol, A. H., 539, 558
Crocker, J., 614–615
Cromwell, R. L., 511
Cronbach, L. J., 419
Crook, J. H., 628
Cross, P. G., 445
Crowder, R. G., 310, 311, 327
Cruccu, G., 145
Culbertson, S., 248
Culver, C., 197
Cummins, R. A., 95
Cunitz, A. R., 327
Cunningham, J. W., 447
Curtis, S., 82
Cutillo, B. A., 100

D

Dahlstrom, L. E., 435
Dahlstrom, W. G., 435
Dali, S., 159
Dalrymple, S., 624
Danks, J. H., 48
Darwin, C., 269, 295, 391, 412, 445
Dauber, R. B., 385
Davert, E. C., 210
Davidson, G. C., 517
Davidson, J. M., 283
Davis, G. E., 481
Davis, J. M., 496
Davis, K. E., 576, 577
Davison, G. C., 560
Davison, L. A., 483
Dawes, R. M., 634, 636
Dawin, C. J., 311
D'Azevedo, W. L., 314
de Baca, P. C., 244
de Bono, F., 363
De Charms, R. C., 16, 287, 293
Deci, E. L., 292
Decker, S. N., 44
De Fries, J. C., 40, 44
De Ghett, V. J., 56
DeGroot, A. D., 367
Dehen, H., 460
Dellas, M., 443–444
De Loache, J. L., 369
Demarest, R. J., 94
Dembroski, T. M., 478
Dement, W. C., 190, 203, 205, 206
Dennerstein, L., 210
Depue, R. A., 554
Deregowski, J. B., 184
Descartes, R., 75, 82, 197, 340
DeSilva, R. A., 473
De Sota-Johnson, D., 299
Deutsch, G., 100, 198
Deutsch, M., 572

De Valois, K. K., 130
De Valois, R. L., 127, 130
Devine, J. V., 244
DeVries, R., 52
Dewey, J., 355
Diamond, J. M., 556
Diamond, M. C., 336
Diamond, M. J., 210
Diamond, W. D., 596
Dias, R. D., 335
Dickinson, A., 253
Dickman, H., 468
Dicton, T. W., 521
Diener, E., 616
Dion, K. L., 588
Doane, J., 520
Dobelle, W. H., 144
Dohrenwend, B. P., 508
Dohrenwend, B. S., 508
Dollard, J., 404–405, 467, 516, 629
Dominowski, R. L., 364
Donchin, E., 345
Donne, J., 569
Donnerstein, E., 394, 634
Doob, A. N., 614, 630
Doob, L. W., 467, 629
Dooling, D. J., 328–329
Dorfman, D. D., 272
Dorosin, D., 578
Doyle, J. C., 100
Drabman, R. S., 633
Dragoin, W. B., 252
Draguns, J. G., 513
Drambarean, N. C., 181
DuBois, P. H., 435
Duda, R. O., 368
Dudek, S. Z., 463
Dudycha, G. J., 390
Dugdale, R. L., 428
Dumont-Driscall, M., 43
Dunbar, F., 463
Duncker, K., 363
Duval, S., 615
Dweck, C. S., 290
Dyk, R. B., 182

E

Eagleston, J. R., 457, 478, 484
Eastwell, H. D., 459
Ebbesen, E. B., 636
Ebbinghaus, H., 322, 333
Ebenholtz, S., 166
Eckert, E. D., 496
Edwards, A. E., 231
Edwards, B., 199
Edwards, D. A., 629
Egeth, H. E., 332
Ehrlich, B. E., 556
Eichmann, A., 621
Eichorn, D. H., 70
Eimas, P. D., 47
Einstein, A., 351, 442
Eisler, R. M., 545

Ekman, P., 295, 297
Ekstein, R., 512
Eliot, T. S., 583
Elisaretsky, E., 335
Elliot, J., 604
Ellis, A., 549
Ellsworth, P. C., 297, 636
Emerson, R. W., 3
Emery, A. E. A., 554
Emery, G., 548
Emmelkamp, P. M., 541
Emurian, H. H., 592
Endler, N. S., 391
Enright, M., 333–334
Epstein, S., 391
Epstein, W., 372
Erdelyi, M. H., 183
Ericksen, C. W., 183, 523
Erickson, R. P., 141
Ericsson, K. A., 316, 365
Erikson, E., 24, 55, 64–65, 67, 69, 71, 397
Eron, L. D., 633
Ervin, F., 628–629
Escalona, S., 474
Escher, M. C., 158
Esveldt-Dawson, K., 546–547
Evans, J. G. M., 95
Evans, M. M., 43
Eysenck, H. J., 387, 412, 429, 557, 558

F

Fagen, J. W., 333–334
Fagot, B. I., 61
Fairweather, G. W., 547
Falcoon, S., 365
Fanelow, M. S., 89
Fantz, R. L., 45
Faraday, M., 351
Farina, A., 523, 524
Farr, M. J., 353, 367
Fass, P. S., 425
Faterson, H. F., 182
Faucheux, C., 599
Fazio, R. H., 581
Fechner, G., 118, 119
Feigenbaum, E. A., 368
Feinleib, M., 478
Feirtag, M., 84
Feld, S., 531
Feldman, A., 354
Feltovich, P. J., 367
Ferguson, P., 482
Fernald, D., 339
Ferrare, N. A., 14, 481
Ferster, C. B., 248, 249

Festinger, L., 582, 585, 615
Fink, A., 16
Fink, H., 148
Fink, M., 553
Finn, S., 436
Fireman, B., 626
Fish, H., 560
Fish, J. M., 558
Fishbein, M., 580
Fishbein, S., 300, 591
Fisher, A. E., 278
Fisher, R. J., 634
Fishman, R., 500
Fiske, S. T., 359, 579, 614–615
Fitts, P. M., 364
Flavell, E. R., 54
Flavell, J. H., 51, 52, 54, 369–370
Fleck, S., 520
Fleischman, P. R., 522
Fletcher, H., 137
Floderus-Myrhed, B., 44
Flood, R. A., 506
Fogarty, S. J., 320
Foley, V. D., 552
Folkin, D. H., 483
Folkman, S., 476
Fontaine, G., 290
Ford, C. S., 280, 283
Fordyce, W. E., 147
Forest, D. V., 512
Forgas, J. P., 323
Formica, R., 586
Foss, C., 587
Fothergill, L. A., 89
Foucault, M., 532
Fouts, R. S., 374
Fowler, H., 268
Fox, M. W., 3
Foy, D. W., 545
Frank, J. D., 559
Frank, R., 285
Franke, R. H., 287
Frankel, A., 574
Franks, C. M., 516
Fraser, S. C., 584, 616–617
Fredericksen, L. W., 545
Freedman, J. L., 584, 614
Freeman, R. R., 206
Freud, S., 16, 24, 55, 62, 64, 71, 181, 196, 206–207, 216, 219, 220, 265, 269–270, 271, 280, 334, 344, 357, 382, 383, 391–397, 398, 399, 404, 412, 413, 442, 477, 516, 525, 534–535, 536, 537, 563, 564, 627, 628, 629, 632, 639
Frey, W. H., II, 299
Friedel, R. O., 505
Friedman, M., 478
Friedman, S., 56
Friedricks, A. G., 370
Friesen, W. V., 295, 297
Frieze, I. H., 290
Frisby, J. P., 122, 131
Fromkin, H. L., 600, 614
Fromkin, V. A., 344

Fromm, E., 210, 397
Fromson, M. E., 618
Frumkin, B., 313
Fry, W. F., 477
Fujioka, T. A., 615
Fulcher, R., 10
Fuller, J. L., 40
Funder, D. C., 384
Funt, A., 356
Furman, W., 448, 546
Fyer, A. J., 499

G

Gage, P., 103
Gagné, R. M., 637
Gagnon, J. H., 284
Gaier, E. L., 443–444
Galaburda, A. M., 99
Galambos, R., 345
Galanter, E., 114, 115, 190
Galen, 74–75
Gallagher, J. M., 51
Galton, F., 380
Gammon, C. B., 631, 632
Gamson, W. A., 626
Garcia, J., 251
Gardner, B. T., 374
Gardner, H., 430–431
Gardner, L., 57, 82
Gardner, R. A., 374
Garfinkel, P. E., 496
Garmezy, N., 511, 521
Garner, D. M., 496
Garner, K., 289
Garner, W. R., 164
Garrison, V., 533
Gatchel, R. I., 517
Gatchel, R. J., 481
Gates, D. W., 176
Gazzaniga, M. S., 190, 197, 198, 200–201
Gebhard, R. H., 282
Geer, J. H., 517
Geis, F. L., 601
Gelade, G. A., 194
Gelb, L., 523
Gelber, E. R., 45
Geldard, F. A., 141, 143
Gelfand, D. M., 631
Gerbner, G., 632
Gergen, K. J., 617
Gergen, M. M., 617
Gervarter, W. B., 368
Geschwind, N., 99, 101
Getman, J., 636
Getty, D. J., 248
Gevins, A. S., 100

Gibson, E. J., 43
Gibson, J. J., 159–160, 170, 172
Gift, T. E., 508
Gill, M. M., 516
Gillig, P. M., 584
Gilligan, C., 63, 69
Gilman, A., 216
Gilmartin, K., 367
Gilmore, G. C., 521
Gilmore, R., 596
Gist, R., 473
Glanzer, M., 327
Glaser, R., 637
Glass, D. C., 481
Glass, G. V., 558–559
Glasser, R., 367
Glassman, R. B., 76
Glazebook, A. H., 579
Gleitman, H., 343
Gliha, D., 524
Glucksberg, S., 48
Goddard, H. H., 428
Goffman, E., 614
Gold, P., 335
Goldberg, S. C., 496
Goldman, R., 278
Goldstein, E. B., 139
Goldstein, M., 520
Goldston, S. E., 562
Gomes-Schwartz, B., 558
Gonzalez, A., 294
Goodenough, D. R., 176, 177, 182
Goodman, C. C., 181, 182
Goodman, D. A., 97
Goodman, L. S., 216, 372
Goodwin, D., 496
Goodwin, F. K., 335
Gordon, A., 278
Gorman, B. S., 294
Gorney, R., 633
Gosselin, J. Y., 521
Gottesman, I. I., 429, 518, 554
Gottlieb, B. H., 480
Gottlieb, G., 56, 95
Gottlieb, J., 514
Gough, H. G., 438, 439, 444
Gould, S. J., 424, 432
Gowing, J., 208
Graves, N., 624
Gray, C. R., 323, 324
Gray, W. D., 347
Green, D. M., 115
Greene, D., 292
Greenfield, P. M., 53
Greengard, P., 89
Greenwald, A. G., 584
Greenwood, M. M., 45
Gregory, M., 183
Griffith, D., 193
Grinnell, A., 85
Gross, A. E., 601
Grossman, M. I., 276
Grossman, S. P., 276
Grusec, J. E., 240

Guilford, J. P., 428
Guillemin, R., 146
Guisewife, C., 484
Gummerman, K., 323, 324
Gumpert, P., 289
Gur, R. C., 100, 210
Gur, R. E., 100, 210
Gurin, G., 531
Gurman, A. S., 552
Guze, S., 496
Gynther, M. D., 439, 450
Gynther, R. A., 439

H

Haas, H., 148
Haas, K., 523
Haber, R. B., 324
Haber, R. N., 324
Habot, T. B., 69
Hackman, J., 601
Hadley, S. W., 558
Hagalauer, H. D., 524
Haier, R. J., 510
Hale, R. L., 424
Haley, J., 521
Halliday, M., 48
Halmi, K. A., 496
Halpin, A., 601
Hamburg, D. A., 554
Hamill, R., 360
Hamilton, D. L., 329, 575
Hamilton, W. J., 142
Hamlin, P., 279
Hammen, C. L., 506
Haney, C., 610, 636–637
Hanna, S. D., 474
Hanson, D., 518
Harackiewicz, J. M., 334
Hardin, G. R., 635
Hardy, A. B., 548
Harlow, H. F., 58–59, 268
Harlow, M. K., 59
Harlow, T. M., 103
Harner, M. J., 217
Harrington, D., 61
Harrington, D. M., 444
Harris, V. A., 578
Harsha, D .W., 203
Harshman, R. A., 217
Hart, R., 60
Hart, R. A., 354
Hartfelder, G., 148
Hartman, D. P., 439, 631
Hartmann, E. L., 204
Hartshorne, H., 61, 389
Hartup, W. W., 448, 546
Harvey, E. N., 203
Harvey, O. J., 601–602, 604–605
Hasenfus, N., 445
Hasher, L., 328

Hastorf, A., 601
Hastorf, A. H., 523
Hathaway, S. R., 435
Hauri, P., 204
Haviland, S. E., 355
Hayes, C., 374
Hayes-Roth, B., 342, 354
Hayes-Roth, F., 342
Haynes, S. G., 478
Haynes, S. N., 422, 423, 439
Heath, R. G., 102
Hebb, D. O., 76, 272, 335, 466
Heber, F. R., 563
Heber, R., 432
Hecht, B. F., 49
Hecht, E., 217
Hedlund, J. L., 437
Heider, F., 275, 576
Heider, R., 576
Heinroth, J. C., 533
Helmholtz, H., 76, 139, 173, 345
Henderson, N. D., 66
Henning, H., 141
Henry, G. W., 532
Hensel, H., 143
Hering, E., 127, 128
Herold, E., 202–203
Heron, A., 67
Herren, R., 197
Hersen, M., 545, 546–547
Hersh, S. M., 621
Herz, M. J., 335
Hesley, J. W., 410
Heslin, R., 284
Hess, W., 102
Heston, L. L., 518
Hetherington, E. M., 55
Hildegard of Bingen, 207, 208
Hilgard, E. R., 148, 190, 209, 210, 211
Hilgard, J. R., 148, 210
Hillyard, S. A., 104, 345
Hinkle, L., 276
Hippocrates, 386
Hirsch, E., 279
Hirsch, H. V. B., 95
Hirst, W., 194
Hitch, G., 313
Hitler, A., 583, 596, 597, 602, 606, 625
Hobart, G. A., 203
Hobbes, T., 611–612, 627
Hobson, J. A., 206
Hochberg, J., 165
Hockett, C. F., 373
Hodgson, R., 500
Hofer, M., 41
Hoffman, C., 299
Hoffman-Ahern, C., 299
Hofling, C. K., 624
Hofstede, G., 16, 287
Hogarth, W., 532
Holahan, C. J., 480
Holden, C., 216, 244
Holen, M. C., 327
Holland, P. C., 232
Hollander, M. H., 535
Hollister, L. F., 210

Holmes, D. S., 482
Holmes, S., 399
Holmes, T. H., 471, 472
Holstein, C. B., 62
Holt, R. R., 438
Holz, W. C., 240
Homme, L. E., 244, 405, 413
Honzig, C. H., 256, 257
Honzik, M. P., 35, 70
Hood, W. E., 604–605
Hopson, J. L., 281
Horner, M. S., 289
Horney, K., 397
Hornstein, H. A., 572
Horton, L. E., 630–631
Hosobuchi, Y., 146
Houghton, J., 523
Hovland, C. I., 583
Howarth, E., 387
Howells, G. N., 548
Hoyt, J., 370
Hubbard, J. L., 336
Hubel, D. H., 24, 88, 129, 133, 162
Huesmann, L. R., 633
Hughes, J., 89
Hull, C. L., 264, 270, 272, 404–405
Humphrey, T., 42
Hungerbuhler, J. P., 100
Hunt, E., 424, 430
Hunt, M., 340, 343
Hurlburt, R., 190
Hurvich, L. M., 127
Hutchins, D., 187
Huxley, A., 213
Hyman, I. A., 240

I

Ickes, W., 614
Ickowicz, R. K., 88
Inglis, J., 100
Inhelder, B., 52
Insko, C. A., 596
Itani, J., 4
Itard, J. M., 33, 34, 47, 425
Iversen, L. L., 88
Izard, C. E., 296, 297
Izquierdo, I., 335

J

Jackaway, R., 289
Jackson, D. D., 521
Jacob, F., 90, 94
Jacobs, B. L., 217
Jacobs, G. H., 127

Jacobs, J., 603
Jacobsen, B., 518
Jacobson, E., 482
Jacobson, L. F., 18
James, W., 6, 39, 190, 269, 297, 401
Jameson, D., 127
Janis, I. L., 271, 358, 469, 583
Janowitz, H. D., 276
Janus, S. S., 477
Jeannerod, M., 195
Jenkins, C. D., 478
Jenkins, J. O., 545
Jenni, D. A., 44
Jenni, M. A., 44
Jensen, A. R., 327, 429
Jodelet, D., 354
Joffe, J. M., 562
John, E. R., 104
Johnson, D. L., 210
Johnson, D. M., 347
Johnson, G. B., 399
Johnson, J. H., 471
Johnson, M. K., 329, 356
Johnson, R. A., 299
Johnson, T. D., 56
Johnson, V. E., 282–283, 284
Johnsone, K., 575
Johnson-Laird, P., 219
Johnston, L. D., 214
Jones, E., 216, 391
Jones, E. E., 523, 576, 577, 578
Jones, J., 507, 603, 621
Jones, M. C., 233, 539
Jones, R., 596–597
Joseph, N., 80
Julesz, B., 162
Jung, C. G., 23, 397, 398, 413, 439
Jusczyk, P., 47
Just, H. A., 344

K

Kabat, L. G., 134, 509
Kagan, J., 57, 66
Kahn, M., 632
Kahn, S., 478
Kahneman, D., 358–359, 360
Kahneman, S., 194
Kalat, J. W., 85, 229, 278
Kallmann, F. J., 517
Kamin, L. J., 252, 429
Kandel, D., 214
Kandel, E., 92
Kanellakos, D. P., 482
Kanigel, R., 315
Kaplan, J., 216
Kaplan, R. M., 616
Karlsson, J. L., 445
Karp, S. A., 182
Katz, L. B., 329
Kaufman, L., 109
Kaufmann, Y., 536–537
Kaushall, P. I., 305
Kazdin, A. E., 541, 542, 544, 559

Kazdin, A. W., 539
Keane, S. P., 545
Keesey, R. E., 278
Kekulé, F. A., 351
Kelem, R. T., 616
Kellerman, H., 397
Kelley, H. H., 576, 577, 583, 588
Kellogg, J. H., 281
Kellogg, L. A., 374
Kellogg, W. N., 374
Kelly, G. A., 409–410, 411, 413
Kelman, H., 598
Kemper, T. L., 99
Kennedy, G. C., 278
Kennedy, J. F., 358
Kenney, M. D., 56
Kesey, K., 555
Kessler, S., 514, 517, 554
Ketron, J. L., 428
Ketterer, R. F., 562
Kety, S. S., 88, 518
Kiernan, R. J., 616
Kiess, H. O., 319
Kihlstrom, J. F., 334
King, H. E., 469
King, M. L., Jr., 592
King, R. G., 624
Kinsey, A. C., 282
Kintsch, W., 347, 350
Kirasic, K. C., 354
Kite, W. R., 601
Klein, D. C., 562
Klein, G., 177
Klein, G. S., 181
Klein, R. E., 57
Klein, R. H., 551
Kleinginna, A. M., 294
Kleinginna, P. R., 294
Kleitman, N., 203
Klima, E. S., 313
Klinger, E., 190
Kniskern, D. P., 552
Knoll, E., 62
Knox, V. J., 211
Kobasa, S. C., 478
Kobre, K. R., 45
Koelling, R. A., 251
Koestler, A., 444
Koffka, K., 157
Kogan, N., 442
Koh, S. O., 508
Kohlberg, L., 62, 63, 69, 71, 274
Köhler, W., 157, 159, 257
Kolata, G. B., 559
Kolb, L. C., 216
Konečni, V. J., 630, 636
Konner, M. J., 296
Koop, E., 633
Korchin, S. J., 417, 546
Kornreich, M., 558
Kosecoff, J. B., 16
Kosslyn, S. M., 323, 352
Kosterlitz, H. W., 89
Kraemer, H. C., 482

Kraft, W. A., 493
Kral, P. A., 252
Kramer, J. C., 216
Krasner, L., 521
Krebs, J. R., 247
Kübler-Ross, E., 70
Kucala, T., 469
Kuhn, M. H., 402
Kuhn, T. S., 357
Kuipers, A., 541
Kutas, M., 104

L

LaBerge, S. P., 206
Lachman, J. L., 357
Lachman, R., 328–329, 357
Lachman, S. J., 459
Laing, R. D., 522
Lambert, N. M., 434
Lambo, T. A., 533
Landis, C., 296
Lane, H., 34
Lang, P. J., 344
Lange, C., 297
Langer, E., 196
Langfeld, H. S., 137
LaPiere, R., 581
Lashley, K. S., 159, 336
Lasswell, H. D., 583
Latham, G. P., 293
Laties, V. G., 216
Lavond, D. G., 336
Lawson, J. S., 100
Lawson, K. D., 483
Layden, M. A., 614
Layzer, D., 432
Lazar, J. B., 523
Lazarus, R. S., 299, 301, 456,
  457, 462, 472–473, 476, 478,
  483
Leask, J., 324
LeDoux, J. E., 190, 200–201
Lee, M., 642
Lee, M. T., 575
Lefkowitz, M. M., 633
Leiderman, P. H., 56
Leiman, A. L., 87, 94, 129
Leirer, V. O., 329
LeMay, M., 99
Lemert, E. M., 524
Lemke, S., 480
Lemmons, P., 293
Lempers, J. S., 54
Lenneberg, E. H., 48, 50
Lepper, M. R., 291, 292, 637
Lerman, D., 288
Lerner, N. D., 248
Levenson, R., 297
Leventhal, H., 271, 300
Levesque, M. J., 480
Levine, J. D., 148
Levine, M., 349
Levinger, G., 591

Levinson, B. W., 187
Levinson, D. L., 67, 68
Levis, D. J., 541
Levy, J., 198
Levy, L. H., 440
Lewin, K., 572, 602–603
Lewine, R. R., 508
Lewinsohn, P. M., 505
Lewis, C., 58
Lewis, D., 281
Lewis, J. W., 146
Leyens, J. P., 633
Leyland, C. M., 233
Liang, M. H., 464
Libow, L. S., 69
Lidz, T., 520
Lieberman, L. R., 522
Lieberman, M. A., 550–551
Liebert, R. M., 383, 403
Liebeskind, J. C., 146
Liem, J. H., 520
Liem, R., 474
Lifter, M., 285
Lifton, P., 63
Lindhagen, K., 46
Lindsay, P. H., 123, 139
Lindsley, D. B., 298
Lindzey, G., 430, 439
Linsenmeier, J. A. W., 448
Lipsitt, L. P., 35, 36, 45
Lipsitz, A., 596
Little, M. I., 537
Livesey, P. J., 95
Locke, E. A., 293
Locke, J., 33, 43, 224
Lockhart, R. S., 326
Loehlin, J. C., 430
Loevinger, J., 62
Loftus, E. F., 331, 364, 637
Logan, F. A., 272
Loomis, A. L., 203
Lorenz, K., 56
Lovaas, O. I., 246, 544, 545
Lovibond, S. H., 610
Lowell, E. L., 286
Lown, B., 473
Loye, D., 603
Lubetkin, A. I., 631, 632
Lublin, S. C., 615
Luborsky, L., 183
Lubow, R. E., 229
Lucas, D., 333–334
Luchins, A. S., 361, 363, 571,
  573
Ludwig, A. M., 218
Luker, K. C., 358
Lumsdain, A., 583
Luria, Z., 60, 572
Lydden, D. T., 299
Lynch, G., 336

M

Maccoby, E. E., 55
Mace, W. M., 160
Machiavelli, 601
Machlowitz, M., 293
Mack, J. E., 474
MacKinnon, D. W., 444
Mackintosh, N. J., 233
Maddi, S. R., 478
Magaro, P., 445
Magnusson, D., 391
Maher, B. A., 349, 508, 512
Maier, N. R. F., 363
Maier, S. F., 246
Mair, A., 136
Malamuth, N. E., 633–634
Malone, T. W., 291, 637
Maloney, M. P., 416
Mandler, G., 296, 300, 324, 469
Manfredi, M., 145
Manson, C., 507
Mansson, H. H., 620
Marcel, A. J., 151, 188
Marek, G. R., 332
Mark, V. H., 628–629
Marks, I., 101
Marks, R., 425
Markus, H., 523
Marlatt, G. A., 218
Marler, P. R., 142
Marquis, J. N., 503
Marr, D., 162
Marshall, J., 195
Martin, C. E., 282
Martin, J. A., 45, 55
Marx, J. L., 519
Maslach, C., 300, 468, 614, 615
Maslow, A. H., 26, 27, 273–274,
  400
Mason, J. W., 462
Mason, W. A., 56
Masters, J. C., 46
Masters, W. H., 281, 282–283,
  284
Masuda, M., 471
Matarazzo, J. D., 421, 429, 446
Matlin, M., 579
Matossian, M., 514
Matson, J. L., 546–547
Matthysse, S., 243, 511
Maugh, T. H., 205
Maughan, B., 62–63
May, M. A., 62, 389
May, R., 26, 27, 400, 549–550
Mayer, G. R., 637
Mayer, J., 278
Mayer, R. E., 341
Maynard, R. F., 547
McArthur, L., 359
McCall, R. B., 429
McCarley, R. W., 206
McCarthy, S. J., 626
McClelland, D. C., 286, 440
McClintock, M. K., 142
McCloskey, M., 332
McCorduck, P., 368
McCormick, D. A., 336

McCrae, R. R., 392
McCrary, J. W., 327
McCraven, V. J., 202
McDougall, W., 269–270
McDowell, E., 240
McGaugh, J. L., 335
McGhee, P. E., 477
McGinnies, E., 182
McGregor, D., 293
McGuigan, F. J., 345
McGuire, C. V., 615
McGuire, W. J., 583, 615
McKenzie, B., 432
McKinley, J. C., 435
McLearn, G. E., 40
McNeil, D., 325
McPartland, T. S., 402
Mead, M., 270
Meador, B. D., 550
Medin, D. L., 347
Medolago, L., 145
Meehl, P. E., 419, 438, 518
Mees, H., 245
Mehrabian, A., 371
Meichenbaum, D., 26, 484, 485, 547–548
Meisner, W. W., 506–507
Meltzoff, J., 558
Melville, J., 498
Melzack, R., 146
Menzel, E. M., 256
Merrill, M. A., 426
Merton, R. K., 572
Mervis, C. B., 346, 347
Meyer, D. L, 300
Meyer, M. M., 512
Meyer, W. U., 275
Meyerhoff, J. L., 592
Michael, J., 544
Milgram, S., 354, 622–624, 625, 626, 639
Miller, D. T., 523
Miller, G. A., 313, 372
Miller, J. Z., 43
Miller, N. E., 29, 264, 271, 404–405, 464, 467, 516, 556, 629, 640
Miller, T. I., 559
Milner, B., 327, 335
Milner, P., 102
Milojkovic, J. D., 367
Minuchin, S., 552
Mischel, H. N., 390
Mischel, W., 329, 389, 390, 391, 406–408, 410, 411, 413, 505, 574
Mishkin, M., 321, 336
Moar, I., 256
Moehle, D., 596
Moeller, G., 16, 287
Modofsky, H., 496
Monahan, J., 562, 637
Monat, A., 456
Moncrieff, R. W., 141
Moniz, E., 553
Monroe, S. M., 554

Monson, T. C., 410
Montague, W. E., 319
Montessori, M., 34
Montgomery, K. D., 266
Moore, C. A., 177
Moore, G. I., 354
Moore, R. Y., 305
Moos, R., 406–407, 480
Mordkoff, A. M., 483
Morgan, A. H., 210, 211
Morgan, B. A., 89
Morgane, P. S., 204
Morris, C., 601
Morris, H. R., 89
Morris, J. J., 429
Morrissey, P., 285
Morton, J., 310
Moscovici, S., 184, 599
Moskowitz, B. A., 49, 50, 371
Motulsky, A. G., 554
Mougey, E. H., 592
Movahedi, S., 614
Movshon, J. A., 95
Mower, O. H., 467, 629
Mowrey, D. D., 543
Moyer, K. E., 629
Muir, M. S., 293
Müller, J., 76
Munroe, R. L., 391, 535
Murawski, B. J., 473
Murphy, J. M., 513
Murray, F. B., 54
Murray, H. A., 286, 440
Muskin, P. R., 499
Mussen, P. H., 70
Muzio, J. N., 205
Myers, R. E., 197

N

Nafpaktitis, M., 637
Nagel, L. E., 206
Nathanson, J. A., 89
Natsoulas, T., 189
Naus, M. J., 319
Nauta, W. J. H., 84
Neale, J. M., 383
Neisser, U., 194, 310
Nelson, K. E., 48, 343
Nelson, Z. P., 543
Nemeth, C., 599
Nerem, R. M., 480
Nerenz, D., 300
Nesselroade, J. R., 37
Neufeld, R. W. J., 457
Neugarten, B. L., 69–70
Newcomb, T. M., 390, 597, 615
Newell, A., 341, 362
Newman, L. S., 581
Nguyen, M. L., 284
Nguyen, T., 284
Nideffer, R. M., 218
Nijinsky, W., 445
Nisbett, R. E., 194–195, 278, 292, 360, 577, 578
Nixon, R., 465, 466

Noback, C. R., 94
Nobles, W. W., 513, 533
Norman, D. A., 123, 139, 193, 344, 350
Norwood, R. M., 447
Noyes, R., 80

O

Oaster, T. R., 327
Obrist, W. D., 100
Oden, M. H., 37, 444
Oden, S., 545
Oeltjen, P. D., 446
Ofshe, R., 575
Okanes, M., 601
Olds, J., 102
Ollendick, T. H., 546–547
Olton, D. S., 256
Olver, R. R., 53
O'Malley, P. M., 214
Opton, E. M., 621
Opton, E. M., Jr., 483
Orkand, R., 85
Orlando, N. J., 547, 619
Orne, M. T., 209, 211
Ornstein, P. A., 319
Ornstein, R. E., 189, 198
Orr, T. B., 440
Orwell, G., 314, 580
Oskamp, S., 634
Ouchi, W., 293

P

Paivio, A. V., 323, 352
Palmer, J. P., 331
Palmer, S. E., 165, 180
Palmonari, A., 67
Pankove, E., 442
Pappenheim, B., 534–535
Park, B., 604
Park, R. D., 240
Parke, R. D., 55, 60, 633
Parlee, M. B., 589
Parrott, J., 343
Partridge, A. J., 464
Pass, J. J., 447
Pasteur, L., 357
Patterson, F., 374, 375
Patty, R. A., 289
Paul, G. L., 541
Pavlov, I., 25, 226, 227, 236, 243, 258
Paykel, E. S., 467
Peake, P., 410
Pearlstone, Z., 324
Pearson, J., 136
Pearson, R. E., 187

Pedersen, N., 44
Pelletier, K. R., 462
Pelletier, L., 202–203
Penfield, W., 73, 101
Penick, S., 276
Peper, E., 462
Pepitone, A., 615
Peplau, L. A., 591
Perenin, M. T., 195
Perlin, S., 506
Perls, F. S., 551
Perrott Boren, M. C., 248
Perry, M. L., 335
Pershod, D., 500
Peters, T. J., 293
Peterson, J. L., 632
Peterson, L. R., 315
Peterson, M. J., 315
Peterson, R. A., 508
Petter, G., 67
Petti, T., 546–547
Pfaffman, C., 141
Pfefferbaum, A., 216
Pfungst, O., 339
Phares, E. J., 418, 428, 438
Phelps, B. H., 554
Phillips, L., 327
Piaget, J., 50–54, 62, 71, 341, 355
Pierce, C. M., 624
Pikonis, P. A., 447
Pilisuk, M., 480
Pilkonis, P. A., 448
Pinel, P., 532, 533
Pines, M., 54
Pinkerton, J., 458
Pinkston, S., 545
Pitts, F. N., 492
Pitz, G. F., 636
Place, E. J. S., 521
Platt, J., 636
Plutchik, R., 295, 397
Pomeroy, W. B., 282
Porter, L. W., 293
Posner, J. K., 54
Posner, M., 364
Posner, M. I., 193, 196
Post, D., 359
Post, F., 134
Post, R. M., 335
Postman, L. J., 327, 328, 357
Potkin, S. G., 554
Pound, E., 445
Powell, L. H., 457
Powley, T. L., 272, 278, 279
Premack, D., 244, 374
Prentice-Dunn, S., 615
Prentky, R. A., 445
Presty, S. K., 88
Pribram, K. H., 516
Price, R. H., 562
Printz, A. M., 494, 495
Proshansky, H. M., 638
Provanzano, F. J., 60, 572
Proxmire, W., 589–590
Psotka, J., 324
Pushkar, D., 208
Putnam, F. W., 212
Pylyshyn, Z. W., 323

Q

Quattrone, G. A., 578, 604

R

Rabbie, J. M., 603, 604
Rabkin, J. G., 523
Rachman, S., 283, 500
Rachman, S. J., 239
Radl, S., 447, 545
Rahe, D., 448, 546
Rahe, R. H., 471, 472
Raines, B., 240
Rasmussen, I., 44
Rawtich, A. B., 631, 632
Ray, R. L., 592
Ray, W. J., 247
Rayman, P., 474
Rayner, R., 231, 232–233
Raynor, J. O., 288
Reese, H. W., 35, 36
Reeves, A., 197
Regan, D. T., 581
Reich, P., 473
Reid, D. K., 51
Reilly, B., 45
Reinisch, J. M., 629
Reisenzein, R., 300
Reish, T., 500
Reiterman, T., 603
Rennick, P. M., 511
Rescorla, R. A., 229, 232
Reyhen, J., 210
Rice, L. N., 274
Ricci Bitti, P., 67
Richter, C. P., 204, 459
Rickert, E. J., 244
Ricks, D. F., 379
Rieder, R., 518
Rifkin, B., 229
Rigby, R. L., 374
Risley, T., 245
Rivers, L. W., 434
Robbins, I., 500
Robbins, L. C., 334
Roberts, T. B., 403
Roberts, W. A., 247
Robeson, J. G., 130
Robinson, T. E., 88
Roby, T. B., 272
Rock, I., 109, 166
Rodin, J., 14–15, 464, 481
Rodnick, E. H., 520
Roediger, H. L., 327
Roffwarg, H. P., 205
Rogers, C. R., 26–27, 274, 400–401, 404, 550
Rogers, M. P., 464
Rogers, R. W., 615
Rogoff, B., 54
Rokeach, M., 581
Roohey, M. L., 520

Roper, B. L., 439
Rorschach, H., 439–440
Rosch, E. H., 179, 346, 347, 348
Rose, R. J., 43
Rose, S., 88
Rosen, H., 62
Rosenbaum, L., 470
Rosenbaum, R. M., 290
Rosenhan, D. L., 492, 522, 625
Rosenman, R. F., 478
Rosenthal, D., 518, 519
Rosenthal, R., 17–18, 339
Rosenzweig, M. R., 87, 94, 95, 129, 336
Ross, D., 254, 631
Ross, L., 360, 577, 578, 593
Ross, M., 579
Ross, S. A., 254, 631
Rossetti, C., 337
Rossier, J., 146
Rothbart, M., 604
Rothman, D. J., 532
Rotter, J. B., 274, 389
Rousseau, J. J., 33, 43, 612
Routtenberg, A., 336
Rovee-Collier, C. K., 333–334
Rowland, N. E., 278
Rozin, P., 54, 278
Rubin, J. Z., 60, 572
Rubin, L. B., 286
Rubin, Z., 590
Rubinow, D. R., 335
Rudy, J. W., 252–253
Rumbaugh, D. M., 374
Rumelhart, D. E., 350
Rush, A. J., 548
Russell, D., 288
Russell, J. A., 638
Rutstein, J., 300, 591
Ryan, W., 578
Rychlak, J., 75
Rytina, S., 626

S

Saari, L. M., 293
Sabini, J., 627
Sachs, N. J., 636
Sacks, O., 207
Saegert, S., 61
Salzman, C., 555
Sanders, D. H., 547
Sanders, M. D., 195
Sanders, R. S., 210
Sansom, W., 208
Santee, R. T., 615
Saraf, K., 449
Sarason, I. G., 471
Sarason, S., 501
Sarnoff, I., 399, 586
Satir, V., 552
Sattler, J. M., 424
Saunders, F. A., 144
Sawin, D. B., 60
Sawyer, J., 438
Saxe, L., 637

Scadden, L., 144
Schachter, S., 278, 299–300, 585
Schaie, K. W., 69
Schank, R. C., 351
Scheier, M. F., 190
Schell, J., 621
Schiffman, S. S., 141
Schimek, J. G., 183
Schlenker, B. R., 574
Schlesinger, H. J., 181
Schlossberg, H., 296
Schneider, A., 335
Schneider, D. J., 574
Schneider, G. E., 121
Schneider, J. A., 482
Schneider, W., 54
Schneidman, E. S., 70, 506
Schrag, P., 580
Schreiber, F., 212
Schroeder, D. A., 635
Schulsinger, F., 518
Schwartz, G. E., 482
Schwartz, P., 285
Scott, J. P., 38, 56
Scott, R. A., 522, 523
Scott, V., 491
Seager, C. P., 506
Sears, P., 37, 70
Sears, R. R., 37, 70, 467, 628, 629
Sebastian, R. J., 633
Seboek, T. A., 339
Selby, J. W., 469
Seligman, M. E. P., 246, 251, 492, 506
Selman, R., 54
Selye, H., 460, 461–462, 464, 465
Semes, J., 159
Shafer, R., 399
Shaffer, R. E., 100
Shakespeare, W., 78, 189, 442, 500, 614
Shapiro, A. K., 464
Shaw, B. F., 548
Shaw, J. C., 341
Shaw, K. N., 293
Sheehy, G., 67
Sheffield, F., 583
Sheffield, F. D., 272
Sheingold, K., 332
Sheldon, W., 386–387, 412
Shepard, R. N., 351, 352, 442
Sheridan, C. L., 624
Sherif, C. W., 568, 604–605
Sherif, M., 183–184, 595–596, 604–605
Sherman, J. A., 542
Sherman, M., 524
Sherman, S. M., 128
Sherrington, C., 76–77
Sherrod, K., 56

Shettlesworth, S. J., 251
Shields, J., 554
Shields, J. L., 478
Shiffrin, R. M., 326
Shigetomi, C. C., 562
Shor, R. E., 210
Shortliffe, E. H., 368
Shotter, J., 571
Siegel, A. W., 354
Siegel, J. M., 471
Siegel, S., 243
Sikes, J., 637
Silberfeld, M., 480
Silver, M., 627
Silver, R., 468
Silverman, L. H., 399
Simmel, E. C., 66
Simmel, M., 576
Simon, H. A., 26, 341, 362, 367
Simon, N. G., 629
Simon, T., 424, 425
Sinclair, J. D., 307
Singer, J., 299–300
Singer, J. E., 481, 615
Singer, J. L., 190, 202
Siple, P. A., 313
Siqueland, E. R., 47
Sjoberg, B. M., 210
Skeels, H. M., 46, 432
Skinner, B. F., 25, 49, 235, 237–238, 247, 249, 259, 264, 372, 402, 409
Slater, P. C., 305
Sloane, R. B., 539, 558
Slobin, D., 373
Slovic, P., 360
Smallberg, S. A., 335
Smith, D., 493, 550
Smith, E. E., 347
Smith, G., 276
Smith, J., 497
Smith, M. L., 558–559
Smith, R. S., 57
Smith, S. M., 372
Smith, T. W., 89
Snapp, M., 637
Snow, C. P., 621
Snowden, C. T., 279
Snyder, C. R., 600, 614
Snyder, C. R. R., 196
Snyder, M., 320, 349, 574, 575
Snyder, S. H., 89, 243, 517, 556
Socoly, F., 579
Solomon, M. R., 596
Sorenson, E. R., 295
Souza, D. O., 335
Spanos, N. P., 514
Spelke, E., 194
Spence, D. P., 183
Sperling, G., 310–311
Sperry, R. W., 24, 95, 190, 197
Spiegler, M. D., 403
Spiesman, J. C., 483
Spinelli, D. N., 95
Spiro, R. J., 328, 330
Spitz, R. A., 57
Spitzer, R., 494
Springer, S. P., 100, 198

Sprinzen, M., 614–615
Spuhler, J. N., 430
Squire, L. R., 305
Staats, A. W., 233
Staats, C. K., 233
Stalin, J., 360
Stampfl, T. G., 541
Stang, D., 579
Strangler, R. S., 494, 495
Stanley, J., 427
Staples, F. R., 539, 558
Stapp, J., 10, 615
Staub, E., 406
Steers, R. M., 293
Steinhorst, R., 244
Steinmetz, J., 593
Steller, E., 276
Stenback, A., 69
Stenham, U., 193
Stephan, C., 637
Stern, P., 581
Stern, R. M., 247
Stern, W. C., 204
Sternbach, R. A., 147
Sternberg, R. J., 428
Sternberg, S., 316–317, 343
Stevens, C. F., 77, 85
Stevens, S. S., 118, 119
Stewart, J. M., 56
Stinson, J., 601
Stolz, S. B., 473
Stone, G. C., 465
Stoppard, T., 640
Storms, M., 579
Storms, M. D., 283
Strauss, J. S., 508
Strauss, M. S., 48
Strom, D., 285
Stromeyer, D. F., 324
Strong, E. K., 446
Stroop, J. R., 196
Strupp, H. H., 537, 558
Stuart, R. B., 543
Suedfeld, P., 208, 586
Sullivan, H. S., 397, 538, 564
Sullivan, M. W., 333–334
Sulzer-Azaroff, B., 637
Summers, R., 335
Sundberg, N. D., 428, 446
Swann, W. B., Jr., 349
Sweet, W. H., 628–629
Swets, J. A., 115
Swift, J., 611
Syme, S. L., 480
Szasz, T. S., 522, 530, 533

T
Tannehill, R. S., 100
Tart, C. T., 201, 217
Taylor, B., 626
Taylor, C. B., 482
Taylor, D., 591
Taylor, J. A., 267

Taylor, R., 320
Taylor, S. E., 359, 465, 579, 614–615
Taylor, S. P., 631, 632
Taylor, W., 136
Teasdale, J., 239
Teasdale, J. D., 246, 320
Teevan, R., 289
Teitelbaum, P., 102, 104, 250
Telch, M. J., 484
Tellegen, A., 203
Tenney, Y. J., 332
Tenopyr, M. L., 446
Terman, L. M., 16, 36–37, 70, 425, 426, 444
Terrace, H., 374
Thatcher, M., 177, 178
Thibaut, J. W., 588, 596
Thienes-Hontos, P., 469
Thigpen, C. H., 212
Thomas, C. B., 479
Thomas, M. H., 633
Thompson, D. A., 278
Thompson, M. J., 203
Thompson, R. F., 336
Thoresen, C. E., 478, 484
Thorndike, E. L., 235–236, 238, 257, 258, 425
Thorndyke, P. W., 354
Thornton, E. M., 535
Timiras, P. S., 465
Tinklepaugh, O. L., 256
Titchener, E. B., 189–190
Toch, H., 630, 637
Tolman, E. C., 255–256, 257, 346, 353
Toman, J. E. P., 372
Tompkins, S., 297, 301
Tontlewicz, J., 95
Toscanini, A., 332
Tourangeau, R., 297
Townsend, J. T., 317
Treisman, A. M., 192, 194
Tresemer, D. W., 289
Trevarthen, C., 198
Triandis, H. C., 67, 513
Triplett, N., 594
Tronick, E., 45
Trulson, M. E., 217
Tryon, W. W., 389
Tuason, V. B., 299
Tucker, O. M., 101
Tulving, E., 321, 324
Turnbull, C., 174–175
Turner, J. A., 583, 584
Tursky, B., 147
Turvey, M. T., 311
Tversky, A., 358–359, 360
Tversky, B., 354
Twain, M., 393
Tyler, L. E., 386, 429, 446

U
Ullmann, L. P., 521
Ultan, R., 372
Underwood, B., 618
Underwood, B. J., 333
Uranowitz, S. W., 575

V
Vaillant, G. E., 67, 68
Valins, S., 480, 560
Valle, V. A., 290
Valsinger, J., 38
Van Doren, T., 500
Van Gogh, V., 445
Van Riper, C., 19
Van Sluyters, R. C., 95
Van Wagener, W., 197
Vardaris, R. M., 631, 632
Vasareley, V., 158
Vasari, G., 172
Vaughan, E., 7, 9
Vaughan, F., 401
Verma, S. K., 500
Verma, V. K., 500
Vernon, P. E., 432
Veroff, J., 531
Vietze, P., 56
Vigorito, J., 47
Vinsel, A., 587
Vogel, F., 554
Voltaire, 508
von Békésy, G., 23, 139
von Hofsten, C., 46
Vonnegut, K., 508
Vonnegut, M., 508–509
Von Wright, J. M., 193

W
Wachtel, P. L., 182
Wagner, A. R., 229, 252–253
Walder, L. O., 633
Waldron, I., 478
Waldvogel, S., 334
Wallach, L., 538
Wallach, M. A., 429, 538
Wallis, C., 145
Walsh, R. N., 401
Walster, E. H., 588, 591
Walster, G. W., 591
Walters, C. C., 240
Walters, R. G., 281
Walters, R. H., 240
Wanous, J. P., 447
Ward, L. M., 638
Ward, M. P., 416
Ward, W. C., 442
Warington, E. K., 195
Warnick, R. K., 88
Warshaw, L., 456
Washburn, A. L., 276
Wason, P. C., 349
Waterman, R. H., Jr., 293
Watson, C. G., 469
Watson, J., 74
Watson, J. B., 25, 190, 231, 232–233, 270, 371–372
Watson, R. I., Jr., 617
Watson, S. J., 519
Watzlawick, P., 560
Weakland, J. H., 521, 560

Weaver, R. G., 79
Webb, W. B., 190, 204
Weber, A. W., 448
Weber, E., 116–117
Wechsler, D., 427
Weigel, R. H., 581
Weil, A. T., 200, 465
Weil, E., 213
Weiner, B., 288, 290
Weiner, M. J., 604
Weingartner, H., 335
Weins, A. N., 421
Weisenberg, M., 146
Weiskrantz, L., 195
Weiss, B., 216
Weiss, M., 5
Weiss, R. S., 587
Weiss, S. M., 478
Weiss, W., 583
Weld, H. P., 137
Welker, R. L., 252
Wells, H. G., 435
Welner, A., 500
Welner, J., 518
Wender, P. H., 518
Werner, E. E., 57
Wertheimer, M., 157, 163
Wessman, A. E., 294, 379
West, S. G., 633
Wever, E. G., 140
Whalen, R., 629
Wheatley, K. L., 252
Whipple, K., 539
White, B. J., 604–605
White, B. W., 144
White, C. A., 533, 560
White, D., 5, 641
White, G. L., 300, 591
White, M. D., 533, 560
White, P., 320
Whitlow, T., 609–610
Whitman, C., 628–629
Whorf, B. L., 372
Wickelgren, W. A., 361
Wicker, A. W., 581
Wicklund, R. A., 582, 615
Wienske, K., 276
Wiesel, T. N., 24, 129, 133, 162
Wig, N. H., 500
Wiggins, J. S., 416
Wilcoxin, L. A., 541
Wilcoxon, H. G., 252
Wilder, D. A., 604
Wilkins, G., 604
Willer, J. C., 460
Williams, J. H., 60
Williams, R. L., 434
Wills, T. A., 586
Wilson, C. C., 423
Wilson, D. H., 200–201
Wilson, E. D., 197
Wilson, E. O., 628
Wilson, G. T., 559
Wilson, J. M., 324
Wilson, J. P., 468
Wilson, M., 596
Wilson, T. D., 194–196, 360
Winer, B., 601
Wing, C. W., 429
Wingfield, A., 317, 327
Winkler, J. D., 614–615

Wintrob, R. M., 513
Wise, C. D., 554
Wispé, L. G., 181
Witkin, H. A., 176, 177, 182
Wittkower, E. D., 463
Wolf, K., 57
Wolf, M., 245
Wolitzky, D. L., 182
Wolk, R. D., 43
Wolman, C., 562
Wolpe, J., 540, 541
Wood, R. D., 620
Woods, D. L., 345
Woodworth, R. S., 265, 296
Woolridge, D. E., 90
Wortman, E., 468
Wright, F. E., 604
Wundt, W., 6, 25, 189, 341, 380, 638
Wurtman, R. J., 38, 82, 94
Wyatt, R. J., 554
Wylie, R. C., 401
Wynne, L. C., 520

Y

Yahraes, H., 518–519
Yarrow, L., 60
Yerkes, R. M., 425
Yorkston, N. J., 539, 558
Young, P. T., 294
Younken, D., 100
Yudkin, M., 474
Yukl, G. A., 239

Z

Zadeh, L. A., 347
Zajonc, R. B., 300–301, 411, 588, 594
Zanchetti, A., 298
Zanna, M. P., 581
Zarcone, V. P., Jr., 206
Zborowski, M., 147
Zeiss, R. A., 468
Zeman, B., R., 54
Zetin, M., 305
Zilboorg, G., 532
Zill, N., 632
Ziller, R. C., 614
Zimbardo, P. G., 13, 134, 266, 294, 447, 449, 509, 545, 585–586, 610, 616, 627, 640, 642
Zimmerman, R. R., 58
Zubeck, J. P., 208
Zuckerman, M., 272
Zurcher, L. A., 403

SUBJECT INDEX

A

Ability, assessing, 428, 430, 446, 447, 452
Abnormal behavior, 488–525, 546; and culture, 513; defining, 492–493; and judgments, 521–524; models of, 512–521; therapy for, 526–564; types of, 494–512. *See also* Psychopathology, Social Pathology
Abortion, 554
Absolute threshold, 113–114, 116, 132, 135, 136, 148
Abstract thinking, 53, 71, 318, 321, 323, 428, 452, 511
Academic success, predicting, 417, 419, 429, 452
Acceptance, 295, 538, 551
Accommodation: in thinking, 51, 54, 355, 375; in vision, 120
Acetylcholine, 87
Achievement, 286–294, 302, 428, 429, 478, 506; intrinsic/extrinsic motivation, 290–292; need for, 263, 286–290, 302, 440; and situation, 406–407; testing, 419, 420, 446, 452
Acoustic encoding, 313, 326, 327, 337
Acquired drives, 271
Acquisition, in conditioning, 228–229
Acromegaly, 261
ACTH, 335, 460, 462
Action, and coping with stress, 458–461, 476, 478
Action potential, 85, 86
Activity level, 266, 271
Actor-observer bias, 578–579, 606
Actual self, 401
Acupuncture, 146
Acute schizophrenia, 509
Adaptive flexibility, 410
Adaptiveness, and intelligence, 428, 430, 452
Addiction, 89, 214, 216, 220, 242, 243, 494, 539, 542, 557, 564
Adequacy, feelings of, 65, 408
Adolescence, 403, 495, 520, 543; and cognition, 53–54; and development, 35, 39, 53–54, 60, 66–67, 71; and drug usage, 213–214; and hypnotizability, 210; and parents, 214, 596; and peer pressure, 214, 596; and psychopathology, 496, 510, 520; and shyness, 448
Adrenal cortex, 81, 460, 462
Adrenal gland, 261, 460
Adrenal medulla, 81, 459
Adrenalin, 81, 459
Adrenocorticotrophic hormone, 335, 460, 462
Adulthood: and hypnotizability, 210; and personality, 403; and sleep, 205; tasks of, 35, 39, 67–69, 71, 519
Affect, 45, 504, 512. *See also* Emotions
Affection, 585, 589, 591, 606
Affective disorders, 497, 504–506, 524, 525, 554

Afferent neurons, 83, 90, 106
Affiliation, 568, 585–587, 606
Afterimages, 126, 127, 133
Age: and development, 35–39; and sleep needs, 205
Aggression, 419–420, 500, 539, 627–634, 639; and alcohol or drugs, 631–632; and anonymity and dehumanization, 615–617, 618; and the brain, 27, 97, 628–629, 639; causes of, 27, 627–634, 639; defined, 627; displaced, 467, 630, 639; and frustration, 467, 627, 639; and human nature, 24, 270, 546, 610, 611, 613; and hormones, 283, 629; as instinct, 394, 627–628, 639; intergroup, 604, 605, 607; as learned, 254, 255, 627, 630–633, 639; physiological basis of, 627, 628–629; and pornography, 633–634; in prison, 609–610, 613; in psychodynamic theory, 270, 392, 394, 397, 398; sexual, 633–634; and stress, 466–467, 482, 486; and sudden murderers, 641; and TV, 632–633, 639. *See also* Violence
Aging, and stress, 464–465, 486
Agoraphobia, 498, 530, 541
Alcohol and alcohol abuse, 189, 208, 213, 215, 216, 217–218, 220, 283, 335, 491, 494, 556; and aggression, 631–632; and stress, 464, 468, 474, 476, 477, 487
Algorithms, 364
Alienation, 450, 468, 617, 619, 639
Alpha temperament, 479
Alzheimer's disease, 336
Ambiguity: in perception, 156, 158–159, 168, 185; in projective tests, 439, 440, 452
American Psychological Association (APA), 9, 10, 436
"Ames chair," 168–169, 173
"Ames room," 173
Amino acids, 87, 89
Amnesia, 305–306, 327, 333, 335, 501–502, 525; hypnotic, 209, 220, 337
Amphetamines, 88, 215, 216, 335
Amplitude: of sound wave, 135, 140, 149; of variables, 228
Amygdala, 97, 98, 335, 336, 629
Anal fixation, 65, 382
Anal stage of development, 64, 71
Analgesia, 146, 147
Analysis, level of, 22–23, 27
Analysis of resistance, 535, 536, 563
Analysis of transference, 535, 546, 563
Analytic psychology, 398
Analytical processing, 197, 198, 220
Androgens, 280, 283
Angel dust (PCP), 88
Anger, 295, 297, 299, 455, 467, 470, 473, 474, 484, 487, 508
Animals: aggression in, 628; communication among, 339–340; and stress, 460, 462

Animistic approach, 74
Anonymity, 614, 615–617, 639
Anorexia nervosa, 277, 279, 496, 527
Anterior pituitary, 462
Anterograde amnesia, 335
Antianxiety drugs, 556–557, 564
Antibody production, 464
Anticipation, 295, 343
Anticipatory anxiety, 500
Anticonformity, 600
Antidepressant drugs, 556, 557, 564
Antipsychotic drugs, 556, 564
Antisocial behavior, 609, 616, 618, 628, 639
Antisocial personality disorders, 495–496
Anxiety, 35, 69, 187, 196, 216, 283, 448, 586, 612; anticipatory, 500; hierarchy of, 540–541; and motivation, 267, 274; and personality, 403, 408; in psychodynamic theory, 396, 397, 399, 413, 534, 563; as psychopathology, 489, 496, 497–500, 504, 507, 516, 521; and stress, 460, 467, 470, 474, 478, 482, 487; treatment of, 540–541, 553, 556–557, 558–559, 563
Anxiety disorders, 491, 492, 497–500, 517, 524–525
Anxiety states, 498, 499–500, 525
Apathy, 69, 290
Aplysia, 91–92
Apparent motion, 166
Appearance, physical, 447
Appeasement gestures, 628
Appetite, 216, 461, 496, 504
Appetitive conditioning, 231
Applied research, 10
Apprehension, feelings of, 498, 499, 525
Aptitudes, 416, 417, 420, 428, 446, 452
Archetype, 398, 413
Archival data, 15–16, 30, 421, 451
Arousal: and aggression, 630–631, 632; and burnout, 467–468; emotional, 97, 298, 299–300, 301, 586, 630; and loving, 590–591; and motivation, 261, 271, 272, 290, 294, 302; and personality, 378, 396, 399; sexual, 280–282, 283, 284, 285, 302, 399, 503; and stress, 458–462, 463, 466, 467, 469–470, 482, 483.
Artificial intelligence (AI), 367–368, 369
Artificial languages, 371, 376
Assertiveness, 287, 447, 545, 546
Assessment, 380, 414–452; of behavior, 439; in China, 416; of creativity, 441–445; ethics of, 450–451; formal vs. informal, 418, 451; of IQ, 424–434; methods of, 418–423; of personality, 379, 435–441; of shyness, 447–450; vocational, 446–447

Assimilation, 51, 54; in memory, 331; in thinking, 355, 375

Association areas, of brain, 97

Associational stage, and skills, 364, 365

Associations: and conditioning, 223–224, 243, 247, 253, 254, 255–257, 258, 259, 387; law of, 224, 258; and memory, 319–320, 327; and motivation, 271; and personality, 410; and sex, 283–284; and skills, 365; and thinking, 339. See also Conditioning

Atomism vs. holism, 157

Attachment, 55–59, 63, 64, 69, 71

Attachment needs, 273

Attention: and affiliation and attribution, 579, 585; desire for, 241, 393, 495; and memory, 312, 313, 337, 353; narrowing of, and stress, 469, 487; and perception, 183, 190–194, 219, 220; and psychopathology, 499, 501, 511, 521

Attentive processing, 194

Attitudes, 55, 225, 359, 456, 572, 637, 644; assessing, 416; changing, 582–584, 597, 606; and society, 568, 572, 580–584, 592, 594–595, 597, 606, 607; and stress, 456, 457, 477, 478, 487; and therapy, 547–549, 557–558, 564

Attraction, interpersonal, 585–591, 606

Attribution theory, 275, 302

Attributions: biases and errors in, 577–579, 593, 606; and motivation, 274, 275

Audition. See Hearing

Auditory cortex, 98, 139

Auditory memory, 310, 311

Auditory nerve, 139

Authoritarian personality, 382

Authority: obedience to, 609, 611, 612, 621–627, 639; power of, 609–610; resentment of, 609; structure, 625–627

Authority figure, 622, 625

Autism, 466, 491, 544, 545

Autocratic leadership, 602, 603, 607

Autohypnosis, 209, 212

Autokinetic effect, 183, 596

"Automatic thoughts," 548–549

Automatic writing or talking, 211

Autonomic hyperactivity, 499

Autonomic nervous system, 79, 80, 81, 106, 231, 279, 298, 382, 387, 458–461, 463, 469, 483, 486

Autonomous stage, and skills, 364, 365

Autonomy, 14–15, 287, 403, 481, 560, 614; and psychopathology, 496, 507, 519; vs. self-doubt, 65, 71

Availability heuristics, 359, 360, 376

Aversion therapy, 542, 564

Aversive conditioning, 231, 259

Avoidance behavior, 145, 240, 241, 267

Axon, 83, 84, 85, 86, 87, 88, 94, 106, 121, 336

B

Babbling stage, 47–48, 71

Backward conditioning, 229

Backward masking, 311

Bait shyness, 251, 279

Bar graphs, 647

Barbiturates, 88, 215, 216, 556

Basal ganglia striatum, 336

Baseline rate, 423, 439

Basic levels, of concepts, 348

Basic reaction tendencies, 43

Basic research, 10

Basilar membrane, 136, 138, 139

Bayley Scale of Infant Development, 35

Bedlam, 532

Behavior: abnormal, 488–525; aggressive, 27, 627–634; and attitudes, 580–583, 606; and biological factors, 23, 43, 80–82, 106, 265, 270, 277–279, 514–515, 525, 553, 629; and the brain, 92–106; determinants of, 21, 27; and development, 32–71; group, 592–607; historic views of, 74–76; innate, 295–296, 302, 393, 394–395, 397, 411; laws of, 6; and role playing, 596–597, 613–614; and social learning theory, 405–409, 410, 413, 630–633; and status, 574–575; and stress, 466–467, 470, 486; therapy to modify, 421, 516, 526–564; variability in, 265, 390–391

Behavior assessment, 439, 452

Behavior dispositions, 580

Behavior genetics, 40

Behavior modification, 539. See also Behavior therapy

Behavior potential, 225

Behavior ratings, 448–449

Behavior sampling, 443, 452

Behavior therapy, 529, 530, 539–547, 558, 559, 564

Behavioral contingency, 238, 245, 247, 250

Behavioral contracts, 543, 545, 564

Behavioral medicine, 464, 465, 563

Behavioral reactions, and emotions, 297, 302

Behavioral rehearsal, 545, 564

Behavioral-situational specificity, 390

Behaviorism, 23, 24–25, 27, 31; and consciousness, 190; and motivation, 264, 301; and personality theories, 402–403, 404–405, 409, 411, 413; and psychopathology, 516, 517

Beliefs, 410, 465, 506, 525, 580, 582, 606; changing, 548–549, 598; and groups, 580, 582, 598, 606. See also Attitudes

Belonging, feeling of, 551

Bem Sex-Role Inventory (BSRI), 642, 645–649, 653

Benzene, 351

Benzodiazepines, 556

Beta-endorphin, 87, 89

Beta temperament, 479

Bias, 386, 393, 424, 436; in attribution, 577–579, 606; in assessment, 422, 429, 434, 450; in decision making, 358–360, 575, 627; experimenter, 17–18, 30; in-group, 603–605; in recall, 330, 332, 337, 471; and mental illness, 521, 522, 524

Bilateral speech control, 100

Binocular cues, 168–169

Binocular disparity, 168–169, 170, 173, 175, 185

Biochemical factors: and behavior, 23, 78, 80–82, 106, 553, 629; and memory, 327, 334, 335–336, 337; and psychopathology, 504–506, 514–515, 517, 519, 521, 525; and stress, 459–464

Biofeedback, 246–247, 259, 482–483, 487

Biological clock, 203–204

Biological factors: and aggression, 628–629; and behavior, 43, 265, 270, 277–279, 479, 514–515, 525; and conditioning, 250–252; and language, 50; and sex, 280–283

Biological needs, 273, 274, 302

Biological model of mental illness, 514–515, 525

Biomedical therapy, 529, 530, 533, 553–557, 560, 563, 564

Bionic ear, 139

Bipolar cells, 121

Birth cohort, 37

Blacks, 425, 430, 434, 450, 470, 620

Blind responses. See Rote responses

Blind spot, 121

Blindness, 134, 144, 393, 501

Blindsight, 195

Blocking, and learning, 252, 253, 254, 255, 259

Blood-brain barrier, 214

Blood pressure, 216, 246, 283, 459, 482, 483. See also Hypertension

Bodily-kinesthetic ability, 430, 431

Body humors, 386

Body image, 217, 218, 496

Body language, 50, 371, 574–575

Body senses, 142–145, 149

Body temperature, 89, 97, 144

Boehm Test of Basic Concepts (BTBC), 434

"Bottom-up" processes: and attention, 193, 220; and memory, 307, 312; and perception, 155, 176–177, 184; and thinking, 367

Bradykinin, 145

Brain, 92–106, 142, 494; and aggression, 27, 628–629, 639; and behavior, 76, 92–106; and biomedical therapies, 553–557, 560; and consciousness, 197–198, 219, 220; and deprivation, 38, 94, 208; and drugs, 88, 89, 208, 214, 217, 553, 556; and emotion, 101, 296, 297, 298; evolution and development of, 42, 92–95, 219; and food intake, 276–278; functions of, 95–102; and hearing, 138–139; hemisphere specialization in, 98, 99–101, 106, 197–199; and language, 98, 100, 101; and memory, 73, 92, 101, 106, 305, 307, 309, 321, 327, 334–335, 336; and neural activity, 76, 78–79, 84, 86, 90, 104, 106; and pain, 97, 145–146; and perception, 152, 159, 166; and psychopathology, 494, 504, 508, 514–515, 516, 519, 524, 525; during sleep, 203, 204–205, 206; and stress, 459–461, 482; structure of, 95–102; tumors, 261, 294, 628–629, 639; and vision, 98, 104, 121–122, 128

Brain damage, 99, 100, 102, 103, 337, 494, 504, 508, 515, 525; and consciousness, 197; and perception, 151, 156–157
Brain lesions, 101, 102, 106, 299, 336
Brain opiates, 89, 146, 460, 519
Brain scans, 104–105, 190
Brain stem, 97, 139, 206
Brain surgery, 100–101, 189, 197–198, 200
Brain-wave patterns, 104, 190, 203, 341; controlling, 246–247; and memory, 327; and schizophrenia, 511; and sleep, 203, 204; and thought, 345, 375
Brightness, 111, 123, 124, 125, 128, 149
Bulimia, 277, 279, 496
Burnout, 465, 467, 470, 487, 618

C

Caffeine, 88, 215, 216
California Personality Inventory (CPI), 435, 438–439, 452
Calpain, 336
Cancer, 369, 464, 456, 479
Cardinal traits, 388, 412
Cardiovascular problems, and stress, 471, 473, 474, 477, 478, 479, 484, 487
Career choice, 435, 445, 446–447
Caring, 63, 284, 467–468, 538, 550
Case study approach, 383–384, 412
Castration anxiety, 399
Catastrophes, 473, 487
Catatonic schizophrenia, 510, 511
Catch trials, 115
Catecholamines, 87, 629
Categorizing, 46, 346, 347–348, 350, 359, 410
Catharsis: and aggression, 628, 630, 632–633, 639; in therapy, 535, 536, 563
Causality, 18, 19–20, 650
Cell body, 83, 85, 86, 87, 94, 97, 106
Cell differentiation, 77, 106
Central nervous system (CNS), 73, 74, 76, 78–79, 83, 106, 146, 278, 482; and attention, 190; and biomedical therapy, 529, 553, 554; and the brain, 92–106, 111; and conditioning, 234–235; and drugs, 88, 214, 215; and eating, 278, 279; and schizophrenia, 219
Central tendency, 647–648
Central traits, 388, 412
Centrism, in thinking, 52
Cephalic responses, 272
Cerebellum, 97, 336
Cerebral cortex, 113, 336. See also Cortex
Cerebral dominance, 99–101
Cerebral hemispheres, 96, 97, 98–101, 106, 197–199, 200–201, 217, 220
Cerebrospinal fluid, 97
Cerebrum, 94, 96, 97
Chaining, 245–246, 259
Character and character types, 382
Checklists, in assessment, 423, 449
Chemical senses, 141–142, 149

Chemotherapy, 335, 519, 529, 555–557, 560, 564
Children and childhood: abused, 212, 491, 502, 514, 626; adopted, 433, 517; aggression in, 628, 632–633; aggression toward, 630; and attractiveness, 588; autistic, 466, 491, 544; cognitive development of, 51–53, 71, 354, 369–370; and conditioning, 231, 236, 244, 245; development in, 39, 47–53, 55–65, 393–394, 534, 538; and hypnotizability, 210; and IQ tests, 429–432, 434, 452; language development of, 47–50, 219; and memory, 312, 319, 334; modeling, 406–408; moral development of, 61–63, 71; and mothers, 45, 538; and parents, 55–60, 572; and personality, 382, 384, 403, 411; and psychopathology, 503; of retarded mothers, 562–563; schizophrenic, 245, 538; and sleep, 205; and social isolates, 545–546; socialization of, 55–61, 71, 545–547; and stress, 470, 474
Chlorpromazine, 9, 555, 556, 564
Choice: importance of, 26, 29, 31, 439, 612; and death, 14–15, 481
Chromosomes, 40
Chronic stress, 457, 461–462, 486
Chronological age (CA), and IQ tests, 38, 425, 426
Chronoscope, 345
Chunking and chunks, 313, 314–315, 316, 318, 322, 326, 337, 365, 367
Circadian rhythm, 203, 220
Classical conditioning, 226–233, 238, 239, 242, 243, 247, 250, 258
Classification: and expert systems, 368, 376; and memory, 312; and mental disorders, 490, 493–494, 495, 497, 499, 504, 510, 521, 524; and perception, 112, 148, 152–153, 154–155, 156, 176–184, 185, 194
Clever Hans, 339–340, 374
Client-centered therapy, 400, 550, 559
Clinical psychologist and psychology, 10, 212, 416, 417, 427, 490, 492, 521, 524, 531, 563
Closure, 162
Co-acting group, 594
Cocaine, 215, 216
Cochlea, 138, 140, 149
"Cocktail party effect," 192
Codeine, 215
Cognition, 50–55, 396; in adolescents, 53–54; and behavior, 25–26; and the brain, 101; and conditioning, 252–256, 257–258, 259; distortion in, 505–506; of elderly, 69–70; and emotion, 294–295, 297–298, 299–300, 302; images in, 323–324; in infants, 50–55, 71, 343, 354; and language, 371–374; and motivation, 274–275, 302; and personality, 405, 409–411, 413; and psychopathology, 505–506, 516–517, 520, 525; and reasoning, 53; and shyness, 447; and stress, 456–458, 469–470, 483–484, 486, 487; and thinking, 51, 340–346
Cognitive appraisal, and stress, 456–458, 462, 470, 475, 483, 486, 487
Cognitive behavior modification, 547–548
Cognitive development, 50–55, 71
Cognitive dissonance, 582, 606
Cognitive distortion, and depression, 505–506

Cognitive interference, 196
Cognitive maps, 256, 346, 353–354, 375
Cognitive model: and development, 23, 25–26, 27, 31; and psychopathology, 516–517, 525
Cognitive needs, 273
Cognitive preparation, 547
Cognitive psychology, 340, 346, 354, 367, 368, 372–373, 375, 376
Cognitive rational-emotive therapy, 547, 549, 559, 564
Cognitive reorganization, 450
Cognitive restructuring, 484–485, 487
Cognitive science, 341
Cognitive skills, 364–370, 376, 430
Cognitive social learning therapy, 384, 410, 411
Cognitive style, 177
Cognitive theories: of personality, 409–411, 412, 413; of thinking, 340–341
Cognitive therapies, 529, 547–549, 558, 559, 560, 564
Cognitive triad of depression, 505
Collective unconscious, 398, 413
Color, 122–128, 148–149
Color blindness, 126, 127
Common traits, 388
Communication, 371–375, 376, 480, 612; animal, 373–375, 376; and development, 58–59; faulty, and schizophrenia, 520–521; and group, 571, 592, 595, 606; improving, 552, 560; and persuasion, 580, 583–584; through smell, 141–142
Community treatment centers, 547, 561, 563
Companionate love, 591
Compartmentalization, 396
Compensation, 396, 398, 413
Competencies, 290, 291, 292, 424, 457, 505, 612; vs. inferiority, 65, 68, 71; and personality, 408, 410, 411, 413
Competitiveness, 406–407, 478, 479, 481, 487, 603, 604, 637
Complementary colors, 125–126
Complementary traits, 587–588, 606
Completion, in assessment, 439
Complexity; and creativity, 444; of sound wave, 135, 149
Compliance, 196, 598, 606, 614, 626, 639
Comprehension, 355–357, 373, 375
Compulsions, 496, 497, 500, 539, 553
Compulsive personality disorder, 495
Computer: compared to human mind, 307, 341, 342, 366, 367–368, 375, 376, 613, 637; use of, in assessment, 435, 452
Concentration, and problems in, 216, 466, 468, 499, 504
Concept formation, 348–349
Concepts, 346–349, 350, 372, 375, 428
Concordance rates, and schizophrenia, 518
Concrete operational stage, 51, 53, 71
Conditional positive regard, 400
Conditional rules, and concepts, 349
Conditioned reinforcers, 242, 244, 245, 246, 259, 280

Conditioned response (CR), 229, 230, 234, 247, 253, 258, 336

Conditioned stimulus, 227–234, 242, 243, 246, 252, 253, 258, 267, 283, 302

Conditioning, 221–259; aversive, 231, 259; and biofeedback, 246–247, 259, 482–483; biological factors in, 250–252; classical, 226–233, 238, 242, 243, 247, 250, 258; cognitive influences on, 252–256, 257–258, 259; and immunological system, 234; instrumental, 236–237, 258; operant, 234–249, 250, 256, 258, 259; paradigms of, 227, 238–242; second-order, 231–233, 252, 253, 254; and sexual deviance, 503

Conditioning trial, 228

Conflict, 623, 624, 632; and humanistic model, 400, 403, 551; intergroup, 598–599, 603, 604, 605, 637; in psychodynamic model, 24, 270, 379, 395, 397, 398, 399, 529, 534, 546, 563; and psychopathology, 501, 502, 516, 525, 612

Conformity, 392, 592, 593, 597, 598, 599, 601–602, 607, 621–627

Conjunctive rules, and concepts, 349

Conscience, 395

Consciousness, 73, 76, 88, 186–220, 283, 501, 525, 533, 535, 536; characteristics of states of, 218; defined, 188, 189, 219; duality of, 197–199; and forgetting, 332, 333, 334; and motives, 264, 270, 301; and perception, 181, 183; and personality, 395, 396, 411, 413; and thought, 341–342, 353

Consensual validation, 189, 207, 585, 606

Consensus criterion, 577, 606

Conservation: and cognition, 53, 54, 357; group norms, 597

Consistency: internal, 419; and perception, 172–175; in personality, 381, 383, 388, 389–391, 392–393, 401, 404, 412, 413, 417; and thinking, 355, 357, 361

Consolidation and memory, 335, 337

Constancies, in perception, 172–175, 185, 511

Constitutional factors, 43. See also Vulnerability

Construct validity, 419–420, 449

Construction, in assessment, 439

Constructions of reality, 189, 219

Constructs, 409–410, 411, 413

Context: and behavior, 522, 525; dependence, 320; and drug effects, 217–218; and memory, 312, 320, 321, 324, 328, 337; and perception, 179–180, 185; social, 568, 569, 570–571, 578, 581, 606; therapeutic, 529–531

Contingency management, 539, 542–544, 564

Contingent relationships; and conditioning, 238, 245, 247, 250; and depression, 505–506

Continuity: of development, 38; in vision, 132–133

Control: biofeedback, 246–247, 259, 482–483, 487; external vs. internal, 288, 290, 291, 302, 587; loss of, and death, 14–15, 464; lack of, in research, 383–384; need for, 14–15, 246, 464, 465, 516, 560; by psychologist, 9–10; in research, 383, 384; of stress, 456, 464, 481–486, 487

Control group, 14, 15, 30, 291, 385

Control procedures, 13–16, 25

Conventional morality, 63

Convergence, and perception, 169, 173, 185

Convergent thinking, 443

Conversion disorder, 501, 525

Convulsive therapy, 553

Cooperation, 481, 585, 592, 603, 604, 612, 634, 636

Coping strategies, 290, 531, 563; dysfunctional, 476, 478; and psychopathology, 497, 516; and stress, 475–479, 487

Corpus callosum, 96, 97, 197

Correlation, 20–21, 30, 471, 473, 480, 649–650; in assessment, 419, 430–431, 433; and personality traits, 383, 384, 385, 389, 391, 412

Correlation coefficient, 419, 649–650

Correspondent inference, 577, 606

Cortex, 73, 97, 98, 99, 101–102, 106, 122, 130, 142, 143, 146

Corticosteroids, 464

Cortin, 462

Cortisone, 462

Counseling, 416, 552

Counterconditioning, 539, 540–542, 564

Countertransference, 537, 563

Covariation principle, 576–577, 606

Coverants, 405, 413

Covert behaviors, 9

Creativity, 29, 398, 442, 522; assessing, 441–445, 452; and thinking, 357, 363, 376, 469, 470

Credibility, and persuasion, 583–584

Crime and criminals, 215, 387, 428, 496, 532, 617, 627, 630, 640–653

Criterion, and test, 420

Criterion performance, 322

Criterion validity, 419, 420

Critical features theories, 178–179, 185, 347

Critical flicker frequency, 133

Critical period, 34, 38, 94, 278

Critical set point, and hunger, 277, 278

Cross-cultural research, 16, 30, 41, 67, 270

Cross-modal integration, 152, 167

Cross-sectional design, 36, 37, 71

Cues: and aggression, 630, 639; and memory, 302, 324–325, 328, 333, 334, 337; and perception, 168–172, 185, 299–300; and personality, 405, 410; and thought, 339, 355, 375

Cultural relativity, 513

Culture: and abnormality, 513–514, 525; and achievement, 287; and aggression, 617; and anonymity, 617; and altered consciousness, 207, 213; and cross-cultural studies, 16, 30, 41, 67, 270; and development, 66–67, 397, 398; and drug usage, 213, 217; and eating habits, 277, 279; and emotions, 295–296, 297, 302; and gender differences, 406; and intelligence or IQ tests, 429, 430–431, 432, 434, 452; and language, 372, 434; and normality, 270, 273, 513; and norms, 595; and sexuality, 283; and role of society, 569; and therapy, 532–533

"Culture-free" test, 434, 452

Curare, 88

Curiosity, as a motive, 264, 268

Cutaneous sense, 143, 144, 145, 149

Cyclic AMP, 89

Cytoplasm, 77, 83

D

Danger, response to, 458–461

Dark adaptation, 132

Data, analysis of, 8, 22, 25, 30, 645–653

Data-driven processes, 176–177. See also "Bottom-up" processes

Daydreaming, 189, 190, 202–203, 220, 283–284, 396

Deafness, 134, 136, 139, 313, 508–509

Death: as development, 39, 69, 70, 72; fear of, 399; instinct, 270, 394, 628, 629; and life-style, 464; sex differences and, 478–479; and stress, 462, 464, 470, 472, 479, 591; and support systems, 479–480; voodoo, 458–459

Debriefing, 644

Decay, in memory, 311, 326, 332–333, 337

Decentration, in thinking, 52

Decision making, 26, 29, 340, 358–360, 367–368, 376, 411, 428, 446, 469, 635–636

Declarative knowledge, 637; and memory, 305, 321, 326, 337; and thought, 350–351, 364, 365, 367, 375, 376

Decoding, of language, 50

Deep structure, 350, 373, 376

Defenses, 379. See also Ego defense mechanisms

Deficiency and growth motivation theory, 273–274, 302, 409, 413

Dehumanization, 467, 611, 618–621, 633, 639

Deindividuation, 613, 614–617, 621, 639

Delayed forward conditioning, 229

Delayed-reward conditioning, 247

Delinquency, 539

Delirium tremens (DTs), 208

Delta sleep, 204, 205. See also Non-REM sleep

Delusions, 110, 189, 349, 506–507, 509, 510, 525, 556

Democratic leadership, 602, 603, 607

Demonic possession, abnormality as, 512, 514–515, 532, 533

Dendrites, 83, 85, 86, 87, 94, 95, 106, 121, 336

Denial of reality, 393, 396, 399, 469

Dependency, 393, 603; and development, 66; on drugs, 214, 215, 216, 220

Dependent variables, 14–15, 21, 30, 570, 622

Depressants, 215–216, 220

Depression, 246, 385, 491, 504–505, 514, 517, 521, 587, 604, 609; and drugs, 88, 216; in elderly, 69; incidence of, 505; neurotic, 496, 504–505; psychotic, 504, 505, 525; and shyness, 447, 587; and stress, 455, 467, 474, 476, 478, 487; and suicide, 506, 557; treatment for, 539, 548–549, 557, 559, 564; and unconscious, 187–188

Depressive episode, 489, 504

Deprivation: and development, 56–57, 82; and dwarfism, 82; emotional, 82; and humor, 477; and IQ, 432; and motivation, 264, 266, 267–268, 272, 301; and perception, 181, 182; sensory, 208, 210, 272; social, 267, 545–546. See also Social isolation

Depth perception, 167–172, 185, 217
Descriptive statistics, 646–650
Desensitization. See Systematic desensitization
Desynchronized sleep, 204–205. See also REM sleep
Determinism, 549; psychic, 393, 411, 412; reciprocal, 405, 413. See also Behaviorism.
Development, 32–71; and age, 38; of brain, 93–95; childhood, 39, 47–53, 55–65, 393; cognitive, 50–55, 71; concepts in, 38–39; emotional and social, 55–61, 71; language, 47–50, 71; life-span, 28, 35–72; moral, 61–63, 71; motor, 36, 51, 71; and nutrition, 38, 41; perceptual, 43; prenatal, 41–43, 93–95; psychosexual, 64–65, 71; research on, 35–37; sex differences in, 60–61, 62–63; stages in, 38, 39, 50–55, 61–63, 64–65, 71
Developmental age, 38
Developmental disorders, 494
Developmental stages, 38, 47–65
Deviation score, 649
Diagnosis: assessment and, 435–438; of disorders, 492, 493, 496
Diagnostic and Statistical Manual of Mental Disorders (DSM-III), 490, 493–494, 495, 497, 499, 504, 510, 524
Dichotic listening, 192
Diencephalon, 93, 97
Diet, 38, 41, 465, 477
Dieting, 278
Difference thresholds, 116–117, 148
Differential reinforcement, 249
Digit span, 365
Dilemma games, 636
Disaster, reactions to, 473
Discipline, 58, 449
Discounting rule, 577
Discrepancy, reducing, 355, 357, 361, 375, 582. See also Distortion
Discrimination: in concept formation, 348–349; and conditioning, 230–231; and prejudice, 604; sexual, 535
Discriminative stimuli, 241–242, 245, 256, 259
Disease, and stress, 457, 460, 462–465, 471, 480
Diseases of adaptation, 462, 463, 486
Disjunctive rules, and concepts, 349
Disobedience, 609, 626
Disorganized schizophrenia, 510
Displacement: of aggression, 467, 630, 639; and language, 373; and personality, 396, 397
Display rules, 295–296, 302
Disposition, 382, 400, 412, 413, 577
Dispositional factors, and attribution, 569, 577–579, 580, 621–622
Dissent, 526, 639
Dissociation, and hypnosis, 210, 211
Dissociative disorders, 211–212, 497, 501–502, 524, 525
Distal stimulus, 154–155, 172–173, 185
Distancing, 485
Distinctiveness criterion, 577
Distortion: in attribution and impressions, 573–579; in memory, 312, 328, 329–330, 331–332, 357, 375, 471; and psychopathology, 516–517

Distributions, statistical, 646–647, 648, 651, 652
Divergent thinking, 443, 452
DNA (deoxyribonucleic acid), 40, 74, 77
Dopamine and dopamine hypothesis, 87, 88, 519, 554
Double bind, 520
Double-blind procedure, 385
Double consciousness, 211
"Drapetomania," 522
Dreams, 189, 190, 203, 206–207, 219, 220; analysis of, 394, 412, 468, 535, 536–537, 551, 563; day-, 189, 190, 202–203, 220, 396
Drives and drive theory, 24, 29, 263, 265, 270–272, 302, 393, 394, 395, 397, 405, 412
Drugs: addiction to, 89, 214, 216, 220, 243, 494, 539, 542, 557, 564; and aggression, 632–633; antianxiety, 556–557; antidepressant, 557; antipsychotic, 556; and the brain, 88, 94, 243, 494, 553; and conditioning, 242, 243; and consciousness, 213–218; dependency on, 214, 215, 216, 220, 464, 482, 494, 557, 560; effect on fetus, 41; effect on memory, 215, 335, 337; and the nervous system, 88; psychedelic, 216–217, 218, 220; psychoactive, 189, 190, 208, 214, 215–217, 220; in therapy, 335, 519, 529, 555–557, 564; tolerance of, 214, 220, 243; withdrawal from, 214–215, 216, 220, 466. See also the names of individual drugs
Dual-code model of memory, 323
Dual hypothalamic theory of hunger, 276, 302
"Dual unity" of mother and child, 538
Dualism: and behavior, 75, 76; and consciousness, 190, 197–198, 220; and emotions, 297–298
Duplex theory of memory, 326, 327
Dwarfism, 82
Dyscontrol syndrome, 629
Dysphoric mood, 504

E

Ear, structure of, 137–139
Echo, and memory, 310, 311
Ecological approach, 638
Ecological Optics, 157, 159–160, 170, 185
Education, 10, 69, 429, 501, 617, 637, 639
Efferent neurons, 83, 88, 106
Efficacy based expectations, 408
Ego, 394, 399, 413, 517, 534, 563
Ego-centrism, 53, 449
Ego control, 384, 385, 546
Ego defense mechanisms, 396, 397, 413, 467, 470, 478, 487, 516, 537, 618
Ego-dystonic feelings, 497
Ego ideal, 395
Ego-integrity, 69, 71; vs. despair, 65, 69
Ego-overcontrol scores, 642, 645, 648, 649, 650, 651, 653
Ego-syntonic feelings, 497
Ego-transcendence, 218
Egocentric recall, 579
Eidetic imagery, 323–324
Einstellung, 363
Elaborative rehearsal, 316, 318, 326, 337

Elderly, 136, 530; brain functioning of, 84; and cognitive ability, 69–70; and death, 70, 464; and development, 39, 69–70, 71; and health, 14–15, 69, 464; institutions for, 14–15, 481; life expectancy of, 481; and paranoia, 507, 508–509; and sleep, 205; and stress, 480, 481
Electroconvulsive therapy, 335, 337, 529, 553, 555, 560, 564
Electroencephalogram (EEG), 104, 106, 159, 203, 204
Electromagnetic spectrum, 122, 123, 124
Electromyogram (EMG), 344
Emotion, 263, 294–301, 302, 353, 382, 397, 410–411; and the brain, 101, 261; and disease, 463; and memory, 21–22; negative, 467; and personality, 410–411; and physiological changes, 294–295, 297–298, 299–300, 301, 302; in psychopathology, 489, 495, 504, 507, 509, 521, 525; and states of consciousness, 213, 218; and stress response, 467–469, 470, 486, 487; theories about, 297–301, 302
Emotion regulation, 476, 478
Emotional inoculation, 483
Emotional insulation, 396
Empathy, 495, 550, 604, 615, 618
Empirical criterion method, 435, 439, 446, 452, 539
Empiricism, 33, 157, 158–159
Encephalization, 90
Encoding, 50, 307, 308, 326, 328, 333, 335, 336, 337, 430; acoustic, 313, 326, 327, 337; and language, 50; in long-term memory, 318–320; and personality, 410, 411; physical, 326–327; semantic, 313, 326, 327, 337; in sensory memory, 310; in short-term memory, 313
Encoding specificity principle, 320, 324
Endocrine system, 78, 80–82, 106, 261, 529
Endorphins, 89, 142, 146, 149, 460, 519
Energy: and arousal, 460, 464, 466, 486; and manic state, 556; psychic, 394, 628, 632
Engram, 336
Enkephalin, 87, 89
Environment, 24, 46, 82, 95, 439; and aggression, 617, 630; and crowding, 635; and social dilemmas, 634–636; vs. heredity, 22, 24, 33–34, 43–44, 46, 49, 71, 157, 411, 413, 429–432, 451, 452; of job, 619; and motivation, 268, 269, 301; and perception, 157, 160, 185; and personality, 388, 404, 405, 409, 410, 413; and psychology, 634, 635–636, 637–638; and schizophrenia, 518–519; social, 569–571; and stress, 474–475, 487, 562, 564; support from, 479–481, 561
Environmental psychology, 10, 634, 635–636, 637–638, 639
Environmental variable, 569. See also Situational variables
Epilepsy, 89, 100, 102, 197, 207, 335, 553
Epinephrine, 87, 298, 299, 335, 337, 459
Episodic memory, 321, 323, 326, 332, 337
Equity theory, 588–589, 606
Ergot fungus hypothesis, 514–515
Eros, 270, 394, 398, 628
Errors, in thinking, 344, 345, 358–360, 375, 557–559, 593, 606

Escape, in conditioning, 241, 246, 259, 267
Esteem needs, 273
Esthetic needs, 273
Estrogen, 82, 280
Estrus, 280
Ethics: of psychologists, 233; in research, 644–645
Ethnic group, and pain, 146–147
Etiology of disorders, 493, 530
Euphoria: drug-induced, 216, 243; and psychopathology, 489, 495
Eustress, 457, 486
Evaluation research, 16, 30
Event-related potentials, 345
Evil: abnormal behavior as, 513; and human nature, 611–612, 613; redefining, 625
Evoked potentials, 104, 345
Evolution, 263, 569, 613
Excitation, of neuron, 77, 106, 128
Exhilaration, and stress, 457, 467
Existential-humanistic therapies, 529, 549–552, 559, 560, 564
Existential neurosis, 550
Existentialism, 400, 413, 549
Expectations, 410, 413, 593, 595; and memory, 328–329, 337; and motivation, 274–275, 302; outcome-based vs. efficacy-based, 408; and pain, 148; parental, 572; and perception, 155, 179–180, 185; and social reality, 572, 606; and therapy, 547, 548, 557–558, 559, 564; and thinking, 350–351, 375
Experience, 225, 271, 337, 581–582, 606, 629; and perception, 157, 174–175, 185; and personality, 393–394, 401; and thinking, 343, 359, 364, 368, 376
Experimental approach, and personality, 383, 384–385
Experimental method, 13–16, 30, 35, 383, 384–385, 412
Experimenter expectancy bias effect, 18
Experts and expert systems, 366–367, 368, 369, 376
Exploration, as a motive, 264, 268
Expressive technique, in assessment, 439
Extinction, 229, 231, 233, 235, 239, 241, 243, 246, 248, 249, 258, 259
Extinction strategies, in therapy, 542, 543–544, 564
Extracellular recordings, 104
Extramarital sex, 242
Extraversion, 387, 448, 449, 496
Extrinsic motivation, 290–292, 293, 302
Eye contact, 447, 546, 595
Eye/hand coordination, 197
Eye movements, 341, 344–345, 375
Eyes, structure of, 119–121. *See also* Vision
Eyewitness testimony, 331–332

F

Facial feedback hypothesis, 297
Fact memories, 321, 326, 336, 337
Factor analysis, 388, 428, 439, 452
Failure, 288, 289, 290, 302, 506, 587, 612; expectation of, 408; predicting, 417

Faith healers, 533
Familiarity, and liking, 588
Family: and achievement, 287; deprivation within, 82, 477; and norms, 596, 597, 600; and schizophrenia, 518, 519–521, 525; and stress, 459, 477, 479; studies, 517, 518–519; and therapy, 533, 551, 552, 560
Family resemblance concept of abnormality, 492–493, 496
Fantasy, 189, 202–203, 220, 283, 286–287, 302, 306, 379, 440, 444, 551; as a defense mechanism, 394, 396; and psychopathology, 495, 502
Fat cells, and eating, 277, 278, 302
Father, 429, 432, 433
Fatigue, 88, 216, 283, 461, 499, 500
Faulty thinking, 548–549, 564
Fear, 216, 231, 232–233, 277, 295, 296, 297, 301, 363, 459, 460, 491, 562; of death, 399; as a drive, 271; and eating, 277, 279, 496; and interpersonal factors, 585–586; sexual, 283; and stress, 469, 470, 473, 474; of success, 289
Feature-detection model, 130, 149
Feature-integration processes, 194
Fechner's law, 118, 119, 135
Feedback, 177, 293, 297, 349, 408, 482–483; biological, 246–247, 259; perceptual, 183–184, 195, 208; and skill acquisition, 364, 365–366, 376, 529
Feeling, and cognition, 294, 300–301, 302
Femininity/Masculinity scale, 642, 645, 646, 648–651, 653
Fetishism, 283, 503
Fetus, 42, 92–93, 94, 629
Field dependence vs. field independence, 176–177, 182
Field experiments, 624, 643–644
"Fight-or-flight" syndrome, 458–461, 486
Figural goodness, 164
Figure and ground, 162, 196
Filter theory, 191–193
First impressions, 573
Fixation: and eye movements, 344; in psychodynamic theory, 65, 71, 399, 534, 538, 546
Fixed action pattern, 3, 9, 41, 196, 269, 302
Fixed interval schedule (FI), 248–249
Fixed ratio schedule (FR), 248, 249
Flashbacks, 217, 468
Flexibility, 189, 410, 469; assessing, 439; and intelligence, 428, 430
Flicker fusion, 133, 149
Flooding, in therapy, 541
Flow charts, 353
Forebrain, 93–94, 96, 97
Foresight, 219
Forgetting, 322, 332–337, 504
Formal assessment, 418, 451
Formal operational stage, 51, 53–54, 71
Forward conditioning, 229, 233
Fourier analysis, 130
Fraternal twins, 210, 518
Free association, 534, 535, 536, 563
Free fatty acids, 277, 278, 279
Free-floating anxiety, 498, 525
Free recall, 318
Frequency: distributions, 646–647; of soundwaves, 135, 136, 137, 139, 140, 149; theory, 139–140, 149
Freudian slips, 344, 394

Friendliness, as a trait, 390–391
Friends: and attraction, 587–589; and groups, 604, 605; support from, 459, 469, 470, 479–480, 485, 561
Frigidity, 283, 541
Frontal lobes, 96, 98, 102, 142, 553
Frustration, 24, 273, 467, 471–472, 520, 537, 629–630, 639
Frustration-aggression hypothesis, 467, 629–630, 639
Functional fixedness, 363, 376
Functional psychoses, 504, 512, 525
Fundamental attribution error, 577–578, 593, 606, 621, 624, 627
Future, and stress, 474, 505
Future orientation, 293–294, 302

G

"G-factor," in intelligence, 428, 429, 452
Gain-loss principle of attraction, 589, 606
Galvanic skin response (GSR), 231, 483
Games, in relationships, 551
Gamma temperament, 479, 487
Ganglia, 80, 90, 91
Ganglion cells, 120, 121, 127, 128, 129, 148
Ganzfeld, 128
Gate-control theory, of pain, 146
Gender differences, 60–61, 62–63, 69, 287, 289, 406. *See also* Men, Women
Gender identity, 60, 71, 406, 503, 510; disorders of, 503–504
Gender roles, 22, 60–61, 63, 71, 503
General adaptation syndrome, 298, 461–462, 463, 486
Generalization: in conditioning, 229–230, 231, 232, 256–257, 258, 541; and impressions, 573, 575; in research, 11, 19, 22, 383–384, 644; in therapy, 539–540, 547, 564; and thinking, 348–349, 355
Generalized anxiety disorder, 499
Generativity vs. stagnation, 65, 67, 68
Genes, 40–41, 71
Genetic engineering, 553, 554
Genetics: and the brain, 514–515, 553; and development, 24, 40–45, 71; and emotion, 264; and hypnotizability, 210; and IQ, 429–432, 451, 452; and personality, 411, 413; and schizophrenia and affective disorders, 514, 517–519, 521, 525, 554; and vulnerability, 463, 465, 517–519
Genital stage of development, 64–65, 71
Genitals, 280, 282, 283, 503
Genotype, 40, 41
Germ cells, 40
Gestalt therapy, 551, 559
Gestaltism, 157–159, 163, 164, 185
Gestures, in communication, 371, 376, 448
Glial cells, 83, 84, 94, 95
Global properties, and perception, 178, 179
Glucose level, and eating, 277, 278, 279
Glutamic acid, 87
Goal state, in problem solving, 362, 363, 376

Goals, 287–288, 289, 290, 293, 299, 302, 406–407; and dehumanization, 620–621; and groups, 601, 604, 605, 606, 607; and motivation, 263, 274, 275, 293, 301; and personality, 379, 406–407, 410, 411, 601; and stress, 457, 467, 485, 486; superordinate, 604, 605, 607; of therapy, 530–531, 532, 543, 546, 548, 549, 550, 563

Gonads, 280

Graded potentials, 85, 87, 89

Grammar, 47

Gratification, delay, of, 384, 406–408

"Gregarious instinct," 585

Ground, in perception, 162

Group, 568, 569, 592–605, 606; conflict in, 598, 599–600, 603, 604; and deindividuation, 613, 614–617, 639; influence of, 593–600, 606–607; and leadership, 600–603, 607; and stress management, 479–480, 485, 487; norms of, 593, 594–597; structure of, 592–593, 607; and perception, 183–184

Group influence, 593–600, 607

Group therapies, 550–551

Grouping, 162–164

Growth, personal, 26–27, 401, 402, 406, 407, 413, 529, 549, 550, 564

Growth motivation, 273–274, 302

Guilt, feelings of, 62, 65, 67, 274, 385, 468, 504, 535, 553, 612

Gustation, 141, 142, 149

H

Habits, 24, 271, 363, 382, 404, 405, 483

Habituation, 92, 106, 132

Hair cells, of ear, 136, 138, 143, 149

Hallucinations, 88, 110, 189, 207–208, 216–217, 220, 508, 510, 514, 525, 555, 556

Hallucinogens, 216–217, 218, 220

"Halo" effect, 422, 451

Happiness, 37, 70, 297, 299, 379

Hashish, 217

Head Start, 451

Headaches, 195, 207, 261, 455, 461, 483, 499

Health: of elderly, 14–15, 69, 464; overconcern for, 491, 501; and sense of control, 14–15, 464, 465; and stress, 462–465, 471–473, 474

Health psychology, 10, 464, 465, 563

Hearing, 134–140, 149, 154; loss of, 136; physiology of, 137–139; and paranoia, 508–509; theories of, 139–140

Heart disease, 462, 470, 473, 478, 479, 484, 487, 499

Heart rate, 231, 246, 283, 297, 459, 460, 482, 498

Hebephrenia. See Disorganized schizophrenia

Hedonism. See Adaptive hedonism

Helplessness, feelings of, 393, 466, 474

Hemispheres, cerebral, 97, 98–101, 106, 122, 197–199, 200–201, 210

Heredity vs. environment, 22, 24, 27, 33, 43–44, 46, 49, 71, 157, 411, 413, 429–432, 451, 452. See also Genetics

Heritability rates, and IQ, 430–431, 432, 452

Hermann grid, 111, 112, 128

Heroin, 215, 216, 243, 491

Heuristics, 358, 359–360, 364, 367, 376, 445

"Hidden observer" phenomenon, 211, 220

Hierarchy: of anxiety-producing stimuli, 540–541; of concepts, 347–348, 375; of needs, 273–274, 302

Higher-order conditioning, 231–233, 252, 253, 254

Hindbrain, 93, 94, 96

Hippocampus, 97, 98, 335, 336

Histogram, 647

Homeostasis, 81–82, 266, 275, 276, 461

Homosexuality, 501, 510, 575

Honesty, 61–62, 389

Hopelessness, and death, 459

Hormones, 78, 80, 82, 84, 88, 97, 106, 553; and aggression, 629; and emotions, 261, 298; and memory, 335; and motivation, 261, 264, 278, 280, 294; and sex, 280, 283, 302; and sleep, 203–204; and stress, 459, 460–461, 462, 464, 481

Hospitalization: historic context of, 532–533; and psychopathology, 497, 504, 506, 507–508, 523, 525, 556; and therapy, 542, 544, 555, 556, 560, 564

Hostility, 57, 273, 283, 396, 482, 520, 521; and groups, 603, 604, 605, 607; and type A behavior, 478, 487

"Hot lines," 460

Hue, 123, 124, 125, 127, 128, 149

Human nature, adaptability of, 611, 614; and anonymity, 615–617; assumptions about, 24–27, 411–412, 413; and behavioristic model, 24–25, 27, 404–409, 546; cognitive model, 25, 27, 409–411; complexity of, 611–617, 624; evolution of, 613; humanistic model, 26, 27, 400–403, 549; and learning, 409; psychodynamic model, 24, 27, 269–270, 391–399, 516, 546; psychophysiological model, 27; and personality theories, 385

Human potential. See Potential

Human potential movement, 550, 564

Human sexuality, 282–286

Humanistic model, 23, 26–27, 31, 274, 302

Humanistic theories of personality, 400–403, 409, 411, 412, 413

Humor, and stress, 476, 477

Hunger, 181, 263, 264, 266, 273, 275–280, 302

Hyperattentiveness, and anxiety, 499

Hypermetropia, 120

Hypersensitivity, and schizophrenia, 511–512, 525

Hypersomnia, 504

Hypersuggestibility, 208–209, 210

Hypertension, 89, 462, 463, 481, 482

Hypnosis, 187, 188, 190, 196, 208–213, 220, 482, 502, 508–509; and memory, 333; and pain, 146–147, 211; in therapy, 534, 535

Hypnotizability, 209, 210, 220

Hypochondriasis, 491, 501, 525

Hypothalamus, 82, 97, 98, 104, 261; and emotion, 297, 298; and hunger, 276, 302; and stress, 459, 460, 486

Hypothesis, in scientific method, 9, 12, 13, 15, 19, 30, 642, 643, 644, 650–651

Hypothesis-driven processes, 177. See also "Top-down" processes

Hysterical conversion, 393, 534–535

I

Icon, 310, 311

Id, 395, 396, 399, 413, 517, 534, 538, 563

Ideal self, 401

Identical twins, 210, 518, 554

Identification, 396, 546, 592, 595, 598, 606, 625

Identity, 66, 67, 71, 401, 430, 502, 538; and group, 569, 600; loss of, 502, 525; vs. role confusion, 65

Ideology, and attribution, 578

Idiographic approach, 381, 384, 388, 390–391, 392, 412

Idiosyncratic traits, 388

Illusions, 109, 110–111, 112, 134, 145, 148, 162, 166, 168–169, 171, 172, 173, 178, 360, 465, 596, 598

Images: and creativity, 442, 452; and memory, 319, 321, 323–324, 344; obsessive, 500; and thinking, 351–354

Imitation: and learning, 254–255, 631–632, 639; in therapy, 544–545, 546, 551, 564

Immaturity, 57–58

Immediate memory span, 313, 314–315

Immigrants, and assessment, 424, 425–426, 451

Immunological system, 234–235, 464

Implicit personality theory, 574, 606

Implosive therapy, 540, 541, 564

Impotence, 216, 283

Impression formation, 573–576, 606

Impression management, 401

Imprinting, 56

Impulsiveness and impulses, 5, 384, 385, 450, 496, 516, 630, 639

In group, 603, 604, 605, 607

Inadequacy, feelings of, 408, 478, 587, 606, 612

Incentives, 268, 271–272

Inconsistencies, and thinking, 355, 357

Independence, 61, 66, 67, 68, 71, 287, 406–407, 444, 598, 600

Independent variable, 14–15, 21, 30, 31, 228, 570, 606

Index variable, 38, 266, 301

Individual differences and individuality, assessing, 416, 417, 430; and personality, 345, 380, 388, 400, 402, 409, 410, 413; and society, 549–550, 569, 611

Individuation, 538, 614–617

Induced motion, 166

Infants: brain growth of, 38, 93–95; cognitive development of, 52, 71, 343, 354; conditioning of, 232–233; and development, 35, 39, 45–47, 61, 71, 432; and emotions, 296, 301; and language, 47–48, 71; and memory, 333–334; and mothers, 46, 56–57, 71; need for love, 56–57, 71; parents' perception of, 572; perception by, 43, 357; and psychosexual development, 64, 71, 393–394, 534; sexuality of, 394; and sleep, 205; and stranger anxiety, 35; and thinking, 343
Inferences, 8, 350, 368, 573–574, 576–579
Inferential statistics, 650–653
Inferiority, feeling of, 65, 398, 413, 449
Influence: of group, 593–600, 607; of minority, 598–600, 607
Information processing: and attribution, 578, 579; and cognition, 340–341, 350–351, 353, 364–370, 372, 375; feedback, 364, 365–366; and intelligence, 430; and memory, 307, 334–336; and neural networks, 335–336; and personality, 410–411, 413; and schizophrenia, 521
Initial state, of problem solving, 362, 363, 376
Initiative vs. guilt crisis, 65, 71
Inkblot tests, 439–440, 443
Innate behavior: emotion as, 295–296, 302; and personality, 393, 394, 395, 397, 411
Innate stimulus elicitors, 296
Insecurity, feelings of, 65, 67, 538
Insight therapies, 535, 557. See also Psychoanalysis
Instinct theory, 268–270, 301
Instincts, 24, 25, 264, 268–269, 274, 391, 393, 394, 546, 585
Instinctual drift, 251
Instrumental conditioning, 236–237, 258
Insulin, 81, 553
Integration: cross-modal, 152, 167; in thinking, 355–357
Intellectualization, 621, 639
Intelligence and IQ, 29, 424–434; artificial, 367–368; and creativity, 444; and environment, 46, 429–432, 451, 563; and happiness, 37, 70; measuring, 419, 424–426; as multiple, 428, 430–431; and psychopathology, 506; and stress, 470; tests, 426–427, 429–434, 443, 451, 452, 563, 651
Interaction approach to leadership, 600, 601
Interaction effect, 21–22
Interests, assessing, 416, 446, 452
Interference, and forgetting, 315, 322, 326, 332, 333, 337
Intergroup relations, 603–605
Intermittent reinforcement, 247–248, 259
Internal representation of problem space, 363
Internalization, 598
Interneurons, 83, 90, 91, 93, 106

Interpersonal ability, 430, 431
Interpersonal factors: and personality, 401–402, 405, 406–407, 538, 564; and sex, 283–284; and stress, 472, 473
Interpersonal relations: affiliation, 585–587; attraction, 585–591, 606; improving, 529, 538, 545–547, 551; liking, 587–589; loving, 589–591; and shyness, 447–448, 545–547, 587
Interposition, and perception, 171, 185
Interrater reliability, 422–423
Interval schedules, 248–249
Intervening variable, 8, 14–15, 25, 263, 265, 301, 385, 388, 570, 606
Interviews, 12–13, 16, 30, 383, 421, 451
Intimacy, 55, 67, 448, 587, 591, 617
Intimacy vs. isolation, 65, 67
Intracellular recordings, 104
Intrapersonal ability, 430
Intrapsychic events, 392
Intrinsic motivation, 290–292, 293, 294, 302
Introjection, 396, 507
Introspection, 25, 151, 189–190, 195, 341–342, 375, 535
Introversion, 387, 448, 496
Intuition, 381, 398, 444, 445
Intuitive strategy, in assessment, 435
Inventories, and assessment, 389, 435–439, 446–447, 452
Inverted-U function, 266
Involvement, 406, 407
Ions, 83, 84, 85, 87, 106
Irritability, 216, 466, 467, 484, 487, 504, 508
Islets of Langerhans, 81
Isolation: as a defense mechanism, 396; emotional vs. social, 586–587, 606; vs. intimacy, 65; therapy for, 545–546. See also Social isolation
Iteration, 373–374, 376

J

James-Lange theory of emotion, 297, 302
Jealousy, 591, 612
"Jig-saw" technique, 637
Job assessment, 446–447
Jobs. See Work
Judges' ratings, 411–412, 421, 439, 443, 448, 449, 451
Judgments: about abnormality, 493, 521–522, 524, 525; and assessment, 422–423, 450; by the depressed, 505; of self-efficacy, 408; and society, 576–579, 596, 598; and stress, 469, 487; and thinking, 215, 217, 358–360, 367, 376, 381, 425
Just noticeable difference (jnd), 116–117, 118, 148

K

Kinesthetic sense, 143, 149, 176
Knowledge: dilemmas, 636; and expert systems, 367–368, 376; and memory, 332; metacognitive, 364, 369, 376; procedural vs. declarative, 305, 321, 326, 637
Knowledge base, and computers, 367, 368
Knowledge stage, and skills, 364–365

L

L-dopa, 88
Labeling, 450, 496–497, 522, 524
Laissez-faire leadership, 602, 607
Language: and animal communication, 373–375; and attribution, 578; and the brain, 50, 101, 198, 200–201, 220; and cognition, 49, 54, 341; criteria for, 373–374; dehumanizing, 619–620; and development, 47–50, 219, 317, 612; in IQ tests, 434; natural, 371, 376; schizophrenic, 507, 509, 510, 511–512, 521, 525; and speech, 344, 348; structure of, 47; theories of, 371–373, 376; and thought, 731–733, 736
Latency, of variable, 228
Latency stage of development, 64, 71
Latent content, 206, 394, 536–537
Latent learning, 225
Lateral geniculate nucleus, 121, 122, 129, 148
Lateral hypothalamus, 276, 277, 278
Laughter, and stress, 476, 477
Law, and psychology, 10, 636–637, 639
Law of association, 224, 258
Law of common fate, 164
Law of effect, 235–237
Law of forward conduction, 83, 106
Law of proximity, 163
Law of similarity, 163, 164
Law of the specific energy of nerves, 76
Laws of grouping, 163–164
Leadership: assessing, 423, 425, 626; and groups, 592, 600–603, 605, 606; learning, 546
Learned helplessness, 246, 256, 506
Learning, 4, 21–22, 29, 106, 340, 637; of abnormal behavior, 539; of aggression, 254, 255, 628, 629, 630–633; associational, 235–236; biological constraints on, 250–252; and conditioning, 221–259; cognitive influences, 252–256, 257–258; defined, 225, 258; and drug usage, 242, 243; and emotions, 295–296, 302; and experience, 225; and human nature, 611–612, 613; as imitation, 254–255; latent, 225; and memory, 320, 336, 337; and motivation, 264, 270–271, 301, 302; observational, 252, 253–255, 256, 405–406, 413; operant, 234–236; overt vs. covert, 225, 255–256, 413; and personality, 383, 404–409, 411; and relearning, 322; theory (see Learning theories). See also Conditioning
Learning disabilities, 336, 418, 425, 491
Learning theories: of personality, 404–409, 411, 412, 413; and psychopathology, 516, 517. See also Social learning theory
Lesch-Nyhan syndrome, 554
Leveling vs. sharpening, 183; in remembering, 331
Levels of processing theory, 326–327
Libido, 394, 397, 398, 399
Life change units (LCU), 471, 472
Life Experiences Survey (LES), 471
Life instinct, 270, 394, 628
Life-span development, 32–72

Life stress, 403, 464, 471–473, 478, 487, 516
Life-style, 464, 465, 477, 483, 485, 487
Light, 114, 122–123
Liking, 585, 587–589, 590, 606
Liking Scale, 590
Limbic system, 97, 98, 102, 296, 298–299, 335, 336, 629
Linear perspective, 172, 185
Linear relationships, 650
Linguistic ability, 430
Linguistic determinism, 372
Linguists, and language, 372–373
Lipostatic theory of hunger, 278
Lithium salt, 557, 564
Little Albert, 231, 236
Locus of control orientation, 275, 288, 290, 478, 587
Logic, 197, 198, 199, 220, 342, 347
Loneliness, 69, 447, 469, 586–587, 606
Long-term inhibitors, and eating, 279
Long-term memory, 309, 311, 312, 316, 318–326, 327, 333, 336, 337, 344, 346, 350, 353, 367, 373
Longitudinal studies, 16, 30, 36–37, 70, 71, 425, 429, 444, 477, 479, 632–633
Loudness, 135, 137, 139, 149
Love Scale, 590, 606
Loving, 284, 589–591, 606, 612
Lymph nodes, 462
Lysergic acid amide, 217
Lysergic acid diethylamide (LSD), 208, 210, 217, 514

M

Machiavellianism, 601
Maintenance rehearsal, 315–316, 319, 326, 333, 337
Malnutrition, 38, 41, 94, 283, 515
Mandala, 398
Manic depressive disorders, 504, 554, 557, 564
Manifest content, 206, 394, 536–537
Marijuana, 214, 217, 220, 596, 631–632
Marital therapy, 552, 560
Marriage: and attribution, 579; as a developmental task, 67; and divorce, 468, 472; and health, 67; and life satisfaction, 70; stress in, 472
Masculinity-Femininity (MF) scale, 436
Masking, 311
Masochism, 503
Mass murder, 507, 514, 621
Masturbation, 281, 282, 283, 503
Maternal behavior, 3, 8, 14, 266
Maturation, 41, 42, 49–50, 71, 225
Maturity, 57–58, 66, 68
Mean, statistical, 647, 648, 649, 651
Meaning: and attention, 192–193; and memory, 312, 316, 318–319, 321, 328, 332, 333, 337; and thinking, 350–351
Mechanistic approach, 75
Median, statistical, 647, 648, 651

Mediating variables, 570
Medical model of abnormality, 514–515, 539
Meditation, 481, 482, 486
Medulla, 97
Melatonin, 82, 203–204
Memory, 25, 29, 49, 54, 304–337, 340, 353, 411, 612; and the brain, 73, 92, 101, 102, 106, 305, 307, 309, 321, 327, 334–335, 336, 553, 564; and chunking, 313, 314–315, 316, 367; and conditioning, 247, 252; and consciousness, 187, 189, 193, 219; and drugs, 215; of elderly, 69; emotional, 336; episodic and semantic, 321; and expectations, 328–329, 337, 350–351, 375; and forgetting, 322, 332–337; long-term, 309, 311, 312, 316, 318–326, 327, 333, 336, 337; loss of, 305–306, 553 (see also Amnesia); and meaning, 312, 316, 318–319; mnemonic strategies of, 319–320; and perception, 157, 180, 183, 185; photographic, 323–324; recall, 54, 306, 307, 308, 310, 313, 315, 319, 321; rehearsal, 309, 314, 315–316, 319; and semantics, 321, 322, 327; and schizophrenia, 521; sensory, 309, 310–312, 326, 333, 337; short-term, 309, 311, 312, 313–317, 326, 327, 333, 337; and sleep, 205, 206; spacial, 336; and state-dependent learning, 320; and stress, 469, 471, 487; theories of, 326–327
Memory code, 312, 337
Memory set, 316–317
Memory span, 313, 314
Memory trace, 335, 336, 337
Men: and acceptance of mentally ill, 524; and achievement, 289; aggressiveness of, 57, 629, 632, 633–634; and the brain, 100, 101; and competition, 478; and crying, 299; and drug usage, 214; genetic differences of, 43; hormones of, 280; intellectual functioning of, 70; and left-handedness, 100; life expectancy of, 478–479; and personality studies, 68; and pornography, 633–634; psychodynamic theory, 399; and psychopathology, 495, 508; sexual response of, 282–283, 284–285; and shyness, 448; in social settings, 406–407; socialization of, 57, 60–61, 284–285; and stress, 474, 478, 487; and suicide, 69, 506, and therapy, 530; and values, 62–63, 67, 69, 71
Menstruation, 142, 496
Mental age (MA), 425, 426, 451
Mental disorders, 488–525; classifying, 492–494, 521, 524; disease model of, 532–533; historical views of, 512–513, 514–515, 532–533; hospitals for, 497, 504, 506, 507–508, 523, 525; incidence of, 490, 491, 497, 505, 506, 507–508, 524, 554, 562; major types of, 494–512; models of, 512–521; myth of, 522; problem of, 490–491; and rights, 560; stigma of, 522–524; treatment of, 526–564. See also Psychopathology, Therapy
Mental health, promoting, 562–563
Mental retardation: determining, 424, 425, 427, 434, 451, 491; and genetics, 554; preventing, 554, 562–563

Mental set, 180, 217–218, 363, 376
Mere exposure effect, 588
Mescaline, 210, 213, 217
Metabolism, 77, 82, 553, 554
Metacognitive knowledge, 364, 369–370, 376
Method of loci, and memory, 319
Micro level of analysis, 22, 23
Midbrain, 93, 96
Middle age, 39, 67, 472–473, 476–477
Mid-life crisis, 67
Migraine headaches, 207, 463
Mind, 219, 220; and drugs, 190, 213–218; theories about, 74–76
Minnesota Multiphasic Personality Inventory (MMPI), 435–437, 446, 450, 452, 509, 642, 645, 646, 648, 649, 653
Minority groups: aggression toward, 630; and assessment bias, 434, 451
Minority influence, 598–600, 607
Mnemonics, 319–320
Mode, statistical, 647–648
Modeling: and aggression, 253–255, 256, 631–632, 639; participant, 544–545, 564; and personality, 405, 406–408, 410; and skill development, 366; symbolic, 544–545; in therapy, 544–545, 547, 550, 564
Models: of human nature, 23–27, 546, 549; of mental illness, 512–521, 546; of stress, 470
Moderator variables, 475, 479, 487
Modifiability of behavior, 404–408, 411, 413
Molar level of analysis, 22, 24, 26
Molecular level of analysis, 22, 23, 24, 26
Monamine oxidose (MAO), 554, 557
Mood, 382, 638; in affective disorders and schizophrenia, 504, 506, 509, 525, 556; and drugs, 243, 556; and recall, 21–22, 320, 337
Moral development, 61–63, 69, 71, 274
Morality principle, 395, 413
Morphine, 89, 215–216, 243, 460, 466
Mother: and infant, 45, 56–57, 58–59, 71; and nutrition, 434; retarded, 68; and schizophrenia, 520, 538; working, 68
Motion, perception of, 132, 133, 134, 166
Motion cues, in depth perception, 169–170
Motion-detector hypothesis, 133
Motivated forgetting, 326, 332, 334, 337
Motive to avoid success (MAS), 289
Motives and motivation, 5, 29, 225, 260–302, 353, 482; achievement, 286–289, 302; biological, 273, 274, 302; cognitive control of, 274–275; concept of, 24; and conditioning, 263–265, 267–268; deficiency vs. growth, 273–274, 409; and emotions, 294–295; and feedback, 365; and the future, 293–294; hierarchy of, 273–274, 302; humanistic view, 400, 402; incentive, 268; intrinsic vs. extrinsic, 290–292, 293, 302; and learning, 264; and perception, 155, 180–184, 185; in psychodynamic model, 24, 62, 392, 394–395, 404, 412, 534, 563; social, 585, 592, 593; theories of, 268–275, 292–293; unconscious, 24, 31, 392, 394–395, 403, 534; and work, 292–293, 302

Motor activity, and psychopathology, 504, 510, 519, 556
Motor cortex, 73, 97, 98, 99, 297
Motor development, 36
Motor neurons, 83, 84, 88, 90, 91, 93, 106
Motor set, 180
Motor skills, 364, 365, 637; and drugs, 215, 218; and memory, 305, 321, 333
Müller-Lyer illusion, 111
Multiaxial evaluation system, 494, 524
Multiple intelligences, 428, 430–431
Multiple-levels of memory, 326–327, 337
Multiple personalities, 211–212, 219, 220, 333, 502, 525
Multiple-system approach, and eating, 277–279
Murderers, 641–643, 645–651, 653
Muscle contractions, 246–247, 341, 344–345, 375
Muscle tension, 458, 460, 461, 481, 482, 498, 499
Mutable self, 403
Myelin sheath, 86, 90, 94, 146, 296
Myelinization, 94, 106
Myopia, 120
Mysticism, 207, 208, 213, 218

N
n Ach, 286–287, 288, 289
Naloxone, 89
Narcissistic personality disorders, 495
National Association for Mental Health, 562
National Institute of Mental Health, 212, 556, 559
Nativism, 33, 157, 158–159, 160
Natural language mediators, 319
Natural languages, 371, 376
Nature vs. nurture. See Heredity vs. environment
Nazism, 583, 596, 620, 621, 625
Necker cube, 156, 168
Needs, 29, 181, 264, 273–274, 302; for achievement, 286–292; for approval, 400; biological, 3–4, 273, 274, 302; hierarchy of, 273–274, 302; in psychodynamic model, 24; sexual, 280; social, 585–587, 592, 607; and work, 292–293, 302
Negative emotions, 467
Negative hallucination, 210
Negative identity, 66
Negative reinforcer or reinforcement, 239, 241, 243, 246, 259
Negative transference, 537
Negativity bias, 579, 606
Neocortex, 97, 299
Neo-Freudian theories, 397–399, 413, 537–538, 546, 564
Neonate, 45
Nerve cells, 23
Nerve energy, 76–78
Nervous system. See Autonomic, Central, and Peripheral nervous system

Network therapy, 533
Networks: in memory, 321, 323; for support, 479–480, 485, 487, 513, 523–524, 586–587; in thinking, 350, 375
Neurobiology, 515
Neurons, 78, 83–92, 94, 95, 98, 104, 106, 116, 140
Neuropeptides, 87
Neuroregulators, 88
Neurosis, 387, 397, 399, 497, 507, 516, 524, 534, 535, 550, 558, 563. See also Anxiety, Somatoform, and Dissociative disorders
Neurotransmitters, 78, 86, 87, 88, 89, 92, 106, 204, 214, 217, 336, 337, 519, 554, 557, 629
Newborns, 382
"New Look" school of perception, 181–182
Nicotine, 215, 216
Nightmares, 216
Nodes of Ranvier, 86
Noise, 136, 188
Nomothetic approach, 381, 384, 390–391, 412
Nonconformity, 445, 450, 598–600
Nonconscious processing, 195–196, 211, 220; controlling, 246–247; and motives, 264, 301
Nondirective therapy, 550
Nonrational factors in decision making, 358
Non-REM sleep, 204, 205, 206, 220
Nonspecific stress response, 461–462
Nonstandard English, 434
Nonverbal communication, 371, 374, 376
Nonverbal tests, 427, 452
Noradrenalin, 81, 459
Norepinephrine, 87, 88, 298, 459, 557
Normal curve, 651–652
Normalcy, 626
Normative studies, 35, 71
Norms: in assessment, 35, 420, 438, 450, 451; and aggression, 631–632; social, 492, 497, 593, 594–597, 599, 607, 625
Nuclear era, and stress, 474, 475, 635
Nucleus, of cell, 77, 83, 90
Nutrition, 432, 434

O
Obsessive-compulsive disorder, 489, 499, 500, 504, 525
Obedience, 609, 611, 621–627, 639
Obesity, 276, 278, 463, 464, 466
Object permanence, 51, 52
Objective tests, 435–439, 440, 449, 452
Objectivity: and abnormality, 521–522; and research, 17–18, 22, 30; sense of, 218
Observation: in assessment, 421–422, 431, 448–449, 451; and cognition, 341, 343, 364–366, 375; in research, 12, 13, 16, 30, 383, 384, 643
Observational learning, 252, 253–255, 256, 405–406, 413
Occipital cortex, 195
Occipital lobes, 96, 98
Occlusion, and perception, 171
Occupational Analysis Inventory, 447, 452

Occupational status, and IQ, 429, 452
Old age. See Elderly
Olfaction, 141–142, 149
Operants and operant conditioning, 234–249, 250, 256, 258, 259, 405, 539, 570; principles of, 238–242; and reinforcement, 242–249; in therapy, 542–544
Operations, in problem solving, 362, 363, 376
Opium and opiates, 89, 215–216, 243
Opponent-process theory, 127, 140, 149
Optic chiasma, 99, 121, 148
Optic nerve, 120, 121, 148
Optical image, 153–154, 160
Oral fixation, 65, 382
Oral stage of development, 64, 71
Organic mental disorders, 494, 504
Organization: and memory, 318–319, 324, 328–330, 332, 337; and perception, 161–175, 188; and thinking, 350–351
Organizational psychologists, 292
Orgasm, 203, 216, 282, 283, 285, 503, 549
Orientation constancy, 175, 185
Orienting response, 92, 106, 227
Out-group, 603, 604, 605, 607
Ovaries, 81
Overcompensation, 398, 413
Overcrowding, 466, 474
Overeating, 276, 278, 464, 466, 467, 486, 496
Overload: and burnout, 467, 468, 470; sensory, 189, 194, 272
Overregularization, 48–49
Overt and covert learning, 225, 255–256, 413

P
Pain, 89, 145–148, 149, 224, 258, 387, 460, 503
Panic disorders, 489, 499–500, 525
Paradigm: of classical conditioning, 227, 250, 258; of discriminative stimuli, 241–242; of operant conditioning, 238–242, 250
Parallel processing scanning, 316–317, 343
Paranoia, 349, 506, 508, 514, 558
Paranoid disorders, 504, 506–507, 508, 525, 530
Paranoid schizophrenia, 510, 522
Paraphilia disorder, 503
Parasympathetic division, 79, 80, 106, 298, 459
Parathyroid glands, 81
Parenting style, 57–60
Parents, 55–60, 64–65, 67, 71, 212, 379, 395, 477, 528, 538, 572; and adolescence, 214, 596; and attachment, 55–57, 71; and drug usage, 214; and intelligence, 431, 432, 433, 434; interference of, 196; and perception, 571–572; and personality, 397; schizophrenic, 518, 519–521
Parietal lobes, 96, 98
Parkinson's disease, 88, 104, 491, 519
Partial reinforcement effect, 247–248, 249, 259

Partial-report procedure, 310–311
Participant modeling, 544–545, 564
Patients' rights, 560
Pattern recognition: and memory, 310, 311, 312, 316, 326, 337, 346; and perception, 45, 178, 185, 198, 199, 220, 340; and thought, 346, 347, 353
Pedophilia, 503
Peers and peer pressure, 44, 66, 214, 397, 595, 596
Penis envy, 399
Perception, 29, 97, 108–149, 150–185, 188, 340, 504, 547, 564; and altered consciousness, 194, 196, 217, 218; and brain, 100, 101, 110, 111, 148, 152, 156–157, 159; and cognition, 51, 53, 350–351, 375; and group influence, 596, 598; in infants, 43; influences on, 363, 456; and memory, 306, 310, 312, 313, 328, 334; and organization, 161–175; of pain, 145–148; personal and social factors in, 180–184; and personality, 409–411, 413; and psychopathology, 504, 506, 507, 516–517, 521, 524, 525; social, 568, 573–579, 606; and stress, 466, 469, 470, 471; thresholds and scaling, 181, 182, 183; visual, 153–160
Percepts, 161, 185, 193
Perceptual defense, 181, 182–183, 334
Perceptual set, 180, 185
Perceptual synthesis, 152
Perfectionists, 495, 496, 527, 528
Peripheral nervous system (PNS), 79, 83, 106, 146
Permissiveness, 57–58, 60, 71
Persistence: and motivation, 266, 287, 301; of variable, 228
Person-centered theory, 400–401
Person-driven scripts, 351, 593
Person variables, 410, 411, 413, 569, 570
Personal construct theory, 409–410, 411, 413
Personal equation, 345
Personal factors, and attribution, 569, 577–579, 606, 621–622, 624
Personality, 24, 67–68, 204, 298, 351, 377–413, 455, 553, 623–624; assessing, 417, 435–441, 451, 452; and attitudes, 548–549; changing, 549, 559–560, 564; Cognitive theories of, 409–411, 412, 413; defined, 381; and dehumanization, 609–610; humanistic theories of, 400–403, 409, 411, 412, 413; ideographic approach to, 381, 384, 388, 390–391, 392, 412; and job, 438, 446; and learning theories, 404–409, 411, 412, 413; and leadership, 600–601, 602, 603; nomothetic approach to, 381, 384, 390–391, 412; and perception, 176–177, 181–183, 185; in psychodynamic theory, 24, 391–399, 403, 404, 411, 412, 534–535; and stress reactions, 476, 478; of sudden murderers, 641–643; type and trait theories of, 385, 386–391, 412
Personality disorders, 494, 495–497, 524
Personality structures, 388
Personality tests, 379, 383, 384, 387, 389, 412, 417, 509

Persuasion, 184, 578, 580, 583–585, 606
Peyote, 208, 213, 217
Phallic stage of development, 64, 71
Phantom limb phenomenon, 146
Phenomenological perspective, 400, 413, 570–571, 606
Phenothiazine tranquilizers, 519
Phenotype, 40
Phenylketonuria (PKU), 554
Pheromones, 142, 149, 280
Phi phenomenon, 166
Phobias, 189, 496, 497, 498–499, 517, 525, 539, 541, 544–545, 560
Phonemes, phonetics, phonology, 47
Photographic memory, 323–324
Photoreceptors, 120, 123, 148, 157, 161
Physical attraction, 588, 606
Physical illness: and attitude, 457, 465, 477, 478, 486; and stress, 459, 461, 462–465, 470, 471, 472, 474, 477, 478, 479, 486, 487, 499, 501
Physiological changes: and aggression, 628–629; and anxiety disorders, 497–498, 499, 525; and emotions, 294–295, 297–298, 299–300, 301, 302, 463, 591; and love, 590–591; and sex, 282–283; and shyness, 447; and stress, 458–465, 470, 473, 486
Physiological dependence, 214
Physiological nystagmus, 132
Physiological psychology, 74, 75–76, 105, 106, 334
Physiological zero, 143
Physique, and personality, 386–387
Pineal gland, 75, 81, 82, 197, 203–204
Pitch, 135, 139–140, 149
Pituitary gland, 75, 81, 82, 89, 261, 278, 280, 459, 460–461, 462, 486
Place learning, 256
Place theory, 139, 149
Placebos, 148, 243, 557, 559
Pleasure, desire for, 24, 224, 258, 394, 404, 413
Pleasure centers of brain, 102, 268
Pleasure principle, 394, 395, 398
Pollution, 475, 635
"Pollyanna" principle, 579
Polygenic characteristics, 40
Ponzo illusion, 172
Pornography, 283, 285, 394, 633–634, 639
Positive reinforcer or reinforcement, 239, 240, 241, 244, 246, 259, 542–543, 544, 564, 637
Positivity bias, 579, 606
Positron emission tomography (PET), 104–105, 106
Postsynaptic membrane or cells, 86, 87, 88, 106, 204, 336, 337
Posttraumatic stress disorders, 467, 468–469, 487, 499, 525
Potential, 273–274, 292, 302, 400, 409, 611–617, 639
Poverty, 428, 434, 563, 617
Power, effect of, 613–614
Praise, 585, 589, 606, 637
Preattentive processing, 194–195, 220, 307
Precategorical form, of memory, 310
Preconditioning, 252, 253, 254, 255, 259
Preconventional morality, 63
Predictability, need for, 464, 525
Predisposition. See Biological factors

Prefrontal lobotomy, 102, 553
Prejudice, 57, 349, 425, 576, 604
Prenatal period, 36, 41, 42, 431, 434; and aggression, 629; and brain, 93–94
Preoperational stage, 51, 52, 62, 71
President's Commission on Mental Health, 491
Pressures, 392, 398, 631–632
Presynaptic membrane, 86, 87, 88, 106
Prevention of mental illness, 562–563, 564
Primary effect, 573
Primary drives, 271, 275, 302
Primary gain, 501
Primary process thoughts, 445
Primary reinforcers, 242, 244, 245, 259
Principle of adaptive hedonism, 224, 236, 258
Prior knowledge, and perception, 155, 174–175, 185
Prisoner's dilemma game, 481
Prisons, 267, 542, 570, 609–610, 614, 636–637, 642, 644
Proactive interference (PI), 333
Probability, 18–19, 358, 359, 360, 376
Problem solving, 53, 69, 198, 220, 318, 517, 548, 630; and intelligence, 428, 430, 452; and stress, 469, 470, 476–478, 487; and thinking, 339–340, 342, 361–364, 367, 376
Problem space, 362, 363
Procedural knowledge: and memory, 305, 323, 326, 337; and thought, 321, 350–351, 364, 365, 367, 375, 376, 637
Processing, 326–327, 337, 410, 413; and attention, 193–194; and short-term memory, 312, 314–316
Progestin, and aggression, 629
Projection, 396, 397, 399
Projective tests, 286–287, 399, 439–441, 443, 452
Propaganda, 583, 606
Propanediols, 556
Propositions, 323, 346, 350, 375
Propranol, 80
Prosocial aggression, 628
Prostaglandins, 145–146
Prostitution, 215, 285
Prototype theories, 178, 179, 185
Prototypes, and personality, 347, 574–575
Proximal stimulus, 154–155, 160, 172, 173, 185
Proximity, and liking, 588, 606
Psilocybin, 217
Psychedelic drugs. See Hallucinogens
Psychiatrists and psychiatry, 212, 492, 493, 521, 531, 563
Psychic determinism, 393, 411, 412
Psychic energy, 270, 394, 412
"Psychic numbness," 473, 633
Psychoactive drugs, 189, 190, 208, 214, 215–217, 220
Psychoanalysis, 529, 531, 534–538, 546, 557, 558, 559, 560, 563, 564
Psychodynamic model, 23, 24, 27, 31, 181, 196, 206–207, 220, 516; and personality, 24, 391–399, 403, 404, 411, 412, 439; and psychopathology, 516, 517, 520, 525; and therapy. See Psychoanalysis

Psychogenic amnesia, 502, 525
Psychoimmunology, 464
Psychological dependence, 215
Psychological factors; and eating, 277, 279; and sex, 283–284
Psychology: assumptions in, 22–23; defined, 6, 493; environmental, 10, 634, 635–636, 637–638, 639, ethics in, 9, 233, 644–645; and experimental model, 13–16, 30, 35; goals of, 7–11, 30; methodology of, 11–22; perspectives in, 22–27; responsibility of, 9, 233, 439, 446; specialty areas, 9, 10
Psychometric function, 113–114, 116
Psychometric theory of intelligence, 428, 452
Psychopathology, 488–525, 546; classifying, 492–494; incidence of, 490, 491, 497, 505, 506, 507, 508, 524, 554, 562; models of, 512–521
Psychopharmacology, 555–557
Psychophysiological model, 23–24, 27, 31
Psychophysical scales, 117–119, 148
Psychophysics, 113–119, 135, 148
Psychosexual development, 64, 71, 546
Psychosexual disorders, 497, 502–503, 524, 525
Psychosis, 216, 491, 504–507, 514, 522, 525, 538, 543, 544, 555
Psychosocial development, 64–65, 68, 71
Psychosocial dwarfism, 82
Psychosomatic disorders, 462–464, 486
Psychosurgery, 529, 553, 560, 564
Psychotherapy, 529, 533, 534–552, 557, 563–564; behavioristic, 539–547, 558, 559, 560; cognitive, 547–549, 559; cost of, 559–560, 561; effectiveness of, 16, 557–561; existential/humanistic, 549–552, 559, 560; psychoanalytic, 533, 534–538, 546, 557, 558, 559, 560
Public health model, 562
Punishment, 239, 240, 241, 243, 246, 259, 267, 523, 542, 543, 609, 614, 615
Pupil, of eye, 119–120

Q
Q-sort test, 384

R
Racial group, and IQ, 425, 430, 432
Radiation, and development, 41, 94
Random assignment, 14–15, 30, 610, 613, 644
Random sample, 644
Range, in research, 648–649
Rank ordering, 646
Rape, 468, 469, 502, 503, 633
Rapid eye movement (REM) sleep, 203, 204–205, 206, 216, 217, 220
Ratio schedules, 248, 249
Rationalization, 396
Raw data, 645, 646
Reaction formation, 396, 397, 399
Reaction time, 76, 316, 317, 343–344, 345, 347, 352, 367, 375, 411

Reality: and altered consciousness, 207, 208, 210, 213, 214, 220; constructs of, 188, 189, 219, 220; and memory, 306; perceptual and objective, 110, 400; and personality, 395, 396, 397, 411, 413; physical vs. social, 571–572, 598; and psychopathology, 497, 504, 508, 509, 512, 517, 520, 521; social, 571–572, 576, 579, 585, 606, 610, 632, 639
Reality principle, 395, 396, 413
Reality testing, 548
Reasoning, 318, 340, 374, 425
Rebellion, 66, 614, 617, 626, 627
Recall, 21–22, 54, 187, 196, 306, 307, 308, 310, 313, 315, 319, 321, 322, 324, 325, 326, 327, 329, 331, 337, 357, 369–370, 575, 579
Receptive field, 128, 129
Reciprocal determinism, 405, 413
Reciprocal liking, 588, 606
Recognition: and memory, 325–326, 333; and reward, 614–615
Reconstructive processes, 328–332, 337
Recursion, 373, 376
Re-education, in therapy, 537, 560
Reference frame, 164–165, 166, 173, 185
Reference groups, 596
Reflex arcs, 77, 90
Reflex behavior, 75, 90, 93, 145, 226–227, 238
Refractory period, 283
Region segregation, 161
Regression, 211, 396, 517
Rehearsal: behavioral, 545, 564; and memory, 309, 314, 315–316, 319, 322, 326, 337, 369–370; strategies, 370; and stress, 483; in therapy, 545, 547
Reinforcement, 239–241, 242–250, 254, 256, 259, 546, 564; and aggression, 630–631, 639; distribution of, 247–250; and feedback, 246, 365, 482; in interpersonal relations, 588–589; and liking theory, 588, 606; in motivation, 264, 271; and personality, 404, 405, 408, 409, 411, 413; positive, 239, 240, 241, 244, 246, 259, 543, 544, 564; primary, 242, 244, 245, 259; and psychopathology, 517; schedules of, 248–249, 404; of self, 405, 408
Rejection, 69, 397, 485, 495, 576, 595, 600
Relabeling, 621, 639
Relative motion parallax, 170, 185
Relative size, 171–172, 185
Relaxation, 481–482, 483, 486, 487, 540
Relaxation response, 482
Relearning, 322
Releasers, and response, 269, 302
Reliability, 16, 391, 418–419, 422–423, 426, 436, 438, 440, 441, 451, 493, 643
Remembering, 306, 309, 328–332, 337
Repeated reproduction, 331
Repetitive actions, 466, 486, 500
Replication, 18, 19, 30, 653
Representativeness heuristics, 359–360, 376
Repression, 181, 196, 334, 392, 394, 395, 396, 399, 413, 516, 534–535, 536, 563
Repressors, and perception, 183
Research methods, 11–22, 641–653; and development, 35–37; and ethics, 644–645
Residual stress pattern, 468

Respondent conditioning. See Classical conditioning
Response bias, 114–115, 116, 148, 183, 184
Response contingent punishment, 146
Response criterion, 116
"Response suppression" hypothesis, 183
Responsibility, 265, 275, 284, 612, 615, 618, 621, 625; and assessment, 439, 446; of psychologists, 233; in therapy, 549, 564
Resting potential, 84, 85, 106
Reticular activating system, 298
Reticular formation, 97
Retina, 99, 119, 120–121, 122, 127, 128, 131, 132, 133, 148, 149, 153–155, 157, 161, 166, 169, 172, 173
Retrieval, 307, 308, 328, 333, 334, 335, 337; cues, 324–325, 331, 333, 334, 337, 355, 469; failure, 326, 332, 333–334, 337; in long-term memory, 318, 320, 324–326; in short-term memory, 316–317, 343, 469
Retroactive interference (RI), 333
Retrograde amnesia, 335
Reuptake, 86, 88
Rewards: in attraction, 585, 588–589; and aggression, 616–617, 630–631; in conditioning, 27, 247, 256; and motivation, 290–292, 293, 302, 614
Rheumatoid arthritis, 463–464
Rigidity, and stress, 469, 470, 487, 516
Risk: and decisions, 358–359; genetic, 517–519, 520; -taking, 287, 288, 450
Rod-and-frame test, 176–177
Role: -confusion, 66, 403; -driven scripts, 351, 593; -playing, 485, 549, 575, 596–597, 613–614
Roles, 351; and adolescence, 66, 403; and authority, 613–614, 622, 625, 627; and development, 402–403; and norms, 593, 599. See also Sex roles
Romantic passion, 590–591
Rorschach test, 439–440, 452
Rote responses, 257
Routinizing, and attention, 194

S
"S-factors" in intelligence, 428, 452
Sadism, 503
Safety needs, 273
Sample, in research, 644, 651
Satiation, 276, 277, 279
Saturation, of color, 123, 124, 125, 128, 149
Savings method, and memory, 322
Scales, in assessment, 435–439, 452
Scapegoating, 603, 630
Schemas: and perception, 180, 185; and remembering, 328–331, 337, 346; social, 573–576, 580, 606, 614; and thinking, 51, 346, 350–351, 355–357, 360, 363, 367, 375

Schizophrenia, 445, 491, 504, 507–512, 517–521, 522, 525; childhood, 245, 538, 564; genetic factors in, 517–519, 554; treatment for, 88, 553, 554, 558, 564; types of, 510
Scientific method, 11–22, 30, 63, 641–653
Scripts: sexual, 282, 284–285, 302, 351; and thinking, 346, 350–351, 367, 375, 614
Second-order conditioning, 231–233, 252, 253, 254
Secondary drives, 271, 302
Secondary gains, 241, 393, 501
Secondary process thoughts, 445
Secondary traits, 388, 412
Sedatives, 216, 217
Selective amnesia, 502
Selective attention, 312, 410, 511, 521
Selective filtering, 191–192, 220, 310
Self, 189, 218, 220, 401–402, 403; -actualization, 27, 273–274, 302, 398, 400, 403, 413, 529, 549, 550, 564; -awareness, 550, 551, 615; -concept, 27, 401–402, 403, 413, 505, 538, 600, 615; -confidence, 57, 408; -consciousness, 447, 449; -consistency, 401; -control, 57, 384, 389, 439; -disclosure, 591; -efficacy, 290, 292, 302, 408, 409, 413, 450, 516, 547, 548, 563; -esteem, 59–60, 289, 401, 403, 408, 413, 447, 449, 457, 501, 504, 507, 516, 615, 630, 650; -fulfilling prophecies, 18, 408, 457, 499, 572, 606; -gratification, 618, 619–620, 639; -hypnosis, 209, 212, 502; -identity, 69; -image, 396, 491, 521, 527, 579, 584, 606, 624, 638, 644; -integrity, 63, 334; -inventories, 422 (see also Self-reports); -monitoring, 369–370, 484–485; -protection, 476, 478; -regulation, 405, 410; -reinforcement, 485; -reliance, 57; -report, 389, 390, 392, 393, 399, 421, 422, 435–439, 449, 451, 521; -serving bias, 579, 606; -statements, 405, 484–485, 529, 547, 548, 564; -system, 538, 564; theory, 401–402; -worth, 63, 286, 549, 550, 563
Semantic encoding, 313, 326, 327, 337
Semantic memory, 321, 323, 326, 332, 337
Semantics, 47, 372, 373
Senility, 507, 508
Sensation, 28, 29, 112, 148, 152–153, 154, 155, 156, 157, 185, 309, 310–312
Sensitivity, 369, 370, 398, 442, 452
Sensitizers, and perception, 183
Sensorimotor stage, 51, 71
Sensory adaptation, 132, 134, 143, 149
Sensory deprivation, 208, 210
Sensory gating, 310, 312
Sensory memory, 192, 309, 310–312, 326, 333, 337, 346, 353
Sensory neurons, 83, 90, 91, 93, 106
Sensory overload, 189, 194, 272
Sensory physiology, 113, 148
Sensory preconditioning, 252, 253, 254, 255, 259
Sensory projection areas, 97, 98, 99
Sensory psychology, 113, 148

Sensory testing programs, 415, 416
Separation, 472, 591
Separation-individuation conflict, 538
Sequential design, 37, 71
Serial learning, 322
Serial position effect, 327
Serial reproduction, 331
Serial self-terminating scanning, 317
Serotonin, 87, 88, 217, 554, 557, 629
Set, and perception, 180
Set point, and eating, 277, 278, 302
Severe stress, 466, 473, 486, 487
Sex and sexuality, 41, 42, 280–285, 440, 500; attitudes about, 281, 282, 284–285, 549; and the brain, 261; as a drive, 263; and drugs, 216; in Freudian theory, 392, 394, 395, 396, 397, 398, 536; physiology of, 280–284; and psychopathology, 500, 501, 502–503; and psychosexual development, 64, 71; scripts, 282, 284–285, 302, 351
Sex differences: and aggression, 629; and the brain, 100, 101; and cognition, 70; and development, 57; genetic, 43; and life expectancy, 478–479; and psychodynamic theory, 399; and sexual response, 60, 280, 282–283
Sex roles, 66, 406, 642, 645, 646, 650, 653
Sexism, 535
Sexual dysfunctions, 503, 525, 527
Sexual fantasies, 202–203, 283, 503
Shadows, and perception, 171, 185
Shape constancy, 173, 175, 185
Shaping, 245–246, 259, 544
Sharpening, in remembering, 331
Shock, 459, 468, 469, 473
Shock therapy. See Electroconvulsive therapy
Short-term inhibitors, 279
Short-term memory, 309, 311, 312, 313–317, 326, 327, 333, 337, 343, 344, 346, 353
Shyness, 13, 388, 402, 435, 445, 447–450, 452, 545–546, 587, 642–645, 647, 649, 651, 653
Siblings, 55, 433, 629, 630
Sign language, 374, 375, 376
Significant differences, 19, 20
Similarity: and forgetting, 322, 333; and liking, 587–588, 606
Simulation modeling, 367
Simultaneous conditioning, 229, 233
Sine-wave, 130, 135, 140, 149
Situation: and attribution, 577, 578–579, 606, 621–622; and leadership, 600, 601; and personality, 400, 406–407, 412, 413, 601; and social behavior, 569, 570, 581, 601, 613–614, 621–625, 639
Situation-driven scripts, 351
Situation-specific behavior, 389, 390, 391
Situational observations, 421–422, 451
Situational variables, 410, 411, 412, 413
Sixteen Personality Factor Questionnaire (16PF), 435, 439, 452
Size constancy, 173–175, 185
Size/distance relation, 171–172, 173
Skewed distribution, 651
Skill development, 364–370, 376, 446, 447, 545–548, 550, 560
Skill memories, 321, 333, 336, 337

Sleep, 190, 203–207; and the brain, 203, 204–205, 206, 220; deprivation of, 205; disturbances in, 499, 500, 504; and dreaming, 206–207, 220; and drugs, 216, 217; stages of, 204–205, 206; and stress, 82, 468
Sleeper effect, 584
Slip of the tongue, 344, 412
Smell, 114, 141–142, 149
Smoking, 464, 465
Social comparison, 585–586, 606
Social context, 568, 569, 570–571, 578, 581, 606, 614
Social dilemmas, 634–636, 639
Social deprivation, 267
Social-emotional leader, 601, 603, 607
Social exchange theory, 588, 606
Social facilitation, 594
Social factors: in drug effects, 217–218; and eating, 279; and perception, 183–184, 185
Social influence, 568, 592, 606, 611–617
"Social isolates," 545–546
Social isolation, 586, 600, 606; effects of, 34, 38, 466, 479–480; and psychopathology, 513–514, 520, 523–524, 569
Social learning: aggression as, 630–633; and sex, 284–285
Social learning theories: and aggression, 630–633; and assessment, 421; cognitive, 410; and motivation, 274–275; and personality, 404, 405–409, 413
Social learning therapy, 539, 544–547, 564
Social network index, 480
Social norms, 284, 513, 522–523, 594–597, 599, 625, 631–632, 639
Social pathology, 618–639
Social payoff, 634–635, 636
Social perception, 568, 573–579, 598–599, 606
Social phobia, 498–499
Social pressure, 592–593, 596, 597, 598, 599, 607
Social psychology, 566–640; and perception, 573–579, 606
Social Readjustment Rating Scale (SRRS), 471, 472
Social reality, 571–572, 576, 579, 585, 598, 606, 610, 632, 639
Social schemas, 573–576
Social service professions, 467–468, 619
Social skills, 447, 448, 450, 544, 545–547, 560, 564
Social status, 574–575
Social support networks, 479–480, 485, 487, 513, 523–524, 586–587
Social traps, 635
Social worth, 428
Socialization: in adolescence, 214, 596; in childhood, 34, 55–61; in infancy, 45–46; by norms, 594–597; sex differences in, 60–61, 62–63, 69; and shyness, 587; and social needs, 585–587, 592, 607

Society: and creativity, 445; and deviants, 522–523; and deindividuation, 617; and personality, 395, 402–403; and sex, 503; and stress, 474–475

Socioeconomic level: and education, 429; and IQ tests, 431, 432, 434; and language development, 49, 434; and paranoia, 506; and perception, 181, 182; and sex, 242, 285; underclass, 617

Solitary confinement, 267, 586, 609

Somatic nervous system, 79, 106

Somatoform disorders, 497, 501, 524, 525

Somatosensory areas of brain, 97, 98, 99

Somatotypes, 386–387

Sound spectrum, 136

Sounds: and hearing, 114, 134–140, 149; and memory, 323–324, 344

Spatial-frequency model, 130, 131, 149

Spatial integration, 165, 185

Spatial relationships: and brain, 101, 106, 198, 217, 220; and cognition, 351, 353, 354, 375; and perception; 112, 128–131

Specialization, and language, 373

Species-specific behaviors, 250–251, 259, 269

Speech, 98, 100, 101, 106, 344, 509, 510, 511–512. See also Language

Spinal cord, 79, 80, 93, 97, 106, 146

"Split-brain" research, 100–101, 197–199, 200–201, 220

Spontaneous recovery, 229, 258, 557, 558, 564

Stability: and achievement, 288, 290; -instability approach, 387, 412

Stages of development, 47–65

Standard deviation (SD), 648–649, 651, 652

Standardization, 17, 418, 420, 435, 436, 438, 451, 452

Stanford-Binet Intelligence Test, 426, 427, 452, 651

Stanford prison experiment, 609–610, 622

Stanford Hypnotic Susceptibility Scale, 210

Stanford Shyness Survey, 449, 642, 645, 646

State dependence, and memory, 320

Statistical significance, 19, 20, 651, 652–653

Statistics, 438, 646–653; descriptive, 646–650; inferential, 650–653

Status, 574–575, 579, 609, 613–614

Stereochemical theory, 142

Stereotyped behavior: of animals, 280, 302; and compulsions, 500; and stress, 466, 469, 470, 486

Stereotypes, 289, 360, 386, 422, 451, 575–576, 588

Stigma, of abnormality, 486, 522–524, 525, 530

Stimulants, 216, 220

Stimulation: and affiliation, 585, 606; of the brain, 73, 95, 101–102, 106, 299; and motivation, 267–268, 272, 310

Stimulation deafness, 136

Stimuli, discriminative, 241–242, 245, 256; distal vs. proximal, 152–155, 160; emotional, 295–296; and psychophysics, 113–119

Stimulus, 8, 9, 21, 31, 223–224, 226; contrast, 128; control, 241–242; discrimination, 230–231, 258; generalization, 229–230, 231, 258; input, 264; variables, 228. See also Conditioned and Unconditioned stimulus

Storage, 307, 308, 326, 327, 328, 333, 335, 337; in long-term memory, 318, 320–324, 326; of sensory memory, 310–311, 326; in short-term memory, 313, 326

Strategy, and metacognition, 369, 370

Stress and stressors, 278, 283, 453–487, 554; appraisal of, 457, 480; chronic, 457, 461–462, 486; and decision making, 358; defined, 456; dysfunctional coping with, 211–212; emotional, 467–469, 470, 486, 487; and humor, 476, 477; managing, 420, 464, 481–486, 562; model of, 470; and personality, 397; physiological reactions to, 458–465, 470; psychological reactions to, 466–470; resources against, 476–478, 479–481, 487; sources of, 471–475; and vulnerability, 475–481

Stress index, 470

Stess-induced analgesia, 460

Stroboscopic motion, 133, 149, 166

Strong-Campbell Interest Inventory, 446, 452

Stroop task, 196

Structuralism, 157, 160, 164, 185

Subconscious processing, 196, 220, 307, 321

Sublimation, 396

Subliminal perception, 385

Substance-use disorders, 494

Success, 485, 569, 587, 592; fear of, 289; and motivation, 287–288, 290, 302, 379, 408; predicting, 417, 429, 439

"Sudden death" phenomenon, 458–459

Sudden murderers' study, 641–653

Suggestibility, hypnotic, 209–210, 211, 220

Suicide, 69, 216, 460, 467, 468, 470, 474, 496, 504, 506, 514, 559, 603, 621

Superego, 395, 396, 399, 413, 534, 538, 563

Superior colliculus, 121, 148, 195

Superordinate goals, 604, 605, 607

Support, 147, 406–407, 469, 470, 478, 479–481, 561, 589

Suppression, and conditioning, 239

Surface structure, 350, 373, 376

Surveys, 12, 16, 30

Symbolic langue, 374, 375, 376

Symbols: in dreams, 206–207; in thinking, 428

Sympathetic division, 79–80, 106, 298

Sympathy, 147, 241, 299, 393, 501, 528

Symptom substitution, 539

Synapses, 86–88, 89, 92, 94, 106, 122, 307, 308, 336

Synesthesias, 217

Syntax, 47, 372, 373

Systematic desensitization, 482, 539, 540–541, 544, 545, 558, 564

Teleological motivation, 264

Television: and aggression, 254–255, 632–633, 639; and test scores, 21

Temperament, 43, 44, 382, 386, 479, 487

Temperature, 143, 149, 246

Temporal integration, 165, 185

Temporal lobes, 96, 98, 139, 629

Tension, 270, 271, 280, 302, 404–405, 481, 498, 499, 500, 534, 556–557

Terminal buttons, 83, 85, 86, 87, 106, 121

Territoriality, 628, 639

Testes, 81, 261, 281, 282

Testosterone, 82, 283

Test-retest reliability, 419

Tests, 13, 16, 17, 30, 418–420; achievement, 21, 419; intelligence, 424–434, 451; personality, 379, 383, 384, 435–441; projective, 286–287, 399, 439–441, 443; and TV viewing, 21; vocational interest, 446–447

Texture gradient, 160, 172, 185

Thalamus, 97, 98, 121, 146, 335, 553

Thanatos, 270, 394, 628

Thematic Apperception Test (TAT), 439, 440–441, 452

Theories V, X, Y, and Z, 293

Theory of signal detectability (TSD), 115–116, 148

Therapeutic contract, 561

Therapeutic process, 530–531

Therapists, 531, 546, 558, 559, 561, 563

Therapy, 29, 482, 484, 526–564; behavioristic, 539–547, 558, 559, 560, 564; biomedical, 553–557, 560, 564; cognitive, 547–549, 559, 564; effectiveness of, 16, 557–561, 564; existential/humanistic, 549–552, 559, 564; goals of, 530–531, 563; history of, 532–533; informal, 531; network, 533; placebo, 557–558; psychoanalytic, 333, 534–538, 546, 557, 558, 559, 563–564

Think-aloud protocols, 341, 342, 375

Thinking, 76, 95, 97, 338–376, 504, 547–549; in childhood, 50–55, 357; creative, 445, 470; divergent and convergent, 443; faulty, 548–549, 564; images in, 351–354; in infants, 52, 343, 357; and language, 51, 371–373, 376; and making decisions, 26, 29, 340, 358–360, 367–368; and problem solving, 220, 318, 339–340, 361–364, 367; schizophrenic, 445, 507, 510, 511, 521, 525; silent speech in, 345, 371; and stress, 456–458, 463, 469–470; structure for, 346–354

Thirst, 266, 270, 273

Thorazine, 555

Threshold: and feelings, 300–301; and perception, 181, 182, 183; and sensation, 113–115, 116, 117, 132, 148

Thymus, 81, 462

Thyroid glands, 82, 261, 460

Thyrotrophic hormone (TTH), 460

Timbre, 136, 149

Time-based designs, 35, 36–37

Time orientation, 293–294

Time sense, 131–132, 612

Token economies, 242, 244, 542–543, 547, 564

T

T-test, 653

Tactile sense, 144–145, 149, 154

Tardive dyskinesia, 556, 560

Task leader, 601, 607

Taste, 114, 141, 142, 149, 251

Technology, 474, 475, 634, 637

"Top-down" processes; and attention, 193, 220; and memory, 307, 312, 318; and perception, 155, 177, 178, 180, 184, 185; and thinking, 346, 347, 355, 367
TOT phenomenon, 325
Touch, 114, 143, 145, 149, 283, 284, 302
Trace forward conditioning, 229
Tragedy of the commons, 635, 639
Traits, 41, 44; assessment of, 417, 435, 436, 439, 451, 452; complementary, 587–588, 606; and creativity, 444; and leadership, 423, 425, 600–601, 602, 603; and personality, 210, 345, 382, 383, 385, 386, 387–391, 392, 400, 406, 411, 412, 449, 574–575, 577, 580, 624
Trance logic, 210–211, 220
Tranquilizers, 69, 476, 519, 555, 556–557
Transactional analysis, 551
Transcendance needs, 273
Transcendental Meditation (TM), 482
Transference, in analysis, 535, 537, 546, 563
Transsexualism, 60, 503
Trauma: and memory, 334, 335; and personality, 394, 397, 399, 529; reaction to, 463, 468–469
Trial and error learning, 257–258
Trichromatic theory, 126, 140, 149
Tricyclics, 557, 559
Trust, 64, 65, 71, 284, 591, 601, 636
Twin studies, 44, 210, 433, 517, 518–519
Two-component theory of emotion, 299–300, 302
Tympanic membrane, 138
Type, and personality, 382, 386–387, 417
Type A behavior, 382, 464, 478–479, 484, 487
Type theories of personality, 385, 386–387, 412
Typicality, 347

U

Ulcers, 462, 463
Unconditional positive regard, 550
Unconditioned response (UR), 227, 232, 258
Unconditioned stimulus (US), 227–234, 239, 242, 252, 253, 258, 267, 283, 302, 540
Unconscious, 110, 206, 500, 546; collective, 398; interference, 173, 175; and mental processing, 187–188, 194, 196, 219; and motives, 265, 274, 392, 516; and perception, 173, 175, 180, 183; and personality, 392, 393, 394–395, 398, 399, 403, 411, 412, 413, 439, 467, 536; and psychoanalysis, 534, 536, 537, 546, 560, 563; and stress, 463, 478
Underclass, 617
Undifferentiated schizophrenia, 510
Undoing, 396
Unemployment, 472, 474, 475, 490, 507, 523, 617
Unique traits, 388
Uniqueness, 381, 384, 388, 409, 410, 412, 435, 485, 600, 614

University Residence Environment Scale (URES), 406–407
Urban life, 472–473, 481, 532, 637, 638
Utility, and decisions, 358, 359, 376
Utricle, 138, 143

V

Validity, 16, 392, 418, 419–420, 424, 435, 436, 440, 441, 451, 643; and judgments of abnormality, 493–494, 522; scales, 436; social, 585–587
Values, 244, 287, 293, 299, 328, 359; forming, 55, 57, 61–63; in humanistic model, 26, 27; and obedience, 621–622, 624; and personality, 382, 410, 413; of psychology, 10, 18; and society, 580, 582, 606, 607, 638; and therapy, 529, 549; of women, 62–63, 67–68, 71, 597
Vandalism, 270, 467, 637
Variability: and assessment, 430–431, 432, 452; and personality, 390–391; and research, 648–649, 652
Variable interval schedule (VI), 249
Variable ratio schedule (VR), 248, 249
Variables, 12, 13–14, 15, 17, 20, 21, 30, 238, 384, 419, 429, 643, 649–650; dependent and independent, 14, 21, 30, 38, 228, 570, 606; index, 38, 266, 301; intervening, 8, 14–15, 263, 265, 301, 385, 388, 570, 606; moderator, 475, 479, 487; and motivation, 263, 264, 265; person and situational, 410, 411, 569; in personality theories, 384, 388, 404, 410, 411, 413, 447; psychological, and drugs, 217–218, 220; types of, 14
Vasopressin, 335
Ventromedial hypothalamus, 276, 277, 279
Verbal abilities, 428
Verbal communication, 371–375
Verbal skills, and the brain, 197, 198, 200–201
Verbal tests, 417, 452
Vestibular sense, 142–143, 149, 175, 176
Vietnam War and veterans, 468, 621
Violence, 5, 495–496, 542, 627; cause of, 24, 617, 630; and group, 631; and pornography, 633–634, 639; and sudden murderers, 641, 642; and TV, 632–633, 639; and the underclass, 617
Vision, 110–112, 119–133, 148–149, 153–160, 415
Visual capture, 167
Visual communication, 371
Visual cortex, 98, 104, 121, 128, 129, 162, 195, 336
Visual encoding, 313, 326–327, 337
Visual imagery, 319, 323–324, 344, 351–354, 367, 375
Visual memory, 310–311, 324
Visual substitution system, 144
Visual thought, 351–354
Visual tracking, 343
Vocational interests, 446–447, 452
Volley principle, 140
Voodoo, 458–459, 513
Vulnerability: to schizophrenia, 517–519, 520; to stress, 463, 465, 470, 475–481, 487

W

Wavelength, of light, 122–123, 124, 125, 126, 127, 130
Weber's law, 116–117
Wechsler Adult Intelligence Scale—Revised (WAIS—R), 427
Wechsler Intelligence Scale for Children—Revised (WISC—R), 427
Whole-report procedure, 310, 311
Wild boy of Aveyron, 33–34, 43, 47, 425
Witchcraft, mental illness as, 513, 514–515, 532
Withdrawal, 147, 243, 396, 468, 481, 509, 510, 545–546, 556, 633
Withdrawal symptoms, 214–215, 216, 220, 466
Woodworth Personal Data Sheet, 435
Women: and acceptance of mentally ill, 524; achievement-oriented, 289; and aggression, 629, 630, 633–634; and drug usage, 214; and ERA, 580, 581; and genetic differences, 43; and hysteria, 393; hormones of, 280; and intellectual functioning, 70; life expectancy of, 478–479; and morality, 62–63; as mothers, 68; and multiple personalities, 212; and pornography, 633–634, 639; in psychodynamic theory, 399; and psychopathology, 495, 496, 508; sexual response in, 282–283, 284–285; and shyness, 448; and social factors, 57, 60–61, 284–285, 406–407, 571; and stress, 478, 479, 487; and suicide, 506; and values, 62–63, 67–68, 71, 597
Work, 66, 68, 70, 286, 287, 472–473, 563; dehumanizing, 618–619; motivation for, 292–293, 302
Working memory, 313, 326, 337, 430. *See also* Short-term memory

Y

Yin and yang, 198, 199
Yoga, 481
Young-Helmholtz trichromatic theory, 126, 140, 149

Z

Zen, 481

STUDY-WARE

School is tough enough. Get an edge on studying this semester with Study-Ware.

Study-Ware is an electronic learning system that not only evaluates your knowledge of text content but also helps diagnose your specific learning skills. Designed for the Apple II+, IIe, and 11c and the IBM PC computers, Study-Ware is keyed directly to PSYCHOLOGY AND LIFE, 11/e, for easy reference and learning.

After reading each chapter in the text, Study-Ware allows you to check how much you have learned with fill-in-the-blank, multiple-choice,

and matching review exercises and self-tests, and then assists you in diagnosing your problem areas.

Automatic scoring allows you to check yourself as you learn.

And Study-Ware is easy to use. Three simple keystrokes are all you need to get started.

The system was designed for use on your own computer or any computer available to you on campus.

To order, complete and mail the card below. Be sure to indicate the type of computer disk you want and your method of payment.

Mail to:

Soft Productions, Inc.
P.O. Box 55055
Madison, WI 53705

Cut out for use with Close-up demonstration on motion aftereffects (p. 134).

Cut out for use with Close-up demonstration on motion aftereffects (p. 134).